INTERNATIONAL ENCYCLOPEDIA OF DANCE

INTERNATIONAL ENCYCLOPEDIA OF

DANCE

A project of Dance Perspectives Foundation, Inc.

FOUNDING EDITOR

Selma Jeanne Cohen

AREA EDITORS

George Dorris   Nancy Goldner   Beate Gordon
Nancy Reynolds   David Vaughan
Suzanne Youngerman

CONSULTANTS

Thomas F. Kelly   Horst Koegler   Richard Ralph
Elizabeth Souritz

VOLUME 1

OXFORD UNIVERSITY PRESS

New York   1998   Oxford

OXFORD UNIVERSITY PRESS

Oxford   New York
Athens   Auckland   Bangkok   Bogotá   Bombay
Buenos Aires   Calcutta   Cape Town   Dar es Salaam
Delhi   Florence   Hong Kong   Istanbul   Karachi
Kuala Lumpur   Madras   Madrid   Melbourne
Mexico City   Nairobi   Paris   Singapore
Taipei   Tokyo   Toronto   Warsaw
and associated companies in
Berlin   Ibadan

Published by Oxford University Press, Inc.,
198 Madison Avenue, New York, New York 10016

Oxford is a registered trademark of Oxford University Press

This work was initiated with funds granted by the
National Endowment for the Humanities,
a federal agency

Library of Congress Cataloging-in-Publication Data
International encyclopedia of dance : a project of Dance
Perspectives Foundation, Inc. / founding editor, Selma Jeanne Cohen;
area editors, George Dorris et al.; consultants, Thomas F. Kelly et al.
p.   cm.
Includes bibliographical references and index.
1. Dance—Encyclopedias.   2. Ballet—Encyclopedias.   I. Cohen,
Selma Jeanne, 1920-.   II. Dance Perspectives Foundation.
GV1585.I586   1998   97-36562   792.6'2'03—dc21   CIP
ISBN 0-19-509462-X (set)
ISBN 0-19-512305-0 (vol. 1)

Printing (last digit): 9 8 7 6 5 4 3 2

Printed in the United States of America
on acid-free paper

EDITORIAL AND PRODUCTION STAFF

Managing Editor
Elizabeth Aldrich

Assistant Project Editor
Christopher Caines

Editorial and Administrative Assistants
Ariane Anthony, Brent Gardner, Andrew Fearnside, Susan McMichaels, Jack Rappaport

COPY DEPARTMENT

Copy Chief   *Editorial Consultant*
Martha Goldstein   Barbara Palfy

Copyeditors
Constantina Rhodes Bailly, Frank Caso, Debra Elfenbein, Anita Finkel, Yaël Lewin,
Jennifer L. MacAdam, Roberta Maltese, Jane McGary, Molly McQuade, Regina C. Paleski,
Mara Peets, Anh-Thu Phan, David J. Schechter, James Waller, Leslie Watkins

Bibliography Editor
Philomena Mariani

Proofreaders
Sandra Buch, Sylvia Juran, Pamela Marshall, Marion Osmun,
David Robinson, Judith Sandman, Ellen Thorn

Translators
Helen Ackerman, Irene Huntoon, Galen Joseph, Irina Klyagin,
Jacqueline Bell Mosio, Miwa Nagura, Rita Signorelli Pappas, Alan Stark, Yuri Sviridov

Keyboarders
Victoria Dittman, Liz Ferris, Judith Hancock, Susan McMichaels

ILLUSTRATIONS DEPARTMENT

Illustrations Editor
Jody Sperling

Illustrations Coordinators
Cynthia L. Millman, Naomi Weinstein

Photo Researchers
Reynaldo Gamboa Alejandro, Maria Vencenza Aloisi, Nicole Dekle, Gloria Fokine, Ann Jacoby,
Robert Johnson, Howard Kaplan, Lisa Kirchner, Irina Klyagin, Jenny Lynn McNutt

INDEXING

Cynthia Crippen, AEIOU, Inc.

PRODUCTION AND MANUFACTURING STAFF

Production Manager
Jeffrey Edelstein

Art Director and Book Designer
Joan Greenfield

Manufacturing Controller
Genieve Shaw

CONTENTS

Foreword *by Curtis L. Carter*
volume 1, page ix

Preface *by Selma Jeanne Cohen*
volume 1, page xvii

Introduction *by Elizabeth Aldrich*
volume 1, page xxi

Directory of Contributors
volume 1, page xxxiii

INTERNATIONAL ENCYCLOPEDIA OF DANCE

Alphabetical List of Entries
volume 6, page 457

Synoptic Outline of Contents
volume 6, page 477

Index
volume 6, page 493

FOREWORD

THE GENESIS OF THE *INTERNATIONAL ENCYCLOPEDIA OF DANCE* WAS IN 1974 AT A meeting of the Dance Critics' Association when conference speakers Arlene Croce, dance critic for the *New Yorker,* and Selma Jeanne Cohen, then editor of *Dance Perspectives,* independently cited the need for a comprehensive scholarly encyclopedia for the field of dance. Shortly thereafter, an *ad hoc* committee chaired by Selma Jeanne Cohen met in New York to begin to define the parameters of a world dance encyclopedia. Members of the committee included Selma Jeanne Cohen (chair), Leon Braun, Nancy Goldner, Marcia Marks, and Nancy Reynolds.

HISTORY OF THE PROJECT

In 1976, Dance Perspectives Foundation, Inc., the publisher of *Dance Perspectives,* established by A. J. Pischl and Selma Jeanne Cohen as a series of monographs in 1960 and continued until 1976, was awarded a grant of $24,859 by the National Endowment for the Humanities (NEH) to fund a planning conference of leading dance scholars. The conference was held in December 1976 in New York. A questionnaire had been circulated to approximately twenty-five consultants from around the world prior to the conference, inviting their responses to the project and a series of questions concerning its structure and content. A compilation of the results had been sent to conference participants for study prior to their arrival, and conference attendees had been asked to come prepared to comment on the proposed outline for the encyclopedia, to consider illustrations, and to identify experts to serve as advisers and authors for the project. Lincoln Kirstein, general director of the New York City Ballet, gave the conference keynote address. Mr. Kirstein expressed the hope that the encyclopedia would represent the views of consultants with expertise in various fields. He warned against basing the encyclopedia "either on the rarefied euphoria of dance buffs and balletomanes or on the amateurism of critics whose overly specialized monologues speak mainly to themselves" (*New York Times,* 3 January 1977).

Among those participating in the planning conference were international scholars such as Erik Aschengreen (University of Copenhagen), Marie-Françoise Christout (Bibliothèque Nationale, Paris), and Horst Koegler (dance critic, Berlin) as well as American representatives, including Genevieve Oswald, curator of the Dance Collection of the New York Public Library, Martha Hill, director of dance at the Juilliard School in New York, anthropologists, and scholars from various disciplines relating to dance. Others such as Elizabeth Souritz and Vera Krasovskaya (Russia), Yasuji Honda (Japan), Mohan Khokar (India), Ivor Guest (England), and Gedeon P. Dienes (Hungary) responded to the questionnaire but were unable to attend the conference.

The meeting set the tone for what would become the guiding philosophy of the encyclopedia. The following criteria were established for the future development of the encyclopedia:

1. The encyclopedia would be a multivolume work.
2. Coverage would be international, with entries on all forms of dance in all countries of the world, but entries on persons would be selective.
3. Editorial control would be vested in a small board of American dance historians, supported by consultants with expertise in worldwide geographic and thematic areas.
4. The encyclopedia would be designed to bring joy as well as enlightenment.

The conferees determined three major areas of dance to be covered in the encyclopedia: Western theatrical dance, theatrical dance in the non-Western world, and ritual and recreational forms of dance. An extensive list of consultants representative of the many aspects of dance to be included was established to assure the fullest range of knowledge of the field. The consultants were intended to form a link between the broader perspectives of the editorial board and the expertise of specialized writers. The initial proposal called for an encyclopedia consisting of eight volumes of 848 pages each with five thousand illustrations. In 1977 the NEH made a supplemental grant of $13,464 for additional small-group meetings to refine the concepts and subject matter.

The Dance Perspectives Foundation undertook sponsorship of the *International Encyclopedia of Dance (IED)* in fulfillment of its mission to encourage awareness and understanding of dance as an artistic tradition of great historical import and as a significant cultural force in contemporary life. The Foundation is concerned with aiding students, scholars, and the general public in their efforts to provide accurate information on dance in all of its forms, including theatrical, ritual, recreational, therapeutic, folk, social, and popular dance from cultures throughout the world. The encyclopedia is intended to address a need arising from the growing popularity of dance and the number of readers seeking information about dance.

One of the first tasks of the Foundation was to constitute an editorial board for the encyclopedia. Selma Jeanne Cohen was appointed editor in chief, and George Dorris, Nancy Goldner, Beate Gordon, Nancy Reynolds, David Vaughan, and Suzanne Youngerman were appointed to assist her as area editors. This board was empowered to plan the contents of the encyclopedia, covering all forms of dance throughout the world. Areas of editorial responsibilities were divided as follows: Cohen (aesthetics, reference, Russia, and various countries); Dorris (dance and music, 1400–1800); Goldner (modern dance and twentieth-century ballet), Gordon (Asian dance); Reynolds (dance and technique up to 1400 and modern ballet), Vaughan (British ballet, avant-garde dance, film and video, and social dance), Youngerman (anthropology and folk dance).

As the project evolved, the subsequent plan for the encyclopedia called for a four-volume work, containing between seven hundred and a thousand illustrations, with a fifth volume to include an index and chronologies. Its contributors were to include some 230 scholars. The contents were to consist of articles on the history of dance in various countries, interpretive essays on historical subjects and thematic motifs, including such topics as aesthetics, criticism, dance works, film, music, lighting, genre, education, companies, and dance organizations, and biographical sketches of dancers, choreographers, composers, designers, impresarios, and writers.

In 1980, the Dance Perspectives Foundation entered into conversations with publisher Charles Scribner's Sons, which resulted in development of a project budget and an agreement to publish the encyclopedia. In addition to planning the contents, the *IED* editors were charged with the following duties: to identify qualified contributors for the articles planned; to commission the articles; to review, edit, and approve manuscripts submitted; and to deliver approved manuscripts to the publisher. Of the initial project budget of $738,000, Scribner's agreed to bear $562,000. To complete the project, the Dance Perspectives Foundation would be required to raise an additional $221,000. The National Endowment for the Humanities again came forth with $109,883 to launch the project, and the Foundation made plans to secure the additional support required. Major grants from several national foundations, a bequest from Mr. Frank Tick, and generous contributions from other foundations and many individuals (all of whom are acknowledged below) rounded out the necessary funding to complete the project.

Work on the *International Encyclopedia of Dance* began with high enthusiasm and expectations on the part of the editorial board, the publisher, and the Foundation. Endorsements for the project came from scholars and artists in the field including Rudolf Arnheim, Agnes de Mille, Dame Margot Fonteyn, Gene Kelly, Lincoln Kirstein, Jerome Robbins, and Walter Terry. A reception at the Century Club in New York, hosted by Scribner's on 11 January 1982, celebrated the launching and heightened interest among potential funding sources and the press. The guest list included Charles Scribner, Jr., members of the *IED* editorial board and the board of directors of the Dance Perspectives Foundation, members of the press, and various luminaries of the dance and philanthropic communities, including Lincoln Kirstein and Jerome Robbins, as well as representatives of the Ford, Mellon, and Kress Foundations and others interested in the success of the project.

The encyclopedia stirred excitement because it was a pioneering venture. There was in fact no deep tradition to draw upon in the newly emerging field of dance scholarship. The enthusiasm of the *IED* editors and authors was refreshing to the NEH program officers, who normally worked in more established scholarly disciplines. The writers commissioned for the encyclopedia included acclaimed international authors in dance history. Others were scholars in fields other than dance with an interest in some aspect of dance. In some instances it was necessary to draw upon authors who were expert practitioners but who had less experience as writers or scholars.

With publication initially anticipated in 1983, work had begun in earnest upon the awarding of the third grant from the NEH. Manuscripts were edited by the *IED* editorial board, approved, and eventually delivered to the managing editor at Scribner's. It then became apparent that the emergent state of dance history was having an unexpected, adverse effect on the project. Because much of the research was original material, completed manuscripts frequently posed problems for the Scribner's copyeditors, who were accustomed to "fact checking" by verifying information from exisiting sources. Apart from varying standards of scholarship among English writers, no consistent standard for scholarly content or format existed among the writers of different nations, some of whom did not write in English. These problems needed to be addressed through costly translation and sometimes extensive rewriting. As the project grew, the editorial board found it necessary to expand the number of commissioned articles to adequately meet its objective of worldwide coverage. As the complexities of the project became more apparent, and as problems of communicating with contributors in distant parts of the world became increasingly difficult, the anticipated publication date was advanced, as it would be many times over the next decade.

The project ultimately passed through two publishing houses before it came to fruition in 1998 at Oxford University Press. The project remained with Charles Scribner's Sons from 1981 to 1986, when Scribner's was sold to Macmillan Publishing Company. During this period the project passed through the hands of three managing editors: Kirk Reynolds, James F. Maurer, and Michael McGinley. In 1985, Marshall de Breuhl resigned his post as head of the Reference Department at Scribner's. A physical move of the Scribner's offices to the Macmillan building resulted in the loss of manuscripts and important mail concerning the project. These changes, together with other problems, did not bode well for the encyclopedia.

Differences intensified between the *IED* editorial board and the editors at Scribner's, who apparently lacked the necessary background in dance to give the project proper direction. The publisher became increasingly discontented, citing problems relating to progress with copyediting and costly rewriting, disagreement over editing responsibilities, an expanding list of manuscript commissions, and delays in the delivery of the final manuscript. On its side, the editorial board found unsatisfactory Scribner's administration of the project, editing, and the failure to provide constructive feedback as to the publisher's expectations. By the end of the year, the editorial board had expressed serious doubts about remaining with Scribner's. When negotiations failed to resolve the difficulties, Allan Wittman, a senior vice-president of Macmillan Publishing Company, notified the Foundation in March 1987 that the agreement to publish the encyclopedia was terminated.

Although disappointed, the Dance Perspectives Foundation and the *IED* editorial board were determined to find another publisher and to complete the project. Various options were explored, including the possibility of turning over the project to the Society of Dance History Scholars for completion. This was a low point for the project. Tensions between the Foundation board and the *IED* editorial board emerged; fundraising and editorial progress were at issue. Editors and contributors alike began to feel that the project might never be completed, and their interest languished.

Hope was restored in 1988 when the University of California Press agreed to publish the encyclopedia. Alain Hénon, senior vice-president, and Doris Kretchmer, project manager, were responsible for overseeing the project at the press. Jane-Ellen Long was named managing editor, and was subsequently replaced by Sandria Freitag. The terms of the contract with the University of California Press provided for additional compensation for the *IED* editorial board as well as funds to pay for illustrations, indexing, and all other anticipated costs. Joint funding efforts of the Foundation and the press produced additional revenues for the project. Based upon the prior years' experience, the agreement clearly delineated the respective duties of the Foundation and the press with respect to future costs for illustrations, editing, and other administrative details that had plagued the previous publishing agreement with Scribner's and Macmillan.

The manuscript moved toward completion at the University of California Press, and additional funding was provided to the *IED* editors from the press and the Foundation. These advancements were nevertheless accompanied by continuing problems centering on communication between the *IED* editorial board and copyeditors at the University of California Press over substantive questions, matters of usage, copyeditorial style, timely return of copyedited manuscripts, and other issues. These matters, exacerbated by the familiar, basic problem of copyeditors' lack of knowledge of dance history and coupled with other, serious problems with the selection and sizing of illustrations, securing permission for use, and writing appropriate captions further delayed production. In July 1991, the project again came to a halt, as communications had further deteriorated, and it was apparent to the University of California Press administration that continuation would require additional funding on the part of the press. An agreement was reached between the Foundation, the editorial board, and the press to continue the project. The project remained with the University of California Press until budget cuts by the state reduced funds for the university system and forced the press to abandon the project in August 1993.

Upon termination of the publishing agreement with the University of California Press, Selma Jeanne Cohen contacted Claude Conyers, an editor knowledgeable in dance who had become editorial director of the Scholarly and Professional Reference Department at Oxford University Press. Encouraged by his interest, the Foundation entered into formal negotiations with him, and an agreement between the Foundation and Oxford was signed in April 1994. Elizabeth Aldrich, a respected dance historian, was named managing editor. Three distinguished dance historians—Elizabeth Souritz, in Russia; Horst Koegler, in Germany, and Richard Ralph, in England—and Thomas F. Kelly, a noted music historian in the United States, were formally engaged as editorial consultants to the project, and a large international group of scholars was enlisted in an advisory capacity.

The agreement between the Foundation and Oxford called for additional subventions for the *IED* editorial board and provided for all costs of continuing and completing the project to be covered by Oxford, with only a modest sum to be charged against the Foundation's royalties. While at Oxford, the project was substantially revised and expanded: virtually all manuscripts were retyped to restore articles to their original state; articles were then copyedited in accordance with a well-developed, rigorous style scheme and returned to contributors for review, approval, and updating; bibliographies were reconstructed and updated; an entirely new illustrations program of more than two thousand illustrations was created; and approximately three hundred new articles were commissioned to fill gaps in the initial program. The result was the expansion of the encyclopedia from four volumes of moderate size to six large volumes in oversize format.

ACKNOWLEDGMENTS

An undertaking of the magnitude of the *International Encyclopedia of Dance* is the result of years of work by many people. First among these is the founding editor in chief, Selma Jeanne Cohen, whose pioneering vision and initiative on behalf of dance scholarship launched the encyclopedia. On behalf of the board of directors of the Dance Perspectives Foundation, I would like to express particular gratitude to Selma Jeanne Cohen for her steadfast determination to ensure excellence for dance regardless of obstacles, and to the other area editors, George Dorris, Nancy Goldner, Beate Gordon, Nancy Reynolds, David Vaughan, and Suzanne Youngerman, for their scholarly efforts and perserverance, and to Brian Rushton, who served briefly as managing editor in 1986. The members of the editorial board frequently provided expertise in publishing, fundraising, and other matters well beyond their editorial duties. They leaped into the project, learning over the years the demands of time and the financial resources required to produce an encyclopedia of the scope envisioned. The emerging state of scholarship twenty years ago when the project began, and the lack of experience of writers and publishers alike with the demand of melding so many aspects of dance from so many cultures, as well as limited funding, undoubtedly contributed to the arduousness of completing the project. The process has been a laborious, sometimes infelicitous process for all who were involved. Nevertheless, through such efforts, the field of dance as an area of knowledge has been substantially advanced.

Without the willingness of the three publishers to chance their fortunes on an uncharted field whose scholars were still finding their way, this project could not have proceeded. For their courage and support of the developing field of dance scholarship, Charles Scribner's Sons, the University of California Press, and Oxford University Press deserve high praise. Thanks are due to Charles Scribner, Jr., Marshall de Breuhl, James Mauer, Michael McGinley, and Kirk Reynolds at Scribner's and to Alain Hénon, Doris Kretschmer, Jane-Ellen Long, and Sandria Frietag at the University of California Press for the various roles they played in moving the project forward. But of course the highest honor accorded to the publishers is reserved for Claude Conyers, Elizabeth Aldrich, and the project staff at Oxford University Press, who, building upon the considerable achievements of the editorial board and the authors, have succeeded admirably in bringing to fruition a most challenging project. Their commitment to the project and their professionalism based on Oxford's long tradition of excellence in publishing have brought to the encyclopedia the highest standards for the production of scholarly reference works. Given their efforts, I am confident that the encyclopedia accurately represents the state of dance scholarship as an evolving field and that it provides a framework into which future disclosures of knowledge concerning dance can easily be incorporated.

The participation of the National Endowment of the Humanities as the major funding source, apart from the publishers, represents an enlightened gesture toward the advancement of knowledge. Surely without this funding for the research and editing, the project would never have attracted the interest of publishers or of other major contributors. The grants and gifts of Mr. Frank Tick, The Ford Foundation, The L. J. and Mary C. Skaggs Foundation, Philip Morris Companies, Inc., and The Rockefeller Foundation were instrumental in keeping the project moving forward. Additional generous grants were received from Capezio/Ballet Makers Dance Foundation Inc., The Capezio Foundation, The Harry De Jur Foundation, The Howard Gilman Foundation, International Research and Exchanges Board, The Jerome Robbins Foundation, and The Roth Family Foundation. Other corporate donors were the Associates of the University of California Press, The Schwarz School of Dance, and Zivili: Dances and Music of the Southern Slavic Nations. Individual donors included Lynn Price Ager, Allen Albert, Robyn A. Bissell, Helene Breazeale, Mary Alice Brennan, Elizabeth Burtner, Curtis L. Carter, Judith Chazin-Bennahum, Lila Cheville, Andrew Crystal, Janice E. Day, Timothy J. Debaets, Jerry C. Duke, Judy Dworin, Patricia Egan, Vera L. Embree, Lynne Emery, F. Mary Fee, Mary J. Freshley, Leslie Getz, Janet Goodridge, Olive Holmes, Dawn Lille Horwitz, Judith Brin Ingber, Charlotte Irey, Nancy Celeste Nix Jones, Elizabeth Kagan, Ruth C. Lert, Greta A. Levart, Gertrude Lippincott, Valentina Litvinoff, Billie Mahoney, Mary Ann O'Brian Malkin, P. W. Manchester, Richard Marcuse, Kennetha R. McArthur, Katia McClain, Raphael F. Miller, Ruth L. Murray, Shirley C. Murray, Nadia Nahumck, Patricia Nanon, Anna Nassif, Karen Nelson, Martha Nishitani, Constance Old, Helen Priest Rogers, Bernice M. Rosen, Patricia Sandback, Luise E. Scripps, Sylvia J. Shaw, Barbara B. Smith, Estelle Sommers, Manon Souriau, Leslie Steinau, Ernestine Stodelle, Rose L. Strasser, Gloria Strauss, Lawrence Sullivan, Rouben Ter-Arutunian, Carol Téten, Rose

Anne Thom, Anne Tolbert, Muriel Topaz, Alice E. Trexler, Maria Butler Troiano, Margery J. Turner, Catherine Turocy, Judy Van Zile, Bessie Schönberg Varley, Lucy Venable, Patricia Welling, Shirley Wimmer, and Carl Wolz. To all of the foregoing, we extend our thanks.

The role of the Dance Perspectives Foundation officers and board of directors has been to oversee the legal and fiscal aspects of the arrangement with the publishers, to encourage and monitor editorial progress, and to assist with raising funds from foundations, corporations, and individual contributors. At the beginning of the project in 1981, the officers of the Dance Perspectives Foundation were Timothy DeBaets, president, Curtis L. Carter, vice-president, and Selma Jeanne Cohen, secretary. Beginning with the presidency of Timothy DeBaets (1980–1984), the board has actively guided the project. Robin Woodard, president (1985–1987), was particularly instrumental in seeking corporate funding and in steering the project carefully through troubled waters at the end of the Foundation's agreement with Scribner's. Curtis L. Carter, president (1988 to the present), led the negotiations leading to publishing agreements first with with the University of California Press and subsequently with Oxford University Press. Through the years, numerous Dance Perspective Foundation board members have contributed to the completion of the encyclopedia. I would like to thank our present board members, Madeleine M. Nichols, vice-president; Hugh Timothy Dugan, treasurer; Patricia Egan; Jonnie Greene; Donald F. McDonagh; and Nancy Walters-Yvertes, along with our predecessors Allan Alberts, Reynaldo Gamboa Alejandro, Mary Bueno, Constance Old, Barbara Palfy, Audrey Ross, Brian Rushton, Fredrika Santos, and Violette Verdy, now honorary director, for their efforts.

—CURTIS L. CARTER
President,
Dance Perspectives Foundation, Inc.

PREFACE

───────────── ⌘ ─────────────

IN A WORLD THAT IS BECOMING INCREASINGLY AWARE OF THE IMPORTANCE OF intercultural understanding, dance has begun to play a role of growing significance. After all, one does not need to learn an entirely new language, full of strange words and complicated grammar, to comprehend the message conveyed by the moving body. True, the message may involve some ideas that seem rather bizarre at first, but the familiarity of the figure signifying them encourages the viewer to try to understand. More and more these days, we are recognizing how important that intercultural understanding can be. Dance has been waiting for this and is ready to serve the cause.

Just a few decades ago it would have been quite inconceivable that a major publisher would consider undertaking a six-volume, international dance encyclopedia. A few American universities might have been willing to buy it, but most of them would have thought twice. After all, apart from a few classes in dancing—discreetly absorbed in departments of physical education—there were no courses here in the history or theory of dance. Other countries did not fare much better, although some state-supported ballet schools, especially in Russia, did offer future performers a chance to learn something about the sources and importance of their art. But interest in the academic aspects of dance was severely limited.

Of course, there were some sporadic attempts, most of them by scattered individuals who became obsessed with an unanswered question about the structure of a seventeenth-century masterpiece or the tours of a nineteenth-century ballerina. Or, traveling to an exotic land, they became fascinated by the survival of an ancient ritual and were induced to learn more. As an occasional book was published, a fascinated reader wrote to the author; correspondence led to meetings and encouragement to go on. In time, a few universities decided to give dance a chance in academia, so an occasional survey course began to appear, stimulating independent research that led to articles in journals such as *Dance Index* and *Dance Perspectives,* and then to books. Eager students were turning into authors and teachers.

At the middle of this century, progress was sporadic, since there were no programs leading to academic degrees in dance history or theory. Individuals, unwilling to settle for other careers, obstinately pursued their goals in their own ways. Eventually, they found one another. In my case, it was meetings with Lillian Moore in New York, then with Ivor Guest in London and Vera Krasovskaya in Leningrad. There were visits to the New York Public Library's Dance Collection, then a small room at one end of the Music Division, but presided over by the energetic Genevieve Oswald, who led me to some fascinating treasures. Then those involved in related fields—in anthropology, visual arts, music, theater, philosophy, and cultural studies—came to recognize the appeal of dance and launched on research, bringing with them the relevant skills and methodologies of their original disciplines. Conferences and journals in their respective areas began to find time and space for dance. In 1965 the Congress on Research in Dance was founded, and in 1978 the Society of Dance History Scholars. Their memberships grew slowly but steadily.

As the word spread, colleges and universities began to add specialized courses for students who wanted to go beyond the general survey; more well-researched publications appeared. Then one day, at a meeting of dance writers, Arlene Croce, editor of *Ballet Review,* remarked that what dance really needed was a thorough, scholarly encyclopedia. And—horrors—everyone in the room looked at me.

BACKGROUND

The National Foundation for the Humanities provided a grant for a plannning conference and later funded the initial work that established the plan of our volumes. Most important, we felt, was comprehensive coverage. We already had dance dictionaries that provided useful, but brief, articles concentrating on individual persons, companies, and choreographed works. What we found lacking were thoughtful, analytic discussions. We began with what we considered the core of the work: extensive historical surveys of the evolution of all kinds of dance in countries throughout the world. Of course we wanted to tell what had happened and who made it happen. But we also wanted to tell how and why dance had assumed such different forms, different values, related to the various cultures in which it evolved. We also felt it important to cover all types of dance, a form of human movement that can serve any one of three functions: people may dance for the gods (ritual), for one another (social), for an audience (theatrical). Different countries have realized these functions in different ways at different times, and we wanted to describe the diversity as thoroughly as possible.

This much decided, we then had to locate those authors throughout the world who were best qualified to write about the history of dance in their respective countries. Ideally, we had hoped to find a single author for each country article. But this was hardly ever possible, since the recognized expert in ballet was most likely to know little about ceremonial or folk dance. Most of the time, we had to choose multiple authors. In some cases, unfortunately, even after industrious searching, we could not locate anyone with sufficient knowledge of a certain style or genre that we knew to be important in a particular country. Then the subject had to be omitted. Our one consolation here is knowing that other encyclopedias have encountered similar problems. Now we hope that there will be readers who, spotting the lacunae, will undertake the research needed to correct them.

In addition to the historical surveys, we wanted to focus on analytical essays. Thorough descriptions of various dance techniques were obviously essential. We were also concerned with the development of music for dance, of costume and scenic design used for dance, of dance films and dance writing. In addition, we planned to cover theories of aesthetics and methodologies that have been applied to dance. For these diverse subjects we had to find not only dance critics and historians but also anthropologists, art historians, musicologists, and philosophers. To cover recent developments we also needed experts in gender and culture studies, as well as the full range of performance arts. To our delight, we found that many people in related fields were already interested in dance and could shed fresh light on our subjects.

In addition to these very broad surveys, we also planned a limited number of specific pieces. The reader will find articles on major personalities, companies, and dance works of influential significance. In each case, again, we asked the authors to look not only at the what but at the how and the why of the enduring importance of the contribution.

Because we are not only living in a multicultural world but learning from the differences we find around us, the encyclopedia has been designed to tell us about the many forms of body movement that are called dance. Learning why different people move in different ways can help us to understand one another. While our body movements show that we have different ideas, different tastes, they also show that we still share many concerns and many values. In this way, dance can serve the development of a truly intercultural world.

ACKNOWLEDGMENTS

I would like to give special credit to Manfred Linke, who organized the first international meeting of workers in our discipline: "Beyond Performance: Dance Scholarship Today" in Essen, Germany, in 1988. Because of him, many of us have been working with friends, not just names on pieces of paper. In addition, I extend my thanks to Erik Aschengreen, Gedeon P. Dienes, Janina Pudełek, Jacqueline Robinson, Elizabeth Souritz, and Anna Greta Ståhle.

I want especially to thank the six area editors, who each contributed special expertise to the realization of the project. Without them, it could never have happened. Each of them also has helpers to thank:

George Dorris acknowledges, with thanks, the helpful advice of Régine Astier, Ingrid Brainard, Marie-Françoise Christout, Noël Goodwin, and Julia Sutton.

Nancy Goldner wishes to thank George Jackson and Gunhild Oberzaucher-Schüller.

Beate Gordon expresses her gratitude to Ritha Devi, Indrani, Samuel L. Leiter, and Benito Ortolani.

Nancy Reynolds extends her thanks to Robert Bianchi, Ingrid Brainard, Lloyd Burlingame, Philip Dyer, Richard Glasstone, Sandra Noll Hammond, Anne Kilmer, Cynthia McCabe, Malcolm McCormick, Libby Smigel, Roy Strong, and Dianne Woodruff.

David Vaughan is grateful for the help of Peter Brinson, Angela Kane, Michelle Potter, Jane Pritchard, Richard Ralph, and Peter Williams.

Suzanne Youngerman wishes to acknowledge the help and advice of Najwa Adra, Richard Crum, Steven Feld, Ann Hutchinson Guest, Judith Lynne Hanna, Adrienne L. Kaeppler, Joann W. Kealiinohomoku, Samuel L. Leiter, William C. Reynolds, and Stephen A. Wilde.

—SELMA JEANNE COHEN
Founding Editor

INTRODUCTION

IN NOVEMBER 1993, BARBARA PALFY AND I WERE INVITED TO SURVEY THE CONTENTS of some twenty-five cartons of materials related to the *International Encyclopedia of Dance* that had been transferred to the Scholarly and Professional Reference Department at Oxford University Press. We were charged with analyzing a substantial sample of the materials to determine the editorial and physical state of the manuscripts and with preparing a general report of the status of the project so that the Oxford staff could consider it for publication. Our task was essentially to provide information that would allow the Oxford staff to judge the worth of the project, to estimate the time, money, and editorial effort required to complete it, and to decide whether to add it to their reference publishing program. After we had reviewed the contents of nearly four hundred article files, we were dismayed to discover that considerable effort would be required to make the manuscripts ready for publication, but we were certain that the *International Encyclopedia of Dance* held promise of being a monumental work of dance scholarship, unparalleled in its magnitude. Although we realized that the cost of completing it would be great, we were pleased to report that its potential value to the field of dance history was immeasurable.

Shortly after Oxford University Press and Dance Perspectives Foundation signed a contract to complete the work, in April 1994, I was appointed managing editor of the project and was charged with the responsibility for coordinating all editorial and administrative tasks necessary to bring it to fruition. As the remaining cardboard boxes were emptied of their contents, it became clear that a carefully constructed work plan would be necessary and that all materials would have to be handled with meticulous attention to detail. Many manuscripts, written in the early 1980s, bore the marks of several rounds of editing, copyediting, and annotation, having become, in the process, virtually illegible. Other articles had been severely abbreviated, and, frequently, a number of articles by various contributors had been "melded" into one. Throughout, bibliographic information had been truncated, and illustrations were inadequately identified.

In consultation with my new colleagues at Oxford, it was decided that the goal of our work plan would be threefold: (1) to restore the integrity of the articles as originally envisioned by the editors and as intended by the authors, (2) to update the work by amending existing materials and by adding a number of new commissions, and (3) to create a user-friendly reference work that would meet the scholarly standards of Oxford University Press. To indicate the extent of our endeavors to reach this goal, I shall here review some of the editorial policies we established, some of the editorial decisions we made, and some of the editorial practices we followed.

To meet the administrative and editorial challenges posed by the project, a course of action was eventually defined that involved the following basic tasks:

- To establish a database of records of information on each contributor, including current addresses, and on the status of each article,
- To restructure major entries by "unmelding" manuscripts into their original component parts and by retitling the components to show the systematic relationships of entries and subentries,
- To create legible manuscripts by retyping them to include authors' and area editors' alterations and to restore text to severely abbreviated articles,
- To create a new bibliographic program, to be verified by online database searches,
- To commission new articles to address gaps in coverage and areas of imbalance,
- To establish authority files for editorial style, personal names, titles of works, and names of performing groups and performance venues,
- To recopyedit every existing article and to formulate a plan for updating,
- To plan and implement a cross-referencing system,
- To build an entirely new illustration program, with appropriate captions and full credits of sources and notices of proprietary rights.

Project Database. The first requirement was to create a database of electronic records for use in project management. Using a customized version of Paradox software, we created a set of relational tables containing records of each article and each contributor in the *International Encyclopedia of Dance*. This database was essential to the day-to-day management of the project. We also created a taxonomy for systematic classification of each article in the encyclopedia and entered that information into our database. Thus, we were able to produce classified reports that allowed reexamination of the conceptual structure of the encyclopedia. Paralleling the records in our database was an extensive set of paper files, which grew to occupy an entire file room at Oxford and a couple of adjacent offices as well. By the end of the project, our database, which had been expanded to include information of all facets of the illustrations program, contained records for 2,157 entries, 650 contributors, and 2,200 illustrations.

Review and Reconstruction of Materials. After establishing a database, we set about reconstructing the entries by unmelding articles and restoring text. We found that manuscripts for some of the melded articles had been cut and pasted and then retyped or photocopied. Unmelding such material was tricky business. But it was essential, so that each article could be presented as a discrete essay, accompanied by its own bibliography and signed by its contributor's name.

The practice of melding was especially evident in entries on countries and regions, which had originally been conceived as comprising several articles written by different scholars. For example, in unmelding the entry JAPAN, we restored the integrity of five independently commissioned articles, written by five different authors. From an enormous file for an entry entitled AFRICA eventually emerged twenty-one separate entries, which appear herein at various logical points in the alphabetical order, all linked by cross-references.

Throughout the unmelding and reconstruction process, we took special care to follow the area editors' instructions and to incorporate their alterations and the contributors' amendments. To facilitate the work of our copyeditors, we restored the contributors' original texts wherever appropriate. For articles not originally written in English, we also took the opportunity to examine original texts and to verify the accuracy of as many translations as possible. At the end of this phase, more than twelve hundred manuscripts required retyping before they could be submitted to copyediting.

Bibliographic Research and Verification. We understood that it was the editors' intention that each article be accompanied by a bibliography to cite principal sources of information that support the article. However, by the time the encyclopedia arrived at Oxford, bibliographies had been reduced to brief lists of basic information: author name, title of work, and date of publication. The inclusion of other sources such as archives, films and videotapes, interviews, and unpublished materials had been discouraged. In general, the bibliographies were deemed inadequate to serve the needs of the scholarly community. With the assistance of a professional bibliographic specialist, we created a new bibliographic program, built on the foundation of the contributors' original bibliographies. We established a stylistically consistent format that would accommodate citation of publications in either list or expository form as well as permitting notation of other sources of research materials.

All bibliographies were entered into electronic files to facilitate checking against online databases of the holdings of various libraries in the United States and other countries. This not only allowed us to verify existing data but also provided opportunity to supply missing information (e.g., subtitles, editors' or translators' names, series titles, language of publication, place of publication, page numbers) and to suggest citations of pertinent works that had been overlooked or that had been recently published. For the bibliographies of articles written by deceased or unlocatable contributors, we took particular care to make judicious additions of recently published works. For bibliographies of articles written by non-English speakers, we tried to suggest the addition of available and appropriate English-language sources.

It should be noted that we discouraged bibliographic citations of articles in major encyclopedias and dictionaries such as *Die Musik in Geschichte und Gegenwart*, 16 volumes (Kassel, 1949–1979), *Enciclopedia dello spettacolo,* 12 volumes (Rome, 1954–1968), *The New Grove Dictionary of Music and Musicians,* 20 volumes (London, 1980), *Kodansha Encyclopedia of Japan,* 9 volumes (Tokyo, 1983), *International Dictionary of Ballet,* 2 volumes (Detroit, 1993), and *Russkii balet entsiklopediya* (Moscow, 1997). Interested readers can readily find these valuable works on the shelves of university and large public libraries. Additionally, we made no attempt to provide inclusive lists of available videotapes. For current listings of available videotapes, the reader is urged to consult listings in current issues of dance periodicals and commercial catalogs published in various countries as well as listings that may be found at numerous and various sites on the World Wide Web.

New Commissions. We generally understood the conceptual framework of the *International Encyclopedia of Dance* to be based upon the country entries, with topical essays to complement them, support them, and provide detailed information on particular dance types, performing groups, and important theatrical works. In their original plans, the editors believed that they had achieved a justifiable balance in their choice of subjects and in overall coverage. Nevertheless, it was recognized that many advances in dance history had taken place since the conceptual structure of the encyclopedia had been developed. It was plain to all concerned that we were faced with a body of dated material, for the articles had been planned, commissioned, and written some twelve to fifteen years earlier. Articles on some topics that the editors had wanted to include had been impossible to commission because knowledgeable scholars were not then available.

In planning a program for commissioning new articles, we understood that it was not the intent of the Dance Perspectives Foundation to address every anticipated gap in coverage. However, many aspects of the field had changed during the dozen or so years the *International Encyclopedia of Dance* had passed from publisher to publisher. Because constraints of time and money required that supplementing the contents of the work be kept within the bounds of reason—that is, within the bounds of our schedule and our budget—we decided to focus our commissioning efforts on four main objectives: (1) to address new areas of research; (2) to add entries on choreographers and company directors who had recently achieved prominence; (3) to enhance coverage of popular culture; and (4) to augment coverage on non-Western dance traditions, especially those of sub-Saharan Africa, South Asia, and East Asia. Suggestions for new commissions came principally from the area editors and from advisers and contributors; other suggestions were offered by managing directors of Oxford University Press offices around the world and by members of editorial and marketing staffs at Oxford's New York office.

In considering possibilities for new commissions, we and the area editors remained highly selective in choosing subjects for new biographies. The editors were quite clear in explaining that they never intended the encyclopedia to be a biographical dictionary, including entries on thousands of performers in the history of dance. The subjects of biographies had been chosen because they had significantly affected the course of dance history, in some way, in the country of their career or because they had become a cultural icon. Choices of all new biographees were made on these criteria. Thus, biographical entries on contemporary performers, however brilliant and however famous, are few indeed; most must await the judgment of history upon the completion of their performing careers.

As a result of the collective effort of all concerned, we eventually commissioned more than three hundred new articles, each of which was routed to an area editor for review and approval upon receipt. We trust that these additions serve to extend, expand, and update the original concept of the *International Encyclopedia of Dance*. We recognize, however, that even in a work of such broad scope as this, it is not possible to cover every aspect of the vast world of dance, nor is it possible to please every reader. Realizing that other editors and scholars would have made different choices, we hope that part of the legacy of this work will be to encourage future generations of scholars to pursue research on topics and figures not included herein.

Editorial Style. Early on, we set out to create a manual of editorial style that would be appropriate to an international dance encyclopedia, intended to be user-friendly to readers of English all over the world. This task included writing a set of guidelines for basic copyeditorial style and compiling extensive authority files for technical terms and special usage, personal names, titles of works, and names of performing groups and performance venues. These guidelines and authority files proved to be indispensible tools in establishing consistency of editorial format and style throughout the encyclopedia.

In our Guidelines to Editorial Style, for example, we created standard formats for presentation of data in the opening lines of articles on persons and on theatrical dance works; we made note of special points of grammar and rhetoric; and we set forth basic principles of capitalization, punctuation, italicization, and other such minutiae of editorial style. We also addressed more general editorial issues, providing guidelines on standard ways of naming musical compositions, on conventions for presenting data in run of text, on preferred ways of treating quotations from published works, and on use of different systems of measurement and different systems of dating.

Measurement and dating. Measurements, for instance, are generally given in imperial units (e.g., feet, miles), which are followed by metric equivalents in parentheses. Dates are given according to the Gregorian calendar widely used in the West, with appropriate indications for "of the common era" (CE) and "before the common era" (BCE). In the context of Russian history, when dates are given according to the Julian calendar ("old style"), equivalent dates according to the Gregorian calendar ("new style") are given in square brackets immediately following (e.g., 3 [15] September 1897; 27 June [10 July] 1904).

Technical terms. In creating an Authority List of Technical Terms and Special Usage, we generated a lengthy list of words, phrases, and names of dance types, dance steps, venues, and organizations likely to be found within the entries. This authority list, which was fully glossed with helpful definitions, indicated appropriate spelling, diacritical markings, plural forms, capitalization, and italicization for more than fifteen hundred words, phrases, and names—from *aak* to the Black Bottom to *pas de bourrée* to the Queen of the Dryads to *seguidillas* to Zurich.

Personal names. Wishing to identify people by their professional names and in the spellings most commonly encountered in scholarly writing in English, we created an Authority List of Personal Names consisting of more than 3,500 entries. This list, of course, does not include the name of every person mentioned in the encyclopedia, only those encountered with some frequency. We paid particular attention to names transliterated from languages not written in the Latin alphabet, such as Chinese and Russian, and to names in languages normally bearing numerous diacritics, such as Polish and Czech.

Except for names in Russian and other Slavic languages, which have been variously romanized, altered, and simplified in the twentieth-century diaspora of Slavic peoples, we have preferred to romanize names according to accepted scholarly principles, including full use of diacritics in such languages as Arabic and Sanskrit. For Slavic names, we have tried to use the forms and spellings by which their bearers are generally known in the West (e.g., Vaslav Nijinsky, not Vatslav Nizhinskii; Léonide Massine, not Leonid Miasin). For persons who are subjects of biographical entries, we have given their full names, when known, in correct transliterations, where appropriate, in parentheses following the headword of each entry.

Theatrical works. To systematize the titles of theatrical works, we created an Authority List of Theatrical Works that contains a thousand titles of works frequently mentioned in the encyclopedia. Works commonly known by titles in French (e.g., *La Fille Mal Gardée, Médée et Jason, Les Sylphides, La Boutique Fantasque*) or other European languages (e.g., *El Amor Brujo, Le Nozze degli Dei, Das Lied von der Erde*) have generally been named in those languages. The titles of classic ballets known in many languages (e.g., *Lebedinoe Ozero, Le Lac de Cygnes, Schwanensee, Swan Lake*) have usually been given in English. When faced with alternatives, English has been our language of first choice, although we have tried to give alternative titles wherever appropriate. For example, titles of most ballets by August Bournonville appear in English throughout the encyclopedia except in the article on Bournonville himself, where Danish titles are also given at the first mention. Conversely, English translations of titles cited in other languages are frequently given in parentheses following first mention (e.g., *Takahime* (The Hawk Princess); *Die Puppenfee* (The Fairy Doll); *El Niño Brujo* (The Witch Boy)).

Performing groups. Our Authority List of Names of Performing Groups includes some four hundred entries of names of companies frequently mentioned. This list was invaluable to copyeditors in sorting out the variety of names used by the many companies in Western dance history that were billed as Ballets Russes, Le Grand Ballet, National Ballet, Ballet International, and International Ballet.

Translation, Transliteration, and Romanization. With many non-English-speaking contributors, this encyclopedia has presented numerous problems of translation ever since its earliest years of creation. Many of the articles submitted in languages other than English were originally translated by a professional service bureau unfamiliar with dance terminology. A number of other articles had been written in English by contributors who knew it only imperfectly, as a second or third language, but who valiantly tried to accommodate requests to submit materials in English. Over the years of copyediting, the original ideas of these authors had sometimes been lost. When we found in the files an article manuscript in the original language of submission, we reviewed and, if necessary, corrected the translation. Throughout the encyclopedia, notations of translation from another language are given in minuscule type following the contributor's name.

Special problems arose from a number of articles written by some fifty authors in the states of the former Soviet Union. Most of these articles had been originally commissioned, translated from Russian and other languages, and edited by Vsesoyuznoye Agentstvo po Avtorskim Pravam (VAAP), the central Soviet copyright agency. Except for a handful of addresses, we had no information on the contributors of these articles, rendering it impossible to request updates. As an additional challenge, many of the articles, especially articles on traditional and folk dance for the various countries, had been written from a conspicuously Soviet point of view. We were fortunate to be able to recommission some of these articles and, for others, to find scholars with knowledge of the languages involved and with access to relevant literature who were willing to review, emend, and update them for us. Throughout the encyclopedia, acknowledgments of persons who amended an article or who assisted in research, writing, or updating are given in minuscule type following the contributor's name.

Given the international scope of the encyclopedia, we knew from the beginning that we would be dealing with many of the world's languages. To my great relief, I learned that the staff of the Scholarly and Professional Reference Department at Oxford is accustomed to solving linguistic problems as a matter of daily routine. My colleagues willingly nominated linguists from whom we sought assistance in clarifying the vocabulary of dance in numerous languages, including Arabic, Armenian, Chinese, Czech, Gaelic, Greek, Hebrew, Indonesian, Japanese, Korean, Polish, Russian, and Sanskrit. Although we strove for consistency in our systems of spelling of technical terms, it sometimes eluded us, and we have often provided variant spellings parenthetically. Moreover, we tried to remain flexible and, wherever we could do so without generating confusion, to accommodate contributors' preferences (e.g., in the orthography of Polynesian languages).

Review of Copyedited Manuscripts by Contributors. One of our major responsibilities was to recopyedit every article and to create a plan to return manuscripts for updating to all contributors for whom we had current addresses. We focused particularly on three areas for updating: biographies of living subjects, extant performing groups, and individual country entries. Virtually all copyedited manuscripts, many of them reconstructed and all of them accompanied by new, verified bibliographies, were returned to contributors with a request that they be reviewed, emended, and updated. We were hopeful that our request would be fulfilled but were fearful that it would not; after all, the contributors had been asked to update their articles several times before and many of them had expressed exasperation with what seemed to be a fruitless process. We were thus totally unprepared for the outpouring of good will toward our efforts and by the genuine desire of many contributors to update and revise their articles. Unfortunately, a few authors remained disillusioned and declined our request; others could not be located, and, regrettably, still others had died. Nevertheless, our worries about publishing outdated materials evaporated in the warmth of contributors' responses as they returned their copyedited articles approved for publication.

Our efforts in constructing bibliographies were also generally approved by contributors, most of whom updated and improved the bibliographic manuscripts submitted to them. As a result, the reader will find herein qualitatively selective bibliographies deemed, in the judgment of contributors and editors, to be the best available literature on the subject.

Illustration Program. Not long after the encyclopedia project was transferred to Oxford University Press, it became apparent that the illustration program that had been assembled was unusable: presized negatives existed but original prints had been lost; images were only sketchily identified, and records of permissions to use the materials could not be located. We had no choice but to build a new illustrations program from scratch. With professional help, we devised a work plan and established a records-management system. Through the several phases of research, review, and selection, twelve photo researchers worked to complete the program; captions were written by various members of the project staff. Sources for illustrations ranged from the encyclopedia's contributors and the archives of numerous photographers to major repositories in New York, London, Paris, Copenhagen, Stockholm, and Moscow. Additionally, special efforts were made to tap the resources of smaller archives, museums, and libraries as well as performing groups, embassies, and information services in the United States and abroad. In the end, well over two thousand images were chosen to be included in the encyclopedia. The source of each is noted in its accompanying caption, as is, where appropriate, acknowledgment of permission to reprint.

Organization and Presentation of Materials. Once we were able to unmeld materials in the files and to create discrete entries, we were able to implement Oxford University Press policies regarding the overall organization of scholarly encyclopedias. The object is to present the contents of such a work in a way useful and logical to both general readers and specialists. Accordingly, entries in the *International Encyclopedia of Dance* are alphabetically arranged, strictly letter by letter. Most articles are entered in alphabetical order under their own headings. However, in order to make use of the specialized expertise of individual scholars while ensuring that diverse aspects of broad topics are fully covered, composite entries are employed to group two or more articles under one headword. In such cases, each component article of a composite entry is preceded by its own heading, is followed by its own bibliography, and is signed by its contributor's name.

Composite entries can be subdivided in several ways. Thematic subdivision is common, as in the entry LIGHTING FOR DANCE, which comprises two articles: one providing a historical overview; the other discussing theory and practice. Geography offers another principle of subdivision, as in the entry MASK AND MAKEUP, which consists of three articles on the practices in three broad areas: Africa, Asia, and Europe. Chronology offers yet another option, as in the entry GERMANY, where two of the several component articles are entitled "Theatrical Dance, 1600–1945" and "Theatrical Dance since 1945." Each composite entry begins with a headnote that explains its organization and, where appropriate, offers a rationale for its division.

To guide readers from one article to related discussions elsewhere in the encyclopedia, we have established an extensive system of cross-references. These will be found in headnotes to composite entries, at appropriate spots within the text of articles, and at the ends of articles. Under INDIA, for example, in the article on "History of Indian Dance" cross-references to entries on pertinent topics will be found throughout the text; at the end of the article appear cross-references to entries on the principal genres of classical Indian dance. At the end of the entry BOURNONVILLE COMPOSERS, the reader is directed to a related article, "Western Music, 1800–1900," under the entry MUSIC FOR DANCE.

In addition to these forms of cross-reference, "blind entries" occur throught the alphabetical range of headwords, providing cross-references to relevant articles under headwords located elsewhere in the alphabet. For example, a reader who looks up AMERICAN INDIAN DANCE will be directed to NATIVE AMERICAN DANCE; a reader who looks up CAMPANINI, BARBARA will be directored to BARBARINA, LA; a reader who looks up LILAC GARDEN will be directed to JARDIN AUX LILAS. A reader who looks up JAVA will be directed to two entries: INDONESIA, where an article on "Javanese Dance Traditions" appears, and ASIAN DANCE TRADITIONS, which provides a general discussion. For subjects that are not headwords, readers are encouraged to consult the index as a further resource, as it contains a wealth of names, titles, and topics.

ACKNOWLEDGMENTS

The completion of this encyclopedia has been a collective endeavor of massive proportions. With the cooperation of the editors and the support of the officers of the Dance Perspectives Foundation, it has been accomplished by the extraordinary efforts of the contributors, the staff at Oxford University Press, and numerous independent scholars and professional experts in various editorial and graphic fields. My gratitude to all these persons is beyond measure.

I wish particularly to thank Alison Arnold, Stephen Comee, Joan Erdman, Edward Herbst, Alan C. Heyman, Sunil Kothari, Paula Lawrence, Samuel E. Leiter, Ou Jian-ping, Jonah Salz, and Bonnie Sue Stein for editorial input on the East Asian, Indonesian, and South Asian articles. A special note of appreciation must also be extended to James Waller and Constantina Rhodes Bailly for their fine editing and copyediting of these materials. All the new commissions in these areas were undertaken under the guidance of area editor Beate Gordon, who also reviewed the illustrations and captions for all Asian articles. Our debt to her is immense.

I also wish to thank Elizabeth Souritz for updating many of the Russian articles, for resolving a number of puzzles and mysteries along the way, and for her continued support of this project. Grateful mention must also be made of Barbara Palfy, who not only copyedited all the Russian materials and assisted in gathering illustrations for the Russian entries but who, early on, recommended me as her partner in assessing the project materials for Oxford and who subsequently served us faithfully as special editorial consultant, answering myriad questions of both style and substance.

Of many other colleagues who offered assistance on editorial matters, I wish to thank María Susana Azzi for her aid on Argentina, Valda L. Craig and Michele Potter for their contributions of a variety of Australian articles, Luz Marmentini and Sara Vial for assistance on Chile, Susan Homer for advice on the Caribbean region, Margareta Barbutza for the Romanian articles, and Alan Stark for Spanish translations. Other contributors who graciously assisted include Ingrid Brainard, Jerry Duke, Rusty E. Frank, Laurel Victoria Gray, Camille Hardy, Angela Kane, Frances MacEachen, T. Davina McClain, Xenia Rakič, Libby Smigel, Sally R. Sommer, and Anna Greta Ståhl. William C. Reynolds reviewed all the folk and traditional dance entries and assisted in obtaining new commissions. Area editor George Dorris cheerfully offered advice and expertise on a number of entries, and, for a few happy weeks before her final illness, Anita Finkel joined us at Oxford and made a substantial editorial contribution.

What began as an illustrations program with a goal of one thousand illustrations rapidly grew into a program that exceeded two thousand. Cynthia R. Millman set up our first administrative system and sent photo researchers into the field. Oxford staff member Naomi Weinstein continued to develop the program, and Jody Sperling concluded the editing and administrative work and wrote many of the captions. They and, indeed, the entire project staff at Oxford owe a debt of gratitude to the staff of the Dance Collection of the New York Public Library for the Performing Arts. For good advice and steady support, we thank Genevieve Oswald and Madeleine Nichols, past and present curators of the collection. For cheerful assistance in locating, assembling, and filing visual materials, we are grateful to Derrick Damon, Irina Klyagin, Dorothy Lourdou, Lacy McDearmon, Monica Moseley, Karen Nickeson, Grace Owen, Else Peck, Charles Perrier, Patricia Rader, Danielle Rogers, Alice Standin, and Rita Waldron. For her splendid photographs of materials in the Dance Collection, we are deeply grateful to Julia Smith.

In addition, we must express our appreciation to many other people who graciously assisted us, in various ways, in assembling the illustrations program: Reynaldo Gamboa Alejandro; David Amzallag; Catherine Ashmore at Dominic Photography, London; Aziz Bassier at the Argus Library, Cape Town; Erik Berg; Ludmilla Chiriaeff; Jed Downhill; Johan Elbers; Mrs. Fred Fehl; Celia Franca; Hannie Gillman and Carol Grenke at the Max Waldman Archive, New York; Jane Jackson and Amanda Jones at the Royal Opera House, London; Lisa Kirchner; Winnie Lee at The Asia Society, New York; Lloyd Morgan at the Barbara Morgan Archive, Hastings-on-Hudson, New York; Norton Owen at Jacob's Pillow, Becket, Massachusetts; Louise Pederson at the Archives and Library of the Royal Theater, Copenhagen; Jane Pritchard at the Rambert Dance Company and English National Ballet, Markova House, London; Jerome Robbins; Beatriz Schiller; LaDena Schnapper at the Center for Ethiopian Arts and Culture, Washington, D.C.; Sally R. Sommer and William G. Sommer; Madison U. Sowell and Debra H. Sowell; Penny Swain; Martha Swope; Hugh Tracey; and Randi Urdal. A special note of thanks must be added to Jack Vartoogian and Linda Vartoogian, whose generosity in allowing us access to their collections of splendid photographs was indeed unbounded. Finally, on behalf of the entire staff at Oxford University Presss, I gratefully acknowledge all contributors who provided photographs for their articles and, in many cases, for other entries as well.

Swelling our litany of thanks, Claude Conyers wishes me to express his appreciation for the support of his colleagues in offices of Oxford University Press around the world as well as his gratitude for favors done by friends in the world of dance. Among the former are Bruce Phillips (OUP UK & Europe), Susan Froud and Katherine Barber (OUP Canada), Kate McCallum (OUP Southern Africa), Ameena Saiyid (OUP Pakistan), Manzur Khan (OUP India), Marek Palka (OUP Australia & New Zealand), and Steve Zilkowski (OUP Japan). Among the latter are Cristian Addams in England; Judith Karstens and Sofia Karstens in the United States; Linda Stearns and Vincent Warren in Canada; Heinz Spoerli in Switzerland; Wayne McKnight in Norway; Jorge Salavisa in Portugal; Andris Toppe and Shane Hewitt in Australia; Dawn Weller and Veronica Paeper in South Africa; and Jayne Torvill and Christopher Dean in England.

For myself, I must acknowledge that my work on this project has been a richly rewarding experience, for I was blessed with a talented, devoted staff and with wonderfully supportive colleagues at Oxford University Press. I wish to thank especially Christopher Caines, Jody Sperling, and Naomi Weinstein for their assistance with the illustrations program and the encyclopedia's daily administrative demands. Additionally, I would have floundered under the burden of masses of apparently insoluble editorial problems had not Jeffrey Edelstein, Martha Goldstein, and Marion Osmun gently intervened with excellent advice and good humor. I owe a profound debt of thanks to them all, as I do to Joan Greenfield, graphic designer and art director for the project, who skillfully resolved hundreds of problems of page layout and who served as our principal morale booster when our spirits flagged. I also wish to express gratitude to Cynthia Crippen, our indefatigable indexer, for her active help in routing out inconsistencies in page proofs, and to Jean Walker, customer service representative at the Clarinda Company, for her patience and cheerful assistance in solving numerous problems in typesetting and page makeup. In addition to the help of all these good people, I must not fail to acknowledge the support of the staff members of the Scholarly and Professional Reference Department at Oxford and to thank them for their understanding and forbearance when the frantic activity on this encyclopedia threatened to overwhelm other projects in progress.

It remains only to thank Claude Conyers, editorial director of the department, who proved to be a generous and supportive mentor. He spent countless hours serving the encyclopedia as contributor, manuscript editor, researcher, photo editor, caption writer, and adviser and friend to the entire staff, never wavering in his conviction that this project would result in a work of superlative scholarship. I extend my sincere gratitude and affection in appreciation of his knowledge, wisdom, and generosity.

ENVOI

Lamenting the lack of an inclusive reference work on dance, Agnes de Mille once noted, "Nothing is comprehensive, nothing catholic, nothing sweeping, and this we must have." Now, four years after the *International Encyclopedia of Dance* came to rest at Oxford University Press, and following a long and troubled history that spanned more than twenty years, we have that work. And while professional standards and achievements in research and writing about dance have advanced and will continue to grow in the coming years, this work must be recognized as a milestone in dance history, a permanent marker of an emerging field and a monument to the extraordinary achievement of all who took part in its creation.

—ELIZABETH ALDRICH
Managing Editor

DIRECTORY OF CONTRIBUTORS

Joan Acocella
Dance critic, New York
L'Après-midi d'un Faune • Alexandra Danilova • Mark Morris • Vaslav Nijinsky • Le Sacre du Printemps • Lydia Sokolova

Katherine M. Adelman
Whereabouts unknown
Cyril W. Beaumont

Reba Ann Adler
Adjunct Lecturer, Marymount Manhattan College, New York
Agon • Apollo • Ballet Imperial • Billy the Kid • Concerto Barocco • Divertimento No. 15 • William Dollar • Don Quixote, *article on* Balanchine Production • The Four Temperaments • Liebeslieder Walzer • Eugene Loring • Serenade • Symphony in C

Najwa Adra
Adjunct Assistant Professor of Anthropology, Hofstra University, Hempstead, New York
Middle East, *overview article and* Dance Research and Publication • Yemen • Zār

Boris B. Akimov
Former dancer and teacher, Moscow
Aleksei Yermolayev

Gennady G. Albert
Ballet teacher, Saint Petersburg
Aleksandr Pushkin

Evan Alderson
Associate Professor, School for the Contemporary Arts, Simon Fraser University, Burnaby, British Columbia
Canada, *article on* Dance Research and Publication

Elizabeth Aldrich
Independent scholar and film choreographer, Washington, D.C.
Révérence, *article on* Nineteenth-Century Modes

Reynaldo Gamboa Alejandro
President, Filipino American National Historical Society, New York
Bayanihan Philippine Dance Company • Philippines • Tinikling

Alisha Ali
Dance ethnologist, Los Angeles
Algeria • Morocco • North Africa • Ouled Naïl, Dances of the • Tunisia

Mindy Aloff
Dance writer, New York
Photography

Judith B. Alter
Associate Professor of Dance Education, Department of World Arts and Cultures, University of California, Los Angeles
Aerobic Dance

Saga Mirjam Vuori Ambegaokar
Choreographer and dance historian; Artistic Director, Saga Dance Company/Troika Association, Ithaca, New York
Maggie Gripenberg

M. M. Ames
Professor of Anthropology and Director, Museum of Anthropology, University of British Columbia
Tovil

Andrea Amort
Dance critic, artistic adviser, and lecturer, Vienna
Die Josephslegende • Margarete Wallmann

Metin And
Dance and theater critic (retired); member, Turkish Academy of Sciences
Turkey

Jack Anderson
Dance critic, New York Times; *coeditor,* Dance Chronicle, *New York; New York correspondent,* The Dancing Times, *London*
Ballet Russe de Monte Carlo

Janet Anderson
Writer, Claremont, California
Edgar Degas

James R. Anthony
Professor Emeritus of Musicology, University of Arizona, Tucson
Opéra-Ballet and Tragédie Lyrique

Hans-Christian Arent
Artistic consultant, Riksteateret, Oslo; Associate Editor, Store Norske Leksikon, *Oslo*
Norway, *articles on* Theatrical Dance before 1919 *and* Theatrical Dance since 1958

Alison Arnold

Instructor of piano and flute, Community Music School, Trappe, Pennsylvania; editor, Garland Encyclopedia of World Music: South Asia

Film Musicals, *article on* Bollywood Film Musicals

Arnold Aronson

Professor of Theatre Arts, Columbia University

Scenic Design

Erik Aschengreen

Professor of Dance, Københavns Universitet

Fredbøjrn Bjørnsson • Valborg Borchsenius • Erik Bruhn • Jean Cocteau • Denmark, *articles on* Theatrical Dance *and* Dance Research and Publication • Flemming Flindt • Mette Hønningen • Gerda Karstens • Niels Kehlet • Henning Kronstam • Margot Lander • Kirsten Ralov • Royal Danish Ballet • Schaufuss Family

Wayne Ashley

Adjunct faculty, Antioch University, Seattle

Teyyam

Régine Astier

Independent scholar; Director, The Beauchamps Conservatory of Baroque Dance, Santa Barbara, California

Académie Royale de Danse • Claude Ballon • Pierre Beauchamps • Michel Blondy • Marie Camargo • Dumoulin Brothers • Feuillet Notation • Michel Gaudrau • Marie-Catherine Guyot • Mademoiselle de La Fontaine • Antoine Bandieri de Laval • Anne-Louis Lestang • François Marcel • Guillaume-Louis Pecour • Françoise Prévost • Pierre Rameau • Adrien Merger de Saint-André • Marie Sallé • Marie-Thérèse Subligny

Martha Bush Ashton-Sikora

Research Associate, University of California, Berkeley

Kṛṣṇāṭṭam • Yakṣagāna

Susan Au

Dance historian, New York

Afternoon of a Faun • Monsieur Albert • Alma • Jean-Auguste Barre • Nadine Baylis • Cecil Beaton • Émile-Antoine Bourdelle • Carey Family • Caricature and Comic Art • Catarina • Fanny Cerrito • Alfred Chalon • Character Dancing • Pierre Ciceri • Jean Coralli • Dances at a Gathering • André Deshayes • Le Diable à Quatre • Le Diable Boiteux • Elssler Sisters • Fancy Free • Sophie Fedorovitch • The Firebird, *article on* Later Productions • Fitzjames Sisters • Footwear • Giselle • La Gitana • Ivor Guest • La Jolie Fille de Gand • Eugéne Louis Lami • Hippolyte Lecomte • Libretti for Dance, *article on* Nineteenth- and Twentieth-Century Libretti • Augusta Maywood • Joseph Mazilier • Mazurka • Médée et Jason • Oliver Messel • Hippolyte and Adèle Monplaisir • Ondine • Paquita • La Péri • Polonaise • Practice Clothes • Prints and Drawings • Psyché et l'Amour • The Sleeping Beauty, *article on* Later Productions • George Washington Smith • La Somnambule • La Sonnambula • La Sylphide • Tarantella • Pavel Tchelitchev • Tutu

Patricia Aulestia

Investigadora Titular B, Instituto Nacional de Bellas Artes, Centro Nacional de Investigación, Información y Documentación de la Danza José Limón, Mexico City

Mexico, *article on* Dance Research and Publication

Lubov Avdeeva

Researcher, Tashkent Institute of Arts Research, Uzbekistan

Galiya Izmailova • Tamara Khanum • Uzbekistan

Ann M. Axtmann

Adjunct Professor of Dance and Performance Studies, Gallatin School of Individualized Study, New York University

Mexico, *article on* Dance Companies

María Susana Azzi

Social anthropologist; board member, Academia Nacional del Tango, Buenos Aires

Nieves and Copes • Plebs and Zotto • Tango

Monique Babsky

Independent scholar and writer; Treasurer, Centre International de Documentation de la Danse, Paris (deceased)

Jean-Louis Aumer • Albert Aveline • Ballet-Théâtre Contemporain • Vittoria Biagi • Fanny Bias • Émilie Bigottini • Blache Family • Félix Blaska • Lycette Darsonval • Michel Descombey • France, *articles on* Theatrical Dance, 1789–1914 *and* Ballet since 1914 • Pierre Lacotte • Emma Livry • Louis Mérante • Louis Milon • Lise Noblet • Jean-Antoine Petipa • Lucien Petipa • Arthur Saint-Léon • Schwarz Family • Léo Staats • Sylvia • Ludmila Tcherina

Nancy Van Norman Baer

Curator, Theatre and Dance Collection, The Fine Arts Museums of San Francisco

Auguste Rodin • Abraham Walkowitz

Avener Bahat

Director, Feher Jewish Music Center, Beit ha-Tefutsot, Museum of the Jewish Diaspora, Tel-Aviv

Israel, *article on* Ethnic Dance

Naomi Bahat-Ratzon

Head, Dance and Movement Department, State Teachers College, Seminar ha-Kibbutzim, Tel-Aviv

Israel, *article on* Ethnic Dance

Egil Bakka

Director of Dance, Norwegian Council for Folk Music and Dance, Universitetet i Trondheim, Norway

Denmark, *article on* Dance in the Faeroe Islands

Sally Banes

Marian Hannah Winter Professor of Theatre and Dance Studies, University of Wisconsin–Madison

Avant-garde Dance • Ballets Suédois • Break Dancing • Trisha Brown • Lucinda Childs • Douglas Dunn • Simone Forti • David Gordon • Grand Union • Anna Halprin • Judson Dance Theater • Kenneth King • Steve Paxton • Yvonne Rainer • Relâche

Barbara Barker
Associate Professor of Dance, University of Minnesota, Minneapolis
Marie Bonfanti • Kiralfy Family • Giuseppina Morlacchi • Domenico Ronzani • Rita Sangalli

Patricia Barnes
Dance critic, New York and London
Royes Fernandez • Cynthia Gregory • Gelsey Kirkland • Hugh Laing • Dimitri Romanoff • Lupe Serrano

Raquel Barros Aldunate
Director, Departmento de Cultura, Santiago, Chile
Chile, *article on* Folk and Traditional Dance

Ann Barzel
Dance writer and critic, Chicago
Patricia Bowman • Mary Day • Nora Kaye • Sybil Shearer • United States of America, *article on* Ballet Education

Ana Paula Batalha
Professor, Universidade Técnica de Lisboa
Portugal, *article on* Traditional Dance

Nancy Becker Schwartz
Writer, Cleveland, Ohio
Busby Berkeley • Film and Video, *article on* Choreography for Camera

Louise Bedichek
Foreign Service Officer, United States Information Agency, New York
Les Ballets Africains • Kemoko Sano

Galina V. Belyayeva-Chelombitko
Board member, Balet, *Moscow*
Sergei Koren • Raisa Struchkova • Vladimir Vasiliev • Rostislav Zakharov

Ninotchka Bennahum
Independent scholar, New York
Flamenco Dance

Viktor I. Berezkin
Leading researcher, State Arts Research Institute, Moscow
Vladimir Dmitriev • Valery Leventhal • Petr Williams

Judith Bettelheim
Writer, Oakland, California
Jonkonnu Festival

Megan Biesele
Writer, Cambridge, Massachusetts
!Kung San Dance

Larry Billman
Vice President, Creative Entertainment, Walt Disney Attractions, Los Angeles
Cyd Charisse • Chita Rivera • Gwen Verdon

Susan F. Bindig
Independent scholar, New Hope, Pennsylvania
Gigue

Edwin Binney, 3rd
Writer, Princeton, New Jersey (deceased)
Théophile Gautier

John Blacking
(deceased)
Southern Africa • Venda Dance

Jeffrey Blanchard
Academic Coordinator, Cornell-in-Rome Program, Italy
Jacques Callot

Jan-Petter Blom
Professor of Social Anthropology, Universitetet i Bergen
Norway, *article on* Folk, Traditional, and Social Dance

Magnus Blomkvist
Professor of Historical Dance, Stockholms Universitet
Sweden, *articles on* Theatrical Dance before 1771 *and* Court Theaters

Ella V. Bocharnikova
Former dancer and teacher, Moscow
Asaf Messerer • Malika Sabirova

Chrystelle Trump Bond
Professor of Dance History and Chair, Dance Department, Goucher College, Towson, Maryland
Lillian Moore

Richard Bonynge
Conductor, Les Avants, Switzerland
Adolphe Adam

Ludmila I. Borel
Dance critic, Moscow
Viktorina Kriger

Erika Bourguignon
Professor Emerita of Anthropology, Ohio State University
Trance Dance

John E. Bowlt
Professor of Slavic Languages, University of Southern California, Los Angeles
Léon Bakst • Alexandre Benois • Eugene Berman • Mstislav Dobujinsky • Aleksandr Golovin • Natalia Goncharova • Konstantin Korovin • Mikhail Larionov • Nikolai Roerich • Serge Soudeikine

Ingrid Brainard
Independent scholar, dance historian, and musicologist; Director, The Cambridge Court Dancers, Boston
Annual Collections • Antonius de Arena • Banquet • Barriera, Torneo, and Battaglia • Bassedanse • Antonio Cornazano • Dance of Death • Dancing Master • Domenico da Piacenza •

Don Juan • Entrée • Figure Dances • Guglielmo Ebreo da Pesaro • Guild Dances • Hey • Longways • Medieval Dance • Mommerie • Moresca • Music for Dance, *article on* Western Music before 1520 • Michael Praetorius • Renaissance Dance Technique • Révérence, *article on* Origins of Modes and Manners • Sarabande • Social Dance, *article on* Court and Social Dance before 1800 • Technical Manuals, *article on* Publications, 1445–1725 • Wirtschaft

Ellen Breitman
Independent arts educator and consultant, Irvine, California
Pablo Picasso • Henri de Toulouse-Lautrec

Valerie A. Briginshaw
Independent scholar, London
Digo Dance • Giriama Dance

Peter Brinson
Consultant, Laban Centre for Movement and Dance, London (deceased)
Great Britain, *articles on* Dance Education *and* Dance Research and Publication • Royal Ballet • Mary Skeaping • Peggy van Praagh

Alan Brissenden
Honorary Visiting Research Fellow in English, University of Adelaide; dance critic, The Australian, Dance Australia
Great Britain, *article on* Theatrical Dance, 1460–1660

Lynn Matluck Brooks
Associate Professor, Department of Theatre, Dance and Film, Franklin and Marshall College, Lancaster, Pennsylvania
Christianity and Dance, *article on* Medieval Views • Spain, *article on* Dance Traditions before 1700

Virginia Loring Brooks
Professor of Film, Brooklyn College, City University of New York; independent filmmaker and videographer, New York
Film and Video, *article on* Documenting Dance

Carolyn Brown
Former principal dancer, Merce Cunningham and Dance Company; choreographer, dance writer, and lecturer, New York
Canfield • Suite for Five • Summerspace • Walkaround Time • Winterbranch

Lise Brunel
Dance writer and critic, Paris
France, *articles on* Modern Dance since 1970 *and* Contemprary Criticism

Theresa Jill Buckland
Director, Master of Arts Dance Studies, University of Surrey, Guilford, England
Great Britain, *article on* English Traditional Dance

Judy Farrar Burns
Dance historian, Brooklyn, New York
La Argentinita • José Greco • Harkness Ballet • Pilar López • La Meri • Ximénez-Vargas Ballet Español

Christopher Caines
Performer, choreographer, composer, and writer, New York
American Dance Festival • Remy Charlip • Viola Farber • Ginger Rogers

Helen Caldwell
Whereabouts unknown
Michio Ito

Henry J. Calkins
Independent scholar, Urbana, Illinois
Native American Dance, *article on* The Northwest Coast

Katia Canton
Professor of Contemporary Arts, Universidade de São Paulo; Curator of Art and Performance, Museu de Arte Contemporânea Arte da Universidade de São Paulo
Brazil, *articles on* Ballet; Modern Dance; *and* Dance Research and Publication • Samba • Nina Verchinina

Suzanne Carbonneau
Dance writer and critic, Washington, D.C.
Le Carnaval • Ivan Clustine • The Dying Swan • Michel Fokine • Theodore Koslov • Mikhail Mordkin • Le Pavillon d'Armide • Schéhérazade • Pierre Vladimiroff

John Cargher
Ballet critic (retired), The Bulletin; *Managing Director (retired), Australian National Memorial Theatre*
Australia, *article on* Ballet

Gerald L. Carr
Writer, Hudson, New York
Bibiena Family • Inigo Jones

Marta Carrasco Benítez
Independent scholar and dance historian, Seville
Spain, *article on* Dance Research and Publication

Curtis L. Carter
Professor of Aesthetics and Philosophy, Marquette University; Director and Chief Curator, Patrick and Beatrice Haggerty Museum of Art, Marquette University, Milwaukee
Aesthetics, *article on* Western Dance Aesthetics • Robert Ellis Dunn • Jan Fabre

Estrella Casero García
Director, Dance Division, Universidad de Alcalá de Henares; dance critic and historian, Madrid
Escuela Bolera

Terry Castle
Professor of English, Stanford University, California
Masquerades

Amy Catlin
Visiting Assistant Professor and Research Associate, Department of Ethnomusicology, University of California, Los Angeles
Cambodia • Laos

Claudia Celi

Professor of Dance History, Accademia Nazionale di Danza, Rome

Filippo d'Aglié • Luigi Albertieri • Caterina Beretta • Pasquale Borri • Giuseppe Canziani • Enrico Cecchetti • Francesco Clerico • Antonio Cortesi • Claudina Cucchi • Amalia Ferraris • Cia Fornaroli • Sofia Fuoco • Gaetano Gioja • Italy, *articles on* Dance Traditions before 1800 *and* Dance Research and Publication • Giovanni Lepri • Giovanni Pratesi • Giuseppe Rota • Salvatore Viganò

Ercilia Moreno Chá

Ethnomusicologist, Instituto Nacional de Antropología, Buenos Aires

Argentina, *article on* Folk and Traditional Dance

Phebe Shih Chao

Lecturer, Arts and Humanities Department, Babson College, Babson Park, Massachusetts

Ye Shaolan

John V. Chapman

Associate Professor of Dance, University of California, Santa Barbara

Jean Dauberval • James Harvey D'Egville • La Fille Mal Gardée • Gosselin Family • Great Britain, *article on* Theatrical Dance, 1772–1850 • Pas de Quatre

Sarah Alberti Chapman

Whereabouts unknown

Jane Dudley • Pearl Lang

Judith Chazin-Bennahum

Professor of Theatre and Dance, University of New Mexico

Libretti for Dance, *article on* Eighteenth-Century Libretti

Natalia Y. Chernova

Senior Researcher, State Arts Research Institute, Moscow (deceased)

Nikolai Boyarchikov • Ekaterina Geltser • Kasyan Goleizovsky • Ekaterina Sankovskaya

Lila R. Cheville

Instructional Specialist, Department of Defense Education Activity, Arlington, Virginia

Panama

Aleksandra E. Chizhova

Independent scholar and critic (retired), Moscow

Nadezhda Nadezhdina

Marie-Françoise Christout

Curator Emerita, Départment des Arts du Spectacle, Bibliothèque Nationale de France; consultant and writer, Paris

Apache Dance • Josephine Baker • Ballet de Cour, *article on* Ballet de Cour, 1643–1685 • Ballet du XXᵉ Siècle • Maurice Béjart • Isaac de Benserade • Can-Can • Jean-Baptiste De Hesse • France, *articles on* Theatrical Dance, 1581–1789; Classical Dance Education; *and* Dance Research and Publication • Icare • Serge Lifar • Louis XIV • Marie-Françoise Lyonnois • Molière • Music Hall, *article on* French Traditions • Paris Opera Ballet

Hazel Chung

Writer, Cantonsville, Maryland

Asian Dance Traditions, *overview article*

Yulia M. Churko

Researcher, Minsk Institute of Culture, Belarus

Belarus • Valentin Elizariev

Paweł Chynowski

Director, Literary Department, National Theater, Poland; editor-in-chief, Taniec, *Warsaw*

Daniel Curz • Conrad Drzewiecki • Witold Gruca • Woytek Lowski • Stanisław Miszczyk • Eugeniusz Papliński • Poland, *article on* Dance Research and Publication • Henryk Tomaszewski

Paula Citron

Dance critic, Classical 96 FM Radio, Canadian Broadcasting Corporation, Toronto

James Kudelka • Television, *article on* Dance on Television in Canada

Adrienne Clancy

Dancer, Bella Lewitzky Company, Los Angeles

Native American Dance, *article on* The Southwest

Vèvè A. Clark

Associate Professor of African and Caribbean Literatures and Cultures, University of California, Berkeley

Katherine Dunham

Mary Clarke

Editor, The Dancing Times, *London*

Svetlana Beriosova • Espinosa Family • Tamara Karsavina • Marie Rambert • Doreen Wells

Roy M. Close

Music critic and writer, Minneapolis, Minnesota

John Cage • Music for Dance, *article on* Western Music since 1900

Margaret Clunies Ross

McCaughley Professor of English Language and Early English Literature, University of Sydney

Australian Aboriginal Dance, *article on* Aborigines of Arnhem Land

Carlos Alberto Coba Andrade

Director, Department of Ethnomusiciology, Instituto Otavaleño de Anthropología; ethnomusicologist and folklorist, Ortavala, Ecuador

Ecuador

Ginnine Cocuzza

Independent scholar, New York

Angna Enters

Selma Jeanne Cohen

Dance historian, New York

Peter Brinson • Marie-Françoise Christout • Genres of Western Theatrical Dance • John Martin • Mai-Ester

Murdmaa • Organizations • The Prodigal Son • Elizabeth Souritz • United States of America, *article on* Dance Research and Publication

Stephen Comee

Editorial Director and special consultant, Japan Foundation; Nō actor of the Kanze School; Administrative Director, Umewaka Nō Foundation; Managing Director, World Institute of Nō Drama, Tokyo

Hōshō School • Kan'ami • Kanze School • Kita School • Kongō School • Konparu School • Konparu Zenchiku • Otozuru • Umewaka Makio

Thomas Connors

Dance critic and writer, Chicago

Valerie Bettis • Lucia Chase • Sol Hurok

Claude Conyers

Vice President and Editorial Director, Scholarly and Professional Reference Department, Oxford University Press (USA), New York

Ballet Technique, *article on* Major Schools • Ludmilla Chiriaeff • Coppélia • Don Quixote, *articles on* Early Productions *and* Other Productions • Eric Hyrst • Kshessinsky Family • Fernand Nault • Brydon Paige • Kirsten Simone • Frank Staff • Sonia Taverner • Stanley Williams

Ray Cook

Associate Professor of Dance, Vassar College, New York

Reconstruction, *article on* Use of Modern Scores

David Coplan

Associate Professor of Social Anthropology, University of Cape Town

Sub-Saharan Africa, *article on* Popular Dance

Mary Coros

National Director of Education and Culture, PanCretan Association of America; independent scholar and choreographer, Toronto

Crete, *article on* Dance in Modern Crete

Constantin Costea

Scientific researcher, Institutul de Etnografie şi Folclor, Bucharest

Romania, *article on* Folk Dance Research and Publication

Michael Crabb

Senior Producer, Radio Arts, Canadian Broadcasting Corporation; dance critic and writer, Toronto

Frank Augustyn • Celia Franca • Les Grands Ballets Canadiens • Evelyn Hart • Christopher House • Karen Kain • Brian Macdonald • National Ballet of Canada • Arnold Spohr • Grant Strate • Veronica Tennant • Vincent Warren

Valda L. Craig

Head, Department of Visual and Performing Arts, Australian Catholic University, New South Wales Division

Australia, *articles on* Modern Dance *and* Dance Research and Publication • Graeme Murphy

Carole Crewdson

Certified Movement Analyst, New York

Movement Choir

Clement Crisp

Writer, London

Natalia Makarova • Alicia Markova • Nadia Nerina • Lynn Seymour

Arlene Croce

Dance critic, The New Yorker

George Balanchine • Edwin Denby

Gerhard Croll

Musicologist, Faculty of Arts, Institut für Musikwissenschaft, Universität Salzburg

Gaspero Angiolini • Christoph Willibald Gluck

Richard Crum

Writer, Santa Monica, California

Albania • Faeroe Step • Yugoslavia, *article on* Traditional Dance

Kitty Cunningham

Dance writer, New York

John Butler • Carmen de Lavallade • Jean Erdman • Jacob's Pillow • Murray Louis • Alwin Nikolais • Bertram Ross

Grażyna Dąbrowska

Adjunct (retired), Instytut Sztuki, Polska Akademi Nauk; Founder, President, and Chair, Polskic Towarzystwo Etnochoreologiczne, Warsaw

Krakowiak • Poland, *article on* Traditional and Social Dance

Sibylle Dahms

Institut für Musikwissenschaft, Universität Salzburg

Franz Hilverding • Eva Maria Violette

Megan Llinos Dail-Jones

Writer, Palmdale, California

Australian Aboriginal Dance, *article on* Warlpiri Dance

Alberto Dallal

Dance critic and writer, Mexico City

Guillermina Bravo • Mexico, *articles on* Theatrical Dance *and* Dance Companies • Pilar Rioja • Waldeen

Robert G. Dalsemer

Coordinator, Music and Dance Programs, The John C. Campbell Folk School, Brasstown, North Carolina

Clogging, *article on* Clogging in Appalachian Dance Traditions

Nancy Dalva

Dance writer, New York

Ocean

David Daniel

Dance writer, New York

Suzanne Farrell • Rudolf Nureyev

Margaret Daniels
Independent choreographer, dancer, and dance historian, Boston (deceased)
Musette

Iria d'Aquino
Dance writer, Urbana, Illinois
Capoeira

Steven A. Darden
Dance historian and lecturer, Flagstaff, Arizona
Navajo Dance

Robert W. Davidson
Faculty member, University of Washington, School of Drama; Artistic Director, Robert Davidson Dance Company, Seattle
Body Therapies, *article on* Skinner Releasing Technique

J. G. Davies
Professor of Theology, University of Birmingham, England (deceased)
Christianity and Dance, *article on* Early Christian Views

Martha Ellen Davis
Faculty Research Associate, Latin American and Caribbean Studies, Indiana University
Dominican Republic

Candi de Alaiza
Dance historian and writer, Alhambra, California
Basque Dance

Marília de Andrade
Professor of Dance, Instituto de Belas Artes, Universidade Estadual de Campinas, Brazil
Brazil, *article on* Dance Research and Publication

Arsen B. Degen
Dance critic, Moscow
Oleg Vinogradov

Jérôme de La Gorce
Centre National de la Recherche Scientifique, Paris
Jean Berain • Louis Boquet • André Campra • Henry Gissey • Les Indes Galantes • Jean-Baptiste Lully • Jean-Joseph Mouret • Jean-Philippe Rameau

Jerome Delamater
Professor of Communication, Hofstra University, Hempstead, New York
Film Musicals, *article on* Hollywood Film Musicals • Bob Fosse • Gene Kelly • Michael Kidd • Herbert Ross

César Delgado Martínez
Dance writer, Mexico City
Concheros • Matachins, *article on* Danza de Matlachines • Mexico, *article on* Dance Companies

Sophia Delza
Director, Delza School of T'ai-Chi Ch'uan and Chinese Theatre Arts; independent scholar and writer, New York (deceased)
China, *article on* Dance in China • Mei Lanfang

Alexander P. Demidov
Dance critic and historian, Moscow (deceased)
Natalia Bessmertnova • Le Corsaire • The Nutcracker, *article on* Productions in Russia • Swan Lake, *article on* Productions in Russia

Nancy de Wilde
Instructor of dance history, Rotterdamse Dansacademie and Theater School Amsterdam
Netherlands, *article on* Theatrical Dance before 1900

E. Mildred Merino de Zela
Coordinator of Folklore, Instituto Riva-Agüere, Pontificia Universidad Católica del Lima
Peru

Gedeon P. Dienes
President, Magyar Tánctudományi Társaság; President, EuroDance Foundation, Budapest; Director, CID-UNESCO for Research and Communication, Paris
Ballet Sopianae • Béla Bartók • Valéria Dienes • Imre Eck • Győr Ballet • Hungary, *articles on* Theatrical Dance before World War II; Theatrical Dance since World War II; Modern Dance; *and* Theatrical Dance Research and Publication • Iván Markó • Viktor Róna

Galina N. Dobrovolskaya
Leading researcher, Russian Institute of the History of Arts, Saint Petersburg
The Firebird, *article on* Fokine Production • Fedor Lopukhov • Les Sylphides, *article on* Russian Origins • Leonid Yakobson

Nikita A. Dolgushin
Dancer and choreographer; Head, Department of Choreography, Saint Petersburg State Conservatory
Petr Gusev

Penelope Reed Doob
Professor of English and Multidisciplinary Studies, York University, North York, Ontario
Labyrinth Dances

Femke van Doorn-Last
Head (retired), Department of Folk Dance Education, Rotterdamse Dansacademie; dance writer, Amsterdam
Netherlands, *article on* Folk and Traditional Dance

George Dorris
Coeditor, Dance Chronicle, New York; Associate Professor of English, York College, City University of New York
Leonard Bernstein • Robert Irving • Romualdo Marenco • Adrien Merger de Saint-André • William Schuman

Jeannine Dorvane

Dance critic and writer, Paris

Marie Allard • Ballet de Collège • Les Caractères de la Danse • La Carmagnole • Duport Family • Louis Dupré • Peter van Dyk • Sébastien Gallet • Gardel Family • Victor Gsovsky • Marie-Madeleine Guimard • Anna Heinel • Hus Family • Lany Family • Joseph Lazzini • Charles Le Picq • Serge Peretti • Antoine-Bonaventure Pitrot • Jacqueline Rayet • Olga Spessivtseva • Vestris Family • Nina Vyroubova • Carlotta Zambelli

Irene Dowd

Faculty member, The Juilliard School; guest faculty member, The National Ballet School of Canada, Toronto; private practicioner in neuromuscular education, New York

Body Therapies, *article on* Ideokinesis

Henry John Drewal

Evjue-Bascom Professor of Art History and Afro-American Studies, University of Wisconsin–Madison

Costume in African Traditions

Jerry C. Duke

Professor of Dance Ethnology and History, San Francisco State University

Cajun Dance Traditions • Clogging, *historical overview article* • Country-Western Dance

Éteri A. Dumbadze

Dance critic and historian, Tbilisi, Georgia

Vakhtang Chabukiani

Elsie Ivancich Dunin

Professor Emerita of Dance Ethnology, University of California, Los Angeles

Gypsy Dance • Yugoslavia, *article on* Traditional Dance

Jennifer Dunning

Dance critic and reporter, New York Times

United States of America, *article on* Contemporary Criticism

Hans Ehrmann

Dance critic, La Nación, *Santiago; Chile correspondent,* Dance Magazine

Chile, *article on* Dance Research and Publication • Ernst Uthoff

Catherine J. Ellis

Ethnomusicologist, Adelaide, Australia

Australian Aboriginal Dance, *article on* Antakirinya Dance

Nikolai I. Elyash

Dance critic and historian; professor, Moscow Theater Institute (deceased)

Vladimir Burmeister • The Fountain of Bakhchisarai • Adam Glushkovsky • Avdotia Istomina • Evgenia Kolosova • Russia, *article on* Dance Education • Ivan Valberkh

George S. Emmerson

Professor Emeritus of Engineering, University of Western Ontario

Great Britain, *article on* Scottish Folk and Traditional Dance

Joan Erdman

Professor of Anthropology, Columbia College, Chicago; research associate, Committee on South Asian Studies, University of Chicago

Uday Shankar

Veit Erlmann

Professor of Anthropology, Freie Universität Berlin

Hausa Dance

Liza Ewell

Associate Editor, Microsoft, Inc., Seattle, Washington

Vera Zorina

Hansel Ndumbe Eyoh

Associate Professor of Drama, University of Buea, Cameroon

Cameroon

Iris M. Fanger

Drama critic, The Boston Herald; *former director, Harvard Summer Dance Center*

Adolphe Appia • Irene and Vernon Castle • Swan Lake, *article on* Productions outside Russia

James C. Faris

Professor Emeritus of Anthropology, University of Connecticut

Nuba Dance

Leslie Farlow

Independent scholar, Lee, Massachusetts

José Limón • The Moor's Pavane

Lois Lamya' al-Faruqi

Independent scholar, Toronto (deceased)

Aesthetics, *article on* Islamic Dance Aesthetics

Elena G. Fedorenko

Dance critic, Moscow

La Esmeralda • Sofia Fedorova • The Little Humpbacked Horse • Russia, *article on* Theatrical Dance before 1917

Rita Felciano

Dance critic, San Francisco Bay Guardian, *California*

Romeo and Juliet

Steven Feld

Professor of Anthropology, University of California, Santa Cruz

Papua New Guinea, *article on* Kaluli Dance

Martie Fellom

Associate Professor of Dance, Southeastern Louisiana University

Skirt Dance

Angene Feves

Independent scholar and dance historian, Pleasant Hill, California

Intermedio • Reconstruction, *article on* Use of Historical Notations

Celso A. Lara Figueroa
Centro de Estudios Folkloricos, Guatemala City
Guatemala

Paul Filmer
Coordinator of Taught Postgraduate Studies in Sociology, Goldsmiths' College, University of London
Methodologies in the Study of Dance, *article on* Sociology

Anita Finkel
Dance writer, critic, and publisher, New York (deceased)
Diana Adams • American Ballet • Ballet Caravan • Pina Bausch • Patrick Dupond • New York City Ballet, *article on* History since 1983 • Kyra Nichols

Catherine Foley
Assistant Lecturer in Ethnochoreology, Irish World Music Centre, University of Limerick
Ireland, *article on* Traditional Dance

John Forrest
Professor of Anthropology, State University College at Purchase, New York
Great Britain, *articles on* Welsh Folk and Traditional Dance; *and* Manx Folk and Traditional Dance • Matachins, *article on* Matachines Dances in the Southwestern United States • Morris Dance • Sword Dance

Susan Leigh Foster
Professor of Dance, University of California, Riverside
Methodologies in the Study of Dance, *article on* New Areas of Inquiry

Henry Frank
Executive Director, Haitian Centers Council, New York
Haiti • Vodun

Rusty E. Frank
Dancer, writer, and producer, Los Angeles
Peg Leg Bates • Berry Brothers • Four Step Brothers • Gregory Hines • Ann Miller • Donald O'Connor • Eleanor Powell • Shirley Temple

Mark Franko
Associate Professor of Theater Arts, University of California, Santa Cruz; Artistic Director, Novantiqua Dance Company
Libretti for Dance, *article on* Sixteenth- and Seventeenth-Century Libretti

Allan Fridericia
Dance writer, Copenhagen (deceased)
Hans Beck • Antoine Bournonville • Études • Vincenzo Galeotti • Harald Lander • Børge Ralov

Zvi Friedhaber
Dance writer, Kiryat Haim, Israel
Jewish Dance Traditions

LeeEllen Friedland
Folklorist, Washington, D.C.
Folk Dance History • Square Dancing

Katherine Friedman
Ph.D. candidate, Department of History, New York University
Dance as Sport

Lisa A. Fusillo
Professor of Dance and Director of Dance Program, College of Fine and Performing Arts, University of Nebraska–Lincoln
Gaîté Parisienne • Léonide Massine • Nobilissima Visione • Le Tricorne

Joseph Gale
Dance critic and writer, Millburn, New Jersey
Riccardo Drigo • Aleksandr Glazunov • Aram Khachaturian • Léon Minkus

Judy Gantz
Certified Movement Analyst and dance kinesiologist, Los Angeles
Kinesiology, *article on* Therapeutic Practices

Lynn Garafola
Editor, Studies in Dance History, New York
Adolph Bolm • Serge Diaghilev • Lubov Egorova • Serge Grigoriev • Stanislas Idzikowski • Lydia Lopokova • Boris Romanov • Ludmilla Schollar • Lubov Tchernicheva • Vera Trefilova • Anatole Vilzak • Alexandre Volinine • Leon Woizikowski

Robert Garfias
Professor of Anthropology, University of California, Irvine
Gagaku • Myanmar

Robert Garis
Katharine Lee Bates Professor of English, Wellesley College, Wellesley, Massachusetts
New York City Ballet, *article on* Origins to 1983

K. Gasanov
Dance critic, Baku, Azerbaijan
Azerbaijan

Klaus Geitel
Ballet Critic, Die Welt, Berlin
Hans Werner Henze

Beth Eliot Genné
Assistant Professor of Dance History and Lecturer, Department of History, Arts and Ideas Program, University of Michigan, Ann Arbor
Phyllis Bedells • Ninette de Valois • Great Britain, *article on* Theatrical Dance since 1850 • Philip Richardson

Richard Glasstone
Artistic adviser, Cecchetti Society, London; fellow of the Imperial Society of Teachers of Dancing, London
Adage • Allegro • Ballet Technique, *articles on* Directions; Linking Movements; *and* Jumping Movements • Ballet Technique, History of, *article on* Ballet since the Mid-Nineteenth Century • Batterie

Moira Goff

Dance historian, London

Thomas Caverley • John Essex • Hester Santlow

Jane Goldberg

Associate Professor, New World School of the Arts, Miami, and New York University; Director, Changing Times Tap Dancing Company, Inc., New York

Baby Laurence • John W. Bubbles • Honi Coles • Paul Draper • Chuck Green

K. Meira Goldberg

Independent scholar, New York

Carmen Amaya

Elizabeth Goldblatt

Writer, Portland, Oregon

Sikkim

Nancy Goldner

Dance critic and writer, New York

Rond de Jambe

Seth Goldstein

Writer, New York

Robert Wilson

Noël Goodwin

Dance critic and writer, London

Ernest Ansermet • Lord Berners • Arthur Bliss • Claude Debussy • Léo Delibes • Manuel de Falla • Yuri Fayer • Constant Lambert • John Lanchbery • Music for Dance, *article on* Western Music, 1800–1900 • Maurice Ravel • Petr Ilich Tchaikovsky

Mel Gordon

Professor of Dramatic Art, University of California, Berkeley

Nikolai Foregger

Brenda Dixon Gottschild

Professor of Dance History and Criticism, Temple University, Pennsylvania

Buddy Bradley • Cakewalk • United States of America, *article on* African-American Dance Traditions • Lavinia Williams-Yarborough

Andrée Grau

Senior Research Fellow, Dance Studies, Roehampton Institute, London

Australian Aboriginal Dance, *article on* Tiwi Dance • Central and East Africa • South Africa, *article on* Indigenous Dance

Laurel Victoria Gray

President, Uzbek Dance and Culture Society, Washington, D.C.

Georgia • Uzbekistan

Doris Green

President, Pan African Performing Arts Preservation Association, Inc., Uniondale, New York

National Ballet of Senegal

Robert Greskovic

Dance critic and writer, New York

Arabesque • Attitude • Ballet Technique, *articles on* Body Positions *and* Turning Movements • Mikhail Baryshnikov • Donald Byrd • Peter Martins • Partnering • Pointe Work • Edward Villella

Elena Grillo

Writer, Rome

Pompeo Diobono • Antonio Rinaldi • Carolina Rosati

Mayer I. Gruber

Senior Lecturer in Bible, Ben-Gurion University of the Negev, Beersheva, Israel

Dance in the Bible

Marina Grut

Former lecturer in ballet history and Spanish dance, University of Cape Town; independent scholar, London

CAPAB Ballet • Vicente Escudero • David Poole • Alexis Rassine • South Africa, *article on* Ballet • Frank Staff

Örn Gudmundsson

Writer, Reykjavik

Iceland, *article on* Theatrical Dance

Ann Hutchinson Guest

Director, Language of Dance Centre, London

Labanotation • Notation • Saint-Léon Notation • Stepanov Notation • Zorn Notation

Ivor Guest

Dance historian, London

Adeline Genée • Adèle Grantzow • Carlotta Grisi • Jules Perrot • Cesare Pugni

Yves Guilcher

Writer, Paris

France, *article on* Recreational Dance

Galina A. Gulyaeva

Musicologist, Balet, Moscow

Reinhold Glière • Shurale

Elena L. Gvaramadze

Dance critic and historian, Tbilisi, Georgia (deceased)

Georgia

Peggy Hackney

Writer, Seattle, Washington

Body Therapies, *article on* Bartenieff Fundamentals

Bengt Häger

Founder, Dansmuseet, Stockholm

The Green Table • Kurt Jooss

David Hahn

Musician, Seattle, Washington

Cascarda • Music for Dance, *article on* Western Music, 1520–1650 • Tordion

Gerlinde Haid
Whereabouts unknown
Austria, *article on* Dance Research and Publication

Darcy Hall
Writer, Hoboken, New Jersey
Anna Sokolow

David Hamilton
Faculty member, The Juilliard School; music critic, New York
Igor Stravinsky

Lena Hammergren
Teatervetenskapliga Institutionen, Stockholms Universitet
Birgit Åkesson • Margaretha Åsberg

Sandra Noll Hammond
Former Professor of Ballet and Dance History, Department of Theatre and Dance, University of Hawaii at Manoa
Ballet Technique, *articles on* Feet Positions *and* Arm Positions • Ballet Technique, History of, *article on* Ballet in the Late Eighteenth and Early Nineteenth Centuries • Pas de Deux • Plié • Port de Bras • Technical Manuals, *article on* Publications, 1765–1859 • Turnout, *article on* History and Aesthetics

Barbara L. Hampton
Director, Graduate Program in Ethnomusicology and Professor of Music, Hunter College, City University of New York
Music for Dance, *article on* African Music

Judith Lynne Hanna
Senior Research Scholar, University of Maryland at College Park
Methodologies in the Study of Dance, *article on* Cultural Context • Ubakala Dance • West Africa

Kathleen Kuzmick Hansell
Music editor, University of Chicago Press
Jean-Georges Noverre

Valdemar Hansteen
Dance writer, Oslo
Norway, *article on* Dance Research and Publication

Jan Michael Hanvik
Executive director, Pan American Musical Art Research, Inc., New York
Caribbean Region

Cathryn Harding
Dance critic and writer, Charlottesville, Virginia
Liz Lerman

Camille Hardy
Dance critic and writer, New York
Michael Bennett • The Black Crook • Fan Dancing • Lighting for Dance, *historical overview article* • Marilyn Miller • Tommy Tune • United States of America, *article on* Musical Theater • Ned Wayburn • Florenz Ziegfeld

Peggy Harper
Associate, African Studies Centre, University of Cambridge
Sub-Saharan Africa, *overview article* • Tiv Dance

Dale Harris
Professor of Humanities and Art History, Cooper Union for the Advancement of Science and Art, New York (deceased)
Ballets Russes de Serge Diaghilev • Margot Fonteyn • Ballet in Opera

Melissa Harris
Writer, New York
Artists and Dance, *articles on* Artists and Dance, 1930–1945 *and* Collaboration • Jasper Johns • Robert Rauschenberg

Rebecca Harris-Warrick
Associate Professor of Music, Cornell University, Ithaca, New York
Allemande • Anglaise • Chaconne and Passacaille • Forlana • Pastorale • Tambourin

Corrie Hartong
Writer, Rotterdam
Netherlands, *article on* Dance Research and Publication

Hasegawa Roku
Independent scholar, Tokyo
Amagatsu Ushio • Butō • Eiko and Koma • Fujima Kanjūrō • Hanayagi Suzushi • Hijikata Tatsumi • Isii Kaoru • Kamizawa Kazuo • Kasai Akira • Maro Akaji • Ōno Kazuo • Tanaka Min • Teshigawara Saburō • Yamada Setsuko

Baird Hastings
Conductor, Mozart Festival Orchestra, Inc., New York
André Eglevsky • Francis Poulenc • Henri Sauguet

Nancy Mason Hauser
Writer, Los Angeles
Hanya Holm • Trend

Katrina Hazzard-Donald
Associate Professor of Sociology, Rutgers, The State University of New Jersey
United States of America, *article on* African-American Social Dance

Philippa Heale
Independent scholar, Melbourne
Antonio and Rosario • La Argentina • Ballet Nacional Español • Luisillo • Pericet Family • Sardana • Seguidillas • Spain, *article on* Theatrical Dance, 1700–1862

Edward Herbst
Visiting Assistant Professor of Music, Middlebury College, Vermont; Co-director and composer, Thunder Bay Ensemble, Thunder Bay, Ontario
Baris • Gamelan, *article on* Balinese Traditions • Indonesia, *overview article and articles on* Balinese Dance Traditions; Balinese Ceremonial Dance; Balinese Dance Theater; *and* Balinese Mask Dance Theater • I Nyoman Kakul • Kebiar • Légong • I Ketut Mario • Sardono • Wayang

Doris Hering
Senior editor, Dance Magazine, *New York*
Cleveland–San Jose Ballet • Dayton Ballet • Dayton Contemporary Dance Company • Lotte Goslar • Houston Ballet • Ohio Ballet • Pacific Northwest Ballet • Pittsburgh Ballet Theatre • Jerome Robbins • Tulsa Ballet Theatre • United States of America, *article on* Regional Dance Companies • Washington Ballet • E. Virginia Williams

Mary Ann Herman
Independent scholar, New York (deceased)
Folk Dance Sounds

André Philippe Hersin
Writer, Paris
Cyril Atanassoff

Charlotte Heth
Writer, Tulsa, Oklahoma
Native American Dance, *articles on* Northeastern Woodlands *and* Southeastern Woodlands

Alan C. Heyman
Independent scholar and writer, Seoul
Ch'oi Seung-hee • Cho T'aek-won • Han Young-sook • Hong Sin-cha • Kim Ch'un-heung • Kim Paik-bong • Korea, *overview article and articles on* Modern Dance *and* Dance Research and Publication • Lee Mae-bang • Lee Sun-ock

Constance Valis Hill
Coordinator of the dance history program, Alvin Ailey School of American Dance; dance critic and writer, New York
Nicholas Brothers • Whitman Sisters

Wendy Hilton
Faculty member, The Juilliard School; consultant in Baroque dance, New York
Ballet Technique, History of, *article on* French Court Dance • Courante • Entrée Grave • Loure • Minuet • Révérence, *article on* Eighteenth-Century Modes

Frank Hoff
Writer, Toronto
Japan, *article on* Folk Dance

Kirsten Gram Holmström
Professor Emerita of Theater Science, Stockholms Universitet
Attitude and Shawl Dance • Sweden, *article on* Theatrical Dance, 1771–1900

Susan Homar
Professor of Comparative Literature and Dance History, Universidad de Puerto Rico, Río Piedras
Puerto Rico

Mantle Hood
Ethnomusicologist, Cantonsville, Maryland
Asian Dance Traditions, *overview article*

Petri Hoppu
Dance writer, Tampere, Finland
Finland, *article on* Traditional Dance

Dawn Lille Horwitz
Dance historian and writer, New York
Ray Bolger

Jana Hŏsková
Editor-in-Chief Emerita, Taneč Listy; *dance critic and writer, Prague*
Czech Republic and Slovakia, *article on* Dance Research and Publication

Victoria Huckenpahler
Independent scholar, Washington, D.C.
Felia Doubrovska • Violette Verdy

Jo Humphrey
Executive Director, Gold Mountain Institute for Traditional Shadow Theatre, Inc., New York
Asian Dance Traditions, *article on* The Influence of Puppetry

Marilyn Hunt
Senior editor, Dance Magazine, *New York*
Alicia Alonso • Leon Danielian • Eliot Feld • Genevieve Oswald • Donald Saddler • Jens-Jacob Worsaae • Igor Youskevitch

Jonathan Hurwitz
Senior publicist, PACT Ballet, Pretoria
PACT Ballet

Geoffrey William Hutton
Dance critic, The Age, *Melbourne* (deceased)
Lucette Aldous • Australian Ballet • Edouard Borovansky • Kathleen Gorham • Marilyn Jones • Laurel Martyn • Marilyn Rowe • Margaret Scott

Marina A. Ilicheva
Dance critic and historian, Saint Petersburg
Irina Kolpakova • Maryinsky Ballet, *historical overview article*

Anna Ilieva
Dance writer, Sofia
Bulgaria, *article on* Folk and Traditional Dance

Pascal James Imperato
Distinguished Service Professor and Chair, Department of Preventive Medicine and Community Health, State University of New York, Health Science Center at Brooklyn
Bamana Dance • Dogon Dance

Judith Brin Ingber
Independent scholar; Co-director and resident choreographer, Voices of Sepharad, Minneapolis, Minnesota
Fred Berk • Israel, *overview article* • Gurit Kadman • Sara Levi-Tanai

Tania Inman
Librarian, The Benesh Institute, London
Benesh Movement Notation

Galina V. Inozemtseva
Dance writer, Moscow
Violette Bovt • Mikhail Gabovich • Sofia Golovkina • Marina Kondratieva • Russia, *article on* Theatrical Dance before 1917

Margarita I. Isareva
Dance critic and editor, Balet, *Moscow*
Igor Moiseyev

Marcelo Isse Moyano
Professor of Dance Theory, Universidad de Buenos Aires
Oscar Araiz • Argentina, *article on* Modern Dance

Sachiyo Ito
Dance historian, New York
Geisha Dance • Okinawa

Allison Jablonko
Independent scholar, Perugia
Papua New Guinea, *article on* Maring Dance

George Jackson
Dance critic and writer, Washington, D.C.
Josef Hassreiter • Tilly Losch • Die Puppenfee • Mia Slavenska

John A. Jackson
Writer and historian, New York
American Bandstand

Silas Jackson
Writer, New York
Robert Wilson

Laura A. Jacobs
Dance writer, New York
The Nutcracker, *article on* Productions outside Russia

Carol Jenkins
Principal Research Fellow, Papua New Guinea Institute of Medical Research, Goroka
Belize • Garifuna Dance

Ron Jenkins
Writer, Cambridge, Massachusetts
Mask and Makeup, *article on* Asian Traditions

Claudia Jeschke
Professor of Dance History, Notation, and Theory, Universität Leipzig
Germany, *article on* Dance Research and Publication

Suki John
Dance writer and choreographer, New York and Havana
Cuba, *article on* Modern Dance

Matthew Johnson
Kabuki researcher and commentator, Tokyo
Azuma Tokuho • Fujima Fujiko

Thomas F. Johnston
Music Department, University of Alaska, Fairbanks (deceased)
Native American Dance, *article on* The Far North • Shangana-Tsonga Dance

Betty True Jones
Dance writer, Santa Rosa, California
India, *article on* Dance Research and Publication

Clifford Reis Jones
Co-director, International Dance Theatre, Lincoln Arts Center, Santa Rosa, California
Bangladesh • India, *articles on* History of Indian Dance *and* Epic Sources of Indian Dance • Kathakali • Manipur • Nautch • Shanta Rao • Rās Līlā • Mrinalini Sarabhai • Tamasha

Stephanie Jordan
Professor of Dance Studies, Roehampton Institute, London
Christopher Bruce • Siobhan Davies • London Contemporary Dance Theatre

Milica Jovanović
Independent scholar, Belgrade
Margarita Froman • Pia and Pino Mlakar • Dimitrije Parlić • Yugoslavia, *article on* Ballet

Deborah Jowitt
Dance faculty, Tisch School of the Arts, New York University; dance critic, The Village Voice, *New York*
American Document • Appalachian Spring • Clytemnestra • Dark Meadow • Deaths and Entrances • Martha Graham • Letter to the World • Modern Dance Technique • Night Journey • Primitive Mysteries • Bessie Schönberg • Seraphic Dialogue

Knud Arne Jürgensen
Dance and music historian, Kongelige Bibliotek, Copenhagen
Bournonville Composers

Adrienne L. Kaeppler
Curator of Oceanic Ethnology, National Museum of Natural History, Smithsonian Institution, Washington, D.C.
Melanesia • Methodologies in the Study of Dance, *article on* Linguistics • Micronesia • Music for Dance, *article on* Oceanic Music • Oceanic Dance Traditions • Polynesia • Rapanui • Tonga

Garrett Kam
Writer, Honolulu
Indonesia, *article on* Dance Research and Publication

Angela Kane
Principal Lecturer in Dance, Roehampton Institute, London
Esplanade • Great Britain, *article on* Modern Dance • Musical Offering • Northern Ballet Theatre • Spindrift • Paul Taylor • Three Epitaphs

Howard Kaplan

Dance writer, New York

Alvin Ailey American Dance Theater, *article on* History since 1979 • Judith Jamison

Richard Katz

Writer, Cambridge, Massachusetts

!Kung San Dance

Joann W. Kealiinohomoku

Executive Director, Cross-Cultural Dance Resources, Inc., Flagstaff, Arizona

Hopi Dance • Gertrude Prokosch Kurath • Primitive Dance

Richard Keeling

Writer, Van Nuys, California

Native American Dance, *article on* California and the Intermountain Region

Elizabeth Kendall

Dance critic and writer, New York

Katherine Litz

Don Kenny

Co-founder and director, Kenny and Ogawa Kyōgen Players, Tokyo

Kyōgen, *article on* Kyōgen Schools • Nomura Mansaku II • Nomura Manzō VI

Genja Khachatrian

Professor of Ethnochoreology, Institute of Archaeology and Ethnography, Armenian Academy of Sciences, Yerevan

Armenia, *article on* Traditional Dance

Theresa Ki-ja Kim

Assistant Professor of Theatre Arts, State University of New York at Stony Brook

Shamanism

Cynthia Tse Kimberlin

Writer, Berkeley, California

Ethiopia

Musa S. Kleimenova

Dance critic, Moscow (deceased)

Leonid Lavrovsky • Olga Lepeshinskaya

Irina Klyagin

Dance Collection, New York Public Library for the Performing Arts

Nina Ananiashvili • Andris Liepa

Donald Knight

Ethnomusicologist, New York

Lakshmi Knight

Horst Koegler

Co-publisher, Ballet International / Tanz aktuell, *Berlin*

Abraxas • Richard Adama • Bavarian State Ballet • Ludwig van Beethoven • Nicholas Beriozoff • Berlin Opera Ballet • Boris Blacher • Gustav Blank • Heinz Bosl • Jean Cébron • Richard Cragun • John Cranko • Werner Egk • Eva Evdokimova • William Forsythe • Germany, *articles on* Theatrical Dance, 1600–1945 *and* Theatrical Dance since 1945 • Tatjana Gsovsky • Hamburg Ballet • Marcia Haydée • Reinhild Hoffmann • Birgit Keil • Johann Kresnik • Susanne Linke • Egon Madsen • John Neumeier • Carl Orff • Gert Reinholm • Stuttgart Ballet • Jochen Ulrich • Erich Walter

Marina E. Konstantinova

Dance historian, Moscow

Ekaterina Maximova

Violetta Konsulova

Whereabouts unknown

Bulgaria, *article on* Theatrical Dance • Anastas Petrov

Elfrida A. Koroleva

Dance critic and historian, Kishinev, Moldova

Vladimir Kurbet • Laurencia • Moldova

Géza Körtvélyes

Professor of Dance History, Hungarian Dance Academy; dance writer, Budapest

Hungary, *articles on* Theatrical Dance before World War II; Dance Education; *and* Theatrical Dance Research and Publication • Zsuzsa Kun • István Molnár • Ferenc Nádasi • Miklós Rábai • Lázló Sergi

Sicille P. C. Kotelawala

Director, Ceylinco Group; dancer and researcher; Columbo, Sri Lanka

Kandyan Dance • Kandy Perahera; • Kohomba Kankariya • Ves Dance

Sunil Kothari

Professor of Dance and Head, Department of Dance, Rabindra Bharati University, Calcutta

Manjusri Chaki-Sircar • Chandralekha • C. V. Chandrashekhar • V. P. and Shanta Dhananjayan • Durgalal • Ram Gopal • India, *article on* New Directions in Indian Dance • Jhaveri Sisters • Yamini Krishnamurthi • Kumudini Lakhia • Kelucharan Mahapatra • Sonal Mansingh • Mudrā • Nātyaśāstra • Odissi • Sanjukta Panigrahi • Raja and Radha Reddy • Leela Samson • Mallika Sarabhai • Malavika Sarukkai • Saswati Sen • Uma Sharma • Bipin Singh • Sitara Devi • Valli • Vedantam Satyam • Vempati Chinna Satyam

Zsuzsa Kővágó

Dance writer, Budapest

Gyula Harangozó • Hungary, *article on* Theatrical Dance since World War II • Szeged Contemporary Ballet

Vera M. Krasovskaya

Head of Research, Saint Petersburg State Theater Arts Academy, Saint Petersburg

Lev Ivanov • Maryinsky Ballet, *article on* Maryinsky Style • Marius Petipa • The Sleeping Beauty, *article on* Petipa Production

Sali Ann Kriegsman

Executive Director, Jacob's Pillow Dance Festival and School, Becket, Massachusetts

Bennington School of the Dance

Eva Krøvel
Dance critic, Oslo
Norway, *article on* Theatrical Dance, 1920–1958

Valery A. Kulakov
Institute of the Theory and History of Fine Arts, Moscow
Elena Andreyanova • Bogdanov Family • Christian Johansson • Olga Preobrajenska • Agrippina Vaganova • Vasily Vainonen

Laura Kumin
Dance adviser, Madrid Regional Cultural Council, Spain
Nacho Duato • Spain, *article on* Theatrical Dance since 1862

Gertrude Prokosch Kurath
Independent scholar, Dance Research Center, Ann Arbor, Michigan (deceased)
Native American Dance, *overview article and article on* Northeastern Woodlands

Elena N. Kurilenko
Musicologist, State Arts Research Institute, Moscow
Rodion Shchedrin

László Kürti
Associate Professor of Cultural Anthropology, Eötvös Loránd Tudományegyetem, Budapest; Director, European Centre for Traditional Culture, Budapest
Czardas • Hungarian State Folk Ensemble • Hungary, *articles on* Traditional and Popular Dance *and* Folk Dance Research and Publication

Elizabeth Kurtz
Ballet teacher, New York
Matachins, *historical overview article*

Billai Laba
Independent scholar, Boroko, Papua New Guinea
Papua New Guinea, *article on* Gizra Dance

Kenneth LaFave
Arts writer, The Arizona Republic, *Scottsdale*
Leonard Bernstein • Aaron Copland

Andrew Lamb
Musicologist, London
Strauss Family

Frederick Lamp
Curator, Arts of Africa, the Americas, and Oceania, The Baltimore Museum of Art
Aesthetics, *article on* African Dance Aesthetics

Roderyk Lange
Professor of Dance Anthropology, Uniwersytet im Adama Mickiewicza w Poznaniu; Director, Centre for Dance Studies, Jersey, Channel Islands
Albrecht Kunst

Pierre Lartigue
Writer, Paris
Antonio Gades

Donna La Rue
Program Co-ordinator, Liturgy, Worship, and Arts Program, Boston Theological Institute
Tripudium

Hannah Laudová
Faculty member (retired), Institute of Ethnography and Folklore, Česká Akademie Véd, Prague
Czech Republic and Slovak Republic, *article on* Folk and Traditional Dance

Kenneth Laws
Professor of Physics, Dickinson College, Carlisle, Pennsylvania
Physics of Dance

William James Lawson
Dance writer, Pittsburgh
Todd Bolender • Jacques d'Amboise • Melissa Hayden • Allegra Kent • Tanaquil Le Clercq • Francisco Moncion • Patricia Wilde

Roberta Lazzarini
Curator, Pavlova Museum, Ivy House, London
Anna Pavlova

Thomas G. Leabhart
Associate Professor of Theatre and Resident Artist, Pomona College, California; Editor, Mime Journal
Mime

Dorothy Sara-Louise Lee
Diocese of Indianapolis, Indiana
Fiji

Du-hyon Lee
Writer, Seoul
Korea, *articles on* Masked Dance Drama *and* Dance Research and Publication

Norma Leistiko
Writer, San Francisco
Body Therapies, *article on* Feldenkrais Method

Samuel L. Leiter
Professor of Theatre, Brooklyn College and the Graduate School and University Center, City University of New York
Bandō Mitsugorō • Bandō Tamasaburō • Bunraku • Hanamichi • Ichikawa Danjūrō • Ichikawa Ennosuke • Japanese Traditional Schools • Jidaimono • Kabuki Theater • Kataoka Takao • Matsumoto Kōshirō • Nakamura Ganjirō • Nakamura Kankurō • Nakamura Kanzaburō • Nakamura Kichiemon • Nakamura Tomijūrō • Nakamura Utaemon • Okuni • Onnagata • Onoe Baikō • Onoe Kikugorō • Onoe Shōroku • Shishimai

Lin Lerner
Writer, Rosendale, New York
Bhutan • Black Hat Dance • Tibet

Fran Levy
Writer, Brooklyn, New York
Dance and Movement Therapy

Yaël Lewin
Dance writer; Artistic Director, Penumbra Dance, New York
Janet Collins

Daniel Lewis
Dean of Dance, New World School of the Arts, Miami
José Limón • The Moor's Pavane

Irène Lidova
Dance critic and writer, Paris
Jean Babilée • Ballets de Paris de Roland Petit • Ballets des Champs-Élysées • Janine Charrat • Yvette Chauviré • Grand Ballet du Marquis de Cuevas • Rosella Hightower • Zizi Jeanmaire • Le Jeune Homme et la Mort • Milorad Miskovitch • Roland Petit • George Skibine

Tullia Limarzi
Writer, Staten Island, New York
Gerald Arpino • Andrée Howard • Joffrey Ballet • Robert Joffrey • Metropolitan Opera Ballet

Meredith Ellis Little
Dance historian, Tucson, Arizona
Bourrée • Folia • Rigaudon

Liu Feng-Shueh
Choreographer, dance historian, and founder, Neo-Classic Dance Company, Taiwan
Taiwan

Belén Lobo
Director of Dance Department, Consejo Nacional de la Cultura; Caracas
Venezuela

Bob Lockyer
Executive Producer, Dance Programmes, BBC Television, London
Television, *article on* Dance on Television in Europe

Sophia D. Lokko
Head, Department of Theatre Arts, School of Performing Arts, University of Ghana
Ghana, *article on* Dance Research and Publication

Sondra Lomax
Ballet specialist, University of Texas at Austin
Les Sylphides, *article on* Diaghilev Production

Glenn Loney
Professor of Theatre, Graduate School and University Center, City University of New York
Jack Cole

Jacob Wainwright Love
Writer, Washington, D.C.
Samoa

Carlos Lozano
Writer, Flagstaff, Arizona
Tigua Dance • Yaqui Dance

Henrik Lundgren
Writer, Copenhagen
Lucile Grahn • Toni Lander • Elna Lassen • Ulla Poulsen • Price Family • Inge Sand • Margrethe Schanne

Lu Wenjian
Professor of Character Dance, Foreign Folk Dance, and Ballet, Beijing Dance Academy (deceased)
China, *article on* Classical Dance

Boris A. Lvov-Anokhin
Stage director, critic, and writer, Moscow
Nikolai Fadeyechev • Galina Ulanova

Alistair Macaulay
Dance writer, London
Richard Alston • The Dream • Enigma Variations • Illuminations • Monotones • A Month in the Country • Rambert Dance Company • Scènes de Ballet • Symphonic Variations • Two Pigeons

Frances MacEachen
Editor and general manager, Am Bráighe, Mabou, Nova Scotia
Step Dancing, *article on* Step Dancing in Cape Breton

Billie Mahoney
Writer, New York
Jazz Dance

Vera Maletic
Professor of Dance, Ohio State University
Laban Principles of Movement Analysis

Barbara Ferreri Malinsky
Dance historian and critic, Philadelphia
John Durang • Mary Ann Lee • Catherine Littlefield

William P. Malm
Professor Emeritus of Ethnomusicology, University of Michigan, Ann Arbor
Bugaku • Malaysia • Mayong • Music for Dance, *article on* Asian Music • Nagauta • Rāga

P. W. Manchester
Former Adjunct Professor of Dance History, Dance Division, College-Conservatory of Music, University of Cincinnati
Merle Marsicano

Muriel Manings
Former Associate Professor of Dance, Queensborough Community College, City University of New York
Cuba, *article on* Modern Dance

Susan A. Manning
Associate Professor of English and Theatre, Northwestern University, Evanston, Illinois
Isadora Duncan • Jean Weidt • Mary Wigman

Giora Manor
Editor-in-Chief, Israel Dance Quarterly, Tel Aviv
Inbal Dance Theatre • Gertrud Kraus • Ohad Naharin

Yvonne Marceau
Co-Founder and Co-Artistic Director, American Ballroom Theater, New York
Ballroom Dance Competition

Morton Marks
Folklorist and musicologist, New York
Brazil, *article on* Ritual and Popular Dance • Cuba, *article on* Folk, Ritual, and Social Dance

Luz Marmentini
Independent scholar and choreographer, Santiago
Chile, *article on* Theatrical Dance

Carol G. Marsh
Professor of Music, University of North Carolina at Greensboro
Galliard • Gavotte • Passepied • Pavan

Carol Martin
Assistant Professor of Drama, Tisch School of the Arts, New York University
Dance Marathons

Kenneth K. Martin
Associate Professor of English, Community College of Philadelphia
Asadata Dafora

Marianne W. Martin
Writer, Milton, Massachusetts (deceased)
Artists and Dance, *article on* Artists and Dance, 1760–1929 • Parade

Katy Matheson
Dance historian, New York
Hilda Butsova • Nikita Dolgushin • Improvisation • Bruce Marks • Helgi Tomasson

Marie Matoušová-Rajmová
Independent scholar, Prague
Mesopotamia

Matteo
Artistic Director, Foundation for Ethnic Dance, Inc., New York
Castanets

Charles S. Mayer
Professor of Art History and Humanities, Indiana State University
Ida Rubinstein

Joseph H. Mazo
Dance critic and writer, New York (deceased)
Alvin Ailey American Dance Theater, *article on* Origins to 1979 • Revelations

Patricia McAndrew
Independent scholar, Bethlehem, Pennsylvania
August Bournonville • A Folk Tale • Kermesse in Bruges • Konservatoriet

Kennetha R. McArthur
Principal, Dancespace Professional School, Toronto
Battement • Technical Manuals, *article on* Publications since 1887

Debra McCall
Director, Choreographic Research, New York; Director of Curriculum, The Ross School, East Hampton, New York
Bauhaus, Dance and the

T. Davina McClain
Assistant Professor of Classical Studies, Loyola University, New Orleans
Mimus • Pantomimus • Roman Empire

Veronica Ann McClure
Independent scholar, Watertown, Massachusetts
Round Dancing

Malcolm McCormick
Costume designer and dance historian, Canton, New York
Costume in Western Traditions, *overview article and articles on* Modern Dance *and* Film and Popular Dance • Barbara Karinska • Arch Lauterer • Mask and Makeup, *article on* European Traditions • Isamu Noguchi • Travesty

Lacy H. McDearmon
Librarian, Dance Collection, New York Public Library for the Performing Arts
Maud Allan

Don McDonagh
Adjunct Associate Professor of Humanities, New York University
Social Dance, *article on* Twentieth-Century Social Dance to 1960

Margaret M. McGowan
Professor of French, University of Sussex, Falmer, England
Académie de Musique et de Poésie • Le Balet Comique de la Royne • Ballet de Cour, *article on* Ballet de Court, 1560–1670 • Balthazar de Beaujoyeulx

Deirdre McMahon
Writer, Brooklyn, New York
Ireland, *article on* Theatrical Dance

Molly McQuade
Dance critic and writer, New York
Cinderella • Petrouchka

Karina L. Melik-Pashayeva
Professor of Musicology, Theater Union of the Russian Federation, Moscow
Raymonda

Nan Melville
Photographer, New York
Veronica Paeper • Dawn Weller

Richard Merz
Dance critic, Neue Zürcher Zeitung
Basel Ballet • Trudi Schoop • Heinz Spoerli • Susana •
Switzerland • Hans Züllig • Zurich Ballet

Azary Messerer
Independent scholar, Valley Stream, New York
Maya Plisetskaya

Judith Milhous
*Distinguished Professor of Theatre, Graduate School and
University Center, City University of New York*
Great Britain, *article on* Theatrical Dance, 1660–1772

Cynthia R. Millman
Dance historian, New York
Big Apple • Lindy Hop • Frankie Manning • Arthur Murray

Miyabi Ichikawa
Visiting professor, Waseda University, Tokyo
Japan, *article on* Modern Dance

Pia Mlakar
Choreographer and dance historian, Novo Mesto, Slovenia
Horschelt Family • Heinrich Kröller • Milko Šparemblek •
Yugoslavia, *article on* Ballet

Pino Mlakar
Choreographer and dance historian, Novo Mesto, Slovenia
Horschelt Family • Heinrich Kröller • Milko Šparemblek •
Yugoslavia, *article on* Ballet

Nèlida Monés i Mestre
Dance historian, Barcelona
Cesc Gelabert • Spain, *article on* Dance Research and
Publication

Sarah Montague
Arts critic, New York
John Curry • Pennsylvania Ballet

Ebbe Mørk
Editor, Politiken, *Hellerup, Denmark*
Hans Brenaa • Niels Bjørn Larsen • Vera Volkova

James E. Morrison
Independent scholar and writer, Charlottesville, Virginia
Jig • Reel

Jane Freeman Moulin
*Associate Professor of Ethnomusicology, University of Hawaii
at Manoa*
Tahiti

Robert D. Moulton
*Professor Emeritus of Theatre Arts, University of Minnesota,
Minneapolis*
Precision Dancing • Radio City Music Hall

John Mueller
*Professor of Film Studies and Political Science, University of
Rochester, New York*
Fred Astaire

William Mullen
*Professor of Classical Studies, Bard College, Annadale-on-
Hudson, New York*
Choral Dancing • Dithyramb

Grete Müller
Director, Sigurd Leeder School of Dance, Herisau, Switzerland
Sigurd Leeder

Hedwig Müller
*Dance historian, Institute of Theater Research, Universität zu
Köln*
Yvonne Georgi • Valeska Gert • Dore Hoyer • Niddy
Impekoven • Harald Kreutzberg • Gret Palucca • Alexander
Sakharoff • Alexander von Swaine

Sal Murgiyanto
Senior Lecturer, Jakarta Institute for the Arts
Indonesia, *articles on* Javanese Dance Traditions; Sumatran
Dance Traditions; Sundanese Dance Traditions; Dance
Traditions of the Outlying Islands; *and* Dance Research and
Publication • Pencak

Anne Murphy
Writer, New York
Nicholas Magallanes • Patricia McBride

James Briggs Murray
*Curator, Moving Image and Recorded Sound Division,
Schomburg Center for Research in Black Culture, New York
Public Library*
Pearl Primus

Betty June Myers
Writer, Washington, D.C.
Katti Lanner

Jasna Peručić Nadarević
Writer, Belgrade
Yugoslavia, *article on* Modern Dance

Andriy Nahachewsky
*Associate Professor of Ukrainian Folklore, Huculak Chair of
Ukrainian Culture and Ethnography, University of Alberta*
Ukraine, *article on* Traditional Dance

Erik Näslund
Director, Dansmuseet, Stockholm
Carina Ari • Birgit Cullberg • Ulf Gadd

Maureen Needham
*Associate Professor of Dance History, Vanderbilt University,
Nashville, Tennessee*
Jean-François Arnould-Mussot • Suzanne Douvillier • Jean-
Baptiste Francisqui • Anna Gardie • Alexandre Placide

Rex Nettleford
Professor of Continuing Studies and Pro Vice Chancellor, University of the West Indies; Artistic Director, National Dance Theatre Company, Kingston
Jamaica

Henrik Neubauer
Assistant Professor of Period Movement and Historical Dances, Academy of Music, Universa v Ljubljani
Yugoslavia, *article on* Dance Research and Publication

Barbara Newman
Dance critic, Country Life, *London*
David Blair • Kathleen Crofton • Margaret Dale • Anthony Dowell • Leslie Edwards • Violetta Elvin • Julia Farron • John Field • Alexander Grant • John Hart • The Invitation • Molly Lake • Anya Linden • Manon • Monica Mason • Pamela May • Ursula Moreton • Norman Morrice • Merle Park • The Red Shoes • Elisabeth Schooling • Moira Shearer • Antoinette Sibley • Michael Somes • Harold Turner • David Wall • Peter Wright

Don Niles
Ethnomusicologist, Papua New Guinea National Research Institute, Boroko
Papua New Guinea, *overview article and* Melpa Dance

Mats Nilsson
Junior Lecturer, Department of Ethnology, Göteborgs Universitet
Sweden, *article on* Traditional Dance

Ole Nørlyng
Art and dance critic, Hellerup, Denmark
Friedrich Burgmüller • Christian Cannabich • Ferdinand Hérold • Rodolphe Kreutzer • Knudage Riisager • Jean-Joseph Rodolphe • Claus Schall • Jean Schneitzhoeffer • Joseph Starzer

Cynthia J. Novak
Associate Professor of Dance, Wesleyan University, Middletown, Connecticut (deceased)
Native American Dance, *article on* Dance Research and Publication • Ritual and Dance

Alfred Oberzaucher
Dance historian, Vienna
Austria, *article on* Theatrical Dance • Rosalia Chladek • Erika Hanka

Gunhild Oberzaucher-Schüller
Forschungsinstitut für Musiktheater, Universität Bayreuth
Les Biches • Louise Bodin • Bronislava Nijinska • Les Noces • The Swiss Milkmaid • Viennese Kinderballet • Gret Wiesenthal

Selma Landen Odom
Associate Professor of Fine Arts, York University, North York, Ontario
Mary Wood Hinman • Émile Jaques-Dalcroze

Michael Oliver
Writer, London
Sergei Prokofiev • Dmitri Shostakovich

Albert Mawere Opoku
Technical adviser, Senior Fellow, and Consultant, International Center for African Music and Dance, Accra; founder and Artistic Director, Ghana Dance Ensemble
Ghana, *overview article*

Benito Ortolani
Professor of Theatre, Brooklyn College and the Graduate School and University Center, City University of New York
Gigaku • Japan, *overview article and* Ritual Dance • Kagura • Nō • Zeami

Hilary B. Ostlere
Contributing Editor, Dance Magazine, *New York*
Dance Theatre of Harlem • Arthur Mitchell

Vittoria Ottolenghi
Coordinator for dance, Spoleto Festival of Two Worlds, Spoleto, Italy; ballet critic and television producer, Rome
Amedeo Amodio • Aterballetto • Ugo Dell'Ara • Susanna Egri • Carla Fracci • Italy, *article on* Theatrical Dance since 1940 • Mario Pistoni • Rome Opera Ballet • Jia Ruskaja • Luciana Savignano • Teatrodanza Contemporanea di Roma • Elisabetta Terabust

Ou Jian-ping
Associate Research Fellow and Director, Foreign Dance Studies, Dance Research Institute, China National Arts Academy, Beijing; critic and China correspondent, Dance Magazine
Chen Weiya • China, *articles on* Contemporary Theatrical Dance *and* Dance Research and Publication • Wu Xiaobang • Yang Meiqi

Barbara Palfy
Associate Editor, Dance Chronicle, *New York*
Pyrrhic

Célida Parera Villalón
Dance writer and critic, New York
Cuba, *article on* Ballet before 1959

Margaret Pash
Dance historian, Springfield, Massachusetts
Branle

Mara J. Peets
Senior Library Administrative Associate, Dance Collection, New York Public Library for the Performing Arts
Pilobolus Dance Theatre

George Perry
Writer, London
Miss Bluebell

Kurt Petermann
Dance writer, Leipzig (deceased)
Germany, *article on* Traditional and Social Dance • Étienne Lauchery

Kurt Peters
Dance critic, writer, and founder-editor, Das Tanzarchiv, *Cologne* (deceased)
Germany, *article on* Dance Education

Ted Petrides
Folklorist; Hellenic American Union, Athens (deceased)
Anastenáridēs • Greece, *article on* Ritual and Carnival Dance Traditions

Emma Petrossian
Professor of Dance and Head, Department of Dance, Armenian Academy of Sciences, Yerevan
Armenia, *article on* Traditional Dance

Oleg A. Petrov
Dance critic, historian, and writer; Artistic Director, Yekaterinburg Ballet, Sverdlovsk, Russia
Yuri Slonimsky

Janis Pforsich
Senior faculty, Laban Institute of Movement Studies, New York; Director, Courante Dance Foundation, Athens, New York
Hornpipe

Claudia Roth Pierpont
Dance writer, New York
Nicholas Georgiadis • Santo Loquasto • Jürgen Rose • Jean Rosenthal • Oliver Smith • Rouben Ter-Arutunian • C. Wilhelm

Margaret Pierpont
Writer and editor, New York
Body Therapies, *overview article*

Julian Olivier Pilling
Leader (retired), Colne Royal Morris Men, Lancashire, England
Step Dancing, *article on* Step Dancing in Great Britain and Ireland

Vladimir N. Pletnev
Dance teacher, Baku, Azerbaijan (deceased)
Gamer Almaszade

Michelle Potter
Founder and editor, Brolga: An Australian Journal about Dance; *dance critic,* Dance Australia; *Oral Historian, National Library of Australia, Canberra*
Lucette Aldous • Australian Ballet • Edouard Borovansky • Kelvin Coe • Kathleen Gorham • Marilyn Jones • Hélène Kirsova • Laurel Martyn • Marilyn Rowe • Margaret Scott • Sydney Dance Company • Meryl Tankard • Garth Welch

William K. Powers
Professor of Anthropology, Rutgers, The State University of New Jersey
Native American Dance, *article on* The Great Plains • Powwow

Tea Preda
Dance critic; editor, Secolul XX, *Bucharest* (deceased)
Oleg Danovschi • Vera Proca Ciortea • Romania, *article on* Theatrical Dance

Valerie Preston-Dunlop
Adviser for postgraduate study and research in dance, Laban Centre for Movement and Dance, London
Rudolf Laban

Curtis A. Price
Writer, Saint Louis, Missouri
Henry Purcell

Fernanda Prim
Faculty member, Universidade Técnia de Lisboa
Portugal, *article on* Traditional Dance

Jane Pritchard
Archivist, English National Ballet and Rambert Dance Company, London
English National Ballet • Ronald Hynd

Vera Proca Ciortea
Professor of Dance, Theatre and Film Academy; former Head, Choreography Department, Institutul de Ethnografie şi Folclor, Bucharest
Romania, *article on* Folk Dance

Valentina V. Prokhorova
Dance critic, Saint Petersburg (deceased)
Natalia Dudinskaya • Konstantin Sergeyev

Janina Pudełek
Professor of Dance History, Akademia Muzyczna im. Fryderyka Chopina w Warszawie
Jan Cieplinski • Jerzy Gogół • Feliks Parnell • Maurice Pion • Poland, *article on* Theatrical Dance • Roman Turczynowicz • Warsaw Ballet • Piotr Zajlich

Patri J. Pugliese
Co-director, Commonwealth Vintage Dancers, Boston
Country Dance

Helen M. C. Purkis
Professor Emerita of French, University of British Columbia
Renaissance Fêtes and Triumphs

Denise Puttock
Whereabouts unknown
Bodenwieser Technique

Colin Quigley
Assistant Professor and Vice Chair, Department of World Arts and Cultures, University of California, Los Angeles
Methodologies in the Study of Dance, *article on* Ethnology

Ali Jihad Racy
Professor of Ethnomusicology, University of California, Los Angeles
Music for Dance, *article on* Arab Music

Barbara Racy
Dance ethnologist, Los Angeles
Music for Dance, *article on* Arab Music

Patricia Weeks Rader
Cataloging Assistant and Reference Librarian, Dance Collection, New York Public Library for the Performing Arts
Alta • Branle • Volta

N. P. Radkina
Dancer, Ashkhabad, Turkmenistan
Turkmenistan

Alkis Raftis
Associate Professor of Sociology and Management, University of Patras
Greece, *articles on* Dance in the Roman and Byzantine Periods; Dance in Modern Greece; *and* Dance Research and Publication

Xenia Rakič
Dance critic and writer, New York
Yugoslavia, *article on* Theatrical Dance since 1991

Richard Ralph
Principal, Westminster College, Oxford, England
Richard Baxter • Thomas Caverley • Philip Desnoyer • John Essex • Giovanni Gallini • Mister Isaac • Anthony L'Abbé • Médée et Jason • Josiah Priest • Psyché et l'Amour • Kellom Tomlinson • John Weaver

Carlynn Reed
Instructor, director, and playwright, Imagiscape Drama Learning Centre, Unionville, Ontario
Liturgical Dance

Hartmut Regitz
Writer, Stuttgart
Hannelore Bey • Tom Schilling

Theresa M. Reilly
Professor, Fashion Design Department, Fashion Institute of Technology, New York
Costume in Asian Traditions

Susan Reiter
Writer, New York
Lucas Hoving • John Kriza • Sallie Wilson

Nancy Reynolds
Director of Research, The George Balanchine Foundation, New York
Ballets 1933 • Madame Céleste • Alfredo Edel • Lincoln Kirstein • Boris Kochno • Carmelita Maracci • Henri Matisse • Alessandro Sanquirico • Maria Tallchief

William C. Reynolds
Executive Director, European Centre for Traditional Culture, Etgved, Denmark
Denmark, *article on* Dance in the Faeroe Islands • European Traditional Dance

Kenneth Richards
Professor of Drama and Director of the University Theatre, University of Manchester
Commedia dell'Arte

Sylvia Richards
Writer, State University, Arkansas
Charles Weidman

Farley Richmond
Professor and Chair, Department of Theatre Arts, State University of New York at Stony Brook
Chhau • Kūṭiyāṭṭam

Frank W. D. Ries
Professor of Dance and Chair, Department of Dramatic Art, University of California, Santa Barbara
Carmen Miranda • Albertina Rasch

Ine Rietstap
Dance critic and writer, Amsterdam
Ballet der Lage Landen • Netherlands, *articles on* Social Dance *and* Dance Education • Alexandra Radius • Scapino Rotterdam • Hans Snoek • Mascha ter Weeme

Cormac Rigby
Dance writer; assistant priest, Church of the Most Sacred Heart, Ruislip, England
David Bintley

James Ringo
Writer, New York
Darius Milhaud

Ritha Devi
Indian classical dancer; founder and Director, Ritham-Chhandra Dance Academy, New York
Bharata Nāṭyam • Devadāsi • Kathak • Kuchipudi • Birju Maharaj • Mōhiniāṭṭam • Yoga

Jorge Riverón
Ballet master, State University College at Purchase, New York; and National Ballet of Cuba, Havana
Cuba, *article on* Ballet since 1959

Martha E. Robbins
Writer, East Lansing, Michigan
Pokot Dance

Allen Robertson
Dance editor, Time Out, *London*
Meredith Monk • Sara Rudner • Glen Tetley

Jacqueline Robinson
Dancer and dance writer; founder, L'Atelier de la Danse, Paris
Dominique and Françoise Dupuy • France, *articles on* Modern Dance before 1970 *and* Modern Dance Education

Mardi Rollow
Dance researcher and folklorist, Los Angeles
Algeria • Morocco • North Africa • Ouled Naïl, Dances of the •
Tunisia

Arnold Rood
Writer, New York (deceased)
Gordon Craig

Brian Rose
*Professor of Communication and Media Studies, Fordham
University, New York*
Television, *article on* Dance on Television in the United States

Bernice M. Rosen
Professor Emerita of Dance, Arizona State University
Ann Hutchinson

Diane J. Rosenthal
Writer, Brooklyn, New York
Cotillon

Jane Mink Rossen
*Independent scholar and lecturer in ethnomusicology,
Copenhagen*
Bellona

Luigi Rossi
Dance critic and writer, Milan
Scala Ballet

Patricia A. Rowe
*Director, Program in Dance and Dance Education, New York
University*
Ritha Devi

Bonnie Rowell
*Senior Lecturer in Dance Studies, Roehampton Institute,
London*
Christopher Bruce • Siobhan Davies • London Contemporary
Dance Theatre

Anya Peterson Royce
Professor of Anthropology, Indiana University
Ethnic Dance

Olga Rozanova
Dance critic, Saint Petersburg
Elena Lukom

Mattani Mojdara Rutnin
*Professor and Head, Department of Fine and Applied Arts,
Thammasat University, Bangkok*
Khōn • Lakhǫn • Manōhrā • Thailand

Nancy Lee Chalfa Ruyter
Associate Professor of Dance, University of California, Irvine
Delsarte System of Expression • Margaret H'Doubler • Martha
Hill • United States of America, *article on* Social, Folk, and
Modern Dance Education

Aliodija Ruzgaitė
Dance historian, Vilnius
Lithuania, *article on* Theatrical Dance

Allan J. Ryan, M.D.
*Secretary, International Association for Dance Medicine and
Science, Minneapolis, Minnesota*
Dance Medicine

Andrew J. Sabol
*Adjunct Professor of English, Brown University, Providence,
Rhode Island*
Masque and Antimasque

A. W. Sadler
Writer, Bronxville, New York
Asian Dance Traditions, *article on* Religious, Philosophical,
and Environmental Influence

Shayma Saiyid
*Consultant, Latin America and Caribbean Region, Economic
Advisers Unit, World Bank, Washington, D.C.*
Rafi Anwar • Ghulam Husain • Sheema Kermani • Pakistan •
Nahid Siddiqui

Magda Saleh
President, Performing Arts International, Inc., New York
Egypt, *articles on* Dance in Ancient Egypt; Traditional Dance;
and Contemporary Dance Companies

Jonah Salz
*Associate Professor, Faculty of Intercultural Communications,
Ryukoku University*
Hanako • Kanze School • Kyōgen, *overview article* • Matsui
Akira • Shigeyama Family • Yakko and Kawakami

Ruth Sander
Writer, Vienna
Fränzl Family • Horse Ballet

Vivia Săndulescu
Lecturer, Theater and Film Academy; ballet critic, Bucharest
Romania, *article on* Theatrical Dance

Claudio Sanguinetti Gambaro
President, The Uruguayan Dance Committee, Montevideo
Uruguay

Ekaterina L. Sarian
Independent scholar, Yerevan
Armenia, *article on* Theatrical Dance • Gayané

Lydia P. Sarynova
Independent scholar, Alma-Ata, Kazakhstan
Kazakhstan

José Sasportes
Director, La Danza Italiana, Rome
Portugal, *article on* Theatrical Dance

David Sassian
Independent scholar, Brooklyn, New York
Estonia

Gabriele Schacheri
Writer, Vienna
Gertrud Bodenwieser

Maria Josefa Schaffgotsch
Writer, Bad Vöslau, Austria
Wiesenthal Technique

Eva van Schaik
Writer, Amsterdam
Hans van Manen • Netherlands, *articles on* Theatrical Dance, 1900–1945 *and* Dance Research and Publication • Netherlands Dance Theater

Edward L. Schieffelin
Professor of Anthropology, University College, London
Papua New Guinea, *article on* Kaluli Dance

Christena L. Schlundt
Professor Emerita of Dance History, University of California, Riverside
Denishawn • Daniel Nagrin • Ted Shawn • Helen Tamiris

Gretchen A. Schneider
Consultant and director, Granada History Productions, Berkeley, California
Ball • Ravel Family • Social Dance, *article on* Nineteenth-Century Social Dance • United States of America, *overview article*

Herbert Schneider
Professor of Musicology, Hochschule für Musik und Darstellende Kunst, Frankfurt
Music for Dance, *article on* Western Music, 1650–1800

Tim Scholl
Assistant Professor of Russian, Oberlin College, Oberlin, Ohio
Lubov Blok

A. C. Scott
Writer, Aix-en-Provence (deceased)
Aesthetics, *article on* Asian Dance Aesthetics • China, *overview article*

Trudy Scott
Professor of Theatre and Dance, Community College of Allegheny County, Pittsburgh, Pennsylvania
Orientalism

Luise Elcaness Scripps
Writer, New York
Balasaraswati • Indrani • Ragini Devi

David Sears
Writer, New York
Erick Hawkins • Pauline Koner • New Dance Group

Eva Selzer
Writer, Vienna
Chladek Technique

Laurence Senelick
Fletcher Professor of Drama and Oratory, Tufts University, Medford, Massachusetts
Circus • Music Hall, *article on* British Traditions • Pantomime • John Rich • Vaudeville

Norbert Servos
Writer, choreographer, and dance historian, Berlin
Ausdruckstanz • Folkwang Tanzstudio

Amparo Sevilla
Instituto Nacional de Antropologia e Historia, Mexico City
Mexico, *article on* Traditional Dance

Laura Shapiro
Senior writer, Newsweek, New York
Twyla Tharp

Roger Shattuck
University Professor and Professor of French, Boston University
Erik Satie

Anthony Shay
Artistic Director, Avaz International Dance Theatre, Los Angeles
Afghanistan • Arabian Peninsula • Danse du Ventre • Iran • Kurdish Dance • Lebanon

Suzanne Shelton
Joint Secretary, Atma Vidya Educational Foundation, Kerala, India
Radha • Ruth St. Denis

Jennifer Shennan
Librarian and tutor, New Zealand School of Dance; dance critic, The Evening Post and Radio New Zealand; dancer, Concordance, Wellington
Maori Dance • New Zealand, *overview article and article on* Dance Research and Publication

Natalia P. Sheremetyevskaya
Independent scholar and dance critic, Moscow
Boris Fenster

Ellen Shifrin
Writer, Toronto
Canada, *article on* Folk and Traditional Dance in French Canada

Ammon Shiloah
Professor of Musicology, Hebrew University of Jerusalem
Bedouin Dance • Islam and Dance

Genevieve Shimer
Independent scholar, New York (deceased)
John Playford

Adrienne Sichel

Dance critic and writer, The Star, Johannesburg

South Africa, *article on* Contemporary Theatrical Dance

Marcia B. Siegel

Associate Professor of Performance Studies, Tisch School of the Arts, New York University

Day on Earth • Doris Humphrey • New Dance Trilogy • The Shakers • Water Study

Sigridur Valgeirsdóttir

Professor of Educational Psychology, University Teachers College of Iceland; Former director, Institute of Educational Research in Iceland

Iceland, *article on* Traditional Dance

Anna Lee Skalski

Dance historian, Orono, Maine

Federal Dance Project

Libby Smigel

Independent scholar, Washington, D.C.

Cheironomia • Emmeleia • Greece, *article on* Dance in Ancient Greece • Hypochēma • Kallinikos • Kordax • Schēma • Sikinnis • Terpsichore

Amanda Smith

Lecturer in Dance, Coe College, Cedar Rapids, Iowa; dance critic and writer, New York

Laura Dean • Phyllis Lamhut • Valda Setterfield

Ronald R. Smith

Associate Professor of Folklore, Ethnomusicology, and Music and Associate Dean, Research and University Graduate School, Indiana University

Congo Dances

Allegra Fuller Snyder

Professor Emerita of Dance and Dance Ethnology, University of California, Los Angeles

Film and Video, *article on* Ethnographic Studies

Janet Mansfield Soares

Senior Lecturer in Dance, Barnard College, Columbia University

Louis Horst

Arkady A. Sokolov-Kaminsky

Dance critic; teacher, Saint Petersburg N. A. Rimsky-Korsakov State Conservatory

Igor Belsky • Gabriella Komleva • Leningrad Symphony • Yuri Soloviev,

Sally R. Sommer

Associate Professor of Dance, Duke University, Durham, North Carolina; dance writer, New York

Loie Fuller • Master Juba • Bill Robinson • Sandman Sims • Social Dance, *article on* Twentieth-Century Social Dance since 1960 • Tap Dance

Kathrine Sorley Walker

Dance critic and historian, London

Ballets Russes de Monte Carlo • Irina Baronova • René Blum • Beryl Grey • Robert Helpmann • Anna Northcote • Tatiana Riabouchinska • Tamara Toumanova

Elizabeth Souritz

Leading scholar, State Arts Research Institute, Moscow

Georgi Aleksidze • Bolshoi Ballet • Dmitri Briantzev • Boris Eifman • Viacheslav Gordeyev • Aleksandr Gorsky • Joseph the Beautiful • Vera Krasovskaya • The Red Poppy • Russia, *articles on* Secondary and Provincial Dance Companies; Twentieth-Century Plastique; *and* Theatrical Dance Research and Publication • Vasily Tikhomirov

Debra Hickenlooper Sowell

Adjunct Assistant Professor, Brigham Young University, Provo, Utah

Carlotta Brianza • Christensen Brothers • Nicola Guerra

Barbara Sparti

Dance historian, Rome

Ballo and Balletto • Saltarello

Paul Spencer

Professor of African Anthropology, School of Oriental and African Studies, London

Samburu Dance

Jody Sperling

Dance writer, dancer, choreographer, and videographer, New York

Film and Video, *article on* Choreography for Camera

Emte Stag

Writer, Førd, Norway

Norway, *article on* Classical Dance Education

Anna Greta Ståhle

Dance critic, Dagens Nyheter, Stockholm; Lecturer in Dance, Stockholms Universitet

Regina Beck-Friis • Anna Behle • Mats Ek • Sweden, *articles on* Theatrical Dance since 1900 *and* Dance Research and Publication

Yuri A. Stanishevsky

Scholar in Folklore and Ethnography, Kiev State Institute of Fine Arts, Ukraine

Elena Potapova • Ukraine, *article on* Theatrical Dance • Pavel Virsky

Bonnie Sue Stein

Executive Director, GOH Productions, New York

Yoshiko Chuma

Omer C. Stewart

Professor of Anthropology, University of Colorado at Boulder (deceased)

Ghost Dance

Amy Ku'uleialoha Stillman
Assistant Professor of Music, University of California, Santa Barbara
Hula

Robynn J. Stilwell
Lecturer in Music, University of Southampton
Sonja Henie • Ice Dancing • Torvill and Dean

Andrew J. Strathern
Andrew W. Mellon Professor of Anthropology, University of Pittsburgh
Papua New Guinea, *article on* Melpa Dance

G. B. Strauss
Independent scholar, New York
Margaret Craske

Desmond F. Strobel
Former Assistant Professor of Historical Dance, University of Southern California, Los Angeles; Director, The Antique Academy of Genteel Dance, Los Angeles
Assemblies • Cotillon • Écossaise • Polka • Quadrille • Waltz

Mary R. Strow
Associate Librarian, Indiana University
Libraries and Museums

Raisa S. Struchkova
Chair, Russian Academy of Arts, Moscow
Gerdt Family • Nikolai Tarasov

Otis Stuart
Dance writer, New York (deceased)
Ballet Competitions

Igor V. Stupnikov
Professor, Saint Petersburg State University
Nina Anisimova • The Flames of Paris

Javier Suárez-Pajares
Instituto Complutense de Ciencias Musicales, Madrid
Bolero • Escuela Bolera

Tiina Suhonen
Dance historian, Helsinki
Finland, *article on* Dance Research and Publication

Lawrence Sullivan
Associate Professor of English Literature, State University College at New Paltz, New York
Elizabeth Anderson-Ivantzova

Sumarsam
Adjunct Professor of Music, Wesleyan University, Middletown, Connecticut
Gamelan, *article on* Javanese Traditions

Susan Cook Summer
Dance writer, New York
Fedor Koni • André Levinson • Valerian Svetlov • Akim Volynsky • Rafail Zotov

William H. Sun
Associate Professor of Drama, Macalester College, Saint Paul, Minnesota; Contributing Editor, The Drama Review, *New York*
Pei Yanling • Yuan Xuefen • Zhou Xinfang

Elisabeth Sussman
Curator, Whitney Museum of American Art, New York
Artists and Dance, *article on* Artists and Dance since 1945

Julia Sutton
Professor Emerita of Musicology, New England Conservatory of Music, Boston
Alta • Thoinot Arbeau • Ballo and Balletto • Branle • Canary • Fabritio Caroso • Cascarda • Galliard • Matachins, *historical overview article* • Music for Dance, *article on* Western Music, 1520–1650 • Cesare Negri • Passo e Mezzo • Pavan • Pavaniglia • Saltarello • Spagnoletta • Tordion • Volta

Lulli Svedin
Professor Emerita of Classical Ballet, University College of Dance, Stockholm; Sweden correspondent, Dance Magazine
Ivo Cramér • Ronny Johansson • Mariane Orlando • Elsa-Marianne von Rosen • Sweden, *article on* Dance Education

Jill D. Sweet
Professor of Anthropology, Skidmore College, Saratoga Springs, New York
Pueblo Dance

Mary Grace Swift
Professor of History, Loyola University, New Orleans
Madame Augusta • Hermine Blangy • Charles-Louis Didelot • Eugénie Lecomte

Karl Heinz Taubert
Dance writer and historian, Berlin (deceased)
La Barbarina

Katherine Teck
Writer, New York
Accompaniment for Dance

Iro Valaskakis Tembeck
Professor of Dance, Université du Québec à Montréal
Canada, *article on* Contemporary Theatrical Dance

Rouben Ter-Arutunian
Stage designer, New York (deceased)
Designing for Dance

Alberto Testa
Dancer, choreographer, teacher, critic, and writer, Rome
Carlo Blasis • Italy, *article on* Theatrical Dance, 1801–1940 • Pierina Legnani • Luigi Manzotti • Romulado Marenco • Aurelio Milloss • Atilia Radice • Taglioni Family • Virginia Zucchi

Emma Lewis Thomas
Professor of Dance and Director, Intercampus Arts Program, University of California, Los Angeles
Bergamasque

Margaret Thompson-Drewal
Writer, Chicago
Mask and Makeup, *article on* African Traditions • Sub-Saharan Africa, *article on* Dance Research and Publication • Yoruba Dance

Jennifer Thorp
Archivist, Regent's Park College, University of Oxford
Mister Isaac • Josiah Priest • Kellom Tomlinson

Edward Thorpe
Dance critic and writer, London
Kenneth MacMillan

Jennifer Tipton
Lighting designer, New York
Lighting for Dance, *article on* Theory and Practice

Erik U. Tivum
Dance critic, Riga
Latvia

Linda J. Tomko
Associate Professor of Dance, University of California, Riverside
Reconstruction, *article on* Beyond Notation

Lea Tormis
Associate Professor of Performing Arts, Higher School of Drama, Estonian Academy of Music, Tallinn
Estonia

Lisbet Torp
Assistant Curator, Musikhistorisk Museum of Carl Claudius' Samling, Copenhagen
Chain and Round Dances

Robert Tracy
Dancer and writer, New York
Bill T. Jones

Trân Van Khê
Professor of Ethnomusicology, Université de Paris (Sorbonne)
Vietnam

Colin M. Turnbull
Professor of Anthropology, George Washington University, Washington, D.C. (deceased)
Mbuti Dance

Yuri P. Tyurin
Dance critic, Moscow
Makhumd Esambayev • Tajikistan • Nina Timofeyeva

Juan Ubaldo Lavanga
Writer, Buenos Aires
Argentina, *article on* Ballet • Olga Ferri

Ayako Uchiyama
President, Ayako Uchiyama Dance Theatre, Inc., New York
Ainu Dance Traditions

Ani Udovicki
Dancer and independent scholar, New York
Yugoslavia, *article on* Theatrical Dance since 1991

Ueno-Herr, Michiko
Writer, Honolulu
Japan, *article on* Dance Research and Publication

Valeria I. Uralskaya
Editor in Chief, Sovetsky Balet, *Moscow*
Mikhail Lavrovsky • Russia, *articles on* Traditional Dance; Theatrical Dance before 1917; *and* Folk Dance Research and Publication • Marina Semenova • Tatiana Ustinova

Robert K. Urasguildiyev
Independent scholar, Dushanbe, Kyrgyzstan
Kyrgyzstan

Dalia Urbanaviciené
Head, Department of Ethnomusicology, Lietuvos Musikos Akademija, Vilnius
Lithuania, *article on* Traditonal Dance

Henning Urup
Archivist, Danish Dance History Archives, Virum, Denmark
Denmark, *article on* Traditional and Social Dance

Usui Kenji
Dance writer, Osaka
Japan, *article on* Ballet • Takarazuka

Luuk Utrecht
Dance historian and critic, Amsterdam
Rudi van Dantzig • Dutch National Ballet • Sonia Gaskell • Corrie Hartong • Jiří Kylián • Netherlands, *article on* Theatrical Dance since 1945 • Netherlands Ballet • Toer van Schayk

Elisa Vaccarino
Dance critic, Il Giorno, Balleto Oggi, *and* Ballet 2000, *Rome*
Louis Henry • Italy, *article on* Classical Dance Education

Ann Vachon
Professor of Dance, Temple University, Philadelphia
Sophie Maslow

Victor V. Vanslov
Director, Research Institute on Theory and History of Fine Arts, Moscow
Boris Asafiev • La Bayadère • Don Quixote, *articles on* Petipa Production *and* Gorsky Production • The Golden Age • Yuri Grigorovich • Legat Family • Legend of Love • Maris Liepa • Russia, *article on* Theatrical Dance since 1917 • Spartacus • The Stone Flower • Simon Virsaladze

Judy Van Zile
Professor of Dance, University of Hawaii at Manoa
Bon Odori • India, *article on* Dance Research and Publication

Vladimír Vašut
Professor of Ballet Dramaturgy, Akademie Múzických Umění, Prague
Augustin Berger • Brno Ballet • Czech Republic and Slovak Republic, *article on* Theatrical Dance • Emerich Gabzdyl • Miroslav Kůra • Saša Machov • Jiří Němeček • Luboš Ogoun • Prague National Theater Ballet • Ivo Vána Psota • Slovak National Theater Ballet • Pavel Šmok

Kapila Vatsyayan
Academic Director, Indira Gandhi National Centre for the Arts, New Delhi
India, *articles on* Philosophy of Indian Dance *and* The Rādhā-Kṛṣṇa Theme in Indian Dance

David Vaughan
Archivist, Cunningham Dance Foundation, Inc., New York
Frederick Ashton • Carolyn Brown • Checkmate • Lesley Collier • Merce Cunningham • Dark Elegies • Audrey de Vos • Garth Fagan • Great Britain, *article on* Contemporary Criticism • Horoscope • Jardin aux Lilas • Job • Chris Komar • Jessie Matthews • Anatole Oboukhoff • Les Patineurs • Pillar of Fire • The Rake's Progress • Les Rendezvous • Dan Siretta • Antony Tudor • James Waring • A Wedding Bouquet

Ursula Vaughan Williams
Writer, London
Cecil Sharp

Lucy Venable
Professor Emerita of Dance, Ohio State University
Body Therapies, *article on* Alexander Technique

Luc Vervaeke
Independent scholar, Oud-Heverlee, Belgium
Belgium, *articles on* Theatrical Dance *and* Dance Education • Jeanne Brabants • Charleroi/Danses • André Leclair • Royal Ballet of Flanders

Mercedes Viale Ferrero
Independent scholar, Turin
Le Nozze degli Dei

Vojko Vidmar
Ballet dancer, Ljubljana, Slovenia
Yugoslavia, *article on* Theatrical Dance since 1991

Irma Vienola-Lindfors
Dance critic and editor (retired), Helsingin Sanomat
Finland, *article on* Theatrical Dance

Stanimir Visinski
Whereabouts unknown
Yugoslavia, *article on* Traditional Dance

John von Sturmer
Independent scholar, Canberra City
Australian Aboriginal Dance, *article on* Aborigines of Cape York Peninsula

Ann Wagner
Professor of Dance, Saint Olaf College, Northfield, Minnesota
Christianity and Dance, *article on* Modern Views

John Dademo Waiko
Member of National Parliament, Papua New Guinea
Papua New Guinea, *article on* Binandere Dance

J. Michael Walton
Professor of Drama and Head, Department of Drama, University of Hull, England
Orchestra

MaryJane Warner
Associate Professor of Dance, York University, North York, Ontario
Canada, *article on* Dance Education

Larry Warren
Professor Emeritus of Dance, University of Maryland at College Park; dance writer, University Park, Maryland
Lester Horton • Bella Lewitzky

Robin Woodard Weening
Independent scholar, Hartland, Wisconsin
Elizabethan Progresses • Revels

Andrew Mark Wentik
Dance writer and critic, New York
Frederic Franklin • Ruth Page

Geoffrey West
Dance writer, Edinburgh
Scottish Ballet

Melanye White-Dixon
Associate Professor of Dance, Ohio State University
Talley Beatty • Donald McKayle • Jawole Willa Jo Zollar

Stephen A. Wild
Research Fellow in Ethnomusicology, Australian Institute of Aboriginal and Torres Strait Islander Studies, Canberra
Australian Aboriginal Dance, *overview article*

R. F. Willetts
Professor Emeritus of Greek, Institute for Advanced Research in the Humanities, University of Birmingham, England
Armed Dances • Crete, *article on* Dance in Ancient Crete

Peter Williams
Dance writer, London (deceased)
Christian Bérard • William Chappell • Peter Darrell • Anton Dolin • Sally Gilmour • John Gilpin • Walter Gore • Jean Hugo • Ronald Hynd • Mona Inglesby • International Ballet • Keith Lester • Maude Lloyd • Metropolitan Ballet • Northern Ballet Theatre

John M. Wilson
Professor of Dance, University of Arizona, Tucson
Kinesiology, *overview article* • Turnout, *article on* Physical Mechanics

Leland Windreich
Copyeditor, Dance International, *Vancouver*
Ruthanna Boris • Agnes de Mille • David Lichine • Rodeo • San Francisco Ballet

Carl Wolz
Professor of Dance, Graduate School, Japan Women's College of Physical Education, Tokyo
Japan, *article on* Dance Research and Publication • Shimai

Leona Wood
Founder and Artistic Director, Aman International Dance Company, Los Angeles
Algeria • Morocco • North Africa • Ouled Naïl, Dances of the • Tunisia

Dianne L. Woodruff
Adjunct Associate Professor of Dance, York University, North York, Ontario
Theaters for Dance

Max Wyman
Dance historian, critic, and writer, Vancouver
Canada, *article on* Theatrical Dance • Royal Winnipeg Ballet

Xu Suyin
Professor of Dance, Beijing Dance Academy
China, *article on* Folk and Minority Dance

Ye Shaolan
Actor, Zhan You Beijing Opera Company; member, Board of Directors, All-China Association of Dramatists, China
Kunqu

Suzanne Youngerman
Program Director, Young Audiences/New York
Methodologies in the Study of Dance, *article on* Anthropology • Shaker Dance

Phillip B. Zarrilli
Professor of Theatre and Drama, Folklore, and South Asian Studies, University of Wisconsin–Madison
Asian Martial Arts

Maria I. Zhornitskaya
Independent scholar, Moscow (deceased)
Russia, *article on* Siberian Dance Traditions

Zhu Liren
Professor of Dance History, Beijing Dance Academy; Managing Director, Beijing Dance Academy Journal
The Red Detachment of Women • The White-Haired Girl

INTERNATIONAL ENCYCLOPEDIA OF DANCE

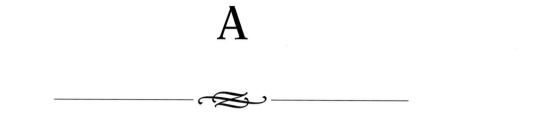

A

ABRAXAS. Ballet in five scenes. Choreography: Marcel Luipart. Music and libretto: Werner Egk. Scenery: Wolfgang Znamenacek. Costumes: Elly Ohns. First performance: 6 June 1948, Prinzregenten Theater, Munich, Bavarian State Opera Ballet. Principals: Marcel Luipart (Faust), Solange Schwarz (Bellastriga), Irina Kladivova, Nika Nilanowa-Sanftleben.

Abraxas was inspired by Heinrich Heine's *Der Doktor Faust: Ein Tanzpoem* (1847), written for Benjamin Lumley in London but never produced. The title of the ballet is a reference to the mystical teachings of the Kabbalah (Abraxas was the name of the great mystery of the Gnostics), and the libretto is a variation of the familiar German story of Doctor Faustus. The first scene introduces the ag-

ABRAXAS. Janine Charrat and an unidentified partner in her 1949 revival of *Abraxas*, staged in West Berlin. (Photograph by Siegfried Enkelmann; from the Dance Collection, New York Public Library for the Performing Arts.)

ing Faust signing a contract with Bellastriga, a voluptuous witch. In exchange for his soul, she grants him youth and guides him into the arms of the arch-courtesan Archisposa, then to a pandemonium in Hell, and finally to Helen of Troy. When he later meets the innocent Margarethe at a German carnival ground and tears up the contract in disgust, he becomes his former self but still draws Margarethe into his deadly downfall.

Abraxas was the first full-length German ballet choreographed and performed after World War II, and its premiere was considered a landmark in Germany's return to classical ballet. After four performances the production was banned by Alois Hundhammer, cultural minister of Bavaria, who accused the producers of presenting satanism in the pandemonium scene. (Hundhammer's name consequently became well known in Germany as a synonym for bourgeois pettiness.) However, the West Berlin revival in October 1949, rechoreographed by Janine Charrat, received more than a hundred performances, making *Abraxas* the most successful ballet of the postwar German repertory. Productions were staged throughout Germany, Austria, and Switzerland as well as in Prague, Helsinki, and Havana. Tom Schilling's production for the East Berlin Komische Oper remained a staple in the repertory until the mid-1980s, after which its popularity slowly faded.

BIBLIOGRAPHY

Nevill, Timothy, trans. *Ballet and Dance in the Federal Republic of Germany.* Bonn, 1988.
Peters, Kurt, ed. *Abraxas.* Special issue of *Die Tanzarchiv-Reihe*, 2. Hamburg, 1964.

HORST KOEGLER

ACADÉMIE DE MUSIQUE ET DE POÉSIE. The institution dubbed the Académie de Musique et de Poésie was founded by royal patent in 1570 by Charles IX of France. The king, a poet and a great lover of music, responded eagerly and authoritatively to the joint request by the poet Jean-Antoine de Baïf and the composer Joachim Thibault de Courville that, following the example of Francis I in founding the Collège de France in 1529, Charles should establish in Paris an institution to foster the study of all the arts that could serve to improve the minds and souls of his subjects. Recognizing that the prestige of the crown was at stake, the king consulted his mother, his two brothers, and other members of the royal family before giving his approval to the project. The University of Paris, fearing the erosion of its role and influence, refused to recognize the academy, but the king was determined; he issued a second set of *lettres patentes* early in 1571, overruling the university.

After Charles's death in 1574, Henri III returned precipitately from Poland to claim his throne. At first it was not clear that he would support his elder brother's foundation, but he not only gave continuing support to the work of the academy but also extended it by founding the Académie du Palais. Discussions on artistic, moral, and intellectual themes took place twice weekly at the latter, located in the Louvre, and Henri expected all members of the court to attend.

To understand the aims of these institutions it is necessary to recall, first, Jean Dorat and his Collège de Coqueret, where he taught the rudiments of Greek to pupils such as Baïf and Pierre de Ronsard and initiated them into the marvels of Greco-Roman civilization; and second, the writings of Pontus de Tyard, especially the *Solitaire premier* (1552), a discourse on poetry, and the *Solitaire second* (1552), a dialogue on music in which he set out the mysterious powers of poetry and music and showed how they fitted into the general frame of encyclopedic knowledge. Baïf and Courville, inspired by their early studies, determined that the academy would bring to France the kind of poetry known to the ancient world, as well as its musical systems and choreography.

To achieve these goals, rules regulating the academy's activities were strict and numerous. Composers, singers, and players were obliged to perform in public for two hours every Sunday. Auditor members and their subscriptions were registered. The texts or scores of compositions could not be sold without permission. Musicians had to meet for regular practice, having fully studied their separate parts beforehand. Other rules guaranteed provision for the members' practical needs and ensured that performances were held in the best possible conditions; for example, auditors were not allowed to make noise during a concert or to enter the auditorium while a work was being played. In France at this time, such a degree of professionalism was unique.

The primary purpose of the academy was to create works of art that, like those of ancient Greece and Rome, would improve, refine, and purify the mind, since this process was believed to afford access to the realms of higher knowledge. From reading classical works (especially Plato's *Timaeus* and Plutarch's *De musica*), members were persuaded that music and poetry, harmoniously combined, had the power to arouse the mind and soul and cause the listener to feel edifying emotions. The literary and musical models were the mythological Orpheus and Amphion, chosen for their capacity to arouse feelings through the exercise of musical and poetic gifts. Charles IX's *lettres patentes* clarify these views: "Where music is disordered, there morals are also depraved, and where it is well ordered, there men are well tutored." Here music represents all the arts fostered by the academy and the general educational role is clear.

The practical means of ensuring such a result are less easy to determine, although the essentials can be found in Marin Mersenne's *Harmonie universelle* (1636). Sixteenth-century musicians argued for the use of Greek musical modes, each of which had a corresponding ethos: thus the Dorian mode represented sobriety, the Phrygian mode called forth enthusiasm, and the Lydian and Ionian modes suggested sweet sounds and a subdued mood respectively. In addition, Baïf thought that French verse had to be modified so that it would blend more effectively with music, so he tried to substitute vowel quantity (the metrical determiner in Latin verse) for stress accent (the principal metrical feature in French).

The academy's activities were integrated into court festivals, which had multiplied extravagantly during the long regency of Catherine de Médicis (1560–1574). Measured dancing followed from measured poetry and music to re-create what was intended to be a reenactment of Greek drama, with its full choreographic dimensions. Dance had to obey the same principles as music, and it was regulated by the same tunes and timing. Musicians from the academy were involved in the production of *Le Balet Comique de la Royne* (1581), which was also concerned with the themes of reason, order, and harmony debated in the academy. In the poems that form the preface to the published edition of *Le Balet Comique*, contemporaries of Balthazar de Beaujoyeulx, its chief composer, stress his attempt to reconstruct composite forms of art, like those of Greek drama—a combination of poetry, music, and dance to create powerful therapeutic effects on the spectators. Frances Yates (1947) has established that Beaujoyeulx was inspired by work that had been going on for several years at the academy. Thus the academy contributed significantly to the introduction in France of a new genre, court ballet, which in turn strongly influenced the beginnings of opera in France.

After Charles IX's death, the academy continued to flourish for a few years, although its activities were transformed. Henri III favored argument over the arts, and until about 1585, when the religious wars put an end to much of the cultural life of Paris, debates on philosophical and moral themes replaced music and poetry. Modern historians recognize this change by renaming the institution of this period the Palace Academy.

[*See also* Balet Comique de la Royne, Le.]

BIBLIOGRAPHY
Frémy, Édouard. *L'Académie des derniers Valois.* Paris, 1887.
Sealy, Robert J. *The Palace Academy of Henry III.* Geneva, 1981.
Walker, D. P. "Musical Humanism in the Sixteenth and Early Seventeenth Centuries" (parts 1–5). *Music Review* 2.1–3.1 (1941–1942).
Yates, Frances A. *The French Academies of the Sixteenth Century.* London, 1947.

MARGARET M. MCGOWAN

ACADÉMIE ROYALE DE DANSE. As the first dance institution established in the Western world, the Académie Royale de Danse is widely known by name only, for the loss of its archives has thus far prevented a fair assessment of its activities and achievements. Founded in March 1661 by letters of patent granted under Louis XIV and ratified by Parlement in March 1662, the academy is generally thought to have been the king's brainchild. In the preamble to the letters, Louis stated that the purpose of the academy was "to restore the art of dancing to its original perfection and to improve it as much as possible," since "as the result of the disorders caused by the lat-

ACADÉMIE ROYALE DE DANSE. An engraving by H. Bonnart depicting Claude Ballon, one of the most distinguished dancers of the first half of the eighteenth century. Ballon became head of the Académie Royale de Danse in 1719, replacing Pierre Beauchamps. (University of Bristol Theatre Collection.)

est wars, many people were now teaching dance without qualifications," so that "the time had come to correct these abuses which may otherwise ruin the art altogether and forever."

The academy was to consist of thirteen dancers, "chosen among the most experienced in the art of dancing." They were François Galand du Désert (dancing master to the queen), Guillaume Raynal (dancing master to the prince [dauphin]), Jean Renaud (dancing master to Monsieur, the king's brother, and later to the king himself), Guillaume Quéru, Hilaire d'Olivet, Jean Raynal, Nicolas de Lorges, Guillaume Renaud, Jean-François Piquet, Florent Galand du Désert, Jean de Grigny, and Thomas Le Vacher. The missing thirteeth academician may have been Henri Prévost, Louis XIV's dancing master, who died the year after the academy was founded.

The academy's twelve articles outlined the program for the academicians' future activities, throwing some light on their functions and privileges. They were to meet monthly at a place chosen by them and rented at their own expense. Every Saturday, in turn, two members were to instruct a class of aspiring dance teachers, as well as anyone else who wished to learn new dances and go over the old ones. To fill a vacancy, the Elders, as the academicians called themselves, would set up an audition, where candidates were requested "to perform all manners of steps, dances old and new, as well as sections of the ballet repertory." Any new member, elected by a majority of votes, paid the sum of 150 livres if he was already a master's son or 300 livres if not. These funds went toward the academy's upkeep. Apart from these duties, the academicians also kept a register of all the Parisian dancing masters and could enforce their decisions throughout the kingdom. In the matter of choreography—their own or their colleagues'—they vouched for absolute integrity in judging the quality of the work presented. New dances would be accepted or rejected after much careful deliberation.

The academicians' privileges were those of the king's officers. They included the *droit de committimus,* that is, the right to appeal directly to the king in cases of litigation; exemption from taxes, such as *taille, curatelle, guet,* and *garde;* and, above all, exemption from the costly *maîtrise* ("mastership") necessary to open a school. In addition, they were allowed to confer teaching credentials on their students.

With the creation of an independent center for the study of dance, Louis had unwittingly unleashed a controversy that was to bitterly confront musicians and dancers for decades. Indeed, since its foundation in 1321, the minstrels' guild had supervised the training of dancers throughout France, granting them the mastership that allowed them to teach. Thus, an autonomous dance academy that not only exempted its members from taking the mastership but also authorized them to dispense their own was a direct threat to the guild's supremacy and privileges. The academy's very existence raised disturbing questions as to the competence of the guild's head, known as "king of the violins." In 1662 Guillaume Dumanoir, holder of that powerful position, marshaled opposition to the creation of the injurious academy. He lost the battle on 3 August 1662 but went on with the war. Several judgments between 1682 and 1683 attempted to settle the dispute, which ended with the dismissal of Dumanoir and the complete reorganization of the guild on 2 November 1692.

In the midst of this turbulence, the indomitable academicians went on with their duties, as articles published in *Le Mercure galant* or the *Almanach des spectacles* periodically testified. Abraham Du Pradel wrote in his 1690 book on Paris, *Le livre commode des adresses de la Ville de Paris,* that "three masters come every Thursday to the Academy to give free lessons to those people of condition who requested it and to the academicians' regular students who hoped to be admitted one day to the academy and have, to this effect, their own protectors . . . as guarantee of their competence when the time of their admission had come." At such times, several academicians would gather together with other qualified persons to examine the candidate and judge his *chef d'oeuvre.* The first Thursday of each month and on 1 May, the entire academy gathered to deliberate its members' common affairs. By 1690 the number of academicians had appreciably increased, "for the king was easily led to bestow this distinction on some of his best ballet dancers."

From the outset, the academy had been placed under the king's protection and the vice-protection of the duke of Saint-Aignan. First housed in the Tuileries palace, the sessions were held in the dauphin's antechamber. With the appointment of Pierre Beauchamps as the academy's chancellor in 1680, it was moved to his house, at 5 rue de Bailleul, and subsequently to the house of each of its heads. Although the academicians elected their members by a majority, they did not elect their head, or director, who was appointed by Saint-Aignan—a mere formality, for it was soon established that the king's own dancing master and/or the composer of his ballets would automatically become head of the academy.

Among the rare documents concerning the academicians' activities, one dated 16 April 1662 relates in great detail the election of a new member, Bernard De Manthe, a replacement for Le Vacher. Another, from 9 March 1693, also concerns an election—less peaceful this time—for the whole academy ended its session at the police station, where clerks on duty recorded for posterity the academicians' black eyes, bruised noses, and swollen lips. In Jean-Georges Noverre's *Lettres sur la danse et sur les ballets* (1760), he sarcastically reports that the academicians were prone to hold their sessions in the pub L'Epée de Bois, which may account for their sometimes less than dignified behavior. Noverre went on to attack the academicians, "who never issued or wrote anything," until he finally joined their ranks in 1775 and "felt of his honor and duty, to give them the praises they deserve."

Altogether, it is impossible to determine the academy's achievements. The first dance notation system was entrusted to Beauchamps, who was not at that time the academy's director; and Jean le Rond d'Alembert and Denis Diderot assigned the technical articles on dancing in their *Encyclopédie* (1751–1772) to Louis de Cahusac but not to the academicians, to whom they should have been given. Without rushing to any conclusion, it is possible that, in the words of the Italian dancer and choreographer Gaspero Angiolini, "the academy's duties were not to write out statutes or publish anything. Its duties were to teach and to produce good dancers and good teachers for the ballets. It has not failed in its mission" (Cordey, 1952, p. 184).

As with other royal institutions, the academy ended with the fall of the monarchy in 1789. In 1778 the *Almanach des spectacles* had published, for the last time, the list of current academicians. With the restoration of the monarchy, a petition for the academy's resurrection was filed in 1819 by the dancer André Deshayes and endorsed by his colleagues of the Académie Royale de Musique: Auguste Vestris, Monsieur Albert, Louis Nivelon, and Louis-Marie Beaupré. The project's objectives were in Deshayes's words "the preservation of our great masters' work" and "the training of young dancers." Yet these dancers "were frustrated in [their] expectations and [their] request never met an answer."

The following is a list of the academy's directors from its creation to its demise (the dates are those of official appointment): François Galand du Désert (1661), Pierre Beauchamps (1680), Claude Ballon (1719), Antoine Bandieri de Laval (1744), and Michel Jean Bandieri de Laval (1770).

[*See also* France, *article on* Theatrical Dance, 1789–1914; *and entries on the principal figures mentioned herein.*]

BIBLIOGRAPHY

Almanach des spectacles de Paris, ou Calendrier historique et chronologique des théâtres. Paris, 1752–1778.

"Archives du Roy: Administration, Minutes et Arrêts du conseil, arrêt du 30 août 1662, arrêt du 28 avril 1682, arrêt du 21 décembre 1682, arrêt du 3 juillet 1683, arrêt du 26 juillet 1683." Bibliothèque Nationale, Paris.

"Arrest du Parlement de Paris: Qui démet les Maîtres Violons, de l'opposition par eux formée à l'enregistrement des Lettres d'établissement de l'Académie de Danse, du 31 août 1662, Extraits des registres du Parlement, signé Du Tillet." Bibliothèque de l'Opéra, Paris.

Cordey, Jean. "L'Académie de Danse, 1661–1778." *Bulletin de la Société de l'Histoire de l'Art Français* (1952).

"Délibération de l'Académie Royale de Danse: Contenant la Reception du Sieur Bernard de Manthe, en la place du feu Sieur le Vacher, et le Réglement des Rangs et Séances des Académistes, du 16 avril 1662." Bibliothèque de l'Opéra, Paris.

Deshayes, André-Jean-Jacques. *Idées générales sur l'Académie Royale de Musique et plus spécialement sur la Danse.* Paris, 1882.

Discours académique pour prouver que la danse, dans sa plus noble partie, n'a pas besoin de musique et qu'elle est tout absolument indépendante du violon. Paris, 1663.

Dumanoir, Guillaume. *Le mariage de la musique avec la danse, contenant la réponce au livre des treize prétendus académistes, touchant ces deux arts.* Paris, 1664.

Du Pradel, Abraham [Nicolas de Blegny]. *Le livre commode des adresses de la Ville de Paris.* 4 vols. Paris, 1690–1693.

Kunzle, Régine [Astier]. "In Search of L'Académie Royale de Danse." *York Dance Review*, no. 7 (Spring 1978): 3–15.

Le Mercure galant (June 1680).

"Lettres patentes du Roi pour l'établissement de l'Académie Royale de Danse de la Ville de Paris, données à Paris au mois de mars 1661, verifiées au Parlement le 30 mars 1662." Bibliothèque de l'Opéra, Paris.

Needham, Maureen Danielle. *"Patent Letters of the King to Establish the Royal Academy of Dance in the City of Paris, 1661:* A Commentary and Translation." *Dance Chronicle* (1997).

Noverre, Jean-Georges. *Lettres sur la danse et sur les ballets.* Stuttgart and Lyon, 1760. Translated by Cyril W. Beaumont as *Letters on Dancing and Ballets.* London, 1930.

Noverre, Jean-Georges. *Lettres sur la danse, sur les ballets et les arts.* 4 vols. St. Petersburg, 1803–1804.

Noverre, Jean-Georges. *Lettres sur les arts imitateurs en général et sur la danse en particulier.* 2 vols. Paris, 1807. Edited by Fernand Divoire as *Lettres sur la danse et les arts imitateurs.* Paris, 1952.

La plainte et les sentimens de la Musique contre les entreprises et contre le livre de la prétendue Académie de la Danse. Paris, 1664.

Pour Guillaume Du Manoir, Joüer de Violon du Cabinet de Sa Majesté, l'un des Vingt-cinq de sa grand' bande, et pourveu aussi de l'Office de Roy des joüers d'instruments et des Maîtres à Danser de France; et encor pour les Maîtres de la Communauté et de la confrairie de S. Julien, déffendeurs. Contre Jean-François Desairs, Jean Regnault, Claude Quèru, Jean-François Piquet, Jean Grigny, Hilaire d'Olivet, Jean et Guillaume Reynal, Fleurand Galand Desairs, Guillaume Regnault et autres, Opposans. Paris, 1664.

RÉGINE ASTIER

ACCOMPANIMENT FOR DANCE. [*This entry is limited to discussion of musical accompaniment for Western theatrical dance. For related discussion in a broader context, see* Music for Dance.]

In its widest sense, accompaniment for dance implies music—in a multitude of global styles, sometimes sung, sometimes played on various instruments, sometimes improvised, sometimes composed. Such a broad definition includes the music heard during ritual, social, and theatrical dancing as well as during rehearsals and dance-instruction classes.

The very word *accompaniment* suggests some clear division of labor: there are those who dance and those who make music for dancers. In traditional styles throughout the world, the distinction may involve other elements as well. Thus, in Australia only Aboriginal men play the *didjeridu* for dancers; in Ghana, only a male master drummer leads dance music. Such division of labor is by no means universal in the history of music for dance. In the first place, dancers have often provided their own aural accompaniment, by vocalizing or singing; including bodily percussive sounds such as clapping or stomping; and using percussive sticks, drums, bells, rattles, and/or other instruments as an important element in the dance itself. Self-accompaniment continues to be a significant aspect of contemporary theatrical dance, for both classwork and choreographed performance.

Europe. For centuries in Europe, the purposes of dance instruction and performance were closely intertwined for aristocrats at the royal courts. In requiring precision and display, by the Renaissance much court dance became the equivalent of what today constitutes a theatrical performance. For court occasions, polished dances would often be demonstrated by one or more couples before the king or local notables. To prepare for such occasions, couples practiced to the music to learn the steps and patterns.

In both Europe and in the European colonies of the New World during the sixteenth, seventeenth, and eighteenth centuries, the custom was for the resident or itinerant dance master to provide his own music when giving private lessons to adults and children in their homes. In France, dance masters operated originally under the aegis of the musicians' guild, and it was expected that anyone seriously studying dance would also master music. Engravings from the seventeenth century attest to the practice of using a pocket-sized bowed instrument called in French the *pochette* (it was at first strung like a rebec and later like a violin); in England this was called the *kit* and in Italy, the *sordino*. The treatises of leading dance masters of the time suggest that, for instructional purposes, familiar tunes accompanied learning steps. Yet, it is also likely that dance masters improvised new tunes or composed their own, retaining the characteristic rhythms, phrasings, and tempos of the various musical forms that were current before Haydn's and Mozart's time.

Among the musical legacies of those leading dance masters are the tunes they included in their treatises, often presented in a way that relates to their written notations for dance steps. In addition, separate collections exist consisting only of the single melodic lines intended for violin. For example, in the Library of Congress in Washington, D.C., the manuscripts of the dance master Pierre Landrin Duport include minuets performed at balls in the presence of George and Martha Washington. Perhaps the most widely used set of country dance tunes was that sold in the multiple editions of English music publisher John Playford (1623–1686)—still used for social dancing as well as by troupes that do historical dancing.

Other instruments besides the violin accompanied dance instruction. The playing of both the tabor (a medieval small drum) and a vertical flute, simultaneously by one performer—as had been done since pre-Christian times in Europe—was very popular in France. These sounds, which accompanied the forerunners of French ballet, have also continued in the contemporary performance of traditional Provençal dance. In Italy, the lute and guitar were also employed in formal dance instruction, along with the harp and keyboard instruments.

In the seventeenth and eighteenth centuries, as European theatrical dance became professionalized and schools were established for elite specialists, it was still mainly the solo violin that accompanied the students' daily classes and rehearsals. A dichotomy was introduced however between the teaching of dance and the production of music; ballet masters began to employ assistants, so accompanists were likely to be specialist musicians rather than the multifaceted artists of former times. The dual virtuosity of Arthur Saint-Léon (who both danced and played the violin onstage in *Le Violon du Diable*) became noteworthy for its rarity.

In rehearsals for the ballet repertory, the tradition of a single violin persisted for a remarkably long period. The presence of the solo violinist is documented hauntingly, for example, in the painting by Edgar Degas titled *The Rehearsal* (now in the Frick Collection in New York City). The violin was not replaced by the piano at the Royal Danish Ballet until the 1930s. At the Paris Opera Ballet, the single violin was sometimes joined by a second violin or a viola. With the mid-nineteenth-century perfection of mass-produced pianos that retained their tuning and were affordable, Parisian dancers were accompanied at times by both the solo strings and a piano. Apparently, the first use of the piano by itself for rehearsal purposes at the Opera Ballet was for André Messager's score to *Les Deux Pigeons* in 1886.

In the twentieth century, for both ballet and modern dance, the use of the piano has dominated studio instruction and rehearsal, despite eventual competition from recorded music. Modern dance pioneer Martha Graham, for example, preferred to hear the structural bones of an orchestral work reduced for piano as she prepared her choreography. The piano has many advantages: it can present melodies with a wide range of expressive nuance; fill out harmonic underpinnings and present percussive rhythmic patterning; project soft sounds as well as fill a studio with degrees of volume; and, perhaps most importantly, suggest a complex orchestral texture. Consequently, among the skills demanded of rehearsal pianists are sight reading a published or manuscript piano reduction and/or reading from a full orchestral score and instantly improvising a piano rendition.

For technique classes in ballet, it has long been customary for musicians to draw from the repertory of music used for theatrical performance. This tradition continues, notably, for example, at the Russian Academy of Ballet in Saint Petersburg. There, studio pianists are expected to memorize vast quantities of melodic material from the school's library (much of the music in unpublished manuscript form). The musicians for class have the double duty of tastefully selecting repertory material suitable for the expressivity of a particular dance combination and of improvising musical textures, accents, and phrase structure supportive of the instructional purpose of each exercise.

Perhaps the most creative challenge for musicians in the field of dance is improvising music for modern dance classes. Unlike the tradition of ballet training (with its fairly predictable patterns of exercises plus a rather universal sense of expressivity), the flow and the exercises in modern dance classes can vary enormously in both technical details and aesthetic style.

Yet, modern dance does have its own distinct tradition of accompaniment, stemming from the summer programs at Bennington College in Bennington, Vermont. Articles published in Louis Horst's *Dance Observer* attest to the lively interchange about the type of new music considered appropriate for the new dance. A number of postmodern dancers have even rebelled against their perceptions of music's constrictions and many have opted to carry on both classes and performances in silence. Some modern dance teachers have come to favor accompanists who, in a single class session, can offer percussion, sing, and both play the piano traditionally and "prepare" its strings to provide a wide variety in timbre. Some musicians use solo cello, flutes, and other traditional melodic instruments quite effectively in the studio classroom. Others have introduced the latest electronic synthesizer equipment to take advantage of the great potential of tone colors and special patterning effects.

An important thrust in modern dance has been an exploration of percussion instruments drawn from various cultures of the world. In fact, studio accompanists favor Latin drums such as conga and bongo sets as well as the table drums of India. For jazz-based styles, several musicians might be employed as a small combo—often, a pianist plus a drummer playing a trap set (bass drum, high-hat cymbal, ride drums, tom-tom, cowbell, triangle, wood block, and smaller percussion). Caribbean- and African-based contemporary styles are apt to include the teacher providing an impelling beat by pounding a large cane while the musician in the corner provides elaborate rhythmic patterns on conga or African drums.

With such a variety in equipment and musical styles upon which to draw, the question of aesthetic appropriateness becomes important, as is the need for effective communication between teacher and musician. The main concerns of dance accompanists are the following:

- The establishment of a correct tempo and mood, an appropriate general musical style that relates to the dance movement, and effective rhythmic patterning to impel the dancers to move in the desired way.
- The use of dynamics that support the movement but do not unduly distract attention.
- The provision of an accurate number of counts and phrases and overall form.
- The selection of an underlying metric structure or doing without one.
- The provision, on demand, of a wide-ranging melodic repertory of musical styles, including Renaissance, classical, baroque, romantic, popular, and jazz.
- The provision of material from the repertory of theatrical dance music.
- Improvisation in multiple styles to fit the needs of any dance aesthetic and to support the instructional purposes of each movement combination.

Above all, the musicians must remain alert and cognizant of what the dancers are doing at each moment. There may be times when pianistic virtuosity is appropriate, but, as choreographer George Balanchine suggested to his pianists, it is more likely that the dancers can do their job and shine when there are not too many musical notes.

Given all these challenges, it is obvious that highly skilled musicians are an advantage, as well as effective modes of nonverbal and verbal communication between dancers and musicians. Because of the lack of formal specialized training available to musicians who wish to work in the field of dance, many dance teachers train their own accompanists, and some use recordings.

An important development in accompaniment was the 1991 founding by William Moulton of the International Guild of Musicians in Dance. Dedicated to encouraging original live music for both theatrical dance performance and instructional studio classes, the guild has become influential through its annual journal and workshop conferences and its newsletters. All its public proceedings are videotaped for the organization's archives (now housed at the State University of New York [SUNY] at Brockport). These serve both to document current practices in music for dance and to set high standards in the field. A European branch of the guild was founded in 1993 by Elina Lampinen in Finland. On both sides of the Atlantic Ocean, membership includes musicians who function in multiple roles for dance: as collaborating composers, educators, conductors, electronic sound engineers, and instrumentalists for theatrical performance—all in addition to working as rehearsal musicians and improvising accompanists for studio classes.

BIBLIOGRAPHY

Brainard, Ingrid. "The Role of the Dancing Master in Fifteenth-Century Courtly Society." *Fifteenth-Century Studies* 2 (1979): 21–44.

Chapman, John V. "The Paris Opéra Ballet School, 1798–1827." *Dance Chronicle* 12.2 (1989): 196–220.

Guest, Ivor. "Les Deux Pigeons." *The Dancing Times* (February 1961): 286–287.

Hammond, Sandra Noll. "A Nineteenth-Century Dancing Master at the Court of Württemberg: The Dance Notebooks of Michel St. Léon." *Dance Chronicle* 15.3 (1992): 291–315.

Hilton, Wendy. *Dance of Court and Theatre: The French Noble Style, 1690–1725*. Princeton, 1981.

International Guild of Musicians in Dance. *Journal* and *Newsletter*. Las Vegas and Los Angeles, 1991–1994.

Kriegsman, Sali Ann. *Modern Dance in America: The Bennington Years*. Boston, 1981.

Moore, Lillian. "The Duport Mystery." *Dance Perspectives* 7 (1960).

Saint-Léon, Arthur. *Letters from a Ballet Master: The Correspondence of Arthur Saint-Léon*. Edited by Ivor Guest. New York, 1981.

Teck, Katherine. *Music for the Dance: Reflections on a Collaborative Art*. Westport, Conn., 1989.

Teck, Katherine. *Movement to Music: Musicians in the Dance Studio*. Westport, Conn., 1990.

Teck, Katherine. *Ear Training for the Body: A Dancer's Guide to Music*. Pennington, N.J., 1994.

KATHERINE TECK

ADAGE. In the context of a classical ballet class, *adage* (It., *adagio,* "slowly," "at a leisurely pace") covers a wide range of movements that are performed slowly and used as exercises to strengthen the carriage and to control the back and legs. Through the practice of *adage,* the dancer develops aplomb, or the stability and sense of perpendicularity that produces ease of equilibrium.

In the context of a theatrical performance, *adage* is a slow, expressive dance. This can be a solo (or even a group dance), but more often it takes the form of a pas de deux, usually the choreographic stylization of a love duet.

In their classroom form, the basic exercises of *adage* can be enhanced by the rotation or inclination of the upper body, as well as by a great variety of arm and head movements. This helps to develop the dancer's coordination and grace. Characteristic balletic poses such as the arabesque and attitude are essential components of *adage* exercises, as are *développés,* the slow, smooth unfolding of the leg into the various positions and alignments of the body. The dancer's equilibrium is tested by rising in these positions, consciously controlling the use of the quarter and the half pointe.

By an almost imperceptible pivoting action of the supporting foot, the dancer can revolve slowly *sur place* in a variety of poses: this movement, called *promenade,* is much used in phrases of *adage,* as is the *penché,* an inclining or tilting of the body forward, backward, or sideways in a given pose. Other common movements are the full *plié,* the *grand rond de jambe en l'air,* the *fouetté,* and the *rotation.* In the more advanced forms of *adage, renversé* movements, pirouettes, and even jumps, are introduced.

Not until the nineteenth century did the concept of line, in the sense of the shapes made in space by the specific disposition of the dancer's limbs, begin to gain ground as an important aspect of theatrical dancing. It is from this search for line—as well as from a desire to emulate sculptured poses and the expressive, yearning gestures characteristic of Romantic ballet—that the balletic *adage* gradually evolved. The second act of *Giselle* (1841) contains clear examples of *adages* performed both individually and as pas de deux. The latter form, which has become an integral part of the choreographic vocabulary of ballet, developed initially as a direct result of the evolution of pointe work. When she rises onto full pointe, the dancer's ability to control or adjust her own equilibrium is much reduced, necessitating the support of a partner.

At first, the partner's role in an *adage* was primarily functional and essentially self-effacing; subsequent choreographic development, however, has often placed equal emphasis on the role of the partner so that both dancers' movements and lines are complementary, both expressively and pictorially.

In his description of "the lesson" in *The Code of Terpsichore* (1828), Carlo Blasis did not use the word *adage.* However, for the section of the class immediately following the preparatory exercises, he listed movements and combinations of movements closely related to those found in what came to be called *temps d'adage*—for example, the practice of attitudes, of *grands ronds de jambes,* and of *grands fouettés,* all of them found in present-day ballet classes. Blasis also included *temps de courante simples et composés* and *temps de chaceone,* movements that are clearly a link with, and presumably a development of, earlier dance forms.

In *Théorie de la gymnastique de la danse théâtrale* (1859), Léopold Adice, who taught at the Paris Opera from 1848 to 1863, deplored the rejection of such exercises as *temps de courante:* "There are even those who are literally ignorant of the sequence." According to Adice, "These sequences were meant to prepare the arms, the body, and above all the hips, the knees, and the insteps, for the *temps d'aplomb* that were to follow." (The sequences of exercises now known as *temps liés*—of great importance in developing the smooth coordination of arms, legs, head, and body—would appear to be a development of such forms.)

Adice then listed several exercises designed to develop strength and control, extolling the virtues of the "old school," which prescribed that the exercises be practiced in long series and "not in ornamental poses, as students say now, or in detached steps, but . . . [in] an extended sequence." Thus, by the middle of the nineteenth century,

ADAGE. Tamara Toumanova performs a *développé à la seconde*—a slow movement of the leg requiring a combination of strength, flexibility, and balance—in the solo *adage* from *Giselle,* act 2. (Photograph by Fred Fehl; used by permission.)

the few remaining links with early dance forms would seem to have been lost in all but name. *Exercises d'aplomb* were becoming less a test of endurance and more a study in decorative poses.

August Bournonville, in *Études chorégraphiques* (1861), started with a list of *pas et temps fondamentaux.* Under the subheading *école ancienne,* he listed *temps de courante* and other exercises related to early dance forms. However, later in that book, he dealt with *exercises d'adagio,* subtitled *études d'aplomb.* The exercises listed there, and the use of the term *adagio* to describe them, are clear evidence of the emergence and codification of this particular element of training and of its acceptance as an integral section of a ballet class in the first half of the nineteenth century.

Enrico Cecchetti was noted for his prolific and varied invention of *temps d'adage,* twenty-seven of which are listed and described in detail by Cyril W. Beaumont and Stanislas Idzikowski in *A Manual of the Theory and Practice of Classical Theatrical Dancing* (1922). These *adages* are generally recognized as being among the most demanding and most beautifully composed examples of this genre. They include exercises that, in spite of the appellation *temps de courante Cecchetti* and *pas de chaconne,* would appear to lack much resemblance to the old forms bearing those names. However, Cecchetti's exercise called *temps de courante sur les pointes,* with its difficult transferences of weight and subtle changes of dynamics, seems to bear more of a relationship to sequences described by the old masters, although adapted to the technique of pointe work.

[*See also* Ballet Technique.]

BIBLIOGRAPHY

Adice, G. Léopold. *Théorie de la gymnastique de la danse théâtrale.* Paris, 1859. Excerpts translated by Leonore Loft in *Dance as a Theatre Art,* edited by Selma Jeanne Cohen (New York, 1974).

Beaumont, Cyril W., and Stanislas Idzikowski. *A Manual of the Theory and Practice of Classical Theatrical Dancing.* London, 1922.

Blasis, Carlo. *The Code of Terpsichore: A Practical and Historical Treatise on the Ballet, Dancing, and Pantomime.* London, 1828.

Bournonville, August. *Études chorégraphiques.* Copenhagen, 1861.

Glasstone, Richard. *Better Ballet.* London, 1977.

Kostrovitskaya, Vera, and Alexei Pisarev. *School of Classical Dance.* Translated by John Barker. Moscow, 1978.

Meunier, Antonine. *La danse classique (école française).* Paris, 1931.

Prudhommeau, Germaine, and Geneviève Guillot. *The Book of Ballet.* Translated by Katherine Carson. Englewood Cliffs, N.J., 1976.

Vaganova, Agrippina. *Basic Principles of Classical Ballet: Russian Ballet Technique* (1934). Translated by Anatole Chujoy. Edited by Peggy van Praagh. 2d ed. London, 1953.

RICHARD GLASSTONE

ADAM, ADOLPHE (Adolphe-Charles Adam; born 24 July 1803 in Paris, died 3 May 1856 in Paris), French composer. Composer of *Giselle,* Adolphe Adam was the son of Louis Adam, founder of the nineteenth-century school of French piano playing. Adam's father firmly opposed a musical career for his son, who studied secretly and alone. At the age of fifteen, he was allowed to enter the Paris Conservatory after promising his father never to write for the theater—a promise soon breached.

Adam's teachers included François Benoist and Anton Reicha, but it was François-Adrien Boieldieu, the foremost composer of *opéra comique* of the day, who befriended him and aided his start in the theater. His first instrument was the organ; he then went on to play the triangle in the orchestra of the Théâtre du Gymnase, where he became successively timpanist, chorus master, and répétiteur. Many of the songs he wrote for his actor friends were incorporated in the *vaudeville* routines performed at the theater. In 1824 an aria of his was among the first compositions sung in *Pierre et Marie, ou Le Soldat Ménétrier.*

A year later Boieldieu, whose favorite pupil he was, introduced him to editors and gave him the job of working on the overture of *La Dame Blanche,* which was to become a staple of the *opéra comique* repertory. He helped to develop Adam's extraordinary melodic gifts and sure instinct for the stage.

Adam's first complete work for the theater was produced under very auspicious conditions. With a libretto written for him by Eugène Scribe, he composed a one-act comic opera, *Le Mal du Pays, ou La Batelière de Brientz* in 1827, in which the leading role was played by the famous actress Virginie Déjazet. The piece was a success, and the overture and eight of the eleven numbers were published in a piano-vocal score by Maurice Adolphe Schlesinger.

From then on, Adam produced theatrical pieces at a remarkable rate. (During his relatively short life, Adam wrote about 455 *opéras comiques,* mostly for the Théâtre de l'Opéra-Comique and the Théâtre Lyrique.) He worked best under stress and wrote amazingly quickly. Meanwhile he augmented his income by writing transcriptions for the piano of famous operatic arias of the day.

The one-act *Pierre et Catherine,* written for the Opéra-Comique in 1829, was followed in 1830 by the three-act *Danilowa* for the same theater. That year Adam wrote his first ballet music, collaborating with the composer Casimir Gide on the pantomime *La Chatte Blanche* for the Théâtre des Nouveautés. *La Sylphide* was first performed at the Opéra-Comique in March 1832, with Jean Schneitzhoeffer credited with the score, but when the ballet opened at the Drury Lane in London (with Marie Taglioni again in the title role) in July 1832, Adam's name was listed with Schneitzhoeffer's as composer. How much he adapted and how much he rewrote is not known. [*See* Sylphide, La.]

About this time, Adam married the sister of Pierre Laporte, director of the Covent Garden and King's Theatre in London. Through his brother-in-law Adam was commissioned to write two operas for Covent Garden in 1832, *His First Campaign* (two acts) and *The Dark Diamond* (three acts).

His first three-act ballet was *Faust* (1833), written for the King's Theatre in London, choreographed by André Deshayes, and danced by Jules Perrot, Monsieur Albert, and Pauline Leroux. Most of the music is lost, although Adam incorporated some of it in later works, notably *Le Chalet* (one act) and *Giselle. Le Chalet,* written to a libretto by Scribe for the Opéra-Comique in 1834, is one of his finest and freshest works.

La Fille du Danube (1836), Adam's first ballet for the Paris Opera, was created for Marie Taglioni; this melodious and elegant score launched Adam as the foremost French ballet composer of the nineteenth century. The tradition of Romantic ballet music was begun by Ferdinand Hérold and Schneitzhoeffer but Adam raised the art to a high plane, an elevation perpetuated by his pupil Léo Delibes. Adam may thus be considered the father of Romantic and lyrical ballet music, his influence descending through Delibes and Léon Minkus to Tchaikovsky.

His second ballet for the Opera, *Les Mohicans* (1837), choreographed by Antonio Guerra, was loosely based on the story by James Fenimore Cooper. It was mounted as a vehicle for the budding ballerina Nathalie Fitzjames but proved a fiasco and had only two noisily received performances.

Adam's next excursion into ballet was written during his Russian tour in 1840, the two-act *Morskoï Rasbonick.* Mounted for Taglioni, it was reputed to be the most opulent spectacle seen to date on the ballet stage, and was a triumph for both dancer and composer. The empress of Russia was so enchanted that she accepted the dedication of the score.

Nicholas I invited Adam to remain and become *Kapellmeister,* but he wanted to return to France. He went by way of Berlin, where Frederick William IV of Prussia invited him to compose a work for the Royal Theater there. The result was an *opéra-ballet, Die Hamadryaden,* in two acts and four scenes. It was splendidly mounted and well received, and Adam was fêted continuously.

After returning to Paris, Adam began work on *Giselle,* arguably the greatest of all Romantic ballets and perhaps the most perfect of all ballet scores. Yet this two-act ballet is still presented more often than not in bastardized orchestrations that give a false impression of the music's structure. Adam's own orchestration is original, very full when necessary, imaginative, and apt. [*See* Giselle.]

The first performance took place at the Paris Opera on 28 June 1841, with choreography by Jean Coralli and Jules Perrot. The leading role was danced by the extraordinary new star Carlotta Grisi. Adam was on such friendly terms with Perrot and Grisi that he claimed the ballet was almost produced in his drawing room. He himself added a few suggestions, being dissatisfied with the way Giselle returned to her grave at the end. He thought that Albrecht should carry her to a bed of flowers, where she would sink slowly into the ground—this ending is featured in many productions. *Giselle* was an instant and triumphant success.

Although none of Adam's later ballet scores equals *Giselle,* many are highly accomplished. *La Jolie Fille de Gand* (22 June 1842), choreographed by Monsieur Albert for the Opera, was a successful follow-up to *Giselle,* with a brilliant and warmly orchestrated score. Equally successful was Mazilier's *Le Diable à Quatre,* first performed at the Opera on 11 August 1845. The elaborately staged production featured one of Adam's wittiest scores. [*See* Diable à Quatre, Le; *and* Jolie Fille de Gand, La.]

London saw the next ballet premiere. Adam was invited by Albert to create a ballet for the Drury Lane. *The Marble Maiden* (27 September 1845), danced by Adèle Dumilâtre, Lucien Petipa, and Albert, was lavishly staged, but was considered too long and had only modest success.

Adam's next major venture was the establishment of the Théâtre National in Paris. However, political events—namely, the 1848 Revolution—led to its almost immediate demise, causing much financial distress. That same year, he scored the three-act *Griseldis, ou Les Cinq Sens,* performed at the Opera. The flying visions created a sensation, and the work's appeal was enhanced by Grisi appearing on horseback and singing a ballad at the end of the ballet. Adam collaborated again with Perrot and Grisi on *La Filleule des Fées* (1849), one of the most ambitious productions to be seen at the Opera. Lit by electricity with fountains of real water, this spectacle was Grisi's farewell to ballet.

Adam's last productions were choreographed by Mazilier. Much of the success of *Orfa* (29 December 1852), which included Fanny Cerrito in her first appearance at the Opera in an Adam ballet, was due to the grandeur of his score. His final ballet, *Le Corsaire* (23 January 1856), premiered at the Opera in the presence of Emperor Napoleon III and Empress Eugénie. The advanced orchestration, in which Adam introduced saxophones, earned him much praise. *La revue musicale* stated,

> The music of Adolphe Adam is worthy of him. The most graceful and captivating themes succeed one another in rare profusion. The whole of the last scene is the work of a master; it is not only ballet music, it is dramatic inspiration of the first rank. (Beaumont, 1937)

Le Corsaire was also a triumph for Carolina Rosati as Medora and for the technicians of the Opera, who produced storms and a shipwreck more prodigious than anything seen before. [*See* Corsaire, Le.]

Adam's final work was *Les Pantins de Violette* in one act, written for Offenbach's Théâtre des Bouffes-Parisiens in 1856. He completed an opera, *Le Dernier Bal* (The Last Ball), that has never been performed or published. Apart from his theatrical output, he also wrote many songs, including the beloved "Cantique de Noël" ("O Holy Night"), piano music, arias for the voice, and many masses. He wrote criticism for major French journals, and two volumes of memoirs were published posthumously. Adam died quietly in his sleep in May 1856.

Despite some financial setbacks, due mostly to the failure of his Théâtre National, Adam's work was a great success during his own lifetime. His art was facile; but when reproached with writing too hurriedly, he replied, "I composed *Le Chalet* in fifteen days, *Le Toréador* in eight, *Giselle* in three weeks, and *Si J'étais Roi* in two months. Are these my weakest works?" (Adam, 1859). He wrote from pure inspiration and seldom corrected or revised, and his inspiration was frequently of a very high order.

Although in the twentieth century Adam has been considered a secondary talent, both melodically and dramatically he wrote much that compares favorably with works by Giuseppe Verdi and Gaetano Donizetti written during the same period. Adam's lyrical and dramatic gifts and his sure theatrical instinct put him in the first rank of French composers.

[*For related discussion, see* Music for Dance, *article on* Western Music, 1800–1900.]

BIBLIOGRAPHY

Adam, Adolphe. *Souvenirs d'un musicien.* Paris, 1857.

Adam, Adolphe. *Derniers souvenirs d'un musicien.* Paris, 1859.

Beaumont, Cyril W. *Complete Book of Ballets.* London, 1937.

Binney, Edwin, 3rd. *Les ballets de Théophile Gautier.* Paris, 1965.

Clément, Félix, and Pierre Larousse. *Dictionnaire des opéras.* 2 vols. 2d ed. Paris, 1877.

Clément, Félix. *Les musiciens célèbres.* 3d ed. Paris, 1878.

Grove, George. *A Dictionary of Music and Musicians, 1450–1880.* London, 1879.

Guest, Ivor. *A Gallery of Romantic Ballet: A Catalogue of the Collection of Dance Prints at the Mercury Theatre.* London, 1965.

Guest, Ivor. *The Romantic Ballet in England.* London, 1972.

Guest, Ivor. *The Ballet of the Second Empire.* London, 1974.

Guest, Ivor. *The Romantic Ballet in Paris.* 2d rev. ed. London, 1980.

Guest, Ivor. *Jules Perrot: Master of the Romantic Ballet.* London, 1984.

Jordan, Stephanie. "The Role of the Ballet Composer at the Paris Opera, 1820–1850." *Dance Chronicle* 4.4 (1982): 374–388.

Lifar, Serge. *Giselle: Apothéose du ballet romantique.* Paris, 1942.

Lifar, Serge. *Carlotta Grisi.* Translated by Doris Langley Moore. London, 1947.

Poesio, Giannandrea. "Giselle" (parts 1–3). *The Dancing Times* (February–April 1994).

Pougin, Arthur. *Adolphe Adam.* Paris, 1877.

Riemann, Hugo. *Dictionnaire de musique.* Paris, 1899.

Smith, Marian E. "Music for the Ballet-Pantomime at the Paris Opéra, 1825–1850." Ph.D. diss., Yale University, 1988.

Studwell, William E. *Adolphe Adam and Léo Delibes: A Guide to Research.* New York, 1987.

RICHARD BONYNGE

ADAMA, RICHARD (Richard Holt; born 8 August 1928 in Long Beach, California), American dancer, choreographer, and ballet master. Richard Adama received his training in ballet from Bronislava Nijinska in Los Angeles. In 1948 he performed with Colonel Wassily de Basil's Original Ballet Russe, and from 1949 to 1954 he danced with Le Grand Ballet du Marquis de Cuevas. Between 1955 and 1961 he was principal dancer—the first and only American to hold this position—at the Vienna State Opera Ballet, where he appeared in all the traditional *danseur noble* roles of the gradually reconstructed repertory. Admired for his insouciant elegance, he became a mainstay of the company, creating important roles in several of Erika Hanka's ballets: Iago in *The Moor of Venice* (1955), Lieutenant von Sandor in *Hotel Sacher* (1957), and the Blind Sailor in *Medusa* (1957). From 1961 to 1965 Adama was principal dancer and assistant ballet master to Yvonne Georgi at the Hanover Opera Ballet, where he staged the 1961 production of *Giselle,* using the original score and restoring all traditional cuts.

Adama subsequently served as ballet master at the Bremen State Opera Ballet (1965–1968) and at the Hanover Opera Ballet (1970–1973), where he succeeded Georgi. In both cities he attracted attention with his meticulously researched productions of the classics, such as *La Sylphide* (the Schneitzhoeffer version), *Swan Lake* (with the Black Swan pas de deux in the first act), and *Coppélia.* Adama's other highly individual stagings include *The Prodigal Son* (Bremen, 1965), *Concert Champêtre* (Bremen, 1965), and *Don Juan* (Vienna Festival, 1969). After returning to the United States, he taught at the Los Angeles Dance Center. In the late 1980s he retired from dance and settled in Vienna.

BIBLIOGRAPHY

Adama, Richard. "Zur Choreographie und Inszenierung von 'La Sylphide.'" *Spielzeit* 10 (1964–1965).

Cohen-Stratyner, Barbara Naomi. "Adama, Richard." In *Biographical Dictionary of Dance.* New York, 1982.

Koegler, Horst. "Adama, Richard." In *Friedrichs Ballettlexikon.* Velber bei Hannover, 1972.

HORST KOEGLER

ADAMS, DIANA (born 29 March 1929 in Staunton, Virginia, died 10 January 1993 in San Andreas, California), American dancer and dance administrator. Adams was a dancer whose tall, long-legged proportions and aura of cool detachment made her the embodiment of the "Balanchine ballerina," but her career embraced many aspects of dance beyond George Balanchine's New York City Ballet. She was a soloist with the early Ballet Theatre and also appeared in feature films with Danny Kaye (*Knock on Wood,* 1954) and Gene Kelly (*Invitation to the Dance,* 1956). Later, Adams became a dance administrator.

Adams had received her early training from her stepmother, Emily Hadley Adams. In New York, she studied at the Ballet Arts School with Edward Caton and Agnes de Mille, who cast her in the corps de ballet of the Broadway musical *Oklahoma!* (1943). The following year Adams joined Ballet Theatre, where she became a member of the circle around Antony Tudor and created the role of Cybele in *Undertow* (1945). In 1947 she married Tudor's close friend Hugh Laing. (They were divorced in 1953. She later married lighting designer Ronald Bates.)

In 1950 Tudor, Adams, and Laing, along with Nora Kaye, joined Balanchine's New York City Ballet. While this would be a passing phase for the others, Adams connected deeply with the emerging Balanchine style; she has been called "Balanchine's most important ballerina between 1957 and 1962" (*New Yorker,* January 1993). The many roles created for her included parts in *Western Symphony* (1954), *Ivesiana* (1954), *Divertimento No. 15* (1956), *Stars and Stripes* (1958), *Episodes* (1959), and *Monumentum pro Gesualdo* (1960). Her lyrically dramatic quality was successfully blended with Balanchine's abstraction in *Liebeslieder Walzer* (1960). Adams's most important role was certainly that in *Agon* (1957), the groundbreaking, modernist Balanchine–Igor Stravinsky collaboration, in which Adams's ability to combine geometric investigation with musicality and sensuality had a transforming influ-

ADAMS. Admired for her elegant line and cool assurance, Adams is associated with the development of George Balanchine's style in the late 1950s and early 1960s. She is pictured here with Arthur Mitchell in the pas de deux from Balanchine's neoclassical masterpiece *Agon* (1957). (Photograph by Martha Swope © Time, Inc.; used by permission.)

ence on the course of Balanchine's future work. Almost as important are two roles created on her but that, because of pregnancies, she never actually performed—Titania in *A Midsummer Night's Dream* (1962) and the leading role in another Balanchine-Stravinsky experiment, *Movements for Piano and Orchestra* (1963).

While Adams was still dancing with his company, Balanchine appointed her a talent scout to identify promising students in ballet schools around the country. Watching a class in Cincinnati, she spotted Suzanne Farrell, who had long admired and identified with Adams. Adams arranged for Balanchine to audition her in New York.

When Adams became pregnant prior to the premiere of *Movements for Piano and Orchestra*, she and her partner, Jacques d'Amboise, taught the role to Farrell (while Adams was confined to the sofa in her living room). It was Farrell's successful conquest of this part that confirmed her ascension to ballerina status; the incident also marked the end of Adams's dancing career.

Adams remained affiliated with the School of American Ballet until 1971. In 1982 she assisted American Ballet Theatre in reviving *Symphonie Concertante*, which she had often danced with the New York City Ballet. Eventually she retired to northern California.

BIBLIOGRAPHY
Coleman, Emily. "Hallmark: American." *Dance News Annual* (1953): 54–63.
Denby, Edwin. *Dance Writings.* Edited by Robert Cornfield and William MacKay. New York, 1986.
Farrell, Suzanne, with Toni Bentley. *Holding on to the Air: An Autobiography.* New York, 1990.
Perlmutter, Donna. *Shadowplay: The Life of Antony Tudor.* New York, 1991.
Russell, Francia, et al. "Recollecting Diana Adams." *Ballet Review* 21 (Fall 1993): 18–27.
Tracy, Robert, and Sharon DeLano. *Balanchine's Ballerinas: Conversations with the Muses.* New York, 1983.

ANITA FINKEL

AERIAL BALLET. *See* Circus.

AEROBIC DANCE is a physical conditioning that uses movement routines composed of simple steps from jazz, folk, and social dance, synchronized with popular music chosen for its tempo. This activity is called by various names, such as aerobic patterns, jazzercise, and aerobic conditioning. Jacki Sorensen's aerobic dancing was the first of these to become popular. Because of the absence of the creative and performance aspects of dance, some dancers maintain that a phrase such as "rhythmic aerobic exercise" would be a more appropriate name for the activity.

Knowing how fitness contributes to general health, Jacki Sorensen designed her aerobic dance routines to combine the pleasure and challenge of dancing with the continuous vigorous activity required to produce a training effect on the heart and lungs. Among the benefits claimed for aerobic dance are lowered blood pressure, increased lung capacity, and a strengthened heart muscle. Other purposes include the burning of calories to facilitate weight control and the exercising of all parts of the body to tone muscles. In the 1970s, Sorensen was appointed to the President's Council on Physical Fitness and Sports because of her work in popularizing this kind of conditioning.

Aerobic dance offers an alternative to other popular aerobic fitness activities, such as jogging, bicycling, racket sports, and swimming; it has attracted large numbers of people, especially in the United States, where participants usually work out three or four times a week. The fact that aerobic dance is a group activity accompanied by lively music may explain its popularity. The movements used in aerobic dance routines are simple, although the routines themselves are carefully modulated to allow for a buildup to the most vigorous routines and a cool-down afterward. Movements include variations of running in place, forward, backward, and to each side. Skips, hops, and jumps are used with kicks, leg swings, and turns. Arms are swung with the legs and often raised above the head. At times, the routines include quick bending so that hands can touch the floor. The movements come from a variety of popular dance sources and often include tap, jazz, and ballroom dance steps as well as the gestures and postures used by cheerleaders.

Aerobic dance classes are taught in many European countries. Because of their popularity and the introduction of these kinds of classes into high school and college physical-education programs in the 1980s, certification standards and training classes were instituted for instructors by organizations such as the American College of Sports Medicine and the Aerobics and Fitness Association of America. At his Aerobics Center, Kenneth Cooper not only certifies instructors, he and his colleagues determined and published the level of intensity, number of minutes per session, and number of sessions per week necessary for a participant to achieve and maintain good or excellent levels of fitness. Thus, the activity of aerobic dancing has been accepted by the leaders in the fitness and sports medicine communities as a viable method for gaining cardiorespiratory fitness.

[*See also* Dance as Sport.]

BIBLIOGRAPHY
Alter, Judy. *Surviving Exercise.* Boston, 1983, 1990.
Alter, Judy. *Stretch and Strengthen.* Boston, 1986, 1990.
Cooper, Kenneth H. *Aerobics.* New York, 1968.
Cooper, Kenneth H. *The New Aerobics.* New York, 1970.
Cooper, Kenneth H. *The Aerobics Program for Total Fitness.* New York, 1982.
Eikoff, Johann, et al. "Selected Physiological and Psychological Effects of Aerobic Dancing among Young Adult Women." *Journal of Sports Medicine and Physical Fitness* 23 (September 1983): 273–280.
Pryor, Esther, and Minda Goodman Kraines. *Keep Moving! It's Aerobic Dance.* 3d ed. Mountain View, Calif., 1987, 1992, 1996.
Sorensen, Jacki, with Bill Bruns. *Aerobic Dancing.* New York, 1979.
Vaccaro, Paul, and Mary Clinton. "The Effects of Aerobic Dance Conditioning on the Body Composition and Maximal Oxygen Uptake of College Women." *Journal of Sports Medicine and Physical Fitness* 21 (September 1981): 291–294.

JUDITH B. ALTER

AESTHETICS. [*To explore aesthetic issues in dance in broad areas of world culture, this entry comprises four articles:*

African Dance Aesthetics
Asian Dance Aesthetics
Islamic Dance Aesthetics
Western Dance Acsthetics

For further discussion of related issues, see Costume in African Traditions; Costume in Asian Traditions; Costume in Western Traditions; Mask and Makeup; *and* Music for Dance.]

African Dance Aesthetics

[*This article is limited to discussion of dance aesthetics in the cultures of sub-Saharan Africa. See also* North Africa.]

The exuberance of African dance has long fascinated the West, but it is primarily some superficial elements that have had an impact on the vocabulary of Western dance—as has happened as well in the cases of Western music and sculpture. Western knowledge of dance throughout the diverse cultures of the African continent suffers from the paucity of focused field study by dance historians and dancers. Western study of African dance is challenged by the difference between European and African concepts of the nature of space, metaphysics, and rhythmic dissonance.

Dance in Africa cannot be considered apart from other art forms. In contrast to the compartmentalization of the arts in the West, in much of Africa, particularly in rural villages, all the arts are brought together in one form designated by a single term. Such terms may be translated as "the sacred," "medicine" (as something that affects), or "the play." Westerners now have theaters for drama, museums for painting and sculpture, concert halls for music, and so forth. The holistic form of African arts has the village square or town plaza and environs, within which art incorporates not only dance, music, mime, narration, costume, and sculpture but also a great many incidental elements—the plan of the village or town, the position of the sun or moon, the dust and heat, the ecstasy or impatience of the mass of children encircling the performers, or the interference of stray dogs or fowl. All this contributes to an art that is a part of daily life yet transforms the ordinary into the special, transporting the actors and audience.

"To dance" in Africa is a transitive linguistic concept. Although dance takes many forms in many different contexts, it is said in some cultures that one "dances" a mask, a headdress, a musical instrument, a staff, or the parts of one's body. One may dance a spirit, an ancestor, the threat of a powerful animal, the affecting image of an onomatopoeic word, or a vital force. As Henry and Margaret Drewel were told by the Yoruba of Nigeria, "We dance *gelede* (the supernatural power of women)" (1983, p. 105). It is the thing that is danced, and the efficacy of a dance is gauged by how well the essence of that thing is communicated—how well the dancer solves, as John Blacking has said, the "problem of capturing force with form" (1970, p. 11).

The Baga of Guinea, for example, dance a headdress known as a-Bemp (the Bird). The carved wooden figure of a bird may be worn on the head of the dancer, who is hidden under a large cloth costume, or the dancer may remove the headdress and "dance it" in the air. Its swift, swirling movements relate to concepts of human and spiritual energy and initiative, as opposed to the sloth and indifference symbolized by another droll mask called Dudu. The Bird dances figures of infant birds and miniature houses on its back, suggesting the importance of creative balance to domestic development.

To dance in Africa is to effect a state of being. As an instrument of power, dance integrates acts and ideas. Just as the special utterance of words in ritual is known to have power beyond the explicit meaning of those words, the dancing movement of the body is known to have power to change the lives of its participants. Dance is capable of transforming ordinary farmers into spiritual mediums, evildoers into religious devotees, or children into adults.

Among the Temne of Sierra Leone, girls in their sacred initiation into adulthood perform a dance for two consecutive days. During the ritual they move through chaos to tranquility, beginning with the sweeping of debris and the uprooting of imaginary rice seedlings and ending with the descent of a serpentine line moving from the east (the source of ancestral regeneration) to the central meetinghouse in the village plaza, where the seedlings are deposited in its darkness and left to "germinate." Their initiation dance is not only a performance in the sense of theater; it is also an instrumental act that performs an operation, a work that causes a fundamental change in their lives. Without the dance, they cannot be considered as adults. The counterclockwise spiral of their final procession is a kinetic glyph reproducing the West African ideograph that represents creative development and metamor-

phosis—appropriately, the masked dancer who precedes them wears a mask whose form is based on that of the butterfly chrysalis.

During recent decades, especially in urban areas, dances imported from the United States, the Caribbean, and Europe have become common in social contexts. With regard to indigenous dance, however, any debate about whether there is secular dance as opposed to sacred dance is useless. For most Africans an opposition between the sacred and secular simply does not exist in the Western sense. Certainly some dances are more sacred than others; some are performed under heavy prohibitions, and others are recreational rather than ritual. Nevertheless, a traditional African life is on every level a life of spiritual communion. Existential meaning is abstracted into even the functional modes of building a house, preparing a dish of rice, constructing bridges across water, balancing loads on the head, or moving in ritual procession. Artistic performance, as John Chernoff has said, "is above all an occasion for the demonstration of character" (1979, p. 151). In dance, whether within the context of sacred initiation or in ordinary display, artistic forms are drawn from an acknowledgment of a daily relationship between cosmological forces and the routine acts of humans.

The human body and its relationship to space are measured and evaluated according to culturally defined conceptions. Numerous studies of African thought reveal that the body is seen as a microcosm, a symbol of universal existence. This human-cosmological paradigm was also expressed by medieval Muslim philosophers such as the Ikhwān al-Ṣafā' (Brethren of Purity), as stated by Seyyed Hossein Nasr:

> Man can be considered as a small world. . . . The body itself is like the earth. . . . From its face to its feet, the body is like a populated state, its back like desolate regions, its front like the east, back the west, right the south, left the north."
> (Nasr, 1978, pp. 68, p. 101).

Head and torso are often opposed in analogy, as are the spiritual and the physical or creation and pollution. Symmetry relates to spiritual balance—spiraling and twisting to spiritual deviance and deception. Gestures convey social and spiritual meaning—a hand to the mouth signifies the necessity of mediating the power of words between a commoner and a dignitary in Cameroon; crossed legs among the Kongo suggests the negation of the spiritual state or the righteous enclosure of the self.

Dance is principally a social act that unites the community, effecting the well-being that springs from harmony and cohesion. An African does not merely dance a "fertility dance"; African metaphorical imagery is much too complex for that. A people dance to create a society that is whole, to gauge the sense of community, and to expand on public and private concerns. Such a society is capable of healthy production and reproduction. The large percentage of the annual budget in any small African community that is appropriated for the performance of rituals attests to the importance it is given. As Hugo Zemp was told by the Dan of Liberia, "The village where there is no musician is not a place where man can stay" (1971, p. 7).

Probably the most elusive aspect of African performance for the non-African student is the incorporation of several different rhythms in the orchestra of drums and in the use of the parts of the body in dance. The dance event is essentially a coordination and complementation of variant motifs expressed through the mode of multiple meter. The ability to handle rhythmic oppositions with balance, said Robert Thompson, "is an aesthetic acid test. . . . Multiple meter is, in brief, a communal examination of percussive individuality" (1966, p. 91). For the African, it reflects "a method of actively tolerating, interpreting, and even using the multiple and fragmented aspects of everyday events to build a richer and more diversified personal experience" (Chernoff, 1979, p. 156). James Fernandez found among the Fang of Gabon that "the fundamental principle at work . . . is that in doubleness, duality, and opposition lies vitality, in oneness and coincidence, death" (1971, p. 373).

The vital dialogue of conversational elements, which we label "call and response" in African music and dance, permeates an artistic event in a way not often seen in the West, where dancers perform onstage, the audience remains hushed in its seats, and the orchestra is confined to its pit. In Africa, each participant reinforces and molds the others' performances. Dancers challenge the drummers and even the audience to match their intensity. Musicians lead or follow the dancers, taunting them to a pitch of creative ecstasy. Members of the audience may move in and out of the dance or offer an ongoing critical commentary of approval or disdain. One of the musicians in Chernoff's study compared these confrontations to the machinations of male and female preparing for the first sexual contact, involving explorations, monitoring of feelings, tactical adjustments, and coordinated solutions.

The African manipulation of cross-rhythms—a phenomenon that is unparalleled elsewhere in the world—is studied and internalized in the body and mind from birth. The baby is carried continually on the back of its mother, sister, brother, or aunt, whether the carrier is working in the fields, pounding rice, or dancing in a ritual procession. There can be no doubt that this childhood experience produces a sensitivity to movement uncultivated in a child who resides in a baby carriage and playpen. African children learn to drum and dance as early as they learn to walk, and children are often encouraged to participate with master drummers and dancers in public ceremonies. We are reminded by A. M. Jones that "if from childhood you are brought up to regard beating three against two as being just as normal as beating in synchrony, then you develop a two-dimensional attitude to rhythm which we in the West do not share" (1959, vol. 1, p. 102).

The sensory experience afforded by the ephemeral aspects of the African arts appears to take supremacy in Africa over that of the plastic and permanent forms of sculpture. In a female initiation ritual in Sierra Leone, it is the movement and sound of the gourd rattles worn by the women, not their masks or their staffs, on which the most sacred oaths are sworn. Their most sacred spirit is represented not by masking (such as the Sande Sowo mask), which most impresses Western observers, but by the pure movement and sound of a woman who dances in the darkness without a costume. In most of Africa, "it is a drum and not a scepter which is the symbol of the king and the voice of the ancestors" (Chernoff, 1979, p. 35).

With the rapid westernization of Africa in the late twentieth century, the most enduring elements of the African arts have been the forms of music and dance. Where the ancient masks have been abandoned or sold to the West, the dance traditions continue and add to the flow of cultural change, often with little alteration or loss of integrity.

BIBLIOGRAPHY

Blacking, John. "Tonal Organizations in the Music of Two Venda Initiation Schools." *Ethnomusicology* 14.1 (1970).

Blum, Odette. "Dance in Ghana." *Dance Perspectives*, no. 56 (Winter 1973).

Chernoff, John Miller. *African Rhythm and African Sensibility: Aesthetics and Social Action in African Musical Idioms.* Chicago, 1979.

Drewal, Henry John, and Margaret Thompson Drewal. *Gelede: Art and Female Power among the Yoruba.* Bloomington, 1983.

Drewel, Margaret Thomson. Yoruba Ritual: Performers, Play, Agency. Bloomington, 1992.

Fernandez, James W. "Principles of Opposition and Vitality in Fang Aesthetics." In *Art and Aesthetics in Primitive Societies,* edited by Carol F. Jopling. New York, 1971.

Jones, A. M. *Studies in African Music.* 2 vols. London, 1959.

Lamp, Frederick. "Cosmos, Cosmetics, and the Spirit of Bondo." *African Arts* 18 (May 1985).

Lamp, Frederick. "Heavenly Bodies: Menses, Moon, and Ritual Sanction among the Temne." In *Blood Magic: The Anthropology of Menstruation,* edited by Thomas Buckley and Alma Gottlieb. Berkeley, 1988a.

Lamp, Frederick. "An Opera of the West African Bondo: The Act, Ideas, and the Word." *Drama Review* 32.1 (1988b).

Lamp, Frederick. Art of the Baga: A Drama of Cultural Reinvention. New York, 1996.

Nasr, Seyyed Hossein. An Introduction to Islamic Cosmological Doctrines. Rev. ed. London, 1978.

Thompson, Robert Farris. "An Aesthetic of the Cool: West African Dance." *African Forum* 2.2 (1966).

Thompson, Robert Farris. African Art in Motion: Icon and Act. 2d ed. Los Angeles, 1979.

Thompson, Robert Farris, and Joseph Cornet. The Four Moments of the Sun: Kongo Art in Two Worlds. Washington, D.C., 1981.

Zemp, Hugo. Musique Dan: La musique dans la pensée et la vie sociale d'une société africaine. Paris, 1971.

FREDERICK LAMP

Asian Dance Aesthetics

The aesthetic principles that are embodied in Asian choreographic styles were first realized by generations of anonymous dancers. Precedents were set in performance for canons that were later formulated by literati working within metaphysical frameworks. The truths of these principles remained constant but were conveyed in various modes of expression, because continental Asia comprises many national territories, each with its own dance style.

These observations refer to the great Asian classical modes that originated in temple and court ceremonies. Apart from these, innumerable folk-dance genres had their origins in animistic, tribal, or agricultural rites. In their later phases, they both drew on and contributed to classical forms. The formulation of aesthetic standards, however, inevitably resulted from classical sophistication.

Dance and music in Asia have always been recognized as inseparable—a rhythmic whole in which song, recitative, mime, gesture, and mask-play become integrated elements of a single expressive structure. The dancer is a matrix for the reciprocal interplay of sound and movement that awakens mood. Space is the dancer's medium but, in Asian dance, space is more intensely realized through the transcendent nature of auditory space, in which the movement of sound commands a multipresent impact on the senses. The emotional depth of Asian dance lies explicitly in this capacity to function at many levels.

Like other crafts in which learning comes through doing, Asian dance has followed a principle of heredity central to the social order. The transmission of function from parent to child and from master to apprentice ensured a continuity of accomplishments and standards through successive generations, thus acknowledging the eternal rhythm of existence that is a central concept of Asian philosophy. Such continuity was manifest in the binding ethic of the teacher–pupil relationship deeply ingrained in all Asian artistic instruction. A teacher was honored as the guardian of an artistic trust to be passed along. The way the artistic act was done, not who did it, was the criterion.

India and China were the sources of philosophical and metaphysical teachings that, over time, generated aesthetic codes throughout Asia. In large part, this resulted from the widespread propagation of the Hindu and Buddhist faiths from India and the Confucian and Daoist philosophies from China. A dominant theme at the core of all these teachings, though diversely interpreted by various schools and sects, held that humanity and nature were an inseparable whole and, within this absolute, the individual sought the meaning of self.

India. Early Indian philosophers of Hinduism defined that which lay beyond the boundaries of empirical existence as *brahman*—omnipresent but transcendent in the flux of the universe. Perceiving *brahman*, the individual achieved self-realization through spiritual sublimation: "I live, yet it is not I, but *brahman*, that lives in me." This basic Hindu belief was interpreted further by Buddhist teachings propagated through central and southeastern Asia to China, Korea, and Japan. The spread of these beliefs led to a direct and intuitive vision of the meaning of existence and the advocacy of psychophysical disciplines as aids in attaining self-realization.

The metaphysical proposition that those who know become the object of their knowledge anticipated the development of an artistic criterion, one that proved to be a step toward the assertion that an artist possessing true outer perception holds the power to express the inner reality of the world through art. The concepts of the individual mind and the universal mind provoked the analogy of the creator and the created. Aesthetic sublimation became accepted as contiguous to spiritual consummation, even though evanescent. Nevertheless, if regularly experienced, it prepared the way for self-realization, an objective that explains the relationship between Indian dance and the temple.

An early attempt to define aesthetic experience is found in the *Nāṭyaśāstra* of Bharata, a treatise in ancient Sanskrit that influences Asian dance and theater much as Aristotle's *Poetics* has influenced the Western dramatic arts. Although this work was revered as a book of divine origin in the past, Indian authorities now consider it a compilation dating from the years 2 to 8 CE. It documents in great detail the technical components and aesthetic basis of Sanskritic dance and drama. Central to its text is an exposition of *rasa*, a principle as significant to Asian aesthetics as the Greek *katharsis* ("purification") is to Western theory. It describes the reactions that must take place between performer and spectator if the dramatic experience is to be consummated. The process is analyzed for its sequential stimulation of emotional responses arising from basic human sensibilities. The gradual disclosure of moods incited by dramatic symbol and suggestion, complemented by the spectator's artistic sensitivity, finally brings about total aesthetic realization. *Rasa* therefore implies that artistic creation is complete and fulfilled only when perceived in the mind of the informed onlooker.

China. Like India, ancient China also implicitly accepted the human affinity with nature but saw it as a unity governed by reciprocal relationships. From the sixth-century BCE Chinese philosopher Laozi (Lao-tzu) came Daoism (Taoism), in which beyond earthly existence is the universal order of the *dao* ("the path," "the way"), manifested in the concepts of *yang* and *yin*—the positive and the negative cosmic forces, respectively, from which all things have evolved. Although opposite in nature, these two forces are considered equally indispensable in the functioning of the universe. Confucianism accepted this as the underlying truth of existence, as reflected in the harmonious kinship of human with nature and human within society. The Confucian worldview, introduced in the sixth and fifth centuries BCE, was concentric, with the family at the center and all human relationships proceeding outward from it.

Confucianism. As a moral order, Confucianism laid stress on the proper conduct of the individual, and so rites and ceremonies were important adjuncts to living. Dance and music were necessary accomplishments for all persons of standing as well as aids to a balanced mind. According to Chinese sages, the will was purified, and conduct attained perfection through the practice of dance and music. Dancing was regarded as a fundamental element of education, and the *Li ji* (Book of Rites) enjoined all boys of good family to begin instruction at the age of thirteen.

Ancient Confucian dance favored elaborate formation pieces characterized by stately movements and dignified postures. Dances were identified as civilian or military—the civilian used long pheasant plumes and yak-tail switches as props and the military used shields and battleaxes. The most complete record of these choreographic forms is contained in the ancient treatise *Yuelü quanshu* (A Collected Edition of the Books of Music and Dance Rules). The author, Zhu Zaiyu (1536–1611), was a renowned musicologist and mathematician. The collection consists of twelve studies published at different times; it comprehensively documents all relevant material, including notations of dance steps and musical scores for accompaniment.

Daoism. Roughly contemporary with the Confucian philosophical mainstream, Daoism argued that the *dao*, as the inner nature of all things, was entirely independent of any external process. The universe's unchanging infinity was reflected in humans. The enlightened individual attained self-realization through a spontaneous and immediate perception. It was a fusion of the one with the many and was beyond the scope of intellectualism. Intuitive knowledge and quiescence were offered as the two means to self-enlightenment, and meditative breathing disciplines were developed as vehicles. Daoists early experimented with such disciplines for therapeutic purposes; they later expanded them into physical training and methods of combat, such as *taijiquan (t'ai-chi ch'uan)*, which were closely related to dance and theater in both China and Japan.

Buddhism. In the first century CE, Buddhism reached China as a reinterpretation of Indian ideas; adapted to Chinese attitudes, it led to the rise of a new school of Buddhist thought known as Chan. This new form drew heavily from Taoism, especially the latter's theory of sudden enlightenment. Calisthenic systems based on methods of respiratory control, kinetic restraint, and stillness became widely practiced in Chan Buddhist monasteries.

The discipline known as *taijiquan* had its beginnings in these methods. Its name derives from a Daoist metaphysical theorem that proposed the existence of a continuum between polarized *yang* and *yin* energies, establishing an effortless relationship between body and space. This theorem exemplifies the primary nature of rhythm in Asian dance forms.

Japan. Chan Buddhism eventually reached Japan, where its parent religion had taken deep root in the sixth century CE. *Chan* became *Zen* in Japanese, and its metaphysical concepts had an enormous impact on the nation's arts, including the dance of the *nō* theater. *Nō* is essentially a highly ritualistic and symbolic dance form which also emphasizes the eternal balance between *yang* and *yin*. It has reached an extreme point of aesthetic refinement and reduction and demands the complete attention of the spectator. A *nō* performance treats silence as a provocative element within a progression of interlocking, highly formalized rhythmic units of song, music, and dance—all of which build toward a choreographic climax in which time and space are transcended.

A series of aphoristic texts, *Zeami nijusan bushi* (The Twenty-three Books of Zeami), provides an aesthetic guide to *nō* methods comparable to the Indian *Nāṭyaśāstra* in historical importance. In these texts, the master actor and dramatist Zeami (or Seami) Motokyo (1363–1443) recorded and refined his craft's art as it had been passed to him orally by his actor father, Kan'ami Kiyotsugu (1333–1384). The texts emphasize a principle that Zeami called *hana* ("flower"): "*Hana* is mind, technique is the seed." By this principle, he implied that an artist transcends technique by utterly mastering it. Then, although technical forms remain constant, the long discipline of mind and body results in a new revelation for the audience at each performance. Through this, *yūgen*—the inner beauty of a passing moment that cannot be expressed in words—is achieved. In *nō* theater and dance, *yūgen* signifies the point or instant of aesthetic revelation when the total act of performance makes its impact on the spectator's mind.

Through the Buddhist concept of the impermanence of all things, the *nō* form has explored the transitory nature of aesthetic experience as it is realized through the classic choreographies of greater Asia. Asian dance has been constantly treated as the expression of a worldview and as a stimulant to human spiritual aspirations.

BIBLIOGRAPHY

Bharata-Muni. *The Nāṭyaśāstra Ascribed to Bharata-Muni.* Translated by M. M. Ghosh. 2 vols. Calcutta, 1951–1961.

Chang Chung-yüan. *Creativity and Taoism: A Study of Chinese Philosophy, Art, and Poetry.* New York, 1970.

Feng Yu-lan. *A Short History of Chinese Philosophy.* Edited by Derk Bodde. New York, 1974.

Gaston, Anne-Marie. *Śiva in Dance, Myth, and Iconography.* Delhi, 1982.

Kale, Pramod. *The Theatric Universe: A Study of the Nātyaśāstra.* Bombay, 1974.

Kawatake, Toshio. *Japan on Stage: Japanese Concepts of Beauty as Shown in the Traditional Theatre.* Tokyo, 1990.

Kliger, George. "Indian Aesthetics and Bharata Nātyam." In *Bharāta Nātyam in Cultural Perspective,* edited by George Kliger. Manohar, 1993.

Lao-tzu. *Tao Te Ching.* Translated by D. C. Lau. Baltimore, 1963.

Nandikeśvara. *Nandikeśvara's Abhinayadarpanam: A Manual of Gesture and Posture Used in Hindu Dance and Drama.* Translated by M. M. Ghosh. 2d ed. Calcutta, 1957.

Sharma, Chandradhar. *Indian Philosophy: A Critical Survey.* New York, 1962.

Stcherbatsky, F. T. *Buddhist Logic.* 2 vols. New York, 1962.

Suzuki, D. T. *Zen and Japanese Culture.* Princeton, 1970.

Zeami. "Seami juroku bushi—Seami's Sixteen Treatises." Translated by Shidehara Michitaro and Wilfred Whitehouse. *Monumenta Nipponica* 4 (1941).

Zeami. *Kadensho.* Translated by Chūichi Sakurai et al. Kyoto, 1968.

A. C. SCOTT

Islamic Dance Aesthetics

Islam is a determining factor in the lives of approximately one billion people who form majority populations in North Africa, the Middle East (Turkey, the Arab nations, and Iran), in Central Asia (Afghanistan, Pakistan, and Bangladesh and the southern republics of the former Soviet Union), and in Southeast Asia (Malaysia, Indonesia, and the southern Philippines). In addition, Muslims are minority populations in other regions. A dance aesthetic for Islam, as for any other tradition, emerges from its cultural base.

Since its seventh-century beginnings, Islamic culture has been based on the concept of *tawḥīd* ("unity"), a strict monotheism that perceives two realms of existence: the realm of nature, which is knowable and malleable by human effort, and the realm of the Creator, which is beyond humans to influence or fully comprehend. Countenancing no separation of the secular from the sacred, *tawḥīd* has permeated all aspects of Islamic culture. Its aesthetic products follow the ideology; all evidence the following characteristics: abstraction, infinite patterns, modular structure, and small intricate movements.

Abstraction. Because God (Allāh) is utterly transcendent and beyond nature, the aesthetic of beauty in Islamic culture is to disguise nature or to avoid it completely. In the visual arts, this aesthetic has resulted in stylization based on the rejection of figural representation. In dance, it brought the avoidance of programmatic choreography—no coordination of steps, formations, movements, or gestures with a story, description of events or things, or portrayal of moods and emotions. Because there is no related drama, no personification, the costumes mirror local customs of dress and tend to obscure the dancer's body as an additional means of transfiguring nature.

Dance, an art that comprises movements of the human body does not lend itself easily to abstraction; this has led to lack of interest in dance in certain segments of Muslim society and even, at times, to its condemnation.

Infinite Patterns. The Islamic work of art seeks to draw the mind of the perceiver toward God and away from nature through the creation of complicated designs that give an impression of never-ending continuity. The dances of the various Muslim peoples exemplify these infinite patterns by their seemingly endless succession of improvised movements. There is no single climactic moment or definite conclusion, no fixed choreography, no predetermined sequence of steps or performance units. This does not preclude preferences for certain steps, body movements, and/or sequences within a regional or local dance culture. Such elements, however, are treated as motifs to be woven extemporaneously into the dance fabric rather than as elements planned by the performer or choreographer. A dance may continue for minutes or hours, depending on the inspiration of the performer and the interest of the audience. A spectator may enjoy one unit of the dance or any number of successive units. As in Islam's visual, literary, or musical arts, any intermediate or final stopping point implies that another module or another pattern might be added, either onstage or in the mind's eye of the performer or spectator. Therefore, a dance performance is not concluded with a grand finale at center stage. The soloist or group seems to continue the dance as it moves offstage, just as the half or quarter medallions at the edge of an oriental carpet imply a continuation of the pattern beyond its borders.

Modular Structure. Dances are like other aesthetic creations in Islamic culture: they are modular in structure. This means, first, that a performance is composed of a series of more-or-less distinct parts whose boundaries are delineated by the alternation of performers; changes of movements, tempos, or rhythms; separation of musical interludes; or repetitive miniclimaxes. Second, there is an additive rather than a developmental organization of the dance modules. Each segment may be appreciated on its own, and no particular ordering of modules is essential to the success of the performance.

Every dance module carries its own buildup and subsequent release of aesthetic tension. This segmented emotional experiencing of the artistic product predominates in all Islamic arts. For example, in each line or couplet of a poem, a gathering of aesthetic and mental tension is resolved only at the point where the completion of the idea, the end of the metric pattern, and the recurrence of the sound pattern, or rhyme, coincide at the end of a module. Similarly, as the spectator focuses attention on one module within an Islamic visual design, there is a search for its constituent motifs and their organization. When comprehension of that module of the pattern is achieved, a feeling of satisfaction, an aesthetic miniclimax, is experienced; then the eye and mind move on to explore the next design module. The dance performance is no less a series of progressions toward points of aesthetic tension and resolution. A particularly skillful "attack" may mark the end of a unit in a combat dance. Solo and chain dances are composed of crescendos of activity and excitement followed by interruptions and new beginnings. Even the religious dances emphasize a succession of emotional and physical climaxes. Because performances usually present a series of music and dance numbers, the artistic event is a multilevel organization of separate entities.

Movements. Just as the patterns of Islamic visual art are characterized by a proliferation of complex details, the dances of Islamic peoples emphasize small and intricate movements. Performers operate in a fairly confined area, displaying shivering, shaking, jerking, or rolling movements rather than wide leaps and open leg movements. In some parts of the Muslim world, whole dances are performed in a sitting or kneeling position. The viewer's appreciation can result only from a careful following of the intricacies of interplay between accompaniment and movement.

Each of the prominent Islamic dance genres—combat dances, solo improvisations, chain dances, and the religious dances of the mystical (Sufi) brotherhoods—has its special movements and flavor. In addition, each part of the Muslim world evidences certain regional preferences for particular movements, accompaniment practices, and costuming. Yet, underlying these elements of variance, the four core characteristics prevail, testifying to a basic artistic unity in the dances of the Muslim peoples.

[*See also* Islam and Dance.]

BIBLIOGRAPHY
Arabesque. New York, 1975–.
And, Metin. "Dances of Anatolian Turkey." *Dance Perspectives,* no. 3 (Summer 1959).
Berger, Morroe. "A Curious and Wonderful Gymnastic: The Arab Danse du Ventre." *Dance Perspectives,* no. 10 (Spring 1961): 4–41.
Faruqi, Lois Lamya' al-. "Dances of the Muslim Peoples." *Dance Scope* 11.1 (1976–1977): 43–51.
Faruqi, Lois Lamya' al-. "Dance as an Expression of Islamic Culture." *Dance Research Journal* 10.2 (1978): 6–13.
Haq, Sirajul. "Samāʿ and Raqṣ of the Darwishes." *Islamic Culture* 18.2 (1944): 111–130.
Masʿūdī, Abū al-Ḥasan ʿAlī al-. *Les prairies d'or (Murūj al-dhahab wa maʿādin al-jawhar).* Vol. 8. Translated by C. A. C. Barbier de Meynard. Paris, 1874.
Molé, Marijan. "La danse extatique en Islam." In *Les danses sacrées,* edited by Jean Cazeneuve. Paris, 1963.
Rezvani, Madjid K. *Le théâtre et la danse en Iran.* Paris, 1962.
Shiloah, Amnon. "Réflexions sur la danse artistique musulmane au moyen âge." *Cahiers de civilisation médiévale* 6 (October–November 1962): 463–474.
Tabbārah, Shafīq. *Al-raqṣ fī lubnān.* Beirut, 1957.

LOIS LAMYA' AL-FARUQI

Western Dance Aesthetics

Western philosophers since the time of Plato have discussed the nature of dance, its varieties and purposes, its connections with music, drama, and poetry, and its distinctive features as a form of creative achievement. Interest in dance aesthetics as an independent subject is a relatively new phenomenon, however. Consequently, few major treatises are devoted entirely to it. The paucity of sources is attributable in part to the fact that for centuries dance was frequently integrated so thoroughly with music and/or drama that it did not command separate treatment in philosophical discussions of the arts.

Some periods in Western culture, particularly those influenced by medieval or puritanical attitudes in which dancing was perceived as sinful, were not sympathetic to discussing dance as an art form because dancing, except for religious purposes, was considered a diversion from the spiritual purposes of life. In the seventeenth century, however, writers began to show an awareness of the importance of dance, particularly in regard to its affinities with and differences from poetry, music, and painting. Twentieth-century philosophers have engaged in the aesthetic problems unique to dance.

Antiquity. The records of Western philosophical writings on the dance as a form of art begin with the ancient Greeks. Their commentaries on the nature and functions of dance are frequently commingled with discussions of music and drama and often appear in treatises on education, moral conduct, and cultural life in general. Although the remarks found in these writings often pertain to dancing as a means of education or of socialization, the authors also consider it to be a mode of artistic performance.

Plato's *Republic* examines the theory that all art is "imitation," either of human passions and actions or of things and events as they appear to the senses. In the *Laws,* Plato considers dance under two separate aspects: its relation to education and virtue, and its relation to the general theory of imitation. For the Greeks of his time, dance was important both in training the body through gymnastics and as a principal means of cultivating the soul. Plato is careful to distinguish between dancing as an educational activity in which every well-educated citizen is expected to participate and dancing as performance in the theatrical spectacles that mark the annual festivals. According to Plato, an amateur who undertakes dance as a form of physical and cultural education would not enter into it to the same degree as one totally committed to the art. The aim of the citizen is to develop his own body and mind by dancing. In contrast, the performer's aim is to create mimetic images that will provide edifying models of virtuous living for the community. A dance edifies when it correctly imitates persons and actions that exemplify such properties as moral goodness and artistic beauty. Pleasure is thus subordinated to moral and artistic worth as a measure of value.

Aristotle refers only briefly to dance in his major aesthetics treatise, the *Poetics*, but provides a fuller treatment in the *Politics*, where he questions the end the arts serve and the benefits derived from participating in an art form. The end of all mimetic arts, including dancing, is imitation of human characters, actions, and experiences. The distinctive end of dance is achieved by means of "rhythm without harmony" (*Poetics*, chapter 1). It is natural for human beings to enjoy both the act of dancing and the process of learning that takes place on viewing imitative actions in an artistic performance. The broader educational ends of such activities are spelled out more fully in book 8 of the *Politics*, where dance is discussed under the term *mousikē*. There, the end of dancing is the development of intellectual culture and, ultimately, of moral character. Aristotle's influence extends into the twentieth century. Writers in each generation have modified his basic concept of imitation to suit their own purposes.

In the Hellenistic period, Plutarch, Lucian, and Athenaeus, while continuing in the tradition of Aristotle, contributed their own additions to or modifications of a theory of dance aesthetics. Plutarch further defines the elements though which imitation can take place. Dancing, he says, consists of three elements: moments, positions, and pointing. The moments constitute phrases that express some emotion, action, or potentiality. Poses are the names of the representational positions, as when the dancers compose their bodies to represent a being such as Apollo or Pan. Pointing functions rather like a proper name—literally to indicate or denote through the dance what is being represented (*Moralia: Table Talk*, book 9). Plutarch's analogies between dance, painting, and poetry invite analysis from the point of view of modern semiotic and linguistic theories of artistic symbols.

Lucian's dialogue *The Dance* underscores the legitimacy of dance as an imitative art with historical traditions comparable to those of music, rhetoric, and philosophy. As with these arts, dance reveals what is in the mind, whether by depicting characters, by imitating rhythmic patterns, or by expression through bodily movements and gestures.

Lucian recognizes the intellectual character of dance as well as its technical requirements and benefits. He emphasizes that a dancer must be able to express his or her ideas and sentiments through the intelligibility of movements and postures. This knowledge is the product of a thoroughly prepared mind that is aware of the important ideas and sentiments of past and present cultures. The dancer also knows how to generate rhythmical and graceful imitations through bodily movements and gestures so as to give the viewer both pleasure and understanding.

In book 14 of *The Deipnosophists* Athenaeus argues that composers and performers of dances in ancient times were as much concerned with the qualities of the movement itself as with the imitative aspects of dancing. The poets, who frequently invented dances for stage performances, composed them to suit the form of their poetry and music. Athenaeus observes that in ancient dances movements of the arms were shaped with great care and that the ancients sought movements that were beautiful as well as becoming to decent people. He shares their view that noble and beautiful dances are the product of beautiful souls and are likely to enhance the souls of both performers and spectators.

Athenaeus classifies more than sixty types of dances. He distinguishes three kinds suitable for the state, each with its own particular aesthetic properties of style and expression: tragic, comic, and satyric. Tragic dance is exemplified by the "naked boy dance," which uses hand gestures like those of wrestlers and is characterized by gravity and solemnity. Comic dance is associated with *hyporchēma*, a dance for men and women in which the chorus sings as it performs dances with lively, fun-filled moments. Satyric dance, exemplified by the war dance, emphasizes rigor and speed but lacks depth of feeling. [*See* Greece, *article on* Dance in Ancient Greece.]

Middle Ages. The dominant medieval aesthetic theories governing dance were drawn from three principal sources—the Bible, the works of ancient and contemporary philosophers, and the writings of the Greek and Latin church fathers—as well as from actual practice. In the absence of any substantial primary treatises, what is known of the aesthetic principles governing dance as an art is based on the general principles applied to the arts and occasional textual references to dancing.

In the Bible, dancing is generally perceived in a favorable light when it is an expression of praise and a celebration of Yahweh, or God. One account describes Miriam, the sister of Moses and Aaron, leading a dance of celebration (*Exodus* 15.20), and David is mentioned on several occasions as dancing in praise of Yahweh (*1 Chronicles* 15.29; *2 Samuel* 6.14–16). Dancing in the Bible is also mentioned in conjunction with, although not necessarily as the cause of, certain ominous episodes: the golden calf (*Exodus* 32.19), which signified idolatry; the sacrifice of Jephthah's daughter (*Judges* 11.34), and Salome's dancing before Herod (*Matthew* 14.6; *Mark* 6.22). Similarly, writers in the Middle Ages—Augustine and other church fathers who otherwise perceived dancing as a violation of virtue—uniformly sanctioned dance that centered on the praise of God. [*See* Bible, Dance in the.]

In book 6 of *On Music*, Augustine considers form and beauty of movement with reference to harmony and proportion. He relates these notions to bodily rhythms, observing that they also influence the rhythms of the soul.

Rhythms emanating from God, impressed on the body through the actions of the soul, are preferable to those originating in the actions and passions of the body.

The sixth-century writer Dionysius the Areopagite transmitted to the Middle Ages the ideas and images of Plotinus concerning the movements of the heavenly and earthly hierarchies. Dionysius's analysis of straight lines and of circular and spiral movements of celestial inhabitants describes the three principal forms of dance—circular, processional, and whirling—mentioned in medieval sources.

For the church fathers, aesthetic considerations such as form, expression, and style were subordinated to religious and moral issues. Many recognized that dancing, modeled on biblical acts of praise and thanksgiving in the forms ascribed to celestial figures by Platens and his followers, could be, as Ambrose observed, "an ally of faith and an honoring of grace."

During the mid- to late Middle Ages, many philosophers came to recognize that a completely satisfactory aesthetic experience requires what Hugh of Saint-Victor (early twelfth century) called a union of the "light of the higher senses and the pleasure of physical gratification." According to Hugh, this union is best achieved in works that incorporate music, poetry, dancing, and the visual arts through the harmonization of sounds, smells, lights, colors, movements, and expressive gestures, with their deeper symbolic meanings.

In the late Middle Ages, Thomas Aquinas considered dance to be an art of "pure play," one directed primarily toward pleasure. He adopted a more liberal view of the arts than did Augustine. Aquinas found dance acceptable provided it did not directly endanger morality or upset the equilibrium of life as a whole; pleasures inspired by beautiful artistic images may in fact be necessary to spiritual well-being. Aquinas's liberal views are grounded in his philosophical principles. Following Aristotle, he argues that an artist's primary aim is to actualize his image or idea in matter. The body in dance thus becomes a necessary vehicle for realizing the images of the soul. Aquinas recognizes the primacy of properties of movement in a dance work; moral and religious intentions are secondary to essential artistic considerations. He recognizes that the body is outside the soul and therefore incapable of corrupting it. These concepts allow Aquinas to accept some dances that directly produce bodily pleasure because they do not threaten to corrupt the soul.

During the Middle Ages, dance—whether within the church, in a theatrical setting (such as a mystery play), or in other independent settings intended for entertainment—was judged according to religious and moral criteria as well as aesthetic merit. The church fathers' condemnations were directed at the debasement of dance rather than at dance itself. [*See* Christianity and Dance, *article on* Medieval Views.]

Renaissance. During the Renaissance, dance took on new refinements and began to occupy an increasingly prominent place in the cultural life of the courts. Humanistic notions gradually assumed a prominent place among the pluralistic views of philosophers and arts theorists, but there was no abrupt shift away from the medieval aesthetic principles governing dance.

The major sources of dance aesthetics for the period are the works of the Renaissance philosophers Giovanni Pico della Mirandola, Marsilio Ficino, and Baldassare Castiglione. Building on Aristotle, Pico claimed that imagination has its own inventive function. It conceives and fashions particular images with sensory properties, whereas the intellect functions at the level of abstraction. Imagination, for instance, would produce the artistic forms of movement created by the dance composer. Aware that imagination could be directed to evil as well as good, Pico added that the wise practitioner should "direct the eye of the mind to God" (Pico, 1930).

Ficino's Platonic ideas on beauty and the arts serve as a source of the theory underlying much of the artistic activity of the Renaissance. In Ficino's terms, a dance might exemplify human striving for beauty. "The beauty of the body lies," he wrote to Giovanni Cavalcanti, "not in the shadow of matter, but in the light and grace of form; not in dark mass, but in clear proportion; not in sluggish and senseless weight, but in harmonious number and measure" (Ficino, 1975–1988). For Ficino, the visible marks of beauty expressed in artistic forms are the signs of invisible beauties characteristic of the soul and ultimately of divine beauty itself.

Of all Renaissance theories, Castiglione's has the most direct relationship to dance. In *The Book of the Courtier*, he bases his advice on an aesthetic model that might also have guided dance composers of the period. The courtier's art should arrange the elements of life so that they meet three essential requirements: to appear natural, to satisfy the rules of social decorum, and to reveal a fundamental beauty.

Grace, *sprezzatura*, and *beauty* are the principal terms of Castiglione's aesthetic. Grace is the harmonious elegance and refinement characteristic of true art, which does not appear to be art. It is the result of taking great care to conceal both the effort and the conformity to rules necessary for its achievement. Ease and spontaneity in accomplishing difficult acts, together with lack of affectation and an observable reserve of energy, are the marks of a graceful action. *Sprezzatura* is the "slightly superior disdain," or studied nonchalance, that accompanies a graceful action, giving the impression that it has been accomplished almost without thought or attention. Both assume a certain freedom, an independence gained not from rebelling against rules but by mastering them.

The Renaissance also witnessed the appearance of the important dance manuals of Domenico da Piacenza, Fabritio Caroso, and Thoinot Arbeau. Although intended to give instructions for performing certain dances, these manuals also reflected contemporary theories of imagination, beauty, and grace. Not all Renaissance scholars saw dance in favorable terms, however. Heinrich Cornelius Agrippa, for example, attempted to discredit ancient, medieval, and contemporary supporters of dance by attributing its popularity to the work of the devil, preferring instead to advance the arts of magic and the occult.

Seventeenth Century. A preoccupation with the developing ideas of science and mathematics and their implications for philosophical issues drew the attention of the major seventeenth-century philosophers away from questions of aesthetics. A notable exception was Thomas Hobbes, who recognized the importance of the fine arts. Nevertheless, Hobbes attempted to "despiritualize" them by reducing matters of the soul and the passions to mechanical terms. Despite their disparaging references to the fine arts, the seventeenth-century rationalists exerted a profound influence on writers of aesthetics, who now urged that the arts should be developed by the application of rational methods analogous to the principles of mathematics and logic.

A principal spokesman for dance in this era was the Jesuit philosopher and dancing master Claude-François Ménéstrier, whose *Des ballets anciens et modernes selon les règles du théâtre* (1682) is a paradigm of neoclassical aesthetics. Ménéstrier sets forth rules for composing dances, basing his theories on classical sources and on firsthand knowledge of approximately two hundred ballets of his own time. He begins his definition of ballets with Aristotle's succinct statement in the *Poetics* that representational dances express actions, characters, and passions by means of harmonious rhythms and the controlled movements of gestures, actions, and patterns. Ménéstrier expands on and illustrates this definition, setting forth in considerable detail the qualitative or formal requirements and the quantitative or necessary components of a ballet, including the ways in which it differs from dance in general or from a poem or painting. Because ballet uses human movement and has greater flexibility of subject matter, Ménéstrier throughout his treatise attributes to it a greater range of representational skills than is found in poetry or painting.

A ballet must have unity of design, for example, but it does not require unity of action or of time and place. Its essential qualitative parts are invention, or the choice of a subject and its development in the ballet composer's imagination; character; movements; harmony; and decoration. Throughout his discussion, Ménéstrier emphasizes the ballet composer's inspiration and skill in shaping these parts, but he is careful to say that native wit or inspiration does not eliminate the need for the rules. Like the rationalist philosophers of the day, he assumes that the rules for making ballets are not arbitrary; they have their roots in the classical models and in a reasoned interpretation and use of nature.

Eighteenth Century. Major developments in philosophical aesthetics and proliferations of treatises on dance provided the basis for dance aesthetics in the eighteenth century. The British aesthetician David Hume and his English colleagues stressed the importance of aesthetic feeling and inner sense, with which they intended to supplant the neoclassical ideal of rules as the criteria for judgments of aesthetic taste. Hume's "inner sense" corresponds to the "natural" values of order, elegance, and harmony in the forms of art; however, inner sense would not necessarily dictate aesthetic choices differing from those based on rules.

The German philosopher Alexander Baumgarten's desire to establish a special domain for the arts led him to separate them from the domain of rationalist thinking. He advanced the idea that the fine arts are unique and nonintellectual in form and content. In this domain, sensuous richness and clarity of form are as important to the fine arts as logical truth and certainty of observation are to philosophy and science.

Among the eighteenth-century philosophers who wrote about dance are Abbé Dubos (Jean-Baptiste Du Bos), Charles Batteux, Denis Diderot, and Adam Smith. These authors agree in general that dance, along with music and poetry, has as its principal end to create pleasure through imitation. They also hold in common the corollary that dance expresses sentiments and feelings along the lines that Hume suggested. Certain questions important to the future of dance aesthetics emerge in the writings of this period—for instance, over such issues as whether imitation is an essential feature of dance, the relative importance of formal concerns versus expressive and narrative components, and the choice of subjects. Batteux and Diderot argue that dance is essentially an imitative or representational art form. Dubos, while recognizing the role of imitation, argues that motion is the principal artistic means of creating pleasure in a dance. Smith (1795), who defines dancing in a formalist manner as "a succession of a certain sort of steps, gestures, and motions, regulated according to time or measure" and formed into a system, suggests that imitation is not necessarily required of dance. As to appropriate subjects for dances, Diderot (1970) advises composers of dances to draw their subjects from domestic and bourgeois life, and, as Batteux (1746) suggests, to present them with "natural unaffected movements." On the other hand, Smith anticipates the modernist need to accommodate dances with no subject other than movement itself.

Paralleling the theories of the eighteenth-century philosophers were writings of choreographers such as John Weaver and Jean-Georges Noverre. For Weaver, the excellence of dance was found in its imitative powers, to explain things conceived in the mind by means of bodily gestures and motions, thus "plainly and intelligibly" representing actions, manners, and passions so that the audience could perfectly understand the performer "by these his Motions, tho' he say not a Word." However, Weaver claims, dance may be beautiful as well as excellent. For Weaver, it achieves beauty when it is "consonant to the Rules of harmonical Proportion and adorn'd with the Beauty of a natural and cultivated Gracefulness" (Weaver, 1960, p. 40). Still, these beautiful motions must be appropriate to the actions and passions that are imitated.

Noverre's discussions parallel those of the philosophers who believed that successful theatrical representations must touch the heart, move the soul, and influence the imagination. His statement that "a well-composed ballet is a living picture of the passions, manners, ceremonies, and customs, of all nations" (Noverre, 1930) underscores the need for expression and universal appeal. He agrees with Diderot that technical facility in dancing, even when it results in grace and nobility of movements, is insufficient without imitation. [*See* Christianity and Dance, *article on* Modern Views.]

Nineteenth Century. Romanticism emerged as a literary-philosophical movement in Germany as early as the mid-eighteenth century with the aesthetics of *Sturm und Drang*. It became a major force in the arts of the nineteenth century throughout Europe and America, stressing originality of genius over elegance and intensity of feeling over conformity to neoclassical rules. As a complex cultural phenomenon, romanticism embraces many different elements—sublime nature; scientific investigation of the past; myth and magic; a demand for free exercise of imagination; a merging of sense, feeling, and intellect; and the elevation of the subjective and spiritual elements of experience. Contrary to the views of the Enlightenment rationalists, the Romantic thinkers and artists considered the fine arts a primary means of ascertaining the true nature of reality. The fine arts were thus, in some instances, elevated above philosophy itself.

Although G. W. F. Hegel failed to include dance in his pantheon of the major fine arts, his brief remarks on dance, together with his views on sculpture and theater, suggest a philosophical approach to the art. In contrast to Théophile Gautier, Hegel offers a metaphysical view wherein dance is judged according to its ability to express mind or spirit.

To Gautier (1947), "dancing consists of nothing more than the art of displaying beautiful shapes in graceful positions and the development from them of lines agreeable to the eye." To him, the Romantic ballet encompassed a formalist aesthetic that depended on a strong commitment to technique; it was a form of dance more suited to expression of the passions than to dealing with metaphysical themes. Still, ideas of striving toward unattainable ideals of beauty and pleasure cannot be entirely divorced from their metaphysical grounding in the philosophies of German romanticism. Although Romantic ballet does not necessarily encompass all the philosopher-aestheticians' ideas, ballet and the literary-philosophical movement share certain points: the predominance of spiritual and emotional elements over rationalist principles; the blending of dreams and reality; the mixing of supernatural and magical elements with natural experiences; and the use of imagination to forge a new vision of the world with new artistic and scientific means of exploring it.

Toward the end of the Romantic period, the symbolist poet Stéphane Mallarmé offered his philosophical expression of the Romantic ballet, calling it "the supreme theatrical form of poetry" (Mallarmé, 1956). For Mallarmé, the ballet is a symbolic form that enables a ballerina, who stands at the edge of fantasy and reality, to be the unconscious revealer of truths inexpressible in any other medium. It differs from its sister art of mime through its use of steps, rather than gesture, as the foundation of its structure. According to Mallarmé, mime characters are the medium for depicting "reality," but dance steps express the fantasy aspects of a theme.

Both Gautier and Mallarmé accept the doctrine of "art for art's sake" and the formalist tendencies that evolved from romanticism. This legacy and romanticism's emphasis on subjective feeling and intuition, leading to a proliferation of expression theories of art, established the two main foundations of twentieth-century aesthetics. Neither Friedrich Nietzsche's dichotomous tension between Dionysian and Apollonian forces nor the social demands of Marxist aesthetics have been able to offset these powerful tendencies of the modern era that began in the mid-nineteenth century.

Twentieth Century. The diversity of modern aesthetic views parallels the emergence of widely varied developments in dance itself. Early in the century, Akim Volynsky, Paul Valéry, André Levinson, Adrian Stokes, and Rayner Heppenstall were especially notable for their contributions to a formalist approach to ballet. Valéry focused attention on the dance itself, considering that the dancers' actions, consisting of steps and gestures arranged in a certain order, are to be admired principally for their inherent qualities of movement.

Levinson based a similar concept of pure dance on the principle of the "turned-out body," rather than on any imitation of human action or features. This principle, the foundation of classical ballet training, calls for "turning the limbs" of the dancer outward from the torso, its "center," to facilitate balance, sideways movement, extensions, and turns. Freed from its usual limitation to forward and backward motion, the body can then move with ease and grace in any direction. This greater flexibility in movement "frees" the dance from dependence on imitation and allows for the fuller development of interest in the movement itself. [*See the entry on Levinson.*] Volynsky further defines the elements—turnout, vertical line, and elevation—that are characteristic of ballet and its aesthetic means. Heppenstall interprets these formalist principles as symbols of order and perfection in a confused world.

Expression as an independent theory applied to dance and the other arts emerged at the turn of the twentieth century in the works of Eugène Véron, Leo Tolstoy, and others and underwent many variations, most prominently in the writings of such philosophers as Robin George Collingwood, Susanne K. Langer, Monroe Beardsley, Rudolf Arnheim, and Nelson Goodman. Common to these is the belief that a primary aim of dance is to communicate, present, or exhibit the expressive properties of the movement—the feelings, moods, and dynamic qualities and their symbolic features that are intended or perceived to be part of a dance.

Véron agrees with Valéry in rejecting imitation as the principal consideration in dance aesthetics. Like Tolstoy and Collingwood, he believes that all art—including dance—consists primarily of the expression of emotion. Collingwood, Langer, Arnheim, and Goodman argue that expression in dance is a form of human symbolic behavior. According to Langer, the feeling in a work of art represents the artist's idea of the feeling; dance is virtual, not actual, gesture; and the feeling that governs the dance is imagined, not actual. Arnheim defines expression as an essential property of physical and mental processes. The expressive properties, including feeling and perceived bodily muscular tensions in a dance movement, are experienced through corresponding acts in the mind of the spectator.

Contemporary philosophers, including Beardsley, Goodman, and Joseph Margolis, have applied the methods of analytic philosophy to the meaning of "expression" in dance. Beardsley makes expressiveness a requisite property for a motion to be accepted as dance. Goodman (1968) understands expression as "metaphorical exemplification," a form of symbolism requiring that the symbol—a dance—assumes certain properties that it cannot literally possess. According to Goodman, his own theater piece *Hockey Seen, A Nightmare in Three Periods and Sudden Death* (1972) expresses various aspects of competition, conflict, violence, frustration, and the struggle between aggression and authority without the dancers being literally violent or frustrated. Goodman considers dance in relation to his theory of symbols and notational symbol systems as outlined in his book, *Languages of Art.* In contrast to Goodman, Margolis argues that a theory of the dance cannot be completely formulated without attention to the literal expressive features of bodily movement, which he believes are passed over in Goodman's conception.

Other recent philosophers who have contributed ideas on topics in dance aesthetics include Étienne Gilson, Mikel Dufrenne, Graham McFee, David Michael Levin, and, most notably, Francis Sparshott. Levin invokes modernist formalism, as exemplified in the choreography and performances of George Balanchine (for example *Agon* and *Violin Concerto*), to develop an aesthetic theory of dance. Formalist dance aesthetics suppresses representational and theatrical elements of dance in favor of the "pure" formal expressiveness of an abstract syntax of movement.

Sparshott applies analytic philosophy to the practices of dance in all cultures in an effort to lay the groundwork for future dance aesthetics. His two books, *Off the Ground: First Steps to a Philosophical Consideration of the Dance* (1988) and *A Measured Pace: Towards a Philosophical Understanding of the Arts of Dance* (1995), represent the most comprehensive efforts to date to examine the philosophical problems of dance. Sparshott focuses on dance as consisting of a broad range of dances including Western ballet, modern dance, and contemporary theater dance, as well as selective artistic and non-art dances of other cultures. While disavowing any general theory of dance, Sparshott suggests that inquiry might focus on how dance has meaning in the lives of humans as the perpetrators of culture in general. Two central concepts guide Sparshott's inquiry: "The concept of a practice" and "dance as a means of transformation of the person dancing." According to Sparshott, dance exists as a practice when persons knowingly engage in bodily movements with a recognizable form that can be identified by conventions such as cultural values expressed in rules, standards, or ideals (*A Measured Pace*, 301–305). For Sparshott, dance's capacity for transforming the person dancing by altering his/her being distinguishes dance from other arts and other forms of human activity.

Apart from philosophers, numerous writers from other fields have enriched contemporary dance aesthetics. Selma Jeanne Cohen has served as a catalyst in dance criticism, history, and aesthetics, stimulating philosophers and others to explore in greater depth questions concerning the identity of the dance work, expression, and style.

Critics such as George Beiswanger, Edwin Denby, and John Martin have also added to the discussion of dance aesthetics. Beiswanger's essays on dancemaking describe dances that "raise the eventful high above the threshold of perception" (Beiswanger, 1973). Denby's remarks uniquely combine theory and visual observations. His writings on dance exemplify the very essence of the dance experience as seen by him. Martin (1933) attempts to define an aesthetics of "the new modern dance." He characterizes the primary purpose of modern dance as a desire to externalize personal experience "in the direction of individualism and away from standardization." His approach is based on negating the classical and the Romantic approaches to dance, with their adherence to a set vocabulary of movements and attitudes favoring abstract over natural bodily movements.

An additional source is the writings of choreographers. Michel Fokine called for a variety of choreographic approaches instead of reliance on a single method of fixed movements and poses. He recommended movements based on naturalistic expression combined with stylistic consistency reflecting national character and period style. George Balanchine's writings state with pristine clarity the essence of the art of choreographing movement. To him, ballet was about the movement of bodies in time and does not represent anything beyond itself. He liked to compare dance to a flower: a beautiful thing that does not need to tell a story.

The writings of such modern dance pioneers as Isadora Duncan, Ruth St. Denis, Mary Wigman, Martha Graham, and Doris Humphrey are also useful for the story of dance aesthetics. Duncan's rejection of ballet and her endorsement of natural bodily movements marked the beginning of a plurality of approaches to Western dance. Although they shared a desire to create expressive forms, Wigman, Graham, and Humphrey each developed an individualized aesthetic based on a specific theory and technique of body movement.

New approaches leading to postmodern dance aesthetics emerged during the 1960s to 1970s and called for fresh approaches to dance aesthetics. The available sources include the writings of and interviews with such American choreographers as Merce Cunningham, Meredith Monk, Yvonne Rainer, Judith and Robert Dunn, and Pooh Kay. In general, however, philosophical discussion of dance has not caught up with existing practice.

In the 1980s and 1990s Western theater dance continues to evolve through the creative efforts of choreographers such as John Neumeier, William Forsythe, Pina Bausch, Mark Morris, Anne Teresa de Keersmaeker, Jan Fabre, and others. Their choreography invites additional contributions to dance aesthetics.

[*See also the entries on the principal figures mentioned herein.*]

BIBLIOGRAPHY

Agrippa, Heinrich Cornelius. *Of the Vanitie and Uncertaintie of Artes and Sciences.* Edited by Catherine M. Dunn. Northridge, Calif., 1974.

Alter, Judith B. *Dancing and Mixed Media: Early Twentieth-Century Modern Dance Theory in Text and Photography.* New York, 1994.

Anderson, Richard L. *Calliope's Sisters: A Comparative Study of Philosophies of Art.* Englewood Cliffs, N.J., 1990.

Aristotle. *The Poetics.* Book 1. *The Politics.* Book 8. In *The Basic Works of Aristotle.* Edited by Richard McKeon. New York, 1941.

Arnheim, Rudolf. *Art and Visual Perception: A Psychology of the Creative Eye.* Berkeley, 1954.

Athenaeus. *The Deipnosophists.* Book 14. Translated by Charles Burton Gulick. London, 1937.

Augustine. *On Music.* Books 1–6. Translated by R. Catesby Taliaferro. Annapolis, 1939.

Backman, Eugène Louis. *Religious Dances in the Christian Church and in Popular Medicine.* Translated by E. Classen. London, 1952.

Balanchine, George. "Notes on Choreography." *Dance Index* 4 (February–March 1945): 20–31.

Batteux, Charles. *Les beaux-arts réduits à un même principe.* Paris, 1746.

Beardsley, Monroe C. "What Is Going On in a Dance?" *Dance Research Journal* 15 (Fall 1982): 31–36.

Beaumont, Cyril W. "Appendix A: Fokine's Theories on the Art of Ballet." In *Michel Fokine and His Ballets.* London, 1935.

Beiswanger, George. "Doing and Viewing Dances: A Perspective for the Practice of Criticism." *Dance Perspectives,* no. 55 (1973).

Bruyne, Edgar de. *The Esthetics of the Middle Ages.* Translated by Eileen B. Hennessy. New York, 1969.

Carroll, Noël. "Theatre, Dance, and Theory: A Philosophical Narrative." *Dance Chronicle* 15.3 (1992): 317–331.

Carter, Curtis L. "Arts and Cognition: Performance, Criticism, and Aesthetics." *Art Education* 36 (March 1983): 61–67.

Carter, Curtis L. "Two Views of Dance: Aesthetic Theory and Performance." In *Art in Culture 2.* Edited by A. Balis, L. Aagaard-Mogensen, R. Pinxton, and F. van Damme. Ghent, 1985.

Castiglione, Baldassare. *The Book of the Courtier.* Translated by Leonard E. Opdycke. New York, 1903.

Chapman, John V. "XXX and the Changing Ballet Aesthetic, 1828–32." *Dance Research* 2 (Spring 1984): 35–47.

Cohen, Selma Jeanne. *Next Week, Swan Lake: Reflections on Dance and Dances.* Middletown, Conn., 1982.

Copeland, Roger, and Marshall Cohen, eds. *What Is Dance?* Oxford, 1983.

Croce, Arlene. *Going to the Dance.* New York, 1982.

Denby, Edwin. *Looking at the Dance* (1949). New York, 1968.

Denby, Edwin. *Dancers, Buildings, and People in the Streets.* New York, 1965.

Diderot, Denis. *Entretiens sur le fils naturel.* In *Oeuvres complètes.* Edited by Roger Lewinter. Paris, 1970.

Dionysius the Areopagite. "On Divine Names, VIII" and "On the Heavenly Hierarchies, IV." In *The Works of Dionysius the Areopagite* (1897–1899). Translated by John Parker. Merrick, N.Y., 1976.

Du Bos, Jean-Baptiste. *Réflexions critiques sur la poésie et sur la peinture.* 2 vols. Paris, 1719.

Dufrenne, Mikel. "Dance: The Performer's Role." In Dufrenne's *The Phenomenology of Aesthetic Experience.* Translated by Edward S. Casey et al. Evanston, Ill., 1973.

Duncan, Isadora. *The Art of the Dance.* New York, 1928.

Ficino, Marsilio. *Commentary on Plato's Symposium.* Columbia, Mo., 1944.

Ficino, Marsilio. *The Letters of Marsilio Ficino.* 4 vols. London, 1975–1988.

Fletcher, Ifan Kyrle, Selma Jeanne Cohen, and Roger Lonsdale, eds. *Essays on the Theory and Practice of Theatrical Dancing in England 1660–1740.* New York, 1960.

Gautier, Théophile. *The Romantic Ballet.* Edited and translated by Cyril W. Beaumont. Rev. ed. London, 1947.

Giles, Jeffrey. "Dance and the French Enlightenment." *Dance Chronicle* 4.3 (1981): 245–263.

Gilson, Étienne. "The Dance." In Gilson's *Forms and Substances in the Arts.* Translated by Salvator Attanasio. New York, 1966.

Goodman, Nelson. "Dance." In Goodman's *Languages of Art.* Indianapolis, 1968.

Gradinger, Malve. "Dances of Disillusion." *Ballett International/Tanz Aktuell* (October 1995): 24–28.

Graham, Martha. "A Modern Dancer's Primer for Action." In *Dance: A Basic Educational Technique,* edited by Frederick R. Rogers. New York, 1941.

Heidegger, Martin. "Hölderlins Erde und Himmel." In *Erläuterungen zu Hölderlins Dichtung,* 4th ed. Frankfurt-am-Main, 1971.

Heppenstall, Rayner. "A Philosophy of Ballet." In Heppenstall's *Apology for Dancing.* London, 1936.

Humphrey, Doris. *The Art of Making Dances.* New York, 1959.

Jowitt, Deborah. *Time and the Dancing Image.* New York, 1988.

Kerkhoven, Marianne van. "Merging of All Boundaries: On the Autonomy of Dance." *Ballett International* 12 (January 1989): 13–19.

Khatchadourian, Haig. "Movement and Action in the Performing Arts." *Journal of Aesthetics and Art Criticism* 31 (1978).

Laban, Rudolf. "Movement Notation and the Field of Its Application." In Laban's *Principles of Dance and Movement Notation.* London, 1956.

Langer, Susanne K. *Feeling and Form.* New York, 1953.

Langer, Susanne K. *Problems of Art.* New York, 1957.

Levin, David Michael. "Balanchine's Formalism." *Dance Perspectives,* no. 55 (1973).

Levin, David Michael. "Postmodernism in Dance." In *Postmodernism: Philosophy and the Arts,* edited by Hugh J. Silverman. New York, 1990.

Levine, Mindy N. "An Interview with Pooh Kay." *Millennium Film Journal* 10–11 (1981–1982).

Levinson, André. "The Idea of the Dance: From Aristotle to Mallarmé." *Theatre Arts* 8 (August 1927): 571–583.

Levinson, André. "The Spirit of the Classic Dance" (1925). In *Dance as a Theatre Art,* edited by Selma Jeanne Cohen. New York, 1974.

Lucian of Samosata. *The Dance.* In *The Works of Lucian of Samosata.* Translated by H. W. Fowler and F. G. Fowler. Oxford, 1905.

Mallarmé, Stéphane. "Ballets." In *Selected Prose, Poems, Essays, and Letters.* Translated by Bradford Cook. Baltimore, 1956.

Margolis, Joseph. "The Autographic Nature of the Dance." *Journal of Aesthetics and Art Criticism* 34 (1981): 419–427.

Martin, John. *The Modern Dance.* New York, 1933.

Martin, John. *Introduction to the Dance.* New York, 1939.

Massine, Léonide. *Massine on Choreography: Theory and Exercises in Composition.* London, 1976.

McFee, Graham. *Understanding Dance.* New York, 1992.

Ménéstrier, Claude-François. *Des ballets anciens et modernes selon les règles du théâtre.* Paris, 1682.

Monk, Meredith. "Vessel: An Opera Epic." *Drama Review* 16 (1972).

Muchow, H. H. "Tans." In *Die Religion in Geschichte und Gegenwart.* 3d ed. Tübingen, 1957–.

Nietzsche, Friedrich. "The Dancing Song." In *Thus Spoke Zarathustra.* Translated by Walter Kaufmann. New York, 1954.

Noverre, Jean-Georges. *Lettres sur la danse et sur les ballets.* Stuttgart and Lyon, 1760. Translated by Cyril W. Beaumont as *Letters on Dancing and Ballets* (London, 1930).

Pico della Mirandola, Giovanni. *On the Imagination.* Translated by Harry Caplan. New Haven, 1930.

Plato. *The Laws.* Books 2 and 8. *The Republic.* In *The Collected Dialogues of Plato.* Edited by Edith Hamilton and Huntington Cairns. Princeton, 1961.

Plutarch. *Moralia: Table Talk.* Book 9. Loeb Classical Library. Cambridge, Mass., 1961.

Rainer, Yvonne. *Work, 1961–1973.* Halifax, N.S., 1974.

Rebhorn, Wayne A. *Courtly Performances: Masking and Festivity in Castiglione's Book of the Courtier.* Detroit, 1978.

Saint-Hubert, Monsieur de. "How to Compose a Successful Ballet" (1641). Translated by Andrée Bergens. *Dance Perspectives,* no. 20 (1964).

Smith, Adam. "Of the Imitative Arts." In Smith's *Essays on Philosophical Subjects.* London, 1795.

Sparshott, Francis. *Off the Ground: First Steps to a Philosophical Consideration of the Dance.* Princeton, 1988.

Sparshott, Francis. *A Measured Pace: Towards a Philosophical Understanding of the Arts of Dance.* Toronto, 1995.

Spencer, Herbert. "Gracefulness." In Spencer's *Essays Scientific, Political, and Speculative.* Vol. 2. New York, 1892.

Stokes, Adrian. *To-Night the Ballet.* London, 1934.

Thomas Aquinas. *The "Summa Theologica" of St. Thomas Aquinas.* Question 168. Translated by the Fathers of the English Dominican Province. 2d rev. ed. London, 1927–.

Valéry, Paul. "Philosophy of the Dance." In *The Collected Works.* Edited by Jackson Mathews. Princeton, 1964.

Véron, Eugène. *L'esthétique.* Paris, 1878.

Volynsky, Akim. "The Book of Exultation." Translated by Seymour Barofsky. *Dance Scope* (Spring 1971): 16–35.

Wagner, Richard. "The Art of Dance." In *Richard Wagner's Prose Works,* vol. 1, *The Art-Work of the Future.* Translated by William Ashton Ellis. London, 1895.

Weaver, John. "Anatomical Lectures 2." In *Famed for Dance: Essays on the Theory and Practice of Theatrical Dancing in England 1660–1740,* edited by Ifan Kyrle Fletcher, Selma Jeanne Cohen, and Roger Lonsdale. New York, 1960.

Wigman, Mary. *The Language of Dance.* Translated by Walter Sorell. Middletown, Conn., 1966.

CURTIS L. CARTER

AFGHANISTAN. A very conservative Islamic country, Afghanistan lies on the eastern edge of the Middle East, to the west of Pakistan and India. Afghanistan is at the confluence of Iranian, Central Asian, and Indian cultural currents, and most groups within Afghanistan have ethnic ties across the borders. Indian elements are the least felt, but the rhythmic footwork of some solo dancing is highly reminiscent of classical Indian traditions. A variety of ethnic and linguistic groups, each with its own choreographic tradition, reflects Afghanistan's enormous cultural diversity. Its dance traditions, however, are scarcely documented. As in most Islamic countries, dancers are paid performers who are often regarded askance. According to Mark Slobin (1980) "both male and female dancing is often associated with potential or actual moral laxity. Dancing boys have long been a feature of Afghan entertainment."

Because of Islamic mores, dancing, like most socializing, is sexually segregated, except in a few urban situations. It is currently being banned by the Mujahidin (the political faction sometimes called "freedom fighters" in the U.S. press) and the government (St. John, 1995). The music for female dancing is generally played by women on instruments that are particularly associated with women. The *chang* (a jaw harp) and hand-held frame drums, such as the *daireh*, are the most widely used. Men's dancing is accompanied by a wide range of stringed and percussion instruments: the ubiquitous *sorna* (a regional oboelike double-reed instrument) and *dohol* (large double-headed drum) are used especially for large outdoor dance gatherings. The most popular dance rhythm is 7/8 (shading into 6/8), although 4/4 and 6/8 are also common.

There are two types of Afghan dances: solo improvised dances and group dances. Solo dances are related to those found in Iran and central Asia, particularly Tajikistan and Uzbekistan; these are performed by dancing boys. Performances run from informal to professional, and the range of performance style, skills, and ability is wide. As in Iranian solo dancing, particular emphasis is given to expressive articulation of the head, shoulders, hands, fingers, and facial features. Indian elements, such as rapid whirling and rhythmic stamping, may also be present. The dance style of the Afghan province of Logar, near Kabul, is particularly esteemed. The Tajik dancers of Badakhshan in extreme eastern Afghanistan use masks and tell stories; similar theatrical dances are also performed across the border in Tajikistan.

The largest ethnic group in Afghanistan, comprising about half the population, is the Pashtun, who speak the Pashto (Pashtu) language. They are concentrated in the south and are both nomadic and sedentary. The group extends well across the eastern border into Pakistan, where the people are known as the Pathan. The most popular Pashtun group dance is the *attan* or *attan melli*, which has both male and female versions. The male's *attan*, considered by many Afghans to be the national dance, can have one hundred or more participants. It begins quietly but works into a frenzy as the dancers remove their turbans and whip their hair around with head gyrations. The performers often carry scarfs and do not hold on to one another. The dance can take on an ecstatic trancelike character, and variations of it can be seen throughout much of Afghanistan.

The Tajik, primarily sedentary Persian-speaking groups living in the region from the border with Iran and the city of Herat in the west to the border of China in the east, comprise about 30 percent of Afghanistan's population. Solo dance is their favorite form of expression. Women dance separate from men, primarily at weddings and other family gatherings. Professional female soloists began to appear in government-sponsored performances in Kabul in the 1960s.

The Turkic-speaking groups in Afghanistan (Uzbek, Turkoman, and a few Kirghiz) live principally in the north and have ethnic ties in the former Soviet republics and in Iran. The Uzbek are culturally related to the Tajik and share musical and choreographic elements with them. As with the Tajik, solo dancing is the most popular dance form. Professional dancing boys are most often Uzbek. The Turkoman are largely nomadic and have few dances. The men perform a round dance with staves, and the women perform both a round and a solo dance.

The Nuristani (also known as the Kafir) live in a remote mountainous region north of Jalalabad. Little is known of their dances, but a women's round dance and male and female solo dancing have been observed. While it cannot be considered dance, the Baluchi in southwestern Afghanistan and in Iran perform the *gwat* (wind) to mediate among evil spirits and afflicted individuals; it is similar to the Egyptian *zār*.

[*See also* Islam and Dance.]

BIBLIOGRAPHY

Hoerburger, Felix. *Volksmusik in Afghanistan*. Regensburg, 1969.

Malgari, Gholam Maha-El Din Ghalji. *Pastoni melli atuheh* (in Pashtu). Kabul, 1974.

Nurdzhanov, N. K. "Razvlecheniia Nardony Teatr Tajikov Karateginai Darvaza." In *Iskusstvo tadzhikskogo naroda*, edited by N. K. Nurdzhanov. Stalinabad, 1965.

Slobin, Mark. *Music in the Culture of North Afghanistan*. Tuscon, 1976.

Slobin, Mark. "Afghanistan." In *The New Grove Dictionary of Music and Musicians*. London, 1980.

St. John, Katherine. "Music and Dance of Afghanistan: The Concept of *Kesbi/Shauqi* (Professional Amateur)." *UCLA Journal of Dance Ethnology* 19 (1995): 61–67.

Tkachenko, Tamara. *Narodnyi tanets*. 2d ed. Moscow, 1967.

ANTHONY V. SHAY

AFRICAN-AMERICAN DANCE TRADITIONS. *See* United States of America, *articles on* African-American Dance Traditions *and* African-American Social Dance.

AFRICAN DANCE TRADITIONS. *For broad overviews of the two major cultural regions of Africa, see* North Africa *and* Sub-Saharan Africa. *For more detailed discussion of dance traditions in sub-Saharan Africa, see* Central and East Africa; Southern Africa; *and* West Africa. *For related discussion of dance traditions in sub-Saharan Africa, see* Aesthetics, *article on* African Traditions; Costume in African Traditions; Mask and Makeup, *article on* African Traditions; *and* Music for Dance, *article on* African Music.

AFTERNOON OF A FAUN. Choreography: Jerome Robbins. Music: Claude Debussy, *Prélude à l'Après-midi d'un Faune* (1892–1894), inspired by a poem by Stéphane Mallarmé, "L'Après-midi d'un Faune" (1876). Scenery and

AFTERNOON OF A FAUN. Two dancers, Francisco Moncion and Kay Mazzo, in a sunny studio appear to gaze in the mirror as they partner each other in Jerome Robbins's popular ballet. (Photograph by Martha Swope © Time, Inc.; used by permission.)

lighting: Jean Rosenthal. Costumes: Irene Sharaff. First performance: 14 May 1953, New York City Center, New York City Ballet. Principals: Francisco Moncion and Tanaquil Le Clercq.

Mallarmé's powerful image of a faun pursuing elusive nymphs on a sultry summer afternoon and Debussy's evocative score have proved irresistible to a number of choreographers since the first, scandalous performance of Vaslav Nijinsky's ballet in Paris in 1912. [*See* Après-midi d'un Faune, L'.] In 1922 Kasyan Goleizovsky choreographed a version for his Moscow Chamber Ballet in which a faun and his chosen nymph executed acrobatic and "eccentric" choreography on a platform while below them three other nymphs danced and two satyrs commented ironically on the action. At the Paris Opera in 1935 Serge Lifar danced the faun as a solo, in which the nymphs existed only in the imagination of the faun and his audience. In Norman Maen's ice-skating version in 1976, the faun (John Curry) encountered a sole nymph on an expanse of sun-dappled ice.

With *Afternoon of a Faun*, however, Jerome Robbins transposed the theme into the modern age with such truth and poignancy that his ballet rapidly became a classic in its own right. He derived his inspiration from his observations of dancers in the studio, in particular Edward Villella's stretching exercises and a rehearsal by two young dancers who seemed unaware of the sexual resonances of their pas de deux. Robbins's *Faun* is set in a sunny dance studio. An imaginary mirror forms its fourth wall, through which the audience watches the action. A boy in tights lies asleep on the floor; rousing, he languidly begins to stretch. A girl in a practice tunic enters and starts to warm up at the *barre*. They fall into a trancelike pas de deux, concentrating their attention on their reflections in the "mirror." At the end of their dance the boy gently kisses the girl's cheek; she raises her hand to her face and hurriedly leaves. The boy lies down once more to sleep.

This ballet is often interpreted as a commentary on the self-absorbed narcissism of dancers; an alternative but equally valid reading sees it as a young girl's awakening to her sexuality. Though Robbins's ballet is less overtly erotic than was Nijinsky's, the boy's bare chest and the girl's loosened hair implicitly create an atmosphere of sexual readiness. Tanaquil Le Clercq, who first danced the girl, gave her portrayal a subtle aura of sensual awareness; her reaction to the kiss was less an awakening than a denial. In describing their characters' relationship as neurotic, her partner, Francisco Moncion, implied that they could not or would not cope with love in the real world beyond the studio mirror. Other dancers have emphasized the girl's innocence: the kiss is her first intimation of carnal knowledge.

Since its premiere, *Afternoon of a Faun* has rarely been absent from the New York City Ballet repertory, where it has been danced by successive generations of principals and soloists. Edward Villella, Peter Martins, and Peter

Boal have all made the faun a signature role; Allegra Kent, Patricia McBride, Kay Mazzo, and Darci Kistler have all left lasting impressions as the girl. Since the early 1970s the work has been staged for numerous other companies, including the Royal Ballet, London; Dance Theatre of Harlem; Paris Opera Ballet; National Ballet of Canada; Royal Danish Ballet; Australian Ballet; La Scala Ballet, Milan; San Francisco Ballet; and Norwegian National Ballet.

BIBLIOGRAPHY

L'Après-midi d'un Faune. L'Avant-Scène/Ballet-Danse, no. 7. Paris, 1982.

Balanchine, George, with Francis Mason. *Balanchine's Complete Stories of the Great Ballets.* Rev. and enl. ed. Garden City, N.Y., 1977.

Reynolds, Nancy. *Repertory in Review: Forty Years of the New York City Ballet.* New York, 1977.

SUSAN AU

AGE OF GOLD, THE. *See* Golden Age, The.

AGLIÉ, FILIPPO D' (Filippo San Martino d'Aglié; born 27 March 1604 in Turin, died 19 July 1667 in Turin), Italian diplomat, poet, musician, and choreographer. Comte Filippo d'Aglié, a descendant of the noble house of Arduino d'Ivrea, succeeded his uncle, Marquis Ludovico d'Aglié, as organizer of entertainments at the court of Carlo Emmanuele I, duke of Savoy. In 1637, on the death of the next duke, Vittorio Amedeo I, Aglié became the favorite of the duchess, Maria Cristina, and a prominent figure in the politics of the state, which was in danger of being crushed between France and Spain during the Thirty Years' War.

Aglié's productions are recorded in the works of Claude-François Ménéstrier, a French Jesuit and dance theorist. Ménéstrier's *Traité des tournois, joustes, carrousels et autres spectacles publics* (1669), *Des représentations en musique* (1681), and *Des ballets anciens et modernes selon les règles du théâtre* (1682) list many court entertainments—ballets, banquets, plays with music, festivals—designed by Aglié. These productions include *Bacco Trionfante dell'Indie* (Rome, 1624); *Circe Scacciata* and *Il Prometeo che Rubba il Fuoco al Sole* (Turin, 1627); and *L'Eternità* (Turin, 1629). Aglié's *Gli Habitatori de' Monti* was presented in Paris in 1631 as a rebuttal to the allegation by Louis XIII's courtiers that the Piedmontese were "rude mountain people." According to the eighteenth-century dance historian Louis de Cahusac, the performance disproved the false opinion of the courtiers.

Aglié had begun his career in the service of Cardinal Maurizio of Savoy, to whom he owed both his political and artistic advancement. In 1634 in Turin, for the birthday of the cardinal, Aglié staged *La Verita Nemica dell'Ap-parenza Sollevata dal Tempo,* an allegorical ballet. In 1640 he followed the cardinal to Paris, where, caught in the conflict between France and the Holy Roman Empire, he was arrested by order of Cardinal Richelieu. He was detained in France until after Richelieu's death in 1642. Upon returning to Italy, Aglié staged several other celebratory productions, including *La Fenice Rinovata* (Fossano, 1644), in which Aglié and the young duke, Carlo Emmanuele II, dressed as the Sun, danced to celebrate the birthday of Maria Cristina. The ballet-banquet *Il Dono del Re dell'Alpi a Madama Reale* (Rivoli, 1645), also commemorating the duchess's birthday, returned to the political theme that Aglié had dealt with in *Hercole e Amore* (Chambéry, 1640), in which the five-year-old duke had impersonated Love restoring peace after the troubles and the dynastic crisis following the death of Vittorio Amedeo I.

After returning to the court at Turin, Aglié continued his rich and varied productions on themes ranging from the political and mythological to the exotic, as in *Il Tabacco,* and the marvelous, treated with inventiveness and humor, as in *Il Gridelino. Il Tabacco,* first presented in Turin in 1650, lauded the tobacco leaf, the use of which had just been legalized. The action took place on the Island of Tobacco, where natives chanted praises to the leaf. The final scene showed Turks, Moors, Spaniards, and Poles smoking and enjoying tobacco. *Il Gridelino* was staged in Turin in 1653 and was also presented in Paris (as *Ballet du Grisdelin*) at the request of Anne of Austria, then queen of France. Of this ballet, and of other productions by Aglié, rich illustrated codices attributed to the ducal secretary Tommaso Borgonio survive at the Biblioteca Nazionale Universitaria (I-Tn) and the Biblioteca Reale (I-Tr) in Turin, together with the music for several ballets, partly written by Aglié.

The comte d'Aglié was a representative figure of the complex cultural and political exchanges that took place between France and Italy during the first half of the seventeenth century and that found a harmonious synthesis in his spectacular productions. Almost a century after Aglié's death, Cahusac compared him to Jean-Baptiste Lully and even went so far as to declare that "his genius is perhaps the most fertile that has ever existed with regard to theatrical and gallant inventions" (Cahusac, 1754). Later historians have credited him as the first genuine choreographer of the Italo-French court ballet.

BIBLIOGRAPHY

Aglié, Comte d'. *Le ballet du tabac: Ballet burlesque dansé le dernier jour du carnaval à Turin, le premier mars 1650.* Facsimile text in Italian, with French translation by Claude Thibaut and an essay by Jean Baudry. N.p., 1973.

Bouquet-Boyer, Marie-Thérèse. "Il teatro di corte dalle origini al 1788." In *Storia de Teatro Regio di Torino,* edited by Alberto Basso, vol. 1. Turin, 1976.

Bouquet-Boyer, Marie-Thérèse. "Musical Enigmas in Ballet at the Court of Savoy." *Dance Research* 4.1 (Spring 1986): 29–44.

Bouquet-Boyer, Marie-Thérèse. "Cronologia degli spettacoli di corte, 1585–1740." In *Storia del Teatro Regio di Torino*, edited by Alberto Basso, vol. 5. Turin, 1988.

Cahusac, Louis de. *La danse ancienne et moderne: Traité historique de la danse*. 3 vols. The Hague, 1754.

McGowan, Margaret M. *L'art du ballet de cour en France, 1581–1643*. Paris, 1963.

McGowan, Margaret M. "Les fêtes de cour en Savoie: L'oeuvre de Philippe d'Aglié." *Revue d' histoire du théâtre* 3 (1970): 183–239.

Prunières, Henry. *Le ballet de cour en France avant Benserade et Lully*. Paris, 1914.

Solerti, Angelo. "Feste musicali alla corte di Savoia nella prima metà del XVII secolo." *Rivista musicale italiana* 11 (1904): 675–724.

Solerti, Angelo. *Gli albori del melodramma*. 3 vols. Milan, 1904–1905.

Sparti, Barbara. "'Baroque or Not Baroque—Is That the Question?' or Dance in Seventeenth-Century Italy." In *L'arte della danze ai tempi di Claudio Monteverdi*, Proceedings of the International Congress, Turin, 6–7 September 1993, pp. 73–93. Turin, 1996.

Tani, Gino. "Le comte d'Aglié et le ballet de cour en Italie." In *Les fêtes de la Renaissance*, vol. 1, edited by Jean Jacquot. Paris, 1956.

Viale Ferrero, Mercedes. *Feste delle Madame reali di Savoia*. Turin, 1965.

Winter, Marian Hannah. *The Pre-Romantic Ballet*. London, 1974.

CLAUDIA CELI
Translated from Italian

AGON. Ballet in three parts and twelve movements. Choreography: George Balanchine. Music: Igor Stravinsky. Lighting: Nananne Porcher. First performance: 1 December 1957, City Center for Music and Drama, New York, New York City Ballet. (Preview: 27 November 1957, March of Dimes benefit performance, City Center, New York.) Principals: Diana Adams, Melissa Hayden, Barbara Walczak, Barbara Milberg, Todd Bolender, Roy Tobias, Jonathan Watts, Arthur Mitchell. Supporting cast: Roberta Lubell, Francia Russell, Dido Sayers, Ruth Sobotka.

The most rigorous, taut, and profound collaboration between Stravinsky and Balanchine, *Agon* defined the classical dance as they had developed it. Mounted for four men and eight women on a dodecaphonic (twelve-tone) score, it appears compulsive and mechanistic, an "IBM device," according to Lincoln Kirstein. Yet it is a machine "that thinks and smiles . . . offering the epoch's extreme statement of its craft" through sophisticated musicianship, discipline, and wit.

Agon completes a triptych of related works created by Balanchine and Stravinsky that began with *Apollo* (1928) and continued with *Orpheus* (1948). The score's structure, devised in detail by both collaborators, is somewhat impersonal and fragmented both rhythmically and melodically, thus differing from its more resonant predecessors. The ballet itself, though courtly in demeanor, lacks the plastic grandeur of *Apollo* and the specific sculptural and ritualistic landscape that scenic designer Isamu Noguchi provided for *Orpheus*. Instead, its dangerously insistent rhythm and precipitous asymmetry necessitated that Bal-

anchine realign traditional dance forms to illustrate Stravinsky's musical inventiveness. Surprisingly, for such an uncompromising work, the ballet was hailed as a masterpiece at its first public performance.

The score, commissioned by the company, was based on twelve seventeenth-century French melodies filtered through Stravinsky's twentieth-century sensibilities. Indeed, traces of jazz, specifically boogie-woogie, are evident, accenting the ballet's wholly contemporary mood.

There is neither setting nor elaborate costuming for *Agon;* the dancers wear practice clothes, which do not detract from the complexity of movement. Lighting, an important structural element, constantly redefines the arena in which the dancers move, adding to the rhythmic and spatial drama.

As the curtain rises, four men with their backs to the audience set the work into motion by swiftly turning to face the viewers in silence. At the end, they return to their original positions, again in silence. Within this framework, Balanchine develops intricate phrases from a limited number of choreographic "building blocks," propelled by the relentless drive of the pulsating score. Movement ideas are compressed and permutated with each recurring musical fanfare (fundamentally a scalar passage for muted strings and trumpets punctuated by timpani) so that, as Kirstein discerns, their nearly unbear-

AGON. Members of the New York City Ballet in a 1958 production of *Agon*. Standing, in the center, are Diana Adams, Melissa Hayden, Arthur Mitchell, Edward Villella, Roy Tobias, and Jonathan Watts. (Photograph from the Dance Collection, New York Public Library for the Performing Arts. Choreography by George Balanchine © The George Balanchine Trust.)

able pressure becomes "an existential metaphor for tension and anxiety."

The title, *Agon,* which in Greek means "gathering" or "prize contest," hints at zestful combativeness as, for example, in the competitive canon for the two cavaliers in the second pas de trois, or in the precarious balances and tossing of the ballerina in the same section. Ultimately, however, the work contains little contextual reference except to the relationship between the dancers and their spatial and temporal environment. (The title is the only allusion to Greece in the work.) The range of expression is wide, from the elegance and simplicity of the first pas de trois to the intimacy and intensity of the central pas de deux. Seemingly one continuous phrase for two like bodies, the latter—with its majesty, boldness, and stark rhythmic exactitude—transcends any struggle of defeat implicit in *Agon* and transforms the struggle into magnitude and beauty.

With the sanction of the Balanchine Trust, *Agon* has also been performed by a number of companies in the United States and in Europe, including Dance Theatre of Harlem, Ballet Oklahoma, Pacific Northwest Ballet, the Pennsylvania Ballet, the Paris Opera Ballet, the Royal Ballet (London), the German Opera Ballet (Berlin), and the Hungarian State Opera Ballet.

BIBLIOGRAPHY

Alm, Irene M. "Stravinsky, Balanchine, and *Agon:* The Collaborative Process." Ph.D. diss., University of California, Los Angeles, 1985.

Balanchine, George, with Francis Mason. *Balanchine's Complete Stories of the Great Ballets.* Rev. and enl. ed. Garden City, N.Y., 1977.

Choreography by George Balanchine: A Catalogue of Works. New York, 1984.

Croce, Arlene. "The Spelling of *Agon.*" *New Yorker* (12 July 1993).

Daniels, Don. "Stravinsky III." *Ballet Review* 10 (Fall 1982): 37–46.

Denby, Edwin. "Three Sides of *Agon.*" *Evergreen Review* 2 (Winter 1959): 168–176.

Garis, Robert. "Balanchine-Stravinsky: Facts and Problems." *Ballet Review* 10 (Fall 1982): 9–24.

Goldner, Nancy. *The Stravinsky Festival of the New York City Ballet.* New York, 1974.

Gruen, John. "Balanchine and Stravinsky: An Olympian *Apollo.*" *Dance Magazine* 55 (April 1981): 84–87.

Hodgins, Paul. *Relationships between Score and Choreography in Twentieth-Century Dance.* Lewiston, N.Y., 1992.

Jordan, Stephanie. "*Agon:* A Musical/Choreographic Analysis." *Dance Research Journal* 25 (Fall 1993): 1–12.

Kirstein, Lincoln. *Movement and Metaphor: Four Centuries of Ballet.* New York, 1970.

Reynolds, Nancy. *Repertory in Review: Forty Years of the New York City Ballet.* New York, 1977.

Reynolds, Nancy. "Balanchine: An Introduction to the Ballets." *Dance Notation Journal* 6 (Winter–Spring 1988–1989): 15–74.

Sherr, Laurence E. "The Genesis of *Agon:* Stravinsky, Balanchine, and the New York City Ballet." Master's thesis, University of Illinois, Urbana-Champaign, 1988.

Thompson-Drewal, Margaret. "Constructionist Concepts in Balanchine's Choreography." *Ballet Review* 13 (Fall 1985): 42–46.

FILM AND VIDEOTAPE.   Excerpt from *Apollo* in *America Applauds Soviet Ballet* (1959), available in the Dance Collection, New York Public Library for the Performing Arts. Peter Martins, *A Dancer*

(1978), produced for Danish television. *The New York City Ballet* (1965), containing the pas de deux from *Agon,* available in the Dance Collection, New York Public Library for the Performing Arts. "Balanchine Celebrates Stravinsky," *Great Performances* (WNET-TV, New York, 1983).

REBA ANN ADLER

AILEY, ALVIN. *See* Alvin Ailey American Dance Theater.

AINU DANCE TRADITIONS. As the prehistoric inhabitants of the Japanese islands, the Ainu lived as hunters and fisherfolk; they belonged to the widespread Caucasoid peoples of northern Asia. When the prehistoric Mongoloid peoples from the southern Asian mainland settled the islands, the Ainu were forced to retreat from south to north; for centuries they gave the Japanese opposition, and campaigns against them are often mentioned in early historic documents of the Japanese empire. The Ainu now live on the Japanese island of Hokkaido and in Sakhalin and the Kuril Islands of Russia; tourists visit their settlements, buy souvenirs, and watch their ceremonies. Their ancient animistic religion centers on the bear cult—which was widespread among the northern and polar peoples of Europe, Asia, and North America.

Among the many hundreds of dances performed by the Ainu people in ancient times, knowledge of only about twenty-five remains today. All were "northland" in color and spirit, expressions of their keenest emotions—from deep sadness to great happiness. Some are ceremonial and others folk dances; all were handed down by the elders. For the Ainu, the dances and accompanying songs were considered as important as food. The only musical instrument used was the *mukkuri*—a type of jew's-harp made of iron and bamboo. Some dances were for men only or for women only, others were for men, women, and children.

A few dances may be described as follows:

1. Wheel Dance (*rimuse*)—Men, women, and children formed a circle; as they turned counterclockwise, their torsos were bent backward and forward. Then their bodies moved up and down by bending the knees, all the while clapping their hands to the rhythm of the songs.

2. Wine Dance—This was performed by women, who sang and danced as they made *amasake,* a sweet wine.

3. Sequel to the Wine Dance—The women sang and danced while filling kegs with wine as it was prepared.

4. Bow Dance (*chikkappu rimuse*)—This ceremonial dance was performed by men, depicting bird hunts, often cranes or geese, with bow and arrow. The movements were very strong and energetic.

5. Crane Dance (*sarolon rimuse*)—Two women imitate the courtship of cranes. The sleeves of their kimonos were waved to imitate the wings of the cranes.
6. Contest Dance—This dance was performed by women forming two teams. It was accompanied by fierce chanting. The very dynamic dancing continued until exhaustion and one team could no longer move.

These dances and others were included in the Ainu's most important ceremony, the Bear Festival—a three-day event. The first day began with a prologue. On the second day a bear was sacrificed to return it to heaven. On the third day the festival ended with an epilogue, busy with dancing, chanting, and feasting on various foods, including bear meat, some of which the villagers were invited to take back to their thatched huts.

The Ainu did not employ masks, but the girls and women displayed tatoos of wide dark blue lines outlining their mouths and wore decorated headbands. The costumes (*atushi*), on fabric woven from the bark of trees, had embroidery and appliqué work, creating colorful patterns. Various hard stones, such as jade, were used in Ainu necklaces and earrings, which completed the costumes.

BIBLIOGRAPHY

Hilger, M. Inez. *Together with the Ainu*. Norman, Okla., 1971.
Munro, N. G. *Ainu Creed and Cult*. London, 1962.
Munro, N. G. *Ainu Material Culture from the Notes of N. G. Munro*. Edited by Birgit Ohlsen. London, 1994.
Ninth Festival of Asian Arts, 18 October–4 November 1984, Hong Kong. Hong Kong, 1984.

AYAKO UCHIYAMA

ÅKESSON, BIRGIT (born 1908 in Malmö, Sweden), dancer and choreographer. Åkesson started dancing in 1929 at the Mary Wigman School of modern dance in Dresden; she never studied classical ballet. After three years she moved to Berlin and studied under Max Reinhardt. She also devoted time to studying in solitude, seeking her own authentic dance language.

She traveled on to Paris, where in 1934 she made her self-choreographed, solo and unaccompanied debut at the Théâtre Vieux Colombier. In the same year she performed dances, again unaccompanied, for a Swedish audience. Åkesson felt that dance without music permitted her to expand her ideas solely through the moving body, her only source of inspiration.

During World War II she did not compose any new works but taught at her dance school and single-mindedly developed her own technique. Her fundamental idea was to train each part of the body to move independently. She used the floor in a then unconventional way; for example one dance included a section performed with the body sup-

ÅKESSON. The solo *Movement* (1949) was an important work in the development of Åkesson's career. (Photograph by Beata Bergström; from the archives at Jacob's Pillow, Becket, Massachusetts.)

ported by one shoulder, the head, and one foot on the floor.

In 1946 Åkesson returned to performing. For the next ten years she often toured abroad, visiting New York, London, and Rome. She was also active in lecturing and writing articles on her theory of choreography. She did not create dance in order to express or repeat everyday life. Her choreography did not tell a story but made poetry through movement, "a listening to an inner voice" as Åkesson herself described it.

The postwar years in Sweden brought an increasing interest in multimedia work. It seemed possible to combine all art forms, and artists looked to one another for inspiration. Åkesson came into contact with composers, authors, and painters who together started several cultural magazines in which contemporary arts were enthusiastically debated. A cooperation among the poet Lindegren, the composer Blomdahl, and Åkesson resulted in a number of ballets with Greek mythology as the theme. *Sysyfos* (1957) and *Minotauros* (1958), among others, were performed by the Royal Swedish Ballet. They were all born out of unique teamwork in which intensive discussion played an important role. The performances were increasingly praised by the critics for the way in which the creators had combined their various talents.

In 1964 Åkesson was one of the founders of the Swedish Choreographical Institute, where she was for some years responsible for choreographic education. Despite her successes with the Royal Swedish Ballet, she was still a freelancer. Over the years it became more and more difficult for her to introduce her choreography into the more conventional repertory. During the 1960s, Swedish television presented some of her shorter ballets; those commissioned for television reveal her remarkable insight into that medium.

Åkesson did not choreograph during the 1970s and 1980s, instead interesting herself in African rituals. Her research in Africa led to a publication on the African origins of dance.

In 1989 Swedish television broadcast two new solo dances by Åkesson—*Höstlöv* and *Dagrar*—performed without music by the Chinese dancer Chiang Ching. The dances stress the principles of Åkesson's choreographic form; the dancer moves organically through a multitude of body shapes, creating rhythms by varying movement qualities and tempi and using elaborate foot-stamping.

BIBLIOGRAPHY

"Åkesson, Birgit." In *Sohlmans musiklexikon.* 2d ed. Stockholm, 1975–.

Åkesson, Birgit. *Källvattnets mask: Om dans i Afrika.* Stockholm, 1983.

Bohlin, Peter. "Swedish Contemporary Dance: Concentrated, Effective Energy." *Ballet International* 12 (March 1989): 9–15.

Engdahl, Horace. "Birgit Åkesson: A New Dimension in Dance." *Ballett International* 12 (October 1989): 10–15.

Hall, Fernau. "Birgit Åkesson: Post-Expressionist Free Dance." In Hall's *An Anatomy of Ballet.* London, 1953.

Hammergren, Lena. *Birgit Åkesson: Koreograf.* Stockholm, 1983.

Hammergren, Lena. *Form och mening i dansen: En studie av stilbegreppet med en komparativ stilanalys av Mary Wigmans och Birgit Åkessons solodanser.* Stockholm, 1991.

LENA HAMMERGREN

ALBANIA. A mountainous country on the Balkan Peninsula bounded by the Adriatic Sea, the former Yugoslavia, Macedonia, and Greece, Albania is inhabited by descendents of the Thraco-Illyrian tribes that once occupied the Central Balkans, who speak a language that forms a separate branch of the Indo-European family. The modern population is about 97 percent ethnic Albanian; 70 percent are Muslims, with Greek Orthodox and Roman Catholic minorities. Albania became independent in 1912 after four centuries of Turkish Islamic rule with the collapse of the Ottoman Empire, the last in a centuries-long sequence of foreign regimes. The young nation was the least developed country in Europe, an impoverished, backward, illiterate feudal society. In 1944 Albania became a communist people's republic and followed a Stalinist economic and social policy dominated by the personality cult of Enver Hoxha, who led the country in almost total isolation from the rest of the world until his death in 1985. Although Albanians boast a rich oral tradition of folk tales and epic and lyric poetry, the "fine arts," as understood in the rest of Europe, were practically nonexistent in Albania until they were promoted for nationalistic reasons by the communist regime. Albania has been in a state of profound transition since the revolution of 1992, which installed a quasi-democratic government. In 1997, the collapse of a nationwide pyramid scheme, in which many members of the regime were implicated, led to widespread protests that escalated rapidly to civil war.

Traditional Dance. The formations of Albanian traditional dance include solo, duo, trio, open or closed circle, and opposing lines. Men's and women's dance traditions are essentially separate, especially in historically Muslim areas. A large number of dances are done without instrumental accompaniment, to singing or in silence. There are a variety of rhythms and metric patterns, including free rhythm, beats of equal length (e.g., 2/4, 3/8) and of unequal length (e.g., 3/8 + 2/8 + 2/8, 2/8 + 2/8 + 2/8 + 3/8); tempos range from slow, to moderate, to steadily accelerating, and fast. Albanians use the terms *valle* and *kërcim* to refer to the activity designated by the English word *dance.* The two are practically interchangeable, though *kërcim* may also mean "jump," "hop," "bound," or "leap." Where they are contrasted (notably in the north), *valle* tends to denote a group dance done in a linked circle or two parallel lines, while *kërcim* refers to free-style solos or unlinked circle or group dances.

Most dance formations found in Albania are common to the entire Balkan area. The so-called *valle dyshe* ("duo dance"), however, appears to be unique to Albanian ethnic dance; it is widespread across the central and southern regions and among Albanians in the former Yugoslavia. Two dancers of the same sex dance side by side, facing forward, with adjacent hands joined. In women's variants, the dancers synchronize their steps in mirror image; this is sometimes the case in men's duo dances, though more often the man at the right spins, does deep knee bends, and performs other virtuosic movements while his partner supports him and marks time.

There is no specific national dance known and practiced by all Albanians; however, there is one step pattern that occurs throughout the Albanian ethnic area. This is a repetitive six-count sequence, popularly called *treshe* ("triple"), named *asimetrik* ("asymmetric") by Albanian dance researchers, and known internationally among ethnic dance scholars as the Faeroe step. Schematically, its Albanian form consists of three steps moving to the right (right, left, right with the feet) plus a gesture with the free left foot, followed by one step moving left plus a gesture with the free right foot; it is subject to much stylistic variation. [*See* Faeroe Step.]

Until recently women's role in Albanian society was dictated by stringent codes of behavior stressing modesty, domesticity, fidelity, and unquestioning obedience to parents and husband. With few exceptions, Albanian women's dances are simple in structure and restrained in style. In the central and southern regions they are done in *valle dyshe* and open-circle forms with various walking patterns, the *asimetrik* predominating. Formerly these dances were accompanied exclusively by singing; instrumental or combined vocal and instrumental accompaniment have become common since the end of the first World War. The women of the Korçë district are well known for their graceful linked open-circle dances performed to the dancers' own polyphonic singing. In the northern areas, women's dances are primarily of the solo type and involve simple footwork, gentle movements of arms and hands, and swaying of the torso. Typically, one woman dances (often flourishing a handkerchief) while the others accompany her, singing monophonically or tapping a *dajre* (tambourine), or both.

Readiness to defend the honor of family and clan is essential to the traditional role of the Albanian male, and the romanticized image of the fierce warrior-hero pervades the country's folklore. The men's dances reflect stamina, self-assurance, and agility and include a number of weapon dances. In the open-circle and *dyshe* dances of the central and southern areas, performed to polyphonic epic songs celebrating the exploits of folk heroes, and in the open-circle dances of eastern Albania, accompanied by the *curle* (a type of shawm) and *lodër* (large drum), the leader executes turns, knee bends, abrupt freezes, and slow, tense, highly plastic movements of the entire body. In the best-known weapon dance, *presja me tagana* ("sword slashing"), of the northern mountains, two men circle each other with broad movements, brandishing and striking their swords in intense mock combat. The dance ends with the "victor" seizing his opponent by the hair and mimicking a death stroke. According to old tribal law, serious disputes between tribes were settled in a sword duel that ended in the decapitation of the defeated combatant. *Presja me tagana*, a traditional reenactment of this custom, is the standard conclusion of local dance events.

Before World War II, mixed dancing was rare in Albania, limited to the Christian populations of the extreme north and south. In the north there are free-style native couple dances, without physical contact and done in any combination of sexes, though traditionally only a married person or close relative would perform such a dance with a member of the opposite sex. Since World War II, in response to official efforts to equalize the status of the sexes, mixed dancing in most traditional formations has become more common, especially among the youth. Dance events in the past took place on religious holidays and at family gatherings, especially weddings. Since World War II new occasions have been instituted, including national and regional folk festivals, at which rehearsed village groups perform their local dances on stage.

The professional Albanian State Folk Song and Dance Ensemble (Ansambli Shtetëror i Këngëve dhe i Valleve Popullore) performs stage adaptations of Albanian ethnic dances and has toured abroad. The repertory of the State Opera and Ballet Theater (Teatri Shtetëror i Operës dhe Baletit) includes original ballets based on folk themes and choreographed using combined classical and ethnic dance techniques. Systematic ethnic dance research began in Albania after World War II and is still in its early stages, hence comprehensive historical and contextual analysis is not possible.

Theatrical Dance. Marked by a turbulent history of foreign exploitation and internecine strife, Albania won nationhood only in 1912. It had no theater, opera or ballet until after World War II. The communist regime established in 1944 initiated a program for the development of the performing arts, some milestones of which were the founding of the State Opera and Ballet Theater (1953) and the State Folk Song and Dance Ensemble (1957). The first ballet produced was Rostislav Zakharov's *The Fountain of Bakhchisarai*, staged in 1953 by Soviet choreographer G. Perkun. There followed *La Fille Mal Gardée*, *Fadetta*, *Romeo and Juliet*, Vakhtang Chabukiani's *Laurencia* and others, all mounted by guest choreographers from the USSR. Several young dancers were sent to study in Moscow and other schools in socialist countries during this period. Among them were Agron Aliaj and Panajot Kanaçi, Albania's most prominent choreographers in the 1980s, and Zoica Haxho, who returned to become a leading ballerina and teacher.

After Albania broke with the Soviet bloc in 1961, it embarked on its own introverted cultural revolution, rejecting most foreign works and demanding of its artists new works based on Albanian nationalist and socialist themes, notably the country's historical struggles, eradication of prerevolutionary social values, and optimistic portrayal of Albania's socialist future. The first native ballet, *Halil and Hajria*, based on a folk ballad relating an episode from the times of Turkish oppression, premiered in 1953 (music by Tish Daija, choreography by Panajot Kanaçi). The next two decades witnessed a succession of original works, of which the best received were *The Mountain Girl* and *Shota and Azem Galica*.

Albanian theatrical dance is unique in Europe in that from its very beginning it developed exclusively within the framework of a conservative Marxist-Leninist-Stalinist ideology and in strictly enforced accord with the principles of socialist realism. Choreographers strove to create "Albanian national ballet," the definition of which is best sought in their works: Albanian-socialist themes; dramatic, didactic libretti in which good and evil are unambiguously delineated; and an aim to inspire ideologically first and to entertain second. The kinetic vehicle for all this is a curious fusion of classical technique and Albanian ethnic dance movements. In a modern Albanian pas de deux, for example, the ballerina executes pure classical variations on pointe while her partner performs rugged, angular movements in Albanian traditional style. This stylistic fusion also permits the Ballet Theater regularly to borrow dancers from the Folk Ensemble when a large corps is required.

BIBLIOGRAPHY

Agolli, Nexhat. *Valle nga rrethi i Shkodrës.* Tirana, 1983.

Bogdani, Ramazan. "Sprovë për një klasifikim shkencor të folklorit koreografik në vështrimin gjinor, krahinor dhe strukturor." *Studime Filologjike,* no. 2 (1975).

Sokoli, Ramadan. *Les danses populaires et les instruments musicaux du peuple albanais.* Tirana, 1958.

RICHARD CRUM

ALBERT, MONSIEUR (François Decombe; born 10 April 1787 in Bordeaux, died 19 July 1865 in Fontainebleau), French dancer and choreographer. Known professionally by the single name Albert, François Decombe began his career as a dancer at a time when many eighteenth-century ideas were still current, and the male dancer was still an imposing if not dominant figure on-

ALBERT. A contemporary lithograph depicting Albert as Le Duc Mevilla in Louis Milon's ballet *Clari*, which premiered in 1820 at the Académie Royale de Musique in Paris. (Courtesy of Madison U. Sowell and Debra H. Sowell, Brigham Young University, Provo, Utah.)

stage. He was a *premier danseur* of the *noble* genre, the most highly esteemed of the three genres of dancer, which also included the *demi-caractère* and the *comique.* He was an object of adulation, but as the Romantic era dawned, he found himself in the uncomfortable position of being the last representative of what was increasingly looked upon as an outmoded style of dancing. He lived to see the triumph of Romanticism on the ballet stage and the eclipse of the male dancer by the ballerina.

Albert began his study of dance in his native Bordeaux and first performed in Paris at the Théâtre de la Gaîté. Engaged by the Paris Opera in 1808, he danced in the ballets of Pierre Gardel, among them *Paul et Virginie* and *La Servante Justifiée.* He frequently partnered the noted actress-dancer Émilie Bigottini, and performed opposite her in Louis Milon's *Nina, ou La Folle par Amour* (1813), a precursor of the Romantics' fascination with madness.

In 1815, Albert danced the role of Zéphire in the Paris Opera staging of Charles-Louis Didelot's *Flore et Zéphire.* Another harbinger of the Romantic period, this staging used flying machines to sail the dancers through the air. His partner in the ballet was Geneviève Gosselin, one of the first ballerinas to experiment with pointe technique. When the Paris Opera revived the ballet in 1831, Albert taught the principal roles to two young dancers who were to become leading figures of the Romantic ballet, Marie Taglioni and Jules Perrot.

During the 1820s Albert made many guest appearances at the King's Theatre in London, partnering ballerinas such as Lise Noblet and Maria Mercandotti. At the Paris Opera, his home company, he created leading roles in several ballets during this period. In Milon's *Clari, ou La Promesse de Mariage* (1820), which he danced with Bigottini, he played the role of a seducer who, contrary to the ballet's source (Baculard d'Arnaud's novel *Clary, ou Le Retour à la Vertu Récompensé),* turns virtuous in the end and marries his hapless victim. In the title role of Jean-Louis Aumer's historical ballet *Alfred le Grand* (1822), Albert had the dubious honor of heading "the last ballet produced at the Opéra for more than a hundred years in which the principal character was a male hero played by a male dancer" (Guest, 1980). He won considerable praise for both his dancing and his miming in this ballet, which depicted the struggle of the Saxons against the Viking invaders of England. In 1828 he partnered Marie Taglioni in Aumer's *Lydie,* a ballet about a shepherdess who incurs the wrath of Cupid. He also danced in operas such as Daniel Auber's *La Muette de Portici* (1828) and Gioacchino Rossini's *William Tell* (1829).

Albert's classification as a *danseur noble* indicates that he was tall and well proportioned, with a special gift for adagio movement and the requisite qualities of majesty, elegance, and refinement. Although the genre was less strictly defined in the 1820s, and noble dancers began to add *entrechats* and steps of elevation to their repertories, Albert apparently maintained the purity of the noble style; a contemporary wrote of him, "Albert does not jump, he prefers the God of Grace to the God of Entrechats" (Guest, 1980). The remarks of an English observer, however, hint that the noble style was considered rather cold by the 1820s, perhaps because Romantic emotionalism was already beginning to color the audience's expectations of the dance. Guest describes Albert as

> unrivalled for the free and yet stately pride of his attitudes, which his uncommon strength of muscle enables him to sustain with a firmness that never trembles from the line of beauty, but there is always an appearance of study about him, which seems never to permit him to enter into the spirit of the dance. His efforts are undoubtedly of the first order; but they are uniformly so conformable to his principles of art, that art alone seems to be his idol.
>
> (Guest, 1972)

Some illuminating comments about Albert's qualities as a dancer occur in comparisons between him and his contemporary Antoine Paul, a *demi-caractère* dancer whose nickname, "the Aerial," points up the contrast between his virtuosic, airborne dancing and Albert's more *terre-à-terre* style. The nineteenth-century Danish choreographer August Bournonville wrote,

> The word "gentlemanlike" fully describes Albert's demeanor as a dancer: noble, vigorous, gallant, modest, ardent, friendly, gay, but seldom inspired. He won the applause of the connoisseurs but failed to move the masses as Paul did. The difference between these two artists was as if they were both at a party, where Albert was the dignified host and Paul the jovial guest. . . . Paul belonged to the air and Albert to the salon.
>
> (As given in McAndrew, 1979)

Another observer contrasted them in literary terms, characterizing Albert as the Virgil of the dance and Paul as the Ariosto.

Despite the dignity and restraint of his dancing style, Albert was generally considered to be a convincing mime. Probably he was careful not to step outside his rather limited range; in *Alfred le Grand*, for example, he wore a kingly air even when in disguise. He was less successful as Alfonso in Anatole Petit's *Le Sicilien* (1827); this role, which is perhaps more familiar today in its operatic incarnation of Count Almaviva in Rossini's *The Barber of Seville*, required of Albert comic gifts that he apparently did not possess in adequate measure.

Albert's first choreographic effort was the ballet *Le Séducteur au Village*, produced at the Paris Opera in 1818. His next ballets, which were staged at the King's Theatre in London in 1821, included *Oenone et Paris* and *Alcide*, the latter choreographed with André Deshayes. The titles of these works suggest that Albert made little attempt to break away from the sentimental and mythological themes that were popular at the time.

His first major work, *Cendrillon*, was created for London in 1822 and restaged at the Paris Opera the following year. Its score was written by the Spanish composer Fernando Sor. Maria Mercandotti danced the title role in London, Bigottini in Paris; Albert himself played the prince in both productions. In selecting the story of Cinderella, Albert may have been influenced by two contemporaneous operas on the same theme, one of them Rossini's *La Cenerentola*, which had been produced in Paris in 1822. Albert's version, however, was based more closely on the story as told by Charles Perrault. Although the dances themselves were praised, his ballet was faulted for dramatic weakness. Bigottini was particularly well cast in the role of Cinderella, for she was able to create a naturalistic portrait of a young girl's sweet, gentle, yet slightly gauche manner. Pierre Ciceri designed the sets and effects, including a Gothic-style castle in the first act and a ballroom scene in the second. Cinderella's carriage, drawn by white horses made to look like unicorns, was especially admired. Albert designed the costumes.

Albert did not create many works immediately following the triumph of *Cendrillon*, though he occasionally choreographed a *pas* in another choreographer's ballet, for example, in Anatole Petit's *Le Sicilien*. He became more active as a choreographer in the 1830s, perhaps as his powers as a dancer began to wane. In 1830 he created two works at the Vienna Hofoper: *Daphnis und Céphise* and *Der Zauberring*. The latter he restaged under the title of *L'Anneau Magique* during his tenure as ballet master of the King's Theatre in London in 1832. Other ballets staged during that time included *Une Heure à Naples* and *Amynthe et Amour*, the latter possibly a version of Aumer's *Lydie*. His leading dancers included the husband-and-wife team of Paolo Samengo and Amalia Brugnoli.

Albert choreographed a ballet version of Byron's poem *The Corsair* in London in 1837, nearly twenty years before Joseph Mazilier's better-known version was staged in Paris in 1856. (Both used the French title *Le Corsaire*.) The cast included Pauline Duvernay as Gulnare. Albert later restaged this ballet in 1844 at Drury Lane, with Adèle Dumilâtre and Henri Desplaces.

The crowning achievement of Albert's choreographic career was *La Jolie Fille de Gand*, which he created in 1842 for a rising young star of the Paris Opera, Carlotta Grisi. Albert himself danced the role of her would-be seducer, the Marquis de San Lucar. The ballet, which was lavishly produced by the Paris Opera, was a great success. Deviating from his usual practice of writing his own libretti, Albert accepted a libretto by a professional, Jules-Henri Vernoy de Saint-Georges. The plot, much praised for its human and moral interest, portrayed the dilemma of a girl who is torn between a humble but honest suitor and an aristocrat who offers her a more luxurious if unsanctified union. Albert created a number of interesting dances, among them a *cracovienne* and a comic "three-legged" dance, but the acknowledged high point of the ballet was the *pas de Diane chasseresse*, in which Grisi mimicked the poses of the ancient Roman goddess of the hunt, Diana. [*See* Jolie Fille de Gand, La.]

In the 1840s Albert choreographed or restaged several ballets in London at the theatres of Drury Lane and Covent Garden. Among his ballets was *The Marble Maiden,* created at Drury Lane in 1845. The ballet was a variation on the Pygmalion theme, set in the Florence of Lorenzo de' Medici. Albert played the role of the sculptor Massachio, whose statue of Hebe (danced by Adèle Dumilâtre) comes to life by day but must return to marble by night. Despite her dual nature, Hebe is torn between Massachio and a second lover, one of the Medicis, and this triangular situation is resolved only when Massachio takes a hammer to the statue, thus freeing the soul of Hebe to rise to heaven like many another heroine of the Romantic ballet. The ballet was considered too long and occasionally tedious and had to be cut in later performances. It is of interest today primarily for its resemblance to two other ballets of the era, Jules Perrot's *Alma* (1842) and Arthur Saint-Léon's *La Fille de Marbre* (1847).

Albert's ability as a teacher was praised by G. Léopold Adice in his *Théorie de la gymnastique de la danse théâtrale* (1859), where he is cited along with Filippo Taglioni as one of the most progressive teachers of the century, and credited with improving the course of training and preparing dancers for the increasing technical demands of the period. Albert's most famous pupil was Arthur Saint-Léon, whose *sténochorégraphie,* a system of dance notation, may have been inspired by Albert's principles. Other notable pupils were Félicité Hullin-Sor and Louise Fleury.

In private life Albert was known as a man of culture and education: Bournonville described him as "a theoretician, musician, and composer. . . . Music and painting had formed his taste, and study of the classics had clarified his aesthetic views." Albert possessed a library of technical manuals in several languages, and his art collection included works by Van Dyck, Rembrandt, Teniers, Watteau, and Boucher. He was married to the opera singer Louise Himm, and two of their children became dancers who used his surname: Auguste Albert and Elisa Albert-Bellon.

BIBLIOGRAPHY
Albert, Monsieur. *L'art de la danse à la ville et à la cour, manuel à l'usage des maîtres à danser, des mères de famille et maîtresses de pension.* Paris, 1834.
Adice, G. Léopold. *Théorie de la gymnastique de la danse théâtrale.* Paris, 1859.
Bournonville, August. *My Theatre Life* (1848–1878). Translated by Patricia McAndrew. Middletown, Conn., 1979.
Chapman, John V. "Auguste Vestris and the Expansion of Technique." *Dance Research Journal* 19 (Summer 1987):11–18.
Guest, Ivor. *The Romantic Ballet in England.* London, 1972.
Guest, Ivor. *The Romantic Ballet in Paris.* 2d rev. ed. London, 1980.
Guest, Ivor. *Jules Perrot: Master of the Romantic Ballet.* London, 1984.
Saint-Léon, Arthur. *Letters from a Ballet Master: The Correspondence of Arthur Saint-Léon.* Edited by Ivor Guest. New York, 1981.

SUSAN AU

ALBERTIERI, LUIGI (born c.1860 in Milan, died 25 August 1930 in New York City), dancer, choreographer, and teacher. By the age of nine Albertieri was a regular performer of comic roles with a juvenile opera company and had already toured Italy, England, France, Spain, and Belgium. Enrico Cecchetti, recognizing Albertieri's potential as a dancer, adopted the boy and made him his protégé. Albertieri was ten years old when he began a decade of training with the master. They appeared together in the London premiere of Luigi Manzotti's *Excelsior* in 1885 and subsequently went to Russia.

When Albertieri began his independent career, he was engaged by the Empire Theatre in London, where he partnered Malvina Cavallazzi, Adeline Genée, and Katti Lanner. With Lanner, he appeared in the ballet spectacle *The Paris Exhibition,* and he garnered excellent reviews for his performance as Pharam in *Cleopatra.* From 1895 to 1902, Albertieri was a choreographer at Covent Garden, London, producing and appearing in several works, including the Drury Lane Christmas pantomimes.

Albertieri first danced with the Metropolitan Opera Ballet in New York City in 1895. He returned in 1902, then in 1910 became ballet master and choreographer at the Chicago Opera, a post he held for three years. Maurice Grau, impresario of the Metropolitan Opera, hired Albertieri as stage manager and ballet master in 1913. During his fourteen years there, he staged the ballets *The Fairy Doll* and *Coppélia* and such operas as Luigi Mancinelli's *Ero e Leandro,* Jules Massenet's *Le Cid,* Jan Paderewski's *Manru,* and Ermanno Wolf-Ferrari's *I Gioielli della Madonna.* He also worked as stage manager and ballet master with the Manhattan and Philadelphia opera companies.

In 1915 Albertieri founded a school in New York City; Rosina Galli, Maria Gambarelli, Albertina Rasch, and Fred Astaire were among his students. His principles are presented in his handbook *The Art of Terpsichore* (1923).

BIBLIOGRAPHY
Albertieri, Luigi. *The Art of Terpsichore.* New York, 1923.
Barzel, Ann. "European Dance Teachers in the United States." *Dance Index* 3/4–5–6 (April–May–June 1944): 56–100.
Cather, Willa. "Training for the Ballet." *McClure's Magazine* (October 1913): 85–95.
"The Death of Luigi Albertieri." *American Dancer* (November 1930): 16.
Guest, Ivor. *Ballet in Leicester Square: The Alhambra and the Empire 1860–1915.* London, 1992.
"Luigi Albertieri: The Last of the Great Ballet Masters." *The Dancing Times* (December 1930): 258–260.

Moore, Lillian. "The Metropolitan Opera Ballet Story." *Dance Magazine* (January 1951): 20–48.

Page, Ruth. "Classwork: Luigi Albertieri." In Page's *Class: Notes on Dance Classes around the World, 1915–1980*. Princeton, N.J., 1984.

Rossi, Luigi. *Enrico Cecchetti, il maestro dei maestri*. Vercelli, 1978.

Tani, Gino. "Albertieri, Luigi." In *Enciclopedia dello spettacolo*. Rome, 1954–.

CLAUDIA CELI
Translated from Italian

ALDOUS, LUCETTE (born 26 September 1938 in Auckland, New Zealand), dancer and teacher. Trained in Brisbane, Queensland, and Sydney, New South Wales, Lucette Aldous entered the Royal Ballet School in London in 1955 on a Royal Academy of Dancing scholarship. In 1957 she joined the Ballet Rambert as a soloist and was a ballerina with the company until 1963. Moving to the London Festival Ballet, she danced with that company until 1966, when she joined the Royal Ballet as a principal dancer.

In 1970 Aldous returned to Australia, where she made her debut with the Australian Ballet as a guest artist. She became resident principal ballerina in 1971. When Rudolf Nureyev visited Australia to produce and star in his version of *Don Quixote*, he chose Aldous to perform the female lead role of Kitri. She repeated the role in a film made in Melbourne in 1973.

Of small physique and light on pointe, Aldous developed and polished her technique and added vivaciousness and a sense of *demi-caractère* that projected naturally to audiences. In addition to the standard nineteenth-century classics such as *Giselle* and *The Sleeping Beauty*, she danced leads in Frederick Ashton's *Cinderella*, *The Dream*, and *La Fille Mal Gardée;* Kenneth MacMillan's *Romeo and Juliet;* Robert Helpmann's *Yugen;* Léonide Massine's *Mam'zelle Angot;* and Roland Petit's *Carmen*. She also created the role of Valencienne in Ronald Hynd's *The Merry Widow* (1975).

Especially popular in the United States, Aldous performed as a guest artist with Nureyev and Helpmann and appeared at Expo 74 in Spokane, Washington. She also appeared in the feature film *The Turning Point* (1977), dancing with Fernando Bujones.

Aldous married Alan Alder, a principal dancer in the Australian Ballet, and retired to have a baby in 1977. Two years later, she was appointed to the teaching staff of the Australian Ballet School; in 1982 she transferred to the West Australian Academy of Performing Arts, where she and her husband joined the faculty.

BIBLIOGRAPHY

Herf, Estelle. "Lucette Aldous." *Ballet Today* (November–December 1967): 18–21.

Potter, Michelle. "Dance Greats: Lucette Aldous." *Dance Australia* no. 85 (August–September 1996): 34–35.

Williams, Peter, and Noël Goodwin. "The Merry Widow." *Dance and Dancers* (September 1976): 14–19.

Woodcock, Sarah C. *The Sadler's Wells Royal Ballet*. London, 1991.

GEOFFREY WILLIAM HUTTON
Amended by Michelle Potter

ALEKSIDZE, GEORGI (Georgii Dmitrievich Aleksidze; born 7 January 1941 in Tbilisi, Georgian Soviet Socialist Republic), dancer and choreographer. Upon graduating in 1960 from the Moscow ballet school, where he trained under Asaf Messerer, Aleksidze returned to Tbilisi to dance at the State Theater of Opera and Ballet, named after Zakhary Paliashvili, where he remained until 1962. In 1966 he graduated from the choreography department of the Leningrad Conservatory, having studied with Fedor Lopukhov; from 1967 to 1978 he taught in the department. Aleksidze worked for the Leningrad (now Saint Petersburg) Chamber Ballet from 1966 to 1968, staging three programs using the music of various sixteenth- to eighteenth-century composers. During the same period he choreographed for the Kirov Ballet *Oresteia* (1968) to music by Yuri Falik, Prokofiev's *Scythian Suite* (1969), *Theme and Variations* (1970) to Brahms, Vivaldi's *Concert in F Dur* (1970), and *Ballet Divertissement* (1974) to Mozart.

From the beginning Aleksidze displayed a talent for interpreting classical music and was one of the few Soviet choreographers to work in the style of plotless ballet, never inclined to attach a story to the music, as did most of his contemporaries even when they were dealing with symphonies. As Aleksidze began composing his plotless ballets soon after New York City Ballet's first visit to the Soviet Union in 1962, he was considered a "Balanchine choreographer." However, he was obliged to stage some multiact story ballets while working in Tbilisi, where the style of the Georgian dancers was dramatic and the company repertory consisted solely of narrative works.

Aleksidze was chief choreographer of the Tbilisi Theater of Opera and Ballet from 1972 to 1980. Here he revived some of his early works but also choreographed new ballets to music by Georgian composers: *Beriocaba* (1973) by Aleksandr Kvernadze; *Choreographic Suite* (1976) by Otar Taktakishvili; *The Svanetish Legend* (1977) by Sulkhan Tsintsadze; and a big dramatic ballet, *Medea* (1978), by Ravaz Gabichvadze. He also restaged a number of classics.

From 1980 to 1983 Aleksidze was chief choreographer of the ballet company of the Perm Theater of Opera and Ballet, and from 1983 to 1985 he worked at the opera studio of the Leningrad Conservatory. He returned to Tbilisi in 1985, where he remains, producing *Pirosmani* (1988) to music by Sulkhan Nasidze, Sibelius's *The Swan of Tuonela* (1989), *Concerto Grosso* (1989) by Alfred Schnitke, and another *Medea* (1989), this time to music by Aleksandr Knaifel. In 1992 Aleksidze was also choreographer for a small company attached to the Saint Petersburg Cappella, which had a repertory of church music that he used for *Agnus Dei* by Bach and *Adagio* by Benedetto Marcello.

After Soviet choreographers had seen the works of George Balanchine in the 1960s, many eagerly imitated him by staging plotless ballets and choosing symphonies and concertos for their music. These were seldom successful because of paucity of dance imagination. Aleksidze is one of the few choreographers who is able to create movement that progresses in complete accord with the music but that also possesses great power of poetic expression. Aleksidze was awarded the title People's Artist of Georgia in 1989.

BIBLIOGRAPHY
Prokhorova, Valentina. *Georgi Aleksidze* (in Russian). Tbilisi, 1982.
Souritz, Elizabeth. "Moscow." *Ballet Review* 21 (Winter 1993): 7–12.

ELIZABETH SOURITZ

ALEXANDER, DOROTHY (Dorothea Moses; born 22 April 1904 in Atlanta, Georgia, died 17 November 1986 in Atlanta), American ballet dancer, choreographer, teacher, and company director. Like Isadora Duncan, Dorothy Alexander typified the artist as visionary. Unlike Duncan, Alexander had the tenacity to realize the goals she envisioned. Her primary goal became the seed of the American regional dance movement. As a girl, she found a wasteland of training and performing opportunities in her native city, and she vowed that nobody who came after her would encounter that limitation. Although she constantly left Atlanta to study (notably in New York with Irma Duncan, Tatiana Chamié, Michel Fokine, Beaucaire Montalvo, and Yeichi Nimura; at Colorado College with Hanya Holm; at Jacob's Pillow with Bronislava Nijinska; and in London at the Royal Ballet School), she was determined to make her career in Atlanta. She did so as dancer, choreographer, teacher, and founding director of the Atlanta Ballet.

Dorothea Moses's early childhood was marred by osteomylitis. She was given dance lessons to restore her strength. Enduring the loss of both parents before she had emerged from adolescence, she learned the meaning of responsibility early on and pursued her academic education at the same time as she performed in concert. In 1921 she opened her own dance studio, which she continued to run for the remainder of her professional life. By 1925 she had graduated from Atlanta Normal Training School, and in 1930 she earned a bachelor of arts degree from Oglethorpe College. In the meantime she had married Marion Alexander, an architect, in 1926; originated a Dance Enrichment Program in the Atlanta public schools in 1927; and formed the Dorothy Alexander Concert Group in 1929. This group eventually became the Atlanta Ballet, the nation's oldest regional company.

During the 1930s Alexander performed as guest artist in her own repertory with the Lucile Marsh Concert Group, the Solomonoff-Menzelli Ballet, the Hollywood Ballet, and the Edwin Strawbridge Ballet. But true to her intent to keep her career in Atlanta, she refused to tour with them. By 1941 Alexander's company was named the Atlanta Civic Ballet. No films exist of the more than eighty works that she created, but still photographs of her as a dancer reveal the elegant *port de bras* that became a company hallmark. These photos also reveal a radiant, almost spiritual quality to her dance.

Under Alexander's guidance, the Atlanta Civic Ballet was the founding company of the National Association for Regional Ballet (NARB), later named Regional Dance America. Her company hosted the first regional dance festival in 1956, and it became the first regional company to dance at Jacob's Pillow in 1958. Alexander retired in 1963, but she remained instrumental in the development of NARB, of which she was the first president, and of the Atlanta Ballet. She was founder-consultant to both. Her awards include Atlanta's Woman of the Year in Arts (1947), a *Dance Magazine* Award (1959), the Association of American Dance Companies award (1971), a citation from the National Endowment for the Arts (1973), the Georgia Governor's Award in the Arts (1976), the Capezio Award (1981), and an honorary doctorate in humane letters from Emory University (1986).

[*See also* Atlanta Ballet.]

BIBLIOGRAPHY
Hering, Doris. "Atlanta Civic Ballet, Company of Contrasts." *Dance Magazine* (March 1959): 52–55.
Hering, Doris. "Tickets for the Bug Man." *Dance Magazine* (February 1963): 52–53.
Hering, Doris. "Dorothy Alexander, Guest of Honor." NARB press kit, December 1980.
Hering, Doris. Obituary. *Dance Magazine* (March 1987): 98–100.
Smith, Helen C. "The Atlanta Ballet: Fifty Golden Years." *Dance Magazine* (November 1979): 88–94.
Terry, Walter. "Miss Dorothy's Way." *Ballet News* 1 (March 1980): 14–17.

ARCHIVES.   The holdings of the Atlanta Historical Society and the Emory University library include materials pertinent to Alexander's career.

DORIS HERING

ALEXANDER TECHNIQUE. *See* Body Therapies, *article on* Alexander Technique.

ALGERIA. Like its North African neighbors, Tunisia to the east and Morocco to the west, Algeria shares a rich heritage of Berber, Arab, and Turkish dance traditions.

ALGERIA. A female Ouled Naïl dancer c.1923, adorned in a spangled necklace and headdress. Such jewelry was traditionally fashioned from gold and silver coins as a means of carrying and displaying wealth. (Photograph by Horace D. Ashton; courtesy of Ibrahim Farrah, *Arabesque Magazine*, New York.)

These traditions appear to have flourished during the French colonial period, which began in 1830 and lasted for 132 years, until Algeria's independence in 1962. Once Algeria was a French colony, its capital, Algiers, began to attract a number of visitors, especially from France, including painters, writers, and photographers. They carried home a romantic portrayal of the exotic Algerians.

The cafés of Algiers became a resort for visitors and military personnel as well as for Algerians, and the female dancers seen there have been described in terms ranging from charming to lascivious. Some performed in the same costume worn by respectable women, while others appeared scantily clothed, to better display the isolated muscle contortions that have contributed to giving this dance its French name, *danse du ventre* ("belly dance"). [*See Danse du Ventre.*]

Outside Algiers, women from the Ouled Naïl tribe danced at the military outposts in the high desert. Their performance styles varied according to the occasion and the requests of their patrons. Unlike the dancers of Algiers, with their Turkish costumes, the desert women wore the *palla*, an ancient Roman-style draped garment still worn in much of North Africa.

Many strict Islamic Algerians object to women appearing in public, much less dancing before strangers—an attitude shared in Libya and, to a lesser degree, in Tunisia. Religious attitudes change however, and young girls belonging to an organization similar to the Girl Scouts are learning the regional dances of the country. The regional

ALGERIA. An Algerian rifle dance typical of the genre of mock warfare seen at North African festivals. (Photograph from the collection of Aisha Ali.)

female dances, apart from those performed by professional entertainers, are simple and repetitive. Although few females actually perform the dances in public, on festive occasions women and girls often dance for each other at private gatherings.

In one graceful dance style, a woman dances with a long narrow scarf pulled across her shoulders. Lifting the ends outward, she flutters her fingers as she turns in place. She steps daintily, keeping her feet close together, one foot in front, placed flat and the heel of the other foot raised. Her shoulders move up and down in an expressive manner, enhanced by a delicate side-to-side neck movement or by a provocative tilting of the head.

The most popular dance of the women and girls can best be described as a form of *danse du ventre*. It involves side-to-side, up-and-down, and circular motions of the lower torso; if the dancer is more practiced, these may be combined with vibrations of the hips and shoulders.

One of the basic folk steps used by both men and women appears in most of the Middle East as well as in North Africa. It is a languidly stepped, rather than gliding, *chassé* that alternates the leading foot. The pelvis is shifted slightly forward and back; women sometimes vary this movement by shifting their hips from side to side. The upper torso is lifted gently and held, but a subtle reciprocal sway occurs. Arms are away from the body and may also swing slightly forward and back.

The most distinctive North African folk movement imitates the prancing of a horse and is generally associated with men's martial dances. It is achieved by a series of single-footed hops in which the weight of the body is lifted only enough to allow progress, while the opposite knee is raised and lowered with the toes pointing downward. A rebounding shoulder movement may also be used. The men often drop into a squatting position, where they continue stepping without touching their knees to the ground; or they may spin while crouching and then quickly rise again to a standing position. Most of these martial dances include the use of such paraphernalia as a rifle, sword, or stick, respectively.

Folk-dance movements used throughout Algeria and other parts of North Africa have a great deal in common. Regional dances usually can be distinguished by a particular specialty or by differences in costumes or musical instruments. For example, in Beni Isguem, a town with a large Berber population in the Mzab, south of Bou Saâda near Ghardaïa, the men dance in a group and their lower bodies sway forward and back as they step along. At times they fold their arms across their breasts and open and close their fingers with a flicking motion. From dynamic turns they drop to the ground and dance in a crouching position.

Like most rural Algerians, the men of Beni Isguem wrap turbans around their heads and wear long loose gowns.

ALGERIA. Female dancers holding baskets perform a mimetic dance of the type popular with Algerian folk dance companies, c.1968. (Photograph from the collection of Aisha Ali.)

When they perform their rifle dance, they wear the burnoose, which is pulled up in front and fastened at the waist. Toward the end of the dance they discharge their rifles at random, ending with a final fusillade.

At Bouïra, located at the base of the Kabylia Mountains, there is a lively women's dance that uses movements similar to those associated with the *ghawāzī* of Egypt: a shimmying walk and a step that involves the alternate lifting of the hips. Here the resemblance ends. The Algerian vibrating shoulder movement is more rapid than that used by the Egyptians, and the Bouïra women display none of the coquetries of the *ghawāzī*. The women of Bouria dance in a circle, accompanied by the sounds of iron clackers *(chakchakas)*, a goatskin bagpipe *(mizwiz)*, and *tabl* (a large two-headed drum played with sticks). Their waists are belted, and they fasten yarn sashes at their hips, with a tassel on each side to accent their movements. The rhythm is further marked by handkerchiefs held in both hands, which are waved from side to side.

The men of Oran, on the western coast near Morocco, do a dance with sticks performed to the music of a *tabl* and *ghaytah* (a folk oboe). In a nearby town a charming veil dance is performed by women wearing long dresses fastened at the waist with silver belts and a large square of filmy cloth over their heads and faces; they sometimes lift the corners of the cloth out to the sides as they dance. When not lifting their veils, they may play gracefully with a silk handkerchief.

In Annaba, on the northern coast near the Tunisian border, the dancers still wear nineteenth-century Ottoman (Turkish) costumes—voluminous trousers and velvet jackets embroidered in gold. The women toss the long, trailing sleeves of their lacy blouses to the cadence of the *zorna* (as the *ghaytah* is called in this Ottoman enclave). To the rhythm of the *tabl* they lift their hips and mark the beat with a series of little kicks.

Celebrating a circumcision at Bou Ismail, on the Mediterranean coast west of Algiers, four male dancers hold the corners of a large square of cloth into which money is tossed, while young boys dressed in Turkish-style pantaloons and vests dance with baskets held aloft. Older youths and men dance with swords, which they strike together in passing. The dance is accompanied by a local variation of the *tabl*.

Tamanrasset is a town in the far south of Algeria. Its people are mainly nomadic Tuareg (a Berber group), and the type of warriors' dances they perform can be seen throughout North Africa. In one of the dances, the men wield heavy sticks as they gesture with a large scarf held in the opposite hand. Their movements consist of a series of leaps and crouches accompanied by the beat of a drum made from a shallow bowl covered with a skin and played with two thin sticks.

In the far western part of Algeria, near both the Mauritanian and Moroccan borders, the Tajakant and Tekna tribal areas meet. There, at the oasis of Tindouf, the typical dances of these tribes can be seen. Along with the Tuareg and several other groups, these tribes are often indiscriminately called "blue people" because the indigo dye in their clothing stains the skin. Like the *guedra* dancers of Morocco and Mauritania, the women of Tindouf fashion their hair into many braids embellished with beads and added strands, some of which form a high crest just above the forehead. Also similar is the manner in which their garments are draped. The garments of the Tindouf women are often made of two lengths of different shades of blue, giving the appearance of having contrasting dark tops. The women perform a version of the *guedra* in which the dancers stand rather than kneel; as in other related ecstatic dances, they toss their hair from side to side and move their fingers with a hypnotic, repetitive rhythm.

After Algeria won its independence in 1962, certain forms of entertainment that had been popular during the French occupation began to suffer disapproval. For a conservative Islamic nation adopting socialism, it was important to foster activities to help restore national identity; to this end, Algeria hosted the 1969 Pan African Cultural Festival in Algiers, bringing its regional dance groups together with representatives from many other parts of the African continent. Regional politics and attitudes may change but the music and dance traditions of Algeria endure.

[*See also* Middle East; North Africa; *and* Ouled Naïl, Dances of the.]

BIBLIOGRAPHY

Henricy, Casimir. *Les moeurs et costumes de tous les peuples.* 2 vols. Paris, 1847.

Hofmann, Wilfried. "Folk and Theatre Dancing in Present Day Algeria." *Ballet Today* (April 1962): 16–18.

Isnard, H. *Algeria.* Translated by O. C. Warden. Paris and London, 1955.

Juana. "From the High Atlas to the Desert's Shore." *Dance Magazine* (December 1951): 17–19.

Shawn, Ted. "Dancing in North Africa." *Dance Magazine* (December 1925): 30–32.

AISHA ALI, MARDI ROLLOW, and LEONA WOOD

ALI-BATYR. *See* Shurale.

ALLAN, MAUD (Ulah Maud Durrant; born 27 August 1873 in Toronto, died 7 October 1956 in Los Angeles), dancer. Maud Allan was the daughter of William Allan, a shoemaker, and Isabella Hutchinson Durrant. When Allan was five, the family moved to San Francisco, where she began to study the piano and later gave recitals, both public and private. In 1895 she went to study at the Royal Academy of Music in Berlin. Soon after her arrival there, her brother Theodore was arrested in San Francisco for the murders of two young women; he was convicted and was executed for these crimes in 1898. This personal tragedy was to haunt Allan for the rest of her life, especially after details of the crime emerged during a libel trial initiated by her in 1918.

ALLAN. Maud Allan as Salomé, kneeling beside the severed head of John the Baptist. Set to music by Marcel Rémy, *The Vision of Salomé* premiered in Paris, 1907. (Photograph from the Dance Collection, New York Public Library for the Performing Arts.)

While studying the piano with Ferruccio Busoni in 1900 and 1901, Allan became interested in the kind of dance being done by Isadora Duncan and abandoned her music studies to prepare herself for a career as a dancer. Self-taught, she made her debut, as Maudy Gwendolen Allan, in November 1903 in Vienna in a program of dances to music by Mendelssohn, Beethoven, Bach, Schumann, Chopin, Schubert, and Anton Rubinstein. She subsequently made several tours of Europe, and it was during this period that she developed *The Vision of Salomé*, which was considered sensational for the time and became her best-known work. In 1907, in Paris, she performed it to a score by Marcel Rémy and made her London debut in it in March 1908 at the Palace, where she had a highly successful run of more than a year.

Allan made her American debut in Boston on 19 January 1910 and appeared in New York on 20 January at Carnegie Hall. At both performances she appeared in other works from her repertory, withholding *The Vision of Salomé* for later performances. After touring the United States, she returned to London in 1911, toured Asia in 1914, and in 1915 appeared in the film *The Rug Maker's Daughter*. She appeared again in the United States in 1916, with her own company, in a dance drama called *Nair, the Slave*.

Internationally renowned during this period, Allan was noted for her supple torso, lovely arms, and lyric interpretation of music. Some of her most popular works were Mendelssohn's *Spring Song*, Grieg's *Peer Gynt Suite*, and Chopin's *Funeral March*. In London in 1918, she instituted a libel suit (which arose from her appearance in Oscar Wilde's *Salomé*), against Noël Pemberton-Billing, a right-wing politician who had accused Allan and her producer, J. T. Grein, of perversion for producing the play. Unjustly, Allan lost the case; she was in disrepute, and her career began to decline. For the next twenty years she lived in London and appeared in England, France, and the United States, but she never regained her earlier success. She established a school in London in the mid-1930s, but her performing career was ended by an automobile accident in 1938. She returned to the United States in 1941 and lived in Los Angeles until her death.

BIBLIOGRAPHY

Allan, Maud. *My Life and Dancing*. London, 1908.
Bizot, Richard. "The Turn-of-the-Century Salome Era." *Choreography and Dance* 2.3 (1992): 71–87.
Cherniavsky, Felix. *Did She Dance [computer file]*. Toronto, 1991.
Cherniavsky, Felix. "Maud Allan" (parts 1–5). *Dance Chronicle* 6.1 (1983); 6.3 (1983); 7.2 (1984); 8.1–2 (1985); 9.2 (1986).
Cherniavsky, Felix. "Maud Allan's Tour of India, the Far East, and Australia." In *Proceedings of the Ninth Annual Conference, Society of Dance History Scholars, City College, City University of New York, 14–17 February 1986*, compiled by Christena L. Schlundt. Riverside, Calif., 1986.
Cherniavsky, Felix. *The Salome Dancer*. Toronto, 1991.
Kettle, Michael. *Salome's Last Veil*. London, 1977.
Koritz, Amy. "Salome Unveiled: Imperialism and the Dancing Body in England." In *Proceedings of the Fifteenth Annual Conference, Society of Dance History Scholars, University of California, Riverside, 14–15 February 1992*, compiled by Christena L. Schlundt. Riverside, Calif., 1992.
McDearmon, Lacy H. "Maud Allan: The Public Record." *Dance Chronicle* 2.2 (1978): 85–105.
Weigand, Elizabeth. "*The Rugmaker's Daughter*, Maud Allan's 1915 Silent Film." *Dance Chronicle* 9.2 (1986): 237–251.

LACY H. MCDEARMON

ALLARD, MARIE (born 14 August 1741 in Marseille; died 14 January 1802 in Paris), French dancer. Allard began her career as an actress with the Comédie de Marseille while studying dance. She moved on to the Théâtre de Lyon, where she was named first dancer. In 1756 she moved to Paris and became a member of the corps de ballet of the Comédie Française. She had several liaisons with members of the nobility and lived for a time with the dancer Gaëtan Vestris; their son Auguste Vestris became one of the greatest dancers of the age.

In 1761 Allard made her debut at the Paris Opera in Jean-Philippe Rameau's *Zaïs* to great acclaim. Warm receptions became common for her, particularly in *Sylvie*, which she danced for the first time in 1766 with Jean Dauberval. The choreographer Jean-Georges Noverre wrote, "This pas de deux embellished with the talents of Mlle Allard, a dancer who combines the charms of a most brilliant performance with an extremely authentic and animated expression, won a well-deserved success."

Allard appeared in works from the repertory, Noverre notes, "composing her *entrées* herself with taste and without the assistance of the masters, something very rare in her sex." She performed in Maximilien Gardel's *La Chercheuse d'Esprit* and Noverre's *Médée et Jason* and *Les Petits Riens*.

A small, shapely woman, Allard was admired for her fair coloring and large blue eyes as well as the vivacity and gaiety of her dancing. A contemporary said that she inspired joy the moment she appeared on the stage. Her *rigaudons, tambourines, gargouillades*, and other delightful steps were wildly applauded. With Dauberval, Jean-Barthélemy Lany, and Mademoiselle Pélin she danced a pas de quatre of which Noverre wrote, "[Their] open, innocent gaiety and authentic expression, adapted to the feeling of joy, an admirable ensemble, and a rare precision governed all their movements; these *pas* enchanted the audience without any assistance from the pirouette." Allard retired from the stage on 5 April 1781.

BIBLIOGRAPHY

Campardon, Émile. *L'Académie Royale de Musique au XVIIIᵉ siècle*. 2 vols. Paris, 1884.

Capon, Gaston. *Les Vestris.* Paris, 1908.

Migel, Parmenia. *The Ballerinas: From the Court of Louis XIV to Pavlova.* New York, 1972.

Noverre, Jean-Georges. *Lettres sur les arts imitateurs en général et sur la danse en particulier.* 2 vols. Paris, 1807. Edited by Fernand Divoire as *Lettres sur la danse et les arts imitateurs* (Paris, 1952).

JEANNINE DORVANE
Translated from French

ALLEGRO. A generic term used to describe all lively, brisk dance movements, allegro is the opposite of slow, sustained adagio movements. As an indication of speed and quality of movement, the word *allegro* can be used, for instance, to describe quick, sharp pirouettes, as opposed to *adage* turns. Applied to a dance, it indicates a fast passage, usually the final section leading to a musical and dramatic climax. Examples are the coda of a *grand pas de deux* or the conclusion of a solo, group dance, or ballet. It is usually the moment for displays of virtuosity.

The term *allegro* can also be applied to the final section of a classical ballet class. Used in this sense, it can refer to all quick, lively movements, including turns and various *temps à terre* and *pas battus*, as well as to small and big jumps. Alternately, the term can be taken to mean only jumping movements, divided into *petit allegro*, or *petits temps sautés* (smaller jumping movements), and *grand allegro*, or *grands temps sautés* (big jumps).

Carlo Blasis, writing in the 1820s, used the expression *temps de vigueur* (vigorous movements) to cover the jumping section of the ballet lesson, dividing the previous section—after the *temps d'aplomb*—into pirouettes and *temps à terre*.

By 1861, when August Bournonville published his *Études chorégraphiques*, the section of the class following the *exercises d'adagio* was subdivided into *movements à trois temps* and *temps de pirouettes*. These were followed by *exercises d'élévation*, subtitled *adagio; temps de coude-pied* [sic], subtitled *allegretto; études de ballon; études de taqueté*; and finally, *temps battus*, subtitled *allegretto*. These classifications convey something of the rich variety of movement qualities studied in classes of that period, as does Enrico Cecchetti's scheme of work.

Cecchetti divided the allegro section of his classes into six basic categories, one for each day of the working week. Monday's allegro steps were based on *des assemblés*, basic jumps that land securely on two feet; on Tuesdays there were a variety of steps involving fast, intricate footwork, *des petits battements*; on Wednesdays *des ronds de jambes*; on Thursdays various types of *jetés*; on Fridays *temps de batterie* and *temps de pointes*; and on Saturdays light, bouncy jumps, *des grands fouettés sautés*.

At the beginning of the allegro section of Cecchetti's class, the basic step for that day was first practiced in a series of simple, repeated movements, followed by increasingly complex, choreographed *enchaînments*. Most of these were arranged to incorporate several technical and artistic problems, which the dancers then practiced regularly, as set study sequences. Cecchetti's aim was to have these prepared *enchaînments* repeated regularly, so that the dancers would be able to concentrate on perfecting their execution. This contrasts with the methods of Nikolai Legat, who favored the composition of new allegro *enchaînments* for nearly every lesson. One of his principal aims was to develop the dancer's ability to learn quickly and to be adaptable. Present-day teachers generally favor a combination of these two approaches.

The traditions handed down through Bournonville, Cecchetti, and their heirs call for a far greater variety of qualities of elevation, movement, rhythm, and dynamics than is generally found in ballet classes today. The allegro of the old school called for great speed in *terre à terre* work, in which the feet hardly left the ground; for rhythmic subtlety in a variety of *contra tempo* movements; for the nuances of musicality that produce true *ballon* (the ability to appear suspended in midair at the peak of a jump); and for the pizzicato-like movements *sur les pointes* known as *taqueté*. According to Cyril W. Beaumont (1931), the term *taqueté* (now almost obsolete) comes from the French *taquet* ("peg") and is said to have been coined in 1834. It was used by Charles Maurice in his review of Fanny Elssler's debut at the Paris Opera in the role of the fairy, Alcine, in the ballet *La Tempête*, adapted from Shakespeare's *The Tempest*: "Artistic people call this style of dancing *taqueté*, to explain that it consists mainly of quick little steps, precise, close together, digging into the stage. . . . the *pointes* play a very great part in it" (*Le courier des théâtres*, 16 September 1834).

The gradual evolution of costume from the long ballet skirt, via the short tutu, to today's ubiquitous tights and leotards naturally shifted the focus of choreographic attention away from the feet and ankles—or from the head, shoulders, and hands—to a more expressive use of the body as a whole. This has given much balletic allegro a new choreographic dimension based less on fleetness of foot and more on total body language—an allegro clearly influenced by modern or contemporary dance forms.

Another important influence on changing styles in allegro has been the example of the Soviet school, with its soaring leaps and sustained lyrical passages. Such changes of emphasis depend largely on the work of leading contemporary choreographers and on the degree to which their ballets become part of the standard repertory. Thus, in Denmark, the qualities of elevation and *ballon* have been particularly well developed and preserved, as a result of the demands made on both the women and the men by the richly varied Bournonville repertory still so popular in Copenhagen. Frederick Ashton's lyricism has left its imprint on the English allegro style, as has the elegant clarity of the Marius Petipa and Lev Ivanov classics, which form the cornerstone of the British repertory.

In the United States, George Balanchine's choreography for the New York City Ballet—with the demands for speed, dynamic diversity, and rhythmic contrast it makes on dancers—has been the most influential force in determining American allegro style.

[*See* Ballet Technique.]

BIBLIOGRAPHY

Beaumont, Cyril W., and Stanislas Idzikowski. *A Manual of the Theory and Practice of Classical Theatrical Dancing.* London, 1922.

Beaumont, Cyril W. *A French-English Dictionary of Technical Terms Used in Classical Ballet.* London, 1931.

Blasis, Carlo. *The Code of Terpsichore: A Practical and Historical Treatise on the Ballet, Dancing, and Pantomime.* London, 1828.

Bournonville, August. *Études chorégraphiques.* Copenhagen, 1861.

Craske, Margaret, and Friderica Derra de Moroda. *The Theory and Practice of Advanced Allegro in Classical Ballet (Cecchetti Method).* London, 1956.

Glasstone, Richard. "Changes of Emphasis and Mechanics in the Teaching of Ballet Technique." *Dance Research* 1 (Spring 1983): 56–63.

RICHARD GLASSTONE

ALLEMANDE. The term *allemande* (and the related terms *allemanda, alemana, almain, alman, tedesco,* and *Deutsche*), meaning "German," applies to several different dances or types of movement in use between the fifteenth and the nineteenth centuries. The word seems to have been used primarily to denote characteristics that were either ascribed a German origin or considered to have uniquely German qualities. As a result, the history of the dance called *allemande* is more a history of the application of a term to various movement characteristics than a tracing of a single line of choreographic development.

In the fifteenth century, the writings of the Italian dancing masters Guglielmo Ebreo and Giovanni Ambrosio often applied the term *saltarello tedesco* (the German *saltarello*) to the *quadernaria,* a four-beat type of meter. Thus it would appear that by this time Italians already considered square meters to be a characteristic of German dancing, in contrast to their own preference for triple meters. In the Italian *balli* of this period, the *saltarello tedesco* was generally used as a section of a larger dance, set off from the rest by meter and character. The step associated with this meter consisted of a *doppio* (double) combined with a *movimento,* a gesture of the foot that may be the precursor of the *allemande* step described by Thoinot Arbeau a century later. Robert Coplande's short *bassedanse* treatise, *The maner of dauncyinge of bace daunces . . .* (1521), includes the steps (but no music) for a dance entitled "La Allemande." As it uses the same five steps as all French *bassedanses,* it is difficult to

ALLEMANDE. A couple illustrating a change of arm positions in the *allemande.* This engraving is from Simon Guillaume's *Almanach dansant, ou Positions et attitudes de l'allemande,* Paris, 1770. (Courtesy of Madison U. Sowell and Debra H. Sowell, Brigham Young University, Provo, Utah.)

know what was considered German about this dance. [*See* Saltarello.]

By the middle of the sixteenth century, a number of collections of dance music that included pieces called *allemandes* had been published by several printers, such as Gervaise, Phalèse, and Susato. These dances were all in duple meter and were often followed by after-dances in triple meter based on the same musical material. The first full choreography of an *allemande* was given by Arbeau in his *Orchésographie* (1588) along with its music, and, like the musical *allemandes* printed by Gervaise et al., it is in duple meter. Arbeau's *allemande* is a very simple processional dance for couples, consisting almost entirely of a repeated sequence of three walking steps done either forward or backward, followed by a *grève,* a movement in which the foot was lifted in the air. Arbeau describes it as a sedate dance known to the Germans and one of the oldest in France. Somewhat more complex variants of this basic processional dance can be seen in English instructions for several choreographed "almains" dating from the late sixteenth and early seventeenth centuries. There is also a choreographed *allemande* for two couples ("Alemana d'Amore") in Cesare Negri's *Le gratie d'amore* (1602).

With the development of the suite and related forms, such as the *sonata da camera*, during the seventeenth century, the importance of the *allemande* as an instrumental composition increased dramatically. At the same time, the *allemande* as a dance disappeared. Although the processional form of the *allemande* may have continued to be danced in parts of Europe into the seventeenth century, in France, where developments in dance were occurring that were soon to make it the dance center of the Western world, the *allemande* existed as an instrumental piece only. As early as 1636 the Jesuit theorist Marin Mersenne stated that the *allemande* was not danced in France, and his contention was supported for the next century and more by French lexicographers, who defined the *allemande* as an instrumental form, in clear distinction to other dance types that were defined as dances.

Neither Jean-Baptiste Lully nor Jean-Philippe Rameau, the most important composers of ballet music in their respective periods, wrote a single *allemande* in any of their stage works. Nor is any trace of the *allemande* to be found among collections of dance music for the ballrooms of the French court. The single choreography in Feuillet nota-

tion entitled "L'Allemande" (Guillaume-Louis Pecour, 1702) is set to a tune that has nothing to do musically with the *allemande* of the instrumental suite and is labeled "air anglais" in André Campra's *Ballet des fragments de Mr. de Lully*. The title almost certainly derives from the use Pecour made of types of movement, most notably certain characteristic arm positions, that the French considered to be unique to the Germans. This choreography should thus be seen as a dance *à l'allemande* ("in the German manner"), that was done for a specific scene in a specific ballet. The *allemande* of the instrumental suite pursued its own independent line of development.

About the middle of the eighteenth century, writers on dance began to take note of certain dances originating in southern Germany and Austria that were gaining in social importance and that differed notably from the dominant ballroom dances of the day—the minuet and the *contredanse*—in that the partners often moved in close embrace. Although in their homeland these dances were known by regional and descriptive names such as the *Ländler, Dreher, Schleifer,* and *Weller,* as a group they were called *deutsche Tänze* (German dances), or simply *Deutsche*. Most *Deutsche* were lively, turning dances in triple meter (the *Deutsche* composed by Franz Joseph Haydn and Wolfgang Amadeus Mozart are all in 3/4 time), and they were important elements in the development of the waltz. [*See* Waltz.] Outside German-speaking areas, and sometimes even inside, the *Deutsche* were called *alle-*

ALLEMANDE. Introduced to France by Marie Antoinette, the *contredanse allemande,* as seen in this engraving, was danced by four couples facing in a square. The characteristic elements included figures in which partners turned under each other's arms or turned in place with arms entwined. This famous engraving by Augustin Saint-Aubin is titled *Le Bal Paré.* (Metropolitan Museum of Art, New York [no.33.56.33]; photograph used by permission.)

mandes. According to the Italian ballet master Giovanni Gallini,

> The Germans have a dance called the *Allemande*, in which the men and women form a ring. Each man holding his partner round the waist, makes her whirl round with almost inconceivable rapidity: they dance in a grand circle, seeming to pursue one another: in the course of which they execute several leaps, and some particularly pleasing steps, when they turn, but so very difficult as to appear such even to professed dancers themselves. When this dance is performed by a numerous company, it furnishes one of the most pleasing sights that can be imagined.　　　　　　　　　(Gallini, 1762)

A somewhat different variety was described by the Leipzig dancing master Carl Pauli. According to him, the *allemande* was a triple-meter dance whose lightness, bold turns, pirouettes, and quick changes of arm position foreigners tried in vain to imitate. When the dance was introduced in Paris, where it became popular in the 1760s and 1770s, it was done quite differently from the German way, at least according to the French dancing master Simon Guillaume. The main interest of the French version lay in a series of joined hand positions through which the partners moved by passing under each other's arms, turning each other around, and passing behind each other's back. The steps to the dance were of secondary importance, judging from the perfunctory manner in which they are treated in French books describing the *allemande*, and seem to have been subject to some variation.

In his *Almanach Dansant* (1770), Guillaume described two *allemande* steps out of the several he said existed, the main one in 2/4 time, and another in 3/8. The supplement to Denis Diderot's *Encyclopédie* (1776) described a "limping" *allemande* step that consisted of a *plié* followed by two walked steps, a sequence of movements that strongly suggests a waltz step. French descriptions of the allemande and collections of *allemande* music suggest that the French *allemande*, unlike the triple-meter *Deutsche*, was almost always danced in 2/4 time.

In France the characteristic arm positions and turns of the *allemande* were soon incorporated into the *contredanse*. The figure called the Allemande indicated a turn in place in which the two partners stood shoulder to shoulder facing in opposite directions with the right hand of each crossed behind the back and holding the partner's extended left hand. (This same arm position was among those used by Pecour in his 1702 *allemande* choreography.) *Contredanses* that made extensive use of this and other movements from the *allemande* were known as *contredanses allemandes*, or sometimes simply as *allemandes*. The well-known engraving by Augustin Saint-Aubin called *Le Bal Paré* shows a *contredanse* of this type. The *contredanses allemandes* were immensely successful and were danced into the nineteenth century. The call of "allemand right" in American square dancing has its origin in these French dances.

BIBLIOGRAPHY
Arbeau, Thoinot. *Orchesography* (1589). Translated by Mary Stewart Evans. New York, 1948.
Böhme, Franz M. *Geschichte des Tanzes in Deutschland*. 2 vols. Leipzig, 1886.
Brainard, Ingrid. "Die Choreographie der Hoftänze in Burgund, Frankreich und Italien im 15. Jahrhundert." Ph.D. diss., University of Göttingen, 1956.
Brainard, Ingrid. *The Art of Courtly Dancing in the Early Renaissance*. West Newton, Mass., 1981.
Cunningham, James P. *Dancing in the Inns of Court*. London, 1965.
Dubois. *Principes d'allemandes*. Paris, c.1769.
Gallini, Giovanni. *A Treatise on the Art of Dancing*. London, 1762.
Guilcher, Jean-Michel. *La contredanse et les renouvellements de la danse française*. Paris, 1969.
Guillaume, Simon. *Almanach dansant, ou, Positions et attitudes de l'allemande*. Paris, 1770.
La Cuisse. *Le répertoire des bals*. 3 vols. Paris, 1762.
Little, Meredith Ellis. "Inventory of the Dances of Jean-Baptiste Lully." *Recherches sur la Musique Française Classique* 9 (1969).
Little, Meredith Ellis, and Suzanne G. Cusick. "Allemande." In *The New Grove Dictionary of Music and Musicians*. London, 1980.
Mersenne, Marin. *Harmonie universelle*, bk. 2. Paris, 1636.
Pugliese, Patri J., and Joseph Casazza. *Practise for Dauncinge: Some Almans and a Pavan, England, 1570–1650*. Cambridge, Mass., 1980.
Reichart, Sarah Bennett. "Music for the Renaissance Allemande." *Dance Chronicle* 8.3–4 (1985): 211–218.
V. A. L. "Contredanse." In *Encyclopédie, ou, Dictionnaire raisonné des sciences, des arts et des métiers*, supp. vol. 2. Paris, 1776.

REBECCA HARRIS-WARRICK

ALMA. Full title: *Alma, ou La Fille de Feu*. Ballet in four acts. Choreography: Fanny Cerrito and Jules Perrot. Music: Michael Costa. Libretto: André Deshayes. Scenery: William Grieve. First performance: 23 June 1842, Her Majesty's Theatre, London. Principals: Fanny Cerrito (Alma), Jules Perrot (Belfegor, or Periphite), Henri Desplaces (Emazor).

Alma was Fanny Cerrito's first important role in London and her first collaboration as a choreographer with Jules Perrot. Presented during Benjamin Lumley's first season as manager of Her Majesty's Theatre, it influenced Lumley's decision to hire Perrot as ballet master, a position that he held for six years, producing in that time some of his most successful ballets.

Perrot and Cerrito were responsible for the principal dances in *Alma*. Perrot's *pas de fascination*, a high point of the ballet, conveyed the dramatic action of the plot through dance rather than conventional mime. In this dance, Alma, a statue brought to life under the condition that she will revert to stone should she ever fall in love, charms the inhabitants of a German town, aided by her Mephistophelean mentor Belfegor (also called Periphite).

Alma's travels take her to France and Spain, where she wins the love of Emazor, a Moorish prince, who follows her through various adventures. When she consents to marry him, she turns into a statue once more.

Cerrito's husband, Arthur Saint-Léon, reworked the ballet for Cerrito's Paris Opera debut in 1847. It was retitled *La Fille de Marbre* but maintained the original libretto and score.

BIBLIOGRAPHY
Beaumont, Cyril W. *The Complete Book of Ballets.* London, 1937.
Guest, Ivor. *The Romantic Ballet in England.* London, 1972.
Guest, Ivor. *Fanny Cerrito.* 2d rev. ed. London, 1974.
Guest, Ivor. *Jules Perrot: Master of the Romantic Ballet.* London, 1984.
SUSAN AU

ALMASZADE, GAMER (Gamer Gadzhi Aga-Kyzy Almaszade; born 10 March 1915 in Baku, Azerbaijan), dancer and teacher. Almaszade was the first Azerbaijani ballerina and choreographer. She received an elementary ballet education at Sergei Kevorkov's studio in Baku; after graduating in 1929 she was admitted to the Akhundov Opera and Ballet Theater of Baku. In 1932 she trained at the Bolshoi Ballet School, and from 1933 to 1936 she studied with Maria Romanova at the Kirov Ballet School. From 1936 to 1953 she was *prima ballerina* of the Akhundov Opera and Ballet Theater.

A dancer of strictly academic style, Almaszade was noted for her lyricism and poetry. Among her roles in the classical repertory were Odette-Odile in *Swan Lake,* the playful Kitri in *Don Quixote,* the lyrical Clara in *The Nutcracker,* the regal title role of *Raymonda,* and the poetic Maria in *The Fountain of Bakhchisarai.* In Azerbaijani ballets and operas she achieved recognition for her beauty of movement, charm, and fanciful patterns. "Gamer Almaszade . . . is a brilliant dancer," Olga Lepeshinskaya wrote in 1938. "She exudes charm; her movements are smooth and harmonious. Her image reminds one of a wonderful tale from the *Thousand and One Nights.*" The first Azerbaijani ballet, *The Maidens' Tower* (1940), was created especially for her by Kevorkov.

In 1936 Almaszade began teaching at the Baku ballet school. In 1950 she choreographed and took the leading role in *Gyulshen,* which depicted life on a collective cotton farm. As chief choreographer of the Akhundov Opera and Ballet Theater from 1953 onward, Almaszade produced her own versions of many classical and Soviet ballets. In 1971 she participated in the foundation of the National Dance Ensemble of Iraq and in 1972 was named artistic director of the Azerbaijani ballet.

BIBLIOGRAPHY
Gardner, Christine. "The Baku Opera Ballet Company." *Ballet Today* (March–April 1970): 19–20.
Karasyova, Nina. "News from the World: Moscow." *Ballet Today* (February 1960): 19.
Pletnev, Vladimir. "Napominaya chudesnuyu legendu." *Sovetskii balet,* no. 4 (1983).
Pletnev, Vladimir. *Gamer Almaszade.* Baku, 1985.
VLADIMIR N. PLETNEV
Translated from Russian

ALONSO, ALICIA (Alicia Ernestina de la Caridad del Cobre Martínez y del Hoyo; born 21 December 1921 in Havana), Cuban ballet dancer, choreographer, and company director. Alonso, the daughter of a well-to-do army officer, grew up in Havana. She studied Spanish dancing briefly on a visit to Spain, then began ballet training at age nine with Nikolai Yavorsky at Havana's Sociedad Pro-Arte Musical, making her first stage appearances there. Moving to New York in 1937, she married Fernando Alonso and bore a daughter, Laura, who also became a dancer and ballet mistress. Alicia Alonso studied on scholarship at the School of American Ballet and with Enrico Zanfretta, Aleksandra Fedorova, Anatole Vilzak, Ludmilla Schollar, and Antony Tudor, and later with Vera Volkova

ALONSO. Alicia Alonso in her most famous role, the title character in the Romantic classic *Giselle.* (Photograph by George Karger; from the Dance Collection, New York Public Library for the Performing Arts.)

in London. She appeared on Broadway in *Great Lady* (1938) and *Stars in Your Eyes* (1939), then toured with Ballet Caravan (1939), in which she danced her first major role in Eugene Loring's *Billy the Kid*.

With Ballet Theatre (1940–1948, 1950–1955, and 1958–1959), Alonso quickly rose from corps to leading ballerina, creating roles in *Undertow* (as Ate), *Theme and Variations, Fall River Legend* (as Lizzie Borden, replacing Nora Kaye at the last moment), Bronislava Nijinska's *Schumann Concerto*, and Enrique Martinez's *Tropical Pas de Deux*. She first danced *Giselle*, the role with which she is most closely identified, in 1943 with Anton Dolin, having rehearsed the ballet mentally during a year of forced immobility after the first of several eye operations. (Later she coped with almost total blindness, although in 1972 an operation restored some vision in one eye.) Extremely versatile, she excelled in both classical and contemporary roles, dancing *Pas de Quatre;* George Balanchine's *Apollo;* Antony Tudor's *Jardin aux Lilas, Gala Performance,* and *Romeo and Juliet;* and Léonide Massine's *Aleko.* Her celebrated partnership with Igor Youskevitch, which began in Ballet Theatre and lasted until 1960, was based on ever-evolving dramatic rapport and on the contrast between their feminine and masculine qualities. Within a wide repertory, their signature ballets were *Giselle, Theme and Variations,* and the Black Swan pas de deux.

During a layoff in 1948, Alonso, who had danced as a guest with Pro-Arte in Havana, returned there to found a company, Ballet Alicia Alonso (now Ballet Nacional de Cuba). For it she and others staged contemporary works and the classics; the productions of the latter now in the repertory are all credited to her. Her own ballets for the company include *Ensayo Sinfónico* (1950), also performed by American Ballet Theatre, *Lydia,* a study of an insane woman (1951), *El Pillette* (1952), *Narcissus and Echo* (1955), *La Carta* (1965), *El Circo* (1967), *Genesis* (1978), and *Misión Korad* (1980).

Until 1960, Alonso divided her time between her Havana company and the United States. After leaving Ballet Theatre, she appeared as a guest with Ballet Russe de Monte Carlo (1955–1959), creating the role of Columbine in Boris Romanov's *Harlequinade.* For the Greek Theatre in Los Angeles, she staged and danced in *Coppélia* with André Eglevsky and Niels Bjørn Larsen (1957), and *Giselle* with Youskevitch (1958). For the Paris Opera Ballet, she produced *Giselle* (1972), dancing in the premiere, *Grand Pas de Quatre,* and *Sleeping Beauty* (1974); for the Vienna State Opera, *Giselle* (1980); and for the Teatro alla Scala, Milan, *The Sleeping Beauty* (1983), with Carla Fracci and Jorge Esquivel.

Alonso was the first Western ballerina to dance as a guest in the Soviet Union, from December 1957 to February 1958, appearing in *Giselle* and *Swan Lake* with great

ALONSO. Celebrated stage partners Igor Youskevitch and Alicia Alonso in a pas de deux from *Swan Lake* in the early 1950s. (Photograph from the Dance Collection, New York Public Library for the Performing Arts.)

success. The Soviet ballerina Tatiana Vecheslova wrote of her, "I believe that our young artists should pay attention to the sharpness of her designs and unlimited perfection of her technical movements" (Vecheslova, 1958). Alonso returned to Russia with her company in 1960. In 1959 she received a *Dance Magazine* Award, but because of tension between the U.S. and Cuban governments, her appearances in April 1960 with Ballet Theatre in New York were her last in the United States for fifteen years.

Continuing to dance into the 1990s—two later partners being Azari Plisetsky and Jorge Esquivel—Alonso has been internationally honored. She won the Prix Pavlova for best dancer at the 1966 International Festival of Dance in Paris. The thirty-fifth anniversary of her first *Giselle* was the occasion of a gala in Havana in 1978, with former partners and foreign dignitaries in attendance, as was her fiftieth anniversary on stage (and sixtieth birthday) in 1981. She has frequently served on juries for international ballet competitions. She danced *Giselle* with Les Grands Ballets Canadiens during Expo 67, the world's fair held in Montreal in 1967, and with the Royal Danish Ballet (as one of that company's rare guests, partnered by Flemming Flindt) in Copenhagen in 1969. In 1975, she married Pedro Simón, editor of the magazine *Cuba en el Ballet*.

Beginning in 1975 with a *Swan Lake* pas de deux, Alonso made several appearances with American Ballet Theatre in the United States including Alberto Alonso's *Carmen* (1976), a full-length *Giselle* (1977), and, reunited with Youskevitch, the act 2 pas de deux (1980). They repeated the last for a gala in Youskevitch's honor in Austin, Texas, in March 1982. She also danced with her own company on U.S. tours in 1978 and 1979, appearing in *Giselle*, *Grand Pas de Quatre*, *Carmen*, Alberto Méndez's pas de deux *La Péri*, and his *Ad Libitum* with Antonio Gades. She joined the faculty of the Universidad Complutense, Madrid.

One of the most celebrated ballerinas for fifty years, Alonso has combined a true sense of romanticism with a Latin boldness of feeling, and the suppleness and high extensions of the Russian school with the brilliant footwork of the Italian. In 1952, Walter Terry wrote:

> [She] is a classicist and even a lyricist but she believes in communicating the heat of drama, the warmth of a very real femininity and the excitement of physical effort to her public.
>
> In George Balanchine's *Theme and Variations*, Miss Alonso moves softly through adagio passages and sharply through allegro sequences and in both one is aware of the sensuousness of movement. A leg, for example, may float easily upward but the exhilaration of stretching is also present in its execution just as the daintiest of steps speak of the pleasure of contact as well as of lightness. . . . She is the kind of ballerina for whom the art of balletic display was invented, a feminine virtuoso, an actress, a vivid personality.
>
> (Terry, 1952)

Her virtuoso aplomb showed itself in a secure balance, multiple turns, and—in the Black Swan—*temps levés* on pointe in *arabesque penché*. A byproduct, however, was that purists occasionally complained of her cavalier treatment of the music.

Alonso united spontaneity with a careful study of period style and of motivation—not only for her own character but that of the entire cast, to whom she related effectively onstage. These elements also characterized her own productions and her nurturing of young dancers. Her example, dedication, and hard work have been the motivating forces of Cuban ballet, whose style reflects hers without slavish copying.

[*See also* Cuba, *articles on ballet.*]

BIBLIOGRAPHY

Alonso, Alicia. *Diálogos con la danza.* Edited by Pedro Simón. Buenos Aires, 1988.

Anderson, Jack. *The One and Only: The Ballet Russe de Monte Carlo.* New York, 1981.

Arnold, Sandra Martín. *Alicia Alonso: First Lady of the Ballet.* New York, 1993.

Concepción, Alma. "U.S. Ballet and Modern Dance in the Caribbean: Cuba and Puerto Rico." In *Proceedings of the Fifteenth Annual Conference, Society of Dance History Scholars, University of California, Riverside, 14–15 February 1992,* compiled by Christena L. Schlundt. Riverside, Calif., 1992.

Dallal, Alberto. "Alicia Alonso." In Dallal's *La mujer en la danza.* Mexico City, 1990.

de Mille, Agnes. *Portrait Gallery.* Boston, 1990.

Molina, Antonio J. *Qué pas de trois: Alicia Alonso, la revolución cubana y Jorge Esquivel.* Hato Rey, P.R., 1993.

Newman, Barbara. *Striking a Balance: Dancers Talk about Dancing.* Rev. ed. New York, 1992.

Terry, Walter. "Two Alicias." *New York Herald Tribune* (12 October 1952). Reprinted in Terry's *I Was There* (New York, 1978).

Terry, Walter. *Alicia and Her Ballet Nacional de Cuba.* Garden City, N.Y., 1981. Includes a chronology of the company's repertory.

Terry, Walter. "Alicia Assoluta." *Ballet News* 3 (December 1981): 20–24.

Vecheslova, Tatiana. "Alicia Alonso Dances." *Dance Magazine* (May 1958): 55–56.

FILMS.   *Swan Lake: Act III Black Swan Pas de Deux* and *Giselle: Act II Pas de Deux* (Jacob's Pillow, 1955), both with Erik Bruhn. *Giselle* (1964), with Azari Plisetsky and Ballet Nacional de Cuba. Excerpts from *Giselle*, *Pas de Quatre*, and *Carmen* in *Alicia* (1976). Excerpts from *Apollo* and *Theme and Variations* in Ann Barzel, *Youskevitch Gala* (n.d.), Dance Collection, New York Public Library for the Performing Arts. *Classically Cuban* (1982).

VIDEOTAPES.   *Pas de Quatre, The Bell Telephone Hour* (1960), with Alonso as Taglioni. Tom Slevin, "Alicia Alonso" (1971).

INTERVIEW.   Alicia Alonso, by Marilyn Hunt (1977), Dance Collection, New York Public Library for the Performing Arts.

MARILYN HUNT

ALSTON, RICHARD (born 30 October 1948 in Stoughton, Sussex), British choreographer and teacher. Since founding the dance group Strider in 1972, Richard Alston has had particular importance and influence in dance in Great Britain. Educated at Eton College and at Croydon College of Art, he studied at the London School of Contemporary Dance (LSCD, later London Contemporary Dance School) between 1967 and 1970, and soon after beginning his dance training, he started to choreograph. His first work, *Transit*, to music by Ronald Lopresti, was performed in 1968. One of the dancers, a fellow student, was Siobhan Davies, who became an important dancer in Alston's subsequent work and remained a close friend and collaborator.

In 1970 Alston began to teach dance composition at LSCD and to choreograph pieces for London Contemporary Dance Theatre. His style was unlike the predominant one in the troupe, which was based on Martha Graham's technique. Alston respected both the musical phrasing and objectivity in ballet teaching and the compositional principles of Merce Cunningham.

One of the first dance awards given by the Calouste Gulbenkian Foundation was awarded to Alston. It enabled him to leave LSCD in 1972 to found Strider, initially a group of four dancer-choreographers. This has subse-

ALSTON. Sara Matthews, Ben Craft, Amanda Bulton, and Bruce Michelson of the Rambert Dance Company in Richard Alston's *Zanza* (1986). The backdrop was designed by John Hayland. (Photograph by Catherine Ashmore; used by permission.)

quently been called the starting point for British new dance. Its members used choreographic forms that differed from the musical, physical, and expressionist idioms of more traditional modern dance forms. Alston's choreography, often performed in unconventional spaces, employed unusual, sometimes commissioned accompaniment and avant-garde compositional or improvisatory procedures. Of great value to Alston in this period was his work with fellow dancers Eva Karzcag and Christopher Banner, and his experience of Cunningham technique with Nanette Hassall.

Between 1972 and 1975 Strider performed in Britain and several European cities. Strider's *Tiger Balm* and *Headlong* were later also performed by London Contemporary Dance Theatre. *Lay-out,* revised in 1974 and reti-

tled *Blue Schubert Fragments,* was created for that company. Strider's residency at Dartington College of Arts in 1974 led to Alston's study and collaboration with Mary Fulkerson. In that same year he taught dance technique for the first time; teaching later became an important adjunct to choreography for him. In 1975 Strider ceased performing. Alston left for New York, where for two years he studied with Merce Cunningham, Valda Setterfield, and Alfredo Corvino. There in 1976 he presented a program of an old work, *Unamerican Activities,* and a new work, *Edge.*

Returning to London in 1977, Alston spent almost three years working as a teacher, performer, and choreographer in various contexts and establishments. *Rainbow Bandit* used a text-and-sound recording by Charles Amirkhanian and showed Britain a more accomplished Alston, using a largely Cunningham vocabulary but with individual phrasing. In 1978 he created *Doublework,* which concentrated on the duet form, with three couples dancing in silence. *Rainbow Bandit* and *Doublework* are the oldest major works by Alston surviving in performance in the 1990s.

In a 1978 solo for Maedée Duprès, *Home Ground*, Alston's choreography responded rhythmically to the music of Henry Purcell. This musicality was henceforth the starting point for most of his choreography. After the creation of his first work for Ballet Rambert in 1980, *Bell High*, set to music by Peter Maxwell Davies, he was asked to become the company's resident choreographer. The opportunity to use live accompaniment and to follow his work's development in the context of company repertory led him to accept the offer. His collaboration with dancer Michael Clark, begun in *Bell High* and continuing after Clark's departure from Ballet Rambert in 1981, would be of great mutual benefit over the next two years. *Bell High* was also the first work for which lighting was done by Peter Mumford, who has since done the lighting for most of Alston's works and designed several of them.

With Ballet Rambert, Alston steadily developed a shared stylistic understanding with his dancers. His third choreography for the company, *Rainbow Ripples* (1980), began with the Amirkhanian text-and-sound accompaniment previously used in *Rainbow Bandit*, but the choreography now responded to it with rhythmic precision. The work used other pieces by Amirkhanian before ending with a recorded xylophone rag by George Hamilton Green that continued the dance's rhythms.

The Rite of Spring (1981) received attention for Alston's use of the two-piano version of Stravinsky's score and because the production linked the company to Marie Rambert's association with the original Vaslav Nijinsky version. Alston's choreography, although contemporary, hearkened back to pictorial documents of that production as well as to Bronislava Nijinska's *Les Noces*. In *Night Music* (music by Mozart) a new length and density of phrase was observed, as well as an increasing interest in the intricate coordinations of the Cecchetti ballet system. These characteristics were further emphasized in *Apollo Distraught* (1982; music by Nigel Osborne) and *Chicago Brass* (1983; music by Paul Hindemith). The influences of Ashton and Balanchine are recognizable in the musicality and formalism of these works; Alston incorporated these influences, however, into his individual classicism. The mature Alston style in this period generally included sculptural and spatial development of taut and long phrases, a basis of firmly rhythmic musicality, a lyrical emphasis laid on the abandonment and recovery of equilibrium in movement, and a classicism more of grammar and structure than of vocabulary. Most of Alston's works are pure dance, but specific relationships are developed in many of them.

These qualities were also found in the works made for other companies. In 1982 Alston made *The Kingdom of Pagodas* (m̄   ̄ jamin Britten) for the Royal Danish Ballet. In 19   ̄ e made *Java* (set to songs recorded by the Ink Spots) and *The Brilliant and the Dark* (music by Britten) for Second Stride, and *Midsummer* (music by Michael Tippett) for the Royal Ballet.

Alston has been interested in setting dance to vocal music since his Strider days. As well as several uses of Amirkhanian text-and-sound recordings, Alston has used songs by Mozart *(Night Music)* and the Ink Spots *(Java)* and Monteverdi madrigals in *Voices and Light Footsteps*. Another favored choice is twentieth-century British music, such as that of Maxwell Davies, Britten, Osborne, Tippett, Simon Waters, and Ralph Vaughan Williams.

Night Music and *Midsummer* involved collaborations with painters Howard Hodgkin and John Hubbard, respectively. *Wildlife* (1984) was the product of Alston's collaboration with designer Richard Smith, lighting designer Peter Mumford, and composer Nigel Osborne; this was Alston's first commissioned score since Strider. In much of this work he used a less balletic language than in his recent choreography. That is also true of the 1985 *Mythologies*, an attempt to depict the British Columbian myths that had inspired Osborne. With *Dangerous Liaisons* (1985), set to a recorded electronic score by Simon Waters, Alston again demonstrated the complexity, fluency, and intensity of his choreographic style.

Alston made a new version of *Java* for Ballet Rambert in 1985, again to Ink Spots songs, incorporating three sections of the original. This version proved one of his most popular works. Comical and full of lively footwork and rich upper-body movement, as well as joking about quotations from other ballets and about male-female relations, it has won wide admiration.

In 1986 Alston was appointed artistic director of Ballet Rambert. For the company's sixtieth anniversary season, he quickly commissioned new works from several other choreographers, all using modern music and new designs. Alston's own major choreographic contribution was *Zanza* (music by Osborne). Densely inventive and successfully dramatic, it used several different styles of movement, in particular the angular and floor-based forms Alston had introduced in *Wildlife*.

In 1987 Alston made the comedy *Pulcinella*, his most intricate narrative to date. It used a slightly modified version of the original libretto to Stravinsky's score, with a range of ballet mime and Italianate gesture in addition to a largely balletic language. Two of his most successful works, *Dutiful Ducks* (1986) and *Strong Language* (1987), were extensive revisions of previous works. Varied in tone and intently musical, *Strong Language* is among the most vigorous works Alston has made.

Alston choreographed six more works for Rambert between 1990 and 1992, none as successful as *Strong Language*. The conflicting obligations inherent in the dual role of artistic director and resident choreographer of a repertory company seem to have contributed to the uncertain tone of some of these pieces. In 1993 Alston left Rambert over differences in artistic policy with the board of directors. After a year of freelance teaching, he was appointed artistic director of The Place (formerly the school of the London Contemporary Dance Theatre), home to the newly founded Richard Alston Dance Company. This change in circumstances has yielded a profound artistic renewal for Alston. Since a well-received season at the Aldeburgh Festival in 1994 with a program of new works to music by Benjamin Britten and Igor Stravinsky, the company has toured extensively in the United Kingdom, Europe, and Asia. Several of Alston's new dances have been choreographed to music by Harrison Birtwhistle, most notably *Orpheus Singing and Dreaming* (1996). With such works Alston continues to build on the achievement of his best works of the 1980s and to confirm his belief in what dance is: a strong language.

BIBLIOGRAPHY

Alston, Richard. "Movement and People First." *Dance and Dancers* (December 1977).
Alston, Richard. "Two Recent Dances." *Artscribe* 16 (February 1979).
Croce, Alston. "Artists and Models." *The New Yorker* (1 November 1983).
Jordan, Stephanie. "New, Joyful, Sleek." *New Statesman* (20 March 1981).
Jordan, Stephanie. "Interviews with Richard Alston and Nigel Osborne." *Choreography and Dance* 1.4 (1992): 57–72.
Jordan, Stephanie. *Striding Out.* London, 1992.
Kane, Angela. "Richard Alston: Twenty-one Years of Choreography." *Dance Research* 7 (Autumn 1989): 16–54.
Macaulay, Alastair. "Alston and Ashton." *Performance* (June–July 1982).
Macaulay, Alastair. "The North Collection." *The Dancing Times* (October 1982): 28–29.
Macaulay, Alastair. "The Rambertians." *The Dancing Times* (May 1985): 678–680.
Macaulay, Alastair. "Choreography by Richard Alston." *Dance Theatre Journal* 5 (Summer 1987): 32–34; 5 (Fall 1987): 36–40. Detailed catalog of Alston's choreography through August 1987.
Macaulay, Alastair. "Richard Alston: Back at The Place." *The Dancing Times* (January 1995): 333–339.
Percival, John. "How Richard Alston Came to Be a Pioneer." *The Times* (27 March 1980). Interview with Richard Alston.
Robertson, Allen. "Full Circle." *Dance Now* 4 (Spring 1995): 18–23.
Vaughan, David. "London Contemporary Dance Theatre." *The Dancing Times* (October 1973).
Vaughan, David. "Structures." *Dance Magazine* (July 1976): 25–26.

VIDEOTAPE. "Dancemakers," Danmarks Radio and RM Arts/BBC (1986).

ALASTAIR MACAULAY

ALTA (Sp. and It., "high," "eminent," "lofty," "above the ground") has had various meanings in dance and music since the fourteenth century. Aside from its general descriptive uses in dance, the term referred specifically to both a Renaissance step (or step pattern) and a dance type. It is still in use to designate a court dance—that is, a social dance performed by personages of high rank.

The *altabaxo* step, or *alto baxo, altibajo,* or *altybaxo* (lit., "high to low" or "high-low," meaning bounce, leap, hop, or skip), appears in Spanish literature from the fourteenth to the seventeenth centuries. It is mentioned by Juan Ruiz in 1330 in *Libro de buen amor:* "Ssé de fazer el altybaxo E sotar a qualquier muedo, / non fallo alto njn baxo que me vença según cuydo" (roughly translated: When you do the *altybaxo* you jump whichever way [you wish], whether high or low I won't say, but you will convince me best by being careful [in control]). A more detailed definition of the step was given three hundred years later by Juan de Esquivel Navarro (1642), who equated it with *saltos al lado,* a high, suspended leap to the side, pointing the toes, and landing on one foot. Although the step is quite unlikely to have had the same specific meaning throughout its long history, it seems always to have been vigorous.

Altadanza was the fifteenth-century word for a Spanish dance type equated by Antonio Cornazano (1465) with the Italian *saltarello* and the French *pas de Brabant,* which were lively dance types—that is, off the ground, with hops, jumps, and leaps—in triple or compound duple meter, often with dotted rhythms. These dance types were frequently paired with the Italian *bassadanza* or the French *bassedanse.* In the complex Italian *balli* (multimovement dances) of the fifteenth century, the *saltarello* was also one of the choreographic/tempo/step types recognized and employed: the term could signify any or all of the three different aspects of a *saltarello* section. Whether the *altabaxo* step was equally characteristic of the Spanish *alto baxo* dance type—or had a similar tempo connotation—is unknown because there are no extant fifteenth-century descriptions of step or dance. The precise connection with the French *pas de Brabant* is also unknown (e.g., the dance titled "Le Hault & Bas" in the Toulouse, Brussels, and Salisbury collections of *bassesdanses* contains no instructions for an *hault* dance; the title may, rather, refer to a chanson text unrelated to dance. Compounding the mystery is an *alta morisca* mentioned but not described in the Cervera manuscript (c.1468).

In the sixteenth century, the *alta* continued as a dance type. That it still could be associated with a *bassadanza* is manifested late in the century by the title of Fabritio Caroso's "Bassa et Alta" (two versions: 1581, 1600), a dance whose *bassa* choreography is derived from the *bassadanza* in Pedro de Gracia Dei's *La crianca y virtuosa dotrina* (c.1486; see Feves, 1991); unfortunately, Gracia Dei gives no choreography for an *alta,* while Caroso's *alta* sections of the later dance are not distinguishable in step type or choreography from other dance types.

Beside the continued association of *bassa* and *alta*, the two seem to have separated into discrete dance types sometime during the sixteenth century. The anonymous Spanish source *Reglas de danzar* (c.1540) gives separate choreographies for an *alta* and a *baja;* although there seems to be little differentiation in the step patterns employed (simples and doubles predominate), the *alta* calls for "high" gestures and leaps and also implies that partway through the dance the gentleman and lady, after dancing forward and together in the line of direction, alternate "high-stepping" variations while facing one another. If this pattern was indeed typical of an *alta*, it fell into the same choreographic category as the *galliarde, tordion, passo e mezzo*, and *canario*—all virtuosic "display" dance types involving alternating solo variations in which the partners faced each other, with passages danced together.

The separation of *bassa* and *alta* continues into the seventeenth century with Caroso and Cesare Negri (1602, 1604); both terms were used as titles of individual dances or multimovement *balletti* in their manuals. They titled seventeen dances *alta;* however, it is not certain whether *alta* always referred to a dance type or simply modified the name of the lady to whom the dance was dedicated (e.g., both "Alta Vittoria" [Caroso] and "Alta Mendozza" [Negri] are dedicated to high-born ladies and have high passages; both are multimovement *balletti* incorporating different dance types).

References up to the mid-seventeenth century continue to recognize the *alta* as a separate dance type. In 1611, Sebastián de Covarrubias Horozco (1943) described the *alta* and the *baxa* as dance types brought to Spain by foreigners and currently being danced in Germany. In 1642 de Esquivel Navarro cited the *alta* as the first dance taught in Spanish dancing schools. He stressed its importance but did not describe it. In 1651 the playwright Pedro Calderón also referred to the *alta* as the first lesson in dancing classes but said it was "a dance that is not in use."

In Spain today, *alta danza* refers to the aristocratic dance of the seventeenth and eighteenth centuries, and *a lo alto* is a term "usually applied to social or period . . . dances in which manners and decorum are of primary importance" (Matteo, 1990). Thus, both terms refer primarily to the rank and formal manner of the dancers of "noble" dances of the past.

BIBLIOGRAPHY: SOURCES

Anonymous. *Reglas de danzar*. Circa 1540. Manuscript located in Madrid, Library of the Royal Academy of History, misc.fol.t25, f.149v.

Calderón de la Barca, Pedro. *El maestro de danzar*. Seville, c.1651–1652.

Caroso, Fabritio. *Il ballarino* (1581). Facsimile reprint, New York, 1967.

Caroso, Fabritio. *Nobiltà di dame*. Venice, 1600, 1605. Facsimile reprint, Bologna, 1970. Reissued with order of illustrations changed as *Raccolta di varij balli*. Rome, 1630. Translated into English with eight introductory chapters by Julia Sutton, the music transcribed by F. Marian Walker. Oxford, 1986. Reprint with a step manual in Labanotation by Rachelle Palnick Tsachor and Julia Sutton, New York, 1995.

Cervera, Archivo Histórico. Anonymous dance manuscript, c.1468.

Cornazano, Antonio. *L'arte del danzare* (c.1455–1465). Manuscript located in Rome, Biblioteca Apostolica Vaticana, codex Capponiano, 203. Translated by Madeleine Inglehearn and Peggy Forsyth as *The Book on the Art of Dancing*. London, 1981.

Covarrubias Horozco, Sebastián de. *Tesoro de la lengua castellana o española* (1611). Facsimile reprint, edited by Martín de Riquer, Barcelona, 1943.

Esquivel Navarro, Juan de. *Discursos sobre el arte del dancado* (1642). Facsimile reprint, Madrid, 1947.

Negri, Cesare. *Le gratie d'amore*. Milan, 1602. Reissued as *Nuove invenzione di balli*. Milan, 1604. Translated into Spanish by Don Balthasar Carlos for Señor Condé, Duke of Sanlucar, 1630. Manuscript located in Madrid, Biblioteca Nacional, MS 14085. Facsimile reprint of 1602, New York and Bologna, 1969. Literal translation into English and musical transcription by Yvonne Kendall. D.M.A. diss., Stanford University, 1985.

Ruiz, Juan. *Libro de buen amor* (1330). 17th ed., edited by María Brey Maríno. Madrid, 1987.

BIBLIOGRAPHY: OTHER STUDIES

Brooks, Lynn Matluck. *The Dances of the Processions of Seville in Spain's Golden Age*. Kassel, 1988.

Brown, Howard M. "Alta." In *The New Grove Dictionary of Music and Musicians*. London, 1980.

Crane, Frederick. *Materials for the Study of the Fifteenth-Century Basse Danse*. Brooklyn, 1968.

Feves, Angene. "Fabritio Caroso and the Changing Shape of the Dance, 1550–1600." *Dance Chronicle* 14 (1991): 159–174.

Matteo [Vittucci, Matteo Marcellus] with Carola Goya. *The Language of Spanish Dance*. Norman, Okla., 1990.

Tani, Gino. "Alta." In *Enciclopedio dello spettacolo*. 9 vols. Rome, 1954–1968.

JULIA SUTTON
with Patricia Weeks Rader

ALVIN AILEY AMERICAN DANCE THEATER.
[*This entry comprises two articles focusing on the history of the modern dance company founded by Alvin Ailey. For related discussion, see* United States of America, *article on* African-American Concert Dance.]

Origins to 1979

Founded in December 1958, under Alvin Ailey, director, choreographer, and principal dancer, the Alvin Ailey American Dance Theater was established as a black folkloric company; it soon developed into a modern dance company and a repository for works in a wide variety of styles. Ailey believed the company must serve both "a creative function"—that of producing new pieces—and a "museum function." He also believed in supplying the public with popular, highly theatrical dance: "First get the people into the theater; then you can show them anything you want," he said, "but you can't show them anything at all if they're still outside."

Ailey gave his first New York performance as a soloist on 30 March 1958, and his company made its debut in December at the Ninety-second Street YM-YWHA, with a program that included *Blues Suite,* a vibrant character dance to traditional music. The troupe's success was furthered by the popular and critical acclaim accorded to *Revelations,* which received its premiere on 31 January 1960. [*See* Revelations.]

During its first seasons the company consisted of black performers; beginning in 1962, Ailey deployed a multiracial troupe, having "discovered that there was a kind of reverse chauvinism in being an all-black company or an all-black anything." Similarly, while Ailey made a point of producing the works of black choreographers, musicians, and artists, and of showing dances based on black American themes, he also stressed artistic and ethnic diversity of repertory. Among the choreographers whose dances have been mounted by the company are Talley Beatty, John Butler, Katherine Dunham, Choo San Goh, Geoffrey Holder, Lester Horton, José Limón, Lar Lubovitch, Donald McKayle, Elisa Monte, May O'Donnell, Pearl Primus, Ted Shawn, Anna Sokolow, Glen Tetley, Joyce Trisler, and Hans van Manen. The most successful works often have a strong theatrical element, and the company's style can be recognized by a vitality and intensity of projection rather than by any specific movement technique. By 1984, the company had staged about 155 works, approximately one third of which had been choreographed by Ailey.

Ailey was born 5 January 1931 in Rogers, Texas. At the age of twelve, he moved with his mother to Los Angeles where, as a member of a junior high school class, he was "dragged bodily to see the Ballet Russe de Monte Carlo." After that, he became a frequent visitor to the Los Angeles theater district, where he saw the company of Katherine Dunham, which thrilled him with the theatricality of its productions and "by the idea of black people doing things of that magnitude on stage." In 1949 he began taking class with Lester Horton; he made his debut with Horton's company, where his partner was Carmen de Lavallade, and became the troupe's artistic director for a brief period after the founder's death in 1953. The following year Ailey and de Lavallade danced on Broadway in *House of Flowers.* That summer, two of Ailey's short pieces were performed by the Horton company at Jacob's Pillow.

Ailey worked in the theater as an actor, dancer, and choreographer while studying with Martha Graham, Hanya Holm, Charles Weidman, Karel Shook, Doris Humphrey, and Anna Sokolow. In 1957, while dancing in the musical *Jamaica,* Ailey worked with Jack Cole, who also influenced his style.

Ailey began to choreograph *Blues Suite* (1958) after working with Sokolow, from whom, he said, he learned

ALVIN AILEY AMERICAN DANCE THEATER. Ailey and Carmen de Lavallade in Lester Horton's *To José Clemente Orozco* at Jacob's Pillow, 1961. (Photograph by John Lindquist; used by permission of the Harvard Theatre Collection, The Houghton Library.)

"how to go inside one's self for themes." His first dances were inspired by images of the valley of the Brazos River in Texas, where he lived as a child: "The people in *Blues Suite* were people I actually knew—I could say, 'This was the man who lived around the corner.'"

Despite the success of Ailey's first pieces, the company—like most modern dance companies of the period—had limited resources. It secured only two engagements in 1960 and three (with de Lavallade as guest artist) in 1962; however, in that year it embarked on a series of foreign tours sponsored by the U.S. Department of State, becoming the first black dance company to be sent abroad by the Kennedy administration's International Exchange Program. The troupe toured Southeast Asia and Australia in 1962; participated in the International Arts Festival at Rio de Janeiro, Brazil, in 1963; performed during the First World Festival of Negro Arts at Dakar, Senegal, in 1966; made its first appearance at the Edinburgh Festival in 1968; and won prizes for best company, best choreography, and best male dancer at the International Dance Festival in Paris in 1970. In that year it went on to make a six-city tour of the USSR.

In 1968, the troupe became the resident company of the Clark Center, New York, where it already was a regular visitor. The following year it appeared in a festival of modern dance at the Billy Rose Theater on Broadway; also in 1969, the company performed at the Brooklyn Academy of Music and remained a resident company there from 1970 through 1972. In 1971, it gave its first performances at New York's City Center and in 1972 became a component company of that theater (under the name The Alvin Ailey City Center Dance Theatre), an arrangement that continued until 1976. A special season in tribute to Duke Ellington (including dances Ailey had made for a television special in 1974) was produced at the New York State Theater at Lincoln Center during the summer of 1976. In the years that followed, the troupe continued to give regular New York seasons at City Center and to tour extensively.

Despite the abundance of works introduced into the company's repertory, few of them have managed to hold the stage for more than a few seasons. The popularity of Ailey's company results from the theatricality of its productions, the muscular, extroverted style of its ensemble, and the strong personalities and physical gifts of individual dancers. The company began its existence with an ensemble of seven dancers plus the choreographer, although guest artists, such as de Lavallade and Matt Turney, sometimes appeared with the group. By 1964, the ensemble had grown to include twelve dancers, including Takako Asakawa, Kelvin Rotardier, and Dudley Williams. In 1965, the troupe acquired three more outstanding members: Miguel Godreau, Clive Thompson, and Judith Jamison—who for more than ten years was the company's undisputed star. Her long body, exuberant style of movement,

and warm personality made her a performer of distinction. [*See the entry on Jamison.*] Other Ailey performers who achieved individual recognition include George Faison, Consuelo Atlas, Thelma Hill, Mari Kajiwara, James Truitte, Donna Wood, and Sara Yarborough. Many Ailey dancers have gone on to teach, choreograph, or direct companies of their own. As a result, Ailey not only provided a company and a place for black dancers but helped black performers and theater personnel move into mainstream American dance.

As a choreographer, Ailey employed a rather limited vocabulary, so comparatively few of his dances have earned high critical acclaim. He did, however, create several quality pieces that remain in the company's repertory, including *Streams* (1970, music by Miloslav Kabeláč); *The Lark Ascending* (1972, music by Ralph Vaughan Williams); *Night Creature* (1974, music by Duke Ellington); and *Memoria* (1979, music by Keith Jarret)—this last has been taken into the repertory of the Royal Danish Ballet. Ailey's more balletic works are characterized by the use of arabesques, long diagonal lines, and clear formal patterns. His jazz-inspired and character dances often employ swirling patterns, strong driving arm movements, huge jumps, and steps that thrust deeply onto the floor.

In 1971, Ailey made a twenty-minute, three-part solo for Jamison to popular music, called *Cry*. The dance pays homage to black women and, like *Revelations*, can be seen as a journey from degradation to defiance, pride, and

ALVIN AILEY AMERICAN DANCE THEATER. *Revelations* at Jacob's Pillow in 1961. The dancers are (left to right) Alvin Ailey, Myrna White, James Truitte, Ella Thompson, and Minnie Marshall. For this performance, danced to taped music, Ailey edited *Revelations* from its original length of one hour and five minutes to its present length of thirty minutes. (Photograph from the archives at Jacob's Pillow, Becket, Massachusetts.)

ALVIN AILEY AMERICAN DANCE THEATER. The enormous popularity of Ailey's *Revelations* was unprecedented. By the late 1980s, it was estimated that the dance had been performed more times than the century-old classic *Swan Lake*. Here, Michele Murray, Kelvin Rotardier, John Medieros, Alma Robinson, Harvey Cohen, and Judith Jamison are pictured in a 1969 performance. (Photograph from the Dance Collection, New York Public Library for the Performing Arts.)

survival. The work makes great physical and emotional demands on the performer and has intense physical and emotional impact on the audience. With this kind of direct powerful statement, Ailey has made his greatest contributions as a choreographer.

In addition to Ailey's output for his own troupe, he created dances for several other companies, including the Joffrey Ballet, the Harkness Ballet, American Ballet Theatre, and the Paris Opera Ballet. *The River* (1970, music by Duke Ellington) was for some time one of American Ballet Theatre's standard closing numbers. In 1966, Ailey choreographed the production of Samuel Barber's 1964 opera *Antony and Cleopatra*, which opened the new Metropolitan Opera House at Lincoln Center. He was also the choreographer for Leonard Bernstein's *Mass* (1971), the inaugural work for the 1972 opening of the Opera House of the Kennedy Center in Washington, D.C.

BIBLIOGRAPHY

Ailey, Alvin, with A. Peter Bailey. *Revelations: The Autobiography of Alvin Ailey*. New York, 1995.

Hering, Doris. "Alvin Ailey and Company." *Dance Magazine* (May 1958): 65–66.

Lewis-Ferguson, Julinda. *Alvin Ailey, Jr.: A Life in Dance*. New York, 1994.

Mazo, Joseph H., and Susan Cook. *The Alvin Ailey American Dance Theater*. New York, 1978.

Moore, William. "Alvin Ailey, 1931–1989." *Ballet Review* 17 (Winter 1990): 12–17.

Rogosin, Elinor. *The Dance Makers: Conversations with American Choreographers*. New York, 1980.

JOSEPH H. MAZO

ALVIN AILEY AMERICAN DANCE THEATER. Hope Clarke and Alvin Ailey performing in a revival of *Blues Suite* at the company's Twentieth Anniversary Gala. (Photograph © 1978 by Jack Vartoogian; used by permission.)

History since 1979

The Alvin Ailey American Dance Theater continued to win accolades and applause for its strong dancers and varied repertory, all under the unwavering creative eye of its founder and leader. The opening program of the fall 1979 New York season was dedicated to the memory of dancer Joyce Trisler, a friend of Alvin Ailey since their early days at Lester Horton's studio in Los Angeles. The following night he premiered *Memoria*, his balletic tribute to Trisler, with Donna Wood as the central figure.

In 1979 Ailey received the Capezio Award. His company completed a successful ten-week tour of Europe and enjoyed ever-increasing popularity. In addition, the company moved to expanded facilities in the Minskoff Building in the theater district. The following year, however, was difficult for Ailey, who was admitted to a psychiatric hospital. Judith Jamison, who had left the company to star in *Sophisticated Ladies* on Broadway, was named acting artistic director. In a *Ballet News* article in May 1980, Ailey commented on the difficulties of surviving as an artist and the responsibilities of running a dance company and school, saying, "I feel that this takes place at at enormous personal sacrifice. It is all-engrossing and keeps me in a state of turmoil all the time."

In a review of a revival of *The Mooche*, Anna Kisselgoff referred to one of Ailey's favorite themes, "the contrast between the popular entertainer's public image and private reality." It was a theme that ran through many of his ballets, including *Flowers* (1971), based on the life of Janis Joplin, for the Royal Ballet's Lynn Seymour; *Au Bord du Precipice*, based on the life of rock star Jim Morrison, for

ALVIN AILEY AMERICAN DANCE THEATER. Sarita Allen in a revival of Ailey's *The Mooche*, created for television in 1974. Allen was only seventeen when Ailey cast her in the sexy role of Marie Bryant. (Photograph © 1980 by Jack Vartoogian; used by permission.)

Patrick Dupond and the Paris Opera Ballet; and *For Bird—With Love* (1985), Ailey's tribute to jazz legend Charlie Parker, for Gary DeLoatch. *Dance Magazine* described the final imagery of this ballet, in which "a white-suited Bird [is] surrounded by whirling dancers in red who show how art outlives the artist. But Ailey has given us something else, too—the pain, love and anguish of his own creative act."

Ailey was always giving, and that generosity was reflected in the emotional range of his ballets and the spirit of his dancers. Pain and beauty went hand in hand in many of Ailey's strongest ballets, as did the message of the difficulty of survival. Throughout the 1980s the Alvin Ailey American Dance Theater continued to inspire audiences throughout the world, though many of the later choreographies were not Ailey's strongest. In 1981 he premiered *Landscapes,* as well as *Spell,* a *pièce d'occasion* for guest

stars Judith Jamison and Alexander Godunov; he also staged his Duke Ellington work, *The River,* originally commissioned by American Ballet Theatre (1970), for his company. The balletic Sara Yarborough returned to the company and in *The River* was praised for her performance in the pas de deux "Lake." That year Billy Wilson presented *Concerto in F* to the music of George Gershwin, and Elisa Monte's *Treading,* set to Steve Reich's "Music for Eighteen Instruments," joined the repertory.

In 1983 the company celebrated its twenty-fifth anniversary, and the following year it achieved another milestone by dancing at the Metropolitan Opera House in New York for two weeks. The year 1985 saw the premiere of Ailey's *For Bird—With Love,* the New York premieres of Judith Jamison's *Divining* and Bill T. Jones and Arnie Zane's *How to Walk an Elephant,* and a revival of Louis Johnson's *Lament.*

In 1986 Ailey premiered *Survivors,* dedicated to the passion and spirit of Nelson and Winnie Mandela; *Witness,* danced to spirituals sung by Jessye Norman; and *Caverna Magica.* The 1987 season was dedicated to Katherine Dun-

ALVIN AILEY AMERICAN DANCE THEATER. Donna Wood (center) with the company in *Memoria* (1979), Ailey's choreographic tribute to his late friend Joyce Trisler. (Photograph © 1979 by Jack Vartoogian; used by permission.)

ham, presenting such works as *Afro-Caribbean Suite,
Choros,* and *L'Ag'ya.* That year he received the Samuel H.
Scripps American Dance Festival Award.

On 4 December 1988 Ailey received the Kennedy Center
Honors from President Ronald Reagan for his lifelong
contribution to modern dance, and "for bridging the gap
between modern dance and the general public in the
United States and abroad." In a *New York Times* article
printed the same day, Ailey is quoted by Anna Kisselgoff
as saying, "I am trying to show the world we are all human beings, that color is not important, that what is important is the quality of our work, of a culture in which
the young are not afraid to take chances and can hold
onto their values and self-esteem, especially in the arts
and in dance." A few weeks later Ailey premiered his last
ballet, *Opus McShann,* set to the music of Kansas City
jazz pianist Jay McShann.

On 1 December 1989, a week before the first performance of the company's annual New York season, Ailey
died of a rare blood disorder. For more than thirty years
he had led one of the finest dance companies in the world
and one of the most visible emblems of African-American
culture and pride, creating seventy-nine ballets.

On 20 December 1989 Judith Jamison was appointed
artistic director of the Alvin Ailey American Dance Theater. Under her aegis the company has continued to grow
while maintaining the original vision of its founder and
mentor. The repertory has flourished, and the dancers
are strong and commanding and can still bring audiences
to their feet. The Ailey organization has grown institu-
tionally as well as artistically. Jamison has initiated an
arts-in-education initiative. AileyCamps, summer programs for middle school children which explores movement and creativity to strengthen self-respect and self-
esteem, are thriving in Kansas City and New York City,
with new camps under development in cities around the
country. The company danced at the Paris Opera in fall
1992 and shortly afterward performed for U.S. president-
elect Bill Clinton on the eve of his inauguration. [*See the
entry on Jamison.*]

Donald Byrd created *Folkdance* in 1992 for the senior
members of the company; Dudley Williams, Sarita
Allen, Marilyn Banks, and Gary DeLoatch; Billy Wilson
choreographed *The Winter in Lisbon* (1992). Jamison
has initiated a Women's Choreography Initiative under
which works such as Jawole Willa Jo Zollar's *Shelter*
(Ailey premiere 1993) and Jamison's own *Hymn* (1993,
libretto by Anna Deveare Smith) and *Riverside* (1995)
were featured. The year 1995 brought the company
premiere of Shapiro and Smith's *Fathers and Sons* and
the company premiere of Lar Lubovitch's *Fandango*
(1990). As of 1995, more than 170 works by sixty-three
choreographers had been performed by the Ailey company.

BIBLIOGRAPHY

Finkel, Anita. "The Road and the River." *New Dance Review* 6 (Winter
1994): 3–7.
Hardy, Camille. "Alvin Ailey American Dance Theater." *Dance Maga-
zine* (October 1992): 48–52.
Jamison, Judith. *Dancing Spirit: An Autobiography.* New York, 1993.
Kisselgoff, Anna. Reviews. *New York Times* (13 December 1979, 15
December 1985, 4 December 1988).
Mazo, Joseph H. "Ailey & Company." *Horizon* (July–August 1984):
18–24.
Mitchell, Jack. *Alvin Ailey American Dance Theater.* Kansas City, 1993.
Reiter, Susan. "Company Revelations: Ailey Men Step Forward."
Dance Magazine (December 1991): 40–44.
Sandler, Ken. "Footnotes." *Ballet News* 2 (July 1980): 6–8.
Sorens, Ina. "A Conversation with David Parsons." *Ballet Review* 22
(Winter 1994): 64–75.
Terhoeven, Andreas. "The Exotic Is No Longer Demanded." *Ballett In-
ternational* 13 (June–July 1990): 37–39.
Willinger, Edward. "Come and Get the Beauty of It Hot." *New Dance
Review* 3 (January–March 1991): 11–13.
Wilson, Arthur T. "Dance! Dance! Dance!" *Attitude* 11 (Spring 1995):
12–17.

HOWARD S. KAPLAN

AMAGATSU USHIO (born 31 December 1949 in Yoko-
suka, Kanagawa Prefecture, Japan), *butō* performer and
choreographer. Amagatsu studied ballet and the Martha

AMAGATSU USHIO. The founder of the *butō* company Sankai Juku
in his dance work *Kinkan Shonen.* (Photograph by Jack Vartoogian;
used by permission.)

Graham method from 1968 to 1972. He joined Maro Akaji's Dai Rakudakan in 1972, becoming a principal dancer with the troupe. In 1975 he founded the Sankai Juku company, becoming its sole choreographer and its principal dancer; his company's first works, *Amagatsu Sho* and *Kinkan Shonen* were presented in 1977 and 1978, respectively, in Tokyo.

Sankai Juku toured Europe in 1980 and in 1982 signed a contract with the Théâtre de la Ville in Paris to choreograph and present one piece every other year; works produced under this contract have included *Jomon Sho* (1982), *Netsu no Katachi* (1984), *Unetsu* (1986), *Shijima* (1988), *Omote* (1991), and *Yuragi* (1993). In 1989 Amagatsu was appointed to a term as artistic director of the Spiral Hall performance space in Tokyo and served as chief judge of the Bagnolet international choreography competition in Bagnolet, France.

Sankai Juku's works are influenced by mysticism, the ancient religions of Japan, and ritualistic aspects of Buddhism. Amagatsu's frequent collaboration with the visual artist Nakanishi Natsuyuki and the musician Yaskaz has enhanced these characteristics.

BIBLIOGRAPHY

Adolphe, Jean-Marc. "Pastimes of the Gods: The Mythological Modernity of Ushio Amagatsu." *Ballett International* 8 (August–September 1994): 60–63.

Brissenden, Alan. "Magnet for Audiences." *Dance Australia*, no. 36 (June–July 1988): 53–54.

Christout, Marie-Françoise. "Légendes du XXᵉ siècle." *Saisons de la Danse*, no. 225 (June 1991): 24–25.

Hering, Doris. Review. *Dance Magazine* (January 1991): 93.

Kaplan, Peggy Jarrell. *Portraits of Choreographers*. New York, 1988.

Mackintosh, Peri. "Jomon sho, by Sankai Juku." *Dance Theatre Journal* 1 (August 1983): 29–30.

Paszkowska, Alexandra. *Butō-Tanz: Ushio Amagatsu und die Sankai Juku Gruppe*. Munich, 1983.

Welzien, Leonore. "Was mich interessiert sind Fragen." *Tanzdrama Magazin*, no. 25 (1994): 4–7.

HASEGAWA ROKU
Translated from Japanese

AMAYA, CARMEN (Carmen Amaya y Amaya; born 3 November c.1913 in Barcelona, died 19 November 1963 in Bagur, Spain), Gypsy flamenco dancer. Amaya, in a majestic and creative way, gathered the power of the traditional flamenco art form to bring this dance to an unequaled height of popularity in the 1930s, 1940s, and 1950s. Her innovations left a permanent impression on her contemporaries, as well as on dancers who followed. By the end of her life, those innovations had been completely integrated into the flamenco dance vocabulary.

Amaya spent her early years in the Somorrostro, a Gypsy squatter settlement on the beach near Barcelona. Her mother, Micaela, was an excellent dancer, although she danced only at private gatherings. Her father, José Amaya, "El Chino," was a guitarist. Amaya was the second of six surviving children, all of whom became flamenco artists. Amaya's grandparents were from Barcelona, Aragon, and Andalusia, where Gypsy families had been performing flamenco professionally since the nineteenth century.

Amaya began dancing professionally at the age of four. Her childhood was spent performing alongside her father in the taverns and the music halls of Barcelona. Still a preteenager, she performed in a Paris review, took Madrid by storm, and toured Spain accompanied on the guitar by her father and her older brother Paco. By 1936 she was an emerging star in Spain. She had made two films, *La Hija de Juan Simón* in 1935 and *María de la O* in 1936. She had also appeared in the prestigious Salón Variedades de Sevilla, where legend says that the two most important flamenco dancers of the turn of the century, La Malena and La Macarrona, were moved to tears seeing her perform.

This endorsement of Amaya's popular fame as a continuation of flamenco traditions is surprising, considering the great contrast between her movement and presentational style and that of her illustrious predecessors. Despite the fact that the pronounced gender distinctions of Gypsy culture are evident in the traditional dance, Amaya danced her trademark solo, an *alegrías*, in male costume. Typically, in flamenco, the male dances from the waist down. He holds his chest out, shifting his body weight over the metatarsals, and creates strong, rhythmic patterns with his feet. The female dances from the waist up. She carries her weight back over her heels, in a "seated," bent-knee position. The male dance communicates virility, agility, and skill in sleight of hand. The female dance communicates graciousness, sensitivity, and majesty. In developing a personal, yet commercially viable style, Carmen Amaya drew from both male and female dance styles.

Amaya learned the feminine dance from her mother and from her aunt, La Faraona, as well as from preeminent dancers of the day, such as La Macarrona, La Malena, La Tanguera, and La Salud. She assimilated the male dance from her father and from a family friend, Raphael "El Gato," a principal exponent of a virile dance called the *farruca*. Amaya incorporated male footwork techniques into her dance. The fast footwork was very commercial and had far-reaching effects on her technique. She was forced to shift her weight from the traditional backward leaning of women forward over the metatarsals to achieve velocity. From this center of balance, she could execute sharp, percussive movement that had previously been the province of males. Her speed was, in flamenco terms, a male rather than a female quality. Yet, the constant realignment of weight from back to front caused an undulation along her spine that was reflective of female upper-body sensitivity.

AMAYA. Drawing from both male and female styles of flamenco, Carmen Amaya became a major innovator and exponent of the genre. She is seen here in a typically masculine flamenco costume, c.1955. (Photograph by Alfredo Valente; from the Dance Collection, New York Public Library for the Performing Arts.)

Before Amaya, female dancers from Spain's Golden Age theaters through the Romantic-era ballets of the nineteenth century had occasionally danced *en travesti*, and within the flamenco tradition La Salud and La Cuenca had worn male costumes. However, Amaya's great commercial success in pants strengthened and highlighted a hitherto submerged strain of female flamenco dancing; she personified in her dance the image of the Gypsy woman as a fiery, powerful, indomitable creature. In male costume Amaya performed long, high-speed footwork solos and multiple fast turns. She did not limit herself to male costume or to the male movement vocabulary but also tossed her long black hair and dressed in bright, glittery dresses. She lengthened the train of her Spanish dancer's costume to fifteen feet (4.5 meters, more than three times her height). She used the train to spectacular effect by wrapping it slowly around her and then kicking it so that it would unwind in midair.

In 1936 Amaya was performing in Valladolid when civil war broke out in Spain. She escaped to Lisbon, Portugal, and from there accepted a contract in Buenos Aires, Argentina, eventually bringing her whole family to perform with her in South America. She created a tremendous stir

wherever she performed, and in December 1940 the impresario Sol Hurok contracted her to come to New York City. In January 1941 Carmen Amaya made her debut at a club called the Beachcomber. Her company included Sabícas, the most important flamenco guitarist of his generation. Media and public attention were heaped on Amaya. She was asked to perform for President Franklin D. Roosevelt, and she contracted for Hollywood films and Broadway plays. She debuted at New York City's Carnegie Hall on 13 January 1942 to mixed reviews that called her "exciting," but "wild" and her dancing "not art."

Amaya toured the United States, South America, and Europe for the rest of her life. In 1947 she returned to Spain and was received with great popular and critical acclaim. In 1951 she married Juan Antonio Aguero, a non-Gypsy from an aristocratic family. Amaya returned to the United States in 1955, after a ten-year absence. This time she received unadulterated praise for her "finely etched [stage] portrait" and new "artistic maturity." Amaya had distilled her dancing, removing excessive turns, footwork, and flyaway hair. She had replaced them with the female expression of silence, a stillness in which her upper body was brought into focus by slow, sustained movement of the arms, her face reflecting her inner life with great subtlety.

In 1962 she made the film *La Historia de los Tarantos,* a tragic love story set in the Gypsy neighborhoods of Barcelona where Amaya had grown up. One day on the set, Amaya fainted. She was diagnosed as having sclerosis of the kidneys too far advanced to be healed. When Carmen Amaya died the following year, her funeral was attended by more than two thousand people.

[*See also* Flamenco Dance.]

BIBLIOGRAPHY

Bois, Mario. "Carmen Amaya o la danza del fuego." *Espasa Calpe* (1994).

Goldberg, K. Meira. "Border Trespasses: The Gypsy Mask and Carmen Amaya's Flamenco Dance." Ph.D. diss., Temple University, 1995.

Sevilla, Paco. "Carmen Amaya." *Jaleo Magazine* (November 1980).

Weinzweig Goldberg, Meira. "Through the Eyes of the Critics: Selected American Perceptions of the Evolution in Carmen Amaya's Flamenco Style." *Jaleo Magazine* 8.4 (1986).

Weinzweig Goldberg, Meira. "Carmen Amaya Wore Pants: Flamenco as a Forum for Cross-Gender Identification in Spanish Gypsy Culture." In *Proceedings of the 1987 Congress on Research in Dance,* edited by Ruth Abrahams. New York, 1989.

Weinzweig Goldberg, Meira. "Flamenco Fire: Form as Generated by the Performer-Audience Relationship." In *100 Years of Gypsy Studies,* edited by Matt T. Salo. Cheverly, Md., 1990.

Weinzweig Goldberg, Meira. "A 'Heart of Darkness' in the New World: Carmen Amaya's Flamenco Dance in South American Vaudeville." *Choreography and Dance* 3.4 (1994).

RECORDINGS. *Queen of the Gypsies* (Decca DL 9816), with guitarist Sabícas. *Furia Amaya* (Decca DL 9094), with guitarist Juan Maya "Marote."

MEIRA K. GOLDBERG

AMERICAN BALLET, a short-lived (1934–1938) and controversial company, the first company headed by George Balanchine after his arrival in the United States in 1933. The American Ballet brought Balanchine into conflict with the prevailing artistic sensibility of the time—notably unsophisticated in regard to dance—and in a sense began the process of developing America's understanding and appreciation of ballet.

Lincoln Kirstein first met Balanchine in Europe in the mid-1920s. He arranged, partly through the influence of his own fortune and partly through that of former Harvard classmate Edward M. M. Warburg, for Balanchine to come to the United States and found the first truly American classical ballet company. Another friend, A. Everett Austin, director of the Wadsworth Atheneum, a museum that is part of the Morgan Memorial Library in Hartford, Connecticut, was attempting to make the Atheneum's new three-hundred-seat Avery Memorial Theatre into a center of avant-garde art. When Warburg guaranteed at least two years of financial support, the Morgan Memorial seemed a logical place to locate the Balanchine enterprise. Balanchine, however, balked at this remote provincial locale and, at the end of 1933, established his first organization, the School of American Ballet, on New York's Madison Avenue.

As early as June 1934, students of the school were presenting a ballet by Balanchine, an early version of *Serenade*, at the Warburg estate near White Plains, New York. But the American Ballet had not yet quite come into being, and a program put on in Hartford that December,

AMERICAN BALLET. Lew Christensen and Annabelle Lyon in *Orpheus and Eurydice* (1936). This production, designed by Pavel Tchelitchev, was considered a critical failure. (Photograph from the Dance Collection, New York Public Library for the Performing Arts.)

AMERICAN BALLET. Rabana Hasburgh, Daphne Vane, and Heidi Vosseler (standing), with Hortense Karklin and Helen Leitch (seated) in George Balanchine's *Mozartiana*. Originally created in Paris, this ballet premiered with the company in Hartford, Connecticut, in 1934. (Photograph from the Dance Collection, New York Public Library for the Performing Arts.)

more elaborate and involving a number of works presented over three nights, was still billed as "the Producing Company of the School of American Ballet."

Most critics approved of only one of the works on the program, *Alma Mater*, which conformed to their notion of what "American ballet" meant—that is, Americana subject matter. *Alma Mater*, with a scenario by Warburg, designs by John Held, Jr., and music by a friend of Warburg's, Kay Swift (orchestrated by Morton Gould), was a spoof of college life and football games. It alone was perceived as being wholesomely, productively "American," as opposed to European and "decadent." *New York Times* dance critic John Martin scolded the troupe after its Hartford debut:

> [Balanchine] constitutes a problem. It is too much to expect him to acquire for many years a feeling of [what is] America . . . and he must inevitably put the stamp of Europe upon his pupils and dancers . . . It is incumbent upon you to find and encourage native choreographers at any cost. . . . Let [your audience] see . . . that the American ballet is classless in its appeal, functional rather than decorative and expressive of a home-grown and not an imported outlook.

Three months later, the company, billing itself for the first time as the American Ballet, had a season in New

York City at the Adelphi Theatre, a Broadway house. Ticket sales were strong enough to encourage the young directors of the troupe to extend the season for a week. Although a success with the public, it was not the darling of the critics. John Martin seized the occasion to nominate *Serenade* and three new Balanchine ballets, *Dreams, Errante,* and *Transcendence,* as "evidences of the decadence of the classic tradition." Warburg, Kirstein, and Balanchine invited theater critics and intellectuals to the Adelphi and these, while more tolerant than the dance critics, were likewise bewildered. Writing in *The Nation,* Kenneth Burke ruminated: "Foremost among the processes of vicarious atonement is the ballet." He permitted dance a very few effects: "Courtliness . . . which is a troublesome offering, a thought out of season"; and "allegory, or symbolism, which makes in the end for a few basic patterns of pictorial interest, the *spectacle,* with all that it entails in the way of decadence."

On 12 August and again one week later, the American Ballet performed at the College of the City of New York's outdoor amphitheater, Lewisohn Stadium, and was again enthusiastically received by the public. A surprise result of these performances was the invitation from one impressed spectator, Edward Johnson, the newly appointed general manager of the Metropolitan Opera, that the American Ballet become the opera's resident dance company.

If Balanchine had had trouble awakening the critics to the essence of ballet and establishing his own vision of what could be "American" in ballet, he had even less luck with the hidebound Metropolitan management, which did not allow him the separate ballet evenings he had been led to expect nor approve his experiments with the opera-ballets themselves. Three trouble-fraught seasons (1935–1938) were punctuated by one critical disaster—the Tchelitchev-designed *Orpheus and Eurydice* (1936), featuring singers in the pit and dancers (led by Lew Christensen, William Dollar, and Daphne Vane) onstage and considered a "travesty" by most reviewers—and one triumph, the two-day Stravinsky Festival of April 1937, which saw the American premiere of *Apollo* (with Lew Christensen and Elise Reiman), a production of *Le Baiser de la Fée* (with Dollar, Kathryn Mullowney, and Gisella Caccialanza), and a new ballet commissioned by Warburg, *Card Party* (Dollar, Annabelle Lyon, and Leda Anchutina).

Despite the festival's success, Warburg lost interest in the American Ballet and withdrew his support at the end of September. Balanchine and some of his dancers had spent the time between Metropolitan Opera seasons in Hollywood filming *The Goldwyn Follies.* Balanchine asked Vladimir Dimitriev, director of the School of American Ballet, who also served the American Ballet as an unofficial adviser, to help with the company's management.

Dimitriev invited Jacques Lidji, a French attorney, to become director, but Lidji proved ineffectual; in March 1938 the Metropolitan Opera, by failing to renew Balanchine's contract, essentially put an end to the American Ballet.

In a letter currently in the files of the Dance Collection, Balanchine wrote a judgment that perhaps best expresses the difficulty he and Americans of culture and ideas had in understanding one another: "I accepted my job at the Metropolitan primarily because I felt that perhaps the men inside would help me expand and enrich that noblest and most aristocratic of all theatrical art—THE BALLET." Nobility and aristocracy were not, apparently, valued as classical, timeless values in America in the mid-1930s.

The American Ballet was briefly revived in 1941; it was merged with Kirstein's independent entity, Ballet Caravan, and was sent by Assistant Secretary Nelson Rockefeller on a U.S. State Department tour of South America.

[*See also the entries on Balanchine and Kirstein.*]

BIBLIOGRAPHY

Chujoy, Anatole. *The New York City Ballet.* New York, 1953.

Kirstein, Lincoln. *The New York City Ballet.* New York, 1973.

Reynolds, Nancy. *Repertory in Review: Forty Years of the New York City Ballet.* New York, 1977.

Taper, Bernard. *Balanchine: A Biography.* New rev. ed. New York, 1984.

ARCHIVE.   The clippings and scrapbook files of the Dance Collection, New York Public Library for the Performing Arts, are essential; see in particular, "Lincoln Kirstein" (vols. 1–2) and "New York City Ballet" (vols. 1–2).

ANITA FINKEL

AMERICAN BALLET THEATRE.   The world's major ballet companies tend to have three elements in common. They are usually guided by an artistic director who is also a choreographer. They have a home theater with attendant rehearsal halls, storage space, and technical shops. And they sustain their own training school.

These factors have not been consistently at work in American Ballet Theatre, one of the world's leading ballet companies. Most of its directors have not been choreographers. Richard Pleasant, the founding director, was trained as an architect and, after leaving the company in 1941, turned to press-agentry. Lucia Chase, who with set designer Oliver Smith became co-director in 1945 and remained at the helm until 1980, was a wealthy woman with training in theater and dance. Mikhail Baryshnikov, who had been a principal dancer with the company between 1974 and 1978, succeeded them in 1980. He confined his choreographic talents to restaging existing works. In 1990 Jane Hermann, an impresario, followed Baryshnikov. Oliver Smith returned as her associate. In 1992 Kevin McKenzie, a former principal dancer with the company, became artistic director. Although he had initiated a choreographic career with the Washington Ballet, this was not to be his priority with American Ballet Theatre.

The company does not have a permanent home in New York City, its birthplace. In 1977 it did become the principal attraction at the Metropolitan Opera House once the opera season ended. Before that its New York bases included the Center Theater, the Broadway Theater, the Fifty-fourth Street Theater, the Majestic Theater, the Uris Theater, the original Metropolitan Opera House, the New York State Theater, the Brooklyn Academy of Music, and the City Center of Music and Drama.

Between 1951 and 1982 there was a company school. Its principal teaching style was Russian, with Bronislava Nijinska the founding director and Valentina Pereyaslavec its most influential teacher between 1951 and the demise of the school.

Several significant choreographers, most notably Antony Tudor and Agnes de Mille, devoted much of their output to American Ballet Theatre, but the company style has never been formed by a single choreographic mind. And so its image and the focus of its repertory have undergone many changes. Despite these seeming limitations, American Ballet Theatre is noted for its vitality, its resiliency, and the variety of its repertory.

The name American Ballet Theatre was adopted by the company in 1957, when it undertook its first tour of Europe and the Middle East, sponsored by the American National Theater and Academy (ANTA) and the U.S. State Department. Before that it was called Ballet Theatre, which clearly implied that the company relied on classical technique shaped to theatrical and dramatic purposes. Much of its repertory has gone in this direction.

American Ballet Theatre has not consistently adhered to Richard Pleasant's credo, but its essence seems to have been a subtle guiding factor. It is summed up in this quote from the company's 1941 souvenir program:

> The gallery idea is a translation from museum to dance terms of a system which can comprehend the collection and display of masterpieces of all times, places, and creators, with the provision that they attain a certain standard of excellence.

This credo strongly flavored the early days of Ballet Theatre and prevented the company style and repertory from being merely an extension of nineteenth-century Russia. Aesthetically, this was the Russia of Mikhail Mordkin, whose company, formed in 1937, was the cradle of Ballet Theatre.

Mordkin was from Moscow, and his own dancing style was flamboyant. In 1923 he immigrated to New York and opened a school. The Mordkin Ballet began as a modest performing outlet for his advanced students, notably Lucia Chase, Leon Danielian, Viola Essen, Dimitri Romanoff, and Leon Varkas. Rudolf Orthwine, a printer with

AMERICAN BALLET THEATRE. *Giselle* with (from left to right) Sonia Arova, Alicia Alonso, and Igor Youskevitch, c.1946. Alonso and Youskevitch, who danced together for many years, are perhaps most associated with this Romantic classic. (Photograph from the Dance Collection, New York Public Library for the Performing Arts.)

a lifelong interest in theater and dance, became president of the Mordkin Ballet. Richard Pleasant, a man of taste and vision, was selected to be managing director. He soon began to think beyond Mordkin's old-fashioned ballets, such as *The Goldfish* and *Souvenir of Roses*. He also began to enlarge the roster of principals by adding such dancers as Patricia Bowman, Edward Caton, Karen Conrad, Vladimir Dokoudovsky, and Nina Stroganova.

Lucia Chase generously matched Pleasant's dreams with cash. His dreams were big. He envisaged three wings, or influences, for the repertory. The classical wing would be in the hands of Anton Dolin, who had begun his career in the Ballets Russes de Serge Diaghilev. The American wing would be under the young American choreographer Eugene Loring. The British wing would be directed by a British choreographer as yet unknown in the United States, Antony Tudor. The company's press image was entrusted to Isadora Bennett, a woman of vast theatrical erudition.

The opening night of Ballet Theatre took place on 11 January 1940 at the spacious Center Theater in New York's Radio City. It was a triumph. The curtains parted, as they would innumerable times thereafter, on Michel Fokine's *Les Sylphides*. Fokine had personally rehearsed the ballet, and to perform the Mazurka he had selected Karen Conrad, whose elevation was to become legendary. The touch of novelty on that glorious night was Eugene Loring's *The Great American Goof*, based on a text by William Saroyan. The program closed with Mordkin's *Voices of Spring*, the only one of his works to make the transition into Ballet Theatre.

As that first three-week season went by, it was clear that the promises made in the prospectus were being fulfilled.

AMERICAN BALLET THEATRE. Nora Kaye and Hugh Laing in *Undertow* (1945), choreographed by Antony Tudor to a commissioned score by William Schuman. The costumes and the nightmarish scenery were designed by Raymond Breinin. (Photograph from the Dance Collection, New York Public Library for the Performing Arts.)

The classical repertory was represented by *Giselle* and *Swan Lake* (act 2), both staged by Anton Dolin, and *La Fille Mal Gardée*, staged by Bronislava Nijinska. Antony Tudor provided the American premieres of his *Jardin aux Lilas, The Judgment of Paris,* and *Dark Elegies.* Fokine staged *Le Carnaval.* There were American premieres of British choreographer Andrée Howard's *Death and the Maiden* and *Lady into Fox.* And there were what might be called novelties: Yurek Shabelevsky's *Ode to Glory,* Adolph Bolm's *Mechanical Ballet* and *Peter and the Wolf,* José Fernandez's *Goyescas,* Agnes de Mille's *Black Ritual (Obeah),* which used a black cast; and Anton Dolin's *Quintet, or The Adventures of Don and Dolores from New York to Holly-*

wood and Back. Most of these works and their casting made one believe that perhaps the legend on the title page of the first souvenir program had validity: "Advanced Arts Ballets, Inc. presents The Ballet Theatre, America's First Ballet Theatre staged by the Greatest Collaboration in Ballet History."

Within a year an important administrative change had taken place. Richard Pleasant left his post, and impresario Sol Hurok took the company under his wing. One of his first acts was to reduce the company size from sixty-two dancers to forty-nine. He then resorted to the time-worn device of calling the season "The Greatest in Russian Ballet by the Ballet Theatre." The magic word *Russian* was deemed necessary to sell tickets.

By 1942, Hurok's influence could be strongly seen in the choice of repertory. Fokine revived *Petrouchka* and began working on *Helen of Troy.* His death left the latter unfinished. Léonide Massine contributed *Aleko* (1942); *Don*

Domingo de Don Blas (1942); *La Boutique Fantasque*, billed as *The Fantastic Toyshop* (1943); *Capriccio Espagnol* (1943); and *Le Tricorne*, billed as *The Three-Cornered Hat* (1943). David Lichine revised and completed *Helen of Troy* (1942). The only important respite from this Slavic onslaught was the world premiere of Antony Tudor's *Romeo and Juliet* (1943). Instead of using the familiar score by Sergei Prokofiev, Tudor turned to the delicately textured music of Frederick Delius. Eugene Berman contributed a Renaissance decor simple in structure yet grand in effect. And the ballet was a particularly fine vehicle for ballerina Alicia Markova, who performed with a youthful impetuousness far removed from her usual Romantic style.

In 1945, under the co-direction of Lucia Chase and Oliver Smith, Ballet Theatre became the first American company to visit England. The trip did a great deal for the morale of the dancers and management. At this point Ballet Theatre was beginning to be rich in dancers and reper-

tory, but it was very much an itinerant troupe, still without a New York home and without a company school. Most of its continuity of style came from Dimitri Romanoff, who became *régisseur* in 1948 and was particularly skilled at styling the classical repertory.

Leading a growing cadre of distinctive young American dancers was Nora Kaye. For twenty years she was virtually the symbol of Ballet Theatre. Antony Tudor had plucked her from the corps de ballet to assume the principal role in his *Pillar of Fire* (1942), the first world premiere he created for the company. It would be difficult to say whether he created the ballet for her or created her for the ballet. As the repressed and yearning Hagar in search of enduring love, Kaye performed with heartrending vulnerability. As the man with whom Hagar was to find love, Tudor cast himself in a role whose significance lay in its deliberate understatement. This was conceivably the prototype for the minister in Agnes de Mille's *Fall River Legend* (1948). Tudor used Hugh Laing as the lascivious Young Man from the House Opposite in *Pillar of Fire*. Laing, who had come from England with Tudor, was not a virtuoso dancer, but he was a consummate actor with the ability to make stillness even more significant than move-

AMERICAN BALLET THEATRE. The ensemble with Alicia Alonso and Igor Youskevitch, the original principals, in George Balanchine's landmark ballet *Theme and Variations* (1947). (Photograph from the Dance Collection, New York Public Library for the Performing Arts. Choreography by George Balanchine © The George Balanchine Trust.)

ment. In 1945 Tudor created for him the principal role of the sexually conflicted adolescent in *Undertow.*

While Antony Tudor was embarking upon the most productive part of his long association with Ballet Theatre, two young American choreographers emerged: Jerome Robbins and Michael Kidd. Robbins, a witty and resourceful character dancer with the company, created his first work, *Fancy Free,* in 1944. Drawing upon the most plebeian of themes—three sailors on shore leave and their efforts to impress some girls—it was a genre masterpiece. The ballet's inventive and idiomatic choreography was the work of a young man with a keen eye for the world around him, no matter how prosaic that world seemed to others. Michael Kidd, also a character dancer, began with a genre ballet called *On Stage!* (1945). It featured Kidd as a shy stagehand encouraging Nora Kaye as an equally shy dancer with aspirations to be a ballerina.

The first important classical work to enter the Ballet Theatre repertory was George Balanchine's *Theme and Variations,* which had its premiere in 1947. It featured Alicia Alonso, who, like Nora Kaye, had risen from the corps, and Igor Youskevitch, the first true *danseur noble* acquired by the company. Danced to Tchaikovsky's Suite no. 3 in G Major, the work had a dignity and an amplitude important for a company perhaps too heavily steeped in character ballets. It also made challenging new technical demands on the corps as well as on the soloists.

Ballet Theatre's last important world premiere came in 1948, when Agnes de Mille created *Fall River Legend.* It was typical of the "psychoanalytical forties," and like Antony Tudor's *Pillar of Fire* and *Undertow,* it explored

how an individual solves emotional repression. In this case, de Mille dealt with the New England spinster Lizzie Borden, who was accused of murdering her father and stepmother with an ax, and who in the ballet is shown as guilty of those crimes. Although Alicia Alonso was the first tormented Lizzie, with John Kriza as her understanding pastor, the role was subsequently associated with Nora Kaye, while Alonso moved on to classical roles, notably Giselle.

The first decade of Ballet Theatre contained more world premieres than any other period in the company's history. Moreover, *Pillar of Fire, Romeo and Juliet, Fancy Free, Undertow, Theme and Variations,* and *Fall River Legend* remained almost continuously in the repertory.

During those first years it looked as though Antony Tudor was the resident choreographer, but after 1950 his output was to become more sporadic. In 1956 there was *Offenbach in the Underworld,* a satire on Léonide Massine's *Gaîté Parisienne,* which Tudor had first done for the Philadelphia Ballet Guild. It was not until 1975 that he again created a world premiere for the company. *The Leaves Are Fading* featured Gelsey Kirkland as a woman looking back upon her past. That same year he also added *Shadowplay,* originally done for the Royal Ballet.

One reason for the slackening in Tudor's productivity for Ballet Theatre had to do with the company's unending search for a home. In 1950, Rudolf Bing, general manager of the Metropolitan Opera, offered what seemed like a solution. Ballet Theatre would be in residence there; Tudor would teach at the Metropolitan Opera Ballet School and would be responsible for the opera ballets. Nana Gollner was engaged as *prima ballerina.*

The experiment lasted for one season—just as the Metropolitan Opera's hiring of George Balanchine and the American Ballet in 1935 had ended after a similarly brief interval. But Antony Tudor stayed on as director of the Metropolitan Opera Ballet School until 1967. And because Nora Kaye, Hugh Laing, and Diana Adams had left Ballet Theatre to join the New York City Ballet, Tudor staged *The Lady of the Camellias* in 1951 and *La Gloire* in 1952 for the latter company.

In 1952 the Ballet Theatre repertory shrank to twenty-two works; only five years earlier there had been forty. That same year Agnes de Mille contributed *The Harvest According,* and, in 1956, *Rib of Eve.* Neither outlived the season of its birth.

Immediately following the 1957 tour, for which the company changed its name to American Ballet Theatre, it visited twenty-three cities in the United States. In 1958 it went on to represent the United States at the Brussels World Fair. En route a fire destroyed the sets, costumes, and scores of sixteen ballets. Assisted by several European companies, American Ballet Theatre managed to fulfill its Brussels commitment. This was followed by another gru-

AMERICAN BALLET THEATRE. Members of the company in Frederick Ashton's *Les Patineurs,* which takes as its scenario events at a skating rink. This ballet, originally choreographed in 1937, was first presented by Ballet Theatre in 1946 with new scenery designed by Cecil Beaton. (Photograph from the Dance Collection, New York Public Library for the Performing Arts.)

eling tour of twenty-one cities in North Africa and Europe. The company then numbered between forty-two and forty-nine dancers. The principals were Nora Kaye, who had returned from the New York City Ballet, John Kriza, Erik Bruhn, Lupe Serrano, Violette Verdy, Scott Douglas, Ruth Ann Koesun, Michael Lland, and, by the end of the decade, Royes Fernandez.

In a valiant effort to offset the aridity that had crept into its repertory and structure, the company initiated the first of a series of spring choreography workshops in 1956 at New York's Phoenix Theater. The idea was to produce as many ballets as possible in a modest format and then to mount the successful ones on the company. Herbert Ross was the most promising choreographer to emerge from the project, although he was not new to American Ballet Theatre. In 1950 it had acquired his *Caprichos* after it was produced for an independent project called Choreographers' Workshop, sponsored by German dancer Trudy Goth.

In *Caprichos* Ross had evoked the Spanish Inquisition as seen through the etchings of the Spanish painter Francisco Goya. For the 1951 season Ross had produced a trifle called *The Thief Who Loved a Ghost,* but not until the Ballet Theatre Workshops was he stimulated to create a succession of works. Had he continued beyond the first series of ideational extremes, he might have become the resident choreographer the company so desperately needed. In 1957 Ross produced *Paean* and *The Maids. Paean,* a well-wrought combination of classical formality and Romantic intent, immediately entered the Ballet Theatre repertory. *The Maids,* based on the Jean Genet play, snarled and grappled its way through the pain of sexual ambiguity. Although in some ways it was superior to *Paean,* its subject matter prevented it from being accepted into the repertory. Instead, in 1968 it turned up in Eliot Feld's American Ballet Company. The Ballet Theatre Workshop of 1958 contained three Ross works, *Ovid Metamorphoses, Concerto,* and *Tristan.* In *Ovid Metamorphoses* and *Tristan,* Ross was again concerned with aspects of sexuality. *Concerto* was probably his first and last attempt at nonprogrammatic dance. In 1960 he staged *Dialogues* directly on the company.

That same spring American Ballet Theatre was again on a plateau. The other company premieres, Birgit Cullberg's *Lady from the Sea* and Serge Lifar's *Pas et Lignes,* seemed far indeed from the early dream of a repertory balanced between works that would emphasize dance values and works that would emphasize human values. The company was scheduled for a trip to the Soviet Union in 1960, but the project was almost canceled. It was felt that, drained by excessive touring and with no outstanding new ballets, the company might make a poor showing. It embarked on a European tour, during which a panel of experts went over to decide whether the Russian tour should be included. The company had miraculously pulled itself together. A sold-out tour of Kiev, Moscow, Tblisi, and Leningrad resulted.

Maria Tallchief, Erik Bruhn, and Toni Lander joined the company as guest artists in the Soviet Union. The following season Lander became a principal dancer with the company. Further strength was added when Fernand Nault became ballet master. Like Dimitri Romanoff, he was a meticulous stylist. No world premieres were added after the return from the Soviet Union, but a company premiere of enduring value and charm emerged. It was Harald Lander's *Études,* a lively and demanding exploration of the classic vocabulary, which proved to be a touchstone—and test—for the dancers in virtually every season to follow.

American Ballet Theatre still had no home. But the Washington Ballet Guild, without a company of its own since the death of founding director Lisa Gardiner in 1956, seemed to be coming to the rescue. It offered the Washington School of Ballet as a home for eleven weeks

each year. In the spring of 1962, American Ballet Theatre performed *Billy the Kid* for President and Mrs. John F. Kennedy at the White House. The following November the company moved to its new home, the nation's capital, which, it was hoped, would offer sorely needed geographic stability. But in spring 1963 the bubble burst. The Washington Ballet Guild voted to "back" but not "subsidize" the company. Again the dancers became nomads. By 1964 they had visited more than 350 cities in forty-five countries on five continents. But there were only fourteen works in the repertory.

The year 1965 brought new hope to the arts in the United States with the beginning of the National Endowment for the Arts. It was a year of triple significance for American Ballet Theatre. Celebrating its twenty-fifth anniversary, the company made a decisive step toward reviving full-length works from the past. This had been in its original manifesto, but little had been done about it. First came Harald Lander's staging of *La Sylphide,* with Toni Lander and Royes Fernandez in the principal roles. This was to begin the strongest trend in American Ballet Theatre repertory since the halcyon days of Antony Tudor.

The company also had not had a world premiere in seventeen years. Now Jerome Robbins returned with *Les Noces* to the celebrated Stravinsky score first used by Bronislava Nijinska. While preserving the primitive naiveté of a Russian peasant wedding, the ballet had the transcendent look of a ceremony set in motion by the tempestuous yet sophisticated score and by the backdrop of two huge, thoughtful icons created by Oliver Smith.

La Sylphide and *Les Noces* also exerted a practical influence. The newly formed National Endowment for the

AMERICAN BALLET THEATRE. Members of the company in Harald Lander's *Études.* Originally choreographed for the Royal Danish Ballet in 1948, Lander revised and restaged this work for American Ballet Theatre in 1961. (Photograph from the Dance Collection, New York Public Library for the Performing Arts.)

AMERICAN BALLET THEATRE. Scott Douglas and Lupe Serrano in the Waltz section of Michel Fokine's *Les Sylphides*. (Photograph from the Dance Collection, New York Public Library for the Performing Arts.)

Arts gave the company an emergency matching grant of $1 million. This was supplemented by an additional $250,000 to support its tour. And tour it did, with the longest journey thus far.

The New York City Ballet was considered a classical company. Its director, George Balanchine, came from the nineteenth-century world of Marius Petipa. And yet he was very much a man of the present. With Igor Stravinsky he created a mode that might be called twentieth-century classical. Perhaps because it did not have a Balanchine, American Ballet Theatre was far less oblique in its approach to the nineteenth century. It went directly to the source and acquired, one by one, a roster of museum pieces. Its first version of *La Sylphide* was so valuable that Erik Bruhn was asked to restage it in 1971 and again in 1983.

In 1966 David Blair of the Royal Ballet did a full-length *Swan Lake* for the Atlanta Ballet. Lupe Serrano was Odette-Odile to Blair's Siegfried. Later that year Blair repeated the production for American Ballet Theatre. Serrano was again the Odette-Odile, with Royes Fernandez as her prince. Verismo mime and dramatic logic were Blair touchstones, and they suited the company well. At the same time it began to extend itself, to grow more confident in the classical segments.

The following summer Blair staged *Giselle* for the Atlanta Ballet. Again the version was taken into American Ballet Theatre. In 1968 it replaced Anton Dolin's twenty-eight-year-old version. The most durable and beloved Giselle and Albrecht in American Ballet Theatre history had been Alicia Alonso and Igor Youskevitch. For eleven years they had epitomized the doomed lovers. Now Carla Fracci and Erik Bruhn brought a different luster to the *Giselle* of David Blair. It paired a ballerina who was essentially a romantic with a *premier danseur* who was a consummate classicist. They accentuated the best in each other.

By 1969, according to its president, Sherwin M. Goldman, American Ballet Theatre was no better off than it had been in 1940. It had no home and no broad base of support. It needed new teaching facilities, an expanded scholarship program, and the security of extended touring residencies rather than the constant hopping from city to city. As if to

AMERICAN BALLET THEATRE. Iván Nagy and Natalia Makarova in a pas de deux from act 3 of *La Fille Mal Gardée*, c.1971. (Photograph by Judy Cameron; from the Dance Collection, New York Public Library for the Performing Arts.)

offset this instability, the company continued to build its nineteenth-century repertory with *Coppélia*, staged by ballet master Enrique Martinez. By this time the company was so rich in soloists that it was able to cast four different Swanildas and six Franzes. Again Carla Fracci and Erik Bruhn shone in their blending of chic and simplicity.

The company also continued to look for a possible resident choreographer. Three Americans came into focus: Glen Tetley, Michael Smuin, and Eliot Feld.

Tetley, who began his career as a modern dancer, had performed briefly with American Ballet Theatre. In 1965 the company commissioned his *Sargasso*, with Sallie Wilson and Bruce Marks in the principal roles of a tormented couple. The following year brought Tetley's *Ricercare* for Mary Hinkson and Scott Douglas. Both works attracted attention as much for their unusual set pieces as for their choreography. Both sets were designed by Rouben Ter-Arutunian. The first ballet took place on a staircase reaching into infinity; the second, on a bed resembling a huge crescent moon. Despite his American origin, Tetley remained a "European" guest choreographer for American Ballet Theatre. His most enduring work was *Voluntaries*, a tribute to the late choreographer John Cranko, which had its company premiere in 1977.

Michael Smuin's abilities as a character dancer gave him a penchant for dramatic works. In 1967 he created *The Catherine Wheel*, a dance version of Arthur Schnitzler's play *La Ronde*. The work was dramatically naive and indicated that Smuin might take time to hit his stride as a choreographer. The following year brought his *Pulcinella Variations*, to the music of Stravinsky, and *Gartenfest*, an eighteenth-century romp set to Mozart's Cassation no. 1.

The Eternal Idol (1969), set to Chopin's Concerto no. 2 in F Minor, was a solemn tribute to the mysteries of the creative process. As metaphor Smuin used a Rodin statue coming to life. In 1970 his *Schubertiade* agreeably, if not distinctively, mirrored a series of Schubert waltzes.

Eliot Feld's choreographic debut in 1967 was reminiscent of that of Jerome Robbins. Both were New Yorkers and had functioned as character dancers. For both, the first choreographic attempt produced a ballet of enduring value. Feld's was *Harbinger*, to Prokofiev's Piano Concerto in G Major (op. 55). Oliver Smith supplied the setting; Stanley Simmons, the costumes. Later that same year Feld's *At Midnight* premiered. Set to four Mahler songs, with heroic painted backdrops by Leonard Baskin, and with Bruce Marks, Christine Sarry, Terry Orr, and Cynthia Gregory in the principal roles, the ballet delineated what is for some artists an eternal conflict: the pull between creation and the search for love, fulfillment, and solitude.

Again hopes were raised. Perhaps with Eliot Feld, American Ballet Theatre could develop a resident choreographer of major stature. It was not to be so. In 1968 Feld left the company to form his own group and to engage in

AMERICAN BALLET THEATRE. Bruce Marks and Cynthia Gregory in *The Moor's Pavane*, José Limón's modern dance based on Shakespeare's *Othello*. (Photograph © 1972 by Max Waldman; used by permission.)

freelance choreography. In late 1971 he returned briefly to create *A Soldier's Tale* and *Eccentrique* and in 1972 to add *Theatre* and *Intermezzo,* both of which had already been premiered by Feld's own American Ballet company. Of the four, only *Intermezzo* had the stature of *At Midnight.*

Another young American choreographer to whom American Ballet Theatre gave ample opportunity during this period was Dennis Nahat. Both Nahat and Michael Smuin were to undergo their principal choreographic development after leaving American Ballet Theatre. Smuin became director of the San Francisco Ballet in 1973, and in 1976, with Ian Horvath, another American Ballet Theatre dancer, Nahat founded the Cleveland Ballet.

High production costs had slackened American Ballet Theatre's pursuit of full-length classical ballets. But in 1972 Fernand Nault did stage a new version of *La Fille Mal Gardée.* And in 1974 Natalia Makarova mounted one scene of what eventually would be a major production. It was the Kingdom of the Shades scene from Marius Petipa's *La Bayadère.* Drawing from her own deeply absorbed Kirov tradition, Makarova, who had joined American Ballet Theatre in 1970, worked tirelessly with the corps. Its members not only danced in unison but seemed to breathe in unison. The soloists were Cynthia Gregory as the elegant Nikia and Iván Nagy as Solor, her tender and remorseful suitor.

During the early 1970s, American Ballet Theatre was beginning to effect organizational changes. By 1976 dancers and staff were guaranteed annual employment. The new contract gave the dancers a 60 percent salary increase over a three-year period. And some of the quick-stop touring was exchanged for longer residencies, principally in Los Angeles, San Francisco, and Chicago.

Artistically, the presence of Natalia Makarova as a principal dancer had a strong effect on some of her younger American colleagues. Gelsey Kirkland, in particular, learned much from Makarova's interpretation of classical roles. It combined intelligence, poetry, and meticulous schooling.

The alternative to mounting full-length productions was to purchase or rent productions that had first been staged on other companies. This was a common practice in opera. In 1973, Peter Darrell's *Tales of Hoffmann* briefly entered the repertory. Darrell had originally done the work for the Scottish Theatre Ballet. The charming Offenbach music plus the promise of elaborate sets and costumes by Peter Docherty were strong attractions. It would also serve as a challenging vehicle for Cynthia Gregory. In reality the ballet proved to be overdressed and lacking in the prime ingredient—interesting choreography.

Another short-lived acquisition of this nature was the production of *Raymonda* that had been staged by Rudolf Nureyev for the Zurich Ballet. In November 1975 *Raymonda* was performed in New York for two full weeks

AMERICAN BALLET THEATRE. Erik Bruhn and Cynthia Gregory in Birgit Cullberg's *Miss Julie* at the company's Thirty-fifth Anniversary Gala. (Photograph from the Dance Collection, New York Public Library for the Performing Arts.)

with Raymonda and her crusader-lover Jean de Brienne danced by Cynthia Gregory and Rudolf Nureyev, Gelsey Kirkland and Iván Nagy, Martine van Hamel and Clark Tippet, Eleanor D'Antuono and Ted Kivitt, Gelsey Kirkland and Rudolf Nureyev, Eleanor D'Antuono and Fernando Bujones. It was a tedious, often pompous work that served to prove that American Ballet Theatre had more fine principals than it had challenging repertory for them.

Torn between a need for full-length ballets and the inability to afford its own productions, American Ballet Theatre in 1976 acquired and quickly dropped a plethora of novelties. They included Alvin Ailey's *Pas de Duke,* Twyla Tharp's *Once More, Frank,* Agnes de Mille's *Texas Fourth,* Glen Tetley's *Le Sacre du Printemps,* and Alberto Alonso's *Carmen.* By now the company was again ready to tackle a classic. In June it premiered Mary Skeaping's version of *The Sleeping Beauty.* Oliver Messel, known for his Royal Ballet decor for the same work, was entrusted with the "look" of the ballet. It was a solid, conscientious version, leisurely in tone, properly grand in feeling.

Mikhail Baryshnikov, who had joined the company in 1974, and Makarova were both now seasoned members of

American Ballet Theatre. They performed the principal roles in *The Sleeping Beauty,* bringing to it the stylishness of their Kirov schooling plus their own personal passion. And yet the ballet lacked the warmth and emotional intimacy of the original Royal Ballet version. By the second season, revisions by Robert Helpmann had restored some of the dramatic logic. During that same period Makarova and Baryshnikov also danced a *Giselle* of great emotional depth, and in 1976 they gave full expression to the musical subtleties of *Other Dances,* a pas de deux to a Chopin waltz and four mazurkas, created especially for them by Jerome Robbins. Baryshnikov also began a memorable, though brief, partnership with Gelsey Kirkland. Their portrayals of the principal roles in *Giselle* were transcendently beautiful.

For the U.S. bicentennial in 1976, the company surpassed its own stylistic versatility with Twyla Tharp's *Push Comes to Shove.* Like most of her works, it functioned on two levels. The surface was casual, sinuous, rhythmically unpredictable. Lurking beneath this fragmented layer was an innate respect for classical structure and its expression in movement. Baryshnikov displayed a sure instinct for the dual style. Resembling an impudent boyar newsboy, he romped among the decorous corps members led by Martine van Hamel.

The Nutcracker is an American tradition, and yet American Ballet Theatre remained one of few American companies that did not stage the ballet. The need was acknowledged in 1976, when Baryshnikov was commissioned to create a version that premiered at the Kennedy Center in Washington, D.C. Shortly thereafter, it made its

AMERICAN BALLET THEATRE. Marianna Tcherkassky, Mikhail Baryshnikov, and Martine van Hamel in Twyla Tharp's *Push Comes to Shove.* Tharp choreographed this ballet for the company in 1976 to challenge Baryshnikov's unique talents. (Photograph © 1981 by Jack Vartoogian; used by permission.)

AMERICAN BALLET THEATRE. Mikhail Baryshnikov and Gelsey Kirkland in Baryshnikov's 1976 staging of *The Nutcracker.* (Photograph from the Dance Collection, New York Public Library for the Performing Arts.)

way to the Metropolitan Opera House with Baryshnikov and Marianna Tcherkassky in the principal roles. This version was closer to that of Soviet choreographer Vasily Vainonen (whose Snowflake scene was used intact) than to that of its originator, Lev Ivanov. Here, adults took the roles of children; Herr Drosselmeyer exerted his influence in the final act as well as in the first scene; and there were psychological overtones more typical of the twentieth century than of the nineteenth. Still, the ballet had considerable theatrical charm and remained sensitive to the Tchaikovsky score. The decor was by Boris Aronson; the costumes, by Frank Thompson. One of the most disturbing vagaries in the costuming was to have Clara dance the *grand pas de deux* in her nightgown. It made her resemble the Sleepwalker in Balanchine's *La Sonnambula.*

Although Baryshnikov had yet to face the challenge of original choreography, he did prove himself adept at restaging works with which he was familiar. In 1978 he took on a rousing version of *Don Quixote,* with sets in the mood of El Greco by Santo Loquasto, and choreography after Marius Petipa and Aleksandr Gorsky. That same year, in the midst of developing a wider range of responsibilities with American Ballet Theatre, he suddenly joined New York City Ballet. With Baryshnikov temporarily out of the picture, greater emphasis was put on the other male dancers, notably Fernando Bujones, John Meehan, Patrick Bissell, Johan Renvall, Kevin McKenzie, Charles Maple, and Danilo Radojevic. Anthony Dowell of the Royal Ballet became guest artist and added a polish that some felt was missing in the style of the Americans. The corps in particular came under critical attack. It was felt that the dancers were receiving insufficient coaching.

There were other signs of unrest. A long-awaited 1978 premiere of Antony Tudor's *The Tiller in the Fields* proved to be, despite Gelsey Kirkland and Patrick Bissell in the principal roles, a minor work about a rustic couple who decide to cast their lots together when the girl becomes pregnant. The emotional subtlety characteristic of such early Tudor works as *Jardin aux Lilas* had been replaced by flatly literal images, as when Kirkland strolled on the stage visibly pregnant.

The company suffered practical setbacks as well. The winter season at Kennedy Center had to be canceled because the dancers had gone on strike. One of their new requests was for travel per diems, and they eventually received 89 percent of their demands. They also began to set a precedent for assertiveness in a profession sadly lacking in this trait.

In 1980, Lucia Chase and Oliver Smith were abruptly relieved of their long-held positions. Mikhail Baryshnikov returned from the New York City Ballet to become artistic director. His expanded artistic staff now consisted of Nora Kaye as associate director, Antony Tudor as choreographer emeritus, Richard Tanner as *régisseur general*, Elena Tchernichova, Georgina Parkinson, Susan Jones, and Diana Joffe as ballet mistresses, and Michael Lland, Yurgen Schneider, Terrence Orr, and Scott Douglas as ballet masters.

The triumph of this transitional year was Natalia Makarova's restaging of the full-length *La Bayadère*. With sets by Pier Luigi Samaritani and sumptuous costumes by Theoni Aldredge, it was the grandest of the full-length works acquired by the company during the fifteen years it had been building this aspect of the repertory.

Some resented the dismissal of Lucia Chase, who had given so much of herself and of her financial resources to the company. Others felt a change was needed. Baryshnikov's stated aims were to find a resident choreographer, to commission good contemporary works, and to raise the level of the company's dancing. More attention was immediately placed on the technique of the corps. And a roster of new soloists began to be nurtured, among them, Peter Fonseca, Robert La Fosse, Lise Houlton, Susan Jaffe, Magali Messac, Christine Spizzo, and Cheryl Yeager.

Choo San Goh (*Configurations*), Peter Anastos (*Clair de Lune*), and Lynne Taylor-Corbett (*Great Galloping Gottschalk*) were promptly invited to enrich the repertory. But the prize among Baryshnikov's initial selections was not new. It was Merce Cunningham's elegantly simple *Duets*, previously staged for his own company and restaged for American Ballet Theatre in 1982.

Although Baryshhnikov had come from a venerable school, he did not prevent the closing of the American Ballet Theatre School. Part of its function was for a time absorbed by American Ballet Theatre II. This second company was founded in 1972 as Ballet Repertory Company.

Its name was changed in 1981. By 1985 it was disbanded. The principal purpose of this twenty-member ensemble was to bring dance to cities too small for visits by the parent company and to prepare young artists for the larger company. About 25 percent of them made the transition.

Directed by Richard Englund, with Jeremy Blanton as associate director, American Ballet Theatre II developed a tasteful repertory designed to interest a wide audience while challenging its youthful dancers. A summer scholarship program brought a nucleus of students to New York for an imaginative curriculum and possible company acceptance. Choreographic experimentation was integral to American Ballet Theatre II. Supervised by Englund and Oliver Smith, the Choreography Workshop began in 1980 with Lynne Taylor-Corbett in residence. For the next two years the project was expanded with Helen Douglas, James Kudelka, Nina Wiener, Mary Giannone, Daryl Gray, Dennis Spaight, Victoria Uris, John McFall, Peter Sparling, and Philip Grosser all working with the company.

Again in 1982 the American Ballet Theatre dancers went on strike. The dispute dragged on for nine weeks and resulted in a four-year, forty-week contract including severance pay. A year later Baryshnikov himself signed a new contract that extended his tenure for an indefinite time but left him free to accept outside assignments. These cur-

AMERICAN BALLET THEATRE. Cynthia Harvey as Gamzatti and Anthony Dowell as Solor in Natalia Makarova's staging of *La Bayadère*. (Photograph © 1980 by Jack Vartoogian; used by permission.)

AMERICAN BALLET THEATRE. Paloma Herrera in act 1 of *Don Quixote,* staged for the company by Kevin McKenzie and Susan Jones. (Photograph © 1995 by Jack Vartoogian; used by permission.)

tailed his appearances with the company, as did several injuries.

In order to strengthen the artistic leadership during his absences, Baryshnikov engaged John Taras, a ballet master of the New York City Ballet, to be his associate director. Sir Kenneth MacMillan, a former director of Britain's Royal Ballet, became his artistic associate with duties resembling those of a resident choreographer.

In 1985 MacMillan's *Romeo and Juliet,* originally staged for the Royal Ballet, was added to the American Ballet Theatre repertory. He also created a new work, *Requiem,* to a score by musical theater composer Andrew Lloyd Webber. In 1987 MacMillan gave the company another full-length *Sleeping Beauty,* with sets and costumes by his longtime collaborator Nicholas Georgiadis. The year before, Baryshnikov himself, in collaboration with choreographer Peter Anastos, had staged a full-length *Cinderella.* It was not an impressive addition.

To enhance the company's contemporary wing, Baryshnikov turned, with only mild success, to David Gordon (*Field, Chair and Mountain* and *Murder*), Karole Armitage (*The Molino Room*), and David Parsons (*Walk This Way).*

The most valuable was Mark Morris's poetic *Drink to Me Only with Thine Eyes.*

Perhaps the most productive trend during Baryshnikov's tenure was his interest in the choreography of Twyla Tharp. In 1988 she was invited to become artistic associate, and seven members of her company were added to the American Ballet Theatre roster. The following year four of her works were presented. Two (*Bum's Rush* and *Everlast*) were premieres. The other two (*In the Upper Room* and *The Fugue*) had been in her company's repertory. *In the Upper Room* proved to be the most enduring.

In 1989, Baryshnikov himself essayed one more full-length production, a costly and largely unsuccessful version of *Swan Lake.* By September of the same year, the company's board of trustees announced that Jane Hermann, director of presentations at the Metropolitan Opera, would join Baryshnikov as executive director. He resigned the same month; Taras followed nine months later.

Hermann asked Oliver Smith to return as artistic adviser. The emphasis for the next two years, during which Hermann had to address a $4 million deficit, was on new productions rather than new ballets. Former American Ballet Theatre ballet master Enrique Martinez staged a giddy version of *Coppélia;* Bolshoi principal Vladimir Vasiliev assembled a full-length *Don Quixote* from a variety of sources; former principal dancer Fernando Bujones tackled *Raymonda* (act 3). David Blair's 1966 version of *Swan Lake* was also restored. Twyla Tharp's *Brief Fling* and *Nine Sinatra Songs* were presented in 1990, but Tharp and her dancers were dropped from the roster because despite their strong audience appeal, Hermann considered them to be too expensive.

There was unrest among the company's dancers, who felt that their needs were being sacrificed to administrative concerns. Kevin McKenzie, a well-respected principal dancer, who had recently left the company to become artistic associate of the Washington Ballet, was invited to become American Ballet Theatre's next artistic director. He returned to the company in October 1992. Gary Dunning became executive director.

While the company set about coping with the financial challenges that had taken it perilously close to bankruptcy in 1984, McKenzie made it clear that he would spend a generous portion of time in the studio and rehearsal hall. The dancers and their development were important to him. His artistic staff consisted of former American Ballet Theatre dancer Ross Stretton as his assistant, Terrence S. Orr and David Richardson as ballet masters, and Georgina Parkinson, Irina Kolpakova, and Alaine Haubert as ballet mistresses. Sallie Wilson was in charge of the Antony Tudor repertory. The roster of principal dancers displayed great range. It consisted of Nina Ananiashvili, Victor Barbee, Julio Bocca, Gil Boggs, José Manuel Carreño, Wes Chapman, Jeremy Collins, Christine Dunham, Alessandra Ferri, Guillaume Graffin, Cynthia Harvey, Paloma Herrera, Robert Hill, Susan Jaffe, Julie Kent, Vladimir Malakhov, Amanda McKerrow, Kathleen Moore, Michael Owen, Johan Renvall, and Marianna Tcherkassky.

McKenzie continued to expand the roster of full-length productions with the return to the repertory of Kenneth MacMillan's 1987 version of *The Sleeping Beauty*. Natalia Makarova was invited to stage *Paquita,* and Kenneth MacMillan's *Manon* was given a sumptuously danced production. Twyla Tharp, who had been so essential to the Baryshnikov regime, returned in 1995 with three new ballets: *Americans We, How Near Heaven,* and *Jump Start.* While not so successful as some of her earlier works, notably *In the Upper Room, Brief Fling,* and *Nine Sinatra Songs,* they were still a welcome challenge for both dancers and audiences.

Most important, by 1995 dancer morale was high. Under McKenzie's guidance, American Ballet Theatre was close to weathering the fiscal and structural crises that had so often shown it to be an incredibly resilient artistic entity.

[*See also the entries on the principal figures and works mentioned herein.*]

BIBLIOGRAPHY

Barnes, Clive. "Showing the Flag." *Dance and Dancers* (August 1991): 30–35.

Baryshnikov, Mikhail. *Baryshnikov at Work.* New York, 1976.

Cohen, Selma Jeanne, and A. J. Pischl. "American Ballet Theatre, 1940–1960." *Dance Perspectives,* no. 6 (1960).

Croce, Arlene. *Afterimages.* New York, 1977.

Croce, Arlene. *Going to the Dance.* New York, 1982.

de Mille, Agnes. *Dance to the Piper.* Boston, 1952.

Denby, Edwin. *Looking at the Dance* (1949). New York, 1968.

Fehl, Fred, and Doris Hering. *Giselle and Albrecht.* New York, 1981.

Finkel, Anita. "American Ballet Theatre: A True History." *Ballett International* 12 (December 1989): 10–16.

Fraser, John. *Private View: Inside Baryshnikov's American Ballet Theatre.* New York, 1988.

Giannini, B. F. "An American Dreamer." *Dance Magazine* (January 1990): 32–37.

Hering, Doris, ed. *Twenty-Five Years of American Dance.* Rev. and enl. ed. New York, 1954.

Hering, Doris. "American Ballet Theatre." *Dance Magazine* (June 1960): 43–45.

Hering, Doris. *Wild Grass.* New York, 1967.

Makarova, Natalia. *A Dance Autobiography.* New York, 1979.

Payne, Charles, et al. *American Ballet Theatre.* New York, 1977.

Rosen, Lillie F. "A Fantastic Evening of Old and New Memories." *Attitude* 6 (Spring 1990): 22–26.

DORIS HERING

AMERICAN BANDSTAND. Television program. First performance: 5 August 1957, American Broadcasting Company (ABC). Broadcast in the United States until September 1989: ABC network, 1957–1987; syndicated, 1987–1988; USA Cable, 1989.

Hosted by the personable, photogenic, and preternaturally youthful Dick Clark (sometimes called "America's oldest teenager"), *American Bandstand* projected dance into America's living rooms and brought home-viewer participation in a television show to new heights. Centered around a cadre of good-looking teenagers who danced to popular music after school and watched recording artists lip-synch (mime) their latest records, *Bandstand* was begun in Philadelphia in 1952, hosted by Bob Horn. (In its early years, the teenagers were exclusively white, as the show's policy was one of *de facto* segregation; in later years, a broader racial and ethnic mix was encouraged.) Clark succeeded Horn in 1956, and when ABC-TV began to broadcast the show nationally as *American Bandstand* the following year, millions of teenagers and young housewives across America tuned in each weekday afternoon. While giving rise to such hoary phrases as, "I'll give it a ninety-two because it has a great beat and it's easy to dance to," *American Bandstand* set in motion a national dance revival in which fads arrived and departed faster than ever. Home viewers (many using mop handles, pillows, and refrigerator door handles as partners) learned the latest trendy dance steps within the friendly confines of their homes to late-afternoon television.

AMERICAN BANDSTAND. Jerry Blavat and his partner take center stage on *American Bandstand*, 1955. The preponderance of females in the studio audience was a constant problem in the show's early days, in part owing to the building's proximity to an all-girls high school. (Photograph courtesy of Urban Archives, Temple University, Philadelphia, Pennsylvania.)

In 1960, *American Bandstand* helped usher in an era of open (solo) dancing, in which partners did not touch. The Twist, a dance whose motions mimicked someone extinguishing a cigarette with both feet while drying off his or her derrière with a towel, was heavily promoted on *American Bandstand* and prompted a craze that forever changed the way the world danced. Once the gyrations of the Twist were legitimized, it became acceptable to take the style even further, and dances named for animals (the Pony, the Fly, the Monkey) and for specific dance motions (the Mashed Potato, the Loco-motion, the Swim) abounded. Open dancing soon became acceptable to everyone, and social dance breached generational barriers as well as racial and class lines.

American Bandstand reached its peak as a social dance forum between 1960 and 1963, before a series of events occurred that diminished the show's influence and popularity. In 1963, ABC began broadcasting *American Bandstand* once a week rather than daily. The following year Clark moved the show to California, where it lost much of its urban hominess and charm. About the time Clark abandoned live *Bandstand* broadcasts for less spontaneous videotaped performances, slick, fast-paced competitors such as *Shindig* and *Hullaballoo*, laden with professional dancers, appeared. The late-1960s psychedelic-drug era precipitated a decline in social dancing that caused *American Bandstand* to become even more irrelevant.

Despite such difficulties, Clark's dance show managed to attain new vitality in the 1970s, as an era of black awareness and pride born of the 1960s civil-rights movement wrought a black renaissance that touched virtually all aspects of American popular culture. (*Soul Train*, the black equivalent of *American Bandstand*, was created in Chicago in 1971.) Clark's show—now changing more with the times than influencing them—programmed more black music and encouraged black dancers to come to its studio.

Spirited black dance music gave rise to the disco era, centered around flashy, grandiloquent couple dances, replete with vigorous movements reminiscent of the jitterbug and the fox trot of the 1930s and 1940s. Disco, in the mid-1970s, sparked the biggest dance revival in ten years and provided a potent elixir for *American Bandstand's* reemergence as a dance forum.

New Wave, a musical genre that featured highly danceable music performed by a wide-ranging pop-to-punk array of artists, propelled *American Bandstand* into the 1980s, but it could not sustain the show indefinitely. The show's unofficial death knell sounded on 1 August 1981, the day the Music Television Network (MTV) cable channel began to broadcast flashy music videos around the clock. MTV's arrival triggered a spate of music video shows on conventional television channels that further eroded *American Bandstand's* audience and caused the show to become an anachronistic promotional venue within the music industry. Ironically, as *American Bandstand* entered the *Guiness Book of World Records* in 1987 as television's longest-running variety program, ABC-TV, encountering ratings problems of its own partly from the rise of cable television, decided to reduce the show's weekly air time from sixty minutes to thirty.

Clark refused and syndicated *The New American Bandstand* to independent television outlets for the 1987/88 season. The ratings were disappointing, however, and Clark hitched *American Bandstand*'s falling star to the booming cable-television industry. He stepped down as the show's host (in favor of David Hirsch) when it debuted on the USA network in April 1989, but the days when *American Bandstand* made stars of aspiring young singers and sparked the latest dance crazes were long gone. Save for its longevity, Clark's dance show had become just another cable-television outlet. In September 1989, after thirty-seven consecutive years on local and network television, Clark took *American Bandstand* off the air.

BIBLIOGRAPHY

Clark, Dick, and Richard Robinson. *Rock, Roll and Remember.* New York, 1976.
Jackson, John A. *Dick Clark's American Bandstand: The Making of a Rock 'n' Roll Empire.* New York, 1997.
Shore, Michael, with Dick Clark. *The History of American Bandstand.* New York, 1985.

VIDEOTAPE. *Twist,* a Triton Pictures release, produced and directed by Ron Mann (1993). Selected programs at the Museum of Television and Radio, New York City.

JOHN A. JACKSON

AMERICAN DANCE FESTIVAL. The American Dance Festival is the direct successor to the Bennington School of the Dance, which was founded in 1934 in Bennington, Vermont, and continued there through 1942, with the exception of a one-year sojourn at Mills College in California in 1939. During World War II, despite the end of the Bennington school as such, Martha Graham continued to spend summers with her company at Bennington (1943–1945), and José Limón brought his first company there in 1946. [*See* Bennington School of the Dance.]

New London, 1948–1977. After the war, Martha Hill and Mary Josephine Shelly decided to revive the idea of a summer center for American modern dance. In 1947, the Bennington faculty held a pilot program at Connecticut College in New London, Connecticut, for dance teachers, college dance groups, and young dancers. The success of this experiment led to the founding of the New York University–Connecticut College School of the Dance the following summer, with Hill as director (the dual sponsorship lasted until 1951, when New York University withdrew). As at Bennington, the summer school was housed in the campus of a New England liberal arts college. The school's aims and its program were likewise closely modeled on Bennington, and seventeen of the twenty faculty members were Bennington alumnae. The six-week session concluded with an American Dance Festival, featuring performances by three of the school's resident companies (Graham's, Limón's, and the Dudley–Maslow–Bales trio) in the college's thirteen-hundred-seat auditorium.

The school continued Bennington's custom of integrating the study of all aspects of stagecraft and choreography with technique and performance, as well as Bennington's explicit dedication to grooming professional performers. The school's prospectus announced "an integrated study of the whole art in which the emphasis is on the active relationship between technique and composition, music and staging, practice and performance," with a view to providing "the working contacts vital to an art which is both a force in the contemporary theatre and a medium of education." Hill was assisted in pursuing these aims by fellow administrators Rosemary Park, president of Connecticut College; Ernest O. Melby, dean of the New York University School of Education; and John F. Moore, director of the summer session at Connecticut College. Former student Ruth Bloomer joined Hill as co-director from 1949 to 1958. Jeanette Schlottman became director in 1959, followed by Theodora Wiesner in 1963. She was succeeded in 1969 by Charles Reinhart, who, together with Martha Myers as dean (and later joined by his wife, Stephanie Reinhart, as co-director), inaugurated a period of steady expansion in the depth and scope of the school's mission.

The school's dominant figures for more than two decades were Doris Humphrey (the leading pedagogue until her death in 1958), José Limón (whose company performed in the festival every summer from 1948 to 1968, producing twenty-three premieres), Martha Graham, and Graham's musical director, Louis Horst, together with their disciples and associates. Most of the leading performers of the day taught at the school at some point, including Helen Tamiris, Pearl Primus, Sybil Shearer, and Charles Weidman. The companies of Merce Cunningham and Paul Taylor were invited to perform new works starting in the late 1950s; at the time, this was regarded as a significant, and controversial, aesthetic departure for the festival.

By the mid-1960s, the festival was clearly out of touch with new developments in the field, particularly with a new generation of experimental choreographers loosely organized around Judson Memorial Church in New York City. Beginning in 1969 Reinhart began to welcome the rebels inside the fortress, inviting innovative choreographers such as Twyla Tharp and Yvonne Rainer to teach and perform at the festival, while also beginning a concerted effort to expand the range of artists, audiences, and constituencies served by it. Among the new projects initiated in the 1970s were an annual critics' conference; an emerging artists' commission program; the sponsorship of a variety of collaborative opportunities for choreographers, composers, directors, and performers; and a number of community outreach initiatives. Beginning in the mid-1970s, Merrill Brockway and Emile Ardolino ran a workshop every year for more than a decade to train television directors to shoot dance effectively for live and prerecorded broadcast. The American Dance Festival's distinguished history in television dance also includes nationally televised programs produced with SCE-TV, WUNC, and New Hampshire Public Television.

Durham, since 1978. The American Dance Festival (ADF) acquired independent nonprofit status in 1976. In 1978 the school left New London for the campus of Duke University in Durham, North Carolina, where it has received financial support from the university, community, city, and state, which it had lacked in Connecticut. In 1982 the festival moved its headquarters from New York City to Duke as well, and began to offer certain service programs year round. Since moving to Duke, the festival has sustained constant growth. By the late 1990s, it employed a faculty of fifty each summer, teaching more than four hundred students, about one third of whom came from outside the United States. In addition to ballet, the major modern techniques, repertory, and composition, the curriculum has included dance video, dance medicine, body therapies, jazz dance, tap, vaudeville, the classical and folk traditions of non-European cultures, Native American and regional American dance, and contact improvisation. The festival has also offered professional workshops in dance criticism (since 1970), pedagogy, medicine in dance, dance therapy, body therapy, administration, and management. In 1981 the festival instituted the $25,000 Samuel H. Scripps American Dance Festival Award to pay tribute to American dance masters; Graham was its first recipient. The Balasaraswati–Joy Ann Dewey Chair for Distinguished Teaching, the school's first endowed faculty chair in dance, was established in 1991.

At Duke the festival holds performances in the university's 1,500-seat auditorium, its 570-seat theater, and an 800-seat theater in neighboring Raleigh, as well as in many studios, gymnasiums, school auditoriums, and outdoor spaces. Performances by visiting and resident professional dance companies remain vital to the summer school. With the inclusion of the Bennington period, the ADF has seen more than four hundred premieres. In the Connecticut years, these included Graham's *Wilderness Stair* (later retitled *Diversion of Angels*), Humphrey's *Night Spell*, Limón's *The Moor's Pavane*, Erick Hawkins's *Lords of Persia*, Sophie Maslow's *The Village I Knew*, Cunningham's *Summerspace*, Pearl Lang's *Shira*, Taylor's *Aureole*, Alvin Ailey's *Masakela Language*, Tharp's *Medley*, and an eccentric early outdoor work by Meredith Monk, *Needlebrain Lloyd and the Systems Kid*, as well as important revivals of works by Graham, Weidman, and Humphrey. Among the well-known artists to show new work at the ADF since the move to Duke are Martha Clarke, Mark Morris, and Bill T. Jones—a complete list, indeed, would include almost every major dance artist in the United States. The ADF has commissioned many works from established artists, and nurtured emerging choreographers with such programs as the Young Choreographers and Composers in Residence Program and the Emerging Generation Program.

International Projects. The main developments in the festival's activities since 1980 have focused on international exchange and reflect the Reinharts' determination to earn for the ADF a role of international leadership in nurturing modern dance. Since 1979 the Reinharts have traveled worldwide seeking out worthy choreographers and companies to bring to Durham. In 1982 the ADF introduced Japanese *butō*, among other new Japanese styles, to U.S. audiences by hosting four major Japanese companies at the festival that summer. After hosting five companies from France the following year, the ADF held an international modern dance festival in 1984 as part of its fiftieth anniversary celebration, with companies from India, Indonesia, the Philippines, and Great Britain. The festival has subsequently produced the first North American performances of companies from every continent. The festival's first International Choreographers Workshop was also held in 1984 (the workshop has been called the International Choreographers Residency Program since 1994); by the late 1990s, the program had brought more than two hundred choreographers from around the world to Durham to study and make new works. A commissioning program was added in 1987, offering selected graduates of the residency program the opportunity to return to Durham to create new works using ADF students. Also in 1984, the ADF sent a small number of faculty to Japan together with the companies of Laura Dean and Martha Clarke to produce a miniaturized version of the Durham six-week summer program dubbed ADF/Tokyo. Similar "mini-ADFs," two to four weeks long, have since been held in Japan (in 1986), Seoul (five times in the 1990s), New Delhi (1990), and Moscow (1992); in 1992 there was also an ADF West in Salt Lake City, Utah.

In response to the need of former International Choreographers Workshop participants, many of whom are affiliated with leading dance schools and companies in their homelands, to maintain and renew their contact with American modern dance, the ADF founded the Institutional Linkages Program in 1987. The program comprises a great variety of exchanges, including teaching residencies and repertory acquisition, between international dance institutions and U.S. artists and teachers, made with the assistance of past workshop choreographers and "brokered" by the ADF's administrators; the purpose is always to foster the development of modern dance in each country, which often entails an intense encounter between the country's own classical and/or folk traditions, and the individualist creative aesthetic of modern dance. The first linkage program, whose success made it a model for subsequent initiatives, led to the founding of the first modern dance program in China, at the Guangdong Dance Academy in 1987, and to the establishment of China's first and only modern dance company, the Guangdong Modern Dance Company, by the program's first graduating class in 1990. Other linkages have involved institutions in many countries in South America, Africa, Europe, and Asia; most are ongoing or periodically renewed.

Many older ADF programs have also been internationalized. The annual dance critics workshop became in 1990 the International Dance Critics Conference, under the direction of Linda Belans (dance critic for the Raleigh *News and Observer*), attracting critics and scholars from around the globe. In 1989 the ADF held its second International Modern Dance Festival, with eleven companies from outside the United States, more than one hundred foreign students, and seventeen choreographers in the international workshop. Also in 1989, as part of a joint initiative with the Jacob's Pillow Dance Festival, the ADF hosted five French companies, officially as part of the bicentennial of the French Revolution. The ADF's links with France are particularly strong, as witnessed by the festival's Franco-American Bilateral Young Choreographers/ Dancers Exchange Project (1987–1988, 1989) and its French Dancers in Residence Project (1991). Since 1991 the festival has also experimented with a touring project, ADF on Tour, initially with the Nucleodanza company of Argentina and the Dayton Contemporary Dance Company, arranging touring to the mini-ADFs and ADF-linked venues overseas, as well as throughout the United States. In addition to the performances, the tours include public panels led by ADF-affiliated scholars.

Historical Projects. The ADF has also undertaken several initiatives concerned with preserving American dance traditions. In 1987 the ADF founded its Black Tradition in American Modern Dance project, directed by Gerald Myers, to preserve classic works by African-American choreographers by reconstructing them on major U.S. companies. The project toured the United States, bringing live performances of some of the eighteen reconstructed works together with a lecture series entitled "African-American Perspectives in Modern Dance" to diverse audiences. The project has also issued two publications, *The Black Tradi-

tion in American Modern Dance (1988) and *African-American Genius in Modern Dance* (1993), as part of a larger series of humanities publications that includes *Philosophical Essays on Dance* (1981), *The Aesthetic and Cultural Significance of Modern Dance* (1984), and *Dancing across Cultures* (1995). In 1993 the ADF experimented with a pilot program to preserve masterworks outside the African-American tradition, the Masterworks Residency/ Preservation Project, through which major works by living choreographers are selected, reconstructed on a modern dance company chosen by the choreographer, and performed by them as part of their regular repertory season. The works are recorded in Labanotation and on video, along with rehearsal footage and an interview with the choreographer. The ADF has also begun an Archival Project to document, preserve, order, and make accessible its own extensive and invaluable archives, which incorporate material dating back to the 1930s, including film, videotape in several formats, photographs, and printed documents of many kinds. The archival project, assisted by Duke University's special collections and the Dance Heritage Coalition, is coordinated with other major dance archives throughout the United States. The 1990s has also seen several installments in a projected series of videotapes entitled "Speaking of Dance—Conversations with the Masters," produced in collaboration with the ADF's video director, Douglas Rosenberg, and available in several languages. Each tape, a profile of a master artist such as Talley Beatty, Ethel Butler, Lucas Hoving, Betty Jones, Donald McKayle, or Anna Sokolow, includes footage from interviews, performances, and teaching.

The festival's original statements of mission, which proclaimed a determination to foster a struggling American art form, have been replaced by a utopian rhetoric proposing dance as an international language that speaks across cultures, a unifying force that extends even "beyond culture" itself (Townes, 1994)—although exactly what realm could possibly lie beyond culture is by no means clear. Nonetheless, the intricate, ever-widening web of international projects remains anchored in the ADF's original foundation: an annual summer school, and an accompanying festival of performances; in this, the ADF has remained true to the Bennington heritage. The festival's history reflects the successful transplantation of modern dance from the United States to countries all over the world that have an indigenous tradition of theatrical dance (and to many that do not), even as the ADF has contributed substantially to that process.

BIBLIOGRAPHY
Anderson, Jack. *The American Dance Festival.* Durham, N.C., 1987.
Borek, Tom. "The Connecticut College American Dance Festival, 1948–1972: A Fantastical Documentary." *Dance Perspectives* no. 50 (1982).

McDonagh, Don. "Cross Currents." *Ballet News* (July–August 1979).
Townes, Alta Lu. *Dancing across Cultures: A Decade Plus of International Development in Modern Dance 1982–1994.* Durham, N.C., 1994.

CHRISTOPHER CAINES

AMERICAN DOCUMENT. Choreography: Martha Graham. Music: Ray Green. Scenery: Arch Lauterer. Costumes: Edythe Gilfond. First performance: 6 August 1938, Vermont State Armory, Bennington, Vermont, Martha Graham and Dance Group. Principals: Martha Graham, Erick Hawkins, Housely Stevens, Jr. (The Actor as Interlocutor).

The format of *American Document* was derived from minstrel shows, but the spoken text included the Declaration of Independence, the Emancipation Proclamation, and excerpts from the *Song of Solomon* and Jonathan Edwards's sermons. The dance linked America's past with its present. Initially, the company of thirteen was augmented by ten students from the Bennington School of Dance. The program lists the following sections: Entrance—Walk-Around; Part I—Declaration; Part II—Indian Episode: Native Figure (Graham) and Lament for the Land (group); Part III—Puritan Episode (Graham and Hawkins); Part IV—Emancipation Episode (group, duet for Graham and Hawkins); Part V—The AfterPiece: Cross Fire—Cakewalk, 1938 (Hawkins, Jane Dudley, Sophie Maslow, May O'Donnell), Declaration, Finale, and Exit—Walk-Around.

In *American Document*, a man danced with Graham's formerly all-female company for the first time. The dance is thought to presage Graham's move from abstraction toward more specific characterization and drama. Lincoln Kirstein, writing in *The Nation*, said the work had "the sober, frank sincerity of a Thanksgiving hymn heard in the open air." The work toured to acclaim, but a 1944 revival was not well received. A completely new work bearing the same title, with music by John Corigliano and starring Mikhail Baryshnikov, premiered at the City Center of Music and Drama in New York City on 3 October 1989.

BIBLIOGRAPHY

Costonis, Maureen Needham. "*American Document:* A Neglected Graham Work." In *Proceedings of the Twelfth Annual Conference, Society of Dance History Scholars, Arizona State University, 17–19 February 1989,* compiled by Christena L. Schlundt. Riverside, Calif., 1989.
Costonis, Maureen Needham. "Martha Graham's *American Document:* A Minstrel Show in Modern Dance Dress." *American Music* 9 (Fall 1991): 297–310.
McDonagh, Don. *Martha Graham.* New York, 1973.

FILM. *Martha Graham and Company,* part 3 (1939), Dance Collection, New York Public Library for the Performing Arts.

DEBORAH JOWITT

AMERICAN INDIAN DANCE. *See* Native American Dance.

AMODIO, AMEDEO (born 14 March 1940 in Milan), Italian ballet dancer, choreographer, and company director. Amodio began his dance training in the ballet school of the Teatro alla Scala in Milan, where his principal teachers were Elide Bonagiunta and Marika Besobrasova, and he later studied Spanish dance in Madrid with Antonio Marin. He made his debut in the corps de ballet of La Scala in 1958, at age eighteen. In following years he was cast in roles in the Italian premieres of ballets by Léonide Massine (*Le Tricorne, Jeux d'Enfants, Fantasmi al Grand Hôtel*), George Balanchine (*Symphony in C, The Four Temperaments*), and Roland Petit (*Le Jeune Homme et la Mort, La Chambre, Le Loup*). He left La Scala in 1963 to work in Rome in a series of popular television shows with choreography by Hermes Pan.

In 1966, Aurelio Milloss engaged Amodio as *premier danseur* with the Rome Opera Ballet and in 1967 gave him leading roles in his new work, *Déserts*, set to music by Edgard Varèse, and in revivals of his ballets *Marsia* and *La Follia di Orlando*. Amodio's youthful face, chestnut curls, and ambiguous smile, coupled with a quick-footed, darting athleticism, made him better suited to character parts than to roles requiring a *danseur noble*. He nevertheless became one of the best-known dancers in Italy and an unquestionable star of the ballet stage, noted for his forceful presence and strong technique. He collaborated many times with Carla Fracci and her touring company, dancing with her in such works as Loris Gai's *The Seagull* (1968) and *Pelléas et Mélisande* (1970), and he made successful appearances in two films by Liliana Cavani, *The Night Porter* and *Beyond Good and Evil*.

For the Spoleto Festival of 1967, Amodio choreographed his first ballet, *Escursioni*, a long pas de deux in a modern style set to music by Luciano Berio. A few years later, in 1972, he made another work for the Spoleto Festival, his version of *L'Après-midi d'un Faune*, to Claude Debussy's familiar score. The success of these early works encouraged Amodio to undertake a number of choreographic commissions in the following years, including *Rot* (1973), to music by Domenico Guaccero, for the Rome Opera Ballet, and *Discourses II* (1973), to music by Vinko Globokar, *Ricercare a Nove Movimenti* (1975), to music by Antonio Vivaldi, and *Oggetto Amato* (Love Object; 1976), to music by Sylvano Bussotti, all mounted for La Scala Ballet. As a choreographer, Amodio's style and subject matter were influenced by central European expressionism, by his experiences with modern jazz, and by the restraint and economy he found in the works of Balanchine. In the summer of 1978 he contributed to the Festival of

Nervi a spectacle called *Il Flauto Danzante* (The Dancing Flute), which featured flutist Severino Gazzelloni, dancer Carmen Ragghianti, and percussionist Tullio de Piscopo and which subsequently was performed on a tour of several Italian cities.

In 1979, Amodio became artistic director of Aterballetto, a modern ballet company based in Bologna that was formed by the Associazione Teatri Emilia-Romagna (A.T.E.R.), a collaboration among fifteen public theaters in the province. Within a short time, he had built this young, experimental troupe into an excellent ballet company with a large repertory. In addition to performing such classic works of the modern repertory as Antony Tudor's *Jardin aux Lilas* and Léonide Massine's *Parade* and such contemporary ballets as Glen Tetley's *Mythical Hunters,* Alvin Ailey's *Night Creatures,* and William Forsythe's *Love Songs,* Aterballetto presents a wide range of Amodio's own works. The company repertory includes several of his works from the 1970s as well as *Là Ci Darem la Mano* (1983), an allegory about Don Giovanni and seduction in general, set to the music of Mozart, and *Psiche a Manhattan* (Psyche in Manhattan, 1984), an elegant homage to the great tradition of Broadway musicals, set to the music of Leonard Bernstein.

In the late 1980s, Amodio expanded the company's repertory with two major productions designed expressly as showcases for Aterballetto's favorite guest star, Elisabetta Terabust. In 1987, he staged *Romeo and Juliet,* with music by Hector Berlioz and scenery and costumes by Guido Ceroli, and in 1989 he mounted *The Nutcracker* with spectacular scenery and costumes by Emanuele Luzzati. In general, however, Amodio has continued to build the company's repertory by adding shorter works by himself, by other contemporary European choreographers, and by such acknowledged masters as Balanchine, Petit, and Jiří Kylián.

[*See also* Aterballetto.]

BIBLIOGRAPHY
Bentivoglio, Leonetta. "A.A.A.: Amedeo Amodio Aterballetto." *Balletto oggi* 18 (March 1984).
Bentivoglio, Leonetta. *La danza contemporanea.* Milan, 1985.
Cucchi, Angela Mascimbene, and Patrizia Paterlini, eds. *Trent'anni di balletto a Reggio Emilia, 1956–1986.* Reggio Emilia, 1986.
Ottolenghi, Vittoria. "Aterballetto, la nostra compagnia." *Balletto oggi* 18 (March 1984).
Rossi, Luigi. *Il ballo alla Scala, 1778–1970.* Milan, 1972.
Testa, Alberto, et al. *Il balletto nel novecento.* Turin, 1983.

VITTORIA OTTOLENGHI
Translated from Italian

ANANIASHVILI, NINA (Nina Gedevanovna Ananiashvili; born 19 March 1964 in Tbilisi), Georgian dancer. Ananiashvili began her career as a figure skater, winning the junior championship of Georgia in 1973. The same year she was admitted to the State Choreographic School of Georgia at the Paliashvili Opera Theater in Tbilisi, where she studied until 1977. In 1977, at the age of thirteen, she transferred to the Moscow Choreographic School at the Bolshoi Theater; her first teacher there was Natalia Zolotova. She was still at school when, in 1980, she won her first award, at the Varna International Ballet Competition, and performed her first leading role, Swanilda in *Coppélia,* in a Bolshoi school production. In 1981 Ananiashvili graduated and was accepted into the Bolshoi Ballet as a soloist.

From the beginning of her professional career Ananiashvili was one of the leading young dancers of the Bolshoi Ballet. Through the 1980s her repertory included the major roles of Odette-Odile in *Swan Lake,* Kitri in *Don Quixote,* Aurora in *The Sleeping Beauty,* Masha in *The Nutcracker,* and Juliet in *Romeo and Juliet.* In 1981 she won a gold medal in the junior division of the Moscow International Ballet Competition, and in 1985 a gold medal in the senior division. Her most frequent partners were Andris Liepa and Aleksei Fadeyechev.

Ananiashvili's artistic personality was shaped to a great extent by her teachers at the Bolshoi, two former ballerinas of the company, Marina Semenova and Raisa Struchkova. From Semenova, who was trained at the Kirov school, Ananiashvili inherited the refined academic tradition of classical dancing and strong technique, with pure and clear line in every position and expressive arms, enriched by her natural elevation and lightness. From Struchkova, a typical Moscow dancer, she acquired stage presence, bravado, a sense of drama, and realistic acting. She blended all this with her inborn lyricism and softness. The combination of a radiant personality, exotic beauty, and technical strength and brilliance made Ananiashvili a perfect Juliet; later she triumphed in *The Firebird* at the Royal Ballet and in the 1993 Moscow reconstruction of Michel Fokine's original production.

During her school days Ananiashvili established a successful partnership with another student, Andris Liepa. This long-lasting partnership has won both dancers international recognition. In 1988 they were invited to perform as guest artists with the New York City Ballet. Since that time Ananiashvili, unusual for a Bolshoi ballerina, has been a frequent guest artist with several major companies all over the world, including American Ballet Theatre, the Boston Ballet, the Royal Ballet (London), the Royal Danish Ballet, the National Ballet of Canada, the National Ballet of Finland, and the Maryinsky Ballet.

In 1993 Ananiashvili formed an international touring group of young dancers from all over the world, Nina Ananiashvili and International Stars Company. The group completed its first successful tour, in Japan, in 1993.

ANANIASHVILI. Nina Ananiashvili in the Maryinsky Ballet production of *Romeo and Juliet*. (Photograph © 1992 by Jack Vartoogian; used by permission.)

BIBLIOGRAPHY

Ananiashvili, Nina. "Ballet as Quintessential Theatre." *Dance Now* 3 (Spring 1994): 4–7.

Ananiashvili, Nina. "The Classics Are Alive." *Dance and Dancers* (March 1992): 10–14.

Finch, Tamara. "An Interview with Nina Ananiashvili." *The Dancing Times* (June 1989): 852–853.

Flatow, Sheryl. "Ananiashvili and Liepa at the New York City Ballet: Glasnost in Action." *Dance Magazine* (June 1988): 48–51.

Kaplan, Larry. "A Conversation with Nina Ananiashvili." *Ballet Review* 19 (Fall 1991): 49–56.

Mainietse, Violette. "Birth of the Ballerina." *Muzykal'naia zhizn'*, no. 5 (1985).

Merrett, Sue. "Spotlight on Nina Ananiashvili." *The Dancing Times* (February 1993): 473.

Newman, Barbara. *Striking a Balance: Dancers Talk about Dancing.* Rev. ed. New York, 1992.

Pierpont, Claudia Roth. "Clio's Revenge." *Ballet Review* 16 (Spring 1988): 29–43.

Willis, Margaret E. "Nina Ananiashvili: From Jet to Jetés." *Dance Magazine* (July 1994): 36–43.

IRINA KLYAGIN

ANASTENÁRIDĒS. An Orthodox Christian sect, the Anastenáridēs came mostly from the towns of Kosti and Brodilovo in Kırklareli (formerly Kirk-Kilissa) in northeastern Turkey. Ousted by the Bulgarians in 1914, they now live in Macedonia, Greece. They are particularly devoted to Saint Constantine and Saint Helen, and express this devotion by dancing on live coals, a practice proscribed by the church authorities. The Anastenáridēs claim that these saints, acting through icons and other sacred objects, bestow extraordinary abilities on their devotees.

They dance to a melody rendered by two *lyra* (bowed stringed instruments), assisted by a drum (the *daoúli*) and a bagpipe (the *gaïda*) if available, which helps the dancers attain an ecstatic state. The main step is a simple two-step reminiscent of treading grapes or kneading dough or clay with the feet. The dancers use this step to move forward and back in front of the icons, to carry the icons in a circle (or forward and back), and to dance barefoot across the coals, stamping them out. The musicians play several tunes, all in 2/4 time, the most important being "Little Constantine." The processional dance music is in 7/16 meter (divided 4, 3 or 2, 2, 3). The processional phase uses a rhythmically modified version of the two-step, or a running two-step (quick, quick, slow) known as the Thracian *mantilatos chorós*. The only linked circle dance is the Thracian *syrtós chorós*, done in 2/4 time around the ashes. As with other Greek ritual dance, the steps are unremarkable; it is apparently the Anastenárides' deep faith that enables them to resist pain and injury.

Music and dance figure prominently in the three-day public celebrations held by the sect every May at Langhadá and Aghía Eléne (also occasionally at Melíke, and formerly at Mavrolévke). On the evening of 20 May the Anastenárides meet at the *konáki*, where their icons are lodged. Late the next morning they perform a sequence of rituals: the consecration of water, aspersion (sprinkling) of the icons and the congregation, censing of the congregation and of a sacrificial animal, and finally the animal sacrifice. Later in the afternoon wood is stacked for a bonfire and ceremoniously lit. After a few hours a circle of glowing coals fifteen to twenty feet across is ready. Dancing on the live coals begins around sunset or later. First a dancelike procession with musicians, icons, accessories, two candles, and a censor goes from the *konáki* to the bed of coals, which the Anastenárides circle counterclockwise. After making the sign of the cross they begin to dance across the coals, continuing until only ashes remain. They then dance the Thracian *syrtós chorós* (in Langhadá a Kalamatianós is added as well), followed by a processional back to the *konáki*, where they wash their feet. (In Aghía Eléne the processional from the *konáki* goes from house to house, and there is no dancing on live coals.) Each day's gathering ends with a late meal, breaking up after midnight. On the third night the meal is more formal and may be followed by popular Thracian dances.

In Bulgaria the related Nestinarski celebration seems to have disappeared as a religious phenomenon and is performed today only as a tourist spectacle. It was centered in Bulgari, a village near Kosti, and was celebrated on the days sacred to Saint Constantine and Saint Helen (2 and 3 June, Old [Julian] Calendar). Both the Greek and Bulgarian names for the sect come from a common root meaning "to sigh" and, by extension, "to suffer." In Spain the villagers of San Pedro Manrique in Soria perform a similar ritual on Saint John's Eve (the night before Midsummer Day). Ritual dancing (or walking and running) over hot coals is also known in many parts of Asia in Islamic, Hindu, and Buddhist contexts.

[*For related discussion, see* Greece, *article on* Ritual and Carnival Dance Traditions.]

BIBLIOGRAPHY

Crossland, John, and Diana Constance. *Macedonian Greece.* New York, 1982.

Kakouri, Katerina I. *Dionysiaka: Aspects of the Popular Thracian Religion of Today.* Athens, 1965.

Makrakis, Basil. *Fire Dances in Greece.* Athens, 1982.

Megas, Georgios A. *Greek Calendar Customs.* 2d ed. Athens, 1963.

Mouzaki, Rozanna. "The Anastenaria." In Mouzaki's *Greek Dances for Americans.* New York, 1981.

Petrides, Ted. "Ta Anastenaria." *Anthropos* 6 (1979): 163–179.

TED PETRIDES

ANDERSON-IVANTZOVA, ELIZABETH (Elizaveta Iul'evna; born 21 April 1890 in Moscow, died 11 November 1973 in New York City), dancer, choreographer, and teacher. Born into a professional family, Elizabeth Anderson studied privately with her cousin Ekaterina Geltser before she was admitted to the Imperial Ballet School in Moscow. Graduating in 1906, she entered the Bolshoi company and was promoted to the rank of *coryphée* in February 1907. A soloist by 1910, she appeared abroad at the London Coliseum with Tamara Karsavina in *Giselle* and *Divertissements,* and again in 1911 at the London Alhambra with Geltser in Aleksandr Gorsky's *Dance Dream.* She was partnered by Leonid Zhukov, whom she later married in 1913. Anderson embarked on her teaching career at the Imperial Ballet School in 1912. During the next three years, she appeared with increasing frequency in important roles in the repertory, such as Myrtha, the Lilac Fairy, and Princess Florine. She was promoted to "first rank" in April 1916. Gorsky directed her debut as Aurora in *The Sleeping Beauty* and again during the 1917/18 season as Odette-Odile in *Swan Lake.* She left Russia in the summer of 1918.

During the 1920/21 season in Paris, Anderson was the choreographer for Nikita Baliev's Théâtre de la Chauve-Souris, a variety theater that had evolved out of the Moscow Art Theater. Her choreography included pas de deux from the classical repertory, which she performed with Viacheslav Svoboda; peasant folk dances; and ensemble staging. Anderson's work with the Chauve-Souris linked her to innovative personalities and new developments in the Russian theater: Konstantin Stanislavsky's Moscow Art Theater, Vsevolod Meyerhold, Aleksandr Tairov and the Kamerny Theater, and Serge Soudeikine, who designed sets and costumes for Baliev's first season. In September 1922, she choreographed Arthur Schnitzler's ballet pantomime *The Veil of Pierrette* for the Kikimora Theater Company at Max Reinhardt's Kammerspiele des Deutschen Theater in Berlin, for which Natalia Goncharova designed the scenery and costumes. Anderson divorced her first husband, Zhukov, in December 1922 and in 1923 married Ivan Ivantzov, a baritone from the Maryinsky Opera of Saint Petersburg. She appeared at the Teatro São Carlos in Lisbon during the 1922/23 season and rejoined Baliev's company for its American tour in 1923–1924; she thereafter remained in the United States.

In 1927, Anderson taught body movement for actors at Richard Boleslavsky's American Laboratory Theater, also choreographing Schnitzler's *Bridal Veil* (1928), Jean Cocteau's *Le Boeuf sur le Toit* (1930), and other productions of the Lab Theater. Her greatest choreographic success, however, was Igor Stravinsky's *Les Noces* at the Metropolitan Opera House in New York City in 1929. Her abstract choreography was geometric in design but based on earthy peasant life in every colorful detail. The choreographic effects were intricately meshed with motifs in Soudeikine's scenic, costume, and lighting designs, exemplifying an aesthetic principle derived from Russian experimental theaters.

In 1937, Anderson opened a ballet school, the Anderson-Ivantzova School of Dance in New York City. Her pedagogical method omitted the *grand plié* as a beginning exercise, reduced the number of repetitions in other exercises, and limited practice at the *barre* to about thirty minutes. A hallmark of her teaching was a theory of placement in balance, an emphasis that attracted many distinguished performers of the ballet and Broadway stages. Among her students were Alicia Alonso, Rosella Hightower, John Kriza, and Donald Saddler.

BIBLIOGRAPHY

Horosko, Marian. "Mme. Anderson-Ivantzova: A Little Bolshoi on 56th Street." *Dance Magazine* (June 1965): 54–56.

Horosko, Marian. "In the Shadow of Russian Tradition." *Dance Magazine* (January 1971): 36–37.

Sayler, Oliver. *The Russian Theatre under the Revolution.* New York, 1920.

Sullivan, Lawrence. "*Les Noces:* The American Premiere." *Dance Research Journal* 14.1–2 (1981–1982): 3–14.

Sullivan, Lawrence. "Nikita Baliev's Le Théâtre de la Chauve-Souris: An Avant-Garde Theater." *Dance Research Journal* 18.2 (1987): 17–29.

Sullivan, Lawrence. "Arthur Schnitzler's *The Bridal Veil* at the American Laboratory Theatre." *Dance Research Journal* 25.1 (1993): 13–20.

Sullivan, Lawrence. "Arthur Schnitzler's *The Veil of Pierrette.*" *Europa Orientalis* [Russo a Berlino], 14.2 (1995): 262–280.

LAWRENCE SULLIVAN

ANDREYANOVA, ELENA (Elena Ivanovna Andreianova; born 1 [13] July 1819 in Saint Petersburg, died 14 [26] October 1857 in Paris), Russian ballerina. Andreyanova studied at the Imperial Theater School in Saint Petersburg under Avdotia Istomina and Antoine Titus. Upon graduation in 1837 she joined the Saint Petersburg Imperial Theater company, making her debut at its Bolshoi Theater as Zoloë's friend in a revised version of Filippo Taglioni's *opéra-ballet Le Dieu et la Bayadère.* Andreyanova's first performance coincided with the arrival in Russia of Taglioni and his daughter Marie, who was impressed by Andreyanova's talents and helped to guide her career. The young dancer attended classes conducted

by Taglioni, and the two women danced together in many productions.

An outstanding Romantic ballerina, Andreyanova danced in the Russian premiere of several of Filippo Taglioni's ballets, including *La Gitana* (1838), *La Révolte au Sérail* (1840), *L'Ecumeur des Mers* and *Le Lac des Fées* (both, 1841). In 1842 she was the first Russian to dance the title role in *Giselle,* considered to be her ultimate achievement. She also triumphed in the title role of *La Péri* when the ballet was brought to the Russian stage by Jean Coralli in 1844. In 1847 Andreyanova starred in Marius Petipa's version of *Paquita,* and in 1848 she danced the lead in Petipa's production of *Satanilla, ou L'Amour et l'Enfer.* Both ballets were restaged by Petipa, Andreyanova's regular partner, for her guest appearances at Moscow's Bolshoi Theater in 1848 and 1849. She created the roles of the Black Fairy in *La Filleule des Fées* and Countess Berta in *Le Diable à Quatre,* both choreographed especially for her by Jules Perrot in 1850.

Andreyanova's style was influenced by the aesthetic principles of the narrative *ballet d'action,* introduced into Russia by Charles Didelot in the early nineteenth century. Critics hailed the virtuosity and perfection of her dancing in roles that called for strength, flamboyance, and improvisation. Psychological insight coupled with wit and expressiveness enabled Andreyanova to master roles that included mime elements, such as Hélène in Filippo Taglioni's ballet in Giacomo Meyerbeer's opera *Robert le Diable* and Fenella in Jean Aumer's ballet in Auber's opera *La Muette de Portici.* She also danced leading roles in Taglioni's version of *L'Ombre* (1839), Alexis Blache's *Don Juan* (1840), Didelot's *Flore et Zéphire* (1842), and Perrot's *Ondine, ou La Naïade* (1851). For a benefit performance in 1853 she danced the role of Count Ragotsky's wife in *La Chaumière Hongroise,* which Didelot had choreographed forty years earlier. Concurrently with Fanny Elssler, Andreyanova launched her own bid to promote folk dances, such as the mazurka, *cachucha, bolero,* and *saltarello.* She also performed character dances in operas, including the *lezghinka* in *Ruslan and Ludmila,* by Mikhail Glinka, and the Slavic dance in Aleksei Verstovsky's *Askold's Tomb.*

Andreyanova performed often as a guest artist in Moscow and toured in Hamburg, Paris, Milan, and London between 1844 and 1852. While she was in Milan she attended classes conducted by Carlo Blasis, and in the same city a bronze medal was cast in recognition of her achievements. During the 1853/54 theater season she led a troupe of Moscow and Saint Petersburg ballet dancers on a tour of the Russian provinces of Odessa, Kharkov, Poltava, Kursk, and Voronezh, a venture unprecedented in the country's cultural life. During this tour the company presented *The Fountain of Bakhchisarai,* a ballet choreographed by Andreyanova herself to music of an unknown composer. She retired from the stage in 1855.

BIBLIOGRAPHY

Guest, Ivor. *Fanny Elssler.* London, 1970.

Guest, Ivor. *The Romantic Ballet in Paris.* 2d rev. ed. London, 1980.

Guest, Ivor. *Jules Perrot: Master of the Romantic Ballet.* London, 1984.

Krasovskaya, Vera. *Russkii baletnyi teatr: Ot vozniknoveniia do serediny XIX veka.* Leningrad, 1958.

Petrov, Oleg. *Russkaia baletnaia kritika kontsa XVIII–pervoi poloviny XIX veka.* Moscow, 1982.

Roslavleva, Natalia. *Era of the Russian Ballet* (1966). New York, 1979.

VALERY A. KULAKOV
Translated from Russian

ANGIOLINI, GASPERO (Domenico Maria Gaspero Angiolini; born 9 February 1731 in Florence, died 6 February 1803 in Milan), dancer, choreographer, ballet master. Much uncertainty and many misconceptions abound regarding the life of Gaspero Angiolini, particularly his choreographic, literary, and musical works; even the place and date of his birth as well as his name are often cited incorrectly. His life is characterized by repeated moves between his Italian homeland, chiefly Milan and Venice, and the imperial cities of Vienna and Saint Petersburg.

Angiolini most likely received his first dance and music training in Florence. From 1747 to 1748 he toured northern Italy (Milan, Spoleto, Turin, and Venice) as a dancer, and evidence exists for his presence in Rome as a choreographer in 1752. His real teacher, and the model he admired throughout his life, was his ballet master at the Hoftheater of Vienna, Franz Hilverding, whom Angiolini vehemently defended posthumously against Jean-Georges Noverre's claims of precedence in creating the *ballet d'action.*

Angiolini is thought to have arrived in Vienna in the early 1750s, probably only temporarily but nonetheless in close artistic contact with Hilverding, then ballet master to Empress Maria Theresa. He began dancing as a soloist in Hilverding's ballets in 1752.

In 1754 Angiolini married his partner, Maria Teresa Fogliazzi (1733–1792), who came from a highly regarded Parma family and who had rejected the advances of (Giovanni Giacomo) Casanova. She had been enthusiastically welcomed to Vienna by Pietro Metastasio in 1752 and was greatly admired by Prince Kaunitz, a connection that proved helpful to Angiolini. After her marriage, she gave up her career as a ballerina to a great extent.

Angiolini's success as a dancer in both Vienna and Italy and his favor at the imperial court led him to be named as Hilverding's successor in Vienna after the latter's departure in 1758. In his first productions, from 1758 to 1760, he followed in Hilverding's footsteps, while making the first attempts at finding his own style. His personal successes as ballet master and dancer culminated in the pantomime-ballet *Don Juan, ou Le Festin de Pierre,* adapted from Molière's *Don Juan,* with Angiolini in the title role. With music by Christoph Willibald Gluck and sets by Giulio Quaglio, it was performed for the first time on 17 October 1761 at the Burgtheater and had many performances in Vienna. The work soon traveled to Paris and to various Italian and German cities. Public opinion was divided over its tragic ending.

In 1762 Angiolini produced a ballet version of Gluck's comic opera *La Cythère Assiégée* on 15 September at the Vienna Burgtheater. He also collaborated as ballet master and dancer on Gluck and Raniero de Calzabigi's opera *Orfeo ed Euridice,* which was performed on 5 October. The following year, Count Giacomo Durazzo, director of the court theaters, obtained the emperor's approval of a pension for Angiolini, who nevertheless remained active as a dancer and ballet master. In 1763 he appeared in Tommaso Traetta's opera *Ifigenia in Tauride;* in 1764, in Gluck's comic opera *La Rencontre Imprévue* and, in connection with the coronation of Joseph II, his own ballet *Le Muse Protette dal Genio d'Austria,* a ballet for which he also composed the music. In 1765 he worked with Gluck on the ballet pantomime *Sémiramis,* based on the work by Voltaire and performed on 31 January at the Burgtheater in honor of Joseph II's remarriage, and the ballet *Iphigénie en Aulide,* based on Jean Racine's tragedy and performed on 19 May in the theater of Laxenburg Castle. To three of these ballets—*Don Juan, La Cythère Assiégée,* and *Sémiramis*—he added a statement of his principles and goals. [*See* Don Juan.]

Emperor Francis I died on 18 August 1765. The official mourning and subsequent theater closing proved a turning point for Angiolini. He was already on insecure ground because of the downfall of Durazzo in the spring of 1764 and the depressing failure of *Sémiramis.* In 1766 he seized an opportunity to leave Vienna for Saint Petersburg, once again as Hilverding's successor.

Angiolini made his debut at the tsarist court on 29 September 1766 with his heroic ballet *Le Départ d'Énée, ou Didon Abandonnée,* a ballet version of Metastasio's first drama, *Didone abbandonata.* The poet sent a congratulatory letter in honor of his success. Angiolini staged eight more ballets between 1766 and 1772, some with his own music, for example, *Telemaco* in 1770, of which he was particularly fond, and others with the music of Vincenzo Manfredini, Ernst Raupach, and Dominik Springer. He also choreographed many *divertissements* in connection with Italian opera performances at the Winter Palace.

In 1772 Angiolini resigned his post in Saint Petersburg and left for Venice, passing through Vienna, where Noverre gave him a gift of the programs for his ballets *Agamemnon Vengé, Iphigénie en Tauride,* and *Les Grâces.* In 1773 in Venice, he produced six ballets, which were performed between the acts of larger operas. They included older works, *Sémiramis* and *Didon Abandonnée,* as well as newer ones, including *Il Re alla Caccia* with his own music, which served as the *ballo primo* in Johann Naumann's opera *Solimano*. He also published the printed music for his *Dido* ballet. That same year in Milan, Angiolini published his own ballet scenarios, including *Il Sagrificio di Dirces* and *La Caccia d'Enrico IV*, and opera ballets, including his ballet in Giovanni Paisiello's *Andromeda*, along with his *Lettere . . . à Monsieur Noverre*. It was in this work that Angiolini challenged Noverre's claim of being the originator of the *ballet d'action*, claiming this honor instead for Hilverding. He also discussed in great detail the principles of the dance and choreography from a historical perspective. Noverre's sharply polemical reply was published in 1774 as a "petite réponse aux grandes lettres du Sr. Angiolini," an introduction to the scenario of his ballet *Les Horaces et les Curiaces*. Thus began a long controversy.

In the spring of 1774 Angiolini returned to Vienna as the successor to Noverre, who had been invited to Milan. In the production of his ballets *L'Orphelin de la Chine, Le Roi et le Fermier, Cid*, and *Montezuma, ou La Conquête du Mexique*, Angiolini faced a strong Noverre contingent that jeered the first two ballets, thwarted a revival of *Montezuma* through intrigue, and applauded demonstratively after a forced revival of Noverre's ballet *Les Horaces et les Curiaces* on 10 September 1775. Angiolini's guest performance in Pavia early in June 1775 was also the scene of a confrontation with Noverre, who was working in Milan. In 1776, Angiolini again left Vienna and returned to Saint Petersburg.

Angiolini's second engagement in that city lasted two years. Although he successfully mounted the ballet productions of *Thésée et Ariane* in 1776 and *L'Orphelin de la Chine* in 1777 and contributed to operas by Paisiello, Angiolini had difficulties with the management of the czarist theater, allegedly because of his obligation to supply music for the ballets in addition to the scenario. The dispute was resolved, and Angiolini was promised an annual pension when he left Russia and returned to Italy in May 1779.

From the summer of 1779 through 1782, Angiolini worked in Venice, Verona, Turin, and especially Milan, where his ballets for the Teatro alla Scala included *Annetta e Lubino; Ciacciona; Attila; Lauretta; Alzira, ossia Gli Americani; Il Diavolo a Quattro, o La Doppia Metamorfosi;* and *Teseo in Creta*. By the time Angiolini was around fifty years old, he was no longer active as a dancer, and he adopted the title "Retired Master of the Two Imperial Courts of Vienna and Saint Petersburg."

On 17 December 1782, Angiolini signed a new four-year contract in Saint Petersburg that guaranteed him a salary, free living quarters and firewood, and travel expenses. During the next four years, he created the choreography for many Italian operas in addition to his own productions, which included *Il Diavolo a Quattro*, already per-

formed in Milan in 1781. He also directed a ballet school at the theater. At the end of 1786, he left Saint Petersburg for good with a small pension.

It is likely that Angiolini returned directly to Italy early in 1787. During the 1788/89 season in Milan, he produced seven of his own ballets, including three at the beginning of the season: the tragic ballet *Fedra*, the heroic-comic ballet *Lorezzo*, and *Un Divertimento Campestre*. The heroic pantomime-ballet *Amore e Psiche* in April of 1789 was his last production for Milan. On 17 October 1790 he drew up his will, in which he bequeathed some money to the Maggiore Hospital in Milan and divided the remainder of his estate equally among his wife and three sons. He went to Turin with *I Vincitori dei Giuochi Olimpici* and *Il Tutore Sorpresa* and to Venice with the heroic pantomime-ballet *Tito* and *La Vendetta Ingegnosa, o La Statua di Condillac* for the 1791 Carnival. Little is known of his life after 1792, but his productivity as an artist was over. He became involved in discussions about theater policy as a strong democrat and supporter of republican ideals; he insisted that theater was not merely an entertainment for the audience but was also a sphere for inspiring civic and democratic sensibilities.

In the summer of 1799 Angiolini was imprisoned for his opinions and then exiled from Milan. He returned to Milan, however, in the summer of 1801 and in 1803 died there at the age of seventy-two. Only three of his children, all of them born in Vienna between 1755 and 1764, survived childhood: Francesco, Giuseppe, and Pietro. Other members of the Angiolini family who made names for themselves as dancers and choreographers were sons of Gaspero's brother Romulo: Niccolò (1765–1815), Pasquale (1766–1817), and the most famous bearer of the Angiolini name among the younger generation, Pietro (1764?–after 1830).

As dancer, ballet master, and choreographer, Angiolini saw as his ultimate goal the representation of a theme by combining all the arts into a ballet pantomime that would occupy a place above all other arts. He strove to achieve this in his creative work by composing the music for his own ballets in Saint Petersburg and Italy, a practice that originated in Vienna during his collaborative period with Gluck.

Choreographic notations of the ballet pantomime alluded to by Angiolini have thus far not been found. Already in his first Viennese ballets, especially those on national themes, Angiolini began evolving his own style as a choreographer; he used fewer innovations in works using historical and fabulous themes, relying for their success on highly polished dance performances.

The four years of collaboration with Gluck and Calzabigi from 1761 to 1765 represent the pinnacle in Angiolini's work. He believed that he had achieved his goal of a complete ballet pantomime with *Sémiramis*. Four months after the ballet had been rejected in Vienna by the imperial wedding party of Joseph II (except for a small group that included Princess Eleonore Liechtenstein), Angiolini consented to a happy ending for his now-lost tragic ballet *Iphigénie en Aulide*. Fundamentally, however, he never wavered in his belief in classical Greek theater and the *danza parlante*. Especially in Vienna, this bias put him at a disadvantage in the public taste whenever he was compared with Noverre. Additional weaknesses, predominantly on the musical side, resulted from the merging of choreographer and composer in one person. Nevertheless, Angiolini's artistic sincerity, idealism, and defense of Hilverding have been remembered as much as his work.

[*For related discussion, see* Austria, *article on* Theatrical Dance. *See also the entries on Gluck and Hilverding.*]

BIBLIOGRAPHY

Anonymous. *Riflessioni sorra [sopra] la pretesa risposta del Sig. Noverre all'Angiolini.* N.p., n.d.

Anonymous. *Lettre d'un des petits oracles de Monsieur Angiolini au grand Noverre.* Milan, 1774.

Angiolini, Gaspero. *Le festin de pierre.* Vienna, 1761.

Angiolini, Gaspero. *Citera assediata.* Vienna, 1762.

Angiolini, Gaspero. *Dissertation sur les ballets pantomimes des anciens, pour servir de programme au ballet pantomime tragique de Semiramis.* Vienna, 1765.

Angiolini, Gaspero. *Lettere di Gasparo Angiolini à Monsieur Noverre sopra i balli pantomimi.* Milan, 1773.

Angiolini, Gaspero. *Riflessioni sopra l'uso dei programmi ne'balli pantomimi.* Milan, 1775.

Brainard, Ingrid. "Angiolini." In *Pipers Enzyklopädie des Musiktheaters.* Munich, 1986–.

Brown, Bruce Alan. *Gluck and the French Theatre in Vienna.* Oxford, 1991.

Carones, Laura. "Noverre and Angiolini: Polemical Letters." *Dance Research* 5 (Spring 1987): 42–54.

Croll, Gerhard. "Gluck's Don Juan freigesprochen." *Österreichische Musikzeitung* 31 (1976): 12.

Dahms, Sibylle. "The 'Ballet d'Action' in Theory and Practice." In *Proceedings of the Stockholm Symposium on Opera and Dance in the Gustavian Era, 1711–1809.* Stockholm, 1986.

Dahms, Sibylle. "Choreographische Aspekte im Werk Jean-Georges Noverres und Gasparo Angiolinis." *Tanzforschung Jahrbuch* 2 (1991): 93–110.

Engländer, Richard. Preface to *C. W. Gluck: Don Juan, Semiramis. Sämtliche Werke,* vol. 2.1. Kassel, 1966.

Gruber, Gernot. "I balli pantomimici viennesi di Gluck e lo stile drammatico della sua musica." *Chigiana* 29–30 (1972–1973): 508–512.

Mariani Borroni, F. "Angiolini, Gasparo." *Dizionario biografico degli italiani.* Rome, 1960–.

Mooser, R. Aloys. *Annales de la musique et des musiciens en Russie au XVIIIe siècle,* vol. 2, *L'époque glorieuse de Catherine II, 1762–1796.* Geneva, 1951.

Noverre, Jean-Georges. *Introduction au ballet des Horaces ou petite réponse aux grandes lettres du Sr. Angiolini.* Vienna, 1774.

Sasportes, José. "La parola contro il corpo ovvero il melodramma nemico del ballo." *La danza italiana* 1 (Autumn 1984): 21–41.

Sasportes, José. "Noverre in Italia." *La danza italiana* 2 (Spring 1985): 39–66.

Sasportes, José. "Two New Letters Concerning the Feud between Angiolini and Noverre." In *Proceedings of the Stockholm Symposium on Opera and Dance in the Gustavian Era, 1711–1809.* Stockholm, 1986.

Testa, Alberto. "Il binomia Gluck-Angiolini e la realizzazione del balletto *Don Juan.*" *Chigiana* 29–30 (1972–1973): 535.

Toscanini, Walter. "Gasparo Angiolini." *Metropolitan Opera News* (8 April 1955).

Tozzi, Lorenzo. *Il balletto pantomimo del settecento: Gaspare Angiolini.* L'Aquila, 1972.

Tozzi, Lorenzo. "La poetica angioliniana del balletto pantomimo nei programmi viennesi." *Chigiana* 29–30 (1972–1973): 487.

Tozzi, Lorenzo. "Musica e balli al Regio di Torino, 1748–1762." *La danza italiana* 2 (Spring 1985): 5–21.

Viale Ferrero, Mercedes. "Appunti di scenografia settecentesca, in margine a rappresentazioni di opere in musica di Gluck e balli di Angiolini." *Chigiana* 29–30 (1972–1973): 513.

Winter, Marian Hannah. *The Pre-Romantic Ballet.* London, 1974.

GERHARD CROLL
Translated from German

ANGLAISE (or *angloise*), a French word, meaning "English," was used in France in the eighteenth century to distinguish the English-style *contredanse*, danced with couples facing each other in rows, from the *contredanse française*, or *cotillon* for four or eight, danced in a circle or

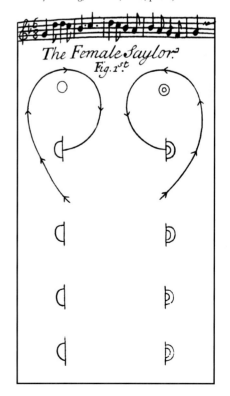

ANGLAISE. Diagram of the first figure of "The Female Saylor," a *contredanse* or *anglaise*. The lady of the head couple moves up the set, around to her right and back to place; the gentleman moves up the set, around to his left, and back to place. (From Raoul-Auger Feuillet's *Recüeil de contredances,* translated by John Essex as *For the Further Improvement of Dancing,* London, 1710, p. 61.)

square. *Anglaises* were written in duple, triple, or compound duple meters.

The earliest *contredanses* in France, introduced at court in the mid-1680s, were all *anglaises* in the sense that they were imported directly from England and were danced in two columns, either for a fixed number of dancers or for "as many as will." However, even in the first French collection of *contredanses*, presented by André Lorin to Louis XIV around 1685, French tendencies were already at work. Lorin suggested the use of steps from the repertory of French social dances, such as *pas de bourrées, jetés,* and *balancés,* in place of the diverse steps and "bizarerie" of the dances he had seen in London. The steps were further codified by Raoul-Auger Feuillet in his *Recüeil de contredances* (1706), which nevertheless still included only progressive longways dances. The adjectives "English" and "French" applied by Feuillet to some of the dances in this collection (and similarly by Jacques Dezais in his collection of 1712) refer only to the nationalities of the choreographers, not to any differences in the fundamental figures. In his *Recüeil de dances de bal pour l'année 1706,* however, Feuillet included a dance for four, entitled "Le Cotillon," that represented an embryonic version of what was soon to become a distinct type of dance.

It is difficult to trace the early development of the *cotillon* because of a gap in the choreographic notation of *contredanses* between 1720 and 1760, but, as the century progressed, collections of dance music included an ever-increasing number of *cotillons* next to the *contredanses anglaises.* In his 1756 book *Élémens de la danse,* the Leipzig dancing master Carl Pauli declared that there existed two types of *contredanse:* the *anglaise* and the *cotillon.* In his opinion, *cotillons* were more amusing because everyone started dancing right away, whereas in the *anglaise* couples down the set were obliged to wait for the dance to progress to them. This point of view appears to have prevailed in France as well, as is apparent from the fact that in the numerous *contredanse* publications of the 1760s and 1770s the *cotillons* outnumbered the *anglaises.* By the end of the century the *anglaise* had been almost entirely eclipsed by its relative.

Certain German music theorists have applied the term *anglaise* to English dancing in general, not simply to country dances. Johann Mattheson divided the *anglaise* into three groups: country dances, ballads (or ballets), and hornpipes. It is in this general sense that the word *anglaise* was sometimes used in the nineteenth century to indicate an English character dance in a ballet. Carlo Blasis, for example, classified the *anglaise* among dances belonging to the lower comic style. Some nineteenth-century European lexicographers, perhaps thinking of the hornpipe, defined the *anglaise* as a solo dance for a sailor.

[*See also* Cotillon; Country Dance; *and* Figure Dances.]

BIBLIOGRAPHY

Blasis, Carlo. *The Code of Terpsichore: A Practical and Historical Treatise on the Ballet, Dancing, and Pantomime.* London, 1828.

Guilcher, Jean-Michel. *La contredanse et les renouvellements de la danse française.* Paris, 1969.

Mattheson, Johann. *Der vollkommene Capellmeister* (1739). Edited by Margarete Reimann. Kassel, 1954.

Pauli, Carl. *Élémens de la danse.* Leipzig, 1756.

Taubert, Karl Heinz. *Die Anglaise . . . mit dem Portefeuille Englischer Tänze von Joseph Lanz.* Zurich, 1983.

REBECCA HARRIS-WARRICK

ANGOLA. *For discussion of dance traditions in Angola, see* Central and East Africa. *For discussion of dance traditions in the African diaspora, see* Brazil, *article on* Popular and Ritual Dance; Cuba, *article on* Folk, Ritual, and Social Dance.

ANISIMOVA, NINA (Nina Aleksandrovna Anisimova; born 23 January 1909 in Saint Petersburg, died 23 September 1979 in Leningrad), Russian dancer, choreographer, and teacher. Anisimova graduated in 1926 from Leningrad's ballet school, where her teachers were Maria Romanova, Agrippina Vaganova, Aleksandr Shiriaev, and A. M. Monakhov. In 1926–1927 Anisimova worked at Leningrad's Maly Opera House before moving to the Theater for Opera and Ballet (later the Kirov Theater) in 1927. At the latter she created the roles of Thérèse in Vasily Vainonen's *The Flames of Paris* (1932) and Nastya in his *Partisan Days* (1937), and Aisha in *Gayané* (1942), which she choreographed to music by Aram Khachaturian. Her other roles included Mercedes in Aleksandr Gorsky's *Don Quixote,* the Siamese Girl in Fedor Lopukhov's *The Bolt,* and Radmila in Vainonen's *Militsa.* A brilliant character dancer, Anisimova appeared in a variety of *divertissements* in standards such as *The Little Humpbacked Horse, Swan Lake, Don Quixote, La Bayadère,* and *Laurencia.* A ballerina of fiery temperament, she created lifelike folk characters.

From 1935 onward, Anisimova also worked as a choreographer. After staging a concert program, *The Spanish Suite,* at the Grand Hall of Leningrad's Philharmonic Auditorium in 1935, she choreographed *The Andalusian Wedding* in 1936 for a graduation performance at Leningrad's ballet school. Her strength as a character dancer informed much of her choreography and was put to especially good use in the provinces. In 1942 she choreographed *Gayané,* which was first presented in Perm, the home of the Kirov Ballet during World War II. Set to the dramatic score by Aram Khachaturian, which includes the well-known "Saber Dance," the ballet takes place on an Armenian collective farm and tells a simple if emotionally charged love story, but in its emphasis on accessible pantomime, use of national dances, and victorious ending it is representative of Socialist principles. Extremely popular, the production remained in the Kirov repertory for many years. While at the Bashkirian Opera and Ballet Theater in Ufa, Anisimova created *Song of the Crane* (1944). The ballet is based on the poetic folk legend of the crane as a symbol of freedom, goodness, and beauty. The corps de ballet in its triangular formations, executing undulating movements and *pas de bourrée couru*, represented the threatened cranes, saved by the hero and heroine, and lent to the overall elegiac quality of the work. At Leningrad's Maly (now Modest Mussorgsky) Theater Anisimova choreographed *The Miraculous Bridal Veil*, also called *The Magic Veil* (1947), and *Weeping Willow, or Willow Tree* (1957), as well as productions of *Coppélia* in 1949 and *Schéhérazade* in 1950.

Anisimova also worked outside the Soviet Union. At the Sofia Folk Opera House in Bulgaria she staged *The Fountain of Bakhchisarai* in 1945 and *The Legend of a Lake* in 1962. She also mounted productions of *Gayané* at the Hungarian Opera House in Budapest in 1959, *Cinderella* at the Yugoslav National Theater of Belgrade in 1963, and *Swan Lake* for the Royal Danish Ballet in 1964. Anisimova retired as a dancer in 1958. From 1963 to 1974 she taught choreography at the Rimsky-Korsakov Conservatory in Leningrad. She was named Merited Artist of the Russian Federation in 1944 and Merited Art Worker of the Russian Federation in 1957. She won the USSR State Prize in 1949.

BIBLIOGRAPHY

Frangopulo, Marietta K. *Nina Anisimova* (in Russian). Leningrad, 1951.
Roslavleva, Natalia. *Era of the Russian Ballet* (1966). New York, 1979.
Sollertinskii, Ivan. *Stati ò balete*. Leningrad, 1973.
Swift, Mary Grace. "The Art of the Dance in the U.S.S.R.: A Study of Politics, Ideology, and Culture." Ph.D. diss., University of Notre Dame, 1967.

IGOR VASILIEVICH STUPNIKOV
Translated from Russian

ANNUAL COLLECTIONS. As the art of refined dancing spread in Europe from the courts to urban ballrooms and assembly halls, the need for rapid expansion of the dance repertory grew. In response to widespread public demand, leading dancing masters and choreographers composed new dances for each approaching season of social activities, publishing them singly or in small groups (usually two or three at a time, sometimes more) in the autumn of each year, early enough to be purchased and learned before the season began. These were the "annual collections," found especially in France and England from about 1700 on. The "Avis au lecteur" (introduction) of the first French *Recüeil de danses de bal pour l'année 1703*, published by Raoul-Auger Feuillet in 1702, states their purpose succinctly:

> As the greater number of persons far away from Paris find it troublesome to obtain knowledge of the new dances for the ball . . . we wish to inform the public . . . that each year at the beginning of November we will offer a small collection of them whose price will be thirty *sols*, beginning with the present one.
> (Feuillet, 1702)

Three years later, lovers of nice books are told that they may acquire calf-bound copies for forty *sols*.

All dances in the French *Petit recueils annuels* (listings in Hilton, 1981, pp. 335–338) are notated in the system developed by Pierre Beauchamps and Feuillet, codified in the latter's *Chorégraphie* (Paris, 1700). Historically noteworthy is the fact that as early as 1700, the year in which Feuillet made Guillaume-Louis Pecour's "Le Passepied Nouveau" available to the public in a format matching that of the subsequent annual collections, even the consumers living in the provinces or abroad could be expected to read Feuillet's dance notation, which obviously was widely known during the latter years of the seventeenth century.

Prior to 1709 the music for the new French ballroom dances (choreographies by Pecour, Feuillet, Claude Ballon, and Dezais) was printed across the top of each page and on one or two separate pages containing only the melodies. From 1710 onward the music pages were left out, and instead the *airs* with their bass parts (*basse de violle*, also *basse continue*, i.e., "figured" or "thorough" bass), suitable for playing on diverse instruments, were published in a companion series, also appearing in early November, at a price of "only" fifteen *sols*.

The repertory reflects the changing tastes of the dancing society. Predominant throughout are the *bourrée, passepied, marche, rigaudon, gavotte*, and *menuet*. In 1705, however, the "Avertissement" to the fourth *Recüeil* speaks of the growing interest in the *cotillon*, "a manner of branle for four that all kinds of persons can dance without ever having learned it," and in the English contradances (Fr., *contredanses*). A *cotillon* was included in the 1706 collection, whose foreword also announced the imminent publication of Feuillet's *Recüeil de contredances* (Paris, 1706). The sixth *Recüeil*, for the year 1708, contained six new *contredanses;* the fourteenth edition, for 1716, contained a large "Cotillon des Fêtes de Thalie" by Dezais; and the seventeenth *Recüeil*, for 1719, contained a sizable *contredanse*, "L'Italienne," also by Dezais.

In England a comparable situation existed. John Playford printed seven editions of his *English Dancing Master* between 1651 and 1686, the year of his death. With the title shortened to *The Dancing Master* after the 1651 edition, each successive volume added new dances and omitted some that had become obsolete (see Beaumont, 1929, pp. 36ff). While Playford's son Henry carried on the family printing business and saw *The Dancing Master* through to its eighteenth and final edition in 1728, a new power arose in the world of music publishing in London: the royal instrument maker, music seller, and publisher John Walsh (c.1666–1736). Walsh, a shrewd businessman, recognized his compatriots' leanings toward dance; nearly half his music collections, many of them annual offerings, beginning with the *Theater Musick* of 1698, contain arrangements of French and English theater and ballroom dances, country dances, and "Entry's Genteel and Grotesque" (Smith, 1968; Smith and Humphries, 1968). Names of famous dancers and choreographers, such as Claude Ballon, Nevelong, Cotine, Isaac, Anthony L'Abbé, Marie-Thérèse Subligny, and de la Garde were mentioned, as were dances of special interest, such as the "Harlequin Chacoone," whose inclusion in *The Fourth Book of the New Flute Master* (1703) may in fact give us an approximate date for the hitherto undated F. Le Roussau choreography.

Walsh's annual dance collections "with directions" or "with figures" are of three types: court dances, such as minuets, *rigaudons*, "French dances," and those composed for royal birthdays (by Isaac, in the editions of 1703 and following; by Anthony L'Abbé, from about 1715 through about 1733; by P. Siris; and by "Monsieur Marcelle of Paris" and others; the notations were the work of John Weaver, de la Garde, and Edmund Pemberton); theater dances; and country dances. The last appeared in sets of twenty-four from 1705 through 1766.

Similar series were initiated by other London publishers, notably the Thompsons, who issued annual collections of twenty-four country dances between 1751 and 1805 as well as a minuet series, in obvious competition with Walsh, who had published collections of minuets, by themselves or in combination with other fashionable dance types, since the 1720s.

In England, as in France, the cotillion began to appear with increasing frequency in the second half of the eighteenth century, side by side with country dances and minuets, as in Francis Werner's *Book 8, for the year 1785, containing 8 Cotillions, 6 favourite Country Dances & two Minuets with their proper figures, for the Harp, Harpsichord & Violin* (London, 1785).

The annual collections periodically presented larger volumes that included the dances of the preceding years. The Thompsons collected their country dances into five cumulative volumes of two hundred dances each; Walsh published his under various titles, such as *The French Dancing Master . . . containing all the French Dances for 3 years past* (1706), *The new Country Dancing-Master . . . containing the Country Dances for the Three last Years* (1709), *The Court Dances for three Last Years* (1709), *A Collection of all the French Dances of the last 7 years, as also the Country Dances of the same Date* (1714), and *20 Books of Figure Dances by Mr. Issacc* (c.1730).

Advertisements for the collections in English and French newspapers (*Mercure de France, Post Man, Daily Courant, Tatler, Evening Post*) stressed the novelty of each successive annual publication, the distinguished provenance of the dances recorded, and their suitability for "Balls, publick Entertainments and Dancing Schools."

[*See also* Social Dance, *article on* Court and Social Dance before 1800.]

BIBLIOGRAPHY

Beaumont, Cyril W. *A Bibliography of Dancing* (1929). New York, 1963.

Brainard, Ingrid. "New Dances for the Ball: The Annual Collections of France and England in the Eighteenth Century." *Early Music* 14.2 (1986): 164–173.

Dean-Smith, Margaret. "Playford, John." In *The New Grove Dictionary of Music and Musicians*. London, 1980.

Guilcher, Jean-Michel. *La contredanse et les renouvellements de la danse française*. Paris, 1969.

Harris-Warrick, Rebecca. "Ballroom Dancing at the Court of Louis XIV." *Early Music* 14.1 (1986): 41–49.

Hilton, Wendy. *Dance of Court and Theatre: The French Noble Style, 1690–1725*. Princeton, 1981.

Kidson, Frank. "John Playford and Seventeenth-Century Music Publishing." *Musical Quarterly* 4 (1918).

Kidson, Frank, et al. "Thompson." In *The New Grove Dictionary of Music and Musicians*. London, 1980.

Little, Meredith Ellis, and Carol G. Marsh. *La Danse Noble: An Inventory of Dances and Sources*. Williamstown, Mass., 1992.

Marsh, Carol G. "French Court Dance in England, 1706–1740: A Study of the Sources." Ph.D. diss., City University of New York, 1985.

Playford, John. *English Dancing Master, 1651*. Edited by Margaret Dean-Smith. London, 1957.

Schwartz, Judith L., and Christena L. Schlundt. *French Court Dance and Dance Music: A Guide to Primary Source Writings, 1643–1789*. Stuyvesant, N.Y., 1987.

Smith, William C., and Charles Humphries. *Music Publishing in the British Isles*. London, 1954.

Smith, William C. *A Bibliography of the Musical Works Published by John Walsh during the Years 1695–1720*. Exp. ed. London, 1968.

Smith, William C., and Charles Humphries. *A Bibliography of the Musical Works Published by John Walsh during the Years 1721–1766*. London, 1968.

Wynne, Shirley S. "The Charms of Complaissance: The Dance in England in the Early Eighteenth Century." Ph.D. diss., Ohio State University, 1967.

INGRID BRAINARD

ANSERMET, ERNEST (born 11 November 1883 in Vevey, Switzerland, died 20 February 1969 in Geneva), Swiss conductor. Ansermet first trained as a mathematician, following his father's profession, and was a professor of mathematics at the University of Lausanne from 1905 to 1909. His interest in music developed during this time, and he took lessons in composition with Ernest

Bloch. In 1910 he decided to make music his career and conducted his first concerts at Lausanne and Montreux. His conducting technique was mainly acquired by observing others. He became conductor of the Montreux Kursaal concerts in 1911 and of the Geneva Symphony Orchestra in 1915.

By 1915, Ansermet had become friendly with several leading composers including Claude Debussy, Maurice Ravel, and especially Igor Stravinsky, whom he met in 1911 at Clarens, Switzerland. Ansermet introduced Stravinsky to the writer C. F. Ramuz, who became the librettist for *The Soldier's Tale* (1918) and wrote the French texts of *Le Renard* (1922) and *Les Noces* (1923). Ansermet also persuaded Stravinsky to conduct his own works, and when conductors Gabriel Pierné and Pierre Monteaux left Serge Diaghilev's Ballets Russes, Ansermet was appointed principal conductor on Stravinsky's recommendation.

In 1916, Ansermet traveled with the company to New York, where he made his U.S. debut and his first phonograph records with the Ballets Russes Orchestra. From 1918 until 1930 he conducted the premieres of most new Stravinsky works, including *The Soldier's Tale* (1918), choreographed by Ludmilla and George Pitoeff; *Le Chant du Rossignol* (1920) and *Pulcinella* (1920), choreographed by Léonide Massine; and *Le Renard* (1922) and *Les Noces* (1923), choreographed by Bronislava Nijinska. His other premieres for Diaghilev included *Parade* (1917), choreographed by Massine to music by Erik Satie; *Le Tricorne* (1919), choreographed by Massine to music by Manuel de Falla; and *Le Chout* (1923), choreographed by Tadeusz (Tadeo) Slavinsky and Mikhail Larionov to music by Sergei Prokofiev.

These performances with the Ballets Russes, together with his increasing concert work with L'Orchestre de la Suisse Romande (which he formed at Geneva in 1918 and directed until his retirement in 1966), laid the basis for Ansermet's international reputation. Besides his understanding and championing of Stravinsky's music (except Stravinsky's later works in the serial idiom), Ansermet showed a particular feeling for the French school of his contemporaries Debussy, Ravel, and Albert Roussel. He was also a persuasive advocate for his Swiss compatriots Arthur Honegger and Frank Martin and was an enthusiastic supporter of Béla Bartók and Benjamin Britten.

In both theater and concert performances, Ansermet was concerned with projecting clarity of line and texture; he exhibited a keen ear for instrumental balance and a scholar's concern for accuracy. He conducted only Stravinsky's original orchestrations of *The Firebird* and *Petrouchka*, refusing to countenance the composer's published "revised versions." A coolness developed between them after some adverse comments by Stravinsky in the late 1940s. Among Ansermet's writings are *Débat sur l'art contemporain* (1948) and the theoretical and philosophical treatise *Les fondements de la musique dans la conscience humaine* (1961), in which he argued strongly against the principles of serial composition.

BIBLIOGRAPHY

Ansermet, Ernest. *Correspondance Ernest Ansermet–Igor Strawinsky, 1914–1967.* Edited by Claude Tappolet. 3 vols. Geneva, 1991.

Ansermet, Ernest. *Correspondances avec des compositeurs européens.* Edited by Claude Tappolet. Geneva, 1994–.

Gavoty, Bernard. *Ernest Ansermet.* Geneva, 1961.

Gelatt, Roland. *Music Makers.* New York, 1972.

NOËL GOODWIN

ANTHROPOLOGY AND DANCE. *See* Methodologies in the Study of Dance, *article on* Anthropology.

ANTONIO AND ROSARIO. Antonio Ruiz Soler (born 4 November 1922 in Seville, died 6 February 1996 in Madrid) and Rosario Florencia Pérez Padilla (born 11 November 1918 in Seville), Spanish dancers. These cousins were dance partners for twenty-two years. They began their dance studies in Seville with Realito, who presented them in recitals beginning in 1927. They also studied in the schools of Angel Pericet and José Otera, and later with Frasquillo. They acquired a broad knowledge of the technique and dances of the *escuela bolera*, regional dances, and flamenco.

In 1928 they appeared in the Liège World's Fair, where their success was so outstanding that they received the nicknames Los Chavalillos Sevillanos ("the kids from Seville"), a name they used professionally for many years. Later in their career they were billed solely as Antonio and Rosario.

Their partnership lasted until 1953. During their touring years they appeared throughout Europe, Latin America, the United States, and the United Kingdom. Their first American tour in 1940 led to Hollywood and an appearance in the film *Ziegfeld Follies* (1946), followed by a United Kingdom debut in 1950 on BBC television.

The repertory by this time included more than thirty dances, including *jotas* from Aragon and Navarre, and the *gaterana* from Toledo (a dance well known in the repertory of La Argentina), *panaderos* from the *escuela bolera*, and *fandango de candil*. Their flamenco repertory featured *alegrías, soleares, bulerías, faruccas,* and the *seguidillas gitanas,* as well as dance adaptations of Federico García Lorca's arrangements for "Ande Joleo" and "Zorango." The music of Spanish composers also featured in their repertory; their choreographies to Enrique Granados's Dance no. 5, *Orgia* by Joaquín Turina, and Manuel de Falla's *El Sombrero de Tres Picos* brought into play lyrical castanets, polished movement, and crystal-clear *zapateados* (heel work). Their travels encouraged them to include regional dances of the countries they visited, and their presentation of the *huayno* from Latin America constantly delighted audiences.

In 1953 their partnership broke up, and in 1954 each formed an independent company. Rosario was partnered by Roberto Iglesias but did not have long-term success. Antonio's company, Ballets de Madrid, had a series of female dancers partnering him, the best known being Rosita Segovia, Carmen Rojas, and Flora Albaicin. Antonio's company was more successful than Rosario's, but it worked spasmodically and its membership was constantly changing.

Although the partnership of Antonio and Rosario was served by good choreography, Antonio was not so successful in his own company. Its best works were probably *La Taberna del Toro* and *Suite of Sonatas* (to music of Antonio Soler).

The contributions of Antonio and Rosario to the art of Spanish dancing can be contrasted sharply with that of Carmen Amaya. Amaya's forte was fantastically dynamic rhythms in flamenco; it was the broad spectrum of their repertory and their presentation that made Antonio and Rosario favorites with audiences. Antonio's interpretation of *zapateados* has never been bettered. They are among the few artists of Spain to be honored (in 1950) with gilded laurel leaves dropped from the flies of Barcelona's theater.

Rosario rejoined Antonio for the 1964 season. Both appeared in films, and Antonio and his Ballets de Madrid made numerous films of his works, some in spectacular settings, such as the caves at Nerja (Málaga) and Arcos de la Frontera.

Rosario has taught in Madrid. Antonio, after the disbanding of his company, appeared as a guest artist with the Ballet de Antologia Española in the 1970s and then took over its directorship in 1980; he died in 1996.

BIBLIOGRAPHY
Antonio [Ruiz Soler, Antonio]. *Mi diario en la carcel.* Madrid, 1944.
"Antonio Scrapbook." *Dance and Dancers* (March 1964): 9–11.
Beaumont, Cyril W. *Antonio.* London, 1952.
Brunelleschi, Elsa. *Antonio and Spanish Dancing.* London, 1958.
Fuentes-Guío, Pedro. *Antonio, la verdad de su vida.* Madrid, 1990.
Hering, Doris. "Antonio and His Ballets de Madrid." *Dance Magazine* (March 1966): 28.
Terry, Walter. "Return of the Kids." *Saturday Review* (24 February 1968).

PHILIPPA HEALE

ANWAR, RAFI (born 1929 in Bombay), Indian dancer, choreographer, and teacher. The son of Syed Sharfuddin, a British army officer, and Najmunnisa Begum. Rafi was attracted to dance at the age of twelve when he saw Rohini Waghle taking lessons at the school of Pundit Sundar Prasad and Mohan Lal Pandae, dancers specializing in the Jaipur school of *kathak.* Knowing that his conservative family would disapprove, he started to learn dancing secretly, initially by observing lessons and reproducing them each day. Rohini Waghle's father was so impressed at his diligence that he began to finance the boy's lessons.

When his father learned of this he was livid, causing Anwar to run away from home. He returned a year later, after his father's death. Soon after, in his first public *kathak* performance, Anwar danced with Rohini Waghle at the Bombay Opera House. The performance was so successful that Anwar joined the dance group of Hema Kaiser Kodi, who encouraged him to branch out into other dance styles. He then spent four years studying *bharata nāṭyam* under Govind Rai Pillai, Chandashekhar Pillai, and Madanlal Rajamani, and two years studying Manipuri under Priya Gopal Sinha and Narendra Kumar.

Anwar financed his dance studies by teaching, through which he met Laila Shahzada, a painter from Pakistan, who invited him there. Anwar moved to Karachi in 1956 and started giving private lessons at Laila Shahzada's house, later moving his classes to the Pakistan American Cultural Center, where he taught for the next ten years. In addition, he gave *bharata nāṭyam* performances with Azuri Begum and Meera Devi Chatterjee and *kathak* performances with Rohini Babli, and he composed ballets with Afroze Bulbul and Shigeko Sasada.

In 1966 Anwar joined the newly opened PIA Arts Academy as instructor, choreographer, and principal dancer. This academy served as a cultural center for advertising the national airline through dance and music. Anwar was in charge of teaching folk dances to a company of thirty dancers. During this time he traveled extensively, performing in Iran, China, Korea, Japan, Tunisia, Morocco, Jordan, France, the Netherlands, and the United States.

Since leaving the academy, Anwar has taught privately and at Karachi schools. He stopped performing in the 1980s but continues to be a prominent member of Pakistan's dance scene as a teacher. His popularity among his students is evidenced by two concerts of his performances organized by his students to raise money for a spacious apartment in which he could live and hold classes. Unfortunately, the conservative neighbors in the apartment building prevented these dance classes from being held, viewing them as immoral. Anwar is now obliged to commute to the traffic-congested metropolis of Karachi to reach his students.

BIBLIOGRAPHY
Anwar, Rafi. "An Introduction to the Indian Dance." *Indian Arts and Letters* 17 (1943): 136–138.
Hakim, Rehana. "The Life and Times." *Newsline* (February 1995).
INTERVIEW. Rafi Anwar, by Shayma Saiyid (Karachi, January 1995).

SHAYMA SAIYID

APACHE DANCE. At the end of the nineteenth century, the fortifications around Paris became shelters for hoodlums known as *apaches* because of their savage practices. They met in popular cafes in Montmartre and later in the rue de Lappe, behind the Bastille, performing lascivious dances in which a man and woman danced closer together than was accepted at the time. Between dances it was customary for the dancers to pay the musicians.

Around 1880, the most famous women dancers—known by such sobriquets as La Goulue (The Glutton), Grille d'Egout (Manhole Grating), Nini-Patte-en-l'Air (Nini Foot-in-the-Air), and La Môme Fromage (The Cheese Urchin)—and their partners, notably Valentin le Désossé (Valentin the Boneless), performed a rowdy dance known as a *quadrille réaliste,* which was depicted by a number of painters, particularly Henri de Toulouse-Lautrec. It included a *développé* with the foot raised to ear level, multiple sweeps of black-stockinged legs, swaying of the hips, and backward thrusts of the torso and pelvis, all done in a great flurry of energetically shaken lingerie and white petticoats.

These activities, which were often watched by wealthy curiosity-seekers, were succeeded around the turn of the century by the *valse chaloupée* ("rocking waltz"), in which the male dancer, wearing a tight-fitting vest and a handkerchief knotted like a tie, held his partner close, his hands on her hips, while she wrapped her arms around his neck. The male dancer then placed his hands on his partner's buttocks or held her by one hand while spinning her rapidly around and then abruptly pulling her back to him.

The reputation of the *apaches,* many of whom were thieves and murderers, made the style fascinating to the public, so some music-hall artists, such as Mistinguett and Max Dearly, did not hesitate to perform close, rocking waltzes before audiences during the years before World War I. The genre ultimately became a tourist attraction and ceased to be the subversive and shocking dance it once had been.

BIBLIOGRAPHY

Cooper, H. E. "A Cycle of Dance Crazes." *Dance Magazine* (February 1927): 28–29.
Verue, Maurice. *Aux usuies du plaisir.* Paris, 1930.

MARIE-FRANÇOISE CHRISTOUT
Translated from French

APOLLO. Original title: *Apollon Musagète;* also known as *Apollo Musagetes* and as *Apollo, Leader of the Muses.* Ballet in two scenes. Choreography: George Balanchine. Music and libretto: Igor Stravinsky. Scenery and costumes: André Bauchant. First performance: 12 June 1928, Théâtre Sarah-Bernhardt, Paris, Ballets Russes de Serge Diaghilev. Principals: Serge Lifar (Apollo), Alice Nikitina (Terpsichore), Lubov Tchernicheva (Calliope), Felia Doubrovska (Polyhymnia), Sophie Orlova (Leto).

Apollon Musagète was the first collaborative venture between George Balanchine and Igor Stravinsky. The ballet was a departure for both composer and choreographer: Stravinsky discarded the folk influences of his earlier ballet scores and developed a polyphonic style governed by the rigors of classical harmony; Balanchine reflected the music's periodicity, its restraint, and its harmonic tensions and resolutions through the classical ballet vocabulary. It was a turning point in the choreographer's creative life, a return to his classical heritage following the modernist experiments of his youth and the avant-garde theatrical works he had earlier produced for Diaghilev.

Stravinsky conceived and composed *Apollo Musagetes* as a ballet. The score was commissioned in 1927 by Elizabeth Sprague Coolidge for a festival of contemporary music in Washington, D.C., where it was first performed on 27 April 1928 with choreography by Adolph Bolm. Balanchine's production for Diaghilev's Ballets Russes was presented in Paris less than two months later, on 12 June 1928. The cast featured Serge Lifar as Apollo and Alice Nikitina as Terpsichore, a role she later shared with Alexandra Danilova. Bauchant's decor and costumes, which derived from the naive school of painting, and Lifar's rough-hewn athleticism prompted Balanchine to create awkward, crude movements for his Sun God and the attendant Muses.

The choreographer's greatest inspiration, however, was the music's rhythmic vitality, with its jazz inflections and

APOLLO. Serge Lifar (Apollo) supports Alice Nikitina (Terpsichore) in the swimming lift in the original production of Balanchine's *Apollo Musagète* (1928) by the Ballets Russes de Serge Diaghilev. (Photograph from the Dance Collection, New York Public Library for the Performing Arts. Choreography by George Balanchine © The George Balanchine Trust.)

its juxtaposition of stasis and propulsion. Stravinsky has stated that the true subject of *Apollo* is versification, reinforcing the impression that the phrase structure is based on iambic and trochaic rhythmic patterns. The isolated movement images—Apollo spreading his arms like the wings of an eagle, Terpsichore "swimming" on the boy-god's back—are sustained by a dance continuity that is supported by the score's rhythmic architecture. *Apollo* also shows the development of the creative imagination through discipline, a theme implicit in many of Balanchine's later works. He augmented traditional classical vocabulary with turned-in legs, contractions, and heel spins. The work is a contemporary *ballet de cour*, an allegory unfolding through classical dance and its inversion.

Scene 1, which serves as a brief prologue, depicts Leto giving birth to Apollo, son of Zeus. Scene 2 reenacts the young god's selection of Terpsichore, personifying dance, over her sister Muses, Polyhymnia, representing mime, and Calliope, the embodiment of poetry. This section consists of two variations for Apollo, a *pas d'action*, a variation for each Muse, a pas de deux for Terpsichore and Apollo, and the final coda and apotheosis. As Apollo is summoned to Olympus, he blesses the pointes of the Muses by touching them with his palm. Their mission is to inspire; they will go forth to show their arts to the world.

Balanchine's *Apollon Musagète* was first presented in the United States in his 1937 production for the American Ballet, with scenery and costumes by Stewart Chaney, at the Metropolitan Opera House in New York. Lew Christensen was Apollo, and Elise Reiman, Holly Howard, and Daphne Vane were the three Muses—Terpsichore, Polyhymnia, and Calliope, respectively. Later revivals by Balanchine include a 1941 production for American Ballet Caravan, with scenery and costumes by Stewart Chaney, and a 1951 production for New York City Ballet, with costumes by Barbara Karinska and lighting by Jean Rosenthal. Since the late 1950s, the work has been called simply *Apollo* and has been danced in practice clothes with minimal scenery. For New York City Ballet's 1979 revival with Mikhail Baryshnikov, scene 1 and Apollo's first variation were omitted, and the ending of the apotheosis was rechoreographed to conclude with the famous pose of the Muses grouped behind Apollo in arabesque, forming a visual image of the sun and its rays. Scene 1 was later restored, as were Apollo's variation and the original ending of the apotheosis, in which Apollo leads the Muses in a stately ascent of Mount Olympus.

In the history of the New York City Ballet, *Apollo* has never been long absent from the repertory. Notable interpreters of the title role have included André Eglevsky, Jacques d'Amboise, Edward Villella, Peter Martins, Ib Andersen, and Peter Boal. D'Amboise, who performed the role for many years, was especially admired for his articulated phrasing and uninhibited attack. In other companies, Donald MacLeary, Rudolf Nureyev, and Michaël Denard made notably successful appearances in the role. Denard was often described as "radiant." Among the ballerinas who have made indelible impressions as Terpsichore are Marie-Jeanne, Maria Tallchief, Svetlana Beriosova, Suzanne Farrell, Kay Mazzo, and Darci Kistler.

With the sanction of the Balanchine Trust, *Apollo* has been staged for many companies around the world. Over the years it has entered the repertories of the Boston Ballet, the San Francisco Ballet, the Miami City Ballet, Britain's Royal Ballet, the Paris Opera Ballet, the Royal Danish Ballet, the Vienna State Opera Ballet, the Australian Ballet, the Maryinsky (formerly Kirov) Ballet in Saint Petersburg, and numerous other companies in Europe, Asia, South America, and the Caribbean.

BIBLIOGRAPHY

Au, Susan. "*Apollo:* The Transformation of a Myth." *Dance Research Annual* 14 (1983): 50–63.

Balanchine, George, with Francis Mason. *Balanchine's Complete Stories of the Great Ballets.* Rev. and enl. ed. Garden City, N.Y., 1977.

Brooks, Virginia Loring. "*Apollo* in Transition." *New Dance Review* 3 (January–March 1991): 7–10.

Choreography by George Balanchine: A Catalogue of Works. New York, 1984.

Denby, Edwin. "Revival of *Apollo.*" *Dance Index* 5 (January 1946): 53–56.

Goldner, Nancy. *The Stravinsky Festival of the New York City Ballet.* New York, 1974.

Gruen, John. "Balanchine and Stravinsky: An Olympian *Apollo.*" *Dance Magazine* 55 (April 1981): 84–87.

Johnson, Robert. "White on White: The Classical Background of *Apollon Musagète.*" *Ballet Review* 13 (Fall 1985): 48–54.

Kirstein, Lincoln. *Movement and Metaphor: Four Centuries of Ballet.* New York, 1970.

Kirstein, Lincoln. *The New York City Ballet.* With photographs by Martha Swope and George Platt Lynes. New York, 1973.

Mickiewicz, Denis. "*Apollo* and Modernist Poetics." In *The Silver Age of Russian Culture,* edited by Carl Proffer and Ellendea Proffer. Ann Arbor, 1975.

Resnikova, Eva. "The Mystery of Terpsichore: Balanchine, Stravinsky, and *Apollo.*" *New Criterion* 2 (September 1983): 22–28.

Reynolds, Nancy. *Repertory in Review: Forty Years of the New York City Ballet.* New York, 1977.

Scholl, Tim. *From Petipa to Balanchine: Classical Revival and the Modernization of Ballet.* New York, 1994.

VIDEOTAPES.   Excerpts from *Apollo* in *The Bell Telephone Hour* (1963), with Jacques d'Amboise and other members of the New York City Ballet, available in the Dance Collection, New York Public Library for the Performing Arts. "Balanchine," parts 1 and 2, *Dance in America* (WNET-TV, New York, 1984). "Stravinsky and Balanchine: Genius Has a Birthday," *Dance in America* (WNET-TV, New York, 1982).

REBA ANN ADLER

APPALACHIAN   SPRING.   Choreography: Martha Graham. Music: Aaron Copland. Scenery: Isamu Noguchi. Costumes: Edythe Gilfond. Lighting: Jean Rosenthal. First performance: 30 October 1944, Library of Congress, Washington, D.C., Martha Graham Dance Company. Principals: Martha Graham (The Bride), Erick Hawkins (The Husbandman), Merce Cunningham (The Revivalist), May O'Donnell (The Pioneering Woman), Nina Fonaroff, Pearl Lang, Marjorie Mazia, Yuriko (The Followers).

Perhaps the best known and best loved of Graham's works, and the one with the finest score, *Appalachian Spring* takes as its pretext a wedding on the American frontier. The dance is like no actual ceremony or party, however. The movement not only expresses individual character and emotion, but it has a clarity, spaciousness, and definition that relate to the open frontier, which must be fenced and tamed.

The stage is defined by Noguchi's spare set: slim timbers that frame a house, a portion of wall, a bench, a platform with a rocker, a piece of fence, and a small, tilted disk. During the dance, the characters emerge to make solo statements; the action of the dance suspends while they reveal what is in their hearts. The Bride's two solos, for instance, suggest not only her joy but her trepidation as she envisions her future. The Followers rush about with little steps and hops and provide a visual chorus of exclamations and amens. As Copland used American motifs in his score, so Graham drew subtly on steps from country dancing to express the frank vigor of these people.

Appalachian Spring has been in the repertory of the Martha Graham Dance Company almost continuously since the work's premiere.

BIBLIOGRAPHY
Gardner, Howard. "Martha Graham: Discovering the Dance of America." *Ballet Review* 22 (Spring 1994): 67–93.
Lloyd, Margaret. *The Borzoi Book of Modern Dance.* New York, 1949.
Reynolds, Nancy, and Susan Reimer-Torn. *Dance Classics.* Pennington, N.J., 1991.
Siegel, Marcia B. *The Shapes of Change: Images of American Dance.* New York, 1979.

FILM AND VIDEOTAPE. *Appalachian Spring* (1958). *Appalachian Spring,* included in "Martha Graham and Dance Company," *Dance in America* (WNET-TV, New York, 1976). "Martha Graham: An American Original in Performance," a Nathan Kroll Production; contains *A Dancer's World* (1957) and *Appalachian Spring* (1958), both directed by Peter Glushanok, and *Night Journey* (1961), directed by Alexander Hammid.

DEBORAH JOWITT

APPIA, ADOLPHE (Adolphe-François Appia; born 1 September 1862 in Geneva, died 29 February 1928 in Nyon, Switzerland), Swiss scenery designer and theoretician. Appia was largely responsible, with English scenographer Edward Gordon Craig, for conceptualizing the three-dimensional suggestive settings of the twentieth century. His designs for abstract shapes in space offered an alternative to the centuries-old stage practice of two-dimensional, realistically detailed scenery that was painted in perspective and positioned behind the proscenium arch.

After early schooling, Appia studied music in Geneva, Paris, Leipzig, and Dresden in preparation for a musical career. Although he attended concerts, he was not allowed to enter a theater because of his strict Calvinist upbringing. Not until age nineteen did he see his first theatrical performance, Charles Gounod's *Faust* at Geneva's Grand Théâtre. In 1882, he attended the premiere of Richard Wagner's *Parsifal* at the Bayreuth Festspielhaus, a new model of theater architecture with a conventional stage behind the proscenium arch. Although Appia was deeply moved by Wagner's music, he disliked the traditional staging. Subsequent summer returns only confirmed his initial impressions.

In 1888, Appia resolved to reform theatrical staging and direction. He spent the next two years as stage apprentice, first at the Dresden Hoftheater, then at the Burgtheater and the Hofoperntheater in Vienna. His theories and designs for Wagnerian music drama initially were set forth in a brief volume, *La mise en scène du drame wagnérian* (The Staging of Wagnerian Music Drama; 1895), and later expanded in a full-length work, *Die Musik und die Inszenierung* (Music and the Art of the Theater; 1899).

Influenced by classical Greek theater, Swiss outdoor theater festivals on national themes, and Wagner's music dramas and writings, Appia proposed a radically changed stage space. Central to his conception was the actor moving in three dimensions rather than in front of a painted scene. He stressed simplicity and suggestiveness and so designed a stage with platforms, steps, and ramps that allowed complete movement through and over the stage space. Thus, a "living" entity of light and shadow molded the actor, provided atmosphere and color, and was rhythmic in its changes. Light was also a unifying element. As had Wagner, Appia called for one director who would interpret the total production, but his designs were turned down at Bayreuth by Cosima Wagner.

Appia's first opportunity to stage his ideas came in 1903 in productions of the first scene of act 2 of *Carmen* and a scene from the Byron-Schumann *Manfred,* which was staged in the private Parisian mansion theater of Countess René de Béarn. Although the production attracted attention, he was given no more directing assignments.

Appia's search for a method of training actors in gesture and movement (which he termed *choreography*) came to an end in 1906 when he attended a lecture-demonstration of rhythmical gymnastics (eurhythmics) arranged by Émile Jaques-Dalcroze. "I found the answer to my passionate desire for synthesis [between music and performer]," Appia wrote in the second preface to the 1918 English edition of his *Music and the Art of the*

Theater. His friendship with Jaques-Dalcroze was based on the mutual appreciation of each other's work. In 1909, Appia made some twenty sketches for "espaces rhythmiques" (rhythmic spaces) to provide a suitable environment for Jaques-Dalcroze's lecture-demonstrations.

When the Bildungsanstalt Jaques-Dalcroze was erected in 1910 at Hellerau near Dresden, Germany, Appia collaborated with Alexander von Salzmann and Heinrich Tessenow in designing the auditorium, stage, and stage lighting. This studio-theater contained steeply raked seating for six hundred people, an orchestra pit, but no curtain or proscenium arch. Parallel rows of approximately three thousand lamps, placed above a cloth ceiling and behind cloth walls for diffuse lighting of stage and audience, directed stage beams masked behind set units and screens, and projectors threw shadows and silhouettes on stage. [*See the entry on Jaques-Dalcroze.*]

Appia's theories of design and staging were first used in 1912 for Hellerau summer festival productions of *Echo und Narzissus*, a dance-drama by Jacques Chenevière with music by Jaques-Dalcroze, and the Hades scene from Christoph Willibald Gluck's *Orfeo ed Euridice.* They were also used again in the June 1913 full-length production of *Orfeo.* These festival pieces were applauded by such luminaries as Serge Diaghilev, Max Reinhardt, and George Bernard Shaw.

Appia served as adviser to Jaques-Dalcroze and French stage director Firmin Gémier for *La Fête de Juin,* a huge pageant staged in July 1914 to celebrate the centenary of the Republic of Geneva's union with the Swiss Confederation. Set up on the northern shore of Lake Geneva, the stage had a rear wall that opened to a view of the mountains, a feature that Appia would have included at Hellerau if costs had not been prohibitive. When World War I began, Jaques-Dalcroze moved to Geneva to open his own institute.

Following the war, Appia provided a sketch for the 1920 production of *Echo und Narzissus* at the Jaques-Dalcroze Institute. In 1923, his design for *Tristan und Isolde* was produced at the Teatro alla Scala in Milan; in 1924 and 1925, he designed three productions that were directed by his protégé, Oskar Waelterlin, at the Basel Stadttheater in Switzerland: *Das Rheingold, Die Walküre,* and *Prométhée.* Appia's book *L'oeuvre d'art vivant* (The Work of Living Art; 1921) contains the most complete explanation of his ideas.

After his death, Appia's work was continued by his pupils Waelterlin and Jean Mercier and by his disciple, French stage director Jacques Copeau. American designer Lee Simonson wrote extensively about Appia's influence on his own work. Following World War II, Appia's theories inspired the Bayreuth productions of Wagner's operas as directed by the composer's grandsons.

[*See also* Lighting for Dance, *historical overview article.*]

BIBLIOGRAPHY

Appia, Adolphe-François. *The Work of Living Art: A Theory of the Theatre* (18—). Translated by H. D. Albright. Coral Gables, Fla., 1960.

Appia, Adolphe-François. *Music and the Art of the Theatre* (1895). Translated by Robert W. Corrigan and Mary Douglas Dirks. Coral Gables, Fla., 1962.

Appia, Adolph-François. *Oeuvres complètes.* Edited by Marie L. Bablet-Hahn. 4 vols. Lausanne, 1983–1991.

Appia, Adolphe-François. *Essays, Scenarios, and Designs.* Translated by Walther R. Volbach. Edited by Richard C. Beacham. Ann Arbor, Mich., 1989.

Appia, Adolphe-François. *Texts on Theatre.* Edited by Richard C. Beacham. London, 1993.

Beacham, Richard C. *Adolphe Appia: Artist and Visionary of the Modern Theatre.* Chur, Switzerland, 1994.

Marotti, Ferruccio. *Adolphe Appia: Attore, musica e scena.* Milan, 1981.

Odom, Selma Landen. "Choreographing *Orpheus:* Hellerau 1913 and Warwick 1991." In *Dance Reconstructed,* edited by Barbara Palfy. New Brunswick, N.J., 1993.

Volbach, Walther R. *Adolphe Appia: Prophet of the Modern Theater.* Middletown, Conn., 1968.

IRIS M. FANGER

APRÈS-MIDI D'UN FAUNE, L'. Ballet in one act. Choreography and libretto: Vaslav Nijinsky. Music: Claude Debussy. Scenery and costumes: Léon Bakst. First performance: 29 May 1912, Théâtre du Châtelet, Paris, Ballet Russes de Serge Diaghilev. Principals: Vaslav Nijinsky (The Faun), Lydia Nelidova (The Principal Nymph).

L'Après-midi d'un Faune was Vaslav Nijinsky's first important ballet, and it established him as a choreographer of note. It also established him, briefly, as the resident choreographer of Diaghilev's Ballets Russes, for Michel Fokine, who had held that post, resigned over what he felt was Diaghilev's preferential treatment of Nijinsky's ballet.

Nijinsky began mounting *Faune* in November and December 1910, working privately with his sister, Bronislava Nijinska. It was set on the company between January and April 1912. Because of the dancers' difficulties in mastering its novel movement style, this twelve-minute ballet required approximately one hundred company rehearsals.

Unlike most of the Fokine ballets that preceded it in Diaghilev's Saison Russe, *Faune* is less narrative than it is poetic, or dreamlike. The libretto, loosely based on Stéphane Mallarmé's poem "L'Après-midi d'un Faune" (which, however, Nijinsky claimed he had not read when he made the ballet), is spare. A young faun, lazing on a rock, observes the arrival of seven nymphs, the tallest of whom proceeds to take a stylized bath. The faun tries to woo the tall nymph; she escapes, leaving a veil behind her. The other nymphs attempt to reclaim the veil, but the faun will not surrender it. Carrying it up to his rock, he lovingly lays it down and then lowers his body on top of it, ending with a spasm suggestive of orgasm.

L'APRÈS-MIDI D'UN FAUNE. A scene from the original 1912 production. Nijinsky as the Faun and Nelidova as the Principal Nymph hook elbows as the other five nymphs look on. The angular movement for this dance may have been inspired by stylized figures on ancient friezes. (Photograph by Baron Adolf de Meyer; from the Dance Collection, New York Public Library for the Performing Arts.)

The premiere was greeted by contending applause and booing, the latter presumably a response to the ballet's final gesture. That gesture also sparked a controversy in the Parisian newspapers, Auguste Rodin and Odilon Redon defending Nijinsky against the charge of obscenity made in a front-page article in *Le Figaro* by Gaston Calmette, editor of the paper.

Bold in its subject matter, the ballet was bolder in its choreography. The dancers moved not to but through the music. And in contrast to the music, Debussy's lush *Prélude à l'Après-midi d'un Faune* (1894)—also in contrast to Bakst's lush backdrop—the movements were angular, often abrupt, and periodically broken by freezes. This last effect, combined with the flatness of the choreographic design—their limbs and heads in profile, the nymphs traveled in horizontal lines across the stage, as if in slots—gave the ballet the look of an antique frieze. (Nijinsky is said to have based the choreography on Egyptian sculpture.) With its freezes and staccato motions, the choreography constituted a dissection of the very process of movement. The steps were utterly anticlassical; indeed, the footwork consisted primarily of flexed-footed walking, much of it heel-toe.

Faune constituted "an absolute break with classic tradition, the first of such impact in four centuries" (Kirstein, 1970, p. 198). Not just its departure from the *danse d'école* but, more important, its analytic approach to movement marks it as the first modernist ballet. Its subject, the discovery of the self via the discovery of sexuality, also aligns it with modernism.

Faune was the only one of Nijinsky's works to remain in the Ballets Russes repertory beyond its premiere season.

In consequence, it is the only ballet of his to survive by unbroken tradition, having been remounted by the (London) Ballet Club (1931), de Basil's Ballets Russes (1933), Ballet Russe de Monte Carlo (1938), Ballet Theatre (1942), Paris Opera Ballet (1976), London Festival Ballet (1979), Rudolf Nureyev and the Joffrey Ballet (1979), and American Ballet Theatre (1982). Other versions, with new choreography, include those of Serge Lifar (1935), Jerome Robbins (1953), and Kurt Jooss (1966). [*See* Afternoon of a Faun.]

BIBLIOGRAPHY
Buckle, Richard. *Nijinsky*. London, 1971.
Choreography and Dance 1.3 (1991). Special issue on Nijinsky's original *L'Après-midi d'un Faune.*
de Meyer, Baron Adolf. *L'Après-midi d'un Faune, Vaslav Nijinsky, 1912: Thirty-Three Photographs.* New York, 1983.
Guest, Ann Hutchinson, with Claudia Jeschke. *Nijinsky's "Faune" Restored: A Study of Vaslav Nijinsky's 1915 Dance Score "L'Après-midi d'un Faune" and His Dance Notation System.* Philadelphia, 1991.
Hellman, Eric. "The Scandal of Nijinsky's *Faune.*" *Ballet Review* 22 (Summer 1994): 10–19.
Kirstein, Lincoln. *Movement and Metaphor: Four Centuries of Ballet.* New York, 1970.
Kirstein, Lincoln, et al. *Nijinsky Dancing.* New York, 1975.
Nijinska, Bronislava. *Early Memoirs.* Translated and edited by Irina Nijinska and Jean Rawlinson. New York, 1981.
Sokolova, Lydia. *Dancing for Diaghilev.* Edited by Richard Buckle. London, 1960.

FILM. *L'Après-midi d'un Faune* (Ballet Club, 1931), is held in the Dance Collection, New York Public Library for the Performing Arts, and the Marie Rambert Film Collection, National Film Archive, London.

ARCHIVES. The private collection of Bronislava Nijinska, which remains in the hands of her family (Pacific Palisades, California), contains several pages of dance notation by Nijinsky, c.1911–1913, as well as a music score annotated by Nijinska, 1922(?). The Rambert Dance Company Archive, London, contains a music score with notes by Antony Tudor, based on Leon Woizikowski's coaching of Ballet Club, 1931. A movement score by Nijinsky, c.1915, is in the collection of the British Library, London.

JOAN ACOCELLA

ARABESQUE. The term *arabesque*, used to describe scrolling and interlacing plant-form motifs, was coined in the sixteenth century. It entered the vocabulary of academic dance in Carlo Blasis's *Traité élémentaire, théorique et pratique de l'art de la danse* (1820). Blasis did not, however, invent the dance designs he called arabesques. Dancers had been striking poses, balancing on one leg (with the other extended back and the knee straight), long enough for Blasis to consider such poses as a group. He found their variety unlimited, because of the innumerable possibilities provided by *épaulement* (the placement of the shoulders) and by arm and leg adjustments.

One of Blasis's illustrations, however, did give rise to a specific term, *arabesque à la lyre*, because it showed a

ARABESQUE. Virginia Johnson of the Dance Theatre of Harlem balances on pointe in a variation of first arabesque. The elevation of the upstage arm dramatically changes the classical line. (Photograph © 1978 by Jack Vartoogian; used by permission.)

dancer pausing on one leg while extending a lifted leg in clear alignment with an upraised arm that held a lyre. This term was then used by the French school to describe arabesques posed with both arms upcurved in front of the dancer's torso. With the palms turned away from the torso in this pose, *arabesque à la lyre* became known, particularly to August Bournonville, as *arabesque à deux bras*.

To distinguish the differences given to arabesques primarily by the legs, the French school identified two specific versions: (1) *arabesque ouverte*, where the downstage leg is extended against a leaning torso and the arms are in corresponding alignment with the legs (i.e., the downstage arm is held in the direction of the working leg and the upstage arm reaches straight out from the body), and (2) *arabesque croisé*, where the upstage leg is extended and the torso leans away from it with the arms arranged in alignment directly related to the legs (i.e., the upstage arm reaches back in line with the extending leg and the downstage arm reaches straight out of a similarly reaching shoulder).

To Enrico Cecchetti, the particulars of the arabesque pose were even more definite. He designated five separate variations.

1. Cecchetti's first arabesque resembles the French *ouverte*, except that the torso is more erect than inclined (as it is in all cases of strict Cecchetti arabesques), and the arms slope gently downward from the slightly raised hand of the upstage, forward arm through to the slightly lowered hand of the downstage, rear arm.
2. Second arabesque retains the open legs of first arabesque but changes the arms and head through *épaulement*. Here the downstage arm reaches forward, from a forward shoulder position, and the upstage arm reaches back, away from the front arm. There is also a related shift of the head, which is slightly inclined and turned, with the gaze toward the audience.
3. Third arabesque relates directly to Bournonville's *arabesque à deux bras*. It keeps the open angle for the legs of first and second arabesques and places both arms in front of the torso, softly extended, with the upstage arm slightly higher than the downstage one.
4. Fourth arabesque is like the French *croisé* in having an extended upstage leg, but Cecchetti's downstage leg supports the pose in *demi-plié*. The carriage of the arms is like that of first arabesque.
5. Fifth arabesque has the legs in fourth-arabesque design, including the *demi-plié* support, but the arms are in third-arabesque position.

In the 1920s Agrippina Vaganova formulated her own principles of classical ballet and in the process designed four different arabesques. When she detailed them for a 1934 volume on her technique, she indicated how her formulations differed from the already established French and Italian versions.

1. Vaganova's first arabesque is akin to Cecchetti's, except that there is a definite forward arch to the torso and the downstage arm, rather than being carried back, is held more to the side of the torso.
2. Second arabesque is also like Cecchetti's, except for the forward arch of the torso and the stronger accent of *épaulement*.
3. Third arabesque is another version of *arabesque croisé*, with the upstage leg as the working leg and the arms positioned as for first arabesque.
4. Fourth arabesque keeps the legs' *croisé* position of third arabesque and changes the arms to the *épaulé* position taken for second arabesque.

Essentially, Vaganova's third and fourth arabesques are *croisé* versions of her first and second designs.

Arabesques are all taught with the dancer standing on the whole foot, but they can acquire distinct inflection when they are taken on the *demi-pointe* or full pointe or are executed with a partner's support. They can also acquire specific graphic variety when they are given an *allongé* or *penché* accent. *Arabesque allongée* is achieved by an elongated reach from the extending leg and the forward extending arm. The repeated arabesques that dominate the entrance of the Shades in Marius Petipa's *La Bayadère* are a notable example. In *arabesque penchée*, the torso reaches downward in direct response to the high raising of the extended leg. With the support of a partner, this arabesque can be executed with continually sustained energy and show finely graded growth, while producing a simultaneously plummeting and soaring line. The opening sequence of the pas de deux in the first lakeside scene of *Swan Lake* includes this dramatic effect.

Arabesque voyagée refers to traveling in arabesque. A striking version of this occurs in act 2 of *Giselle*, when two flanks of wilis cross the stage, one from each side, and proceed in firm first-arabesque pose at an unvaried pace. A signature configuration from George Balanchine's *Apollo* has three Muses braced behind Apollo in variations on arabesque leg heights—one holds a half height *(demi-arabesque)* pose; the next, a full-height, hip-level extension; and the third, an above-the-hip *penché* pose. The image suggests Apollo as the sun and the legs of the Muses as rays of light.

BIBLIOGRAPHY

Grant, Gail. *Technical Manual and Dictionary of Classical Ballet.* Rev. ed. New York, 1982.
Vaganova, Agrippina. *Basic Principles of Classical Ballet: Russian Ballet Technique* (1934). Translated by Anatole Chujoy. Edited by Peggy van Praagh. 2d ed. London, 1953.

ROBERT GRESKOVIC

ARABIAN PENINSULA. The regional dances of the vast but sparsely populated peninsula that includes Saudi Arabia, the Gulf states and emirates, and Yemen are—due to political, religious, economic, and other reasons of access—among the least studied. Historically, the gulf region is one of the most ancient marketplaces, with traders from India, Mesopotamia, Africa, and the Arabian hinterland meeting here for centuries. Influences from all of these groups may be discerned in the dancing.

The dances in this region have their most striking similarities to those on the Iranian side of the gulf as well as those in Iranian and Pakistani Baluchistan. Regional specificity is found throughout the different districts; however, several unifying elements seem to characterize the dancing throughout this area: (1) the accompanying music is often performed vocally with a soloist—more rarely, an instrumentalist—and a response chorus in which the dancers take part; (2) the dancers, musicians, and onlookers perform intricate rhythmic interlocking clapping patterns; (3) opposing lines of dancers sing, clap, and sway together—sometimes the lines move together and away from each other; and (4) simple foot patterns are used.

Soloists often break away from the lines or the circle and perform, in the midst of the group, intricate, individually idiosyncratic movements within the regional stylistic parameters. Both male and female dancers sometimes manipulate their garments with their hands, particularly when wearing tunics with large amounts of fabric; male dancers from districts where full tunics are worn rapidly whirl to create the effect of the garment flaring in a dramatic fashion.

Solo figures within a group context are common and often highly athletic, featuring rapid whirling, often while hopping on one foot, squats, and articulations of the torso, shoulders, neck, and head. Some dancers move slowly about the dance space, swaying almost imperceptibly from side to side, as if in a trance. Such movements remind one that the *zār* (exorcistic ritual) complex of eastern Africa, Egypt, and southern Iran is rumored to be present here as well.

Perhaps one of the most famous male dances, for the king of Saudi Arabia is also known to perform it, is dancing with swords. Rather than combat, the emphasis in these dances is the ceremonial brandishing of the sword. Some dancers perform with two swords, which they deftly manipulate in intricate patterns, crossing the front and back of the body. Men also dance with staves, which they twirl in the manner of a baton. A comic dance with two men dressed as a horse and following the "orders" of the trainer is also known in Saudi Arabia.

Richly dressed women are known for the performance of *raqs al-dawsari*, in which the women execute subtle gestures and articulations of the hands, torso, shoulders, and

ARABIAN PENINSULA. *Bara'* is a men's dance from the highlands of Yemen. Performed to the beat of drums, its intricate steps vary from village to village. Typically, the dancers wield daggers in their right hands as they combine grapevine variations, hops, and deep knee bends and move either in line formations or in groups of two or three. The men pictured here dance on a threshing ground in Al-Ahjur, Yemen. (Photograph © 1979 by Najwa Adra; used by permission.)

head. A similar dance style of the gulf region, known as *kheliji*, with articulations of the torso similar to those found in domestic belly dancing and gyrating of the head, is popular among performing groups outside the region. It is similar to the dancing known as *bandari* in the gulf region, found on the Iranian side.

Musical accompaniment for dancing, in addition to singing, is provided by bagpipes, double-reed wind instruments, and percussion ensembles. In the cities, there are orchestras with oud (a lute) and other stringed instruments.

[*See also* Middle East *and* Yemen.]

BIBLIOGRAPHY

Deaver, Sherri. "Concealment versus Display: The Modern Saudi Woman." *Dance Research Journal* 10 (Spring–Summer 1978): 14–18.

Fujii, Tomoaki, ed. *JVC Video Anthology of World Music and Dance.* Tokyo, 1988. See book V *The Middle East and Africa*, 27–30, and video volume number 16 *Qatar*, 16–19.

Khulaifi, 'Aisha al-. "Al-muradah: Raqsat al nisa' fi al-Khalij al-'Arabi." *Al-Mathurat al-Sh'abiya* 1 (1986): 104–129.

Muslimani, Muhammad al-. "Hawl al-musiqa was al-raqs al-sh'abi fi Qatar." *Al-Mathurat al-Sh'abiya* 1 (1986): 88–103.

ANTHONY V. SHAY

ARAIZ, OSCAR (born 2 December 1940 in Bahía Blanca, Argentina), dancer and choreographer. The state-sponsored modern dance company of Argentina is the Contemporary Ballet of the San Martín Municipal Theater. Its present director, Oscar Araiz, was born in Bahía Blanca in Buenos Aires Province. His birth coincided with the introduction of modern dance in Buenos Aires, the Ar-

gentine capital. At the age of fifteen he began to take lessons in contemporary dance with Elide Locardi, a pioneer, who had decided to bring modern dance to the provinces. Araiz finished his dance training with the Teatro Argentino in the city of La Plata. He studied modern dance with Renate Schottelius and classical dance with María Ruanova, among others.

Early in his youth Araiz knew that he wanted to be a choreographer. His first work was a 1959 duet based on a Gershwin prelude. From the beginning and throughout his career, music was his main source of inspiration. Toward the end of the 1950s he joined a group of seven artists that had been formed by Dore Hoyer at her school, where he also acted as an assistant teacher.

Araiz first traveled abroad in 1960. He composed several dance works in Barcelona, Spain. Upon returning to Buenos Aires, he began active participation in a series presented by the association Amigos de la Danza (Friends of the Dance). Among the numerous compositions he created during this period is an outstanding version of *The Rite of Spring* entitled *Consagración de la Primavera*, which later opened doors for him abroad.

Maurice Béjart visited Argentina in the early 1960s and left a lasting impression on Araiz, particularly in regard to freedom of creation. Araiz has always rejected stereotypes, the distinction between American and German schools, and the exclusive dominance of any single technique. He has always been receptive to a variety of influences, most notably that of José Limón. This permitted him to generate his own style, which today is highly regarded.

During the 1960s Araiz, together with Susana Zimmermann and Ana Labat, co-directed the Hoy Ballet company, where individual works were alternated with collaborative productions. With this company he toured Argentina. In 1966 he created works for the Holland Net National Ballet and the Ballet of the Bonn Opera. In 1967, back in Argentina, he participated in performance events of the Di Tella Institute, presenting his work *Crash*. In 1968, the director of the San Martín Municipal Theater invited Araiz to present a series of programs devoted to modern dance, but Araiz proposed the creation of a permanent group. This resulted in the founding of the first state-sponsored modern dance company in Argentina, which was directed by Araiz until its dissolution in 1973.

In 1974 Araiz began to work steadily abroad. First he went to Brazil; then he was invited by the Royal Winnipeg Ballet of Canada to stage his version of *The Rite of Spring*. In subsequent years he produced works for several companies, including the Joffrey Ballet, where he revived his version of *Romeo and Juliet* to the music of Prokofiev.

In 1979 Araiz returned to Argentina and was commissioned to direct the ballet company of the Colón, a theater devoted to classical dance. He stayed there for a year; in 1980 he accepted an invitation to direct the Ballet du

ARAIZ. Dancers of the Royal Winnipeg Ballet in Oscar Araiz's production of *The Unicorn, the Gorgon, and the Manticore,* set to the music of Gian-Carlo Menotti. (Photograph © 1978 by Johan Elbers; used by permission.)

Grand Théâtre of Geneva. He spent eight years there, combining his employment with the creation of dance works for other companies in Europe and periodic visits to Argentina.

In 1990 Araiz was again appointed director of the Ballet of the San Martín Theater, which had been reestablished in 1978. During the next two years the company revived several of his productions and offered opportunities to other Argentine choreographers. Always starting from the music, especially works of contemporary composers, and sometimes inspired by pictorial or film images, Araiz has presented various choreographic works with the Ballet. He has also staged several musical theater productions, and in 1995 he undertook a new venture, the direction of drama.

BIBLIOGRAPHY

Araiz, Oscar. *Tango: Un espectáculo de Oscar Araiz y Atilio Stampone.* Buenos Aires, 1984.

Buffat, Serge. *Oscar Araiz: Carnets de danse.* Lausanne, 1988.

Falcoff, Laura. *Ballet contemporáneo: 25 años en el San Martín.* Buenos Aires, 1994.

Gregory, John. "*Misia:* A Choreographic Experience." *Dancing Times* (June 1987): 778–789.

Isse Moyano, Marcelo, et al. *Primer cuaderno le danza del Instituto de Artes del Espectáculo de la Universidad de Buenos Aires.* Buenos Aires, 1995.

MARCELO ISSE MOYANO

ARBEAU, THOINOT (Jehan Tabourot; born 17 March 1520 in Dijon, France, died 21 July 1595 in Langres), French cleric and dance-manual author. Arbeau's real name, Tabourot, and his coat of arms (three tabors) suggest an ancient family profession that may explain his intimate knowledge of drumming. As a member of a ranking Burgundian family, a number of whom were writers and architects in the first half of the sixteenth century (an uncle, Jean Pignard, was master of music at the cathedral at Langres), Arbeau studied at Dijon and Poitiers, and perhaps also in Paris, attaining a licentiate of laws. In his manual *Orchésographie* (1588, see bibliography for complete title), Arbeau mentions his dance teacher in Poitiers and his own dancing prowess as a young man. He also refers several times to the dance manual of Antonius Arena, *Ad suos compagnones studiantes* (1528). Arbeau's career in the church is recorded in his promotions: in 1542 he became treasurer of the chapter at Langres; in 1547 he became canon of the cathedral; and in 1565 he was canon-treasurer at Bar-sur-Aube. Succeeding appointments included that of *official* (ecclesiastical judge), *chantre scoliarque* (inspector of diocesan schools), director of cathedral restoration after damage by lightning, and finally, vicar-general of his diocese. He is known to have published two other works under the pseudonym of Jean Vostet Breton: *Kalendrier des bergers* (Langres, 1582)

DE THOINOT ARBFAV. 80
Tabulature du branle d'Efcoffe.

Air du premier branle d'Efcoffe.   *Monuements pour ce premier branle.*

pied largy gaulche.

pied droit approché.

pied largy gaulche.

pied croifé droit.

Ces quatre pas equipolēt vn double a gaulche.

pied largy droit.

pied gaulche approché.

pied largy droit.

pied croifé gaulche.

Ces quatre pas equipolēt vn double a droit.

pied largy gaulche.

pied croifé droit.

Ces deux equipolēt a fimple gaul.

pied largy droit.

pied croifé gaulche.

Ces deux equipolēt a fimple droit.

pied largy gaulche.

pied droit approché.

pied largy gaulche.

pied croifé droit.

Ces quatre equipolent vn double a gaulche.

ARBEAU. The tabulature devised by Thoinot Arbeau, as published in his 1588 treatise *Orchésographie*, correlates dance steps with music more precisely than any other source of the period. This example shows the "Branle d'Escosse". (Dance Collection, New York Public Library for the Performing Arts.)

and *Compot et manuel kalendrier* (Paris, 1588; Langres, 1589). His attitude toward dancing was positive, both in pursuit of good health and in the pleasurable search for a mate. His neo-Platonic view that earthly dance mirrors the harmonious dance of the universe places him squarely in the tradition of those sturdy Renaissance ecclesiastics so vividly represented by Rabelais. Arbeau declares that puritans who oppose dancing "deserve to be fed upon goat's meat cooked in a pie without bacon."

Arbeau's work is of manifold interest. One of the three old men who published important dance manuals in this period (Fabritio Caroso and Cesare Negri are the others), Arbeau represents dance practice beginning in 1550 at least. His *Orchésographie* is the only manual of the time to explain the dances with the aid of a specific kind of tabulation that correlates dance steps quite precisely with music.

Furthermore, *Orchésographie* is the only French manual of the latter half of the sixteenth century. It is also the only manual from northern Europe that provides enough detail to permit reasonably accurate reconstructions of the dance types mentioned by Shakespeare, for example. The only other contemporary northern sources, the so-called manuscripts of the Inns of Court, have cryptic *aides mémoires*—choreographic shorthands that do not describe steps or provide music. Arbeau is also unique in emphasizing the close ties between dance and other manly activities. He frames the book with the martial arts, first by describing a variety of marching and drumming techniques and last with his longest, most complete, and most complex dance and the only known choreography of a well-known sword dance for men, "Les Bouffons." *Orchésographie* is also the only sixteenth-century manual to describe *branles* (an immense family of circle dances) in detail (there are twenty-four types), including with their titles ascriptions of their provenance and calling for actions that seem to point more strongly to peasant origins than the dances in any other source (e.g., "Branle des Lavandières" [Washerwomen]; Negri's three *brandi* are much more elaborate dances that appear to be related to Arbeau's only in title). In addition, Arbeau is the only authority to give brief, but seemingly complete, choreographies of the *volte* and the *morisque*. The latter is the only dance in all the sixteenth-century manuals specified to be performed by a member of the lower classes, a lackey. Arbeau also supplies the first choreographies of a *gavotte*, an *allemande*, and a *courante*. Although his version of the last dance is questionable because it is in duple rather than the normal triple time (Negri's "Corrente" of 1602 is another sixteenth-century example), he does give the only discrete pavan choreography of the century.

Arbeau describes other dances in varying detail: *bassedanse* (though "out of fashion some fifty years"), *tordion* and *galliarde* variations, *canario* (though in duple rather than the normal triple time), and "Pavane d'Espagne." He also refers to the *passo e mezzo* briefly, without supplying a choreography.

Most of the choreographies in *Orchésographie* are typical of all the manuals in that they are predominantly social (or what Arbeau terms recreative) ballroom dances, ranging from circle dances for as many couples as will (*branles*) to dances for a solo couple (such as the *galliarde*), and including playful kissing games (e.g., *gavottes*), simple mixers (e.g., "Branle de la Torche"), humorous miming dances (e.g., "Branles des Hermites"), and that vigorous dance with the most intimate hold of partners described at the time, the *volte*. Exceptions to the initially social purpose occur, however, in a number of dances that originated in more theatrical milieus: several mimed *branles* (e.g., "Branle de Malte"), which Arbeau cites as originating in a masquerade; the *morisque*, a solo dance in blackface and bells; and "Les Bouffons," a show dance for martially costumed, armed men wearing bells at their knees and wielding swords and shields. In certain respects, Arbeau provides a greater variety of dance types than either Caroso or Negri; unlike them, many of his dances are simple enough for beginners. Nevertheless, most of his choreographies are extremely short. They do, however, allow the ever-present option of being expanded through improvised variation. In some cases they are certainly incomplete (e.g., "Branle de Guerre"), so the advantages of his manual are balanced by major problems of reconstruction.

Arbeau has none of the complete, lengthy, and sophisticated choreographies of social-dance types that dominate the Italian manuals—the *balletto* suites of several movements, the complex figure dances for two to as-many-as-will couples, or the long sets of variations on well-known dance types such as the *passo e mezzo, pavaniglia, canario, tordiglione,* and *galliarde*. His technical demands and step vocabulary are simpler than those of any of the Italians (e.g., he only hints at the possibilities of technical feats specified by Negri, such as double turns in the air or multiple pirouettes). Stylistically, Arbeau's knee and ankle are more relaxed in kicking movements, and his arms appear to move more freely. Many of the steps Arbeau describes, however, clearly bear a strong resemblance to those in the Italian manuals (e.g., his second *galliarde* variation is identical to Caroso's basic *galliarde* pattern). There is no question that Arbeau knew the international European dance language of his time. This is even more evident in his strong emphasis on the well-established traditions of improvisation and variation on accepted models.

From the musician's point of view, Arbeau is uniquely informative, for his manual is the only known source to write about and illustrate Renaissance drum rhythms. It is also the only source of music for extemporizing specifically on the fife, with significant details of tonguing techniques. In addition, *Orchésographie* contains many valuable clues to musical performance practice for dancing—including appropriate northern European instrumentation, details of instrumental construction, singing dances, and sources for additional dance music—and for underscoring the strength of the traditional improvisational skills of the musicians ("Those who play improvise to please themselves," he says). It is clear that he fully expected dance musicians to supply a bass and inner or descant parts to the tunes he supplies. He gives important tempo indications for dancers and musicians, both when comparing dance types (e.g., "The *tordion* is danced close to the ground to a light, lively beat and the *galliarde* is danced higher off the ground to a slower, stronger beat"), and when giving a tempo range for a single dance type ("The *galliarde* needs must be slower for a man of large stature than for a small man, inasmuch as the tall one takes longer to execute his steps").

On manners and mores, *Orchésographie* provides much information regarding social ambience in the ballroom, acceptable and unacceptable behavior by dancers, the normal order of dances at a ball, and the interaction of musicians and dancers. The manual is written as a dialogue between master and disciple, and the student, Capriol, is admonished, for example, to keep his "head and body erect and appear self-possessed"; to "spit and blow [his] nose sparingly"; and to "converse affably in a low, modest voice." The well-bred lady is told how to prevent her skirts from flying up during the *volte,* and to "never refuse him who does her the honour of asking her to dance."

Arbeau's manual poses some serious questions. While it is undoubtedly valid for northern European dance in the last half of the sixteenth century, it is not known how far into the seventeenth century it remains a representative source—F[rançois] de Lauze, publishing in London in 1623, presents a markedly changed style. Even for Arbeau's own time, it is uncertain whether his style or his dances truly represent practices at the French court (there is also no evidence that he was ever there). It is known that contemporary Italian dancing masters were active at major courts all over Europe, including those in France. Despite these mysteries, however, *Orchésographie* remains a rich, delightful, and satisfying source of dance and music history.

[*Many of the dance types mentioned herein are the subjects of independent entries.*]

BIBLIOGRAPHY: SOURCES

Arbeau, Thoinot. *Orchésographie et traicte en forme de dialogve, par leqvel tovtes personnes pevvent facilement apprendre & practiquer l'honneste exercice des dances.* Langres, 1588, 1589. Facsimile reprint, Langres, 1988. Reprinted with expanded title as *Orchésographie, metode, et teorie en forme de discovrs et tablatvre povr apprendre a dancer, battre le Tambour en toute sorte & diuersité de batteries, Iouët du fifre & arigot, tirer des armes & escrimer, auec autres honnestes exercices fort conuenables à la Ieunesse.* Langres, 1596. Facsimile reprint, Geneva, 1972.

Arbeau, Thoinot. *Orchésographie.* Copy of 1589 with an introduction by Laure Fonta. Paris, 1888.

Arbeau, Thoinot. *Orchesography.* 1589. Translated into English by Cyril W. Beaumont. London, 1925. Reprint, New York, 1968.

Arbeau, Thoinot. *Orchesography.* 1589. Translated into English by Mary Stewart Evans. New York, 1948. Reprinted with corrections, introduction, and notes by Julia Sutton, and representative steps and dances in Labanotation by Mireille Backer. New York, 1967.

Arena, Antonius. *Ad suos compagnones studiantes.* Lyon, 1528. Translated by John Guthrie and Marino Zorzi in "*Rules of Dancing* by Antonius Arena." *Dance Research* 4 (Autumn 1986): 3–53.

Beaujoyeulx, Balthazar de (Belgioioso, Baldassare de). *Le Balet Comique de la Royne* (1581). Facsimile reprint, Turin, 1965. Translated by Carol and Lander MacClintock, the music transcribed by Carol MacClintock. Rome, 1971.

Caroso, Fabritio. *Il ballarino* (1581). Facsimile reprint, New York, 1967.

Caroso, Fabritio. *Nobiltà di dame.* Venice, 1600, 1605. Facsimile reprint, Bologna, 1970. Reissued with order of illustrations changed as *Raccolta di varij balli.* Rome, 1630. Translated into English with eight introductory chapters by Julia Sutton, the music transcribed by F. Marian Walker. Oxford, 1986. Reprint with a step manual in Labanotation by Rachelle Palnick Tsachor and Julia Sutton, New York, 1995.

Lauze, F[rançois] de. *Apologie de la danse, 1623.* Translated by Joan Wildeblood, and with original text, as *A Treatise of Instruction in Dancing and Deportment.* London, 1952.

LeRoy, Adrian. *Ier livre de tabulature de luth* (1551). Facsimile reprint, Paris, 1960.

Lupi, Livio. *Libro di gagliarde, tordiglione, passo e mezzo, canari e passeggi.* Palermo, 1600. Rev. ed., Palermo, 1607.

Lutii, Prospero. *Opera bellissima nella quale si contengono molte partite, et passeggi di gagliarda.* Perugia, 1589.

Maisse, André Hurault de. *A Journal of All That Was Accomplished by Monsieur de Maisse, Ambassador in England from King Henry IV to Queen Elizabeth* (1597). Translated by G. B. Harrison and P. A. Jones. London, 1931.

Manuscripts of the Inns of Court. Located in Bodleian Library, Rawl.Poet.108, ff.10v–11r; British Library, Harley 367, pp. 178–179; Bodleian, Douce 280, ff.66av–66bv (202v–203v); Bodleian, Rawl.D.864, f.199v, ff.203r–204; Royal College of Music, MS 1119, title page and ff.1–2, 23v–24r; Inner Temple, Miscellanea vol. 27.

Negri, Cesare. *Le gratie d'amore.* Milan, 1602. Reissued as *Nuove invenzione di balli.* Milan 1604. Translated into Spanish by Don Balthasar Carlos for Señor Condé, Duke of Sanlucar, 1630. Manuscript located in Madrid, Biblioteca Nacional, MS 14085. Facsimile reprint of 1602, New York and Bologna, 1969. Literal translation into English and musical transcription by Yvonne Dendall. D.M.A. diss., Stanford University, 1985.

Praetorius, Michael. *Terpsichore.* Wolfenbüttel, 1612. Facsimile reprint of text only in *Gesamtausgabe der musikalischen Werke.* Vol. 15. Edited by Friedrich Blume et al. Wolfenbüttel, 1928–1960.

BIBLIOGRAPHY: OTHER STUDIES

Alford, Violet. *Sword Dance and Drama.* London, 1962.

Barker, E. Phillips. "Master Thoinot's Fancy." *Music and Letters* 11 (October 1930): 383–393.

Barker, E. Phillips. "Some Notes on Arbeau." *Journal of the English Folk Dance Society* 3 (1930): 2–12.

Brainard, Ingrid. "Even Jove Sometimes Nods." *Dance Chronicle* 18.2 (1995): 163–169.

Brown, Alan. "Galliard" and "Pavan." In *The New Grove Dictionary of Music and Musicians.* London, 1980.

Brown, Howard M. *Music in the French Secular Theater, 1400–1550.* Cambridge, Mass., 1963.

Brown, Howard M. *Embellishing Sixteenth-Century Music.* London, 1976.

Brown, Howard M. "Performing Practice, 4: Fifteenth- and Sixteenth-Century Music." In *The New Grove Dictionary of Music and Musicians.* London, 1980.

Carpenter, Nan Cooke. *Rabelais and Music.* Chapel Hill, N.C., 1954.

Donington, Robert. "Volta." In *The New Grove Dictionary of Music and Musicians.* London, 1980.

Feldmann, Fritz. "Historische Tänze der musikalischen und choreographischen Weltliteratur" (parts 1–2). *Volkstanz in Tanzarchiv* 4–5 (1960–1961).

Gudewill, Kurt. "Courante." In *Die Musik in Geschichte und Gegenwart.* 1st ed., vol. 2, 1952. Kassel, 1949–1979.

Guilcher, Yves. "Les différentes lectures de l'*Orchésographie* de Thoinot Arbeau." *Recherche en Danse* 1 (June 1982): 39–49.

Guilcher, Yves. "L'interpretation de l'*Orchésographie* par des danseurs et des musiciens d'aujourd'hui." *Recherche en Danse* 2 (1983): 21–32.

Guilcher, Yves. "L'*Orchésographie* de T. Arbeau en tant qu'essai pour transmettre la danse par l'écriture." *Recherche en Danse* 3 (June 1984): 25–28.

Heartz, Daniel. "Sources and Forms of the French Instrumental Dance in the Sixteenth Century." Ph.D. diss., Harvard University, 1957.

Heartz, Daniel. "The Basse Dance: Its Evolution circa 1450 to 1550." *Annales Musicologiques* 6 (1958–1963): 287–340.

Heartz, Daniel. *Preludes, Chansons, and Dances for Lute Published by Pierre Attaingnant, Paris, 1529–1530.* Neuilly-sur-Seine, 1964.

Heartz, Daniel. *Keyboard Dances from the Earlier Sixteenth Century.* American Institute of Musicology, Corpus of Early Keyboard Music, vol. 8. Dallas, 1965.

Heartz, Daniel. "Tourdion" and "Volte." In *Die Musik in Geschichte und Gegenwart.* 1st ed., vol. 13, 1966; vol. 14, 1968. Kassel, 1949–1979.

Heartz, Daniel. "Basse danse" and "Branle." In *The New Grove Dictionary of Music and Musicians.* London, 1980.

Hudson, Richard. "Canary," "Passamezzo," and "Pavaniglia." In *The New Grove Dictionary of Music and Musicians.* London, 1980.

Hudson, Richard. *The Allemande, the Balletto, and the Tanz.* Cambridge, 1986.

Jacquot, Jean, ed. *La musique instrumentale de la Renaissance.* Paris, 1954.

Lesure, François. "Allemande" and "Branle." In *Die Musik in Geschichte und Gegenwart.* 1st ed., vol. 1, 1949–1951; vol. 2, 1952. Kassel, 1949–1979.

Little, Meredith Ellis, and Suzanne G. Cusick. "Allemande." In *The New Grove Dictionary of Music and Musicians.* London, 1980.

Little, Meredith Ellis. "Courante" and "Gavotte." In *The New Grove Dictionary of Music and Musicians.* London, 1980.

Mary, André. "L'*Orchésographie*' de Thoinot Arbeau." In *Les trésors des bibliothèques de France,* vol. 5, edited by Émile Dacier. Paris, 1935.

Meyer, Ernst Hermann. "Allemande," "Ballo," and "Galliarde." *In Die Musik in Geschichte und Gegenwart.* 1st ed., vol. 1, 1949–1951; vol. 4, 1955. Kassel, 1949–1979.

Poulton, Diana. "Notes on the Spanish Pavan." *Lute Society Journal* 3 (1961): 5–16.

Reichart, Sarah Bennett. "Music for the Renaissance Allemande." *Dance Chronicle* 8.3–4 (1985): 211–218.

Sonner, Rudolf. "Arbeau, Thoinot." In *Die Musik in Geschichte und Gegenwart.* 1st ed., vol. 1, 1949–1951. Kassel, 1949–1979.

Sutton, Julia. "Reconstruction of Sixteenth-Century Dance." In *Dance History Research: Perspectives from Related Arts and Disciplines,* edited by Joann W. Kealiinohomoku. New York, 1970.

Sutton, Julia. *Renaissance Revisited: Twelve Dances Reconstructed [in Labanotation] from the Originals of Thoinot Arbeau, Fabritio Caroso, and Cesare Negri.* New York, 1972.

Sutton, Julia. "Arbeau, Thoinot"; "Caroso, Fabritio"; "Dance, I: Introduction"; "Dance, IV: Late Renaissance and Baroque to 1700"; "Matachin"; and "Negri, Cesare." In *The New Grove Dictionary of Music and Musicians.* London, 1980.

Sutton, Julia. "Triple Pavans: Clues to Some Mysteries in Sixteenth-Century Dance." *Early Music* 14.2 (1986): 174–181.

Sutton, Julia. "Canario." In *Die Musik in Geschichte und Gegenwart.* 2d ed., vol. 2, 1995. Kassel, 1994–.

Tani, Gino. "Allemanda," "Bassadanza," "Branle," "Corrente," "Gagliarda," "Mattaccino," "Moresca," "Passamezzo," "Pavana," "Saltarello," "Tourdion," and "Volta." In *Enciclopedio dello spettacolo.* 9 vols. Rome, 1954–1968.

Tani, Gino, et al. "Danza." In *Enciclopedio dello spettacolo.* 9 vols. 1954–1968.

Tani, Gino. *Storia della danza dalle origini ai nostri giorni.* 3 vols. Florence, 1983.

Viard, Georges, et al. *Jean Tabourot et son temps: Actes des journées d'étude organisées pour le quatrième centenaire de l'Orchésographie.* Langres, 1989.

Ward, John M. "Passamezzo." In *Die Musik in Geschichte und Gegenwart*. 1st ed., vol. 10, 1962. Kassel, 1949–1979.

JULIA SUTTON

ARENA, ANTONIUS DE

ARENA, ANTONIUS DE (also known as Antoine d'Arènes, des Arens, de la Sable, Sablon, du Sablon; born late fifteenth century in Solliès, Provence, died 1544? in Saint-Rémy or 1550? in Solliès), French judge, historian, dance theorist, and poet. In 1519 Arena began to study law at the University of Avignon, dividing his time between his studies and dancing, his main extracurricular activity. The first, until now untraced, copy of his dance manual *Leges dansadi*, later known under the title *Ad suos compagnones studiantes*, was compiled during that first year.

In 1520, when the plague reached Avignon, the university suspended all classes. Arena left temporarily until the danger had passed. He then completed his studies and, in 1527, joined the French army. A struggle for control of Italy was then raging between French king Francis I and Habsburg Holy Roman emperor Charles V, and Arena was soon in Rome, fighting with the forces defending the Castel Sant'Angelo against the onslaught led by the Constable Bourbon, who had defected to the Habsburg side. Poverty-stricken, he reenlisted and returned to Italy under Marshal Odet de Foix de Lautrec and was an eyewitness to the revolt in Genoa and the final defeat of the French under the walls of Naples.

Late in 1528 Arena returned to Provence, firmly resolved never to fight again but to spend his life in the pursuit of poetic and philosophic endeavors. Although he never became a major figure in the legal profession, he was at least able to make a living in it. He spent several years in Aix until he was named *juge ordinaire* of Saint-Rémy in 1536. The place and date of his death are still uncertain (see the works of Bouche, Plattard, Fabre, Dollieule, and Mullally listed in the bibliography for the several opinions).

The most frequently published and best known of Arena's writings is the dance treatise, known either as *Leges dansadi* (Rules of Dancing) or *Ad suos compagnones studiantes* (To His Fellow Students), that he wrote in macaronic Latin verse. It forms the center section of a volume that also contains the author's grim reports of the wars of Rome, Genoa, Naples, and Avignon. The book is preserved in thirty-two different editions, five undated, published between 1528 (1519?) and 1770. (For details regarding the history of Arena's text, see Dollieule, 1885–1886, 1886; Mullally, 1979.)

The main subject of Arena's treatise is the *bassedanse* as it was practiced during the early years of the sixteenth century; the *pavane* and *branle* are mentioned in passing as novelties too recent to warrant full theoretical treatment. Arena gives fifty-eight choreographies, without music, for less common *bassedanses*. He uses the traditional French-Burgundian step tablature, the only notational difference being that the letter *b* (for *branle*) has been replaced by *c* (for *congé*). The spirited theoretical text contains detailed step descriptions (*révérence*, simple, double, *congé*, reprise), among which that of the *révérence* is of particular importance because this gesture of courtesy, routinely executed by all courtiers in the fifteenth century, had never been fully described before. [*See* Bassedanse.]

In addition to dealing with dance technique and with music (meter, tempo, instruments), Arena discusses polished ballroom manners. He explains the handling of the hat, cloak, sword, and gloves in dancing; he warns against pushing and shoving on the dance floor, advocates practice in the art of conversation, and promises much success with the ladies to his "fellow students" who master these and other rules of genteel etiquette.

Arena's second major book, the *Meygra entrepriza* (Great Undertaking; Avignon, 1537), condemns the ravages inflicted on Provence by the armies of Charles V. Here, as in the dance treatise, the author paints a vivid picture of the life and times of his beloved homeland as he witnessed them. His medium, which he also used in a number of smaller occasional poems, is the macaronic language, a mixture of classical Latin, French, Italian, and Provençal. His verse is supple and flowing, his gifts of observation and characterization keen, and his humor irrepressible. Arena would have been a good poet in any conventional medium, but he chose, like his contemporary the Italian poet Teofilo Folengo, to be outstanding in the realm of the ribald and the linguistically absurd.

BIBLIOGRAPHY

Arena, Antonius de. *Ad suos compagnones studiantes.* Lyon, 1528. Translated by John Guthrie and Marino Zorzi in "Rules of Dancing by Antonius Arena." *Dance Research* 4 (Autumn 1986): 3–53.

Bouche, Honoré. *La chorographie, ou, Description de Provence.* 2 vols. Aix, 1664.

Brainard, Ingrid. "Die Choreographie der Hoftänze in Burgund, Frankreich und Italien im 15. Jahrhundert." Ph.D. diss., University of Göttingen, 1956.

Brainard, Ingrid. *The Art of Courtly Dancing in the Early Renaissance.* West Newton, Mass., 1981.

Crane, Frederick. *Materials for the Study of the Fifteenth-Century Basse Danse.* Brooklyn, 1968.

De Bure, Guillaume-François. *Bibliographie instructive, ou, Traite de la connoissance des livres rares et singuliers.* Paris, 1765. [7 vols., 1763–1768]

De Bure, Guillaume-François. *Catalogue des livres de la bibliothèque de feu M. le duc de la Vallière.* Paris, 1783.

Dixon, Peggy. "Reflections on Basse Dance Source Material: A Dancer's Review." *Historical Dance* 2.4 (1984–1985): 24–27.

Dollieule, Frédéric. "Antonius Arena de bragardissima villa de Soleriis: Sa vie et ses oeuvres." *Revue de Marseille et de Provence* 31 (1885); 32 (1886).

Dollieule, Frédéric. *Antoine Arène, poète macaronique et jurisconsulte: Sa vie et ses oeuvres.* Paris, 1886.

Fabre, Antoine. *Antonius Arena: Notice historique et littéraire.* Marseille, 1860.

Feller, François Xavier de, ed. *Dictionnaire historique.* 8th ed. Lille, 1832–1833.

Garavini, Fausta. "Le traité de danse d'un étudiant provençal autour de 1520: Antonius Arena." *Recherche en Danse,* no. 3 (June 1984): 5–14.

Genthe, F.-W. *Geschichte der macaronischen Poesie, und Sammlung ihrer vorzüglichsten Denkmale.* Halle, 1829.

Heartz, Daniel. "Arena, Antonius de." In *Die Musik in Geschichte und Gegenwart.* Kassel, 1949–.

Heartz, Daniel. "The Basse Dance: Its Evolution circa 1450 to 1550." *Annales Musicologiques* 6 (1958–1963): 287–340.

Lalanne, Ludovic. "Arena." In *Dictionnaire historique de la France* (1877). 2d ed. New York, 1968.

Moréri, Louis, ed. "Arena, Antoine de." In *Le grande dictionnaire historique.* Lyon, 1674.

Mullally, Robert. "The Editions of Antonius Arena's 'Ad Suos Compagnones Studiantes.'" *Gutenberg Jahrbuch* (1979): 146–157.

Plattard, Jean. "Antonius de Arena et les danses au XVIe siècle." *Revue des livres anciens* 1 (1913–1914).

Prevost, Michel. "Arena (Antoine)." In *Dictionnaire de biographie française.* Paris, 1930–.

Reboul, Robert. "Antonius Arena: Notice bibliographique." *Revue Sextienne* 5 (1884).

Sachs, Curt. *World History of the Dance.* Translated by Bessie Schönberg. New York, 1937.

Tani, Gino. "Arena, Antonius de." In *Enciclopedia dello spettacolo.* Rome, 1954–.

Wilson, D. R. "Theory and Practice in the Fifteenth-Century French Basse Dance." *Historical Dance* 2.3 (1983): 1–2.

Wilson, D. R. "The Development of French Basse Dance." *Historical Dance* 2.4 (1984–1985): 5–12.

INGRID BRAINARD

ARGENTINA. [*This entry comprises three articles on dance in Argentina. The first article explores indigenous folk and European-influenced traditional dance; the companion articles focus on the history of ballet and modern dance.*]

Folk and Traditional Dance

With an area of some 1.1 million square miles (2.8 million square kilometers), Argentina has a population of about 34 million, of whom 85 percent have European ancestry. The majority is composed of Spanish-speaking Roman Catholics. Natives and *mestizos* (mixed European and Native American) have been pushed aside or absorbed. The most representative dance of Argentina, throughout the world, is the tango, a couple dance with sensual and complex choreography.

Traditional Argentine dances fall into two groups: those that still exist among the small Native American population (about 400,000 people) and the folk dances maintained by rural people of European and *mestizo* descent. The Native American traditional dances, associated with the ceremonies and rituals of several distinct cultural groups, have almost vanished without being systematically documented.

Nowadays there are about twenty folk dances. A few, which retain traces of native traditions, are choral dances in which the dancers move freely or in a circular formation. The rest are couple dances of European origin, performed with the partners embraced, or entirely separated, or with arms joined.

Argentine couple dances were thoroughly studied by the musicologist Carlos Vega (1898–1966), who from 1936 to 1956 developed a model categorization of regional folk dances based on historical documents and fieldwork. His major work is *El origen de las danzas folklóricas* (1956). Vega determined that from the sixteenth century onward, European social dances were continually imported to Argentina, where they were adopted by the elite, modified to local tastes, and transmitted to the lower classes where further adaptation occurred. He identified four historical waves of dance introductions, which are summarized here.

During the sixteenth century Argentina received its dances from the Spanish court, but in the seventeenth and eighteenth centuries the French court and salons had greater influence. The city that diffused the European dances during these years was Lima, Peru, the center of Spanish colonial administration in the region during the seventeenth and eighteenth centuries. Santiago, Chile, was important as a cultural link between Peru and Argentina. When the wars of independence from Spain began in 1810, Buenos Aires assumed supremacy.

The earliest dances imported from Europe were such lively types as the *galliarde* and *courante,* which in Argentina developed into the *gato, chacarera, zamba,* and other dances that survive to the present. In the late seventeenth century, court dances such as the *menuet* and gavotte were imported; their Argentine forms, the *minué, cuando,* and *condición,* became extinct by the mid-nineteenth century.

Eighteenth-century introductions featured contradances and quadrilles, which generated the *cielito, pericón,* and *media caña,* performed until the mid-nineteenth century. In the early nineteenth century, the waltz was welcomed, soon followed by the polka, mazurka, and other embraced-couple dances, some of which are still popular today under the same names.

Choral dances, performed in open or closed circles, barely survive in the extreme northern part of Argentina, which shares the Andean tradition with Peru, Bolivia, and Chile. The majority of choral dances have a ritual function and are associated with Native American fertility rites (such as that of the cattle branding in the province of Jujuy) or with Roman Catholicism (the *adoraciones,* for example, danced during the Christmas season in Jujuy and Salta).

Some vestiges of ritual society dances can be seen in the celebration of the Virgin of Andacollo in San Juan, in which members of a brotherhood called *chinos* dance and play flutes in honor of the holy image. Ancient male combat dances survive in an annual performance in the village of Iruya, Salta, in which a mimed battle between Christians and Moors (Muslims who dominated the Iberian Peninsula from 711 to 1492) proclaims the triumph of Christianity. Dances of competition are represented only in the nearly extinct *malambo,* in which two or more men dance in turn, displaying skill in leaping and foot-tapping, to guitar accompaniment.

European dances were introduced primarily through elite social functions but also through theatrical performances. Immigrants in the early twentieth century also brought regional dances, especially from Spain and Italy.

In nonpatterned or in round dances with a strong Native American element, such as the *huayno,* the music may be in non-European melodic modes. Indigenous instruments, usually flutes and small drums, may be played by the dancers themselves. The basic time unit is duple meter, marked in the dance by knee flexions and torso contractions, and there is no difference between men's and women's movements.

In couple dances, which generally represent courtship, European musical styles prevail. There are fixed genres of composition and lyrics, and the music is provided by a separate ensemble. The most common instruments are guitar, accordion, and harp; duple and triple meters and moderate tempo are usual. Steps tend to be smooth and graceful, often involving variations of the waltz. The body is held erect without pronounced pelvic or hip movements, and the dancer follows a ground pattern of circle, rhombus, or double line. In some dances, such as the *escondido,* both arms are raised to shoulder height and the fingers are snapped throughout the dance; in others, such as the *cueca,* both dancers flourish handkerchiefs. Most of these dances have two equal parts, each preceded by an instrumental introduction that is not danced.

Some choreographic figures show a strong influence of European contradances—for example, different kinds of chains are always present in the *pericón* and related dances. Direct Spanish influence can be seen in the use of finger-snapping, handkerchief-waving, and heel-tapping. The last is performed only by men, while their partners respond with flirtatious gestures of their skirts.

In rural areas the dances are performed for recreation in a spontaneous manner. They can also be seen in clubs or traditionalist centers *(peñas folklóricas)* established by groups of people who have migrated from specific rural regions to the cities. Urban enthusiasts learn folk dances and perform them on such holidays as Independence Day at schools or other public institutions, when they wear traditional nineteenth-century costume.

The government-supported teaching of folk dance began in 1939 in the Conservatorio Nacional de Música y Arte Escénico in Buenos Aires, under the leadership of Antonio Barceló. He also inspired the creation in 1948 of the Escuela National de Danzas Folklóricas. Since then hundreds of dance teachers have been trained to teach in elementary and middle schools all over the country. The Instituto Nacional Superior del Profesorado de Folklore, established in 1988, has taken over this task; in 1993 it began to offer two degree programs, one for dance teachers and one for professional folk dancers. The more nationalist Argentine government, particularly the one from 1945 to 1955, encouraged the practice of folk dancing and even made its teaching mandatory in primary and secondary schools. Today some provinces require it by law.

In addition to government agencies mentioned above, there are the Escuelas Polivalentes de Arte and the private academies that exist throughout Argentina. Many of these possess their own dance troupes, as do some clubs and traditionalist centers. These groups appear in folk music festivals and traditional dance festivals; there are at present about twenty such annual events throughout the country.

In 1990 the Ballet Folklórico Nacional, headed by Norma Viola and Santiago Ayala, was founded by the Ministry of Culture and Education. During its performing season the company presents two shows monthly of choreographed works based on folk customs, stories, and legends. It has toured in Brazil, Chile, Bulgaria, Spain, and Portugal.

The Argentine mass media ignore folk dance, and there is no television or radio program that on a regular basis deals with folk dance. Folk troupes rarely have the opportunity to perform on the stages of major urban theaters.

Young urban Argentines mostly know nothing about folk dance, while the older people remember only a little from the resurgence of folk and dance music that swept Argentina in the 1960s. This movement, which lasted about a decade, resulted in the popularization of folk-style music in many sectors of society; the repertory came mostly from the northern provinces.

Traditional dance remains strong in some northeastern provinces, where it is performed in rural areas during fairs, holidays, and secular or religious festivals. The oldest dances, however, are being supplanted by newer ones, some recently brought from other South American countries; examples are the Colombian *cumbia,* Bolivian *taki-rari,* and Brazilian *chamarrita.* The *chamamé* is the only Argentine traditional dance that seems to be increasing in popularity, having expanded from its original site in the northeast to the rest of the country and also to southern Chile.

Folk dance collections have been compiled by several scholars, notably Ventura Lynch (1883), Vicente Darago

(1908), Jorge Furt (1927), and Andrés Chazarreta (1916, 1941). Carlos Vega devoted more than thirty years to meticulous recording, producing monographs on twenty-six dances, analyzing their history, origin, music, poetry, and choreography; these works were collected under the title *Las danzas populares argentinas* (1952, reprinted 1986). Since Vega, however, there have been only a few isolated contributions on traditional dance.

BIBLIOGRAPHY

Aretz, Isabel. *El folklore musical argentino.* Buenos Aires, 1952.

Aretz, Isabel. *Costumbres tradicionales argentinas.* Buenos Aires, 1954.

Assunção, Fernando O. *Evolución de los bailes populares tradicionales en el Río de la Plata.* Buenos Aires, 1978.

Berruti, Pedro. *Coreografías de danzas nativas argentinas.* 4 vols. Buenos Aires, 1976–1995.

Hanvik, Jan Michael. "An Argentine Folk Dance." *Dance Notation Journal* 1 (Fall 1983): 3–20.

Vega, Carlos. *Las danzas populares argentinas* (1952). 2 vols. Buenos Aires, 1986.

Vega, Carlos. *El origen de las danzas folklóricas.* Buenos Aires, 1956.

ERCILIA MORENO CHÁ

Ballet

In the nineteenth century, theatrical dance in Argentina was dominated by European companies. The first professional dancers to appear in Buenos Aires were Caroline and Jean Touissant, who in 1823 brought ballets from France, including Charles Didelot's *Flore et Zéphire.* In 1830 Juana and José Cañete arrived with excerpts from *La Fille Mal Gardée* and other works. In 1832 Caroline and Philippe Caton brought dramatic and historical ballets based on stories of Napoléon. In 1836 Juana Cañete returned to dance *La Cachucha,* made famous by Fanny Elssler.

The Romantic ballet came to Buenos Aires in 1849 when Enrique and Ana Trabattoni Finart danced in scenes from *La Sylphide.* In 1857 the city saw its first major company. Headed by Jean Rousset, the group presented a number of ballets from the Romantic repertory, including *Giselle* with Carolina Rousset in the title role and her sister Calestina, *en travesti,* as Albrecht. Later the Thierry company came with a similar repertory, and in 1861 Virgina Ferrari and Celestino de Martino brought *Esmeralda* from the Teatro San Carlo of Naples. Other European successes followed. In 1883 the Gran Compañia Coreográfica Italiana brought *Excelsior;* in 1897 the Victoria Theater offered *The Fairy Doll,* and the Ludovico company performed *Coppélia.*

As soon as it was completed in 1908, the Teatro Colón became chiefly a lyric theater, and dance was relegated to the role of a *divertissement* in operas. In 1925, however, three permanent companies were established in the Teatro Colón—chorus, orchestra, and ballet. Previously the theater had been used only for isolated dance presentations, such as those of Olga Preobrajenska, visits of the Diaghilev Ballets Russes in 1913 and 1917, and Anna Pavlova's troupe in 1917. The corps de ballet was established in 1925 under the direction of Adolph Bolm; the first item in its repertory was *Le Coq d'Or.* Its first soloists included Ekaterina de Galanta, Galina Chabelska, and Vera Grabinska, who danced with such guest artists as Elena Smirnova, Felia Doubrovska, Anatole Oboukhoff, Ludmilla Schollar, and Anatole Vilzak.

Bronislava Nijinska and Boris Romanov presented their major works during the 1920s and 1930s. In 1931 the visit of Michel Fokine, with his star Olga Spessivtseva and her partner Keith Lester, was one of the most important events in the development of the theater's repertory. Fokine's assistant, Esmée Bulnes, settled in Buenos Aires and became a great creator of Argentine ballerinas, beginning with Dora del Grande, Leticia de la Vega, and Lida Martinoli; the most notable was María Ruanova, the first Argentine star to grace the world of dance. Her rise to fame began in 1934, when Serge Lifar presented her with the permanent corps of the Teatro Colón.

Margarete Wallmann helped to expand the repertory of Argentine ballet during the 1940s. In 1942, guest director George Balanchine mounted his *Apollon Musagète* and created a new ballet, *Concierto de Mozart,* for the company.

In 1943 the Original Ballet Russe of Colonel W. de Basil merged with the Ballet of the Teatro Colón. In the late 1940s and 1950s the company was graced by Aurelio Milloss, Léonide Massine, David Lichine, Tatiana Gsovsky, and Heinz Rosen, and new choreography was added. In 1960 there was an unforgettable reception for two visiting companies, Le Grand Ballet du Marquis de Cuevas and London's Festival Ballet; the resident ballet of the Teatro Colón presided over the evening's festivities. During the 1950s new choreographic works by Janine Charrat, Antony Tudor, and John Taras were presented. The English choreographer Jack Carter presented works especially created for the Teatro Colón, including *Coppélia, Swan Lake,* and *The Sleeping Beauty,* while William Dollar presented *Constantia, Sebastian,* and *Le Combat.* During this second phase a new generation of Argentine dancers emerged, including Olga Ferri, Esmeralda Agoglia, Victor Ferrari, José Neglia, Enrique Lommi, Norma Fontenla, Antonio Truyol, Adela Adamova, Irina Borowska, and Wassil Tupin. Two of them, Olga Ferri and José Neglia, became the mainstays of the company. Neglia won the Nijinsky Prize and the Gold Star at the 1968 Paris Festival.

Olga Ferri was the first Argentine star to dance with London's Festival Ballet and the Berlin Opera Ballet. She has danced in Europe and the United States and achieved national recognition when she won Argentina's Grand Prize of the National Fund for the Arts. Another impor-

ARGENTINA: Ballet. *(left)* José Neglia and Olga Ferri in Jorge Tomin's *Antiguas Danzas y Areas,* set to the music of Italian composer Ottorino Respighi. *(right)* The same pair in Jack Carter's *El Niño Brujo* (The Witch Boy) at the Teatro Colón in Buenos Aires in 1966. (Photographs by Annemarie Heinrich; used by permission.)

tant step in her career occurred when she danced with Rudolf Nureyev in the first performance of his *The Nutcracker* in 1971 at the Teatro Colón. [*See the entry on Ferri.*]

George Skibine, Pierre Lacotte, Zarko Prebil, Flemming Flindt, and others have provided the resident ballet company with new choreographic works for the third generation of Argentine dancers, among them Nancy López, Gustavo Mollajoli, Violeta Janeiro, Liliana Belfiore, and Rubén Chayan. In the 1980s the leading dancers of the Teatro Colón included Silvia Bazilis, Cristina del Magro, Alicia Quadri, Lidia Segni, Eduardo Caamaño, Daniel Escobar, Alejandro Totto, and the rising star Raúl Candal, who enjoyed a triumph in *Giselle,* partnering his teacher, Olga Ferri. Two young dancers, Julio Bocca and Maximiliano Guerra, were gold medalists in Moscow and Varna, respectively.

Recent masters of the company have included Boris Kniaseff, Alexander Minz, Azari Plisetsky, and Héctor Zaraspe. The Teatro Colón is visited every year by the leading ballet companies and the stars of international ballet. Its permanent company appeared in 1968 at the Paris Dance Festival; in 1974 the national government sponsored a Latin American tour.

BIBLIOGRAPHY
Anderson, Jack. "Concerning Miracles, Sylphs, and Buenos Aires." *Dance Magazine* (November 1974): 22–26.

Basaldua, Emilio. "Hector Basaldua and the Colón Theater." *Journal of Decorative and Propaganda Arts* 18 (1992): 32–53.
Benmayor, Lily. *Nuestro Teatro Colón.* Buenos Aires, 1990.
Bullrich, Silvina. *Mas vida y gloria del Teatro Colón.* Buenos Aires, 1985.
Caamaño, Roberto. *La historia del Teatro Colón, 1908–1968.* 3 vols. Buenos Aires, 1969.
Giovannini, Marta, and Amelia Foglia de Ruíz. *Ballet argentino en el Teatro Colón.* Buenos Aires, 1973.
Heinrich, Annemarie. *El espectáculo en la Argentina, 1930–1970.* Buenos Aires, 1987.
Malinow, Inés. *Desarollo del ballet en la Argentina.* Buenos Aires, 1962.
Malinow, Inés. *María Ruanova.* Buenos Aires, 1993.
Manso, Carlos. *Maria Ruanova: La verdad e la danza.* Buenos Aires, 1987.
Riobó, Julio F., and Carlos Cucullu. *El arte del ballet en el Teatro Colón.* Buenos Aires, 1945.
Valenti Ferro, Enzo. *Los directores: Teatro Colón, 1908–1984.* Buenos Aires, 1985.

JUAN UBALDO LAVANGA

Modern Dance

Before the 1940s, ballet was the only type of theatrical dance represented in Argentina. The Teatro Colón, one of the best-known landmarks in Buenos Aires, was the principal stage for costly productions and was also the home of a traditional school of classical dance. Modern dance had been seen only in sporadic appearances: in 1916, Isadora Duncan danced at the Teatro Colón; in the late 1930s, Alexander and Clothilde Sakharoff stayed in Argentina for a short time, producing shows and teaching. Some years later, they formed a dance group that included some Argentine dancers. The Chilean Inés Pizarro, the Jooss Ballet, and Harald Kreutzberg also performed in

ARGENTINA: Modern Dance. Paulina Ossona in her dance *Germinación* at the Teatro Lineamientos, Buenos Aires, 1962. (Photograph by Lidya Márquez; courtesy of Paulina Ossona.)

Buenos Aires. Margarete Wallmann, Renate Schottelius, and Otto Werberg came from central Europe, remained in Argentina, and were the first dance instructors of this new style of dance. All of them aroused an interest in the new dance and influenced some dance instructors, who started to teach the techniques they had just learned.

The American dancer and choreographer Miriam Winslow, a disciple of Denishawn, arrived in Argentina in 1941. The programs she and her partner Foster Fitz-Simmons offered then and on a return visit in 1943, together with her decision to stay and establish a new company in 1944, marked the beginning of the continuous development of modern dance in Argentina.

Miriam Winslow's first company, the Winslow Ballet, included Renate Schottelius, Ana Itelman, Cecilia Ingenieros, Luisa Grimberg, Celia Tarcia, and Margarita Guerrero. During the company's short existence, Winslow herself was in charge of all the productions. Frequent tours to the provinces and the production of two shows daily in Buenos Aires attracted large audiences, but the company dissolved in 1946 owing to internal problems. Miriam Winslow returned to the United States. Nevertheless, from that group came the pioneer teachers and choreographers of this new art form in Argentina.

Renate Schottelius had been born in Germany, where she had studied with Wigman's pupils. She continued dancing as a soloist and later traveled to the United States, where she had contact with the Humphrey-Limón technique. In the early 1950s, from her students arose the first cooperative contemporary dance group in Argentina. Later she founded Renate Schottelius and the Experimental Group of Contemporary Dance, which performed all over the country.

Ana Itelman founded a group and a school, then went to the United States and studied all the techniques in vogue. Twelve years later she returned to Argentina and became a renowned choreographic composition teacher who influenced generations of choreographers. Other choreographers such as Paulina Ossona, Luisa Grimberg, and María Fux followed her path in both the creative and the pedagogic sense. Thus from the first dance group of Miriam Winslow came pioneers who, from Buenos Aires, dominated the modern dance scene in Argentina during the 1940s and 1950s, always under the influence of German expressionistic dance and American techniques.

In 1952, another key visitor was Dore Hoyer. Her recitals at the Teatro Colón were a tremendous success. During the 1950s this favorite disciple of Mary Wigman visited Argentina on various occasions. In 1959, Hoyer was invited by the government to settle in Argentina and to found a school in the city of La Plata. There she trained some of the most talented figures in modern dance of the following years, such as Oscar Araiz, Iris Scaccheri, and Lía Jelín. Political and financial factors caused her contract to be terminated in 1963, and Hoyer returned to Germany.

By the beginning of the 1960s, modern dance had expanded and many creators and groups were in existence. Now Argentine choreographers trained by the pioneers began to search for new directions. Three significant events took place in those years—the founding of Amigos de la Danza, the opening of the General San Martín Municipal Theater, and the creation of the Di Tella Institute. On 23 November 1961 the General San Martín Municipal Theater was inaugurated in Buenos Aires; in years to come it would house the first state-sponsored modern dance company. On that night the most important figures of the nation's cultural world appeared there, and modern dance was also well represented as the Renate Schottelius group presented her work *Estamos Todos Solos* (We Are All Alone).

The Amigos de la Danza association was founded in

1962. During its ten years of existence its purpose was to promote independent choreographic creation and to unify two tendencies in dance—classical and modern—that until then had appeared irreconcilable. The aim was to offer programs with new choreography and different styles, employing Argentine musicians and designers. Owing to the efforts of this foundation, choreographers with an established reputation as well as young artists were given a space where they could search for their own personal styles.

The Center of Audiovisual Experimentation of the Di Tella Institute provided the right environment for the exploration and research that marked a new form of expression in the world of dance. Working together or individually, Ana Kamien, Marilú Marini, Susana Zimmermann, Oscar Araiz, Iris Scaccheri, and Graciela Martínez turned away from earlier modes of dance to create a new and daring language. The Di Tella productions gave room to satire and absurdity and the free play to work with objects, happenings, and improvisation; it opened a new creative space that competed with the traditional expressionist and American influences in Argentine modern dance.

On 17 March 1968, the San Martín Municipal Theater Contemporary Ballet was created under the direction of Oscar Araiz, a young choreographer who had studied all the trends that had appeared in Argentine dance to that time. He had a background in ballet and had received the influence of Winslow through his first modern dance teacher Elide Locardi. Araiz had been Dore Hoyer's pupil in her La Plata School, had choreographed for the Amigos de la Danza, and had participated in the presentations of the Di Tella Institute. This company, under several directors, has since been the only official one devoted to modern dance. Many remarkable Argentine choreographers have created works for the company; the group also includes in its repertory works by non-Argentine choreographers, such as Donald McKayle and Jennifer Muller.

Since the 1970s several independent companies have formed, with differing results. Because of the repression suffered under military rule in Argentina, those years were the least favorable for the development of modern dance. Creativity was frequently curtailed. It is important to mention, though, the founding in 1975 of a significant group, Nucleodanza, directed by Margarita Ball and Susana Tambutti. Starting from a search through formal language and experimentation with trial and error, they generated a boundary of self-containedness that allowed the company to grow within its own aesthetic, independent of the sociopolitical milieu. Although some elements in its later works could be given a political reading, it managed to survive; today it maintains all its force and has become Argentina's most prestigious independent group, with international recognition. Modern dance emerged again in the early 1980s, in a series called Danza Abierta. Here many talents, recognized as well as new, developed a creativity that challenged the government.

With democracy restored in 1983, Argentine modern dance began to grow in quality and in the number of artists, but it had to respond to a new challenge. Certain intellectuals, particularly critics, reproached this modern art that had developed in Argentina for a lack of national identity. They complained that every choreographer or

ARGENTINA: Modern Dance. Members of Susana Tambutti's company Nucleodanza performing her *Jugar con Fuego* (Playing with Fire) at the Teatro Municipal General San Martín, Buenos Aires, 1990. The dancers are Mariana Blutrach, Inés Sanguinetti, Laura Hansen, Gustavo Lesgart, and Luis Baldassarre. Mónica Toschi designed the sets and costumes. (Photograph courtesy of Susana Tambutti.)

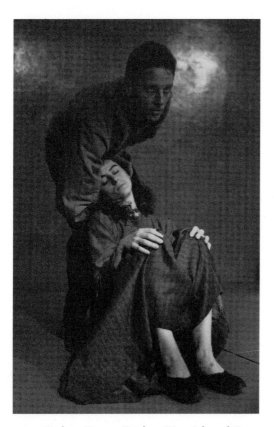

ARGENTINA: Modern Dance. Esteban Wozniuk and Rosana Zelaschi in Oscar Araiz's *Numen* at the Teatro del Sur, Buenos Aires, 1991. (Photograph by Carlos Flynn; courtesy of Oscar Araiz.)

company that had visited the country, whether Maurice Béjart, Merce Cunningham, or Pina Bausch, so influenced the local scene that Argentine artists adopted in turn the style of every visitor. Choreographers responded by falling back on the tango, both in music and in dance. Their mistake was to ignore the Argentine characteristic of eclecticism, an ability to absorb all that comes from other countries, thus becoming at once both international and local.

Finally after decades of learning and of incorporating and adapting all that was taking place in the dance world, Argentine modern dance began to project beyond its national boundaries. The San Martín Theater Contemporary Ballet made tours through Latin America, the United States, and Europe; Nucleodanza toured throughout the world. Oscar Araiz, Mauricio Wainrot, Ana Maria Stekelman, and Susana Tambutti, among others, have directed or choreographed for prestigious foreign companies.

Although modern dance is not yet a very popular art form in Argentina, many young people have started to work, create, and investigate new forms in this field. The generation of the 1990s finds itself confronted by an art with a history that allows for a variety of techniques, methods, and systems, and they are now free to create without cultural pressures and political repression. The major problem remains in economic factors, which sometimes act as a subtle mechanism of censorship.

Among outstanding new figures are Mabel Dai Chee Chang, with her interdisciplinary work; Miguel Robies, who does not identify with defined codes and uses improvisation as a method; Laura Veiga and her comedic innovations; the experimentation carried out by the group El Descueve; and Mariano Patín, with his work within the genre of dance theater. Choreographers like these few mentioned make the future of Argentine modern dance very promising.

Modern dance acquired such importance that since 1987 its history, theory, and aesthetics have been studied at the University of Buenos Aires and important research has been accomplished there.

[*See also the entry on Araiz.*]

BIBLIOGRAPHY

Falcoff, Laura. *Ballet contemporáneo: 25 años en el San Martín*. Buenos Aires, 1994.

Isse Moyano, Marcelo, et al. *Primer cuaderno le danza del Instituto de Artes del Espectáculo de la Universidad de Buenos Aires*. Buenos Aires, 1995.

MARCELO ISSE MOYANO

ARGENTINA, LA (Antonia Mercé y Luque; born 4 September 1890 in Buenos Aires, died 18 July 1936 in Bayonne, France), significant artist in the development of Spanish dance. Born of a Castilian father and an Andalusian mother, Antonia Mercé returned to Spain from Argentina with her parents at the age of two. Years later she was to take the name of her natal country as her professional name and establish herself as one of the most significant artists in the development of Spanish dance in the twentieth century. Her mother was the *première danseuse* of the Teatro Real, Madrid, and her father was ballet master there; she began her dance training under his tutelage at age four. Subsequently she joined the corps de ballet at the Opera House at the age of nine and became *première danseuse* at eleven.

Mercé eventually left to perform in the music halls of Spain, making her first artistic venture outside Spain in 1906 with a visit to Portugal. She traveled to Paris in 1910 to appear at the Moulin Rouge in *L'Amour en Espagne*. Creating her own choreographies, she mounted *La Corrida* (The Bullfight) in 1912. She originally created it as an *alegrías* but eventually set it to the music of Quinto Valverde; the dance was to remain in her repertory throughout her life. She continued to appear without much notice in a variety of musical hall productions in Paris and the French provinces for some years. Early appearances in London and New York also passed without note.

As a child, Mercé found the sound of castanets distressing. At her insistence her father allowed her to request a castanet-maker to experiment with the carving of them so that they would make a more melodious sound. Her experiments with the shape and sound of castanets were to have a dramatic effect on her eventual success as a solo recitalist. Steeped in Spain's folk music from childhood and encouraged by her mother—herself a musician—Mercé began to take an interest in the music of Spain's emerging generation of composers, choreographing numbers to their music. Firm friendships with Enrique Granados, Isaac Albéniz, Manuel de Falla, Ernesto Halffter, and Joaquín Nin bore fruit in dances such as *La Vida Breve* and *Serenade Andalouse* (to music by Falla), *Goyescas* (Intermezzo), *Jota Valenciana, Andaluza,* and *La Danza del Ojos Verdes* (dedicated to her by Granados), *Andalouse Sentimentale* (to music by Joaquin Turina), and *Danse Iberienne* (a dance drama in three parts dedicated to her by Nin). She did not neglect Spain's regional dances or *escuela bolera* in her programs; she also added dances collected during her travels, such as *Cariñosa* to music from the Philippines, and *Suite Argentine,* comprising *Bailecito, Zambra, La Firmeza,* and *Condición.* Flamenco did not feature prominently in her programs, although her *Tango Andalou* was a firm favorite.

In 1923 Argentina met the Russian émigré impresario Arnold Meckel, and under his management her European touring career began. In 1929 she formed her company, Ballets Espagnols d'Argentina, choreographing *El Amor Brujo* to Falla's music, *Triana* to Albéniz's *Suite Iberia,* Halffter's *Sonatina,* Durán's *El Fandango de Candil,* Oscar Espla's *Le Contrebandier,* and Julián Bautista's *Juerga.* The corps de ballet was recruited from the Paris Opera, but soloists came from Spain and included Vicente Escudero, Francisco León (professionally known as Frasquillo) and his wife Francisca González León (La Quica), Carmen de Gomez (La Josalito), and Martinez. Argentina did not continue with the company because of the difficulties of touring. In 1933 in Buenos Aires, she again recruited locally and produced *El Amor Brujo;* its final production was at the Paris Opera in June 1936, just prior to her death.

Argentina's solo recitals, interspersed with piano solos of Spanish music, were her forte, and her 1928 appearance in New York was hailed as a triumph. She returned to North America regularly; in 1935 she appeared on a program with the Vienna Boys Choir at the White House, in Washington, D.C. Her 1929–1930 tour of the Far East took her to Japan, China, the Philippines, and Saigon. On her return to Europe, she undertook additional tours in North Africa. Her first London appearance was in 1931 under the management of Charles B. Cochran, who brought her back to London each succeeding year, always to full houses.

She made an indelible impression on all who saw her. Years later the mention of her name brings back a flood of

LA ARGENTINA. An exceptional figure in the development of Spanish dance, La Argentina founded her own company to perform regional dances and her own solo and group choreographies. She is seen here c.1934. (Photograph by Nicholas Murray; from the Dance Collection, New York Public Library for the Performing Arts.)

memories to those who were in her audiences. The first of her many portraits was painted by Angel Nieto. She inspired poetry in French, Spanish, and English, as well as notation of her castanet work and books. She was honored by France with membership in the Légion d'Honneur in 1930, by Spain in 1932 with the Cruz de Isabel la Católica, by Tunis with the Order of Icham Iftikar in 1933; the press association of Latin America awarded her the Laurier d'Or after she created *Suite Argentine.*

Argentina's career was cut short by a heart attack in July 1936 in the Pyrenees, where she had gone to rest after an exhausting touring program. The Spanish Civil War broke out the day she died.

After her death, the association Les Amis d'Argentina was established to perpetuate her memory. The association fell into a decline during World War II but was reestablished by Monique Paravicini after the war. It holds exhibitions, lends costumes and memorabilia, and marks commemorative dates. Members have instigated the erection of memorial plaques in the Salle Pleysel (Paris), at Mercé's childhood home in Madrid, and at her birthplace in Buenos Aires. A Madrid street has been named Calle Antonia Mercé, and a red floribunda rose was christened "La Argentina" in Barcelona in 1986. The Paris Opera Museum held a major exhibition in 1956 to mark the twentieth anniversary of her death. Her fiftieth anniversary was marked by an exhibition at Canning House in London and a mass in Paris. Other major exhibitions have been held in Madrid under the patronage of Queen Sofia of Spain in 1982, and in Paris in 1984, marking the anniversary of her last performance there.

BIBLIOGRAPHY

Antonia Mercé "La Argentina": Homenaje en su centenario, 1890–1990. Madrid, 1990.

Cordelier, Susanne F. *La vie brève de la Argentina.* Paris, 1936.

García Redondo, Francisca. *El círculo mágico en el centenario de Antonia Mercé, Vicente Escudero y Pastora Imperio.* Cáceres, 1988.

Levinson, André. *La Argentina: A Study in Spanish Dancing.* Paris, 1928.

Levinson, André. *La danse d'aujourd'hui.* Paris, 1929.

Levinson, André. *Les visages de la danse.* Paris, 1933.

Levinson, André. "Argentina." In *André Levinson on Dance: Writings from Paris in the Twenties.* Edited by Joan Acocella and Lynn Garafola. Middletown, Conn., 1991.

Luján, Néstor, and Xavier Montsalvatge. *"La Argentina" vista por José Clara.* Barcelona, 1948.

Moore, Lillian. "La Argentina." In Moore's *Artists of the Dance.* New York, 1938.

Rice, Cyril. *Dancing in Spain (Argentina and Escudero).* London, 1931.

Wright, Dexter. *Notations of Ten Castanet Solos by Spain's Most Famous Dancer La Argentina.* New York, 1931.

FILM. *Les Amis d'Argentina,* featuring *La Corrida* and *Tango Andalou.*

RECORDINGS. Nine 78 r.p.m. recordings were made in the late 1920s, issued in France under the Odéon label and in England and the United States under Parlophone; reissued by Odéon on long-play record No. OD.1023. All records are now out of stock.

PHILIPPA HEALE

ARGENTINITA, LA (Encarnación López Julvez; born 3 March 1895 in Buenos Aires, died 24 September 1945 in New York City), Spanish dancer. Together with La Argentina and Pastora Imperio, La Argentinita was responsible for the initial development of Spanish dance as a concert form. As the critic Margaret Lloyd has observed, at a time when the Italians, Russians, and French seemed more interested in Spanish dance than Spaniards were, La Argentinita more than any other dancer demonstrated the rich diversity of authentic Spanish dance—classical, regional, and flamenco. Her particular vehicle was the *bosquejo,* a little sketch built around a dance with singing, mime, and gentle comedy, which created a cameo impression of a particular region of Spain. In an age of exotic Spanish stereotypes and vaudevillian peas-

ant dances, Argentinita's art was understated, warm, and authentic.

When Encarnación López was four years old, her Castilian-Spanish parents brought her back to Spain, where she acquired the childhood nickname that later served as her professional name. She studied regional dance from early childhood and first performed at the age of six. While still in her teens, she was so well known that Jacinto Benavente dubbed her "the queen of dance."

From the late 1920s until the Spanish Civil War of the 1930s, Argentinita was associated with a circle of Spanish intellectuals and artists including José Ortega y Gasset, Manuel de Falla, and the poet-dramatist Federico García Lorca, who were interested in recovering and preserving Spain's cultural richness. Earlier she had worked with Martinez Sierra's theater group and then formed her own company, reviving nineteenth-century Spanish plays, reportedly with wit and originality. She studied flamenco with Gypsies and in 1927 formed an authentic Gypsy dance troupe with which she toured France and Latin America, learning Spanish-American dances along the way. Encouraged by Lorca, she collected Spanish regional dances; Lorca, at the piano, and Argentinita, singing and dancing, also recorded Spanish folk songs. Her involvement in these projects was as a performer rather than as a scholar; nevertheless, aficionados such as D. E. Pohren (1964) rate her the most authentic performer of the "ballet" period of Spanish dance.

In 1932, Argentinita and Lorca founded the Madrid Ballet to encourage preservation of old-style Gypsy dancing. Argentinita's younger sister, Pilar López, joined the company in 1933, but its main attractions were the legendary Gypsy dancers whom Argentinita coaxed from seclusion. They toured Spain and France performing not only flamenco but also Argentinita's own choreography to Manuel de Falla's *El Amor Brujo.* In 1935 she created a theatrical *cuadro flamenco, Las Calles de Cadiz,* using her company and renowned Gypsy singers and musicians. Each artist not only danced but also acted a role. According to Pohren, the flamenco was pure, and the *barrio* of Cadiz seemed to come alive.

Argentinita made a brief and disastrous U.S. debut in 1930 in Lew Leslie's *International Revue.* Performing against a flashy backdrop of showgirls dressed in Broadway-type Spanish gowns, the modest, authentically costumed Argentinita did not appear to advantage. She recouped a few weeks later with a short series of New York concerts that John Martin in the *New York Times* called "a triumph fully justified."

It was not until Argentinita left Spain, after Lorca's execution in the Civil War, that she gained widespread popularity in England and America. Anton Dolin, a passionate admirer of her work since both had appeared in the *Inter-*

LA ARGENTINITA. Known for her understated performaces that included singing and mime, La Argentinita achieved fame for her interpretations of flamenco and classic regional Spanish dances. (Photograph from the Dance Collection, New York Public Library for the Performing Arts.)

national Revue, arranged for her first London performance in March 1937. The following year, under the auspices of Sol Hurok, Argentinita and her company—Pilar López, Antonio de Triana, and the guitarist Carlos Montoya—toured the United States. Critical and public acclaim brought her back every year until her death. Works that consistently pleased U.S. audiences were *El Huayno,* a Peruvian dance of faith to Inca flute music; the gently comic *Mazurka of 1890; L'Espagnolade,* a satire on stereotypes of Spanish dancing; and *Boléro,* to Maurice Ravel's music. John Martin found the latter particularly effective because as the music intensified, the choreography remained understated, creating a mounting tension.

At Monte Carlo in 1939, Argentinita collaborated with Léonide Massine on Rimsky-Korsakov's *Capriccio Espagnol* for the Ballets Russes. She also danced opposite Massine for one performance of his *Le Tricorne* in New York in 1942. Her company made guest appearances with Ballet Theatre in 1942 and subsequent seasons, performing such works as the dances from *Carmen,* which she had originally choreographed for the Mexican National Opera in 1941.

In 1941 the Dutchman Freddie Wittup (Federico Rey), who had danced with La Meri, became Argentinita's part-ner. By early 1943 he had been replaced by two young dancers of importance, José Greco and Manolo Vargas. With Argentinita and Pilar López they formed a quartet of exceptional talent. Argentinita and López choreographed new works such as *Picture of Goya,* and Argentinita choreographed an expanded version of the slyly comic *Café de Chinitas,* based on the historical rivalry between the two legendary flamenco dancers La Majorana and La Coquinera.

Argentinita's art was essentially an intimate one, small in scale, exact in detail, and dependent on a personal connection between herself and each member of her audience. As she danced, she often sang in a high, expressive voice. In the oversized theaters in which she sometimes performed in the United States, "the nuances of her art," as Martin observed in 1943 in the *New York Times,* "simply evaporated into thin air."

"Only the greatest dancers can awaken so personal a response by as restrained an art as hers was," Edwin Denby eulogized Argentinita when she died of cancer in 1945. She left behind a national treasure—a repertory that was the nearest thing Spain had to the great ballet companies of other countries. Her sister Pilar López took up that legacy, returned to Spain, and formed her own Ballet Español in 1946.

[*See also the entry on López.*]

BIBLIOGRAPHY

Denby, Edwin. "To Argentinita, Passing Star." *New York Herald Tribune* (20 September 1945).
Dolin, Anton. "Some Memories." *The Dancing Times* (November 1945): 58–60.
Martin, John. Articles and reviews. *New York Times* (1930, 1938–1945).
Meri, La [Russell Meriwether Hughes]. *Spanish Dancing* (1948). Pittsfield, Mass., 1967.
Pohren, D. E. *Lives and Legends of Flamencos.* Madrid, 1964.
Thomas, Katherine. "Anda jaleo, jaleo! The Flamenco Song and Dance Lineage of Federico García Lorca and La Argentinita." *UCLA Journal of Dance Ethnology* 19 (1995): 24–33.

RECORDING.   Irving Deakin, "Dances and Rhythms of Spain: La Argentinita," WQXR radio broadcast, 20 March 1941 (tape recording).

ARCHIVE.   Dance Collection, New York Public Library for the Performing Arts.

JUDY FARRAR BURNS

ARI, CARINA (Carina Jansson; born 14 April 1897 in Stockholm, died 24 December 1970 in Buenos Aires), Swedish dancer and choreographer. Ari was a student in the Royal Swedish Ballet School in 1913 when choreographer Michel Fokine chose her to appear in an all-Fokine program in Stockholm. In 1919 she went to study with Fokine in Denmark. Ari created the large ballet included in Mauritz Stiller's film *Erotikon* (1920). From 1920 through 1922 she was one of the principals for Les Ballets Suédois in Paris. She was praised as an extraordinarily expressive artist, with especially beautiful arm movements.

In 1923 Ari left Les Ballet Suédois to launch a soloist career, based in Paris. In 1925 at the Opéra-Comique she produced her own complete program, *Scènes Dansées*, consisting of eight solo dance scenes with full stage designs and symphony orchestra. She toured this spectacular program in various countries until 1939 .

In 1928 Ari had created *Rayon de Lune* for the Paris Opera and danced one of the leading roles. In 1929 she appeared with her own company at the Fête des Narcisses in Montreux; in the 1929/30 season she was ballet mistress at the National Opera in Algeria; in 1932/33 was ballet mistress and ballerina at the Opéra-Comique in Paris. From 1935 to 1937 she staged several of her ballets at the Royal Opera in Stockholm. In 1938 she created the role of the Sulamite in Serge Lifar's *Le Cantique des Cantiques* at the Paris Opera.

Ari left dance in 1939, settled in Buenos Aires in 1941, and later started a second career as a sculptor. In the 1960s she generously supported Swedish dance and cultural life. In her will she endowed the Carina Ari Foundation in Stockholm, which grants scholarships to young dancers and helps support elderly dancers. A gold medal in her name is awarded each year to the person who has made a special contribution to dance life in Sweden. The Carina Ari Library is also situated in Stockholm.

BIBLIOGRAPHY

Näslund, Erik. *Carina Ari: Ett lysande liv.* Stockholm, 1984.
Näslund, Erik. "Carina Ari." *Dance Research* 7 (Autumn 1989): 70–80.

ERIK NÄSLUND

ARMED DANCES. Dances done with weapons originated in early antiquity, flourished in feudal societies, and survive to the present day. Found throughout the history of world dance, they differ from region to region and from period to period. Armed dances from all regions and periods, however, share associations with rituals of fertility, virility, and warfare.

In the Classical period, some of these associations derived from the mythology surrounding the Cretan Zeus. Stories of the god's birth are associated with fertility rituals, stories of his nurture with warfare rituals, and stories of his rebirth with initiation rituals. Hesiod's *Theogony* tells how the Curetes (semidivine beings inhabiting Crete) danced around the infant Zeus, beating drums and clashing spears against their shields so that his cries would not be heard by his father Kronos. Origins of armed dances are also found in myths surrounding the nurturing of

Zeus in a cave on Mount Dikte (identified with Mount Ida). According to tradition, the cave was sacred to bees; neither god nor man could enter. Stories about this cave have prompted the hypothesis that the Curetes represented primitive beekeepers, who attracted bees into the hives with the sound of drums and spears beating against shields.

Presumably, the earliest armed dances—performed as seasonal fertility rites and as victory celebrations—used sticks, spears, and axes. After metallurgy had developed, swords replaced the less sophisticated weapons. The sword possessed a mystique, personality, and power of its own. Many sword dances used the weapon as a symbolic prop. Stylized combat could as easily signify seasonal battles between summer and winter or diurnal ones between night and day as actual battles between tribes. For instance, although the Spanish *morisca* ("Moorish dance"), first noted in 1500, involves the realistic miming of battles, scholars have traced its origins to ancient springtime rites that invoked the return of the sun and of plant life and culminated in a human or animal sacrifice. [*See* Moresca *and* Sword Dance.]

During the Middle Ages, central European sword dances became attached to guilds as well as to male fraternities. This remains true today in Austria. There, as in Spain and Portugal, sword dances have survived as part of an active cultural tradition. In England they were revived after 1900 as a result of the work of Cecil Sharp, the celebrated collector of folk songs and dances.

Among the varied types of sword dances are the solo dances prominent in the Near East, characterized by the performer's brandishing of a sword or saber while dancing. Another type found throughout Europe involves a solo performer, accompanied by pipe music, stepping between two crossed swords, sticks, or a crossed sword and scabbard. Originally a victory dance, this type includes the Scottish "Gille Calluim," the English "Bacca Pipes," the Finnish "Skin Kompasse," and the Hungarian "Kanász Tánc." In China and Japan, sword dances are featured in stylized theatrical presentations of warfare.

Even within types, wide variations occur. The English Morris dance differs from the *morisca* in its extreme stylization, the absence of actual clashing of the sticks, and the presence of side actors who enact a tale of death and resurrection. Like the Morris dance, sword dances in western Europe de-emphasize the element of combat while emphasizing the excitement created by the steady evolution of geometric and rhythmic patterns of the dancers and drummers. Swords serve not to divide but to connect the male performers: each man grasps the hilt of his own sword in one hand and takes the point of his neighbor's sword in the other; except for passages in which the dancers interweave their swords into starlike shapes, the circle never comes undone until the dance's end.

[*For related discussion, see* Asian Martial Arts; Egypt, *article on* Traditional Dance; Matachins; *and* Middle East, *overview article.*]

BIBLIOGRAPHY

Alford, Violet. *Sword Dance and Drama.* London, 1962.

Allenby Jaffe, Nigel. "The Crane and the Pyrrhic Reviewed and Reinterpreted." Paper presented at the Fifth International Conference on Dance Research: Dance and Ancient Greece, Athens, 4–8 September 1991.

Delavaud-Roux, Marie-Hélène. "La pyrrhique en Grèce antique." *Études Indo-Européennes* 9 (1990): 29–47.

Delavaud-Roux, Marie-Hélène. "War-Dances in Ancient Greece." Paper presented at the Fifth International Conference on Dance Research: Dance and Ancient Greece, Athens, 4–8 September 1991.

Sparti, Barbara. "Report on the Fifth International Conference on Dance Research: Dance and Ancient Greece." *Dance Research Journal* 24 (Spring 1992): 52–54.

Willetts, R. F. *Cretan Cults and Festivals.* New York, 1962.

R. F. WILLETTS

ARMENIA. [*To survey traditional and theatrical dance in Armenia, this entry comprises two articles: the first article discusses the history of traditional dance; the second explores the development of staged folk dance and ballet.*]

Traditional Dance

Situated in the southern Caucasus Mountains between the Black Sea and the Caspian Sea, the Armenian Republic occupies a portion of the Armenian highlands, an extension of the Anatolian plateau. In the north and east, it is bordered by the republics of Georgia and Azerbaijan; in the west and southeast by Turkey and Iran. Some 3.4 million people live in 11,500 square miles (30,000 square kilometers); 88 percent are Armenians and the remainder are Russians, Kurds, Ukrainians, and Azeris. Armenians also live in Turkey and Iran as well as in countries beyond the Middle East.

By 6000 BCE, the Anatolian plateau and Armenian highlands were a neolithic farming center, one of those that led to the rise of civilization in the ancient Near East about 3500 BCE. An inscription from 521 BCE on the cliff of Behistun (Bisitun) first mentions Armenia, when it fell to Persia under Darius the Great. In 301 CE, the kingdom of Armenia was the first nation to adopt Christianity as its state religion—this through the missionary work of Saint Gregory the Illuminator. In 405, Mesrop Maštocʿ created the Armenian alphabet. The spread of Christianity throughout the country inevitably caused some destruction of the earlier culture, including temples and libraries.

The Armenian kingdom fell to a series of invaders—the Greeks under Alexander the Great, the Romans in the first century BCE, and the Persians in the fourth century CE. Independent from 886 to 1046, Armenia fell to the Byzan-

tines who lost it to the Seljuk Turks in 1071; with the Mongol invasion of the eleventh century, Armenia's Prince Reuben established the kingdom of Little Armenia in Cilicia to the west, which lasted until the Mamluk conquest of 1375 and the Mongol invasion of Tamerlane from 1386 to 1394. After Tamerlane's death in 1405, the Ottoman Empire ruled Armenia until its demise in World War I.

For being Christian, Armenia suffered under Ottoman rule, and ethnic extermination was attempted between 1894 and 1915. At Lake Van, the Armenians revolted, holding the territory until Russian troops arrived. After World War I, Armenia became an independent republic, but the Russian Revolution resulted in its 1921 incorporation as a Soviet republic. With the dissolution of the USSR in 1991, Armenia became an independent republic having border problems with Azerbaijan.

Traditional Dance. In early times, dances had definite functions in Armenian pre-Christian ritual. The many myths and legends were performed by mime and dance in the temples and ceremonial centers, the most famous of which were Armawir, Yervandašat, Artašat, Bagaran, Ani, and Arsamosata. There, ceremonials included grove prophets, sacred dancers, ritual experts, and leaders of round dances. Armenian historians have recorded some aspects of the pre-Christian society. According to Movsēs Xorenacʿi (fifth century CE) the province of Gokhtn was famous for its narrators, singers, and musicians. A major topic was the procession of Noah down from Mount Ararat—which is in Armenia—and the settlement of his descendants in the country. The historian Pʿawstos Buzand (fifth century CE) described funeral processions, where men and women wept, played musical instruments, danced, and clapped hands. The dead man's wife stood in the center of a round dance and sang.

Dance in the Middle Ages. In the medieval palaces of Armenia's feudal lords, wandering dancers and acrobats were hired to perform; many had trained monkeys and bears. The Christian clergy tried to prohibit the performances, but eleventh-century writer Aristakes Lastiverc'i recorded that at the festivals in Ani (then the capital), the people gathered in the squares and sounded trumpets, cymbals, and other instruments. Theatrical performances and musical instruments are also described in medieval Armenian manuscripts of the twelfth to the seventeenth century, with masked dancing, acrobats, musicians, and trained animals.

Contemporary Dance. Only since the mid-nineteenth century did systematic publications appear on ethnographic research, traditional dance, and theatrical folk productions. The texts of songs and the descriptions of games and performances were also published. Although the names of dances, styles, forms, and the time and place of performances have come down to us, there are no descriptions of the dance movements.

True dance research began in Armenia at the beginning of the twentieth century. The dancer Srbuhi Lisitsian started a studio in Tbilisi in 1923; the program included a theory of movement and the urban dances of the Armenians, Georgians, Chechens, Ossetians, Dagestans, and others. Most were adapted for the stage. About this time, a few other dance schools were started in Erevan, Armenia's capital. Their programs consisted of European and Transcaucasian urban (social) dances—including the polka, *pas de Spain, shalakho, lekuri, mirzai,* and *tarakama.* The dancer and teacher Vahram Aristakessian organized the Ethnographic Ensemble in his studio; both folk dance and staged folk dances were in the repertory. The dances were from the regions of Mush, Sasun, and Van; the dancers wore traditional costumes and the musicians played the *zurna* and drum. Many of the students went to various villages after their training to begin their own ethnographic ensembles. For years these ethnochoreologists recorded dances from village informants as authentic, but some were actually staged dances and not native to many regions.

In 1936, in Erevan, a choreographic middle school was begun where students learned both classic and folk dances from Lisitsian and took part in the ethnographic ensemble. In 1937, the House of Folk Art was opened in Erevan; it systematically organized the fieldwork from Armenia's regions, gave consultations and courses for amateur dance group leaders, and sponsored meetings and festivals. Such authentic folk dance groups were formed in the regions of Talin, Aštarak, Artašat, Kotajk, Lori, and Zangezur. In 1938, the State Ensemble of Folk Singing and Dancing was instituted with Tatul Altunian as leader and Edward Manukian as choreographer. Elements of folk dance were used in many performances, but this was a professional ensemble with dances based on ideas other than folklore.

Real attention and interest in folk dance intensified in Armenia in 1957, with the appearance onstage of the ethnographic dance group from the village of Ashnak, led by Vahram Aristakessian and first dancer Tovmas Kazarian. Their program consisted of authentic dances from the region of Sasun. The mass media inspired great interest in them, so their repertory exerted an ongoing influence on all Armenian dance groups.

Dance Research. Important work has been done in the history and theory of Armenian dance. Since 1924, Lisitsian has been collecting and researching Armenian dances. She devised a system of notation called kinetography to analyze movement and connect dance elements. Others have continued her methodology and classification system, resulting in a rich archive. The dances are categorized as collective, group, duet, or solo. In collective dances, the number of dancers is not limited; sometimes the whole village dances. In group dances, eight or nine

dance; these are difficult dances with complicated movements, and the dancers may form two groups. In duets, a man and a woman or two dancers of the same sex take part. In solos, a man or a woman may dance, but it is most often a woman.

Folk dancers are divided by sex and by age. Dances may be for males and females, all male, all female, or for children. There are two formations for the male/female dances: the old, with the men first and the women following; the modern, with men and women alternating. The lead man and the end man (the "head" and the "tail") must be good dancers; they hold handkerchiefs in their right hands and wave them to establish rhythm. The musicians stand near the dancers—often in the center of a circle—and play without interruption, maintaining the strict order of the dances.

In collective dances, the formations are the round (circle), semicircle, and line. The dancers stand side by side, facing the center, holding hands. When there are large numbers, they form two or more concentric circles, often with the outside circle(s) all men and the inside all women. The semicircular formation is similar to the circle dance, but it winds, leading the dancers around or turning them in a spiral, snake, under bridged hands, into two groups, or into new directions. The line dance is more restricted. The dancers move side by side, one after another, or face to face (if there are two lines). Usually the tempo is slow and dancers hold each other's little fingers, with arms held low, bent at the elbows, or above the waist or shoulders. Slow dances are not difficult, so all ages can join in.

When dancers are connected palm on palm (the "handshake"), they stand shoulder to shoulder and the hands are low, moving forward and back. If the arms are bent, they move to the right and left. The "wing to wing" connection *(tev-tevi)* is used when arms are on the shoulders of the dancers to the right and left—as in the men's fast dances with jumping and squatting. When the arms are behind the partner's back, dancers stand shoulder to shoulder and very close, as if forming a wall; this is specific to some men's dances.

The direction of the line of movement is very important; movement to the right is positive and to the left negative. The right has always been associated with acts of positive (white) magic and the left to negative (black) magic. Usually dance steps are to the right and the left—but the right prevails.

Armenian folk dance has many fixed step combinations that come down from ancient times, and they have names. Each is defined by a series of steps and a mode of using the hands. The names of the dances come from the first line of the accompanying song or from the general form. The traditional dances have been classified by genre: they are road, war, wedding, mourning, ritual, pantomime, and work dances—sometimes it is difficult to differentiate among them. Road dances are for the processions going to festivals, celebrations, and meetings—for seeing off pilgrims, wedding parties, and so on. Road dances are collective, couple, or solo. War dances and games take place at weddings and festivals. These are danced only by men—as a solo, duet, or group. As a genre, pantomimes are very old. Dancers imitate the movements of birds or those of goats, bulls, bears, camels, or monkeys. All the dances have the same form; they show the life, show the death, and then the resurrection. The many bird dances are either collective or solo, and the dancers are men. The birds most imitated are the crane, the goose, and the hen; the elements shown are the mother and young pecking grain, drinking water, and flying.

Some solo dances for women pay homage to fruit trees—apricot, pear, pomegranate. These are lyric dances with three parts: slow–quick–slow. For weddings, Armenians have many dances. Some are compulsory as ritual dances and are both solo and collective. Work dances are for men, such as "Mortar" *(Dngo)*, the "Butcher's Dance" *(Kasab havasi)*, or "Let Us Pound Onion and Garlic" *(Ekek tzezenk sokh u skhtor)*. Dance with song has questions and answers:

> Let us pound onion and garlic!
> How [do we] pound onion and garlic?
> By hand [we] pound [the] onion and garlic.

The dancers then show how they work, and the questions and answers are repeated, using the parts of the body in a systematic and often humorous way (the foot, knee, head, ear, pelvis, and so on). Some solo men's dances imitate work: the dancer shows how to wash, dry, comb wool, twist thread, and weave. Sometimes a man will dress like a woman and try to joke about the work involved. Other topics for dance include everyday routine and comic, lyric, tragic, and epic situations.

The musical instruments that accompany the dancing include the *zurna, duduk,* and *dhol* (drum). These form a classic country group. The *zurna* and *duduk* are wooden wind instruments—types of oboe. The drum is mid-sized, with skins over both sides, and is played by two sticks or by the palms and fingers. In the region of Hamshen, people dance to the *kämani*—a type of violin. When Armenians dance to song accompaniment, either two dancers and then two more sing or all the dancers sing. The dance measures are 6/8, 3/8, 2/4, 6/4, or 12/8.

Contemporary Armenian amateur dance groups are moving in two directions. Rural groups continue the authentic folk or near-folk traditional dances. Urban repertories often mix classical ballet movements and style with the traditional movements. Many urban dance groups are financed by societies, organizations, social clubs, factories, or trade unions. There are also some state-sponsored

dance schools: the Erevan Choreographic School (department of classic and folk dance); the Erevan State Pedagogical Institute (department of Armenian folk dance); and the club-organized dancing schools. There are as well two state dance ensembles: the Armenian State Dance Ensemble and the Armenian State Ensemble for Folk Singing and Dancing. Professional ethnochoreologists of the Institute of Archaeology and Ethnography, Academy of Sciences, Republic of Armenia, continue to collect, describe, analyze, publish, and do fieldwork on folk dance and folk theater.

BIBLIOGRAPHY

Khachatrian, Genja. "Armenian Folk Dances of Javakhk" (in Armenian). *Hay Azgagrutjun ev Banahjusutjun* 7 (1975): 5–104.

Khachatrian, Genja. "Principles of Classification and Form of Armenian Dances." In *Folk Dance: Problems of Study* (in Armenian). St. Petersburg, 1991.

Lisitsian, Srbuhi. *Starinnye pliaski i teatralnye predstavleniia armanskogo naroda.* 2 vols. Erevan, 1958–1972.

Lisitsian, Srbuhi. *The Armenian Old Dances* (in Russian). Erevan, 1983.

Petrossian, Emma, and Genja Khachatrian. *Armenian Folk Dance* (in Russian). Moscow, 1980.

Petrossian, Emma. *Topics and Images of the Armenian Folk Dramatic Art* (in Russian). Moscow, 1985.

Petrossian, Emma. "Totemic Dances of Armenia." In *The Performing Arts,* edited by John Blacking. The Hague, 1979.

GENJA KHACHATRIAN and EMMA PETROSSIAN

Theatrical Dance

The dance of Armenia is associated with the history of an ancient Christian people; because of its location, Armenia has long served as a corridor between the Christian West and the Muslim East. A blending of these cultures gave Armenia some distinctive traditions and, gradually, dance performances associated with Christian holidays acquired a secular content. The traditional accessories—swords, sabers, and spears—were replaced with sticks, banners, and kerchiefs. Through a long history in which their national identity was constantly threatened or suppressed, Armenians preserved their dance heritage.

In the Soviet period, the choreographers Srbuhi Lisitsian, Vahram Aristakessian, and Ilya Arbatov began to record, classify, and perform traditional Armenian dances. Two companies, one founded in 1938 by T. Altunian and the other in 1958 by E. Manukian, also preserve and perform Armenian folk dances. In 1924, a choreographic studio was established in Erevan, Armenia's capital, by Aristakessian and a studio for rhythmic dance was founded in Tbilisi by Lisitsian. These formed the basis for the professional ballet school that was founded in 1937.

The Opera and Ballet Theater was opened in Erevan in 1933 with nineteen dancers from Odessa led by Valentin Presnyakov. Five years later Arbatov took charge of the company and in 1939 created the first Armenian national ballet, *Happiness,* to music by Aram Khachaturian. In the

ARMENIA: Theatrical Dance. Karoun Tootikian (second from left) with dancers of her Armenian Ballet Company in their version of the festive folk dance *Lepo-leh-leh*. (Photograph from the archives at Jacob's Pillow, Becket, Massachusetts.)

following decades, Russian masters staged ballets from the classical repertory in Armenia. In the 1960s, the repertory was enriched with the work of additional Armenian composers, and a national style began to develop. Lively rhythms, rich imagery, and an expressive style were characteristic. Armenian choreographers of the 1960s included Mark Miatsakanian, Evgeny Changi, and Maxim Matirosian. The company also performed classical works.

The Armenian ballet was for many years directed by Vilen Galstian, who was both a choreographer and a dancer. The company made frequent tours abroad. Among Galstian's best works is his *David of Sasun*, a ballet-opera with a score by the Armenian composer Edgar Organisian. The choreographer used the movements and dance patters of the province of Sasun (the mountainous part of Armenia), whose folklore is notable for tales of manliness and where the dynamic war dances are preserved. At the center of the spectacle are the folk scenes.

In the vast scale of the production, the authors achieved monumental expressions; the solo parts contain intricate and subtle detail while remaining visually striking. Ample use is made of the most complicated classical vocabulary and of melodies tuned to the ligature of Eastern dances. The hero, David of Sasun, is a generalized image of the mighty hero. Like the folk tale on which it is based, the ballet-opera is an epic production.

Other important works by Galstian include *Ara the Beautiful* (1982), to music by the Armenian composer G. Egiazarian. In 1990, Galstian choreographed *The Snow Queen*, to music by T. Mansurian, dedicated to the children who died in the earthquake of December 1988.

Since the dissolution of the Soviet Union in 1991, Armenia's social climate, the border war with Azerbaijan, and a faltering economy caused the State Opera and Ballet Theater in Erevan to suspend regular performances.

BIBLIOGRAPHY

Gosudarstvennyi teatr opery i balety Armenii imeni A. A. Spendiarova. Moscow, 1939.
Roslavleva, Natalia. "How Large Is Soviet Ballet?" *Dance Magazine* (November 1963): 35–37, 58–61.
Tigranov, Georgii. *Armianskii muzykal'nyi teatr.* 2 vols. Erevan, 1956–1960.

EKATERINA L. SARIAN
Translated from Russian

ARMS. *For discussion of positions of the arms in ballet, see* Ballet Technique, *article on* Arm Positions. *For discussion of carriage of the arms, see* Port de Bras.

ARNOULD-MUSSOT, JEAN-FRANÇOIS (born 1734 in Besançon, France, died 1795 in Paris), French actor, theater director, author, and librettist. Acknowledged by Henry Lyonnet as "the true creator of melodrama," Arnould-Mussot was an important transitional figure in eighteenth-century French ballet, between Jean-Georges Noverre and Théophile Gautier. Under the stage name François Mussot, he created the majority of ballets and pantomimes produced at the Théâtre de l'Ambigu-Comique in Paris from 1770 to 1795; many of these were adapted for the London stages by George Colman. Arnould-Mussot's works were the first serious ballet-pantomimes imported to the United States.

The son of an *avocat au parlement*, Arnould-Mussot studied law himself until drawn to the stage. A spirited actor, he undertook the *amoureaux* roles in the prince of Conti's private theater, where he met Nicholas Audinot. In 1770 he joined Audinot's new Théâtre de l'Ambigu-Comique, destined to become one of the two great popular theaters of the Paris boulevards. In 1775 he was appointed co-director of the troupe, a position he held for the next twenty years.

Arnould-Mussot's fortune and fame as an author derived from his pantomimes, which were performed throughout the Western world. His first triumph was the ballet-pantomime *Le Chat Botté* (1770); Louis XV's mistress, Madame du Barry, selected it for a program designed to amuse the downcast king. Arnould-Mussot next composed, in the old comic style, a number of short comedies, satires, and pantomimes, which were well received. However, by 1779 he had turned away from the traditional comic pantomimes, which in the preface to his *Les Quatre Fils Aymons* he described as having "like eternity, neither beginning nor end, in which the principal action consists in a score of special scenic effects which are moved into view by means of machines."

Les Quatre Fils Aymons is credited as being the first popular serious pantomime, an innovative genre that changed the course of popular theater in France. Featuring the deeds of Charlemagne, Roland, and other heroes as derived from the tradition of heroic romances, it was imitated by scores of other "historical" melodramas. Another new feature was the character of the maltreated virtuous heroine, who first appeared in this pantomime and who became the focus of more involved complications in Arnould-Mussot's later works as well as the mainstay of many nineteenth-century ballets and melodramas. For example, in *La Belle Dorothée* (1782), a lecherous Spanish inquisitor threatens to burn the noble heroine at the stake as a supposed heretic, and *L'Héroïne Américaine* (1786) concerns an Indian maiden who saves an English sailor's life only to be sold into slavery by the ungrateful villain.

Arnould-Mussot won great fame with the three-act pantomime *Le Maréchal des Logis* (1785). It was based on an actual event in which an old soldier, while walking through a forest, came upon a pretty young girl threatened by two robbers. He attacked the brigands, who seriously wounded him and then fled. When he returned the girl safely to her parents, he was rewarded with her hand in marriage. All Paris was said to have sobbed over Arnould-Mussot's sentimental rendition of the story.

Arnould-Mussot attempted to incorporate realistic costumes and appropriate dance styles in his pantomimes. For example, in the libretto for his heroic pantomime *La Morte du Capitaine Cook* (1788), he suggested that the stage musicians play nose flutes and drums hollowed from tree trunks. The dancers were instructed to dress in imitation of contemporary Hawaiians, "half-naked," garbed in feathers, glass beads, and shells, with long, flowing hair dyed several colors. At one point, two rows of dancers were directed to "perform an entertainment in the style of their [the Hawaiians'] country," accurately described in the libretto as being "very lively; the dancers move their feet with astonishing ability. The females demonstrate much grace and dexterity in the movements of their hands and fingers which they clap to the measured sounds of the drum. The lead singer also directs this same movement by shouts or by clapping his hands." Such attention to authentic detail was virtually unprecedented in eighteenth-century ballet.

The eighteenth-century label "pantomime" may mislead the modern-day reader, for performances at the Ambigu-Comique and other Paris boulevard theaters probably were closer to the current notion of ballet than of mime. Pantomimes were performed rhythmically to orchestral music and, unlike many of the *opéra-ballets* of the time, included no poetry or song. Sometimes the pantomimes boasted more dances than did the *ballets d'action. La Morte du Capitaine Cook,* for example, included four *divertissements,* whereas the libretto for Maximilien Gardel's *ballet d'action Mirza* (1782) gave directions for only one pas de deux and one *divertissement.* One observer cryptically noted in his daily journal that a 1774 production of Gaspero Angiolini's ballet *L'Orphelin de la Chine* had "no dance" whatsoever.

The art of pantomime at the popular theaters was inextricably interwoven with the development of ballet technique and with theatrical reform during the latter half of the eighteenth century. While some dance theoreticians called for ballet's reform by an application of ancient Roman pantomimic principals, others argued that it was not necessary to seek models primarily in the past. Contemporary scholar Charles Compan observed that "All the time we see the Low Comic dancers [the *bas-comique*] render Pantomime Dance albeit in a naive manner." Sarah Goudar, a renowned wit and cultural observer, demanded to know why the *opéra-ballets* could not, with such effective examples before them, achieve the same level of dramatic expressivity as the pantomime dances at the popular theaters.

Conversely, pantomimes at the popular theaters were influenced by Noverre and his court ballets. Indeed, Arnould-Mussot's pantomime-ballets, according to J. F. Michaud, grew directly out of the Noverrian *ballet d'action.* Arnould-Mussot substituted serious themes for comical ones and abolished the printed programs upon which Noverre relied to explain the dramatic action in his ballets. He remained within the classic unities of time, place, and action, which Noverre had categorically denied could be done. He jettisoned the erudite mythological settings that Noverre preferred in favor of a kind of *drame bourgeois* as promulgated by Denis Diderot and the French encyclopedists. Finally, Arnould-Mussot's popular pantomimes touched the hearts of spectators from all social classes—an accomplishment that, if Goudar is to be believed, Noverre tried in vain to achieve.

Viewed as part of a continuum from the works of Noverre to those of Gautier, Arnould-Mussot's pantomimes can be regarded as precursors to the Romantic ballet characters he shaped: the suffering, virtuous heroine, the outcast hero, the innocent child-victim, the manipulative villain, all of whom remained popular throughout the nineteenth century and indeed through Hollywood's silent screen days. Arnould-Mussot skillfully combined the Romantic penchant for local color with high spectacle. His themes—romanesque, historical, exotic—later became staples of the Romantic repertory. However, unlike Gautier's, they always were founded upon a strong realistic base and did not rely upon supernatural or magical plot devices or on the *Sturm und*

Drang ("storm and stress") atmospherics of the German poets.

Lillian Moore has touted the 1794 Philadelphia premiere of *La Forêt Noire* as "an event of the greatest importance in the history of ballet in America," adjudging it "the first serious ballet to be given in this country." Actually Alexandre Placide and Suzanne Douvillier had already presented a number of other Arnould-Mussot pantomimes in several eastern cities. The first such performance of which we have a record was on 14 December 1791, when *Le Maréchal des Logis* was presented under the English title *The Old Soldier.* It was followed over the next three years by *La Belle Dorothée, L'Héroïne Américaine, Le Braconnier, La Morte du Capitaine Cook, Pierre de Provence et la Belle Maguelonne, Les Quatre Fils Aymons* (as *The Four Valiant Brothers*), *Robinson Crusoe dans Son Isle, Le Vétéran, ou Le Bûcheron Déserteur, Le Vice Puni, ou Le Nouveau Festin de Pierre,* and *Geneviève of Brabant* as well as *La Forêt Noire.* Because Arnould-Mussot was given no credit for any of these works, his contribution to the establishment of ballet in the United States has remained for the most part unrecognized.

[*For related discussion on English pantomime, see* Pantomime.]

BIBLIOGRAPHY

Brazier, Nicolas. *Chroniques des petits théâtres de Paris.* 2 vols. Paris, 1837.

Compan, Charles. *Dictionnaire de danse.* Paris, 1787.

Costonis, Maureen Needham. "The French Connection: Ballet Comes to America." In *Musical Theatre in America,* edited by Glenn Loney. Westport, Conn., 1984.

Goudar, Sarah. *Remarques sur la musique et la danse, ou Lettres de M. G. à Milord Pembroke.* Venice, 1773; supp., Amsterdam, 1777.

Lyonnet, Henry. *Dictionnaire des comédiens française.* 2 vols. Paris, 1902–1908.

Mason, James Frederick. *The Melodrama in France from the Revolution to the Beginning of Romantic Drama, 1791–1830.* Baltimore, 1912.

Michaud, J. F. *Biographie universelle.* Paris, 1854.

Moore, Lillian. "John Durang, the First American Dancer." In *Chronicles of the American Dance: From the Shakers to Martha Graham,* edited by Paul Magriel. New York, 1948.

MAUREEN NEEDHAM

ARPINO, GERALD (Gennaro Peter Arpino; born 14 January 1928 in Staten Island, New York), American dancer, choreographer, and director. Gerald Arpino began studying ballet as a nineteen-year-old Coast Guardsman stationed in Seattle, Washington, where his friend Robert Joffrey introduced him to Mary Ann Wells's classes. In 1948 he returned to New York with Joffrey to further his dance career. There he studied with Aleksandra Fedorova, at the School of American Ballet, and with May O'Donnell and Gertrude Shurr.

Arpino's professional performing career began with chorus roles on Broadway in late 1950. In 1951 and 1952 he toured South America with the Ballet Russe of Nana Gollner and Paul Petroff.

When Robert Joffrey founded his school, the American Dance Center, in 1953, Arpino was on the faculty, and in 1954 he became a member of Joffrey's first concert group. He remained one of Joffrey's principal dancers until 1964, when he stopped performing to concentrate exclusively on choreography. He was also a principal dancer with the New York City Opera during Joffrey's tenure there as resident choreographer (1957–1962).

Arpino made his choreographic debut in May 1961 on a program presented at the Ninety-second Street YM-YWHA in New York. Two of his ballets, *Ropes* and *Sea Shadow,* entered the Joffrey company's repertory in 1962. Arpino served as the company's chief choreographer for the rest of Robert Joffrey's life, creating more than one third of the ballets commissioned for the Joffrey. He became associate director of the Joffrey Ballet in 1965.

Robert Joffrey became seriously ill in the mid-1980s. When he died in March 1988, Arpino was named artistic director. From that time forward, he created no new

ARPINO. Dennis Wayne, Christian Holder, and Gary Chryst in Arpino's rock ballet *Trinity,* a signature piece of the Joffrey Ballet throughout the 1970s. (Photograph from the Dance Collection, New York Public Library for the Performing Arts.)

works, meeting the Joffrey Ballet's needs for new choreography by commissioning pieces from outside. His last completed work was *The Pantages and the Palace Present TWO-A-DAY* (1989).

In 1990 it came to light that the company owed a substantial debt to the dancers' union for unpaid health insurance premiums. The ensuing financial crisis prompted the board of directors to remove Arpino from control of the company. The Joffrey was about to open its month-long season at the Los Angeles Music Center; Arpino responded by resigning and withdrawing all his ballets from the repertory. By the end of the season, he had been restored as artistic director.

Financial stability did not return, however. The Joffrey Ballet lost its base as a resident company of the Music Center, and, as result of burdensome debt, was forced to curtail rehearsals and seasons in New York. In 1995 Arpino oversaw the dissolution of the Joffrey Ballet, which declared bankruptcy, and the establishment of the Joffrey Ballet of Chicago, a somewhat different, smaller troupe.

[*See also* Joffrey Ballet.]

BIBLIOGRAPHY

Anawalt, Sasha. "No Compromise: Gerald Arpino and Joffrey Ballet." *Dance Magazine* (May 1992): 40–47.

Laine, Barry. "Crowd Pleaser." *Ballet News* 7 (November 1985): 11–15.

Maynard, Olga. "Arpino and the Berkeley Ballets." *Dance Magazine* (September 1973): 47–61.

Reynolds, Nancy, and Susan Reimer-Torn. "Trinity." In *Dance Classics*. Pennington, N.J., 1991.

Solway, Diane. *A Dance Against Time: The Brief, Brilliant Life of a Joffrey Dancer.* New York, 1994.

TULLIA LIMARZI

ARTISTS AND DANCE. [*To consider the relationship between the visual arts and the performing arts, this entry comprises four articles. The first three articles focus on the dance-related work of visual artists between the years 1760 and 1969; the fourth considers collaborative work among painters, sculptors, film and video artists, composers, choreographers, and writers.*]

Artists and Dance, 1760–1929

Although dance and the visual arts have evolved in close association since earliest times, this kinship continues to be neglected in the histories of both arts. Undoubtedly, the "inferior" status of dance among the fine arts, fully equalized only at the turn of the twentieth century, has largely been responsible for this omission. Complex socioeconomic issues, in part, also determined the historical and critical fate of dance, as did the great cultural and political upheavals of the eighteenth century, which helped call attention to the intrinsic significance of dance as a discipline and its close kinship to the other arts.

By the end of the nineteenth century, the interaction between dance and the visual arts greatly quickened in intensity and deliberateness. The 1909–1929 productions of the Ballets Russes of Serge Diaghilev achieved one of its best-known and most admired interactions. Yet the continuing and much more fundamental interactions between the two media, especially from about 1860 to about 1918, have barely been noted. Many of their motivating ideals have come to be identified with modernism in the arts in general.

The Enlightenment. Much of the credit for initiating the inquiry into dance's aesthetic substance and place among the other arts goes to the thinkers of the Enlightenment, notably Louis de Cahusac, Denis Diderot, and the dancer-theorist, Jean-Georges Noverre. Their views, like those of many other eighteenth-century intellectuals and artists, received powerful stimuli from the fresh reconsiderations of antiquity. They coincided with the incipient Romantic revolution and with the tangentially related investigations of human nature and the natural world. Cahusac dignified dance with an authoritative historical lineage that earlier writers had but vaguely established.

In their reforming zeal, all three men eagerly supported the relatively new *ballet d'action*. This theatrical dance form deliberately sought to free dance from its many stifling usages by means of recourse to ancient pantomime, which greatly enhanced its claim to expressive self-sufficiency and equality as a medium. This claim they justified by comparisons with the other arts; Cahusac even went as far as to assert the superiority of the dance over painting because of its capacity to render more than "one moment" and because "movement . . . is but imitated [in art]. . . . It is always real in dance" (Cahusac, 1754).

Thanks to his broad scope and learning, Diderot probably more than anyone else laid the groundwork for what might be called the modern form of the dialogue between the two media. As a writer, man of the theater, and art critic he was able to range across the various arts and translate his acute insights into general aesthetic terms. His vitalistic viewpoint led him to emphasize gesture and rhythm as essential means of human expression and as basic to the experience of poetry, dance, the plastic arts, and music. Indeed, he identified gesture—the "tool of the heart"—with the vital force inhabiting both human beings and nature and held that "rhythm [was] the image of the soul." Like Stéphane Mallarmé a century or so later, he maintained that the language of poetry was emblematic, like a tissue of hieroglyphs, affecting the imagination like physical gesture because of its similarly synthetic form. Diderot admitted that he looked at paintings as if they were conversations between deaf-mutes, and that on occasion he could render his reactions to pictures only by

ARTISTS AND DANCE. Jean-Baptiste Carpeaux's sculptural relief entitled *Danse* (1868), Musée d'Orsay, Paris. (Photograph from the Dance Collection, New York Public Library for the Performing Arts.)

means of the bodily motions that instinctively accompanied his visual experiences. It is not surprising, therefore, that Diderot could find great artistic merit both in the moralizing "naturalism" of Jean Baptiste Greuze's explicit narrative tableaux, such as *The Village Bride* (1761), and in the preverbal dynamics of Jean-Baptiste-Siméon Chardin's luminous and poetic still lifes.

It was left to the slightly younger Noverre to adapt many of the views of Cahusac and Diderot as well as those of the composer and opera reformer Christoph Willibald Gluck into the specific terms of dance and dance theory. Noverre's celebrated *Lettres sur la danse* (1760) is in many ways an apology for the self-sufficient *ballet d'action* and its freer movements, which he referred to as "expressive dancing." In accord with Diderot, Noverre believed that a step, gesture, movement, and an attitude expressed more than words. Not unjustly was he dubbed by the great actor David Garrick, "the Shakespeare of the dance." In his *Lettres*, Noverre also made much of the kinships between dance and the equally mute visual arts, including architecture. Undoubtedly, he thereby sought again to underline the elevated status of the dance as well as to enlarge its creative scope. He also unintentionally provided justification for the persistent view of the so-called dependence of dance upon art, which helped to prolong the concept of dance's position of inferiority.

Although the plastic arts continued to be very meaningful to dance during (and since) Noverre's day, the inspiration exerted by dance upon art during this time seems to have been largely ignored. Thus, not until 1941 did the art historian Edgar Wind call attention to the more than likely connections between Jacques-Louis David's neoclassic masterpiece *The Oath of the Horatii* (1784) and Noverre's ballet *Les Horaces* (1777).

Early Nineteenth Century. The sculpture of Antonio Canova, David's near contemporary, suggests an even more tantalizing kinship to dance. Not unexpectedly, it was quickly added to the visual models cited in nineteenth-century dance manuals, from those of Carlo Blasis onward. Canova interpreted ancient art in a remarkably vivid, personal way. The incisive gestures of his figures and their subtle dynamic balance suggest an outward release of energy that comes singularly close to what Noverre understood to be expressive dancing. It may even be said that Canova's exquisite *Three Graces* (1810–1812) epitomizes his notion of beauty as graceful movement. Canova evidently distilled this ideal from the actual experience of dancing, as is suggested by his numerous drawings of dancers, some probably taken from life, and his related paintings and sculpture. All of these give testimony to his enduring goal of rendering an internal animation or vital grace, the basis of his entire oeuvre.

At about this time Goethe, so deeply concerned with the renewal of German art, recommended that painters look at dancers for inspiration. Upon seeing Emma Hart (later Lady Hamilton) in 1787 when he was still a young man he, like many others, was smitten by her fluid "attitudes" which, as he noted, "with their finished movements and astounding variety accomplish what many thousands of artists would have liked to have done." Subsequently he eloquently praised Johann Gottfried Schadow's etchings of the dancing Viganòs (1796) and described the etchings as an instance where the pleasure of experiencing the "dynamic presence" of the dance "benefited the other art . . . [because] both arts are mutually responsive to one another in their aim to delight the eye."

Intellectually and creatively the ground had been well prepared during the early nineteenth century for an open and productive exchange between the two disciplines. Contrary to expectations, however, the developing Romantic ballet did not elicit equally spectacular visual responses. In fact, as landscape painting became a major preoccupation of many leading artists during the second quarter of the century, the two disciplines appeared to drift far apart. Yet this temporary divergence was not as fundamental as might be supposed at first: both media perceived nature as a metaphor for eternal rhythms; each in its way looked to nature's mysterious and private corners for evidence of elusive truths, thus establishing the basis for their later, more searching dialogue.

The Romantic Era. The quietly revolutionary art of Camille Corot best exemplifies the underlying concord between the two disciplines during this seemingly infertile moment of their interaction. Corot's deep commitment to the artistic ideals of classicism undoubtedly attuned him to many aspects of the Romantic ballet. At the same time, it allowed him to assimilate its qualities into his penetrating and affectionate insights into nature. This is especially apparent in his later, more loosely brushed paintings, accentuated explicitly in the lovely *A Morning: Dance of the Nymphs* (c.1850). Such pictures are a composite of nostalgic evocations of Italy, dewy ponds near Paris, and probably also the ballets at the Paris Opera, which he attended regularly. Corot always carried a sketchbook with him and at the theater made drawings of dancers, whose seemingly free and spontaneous gestures prophesy the art of Edgar Degas and the dancing of Isadora Duncan.

Late Nineteenth Century. The increasingly vigorous rapprochement between dance and art that took place in the late nineteenth century was furthered by an awareness of additional deep bonds between the two media and by specific historical circumstances. The ever-growing popularity of ballroom dancing and the discovery of non-Western dance genres, through performances at cabarets and at the quickly multiplying world's fairs, account for much of the widespread interest in dance. Furthermore, health and hygienic reforms (which led to the development of Swedish gymnastics) and the gradual discarding of the corset and other confining clothing strengthened a growing concern with physical fitness in general and the dance more specifically. The revival of the ancient Olympic Games in 1896 bracketed many of these cultural and hygienic ideals on a grand international scale.

More erudite and scientific support for the preoccupation with dance came variously from the writings of Richard Wagner, Friedrich Wilhelm Nietzsche, Charles Darwin, and Herbert Spencer. Wagner and Nietzsche emphasized the fundamental expressive and spiritual power of the dance in their highly influential books. Darwin's *Expression of Emotions in Man and Animals* (1872) provided a biological basis for the time-honored notion that seemingly unconscious bodily gestures are symbols of emotions. Spencer's exceedingly popular *First Principles* (1862, 2d enlarged edition, 1869) posited rhythm as a universal attribute of all realms of nature. Much more forcefully than Diderot, Spencer thus argued for a universal vitalism that identified rhythm as an essential structural

ARTISTS AND DANCE. *Carmencita*, an oil painting by William Merrit Chase (1849–1916). Flamenco dancer Carmen Dausset, usually billed as "Carmencita, The Pearl of Seville," was also the subject of a famous painting by the artist John Singer Seargent. (Metropolitan Museum of Art, New York; Gift of Sir William Van Horne, 1906 [no. 06.969]; photograph used by permission.)

principle, not only for poetry and music but also for the plastic arts. Spencer's rhythmic metaphor for the mysteries of the universe has had an enduring appeal until the present. Fortunately, the much more substantial studies on the nature of rhythm in music and poetry undertaken by his contemporaries and heirs (e.g., Westphal, Lussy, Riemann, and, most significantly in this context, Émile Jaques-Dalcroze) gave a much sounder basis to this topic.

Degas. Edgar Degas is the best known of the late nineteenth-century artists whose lifelong dedication to the world of dance may be seen both as coincidental and deliberate affirmations of some of these cultural events and as explorations of the kinship between the two media. His visual ruminations about the dance convey many of his innermost convictions about the nature of art and the artist in general. More specifically, the contemporary ballet's surviving classical notions of beauty and grace helped to focus his ambivalent attitudes toward the cultures of the past and present. At the same time, Degas's studies of the dance forced him to come to grips with the persistent problem of the suggestion of movement in static visual media and challenged him to devise novel spatial and other formal devices to meet this demand.

Degas matured in the realist milieu. His giving expression to the face in his art as well as to the body indicates his awareness of the psychobiological researches of Dar-

ARTISTS AND DANCE. Edgar Degas, who is perhaps more associated with dance than any other visual artist, often portrayed dancers at moments of rest. This famous bronze by Degas is entitled *The Little Dancer, Aged Fourteen* (1880–1881). (Photograph from the Dance Collection, New York Public Library for the Performing Arts.)

win and his predecessors. Teachings on the "semiotics of gesture" by the then much-admired movement coach François Delsarte also seem to have served Degas (and many of his fellow artists) in the quest for a deeply meaningful human gesture—much as they were to serve Isadora Duncan and Ruth St. Denis a few decades later. Degas's numerous studies of women performing the practiced and economic gestures of bathing or drying or combing their hair can therefore be seen both as complements to his studies of classical dance and as endeavors toward discovering succinct preverbal expressions. Ultimately, Degas's vision of the dance appears to have meant a transcendence of the here and now, an intimation of an unrealized and unrealizable ideal—as is suggested also in some of his late sonnets and his increasingly elliptical dance images. These late efforts reveal Degas's unintentional kinship to the symbolists, particularly to his friend, the poet Stéphane Mallarmé. Mallarmé also loved the dance and in the 1890s defined it as a "hieroglyph," a "corporeal writing . . . free from all the apparatus of the scribe." [*See the entry on Degas.*]

Rodin and Hodler. The sculpture of Auguste Rodin is another contemporary example of the intentional and accidental correspondences between art and dance. Many similarities exist between the sculptor's great concern with details of surface, muscles, position, and total gesture of the body and Delsarte's system of oratorical gesture. The initial idea of two of Rodin's most renowned sculptures, *The Burghers of Calais* (1885–1895) and *The Gates of Hell* (1880–1917), derived from a type of round dance. In the final versions of both, the artist's "choreographic" disposition of forms in space creates a novel kind of cohesiveness that supplants the more traditional modes of organization and, hence, affects the resultant meaning. This aspect of his work continues to be misunderstood and criticized. Today, however, anyone familiar with the asymmetrical, seemingly random choreography of Merce Cunningham and his followers can visualize Rodin's instinctive comprehension of dance and, by extension, of sculpture, as continuous articulated motion in space. That Rodin subsequently became a sensitive observer and supporter of the dancers Isadora Duncan and Loie Fuller as well as of others (e.g., Sada Yakko, and Hanako) who employed a highly evolved body "rhetoric" is not surprising. In *Nijinsky* (1912) his comprehension of the explosive genius of the dancer appears unsurpassed. [*See the entry on Rodin.*]

Well before 1900, a much more deliberate working relationship united two residents of Geneva, Switzerland—the painter Ferdinand Hodler and Émile Jaques-Dalcroze, the composer and founder of eurythmics. Their ideals developed from many common bases. These included a knowledge of Rodin's and Delsarte's achievements and, above all, a commitment to rhythm as a fundamental and

ARTISTS AND DANCE. With his *Nijinsky,* Auguste Rodin felt he came closest to his goal of representing in sculpture the abstract essense of a figure in movement. Modeled from life in 1912, after the premiere of Nijinsky's controversial *L'Après-midi d'un Faune,* the work was cast in plaster by the artist. Georges Rudier later cast this bronze in 1959. (Metropolitan Museum of Art, New York; Gift in honor of B. Gerald Cantor, 1991 [no. 1991.446]; photograph used by permission.)

even transcendental creative component. In the hands of Jaques-Dalcroze these ideals led to an exhaustive analytical translation of music into body movements. Hodler incorporated them into a mystical vision of humankind's complementary union with the universe. Powerful, symbolic figural arrangements visualize his views, as those found in the appropriately named *Eurythmy* (1895) and in *Day* (1900), *Truth* (1903), and other works. All of them reveal his partial indebtedness to Jaques-Dalcroze, with whom he also shared a susceptibility to the expressive movements of Far Eastern dancers and, subsequently, to those of Duncan, St. Denis, and their followers.

Loie Fuller. The far-reaching contributions of Loie Fuller—not only to dance and staging but to the visual arts—have been increasingly recognized. In many ways, her performances epitomized the spirit of Art Nouveau in its ephemeral symbolist aspects. In a larger sense, these performances were a fulfillment of the Romantic aspiration, reiterated by the writings of Richard Wagner, for a multimedia spatial and temporal unfolding of visual analogies. Such analogies diminished and even denied the expressive significance of the finite human form, which was seemingly dematerialized and absorbed into its similarly insubstantial surroundings.

Fuller's remarkable achievement and Mallarmé's brilliant evocations of it may well have been a decisive factor in the tacit granting of full equality for which the dance had fought so long. Furthermore, Mallarmé's renewed and convincing argument on the basic concordance of dance with the other arts helped to make it acceptable to those avant-garde artists for whom the ballet represented tradition-bound bourgeois values.

Fuller's Paris debut in 1892 and her subsequent appearances were quickly celebrated by a deluge of small and large objets d'art. Of the early artists who commemorated her performances, Henri de Toulouse-Lautrec and the poster designer Manuel Orazi stand out. Both produced a series of differently hued lithographs (Toulouse-Lautrec in 1893, Orazi in 1900), and both show Fuller as a seemingly weightless, floating shape formed by the voluminous silk draperies she manipulated with long wands. As a group these lithographs present a provocative counterpart to Claude Monet's roughly contemporary series of shimmering haystacks and façades of the Rouen cathedral. Whereas Fuller's changing forms were illuminated by variously colored and shifting electric lights, the light of the sun performed the dance of time in Monet's series. [*See the entry on Fuller.*]

ARTISTS AND DANCE. A poster by Henri Toulouse-Lautrec advertising a cabaret performance by La Troupe de Mademoiselle Églantine, starring Jane Avril, at the Moulin Rouge in Paris. (Photograph from the Dance Collection, New York Public Library for the Performing Arts.)

Twentieth Century. Thanks partly to the influential writings of Mallarmé, Fuller's achievement remained meaningful to many younger modernist artists who matured before World War I, although she herself had passed her prime as a performer. The long list would include exponents of Fauvism, cubism, futurism, expressionism, and synchronism.

The Futurists. It seems that the futurists not only discerned the aesthetic potential of Fuller's craft more completely than almost all of their contemporaries, but they were able to translate it fully into the twentieth-century context propagated by their leader, the poet Filippo Marinetti. This was to be expected, for the futurist artists aimed from the start at rendering "the gesture . . . [as] dynamic sensation itself," as they proclaimed in *Futurist Painting: Technical Manifesto* (1910).

Gino Severini, one of the futurists' artist members, created especially adventurous interpretations of Fuller's dances. His *Bear Dance = Sailboat + Vase of Flowers* (1913–1914) and *Serpentine Dance* (1914) evidently derive from Fuller's "transformations" of herself into writhing snake- or flamelike forms; however, the visual and aural complexities of these works go far beyond the *fin-de-siècle* aspects of her performances. Severini envisaged pictures such as these as analogies to the universal flux, which also

ARTISTS AND DANCE. A lithograph entitled *Galopp* (c.1910) by the German artist Leo Rauth. (Metropolitan Museum of Art, New York; The Elisha Whittelsey Fund, 1959 [no. 59.608.102]; photograph used by permission.)

announced his next, if temporary, step to total abstraction, as seen in *Spherical Expansion (Centrifugal)* (1913–1914). In it, the diaphanous shifting planes of color can be seen as corresponding to his wish to enclose the universe in a work of art, so that objects would no longer exist. In some ways this idea accords with Fuller's virtual disappearance within her moving props and lights. It is also implicit in *Plastic Complex + Dance + Merriment* (1915) by Severini's colleague, Giacomo Balla. This colored, sound-making mobile sculpture exemplified, half humorously, the type of objects to be created for *The Futurist Reconstruction of the Universe*, as Balla put it in his contemporary manifesto by that name.

The futurists' vitalism prompted them to intuit the various abstract rhythms of objects. Shortly thereafter, Balla painted *Rhythms of the Bow* (1912), and Carlo Carrà created *Rhythms of Objects* (1912). The futurists' stress on rhythm as the principal representational and structural element in their creations had, of course, been influenced by many of the sources mentioned above. To these must be added the related protocinematic efforts of Étienne Jules Marey, Eadweard Muybridge, and G. Demeney; early films; physiological studies of professional movement; and pedagogic reforms.

The futurists explored the abstract essentials of the dance as the basis of their art and their perception of the world. By contrast, some painters remained loyal to the human body as their chief expressive tool. For many of these artists other dance pioneers in the United States, notably Isadora Duncan, provided a liberating, if not always acknowledged impetus. Significant parallels between Duncan's highly controlled choreography and the basically "classical" endeavors of Henri Matisse can be made, for example, from Matisse's great pictures *Le Luxe I* and *II* and *La Danse I* and *II* (1907–1908; 1909–1910, respectively). The painter's comparably conscious distillation of past achievements with vital new inspiration is noteworthy; it may explain in part why Matisse, who in 1909 had a studio in the same building as Duncan, refused to recognize her skill.

German expressionism. The powerful expressionism of German and Austrian artists seems to have been furthered, directly or indirectly, by Duncan's art and ideas. Thus, it was no accident that Duncan first achieved enthusiastic acclaim in Germany and Austria and that the term *Ausdruckstanz* (expressive dance) was coined for dancing in the first years of the twentieth century. In those Germanic lands her message, like that of Matisse and his French Fauvist followers, seems to have been understood in rather different ways, falling as it did on ground that had been well prepared by Nietzsche's Dionysian vision. Moreover, the air had been cleared in those countries by dancer-entertainers such as the exceedingly popular Barrison Sisters, who also were from the United States.

ARTISTS AND DANCE. Isadora Duncan's performances inspired works by many artists. This watercolor, ink, and pencil work by Abraham Walkowitz is entitled *Isadora Duncan Dancing*. (Metropolitan Museum of Art, New York; Gift of Abraham Walkowitz, 1940 [no. 40.60.3]; photograph used by permission.)

They are clearly an imaginary blend of the Barrison Sisters, the Valkyries, Duncan, and Fuller; like innumerable other such dancerlike images by Moser and his Viennese colleagues, they suggest a virtual identification of artistic regeneration with the spirit of the evolving "new" dance.

The Viennese dancer Grete Wiesenthal, the daughter of a painter, helped to turn this dream into reality. Inspired by Duncan's example, and with the assistance of the composer Gustav Mahler and the stage designer and painter Alfred Roller, she left the Vienna State Opera Ballet in 1907. Shortly thereafter she participated with her own choreographic inventions in the activities of the Wiener Werkstätte, headed by Moser and the architect Josef Hoffmann. This modernist, experimental arts-and-crafts workshop was annexed to the Viennese School of Applied Art, then a haven for rebellious young artists. Two of these, Oskar Kokoschka and Erwin Lang, especially came under Wiesenthal's spell; Kokoschka found important confirmation and stimulation in her choreography for his much more ominously gesturing figures—as seen in his 1908 poster for his pantomime *Murder, the Hope of Women* and in his roughly contemporary illustrations for the *Dreaming Boys* (published by the Wiener Werkstätte). Lang, Kokoschka's friend, married Wiesenthal in 1910 and in the same year published a set of stark woodcuts of her various dances. These prints help to explain why, later, Mary Wigman stated that the performances of Duncan and Wiesenthal determined her own choice of career.

Dresden Brücke group. The dance in a literal and extended sense also formed a central ingredient of the Dresden Brücke group of artists founded in 1905. Ludwig Kirchner and Erich Heckel were much impressed by the acts of cabaret and circus dancers. In those acts they perceived something of both the driven, harshly ritualistic and redemptive aspects of life, which demanded a brazen front for the fragile psyche beneath. Kirchner's observations of the more or less complex choreographic rhythms of the performers enabled him to fortify his taut, dramatic compositions. It is tempting, therefore, to see his powerful geometric street scenes of 1913 and 1914 as painted developments of his dance experiences.

The older Emil Nolde, who had belonged only briefly to the Brücke group, used dance in his work to symbolize the primitive energies that seemingly control human destiny. *Dance around the Golden Calf* (1910) and the triptych *Mary of Egypt* (1912), especially the scene of the saint's conversion, are outstanding examples of Nolde's understanding of dance. In paintings such as these, the vehement, irregular rhythms that appear to animate the wildly gesturing figures also seem to have guided the artist's brush. As a result, the painting process has become nearly inseparable from the fundamental content of the picture, anticipating surrealist and abstract expressionist procedures.

Thomas T. Heine, a caricaturist and major contributor to the cynical Munich weekly magazine *Simplizissimus*, observed pointedly in 1897 that the Barrisons' absence of harmonious gesture à la the Romantic ballerinas was a virtue and defined their style.

In cities such as Vienna, Dresden, and Berlin, where cultural ferment had reached a high pitch in about 1900, the Barrisons' daredevil spirit and naughty parodies of high art created room for more "serious" artistic ventures. *Ver Sacrum*, the ambitious Viennese vanguard review of the arts (published 1898–1903), and Kolo Moser's many designs for it, demonstrate this. For example, Moser's illustration for the back cover of the second issue shows three barefoot "butterfly girls" in long, floating robes.

ARTISTS AND DANCE. *Pavlova Gavotte*, a tinted wax sculpture, cast in bronze c.1915, by the artist Malvina Hoffman. This statue represents Anna Pavlova in her popular *divertissement* first performed in 1913 under the title *Gavotte Directoire*. (Metropolitan Museum of Art, New York; Rogers Fund, 1926 [no. 26.105]; photograph used by permission.)

Wigman, Palucca, and the Bauhaus. Nolde's approach to art helps to explain why the young dancer Mary Wigman struck up a friendship with him. She listened to his advice to seek out the then little-known dance teacher and choreographer Rudolf von Laban. Subsequently, Wigman followed her own creative dictates, but she remained grateful to Laban for his vision. She also never deviated from her dedication to "absolute" movement—a quest that had initially attracted her to Nolde's related vision.

After World War I, Wigman performed at the Bauhaus, the utopian German art school located in Weimar and later in Dessau. The Bauhaus developed a very lively experimental theatrical program, and many of its faculty—Wassily Kandinsky, Paul Klee, Johannes Itten, Lothar Schreyer, László Moholy-Nagy, Oskar Schlemmer, and Walter Gropius, the director—were deeply receptive to dance. Wigman's expressionist seriousness, however, did not appeal as much to these men as the choreography of Wigman's master pupil, Gret Palucca. Palucca's youthful, boyish litheness and seeming detachment were more in line with the school's aesthetic mission to provide

spiritual and physical furnishings for the modern industrial world. Kandinsky was so enthusiastic about Palucca that he took photographs of her dancing and subsequently made diagrammatic drawings of them to illustrate the various kinds of "points" in his theoretical treatise, *Point and Line to Plane* (1926). It is very likely that a number of his nonobjective geometric works of the later 1920s, such as the suggestively entitled *Sur les Pointes* (On Pointe) (1928), were inspired by dance studies such as those used in his book. [*See the entries on Palucca and Wigman.*]

Mondrian and van Doesburg. One of Piet Mondrian's austere diamond-shaped canvases of 1926 occupied a place of honor above the piano in Palucca's white-walled studio in Dresden. Although she never met the Dutch painter, she seems to have understood instinctively the subtle rhythmic basis and balance of such totally nonobjective pictures. Mondrian's art derived at least in part from his love of jazz, social dancing, and modern music. Indeed, for Mondrian, Palucca's 1926 canvas was a preparatory step toward his climactic works, such as *Foxtrot A* (1930) and *Victory Boogie Woogie* (1943/44).

Theodore van Doesburg, Mondrian's erstwhile associate in *de Stijl* (Dutch for "the Style," an abstract art movement founded in the Netherlands in 1917), shared Mondrian's fascination with the dance. The angular, disciplined movements of exotic dancers provided him with a point of departure for the geometric abstractions he used as designs for stained-glass windows in 1917 and for the lively *Rhythm of a Russian Dance* (1917/18). In the painting, the variously accented, multicolored rectangles suggest, perhaps unintentionally, the movement patterns of dance notation.

Van Doesburg's dance experiences formed one of the sources for the evolution of his own complex design principles, called elementarism, which reinstated the diagonal into his art. The architecture and decor of the now-destroyed structure, the Café Aubette, built in Strasbourg in 1928—for which he was the controlling designer—represented a full-scale application of his elementarist ideals. The Café Aubette, with its multiple uses as civic entertainment center, dance hall, cinema, and theater, signified an appropriate, if perhaps unwitting, closing of the circle in which the rhythmically gesturing human body forms the actual or symbolic radius that measures the vitality of modernism in the arts.

Artists as Stage Designers. It is still impossible to venture a responsible opinion about why direct collaborations between leading artists and the dance—such as those that distinguished the productions of Diaghilev's Ballets Russes in the first decades of the twentieth century—were delayed by so many decades, although their occurrence may of course have depended largely on the developments surveyed above. It is true that highly competent stage and costume designers had helped to produce the elaborate dance spectacles of much of the preceding century, but their role was primarily that of supporting artisans rather than "creative" contributors. The various European antinaturalist stage reforms of the late nineteenth century emphasized, however, the integral partnership between the similarly oriented visual arts and the dance in the unfolding of the spiritual drama. Stage design thus lost its onus as a minor decorative art, and young artists eagerly accepted the chance to participate in theatrical dance ventures.

Joint endeavors did not, however, add anything essential to the more covert interactions between the two media. Rather, they put the different modernist visual tendencies onstage and tested them in public. Nonetheless, the mutual involvement of the two media produced an opportunity for grappling afresh with their shared essence— namely, the expressive articulation of space. This forced the ballet to reconsider its old and established principles in the light of the contemporary aesthetic. The artists, in turn, were newly reminded of the ancient, originative role of the theater in their medium, a role that assumed new and challenging dimensions as the nonrepresentational tendencies of modernism deepened.

Diaghilev's Ballets Russes. At their best, the finely crafted productions of Serge Diaghilev achieved a harmonious marriage between highly disciplined choreography, carefully selected music, and scenarios sensitively integrated by means of appropriately shaped, colored, and spaced decors and costumes. Diaghilev's skill thus resided above all in his capacity to bring about the subjugation of the individual priorities of the collaborative media to the demands of the whole.

Especially at the outset, Diaghilev received considerable assistance along these lines from painter-collaborators such as Alexandre Benois and Léon Bakst. These well-informed, sophisticated artists also had a hand in the preparation of the plots and the development of the choreography. In fact, the theater became the means for realizing their aesthetic vision, and their sets and costumes were essential, dynamic vehicles in the choreographic process. It has frequently been said that subsequently renowned artists like Pablo Picasso tended to dominate Diaghilev's productions at the expense of the dance. This is accurate only with respect to publicity, both planned and accidental, which Diaghilev eagerly sought. Picasso, like many of the other later artist-collaborators—Mikhail Larionov, Natalia Goncharova, Giacomo Balla, Henri Matisse, Naum Gabo, Antoine Pevsner, Giorgio de Chirico, Pavel Tchelitchev—aimed more or less successfully at an artistic immersion in the total production that was comparable to that of Bakst and Benois. As a consequence, adequate adaptations not only of cubism but also of futurism, rayonism, constructivism, metaphysical art, and surrealism were brought to life on the stage in conjunction with the choreography, even if at times the physical presence and traditional skills of the dancers were greatly curtailed or even obliterated.

Other experiments. Two other early twentieth-century approaches to collaborative staging represent extreme positions that have been highly suggestive to younger practitioners. Both evolved, at least partially, in response as well as in opposition to Diaghilev's example. These are the cerebral dance productions of the artist Oskar Schlemmer, which matured mostly in conjunction with his teaching at the Bauhaus, and the much more improvisatory performances sponsored by the futurists and Dadaists from about 1914 to 1924.

ARTISTS AND DANCE. Oskar Schlemmer's *The Triadic Ballet: Figurines in Space* (1924), in gouache with photographs. The figure in the foreground represents the Abstract, a role Schlemmer performed in his 1922 experimental dance work; to the left is the Gold Sphere figurine; and in the upper right corner is the Wire Figure. (Museum of Modern Art, New York; Gift of Lily Auchincloss [no. 60]; photograph used by permission of the Oskar Schlemmer Theater Estate, Badenweiler, Germany)

Hindsight reveals that the most significant aspect of Schlemmer's contribution is the ideational and practical identity of his dance productions and his studio pieces. He was as much the total master of his stagings as of his paintings and sculpture. In addition to producing his ballets, he designed the decors, originated the choreography and its connotations, selected the music, and danced, although he had no professional training. Schlemmer, the visual artist, thus literally shaped the physical ambient as the space of his work. He became a component of it by means of the spatiotemporal relationships his movements established. The renowned *Triadic Ballet* (1922) represents Schlemmer's first and best-documented fulfillment of his theatrical aims. Schlemmer was nourished by many of the same sources that affected the artists discussed above, to which Heinrich Kleist's metaphysical speculations about marionettes belong. [*See* Bauhaus, Dance and the.]

If there was any method in futurist and Dadaist performances, it was the deliberate rejection of all hallowed theatrical and artistic traditions. The assaults on rigid notions about the various artistic disciplines extended also to those about the audience itself. These attitudes had fruitful consequences in the 1950s and 1960s in equally defiant approaches to performance. They led to additional hybrid constellations that reconsidered and enlarged the potential of the diverse arts and of their concerted action.

The futurists and Dadaists shared their aim of spiritual reorientation with most other early twentieth-century creative movements, but they were more vocal and impatient than the rest. The futurists held raucous *serate* (evening performances) in large theaters to make their ideals pertaining to the different arts known to the audience—whom they deliberately incited to vehement reactions. Under the threat of World War I, and in the course of the war, Filippo Marinetti increasingly theatricalized his movement and promulgated novel performance ideals. These incorporated his own literary inventions—"free-word-poetry" and "wireless imagination"—and elements from the work of his associates, such as Luigi Russolo's manifesto "Art of Noises" and Valentine de Saint-Point's antisensuous, geometric dances. The futurist painters' objective of involving the spectator in the work of art and their dynamic notions of simultaneity and randomness became crucial ingredients as well.

Giacomo Balla was an especially adept participant in these futurist performances, such as *Piedigrotta* (1914), of which no visual records are known to have survived. A sense of what these performances were like is obtainable from a few still photographs and scene synopses of the futurist film *La Vita Futurista* (1916), in which Balla also collaborated significantly. The futurists drew considerably upon vaudeville, Loie Fuller, and early films; in turn, they set many precedents for the Dadaists, Schlemmer, Nikolai Foregger's "machine dances," and cinematic efforts—par-

ARTISTS AND DANCE. A constructivist design by Alexandra Exter. (Photograph from a private collection.)

ticularly Fernand Léger and Gerald Murphy's *Ballet Mécanique* (1923/24).

The participants in the Dadaist *serate* devised even more chaotic ways of challenging the spiritual status quo. These interdisciplinary free-for-alls, particularly those of the Zurich phase of Dada, included performances by Laban's pupils, such as Mary Wigman and Sophie Taeuber, whose choreography accorded with the Dadaists' wish to recapture preverbal purity and "primitive," or childlike, directness. No detailed visual accounts of these Dada performances exist; thus, it seems appropriate to regard the ballet *Relâche* (1924), produced by Rolf de Maré's Ballets Suédois, as a good, if somewhat tardy and domesticated, version of Dadaist attitudes and achievements. The painter Francis Picabia, who had a long-standing interest in the dance, was responsible for the script and decor. He was ably assisted and abetted by the artist Marcel Duchamp, the composer Erik Satie, and the young filmmaker René Clair, who had gotten his start with Loie Fuller and the choreographer Jean Börlin.

There was little dance in the academic sense in *Relâche;* but Clair's subtle cinematic enframement and his filmed intermezzo *Entr'acte,* together with Picabia's extraordinary backdrop of blinking headlights, announced and carried the pulsating, if unpredictable, rhythm of *Relâche,* participating more or less blatantly in its choreography. (*Relâche,* which means "no performance" in French, turned out to be literally true for de Maré, who disbanded his company shortly thereafter.) For Picabia and his cohorts it signified the perennial affirmation of creative freedom from stultifying formulas. In its humorous, irreverent way, *Relâche* expressed the vision not only of Dada, but of modernism in all the arts. [*See* Relâche.]

[*For further information, see* Prints and Drawings; Scenic Design. *See also entries on the principal figures mentioned herein.*]

BIBLIOGRAPHY

Amberg, George. *Art in Modern Ballet*. New York, 1946.

Cahusac, Louis de. *La danse ancienne et moderne, ou Traité historique sur la danse*. La Haye, 1754.

Cooper, Douglas. *Picasso Theatre*. New York, 1968.

Elsen, Albert E. *Rodin*. New York, 1963.

Farese-Sperkin, Christine. *Der Tanz als motiv in der bildenden Kunst des 20. Jahrhunderts*. The Hague, 1969.

Garafola, Lynn. *Diaghilev's Ballets Russes*. New York, 1989.

Harris, Margaret Haile. *Loïe Fuller: Magician of Light*. Richmond, Va., 1979. Exhibition catalog.

Hengst, Franzis. "Die Befreiung vom Dekorativen: Über des Zusammenwirken von Tanz und bildender Kunst im 20. Jahrhundert." *Ballet-Journal/Das Tanzarchiv* 42 (December 1994): 50–57.

Kandinsky, Wassily. "On Stage Composition" and "The Yellow Sound: A Stage Composition." In *The Blaue Reiter Almanac* (1912), edited by Wassily Kandinsky and Franz Marc. New York, 1974.

Kermode, Frank. *The Romantic Image*. New York, 1957.

Kirstein, Lincoln. *Movement and Metaphor: Four Centuries of Ballet*. New York, 1970.

Die Maler und das Theater im 20. Jahrhunderts. Frankfurt, 1986. Exhibition catalog, Schirn Kunsthalle.

Martin, Marianne W. *Futurist Art and Theory, 1909–1915*. Oxford, 1968.

Martin, Marianne W. "Modern Art and Dance: An Introduction." In *Art and Dance: Images of the Modern Dialogue*, edited by Marianne W. Martin. Boston, 1982.

McQuillan, Melissa A. "Painters and the Ballet, 1917–1926." Ph.D.diss., New York University, 1979.

Piet Mondrian Centennial Exhibition. New York, 1972. Exhibition catalog, Guggenheim Museum.

Pritchard, Jane. "André Derain in Paris." *The Dancing Times* (February 1995): 479–487.

Rischbieter, Henning. *Art and the Stage in the Twentieth Century*. Translated by Michael Bullock. Greenwich, Conn., 1968.

Vaughan, David. *Diaghilev/Cunningham*. Hempstead, N.Y., 1974. Exhibition catalog, Emily Lowe Gallery, Hofstra University.

MARIANNE W. MARTIN

Artists and Dance, 1930–1945

For both European and American artists, the artistic climate of the 1930s was profoundly influenced by economic and political developments: the financial collapse of 1929 and the start of World War II. With many American artists returning home from Europe and some European artists fleeing to the United States, the 1930s became, as art critic Harold Rosenberg (1972) describes them, "an interval in which history openly revealed its power to tamper with art." Pervasive then in the United States was the desire for an art that felt intrinsically American—in form, content, and spirit. Whether this was evinced through the socially conscious arts projects of the New Deal or the pioneering individualism of, for example, photographer Alfred Stieglitz and the artists associated with his gallery, called

An American Place (founded 1929), American artists were clearly not depending solely on Europe for their inspiration. At the same time, however, surrealism, an art movement and philosophy European in gestation, had emerged as a formidable presence; a major show, *Fantastic Art, Dada, and Surrealism*, was mounted in 1936 by the new Museum of Modern Art in New York City.

Ballet. The Russian emigré choreographer Léonide Massine was collaborating with many artists in the surrealism movement, and these projects often exemplified the nonhierarchical relationship among media called for by Antonin Artaud in *The Theater and Its Double* (1938, English translation 1958). The Spanish painter Joan Miró designed sets and costumes for Massine's ballet *Jeux d'Enfants* (1932), about a child who wakes up one night to find all her toys have come to life. Given the marvelous childlike quality in Miró's work, the tender balance he achieves between reality and abstraction, and his stated desire to "seek the noise hidden in silence, the movement in immobility, life in the inanimate, the infinite in the finite, forms in space" (Penrose, 1969), Miró's vision seems especially suitable for the theater. In 1925 Miró had collaborated with Max Ernst on Serge Diaghilev's production of *Romeo and Juliet;* from 1925 to 1927 he executed many paintings based on a circus theme. His set for *Jeux d'Enfants* consisted primarily of a large white circle and a tall black triangle topped with a much smaller circle. This triangle bent toward the large circle and, according to Massine (1968), resembled a dunce cap. Massine also allowed Miró's design to initiate some of the movement. As art critic Clement Greenberg (1948) pointed out, Miró was "a great constructor in color as well as a great decorator"; his work for the stage may have actually accelerated this development in his painting. Furthermore, the mixed-media and at times disjunctive quality of collaborative theater, fused with the surrealist notion of automatism, may also have inspired, in part, his collages and objects of the mid-1930s, such as *Rope and People* (1935), an oil on cardboard with a coil of rope, and *Objet Poétique* (1936), made from wood, a man's hat, and a stuffed parrot.

Massine, who had previously worked for Diaghilev's Ballets Russes with French painter Henri Matisse on *Le Chant du Rossignol* (1920), collaborated with him again in 1939 on *Rouge et Noir* (also known as *L'Étrange Farandole*). By this time Matisse had already executed a considerable number of paintings that focused on dance. *Rouge et Noir* reflects the purity and simplicity of Matisse's style during the 1930s as well as his paper-cutout technique. In response to Massine's idea for a "vast mural in motion," Matisse chose five colors—white, black, blue, yellow, and red—orchestrating them in costume and configuration as inspired by his mural *La Danse I* (1936). As the dancers moved, the shifting patterns created an animated collage of color and form.

ARTISTS AND DANCE. The full cast of Léonide Massine's *Jeux d'Enfants* (1932), a ballet about toys come to life, performing in front of the abstract set designed by Joan Miró. (Photograph from the Dance Collection, New York Public Library for the Performing Arts.)

In the United States, Massine worked with Salvador Dali on the ballets *Bacchanale* (1939), *Labyrinth* (1941), and *Mad Tristan* (1944). Their work always incited controversy, and Dali's contribution—which often included the book as well as the set and costumes—was criticized for upstaging Massine's. The bizarre surreal themes and images permeating Dali's paintings appeared in these theater pieces. In *Bacchanale*, an enormous swan presides, protected by a golden fish; symbolizing death is a huge black umbrella marked with a luminous skull. In *Labyrinth*, Dali and Massine composed an illusionist scene suggesting a nude girl guarded by white doves. All these works combined the sexual, hallucinatory, and violent with paranoia, madness, and terror.

In 1942 the Russian emigré painter Marc Chagall designed Massine's *Aleko*. Chagall's lyricism, fluid use of color, and often whimsical imagery easily evoked the folkloric qualities of Aleksandr Pushkin's poem "The Gypsies," on which the ballet was based. Many of Chagall's designs recalled his circus works of the 1930s, for example, *The Acrobat* (1930) and *The Circus Horseman* (1931). *Aleko's* decor, as exemplified in scene 4, "A Fantasy of Saint Pe-

tersburg," seemed infused with the disjunctive fairy-tale magic for which his work is noted. Massine and Chagall collaborated closely on the movement and color patterning.

Of Chagall's designs for Adolph Bolm's restaging of *The Firebird* for Ballet Theatre in 1945, the dance critic Edwin Denby (1968) wrote that the decor was "heartwarming and scintillating. . . . You can fly in the sky, you can peer into a magic wood and see people living in a dragon. One sits before it in childlike enchantment."

Modern Dance. By 1935 the "heroic age" of American modern dance had begun. Leading the way was Martha Graham, who advised American dancers (Armitage, 1978) to "know your country. When its vitality, its freshness, its exuberance, its overabundance of youth and vigor, its contrasts of plenitude and barrenness are made manifest in movement on the stage, we begin to see the American dance." Graham felt that movement was "the product not of invention but of discovery" and that "balance" involved "your relationship to the space around you." Thus, Graham's incorporation of Alexander Calder's mobiles in two of her early pieces, *Panorama* (1935) and *Horizons* (1936), seems a natural inclination. For *Panorama*, Calder contributed overhead disks; lines attached these disks to the dancers' wrists, so that their gestures animated the mobile. For *Horizons*, Calder's set of whirling circles and spirals alternated with three sequences of dancing. Calder's circus figures (1926–1932) also embodied notions of spectacle and movement, and his *Dancer and Spheres* (1936) was probably inspired by his experiences with Graham.

In 1935 Graham also worked with the Japanese-American sculptor Isamu Noguchi on *Frontier,* the first of many stage collaborations between the two. Noguchi's composition for *Frontier* extended the stage space through the use of rope to suggest the "vastness of the frontier" (Noguchi, 1968). He would again attempt "through the elimination of all nonessentials, to arrive at an essence of the stark pioneer spirit" for Graham's *Appalachian Spring* (1944). The angular, abrupt immediacy of the choreography, combined with the sparingly designed farmhouse set, led Denby (1968) to write that the work "is a credible and astonishing evocation of that real time and place."

In a different realm altogether were the "boxes" of the

artist and dance lover Joseph Cornell, who seemed to idolize various ballerinas, particularly those of the Romantic era. Along this line, his constructions—poetic assemblages of often unrelated objects, bits of paraphernalia, fragments of the past—bore such titles as *Taglioni's Jewel Casket* (1940), *Homage to the Romantic Ballet* (1941), and *A Pantry Ballet (for Jacques Offenbach)* (1942).

During the 1940s, the French artist Marcel Duchamp was living in New York City and participating with many of the surrealists on projects in which movement was often a central concern. Duchamp's interest in motion (which also extended to film) was apparent from the time of such early paintings as his *Portrait of Chess Players* and *Sad Young Man in a Train* (both 1911); the latter, especially, portrays many phases of movement simultaneously and is often considered a prototype for his famous painting of the 1913 Armory Show in New York City, *Nude Descending a Staircase* (1912). About *Nude Descending a Staircase,* Duchamp stated: "My aim was static representation of motion" (Rubin, 1969).

For artists, the end of World War II seemed to signal a re-

ARTISTS AND DANCE. Salvador Dali's design for the scenery of *Bacchanale* (1939), choreographed by Léonide Massine for the Ballet Russe de Monte Carlo. (Photograph from the Dance Collection, New York Public Library for the Performing Arts.)

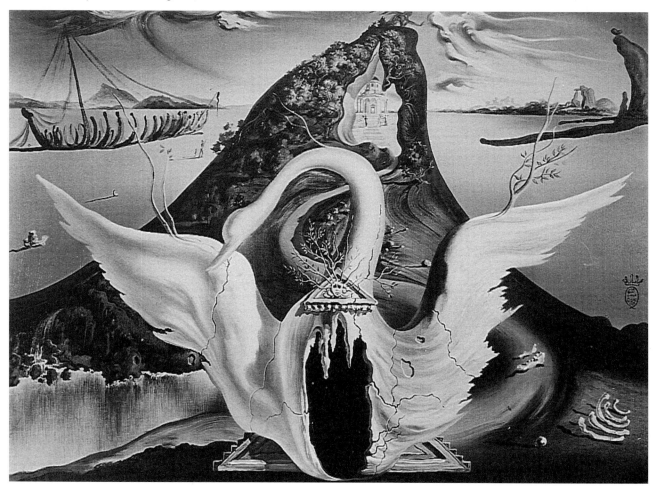

ARTISTS AND DANCE. *Portrait of Nijinsky* (1942), Franz Kline's depiction of Vaslav Nijinsky in one of his most famous roles, the title character in Michel Fokine's ballet *Petrouchka*. (This oil portrait was painted from a photograph taken by the London studio of Elliott & Fry in 1911. Metropolitan Museum of Art, New York; Gift of Dr. Theodore J. Edlich, Jr., 1986 [no. 1986.406.2]; photograph used by permission.)

newed concern with process, as elucidated in the work of the postwar abstract expressionists and other artists—including many who were teaching and studying at Black Mountain College in North Carolina. This institution had been formed in 1933 by a group of educators and students rebelling against the academic, political, and social conventions of "establishment education," with the intent that "the students share in the power and responsibility for running the community," and that "'living' and 'learning' should be intertwined" (Duberman, 1972). The German-American artist and designer Josef Albers and his wife, Anni, who had been teaching at the Bauhaus (1920–1923) in Berlin, were invited; Black Mountain shared the Bauhaus desire to foster a kind of multimedia energy and collective spirit while encouraging each student's individualism. Josef Albers's approach to teaching helped to fuel Black Mountain's reputation as "an advanced place"; in turn, more artists wished to visit the college, including, in the spring of 1948, American composer John Cage and his companion, the American choreographer and modern dancer Merce Cunningham. When Cage and Cunningham were asked back for the summer, they returned

with their friends the Dutch artists Willem and Elaine de Kooning and the American sculptor Richard Lippold.

This confluence of people and events at Black Mountain, from its inception until its closing in 1956, propelled the art–dance connection into previously unimagined territory, further removing this fruitful relationship from the confines of traditional theater.

BIBLIOGRAPHY

Anderson, Jack. *The One and Only: The Ballet Russe de Monte Carlo.* New York, 1981.
Armitage, Merle, ed. *Martha Graham* (1937). New York, 1978.
Denby, Edwin. *Looking at the Dance* (1949). New York, 1968.
Duberman, Martin. *Black Mountain.* New York, 1972.
Greenberg, Clement. *Joan Miró.* New York, 1948.
Massine, Léonide. *My Life in Ballet.* New York, 1968.
Noguchi, Isami. *A Sculptor's World.* New York, 1968.
Penrose, Roland. *Miró.* New York, 1969.
Rosenberg, Harold. *De-definition of Art.* London, 1972.
Rubin, William, ed. *Dada and Surrealist Art.* London, 1969.
Sorley Walker, Kathrine. *De Basil's Ballets Russes.* New York, 1983.
Stodelle, Ernestine. *Deep Song: The Dance Story of Martha Graham.* New York, 1984.

MELISSA HARRIS

Artists and Dance since 1945

The involvement of artists with dance since 1945 has taken several forms. On the one hand, movement, gesture, time, and space (features of dance) have been connotatively referred to in paintings. On the other hand, actual movement, gesture, and time have become expressive and structural features of the art object—in abstract painting and in the evolution of the activities collectively called performance art.

Post–World War II abstract expressionists, according to the theory of one of their most influential critics, Harold Rosenberg, were best described as action painters. To them "the canvas began to appear . . . as an arena in which to act. . . . What was to go on the canvas was not a picture but an event" (Rosenberg, 1959). Such terms as *action, gesture, rhythm, arabesque, environment,* and *arena,* used by critics to describe the new painting and, in some cases, by painters to title their work (as in Jackson Pollock's *Autumn Rhythm,* 1950), suggest that movement (process and action) and space were defining characteristics of abstract expressionism and that appreciation of this new art form demanded the relinquishment of the boundaries between the sister arts. "Since the painter has become an actor," Rosenberg maintains, "the spectator has to think in a vocabulary of actions" (Rosenberg, 1959).

According to the theory of action painting, the signifying marks of the painting on canvas were the records of action: the residue of paint from the artist's gesture, the tracks of dripping paint, or the stain of paint into the structure of the painting. Greatly oversized canvases were a virtual space for the painter's activity. Several painters associated with abstract expressionism were interested or involved in dance, though it is questionable whether the involvement was a direct source for their painting. Franz Kline titled two paintings after Vaslav Nijinsky: *Portrait of Nijinsky* (1942) and *Nijinsky* (1950). Both Kline and Willem de Kooning collaborated with dancers, producing large, abstract backdrops for productions. In 1946 de Kooning designed the backdrop for a dance recital entitled *Labyrinth* by Maria Marchowsky and her company in New York City. Kline, in 1960, painted a backdrop entitled *Queen of Hearts* for a performance of Merle Marsicano's dance company, also in New York. Pollock's interests were not with modern dance or ballet but in ritual: he had been particularly impressed by Navaho sand painters. Like other artists of the New York school, Pollock maintained a strong interest in a variety of primitive arts.

In the late 1950s and early 1960s, two movements—happenings and fluxus—brought many visual artists from static art forms to time-based forms or events more directly related to dance. Happenings made the implied or reflected action of abstract expressionism literal. The structure of happenings did not resemble the modern dance tradition, which was being challenged and transformed during this period. Artists and their friends performed in happenings, which took place in lofts, galleries, and storefronts. Typically, the audience for these events was involved in the process of the performance.

Allan Kaprow, founder of happenings, divided these events into several categories: the pocket drama, or nightclub, in which performers, often with the audience, carry out certain acts, such as cooking, making love, or destroying furniture; the extravaganza, a circuslike presentation on a stage, involving musicians, painters, and poets; events, in which an audience seated in a theater watches a performer in a solitary action or single occurrence; a guided tour, or journey, for a selected group of people in which ordinary things are discovered; and idea art, in which an action or thought is designated as art in the Duchampian sense: art is simply whatever is mentally designated as art, including any commonly executed act, such as shopping in the supermarket.

After Kaprow's *18 Happenings in 6 Parts* was shown at the Reuben Gallery in New York City in 1959, many other artists' events followed in quick succession. The development of pop art was intimately connected with these events. Jim Dine and Claes Oldenburg used and transformed ordinary objects in performance, as in pieces performed at the Judson Memorial Church in 1960: Dine's *Smiling Workman* and Oldenburg's *Snapshots from the City*. Simultaneously, they showed "new art" based on popular sources at the Judson Gallery. Oldenburg transformed common objects into colored plaster, soft sculpture, and eventually colossal monuments.

In 1961, the term *fluxus* was coined to describe an on-going series of events or actions ultimately more international in scope than happenings. Fluxus performers included American, European, and Japanese artists, such as Nam June Paik, George Maciunas, Robert Filiou, and Wolf Vostell. As practiced by the German artist Joseph Beuys, a fluxus-inspired action took place in an environment (stage, gallery) planned by the artist; it included an assemblage of objects and materials, usually of a banal character; and it involved sound, duration, and the artist's participation as performer. (A typical Beuys piece is *The Chief*, performed simultaneously in December 1964 by Beuys in Berlin and by the sculptor Robert Morris in New York City.) Fluxus activity can be seen as an expansion of the definition of sculpture to include a fluctuating phenomenon whose form and actions are concretizations of thought and activities of the spirit.

Yves Klein (active in France, 1958–1962) thought of art forms as the "spiritual marks of captured moments." Klein "events" include the artist's photographed jump off a building (1960) and the "live painting" exhibition (*Anthropometries of the Blue Period*, 1960). In the latter, the audience was invited to a gallery to see naked models, used as "living brushes," press their paint-smeared bodies against prepared canvases. These events involved movement and action as more adequate expressions of such mystical notions as "the void" and color as the "real dweller of space."

Starting in the late 1940s, the synergy of movement, sound, and visual design that constitutes mixed-media theater was distinctively carried forward in the work of

ARTISTS AND DANCE. *Nude Couple Dancing with Young Girl Holding a Mask* (1955), an intaglio etching by Pablo Picasso. (Metropolitan Museum of Art, New York; Gift of Reiss-Cohen, Inc., 1983 [no. 1983.1212.1]; photograph used by permission.)

Alwin Nikolais. He single-handedly provided not only music and choreography, but also costumes, props, and, notably, lighting (including film projections) in a productive career that ended only with his death in 1993. "Nik," as he was fondly known, employed the forms, patterns, and colors created by the deployment of dancers' illuminated bodies in the service of visionary abstractions that, in common with happenings, broke definitively with the Freudian-oriented origins of modern dance.

From the early 1950s onward, Robert Rauschenberg was closely involved with musicians and dancers. He had performed with John Cage and Merce Cunningham at Black Mountain College in North Carolina in 1952. Two years later, in New York City, Rauschenberg resumed his association with Cunningham, creating sets and costumes for the company and collaborating with Paul Taylor. The "combine" paintings of the 1950s and 1960s (such as *Bed*, 1955; *Winter Pool*, 1959; *Third Time Painting*, 1961), in which found objects (a bed, a ladder, a clock) are layered with painted canvas and collage elements, are, arguably, experiences of operational, or "real," time. They suggest the chance quality, disjunction, and layered consciousness of everyday experience. These paintings parallel similar structures in Cunningham's dances. Rauschenberg's paintings appear as the chance accumulations of the studio and thus come closer to tangible experience than does the fixed, framed, static, spatial experience of the classical Renaissance tradition.

Rauschenberg moved easily from a painted analogue of experience (which he has not abandoned) to the making of events—specifically, the creation of choreography for himself and other performers. In *Pelican* (1963), which involved him, Alex Hay, and dancer Carolyn Brown as performers, the movements of the male performers, conditioned by parachutes and roller skates, contrasted with the female dancer's movement in pointe shoes. The exigencies of the particular performance space, the unconventional employment of objects (a carry-over from his paintings), and the aspect of spectacle characterize Rauschenberg's performance pieces. [*See the entry on Rauschenberg.*]

The interest in real versus virtual space and time, which occupied Rauschenberg during the 1950s and 1960s, engrossed other artists, particularly the minimalist sculptors. By the mid-1960s, these artists were pursuing a tendency designated by the influential critic Michael Fried as theatrical. Fried wrote in 1967 that "literalist (minimalist) sensibility is theatrical because, to begin with, it is concerned with the actual circumstances in which the beholder encounters literalist work."

This tendency is clear in the career of Robert Morris (see above), who explored similar ideas in both sculpture and performance. In 1961, as part of a series of performances at the Living Theater in New York City, Morris presented a column eight feet high and two feet deep, made of plywood painted gray, that stood upright for several minutes and then fell. This column looked like the subsequent minimalist sculpture Morris showed in galleries (such as *Untitled, 1965*). The meaning or expressiveness of this piece, as in its performance, is in the viewer's experience in moving around two identical forms (large I beams, similar to the plywood column) placed in different positions. As Morris wrote in 1971,

> The better new work takes relationships out of the work and makes them a function of space, light, and the viewer's field of vision. . . . One is more aware than before that [the spectator] himself is establishing relationships as he apprehends the object from various positions and varying conditions of light and spatial context.

By 1963, Morris was among the group of nondancers who became active as performers and choreographers with the Judson Dance Theater in New York City.

Relationships between performance works (Morris's and others) continued through the decade. For instance, connections between *Check*, a performance choreographed for forty performers moving singly or in groups through a space three hundred feet long at the Moderna Museet in Stockholm, and the film related to it, *Wisconsin* (1970), involve formal and random movements as metaphors for order and decay. The same issues underlie Morris's scatter pieces, such as *Untitled, 1968*, a work of two hundred pieces of felt, copper, zinc, nickel, aluminum, corten steel, and stainless steel arranged or positioned by computer. Morris's *Continuous Process Altered Daily* (1969), an arrangement of earth and metal in the warehouse of the New York art dealer Leo Castelli, which was changed by the artist every day, was a source for choreographer Yvonne Rainer's *Continuous Project—Altered Daily*, an ongoing performance (1969–1970) in which the basic processes of making a dance (teaching, rehearsing, marking, and working out material) were included among the elements of the work's actual performances.

Political activism in the 1960s resulted in the emergence of an ideology among artists that rejected the art-world establishment of galleries, museums, and collectors. During the so-called poststudio movement, which lasted until 1977, time-based forms were positioned (in opposition to tendencies in painting and sculpture) toward extreme reductivism in content and forms (minimalism). Greater numbers of visual artists moved into modes of action (or actions) that conveyed personal and political content (radical theater groups of the 1960s had set an important example). The directions pursued included feminist performance (Mary Beth Edelson, Ulrike Rosenbach), film (Yvonne Rainer), and ritual-based installations (Vito Acconci, Robert Morris).

ARTISTS AND DANCE. Merce Cunningham (center) and company in *Walkaround Time* (1968). This photograph was taken during a rehearsal in Buffalo, New York, before its premiere. Jasper Johns designed the set as a large-scale replica of Marcel Duchamp's sculpture *The Large Glass*. (Photograph © 1968 by James Klosty; used by permission.)

In the world of the proscenium theater *per se*, other manifestations of the continuing dialogue between dance and the visual arts may be cited. In 1946, Lincoln Kirstein and George Balanchine founded Ballet Society. The neo-Diaghilevian venture was to foster the creation of a new and original balletic repertory, featuring commissioned scores and decors by practicing artists. In its brief, unstable existence, the society produced three of Balanchine's most important works: *The Four Temperaments* (1946, with music by Paul Hindemith and scenery by Kurt Seligmann), the American premiere of *Symphony in C* (1948; music by Georges Bizet), and *Orpheus* (1948), a three-way collaboration among Balanchine, Igor Stravinsky, and Isamu Noguchi (Martha Graham's designer). Noguchi's improvisations on archaic Greek motifs removed the action from an anchor in classical antiquity, providing a sense of primeval timelessness that accorded well with the reductive aesthetic of Balanchine and Stravinsky. The production led directly to the establishment of the New York City Ballet.

The visual arts have often inspired choreographers. For Glen Tetley, Rembrandt's *Anatomy Lesson* provided a point of departure for ruminations on modern man on Judgment Day, in his ballet of the same name (1964). Anna Sokolow created pithy dance epigrams from images of the Belgian surrealist painter René Magritte—lovers' heads encased in sacks, a derby hat, an apple (*Magritte, Magritte,* 1970). Martha Clarke brought the world of the painting alive in her bawdy *Garden of Earthly Delights* (1984), inspired by Hieronymus Bosch. The New York City Ballet's American Music Festival of 1988 prompted whimsical or witty musings on the work of Edward Hopper, Henri Rousseau, Fernand Léger, Pablo Picasso, and others in *Into the Hopper* (choreographer, Bart Cook) and Jonathan Barofsky in *Archetypes* (choreographer, Robert Weiss).

ELISABETH SUSSMAN

Collaboration

Since the early 1950s, painters, sculptors, film and video artists, composers, choreographers, and writers have explored the infinite possibilities suggested by collaboration. Many of them at some point participated in happenings, Fluxus projects, Sonic Arts Union (a composers collective), Once Group (a music-theater collective), Judson

Dance Theater, and Grand Union (a choreographers collective).

For more than thirty years, modern dancer and choreographer Merce Cunningham and composer John Cage demonstrated their belief in the coexistence of art, dance, and music for performance as opposed to an interaction in which one medium underscores or illustrates the other. They urged a way of working in which artists and, ultimately, what they create act interdependently. Cunningham's company has in addition had several artistic advisers, beginning with Robert Rauschenberg, who was followed by Jasper Johns. The British painter Mark Lancaster first designed for Cunningham's company in 1974 and served as artistic adviser from 1980 to 1984. In late 1984, William Anastasi and Dove Bradshaw became its artistic advisers; these two artists were interested in introducing certain ideas and processes into their stage work that were already operating in their solo projects. They found especially challenging the ongoing opportunity to bring ideas not initially conceived in terms of theater into a different context and scale.

Collage has been an important aspect of Bradshaw's work, and her ability to weave and build pattern and texture is equally apparent in her costuming of the dance *Phrases* (1984, to music by David Tudor) and her lighting of *Native Green* (1985; to music by John King). In *Phrases,* working mostly with a palette of primary colors, she layered various articles of clothing (shirts, leg warmers, sweaters), creating costumes that seem to be relentlessly reinventing themselves; with Anastasi's composition for this piece (two lines that imply a right angle but do not visibly meet), the effect is a kind of kinetic painting, as by Piet Mondrian. Bradshaw's subtle lighting for *Native Green* also seems intuitively to complement Anastasi's elemental, yet somehow otherworldly, coloring and marking of both set and costumes: the backdrop looks almost tea stained, like an antique map, and the costumes are luminously white. As with *Phrases,* Anastasi also uses, in part, an angular composition in *Native Green.* The horizontal line of the suggested angle parallels the stage and, from the audience, it is difficult to discern whether the "line" is part of the backdrop or the stage floor; as the dance ends, it turns out to be of substance and quite malleable; the dancers twist it into a kind of horseshoe, transforming the shape of the performance space. Anastasi's designs for these two dances indicate a venturing beyond the confines of "wall" and "floor," which he has practiced in his solo work as well, particularly in his wall-removal pieces of the 1960s.

Cunningham has worked with Elliot Caplan on film and video dances. Charles Atlas, who preceded Caplan as filmmaker-in-residence, also collaborated with Karole Armitage and Douglas Dunn (both former Cunningham dancers) as well as with British choreographer Michael

Clark (*Hail the New Puritan,* 1986, a film; and *No Fire Escape in Hell,* 1986, for the stage). Of collaboration, Atlas has said in interview, "Even if all the elements going into it are independently 'good,' the piece still may not work. Each element may be too selfish an object with too little sensitivity to everything else in the piece. However, when everything does work, it becomes a kind of model for an ideal society, because it shows that people can work together . . . with someone else's idea."

Armitage and Atlas created many video projects, such as *Parafango* (1983); Atlas also designed the sets, costumes, and lighting for several stage pieces, including *Drastic Classicism* (1981), *Slaughter on MacDougal Street* (1982), and *The Last Gone Dance* (1983). Armitage also worked with David Salle, who incorporated her into his paintings. Atlas designed costumes for many of Douglas Dunn's dances, including *Coquina* (1978) and *Hitch* (1981). He also teamed with Dunn and poets Reed Bye and Anne Waldman on the videodance *Secret of the Waterfall* (1982). This piece was reworked for a live performance in 1983 with additional designs by the painter Mimi Gross. Gross collaborated with Dunn on many dances, including *Skid* (1981), *Elbow Room* (1984), and the 1984 version of Dunn's joyous *Pulcinella.*

Other artists with whom Dunn created works include Jeffrey Schiff on the site-specific dance *Second Mesa* (1983) for the Institute of Contemporary Art in Boston. The collaborators were interested in kinetically, sonically, and visually articulating the museum's two floors, both of which are architecturally defined by two nonsymmetrical rooms, so that the material Dunn created responded directly to the situations that presented themselves. Dunn worked with David Hannah on *3rd Rotation* (1985); costumed in Hannah's funky black-and-white, buoyantly dotted outfits, trios of dancers seemed to explode within their created spheres of ever-changing centers. In 1986 David Ireland joined forces with Dunn to make *Dances for Men, Women, and Moving Door.*

Power Boothe is another artist who consistently worked with choreographers, especially Charles Moulton (*Step Wise Motion,* 1982, and *Variety Show,* 1984) and David Gordon (*Trying Times,* 1982, *Framework,* 1984, and *My Folks,* 1984/85). For Boothe, while paintings are complete in themselves, collaborations were an opportunity to take his sensibilities into another realm to make things that were meaningful only if they made sense with regard to the whole project. The urgency was to get the joint work right. Boothe's sets and films interact with the dancers and often appear as choreographed as the dance itself. In *Trying Times* he wanted the piece he built to move around the way the dancers moved around. For that work, Boothe constructed, among other visual devices, a frame that Gordon used again in *Framework,* further exploring its possibilities for describing the world in which we move around. Whether it operated functionally and/or symbolically, or purely as a compositional element, the role of this frame was defined in terms of the movement; at the same time, the movement suggested various meanings, depending on the manipulation of the frame. Before entering into the collaboration, Gordon had assumed that he would be giving up something; instead he found that his own vision of what he was doing was expanded.

Like Gordon, Trisha Brown also believes that there is a way of collaborating in which artists can come together and still maintain their independence. Brown has worked with artists such as Nancy Graves (*Lateral Pass*, 1985), Fujiko Nakaya (*Opal Loop*, 1980), Rauschenberg (*Glacial De-*

coy, 1979, and *Set and Reset*, 1983), and Donald Judd. In *Son of Gone Fishin'* (1981) Judd's design of green and blue backdrops revealed itself not just in space but in time. The colors emerge subtly and then gently place each other in shadow, sculpting an ever-changing spectrum of tones and constantly altering the viewer's sense of the stage space.

Choreographer Paul Taylor has also collaborated substantially with painters throughout his career, among them Alex Katz and Ellsworth Kelly. The dance theaters of Pina Bausch and Alwin Nikolais should also be noted. Painter David Hockney often designed for the stage as well.

Certain performance projects, not necessarily rooted in dance yet intricately choreographed, also deserve attention: the Bread and Puppet Theater, the individual and collaborative work of Ping Chong and Meredith Monk, and Richard Foreman's and Robert Wilson's theaters are

ARTISTS AND DANCE. A scene from a revival of Robert Wilson's *Einstein on the Beach* at the Brooklyn Academy of Music. This landmark multimedia work integrated Wilson's sets and stage direction with choreography by Lucinda Childs and music by Philip Glass. (Photograph © 1984 by Johan Elbers; used by permission.)

all situations seemingly conceived and staged in terms of both abstract and text-related movement. In the 1984 revival of Wilson's *Einstein on the Beach,* with choreography by Lucinda Childs (who has worked with Sol LeWitt and the architect Frank Gehry, among others), it was impossible to isolate movement from the entirety of the piece. Childs's choreography involved fast-paced, quirky movement performed over and over, contrasted with long, evolving dances; the score by Philip Glass proceeds similarly—rapid, unrelenting sequences recur, while other themes seem to build in stages. Orchestrated to suit the metamorphic and kinetic nature of Wilson's sets, the elements of image, music, text, movement, and gesture became as inseparable as they are firmly distinct.

Einstein on the Beach and the other projects discussed here involve artists who may differ not only in terms of the media in which they realize their ideas but also in their notions of collaboration and sense of the finished piece. These differences, however, demand neither a compromise of individual sensibilities nor that every serendipitous revelation be incorporated into the work. Rather, collaboration simply offers a working process in which, among other possibilities, decisions may be required about previously unimagined events.

[*See also* Scenic Design. *Many of the principal figures mentioned herein are the subjects of independent entries.*]

BIBLIOGRAPHY

Garafola, Lynn. *Diaghilev's Ballets Russes.* New York, 1989.
Hengst, Franzis. "Die Befreiung vom Dekorativen: Über des Zusammenwirken von Tanz und bildender Kunst im 20. Jahrhundert." *Ballet-Journal/Das Tanzarchiv* 42 (December 1994):50–57.

MELISSA HARRIS

ASAFIEV, BORIS (Boris Vladimirovich Asaf'ev; born 17 [29] July 1884 in Saint Petersburg, died 27 January 1949 in Moscow), Russian composer and musicologist. Asafiev graduated from the History and Philosophy Department of Saint Petersburg University in 1908. Two years later he entered the Saint Petersburg Conservatory, where he studied composition under Anatol Liadov. At the same time, he was a piano accompanist for ballet dancers at the Maryinsky Theater.

Asafiev wrote extensively, using the pseudonym Igor Glebov, on every aspect of music and ballet. He also composed the music for ballet adaptations of some of Aleksandr Pushkin's best-known works, including *The Fountain of Bakhchisarai* (1934), choreographed by Rostislav Zakharov for the Kirov Theater in Leningrad; *The Prisoner of the Caucasus* (1938), choreographed by Leonid Lavrovsky for the Leningrad Maly Opera and Ballet Theater; *Mistress into Maid* (1946), choreographed by Zakharov for Moscow's Bolshoi Theater; and *The Stone Guest,* based on Spanish folk songs recorded and arranged by Mikhail Glinka, choreographed by Leonid Yakobson for the Leningrad ballet school. Even in his lifetime Pushkin had attracted the attention of Russian choreographers, and the Russian ballet's Pushkiniana is fairly large. Asafiev added to it greatly by placing his adaptations in a modern context.

Seeking to bring ballet closer to literary classics, Asafiev provided music for other ballets drawn from Russian literature. These include *Christmas Eve* (1938), after Nikolai Gogol, choreographed by Vladimir Varkovitsky for the Leningrad ballet school; *The Beautiful Radda* (1938), after Maxim Gorky, choreographed by Anatoly Shatin for the Island of Dance Theater in Moscow's Gorky Amusement Park; *Ashik-Kerib* (1940), after Mikhail Lermontov, choreographed by Boris Fenster for Leningrad's Maly Opera and Ballet Theater; and *Sulamyth* (1941), after Aleksandr Kuprin, choreographed by Vladimir Kononovich for the Sverdlovsk Opera and Ballet Theater. Asafiev also composed ballets based on western European literature, including Honoré Balzac's *Les illusions perdues* (1936), presented in 1936 at the Kirov Theater, with choreography by Zakharov, and *Francesca da Rimini,* a 1947 premiere at Moscow's Stanislavsky and Nemirovich-Danchenko Theater, with choreography by Nikolai Kholfin. Asafiev composed a number of ballets on topical contemporary subjects, including two for the choreographer Vasily Vainonen at the Kirov Theater: *Partisan Days* (1937), which focuses on the Russian civil war, and *Militsa* (1947), which deals with resistance to fascism.

In Asafiev's ballet music, leitmotifs characterize the protagonists and dramatic situations. The composer studied history in order to recreate in his music the atmosphere unique to various historical periods. Thus, in Vainonen's ballet *The Flames of Paris* (1932), the action of which is set in Paris during the French Revolution, Asafiev drew heavily on folk tunes and the music of French composers of the era.

Asafiev was also an eminent music scholar and was received as a full member of the Soviet Academy of Sciences in 1943. His selected works were published between 1952 and 1957 in four volumes, plus a fifth volume containing detailed, scholarly bibliographies and notated music scores. Asafiev was one of the first Soviet musicologists to discuss the innovative significance of the ballets of Tchaikovsky, Glazunov, Stravinsky, and Prokofiev. He also substantiated in theoretical terms the principle of symphonism in ballet music. Asafiev was named a People's Artist of the USSR in 1946 and won state prizes in 1943 and 1948.

BIBLIOGRAPHY

Asafiev, Boris. *Izbrannye trudy.* 7 vols. Moscow, 1952.
Kabalevskii, Dmitrii. *B. V. Asaf'ev—Igor Glebov.* Moscow, 1954.
Keldysh, I. V., ed. *B. V. Asaf'ev i sovetskaia muzykalnaia kultura.* Moscow, 1986.

Norris, Geoffrey. "Asaf'yev, Boris Vladimirovich." In *The New Grove Dictionary of Music and Musicians*. London, 1980.

Orlova, Elena M. *B. V. Asaf'ev*. Leningrad, 1964.

Souritz, Elizabeth. *Soviet Choreographers in the 1920s*. Translated by Lynn Visson. Durham, N.C., 1990.

Swift, Mary Grace. *The Art of the Dance in the U.S.S.R.* Notre Dame, 1968.

Titova, N. V., ed. *Problemy sovremennogo muzykoznania v svete idei B. V. Asaf'eva*. Leningrad, 1987.

ARCHIVE. Central State Archive of Literature and Art, Moscow.

VICTOR V. VANSLOV
Translated from Russian

ÅSBERG, MARGARETHA (born 1939 in Stockholm, Sweden), dancer and choreographer. Åsberg began studying classical ballet at the Swedish Royal Ballet school in 1952. Abroad, she studied modern dance with Sigurd Leeder and Anna Sokolow. In 1957 she was employed by the Royal Ballet. She was injured during a tour in China, and during the ensuing period of inactivity she cultivated an interest in choreography. Beginning in 1962, she studied composition at the Juilliard School in New York. At the same time she danced in the Pearl Lang and Anna Sokolow companies and with the Martha Graham Dance Company.

After her return to the Swedish Royal Ballet in 1964, Åsberg danced several solo parts, most notably in ballets choreographed by Birgit Åkesson. Åsberg's increasing interest in modern dance influenced her simultaneously to study at the Stockholm Choreographic Institute, where the senior teacher was Åkesson; her ideas on choreography strongly influenced Åsberg.

Åsberg concluded her dancing career at the Royal Ballet in 1967 but continued teaching modern dance and improvisation. She also worked with nonprofessionals, creating her own special teaching technique. The choreographic themes she wanted to work with now began to crystallize; the fundamental elements were space, time, and energy. She worked closely with several of Sweden's most important artists and composers in cooperative productions combining dance, scenery, and music as independent components, in the Cunningham spirit.

Since 1979 Åsberg has worked as a choreographer and dancer with her group Pyramiderna, Sweden's foremost postmodern dance company. The group, whose membership is fluid according to choreographic requirements, initially presented its works at various art galleries. Since the mid-1980s Pyramiderna has performed at Moderna Dansteatern, an avant-garde venue founded by Åsberg. Åsberg's choreography has developed from using the body and movement in a manipulative relationship with different objects, to a form of movement born out of its own possibilities, and finally to multilayered works including fragments of text. Dance consists, in the main, of forms of communication settled beforehand, something from which Åsberg continually tries to break away in order to reach immediate, uncompromised expression.

BIBLIOGRAPHY

Åsberg, Margaretha. *Pyramiderna*. Stockholm, 1979.

"Åsberg, Margaretha." In *Sohlmans musiklexikon*. 2d ed. Stockholm, 1975–.

Bohlin, Peter. "Swedish Contemporary Dance: Concentrated, Effective Energy." *Ballett International* 12 (March 1989): 9–15.

Bohlin, Peter. "Margaretha Åsberg." *Entré* 16 (1989).

Engdahl, Horace. "Margaretha Åsbergs Fragment av en kub." *Kris* 17–18 (January 1981).

Näslund, Erik. "Dance in Sweden." *Ballett International* 5 (February 1982): 42–47.

LENA HAMMERGREN

ASHTON, FREDERICK (Frederick William Mallandaine Ashton; born 17 September 1904 in Guayaquil, Ecuador, died 18 August 1988 in Eye, Sussex, England), British dancer and choreographer. Ashton grew up in Lima, Peru, where his father was a businessman and minor British diplomat. In 1917 Anna Pavlova toured Peru, and seeing her perform made Ashton determined to become a dancer. He was unable to pursue his ambition for several years, since such a career was then considered unsuitable for a young man from an upper-middle-class British family. In 1919 Ashton was sent to school in England for three years, at the end of which he found an office job. Soon afterward he answered a newspaper advertisement for dance classes taught by Russian choreographer Léonide Massine and became one of his pupils. When Massine had to leave London, he suggested that Ashton continue his studies with Marie Rambert.

Rambert's forte as a teacher was the ability to divine talents in her students that they did not suspect they possessed. In 1925 she cast Ashton, her only regular male pupil, in a small ballet, in the role of a couturier. When he showed her some movements he had devised to suit this character, Rambert insisted that the reluctant Ashton undertake the choreography of the entire ballet. *A Tragedy of Fashion, or The Scarlet Scissors* was added to a London revue, *Riverside Nights*, receiving its first performance on 15 June 1926, with Rambert and Ashton dancing the leading roles. The ballet was designed by Sophie Fedorovitch, a young Polish artist Ashton had met at Rambert's studio, who became one of his most valued collaborators and his dearest friend.

From 1927 to 1929, Ashton began to make a living as a dancer (for example, with the Nemchinova-Dolin Ballet at the London Coliseum and in the Royal Opera season at London's Covent Garden); he continued to choreograph small ballets for his fellow students at Rambert's classes. In the summer of 1928 he went to Paris and auditioned

ASHTON. Frederick Ashton in the Tango from his ballet *Façade* (1931), a lighthearted work satirizing various dance styles. (Photograph from the Dance Collection, New York Public Library for the Performing Arts.)

for the company that Bronislava Nijinska was putting together for wealthy dilettante Ida Rubinstein. Ashton was given some solo roles and had the opportunity to learn the craft of choreography from both Nijinska and Massine.

Ashton returned to London in the spring of 1929 and in the following winter persuaded Rambert to present her students in a matinee performance that incorporated several of his ballets. A new one, *Capriol Suite,* was a set of court and country dances to Peter Warlock's arrangement of musical themes from Thoinot Arbeau's dance collection *Orchésographie,* published in 1588. Although the influence of Nijinska is apparent in some of the groupings, *Capriol* does not have the modishness of most of Ashton's previous works, showing, rather, a robust quality.

The matinee's success encouraged Rambert to present the Marie Rambert Dancers in a two-week season the following June, with Tamara Karsavina as guest artist. Early in 1930 several people in the dance world had joined together to form the Camargo Society, with the object of presenting regular performances; these would, to some extent, make up for the loss of the London seasons of the Ballets Russes de Serge Diaghilev after Diaghilev's death

in 1929. Ashton's *Pomona,* to a score by Constant Lambert, given at the society's inaugural performance in October, was credited in *Dancing Times* with confirming the existence of "a British choreographer of the first rank."

Rambert, wanting her own company to have a permanent footing, formed the Ballet Club, which would give performances on Sunday evenings in its own tiny theater, later to be called the Mercury. Meanwhile, Ninette de Valois had been invited by Lilian Baylis, manager of the Sadler's Wells and Old Vic theaters, to form a small company to provide incidental dances for the operas and classical plays presented. Both women doubtless looked forward to a time when the Vic-Wells Ballet (as the company became known) would have an independent existence, and in May 1931 the first all-ballet evening was given, at the Old Vic.

These various manifestations of burgeoning British ballet were not in competition with one another. There was considerable overlap in personnel among the companies, with each sharing dancers and ballets. For example, de Valois's *Job* went into the Vic-Wells repertory, and Ashton's witty *Façade* was taken into the repertory of the Ballet Club. There was some difference in the audiences the companies attracted: Lilian Baylis wanted to build a popular audience for serious drama and opera, while both the Camargo Society and the Ballet Club catered to the cognoscenti, those Bloomsbury intellectuals and society figures who previously had supported Diaghilev.

All the same, de Valois was determined to build her company into an important one, and she recognized that the nineteenth-century classic ballets would be its indispensable foundation. During the first decade of her company's existence, she added to its repertory *Giselle, Coppélia,* and the three great Tchaikovsky ballets, *Swan Lake, The Nutcracker,* and *The Sleeping Beauty.* Rambert, in contrast, was developing new choreographers—another essential element in the growth of a national ballet (the third is the existence of a school). Not only Ashton but Antony Tudor, Andrée Howard, Frank Staff, and Walter Gore emerged from Rambert's company, but in other ways it remained a small-time operation, giving its weekly performances, with occasional seasons in larger theaters, and eventually both Ashton and Tudor would seek larger opportunities elsewhere.

Ashton not only continued to choreograph for both the Camargo Society and the Ballet Club, he also made two ballets for the Vic-Wells: *Regatta* (1931), a slight comedy piece, and *Les Rendezvous* (1933), a charming suite of dances to music by French composer Daniel Auber. Designed to show off two virtuoso guest artists from Diaghilev's Ballets Russes, Alicia Markova and Stanislas Idzikowski, *Les Rendezvous* incidentally provided a technical challenge to the young dancers of the supporting company.

At the same time, Ashton, in order to augment his relatively meager income (Rambert paid her choreographers £1 a minute of finished choreography, with no royalties) began to work in Britain's commercial theater and cinema, staging numbers for musical comedies and revues. (Between other engagements he often danced in the musicals himself.) He frequently worked in London shows with the American choreographer Buddy Bradley, who would stage the tap and rhythm numbers while Ashton supplied the ballets. This led to their collaboration on a West Indian–style jazz ballet, *High Yellow*, for the Camargo Society, with Markova in the lead.

As a result of this diverse activity, Ashton was beginning to develop a personal style. Its firm grounding was in classic technique—the Cecchetti method—as taught by Rambert and, more authentically, by Margaret Craske; this was modified by the freer *plastique* (especially in the use of the torso) that Ashton had learned from Nijinska. At that time Ashton had only a limited firsthand knowledge of the ballets made by Marius Petipa, having danced only the excerpts from *Aurora's Wedding* that were in Rambert's repertory. Rambert had always insisted on the fundamental importance of Petipa's classicism (with rare perception, she used to refer to its "abstract" qualities). All these elements reached an early synthesis in Ashton's *Les Rendezvous*, which in its modest way was his first statement of a personal classicism.

Of equal importance in the evolution of Ashton's style were influences of a more exotic, or more contemporary, nature than those of classicism. For example, the Englishness of ballets such as *Capriol Suite* or his two Tennyson ballets, *The Lady of Shalott* (for Rambert, 1931) and *The Lord of Burleigh* (for Camargo, 1931), contrasts with a Latin character that derived from Ashton's Peruvian background, which surfaced in the raffish *Rio Grande* (for Camargo, 1931) and in the tango in *Façade* (1931). Bradley's jazz influence was also evident. Finally, Ashton was inevitably affected by the modish, even perverse distortions found in many of the 1920s Diaghilev ballets by Massine, Nijinska, and George Balanchine. One of the characteristics of genius is the ability to absorb outside influences and transmute them into a uniquely personal style. Another 1933 ballet in which Ashton's developing style manifested itself was *Les Masques* (for Rambert), to the trio for piano, oboe, and bassoon by Francis Poulenc, with Art Deco designs in black, white, and gray by Fedorovitch. Witty, sophisticated, elegant, mysterious, *Les Masques* is at once classic and contemporary.

Immediately after the premiere of *Les Rendezvous*, Ashton sailed for New York, having received an invitation to stage the dances and movement for the Gertrude Stein–Virgil Thomson opera *Four Saints in Three Acts*. It was first performed in Hartford, Connecticut, in 1934, with an all-black cast. Ashton's task was made harder by the lack of trained black dancers, but his experience in the commercial theater was helpful here—he was used to making relatively untrained performers look their best. In staging *Four Saints*, Ashton drew upon the feeling for ritual he had acquired as an altar boy in the Cathedral of Lima. *Four Saints* was a box office success. It also played several weeks on Broadway, giving Ashton his first taste of international celebrity.

Before the end of the run, Ashton returned to Britain to continue his work with Rambert and for commercial theater and cinema. His first work after his return was *Mephisto Valse*, a Romantic ballet in miniature for the Mercury stage, to Franz Liszt's music and with designs by

ASHTON. Robert Helpmann (The Poet) lying at the feet of Margot Fonteyn (The Woman in the Ball Dress) at the dress rehearsal of Ashton's *Apparitions* (1936). This ballet marked the beginning of an almost thirty-year collaboration between the choreographer and Fonteyn, his favorite dancer. (Photograph from the Dance Collection, New York Public Library for the Performing Arts.)

Fedorovitch, followed in 1935 by *Valentine's Eve,* to Maurice Ravel's *Valses Nobles et Sentimentales,* also designed by Fedorovitch.

At this time de Valois was reaching a crucial point in the development of her Vic-Wells company. Markova had been its ballerina, making possible the classic revivals and creating roles in such ballets as *Les Rendezvous* and de Valois's own *The Rake's Progress.* (Markova also danced regularly at the Ballet Club, where Ashton created *La Péri, Foyer de Danse, Les Masques,* and *Mephisto Valse* for her.) Now Markova had accepted a proposal to form her own company with Anton Dolin. It was therefore necessary for de Valois to find a new ballerina, and she was determined to do so from the ranks of her own company. The dancer she chose, who was to become known as Margot Fonteyn, was then only sixteen years old. Among Fonteyn's early roles was that of the Creole Girl (created by Markova) in a revival of Ashton's *Rio Grande.*

Equally important in de Valois's eyes was the necessity of finding a choreographer who could make ballets in a contemporary classic style—her own were usually *demi-caractère* or in a vein of central European modernism. Ashton was the inevitable choice, and at the beginning of

ASHTON. Alexander Grant (The Bridegroom) and Merle Park (The Bride) in a revival of Ashton's *Wedding Bouquet* (1937), a dance parody of a French provincial wedding. (Photograph from the Dance Collection, New York Public Library for the Performing Arts.)

the 1935/36 season he joined the Vic-Wells company as resident choreographer and principal dancer. (In the previous season he had revised *Les Rendezvous* and supervised the revival of *Rio Grande.*) On opening night, Fonteyn assumed Markova's role in *Les Rendezvous;* Ashton appeared as Pierrot in Michel Fokine's *Le Carnaval.* He soon mounted a new production of *Façade.* His first new ballet for the company was a version of Igor Stravinsky's *Le Baiser de la Fée* (he had danced it in Nijinska's original production for Rubinstein), designed by Fedorovitch. Fonteyn danced the Bride, performing with Harold Turner Ashton's first full-scale classic pas de deux. Pearl Argyle, a dancer also recruited from Rambert, took the role of the Fairy.

The musical director of the Vic-Wells Ballet was Constant Lambert. As well as being a great ballet conductor, Lambert was a man of enormous culture who had an important voice in the artistic policy of the company and in the development of Ashton as a choreographer. In the next few years Ashton was to produce a series of ballets whose level of artistic collaboration rivaled those of Diaghilev's Ballets Russes in its later years. Most of these were made for Fonteyn, who more than any other ballerina was Ashton's muse.

Apparitions (1936), to music of Liszt selected by Lambert and with designs by Cecil Beaton, was partly produced with the remaining funds from the moribund Camargo Society. A Romantic ballet, the theme was derived from Hector Berlioz's program for his *Symphonie Fantastique* (produced as a ballet by Massine later the same year); it featured Fonteyn as the *idée fixe* of a poet (Robert Helpmann) tormented by drug-induced visions. *Nocturne* (also 1936), to Frederick Delius's tone poem *Paris,* was a *ballet d'atmosphère* with a *fin de siècle, Yellow Book* flavor captured to perfection in Fedorovitch's designs. (*The Yellow Book* [1894–1897] had been a quarterly review, in book form, containing essays, poems, stories, and illustrations, particularly those by Aubrey Beardsley, that expressed the symbolist, decadent aesthetic of the 1890s.) Stylish collaborations such as these and *Les Patineurs* (1937), *A Wedding Bouquet* (1937), and *Horoscope* (1938) enabled the Vic-Wells Ballet to attract the fashionable and intellectual audience that Lilian Baylis had scorned.

In 1939 Ashton collaborated with Lord Berners on *Cupid and Psyche,* a jocular (some thought tastelessly so) treatment of the Greek myth, with designs by Francis Rose. The ballet was not without redeeming features choreographically—in fact, in its pas de deux Ashton began to explore the "walking on air" motif that became a hallmark of his later ballets—but its frivolous portrayal of Jupiter as a fascist leader struck a wrong note in the year that World War II began, and the ballet flopped.

The success of Ashton's previous ballets had not gone unnoticed by the directors of the international Ballet

Russe companies, and both René Blum and Colonel Wassily de Basil at various times announced that they would present ballets by Ashton. In the summer of 1938 the Ballet Russe de Monte Carlo, which Massine had taken over, had presented Ashton with a ready-made score and libretto by Vincenzo Tommasini and designs by Eugene Berman for a ballet then called *Le Diable S'amuse*. Ashton worked on the ballet in Paris in the summer of 1939. The premiere, scheduled for September during a brief season at Covent Garden, was canceled when war broke out; the dancers made their way to New York. Some arrived toward the end of October, on the very day that the company opened at the Metropolitan Opera House, with a program including *Devil's Holiday*, as the title was rendered in English. Ashton never saw it in performance; he might have done so if he had accepted an offer to go to New York to join the newly formed Ballet Theatre later that season, but he decided to remain in Britain. In the first months of the war the Vic-Wells (which in 1941 changed its name to the Sadler's Wells) Ballet toured the British provinces, but when the anticipated air raids failed to materialize, the company returned to its London home immediately after Christmas 1939.

A month later a new ballet by Ashton, *Dante Sonata* (1940), was given in London. Once again he used music by Liszt, orchestrated by Lambert, who collaborated closely on the planning of the ballet. Fedorovitch's designs were based on John Flaxman's illustrations for Dante's *Inferno*. As a schoolboy, Ashton had seen Isadora Duncan dance, and she had made an impression on him almost as strong as that of Pavlova; the idiom of *Dante Sonata* was pure Duncan—the dancers were barefoot; the women's hair, unbound. The ballet did not attempt to depict the content of Dante's poem in a literal sense but was an abstract treatment of the struggle between good and evil, personified as the Children of Light and of Darkness. Remarkably, neither side won; if the ballet reflected Ashton's reaction to the war, as was generally supposed, that reaction was pessimistic, or at any rate realistic. Certainly the piece had a cathartic effect on audiences at that time.

Ashton's next ballet was in complete contrast: a serene work that showed, through its biblical subject matter and ritualistic manner, that Ashton was a devout man. *The Wise Virgins* (1940), to excerpts from cantatas by Johann Sebastian Bach, orchestrated by William Walton, had very little dancing in the conventional sense but was a series of Baroque-style tableaux, exquisitely situated in Rex Whistler's decor.

The Wise Virgins was presented in April. The following month the company embarked on an ill-advised tour of Holland, Belgium, and France. The tour was abruptly cut short by the Nazi invasion of Holland; the company managed to escape but at the cost of abandoning the scenery, costumes, and musical scores of all the ballets it had taken on tour. Of the Ashton ballets lost, only *Horoscope* was never revived; *Les Patineurs* and *Dante Sonata* were immediately remounted, and *Façade* was redesigned and expanded.

The company reopened at Sadler's Wells in July and played there through the summer. De Valois choreographed a new ballet, *The Prospect before Us, or Pity the Poor Dancers*, based on incidents in the history of ballet in London during the eighteenth century. Ashton impersonated his great forebear, the French dancer-choreographer Jean-Georges Noverre. Toward the end of the summer, when the *blitz* (German air raids) began in earnest, the theater closed its doors and the company went on the road. When it returned to London, in January 1941, it was to play matinees only, in a theater in the West End of London, the New (later called the Albery). For the next few years the company alternated long provincial tours with engagements at that theater, adding early evening performances during the summer months, when darkness and air raids came later.

ASHTON. *Symphonic Variations* (1946), with original cast members (left to right) Pamela May, Michael Somes, Margot Fonteyn, and Moira Shearer. This was Ashton's first ballet choreographed for the stage of the Royal Opera House, which had become the Sadler's Wells Ballet's home after World War II. (Photograph from the Dance Collection, New York Public Library for the Performing Arts.)

In January 1941 Ashton's third early wartime ballet was presented, an allegorical-psychological piece called *The Wanderer*, to Franz Schubert's Fantasia in C Major, with design by Graham Sutherland. Robert Helpmann danced the protagonist, a man who recapitulates, in his imagination, his loves, failures, and triumphs. Fonteyn, who had led the Children of Light in *Dante* and performed the chaste Bride in *The Wise Virgins*, here appeared as the embodiment of worldly success. Although the ballet had something in common with Massine's symphonic allegory *Les Présages*, on another level it depicted, in a remarkable way, a neurotic state of mind.

During the following months of 1941 the male ranks of the company were considerably thinned by the military draft. Ashton himself went into the Royal Air Force in June. Early in 1943 he was given special leave to choreograph a new ballet, *The Quest*, a patriotic spectacle based on Edmund Spenser's *The Faerie Queene*, with a commissioned score by William Walton and designs by John Piper. In spite of difficult working conditions (the ballet was rehearsed on tour, with the score being delivered piecemeal) and an unwieldy scenario, which depicts the triumph of Saint George over the forces of evil, Ashton managed to create some passages in which the dance content outweighed the literary: the *divertissement* of the Seven Deadly Sins, the pas de deux for Una (Fonteyn) and Saint George (Helpmann), and the ritualistic final scene.

Ashton was released from the Royal Air Force in May 1945, and in July the company returned to its home at Sadler's Wells for the first time in four years—but not for long. Early in 1946 the Royal Opera House at Covent Garden was reopened and the Sadler's Wells Ballet—now the British national ballet in everything but name—became the resident ballet company. It was decided that the proper vehicle for this transition would be a new production of *The Sleeping Beauty*, which had remained in the repertory during most of the war years in the production first mounted in 1939, with its decidedly meager decorations by Nadia Benois. The new production was sumptuously redesigned by Oliver Messel, and Ashton made several choreographic emendations (more were added as time went on). As in 1939, Fonteyn danced Aurora, with Helpmann as the Prince (doubling as Carabosse, a role Ashton also undertook later).

The production was a triumph and ran for several weeks, during which the rest of the repertory was prepared. Old ballets were adapted to the larger stage, with varying degrees of success. *Nocturne*, *Dante Sonata*, and *Apparitions* were among those that did not survive for long; *The Wanderer* for some reason was not attempted. Ashton was also working on a new ballet, to César Franck's *Symphonic Variations*, which he had been studying for some time. The mystical content he had originally considered was dropped, or rather submerged, and the

ASHTON. The choreographer *en travesti* portrays an Ugly Sister in his three-act ballet *Cinderella* (1948). (Photograph by Anthony Crickmay; used by permission of the Board of Trustees of the Theatre Museum, London.)

ballet that finally reached the stage in April 1946 (a postponement caused by an injury to Michael Somes gave the opportunity for further radical revision) was a pure dance work for six dancers, three women (Fonteyn, Moira Shearer, Pamela May) and three men (Somes, Henry Danton, Brian Shaw), who never left the stage. Fedorovitch designed the vernal setting and the simple costumes.

Symphonic Variations was the equivalent in Ashton's oeuvre of *Apollo* in Balanchine's—a statement of his choreographic credo, in which the dance itself was of paramount importance—without denying the inspiration of what Ashton called "a personal fount of emotion." In part he wanted to offset the prevailingly literary nature of many wartime ballets, particularly those of Robert Helpmann—though Ashton had himself contributed to this trend with *The Quest*. He saw, too, that it was important for the dancers to meet a technical challenge without being able to conceal any shortcomings beneath a costume or characterization.

Ashton's future career, in spite of having passed such a milestone, was not without its setbacks. His next ballet, *Les Sirènes*, given in November 1946, reunited him with two former collaborators, Lord Berners and Cecil Beaton. The result nearly repeated the disaster of *Cupid and Psyche*, and for similar reasons: they tried too hard to be funny and in the process gave rise to the suspicion that they were out of touch with contemporary life. The time for little jokes about Edwardian high life had passed.

Ashton soon hit his stride again. De Valois had established a second company, the Sadler's Wells Theatre Ballet, for which Ashton choreographed in 1947 a new ballet set to Ravel's *Valses Nobles et Sentimentales,* using a decor similar to that of *Valentine's Eve,* his earlier ballet to that music. *Valses Nobles et Sentimentales* had only a slight narrative thread; it was no more than a pretext for a series of dances that continued, among other things, his exploration of the varieties of supported adagio already begun in *Symphonic Variations.*

Exquisite as it was, *Valses* did not mark a new departure in Ashton's work, as did his next ballet at Covent Garden, to Stravinsky's *Scènes de Ballet* (1948), a complex, astringent score that placed greater demands on Ashton than had either Franck's or Ravel's. Ashton later said that he actually worked out his choreographic configurations according to Euclid, but a more important formal element in the ballet derived from his intensive study of Marius Petipa's *The Sleeping Beauty.* The classicism of Petipa is implicit in *Scènes de Ballet,* just as it is, say, in Balanchine's *Agon.*

Ashton's handling of Stravinsky's score was masterly, and the experience enabled him to tackle other important ballet scores with greater assurance. At the end of 1948 the company presented Ashton's first full-length ballet, *Cinderella,* to music by Sergei Prokofiev. Fonteyn, who had created the leading roles in *Symphonic Variations* and *Scènes de Ballet,* was forced to withdraw from the title role when she injured herself during the first performance of Ashton's *Don Juan.* Her place was taken by Moira Shearer. *Cinderella's* structure was openly modeled on Petipa, particularly in the *divertissement* of the Fairies of the Seasons, the *ballabili* of Stars, and the *pas d'action* in the ballroom scene. Otherwise the most notable part of the production was Ashton's performance as one of the Stepsisters, opposite Robert Helpmann—a superb clown's performance, comic and pathetic. *Cinderella* has remained in the repertory and Ashton continued to appear in his role until the 1976 revival.

More than two years elapsed before Ashton's next new ballet for his own company. During that time he supervised further revivals of prewar ballets. *A Wedding Bouquet,* which transplanted successfully in early 1949, and

ASHTON. Svetlana Beriosova (Cinderella), being greeted by Donald MacLeary (The Prince), in the ballroom scene of Ashton's *Cinderella,* c.1959. (Photograph from the Dance Collection, New York Public Library for the Performing Arts.)

Apparitions, which, with its overly elaborate new decor and costumes, did not. He also created a piece for the Ballets de Paris de Roland Petit, *Le Rêve de Léonor,* which like *Devil's Holiday* had a ready-made book and designs, in this case by Léonor Fini. Given the circumstances, failure was predictable, even with Renée Jeanmaire in the title role.

A far more important event was the first New York season and U.S. tour of the Sadler's Wells Ballet, in the fall of 1949, which established the company as one of international stature and Fonteyn as a world-class ballerina. The conquest of New York was accomplished with the great production of *The Sleeping Beauty.* Although it exemplified the British style of classic dance—lyrical, precise, mannerly—largely created by Ashton, his own ballets made less of an impression at the time. In future tours his ballets were often more highly regarded—and more perceptively reviewed—than at home. But in 1949 American audiences were slow to recognize the quality of such ballets as *Symphonic Variations* and *Scènes de Ballet,* perhaps be-

ASHTON. Original cast members Nicholas Magallanes as the Poet and Melissa Hayden as Profane Love in Frederick Ashton's *Illuminations* (1950), created for the New York City Ballet. (Photograph by Baron; used by permission of Camera Press, Ltd., London.)

cause they were already accustomed to the hard-edged classicism of Balanchine.

Ashton returned to New York early in 1950 to choreograph a work for Balanchine's own company, New York City Ballet, at the invitation of Lincoln Kirstein. The ballet was *Illuminations,* to composer Benjamin Britten's settings of Arthur Rimbaud's poems, which Ashton had wanted to use for some time but had hesitated to propose for the Sadler's Wells Ballet because of their "shocking" subject matter. Cecil Beaton was the designer. Kirstein, inspired by a French children's book, suggested dressing the dancers as Pierrots (a notion as irrelevant as it was insipid). Apart from the fact that Beaton's designs prettified the ballet, they also obscured its structure, which as always with Ashton had a classic strength and clarity. In the permissive atmosphere of New York, Ashton felt free to represent the sexual aspect of the ballet's subject more graphically than he might have dared to at home. Yet it is possible to object that he failed to translate these passages into dance terms. *Illuminations* did not enter the British repertory until 1981, following its successful revival in New York by the Joffrey Ballet.

The Sadler's Wells Ballet returned to the United States for another New York season and cross-country tour in the fall of 1950. That summer Ashton had spent his vacation in Greece, partly to prepare himself for his next project. He wanted to rescue from the concert hall Ravel's score for *Daphnis and Chloe,* composed for Diaghilev, and restore it to the stage. He was encouraged in this bold endeavor by Tamara Karsavina, who agreed that a contemporary treatment was called for, rather than an archaeological exercise à la Fokine. Again, the fundamental structure was classic ballet; Ashton even put the women on pointe. Above all, he had the courage to be simple, to work against the lushness of the score, giving the ballet a timeless quality that underlies its contemporaneity.

Technically, *Daphnis* is firmly grounded in the *danse d'école,* with occasional hints of Isadora Duncan and a few references to Greek folk dance. Here, too, the treatment of physical love is entirely in dance terms, both in the innocent sensuality of the two lovers and in the seduction of Daphnis by the temptress Lykanion. Perhaps because, as Ashton anticipated, British audiences had a preconceived idea of how a ballet from the Diaghilev era should look, *Daphnis* was coolly received at first and was not recognized as a masterpiece until it was seen by American critics and audiences in 1953.

Daphnis, first given in April 1951, was followed by another ballet on a Greek theme, *Tiresias.* This was a disaster, with tragic consequences. The score and libretto were by Lambert, who had intended, years before, a satirical treatment of the subject, similar to that of *Pomona,* but who now came up with one that was fatally portentous. Ashton and Fonteyn (as Tiresias in female form) tried

ASHTON. The ensemble of the Sadler's Wells Ballet in Ashton's version of *Daphnis and Chloe* (1951). (Photograph from the Dance Collection, New York Public Library for the Performing Arts.)

hard to save the work—out of love for and loyalty to their old friend and colleague. Fonteyn's pas de deux with John Field had the ambiguous eroticism that the subject called for, but nothing could rescue the ballet as a whole. Lambert was already a sick man; six weeks after the premiere in July 1951, he died, a grievous loss to British ballet.

It was no doubt a relief for Ashton to turn next to the indestructible music of Tchaikovsky's *The Nutcracker*, of which he made a two-act version for the Sadler's Wells Theatre Ballet, led by Svetlana Beriosova. The company toured the United States early in 1952, and Ashton was present at its New York opening, having been commissioned by the New York City Ballet to make *Picnic at Tintagel*, a fanciful treatment of the story of Tristram and Iseult. Both ballets were designed by Beaton.

Before deciding to attempt the Prokofiev score to *Cinderella*, Ashton had considered Léo Delibes's *Sylvia*, and he now took it up as his next project. The three-act ballet opened the 1952/53 season at Covent Garden, in an exquisite production designed by Robin and Christopher Ironside, who, like Ashton himself, revealed an extraordinary sense of identification with the period of the ballet's composition (France's Second Empire), free from any

condescension. Sylvia was another great role for Fonteyn, now in full possession of her powers as a ballerina.

Later in this season Ashton suffered another great personal loss: his beloved friend and earliest collaborator Sophie Fedorovitch died during the preparation of a production of Christoph Willibald Gluck's opera *Orpheus*, which Ashton was mounting for the Royal Opera, with dances featuring Beriosova. Appropriately, Ashton's staging again evoked memories of Duncan, who had danced to Gluck's music.

Perhaps because he felt the loss of Fedorovitch, with whom he had discussed all his projects, Ashton's next few ballets showed little inspiration—products of his craft rather than his genius. *Homage to the Queen* (1953), as its title suggests, was an occasional piece celebrating the coronation of Elizabeth II, with the ballerinas of the company leading the entries for the four elements; Fonteyn was Queen of the Air. Ashton produced no major work at all in 1954, but he made up for this hiatus at the outset of the following year, when he brought out a pair of ballets, *Rinaldo and Armida* and *Variations on a Theme by Purcell*, neither of which was very successful. They were followed a few months later by the charming *japonaiserie* called *Madame Chrysanthème*.

Less than two months elapsed before the premiere of yet another Ashton three-act ballet, *Romeo and Juliet*, to the music of Prokofiev, for the Royal Danish Ballet, in

ASHTON. A scene from Ashton's version of *Sylvia* (1952), with members of the Sadler's Wells Ballet. The scenery was designed by Robin and Christopher Ironside. (Photograph by Felix Fonteyn; from the Dance Collection, New York Public Library for the Performing Arts.)

May 1955. Lavrovsky's great veristic version for the Bolshoi had not yet been seen in the West, and Ashton characteristically cast the piece in the form of a classic ballet, focusing on the intimate tragedy of the lovers. Juliet was created by Mona Vangsaae, opposite whom Ashton cast a young soloist, Henning Kronstam.

On 5 May 1956, to celebrate the twenty-fifth anniversary of the first evening of ballet given by the Vic-Wells Ballet, the Sadler's Wells Ballet—about to receive the royal charter that would confer on it the title of Royal Ballet—gave another occasional piece by Ashton, *Birthday Offering*. This was a grand *divertissement*, to music by Aleksandr Glazunov, for seven ballerinas, again led by Fonteyn, and their partners; it served to define the classic style that Ashton had derived from the masterpieces of Petipa—delicate and precise in footwork and *épaulement* but with nobility of line and amplitude of phrasing.

Ashton's next three-act ballet had a commissioned score, *Ondine*, with music by Hans Werner Henze. The

work reached the stage in October 1958. More than ever Ashton designed this ballet to enshrine the qualities of Fonteyn. Exquisite as her performance was as the wayward water sprite, and in spite of the expertise of Ashton's *mise-en-scène*, aided by Lila de Nobili's designs, *Ondine* had long passages of routine choreography during which Ashton seemed to be dutifully plowing through Henze's emptily eclectic score.

Privately Ashton resolved to make no more three-act ballets. Another serious objection to *Ondine* was that it was yet another attempt to breathe life into subject matter without contemporary relevance. Ashton's answer to the criticism took a surprising form; with the encouragement of Tamara Karsavina, he made a new version of one of the earliest ballets extant, *La Fille Mal Gardée*, first choreographed by Jean Dauberval in 1789. Karsavina herself wrote a program note pointing out the timelessness of this simple tale of a maiden (Lise) in love with a young farmer (Colas); they contrive to outwit her mother's plan for a more advantageous marriage. Karsavina also gave practical assistance to Ashton—she showed him some of the traditional mime passages and other elements from the Maryinsky version, which may have been handed down from the original.

Dance critic Edwin Denby once wrote, "The more trivial the subject, the deeper and more beautiful is Ashton's poetic view of it." The simple libretto and the tuneful score concocted by John Lanchbery from various earlier scores for the ballet released in Ashton a flow of the most personal and profound poetry. The lovers' dances are full of tenderness and passion. Ashton took the idea of the ribbon used in one of the pas de deux in the old ballet and made of it a metaphor for the love of Lise and Colas, which recurs throughout the work. The entire ballet is redolent of Ashton's love of the English countryside—from the comic rooster and his bevy of hens, who open the ballet, to its close, when the cast members dance out into the open air, singing as they go.

The leading roles were made for two younger dancers, Nadia Nerina and David Blair, making full use not only of their sunny personalities but also of their virtuosity. The Widow Simone, traditionally a travesty role, was created by Stanley Holden, who enriched it with a comic instinct originating in the British music hall (his Clog Dance was straight from Lancashire). As Alain, the foolish suitor, Alexander Grant was both funny and touching.

ASHTON. Michael Somes and Margot Fonteyn as the original leading couple in Ashton's *Birthday Offering* (1956), a ballet made for the twenty-fifth anniversary of the Sadler's Wells Ballet, which soon afterward became the Royal Ballet. (Photograph by Jack Blake; from the Dance Collection, New York Public Library for the Performing Arts.)

Fille, a masterpiece, has held the stage since its first performance in January 1960. *The Two Pigeons*, made a year later for the touring section of the Royal Ballet, was in a similar vein. Again Ashton took a simple story and an unpretentious score, composed by André Messager in 1886 (also adapted by Lanchbery), and used them to convey a statement on the nature of love, rising to emotional heights in the final pas de deux of reconciliation. Here, too, Ashton extended a seemingly unimportant idea, the birdlike movements of the heroine in the first scene, into an unexpectedly resonant poetic metaphor. And once more, he worked with young dancers, Lynn Seymour and Christopher Gable. Not as immediately successful as *Fille* and still not as widely known, *Two Pigeons* has nevertheless become a much loved ballet.

At the end of 1960, the main company presented a new work of a very different kind, Ashton's version of Stravinsky's difficult choral ballet *Persephone*, with a text by French author André Gide. Ashton's task was made easier by the fact that Beriosova, in the title role, was not only a great dancer but also had a beautiful speaking voice. *Persephone* never became a popular success, and the large-scale musical forces it demanded made it unlikely to enter the regular repertory, but it showed Ashton as a mature choreographer at the height of his powers.

Ashton had for some time been looking for a subject for Fonteyn. He finally settled on Alexandre Dumas *fils*'s *La Dame aux Camélias*, and by the time he started work on it there was no doubt who would appear opposite her—Rudolf Nureyev. Their partnership began with the 1962 season when Nureyev, recently defected from the Kirov Ballet, gave a performance with Fonteyn of Ashton's 1960 staging of *Giselle*. *Marguerite and Armand*, as the new ballet was known—Ashton's ultimate homage to Fonteyn—was first given in April 1963 by the firmly established partners.

At the end of the 1962/63 season de Valois retired as director of the Royal Ballet and was succeeded by Ashton. (Ashton and Lambert, in 1948, had been named joint artistic directors with de Valois, but these would seem to have been honorific titles, especially in Lambert's case given his state of health, to acknowledge their parts in the company's artistic development.) Although Ashton delegated much of the administrative work to his assistants, Michael Somes and John Hart, he took his job seriously. His own contributions to the repertory became less frequent, but he saw to it that other choreographers received their due. Balanchine's *Serenade* and *Apollo* were added to the repertory. Nureyev staged the Kingdom of Shades scene from Petipa's *La Bayadère*. Antony Tudor was invited to revive his *Jardin aux Lilas* and to choreograph two new ballets. Most important of all, Bronislava Nijinska's masterpieces *Les Biches* and *Les Noces* were brought back to the stage after years of neglect.

ASHTON. The final scene of Ashton's *Ondine* (1958), with the original principals, Margot Fonteyn and Michael Somes (center), and female dancers of the Royal Ballet. Ashton choreographed this water-nymph ballet to highlight the special qualities of Fonteyn's dancing, but after a brief stay in the repertory, it sank under the weight of Hans Werner Henze's leaden score. (Photograph by Roger Wood; used by permission.)

Under Ashton's direction the Royal corps de ballet became the finest in the world, dancing with a new breadth and fullness, a development undoubtedly due in part to their working with Nureyev on *La Bayadère*. In December 1963 the company presented a new staging of *Swan Lake* with choreographic additions by Ashton, notably in the last act, a beautifully elegiac composition in which the corps de ballet played a leading part.

In April 1964, on the four hundredth anniversary of Shakespeare's birth, the Royal Ballet presented a special program that included a revival of Helpmann's ballet *Hamlet;* a new ballet by Kenneth MacMillan, *Images of Love;* and Ashton's *The Dream.* At the time, even Ashton seemed to regard this as a routine assignment, but his ballet proved to be an enduring masterpiece. More than a straightforward translation of *A Midsummer Night's Dream,* his version was another statement on the nature of love, comically depicted in the imbroglio of the mortal couples and in Titania's infatuation with the transfigured Bottom and poetically depicted in the final pas de deux of Titania and Oberon. In the roles of Titania and Oberon, Ashton cast two young dancers, Antoinette Sibley and An-

thony Dowell, thereby initiating another of the great partnerships of modern ballet.

Ashton produced one short work in 1965, a pas de trois for a gala performance, but its importance was out of all proportion to its scale. *Monotones,* to Erik Satie's *Trois Gymnopédies,* danced by three of the purest classical dancers in the company, Dowell, Vyvyan Lorrayne, and Robert Mead, was a further distillation of Ashton's personal classicism as defined in *Symphonic Variations.* A year later Ashton added a second trio, to Satie's *Trois Gnossiennes,* for Sibley, Georgina Parkinson, and Brian Shaw.

As director of the Royal Ballet, Ashton felt an obligation to give its touring section a new ballet, but *Sinfonietta* (1967) proved to be a minor work to an undistinguished score by Malcolm Williamson. So too was *Jazz Calendar* (1968), for the main company, to another inferior score, this one by Richard Rodney Bennett; the most interesting feature of this ballet was the pop art decor by Derek Jarman.

Later in 1968 Ashton created a more personal work, *Enigma Variations,* to a series of musical portraits composed by Edward Elgar in 1899 of his wife and friends. Ashton followed Elgar's scheme; on the face of it, the ballet is an almost naturalistic set of character studies, an impression reinforced by Julia Trevelyan Oman's scenery and costumes, with their wealth of authentic detail. But like nearly all Ashton's ballets, *Enigma Variations* is firmly based on the classic technique, both in the individual dances and in the almost conventional structure of the finale. Ashton's mastery of this language was such that he could use it to express the most subtle nuances of personal relations, as in the Nimrod pas de trois, which encapsulates the relationship of Elgar, his wife, and his best friend. (In dance terms, it is close to the first *Monotones.*) Once again the Royal Ballet revealed itself to be an extraordinary ensemble of dancer-actors, led in this instance by Derek Rencher, as the Composer, and Beriosova, as His Wife.

Only a poet could have conceived a ballet such as *Enigma.* In contrast, Ashton's next large-scale work, his version of Beethoven's *The Creatures of Prometheus,* created for the touring company in 1970, lacked any personal quality. At the time of its premiere, in Bonn on the occasion of the Beethoven bicentennial, Ashton's retirement was imminent. At the end of that Covent Garden season in July, the company held a farewell gala that took the form of a retrospective, including excerpts from Ashton ballets long since dropped from the repertory.

There was no immediate rest for Ashton, however, since he was committed to doing the choreography for a dance

ASHTON. Rudolf Nureyev and Margo Fonteyn as the title characters in *Marguerite and Armand* (1963). Ashton created this ballet specifically to showcase the celebrated Fonteyn-Nureyev partnership; it has never been performed by other dancers. (Photograph from the Dance Collection, New York Public Library for the Performing Arts.)

ASHTON. David Blair as Colas and Nadia Nerina as Lise in a ribbon dance from Ashton's version of *La Fille Mal Gardée* (1960). (Photograph by Houston Rogers; used by permission of the Board of Trustees of the Theatre Museum, London.)

film, *Tales of Beatrix Potter,* with dancers from the Royal Ballet, in which he was to appear as Mrs. Tiggy-Winkle. But for the next five years he confined himself mainly to arranging short numbers for favorite dancers, usually for gala performances. Of these, the "Meditation" from the opera *Thaïs* by Jules Massenet, for Sibley and Dowell in 1971 was in fact a small masterpiece. One larger project in which Ashton became involved was Benjamin Britten's 1973 opera *Death in Venice,* based on Thomas Mann's novella.

In 1976 Ashton came out of retirement to make a full-scale ballet, *A Month in the Country,* from Ivan Turgenev's play; he had considered the idea several years before but had put it aside. Lanchbery arranged three early works of Chopin into a seamless score that supported the action at every turn. The structure of the ballet reduces the action of the play into a series of dances, including several pas de deux, linked by passages of pantomime (a form of silent acting rather than conventional gestures). Again Ashton worked with favorite dancers in the leading roles, Lynn Seymour as Natalia, the *femme de trente ans;* and Dowell as her son's tutor, Beliaev, with whom she falls in love.

Following the production of his ballet, Ashton again restricted himself to making small occasional *divertissements* until 1980, when in honor of the Queen Mother's eightieth birthday he created a brilliant pure dance work, *Rhapsody*, to music by Sergei Rachmaninov, as a vehicle to display the virtuosity of both Mikhail Baryshnikov, who danced as guest artist at the first performance, and his partner Lesley Collier. In 1981 Ashton created the choreography for Stravinsky's opera *Le Rossignol*, which was danced at the Metropolitan Opera House in New York (and two years later at Covent Garden) by Natalia Makarova and Anthony Dowell.

Ashton was always grateful to American audiences for their support during the difficult years of the 1950s and was therefore happy to make a brief *jeu d'esprit* for the opening of the Royal Ballet's New York season in April 1983; *Varii Capricci* was danced by Sibley and Dowell to music by Ashton's old friend William Walton. Both this ballet and *Le Rossignol* were designed by the English painter David Hockney.

Ashton also came out of retirement occasionally to supervise rehearsals of his ballets; in the mid-1980s he entered into a new relationship with the London Festival Ballet, whose artistic director, Peter Schaufuss, was anxious to revive the *Romeo and Juliet* that Ashton had choreographed for the Royal Danish Ballet in 1955—and in which Schaufuss's parents had danced leading roles. The ballet had not been performed in its entirety since 1966

but was revived by Niels Bjørn Larsen with the help of films and notations he had made when the ballet was still in the repertory. Ashton himself made several changes and additions, and the ballet was then given by Festival Ballet in the summer of 1985. In 1987 that company also presented a revival of *Apparitions*, which had been out of the Royal Ballet repertory for almost thirty years; this revival was staged by Jean Bedells. In 1988 Natalia Makarova staged *Swan Lake* for Festival Ballet, incorporating various Ashton additions (the pas de quatre, the Neapolitan dance, and the whole of act 4) that had been dropped from the latest Royal Ballet revival.

George Balanchine is famous for having said "Ballet is woman," and his ballets do indeed show him to have been a worshiper of women. But of all twentieth-century choreographers, Ashton showed the most empathy for women. It has been said of him that every role he wrote for a ballerina was ideally for Anna Pavlova, his first inspiration. At her death, Pavlova was said to have been considering the commissioning of new ballets from both Ashton (having seen his *Capriol Suite* and *Leda and the Swan*) and Balanchine. Although this never came to pass, Ashton made ballets for many of the great *danseuses* of his time: Tamara Karsavina and Lydia Lopokova, Alicia Markova and Alexandra Danilova, Margot Fonteyn, Moira Shearer, Svetlana Beriosova, Antoinette Sibley, Nadia Nerina, Lynn Seymour (for whom in 1976 he made *Five Brahms Waltzes in the Manner of Isadora Duncan*, in homage to the other

ASHTON. Dancers of the Royal Ballet in Ashton's *Enigma Variations* (1968), a ballet structured as a series of character sketches. (Photograph from the Dance Collection, New York Public Library for the Performing Arts.)

ASHTON. Lesley Collier with members of the Royal Ballet in *Rhapsody* (1980), one of Ashton's last ballets. (Photograph by Anthony Crickmay; used by permission of the Board of Trustees of the Theatre Museum, London.)

dancer who had inspired him at the beginning of his career), Renée Jeanmaire, Tanaquil Le Clercq, Melissa Hayden, Diana Adams, and Natalia Makarova.

In addition to the ballets that Ashton created for companies other than his own, works he originally made for the Royal Ballet have been revived by companies all over the Western world. His contribution to British ballet has received official recognition in the form of many awards and titles: Commander of the Order of the British Empire (1950), a knighthood (1962), Companion of Honour (1970), and Order of Merit (1977). France admitted him to the Légion d'Honneur in 1962, and Denmark made him a Commander of the Order of the Dannebrog in 1963. He also received honorary degrees from the universities of Birmingham, Durham, East Anglia, London, and Oxford.

Ashton often used to prophesy that after his death, his works would be considered dated, and it is true that they fell into neglect even at the Royal Ballet, which should have done the most to preserve its heritage. However, there was some improvement in 1994, when the ninetieth anniversary of his birth was celebrated in an important conference at the Roehampton Institute in London and by a number of revivals by the Royal Ballet and other companies.

Ashton was a consummate storyteller in dance whose ballets move spectators to both laughter and tears. But his chief preoccupation was always that of every true choreographer: the movement of bodies in space and time. "The older I get," he once wrote, "the less interested I am in ballets of the pests, persecutions and cynicism of contemporary life, and frankly, I only like ballets which give an opportunity for real dancing. . . . A re-statement of one's own personal idiom of the classical ballet is all I ask to be able to achieve."

[*See also* Royal Ballet *and the entries on principal figures and works mentioned herein.*]

BIBLIOGRAPHY

Dominic, Zoë, and John Gilbert Selwyn. *Frederick Ashton.* London, 1971.

Jordan, Stephanie, and Andrée Grau, eds. *Following Sir Fred's Steps/Ashton's Legacy. Proceedings of the Ashton Conference, Roehampton Institute, London, 12–13 November 1994.* London, 1996.

Kavanagh, Julie. *Secret Muses: The Life of Frederick Ashton.* London, 1996.

Macaulay, Alastair. *Some Views and Reviews of Ashton's Choreography.* Guildford, 1987.

Vaughan, David. *Frederick Ashton and His Ballets.* London, 1977.

DAVID VAUGHAN

ASIAN DANCE TRADITIONS. [*To survey the diversity of dance throughout Asia, this entry comprises three articles:*

An Overview
The Influence of Puppetry
Religious, Philosophical, and
Environmental Influence

The introductory article surveys the cultural implications of epic tales, a comparison of Asian and Western attitudes toward dance, common technical elements, the transmission of dance traditions, and a general discussion on music and costumes. The second article discusses shadow theater and puppetry; the third article examines Asian dance traditions in terms of religion, time and place, climate, culture, and history. For related discussions, see Costume in Asian Traditions *and the Asian-related articles in the entries* Aesthetics; Mask and Makeup; *and* Music for Dance.]

An Overview

In Asia, cultural and social groups identify with "national" epics—long narrative poems about the deeds of a traditional or historical hero or heroes. These oral or written literatures combine history, myth, ethics, mysticism, morals, and social mores. They serve as timeless reminders of an individual's social or ethnic identity, often representing a standard against which the rest of the world and the march of current events are measured.

Cultural Implications of Epic Identity. For millennia and through the generations, epics have been told and retold, as accompanied or unaccompanied song, as ritual enactments, as puppet plays, as fragments of dance dramas, as whole dance cycles, and as dance theater. From the prescribed general movements of religious ritual to the particular gestures, facial expressions, and masks that establish specific characterization, epic identity is the source from which dance in Asia is created and the foundation from which it grows.

Epics such as the Indian *Mahābhārata* and *Rāmāyaṇa* have spread from South Asia to many parts of Southeast Asia, where they have long since been accepted as indigenous. On the Indonesian island of Bali, for example, the religious literature of Balinese Hinduism forms a primary source of epic identity, even though this literature originated in India. Told as puppet plays and dance dramas, episodes from the Hindu epics are durable threads in the fabric of Balinese life. Historical stories, performed by the famous *légong* dancers of Bali, form another part of Balinese identity. The two Indian epics came to Bali via the East Javanese empire known as Majapahit during the fourteenth and fifteenth centuries, but on the island of Java itself, Islam has been the dominant religion for the past three centuries. Even so, the epic identity of earlier times remains so strong that the Hindu-derived *Ma-*

hābhārata and *Rāmāyaṇa* remain the principal literature of the Javanese puppet play and the dance drama, notwithstanding Java's acceptance of Islam.

Likewise, bygone courtly splendor persists in the dances of Thailand, Cambodia, Laos, and Burma (Myanmar)—testimony to the former patronage of royalty and the lasting imprint of an epic identity, also based on the stories from India.

A highly developed dance genre of southern India, *bharata nāṭyam*, contains a rich vocabulary of hand gestures. The dancer interprets Hindu religious poetry line by line, often performing several different danced versions of each line. These performances are rendered with such sensitivity that Indian audiences may be moved to tears by the danced imagery of their epic identity. [*See* India, *articles on* Epic Sources of Indian Dance *and* The Rādhā-Kṛṣṇa Theme in Indian Dance.]

In Japan, the legacy of medieval aristocratic warrior-class samurai culture has become part of the living epic identity of the *nō* drama, the puppet theater called *bunraku*, the courtly dances of *bugaku*, and the popular *kabuki* theater. As in Java and Bali, Japan's puppet theater had an initial and lasting effect on the stories, movements, and costumes of the dance theater. The incredibly humanlike movements of the *bunraku* puppets, the stylized and symbolic movements of the *nō* dancer-actor, and the dramatic gesturing and stances of the *kabuki* performer all awaken latent images of epic identity in Japanese audiences.

Distilled through centuries of artistic expression, the epic identity of a society is indelible and will endure for as long as the society. This sacred link between epic and artistic expression is the primal catalyst of dance in Asia.

Asian versus Western Dance. The strong bond between Asian epics and the dance styles through which they live produces basic differences between Asian and Western audiences, techniques, concepts of performance space, and pedagogy, as well as differences between the ways in which music relates to dance in Asia and the West.

Audiences. In Asia, the terms for *audience* carry a different connotation from the usual meaning of "audience" in Western cultures. Because of their strong personal identification with the stories and characterizations, Asian audiences might better be thought of as indirect participants in the dance dramas themselves. Throughout Asia there is a common belief that the ancestors are watching over society. Particular evidence of this belief in Southeast Asia is a feast held to honor the ancestors as a means of warding off disease, economic disaster, and other evils. Friends and neighbors are invited to witness and share in the event, and dance is a significant part of the occasion.

To explore some of the differences between Eastern and

Western dance audiences, one might compare classical ballet with traditional Asian dance-drama types. In the West, classical ballet, whatever its national stamp, attracts a generally elite audience. As with Western opera, some portion of the audience attends more for social reasons than for the enjoyment of dance. In Asia today, although members of the elite classes often attend performances of dance dramas that in past eras were court-sponsored, these elite spectators are also highly knowledgeable about dance, an art that is part of their aristocratic schooling. In major Asian cities, however, the characteristically large audiences for traditional dance are drawn mostly from the general public. In Tokyo, the high admission price for *kabuki* theater does not discourage sold-out performances, which can begin at 11:00 AM and run into the night. In Beijing, nightly performances of Beijing Opera also result in sold-out houses. Classical-dance performances in India are no longer limited to elite audiences but may attract as many as fifteen thousand spectators when famous dancers perform. And Japanese, Chinese, and Indian audiences are well-qualified critics of the performances they witness.

It is also possible to compare the extent and kind of communication achieved between Asian and Western dancers and audiences. The story and characterizations of *Swan Lake, Les Sylphides,* or *Le Spectre de la Rose* tend not to arouse feelings of personal identity among Western audience members, no matter how superlative the performance. In contrast, for many Asians, the gods and heroes of the *Mahābhārata* represent the story of their own ancestry. A dance drama based on one of the three thousand episodes of the epic, therefore, readily establishes a personal identity in the minds and hearts of the audience.

Moving beyond classical ballet and traditional dance drama, one discovers yet other differences. For the most part, in the West, different kinds of dance—ballet, modern dance, Broadway pop-jazz, and, of course, the array of social dance including ballroom, rock, and disco—attract recognizably different audiences. In Asia, by contrast, audiences for dance tend to be undifferentiated, except in large cities such as Tokyo, where Western ballet, modern dance, traditional *nō, kabuki,* and *bunraku* have noticeably different followings. In Southeast Asia, the classical dance drama, once fostered by the royal courts, continues to be performed in the most remote villages. Formerly, the great clans of southern China sponsored performances of *kunqu,* a form of opera associated with the literati; but these performances, held in connection with sacrifices to clan ancestors, took place outside the family temple, and the populace of the local village would also attend.

Rituals involving dance are communal activities in Asia. "Folk dance" in the Western sense of the term does not exist; rather, one finds religious or secular ritual dance.

Techniques. A goodly number of the members of any Western ballet audience will recognize the standard elements of ballet's movement vocabulary—*grand jetés, entrechats,* and so on. A smaller number will appreciate how well the vocabulary of the ballet is being executed. A few discerning members of the audience will distinguish

ASIAN DANCE TRADITIONS: An Overview. Three young dancers of the Royal Cambodian Ballet, c.1900. Until 1970, the Royal Household at Phnom Penh supported a company of performers, called *lakhon lueng,* or "king's dancers." (Reprinted from Jukka O. Miettinen, *Classical Dance and Theatre in South-East Asia,* Singapore, 1992, p. 145.)

those rare moments when the prima ballerina achieves a quality of movement and height of characterization that transcend pyrotechnic display.

At this technical level of communication there is some similarity between East and West, notwithstanding the contrast in dance vocabularies. But there is a major difference in the subtlety and complexity of technique, and of audience members' understanding. In Asia, the particular style and quality of movement and the multiple stylized elements of the *mise-en-scène*—costumes, facial makeup, hair ornaments, abstract stage properties—are all theatrical conventions and indications of characterization.

In the traditional classical dance genres of Asia, physical movements, gestures, and expressions fulfill general requirements of characterization. At a higher level of characterization, particular dramatis personae require specific movements. The highest level of dance vocabulary establishes the character's mood or state of mind (angry, meditating, in love) and even the specific exigencies of the dramatic situation in which the character is involved—for example, the etiquette appropriate to an audience with a refined king, the demands of valor that weigh on a medieval warrior defending his castle, and so on. Within the tradition of this minutely defined vocabulary, there are also subtle shades of movement that permit the solo dancer freedom for improvisation, individual style, and display of technical skill.

ASIAN DANCE TRADITIONS: An Overview. Ichikawa Danjūrō XII in the *kabuki* drama *Kanjincho*. (Photograph © 1985 by Jack Vartoogian; used by permission.)

Relation to space. Asian and Western dancers relate to space in contrasting ways. In the West, the ballet or modern dancer seeks to defy gravity with leaps and great extensions into space. Space is an element to conquer, to invade, to overcome, to be freely explored and subdued. In the East, despite the variability of basic dance positions from tradition to tradition, the dancer is in all instances earthbound, and space is a contained area in which dance occurs.

Throughout Asian traditions, dancers' feet are anchored to the ground, often with the weight on the heels but toes upturned. In India, for example, *kathakaḷi* requires performers to dance continuously on the sides of their feet—a dramatic contrast (if equally crippling) to the ballerina on pointe.

In South Asia, classical dance, fostered by the elite, was placed in an intimate surrounding for a small audience. The Indian *devadāsī* was a temple dancer whose theatrical space was defined by the place of religious worship. (Ritual dances and processions by the common folk were held in vast outdoor spaces.)

In Southeast Asia, social stratification directly affected the basic body position of the dancer. Javanese dancers performed their roles in a crouching position in the presence of royalty, since no one's head was allowed to be higher than that of the ruler seated on his throne. This custom can still be seen in residual form, when the dancer enters the side of the dance pavilion of a princely residence. At this moment, and in appropriate situations throughout the drama, three levels of formal supplication

are performed. Known as the *sembah*, the lowest level is in recognition of the general audience; the middle level is in recognition of the ancestors, including living royalty; and the highest level is in recognition of the gods. The persistence of the earlier practice can be seen in *langen mandra wanara*, a dance style executed on the knees throughout the drama; it is still performed today on rare occasion. For a thousand years, the court dances of Java have been emulated in the villages in the modest surroundings afforded by local conditions. After the colonial Dutch action in 1908 nearly decimated all royal families in southern Bali, patronage for music and dance gradually became the communal responsibility of the village. Here, the dance area is arranged outside a temple wall, the earthen floor covered with mats and the rectangular dance space defined by four umbrellas.

Music and dance. In Asia, the relationship between dance and music is quite specific. Standard pieces of music accompany standard character types, specific structural sections of the drama, and particular characters and dramatic moods. The court orchestras of Asia perform with predictable regularity according to each type of piece, so that long, medium, and short dance phrases coincide with structural divisons in the music. In Java and Bali the dancer may even "direct" the music by designating changes of tempo, dynamics, phrase lengths, and even when and where to stop—all in the course of an actual performance.

In the West, whether in ballet or modern dance, the relationship between music and dance is more casual, so that it is quite acceptable to create very different choreographies for the same piece of music. Even music composed especially for the choreographer shows considerable latitude in accommodating structural and accentual aspects of the dance.

Professionalism and pedagogy. There is also a considerable difference between Eastern and Western conceptions of the professional or amateur status of the dancer. In East Asia, professional dancers—persons who earn their living solely by dancing—are limited to a few metropolitan centers. Elsewhere, dancers also tend to be teachers of dance, spending much of their time in this occupation, or performers who also ply other trades—as farmers, government clerks, artisans, and the like.

Moreover, there is great contrast between Eastern and Western dance training. Even the personal goals of the dancer show a basic difference, East and West. In Asia, the ultimate achievement of the dancer is to attain recognition as a great teacher. In the West, a dancer's achievements tend to be measured in terms of the number, quality, and locations of performances given.

Fundamental differences also exist in the methods of teaching dance. In the West, strict regimentation in discipline and routines is expected by every serious teacher of ballet, modern dance, or jazz dance. Hours and hours of daily drill are demanded to achieve desired technique and to mold the body and its musculature in attaining a quality that projects across the footlights. Some teachers' shouted dance directions are as loud and fierce as those of an army drill sergeant.

In the East, dancers are chosen according to physical type, selected because of an innate quality, and trained from a very young age—not in technique as such but rather in the total fulfillment of a particular role and characterization. Throughout Asia the approach is nonverbal, learning by rote and imitation. Corrections are made by adjustment through body contact, not verbal reprimands. The adjustments are made again and again, until the pupil is finally an accomplished traditional dancer, who may someday reach the highest plateau of the dance profession and become, in turn, a teacher.

Preservation and continuity. Some in the West incorrectly view the dance traditions of Asia as completely ossified, but, in fact, for several thousand years these dance styles have steadily accommodated change within the continuity of tradition. India has influenced China; China has influenced Korea and Japan; Southeast Asia and Indonesia have continually been a crossroads of external influences; and most of Asia has had cultural influences from the Middle East. No art form, East or West, remains unchanged. Although periods of relative isolation occur, all arts are dynamic and constantly receive greater or lesser infusions from within and outside the cultures in which they live.

The steady encroachment of international audiovisual communications is now producing more rapid change. First, recorded music and radio, then the motion picture industry, and, most recently, television have all made inroads throughout Asia—with many implications for Asian dance traditions.

Since the late 1960s, an increasing number of international dance troupes has been performing throughout the world. The performers and their managers, promoters, and producers are hardly oblivious to the professional hallmarks of dance or to the technological wonders of the world through which they travel. Sequins and flashy decorations are replacing traditional gold thread, ikat cloth, and gold leaf on pierced buffalo hide. Performers adopt a frontal orientation as they address the proscenium arch rather than the confines of a village square, an outdoor temple, or a teahouse. Subtleties that would be lost beyond the tenth row of the concert hall are minimized and gradually omitted altogether. Extracultural borrowings occur in the showy range of dance techniques and acrobatics.

Technology and the global audience have unquestionably accelerated the rate of change. And yet, as in past centuries, there is continuity in the traditions of Asian dance. Even in the face of rapid, bewildering change there is a stubborn tenacity.

East Asia. For centuries, cultural interchange took place among three major areas of East Asia: China, Korea, and Japan. Each of these cultures has also been influenced by forces external to East Asia. These influences and interchanges are visible in many art forms, including dance.

China. The court traditions of China had a profound and lasting influence on both Korea and Japan. Rituals derived from the Zhou dynasty (1027–256 BCE), combined with the philosophical teachings of Confucius (551–497 BCE) became the foundation for development of *yayue*, the ritual music of Confucianism. For two thousand years, until the revolution of 1911, Confucianism was the official religion of every successive Chinese state, and its music the official music. After the decline of the royal courts in China and Korea, *yayue* has been performed only in Confucian temples and in the National Institute of Classical Music in Seoul.

Yayue consisted of two types: one for indoor, the other for outdoor music, which accompanied dance. Instrumental ensembles made up of various types of gong-chime instruments, played outdoors, were used to accompany *wenwu* (civilian dance) and *wuwu* (military dance). The precise instrumentation differed according to the political class. The two types of dance had corresponding specifications according to the rank of the dignitaries who officiated: 64 dancers arranged in a square of 8 by 8 persons was proper for the emperor; 48 dancers, 8 by 6, was appropriate for lords; 32 dancers, 8 by 4, for ministers; and 16 dancers, 8 by 2, sufficed for lower officials. The civilian dancer played a *xiao*, or end-blown flute, and the military dancer performed with a sword or shield.

Nowhere in Asia is the unity of movement, music, and sung speech more perfectly blended than in China. Specific musical categories often included dance; for example, the ancient general term for "banquet music" implicitly included dance. During the Tang dynasty the so-called Ten Kinds of Music referred not only to popular Chinese music and music from India, central Asia, and Korea but also to grand dance productions combining both Chinese and foreign elements. The category known as Two Kinds of Music was established in the eighth century and consisted of fourteen spectacular dance compositions divided into two types, one for outdoor entertainment in the garden and one for indoor entertainment in the great hall. This tradition was maintained until the end of the Qing dynasty (1912).

There are more than three hundred regional forms of Chinese opera with various styles of movement, music, and sung speech. Some types are popular throughout large regions of the country; many are known only in small districts. This bewildering variety of regional theater is sometimes grouped into four categories. *Gaoqiang* developed in the early sixteenth century based on village folk idioms and spread quickly through the trade routes and provinces along the Yangzi. *Kunqu* also developed in the sixteenth century as a much more sophisticated style of opera based on early literary dramas. The clapper opera from northern China was based on popular folk sources; during the eighteenth century it spread south, influencing especially the opera of Sichuan and moving from there to Beijing in 1779. Two forms known collectively as *pihuang* were combined in the eighteenth century to lay the foundation for the development of Beijing Opera in 1790.

All these styles of opera and their local variants and combinations have certain features in common. They are either civilian (*wen*), based on lyrical love stories, or military (*wu*), based on heroic tales and featuring incredible acrobatics. Characters, makeup, costumes, and basic movements tend to be standardized as male roles (*sheng*), female roles enacted by men (*dan*), clown roles (*chou*), and so forth.

By 1790, the two kinds of opera from southern China, known collectively as *pihuang*, were combined to form Beijing Opera; teahouses were the usual theaters for these productions, and socializing and conversing competed with the entertainment. Beijing Opera was also featured in the private parties held in restaurant-theaters, guild halls, and wealthy homes. Young boys were sold under contract to opera companies and trained to play women's roles, a practice that dominated the early years of Beijing Opera. In the late nineteenth century, increasing emphasis was placed on the heroic drama. During this period, the former prejudice held by the royal courts against what had been considered a vulgar form of theater disappeared, and Beijing Opera found royal patronage that sustained it through the close of the Qing dynasty (1912). From the early Republic of China until the formation of the People's Republic, 1912 to 1949, many star performers developed in Beijing Opera; the best known were Mei Lanfang, Cheng Yanqiu, Yang Xiaolou, and You Shuyan. Prominent citizens replaced royal patrons in supporting the continuing popularity of the teahouse theaters where Beijing Opera flourished.

Since 1949, the communist government of the People's Republic of China shifted the emphasis of plot and action away from the lives of feudal aristocracy and the bourgeoisie to the concerns of workers, peasants, and soldiers. Repression during China's Cultural Revolution (1966–1977) eliminated traditional themes, which were replaced by heroic plots lauding class struggle and revolutionary causes. Since the end of the Cultural Revolution, there has been a gradual return to more traditional themes, although modern stories are still popular, especially in the vigorous military style of opera. Methods of training have

ASIAN DANCE TRADITIONS: An Overview. Women from the Performing Arts Company, a contemporary Chinese troupe, in *The Red Silk Dance*, a work inspired by traditional ribbon dances. (Photograph © 1978 by Jack Vartoogian; used by permission.)

been modernized, so that all actors have both a normal schooling and an education in the theater arts. After some years of the communist regime, the earlier restriction to either all-male or all-female casts was finally abolished. The tradition of males playing female roles is no longer seen.

A fertility dance called *yangke,* traditionally performed in the spring in the northwestern province of Shaanxi, became a primary vehicle for the revolutionary ideology of the People's Liberation Army as it combated the Japanese invasion that had begun in 1937. As a folk rite *yangke* was performed by young men and women. The leader carried a rake or hoe, and the girls carried umbrellas; male and female opposing lines danced in a simple but energetic pattern of three steps forward, one swinging step backward and sideways. This basic step had many variations, according to the particular characters being enacted by the dancers, but usually the swinging movements in this fertility dance were sexually suggestive. Songs were essentially questions and answers between the young men and

women about love themes or congratulatory greetings. Solo roles were complemented by the fanciful ground patterns of two weaving lines of boys and girls, accompanied by percussion instruments and the *hu qin,* a two-stringed bowed lute.

Over a period of time, this simple folk rite was adapted by the communist forces for propaganda purposes. The two opposing lines were conjoined as a circle dance. Guns and flags replaced hoes and umbrellas; uniform dress was substituted for male and female attire; love themes were replaced by political messages. As this new version of *yangke* theater developed, it spread over much of China and was finally adopted by the intellectuals, who had formerly scoffed at this type of theater as lowbrow entertainment but who now gave the movement enthusiastic support. By this point, some of China's finest theatrical talent had been enlisted. *Yangke* theater became a regular weekly event in many parts of China, developed an avid following among university students, and reached something of an apex in productions that lasted four or five hours. Today, it has disappeared, but the merger of peasant and intellectual interest in a common dance theater has resulted in communal efforts that have probably affected all types of dance in China.

Some influence of ballet can be seen in modern Beijing Opera productions. Occasionally on television, a greatly modified style of "ballet" is placed in a rural or rustic setting. As the years that separate the disastrous Cultural Revolution from the present grow, new developments will undoubtedly occur in many forms of Chinese dance. [*See* China *and* Kunqu.]

Korea. According to Chinese sources, the earliest forms of Korean music and dance were ritual festivities connected with planting and harvest that were practiced by the tribal states of Korea before 57 BCE. During the period of the Three Kingdoms (57 BCE–633 CE), contacts between northern Korea and China brought Chinese influences in court music and dance. In southern Korea during this period, different Chinese influences resulted in the rise of masked dance dramas, forms of which are still popular today. In the southeast, the Silla kingdom managed the unification of Korea by 668 CE, creating a military alliance with the Tang dynasty of China (618–906). After this time, Chinese influences were even stronger, and the designation *tangak* ("Tang music") was used for Chinese-influenced music that developed after the unification of Korea, as distinct from *hyangak*, indigenous Korean music. Both musical genres included their respective dance traditions.

During Korea's Koryŏ dynasty (918–1392), court ritual music and dance of Chinese origin reached Korea. Called *aak*, it consisted of indoor and outdoor genres, including civilian and military types of ritual dance, *munmu* and *mumu*, respectively. Banquet music and dance of Song-dynasty (960–1279) China were introduced and took their place alongside the native Korean court banquet music and dance. During Korea's early Yi dynasty (1392–1593), greater emphasis was placed on Korean traditions, with a corresponding waning of Chinese forms. In 1493, the *Akhak Kwebom* (Book of Music) was published; it included chapters on Chinese and Korean dances of earlier periods, contemporary Chinese dances, contemporary Korean dances, characteristics of Chinese and Korean dances, and costumes of musicians and dancers.

By the mid-seventeenth century, both *tangak* and *hyangak* were performed by the same orchestra, with a resulting Koreanization of the Chinese music. By the eighteenth century, the court traditions gave way in popularity to aristocratic and folk music, including the dramatic, one-person opera form called *p'ansori* and the related instrumental form *sanjo*, gaining the wide acceptance that persists to this day. During Korea's late Yi dynasty (1593–1910), Japanese and Manchurian invasions destroyed much of Korean culture, and the court tradition of *aak* disappeared. From 1910 until 1945, during which time Korea was annexed by Japan, *aak* was seldom performed and the distinction between *tangak* and *hyangak* became vague.

Since Korean independence, the National Music Insti-

ASIAN DANCE TRADITIONS: An Overview. Korean drummer in *nongak* (farmers' dance), featured in a program arranged by Samul-Nori and Company at The Asia Society, New York. This genre is the oldest extant music and dance tradition in Korea with influences from ritual dance and military drills. (Photograph by Darryl Pitt; used by permission of the Asia Society, New York.)

tute and Seoul National University have developed strong programs of traditional music and dance studies and encouraged new compositions based on traditional materials. Among the early traditional Korean performers were the *kisaeng*, female entertainers schooled in instrumental music, song, and dance. Many were prostitutes or concubines of royalty in former times, but despite low social status that resulted from these roles, the *kisaeng* occupied a central place in Korean culture. Today, the role of the female entertainer is still very strong in Korea.

The guiding aesthetic of Korean dance is controlled by an inner spirit of subtle restraint. Movement is emphasized by the shoulders, with a response from the arms and the head moving in affirmation. A loose-fitting costume reaches to the floor, its sleeves extended by long pieces of cloth called *hansam*, which cover the hands and magnify arm movements. Effective use of the *hansam* and an achievement of quiescence are primary techniques in Korean dance. The classical dancer may move or stand still and at the same time manage to achieve the spiritual exaltation brought by quiescence. Such is the spirit of the dance. Folk dance, on the other hand, is very active in execution.

A key characteristic of Korean dance is the precedence

of rhythm; rather than being accompanied by rhythm, dance creates its own rhythm. Traditionally, all masters of Korean dance were also excellent drummers. It is said that the ancient drummers of Korea could not suppress their feelings as they drummed—they had to stand up and dance.

Korean court dance, or *choyong*, is derived from early royal household festivities in which a narrator led the dancers to the stage, narrated the theme about to be performed, and closed with an epilogue. More than fifty court dances are still known, all typified by slow movements and the suggestion of grandeur: among them, the *chosun* dance of the Koguryŏ period, the sword dance and the *choyong* dance of the Silla period, the *ki-ak* dance of the Paikje period, the ball and crane dances of the Koryŏ period, and the *hangjang* dance and the nightingale-singing-in-the-spring dance of the Yi dynasty. Accompanying songs have explanatory texts, and the costumes reflect Confucian ideas.

In contrast to the elegant, slow, feminine court dances of Korea, Korean folk dances are animated, fast, masculine, and unrestrained in movement. One of the best known is the farmer's dance, performed at times of harvest and planting and on other occasions. Accompanied by drums and wind instruments, the dancers are dressed in brightly striped costumes and spin like tops, beating small drums and tossing long paper streamers attached to their hats in immense loops. This dramatic neck movement is the primary technique of the dance. Another popular dance is the (folk) sword dance, originally a vigorous dance performed by men but now a graceful dance performed by women. Yet another is a famous drum dance

performed with a long, slender *chang-ko* drum slung over the shoulder. The elaborate acrobatic movements suggest a Chinese origin (and the *chang-ko* is said to have been introduced from China during the Koryŏ dynasty). A variant requires the dancer to play as many as nine drums, which are held in racks, while the acrobatic choreography accelerates in tempo and physical challenge. [*See* Korea.]

Japan. Japanese historical development is often divided into five broad periods, which also represent five periods of development in the performing arts.

1. The Neolithic and the early Bronze Age in Japan are known vaguely from archaeological evidence and from written materials of the eighth century CE. A clan system slowly became a unified imperial state, and early shamanism was gradually systematized into the state religion, known as Shintō. Ceremonial music and dance were already part of court ritual by the time this earliest period ended.

2. In the fifth and sixth centuries, foreign styles from continental Asia began to invade Japan. Influences came first from Korea and then from China, greatly altering the nature of Japanese music and dance. The introduction of Korean Buddhism in the sixth century and of Chinese masked dances and pageants, called *gigaku*, in the sixth and seventh centuries had a profound affect. Shortly after this, various kinds of Korean and Chinese court music and dance were introduced; collectively, these are known as *gagaku*. Instruments preserved in the imperial treasure from the eighth century indicate that influence from abroad came not only from Korea and China but also from India, Persia, and Central Asia. During this second historical period, as the aristocracy began to replace the

ASIAN DANCE TRADITIONS: An Overview. A performer of *bugaku*, the imperial court dance of Japan, holding a spear in *Nin'naraku*. (Photograph © 1990 by Jack Vartoogian; used by permission.)

imperial government as sponsors of the arts, foreign aspects of *gagaku* were modified to suit Japanese taste.

3. By the tenth century, feudal society under a shogunate (hereditary military governors) had begun to control the cultural life of Japan. Gradually, court and Buddhist traditions were further modified, and by the fourteenth century the *nō* drama had developed, regarded by many Japanese as the perfect unification of music, dance, drama, and theater.

4. From the late sixteenth to the mid-nineteenth centuries, support for the arts began to arise among the merchant and artisan classes, although the ruling shogunate family continued to dominate the country. By the later part of the Edo period (1603–1868), *gagaku* and *nō* had ceased to function as entertainment and had become formal rituals for the court, temple, or samurai (warrior class) society.

5. After 1868, when Japan opened itself to the world, Western traditions and, more recently, international traditions were enthusiastically embraced. To some extent, this weakened the importance of older traditions, but it also ultimately gave rise to new genres, such as *butō*, that combine Western and indigenous Japanese styles.

A survivor in Japan, from ancient times, is the stately court dance called *bugaku*, still performed in the palace of the imperial household in Tokyo. The music of *gagaku*, which accompanies these slow, formal dances is divided into two repertories: *komagaku*, music derived from Korea, and *tōgaku*, music from China, including foreign music imported into China at the time of the Tang dynasty. The themes of *bugaku* are extremely abstract and may be performed by solo performers, duets, quartets, or larger groups. The performers are also practicing musicians of *gagaku*. The costumes are among the richest and most elaborate in all Asian theater. [*See* Bugaku *and* Gagaku.]

The *nō* drama has experienced a relatively recent revival of interest in Japan and is faithfully attended by enthusiastic intellectuals, who often read the text as it is chanted and sung by the dancer-actors. About 10 percent of the original two thousand dramas still survive. The staging has a beautiful simplicity, with the principal stage marked by four pillars, an adjoining rectangular area for the chorus, an upstage area for instrumentalists, and a long entry ramp. A stylized pine tree is painted on the back wall. There is a principal actor *(shite)*, second principal actor *(waki)*, and comic-relief actor *(kyōgen)*. As the principal figure the *shite* not only acts but also sings and dances. In fact, all movement by the actors is so formalized that it has become dance. The drama is composed of one or two acts; comic *kyōgen* actors perform while the principal actor is changing costumes for the second act, in which he often plays a role that contrasts with his role in the first act. [*See* Kyōgen *and* Nō.]

Popular since the beginning of the seventeenth century,

and today Japan's most widely attended form of theater, *kabuki* began as a theatrical form featuring prostitute performers. This was soon banned and replaced by a theater featuring young boys, also eventually banned. *Kabuki* finally developed into an all-male drama in which female impersonators have become especially famous. There are several genres: semihistorical pieces, stories about life in the Edo period, and modern plays. Complete dramas are quite long, so that, today, excerpts from several plays usually make up the program. The theater and stage are built on a grand scale, with both onstage and offstage orchestras as well as a long side ramp for dramatic entrances.

The usual, three-part form of *kabuki* corresponds to the three-part division common in Japanese music. *Kabuki* costuming is richly varied and elaborate. Principals become famous for the dramatic stances and poses with which they end phrases and sections. Many of these have been immortalized in portraits by Japanese printmakers who, especially in the nineteenth century, produced the style known as *ukiyo-e*. [*See* Kabuki Theater.]

India. For nearly three millennia, the civilization of India has exerted influence throughout Asia. Centuries of Indian philosophical, religious, and artistic thought—preserved in sacred literature and art—have ultimately touched all of the major cultures of the continent.

The earliest literary dance source is the *Ṛgveda* (between 1500 and 1000 BCE), which contains abundant references to dance in the form of epithets, metaphors, and similes. Epic Sanskrit literature, including works such as the *Rāmāyaṇa, Mahābhārata,* and genres such as *nāṭaka* and *kāvya* (eleventh century BCE to eighth century CE), has provided the primary framework for dance, music, and drama as forms of religious expression throughout Southeast Asia and much of East Asia.

The most detailed and comprehensive dance treatise is the *Nāṭyaśāstra,* written by Bharata (c.100–300 CE). Both descriptive and analytical, it presents the 108 *karaṇas* (units of movement), establishing the foundation of a scientific notation system. The *karaṇa*s can also be seen in bas-relief on the temples at Chidambaram, which date from the thirteenth century. (The earliest plastic record of Indian dance is in the bas-reliefs of the eighth-century Borobudur in central Java.) The *Bainaya-darpaṇa,* a treatise devoted exclusively to dance and included in the *Nandi Keśvara* (fifth through tenth centuries), defines dramatic expression and the meaning of postures and of gestures of the hands, feet, and face, and it illuminates the inseparability of dance, music, and poetry. It explains *nṛtta* (pure dance), *nāṭya* (the dramatic elements), *nṛtya* (sentiment and mood), and *abhinaya* (dramatic expression). In the thirteenth century, the *Saṅgīta-ratnākara* was devoted solely to dance; since then, there have been many texts devoted to the regional styles of the many areas of India.

Evidence of the importance of dance in India's religions

ASIAN DANCE TRADITIONS: An Overview. Masked performer of *nō*, the classical Japanese dance drama with origins in the fourteenth century. (Photograph © 1989 by Jack Vartoogian; used by permission.)

is found in the bas-reliefs that decorate countless temples and in paintings and freestanding sculptures of stone, terra cotta, wood, and bronze. In these diverse media, the "dancing gods" Śiva (Shiva), as Nāṭarāja, "Lord of the Dance," and Kṛṣṇa (Krishna) are portrayed in stylized poses.

Dance theory in India. Regional folk dance in India is rich and varied—so varied that it has not yet been systematically documented. In the classical forms of dance, however, a fully developed theory of dance exists.

The concept of *rasa* ("flavor," "root," "sap," "essence") is intrinsic to all forms of artistic expression in India. Dance is considered an art that uses the human body, spirit, and mind to express the deepest emotions and the innermost state of being. Body parts are distinguished as either *aṅga* (the major parts: head, torso, upper and lower limbs) or *upāṅga* (the minor parts, including the facial features from eyebrows to chin). In the concept of *nṛtta* (pure dance), abstract patterns of movement create perfectly designed sculptural postures through movement and music. In *nṛtta*, no facial expressions are used to establish mood or sentiment. In *nṛtya* (mime), mood and sentiment are expressed through an extensive vocabulary of facial expressions and related gestures. *Abhinaya* is the complete manner in which *nṛtya* is conveyed to an audience. The most famous twentieth-century Indian dancer, known especially for her inspirational *abhinaya*, was Balasaraswati. Her dramatic interpretations sometimes included four or five different expressions for a single line of poetry.

Preparation for studies in classical dance includes at least two years of instruction in both executing the vocal patterns of drum mnemonics and in singing. These two disciplines are fundamental in training the dancer in order to provide a sure knowledge of the complex rhythms *(tāla)* and microtonal melodies *(rāga)* for which India is famous.

Principal styles of Indian dance. The oldest and purest dance style in southern India is known as *bharata nāṭyam*. It is a solo dance, and in all but a few villages it is danced exclusively by women. A full program consists of seven sections: *alārippu, jātīśvaram, śabda, varṇam, padam, tillānā, śloka*. Each section emphasizes either *nṛtta* or *nṛtya*, displaying either the technical skill of the dancer or her ultimate artistry, achieved through *abhinaya*. There is no finer showcase for the truly accomplished Indian female artist. [*See* Bharata Nāṭyam.]

Historical and literary sources document the importance of dancers in the temple and the court. The *devadāsī* are professional temple dancers, responsible for a revival of interest in classical dance during the 1930s.

The style known as Kuchipudi influenced three groups of dancers: the *devadāsī*s, who performed devotional dances for festivals inside the temple; the *brahman*s, who stressed ritual dance dramas; and the *rāja nartaki*s, secular dancers who staged their productions outside the temples for various kinds of social occasions. Variations of existing forms, as well as new forms, arose, such as the Kuchipudi dance drama of Parijata Harana, which became the popular *bhama kalapana*, stressing the *abhinaya* or *viraha* (emotional intent) attributed to the god Kṛṣṇa. In this style all three elements appear: *nāṭya* (acting and dancing), *nṛtta*, and *nṛtya*. [*See* Devadāsī *and* Kuchipudi.]

Originating in Kerala, in southwestern India, in about the eighteenth century is the demanding, all-male style known as *kathakaḷi*. Its roots lie in both ritual and folk dance, and it arose from the elite-supported, Nayar military-gymnastic training. The rigorous, almost spartan, technique requires a vigorous physical preparation, which begins at age twelve and continues, for those who manage to survive it, for eight to twelve years.

The *kathakaḷi* student's body is massaged regularly to help him to achieve some of the most difficult and unusual positions known in any dance style. The weight of the body is carried on the outside edges of the soles of the feet. Every muscle of the dancer's face is trained to project an array of emotional expressions. During the prolonged, incredibly wide training period, students lie supine on the floor for long periods, with heavy weights placed on the outer parts of their thighs.

Preparation for a *kathakaḷi* performance requires three to four hours to apply the elaborate makeup. This procedure is a precise ritual in which the psychological and physical transformation of the dancer takes place. *Kathakaḷi* has six basic types of characters, each with its corresponding facial color, makeup design, and costume. These character types are depicted in many carvings and paintings on temple walls. A vegetable seed is placed inside the lower eyelid to color the white of the eye either rose (for a hero) or red (for a demon).

Before the *kathakaḷi* drama itself begins, there is an elaborate preprogram performance of devotional songs that display musical virtuosity and that may last as long as two hours. A full-length *kathakaḷi* drama runs from five to seven hours. The *kathakaḷi* repertory has more than one hundred different plays with texts taken from the *Rāmāyaṇa*, the *Mahābhārata*, and the *Bhāgavata Purāṇa*. The characters' entrances are dramatized by the actors' manipulation of the *tirasila*, a curtain about six feet by nine feet (about 2 meters by 3 meters). The curtain's movements create moods appropriate to the character. Through shaking, concealing, and tantalizing, the actor masks his approach and identity to create a feeling of suspense. [*See* Kathakaḷi.]

Mōhiniāṭṭam, a related style for women, developed in the late eighteenth and early nineteenth centuries. It is based on stories of the goddess Mohini, the seductress in Hindu mythology. *Nṛtta* dominates the style. [*See* Mōhiniāṭṭam.]

Another dance style for women, called Oḍissi, is characterized by sudden shifts in level (in contrast, for example, to *bharata nāṭyam*, which is limited primarily to two levels). Characteristics of the style are a figure-eight movement of the head, a balance of the hip and torso bent in one direction, and a semicircular neck movement. [*See* Oḍissi.]

The Manipuri style of dance has five kinds of dances, which include solo, couple, and group forms. Manipuri uses a mixed cast of males and females and is staged as a ritual in connection with the full moon in spring, autumn, and winter. In contrast to the angular, statuesque poses of *bharata nāṭyam* or the large, powerful dimensions of *kathakaḷi*, Manipuri is characterized by a soft, circular quality of movement as the upper torso traces figure-eight patterns in space.

The Manipuri performance opens with an invocation by

ASIAN DANCE TRADITIONS: An Overview. Performers from the Nomura Kyōgen Theater held captive in the play *Ro-Shibari*. In a typical program, *kyōgen*, stylized Japanese comedies, are performed in alternation with scenes from classical *nō* dramas. (Photograph © 1985 by Jack Vartoogian; used by permission.)

a single drummer, with lyrical singers and accompanying stringed instruments. The dance technique consists of soft, lyrical movements called *pareng* and contrasting vigorous, masculine, energetic movements called *colam*, often performed by men playing drums or cymbals. Manipuri training emphasizes the suspended, sensitive movement of the wrists and hands—especially the languid unfolding of the hands. Foot movements exhibit no physical tension; rhythmic emphasis is given through toe contacts rather than with the heels. The emotions expressed through Manipuri are love, ecstasy, and devotion to the divine. [*See* Manipur.]

Another major dance style of India, known as *kathak*, developed in response to fundamental cultural changes brought about by the arrival of Islam on the subcontinent. The new religion condemned the expressive arts, and, in consequence, the classical Hindu dance drama began to decline as early as 1200 CE. The once-great Hindu temples, which had fostered music, poetry, and dance, grew empty and quiet, and the mighty dancing gods of the Hindu pantheon were stilled.

Miniature painting, Hindi literature, and writings such as the *Nāṭyaratnakośa* (fifteenth century) and *Saṅgīta-Mālika* (seventeenth century) give evidence that the *kathak* dance style of northern India developed in the fifteenth to the seventeenth centuries. The music treatise *Kurtanas* provides detailed descriptions of choreography and dance technique: *maṇḍala*s (dance postures), *bhramaṇa*s (spinning turns), *gati*s (steps), *hasta*s (hand gestures), *abhinaya*, and drum mnemonics.

The word *kathak* derives from *kathakar*, or storyteller, and it is possible that the dance style's origin may be related to the activity of itinerant poets and storytellers who traveled from village to village secretly instructing the people and entertaining them with old sacred legends, mythology, and folklore during the era when Islam was spreading and establishing itself. Dance, music, and mime were gradually added to dramatize the holy words and epic poems. The *kathakar*s, being both musicians and dancers, became renowned in Lucknow and Jaipur, and in other cities of the northwestern provinces of Uttar Pradesh and Rajasthan.

With the spread of the Kṛṣṇa cult, devotees began to worship Kṛṣṇa through dance dramas known as Kṛṣṇa-*līlā*s. Śrī Kṛṣṇa, the divine dancer, became the culture hero, and his adventures provided the central themes for a majority of dance dramas from the fifteenth through the seventeenth century.

Kathak in North India evolved as sacred dances in Mongol times but became associated with the female nautch dancers of the brothels. At one time, young boys were featured in the sacred dances and eventually in their secular presentations. This is the only dance style, therefore, that can be performed by either men or women; it is noted

ASIAN DANCE TRADITIONS: An Overview. Ritha Devi, a well-known Indian dancer, performing *bharata nāṭyam*, a classical dance style of South India. (Photograph from the Dance Collection, New York Public Library for the Performing Arts.)

for grace, masculine strength, and rich interpretive qualities.

One of the most characteristic movements of *kathak* is *chakkar*, a series of fast turns executed while pivoting on one spot or covering space with intricate foot rhythms augmented by one hundred bells fastened around each ankle. Some dancers acquire such technical virtuosity that they can sound a single bell—or just seven, or just twelve—while dancing. Others, blindfolded, can use their feet to trace a picture of a peacock or an elephant on a floor covered with rice powder. A basic pose in the *kathak* style is one in which the torso is held straight with one hand above the head and the other slightly curved on the opposing side at shoulder level (similar to ballet's third position). [*See* Kathak.]

Continuity and change. Among the resources of any viable art are the elements essential to accommodate change. The process of change in Indian dance has been continual and sufficiently enough controlled that the integrity of the art form, whatever the particular style, has been maintained over time. Two factors have had an enormous influence on dance in India over the past few decades. The first is the mass media, particularly the enormous Indian motion picture industry. [*See* Film Musicals, *article on* Bollywood Film Musicals.] The second, related, factor is the huge, mass audiences that the media have brought to dance—unknown until the recent past because the detailed, subtle movements required for characterization in traditional dance had always required an intimate setting. Both factors, whatever contradictory aspects may be present, have stimulated the field of dance. Even with the encroachment of television and the mixed blessings of late-twentieth-century culture in India, the future of Indian dance seems assured. [*See* India *article on* New Directions in Indian Dance.]

Southeast Asia. For more than two thousand years, the diverse cultures of Southeast Asia have been shaped by external forces that have produced lasting influences and certain general common characteristics. Moreover, from the beginning of the Dong Son culture (c.300 BCE) in the area of present-day Vietnam, cultural elements spread out beyond the mainland of Asia to some of the islands of the Indonesian archipelago and possibly as far as the Philippines. The greatest unifying element derived from these early times was what became known as the gong-chime orchestras, which accompany dance dramas based on epic literature originating in India. These court dances, emulated in the villages, have been the dominant elite dance tradition; they have developed alongside indigenous forms of secular and religious ritual dance.

Nowhere in Asia is the viability of an epic identity more in evidence than in Indonesia. Myths associated with the cult of the ancestors, with the culture hero, with semihistorical characters and events, and with different kinds of religious beliefs are the stuff of which epic identities are made in these tropical islands. Especially on those outer islands untouched by major world religions, the variety of provincial secular and religious dance is bewildering. Indonesia has more than three hundred languages, and the cultural expressions representing them underscore the national motto, "Unity in Diversity." Unity, in this instance, is represented by the commonality of dance—in whatever form—as an essential expression of epic identity. The diversity ranges, for example, from the tribal dances of Irian Barat (western New Guinea) to the stately court styles of central Java. The most cultivated and best-known styles are found on the islands of Java and Bali.

From the seventh through the tenth century, colonists from India brought a wealth of cultural infusions to these two islands: the Hindu and Buddhist religions, a written script, a calendar, poetic forms, rules of architecture, rules of governance, a rich variety of musical instruments and dance, and two great epics, the *Mahābhārata* and the *Rāmāyaṇa*.

Indian types of dance and music apparently did not last much longer than the presence of the colonizers who imported them. Bas-reliefs on temples at the eighth-century Javanese sites of Borobudur and the temple Candi Mendut at Prambanan carry a record of the Indian performing arts that had been imported to the island. Dance, puppets, and musical instruments depicted on the temples of the East Javanese empires (eleventh to sixteenth century) are similar to those found in performance among the Balinese today.

Java. Strong circumstantial evidence suggests that the birth and development of gong-chime ensembles occurred in Java, a process that began with the importation of Bronze and Iron Age technologies in an advanced stage of development around the third to second century BCE.

The pertinent artifacts, still extant, are so-called bronze kettle drums (actually a type of horizontal gong kettle). These musical instruments were played in sets, numbering at least sixteen per set, and were precursors of the first gamelan orchestras. By the time Indian colonization was entrenched, in the seventh and eighth centuries, several early forms of gamelan orchestra had developed.

Direct Indian influence on Java disappeared by the tenth century. In the eleventh century, the seat of power moved to eastern Java, and central Java sank into obscurity until the beginning of the seventeenth century. East Javanese temples built from the thirteenth through fifteenth centuries depict many puppet figures. (In both Java and Bali, dance movements derive from their respective—and different—puppet theaters.) By the end of the sixteenth century, the seat of power once again returned to central Java, and Islam replaced Hinduism and Buddhism as the dominant religion. Little is known about dance styles before the nineteenth century, when music and dance received strong patronage from the royal courts, but these arts had probably enjoyed similar royal sponsorship during the golden age of East Javanese culture (thirteenth to sixteenth century).

The most demanding and abstract Javanese stylization in dance occurs in Jogjakarta, one of the two principal cultural centers of central Java. The flat leather puppets used in *wayang* puppet theater are two-dimensional; likewise, the basic dance positions in the Jogjakarta style are as nearly two-dimensional as the human figure can manage. This degree of flatness was sometimes achieved through tortuous means. For example, in the palace of the sultan of Jogjakarta, the bodies of male dancers were altered by bending their hands backwards and strapping them to their wrists and by placing a kind of "spacer" between their knees and legs to hold them in a complete turnout when they went to bed for the night.

In the other principal cultural center of central Java, Surakarta, the style is somewhat more relaxed, and, unlike the practice in Jogjakarta, the roles of highly refined male characters—princes, kings, and warriors—are played by female dancers. In both centers, however, especially in the characterization of strong male roles, body positions resembling those of the flat leather *wayang* puppets are maintained.

Formal training in the palaces and royal courts followed the tradition of imitation and rote learning. Outside the courts, commoners engaged in informal training in an attempt to imitate the royal models in small towns and villages. The first school outside the palace of the sultan was established in Jogjakarta in 1918 by one of the sultan's brothers. Known as Krida Beksa Wirama, it still flourishes today, though formal degree-granting dance academies have since been founded in Jogjakarta and elsewhere. The birth of Krida Beksa Wirama gradually en-

ASIAN DANCE TRADITIONS: An Overview. *Thabal Chongbi* (Jumping in the Moonlight), a Manipuri dance performed in spring during the Yaossang festival. Performed by men and women together, this dance has a light, lyrical quality and expresses a ritual connection to the full moon. (Photograph © 1990 by Jack Vartoogian; used by permission.)

couraged the formation of a number of private dance clubs outside the court.

At every rehearsal many small children watch open-eyed as their older brothers and sisters devote hours to learning new roles and characterizations. This early participation as spectators prompts childish attempts at role-playing and establishes in the very young the underlying spirit and attitude essential to the dedicated Javanese dancer. First by observation and then through participation, the dance student learns the language of signals from the *keprak* (wood block) played by the dance master, the structural roles of the key instruments of the gamelan orchestra, and the musical phrases that correspond to dance movements.

Characterizations are broadly distinguished as *poutra alus* (refined), *putra gagah* (strong or coarse), and *puteri* (female). These categories are further differentiated through stereotypical body attitudes characteristic of each type; through stylized leg, arm, and head movements; and through basic postures and gradations of those postures. Increasing levels of refinement within each style progress from general character-types to specific characters in a particular drama.

Rehearsals and performances occur in a spacious open pavilion *(pendapa)*. In a princely residence, a grand pavilion may have a marble floor; in a village, the pavilion's floor is generally made of concrete. From the moment of entry along the side of this pavilion, even before performing the initial *sembah*, or supplication, the Javanese dancer has already reached a state of spiritual detachment, a kind of intense serenity, in preparation for the demanding responsibility of creating the portrayal of a god,

hero, or demon. It is an intense experience because these roles are those of ancestor-figures who make up the epic identity of Javanese culture.

As the dance drama unfolds, with narrative links supplied by the *dalang,* or puppeteer, the dancer heightens this personal detachment and for some hours becomes other than self. This remarkable artistic elevation beyond self is the hallmark of traditional Javanese dance.

Today, there is a strong trend toward creating dance programs made up of favorite fragments from different episodes of the *Mahābhārata* or the *Rāmāyaṇa;* sometimes the two epics are represented in the same program. On these occasions the attainment of real spiritual detachment is likely to be rare, reached only by the finest dancers.

The classical dance of central Java can be broken down into five categories, depending on the literature or fragment being portrayed. *Wayang purwa wong* has a large cast of characters who enact stories from the *Mahābhārata* or the *Rāmāyaṇa.* In Jogjakarta, when these stories are performed as a kind of opera requiring the dancers to perform on their knees and to sing and act, the style is known as *langen mandra wanara.* In Surakarta the dancers perform the equivalent in standing position, and the style of the dance-opera is called *langendriya.* Here, however, the stories are not *wayang purwa* (the "old stories" from India) but instead are drawn from the exploits of Menak Djinggo, the legendary Red Knight of the East Javanese kingdoms. A masked dance-drama genre based on the stories of the culture hero Panji is called *wayang topéng.* When Arabic stories of the Menak literature form the basis of a dance drama, featuring stiff movements imitative of round wooden puppets, the style is known as *wayang golek* (not to be confused with the puppet theater of the same name).

Two classical court dances performed by women require special mention. *Bedaya* is a highly stylized, lyrical dance depicting an abstract version of a story from the *Mahābhārata* or some other source and performed by five, seven, or as many as nine dancers. *Srimpi*, which is performed by four principal dancers and four attendants, depicts a fight. One pair of the principal quartet represents two quarreling princesses; the second pair is a symmetrical duplication. Rarely, *srimpi* is performed by only two dancers or even by a single dancer (in the latter instance there is no fighting).

Outside these courtly traditions are two kinds of professional female solo-dance styles. *Taledek*, a flirtatious dance used solely for entertainment, borrows from *srimpi* and *bedaya*, but it is not restricted to traditional transition movements between dance postures. *Golèk* combines features of all three of these styles. Two basic types of folk dance drama also deserve mention: *srandul*, based on current events and legendary tales, and *prajuritan* (or *jaran kepang*), based on the Arabic Menak stories.

There are several professional dance theaters in Java; one of the most renowned is Ngesti Pandawa, a touring company whose home theater is in Semarang.

The people of Java belong to several different ethnic groups, the two largest of which are the Javanese, who live mostly in eastern and central Java (and whose traditions have been discussed above) and the Sundanese, of western Java. The Sundanese use the same literature as the Javanese of central Java for their courtly dance styles and puppetry. The basic body attitude is similar to that found in central Java, but the movements are fluid, less formalized, and less restrained. The body is more three-dimensional, and the Sundanese style features more movement of the upper torso, emphasized by a rocking of the shoulders. Basic leg positions are less elevated than those of Central Java, and movements for dancers depicting female characters are not as restrictive.

The Sundanese recognize two kinds of dance *(igel): ébéng,* or classical dance, and *jogéd,* or village dance. There has been some borrowing and cross-influence between the two. The classical dance dramas of the Sundanese are, like those elsewhere in Java, based on stories of the *Mahābhārata,* the *Rāmāyaṇa,* and the *Panji* cycle. Characterizations are divided into two groups, *ngalamba* and *leyepan,* designating the introductory and main sections of the refined type, and *monggawa,* designating the strong or coarse type.

Jogéd includes an amazing variety of village styles and even extends to include the popular *pencak,* a martial-arts fighting dance known generally throughout Indonesia. Some kinds of *jogéd* require a full Sundanese gamelan orchestra for accompaniment; other types may be accompanied by an ensemble of bamboo instruments.

Like the Javanese, the Sundanese may present full dance dramas or, especially in recent years, medleys of fragments from traditional dance dramas combined in a program with new stories based on animal figures or social activities such as planting rice or weaving. *Topéng* (masked dances) are very popular, and the whole art of dance is stimulated by competitions held by local and regional dance clubs. [*See* Indonesia, *articles on* Javanese Dance Traditions *and* Sundanese Dance Traditions.]

Bali. Only the most general correspondence exists between the dance styles of Java and those of Bali. Ten centuries of Balinese Hinduism have made the performing and creative arts an indispensable part of Balinese religion. The traditional role of the arts in Bali is so significant—more than in any other society—that it has been said that if by some magical command the arts should suddenly vanish, the whole society would collapse.

The blending of religion, magic, and superstition in Bali, and especially the Balinese belief in the existence of both good and evil forces, has produced the Balinese conviction that gods and demons occupy the present world. This good–evil duality must be recognized and the forces of darkness neutralized by bringing them out into the sunlight of reality. Music, dance, drama, chants, the graphic and plastic arts, the decorative arts, and religious offerings are all concrete means of mitigating evil.

The ever-present Hindu literature, the culture-hero Pandji, and other legends and historical stories form the basis of a rich variety of dance forms. Body attitudes conform in the most general way to those of Southeast Asian classical dance, but certain particularities define Balinese style.

As in Java, characters in the Balinese dance drama are stereotyped as *alus* (refined) or *manis* (literally, "sweet"), and *keras* (strong or coarse). Whatever their rank, principal female characters are "refined," and whether she is a queen, princess, or demon a female character's vocal delivery is always sweet *(manis)*. At one time, all these roles were portrayed by men, a practice that is still followed in certain types of dance drama such as *topéng,* or masked play, and *wayang wong.* Eccentric female roles are, for example, played by men in a kind of spoken-sung form of opera called *arja.* The famous role of the witch Rangda in the trance dance drama *Calonarang* is considered so dangerous to perform that it is usually played by an older male priest. [*See* Wayang.]

Minor female roles are very important in most forms of Balinese dance-drama. The *condong* is a female attendant of the leading female dancer and has a vital function throughout the drama. Two important male attendants for the principal characters are the *panasar* and the *kartala,* the former acting as a stupid interpreter of his master's high-flown language and serving as a butt for the antics of the *kartala*. The latter is reminiscent of the Shakespearean fool; both attendants' roles enjoy great popularity.

Although eccentric female roles tend to be somewhat mannish in style, they are still *alus* compared to the strong male roles of even such refined and *alus* characters as Arjuna (from the *Mahābhārata*), who moves with great delicacy and speaks in a soft voice. In Bali the distinction between *alus* and *keras* is not as rigidly observed as in Java. On occasion, if the proper mask is not readily available, an *alus* character may wear a *keras* mask and reverse his normal style; this bow to expediency is well understood by the audience.

The Balinese dance teacher maintains much more bodily contact with the student than is customary in Java, pushing an arm into place, shoving a leg forward, enveloping the head in two guiding hands, molding the lithe little body of the child disciple into movements transferred directly from the teacher's body. The experience of this kind of kinetic teaching remains as a permanently imprinted muscular memory and is retained by association with the familiar melodies and rhythms of the gamelan.

As in Java, learning by rote and imitation based on constant observation is preliminary to personal guidance from the teacher. At some point, young students are chosen for special training. Selection is based on typecasting, personality, physical features, and intelligence. Certain dances, such as the famous *légong*, require retirement of by the age of puberty: the little girls who dance *légong* undergo training and perform during a career that lasts only from about age eight to about age twelve. [*See* Légong.]

Body posture for the female Balinese dancer is very different from that found in Java. Shoulder blades are pulled back tightly, the legs are bent in a deep plié, and the hips are released back so that the torso forms an extraordinary, curvaceous figure S. Darting eyes are used for focal emphasis, and vibrating fingers capture the shimmering quality of the gamelan music. Hand gestures are few in type and abstract in meaning.

The temple is the setting and background for Balinese dance dramas. The bare earthen stage is delineated by four umbrellas outlining a square in which the drama unfolds. Sometimes the staging is part of a temple celebration, so that the performance takes place within the open, walled courtyard of the roofless temple. Not infrequently, while the *panasar* and the *kartala* entertain the audience for a considerable length of time, the principals are backstage debating which episode of a given literature will be performed. The whole atmosphere is less formal than in Java, but the performance is completely professional.

There are said to be nearly twenty-five different gamelan traditions in Bali, many with their own dance traditions. Ritual dances are usually slow and sometimes not easily differentiated. *Mendèt* may be performed by old and young women, by priests and boys, or by tiny girls. *Rejang* and *gabor* are usually performed by mature women, but occasionally they may be performed by men. Among the ceremonial forms is a brilliant style of male dance called *baris*, which involves a line of anywhere from four to sixty men in soldier dress, gesturing and posing with spears, bows, or shields. The most dramatic form of *baris* is performed by a solo male dancer who excels in statuesque poses; the dancer's tentative advances and careful withdrawals are abruptly contrasted with outbreaks of violent tension in which all parts of the body quiver and tremble. The *baris* character may be refined, as when representing Arjuna or Rama, or *keras*, as in the role of the *jauk* demon, for which the dancer wears a fierce mask with bulging eyes.

Apparently basic to all forms of dance in both Java and Bali is an ancient form of dance drama known as *gambuh*. This dance-theater form was imported to Bali from the kingdoms of East Java during the golden age of the Majapahit empire in the fourteenth and fifteenth centuries.

ASIAN DANCE TRADITIONS: An Overview. *Wayang wong* performance at the Sultan's Palace in Surakarta, Java. The character Prince Panji (center), flanked by his attendants, exemplifies the Javanese refined male style *(outra alus)*. (Photograph from the Tropenmuseum, Royal Tropical Institute, Amsterdam.)

ASIAN DANCE TRADITIONS: An Overview. A scene from the Balinese *Calonarang* dance drama, a genre best known for depicting battles between Rangda, a witchlike personification of evil, and the *barong*, a magical protective beast. Here, the widow-witch Calonarang (center), who later manifests as Rangda, performs an unsavory magical ritual. (Photograph by Sakari Viika; used by permission.)

The *gambuh* dialogue is still sung and spoken in fifteenth-century Javanese, but the attendants translate the lofty thoughts of their noble masters into colloquial Balinese. The literature is drawn from the *Panji* cycle of stories, from the Javanese historical romance called *Rangga Lawe*, and from the Javanese-Islamic cycle *Amad Muhammad*. This unique dance-theater form is considered pompous and too slow by many contemporary Balinese, who miss the comic relief and sentimentality found in other literature. But the flamboyant style of dancing and the masterful grace and quality of movement make it a significant Indonesian dance form. It had almost died out until a revival of interest was fostered by the dance academy in Bali in the 1960s.

There are many kinds of trance dance in Bali, the most famous being the *Calonarang,* mentioned above. This dance drama, when performed in its proper context and

not as a tourist attraction, results in nearly all the participants falling into deep trance. Especially dramatic is the large number of *keris* dancers, each holding a sharpened dagger *(keris)* at the chest while dancing about vigorously until, in a state of trance, they all fall to the ground in a trembling paroxysm. The most popular dance for tourist consumption is the *kécak,* the "monkey dance" taken from a scene in the *Rāmāyaṇa*; in the *kécak,* the monkey army is represented by a large number of young men chanting and swaying rhythmically as two opposing choruses, while the principals posture and dance in the center of the huge circle of performers.

The most popular dance style in southern Bali today was developed as recently as the 1930s, when the famous dancer I Ketut Mario introduced *kebiar,* based on music borrowed from northern Bali. Although I Mario used the traditional movements of Balinese dance, for the first time the performer was freed from the obligation of stereotyped characterization and could express his own personality as a reflection of the dramatic, animated music. Mario choreographed the solo *Kebiar Duduk,* which he performed entirely in a squatting position, utilizing a fan and manipulating a long train on his costume. He created a number of solos, such as one that required the playing of the *trompong* (a gamelan instrument) while dancing. *Tumullingan, Pandji Semerang,* and *Taruna* are others of his creative inventions, in which women danced male roles and vice versa. The orchestration and even the gamelan instruments were gradually changed from the older *gamelan gong* orchestra to reflect this new, virtuoso form of dance. The new orchestra became known as *gamelan gong kebiar* or *gong kebiar.* [*See* Gamelan *and* Kebiar.]

The rapid expansion of tourism since the late 1960s has had contradictory effects on the Balinese performing and creative arts. Audiences of tourists, and the money they bring, create an abnormally high demand for music and dance (as well as for carvings and paintings) on an island where there has always been a plethora of the arts. Tourists' eyes and ears are insensitive to the refinement of the tradition, and the result has been a higher standard of living but a lowering of artistic standards.

On the positive side, however, so long as Balinese Hinduism and the constant requirements of musical and dance offerings remain essential to Balinese life, the finest elements of the traditional forms will persist. On an island that over time has accommodated the arrival of Hinduism, Javanese colonization, and Dutch imperialism, contemporary tourism is but another in a long series of external forces, and it is likely that the arts of Bali will adapt to it as well. [*See* Indonesia, *articles on Balinese dance traditions.*]

BIBLIOGRAPHY

Bandem, I Made, and Fredrik Eugene DeBoer. *Balinese Dance in Transition: Kaja and Kelod.* 2d ed. New York, 1995.

Bartenieff, Irmgard, with Dori Lewis. *Body Movement: Coping with the Environment.* New York, 1980.

Bowers, Faubion. *Theatre in the East: A Survey of Asian Dance and Drama.* New York, 1956.

Brandon, James R. *Theatre in Southeast Asia.* Cambridge, Mass., 1967.

Brandon, James R., ed. *The Performing Arts in Asia.* Paris, 1971.

Brandon, James R. *Brandon's Guide to Theater in Asia.* Honolulu, 1976.

Brandon, James R., et al. *Studies in Kabuki: Its Acting, Music, and Historical Context.* Honolulu, 1978.

Chen, Jack. *The Chinese Theatre.* New York, 1948.

Cho Won-kyung. *Dances of Korea.* New York, 1962.

Coomaraswamy, Ananda K. *The Dance of the Shiva: Fourteen Indian Essays* (1918). Rev. ed. New York, 1957.

Coomaraswamy, Ananda K. *History of Indian and Indonesian Art.* New York, 1927.

Covarrubias, Miguel. *Island of Bali.* New York, 1937.

Crossley-Holland, Peter. "Tibet." In *The New Grove Dictionary of Music and Musicians.* London, 1980.

de Zoete, Beryl, and Walter Spies. *Dance and Drama in Bali.* London, 1938.

de Zoete, Beryl. *The Other Mind.* London, 1953.

Garfias, Robert, et al. "Burma." In *The New Grove Dictionary of Music and Musicians.* London, 1980.

Gargi, Balwant. *Theatre in India.* New York, 1962.

Gargi, Balwant. *Folk Theater of India.* Seattle, 1966.

Gaston, Anne-Marie. *Siva in Dance, Myth, and Iconography.* Delhi, 1982.

Hall, Fernau. "Noh, Kabuki, Kathakali." *Sangeet Natak* 7 (1968).

Het Serimpi Boek: 20 gekleurde platen en 12 autotypieen van Serimpi-en bedajadansen. Weltevreden, Java, 1925.

Holt, Claire. *Dance Quest in Celebes.* Paris, 1939.

Holt, Claire. "Two Dance Worlds: A Contemplation." *Impulse* (1958).

Hood, Mantle. "The Enduring Tradition: Music and Theatre in Java and Bali." In *Indonesia,* edited by Ruth Thomas McVey. New Haven, 1963.

Hood, Mantle, et al. "Indonesia." In *The New Grove Dictionary of Music and Musicians.* London, 1980.

Huang, Al. *Embrace Tiger, Return to Mountain* (1973). Berkeley, 1987.

"In Praise of Kathak." *Marg* 12 (1959).

Jones, Clifford Reis, and Betty True Jones. *Kathakali.* New York, 1970.

Keith, A. B. *The Sanskrit Drama.* Oxford, 1924.

Kersenboom, Saskia C. *Nityasumaṅgalī: The Devadasi Tradition in South India.* Delhi, 1987.

Kishibe Shigeo, et al. "Japan." In *The New Grove Dictionary of Music and Musicians.* London, 1980.

Kishibe Shigeo. *The Traditional Music of Japan.* New rev. ed. Tokyo, 1984.

Kop, G. G. van der. "The 'Wayang Wong' or 'Wayang Orang.'" *Sluyters' Monthly* 3 (September 1922).

Lee Byong-won. "Korea." In *The New Grove Dictionary of Music and Musicians.* London, 1980.

Lelyveld, Theodore B. van. *De javaansche danskunst.* Amsterdam, 1931.

Le May, Reginald. *The Culture of South-East Asia.* London, 1954.

Maceda, José, et al. "Philippines." In *The New Grove Dictionary of Music and Musicians.* London, 1980.

McPhee, Colin. "Dance in Bali" (1948). In *Traditional Balinese Culture,* edited by Jane Belo. New York, 1970.

Mershon, Katharane E. *Seven Plus Seven: Mysterious Life-Rituals in Bali.* New York, 1971.

Miettinen, Jukka O. *Classical Dance and Theatre in South-East Asia.* New York, 1992.

Miller, Terry E. "Laos." In *The New Grove Dictionary of Music and Musicians.* London, 1980.

Moerdowo. *Reflections on Indonesian Arts and Culture.* 2d ed. Sourabaya, 1963.

Morton, David. "Thailand." In *The New Grove Dictionary of Music and Musicians.* London, 1980.

Ortolani, Benito. "Iemoto." *Japan Quarterly* 16.3 (1969).

Pian, Rulan Chao, et al. "China." In *The New Grove Dictionary of Music and Musicians.* London, 1980.

Rawson, Philip. *The Art of Southeast Asia.* London, 1967.

Scott, A. C. *The Theatre in Asia.* London, 1972.

Scott, A. C. *Actors Are Madmen: Notebook of a Theatregoer in China.* Madison, Wis., 1982.

Survey of Korean Arts, vol. 2, *Folk Arts.* Seoul, 1974.

Thiounn, Samdach Chaufea. *Danses cambodgiennes.* 2d ed. Phnom Penh, 1956.

Tran Quang Hai. "Kampuchea." In *The New Grove Dictionary of Music and Musicians.* London, 1980.

Trân Van Khê. "Theatre in Vietnam." *Sangeet Natak* 8 (1968).

Vatsyayan, Kapila. "India, VII: Dance." In *The New Grove Dictionary of Music and Musicians.* London, 1980.

Vatsyayan, Kapila. *Indian Classical Dance.* 2d ed. New Delhi, 1992.

Wade, Bonnie C. *Music in India: The Classical Traditions.* Englewood Cliffs, N.J., 1978.

Yoshinobu Inoura. *A History of Japanese Theater,* vol. 1, *Noh and Kyogen.* Yokohama, 1971.

Yupho, Dhanit. *Classical Siamese Theatre.* Bangkok, 1952.

Zarina, Xenia. *Classic Dances of the Orient.* New York, 1967.

HAZEL CHUNG and MANTLE HOOD

Influence of Puppetry

A unique Asian contribution to the performing arts, shadow theater developed as a part of religious ritual and was protected by imperial patronage. Asian cultures regarded the human shadow as the soul; two-dimensional figures, such as those projected onto a backlit screen, often depicted the spirits of ancestors and deities. In fact, many Asian dance movements, which are extremely stylized and angular, show the influence of shadow theater.

Asians distinguish between shadow theater (or, as literally translated from Asian languages, "leather shadow show" or "leather shadow dance") and puppetry (which uses three-dimensional dolls). The early relationship between puppetry and dance may be reflected in the word *puppet*, which in English derives from Latin *pupa*, meaning "girl" or "doll." Many scholars connect the word to the Sanskrit *putrika, puhitrika, puttali,* and *puttalika,* all of which mean "maiden." In fact, the earliest descriptions of

ASIAN DANCE TRADITIONS: Influence of Puppetry. Shadow figure of Sitā, from the *Rāmāyaṇa*, the Hindu epic poem, as portrayed in the Tolo Bomalata tradition from Andra Pradash, India. (Photograph by Jo Humphrey; from the collection of the American Museum of Natural History, New York.)

puppets (c.1000 BCE in both India and China) are of animated female forms that sang and danced. In Asia, puppet theater probably began before structured human theater, and, in fact, the Sanskrit *sutradhar,* for "stage manager," reflects this connection: it literally means "thread holder." Throughout early Buddhist writings, there are allusions to dancing puppets. In most Asian countries, dancers perform to recitations of poetry by a storyteller or narrator/chanter. Costumes, poetry, and music are the same as those used in shadow and puppet theater.

Indian shadow theater *(chaya nataka)* dates from the second century BCE. Shadow figures from Andhra Pradesh, Karnataka, Kerala, and Orissa often resemble ancient dancers depicted in the local sculpture, temple murals, and folk paintings. Deities and mortals dance on the screen as their manipulators dance and sing from behind. The all-male *kathakaḷi* dancers of southern India use masks painted like the shadow figures from Andhra Pradesh. Important characters emerge from behind a screen as if the shadow figures were coming to life.

The great Hindu epics, the *Rāmāyaṇa* and the *Māhabhārata,* provide the basic themes for South Asian, Indonesian, and Southeast Asian performing arts. The performers pay homage to the same elephant-headed god, Ganesh, deity of the theater, and to Śiva (Shiva), lord of the dance. When classical Sanskrit drama diminished in the tenth century CE, dancers competed with puppets and shadow figures. From the twelfth to the eighteenth centuries, the itinerant shadow and puppet theaters were again the most popular entertainment; only the wealthy could enjoy the human theater.

Ironically, twentieth-century scholars of dance have used shadow figures and ancient sculptures to help reconstruct ancient costumes and dances. The nautch dance of North India, now performed only by prostitutes, still appears in its pure form as the *putul* nautch (dance of dolls) in West Bengal, with rod puppets that wear costumes similar to those worn in the Jatra theater.

Hindu influence spread through Southeast Asia more than two thousand years ago. In many countries, however, remnants of indigenous dances still exist: devil dances in Sri Lanka, spirit and animal dances in Burma (now Myanmar), introductory *praleng* dances in Thailand, and trance dances in Bali. Although Buddhism and Islam superseded Hinduism in Southeast Asia (Bali being the notable exception), Indian mythology still forms the basis of most performing arts throughout the region, albeit the religious aspects have long disappeared.

Each country has developed its own distinct style of interrelated dance, shadow, or puppet theater. For example, Cambodian palace dancers used the exaggerated extension of arms and fingers to reproduce the double-jointed appearance of the stone *apsaras* on the walls of Angkor Wat. The same hand positions are seen on *nang talung* shadow

ASIAN DANCE TRADITIONS: Influence of Puppetry. The National Bunraku Theater of Japan performing *Sekidera Komachi* (Komachi at Sekidera Temple), a scene from the play *Hanakurabe Shiki no Kotobuki* (The Fortunate Flowering of the Four Seasons). Yoshida Minosuke III is the *omozakai*, or master puppeteer, who controls the puppet's head and right arm. The hood of one of the other two puppeteers is visible to the left of the puppet's head. (Photograph © 1983 by Jack Vartoogian; used by permission.)

China's tremendous wealth of written records provides detailed evidence of early performing arts. Because of the Confucian emphasis on self-determination, dance was not performed as a ritual dedicated to the gods. Still, dancers and acrobats performed for religious festivals as well as for the pleasure of the court as early as 1122 BCE. The ribbon dance, which depicts fairies, dates from the Han dynasty (202 BCE to 221 CE). During the Han, masks were used in battle; not until the sixth century CE were masked dancers and lion dances introduced, coming from India along with Buddhism. *Nō* masked theater is still performed in western China today. The masks used in this ancient type of dance drama resemble the carved faces on various types of puppets. The stylized movements suggest their origins in the puppet world. This art was refined into the highly codified Japanese *bugaku* theater that is now a National Living Treasure in Japan. The first Chinese puppets (probably *budai xi*, or hand puppets) were credited to Yang Shi in the early Western Zhou dynasty (1027–770 BCE). Water puppets also existed. Rod puppets and shadow figures *(piying xi)* first appeared during the Han dynasty.

Court dancing gradually gave way to more dramatic storytelling in China. During the Tang dynasty (618–906 CE), Chinese opera was born. Emperor Ming Huang established the first theater school during the Five Dynasties

ASIAN DANCE TRADITIONS: The Influence of Puppetry. Fujian hand puppets from China depict a scene in which a plate-spinner (left) entertains a government official. (Photograph by Carrillo Gantner; from the archives of The Asia Society, New York.)

figures from southern Cambodia and Thailand and on the northern-style *nang yi*—huge carved panels of water buffalo hide. Held aloft by dancers, they appear in front of and behind a large screen as the story is chanted. Thailand's *khon nah jor* (masked dance) is performed in front of a screen, like a shadow play. Another *khōn* uses paper puppets of large mosquitoes. Classical dance in Burma imitated the leaps, spins, and twirls of Burmese marionettes.

In Indonesia, the leather shadow play known as the *wayang kulit* originated in 907 CE. It still influences the lives of Indonesians, and each shadow master *(dalang)* is regarded as a spiritual leader in his community. In the *wayang wong* court dances, movements, speech mannerisms, stories, music, storyteller, and costumes are the same as those used in the shadow theater, and dancers imitate shadow figures. The Balinese, who do not operate under Islamic strictures (concerning nondepiction of the human form), as do other Indonesians, have created more realistic *wayang* figures; dance movements are smoother and more flowing, and the dances are more abstract. The theme in Balinese shadow and human theater is the balance between good and evil, and everyone belongs to a society *(suka)* of music, dance, or shadow play.

(907–960), which emphasized singing and acting. In the Song dynasty (960–1279), puppet and shadow theater reached their heights of popularity. Several new forms were added, including marionettes and "human puppets" (children on the shoulders of adults). Marionettes and some southern Chinese shadow figures were used ritualistically for funerals and exorcisms. Opera and shadow theater shared the same costumes and stories, which were based on classical literature. Many scholars believe that the stylized movements and painted faces of Chinese opera developed from puppets and shadow figures. Stage entrances and exits still are made from stage right to stage left, probably because early shadow figures, such as those from Fujian province in southeastern China, could perform in only one direction. The direction of onstage movement probably originated because of the right to left reading of Chinese characters.

North and East Asian countries owe large parts of their cultures to China. Ancient Chinese water puppets still float during festivals in Korea and Vietnam, and Thailand has preserved a Chinese fan dance.

Japan's continuing imperial patronage brought seventh-century *gagaku* and *bugaku* into the twentieth century. Hand puppets and marionettes were replaced by the more highly developed *bunraku* rod puppets that are manipulated by three performers. *Bunraku* and *kabuki* (which is similar to Chinese opera) are so closely associated that scripts are exchanged and performing techniques traded.

Shadow figures, puppets, and human performers have coexisted in Asia for a very long time. Basic performing styles, musical language, and costumes reflect the influences that have passed back and forth. As the governments of the Asian countries have stabilized, traditional arts have been revitalized and new forms are developing.

[*See also* Bunraku *and* Wayang.]

BIBLIOGRAPHY

Asian Cultural Center, UNESCO. "The World of Masks." *Asian Culture* 17 (August 1977).
Asian Puppets: The Wall of the World. Los Angeles, 1976.
Awasthi, Suresh. "The Puppet Theatre of India." *Arts of Asia* (September–October 1975).
Bowers, Faubion. *Theatre in the East: A Survey of Asian Dance and Drama.* New York, 1956.
Buurman, Peter. *Wayang Golek: The Entrancing World of Classical Javanese Puppet Theatre.* Singapore, 1988.
Chŏe Sang-su. *A Study of the Korean Puppet Play.* Seoul, 1961.
Delza, Sophia. "The Dance-Arts in the People's Republic of China: The Contemporary Scene." In *Dance in Africa, Asia, and the Pacific,* edited by Judy Van Zile. New York, 1976.
"Gagaku." *Facts about Japan* (July 1969).
Humphrey, Jo. *Monkey King: A Celestial Heritage.* Jamaica, N.Y., 1980.
Malik, Kapila. "Bharatanatyam: Its Origin and Recent Development." *World Theatre* 5 (1956).
Miettinen, Jukka O. *Classical Dance and Theatre in South-East Asia.* New York, 1992.
Pischel, Richard. *The Home of the Puppet-Play.* Translated by Mildred C. Tawney. London, 1902.
Rolfe, Husein. "Drama and Dance in Southeast Asia." *Eastern Horizon* 14 (December 1977).
Scott, A. C. *The Puppet Theatre of Japan.* Rutland, Vt., 1963.
Soedarsono. "Classical Javanese Dance: History and Characterization." *Ethnomusicology* 13 (September 1969).
Sweeney, Amin. *Malay Shadow Puppets: The Wayang Siam of Kelantan.* London, 1972.
Trân Van Khê. *Marionettes sur eau du Vietnam.* Paris, 1984.
Tsuan Chieh Di. *Investigation into Puppet Plays* (in Chinese). Hong Kong, 1948.
Vatsyayan, Kapila. "Kathakali: Dance Theatre of India." *World of Music* 10.1 (1968).

JO HUMPHREY

Religious, Philosophical, and Environmental Influences

Throughout Asia, dance is essentially of three kinds: the dance of form, the dance of myth, and the dance of ritual. Before examining these distinctions, however, the stage on which dance is performed and the time within which it occurs must be considered.

Place, Time, and Typology. A confined space, the stage is usually within a temple or shrine compound, or it may be situated along an avenue leading to a sacred enclosure. It is thus a confined space within or on the periphery of a confined space. Much the same may be said of the time during which the stage is in use, as it is "isolated" from ordinary time; that is, it is in festival time. A festival marks a point that is, in a sense, outside of time—the harvest is just in, and a new season has yet to begin; or the winter season of confinement is ending, and the planting season is about to start. Such transitions are marked by a festival that draws men and women, youths and adults, children and the aged to a place where their aspirations are focused and the spirit of their community celebrated. It is here, at this sacred place, that ground is set aside, a stage is set up, and dancing is done.

If the dancing is done at night or extends into the night, then the darkness of the night adds to the sense of isolation of the place and time. Lanterns are hung about or torches held aloft to signify that something outside the ordinary is taking place. The wooden boards of the stage might be raised and barrels filled to various levels with water placed in the hollow beneath, to resonate to the dancer's steps. The music will likely be simple, or at least of simple instrumentation: reed flutes, drums, gongs, bells, and droning strings. Fittingly, the sounds of the dance are perhaps a bit eerie, otherworldly, and suggestive of transcendence.

Dancers use the stage in different ways—for example, as a large chessboard, on which purely formal, geometric movements are performed. Because the stage is generally square, an even number of dancers (usually two or four) perform, and movement proceeds from the four corners toward the center, or from the four sides to the center, or from the center out toward the sides and corners. This "dance of form" can best be appreciated by looking down from above, as the gods might do. Tang dynasty (618–906) court dances were of this order, as is the Japanese *gagaku;* certain *miko* dances done by young girls on the stages of Shintō shrines are similarly formal and almost purely abstract—that is, they are completely without mythic purport or story content.

Where two rather than four dancers perform, they often represent the opposing forces of *yin* and *yang*—male and female, order and chaos, summer and winter, matter and spirit. Thus, a dance that may at first appear to be purely abstract will eventually reveal a subtle mythic content: the dance reenacts the creation of the world.

Indeed, as the four dancers move in from the corners of the stage, then circle the center, sidestep, and then dance out toward the corners again, they may be executing the vestiges of some ancient ritual of purification of the sanctuary, and hence of the four corners of the earth. "Pure form," on close inspection, may reveal more than form.

Dancers may also use the stage to enact a drama, one that, in all likelihood, will be based on mythology. In this kind of dance, the dancers do not simply relate events from some mythic past; they reenact the myth, thereby recreating the primordial past. For the gods were living at the beginning of time. They lived before time was. Thus in a very real sense they do not and cannot live in our time. They cannot breathe our air or eat our food or enjoy our music because it is not theirs. At festival time, however, we are permitted to hear special music and to eat special foods. With patience, and with the freedom to permit fancy to come into play, we may even see the gods cavort. The stage has been established for their use. The music of the festival is an inducement, an invocation to the gods, asking them to come forth into our time, to make it momentarily their own. They appear as masked dancers, as shadows cast by the puppeteers on a wall or curtain, as goddesses in silk saris with jingling anklets and bracelets.

We view these dances at stage level, for the gods become human this night, and we become as gods. The dancer loses himself in the role, the spirit of the deity enters the dancer's body and costume, and the dancer becomes the god. The form of the dance serves the festival's narrative; but if the young people watching the performance do not quite know the story, the form itself has sufficient power to convey the mythic content.

Finally, the stage may be used as a temple. An altar may actually be on the stage with an image of the deity and offertory vessels and trays, with food and wine and gifts consecrated to the deity. More often, the stage serves as an outer hall or offertory within the temple complex from which the dance itself will be offered up as a festival gift to the god. The stage faces the sanctuary, and often the dancers begin with an act of obeisance toward the holy of holies. Behind them stands the audience or congregants. Serving as intermediaries, the dancers stand between the people and the deity. Making an offering in the name of the assembly, they are as priests, who serve both the god for the people and the people for the god. If the dance is understood to be mythic, then the dancers represent—and in some sense truly become—the deities, assembling there on the stage for a show, a showing, a holy seeing by the populace. This is always and everywhere the role of the priest: to stand as intermediary between human beings and the gods, taking the offerings of men and women to the gods and the communion of the gods to the people. So, for the occasion of the festival, the dancer is a special priest. Through the dancer, sacred time flows into the human world, and the dancer moves as the gods move. The people look up to the dancer as priest; so the dance of form or myth becomes a dance of ritual as well.

Both the nobility and the common people were responsible for drawing dance away from its origins in the sanctuary. It is said that *kathakaļi*—the militant-style male dance of southern India—migrated from Hindu temple precincts to village clearings, in part, because so many people wanted to see the performances and could not be accommodated in so confined a space. In addition, among the devotees of the sacred dance were members of the lower castes who were not permitted inside the temple compounds. The result was not only a revolution in sacred and secular entertainment but also a reformation of religion—if all the people could not go to perform *bhakti* (Skt., "devotion"), then *bhakti* would be brought to the people.

Throughout most of Asian history, theocracy was the norm, since when ancient lands were ruled by kings, the kings gradually came to be revered as gods. Thus, palaces acquired the aura of temples, and temples that of palaces. Dances done by temple dancers in service to the gods were easily transposed into court dances and performed in palaces. But the typology still holds: courtly dance tends away from the mythic toward the formal, since the king presides over the scene from above, just as would a god. Village dance tends toward the mythic and away from the formal since the dancers are on the same plane as the villagers. But the sacred atmosphere, the sense of a time and a place set apart, remains. Sarla Sehgal provides an exemplary description of a performance that is Indian but that could just as easily be Indonesian, Thai, Japanese, or Cambodian:

> Kathakali is an all-night function performed in the open without a backdrop or stage accessories. One large brass lamp filled with coconut oil is all the stage-lighting. Several hours before the performance is due to begin, loud and incessant drumming announces to the neighborhood that a Kathakali dance-drama will take place, and entire families begin to assemble to witness the spectacular performance. When all is ready and darkness has thickened, the expectancy of the atmosphere is im-

measurably heightened by the leaping lamp-flame casting weird shadows, the ear-splitting drumming and the clashing of cymbals. The musicians now appear at the back of the clearing which serves as a stage and the drumming increases in volume. The atmosphere is near-hypnotic. The chanting begins, and two men arrive holding between them a coloured curtain. After invocatory verses in honour of the deities, a devotional dance, *Thodayam*, is done by two dancers behind the curtain. Then follows the *Purappadu* (commencement), which is a pure dance prelude by a "divine pair."

Western observers of Asian dance forms will at times be conscious of watching a purely formal dance and at other times of observing a re-creation of mythic acts. At still other times, Westerners will think they are participating in a ritual before a visible or an invisible altar. But in each case, all three elements will be present, however subtly, within the dance. The dancer's stage is where transitions of cosmic time are noted and celebrated.

When this is properly understood, all dichotomies vanish. Human beings and gods become as one. Distinctions between sacred and secular time fade. The forces whose opposition brings the world into being are discovered to be, in truth, not opposed but harmoniously, although precariously and dramatically, balanced.

Some see in the movements of Asian dancers the gestures of the rice farmer sowing seed and the fisherman casting nets. Asian dancers, it has been said, do not dance as though trying to lift themselves off the earth, as in Western ballet; they dance toward the earth, into the land and the water. Of course, no one legitimately knows the origins of these dance gestures; but the notion of secular movement, of the motions of men and women in their workaday lives finding their way into these dances of ritual, myth, and form should not surprise us. For the very occasion of the dance marks the descent of the gods among their people, with whom they share in the joys and the pains of work and play. As the saying goes, "In the age of the gods, the gods were all human." Asian dances celebrate divinity and humanity simultaneously and as a mysterious confluence. Festival time became the time to ponder that mystery, whereby unity is discovered within duality and transcendence reveals itself in immanence. Dance is, in Asia, a coming to earth.

Locale, Climate, Culture, and History. The terrain of the Asian continent ranges from great river valleys and mountains to vast arid deserts, steppes, tropical plains, and rain forests. A certain vogue in late-nineteenth-century European scholarship regarded climate as a determinative factor in culture. Thus, the dance of southern climes would be predicted to be openly sensual, supple, and voluptuous—as is the *bharata nāṭyam* of India. In the north, dance would be expected to be more arid, cerebral, and angular, such as that used in Japanese *nō* theater. But the society that produced *nō* also produced the vibrant *kabuki*, and the society of the *bharata nāṭyam* also produced *kathakaḷi*. *Kabuki* was the dance of Japan favored by the old merchant class; *nō* was the dance of the Zen sect of Buddhism—monastic, severe, and militaristic. If climate has little or no determinative value in producing culture traits, social class apparently does. Dance types and genres reflect the taste and the ethos of those who support and participate in dance.

Another pattern is worth watching for in Asian dance. The *bharata nāṭyam* may be danced by women, but *nō* is performed only by men. Many dance genres in Asia—north and south, Hindu- and Buddhist-inspired—are traditionally performed only by male dancers. Various reasons have been given for this, but it all comes down to a puritanical ethos, based on patriarchy and a strictness about propriety present in all Asian religious traditions. In India, this puritanism was responsible for the seclusion of women known as purdah, which in turn prevented women from appearing on stage; in Japan, this puritanism took the form of an ascetic suspicion of bright colors, frivolity, and spontaneity of expression of feelings. Puritanism comes and goes in all cultures and religious traditions. When it is ascendant, the dance may find itself pushed toward acerbity and formalism; when it is in decline, the dance may freely move toward the people, toward the mythic, toward openness and sensuality and the full involvement of both men and women.

In the history of Asian religions, one or two developments have been decisive for history and thus for the arts. The first is the emergence—during the millennium that began with the life of the Buddha (c.563–483 BCE) and ended with the life of Muhammad (c.570–632 CE)—of global faith. Until this time, and indeed after it, religious traditions had been (and in much of the world still continue to be) local affairs—matters of village and regional custom. The second development was the arrival of Islam in the seventh and eighth centuries and will be discussed in turn. Global faiths are restless faiths, often not surviving in the lands of their origin but flourishing in other places. They change, often drastically, as they migrate, yet never lose their missionary zeal.

Hinduism is not a global faith; Buddhism is. Indian culture thus powerfully shaped neighboring cultures, although this happened gradually and subtly. The favorite epic of India, the *Rāmāyaṇa*, is danced throughout Southeast Asia, but no brahmin sent out disciples to spread the teachings of the *Rāmāyaṇa*; Indian culture spilled over Indian borders as easily as wandering Aryans from the north spilled in. In the end, it was south Indian, Dravidian lore, usage, and imagery that seeped into the consciousness of the entire subcontinent to form a unified, dynamic civilization. Its vital dance forms drew on the store of mythic wisdom from both northern Aryan and southern Dravidian cultures.

Islam's invasion of India in the seventh and eighth centuries was quite different from the earlier Aryan invasions that united the subcontinent. India's global state already existed, as did the zeal of Buddhism—an Indian-based global faith. Hindu and Buddhist myth and dance had already influenced India's neighbors without destroying anything of the indigenous cultures. In contrast, a militant Islam overtook northern India and shook its traditions to the core; Indian culture was never again the same. Hinduism became devotional in a new way, moving toward a kind of free-form ecstasy. Chant and the pursuit of a vision displaced the mythic consciousness, and ecstasy was extracted from the dance and left to stand on its own. The holy man became a spontaneous dancer. Sri Caitanya (1485–1533) was a kind of Hindu Isadora Duncan, dancing without choreography. He was possessed, and his possession was sufficient for him. Inspiration became all important, tempered only by doctrine—and precious little of that.

Alternatively, consider the impact of Buddhism on Japan's dance drama, which led to the birth of *nō.* The *kagura* was transformed; the shrine priestesses *(miko)* who danced it were replaced by male dancers; a new emphasis on plot was introduced; plays became literary masterworks. Religion and the dance became more concerned with matters of belief. *Nō* depicted the triumph of the new magic of asceticism over the old magic of animism and animatism—of animal spirits and ghosts. Above all, Japan's theater became highly verbal—movement became subordinated to the word.

Modernization has done and is doing new things in Asian theater. Many believe that the best place to see Asia's traditional dance and theater is at the concert hall. For example, *kagura* troupes have performed at New York City's Lincoln Center and in the theater of Tokyo's Mitsukoshi department store, as well as at some of the prestigious Shintō shrines (those with connections to the imperial family) that have been rebuilt since World War II. But one of these troupes has also appeared, and appeared often, at a nightclub. This may tell us more about the impact of modernity than anything else. If the dancers succeed in bringing to the nightclub stage some of the sense of sacred space, they do so only with great difficulty. Optimistically, this may just be another stage in the democratization of dance as traditional dances are being brought into our everyday lives. Pessimistically, such developments signify the undermining of what was essential to the survival of the old forms.

The emergence of folklore as a field of study coincided with the realization that folk culture was withering away; we began to study traditional dances only when we sensed that they were threatened with extinction.

A modern cliché holds that religion and philosophy are separate in the West but one in the East. Nevertheless, a distinction exists in Asia, too. Nowhere is this distinction plainer than in Asian philosphers' descriptions of their music and dance, in contradistinction to what the folk traditions of their lands have to tell us.

For example, Confucius (c.551–c.479 BCE) spoke of dance as a branch of government; his heart was with poetry and with music (he played the *se,* akin to the lute, and the stone gongs). But what does he say of dance? Only that incorrect and inappropriate dances are sometimes used in the courtyard ceremonials of families with overweening political ambitions and that such people thereby make themselves insufferable. But Mozi (Mo-tzu; c.470–391 BCE), who opposed dancing, quoted an ancient and presumably lost court document as saying: "Constant dancing in the palace—this is the way of shamans!"

Japanese tradition makes it clear that Japan's dance indeed had origins in shamanism. According to Japanese mythology, two families of gods exist: the sky gods and the earth gods. The earth gods are obstreperous and rather bawdy; the sky gods are noble and sensitive. Amaterasu, the sun, the source of all light, and the queen of the celestial deities, demonstrates the sky gods' propriety. Early in the creation Amaterasu is so shocked by the bad manners of her earthly brother, Susa-no-o, that she withdraws into a sky cavern and renders the world dark. The earth spirits are remorseful, and the celestial spirits are all atwitter. The resolution of the problem (the first eclipse) is left to a being who commands both realms. She is Ame-no-Uzume, the prototypical shamaness, and she does the trick by doing a dance that brings the overly refined sky gods out of their shell, yet tames the earth spirits with laughter. This is the first dance, and it reconciles heaven and earth, spirit and flesh.

Gods dance; philosophers generally do not. Rangda and Barong dance out their differences annually in Balinese temple courtyards; Śiva dances and brings the universe, in all its complexity and diversity, into being—and then ushers it out of existence again, leaving nothing but the dance. Asian dance has never lost this cosmic dimension or this mythic purport.

[*For further discussion, see entries on specific dance forms mentioned herein.*]

BIBLIOGRAPHY

Caillois, Roger. *Man and the Sacred.* Translated by Meyer Barash. Glencoe, Ill., 1959.

Confucius. *The Analects.* Translated by Arthur Waley. London, 1938.

Coomaraswamy, Ananda K. *The Dance of Śiva.* London, 1918.

Durkheim, Émile, and Marcel Mauss. *Primitive Classification* (1903). Translated by Rodney Needham. London, 1963.

Eliade, Mircea. *Cosmos and History: The Myth of the Eternal Return.* Translated by Willard R. Trask. Princeton, 1954.

Eliade, Mircea. *The Sacred and the Profane.* Translated by Willard R. Trask. New York, 1959.

Eliade, Mircea. *Myth and Reality.* Translated by Willard R. Trask. New York, 1963.

Eliade, Mircea. *Shamanism: Archaic Techniques of Ecstasy.* Translated by Willard R. Trask. New York, 1964.

Lévi-Strauss, Claude. *The Savage Mind.* Chicago, 1966.
Ministry of Information and Broadcasting, Publications Division. *Indian Dance.* Delhi, 1955.
Mo-tzu. *Basic Writings.* Translated by Burton Watson. New York, 1963.
Philippi, Donald L., trans. *Kojiki.* Tokyo, 1968.
Sadler, A. W. "The Form and Meaning of the Festival." *Asian Folklore Studies* 28.1 (1969).
Toynbee, Arnold. *Civilization on Trial, and The World and the West.* New York, 1960.
Waley, Arthur. *Three Ways of Thought in Ancient China.* Garden City, N.Y., 1956.

A. W. SADLER

ASIAN MARTIAL ARTS have contributed to dance and theatrical performance both directly and indirectly—for example, as a source of training technique. This article first reviews the history and underlying philosophy of the martial arts and then considers their relationships to both past and contemporary performance.

Historical Overview. The Asian martial arts comprise a diverse group of specific fighting forms unique to each Asian country; they first developed as systems of combat whose primary purpose was to disarm or kill an enemy or opponent. Some martial forms emphasize the use of weapons, while others developed primarily as empty-hand systems in which the hands and feet become the weapons.

While each of the Asian martial arts is unique, many of them share common features. Most of the martial arts are highly specialized systems of knowledge. Originally, access to the martial arts was carefully restricted, in some cases by class or caste distinctions. Many techniques, especially those considered most dangerous, are secret, disclosed only to the most advanced and trusted students. The techniques of a system are carefully structured to move the novice through a long and difficult course of study, culminating in fighting expertise, achieved only after years of disciplined practice.

Careful and disciplined daily practice is usually required of "forms" (Japanese *kata*), set patterns through which specific techniques are learned by repetition. Such careful and disciplined training is imparted by master to disciple directly through the student's body, which is the vehicle for the combat-effective realization of practice forms. Only repetitive in-body training produces the spontaneous reflex responses necessary to the martial practitioner. Minimum periods of study in a martial discipline range from four to seven years, but life-long study of a martial art is most typical.

The master usually includes schooling not only in the martial techniques but also in concomitant moral and ethical principles. Such principles are not always directly transmitted through verbal instruction, but may instead be absorbed from the demeanor, behavior, and example of the teacher and advanced students. The careful screening process by which a master judges a student worthy of advancement, especially to the most secret parts of a discipline, ensures that only those who have absorbed implicit codes of moral conduct are given advanced knowledge. Often the moral code prohibits the use of the dangerous techniques unless one's life is threatened. In some systems, rules of diet and behavior circumscribe the training, discouraging those weak in mind and body. Such demands shape the personality, demeanor, behavior, and attitude of the long-term student.

In the past, complete fighting artists had to be capable of defending themselves against attacks to the most vulnerable spots (Sanskrit, *marman*) of the body. In addition, a master was often called upon to minister to casualties of the training place or battlefield. It is therefore not surprising that the Asian martial arts developed in close association with the understanding of anatomy, medical sciences, and health care. Three of the most important principles of Asian medical sciences closely associated with martial arts are the role and use of breath; the role and function of proper exercise in health maintenance; and an understanding of the body's vital spots. The English word *breath* does not bear the rich meaning of the Asian terms. The Sanskrit term *prāṇa* refers to the vital energy that is life itself; breath and respiration are only one manifestation of this total life force. The Chinese *qi* and Japanese *ki* similarly denote the vital (life) force. Breath then, or "life force," was considered the very foundation for life and, therefore, of health. By controlling the life force, one could effectively gain power over one's health as well as gain the ability to channel the energy and power of this force into martial techniques.

Techniques of breath control have therefore developed as one of the central practices of many Asian martial systems. Such control is gained by the repetitious practice of breathing exercises, either as part of the forms of physical practice or as a separate set of special breathing exercises. When such control of the vital force is exercised, in conjunction with the physical exercise of the entire body through the practice of forms, the result is the promotion of individual general health and well-being.

The martial practitioner also has to have a fundamental understanding of the body's anatomy, especially the vital spots, which are usually the object of attack and defense. Injury to vital spots results in instant death or serious impairment of the nervous system. Many Asian masters, especially in India and China, became masters of both fighting and medical arts, especially those branches of medicine associated with battle-related injuries.

The Asian cultural and religious environments that shaped the fighting arts nurtured a holistic understanding of the interrelationship between body, mind, and spirit.

ASIAN MARTIAL ARTS. The master of Chinese *taijiquan* allows *qi* (life energy) to circulate through his body. He moves slowly, fluidly through prescribed forms, shifting his weight evenly, imperceptibly from foot to foot. (Photograph © 1981 by Jack Vartoogian; used by permission.)

Body and mind were not opposed as separate, dualistic, or warring enemies; instead, they were most often perceived as working in harmony. For example, in India the ancient *dhanurvedic* ("science of the bow") tradition recognized the importance of one-point concentration in practice. The *Agni Purāṇa* (a seventh- or eighth-century revision of a much earlier and now lost work, the *Dhanurveda*) notes that "the man who has made the vision of both his mental and physical eyes steady can conquer even the god of death." Warriors were expected to have a highly developed steadiness of hand and the ability to concentrate the mind. Such single-mindedness was achieved both through the daily practice of martial forms and through the selective practice of yoga and associated breathing techniques (*prāṇāyāma*). This practice is still followed by a few masters of *kaḷarippayaṭṭu,* a regional Indian martial art.

Like the *dhanurvedic* tradition, other Asian martial systems recognize the necessity of single-point concentration. Spontaneous and immediate reflex reactions are necessary in combat situations: distraction means death. Such single-mindedness is the natural result of the mind–body harmony developed through the in-body process of training. When the body and breath are controlled and the mind is focused completely on the act of doing the technique, then the weapon (or the hand) is filled with directed and controlled energy.

Many Asian systems locate the practitioner's center in the abdominal region. This area below the navel is believed to be the source of breath and, therefore, the origin of the vital force and energy to be applied in movement. Mastery brings a total integration and harmony of body, breath, and manifest energy—qualitatively seen in the tremendous heaviness and power that characterize the martial movements, attacks, and defenses performed by masters.

While such mental and physical integration is characteristic of all Asian martial arts at advanced levels, the explicit use of martial arts—for meditational purposes, or to achieve spiritual enlightenment—has varied with historical circumstances. Indian yoga and some of its martial traditions, such as *kaḷarippayaṭṭu,* share a similar pattern of psychophysical integration, single-minded focus, and concentration developed through in-body techniques. Yoga, the "higher" art, took the individual beyond single-minded concentration into higher meditation, eventually resulting in the attainment of enlightenment and release.

In China, an entirely different set of historical and religious developments combined to produce an organic and explicit relationship between higher spiritual goals and martial practices. It was in China that early systems of health-giving breath and body exercises were developed by Buddhist monks to assist in the rigors of life and in the achievement of meditational goals. Eventually, many of the monasteries developed fighting arts that were based on the breath and body exercises; they were used as a means toward spiritual development.

While many of the Asian martial arts share common

ASIAN MARTIAL ARTS. A practitioner of *kaḷarippayaṭṭu,* the martial art of Kerala, performs one of the beginning exercises that salute the Hindu deities of a *kaḷari*—the place where this form is practiced. (Photograph by Phillip B. Zarilli; used by permission.)

foundations, the manifestation of body–mind harmony, energy flow, and single-mindedness appears to differ qualitatively in the various forms. All the Asian fighting disciplines may be thought of as existing along a continuum. At one end of the continuum we find those forms whose movements appear soft and fluid, that emphasize circular lines and forms supported by a constant and sustained flow of energy. Such curved movements are usually evasive in action, allowing the defender to redirect an attack. At the opposite end of the continuum are those forms dominated by the use of straight-line attacks and defenses, hard or percussive actions supported by quick explosions of energy. Here direct force is usually met by direct force in the application of straight-line moves. This basic distinction is derived from the Chinese, who divided their own martial arts into two main types, soft and hard. However, no martial art is purely soft or hard; all share aspects of both. Between the two extremes are many forms that make equal use of both straight-line and curved movements, both sustained energy and short bursts of energy.

These qualitative dimensions of movements and energy are best illustrated through specific examples. At the curved or soft end of the spectrum is the Chinese *taijiquan* (*t'ai-chi ch'uan*; the ancient Chinese exercise art). Here the master moves in a steady, constant, measured yet continuous flow through curved forms. *Qi* (life energy) circulates through the master's body. The feet are firmly and solidly planted on the ground. The spine remains upright over the solid pillar of the waist, which serves as the axis of the body, facilitating slow and sustained breathing. During the entire sequence of movement in a form, the weight is slowly and alternately shifted from one leg to another as the exercise continues without break for fifteen to thirty minutes.

In India's *kaḷarippayaṭṭu*, equal emphasis is given to circular and straight-line patterns. While practicing the preliminary total body exercise patterns, an advanced student will use sustained energy and diaphragmatic breathing to move quickly through a complex series of wavelike movements, kicks, steps, and high jumps—an acrobatic tour de force. A master practicing with the wooden practice weapon crouches low to the ground in an opening position, feet planted firmly at right angles in the "lion" pose. The abdominal area is bound tightly in yards of wrapped cloth. The master's eyes are focused steadily and intently on the opponent's eyes. Together, the combatants move through an undulating series of serpentine motions that culminate in an exchange of attacks against and defenses of the body's vital spots.

The hard, linear straight-line forms are perhaps best illustrated by Okinawan karate. A karate master executes, in quick succession, a sequence of attacks and defenses across the floor. This sequence is based on the repetitious practice of preliminary forms. A right elbow thrust may be followed by a forearm block and then by a quick succession of kicks, all based on linear movements. Hard, percussive, and angular, the fists or feet lash out with lightning speed, each a burst of hard energy often accompanied by a strong expulsion of breath.

Because of the careful and meticulous process of transmission, many of the Asian martial arts are still practiced today. While they have undergone a gradual process of change and adaptation under individual masters, resulting in the proliferation of numerous schools or styles, the Asian martial arts exhibit a strong continuity of practice over many generations. The fundamental techniques of many of today's numerous forms are centuries old. Since the nineteenth century, a number of new martial arts have been created (especially Japanese forms), all of which are based on adaptations of older techniques. The recent Japanese *do* forms, such as *aikido*, *kendo*, and *kyudo*, developed as the combat efficacy of old weapons forms was no longer needed or emphasized. The main concern of these recent *do* forms is with spiritual development and discipline; a logical development of Zen Buddhist belief, the more recent forms emphasize the use of martial disciplines as a means to self-perfection.

The twentieth-century martial arts world is a complex mosaic of disciplines practiced for widely divergent reasons. Some old combat forms that emphasize weapons practice, such as the Japanese *bugei* (including *iaijutsu*) or the Indian *kaḷarippayaṭṭu*, continue to teach the forms of combat art with live weapons aimed at the body's vital spots, essentially as they were taught centuries ago. Other Asian martial arts, including many of the more recent forms, have been transformed into competitive sports, complete with modern equipment and scoring systems. Still other martial arts are practiced today as self-defense

ASIAN MARTIAL ARTS. A teacher, or *gurukkal* (right), practices spear versus sword and shield with an advanced student of *kaḷarippayaṭṭu*. (Photograph by Phillip B. Zarrilli; used by permission.)

ASIAN MARTIAL ARTS. The *kabuki* theater developed a stylized fight technique called *tachimawari*, seen here, to depict battle scenes, especially those involving samurai characters. (Photograph from the archives of The Asia Society, New York.)

forms for practical use in an often violent world. Some others among the fighting arts are today practiced mainly for their meditational and general health benefits. Finally, a number of martial arts are playing an important role in the training and creative worlds of contemporary performing arts.

Asian Martial Arts and Performance. The Asian martial master is as striking in his effortless virtuosity, the quickness and fluidity of his movements, and the total integration of mind and body concentrated in the moment as is the master Asian performing artist. This is not surprising, since historically in Asia, there has always been a close relationship between the martial arts and a wide variety of performing arts. Indeed, it is often hard to distinguish where the martial art ends and where the performing art begins. Javanese *pencak-silat* is a highly effective self-defense and weapons form which is often practiced to the accompaniment of percussion instruments. Its grounded, fluid solo and partner forms are characterized by light and graceful movements. *Pencak-silat* is often performed at marriages or other social and festive occasions. It serves simultaneously as an absorbing and beautiful performing art and as an effective self-defense and combat art.

Asian martial and performing arts share common principles and practices, such as the centrality of diaphragmatic breathing, psychophysical integration, and long-

term in-body training. Indeed, the martial techniques have often provided a fundamental set of physical training techniques, basic body positions and stances, breathing and centering principles, and choreographic patterns that have been taken over or completely transformed into performing traditions. Not only are the martial art forms as graceful, fluid, and beautiful as dance, the weapons techniques provide a ready means for literal or stylized presentation of stage combat. Such combat forms have been used to enact the great body of mythical, epic, and quasi-historical literatures of all major Asian cultures. What better way to bring alive the courageous heroes and gods than to bring them to the dance or dance-drama stage with the demeanor, movements, and combat techniques of the contemporary combat arts. So close has this relationship been between martial and performing arts that all the major dance-drama forms of Asia have been highly influenced by their respective martial traditions.

The spectacular acrobatic feats and mass stylized combat of the Beijing Opera stage is a direct transference of indigenous fighting arts to the stage. The disciplined training of the Beijing Opera actor involves emphasis on a wide variety of techniques employing both hand-to-hand fighting and manipulation of a wide variety of weapons, including halberds, lances, and swords. Such techniques were probably taken from China's old northern Shaolin Temple boxing and arms traditions, which emphasize graceful movements.

Likewise, the *kabuki* theater of Japan developed its *tachimawari*, or stylized fight scene techniques, especially those associated with the portrayal of the aristocratic warrior class samurai characters. In *kabuki*, the *tateshi* became the acting company's stage fight specialist, responsible for combining various acrobatic moves, poses, and specific fighting techniques derived from the martial arts into *kabuki's* exciting, fast-paced battle scenes.

Even the more reserved and restrained *nō* theater of Japan, the predecessor of *kabuki*, was influenced by the martial tradition and its techniques. The Kita *nō* school, one of the five main family traditions of *nō* acting, originated with the samurai class. Some of today's contemporary Kita school actors compare the concentration and single-mindedness of the *nō* performer to that of the martial artist. Younger Kita school actors often undergo extensive training in a martial art to enhance the overtly martial style of the school. One of many examples of the specific use of martial techniques in *nō* performance is the wholesale use of the traditional sword versus the halberd in the culminating fight of the demon play, *Funa Benkei*, in Kita style. [*See* Kita School.]

Yet another example of the close relationship between Asian martial arts and performance comes from India. As early as the writing of the *Nāṭyaśāstra* (the encyclopedia of Indian stage practice, dating between 200 BCE and 200

CE), the link between martial techniques, performer training, and stage combat has been made. In the eleventh chapter, the performer is enjoined to prepare himself for the stage by taking "exercise on the floor as well as high up in the air, and should have beforehand one's body massaged with the [sesame or *sesamum*] oil or with barley gruel." In addition to practicing such exercises, the neophyte is enjoined to observe dietary restrictions and to be well trained in body movements to be used in stage combat. Specific techniques of weapons' use, drawn directly from the *dhanurvedic* martial traditions, are carefully described.

This legacy of an early Indian connection between martial and performing arts—evidenced as a holistic design for physical exercise, development of health, and specialized skills—is most vividly found today in *kathakaḷi*, the powerful male dance drama of Kerala state in southern India. *Kathakaḷi* originated with Kerala's martial caste, the Nayars (Nairs), who were practitioners of the traditional regional martial form, *kaḷarippayaṭṭu*. The entire preliminary physical-culture training system of *kathakaḷi*, including the full-body massage, is designed to render the actor's body flexible, supple, balanced, and controlled; it is drawn directly from the preliminary exercises of the martial art. In addition, the dance drama's basic body positions, low center of gravity in the abdomen, and dynamic choreography (including leaps, turns, jumps, and circling patterns) are drawn directly from the martial tradition. [*See* Kathakaḷi.]

Contemporary Performance. In the 1950s, Western performing artists began to search Asia for techniques and traditions that could revitalize their own contemporary arts. One of the major sources during the ensuing decades has been the Asian martial arts. Western contemporary performing artists have been drawn to the Asian martial arts because they offer more than simple technical mastery or virtuosity; mental and spiritual dimensions are touched through long practice and thus the martial arts transcend simple physical mimicry. The Asian martial or performing artist presents the Westerner a complete picture of the virtuoso performer: self-possessed, ideally egoless, in absolute control and command of his art, and able to infuse his technique with a vital energy through absolute concentration and focus. The results of long-term practice—new awareness of centering, breath and energy control—make the Asian martial arts an important source of inspiration and of fundamental training techniques for the contemporary Western performing artist.

One of the most important martial arts to have had an early and lasting impact on contemporary performance is China's *taijiquan*. In the early 1960s, A. C. Scott began to use it as a regular part of performer training at the University of Wisconsin. The sustained energy, economy of movement, center in the lower abdomen, directed visual focus, and body–mind integration made *taijiquan* an important resource for the disciplined and controlled training of the performer. Since its early use, other martial arts have been introduced into performer training programs.

The Asian martial arts have made an important contribution to choreography, stage movement, and stage combat. This impact has been both direct, as in the use of martial techniques in dance or theater productions, and indirect, as in the application of principles of movement as a creative catalyst for movement. One example of the literal use of a martial art in contemporary performance is that of Yoshi and Company. In the 1970s, this company created a complete performance piece *Ame-Tsuchi*, based on Japanese *kendo*—the modern sword form in which full-body equipment girds the warrior for exchanges delivered with a mock sword to the opponent's body. The rituals of combat and the full contact exchanges serve as an effective vehicle to transmit the symbolism behind the Japanese origin myth serving as the text for the performance.

One choreographer who has worked with the qualitative dimensions of the martial arts and attempted to use their underlying principles in choreography is Al Huang. Huang, who learned *taijiquan* as a child in China, attempts to apply the concepts and philosophy of fluid movement, solid central torso control, and balance to his own choreography.

The connection between Asian martial arts and performance has deep historical roots within Asia. The underlying principles that inform the Asian martial arts make their specific techniques an important resource for the contemporary and traditional artist alike.

[*See also* China, *article on* Dance Traditions, *and* India, *article on* History of Indian Dance. *For more detailed discussion of Indonesian martial arts, see* Pencak. *For mock combat in Western traditions, see* Armed Dances; Barriera, Torneo, and Battaglia; Capoeira; Matachins; Pyrrhic; *and* Sword Dance. *For similar discussion of Middle Eastern traditions, see* Egypt, *article on* Traditional Forms; Middle East, *overview article; and* Music for Dance, *article on* Arab Music.]

BIBLIOGRAPHY

Draeger, Donn F. *Weapons and Fighting Arts of the Indonesian Archipelago.* Rutland, Vt., 1972.
Draeger, Donn F. *Classical Budo.* New York, 1973.
Draeger, Donn F. *Classical Bujutsu.* New York, 1973.
Draeger, Donn F. *Modern Bujutsu and Budo.* New York, 1974.
Draeger, Donn F., and Robert W. Smith. *Comprehensive Asian Fighting Arts.* New York, 1980.
Herrigel, Eugen. *Zen and the Art of Archery.* New York, 1971.
Huard, Pierre, and Ming Wong. *Oriental Methods of Mental and Physical Fitness: The Complete Book of Meditation, Kinesitherapy, and Martial Arts in China, India, and Japan.* New York, 1977.
Tohei Koichi. *Aikido in Daily Life.* Tokyo, 1973.
Wong, James I. *A Source Book in the Chinese Martial Arts.* 2 vols. Stockton, Calif., 1978.

Zarrilli, Phillip B. "'Doing the Exercise': The In-Body Transmission of Performance Knowledge in a Traditional Martial Art." *Asian Theatre Journal* 1.2 (1984): 191–206.

Zarrilli, Phillip B. "Three Bodies of Practice in a Traditional South Indian Martial Art." *Social Science and Medicine* 28 (1989): 1289–1309.

Zarrilli, Phillip B. "Actualizing Power(s) and Crafting a Self in *Kalarippayattu*, A South Indian Martial Art and the Yoga and Ayurvedic Paradigms." *Journal of Asian Martial Arts* 3.3 (1994): 10–51.

PHILLIP B. ZARRILLI

ASSEMBLIES. The term *assembly* is derived from the French verb *assembler* (to gather or meet). Although it is also applied to meetings for prayer, legal proceedings, or governing, the word has long been associated with gatherings specifically intended for social diversion, music, dancing, and conversation. The French dancing master André Lorin referred to assemblies in England around 1688: "I saw them danced not only at Court, but at Assemblies in town, at schools, Masquerade Balls and at the Comedie, Musicales, and in the country."

In the eighteenth century, assemblies were organized among the British and European upper classes by a committee of social leaders who issued subscription tickets to selected people for a series of gatherings scheduled during the social season. Those chosen then purchased the permitted number of tickets, called vouchers, for their guests, who were expected to be equally socially acceptable. An invitation to the most important assembly of the season was a coveted prize and denoted impeccable antecedents or at least connections of consequence.

As a social institution, the assembly functioned in eighteenth-century society as a genteel setting for members of the upper classes to meet and mingle. Parents could further their children's marriage prospects; young ladies could be displayed before eligible gentlemen; and even business and political interests could be pursued in a setting less crass than the countinghouse and less intimate than one's own drawing room. Precautions were taken to ensure that persons of inferior social standing or less than impeccable reputation were not admitted. Protocol was severe: even the duke of Wellington was refused

ASSEMBLIES. *The Comforts of Bath*, an engraving by Thomas Rowlandson published in 1798, shows the splendor of an assembly room at one of the most popular eighteenth-century English spas. Scenes in several of Jane Austen's novels were based on her intimate knowledge of the Upper and the Lower Assembly Rooms at Bath. (Courtesy of Elizabeth Aldrich.)

entry, once for arriving after midnight and once for appearing in trousers instead of knee breeches.

By the early eighteenth century, large public assembly rooms were being built in fashionable cities in Great Britain, on the Continent, and in the colonies. Town halls, country inns, and hostelries often provided an assembly room. Among the most noted in England were those at Almack's, Ranelagh, and the Vauxhall Gardens, all in London.

The most spectacular of the early eighteenth-century assembly rooms, however, were those at Bath, about a day's travel by coach from London. Bath's famous hot springs were dedicated to the gods by the early Celts and extensively developed by the Romans in the first century CE. The spa fell into ruins during the Middle Ages, but the waters drew important royal visitors throughout the Renaissance and Baroque periods. In 1703, the ailing Queen Anne's sojourn at Bath set a fashion that eventually raised the resort far above its ancient splendor.

Beau Nash (1674–1762) was master of ceremonies at the Pump Room in Bath from 1708 until 1761. It was largely due to his eccentric style as arbiter of taste and manners that the Bath Assembly Rooms prospered. Nash decreed "that Elder Ladies and Children be contented with a Second Bench at the Ball, as being past, or not come to Perfection," and that dancing should cease promptly at midnight even if a dance were in progress.

The author Jane Austen (1775–1817) resided at Bath, where the Upper and Lower Assembly Rooms provided inspiration for romantic episodes in her novels *Northanger Abbey* and *Persuasion*.

An Assembly usually commenced with a minuet danced by one couple at a time, in order according to rank. Each man was expected to dance twice, ensuring that all women would have a turn. Women who desired to dance the minuet were given favored seating and were guaranteed the scrutiny of the entire assembly. After several hours, the contredances began. Partners for this lively, less formal dance were often assigned by the ball committee; positions in the sets were regulated by numbered tickets given to each woman on arrival.

Often a dancing master held an assembly at his academy and sold tickets to the prominent families of his pupils. Among the middle classes, professional guilds and trade organizations held assemblies for their members and guests, imitating the protocol practiced by the *haut monde*.

Dancing was an important diversion at an assembly, but gambling proved equally popular, and special rooms were provided for whist, quadrille, and other games of chance. In addition, intervals for the serving of elaborate teas or suppers were customary. Musical recitals and poetry readings were sometimes offered.

Assemblies continued into the nineteenth century, but more emphasis was given to the brilliance of the ball and less to gambling, probably a reflection of growing class conservatism. Eventually gambling was omitted entirely and retreated to the casinos.

During the nineteenth century travel became less difficult, and a general mobility of all economic classes ensued. Seacoast resorts and grand hotels became favorite gathering places for a broad range of people. The exclusivity of large private subscription assemblies was threatened by an influx of new wealth as merchants and manufacturers prospered and sought respectability. Theaters, concert halls, pleasure gardens, restaurants, and public ballrooms flourished. Rather than declining, the institution of the assembly broadened to serve the middle classes. The fashionable attended these popular entertainments but preferred the relative seclusion of private balls and dinner parties. By the mid-nineteenth century the term *ball* (denoting a gathering of one hundred persons or more—fewer constituted an evening party) appeared on fashionable invitations, and the word *assembly* fell into disuse.

[*See also* Social Dance.]

BIBLIOGRAPHY

Emmerson, George S. *A Social History of Scottish Dance*. London, 1972.

Richardson, Philip J. S. *The Social Dances of the Nineteenth Century in England*. London, 1960.

The Upper Assembly Rooms and The Pump Room. Bath, England, n.d. Booklet published by the Bath Museum.

DESMOND F. STROBEL

ASTAIRE, FRED (Frederick Austerlitz; born 10 May 1899 in Omaha, Nebraska, died 22 June 1987 in Los Angeles), American dancer and choreographer. Astaire worked in vaudeville, revue, musical comedy, television, radio, and Hollywood films, especially musicals. He achieved admiring recognition not only from his peers in the entertainment world but also from major figures in ballet and modern dance, such as George Balanchine and Merce Cunningham.

Over the course of his long film career, Astaire appeared in 212 musical numbers, of which 133 contain fully developed dance routines, an amazingly high percentage of which are of the highest artistic value. In quantity and especially in quality, Astaire's contribution is unrivaled in films and, indeed, has few parallels in the history of dance. Because he worked mainly in film, Astaire is that great rarity—a master choreographer, the vast majority of whose works are precisely preserved.

Astaire made an impact in other ways too. He helped enormously to define and develop a motion picture genre; he brought out the best in many composers and lyricists; he influenced a generation of filmmakers and choreographers; he inspired quite a few people to take up dance as an avocation or a profession; and he activated the fancies and fantasies of millions in his audiences—and will continue to do so as long as films are shown.

Astaire's dances are stylistically eclectic. What he called his "outlaw style" is an odd and singularly unpredictable blend of tap and ballroom with bits from other dance forms thrown in, but he denied being a specialist in any form and said he resented any rules and restrictions that would follow from adherence to a specific approach. What held everything together was Astaire's distinctive style and sensibility: the casual sophistication, the airy wit, the transparent rhythmic intricacy, the apparent ease of execution, the consummate musicality—qualities apparently inbred in this most natural of dancers.

If Astaire was not restricted by style, he was perfectly content to work within the considerable restraints posed by the types of films in which he was presented: mostly romantic comedies that explored a limited range of emotions, used popular music exclusively for his extensive and frequent dance numbers, and were designed above all to be financially successful.

Although the creation of many of Astaire's dances involved a degree of collaboration with another choreographer, dance director, or dance assistant—the most important of whom was Hermes Pan—Astaire himself was the guiding creative hand and the final authority on his solos and duets—some of which were filmed in one shot. His choreography is notable for its inventiveness, wit, musicality, and economy. Characteristically, each dance takes two or three central ideas, which might derive from a step, the music, the lyrics, the qualities of his partner, or the plot situation, and carefully presents and develops them.

A perfectionist who was obsessed by the idea of not repeating himself, Astaire spent weeks working out his film choreographies. He was a remarkably efficient planner and worker when the costs were highest; some of his most complicated film routines, planned for months, were shot in a day or two. His courtesy, enormous professionalism, and tireless struggle for improvement earned him the devoted admiration of his co-workers, even if his perfectionism, propensity to worry, shyness, self-doubt, and rages (usually directed at himself) could make him difficult to work with at times.

Once in Hollywood, after a vastly successful stage career with his sister Adele as partner, Astaire quickly focused his attention on the problems and prospects in the filming of dance. He soon settled on the approach he was to follow throughout his career, one that was to dominate Hollywood musicals for a generation; both camera work and editing are fashioned to enhance the flow and continuity of the dances, not to undercut or overshadow them. The dances are captured in a small number of shots

ASTAIRE. *The Story of Vernon and Irene Castle* (RKO, 1939). In their ninth film together, Fred Astaire and Ginger Rogers portray the Castles, the legendary husband-and-wife duo who charmed pre–World War I audiences with elegant and lively ballroom dancing. (Photograph by RKO Studios; private collection.)

(sometimes only one), and the camera is almost always comfortably distant so that it shows the dancers fully from head to toe.

Although his approach was fundamentally cautious and conservative, Astaire was open to new ideas and to development. Once he had gained control over the filming of his numbers in the 1930s, and once he had firmly established his basic aesthetic for filmed dance, he began to open out, to expand, to make wider use of the medium—but always with an eye toward putting the medium at the service of the dance.

Astaire's father was an immigrant Austrian brewery employee and a stagestruck amateur musician. Because Astaire's sister Adele showed such prodigious talent in early dancing school recitals, in 1904 their mother took her to New York City for professional training. Fred, one-and-a-half years younger than Adele, was brought along and enrolled with her in dancing school. In 1905, when he was only six, they began performing together in vaudeville, earning $150 per week at a time when the average skilled worker made less than $10 per week.

In a few years the duo had outgrown their material and could no longer get bookings. For two years they stayed out of show business, attending regular school sessions in New Jersey. Soon they returned to vaudeville and, following the advice of another vaudeville dancer, Aurelio Coccia, whom Astaire considered the most influential man in his dancing career, soon had a "streamlined show stopper." By their last season in vaudeville, while still in their midteens, they had become featured performers, earning $350 per week.

In 1917 the Astaires moved from vaudeville to the musical stage. From then until 1932 they appeared in ten musical productions on Broadway. A few were flops, but most were hugely successful, in particular, two musical comedies with songs by George and Ira Gershwin (*Lady, Be Good!* in 1924 and *Funny Face* in 1927) and a revue with songs by Arthur Schwartz and Howard Dietz (*The Band Wagon* in 1931). Although Astaire was self-effacing around his talented sister, his own gifts did not go unnoticed. Among those with limitless admiration for Astaire was Serge Diaghilev, the great Russian ballet impresario, who was particularly impressed by the dancer's charm and musicality.

As their stage careers progressed, Astaire became more and more involved in the choreography for the routines. Beginning with *Lady, Be Good!* he also started performing in solo numbers devised primarily by himself. Particularly influential on his outlook on dance at this time were, besides Coccia, the great Danish ballerina Adeline Genée and three dancing teams: Vernon and Irene Castle, Eduardo and Elisa Cansino, and Bert Kalmar and Jessie Brown. Astaire was very impressed also by a black tapper, John W. Bubbles, whose sense of invention never seemed to flag.

When in 1932 Astaire's sister retired from show business to marry a British aristocrat, Astaire sought to reshape his career. He settled on the featured role in the show *Gay Divorce*, a "musical play" with songs by Cole Porter. This show was important not only because it proved that Astaire could flourish without his sister but also because it helped to establish the pattern of most of his later film musicals—a light, perky, unsentimental comedy largely uncluttered by subplot and built around a love story for Astaire and his partner (in this case Claire Luce) that was airy and amusing but essentially serious, particularly when the pair danced together. To the show's hit song, "Night and Day," he fashioned his first great romantic duet. However, he never saw himself as a true romantic lead and had an antipathy for "mushy" dialogue scenes: "Saying 'I love you' was the job of our dance routines," he asserted.

In 1933 Astaire married Phyllis Livingston Potter, who came from one of Boston's most aristocratic families and who had never seen him on the stage. (They had two children: Fred, Jr., born in 1936, and Ava, born in 1942. To Astaire's great despair, his wife died of cancer in 1954 at age forty-six.) Shortly after his marriage, Astaire went to Hollywood. For a few days he worked at Metro-Goldwyn-Mayer (MGM), where he had a dancing bit in the Joan Crawford film *Dancing Lady* (1933), and then he went to the financially shaky RKO, where, under contract, he was fifth-billed in the exuberant, fluttery *Flying Down to Rio* (1933), in which he mostly kept the characterization as a juvenile he had used on Broadway with his sister. *Flying Down to Rio* was a massive hit, and Astaire's performance was obviously a major factor in that success. The clearest trumpeting of his potential and the reasons for it came in the review in *Variety:* "He's assuredly a bet after this one, for he's distinctly likeable on the screen, the mike is kind to his voice and as a dancer he remains in a class by himself." The message was clear: the thin, balding, self-conscious, ingratiating, romantically unimpressive tap dancer from the New York stage was a moneymaker.

ASTAIRE. Hermes Pan and Fred Astaire in "Me and the Ghost Upstairs," a number that was cut from the film *Second Chorus* (Paramount, 1941). Although Pan worked closely with Astaire on his material, this was the only time the two appeared together on film. (Photograph from the collection of Rusty E. Frank.)

ASTAIRE. Rita Hayworth and Fred Astaire swinging out in the film *You Were Never Lovelier* (Columbia, 1942). (Photograph by Columbia Pictures; private collection.)

Along for the ride was Ginger Rogers, also a contract player at RKO. Rogers had been chosen to play opposite Astaire in *Flying Down to Rio* more as a comedy foil than anything else. As it turned out, they went together well.

The Gay Divorcee (1934), a film version of *Gay Divorce*, was the first of the major Astaire-Rogers pictures, and it scored even better at the box office than had *Flying Down to Rio*. Despite Astaire's reservations about being tied into another partnership, the Astaire-Rogers team was an almost overnight success, and exhibitors would seek to book all of RKO's pictures just to be assured of the Astaire-Rogers films—nine in all.

Roberta (1935), with music by Jerome Kern, followed, outgrossing *The Gay Divorcee* and firmly establishing Astaire and Rogers as the king and queen of the RKO lot. Moreover, in this film they reached their full development as a team—the breathless high spirits, the emotional richness, the bubbling sense of comedy, and the romantic compatibility are all there in full measure.

Six more films followed to make them one of the legendary partnerships in the history of dance: *Top Hat* (1935), *Follow the Fleet* (1936), *Swing Time* (1936), *Shall We Dance* (1937), *Carefree* (1938), and *The Story of Vernon and Irene Castle* (1939). Rogers was an outstanding partner for Astaire because as a skilled, intuitive actress she was cagey enough to realize that acting did not stop when the dancing began. She seemed uniquely to understand the dramatic import of the dance, and without resorting to style-shattering emoting, she cunningly contributed her share to the choreographic impact of their numbers together. [*See the entry on Rodgers.*]

For these films Astaire created a rich series of romantic and playful duets for the team as well as an array of dazzling and imaginative solos for himself. Although the plots of the films sometimes lurch improbably, Astaire was concerned from the outset that his numbers have motivation in the script. Playing off the feisty yet arrestingly vulnerable Rogers, he gradually expanded beyond the likable, happy-go-lucky, asexual juvenile he played in his earliest films. His screen persona developed more depth, sexual definition, security, and, eventually, maturity.

Astaire's musicality, and the fact that his films had class and were highly profitable, attracted many of the top popular-song composers of the day. As Irving Berlin said to George Gershwin in 1936, "There is no setup in Hollywood that can compare with doing an Astaire picture." The result was a series of films whose musical values often matched their choreographic splendor.

Under such conditions, Astaire was in a very good bargaining position, both creatively and financially. The directors of his films were instructed to give him complete freedom on the dances and as much rehearsal time as he wanted, and he had little difficulty convincing the studio executives to accept his requests for higher fees.

Astaire's lone effort without Rogers during this period, the delightful *A Damsel in Distress* (1937), was his first film to lose money overall. By the end of the 1930s, the revenues of his films with Rogers also had begun to fall; after a disagreement over fees with the studio Astaire left, dissolving his partnership with Rogers, at least temporarily.

The next years were nomadic ones for Astaire. He wandered from studio to studio, appeared with a variety of partners, and prospered. Between 1940 and 1946 he made three films at MGM, two at Columbia, three at Paramount, and one back at RKO.

The dances in these films retain the usual high quality. His tap duets with Eleanor Powell in *Broadway Melody of 1940* (1940) may be emotionally unevocative but are brilliant nonetheless, as are several of his other duets—with Paulette Goddard in *Second Chorus* (1941), Rita Hayworth in *You'll Never Get Rich* (1941) and *You Were Never Lovelier* (1942), Virginia Dale in *Holiday Inn* (1942), Joan Leslie in *The Sky's the Limit* (1943), and Lucille Bremer in *Yolanda and the Thief* (1945) and *Ziegfeld Follies* (1946). In his solos Astaire often seemed to be seeking to expand the tap vocabulary, in part by capitalizing on its capacity for sheer noise-making, an effect maximized in his solo with firecrackers in *Holiday Inn*. This quality was used for emotional purpose as well, to express giddy joy in *You'll Never Get Rich*, rage and frustration in *The Sky's the Limit*, and an arresting sense of audience confrontation in *Blue Skies* (1946).

Musically, Astaire continued to attract the best: Porter,

ASTAIRE. Fred Astaire dips the long-legged Cyd Charisse in *The Band Wagon* (MGM, 1953), one of his later films. (Photograph from the Film Stills Library, Museum of Modern Art, New York.)

Berlin, Kern, Harold Arlen, Harry Warren, and the brilliant lyricist Johnny Mercer. Major musical contributions in these films also came from several on-screen bands whose sounds Astaire often found choreographically invigorating: Artie Shaw, Freddie Slack, Chico Hamilton, Xavier Cugat, and Bob Crosby.

All these early to mid-1940s films are comedies, and the first few mostly seek to emulate the breezy insouciance of Astaire's earlier films with Rogers. Other approaches were, however, tried: *The Sky's the Limit* is a dark comedy about the impact of World War II on life and love; *Ziegfeld Follies* presents a sumptuous, if sometimes overcalculated, opulence, and most of the numbers have an arrestingly hard edge. Astaire seems to have found the latter's precedent-shattering revue form liberating, creating a duet for himself and Bremer that evokes a kind of extravagant, highly charged lovemaking that he had never before explored so richly. *Yolanda and the Thief* attempted to achieve vaporous fantasy, while in the two films with Bing Crosby, *Holiday Inn* and *Blue Skies*, Astaire is content to be a romantic also-ran.

By 1946, when Astaire decided to retire from motion pictures, his films had created a boom in the dancing school business, so he began what turned out to be a difficult but ultimately successful venture to establish his own chain of dancing schools. Astaire made the investment in part because he had no desire to experience a long, pathetic period of decline as an aging dancer. Like most of his apprehensions, this one was considerably exaggerated, as his next films were to demonstrate. But this "retirement" gave him time to reflect and to realize that he was not yet ready to abandon show business.

In 1947 Gene Kelly, who was scheduled to appear opposite Judy Garland in *Easter Parade* at MGM, broke his ankle and was unable to work. At Kelly's suggestion, producer Arthur Freed approached Astaire about taking over, and Astaire found himself once again in the movies.

Of the ten Astaire films released between 1948 and 1957, seven were made at MGM; six of these were produced by Freed. In general the conditions were congenial and the salary—$150,000 per film—generous. Freed was the dominant figure in Hollywood musicals during that era, producing dozens of financially successful films that had a deserved reputation for quality. His productions tended to be slick, colorful, well paced, tasteful, and energetic, with plots that were literate (or at any rate coherent).

Astaire's participation certainly contributed to both the earnings and the reputation of the Freed musicals. *Easter Parade* (1948), co-starring the affectingly vulnerable Garland, was a major hit. Because of illness, Garland was replaced by Ginger Rogers in Astaire's next film, *The Barkleys of Broadway* (1949). The pairing still had plenty of electricity, but it was not tried again. Most of Astaire's other partners in these later musicals were ballet-trained: Vera-Ellen in *Three Little Words* (1950) and *The Belle of New York* (1952), Cyd Charisse in *The Band Wagon* (1953) and *Silk Stockings* (1957), Leslie Caron in *Daddy Long Legs* (1955), and, more limitedly, Audrey Hepburn in *Funny Face* (1957). For variety, Jane Powell, a singer-actress who could move quite well, was paired with Astaire in *Royal Wedding* (1951); and Betty Hutton, a bombastic comedienne, played opposite him in *Let's Dance* (1950). Occasionally Astaire had difficulty using his partners' various talents to advantage but, for the most part, he did quite well; in *The Belle of New York* he seems to have relished the opportunity to choreograph for a dancer who could comfortably keep up with him.

These later films contain a number of masterful dances, but their average quality is not quite as high as in earlier films. The choreography in *Three Little Words* and *Funny Face*, for example, is remarkably undistinguished by the standards Astaire had set earlier, however appealing the films may be in other ways. In some of these films Astaire seems to have been guided more than usual by other choreographers, and it sometimes shows. Also, in some of what should be romantic duets, his partner seems to be intractable. But if the average is lower, the peaks are still there—among them playful duets, sometimes of the screwball variety, and inventive solos. In many of these dances Astaire developed his talents at mime and mimicry, bringing them to new heights.

The songs created for these films are often weak, and it was undoubtedly a sign of the times that four of the films—*Easter Parade, Three Little Words, The Band Wagon,* and *Funny Face*—rely mostly on songs resurrected from the 1920s and 1930s. By the mid-1950s the era of the classic Hollywood musical as Astaire had experienced it—indeed, defined it—was coming to an end. Revenues were declining, costs were rising, the studio system was in trouble, competition with television was growing, and popular music was moving into the age of rock-and-roll.

Undaunted, Astaire moved into other fields. He had a highly successful career in television, where he appeared on numerous shows as host and/or performer and where he produced four carefully crafted, multiple-award-winning musical specials between 1958 and 1968. His partner in the specials was Barrie Chase, a limber young dancer who had had bit dancing parts in two of his films in the 1950s. Major contributions to the television choreography were made by Hermes Pan and Herbert Ross. With some important exceptions the choreography was not of as high a quality as in Astaire's films.

In 1968 Astaire appeared in one more musical film, as the gnarled, dotty title character in *Finian's Rainbow*, and in the 1970s he helped to host *That's Entertainment*, two compilation films by MGM to salute its by-then vanished golden age of musicals.

Astaire also explored other fields. Shattering Hollywood tradition, he wrote his autobiography himself. He also tried his hand at straight acting roles with considerable success. In films he played a misanthropic scientist in *On the Beach* (1959), an irrepressibly debonair playboy in *The Pleasure of His Company* (1961), a diplomat in *The Notorious Landlady* (1962), a British secret agent in *The Midas Run* (1969), a con man in both *The Towering Inferno* (1975) and *The Amazing Dobermans* (1976), a country doctor in *The Purple Taxi* (1977), and a conscience-stricken murderer in *Ghost Story* (1982). He also appeared in numerous dramatic specials and series on television, usually playing a suave gentleman.

As he entered his eighties Astaire, a lifelong horse-racing enthusiast, romanced and in 1980 married Robyn Smith, a successful, thirty-seven-year-old jockey who had never seen any of his films.

In later life, as others honored and feted him for his achievements at glamorous celebrations held in New York City, Los Angeles, and Washington, D.C., Astaire maintained that his dancing past interested him very little. But after looking at some of his old film clips at a gala in his honor in 1981, he did observe with pleasure, and with some apparent surprise, "I didn't realize I did all that stuff . . . but I'm glad to say I liked what I saw."

[*See also* Film Musicals, *article on* Hollywood Film Musicals; *and* Tap Dance.]

BIBLIOGRAPHY

Astaire, Adele. "He Worries, Poor Boy." *Variety* (18 March 1936).
Astaire, Fred. *Steps in Time*. New York, 1959.
Croce, Arlene. *The Fred Astaire and Ginger Rogers Book*. New York, 1972.
Eustis, Morton. *Players at Work*. New York, 1937.
Green, Stanley. *Starring Fred Astaire*. Garden City, N.Y., 1973.
Giles, Sarah. *Fred Astaire: His Friends Talk*. New York, 1988.
Harvey, Stephen. *Fred Astaire*. New York, 1975.
Lewis, Ken. "Hermes Pan." *Dance Pages* 8.3 (1991): 26–29; 8.4 (1991): 26–29.
Mueller, John. "Fred Astaire and the Integrated Musical." *Cinema Journal* (Fall 1984).
Mueller, John. *Astaire Dancing: The Musical Films*. New York, 1985 and London, 1986.
Saltus, Carol. "The Modest Mr. Astaire." *Inter/View* (June 1973).
Satchell, Tim. *Astaire: The Biography*. London, 1987.

JOHN MUELLER

ATANASSOFF, CYRIL (born 30 June 1941 in Puteaux), French dancer. Atanassoff, of Bulgarian descent, entered the Paris Opera Ballet school in 1953, at the age of twelve. He began his training with Roger Ritz, a former *danseur étoile*, and he subsequently worked with Serge Peretti, whom he regarded as his true teacher. His handsome physique and elegant bearing destined him for noble, virile roles. He joined the Paris Opera Ballet in 1957 and was promoted to *premier danseur* in 1962. Named *danseur étoile* in 1964, he became a favorite with the public, choreographers, and ballerinas, who found in him an attentive partner.

In 1965 Atanassoff performed the role of the Chosen One in Maurice Béjart's *Le Sacre du Printemps* (Rite of Spring), in which his strength and sensual intensity were especially impressive. This role was one of the high points of his career, as was his portrayal of Quasimodo in Roland Petit's *Notre-Dame de Paris* in 1966. Michel Descombey, ballet master and choreographer of the Opera Ballet between 1963 and 1969, created numerous ballets for Atanassoff, including *Sarracenia, But,* and *Bacchus et Ariane*. His outstanding classical role was that of Albrecht in *Giselle*, which he danced chiefly with Yvette Chauviré but also with Noëlla Pontois and with Alicia Alonso in 1967, when she revived the ballet for the Opera troupe. He gave the role of the Prince an intense dramatic resonance and density. In 1972, he partnered Chauviré in her final performances.

Atanassoff rarely performed in other countries, remaining faithful to the Paris Opera Ballet, which he officially left in 1986. Since then he has occasionally appeared as a guest artist with the company and at the Opéra-Comique. At his peak, he was an excellent cavalier in the classical mold and executed each of his roles with extreme precision, but above all he is remembered as a great interpreter.

BIBLIOGRAPHY

Cyril Atanassoff: Présenté par Claude Bessy. Paris, 1979.
Goodwin, Noël. "France/Dance." *Dance and Dancers* (July–August 1986):29–33.

Hersin, André-Phillipe. "Cyril Atanassoff." *Saisons de la danse* (November 1968).

Mannoni, Gérard, and Pierre Jouhad. *Les étoiles de l'Opéra de Paris.* Paris, 1981.

Planell, Martine. "L'âme du Chaman." *Pour la danse* (June 1987). Interview with Atanassoff.

ANDRÉ-PHILIPPE HERSIN

ATERBALLETTO. The name *Aterballetto,* or *ATERballetto,* designates the ballet company of the Associazione Teatri Emilia-Romagna (Association of Theaters in Emilia-Romagna, a province in northern Italy), commonly known as A.T.E.R. The company is in the forefront of contemporary Italian ballet, not only because of the overall quality of the small troupe (it has only eighteen to twenty members) but also because of the interesting and innovative nature of its organization and purpose.

Until 1977, when Aterballetto was founded, there were in Italy no independent, well-established ballet companies, only companies attached to municipal opera houses or private companies that, for financial reasons, could perform only for limited periods of time. To overcome this *de facto* slavery of dance, subject to operatic schedules or condemned to a sporadic existence, fifteen community theaters of Emilia-Romagna—including those in the cities of Bologna, Parma, Modena, Reggio Emilia, Piacenza, Cremona, Ferrara, and Ravenna—banded together to form A.T.E.R., and they eventually succeeded in creating an orchestra, a legitimate theater company, and a ballet company. In addition to performances by these groups, A.T.E.R. arranges performances in the historic opera houses of the province by visiting opera and ballet companies, frequently from eastern Europe.

Aterballetto began under the direction of Vittorio Biagi, formerly a dancer with Maurice Béjart's Ballet du XXe Siècle, a *danseur étoile* at the Opéra-Comique in Paris, and ballet director at the opera house in Lyon. His inventive choreographies set the new company firmly on its course. It continued to grow and to establish its unique identity under the direction of Amedeo Amodio, who was appointed to succeed Biagi in 1979. Amodio, who had been *premier danseur* with the Rome Opera Ballet, had also made a name for himself as a choreographer with works mounted for the Spoleto Festival, for La Scala Ballet, and for the Rome Opera Ballet.

Aterballetto's preferred style is the modern classicism that characterizes the work of Glen Tetley, William Forsythe, and Amodio himself. Among the important ballets added to the repertory in the early 1980s were Amodio's *Ricercare a Nove Movimenti,* set to the music of Antonio Vivaldi; Tetley's *Sphinx* and *Mythical Hunters,* set to music by, respectively, Bohuslav Martinů and Oedoen Partos; and Forsythe's *Love Songs,* set to popular songs

sung by Aretha Franklin and Dionne Warwick. The company also presented successful productions of Alvin Ailey's *Night Creature,* to music by Duke Ellington, and of such twentieth-century classics as Léonide Massine's *Parade,* to a score by Erik Satie, and Antony Tudor's *Jardin aux Lilas,* to music by Ernest Chausson.

Although egalitarian in approach, Aterballetto established an ongoing relationship in the early 1980s with two international stars, Elisabetta Terabust and Peter Schaufuss, both of whom were then affiliated with London Festival Ballet. In 1984 Schaufuss mounted on the company a series of *divertissements* based on the Bournonville repertory that contributed substantially to its artistic development and technical rigor. Also in that year Patricia Neary mounted George Balanchine's *Agon,* which the company performed with notable success. During the late 1980s, Terabust danced as guest star in such ballets as *Romeo and Juliet* and *The Nutcracker,* mounted especially for her by Amodio.

From its first season, Aterballetto has been a regular and welcome guest of the Teatro Municipale of Reggio Emilia, a theater that for many years, under the direction of Guido Zannoni, favored dance and provided a measure of economic support. The company also performs regularly in other municipal theaters in Emilia-Romagna and has toured abroad in Great Britain, France, Germany, Hungary, the Soviet Union, and the United States.

[*See also the entry on Amodio.*]

BIBLIOGRAPHY

Bentivoglio, Leonetta. "A.A.A.: Amedeo Amodio Aterballetto." *Balletto oggi* 18 (March 1984).

Cucchi, Angela Mascimbene, and Patrizia Paterlini, eds. *Trent'anni di balletto a Reggio Emilia, 1956–1986.* Reggio Emilia, 1986.

Doglio, Vittoria, and Elisa Vaccarino. *L'Italia in ballo.* Rome, 1993.

Grillo, Elena. "ATERballetto: La danza senza l'ombra della lirica." *La danza italiana* 4 (Spring 1986): 119–128.

Ottolenghi, Vittoria. "Aterballetto, la nostra compagnia." *Balletto oggi* 18 (March 1984).

Ottolenghi, Vittoria. "Aterballetto." Program notes, Teatro Comunale di Bologna, 5–8 February 1986.

VITTORIA OTTOLENGHI
Translated from Italian

ATLANTA BALLET. Founded in 1929, the Atlanta Ballet is the oldest classical ballet company in the United States. It was established by Dorothy Alexander as a performing outlet for the most accomplished students in her school, the Atlanta School of Ballet. Initially called the Dorothy Alexander Concert Group, the company was renamed Atlanta Civic Ballet in 1941 and in 1967 became the Atlanta Ballet. From the outset, Alexander's company served as the paradigm for America's regional or resident companies as they began to develop in the Southeast. [*See the entry on Alexander.*]

Alexander was a gifted teacher and an instinctive, if relatively untrained, administrator. Many of her concepts for dealing with board and company personnel, as well as with fund-raising sources, have remained valid throughout the company's history. More important, however, were her unique characteristics as performer and choreographer.

Alexander was a poetic dancer with natural lightness and elegance. She also radiated a spiritual quality that infused the subject matter of her later choreography. Although she enjoyed creating pure-dance works like *Fireworks Suite* (1956), her concern with the nature of life and her straightforward awareness of death permeated her longer works, such as *Green Altars* (1957), *Deo Gratias* (1959), and *Swan and Skylark* (1962). These also dealt with the redemptive power of love and with dance as the link between death and rebirth. Alexander, who danced at the head of her company until 1947 and created the major portion of its repertory until her 1963 retirement, was a true romantic.

Under Alexander, the company was known for its finely honed lyrical style and for its gracious *port de bras*. The group performed regularly in Atlanta and began to earn recognition outside the city through a 1955 tour of the state sponsored by the Georgia Power and Light Company and annual appearances at the festivals of the Southeastern Regional Ballet Association, which Alexander founded in 1956. By 1958 it had become the first regional company to appear at the Jacob's Pillow Dance Festival in Becket, Massachusetts.

In 1957, New York City Ballet principal dancer Robert Barnett arrived in Atlanta with his wife Virginia, a former Atlanta Civic Ballet member who subsequently had joined the New York City Ballet. Alexander invited the couple into the company and made Barnett its associate director. He became artistic director upon her retirement in 1963 and held the position until 1994. Barnett guided the company through its transition from a nonprofessional structure in which artistic director and dancers had drawn no salary to a professional one in which all were salaried.

Because of his previous connection with George Balanchine, ballet master-in-chief of the New York City Ballet, Barnett had access to Balanchine's ballets. The Atlanta Ballet subsequently performed fourteen of them, beginning with *Serenade* and *The Nutcracker*. Like Alexander, who had drawn upon the choreographic talents of her associates Merrilee Smith, Hildegarde Bennett, and Carl Ratcliff, Barnett gave opportunities to Mannie Rowe and especially to Thomas Pazik. Gradually, full-length ballets such as *Swan Lake*, *The Sleeping Beauty*, and *Giselle* (all staged by David Blair of England's Royal Ballet), plus Pazik's *Romeo and Juliet* and *Cinderella*, were added to the repertory. Outstanding guest choreographers, notably Lynne Taylor-Corbett, John McFall, Toni Pimble, Peter Anastos, and Donald Byrd, were additional resources.

In 1993 Barnett and Dennis Nahat, artistic director of the Cleveland–San Jose Ballet, collaborated on a highly successful, full-length *Swan Lake* that utilized the personnel of both companies and was performed in all three cities. Barnett also occasionally produced his own works, which were characterized by vivacity and physical challenge. His principal strength though lay in his ability to coach his dancers, among them, Anne Burton, Maniya Barredo, and Gil Boggs.

After Barnett's resignation in 1994, the ballet's board of directors selected John McFall to succeed him in January 1995. During his eighteen years as a dancer with the San Francisco Ballet and eight as artistic director of the BalletMet of Columbus, Ohio, McFall had done a generous amount of choreography. However, his initial plans for the Atlanta Ballet stressed organizational and fund-raising priorities, plus a wide range of community-oriented projects and the establishment of new company premises.

BIBLIOGRAPHY
"The Atlanta Ballet." *Atlanta Magazine* (September 1990).
Hering, Doris. "Robert Barnett Resigns from Atlanta Ballet." *Dance Magazine* (July 1994).
Hering, Doris. "Atlanta Ballet Redivivus." *The World and I* (February 1995).
Hering, Doris. "McFall to Direct Atlanta Ballet." *Dance Magazine* (February 1995): 26–28.
Salisbury, Wilma. "McFall Makes Magic." *Dance Magazine* (April 1991): 54–59.
Smith, Helen C. "Swan Song." *Atlanta Journal-Constitution* (1 May 1994).

DORIS HERING

ATTITUDE. The ballet position in which the working leg is raised and bent approximately ninety degrees at the knee is known as an attitude. Classically, the arm on the same side as the working leg is raised in high fifth position. Although many variations in the positions of the arms and the torso have been used, it is the half-bent leg that identifies an attitude. Attitude poses are varied according to the positions of the body—*effacé, croisé,* and *en face*—and also according to the direction of the flexed leg—*derrière, devant,* and *de côté.* Stylistic details differ according to the theory of the pedagogue who designed the poses.

The earliest account of the term, including both general and specific uses, appears in Gennaro Magri's *Trattato teorico-prattico di ballo* (1779). The term entered the dance vocabulary after Carlo Blasis published *Traité élémentaire, théorique et pratique de l'art de la danse* (1820). Almost all of the then familiar standard poses were known as attitudes, but when Blasis wrote of a position that was "an adaptation of the much admired pose of the celebrated Mercury of Bologna" (the sixteenth-century

ATTITUDE. *(left)* Small bronze copy of Giovanni da Bologna's *Mercury in Flight* (1564), in the characteristic bent-leg pose that became known as attitude. *(right)* The Russian ballet dancer Alexander Gudonov holds a similar position, a classical *attitude croisé derrière*. (*Left:* Metropolitan Museum of Art, New York; Bequest of Irwin Untermyer, 1974 [no. 1974.28.145.]; photograph used by permission. *Right:* photograph by Stan Fellerman; from the archives at Jacob's Pillow, Becket, Massachusetts.)

Mercury in Flight sculpted by Giovanni da Bologna), he singled out the pose now defined as attitude. The statue's upcurving torso and upward gaze bear a particular relationship to the arms: the arm on the same side as the raised leg is uplifted and the other arm stretches downward, holding a caduceus. The most distinctive element in the pose is, however, the ninety-degree flex of the raised leg at the knee. The raised leg is clearly turned in.

The major and consistent difference found in post-Blasis attitudes is the use of full turnout. August Bournonville, who preferred attitude to arabesque in both teaching and choreographing, marked a transition from the older to the newer style. Under the long skirts of his day, the attitude was done with a less pronounced turnout—the knee was dropped and the foot flipped up. In the early twentieth century, Agrippina Vaganova's attitudes were described in her *Basic Principles* (1934) as improvements on the versions of the French and Italian schools. Vaganova's principal departures were the use of the distinctly Russian arched torso, the slightly obtuse angle of flex at the knee, and the relationship of the knee to the foot. Her *attitude effacé* differed from her *attitude croisé* not only in the direction of focus but also in the subtlety of the working leg: in *effacé*, it was bent less than ninety degrees, and the foot was higher than the knee. In Enrico Cecchetti's versions of attitude, the leg was in full ninety-degree flex, and the knee was higher than the foot.

As a signature pose, with many variations on the angle of view, the *attitude derrière* for Aurora in Marius Petipa's *The Sleeping Beauty* is as dominant a motif as the arabesque in his *Swan Lake*. A fine example of *attitude devant* appears in a trio from Michel Fokine's *Les Sylphides;* the Young Man supports two of the Sylphs, both posed in *croisé* versions of this attitude. George Balanchine was one choreographer who presented his dancers in *attitude de côté*, often with a flexed foot to accentuate the sideward plane, as in the first movement of *Bourrée Fantasque* and in *Bugaku*. Pirouettes in attitude, or *attitudes en tournant*, look especially serene because the timing mechanism of spotting is not used.

BIBLIOGRAPHY

Blasis, Carlo. *An Elementary Treatise upon the Theory and Practice of the Art of Dancing* (1820). Translated by Mary Stewart Evans. New York, 1944.

Grant, Gail. *Technical Manual and Dictionary of Classical Ballet*. Rev. ed. New York, 1982.

Vaganova, Agrippina. *Basic Principles of Classical Ballet: Russian Ballet Technique* (1934). Translated by Anatole Chujoy. Edited by Peggy van Praagh. 2d ed. London, 1953.

ROBERT GRESKOVIC

ATTITUDE AND SHAWL DANCE. The genre known as attitude, or mimoplastic art, consisted of representing works of art, particularly those based on classical subjects, by means of mime, gestures, and draping. It enjoyed a vogue among aristocrats and intellectuals of the neoclassical period, arising outside the professional theater as an invention of the art-loving Sir William Hamilton, British ambassador to Naples. Hamilton taught Emma Hart (1765–1815), his mistress (who became his wife and the mistress of Lord Nelson), to replicate poses from ancient sculpture and classical Italian art.

By the time Hart arrived in Naples in 1786, the future Lady Hamilton already possessed exceptional qualifications for this art: she had modeled for painter George Romney from 1782 to 1786. Hart performed her attitudes only at entertainments held at the embassy; the audience was composed of artists and aristocrats.

Performances took place in the center of a drawing room. Lady Hamilton appeared as if in an arena, under ordinary lighting and with the spectators gathered around her. She was dressed in a white tunic with a girdle, and her hair was loose or was pinned up with a comb. Her only properties consisted of two or three shawls and some objects—an urn, a lyre, or a tambourine. Taking her place in the center of the room, she covered herself with the shawls. When she was ready, she would suddenly lift the first shawl, which had acted as a kind of curtain. Sometimes she let the shawl fall to the ground, and sometimes she caught it halfway, when it was to serve as drapery for the figure she was representing. Her ability to express emotions and her swift changes of pose to indicate changes of feeling—from grief to joy, from anger to affection—fascinated the spectators. She used no conventional dance movements as connecting links between attitudes and had no musical accompaniment.

Lady Hamilton had two immediate successors: Ida Brun, a young Danish aristocrat, and the German actress Henriett Hendel Schüler. Brun was inspired by and performed to music. Schüler was a professional performer who used a painterly, tableau-like approach, in the spirit of early romanticism.

The shawl dance (Fr., *pas de schall*) is often related to the attitude, but they only share expressiveness and the use of the shawl and tunic. Unlike the attitude, the shawl dance employed dancelike movements accompanied by music. The shawl dance became fashionable after the performances in Paris in 1768 of the Indian *bayadère* Bebaiourn. Performed mainly at private gatherings, it was also found in the professional theater.

The *pas de schall* has received little attention in dance literature. It is not discussed in Carlo Blasis's *Manuel complet de la danse*, for example, although it appears in the illustrations to the chapter "Danse de société." It lived on in occasional performances in drawing rooms and in ballets until about the mid-nineteenth century.

Attitude and shawl dances today survive only in literature. For example, Johann Wolfgang von Goethe, in his novel *Elective Affinities*, and Madame de Staël, in her *Corinne* and *Delphine*, used the dances in connection with their heroines.

BIBLIOGRAPHY
Holmström, Kirsten Gram. *Monodrama, Attitudes, Tableaux Vivants: Studies on Some Trends of Theatrical Fashion, 1770–1815.* Stockholm, 1967.
Jenkins, I., and K. Sloan. *Vases and Volcanoes: Sir William Hamilton and His Collection.* London, 1996.

KIRSTEN GRAM HOLMSTRÖM

AUDEOUD, SUSANA. *See* Susana.

AUGUSTA, MADAME (Caroline Augusta Josephine Thérèse Fuchs; born 17 September 1806 in Munich, died 17 February 1901 in New York), German dancer. Americans had seen ballet since the eighteenth century, but many first developed a taste for the subtle Romantic ballet only after seeing the beautiful Madame Augusta perform. She studied under Filippo Taglioni in her native Bavaria and under Monsieur Albert in Paris. In Paris she began living with a retired army officer, Count Antoine-François-Auguste Collet, comte de Saint-James, whom she later married on 14 August 1841.

Augusta made her debut at Drury Lane, London, in February 1833 as the fairy Nabote in *The Sleeping Beauty*. Later she danced there in *The Maid of Cashmere* and in *The Pages of the Duke of Vendôme* (1833). Augusta's chance to debut at the Paris Opera in *The Pirate's Isle* came in the fall of 1835 when Fanny Elssler was absent; her initial six-month engagement was not renewed.

Augusta and Count de Saint-James arrived in the United States on 7 September 1835. She opened at New York's Park Theatre on 16 September 1836 in the ballet *Les Naïads*. On 3 December 1836 she appeared in the very popular *La Bayadère*. In spring 1837 she began a tour of the eastern United States, and in December she presented *La Somnambule* at the National Theatre in New York.

After Augusta had added the *opéra-ballet* version of *La Sylphide* to her repertory at the Park Theatre in December 1838, *Knickerbocker Magazine* expressed the widely held view that "it is not her magnificent dancing alone, that pleases; it is her graceful ability, united with lady-like modesty and good taste in every movement, which wins golden opinions from all sorts of people."

January 1839 found Augusta in New Orleans. After returning to the East in the late spring of 1839, she became ill during an engagement at Providence. She sailed for Europe in August 1839.

In 1843 Augusta danced at the Paris Opera; later she appeared in Brussels. She returned to the United States to appear at the Park Theatre on 4 November 1845 in *Le Dieu*

AUGUSTA. In Filippo Taglioni's *divertissement* from Daniel Auber's *opéra-ballet Le Dieu et la Bayadère.* This lithograph by Nathaniel Currier was printed in 1836 as the cover of the opera's sheet music. (Courtesy of Madison U. Sowell and Debra H. Sowell, Brigham Young University, Provo, Utah.)

et la Bayadère and *La Rondella.* Later in the month she danced in the ballets *Diane la Chasseresse* and *Nathalie,* as well as in the opera *Le Postillon de Longjumeau.*

Madame Augusta's most noteworthy contribution to ballet in the United States was probably her appearance on 2 February 1846 in *Giselle* at New York's Park Theatre. Playbills state that in the ballet, "produced under the immediate direction of Augusta," William S. Fredericks as Albrecht vied with Charles Parsloe as Hilarion for her love. The *Morning Courier* reported that "her first bounds after she rises from her grave, were the most electrifying movements we ever saw upon the stage." *The Albion* praised her "exquisite delicacy and feminine modesty of execution," noting that "she absolutely appears to float and spring in the air, assuming her poses with an artistic precision and finish that excite universal admiration." Later Augusta danced *Giselle* in Richmond, Philadelphia, Baltimore, and Boston.

After another respite in Europe, Augusta opened in September 1847 at Palmo's Theatre in New York and the

following April in New Orleans, where she danced in *La Polka Comique, La Castilliana, La Tarentule,* and *Le Diable Boiteux.* She performed along the Mississippi River circuit on her way back to New York, where she was engaged again at Palmo's in 1847. At Burton's Theatre in 1849 she danced in *The Pirate's Isle.* In 1850 she appeared at Philadelphia's Walnut Theatre, and in August of that year she danced the leading role in *The Beauteous Captive* at New York's Astor Place Theatre.

Augusta bought the dance studio of Adelaide Ferraro in New York. To allay her financial distress after her husband's death, George P. Norris, editor of the *New York Mirror,* sponsored a benefit for her on 10 May 1855 at Tripler Hall. There she danced the role of Zoloë *La Bayadère.* After this appearance she faded from view as a performer, although she maintained contact with Parisian teachers in order to learn the latest quadrilles, waltzes, polkas, and cotillons to teach her pupils.

BIBLIOGRAPHY

Ludlow, Noah M. *Dramatic Life as I Found It.* St. Louis, 1880.

Swift, Mary Grace. *Belles and Beaux on Their Toes: Dancing Stars in Young America.* Washington, D.C., 1980.

ARCHIVES.   Dance Collection, New York Public Library for the Performing Arts (under Carolina Augusta Fuchs).

MARY GRACE SWIFT

AUGUSTYN, FRANK (Frank Joseph Augustyn; born 27 January 1953 in Hamilton, Ontario), Canadian dancer, director, and producer. Frank Augustyn trained at the National Ballet School of Canada, graduating into the National Ballet company in 1970. He was promoted to soloist in 1971 and to principal dancer in 1972. He was soon paired with the young ballerina Karen Kain, with whom he was to form a memorable partnership. Like her, he quickly fell under the benign influence of Rudolf Nureyev, who arrived in Toronto to stage his production of *The Sleeping Beauty* for the National Ballet in 1972. Augustyn was cast as the Bluebird and understudied Nureyev as the Prince. With his strong stage presence, handsome looks, noble bearing, and exceptional partnering ability, Augustyn came to be acknowledged as the National Ballet's leading classical *danseur noble,* yet he was equally praised as an interpreter of contemporary choreography.

Augustyn's partnership with Karen Kain flourished, particularly after the two took the prize for best pas de deux at the 1973 International Ballet Competition in Moscow. In 1977 they returned to Moscow to dance the leads in *Giselle* as guest artists with the Bolshoi Ballet and other Soviet troupes. Kain and Augustyn became household names in Canada, aided by network broadcasts of *Giselle* (1976) and *La Fille Mal Gardée* (1979). Rumors of an offstage romance, confirmed years later in Kain's autobiography, added to the popular appeal of their partnership. Augustyn was acclaimed as a compelling stage actor, projecting a very masculine romantic ardor in a wide-ranging repertory of full-length ballets from the Russian classics to such twentieth-century works as John Cranko's *Romeo and Juliet* and *Onegin* (televised by CBC in 1986 with Augustyn and Sabina Allemann in the leading roles).

In the mid-1970s, Augustyn performed as a guest artist with such companies as the London Festival Ballet and the Dutch National Ballet. He spent one season, 1981/82, with the Berlin Opera Ballet and was a permanent guest artist of the Boston Ballet from 1984 to 1986. During the early 1980s, Augustyn's and Kain's careers evolved in different directions, and they danced together less frequently. His personal popularity with Canadian audiences, however, never waned, and, while a younger generation of National Ballet men emerged to challenge his technical supremacy, he remained the model of princely elegance and authority.

Augustyn resigned from the National Ballet of Canada in 1989 to become artistic director of a small Ottawa-based company, Theatre Ballet of Canada, which he quickly renamed Ottawa Ballet. He worked hard to rebuild the company as a compact, contemporary ballet troupe touring centers that the larger companies no longer served. He expanded the repertory with works by Canadian and foreign choreographers and produced and performed in *The Tin Soldier* for stage and CBC-TV. When the company folded in 1994, Augustyn decided to resettle in Toronto, where he became a teacher at the National Ballet School.

Among Augustyn's other accomplishments is his production of a series of internationally broadcast educational ballet programs, *Foot Notes: The Classics of Ballet*, for Bravo! television. Since 1986, Augustyn has been artistic director of Le Gala des Etoiles (formerly Le Don des Etoiles), a major annual charity event in Montreal that attracts leading dancers from around the world. His many awards and honors include the Order of Canada, conferred upon him in 1979.

BIBLIOGRAPHY

Bland, Alexander, and John Percival. *Men Dancing.* London, 1984.
Darling, Christopher, and John Fraser. *Kain and Augustyn.* Toronto, 1977.
Kain, Karen, with Stephen Godfrey and Penelope Reid Doob. *Movement Never Lies: An Autobiography.* Toronto, 1994.
Montague, Sarah. *Pas de Deux.* New York, 1981.
Neufeld, James. *Power to Rise: The Story of the National Ballet of Canada.* Toronto, 1996.

MICHAEL CRABB

AUMER, JEAN-LOUIS (born 21 April 1774 in Strasbourg, died July 1833 in Saint-Martin-en-Bosc), French choreographer and dancer. Jean-Louis Aumer was the son of a manual laborer, but nothing else is known of his childhood. He became the protégé of Jean Dauberval, who brought him to Bordeaux. A tall man for his time, Aumer quickly realized that choreography would be a better choice for him than dancing. He observed his mentor very carefully and also studied music and painting. He followed Dauberval to London in 1791–1792 and again in 1794, the second time to participate in Jean-Georges Noverre's last season at the King's Theatre. In 1795 Aumer appeared once again at the King's Theatre, after which he returned to Bordeaux.

Dauberval helped Aumer to make his debut at the Paris Opera in 1798. While continuing to dance—in *Les Noces de Gamache* and *Pygmalion,* both by Louis Milon, in 1801, *Vénus et Adonis* in 1808, and *Alexandre chez Apelles* in 1809, both by Pierre Garden—Aumer also served as ballet master at the Théâtre de la Porte-Saint-Martin starting in 1802. Initially, he staged ballets by Dauberval, such as *La Fille Mal Gardée* (1804) and *Le Page Inconstant* (1806). But he also presented his own creations, the most famous of which are *Rosina et Lorenzo* (1805), *Jenny, ou Le Mariage Secret* (1806), and *Les Deux Créoles* (1806), which was based on Jacques-Henri Bernadin de Saint-Pierre's pastoral romance *Paul et Virginie* (1788). Coincidentally, Pierre Gardel mounted a ballet at the Opera based on the same story at about the same time.

In a letter of 1807 Noverre says,

> Aumer, opera dancer and good mime, also composed ballets and obtained permission to create his own works at the Théâtre de la Porte-Saint-Martin. He began modestly (something that is quite rare) and preferred to be a good copyist of the famous Dauberval than to be a weak and imperfect original. . . . Encouraged by his success, he gave two of his own ballets [*Jenny* and *Les Deux Créoles*], both of which were ecstatically applauded. Moreover, they still attract crowds.
>
> (Noverre, [1807] 1950, no. 33)

The critics' opinions of *Les Deux Créoles* were, however, divided. In the *Journal de l'empire* (4 July 1806), Julien-Louis Geoffroy, an admirer of Gardel, compared the two choreographies (Aumer's and Gardel's) based on the text of Bernardin de Saint-Pierre:

> Aumer's ballet, considered in regard to the theater for which it is intended, seems to achieve its object: It entertains the frequenters of the Porte, but compared to the one [by Gardel] it is a hotch-potch.

The critique written for the *Courrier des spectacles* (30 June 1806) noted of *Les Deux Créoles* that

> the adventures of the two creoles are so moving, and the images offered are so striking and so varied, that this ballet ought to remain in the theater's repertory. Mlle Quériau invests in her part such warmth, abandon, and pathos, I do not know how she can support so many shocks.

Between 1802 and 1806, Aumer presented close to thirty *divertissements* in the melodramas of Guilbert de Pixérécourt, including *Pizarro* (with a sun festival) and the *Jeux d'Eglé*, which the Paris Opera dancers danced at a gala in his honor. In 1807, after Napoleon closed the Théâtre de la Porte-Saint-Martin, Aumer left for Lyon, where he restaged his earlier works. In 1808 he succeeded in presenting *Les Amours d'Antoine et de Cléopâtre* at the Paris Opera, where it had a certain amount of success. Writing in the *Journal de l'empire* (10 March 1808), Geoffroy declared,

> The arrangement and composition reveal the touch of an accomplished master. . . . Mlle Chevigny is a really astounding artist: Her features express tenderness, jealousy, spite, and hatred one after the other. Vestris . . . surpassed himself.

Gardel was, however, jealous of Aumer and prevented him from staging other works at that time. Aumer therefore accepted King Jerome of Westphalia's offer of a post as ballet master in Kassel, where he remained until 1814, with time out for an engagement in Lyon in 1812.

Aumer's next post was in Vienna (1814–1820), where he was assisted by Friedrich Horschelt and his "children's ballet." His two first dancers were Filippo Taglioni and Jean Rozier. He presented a new version of *Le Déserteur* (1814), *Les Pages du Duc de Vendôme* (1815), *La Bayadère* (1815), with music by Adalbert Gyrowetz, *Thétis et Pélée* (1816), *Achille* (1818), and *Le Songe d'Ossian* (1819), to mention only a few. In 1820, he agreed to return to the Paris Opera as ballet master, as Gardel and Milon were both growing older. However, he remained for an additional year in Vienna and also spent time at the Teatro alla Scala in Milan, at which time he mounted *Les Pages du Duc de Vendôme*. The critic for the *Journal des débats* wrote on 20 October 1820 that the ballet was too long and there were too many *divertissements*. The character dances by Ferdinand and Mademoiselle Aimée and a *pas* danced by Émilie Bigottini and Fanny Bias were highly praised. However, the second *divertissement* at the end of the ballet was thought to be superfluous. Despite these shortcomings, the piece achieved a complete success and was frequently revived.

Les Pages was followed by *La Fête Hongroise* (1821). *Alfred le Grand* (1822), which had already been given in Vienna and Milan, was the last ballet mounted at the Paris Opera with a man in the principal role. *Aline, Reine de Golconde*, given in Vienna in 1818, in London, and then in Paris in 1823, was presented with new music. Then came a new version of Dauberval's *Le Page Inconstant*, with different music. Aumer presented *Le Songe d'Ossian* in London in 1824.

In 1827 Aumer's two major ballets were *Astolphe et Joconde*, which he produced for Pauline Paul (later Montessu), Lise Noblet, and Monsieur Albert François

AUMER. Lithograph (c.1820) by Godefroi Engelmann depicting Jean-Louis Aumer as Duke Vendom in his 1815 ballet *Les Pages du Duc de Vendôme*. (Dance Collection, New York Public Library for the Performing Arts.)

Decombe), and *La Somnambule*, which he choreographed to music by Ferdinand Hérold, with Pauline Montessu and Amélie Legallois in principal roles. [*See* Somnambule, La.] By and large, the critics liked *La Somnambule*. The critic for *Le corsaire* said,

> It is a little drama, perfect as a whole, delightful in detail. . . . Mme Montessu dances and mimes with a perfection that our foremost actresses might envy. The success was complete. . . . The first act is perhaps a little too long, composed solely of pas de trois and ensembles.

The year 1828 was an important one for Aumer, highlighted by his staging of the *divertissements* for Daniel Auber's opera *La Muette de Portici*, danced by Lise Noblet, and his mounting of Dauberval's *La Fille Mal Gardée*, with new music arranged by Hérold. In 1829 he presented *La Belle au Bois Dormant* (The Sleeping Beauty), using a libretto by Eugène Scribe and music by Hérold, with Lise Noblet in the title role and Marie Taglioni in the role of a naiad. His last ballet was *Manon Lescaut* (1830), with a libretto by Scribe and music by Fromental Halévy, his first score for ballet.

Aumer resigned his post as ballet master at the Opera in 1831 and retired to Normandy. Finding that he missed his life in the theater, however, he lived in hope of being recalled to Paris. He died of a stroke in the summer of 1833.

BIBLIOGRAPHY

Blyth, Alan, et al. "Manon." *About the House* 4.5 (Spring 1974): 23–29.

Guest, Ivor. "An Earlier 'Sleeping Beauty': *La Belle au Bois Dormant* in the Eighteen Thirties." *Ballet* 12 (April 1952): 36–42.

Guest, Ivor. *The Romantic Ballet in England*. London, 1972.

Guest, Ivor. *The Romantic Ballet in Paris*. 2d rev. ed. London, 1980.

Michel, Marcelle. "Apothéose et décadence de la danse classique sous la Révolution et l'Empire." Ph.D. diss., Sorbonne, 1955.

Noverre, Jean-Georges. *Lettres sur les arts imitateurs en général et sur la danse en particulier*. (1807). Edited by Lieutier. Paris, 1950.

Winter, Marian Hannah. *The Pre-Romantic Ballet*. London, 1974.

ARCHIVE.   Walter Toscanini Collection of Research Materials in Dance, New York Public Library for the Performing Arts.

MONIQUE BABSKY
Translated from French

AUSDRUCKSTANZ. One of the most important stylistic developments of dance in the twentieth century took place in Germany. The principles of *Ausdruckstanz* ("expressionist dance," known in America as "German dance" or "German expressionist dance" and in England as "central European dance) formed the basis for the "new artistic dance" that was influential from around the turn of the twentieth century until World War II.

A general awakening of body consciousness, beginning around 1890, laid the foundation for the *Ausdruckstanz* movement. Youth, especially in Germany, experienced an unmistakable spirit of awakening. The highly stylized model of the youth cult finally gave the entire epoch its name, *Jugendstil* ("youth style").

In the wake of this new body consciousness, an interest in gymnastics developed. Among the influential systems in Germany were that of the American Bess Mensendieck, who used her exercises as a form of therapy, and that of Rudolf Bode, who strove to train the whole body rhythmically. Linking this idea of physical training with artistic sensibility was the school of Emile Jaques-Dalcroze, in which Mary Wigman, the leading spirit of *Ausdruckstanz,* was a student.

The first center of the new "absolute" dance, as it was then called, was Rudolf Laban's colony at Monte Verità on Lago Maggiore (at the Swiss-Italian border). There a new understanding of dance took root in the company of anarchists, communists, vegetarians, theosophists, and anthroposophists influenced by Rudolf Steiner, Freemasonry, and new theories of medicine and psychology, along with artists and writers such as Paul Klee and James Joyce.

Laban moved his base to Munich in 1910; he moved to Zurich and Ascona during World War I. Among his early students were the Swiss Suzanne Perrottet and Berthe Trümpy and the German Wigman. Together, Laban and Wigman developed the basis for the new dance. They wanted to emancipate dance, to release it from both literary and musical bonds; they wanted to work from movement alone, to establish dance as a medium in its own right and to explore its independent capacities for expression.

Ausdruckstanz developed as a movement dominated by soloists who sought venues outside the opera houses, hence its name "podium" or "concert" dance. Spaces ranging from open-air theaters to community halls to sports arenas could serve as performance sites.

The curriculum of the school at Monte Verità aimed at "new forms of a simple and harmonious life." The focus was on individual self-realization. In a movement that owed much to the eurythmics theory of Rudolf Steiner, the highest goal was reconciliation of the division between soul and body, or between the individual and the cosmos.

Wigman's *Witch Dance* (1914) exhibits all the important elements of the new dance: connection to the floor, in contrast to the aerial tradition of the ballet; composition based on the principle of tension and relaxation; and the initiation of expressive movements directly from the emotion of the dancer. Wigman used all the possibilities of the body; for the first time movements streamed out in all directions. She was not limited to the beautiful, brilliant, and virtuosic. The dance could accept and stylize as dramatic expression any gesture, from any cultural or everyday context. Thus, *Ausdruckstanz* extended the scale of expressive possibilities, which until then had constrained dance to the realm of beautiful appearance.

While Wigman concentrated on solos, Laban concerned himself with group choreography. In his belief, humans were connected by means of the body to the natural harmony and unity of the cosmos. Civilization and mechanization have alienated the body, destroying humans' harmonious relation to the world. Laban's work with lay dance groups and movement choirs was designed to restore humanity's eurythmic relation to nature.

Not only the two leaders but also the majority of other *Ausdruckstanz* devotees founded their own schools in which they imparted their theories of understanding through dance. As a result of the individual orientation of the new dance, no single teaching method developed. The number of participants grew rapidly; as well as numerous schools, there were tours and guest performances throughout Germany.

The intensive teaching activity soon created an abundance of dancers, who began to threaten their own resources for existence. The dancers crowded a scene that could hardly absorb their enormous energies. Another consequence for the rising generation was increased dilettantism. What was lacking was an institutional framework in which the dance revolution could establish itself.

Of the numerous schools that were founded, only a few offered self-sufficient teaching methods. Gertrud

Bodenwisser, Gret Palucca, Dorothee Günther, and Rosalia Chladek succeeded. Bodenwisser later emigrated to Australia; Laban joined Kurt Jooss in England.

Others prominent in the period between the wars were striking individual performers but they did not draw disciples. Niddy Impekoven had a childlike, playful charm. Clotilde von Derp and Alexander Sacharoff were known for their poetic expressiveness. The grotesque dances of Valeska Gert were short, satirical portraits of types, such as *Procuress* and *Clown*. Jean Weidt created propagandizing works with his Red Dancers. Others turned, as had Ruth St. Denis, to stylized reproductions of foreign dance traditions. Oskar Schlemmer transformed dancers into kinetic objects. The picture was decidedly pluralistic.

An entire line of concert dancers, however, came directly from the Wigman school. They included Gret Palucca, known for her bounding, lighthearted compositions; Yvonne Georgi, admired for her flowery, gentle fairy-tale mood and mystical ecstasy; and Harald Kreutzberg, noted for his dramatic talents. Dore Hoyer's precisely formulated mime and gesture highlighted the essential elements of *Ausdruckstanz:* emotional intensity, strength of expression, visible tension, and a concentration on the essential.

The influences of *Ausdruckstanz* were manifold and extended well beyond the boundaries of continental Europe. The Wigman studio that Hanya Holm founded in New York City in 1931 became one of the most important educational centers for modern dance there. In England, Laban's analytical studies contributed to the search for identity among a new generation of dancers and choreographers seeking to depart from a classical style based on an aristocratic tradition. With *Ausdruckstanz,* dance passed into other hands; theatrical dance was becoming accessible to other circles. *Ausdruckstanz* was envisioned as a decisive step toward the emancipation and democratization of an art form.

The Nazi era (1933–1945) in Germany abruptly interrupted the development of modern dance there. *Ausdruckstanz* had, however, already passed its innovative peak by the beginning of the 1930s. The emphasis on individual realization, the paucity of institutional support, and the lack of technical method made its survival difficult. Its works were so closely related to the person of the dancer-choreographer who created them that they could not be learned and performed by others. The productions of *Ausdruckstanz* were never viewed as timeless.

In addition, the individualistic attitude of *Ausdruckstanz* allowed it to be readily coopted by the German government's new holders of power. Politically motivated emigration (such as Kurt Jooss) was the exception; the majority of *Ausdruckstänzer* were politically naive. Laban wanted to effect a revolution in society by reintegrating the individual with the rhythm of the community. Fatally, this conception coincided in part with the goal of National Socialism: to achieve the release and coordination of individual identity through the collective experience of the moving mass.

Ausdruckstanz as a movement is a historical example of the problematic situation of dance makers who are not aware of their responsibility in the social context. This does not detract, however, from their importance in the development of a totally new orientation for European dance. They prepared the way for the emancipation of dance as a medium sufficient in itself and proclaimed the expressive power of movement.

[*See also* Artists and Dance, *article on* Artists and Dance, 1760–1929; Germany, *article on* Theatrical Dance, 1600–1945; *and the entry on Wigman.*]

BIBLIOGRAPHY

Bach, Rudolf. *Das Mary Wigman-Werk.* Dresden, 1933.

Blüher, Hans. *Wandervogel: Geschichte einer Jugendbewegung.* Prien, 1922.

Bode, Rudolf. *Ausdrucksgymnastik.* Munich, 1922.

Boehn, Max von. *Der Tanz.* Berlin, 1925.

Brandenburg, Hans. *Der moderne Tanz.* 3d ed. Munich, 1921.

Cohen, Selma Jeanne, ed. *Dance as a Theatre Art.* New York, 1974.

Duncan, Isadora. *Der Tanz der Zukunft.* Leipzig, 1902.

Die Elizabeth Duncan Schule. Jena, 1912.

Feudel, Elfriede. *Rhythmik: Theorie und Praxis der körperlich-musikalischen Erziehung.* Munich, 1926.

Günther, Dorothee. *Der Tanz als Bewegungsphänomen.* Reinbek bei Hamburg, 1962.

Hackmann, Hans. *Die Wiedergeburt der Tanz- und Gesangskunst aus dem Geiste der Natur.* Jena, 1918.

Jaques-Dalcroze, Émile. *Rhythmus, Musik und Erzeihung.* Basel, 1922.

Koegler, Horst. "Tanz in die Dreißiger Jahre." In *Ballett 1972: Chronik und Bilanz des Ballettjahres,* edited by Horst Koegler et al. Velber bei Hannover, 1972.

Koegler, Horst. "Tanz in den Abgrund." In *Ballett 1973: Chronik und Bilanz des Ballettjahres,* edited by Horst Koegler et al. Velber bei Hannover, 1973.

Laban, Rudolf. *Die Welt des Tänzers.* Stuttgart, 1920.

Laban, Rudolf. *Ein Leben für den Tanz.* Dresden, 1935.

Laban, Rudolf, and Mary Wigman, eds. *Die tänzerische Situation unserer Zeit: Ein Querschnitt.* Dresden, 1936.

Lämmel, Rudolf. *Der moderne Tanz.* Berlin, 1928.

Mensendieck, Bess M. *Körperkultur der Frau* (1906). 8th ed. Munich, 1924.

Müller, Hedwig, and Norbert Servos. "Espressionisme? L'Ausdruckstanz e il nuovo Tanztheater in Germania." In *Tanztheater: Dalla danza espressionista a Pina Bausch,* edited by Leonetta Bentivoglio. Rome, 1982.

Müller, Hedwig, and Patricia Stöckemann. ". . . jeder Mensch ist ein Tänzer": Ausdruckstanz in Deutschland zwischen 1900 und 1945.* Giessen, 1993.

Oskar Schlemmer: Das triadische Ballett. Dokumentation, 5. Berlin, 1977. Exhibition catalogue, Akademie der Künste.

Schikowski, John. *Geschichte des Tanzes.* Berlin, 1926.

Szeemann, Harald, et al. *Monte Verità—Berg der Wahrheit.* Milan, 1978.

Thiess, Frank. *Der Tanz als Kunstwerk.* Munich, 1920.

NORBERT SERVOS
Translated from German

AUSTRALIA. [*This entry comprises three articles on the-atrical dance traditions in Australia. The first article focuses on the history of ballet; the second explores modern dance; the third discusses dance research and publication. For discussion of dance in the cultures of indigenous peoples, see Australian Aboriginal Dance.*]

Ballet

The first European settlement of Australia began in the late 1700s; however, only the most basic kind of dancing took place in theaters until the mid-nineteenth century. The fashionable art was then opera, performances of which included dances inserted into the work itself (for example, Mr. Phillips in the "Cracoquick" in Beethovan's *Fidelio* in 1839) or a dance interlude between the opera and the play that always concluded the evening's entertainment. Works were cut heavily or padded with unrelated material at the whim of the promoter or star or by the demands of the audience.

The first theatrical dance work with a title, *The Fair Maid of Perth, or The River Lovers*, was staged at the Theatre Royal in Sydney on 17 January 1835, less than three months after what has been accepted as the first production of an opera in Australia. Nothing is known about this entry in the theatrical annals of the new British colony, but doubts exist as to the validity of any ballet or opera performances then advertised as such. Mrs. Michael Clarke's company began to present regular opera seasons in the Theatre Royal in Hobart, Tasmania, the oldest Australian theater still in existence (now rebuilt in replica after its 1986 fire). Mrs. Clarke's stars of opera in 1842 included Jerome Carandini, a self-styled Italian marquis billed as "a successful professional dancer," who nevertheless made his debut singing in François Boieldieu's opera *Jean de Paris*. The distinction between singers, dancers, and actors was not strongly drawn in colonial Australia. Carandini and the wife of another singer, Mrs. Frank Howson, added various pas de deux from his repertory to the Irish jigs and Scottish reels that for many years remained the principal theatrical dancing activity in Australia. Carandini married a young Hobart contralto, Marie Burgess, who as Madam Carandini later became prominent as "The Tasmanian Nightingale."

Individual European and American dancers and acrobatic troupes regularly undertook the three-month sea journey to Australia where, despite great hardships in traversing the long distances between the cities, considerable money could be made, especially after the discovery of gold in the 1850s and the resulting influx of migrants from all over the world. Ballet proper was as yet unknown, but dance was part of the pantomime tradition, with characterization more important than technique. Ballets uninterrupted by dialogue or singing were not yet

AUSTRALIA: Ballet. David Lichine (The First Junior Cadet) displays Tatiana Riabouchinska (The First Junior Girl) in the climax of the Circus pas de deux from Lichine's *Graduation Ball*. The Original Ballet Russe premiere was in Sydney in 1940; this photograph shows a 1948 performance in Melbourne. (Photograph from the Dance Collection, New York Public Library for the Performing Arts.)

performed, and no distinction was made between acrobatics and dancing. In 1841, the French dancer-choreographer Monsieur Charrière created a sensation by dancing a *pas seul* (solo dance), *La Polichinelle*, on stilts; and as late as 1871 Signor Donato, billed as "the sensation of the 1864/65 Covent Garden season," performed Hungarian and Spanish dances and even a pas de deux with the reigning ballerina, Mademoiselle Thérèse (Schmidt)—even though Donato had only one leg.

Visiting stars were often actresses with a dancing background, who demonstrated the remnants of almost forgotten techniques to audiences hungry for entertainment. Céline Céleste was fifty-six when she arrived in Melbourne in 1867 to play in *The Woman in Red* and other dramas. Her encore piece each night was the cachucha, a widely hailed dance event. The notorious Lola Montez, another dancer who came to Australia as an actress, added the sensuous Spider Dance to her role as Lady Teazle in Sheridan's *The School for Scandal* in March 1856. A month earlier, she had caused a public outcry, a run at the box office, and headlines when she horsewhipped the editor of the *Ballaarat Times* for writing an article on "her true character as a woman."

In 1853, the first attempts of any kind of real ballet performances came to Melbourne, Geelong (May), Launceston (July), and Sydney (September), when Thérèse Ferdinand-Strebinger, who had studied at the Paris Opera School and with Jules Perrot, danced the *cachucha* and the *pas noble*. In 1855, Strebinger and Carandini staged and starred in Australia's first *Giselle* in Melbourne, with a twenty-member corps de ballet and a dozen extras. The real beginnings of professional ensembles employed on a permanent basis came with William Saurin Lyster's various opera companies, which toured the country from 1861 to 1880. Unlike the numerous family groups that appeared throughout Australia at the time, performing mostly in pantomimes and on mixed bills, Lyster attempted to put grand opera in the French manner on a permanent footing by including something approximating classical ballet. His first company was headed by Mademoiselle Thérèse and Jules Schmidt, Strebinger, dancer-pantomimist-trapeze artist J. H. Flexmore, and a corps de ballet of twelve. These performances were supplemented by almost every dancer appearing in Australia during the period of Lyster's reign, the ballet at last becoming a major part of the evening's attraction.

AUSTRALIA: Ballet. Members of the Kirsova Ballet, the first professional ballet company in Australia, forming a tableau from Michel Fokine's *Les Sylphides*, Melbourne, 1942. Dancers featured in this performance included Rachel Cameron, Henry Legerton, Strelsa Heckelman, and Peggy Sager. (Photograph from the Dance Collection, New York Public Library for the Performing Arts.)

Lyster's death in 1880 was followed by theatrical chaos. Grand opera began to yield to comic opera, with chorus girls rather than ballet dancers as the main attraction. The picture stabilized through the efforts of American actor and manager James Cassius Williamson, who first appeared in Australia in 1874 with his play *Struck Oil* and later extended his activities to almost every kind of theater. The empire he founded—J. C. Williamson Theatres Limited—lasted a hundred years and was closely identified with dance.

In 1888, Williamson organized the Royal Comic Opera Company, for which he assembled the first all-Australian dancing troupe, the Royal Ballerinas. Led by Mary Weir, who later became Williamson's second wife, the Royal Ballerinas made their debut in the pantomime *Sinbad the Sailor*. In 1893, Williamson ventured into Lyster's old territory by bringing the operas of Pietro Mascagni and Ruggero Leoncavallo to Australia. Because these works were unsuited for interpolated dances, he arranged to stage a separate attraction—the first Australian ballet—*Turquoisette, or A Study in Blue*, which was presented at the conclusion of each opera. Rosalie Phillipini, then the

AUSTRALIA: Ballet. Scenery for the Borovansky Ballet's production of *Petrouchka*, staged by Edouard Borovansky after Michel Fokine. (Photograph from the Dance Collection, New York Public Library for the Performing Arts.)

director of the Royal Ballerinas, was in charge of a corps of no less than ninety, plus eight imported *coryphées* and two ballerinas—the Russian Catherina Bartho and Enrichetta D'Argo from Italy. *Turquoisette* was little more than a monumental expansion of pantomime dancing, but it ran for months on the backs of Leoncavallo's *I Pagliacci* and Mascagni's *Cavalleria Rusticana* and *L'Amico Fritz.*

The major milestone in developing a public for classical ballet was the visit of Danish dancer Adeline Genée in 1913, when more or less proper versions of *Coppélia, Les Sylphides* (Fokine), and other ballets were presented in Australia. Genée was supported by members of the Imperial Russian Ballet, including Alexandre Volinine and Halina Schmolz, and a corps of twelve Russian and ten Australian women. A visit by Anna Pavlova, announced for 1914, was canceled when World War I broke out. Not until 1926 did Australians see the first of two visits by that legendary ballerina.

Pavlova, though in her declining years, brought a company of forty-two with a varied repertory of her signature works supplemented, surprisingly, by a two-act version of *Don Quixote* that, as much as *The Dying Swan*, enthralled Australian ballet audiences. The vogue for the classical repertory has not dimmed since then and in the years that followed, Williamson's organization brought a steady succession of the world's best dancers to Australia. Pavlova returned in 1929 with an even bigger company and ballets such as *Giselle* (danced by Pavlova and Pierre Vladimiroff, with Ruth French as Myrtha, and Edouard Borovansky as Hilarion).

The Pavlova visits resulted in the founding of numerous ballet schools throughout Australia, many teaching the Cecchetti and other established methods. [*See the entry on*

Cecchetti.] Later, visits by the various post-Diaghilev European Ballets Russes companies continued to fan enthusiasm for classical dance.

The superabundance of touring companies of Russian emigré dancers during the 1930s inhibited the creation of native dance groups. English and American shows were the only outlets for local dancers, and the few serious talents who emerged performed in Williamson musical comedies and revues before drifting overseas. Australian dancers, such as Robert Helpmann, Moyra Fraser, and Gordon Hamilton, who became prominent in overseas companies, were rare indeed.

The Ballets Russes companies that toured Australia under the banner of Colonel Wassily de Basil in the 1930s were in an almost constant state of flux. Nevertheless, the opportunity to see dancers such as Olga Spessivtseva, Leon Woizikowski, Vera Nemchinova, Lubov Tchernicheva, Anton Dolin, Serge Lifar, Irina Baronova, Tamara Toumanova, Tatiana Riabouchinska, David Lichine, and dozens of others in Diaghilev's ballets of the era (many choreographed by Léonide Massine) created a discerning public used only to the best. As the decade drew to a close, Australia became the site of two world premieres, Lichine's *The Prodigal Son* (1938) and *Graduation Ball* (1940). After 1940, the importation of companies stopped completely because of World War II. But two members of the visiting Ballets Russes companies—Hélène Kirsova and Edouard Borovansky—remained to fill the gap, as did one Australian, Laurel Martyn, formerly a soloist with the Rambert and Sadler's Wells ballets.

Hélène Kirsova came to Australia with Colonel de Basil's Monte Carlo Ballet Russe (the de Basil "second company") in 1936, married, and settled in Sydney, where

she opened a school. With four other dancers who remained behind from other seasons, and a dozen local dancers, she started the Kirsova Ballet in 1941. This first professional Australian ballet company continued for only three years, but its brief existence proved that native talent led by an experienced professional could be a viable entity. Strelsa Heckelman, Helen France, and the New Zealander Peggy Sager were among the first native principals to appear. Music and designs were all of local origin, but the choreography and the artistic direction were in the hands of Kirsova. None of her ballets, which included a three-act *Faust* (1941), survived when the Williamson organization decided to back the Melbourne-based Borovansky instead.

Melbourne was also the home of Laurel Martyn, who became a kind of Australian Marie Rambert. In 1940 she started producing intimate ballets, a new medium for Australia. Her Victorian Ballet Guild, launched in 1946, ultimately became Ballet Victoria, which survived until 1975, when an ill-advised attempt to turn it into a full-scale major company caused its collapse. Ballet Victoria was thoroughly Australian, and most of its ninety-four ballets were originals. Martyn was a leading dancer herself, but she encouraged new talent and placed her art above personal ambition. Although she was responsible for many of the company's best ballets, including several on Australian themes (*The Sentimental Bloke, Mathinna*), she gave new choreographers such as Rex Reid, Vassilie Trunoff, Margaret Scott, Garth Welch, and John Meehan a chance to show their work.

Another company that was briefly featured in the postwar boom was Melbourne's National Theatre Ballet, started in 1949 by Joyce Graeme. This failed attempt to establish a genuinely national ballet company (with funding by the Victoria state government) had its highlights, notably the first Australian four-act *Swan Lake* and the best ballet on aboriginal themes to date, Rex Reid's *Corroboree* (1950). In addition, before the troupe folded in 1955, it developed excellent native talent to back its principals, Graeme, Scott, and Reid, who had stayed behind when Ballet Rambert visited Australia in 1947.

Czech-born Edouard Borovansky is considered the father of Australian ballet. He first visited the country with

AUSTRALIA: Ballet. (*top*) Lisa Pavane and Greg Horsman in Maina Gielgud's 1986 staging of *Giselle* for the Australian Ballet. (*center*) Barry Kitcher, as the Lyrebird, hovers over Kathleen Gorham, as the Girl, in *The Display* (1964). Robert Helpmann's ballet was inspired by the mating dance of the Australian lyrebird—named for the shape of its tail arrayed. (*bottom*) Graeme Murphy, longtime director of the Sydney Dance Company, in *Daphnis and Chloe*. (Photographs from the Dance Collection, New York Public Library for the Performing Arts.)

Pavlova in 1929 and in 1938 returned as a minor soloist with the old de Basil company under the name The Covent Garden Russian Ballet; his most notable role was the Strong Man in *Le Beau Danube*. In 1939, Borovansky opened a ballet school in Melbourne and a year later started the Borovansky Australian Ballet Company, an elaboration of his school performances. In 1942, the J. C. Williamson Organization, desperately looking for wartime attractions, offered to back Borovansky's attempt to recreate the successes of the various prewar Ballets Russes companies. Initially using only Australian dancers (Martyn, Dorothy Stevenson, Edna Busse, Martin Rubinstein), Borovansky added *Giselle, Les Sylphides,* and a one-act *Swan Lake* to some of the ballets Martyn had been producing with her friends to create an instant repertory. After the collapse of the Kirsova Ballet, Borovansky acquired most of its dancers and some ballets, and the real Borovansky Ballet was born.

The company had little that was Australian about it. Its repertory was basically identical to what the public had come to love: the choreography of Michel Fokine, Léonide Massine, and the standard classics. After World War II, it

imported some dancers but built its own stars, using such established Australian dancers as Stevenson, Sager, Trunoff, Rubinstein, Kathleen Gorham, and later Marilyn Jones and Welch. Attempts at Australian works such as *Terra Australis* (1946), *The Outlaw* (1951), and *The Black Swan* (1949), based on Dutch sailors capturing black swans in West Australia in 1697, were not successful, but the introduction of British classics such as *Façade* and *Pineapple Poll* began to change the character of the repertory.

On 18 December 1959 Edouard Borovansky died, only hours before the Sydney premiere of a new full-length production of *The Sleeping Beauty*. Plans for 1960 had been completed with extra care, because recent visits by the Royal Ballet and the New York City Ballet had shown that perhaps Australia was not keeping pace with modern developments. The Williamson organization engaged the British Ballet director Peggy van Praagh to manage the planned season but refused to continue backing the Borovansky Ballet without Borovansky. The company's final performance took place in January 1961, and the Australian government subsequently announced that it would back a national company to continue the Borovansky tradition.

The Australian Ballet was born on 2 November 1962 in Sydney with a four-act *Swan Lake* starring guest artists

AUSTRALIA: Ballet. The ensemble of the Australian Ballet arrayed in Serge Lifar's *Suite en Blanc,* originally choreographed for the Paris Opera Ballet in 1942, and staged for this company in 1981. (Photograph by Branco Gaica; used by permission.)

Sonia Arova and Erik Bruhn. Van Praagh had been engaged as artistic director and had talked most of the Borovansky principals into returning. Other Australian ballerinas (Elaine Fifield and Lucette Aldous) were to return later, but the company has basically relied on talent recruited from its own school, which was part of the original charter and was directed by its founder Margaret Scott from 1964 to 1990, when she was succeeded by the former Australian Ballet principal dancer Gailene Stock.

Robert Helpmann's *The Display*, which premiered at the Adelaide Festival of 1964, with music by Malcolm Williamson, decor by Sidney Nolan, scenario by Patrick White, and an Australian bush setting built around the lyre bird, was the Australian Ballet's first work to be completely native in its collaborators and theme. Helpmann followed it with a series of original ballets, and in 1965 he was appointed joint artistic director with van Praagh. At the 1965 International Festival of Dance, van Praagh's production of *Giselle* won the Grand Prix of the City of Paris.

The Australian Ballet achieved international status in the 1970s with a series of regular overseas tours, usually headed by a major star such as Rudolf Nureyev or Margot Fonteyn. A film of Nureyev's version of *Don Quixote*, costarring Aldous and Helpmann, was released worldwide in 1973. For many years, the company relied on its own dancers and repertory to establish its reputation, and as older dancers retired they were replaced by homegrown principals such as Marilyn Rowe, Kelvin Coe, Gaelene Stock, Gary Norman, Michela Kirkaldie, and Dale Baker.

Helpmann ended his association with the Australian Ballet in 1976 with a lavish, full-length *Merry Widow*. Administrative turmoil followed. Anne Woolliams served as the company's artistic director from 1976 to 1977, and van Praagh, who retired in December 1974 because of ill health, returned in 1978. Marilyn Jones took over in 1979, followed by Marilyn Rowe and, in 1983, Maina Gielgud.

The Australian Ballet may have been a continuation of Borovansky's Russian style and repertory, but the influence of van Praagh and Helpmann created an antipodean copy of Britain's Royal Ballet. The brief reign of Woolliams, whose formative influence was the Englishman John Cranko and his Stuttgart Ballet, did not alter this. Internal political problems beset the company during the following years and Gielgud found dispirited ranks, many of the best dancers having left, when she took over. The changes she made were drastic. She had been a principal with the Belgian Maurice Béjart's Ballet du XXᵉ Siècle, and she moulded her raw young dancers in his traditions, producing many of his ballets and those of others, thereby internationalizing the artistic concept of the company.

Box office dictated the continuation of full-length ballets regardless of quality; most were based on brilliant spectacle rather than on fine choreography, not counting the standard classics and the better-known works of Frederick Ashton and John Cranko, but Gielgud kept the fine Woolliams *Swan Lake* and added her own *Sleeping Beauty* and a new version of *The Nutcracker* by Graeme Murphy. The importation of guest artists, which had kept the company going during its barren period, ceased. Gielgud chose to build new principals from the ground up and succeeded brilliantly, if not instantly. A whole new generation of Australian dancers good enough to take New York and London by storm was created by Gielgud.

Australia has always produced good male dancers, and ballets like László Seregi's *Spartacus* were danced worldwide by Australians with a success equal to the Bolshoi's choreographically superior one. Dale Baker, Steven Heathcote, Greg Horsman, David McAllister, and others held their own against British, American, and Russian dancers, as had their predecessors Kelvin Coe, John Meehan, Gary Norman, and Garth Welch. With female dancers, Gielgud was less successful, producing a magnificently disciplined corps de ballet and a series of good-looking ballerinas who danced superbly but who lacked the star quality of the men. Vicki Attard, Miranda Coney, Lisa Pavane, and Fiona Tonkin have the technique, but not the charisma of earlier Australians such as Lucette Aldous, Kathleen Gorham, Marilyn Jones, or Marilyn Rowe.

Gielgud's greatest artistic achievement was in the choreographic field. The Australian Ballet's repertory is more varied than that of most companies, presenting every kind of style—the initial Béjart predominance having been substantially reduced, even though the company is still one of only three to have his full-length *Le Concours* on stage and even television. Almost every major established choreographer is represented (Kylián, Butler, Tetley, Robbins, et al.), and new talent is emerging at regular intervals, most recently the young Australians Stephen Baynes and Stanton Welch. Gielgud's term as artistic director expired at the end of 1996. She was succeeded by Ross Stretton, whose career with American Ballet Theatre was a continuation of his years with the Australian Ballet.

The only "national" ballet company, the Australian Ballet is subsidized by the federal Australian government and tours in many of Australia's states each year. Most other companies in the capital cities of the individual states are based on modern dance. The exceptions are Queensland Ballet in Brisbane, directed since 1978 by Harold Collins, and the West Australian Ballet in Perth, directed since 1983 by Barry Moreland. Collins is presenting standard works like *Romeo and Juliet* with his own choreography and also touring minor cities in Queensland. Moreland has always been a major Australian choreographer, but the West Australian Ballet also presents cash-producing ventures such as *The Nutcracker* and *A Midsummernight's Dream*, both Moreland's own work.

[*See also* Australian Ballet *and entries on the principal figures mentioned herein.*]

BIBLIOGRAPHY

Bellew, Peter, ed. *Pioneering Ballet in Australia.* Sydney, 1945.
Cargher, John. *Opera and Ballet in Australia.* Sydney, 1977.
Cook, Michael. *Swan Lake: The Making of a Ballet.* Sydney, 1978.
Hall, Hugh P. *Ballet in Australia from Pavlova to Rambert.* Melbourne, 1948.
Haskell, Arnold L. *Dancing round the World.* London, 1937.
Laughlin, Patricia. *Marilyn Jones.* Melbourne, 1978.
Macgeorge, Norman. *The Borovansky Ballet in Australia and New Zealand.* Melbourne, 1946.
Pask, Edward H. *Enter the Colonies Dancing: A History of Dance in Australia, 1835–1940.* Melbourne, 1979.
Pask, Edward H. *Ballet in Australia: The Second Act, 1940–1980.* Melbourne, 1982.
Pelly, Noël. *Zita.* Melbourne, 1994.
Salter, Elizabeth. *Helpmann: The Authorised Biography of Sir Robert Helpmann, CBE.* Brighton, 1978.
Sturmer, Caryll von. *Margaret Barr: Epic Individual.* Sydney, 1993.
Tait, Viola. *A Family of Brothers.* Melbourne, 1971.

JOHN CARGHER

Modern Dance

Modern dance in Australia developed from three major streams of influence—central European, North American, and British—although it has cultivated its own characteristics and identity, in large part as a result of the nation's geographic isolation.

Central European Influences. During the 1930s and 1940s, a group of young Australian artists in Melbourne were inspired by individual exponents of central European modern dance: Norda Mata, Anny Fligg, Eve Alwyn, Stephanie Edye, and Gerd Haas. Irene Vera Young (a student of Jan Veen) taught and performed in Australia during this period, while Sonia Revid (a Mary Wigman student), Elizabeth Wiener (an Isadora Duncan student) and Daisy Pirnitzer (a Rosalia Chladek student) opened studios in Melbourne.

The arrival of Gertrud Bodenwieser and her group in Sydney in 1939 consolidated and developed the central European influence on Australian modern dance. Bodenwieser instilled in her students a philosophy of sensuous, fluid movement with well-composed groupings and the power of emotional expression that has had a profound influence on subsequent generations. When she died in 1959, company members Margaret Chapple and Keith Bain continued the work through the Bodenwieser Dance Centre and the Bodenwieser Dancers. In a 1960 tribute to Bodenweiser, Chapple and Bain restaged such major works as *The Blue Danube, The Demon Machine,* and *The Heretic* from the Bodenwieser repertory; Chapple's *Mobiles and Cycles* and Bain's *Primitive Suite* were among their major works of the 1960s. Bodenwieser dancers soon opened studios in Sydney and in Melbourne.

In 1963 Shirley McKechnie (a student of both Daisy Pirnitzer and Johanna Exiner) established the Australian Contemporary Dance Theatre. McKechnie initially drew on the expressionistic style of central Europe, and later developed a more formalized approach to both style and structure. Her 1972 work, *The Finding of the Moon*, inspired by a cycle of poems by Judith Wright and set to a score by Ian Cugley, received critical praise and remains the paradigm of her work. In 1975 McKechnie established Australia's first college program in dance, at Rusden State College (later Deakin University—Rusden Campus).

Also in 1963, Margaret Lasica (a student of Elisabeth Wiener and later, Johanna Exiner) established the Modern Dance Ensemble in Melbourne, producing experimental and imaginative works that retained a strong connection to her early Duncan influences while reflecting the wider theatrical concerns of her dancers. Lasica's outstanding 1971 production was *Another Time, Another Place*, set to the Double Violin Concerto of J. S. Bach. Throughout the 1980s, Lasica continued to create performance opportunities for a significant number of Australia's practicing professional artists through an ongoing series of experimental festivals.

Edouard Borovansky remained in Australia in 1939 at the conclusion of the Covent Garden Russian Ballet tour; he soon inspired the Australian dance community with the theatricality of his productions. Indeed, it was the Borovansky company that provided Laurel Martyn with the opportunity to choreograph new works during the 1940s, and she went on to create challenging and inventive works over the next thirty years for the Victorian Ballet Guild (later Ballet Victoria). [*See the entries on Borovansky and Martyn.*]

Beginning in the mid-1930s, contemporary ballets were created in Perth by Linley Wilson (whose early inspiration was Diaghilev's Ballets Russes) and, from the 1950s, by former de Basil dancer Kira Bousloff, who founded the West Australian Ballet.

North American Influences. Canadian Maud Allan introduced her "free-dance" style to small audiences on an Australian tour as early as 1914. The American influence was not felt until the late 1940s, beginning in 1947 when Ted Shawn, interested in Australian Aboriginal culture, performed in Perth, Darwin, Adelaide, and Sydney. That same year, American dancer Beth Dean settled in Sydney to pursue her interest in Aboriginal music and dance. She contributed to the Australian modern dance scene through production and choreography, lecturing and writing.

In 1952, the Denishawn/Graham–trained Margaret Barr came from a teaching post at Dartington Hall in the United Kingdom to open a school of modern dance in Sydney. Her dance-drama group continued to perform through the 1980s. Barr was uncompromising in her statements on social and political issues. Her movement was idiosyncratic and powerful; she created striking stage pictures and tableaux in works with truly Australian themes, such as *Judith Wright—Australian Poet* and *Portrait of a Lady with the C.B.E.* (1971), set to words from the autobiography of pioneer social worker Daisy Bates (who had been made a Companion of the British Empire).

In 1956, Katherine Dunham toured Australia, creating a surge of interest and excitement in modern dance. Australian dancers Jeanette Liddell and Anita Ardell toured with the company, and later became important teachers of the African-influenced jazz style in Australia. Joe Jenkins, Antonio Rodriguez and his wife Yolande remained in Australia for a period, teaching and performing Dunham material.

In the late 1950s, Coralie Hinkley was awarded a Fulbright Scholarship to study modern dance in New York. From 1957 to 1959 she worked with Martha Graham, Doris Humphrey, Louis Horst, and Merce Cunningham. She returned to Australia in 1960 to dance, choreograph, write, and work mainly within the educational system.

American dancer Ronne Arnold, who settled in Australia after performing in *West Side Story* in 1960, founded the Contemporary Dance Company of Australia, which performed from 1966 to 1972. Some of the best of young Australian modern and jazz dancers of the time joined him, responding to the dynamic energy of the American jazz idiom and contemporary themes.

The Alvin Ailey American Dance Theater toured in 1962, 1964, and again in 1986, each time performing before larger and more enthusiastic audiences. Ailey company dancer James Truitte returned to Australia for the 1969/70 season to teach Horton technique in Sydney, Melbourne, and Adelaide. This project, funded in the early days of the Australian Council for the Arts, was the first of its kind.

The Limón Dance Company toured once, in 1963, winning a dedicated following and inspiring a number of Australian dancers to study the technique in the United States.

The Eleo Pomare Company performed at the Adelaide Festival in 1972, surprising audiences with its daring and its political themes. Pomare company dancer Carole Johnson remained in Australia after the 1972 tour and in 1975 established in Sydney the Aboriginal/Islander School (renamed National Aboriginal/Islander Skills Development Association). This was the first institution for the education and training of indigenous Australian dancers. It laid the important foundation for the development of the Aboriginal/Islander Dance Theatre and Bangarra Dance Theatre.

The Merce Cunningham Company toured in 1976 and

the Cunningham technique and choreographic style made a strong impression. A number of Australian dancers and teachers studied at the Cunningham Studio in New York City.

Australian dancer-choreographers Nanette Hassall and Russell Dumas returned to Australia in the mid-1970s, after substantial North American experience, and initiated far-reaching change and development throughout Australia. Hassall's main North American influences were the Juilliard School and the Cunningham company (1970–1972); Dumas studied at the Martha Graham School and danced with both the Trisha Brown and Twyla Tharp companies. Over the years Dumas has continued to value subtlety and understatement, with kinesthetic interest as his foremost concern. Hassall has maintained a deep interest in abstracting movement from ideas and experiences and has gone on to create more complex collaborative works.

British Influences. Ballet Rambert undertook a fifteen-month tour of Australia and New Zealand from 1947 to 1949. The ensemble was composed of thirty dancers, and a number of Australian dancers were recruited. Twenty-six ballets were performed, including works by Walter Gore, Antony Tudor, Frederick Ashton, and Michel Fokine. After the tour, Rambert dancer Margaret Scott settled in Australia and established the Australian Ballet

School in Melbourne, which she directed from 1964 to 1990.

Peggy van Praagh came to Australia as acting artistic director of the Borovansky Ballet after the death of Edouard Borovansky in 1959; she was appointed the first artistic director of the Australian Ballet in 1962. Van Praagh pursued a policy of creating the opportunity for young dancers to choreograph the company productions. She established annual choreographic workshops and festivals, and developed the Armidale Summer Schools series (which began in 1967) with Bernard James of the Department of Continuing Education at the University of New England at Armidale. At Armidale, the dance community spirit was fostered through classes, discussions, and workshops led by some of Australia's leading artists, and by visitors such as Peter Brinson from the Calouste-Gulbenkian Foundation, Martha Hill from the Juilliard School, and Norman Morrice from Ballet Rambert. [*See the entry on van Praagh.*]

Dame Peggy van Praagh was a mentor for such Australian modern dance choreographers as Graeme Murphy, Barry Moreland, Don Asker, John Meehan, Ian Spink, Leigh Warren, Paul Saliba, Meryl Tankard, and Garth Welch. This fostering of contemporary works within the major ballet company had a strong impact on Australian modern dance in the 1980s.

AUSTRALIA: Modern Dance. A scene from act 2 of Graeme Murphy's *Poppy* (1978), in which nurses subject Jean Cocteau, portrayed by Murphy (center), to a treatment for opium addiction. (Photograph by Branco Gaica; used by permission.)

Australian Modern Dance Companies. Australian Dance Theatre (ADT), in Adelaide, was established by Elizabeth Dalman in 1965. Dalman made many study tours to Europe and the United States; she introduced both audiences and artists to dance that was new to Australia. Eleo Pomare, in whose company Dalman danced and taught during the 1970s, significantly influenced her choreographic style. In 1966 Pomare created *Gin, Woman, Distress* for her, and Dalman continued to perform it in the 1980s as well as to create mature, intense, personal solos such as the earthy, sensual *Earth Dreaming,* accompanied by live *didjeridu* (most ancient Aboriginal wind instrument) from her *Scangiarusca* in 1988; this captured the spirit and splendor of the Australian landscape to the music of a contemporary Australian band, Gondwanaland, that features *didjeridu.* Her company works were mainly about contemporary issues and Australian art, most often featuring music by Australian composers.

After the Australian Dance Theatre board dismissed Dalman in 1976, Jonathan Taylor from Ballet Rambert was invited the next year to reestablish the company. He commissioned works from international choreographers as well as from Australians, although Taylor himself was responsible for most of the Australian Dance Theatre repertory. Taylor embraced the boldness and openness of his Australian dancers and made full use of their ability to adapt European and North American stylistic qualities to suit the Australian energy and attitude toward space.

Leigh Warren was artistic director of the Australian Dance Theatre from 1987 to 1992. Warren focused on new contemporary works with and by young Australians and furthered the valuable education and community work that was an important feature of the company's work under Elizabeth Dalman. He developed a class structure and methodology by adapting stylistic influences from the United States and Europe to contemporary Australian energies. In 1993 Warren was replaced as artistic director of the Australian Dance Theatre by Meryl Tankard. Warren then formed a new company in Adelaide, Leigh Warren and Dancers.

Meryl Tankard left the Australian Ballet to dance as principal soloist with the Pina Bausch Tanztheater Wuppertal from 1978 to 1984. Tankard returned to Australia to choreograph in her own emerging style and in 1989 she became director of the Meryl Tankard Company (formerly Human Veins Dance Theatre) in Canberra. In 1993 Tankard became artistic director of Meryl Tankard Australian Dance Theatre (formerly Australian Dance Theatre). Tankard's work ranges from controlled minimalism to vigorous breathtaking movement. With her partner Regis Lansac's design and photographic projections, Tankard excels in creating a sense of ritual and timelessness. The 1990 work *Nuti* was inspired by the "Civiliza-tion" exhibition at the Australian National Gallery: five clay-whitened dancers in fabric wraps from the waist, with limited movement, brought to life a frieze of images of ancient Egypt. Lansac's projection of pictures from the exhibition washed the entire performing area to match the emotional intensity of the movement and the music. In *Furioso* (1993), Tankard mastered extremes and tensions: the dancers swung from ropes and took risks in exuberant physical and emotional engagement. With movement ranging from savage to tender, they flung themselves to the floor or moved in smooth, controlled phrases. [*See the entry on Tankard.*]

The Society of Dance Arts (SODA) produced a season (1965) of modern dance at the Union Theatre in Sydney. That initiative led former Australian Ballet member Suzanne Musitz to establish, in Sydney in 1966, Ballet in a Nutshell. This was an educational dance group that became Athletes and Dancers (1967–1970). The company was small, flexible, and mobile and serviced the rural areas of New South Wales as well as some major cities. This company paved the way for the formation in 1971 of the Dance Company of New South Wales.

The Dance Company of New South Wales presented works by Australian choreographers Graeme Watson, Jacqui Carroll, John Meehan, Chrissie Koltai, Keith Little, Suzanne Musitz, Garth Welch, Ian Spink, and Ross Coleman. Under Jaap Flier's direction for fifteen months (1975/76), works by Flier, John Butler, Glen Tetley, and Anna Sokolow were featured.

Graeme Murphy became artistic director of The Dance Company of New South Wales at the end of 1976, with Janet Vernon as ballet mistress. The company was renamed the Sydney Dance Company in 1979. The repertory has featured major works by Murphy, who has commissioned Australian composers and designers. Murphy's works, danced by predominantly classically trained dancers, are invariably sensual and theatrical, with quirky inventive movements shifting in focus and direction. They range from narrative full-evening productions such as *Poppy* (1978), concerning the life of Jean Cocteau, to plotless ballets such as *Kraanerg* (1988) set to a ballet score by Iannis Xenakis. For an Australian bicentennial project, Murphy created *Vast* (1988), a four company, seventy dancer work with the varied Australian landscapes of the sea, the coast, the center, and the cities as themes. [*See the entry on Murphy.*]

Kai Tai Chan, a Chinese-Australian architect, studied dance in Sydney with Margaret Barr. After freelancing in Europe and England from 1973 to 1976, Chan returned to Australia to establish The One Extra Company and to become a prolific creator of innovative dance-theater work, often juxtaposing Asian-Australian sensibilities and experience onto his Martha Graham–based training. In *Ah Q Goes West* (1984), he dealt with a Chinese peasant immigrant in Australia; in *The Shrew* (1986), he reworked the theme of Shakespeare's comic *The Taming of the Shrew* and set it in China and in modern Australia; *People Like Us* (1991) was set in contemporary Australia and dealt with social change, migrant life, and living with AIDS.

Graeme Watson (Bodenwieser Dance Center–trained) studied in New York City under James Truitte, Dan Waggoner, and Charles Moore and later freelanced in Europe. Watson, who choreographed for Netherlands Dance Theater, and for most of the contemporary companies in Australia from 1980 onward, became artistic director of The One Extra Company in 1992, with Julie-Anne Long as associate director. Watson's choreography is intellectually challenging, with clear form and structure and with kinetically evocative movement phrases that have a weighty but fluid quality. He acknowledges popular culture, technological advances, and the influence of the Australian landscape in his explorations of Australian social issues. In one of his 1994 works, *Backyard and Beyond*, for the Queensland Ballet, Watson employed peculiarly Australian images and characters such as a clothes hoist and a motorized snake, and historic characters such as the tragic explorers Robert O'Hare Burke and William Wills.

AUSTRALIA: Modern Dance. Bernadette Walong balances atop Pham Anh Phuong as Luisa Barisic (left) and Brett Daffy crouch close by in *Ochre Dusk*, choreographed by Cheryl Stock for the Dance North company. (Photograph by Ned Kelly; used by permission.)

The backdrop for this piece was a real dinosaur skeleton.

Don Asker danced with London Festival Ballet and was house choreographer for Netherlands Dance Theater from 1972 to 1975, after which he freelanced in Europe as a choreographer and an artist-teacher. Asker returned to Australia in 1979 to establish Human Veins Dance Theatre in Canberra from 1979 to 1988. His works for this company explored contemporary themes and were often autobiographical.

Cheryl Stock, featured dancer with Australian Dance Theatre in the 1970s, studied in New York and Europe in 1975 and again in 1979, concentrating on Graham, Cunningham, and Limón techniques. Stock worked with Don Asker, Kai Tai Chan, and on independent multiart-form projects before being appointed artistic director of Dance North in Townsville, Queensland, in 1984. Dance North has extensively toured northern Australia's regional areas presenting a soundly developed educational program and commissioned works, by Australians, dealing with Australian environmental and cultural issues. Among the works presented have been Stock's *Ochre Dusk* (1987) inspired by the "red center" of Australia and *Women's War II* (1992), which captured the mood and role of women in North Queensland in wartime. Stock has also undertaken many projects throughout Southeast Asia, particularly in Vietnam. In 1995, Stock resigned to pursue research and choreography in Vietnam. Graeme Watson left The One Extra Company to become artistic director of Dance North. The One Extra Company then restructured under an executive producer, commissioning artistic teams from the company's core of affiliated artists for each performance season.

From 1989 to 1992, Don Asker's Human Veins Dance Theatre became the Meryl Tankard Company, but in 1993, under the direction of Sue Healey, it became Vis-A-Vis Dance Canberra. Healey worked in a variety of performance projects from 1989 onward, in Australia, New Zealand, New York, China, and Europe. Her works are collaborative and explore the human condition. In *Knee Deep in Thin Air* (1993), Healey referred to fairy tales in an exploration of traditional male-female roles in society. Healy resigned in 1995 and Vis-A-Vis was restructured as The Choreographic Centre, aimed at providing a support organization for choreographic experimentation.

Dance Exchange, a postmodern company, was established by Russell Dumas and Nanette Hassall in Sydney in 1976. Through Dance Exchange, Dumas established a program of workshops in some of the capital cities with prominent postmodern artists such as Steve Paxton, Dana Rietz, Deborah Hay, and Lisa Nelson. In 1983 Hassall established Danceworks in Melbourne, a postmodern company dedicated to the development of Australian choreographers. Helen Herbertson and Beth Shelton became joint directors after Hassall's resignation in 1989 and Herbertson became sole director in 1992. Danceworks has continued Hassall's nonrepertory philosophy, offering artists the stimulation and challenge that is derived from working with peers who have a similar focus but a diversity of backgrounds.

Australia's first dance-in-education company, Tasdance, began under the direction of Jenny Kinder (1984–1994) who developed her artistry with Shirley McKechnie. She later studied at the Cunningham School in New York City. Kinder's policy was to commission provocative choreographers to develop an impressive postmodern repertory. Tasdance has engaged the imaginations of countless children with its school-residency program, in which children participate in workshops on specific thematic material, observe the company in rehearsal of this material, and attend the theater for a performance of the work.

In 1995 Tasdance appointed Karen Pearlman and Richard Allen as co-artistic directors. The couple had been in charge of their own company, That Was Fast, which had toured Europe and the United States as well as Australia. The new directors chose to broaden the role of Tasdance beyond education and to include works with text as well as movement (Allen is also a poet), to add concentration on community work.

In Western Australia, American Derek Holtzinger, with Australian Sue Peacock, founded a dance-in-education company, 2 Dance Plus in 1985, taking quality contemporary dance to regional and remote areas in Western Australia. Teacher-dancer Phillippa Clarke, a former member of Tasdance, became artistic director of 2 Dance Plus in 1991. Two smaller dance-in-education companies—with very small funding bases—Darc Swan (founded in 1982) in New South Wales and Outlet Dance (founded in 1987) in South Australia, have struggled to achieve excellence in, and an understanding of, contemporary dance by touring community centers and regional schools. Tracks, a 1990s project group established by David McMicken and Sarah Calver, has taken performance and workshop to small remote communities in the Northern Territory.

Maggie Sietsma gained experience in theaters in Australia, North America, England, France, and Italy prior to her 1984 founding of Expressions Dance Company in Brisbane. Sietsma choreographed most of the company's works, but commissions also went to several young Australian choreographers. She has in addition developed a strong educational policy.

Jim Hughes performed extensively in Europe with the Gulbenkian Dance Company. Hughes founded Fieldworks Performance Group in 1988 and has explored new performance practices and sites. His productions reflect his research in sociology, anthropology, philosophy, biomechanics and the related arts; he is regarded as an initiator of challenge and extension in the dance theater of the 1990s.

Among the multicultural dance companies, Bharatam Dance Company founded in 1987 by Dr. Chandrabhanu and Kailish Dance Company founded in 1993 by Padma Menon are committed to the practice and promotion of traditional heritage through experimentation in contemporary dance styles.

Chrissie Parrott, former dancer with the One Extra Company and West Australian Ballet, worked in Europe mainly with TanzForum Cologne, before returning to Australia in 1986. From a dancers' collective, the Chrissie Parrott Dance Company was formally established in 1990 in Perth. Much of Parrott's best work has resulted from her collaboration with prominent performing artists: in music with Cathie Travers and David Pye and the Nova Ensemble (*Terminal Velocity, Software Dragon*); in musical theater with Travers and Robyn Archer (*See Ya Next Century*); and with designers Andrew Carter and Mary Moore. In 1994 her company joined with Leigh Warren and Dancers to tour nationally, with joint productions, including William Forsythe's *Enemy in the Figure*. In 1992 her company was nationally recognized with the Sidney Myer Award in the Performing Arts.

Bangarra Dance Theatre, an Australian national indigenous dance-theater company, was founded by Carole Johnson in 1989 as the natural extension of the National Aboriginal and Torres Strait Islander Skills Development Association (NAISDA). Bangarra presents both traditional Aboriginal and modern Australian dance. Modern works are usually narrative in structure with themes taken from social issues of importance to the Aboriginal community. Stephen Page's *Praying Mantis Dreaming* (1992) deals with the struggles of a young Aboriginal-Australian woman to resolve living within both cultures. Here a praying mantis is used to represent the great depth of Aboriginal spirituality and traditional Aboriginal movement qualities are dominant in the choreography. Page, a 1983 NAISDA graduate and member of Sydney Dance Company, became artistic director of NAISDA in 1991.

The Aboriginal/Islander Dance Theatre (AIDT) was formally launched as the professional arm of NAISDA in March 1991, with 1984 graduate Raymond Blanco as artistic director. Its goal has been to educate and inform the general public of the history and evolution of Aboriginal and Torres Strait Islander culture. Tribal custodians from the Yirrkala and Sabai Islands also regularly perform with urban Aboriginal dancers. In the company's modern works, traditional Aboriginal dance qualities are blended with Martha Graham–based technique.

The Australian Choreographic Ensemble, a short-lived project company, was founded in 1992 as a creative forum for a small group of choreographers, with Paul Mercurio, formerly with the Sydney Dance Company, as artistic director.

Several disbanded small companies—Brian Coughran and Ken McCaffrey's Queensland Modern and Contempo-

AUSTRALIA: Modern Dance. Ros Warby, Dianne Reid, and Nicky Fletcher of Danceworks, a postmodern company dedicated to presenting works by Australian choreographers, find themselves wound up in the 1993 piece *In the Company of Angels*. (Photograph by David Simmonds; used by permission.)

rary Dance Company in Brisbane; Philippa Cullen's Electric Dance Ensemble in Sydney; Heather Callandar's Kinetikos Dance Theatre and the Reyes de Lara–Jean Talley company Still Moves in Perth; Ron Bekker's ACDC in Melbourne; and Maggi Phillips's Feats Unlimited Company in Darwin—are deserving of acknowledgment for their valuable contributions to and development of the art form.

Eclecticism and Change. Significant instruments of change came in the 1950s with the introduction of television and (in New South Wales) local recreational clubs. They created an opportunity for small dance companies that, although often short-lived, encouraged and gave increased exposure to modern dance.

Interaction between geographically separated artists was facilitated by Peggy van Praagh's Armidale Summer Schools. With Gulbenkian Foundation assistance, this led to the development of a series of Australia–New Zealand choreographic workshops and to the establishment of the annual Green Mill Dance Project in 1993.

Independent artists of the 1990s and collectives such as Dance House in Melbourne and Dance Base in Sydney continue to present works for short seasons, usually assisted by project grants from the Australia Council or from state arts ministries. The work of independent artists cannot be underestimated and is strongly influencing the shape of modern dance in Australia. Since the late 1980s there has also been an extraordinary growth of physical theater groups, which incorporate circus and acrobatic skills such as Legs On The Wall, Desoxy, and Circus Oz. However their performances are mainly in fringe festival venues. A gradual change in Australian attitudes toward the arts was enhanced by a flourishing of arts festivals along with the building of performing arts complexes in the 1970s and early 1980s. Leading modern companies and artists from Europe, America, and Australia have been given increased exposure.

With the establishment of the Australian Council for the Arts in 1968 (since 1973, the Australia Council), an increasing number of Australian dancers have been awarded grants to spend time in the United States, the United Kingdom and Europe. As a result, a significant number of Australians have joined major American companies.

Competitions, such as the Ballet Australia Choreographic Competitions held annually from 1969 to 1976, were established by the Australian dancer Valrene Tweedie, who had toured extensively with one of the Ballets Russes companies. Cash prizes enabled Australian choreographers to enhance their experience by travel overseas.

The introduction in 1975 of dance programs in colleges and universities, along with the 1977 establishment of the Australian Association for Dance Education (since 1992, Ausdance—The Australian Dance Council) have increased the awareness of and status of modern dance in Australia.

Australian Modern Dance in the 1990s. In 1992, the Australian federal government increased its recognition policy for its creative artists. A major cultural policy, called Creative Nation, was launched in 1994. It focused on promoting Australian works, new technologies for the arts, and providing opportunities for Australian dancers and choreographers.

While Australian modern dance has become more and more eclectic as a result of increased national and international exchange, pride in the Australian artistic identity and in the home product grows. Australian themes are being confidently explored, most often with openness and athleticism in the quality of movement. Australian artists are influenced by, but not subservient to, the major modern dance techniques. Australians are generally pragmatists, who perceive themselves as physical beings in a sporting nation and as bound to the challenges of a harsh and historically isolated land. These perceptions influence most Australian modern dancers in their total acceptance of unrestricted space, demanding light, and strong contrasts.

BIBLIOGRAPHY

Australasian Dance. Crows Nest, N.S.W., 1971–1972.
Australian Dance Theatre: The Modern Dance Company of Australia. Adelaide, 1978.
Brolga, no. 1 (December 1994).
Dance Australia. Melbourne, 1980–1988.
Denton, Margaret Abbie. "Reviving Lost Works." *Brolga* (June 1995): 57–67.
Dyson, Clare. *The Ausdance Guide to Australian Dance Companies 1994.* Canberra, 1994.
Fisher, Lynn. "Irene Vera Young and the Early Modern Dance in Sydney." *Brolga* (June 1995): 7–29.
Formby, David. *Australian Ballet and Modern Dance.* Sydney, 1981.
MacTavish, Shona Dunlop. *An Ecstasy of Purpose: The Life and Art of Gertrud Bodenwieser.* Dunedin, N. Z.,1987.
Pask, Edward H. *Enter the Colonies Dancing: A History of Dance in Australia, 1835–1940.* Melbourne, 1979.
Pask, Edward H. *Ballet in Australia: The Second Act, 1940–1980.* Melbourne, 1982.
Potter, Michelle. *A Passion for Dance.* Canberra, 1997.
Ruskin, Pamela. *Invitation to the Dance.* Sydney, 1989.

INTERVIEWS. Keith Bain, Margaret Chapple, Julie Dyson, Hilary Trotter, Shirley McKechnie, Garry Lester, Michelle Potter, Peter Lucas, Margaret Denton, Jennifer Barry, Janine Kyle, and Elizabeth Dalman.

VALDA L. CRAIG

Dance Research and Publication

Dance research, along with archival collection of works on dance and the development of college degree programs in dance, is relatively in its infancy in Australia. Paul Hammond, archivist with the Australian Ballet Foundation, offered a pertinent comment on the state of dance research in Australia when, at a 1987 seminar in Canberra he said, it is "not until the middle part of this century that an indigenous dance world and the desire to preserve our past, in all facets of human endeavor, has arisen."

The Canberra seminar brought together representatives of major Australian national and state institutions to discuss the objectives of a proposed national dance research center. The issues raised at the seminar virtually presented an overview of the state of dance research in Australia at that date.

Don Asker, former artistic director of Human Veins Dance Theatre, speaking from the perspective of a company director, highlighted the need for current resources and information. The subsequent discussion brought out the difficulty of demarcation between a research center and a resource center, given that today's records become tomorrow's research materials.

Michelle Potter, who had written a thesis on the designers of the Ballets Russes, emphasized that she had been obliged to pursue her studies through a department of art history, since no Australian college offered an advanced degree in dance history. She identified the urgent need for a catalog of primary dance sources and also noted that individual researchers did not have the means to publish or disseminate their work.

The research needs of university-level dance programs were considered by David Roche of the then South Australian College of Advanced Education. He, like Potter, urged the establishment of a comprehensive bibliography of source materials. However, Paul Hammond felt that not much historical material would be found since little information on dance events prior to the 1920s was available. The Canberra seminar clearly identified the need for the support of researchers, an outlet for publication, and a resource publications program.

Funding efforts on behalf of the center proved unsuccessful; the Australian Dance Council (formerly Australian Association for Dance Education), on limited funding, immediately established information-network links through monthly newsletters. From 1991 it published the quarterly journal *Forum* and from 1994 the semi-annual *Brolga,* a dance journal edited by Michelle Potter. Additional office space was obtained and with voluntary help, a print and audiovisual collection was begun and cataloged. Liaison with the Australian National University has resulted in the establishment of Internet access and liaison with the National Film Archives has resulted in the establishment of a video dance collection. In 1994, the Australian Dance Council formed the Australian Chapter of the World Dance Alliance–Asia-Pacific Center.

Prior to the Australian Dance Council publications, there had been only two national dance magazines published in Australia. With a foreward by Dame Peggy van Praagh, *Australasian Dance* had been launched in March 1971 as a monthly magazine, with John L. Groves as managing editor and Victor Carell as editor. A dedicated struggle by a number of editors kept the magazine going until December 1972. Dance enthusiast Dalley Messenger launched a new quarterly magazine *Dance Australia* in September 1980. Campbell Smith became its editor in 1986, with Dalley's role mainly as publisher, and the magazine soon became bimonthly. Karen van Ultzen became editor in 1989 when the magazine was sold to the Yaffa Publishing Group, with James Parker as publisher.

In 1985, with the assistance of the Australia Council for the Arts (equivalent to the U.S. National Endowment for the Arts, NEA), the semi-annual journal *Writings on Dance* was launched. Editors Elizabeth Dempster, Anne Thompson, Jude Walton, and Sally Gardiner have nurtured its development and continuity with themes such as "Ideokinesis and Dance Making," "Critical Issues," "Of Bodies and Power," "Making History," and "Privilege and Presence."

Today, dance research in Australia is growing increasingly important. The multicultural dance scene is strong; for example, the Asian community is prominent and a number of professional Indian dancers live and perform in Australia. Since 1988, the Australian bicentenary year, there has been a greater public awareness of the national culture and projects pertaining to it. Organizations and government agencies exist for the preservation of the heritage of the Australian Aborigines and the Torres Strait Islanders as well as those of Australia's various ethnic groups. Concerned institutions are cooperating in laying a foundation for the collection of information on dance, providing easier access to that information, and helping dance researchers avoid inefficient duplication of effort.

Ausdance-Australian Dance Council has conducted research projects and published reports on issues such as *Safe Dance Practice, Dancers Transition Project, Dance Educators in Australia, Guide to Tertiary Dance Programs in Australia;* in 1994, *The Ausdance Guide to Australian Dance Companies* was researched and produced for Ausdance by Clare Dyson—this guide details the history and repertory of all the contemporary companies.

VALDA L. CRAIG

AUSTRALIAN ABORIGINAL DANCE. [*To explore the dance traditions of indigenous inhabitants of Australia, this entry comprises six articles:*

> An Overview
> Aborigines of Arnhem Land
> Tiwi Dance
> Aborigines of Cape York Peninsula
> Walpiri Dance
> Antakirinya Dance

The introductory article surveys common characteristics, body decorations, and the importance of dance in Aboriginal life. The companion articles focus on practices in various regions and among various peoples of Australia.]

An Overview

The indigenous inhabitants of continental Australia and most of its offshore islands, conventionally termed Aborigines, were hunter-gatherers whose lives were intertwined with nature and what it provided. Before the arrival of British settlers in 1778 to establish a penal colony, Aborigines lived throughout Australia in well-organized, seminomadic groups. They probably migrated from Southeast Asia at least forty thousand years ago, and they spoke more than two hundred languages as yet not definitely related to any other linguistic family. In the late twentieth century in intensely settled regions of the continent some of the original languages are no longer spoken, while in more remote regions many are still spoken as first languages. At this time, Aboriginal people constitute between 1 and 2 percent of the nation's eighteen million people.

Aboriginal dancing has been widely admired by outsiders since the earliest British settlement, and often compared favorably with European dancing. In 1793, John Hunter wrote glowingly of Aboriginal dancing in his account of the early years of the British colony at Sydney Cove, located on the southeastern coast. He introduced the local Aboriginal word *carib-berie,* meaning "a dance," which eventually became standardized in Australian English as *corroboree* and came to mean any public performance of Aboriginal music and dance. However, local ancestral dance traditions are no longer practiced, for the most part, in southeastern Australia, now the country's most densely populated and industrialized region. Nineteenth-century descriptions and illustrations are virtually the only records with which the traditions that survive in other large areas of the country can be compared.

Although caution should be exercised in the interpretation of early European representations of Aboriginal dancing, late eighteenth-century and early nineteenth-century accounts and depictions of dance in southeastern Australia suggest that dancers made extensive use of formal, precise, and complex ground patterns involving many dancers in ranks of straight or curved lines. It appears that the lines may have moved in several directions simultaneously, and individual dancers performed solo movements. A master of ceremonies may have directed public performances of musicians and dancers, standing apart from both. On the other hand, musical analysis indicates that musicians provided musical cues to dancers to determine when the performance should be continued through repetitions and when it should be concluded. In southwestern Australia, another region where the connection with much ancestral Aboriginal culture has been lost, circling and spiraling formations were reported to have been used frequently.

In other regions, where ancestral Aboriginal life continues in less modified forms, dancing is more individualistic than what may have been the case in the south. Indeed, dancing is an activity of Aboriginal life that allows for significant creativity and prowess. In central Australia, interpretations of dance roles tend to be highly individual, in both solo and group performances. In Arnhem Land in central-northern Australia, dancers perform either solo or in flexible groups led by one dancer or more. Here, also, cues are given by singers indicating when to proceed to the concluding section of the dance. In Cape York (northeast peninsula), memorable performances by powerful individuals define anew the spiritual meaning of a dance, and subsequent performers strive to reproduce them. Tiwi Aborigines on Bathurst and Melville Islands, which lie off the central-north coast, particularly encourage individual creativity of dancers.

Men's movements and postures include dancing on all fours, dancing in a sitting position, jumping backward rapidly, jumping or stepping sideways, high leaps, and high-knee stamps (knees raised alternately to the point where the thigh is parallel to the ground, and lowered with a firm stamp). Arm movements are similarly extensive, varied, and vigorous. Women's dance postures and movements are generally less pronounced than the men's. Central Australian women commonly dance with feet wide apart, knees bent, moving slowly forward with small jumps, feet just skimming the ground, heads bowed, and arms held close to the body. In Arnhem Land the characteristic women's stance is feet close together and raised alternately, throwing sand over the other foot. In both traditions meaning is conveyed in different women's dances by various patterns of delicate, graceful, and subtle arm and hand movements.

Dancing is usually performed in a cleared space at a distance from the living area, with a canopy of boughs (commonly called a bough-shade) erected to screen the dancers as they prepare themselves. Women and men usually have separate bough-shades when they perform together. A lot of dancing, particularly public dancing, is performed at night, and firelight is used with dramatic effect. Dancers often emerge from screens of boughs, smoke, or natural vegetation and may appear suddenly in

AUSTRALIAN ABORIGINAL DANCE: An Overview. *(top)* An old print depicting the totemic Kangaroo Dance. In hunting societies, people often imitate the physical characteristics of prey, as a way of identifying with the animals and/or giving thanks to them. *(bottom)* Man from the Ngatatjara tribe in a Kangaroo Dance in 1966. The wide, turned-out stance of this dancer, often accompanied by a trembling of the legs, is a characteristic element in many of the Aboriginal dances performed by men. (Photographs from the Department of Library Services, American Museum of Natural History, New York [no. 250517 and no. 333533]; used by permission.)

the flickering light, their bodies elaborately decorated. These concealment techniques heighten the theatrical impact when the dancers appear.

Styles of body decorations of dancers vary from region to region, but there are some widely shared elements both in materials and designs. Commonly, patterns of red and yellow ochers, white clay, and charcoal are applied to the torso, arms, legs, and face. In some areas, particularly in central Australia, male dancers are decorated with finely chopped white feathers or the white fluff from certain plant species, colored by powdering with ocher (or left naturally white) and glued with blood onto the body in patterns representing the subject of the dance. This kind of decoration, which may continue upward over a high conical headdress, effectively masks the dancer's everyday identity. Men commonly wear leafy eucalyptus branches tied to the upper or lower leg, making a rustling noise in the rhythm of the leg movements. White cockatoo feathers held in place by a headband and pointing either upward or downward are often worn by both male and female dancers.

Most dancers carry ritual or ritualized objects. Sometimes objects used also for other purposes, such as boomerangs, shields, spears, fighting sticks, or digging sticks—often decorated—are used. Other objects are specifically manufactured for the occasion.

Dancing is used in many contexts of Aboriginal social life. Public entertainments (corroborees), consisting of singing, dancing, and other dramatic representations, occur throughout Australia. Dancing always plays an important part in both initiation and mortuary rites of passage, and it is always a key part of local totemic rites. Ceremonies performed for weather control, enhancement of sexual desire, healing, and sorcery often include dancing. Cult ceremonies, which exist in varying forms across several regions, especially feature dancing. Finally, Aboriginal dancing is often an integral part of formalized attempts to resolve family disputes, of ceremonies of diplomacy between groups, of peacemaking activities, and in formal preparations for warfare.

Such categories are not exclusive. Totemism, in particular, is an element of most dance occasions. Cult ceremonies are also frequently rites of passage. Intentions to control weather, enhance sexual desire, heal sickness, or cause personal harm are an element of many ceremonies in which dancing is featured. Formal means of conflict management are also frequently incorporated into performance occasions.

Australian Aboriginal dancing is generally connected with Aboriginal religion to a greater or lesser extent. In most places, Aboriginal people believe that new dances are received from spirits, especially those of recently deceased kin or of totemic figures. The subjects of dances are frequently totemic, sometimes mixed with topical al-

AUSTRALIAN ABORIGINAL DANCE: An Overview. A man of the Gurindji tribe dances in a *corroboree*, celebrating the return to tribal ownership of some three thousand square kilometers of Northern Territory grazing lands. (Photograph by Penny Tweedie; used by permission of the Office of Public Affairs, Australian Consulate General, New York.)

lusions. While public dances tend to be the most secular in content, dances performed in secret are the most sacred. No matter what the occasion, Aboriginal dancing is usually a fusion of religious intent and playful diversion. Australian Aborigines are seldom as serious and joyful simultaneously as when they are dancing.

BIBLIOGRAPHY

Angas, George French. *Savage Life and Scenes in Australia and New Zealand* (1847). New York, 1967a.

Angas, George French. *South Australia Illustrated* (1847). Sydney, 1967b.

Berndt, Ronald M., and Catherine H. Berndt. "Aborigines: Dancing." In *Australian Encyclopaedia*. 2d ed. Sydney, 1962.

Berndt, Ronald M., and Catherine H. Berndt. *The World of the First Australians*. 2d ed. Sydney, 1977. See pages 381–387.

Curr, Edward M. *Recollections of Squatting in Victoria*. Melbourne, 1883. See pages 135–140.

Curr, Edward M. *The Australian Race*. Vol. 1. Melbourne, 1886. See pages 89–93.

AUSTRALIAN ABORIGINAL DANCE: An Overview. Men of the Ngatatjara and Pintupi tribes in the totemic Carpet-Snake Dance, a type of "sitting dance," at the Warburton Range, Western Australia, 1966. (Photograph by R.A. Gould; from the Department of Library Services, American Museum of Natural History, New York [no. 333540]; used by permission.)

Dawson, James. *Australian Aborigines: The Languages and Customs of Several Tribes of Aborigines in the Western District of Victoria, Australia* (1881). Canberra, 1981. See pages 80–84.

Donaldson, Tamsin. "Making a Song (and Dance) in South-Eastern Australia." In *Songs of Aboriginal Australia*, edited by Margaret Clunies Ross, Tamsin Donaldson, and Stephen A. Wild, pp. 14–42. Sydney, 1987.

Elkin, A. P. *The Australian Aborigines.* 5th ed. Sydney, 1974. See pages 284–307.

Eyre, Edward J. "Manners and Customs of the Aborigines of Australia." In Eyre's *Journals of Expeditions of Discovery into Central Australia* (1845). Vol. 2. Adelaide, 1964. See pages 228–243.

Grau, Andrée. "Dreaming, Dancing, Kinship: The Study of Yoi, the Dance of the Tiwi of Melville and Bathurst Islands, North Australia." Ph.D. diss. The Queen's University of Belfast, 1983.

Gummow, Margaret. "Aboriginal Songs from the Bundjalung and Gidabal Areas of South-Eastern Australia." Ph.D. diss. The University of Sydney, 1992.

Hassell, Ethel. *My Dusky Friends: Aboriginal Life, Customs, and Legends and Glimpses of Life at Jarramungup in the Late 1880s.* Fremantle, 1975. See pages 38–39, 110–113, 138–140, and 193–195.

Hodgkinson, Clement. *Australia from Port MacQuarie to Moreton Bay.* London, 1845. See pages 230–235.

Howitt, A. W. "On Some Australian Ceremonies of Initiation." *Journal of the Royal Anthropological Institute* 13 (1884):432–459.

Howitt, A. W. *The Native Tribes of South-East Australia.* London, 1904. See pages 389–393, 413–425, and 534–556.

Hunter, John. *An Historical Journal of Events at Sydney and at Sea, 1787–1792* (1793). Edited by John Bach. London, 1968. See pages 143–145.

Isaacs, Jennifer. "Body Decoration." In *The Encyclopedia of Aboriginal Australia*, edited by David Horton, vol. 1, pp. 136–138. Canberra, 1994.

Mitchell, Thomas L. *Three Expeditions into the Interior of Eastern Australia.* Vol. 2. 2d ed., rev. London, 1839. See pages 4–6.

Moyle, Alice M. "Music and Dance: Master Singers of the Bush." In *The Moving Frontier: Aspects of Aboriginal-European Interaction in Australia*, edited by Peter Stanbury. Sydney, 1977.

Moyle, Alice M. "Aborigines: Music and Dance." In *Australian Encyclopaedia.* 4th ed. Sydney, 1983.

Moyle, Alice M., ed. *Music and Dance of Aboriginal Australia and the South Pacific: The Effects of Documentation on the Living Tradition.* Sydney, 1992.

Roth, Walter E. *Ethnological Studies among the North-West Central Queensland Aborigines.* Brisbane, 1897. See pages 114 and 117–125 and plates 14–16.

Roth, Walter E. *Games, Sports, and Amusements.* Brisbane, 1902. See pages 22–23.

Salvado, Rosendo. *The Salvado Memoirs: Historical Memoirs of Australia and Particularly of the Benedictine Mission of New Norcia and of the Habits and Customs of the Australian Natives* (1851). Translated and edited by E. J. Storman. Nedlands, 1977. See pages 133–135.

Smyth, R. Brough. *The Aborigines of Victoria.* Melbourne, 1878. See pages 166–176.

Von Sturmer, John. "Aboriginal Singing and Notions of Power." In *Songs of Aboriginal Australia*, edited by Margaret Clunies Ross, Tamsin Donaldson, and Stephen A. Wild, pp. 63–76. Sydney, 1987.

Wild, Stephen A. "Australian Aboriginal Theatrical Movement." In *Theatrical Movement: A Bibliographical Anthology*, edited by Bob Fleshman, pp. 601–624. Metuchen, N.J., and London, 1986.

Wild, Stephen A. "Aboriginal Music and Dance." In *The Australian People. An Encyclopedia of a Nation, Its People and Their Origins*, edited by James Jupp, pp. 174–181. Sydney, 1988.

Wild, Stephen A. "Australian Aboriginal Drama." In *The Masks of*

Time, edited by A. M. Gibbs, pp. 177–195. Canberra, 1994.

Williams, Drid "Dance." In *The Encyclopedia of Aboriginal Australia,* edited by David Horton, vol. 1, pp. 255–257. Canberra, 1994.

STEPHEN A. WILD

Aborigines of Arnhem Land

For the Aboriginal people of Arnhem Land, in the northeast of the Northern Territory, Australia, dance is primarily a vehicle for religious expression. It is a major formal component of rituals that mark transitions in an individual's life history, particularly those concerned with male puberty, initiation into secret male cults, and disposal of the dead. Dance is also important in ceremonies of diplomacy, called *rom,* whose purpose is to secure friendly relations between Aborginal communities who may live some distance apart.

Aborigines in this coastal region belong to small communities of three hundred persons or fewer, divided into several clans, each of which owns a separate territory. The clan estates and the natural features and resources that they contain are believed to have been shaped by various zoomorphic and anthropomorphic beings, called *wangarr,* in the time before living memory. Most nonpublic ceremonies celebrate the creating *wangarr,* who are believed to have traveled widely in ancestral times, creating features such as springs, rain forests, and freshwater swamps on various clan estates. Aborigines throughout eastern and central Arnhem Land venerate the *wangarr* in song and dance in rituals such as the *mardaian* or *ngarra* (the latter term is used in eastern Arnhem Land), which the Australian anthropologist Adolphus P. Elkin described as an "All Souls' festival." The *kunapipi,* a fertility cult also known as "old woman," has traveled to north-central Arnhem Land from the south and southeast and is now the most popular of the men's secret cults. It makes great use of revelatory theatrical performance in which dance is a major component.

The main public rituals are mortuary ceremonies and the *rom* rite, sometimes called *maradjiri.* The structures of mortuary and *rom* ritual have much in common and are based on a number of named clan-song series, called *manikay.* Various *manikay* are sung throughout central and eastern Arnhem Land, and each is owned by a consortium of clans. In certain circumstances, each *manikay* may be accompanied by appropriate dances, the combination of song and dance being termed *bunggul.* Each *manikay* and its dances venerates a separate set of *wangarr;* generally speaking, *manikay wangarr* do not overlap with site-creating *wangarr,* though they too may be associated with particular clan estates. An individual song series comprises around twenty to forty song subjects, each realized in performance in a number of short verses. Each song subject, and hence each *bunggul,* is about a particular *wangarr* and usually refers to the *wangarr*'s characteristic behavior and to places, both actual and mythical, that it inhabits. The song series *Djambidj* includes turtle, northwest monsoon, and white cockatoo among its twenty-one subjects; another series, *Bugala,* celebrates crocodile, saltwater, and emu.

Manikay are sung by one or two senior men from the clans that own the songs. The accompaniment is the beating of hardwood clapsticks and the drone of the *didjeridu,* a trumpetlike wind instrument made from a branch. When *bunggul* takes place, performers may include both men and women, who dance the same subject on separate parts of a rectangular dance ground of firm sand. Usually musicians sit at one end, and the male dancers begin from the opposite end of the ground; the women form a line along one side, usually to the singers' left.

Women may dance alone, both within and outside ritual contexts—around the evening campfires, for example. Female dancing is often restricted to delicate gliding movements of the feet just under the surface of the sand (translated as "they throw the sand") and to movements of the arms and hands about the head or in front of the upper body. The head is usually bowed. Only assertive senior women advance any distance into the dance ground during performance. There is a distinctive female dance for every *manikay* subject.

Male dancing is much more vigorous than that of women and utilizes most of the dance ground. Dancers give out series of ritual calls and invocations to the wan-

AUSTRALIAN ABORIGINAL DANCE: Aborigines of Arnhem Land. Young women dancing at a burial rite, Goulburn Island. (Photograph by A. P. Elkin; from the Department of Library Services, American Museum of Natural History, New York [no. 330822.]; used by permission.)

garr. Men, however, dance only a certain number of *manikay* subjects. The chosen subjects are those that belong by convention to a set of dances performed on consecutive evenings during the preparatory parts of public ritual, with those that express the thematic cores of these rites. The evening *bunggul* set of *Djambidj* consists of eight subjects—spangled grunter (a fish *wangarr*), king brown snake, bittern, friar bird, small bird, tuber, small fish, and white cockatoo. *Djambidj* subjects that form the thematic cores of mortuary ritual are crow, wild honey, boomerang, and brown booby (a seabird *wangarr*). All these have complex dances.

Within the evening *bunggul* set, Aborigines distinguish two main dance styles, straight and circle dancing. Circle dancing is reserved for a small number of subjects—only two in *Djambidj* (spangled grunter and king brown snake); these usually begin the evening performance. Circle dances continue through a sequence of several song verses and incorporate lines of men in ever-decreasing spiral formations. Straight dances last for the duration of a single song verse (about a minute). Aborigines usually perform several items of the same subject and then change to a different one, thus building up long sequences from small units. Straight dancing is brisk and vigorous. In the common pattern, dancers approach and retreat from the musicians at a run or a gallop, then clump together in a knot; finally, they raise their knees high and stamp forward toward the musicians, as the dance leader invokes the sacred names of the pertinent *wangarr.*

Dance leaders *(djalagan-nga)* and singers hold complex ceremonies with the skill and apparent ease of long practice. Dance is, however, only one component of many in these performances. It never expresses meaning independently of the other performance elements, though it is usually the most dramatic of them.

BIBLIOGRAPHY
Berndt, Ronald M. *Kunapipi: A Study of an Australian Aboriginal Religious Cult.* Melbourne, 1951.
Borsboom, A. P. *Maradjiri: A Modern Ritual Complex in Arnhem Land, North Australia.* Nijmegen, 1978.
Clunies Ross, Margaret, and Lester R. Hiatt. "Sand Sculptures at a Gidjingali Burial Rite." In *Form in Indigenous Art,* edited by Peter J. Ucko. Canberra, 1977.
Clunies Ross, Margaret, and Stephen Wild. *Djambidj: An Aboriginal Song Series from Northern Australia.* Canberra, 1982. Companion book to a recording.
Clunies Ross, Margaret. "Two Aboriginal Oral Texts from Arnhem Land, North Australia, and Their Cultural Context." In *Words and Worlds: Studies in the Social Role of Verbal Culture,* edited by Stephen Knight and S. N. Mukherjee. Sydney, 1983.
Clunies Ross, Margaret, and Stephen Wild. "Formal Performance: The Relations of Music, Text, and Dance in Arnhem Land Clan Songs." *Ethnomusicology* (1984).
Elkin, A. P. *Two Rituals in South and Central Arnhem Land.* Oceania Monographs, 19. Sydney, 1972.
Hiatt, Lester R. *Kinship and Conflict: A Study of an Aboriginal Community in Northern Arnhem Land.* Canberra, 1965.
Keen, Ian. "One Ceremony, One Song: An Economy of Religious Knowledge among the Yolngu of Northeast Arnhem Land." Ph.D. diss., Australian National University, 1978.
Moyle, Alice M. "Sound Films for Combined Notation: The Groote Eylandt Field Project, 1969." *Yearbook of the International Folk Music Council* 4 (1972): 104–118.
Moyle, Alice M. "North Australian Music: A Taxonomic Approach to the Study of Aboriginal Song Performances." Ph.D. diss., Monash University, 1974.
Moyle, Alice M. "Aboriginal Music and Dance in Northern Australia." In *The New Grove Dictionary of Music and Musicians.* London, 1980.
Stubington, G. J. "Yolngu Manikay: Modern Performances of Australian Aboriginal Clan Songs." Ph.D. diss., Monash University, 1978.
Wild, Stephen, ed. *Rom in Canberra.* Canberra, 1984.

FILMS.   Alice M. Moyle and E. C. Snell, *Groote Eylandt Field Project: Aboriginal Dances* (Canberra: AIAS, 1969), and *Groote Eylandt Field Project: Five Brolga Dances* (Canberra: AIAS, 1969). Ian Dunlop, *Madarrpa Funeral at Gurka'wuy* (Sydney: Film Australia, 1979). Kim McKenzie, *Waiting for Harry* (Canberra: AIAS, 1980). The Australian Institute of Aboriginal Studies holds in its archive considerable footage depicting dance in north-central Arnhem Land, principally from *Waiting for Harry* and from a *rom* ceremony held in Canberra in 1982.

RECORDINGS.   *Djambidj: An Aboriginal Song Series from Northern Australia* (Canberra: AIAS, 1982). *Songs from Arnhem Land* (Canberra: AIAS, 1966).

MARGARET CLUNIES ROSS

Tiwi Dance

The Tiwi people inhabit Melville and Bathurst islands off Australia's north-central coast. Three basic concepts underlie Tiwi dance: first, dance and music are closely interrelated; second, dance competence is expected of every Tiwi; and third, creativity and originality are greatly valued. All dances are very short, rarely lasting longer than a minute.

The word *yoi* refers to the dance, to the songs used for dance, and to the rhythm of these songs, as well as to the actions of dancing and singing for dance. Thus it denotes the concept and act of dancing and the music associated with dance and its performance. All are seen as inextricably related.

Any Tiwi is capable of an acceptable dance performance. The occasion for taking part is usually social. Each person has certain duties to perform toward his or her relatives, including dancing on certain occasions. As soon as Tiwi children are old enough to be aware of the surrounding world, they are exposed to dance. During childhood they are encouraged to dance informally and to take part in all dance events, imitating their elders. All teaching is done in context. By the time children reach adolescence, they have enough knowledge of the basic dance repertory to play their roles competently.

Each Tiwi uses the arts to express individual thoughts and experiences. To be original and creative is important, and so each recognizes the power of the intellect in this process. Tiwi designs, songs, and dances rarely have supernatural origins; they are not dreamed, as they are in many Australian Aboriginal societies, but rather thought. Tiwi artists continually make mental notes, accumulating ideas and comments about people or events until an occasion when they can use this material.

Men and women perform dances together, but they have different styles. Women dance with feet parallel, the head slightly inclined forward, or the eyes looking down, and one foot completely flexed back away from the ground on the beat; they use a regular tempo throughout the performance. Men dance with their feet slightly turned out, with the head upright or inclined slightly back, and with both feet on the ground on the beat; they increase the tempo, almost doubling it toward the end of their performance. These two major types of dance are described by the Tiwi as the "slow dance" (the women's dance) and the "fast dance" (the men's dance). The movements of the feet for both men and women tend to be the same throughout the Tiwi dance repertory, except for a few dances that have distinctive foot movements. Dances are differentiated essentially by arm movements.

All dances are accompanied by singing and clapping. Dances tend to have three parts: a short introduction in which the dancer dances on the spot at the edge of the dancing ground; a longer middle section in which the dancer moves around the dance ground; and a short concluding section, once again danced in place but now somewhere within the dance ground.

In their evaluation of a dance performance, the Tiwi put great emphasis on precision: the movements must be direct, with clear transition from one posture to the next; and timekeeping must be precise, with the transfer of weight from one foot to the other or from one foot to two feet coinciding exactly with the beat. The first type of precision is often termed "dancing strong," and the latter as "punching the ground properly." The dancers are also expected to "throw their bodies into the dance."

Traditionally, dance was used informally for general entertainment, and formally in mortuary rituals and during the annual Kulama (yam ceremony). Today dance is also used formally at official ceremonies, at social clubs, and to some extent in church. The majority of dances are not context-specific. The occasions for which dances may be choreographed are primarily preliminary mortuary rituals. The only people who can choreograph are specific kin of the deceased. In addition, at social clubs anyone can choreograph. Dance events are organized along regular patterns, which lay importance on the chosen performers and order of the dances.

The Tiwi give a name to each individual dance, but this name is rarely restricted to denoting a dance; it can also refer, for example, to the bereavement status of the dancer or to the subject matter of the dance. The dances are divided into those that are owned by the choreographer and his descendants and transmitted patrilineally, and those that have no known choreographer and are said to have always existed. The latter belong to everyone, although not everyone can perform them on every occasion. Usually kinship determines whether a person is eligible to perform a specific dance on a specific occasion.

Many dances are created, but not all are transmitted. Many are forgotten over the years, because they were not successful or popular enough to stand the test of time.

BIBLIOGRAPHY
Attenborough, David. *Quest under Capricorn.* London, 1963.
Brandl, Maria. "Pukumani: The Social Context of Bereavement in a North Australian Tribe." Ph.D. diss., University of Western Australia, Nedlands, 1971.
Dean, Beth. "In Search of Stone-Age Dance." *Walkabout* 21 (May 1955): 15–20.
Ewers, John K. "Pukumani (Northern Territory)." *Walkabout* 14 (June 1948): 29–34.
Ewers, John K. *With the Sun on My Back.* Sydney, 1953.
Goodale, Jane C., and Joan D. Koss. "The Cultural Context of Creativity among the Tiwi." *Proceedings of the American Ethnological Society* (1966): 185–191.
Goodale, Jane C. *Tiwi Wives: A Study of the Women of Melville Island, North Australia.* Seattle, 1971.
Grau, Andrée. "Dreaming, Dancing, Kinship: The Study of *Yoi,* the Dance of the Tiwi of Melville and Bathurst Islands, North Australia." Ph.D. diss., Queen's University of Belfast, 1983.
Grau, Andrée. "Sing a Dance—Dance a Song: The Relationship between Two Types of Formalised Movements and Music among the Tiwi of Melville and Bathurst Islands, North Australia." *Dance Research* 1 (Autumn 1983): 30–42.

FILMS. Francis Birtles, *Coorab in the Island of Ghosts* (Melbourne, 1929). Stewart Scougall, *Pukumani* (Sydney, 195–). John Morris, *Tumanu's People* (Sydney, 1960). David Attenborough, *Buffalo, Geese, and Men* (London, 1963). Jack Rogers, *Dance of the Buffalo Hunt* (Sydney, 1963). Dahl Collings and Geoffrey Collings, *Pattern of Life* (Sydney, 1964). Lee Robinson, *In Song and Dance* (Sydney, 1964). Roger Sandall, *Pukumani for Barney Tuk* (Canberra, 1971). Curtis Levy, *Mourning for Mangatopi* (Canberra, 1975). David MacDougall, *Goodbye Old Man* (Canberra, 1977).

ANDRÉE GRAU

Aborigines of Cape York Peninsula

The dance of the Aborigines of Cape York Peninsula is characterized by great diversity and variation. In this respect it parallels language diversity in the region and, like language differences, serves to mark individual and group identity. It is likely that all dances, even those now regarded as secular, originated in religious life.

Most dances are taught and performed in ritual contexts dominated by senior men. In general, they allude to characters and events recorded in mythology. It is possible to categorize dances into classes that depict the activities of a patri-clan (father's clan) ancestor within his own country; the relationship between the ancestors of neighboring (the proximate) clans; or the activities of culture or creator heroes, who traveled about instructing people in ceremonies but who are not affiliated with any particular patri-clan.

An example of the first class is the Bonefish Dance (lower Archer River, *winychinam* tradition), in which the senior male clansman dances with torch and spears, hunting his totem or *puul waya* (symbolized by two young men bearing carved and painted representations of the bonefish) at night from a bark canoe paddled by a close kinsman. There is an identification between hunter and hunted.

Relationships between clans are displayed in the Taipan Snake–Blue-tongued Lizard Dance (lower Knox River, *apalacha* tradition), which recreates the conflict between these two totemic reptiles. The third category is exemplified by the Wallaby Dance (lower Holroyd River, *wanam* tradition), in which the two *kaa'ungken* hero-brothers argue before reconciling and symbolically spearing the wallabies, enacted by men who appear in line before them.

In the first two classes of dance, individuals represent themselves in more or less heightened ways. They are not bonefish, taipan, or blue-tongued lizard, but rather Bonefish Man, Taipan Man, or Blue-tongued Lizard Man. Although they may exhibit some features of their eponymous animal species, they dance as men—or perhaps more accurately as spirits, or as revealing their own spiritual essence. These dances (which are fairly typical) have little mimetic or even narrative content; they are representational, in a highly formalized way, but of human activities and responses, personal identity, and social relations, not animal behaviors.

Songs accompany most religious dancing and have the power to summon up spirits. In one ritual they are used to call up the spirits of the recently dead; the spirit is then sent to its final abode somewhere in the deceased's clan estate. Songs may variously be interpreted as summoning the ancestral spirits to the performer in the course of the dance, or as bringing the performer's own spirit into play. Great dancers are deemed to be closely in touch with the spirit world, and therefore to be the bearers of true knowledge and the possessors of authorized (if somewhat frightening) power.

Totemic dances are said to be transmitted from one's immediate ancestors, from one's father and one's father's father. This perspective does not permit conscious innovation. A performance can be validated simply by claiming, "I follow from my father"; one also might assert, "Being Bonefish, how can I dance other than Bonefish?" The propriety and integrity of the dance are considered to reside within the performer, however, permitting legitimate but unconscious innovations to be made at any time.

Although anyone may dance, certain dancers are recognized as better than others. In culture-hero dances, this fact is structured into the ceremony and its underlying mythology. Especially brilliant dancers are identified with the hero brothers—even as their incarnate forms. They receive rapid advancement through the initiation grades and assume an authority over dance matters that transcends whatever rights or interests others might have, by virtue of clan affiliation, in the mythological events that occurred within their own clan estates. The superior dancers are determiners as much as keepers of the tradition.

Ceremonies are highly localized. Apart from their specific contents, they exhibit stylistic features that serve to distinguish them, sometimes minimally, from the ceremonies held by neighboring populations, or from other ceremonies held by the same group: the call that terminates each song segment, the body decorations, the nature of the nonvocal musical accompaniment (for example, the presence or absence of drums, the use of boomerangs as clapsticks, or even the way the boomerangs are struck). Differences are jealously guarded, and there are frequent accusations of stealing. Groups worried that their repertory is in danger of being commandeered may threaten to "kill" it. Access even by senior men to another group's ceremonial life is a carefully allocated privilege.

Some ceremonial dances are performed on special grounds in exclusively male contexts; almost all the men present participate, as dancers, as singers, or by providing background support such as clapping, stamping, grunting, or calling. Other men's dances are performed in the general camp, visible to all. In still others, women play a fully complementary role, dancing in parallel with the men or terminating dances men have begun. Women may also play a subsidiary role, either "warming up" the dance before the men appear or dancing alongside the men, using body signs that indicate their relationship to the male participants.

Women have their own dance form, *wuungk*, which is distributed widely throughout the central peninsula. Its main function is in mortuary ritual, when the women carry male hunting paraphernalia they are normally forbidden to touch. There is no secret women's dancing.

Secret dances may, at times, be released into the public arena. If a dance has not been performed publicly for a long time, or if there are people present who have never seen it before, the senior men rub the audience with underarm smell and blow in their hair to protect them from its power. Dances associated with a deceased person remain unperformed until mortuary rituals are completed, or they may be performed as part of the final rites.

Dancing is believed to enhance the sexual attractiveness of performers, both male and female; some *wuungk* songs refer explicitly to "sweetheart business." At Aurukun, missionaries banned *wuungk* at one time because it was said to provoke jealous fights; peculiarly, the injunction was not extended to male dancing.

A popular form of secular Aboriginal dance is referred to either as *corroboree* or *play-about*. A popular form called *shake-a-leg* is probably a remnant of a ceremony *(malpa* or *malgarri)* introduced into the peninsula from the southwest in the early twentieth century. Its standard repertory depicts events that occured historically on cattle stations (ranches), often explicitly self-mocking or aimed at deflating European pomposity. Shake-a-leg also denotes a dance movement which, with various dynamics, is common to many of the major ceremonial styles. The legs are spread wide apart, and the knees are flexed and trembled smoothly, or jerked in and out more or less rapidly.

Since about the 1930s, the so-called island style, introduced via the Torres Straits, has enjoyed an intermittent vogue. Although of lower status than indigenous dance forms, it has been largely "Aboriginalized." At Aurukun, it has been incorporated into contemporary mortuary rituals called "house openings."

Since 1990, attempts have been made to salvage or revive flagging traditions by such strategies as instructing preadolescents, releasing certain secret dances for public performances, staging dance festivals, and undertaking dance tours within Australia and abroad.

BIBLIOGRAPHY

Chase, A. K. "Which Way Now? Tradition, Continuity, and Change in a North Queensland Aboriginal Community." Ph.D. diss., University of Queensland, 1980.

McConnel, Ursula H. *Myths of the Mungkan.* Melbourne, 1957.

Sturmer, John von. "The Wik Region: Economy, Territoriality, and Totemism in Western Cape York Peninsula, North Queensland." Ph.D diss.,University of Queensland, 1978.

Sturmer, John von. "Communicating with Dance: Some Western Cape York Peninsula Examples." Paper presented at the Australian Anthropological Society Conference, Adelaide, August 1983.

FILMS. Ian Dunlop, *Dances at Aurukun* (Sydney, 1964). Ian Dunlop, *Five Aboriginal Dances from Cape York* (Sydney, 1966). Curtis Levy, *Lockhart Dance Festival* (Canberra, 1974). Judith MacDougall, *The House-Opening* (Canberra, 1980).

JOHN VON STURMER

Warlpiri Dance

One of the largest Aboriginal groups, the Warlpiri once occupied around 50,000 square miles (150,000 square kilometers) of semiarid land in central Australia. Today they number approximately 2,500 and live primarily on government reserves in Australia's Northern Territory.

Traditional Warlpiri dances are reenactments of the events of the Dreamtime, when, according to Aboriginal myth, the universe was created by totemic ancestors. Dancing the ritual dramas is intended to remind participants of the source and sustaining power of the universe, to reveal the Dreaming—the Dreamtime knowledge and episodes, and to help maintain the Warlpiri world. As communication with the Dreamtime by linking temporality with eternity, dances are performed within a ceremonial context; style and structure vary with ceremonial function.

Australia's summer season (September through February) brings several important ceremonies: fire ceremonies to resolve conflict, in which participants receive burns; public ceremonies, usually intended for public entertainment; and annual initiation ceremonies, which incorporate the circumcision of pubescent males. The remainder of the year has several important ceremonies that are performed individually or as parts of other rites, including men's private totemic-increase ceremonies and love-management ceremonies, and women's private ceremonies for the physical and spiritual maintenance of land and people.

Dances are learned through observation and participation. They are believed to be supernatural in origin, learned either from the Dreamtime or from ancestral spirits in dreams. Some are borrowed from neighboring cultures. Although choreographic patterns exist, dances are not rehearsed and extensive individual variation exists; gifted dancers are agents of sociocultural innovation. Dances are associated with totemic ancestors and are owned and passed on by their human descendants through paternal clan (patri-clan) lines, thus perpetuating the link between past and present and ensuring the Warlpiri people's continued survival.

Two primary dance and ceremonial roles are that of the performer-owner (*kirda,* or member of the owning patri-clan) and the manager (*kurdungulu,* or descendant of a female member of the owning patri-clan). A person may function in either role, depending on experience, ability, and the Dreaming that is being manifested. A manager is a guardian of the Dreaming and prepares and instructs the performer-owner, who represents the Dreaming. Sometimes these roles are extended to the opposite patri-moiety (half of the clans in a society form each moiety).

Before a ceremonial dance begins, the managers decorate the bodies of the dancers with paints and clays; they prepare the dance paraphernalia and the performance area. Simultaneously, singers chant appropriate song verses to activate the Dreamtime power. Dances usually are performed at sunset or at night, in a clearing, before an audience of performers and observers who provide the music. Dancers frequently wield ritual objects. Occasionally after a dance, managers receive items such as money and blankets from owners in exchange for their management of the performance and transmission of sacred knowledge.

Men's and women's dances are usually segregated in space, although occasionally both sexes dance simultane-

AUSTRALIAN ABORIGINAL DANCE: Warlpiri Dance. Men of the Warlpiri tribe at Yuendumu in the Northern Territory performing a *murrungurru*, a traditional welcoming dance, for visitors from the capital city of Darwin. (Photograph by Michael Jensen; used by permission of the Office of Public Affairs, Australian Consulate General, New York.)

ously within the same general area. Each sex has two dance styles, one sex-specific and the other shared. Sex-specific dance styles, believed to help maintain the cosmos, symbolize relationships between land and people. Dances in the shared style, believed to help maintain the well-being of the family, symbolize fertility and nurturance. A sliding jump, performed with knees bent and feet apart and parallel, is characteristic of women's dance *(wirntinjaku karnta-karnta-kurlangu)*. Men perform this movement to symbolize women.

Mimetic dances *(walaparini* or *panpa)*, in which a dancer mimes the behavior of a Dreamtime ancestor, are performed by owners representing specific Dreamtime figures and are directed by managers. Dancers wear elab-

orate headdresses and have plant or animal designs painted on their bodies, drawn in blood by the managers. Lasting a few minutes, a mimetic dance is performed by as many as five men (women are not allowed to perform this type of dance), who frequently dance solos on a ground painting that is destroyed in the process. At the conclusion of the dance, managers touch each dancer's design and remove his headdress.

Mimetic dances are of four types: running *(pangkaja-kura)*, walking *(wapanja-kura)*, sitting *(nyinanja-kura)*, and on all fours *(kiripikanyi)*. Sitting dances are performed to singing; others may have only rhythmic accompaniment, such as the clapping of two boomerangs struck together. Movements are classified according to body action, such as leg quivering *(pakali)* or looking behind *(kulpari-nyanka)*.

Nonmimetic dances *(mili-mili wirntimi)* are performed by managers, by ritual clowns, or by subincised men during parts of the circumcision rite. Representing the traveling movements of a specific Dreamtime ancestor, nonmimetic dancers usually decorate their bodies but do not wear headdresses.

The private, sacred dances last approximately thirty minutes. Dancers decorate their bodies with grease and ochre designs that are usually applied by managers; they often wear feather bundles in headbands, and they may sing. One dance, performed to vocal accompaniment, focuses on a symbolic ritual stick around which a line of owners (the embodiment of the ancestor) dance under the guidance of managers; the stick is then extracted by dancing managers and handed to observing managers.

Warlpiri women do not have names for their structurally distinct dance styles. Warlpiri women's dances are classified according to the Dreaming (of country or totemic ancestor). A single dance may include sitting, kneeling, walking, and running. Many movements from the large repertory are similar to male mimetic movements. Their public dances are performed by women representing generalized ancestors. To the accompaniment of men's singing, women perform a few motifs repeatedly, sometimes for hours. In some dances they shout calls on alternate jumps.

BIBLIOGRAPHY

Bell, Diane. "Daughters of the Dreaming." Ph.D. diss., Australian National University, 1980.

Bell, Diane. "Women's Business Is Hard Work: Central Australian Aboriginal Women's Love Rituals." *Signs* 7 (1981): 314–337.

Berndt, Catherine H. "Women's Changing Ceremonies in Northern Australia." *L'Homme* 1 (1950): 1–87.

Berndt, Catherine H. "Women and the 'Secret Life.'" In *Aboriginal Man in Australia*, edited by Ronald M. Berndt and Catherine H. Berndt. Sydney, 1965.

Dail-Jones, Megan Llinos. "A Culture in Motion: A Study of the Interrelationship of Dancing, Sorrowing, Hunting, and Fighting as Performed by the Warlpiri Women of Central Australia." Master's thesis, University of Hawaii, 1984.

Glowczewski, Barbara. "Affaire de femmes ou femmes d'affaires: Les Walpiri du Désert Central Australien." *Journal de la Société des Océanistes* 37 (1981): 77–97.

Meggitt, M. J. "Djanba among the Walbiri, Central Australia." *Anthropos* 50 (1955): 375–403.

Meggitt, M. J. *Desert People: A Study of the Walbiri Aborigines of Central Australia*. Chicago, 1962.

Meggitt, M. J. *Gadjari among the Walbiri Aborigines of Central Australia*. Sydney, 1966.

Munn, Nancy D. *Walbiri Iconography: Graphic Representation and Cultural Symbolism in a Central Australian Society*. Ithaca, N. Y., 1973.

Peterson, Nicolas. "Secular and Ritual Links: Two Basic and Opposed Principles of Australian Social Organization as Illustrated by Walbiri Ethnography." *Mankind* 7 (1969): 27–35.

Peterson, Nicolas. "Buluwandi: A Central Australian Ceremony for the Resolution of Conflict." In *Australian Aboriginal Anthropology*, edited by Ronald M. Berndt. Nedlands, 1970.

Shannon, Cynthia. "Walpiri Women's Music: A Preliminary Study." Honors thesis, Monash University, 1971.

Spencer, Baldwin, and F. J. Gillen. *The Northern Tribes of Central Australia*. London, 1904.

Wild, Stephen A. "Walbiri Music and Dance in Their Social and Cultural Nexus." Ph.D. diss., Indiana University, 1975.

Wild, Stephen A. "Men as Women: Female Dance Symbolism in Walbiri Men's Rituals." *Dance Research Journal* 10 (Fall-Winter 1977–1978): 14–22.

FILM. Roger Sandall, *A Walbiri Fire Ceremony: Ngatjakula* (Canberra, 1977).

Megan Llinos Dail-Jones

Antakirinya Dance

Many Aboriginal performers in South Australia, from Port Augusta northwest to the Northern Territory border, claim to be Antakirinya; however, researchers have also found these people identifying themselves with their western neighbors, the Yunkuntjatjara or Pitjantjatjara, who speak closely related languages. Other traditional neighbors, the Aranda in the north and Kokata in the south, have similar dance types. In the literature, little detailed information on their dance is available, but it serves to expand the fieldwork observations.

Certain features seem to be common and essential characteristics of the Antakirinya dances. These performances represent the re-creation of historical or mythic events through the multidimensional channels of song, rhythmic accompaniment, movement, design, and, sometimes, associated ritual objects. The roles of the dancers, singers, and painters, although separate, are interrelated. Some dance steps, song texts, and designs are explicitly representational; others are obscure symbolic statements about which little verbal information can be obtained.

The setting for all performances described in the literature seems similar: skillful use of smoke screens and blazing firelight heighten the drama of the dance, which is performed in a clearing with the dancers moving toward the group of singers seated on the perimeter of the clearing. The dancers are first taken out of sight of the main group of singers to have their bodies decorated with the appropriate designs. The dance commences when the performers appear through the smoke screen; they dance usually in a straight line toward the singers, to the accompaniment of hearty singing and emphatic percussion. The nature of the singing changes markedly from that used to accompany preparatory body-painting. There may be one or two dancers or, less often, a group.

New creations can enter the repertory of any of the non-sacred performances through the process of dreaming. A new dance and song may be dreamed by its creator, whose responsibility it is to remember the detail of the dream, and, on waking, to teach it to those who will perform it. This process is linked with the concept of the Dreaming, or Dreamtime, which preserves the ancestral past. The creator is said to have entered the Dreaming in his or her own dream and to have had revealed the dances, designs, and songs necessary for the new creation.

Men's and women's dance steps differ in character. Men's dancing is more energetic than women's, with greater movement of limbs away from the body. One common Antakirinya male step involves a series of backward jumps, with feet wide apart and knees bent and turned outward; in the course of a backward jump the knees are rapidly moved inward and back several times. Women's dancing is more constrained, with the arms close to the body, often with one hand supporting the breasts, and the legs closer together than in most men's dances. Both men and women have dances performed on the knees, sometimes involving movement over the ground space, and sometimes remaining in the one place, moving the arms and body. Children learn by observation and adopt the appropriate dance steps for their sex at a very early age. Only Ellis (1970), Kartomi (in Berndt and Phillips, 1973), and Strehlow (1971) have described the steps or their related ground patterns in any detail.

Antakirinya terminology for some steps has been given by performers. *Pakani* ("rising") is the generalized term for dancing. Other descriptions of dance steps include terms for "moving along," "standing on knees," "quivering with knees," "stamping the feet when dancing" (men only), "jumping with feet kept on the ground to leave continuous tracks" (women only), and "head down on one side when dancing." There are more.

Only a knowledge of the complete story being represented and the specific musical, graphic, and mimetic symbolism permits comprehensive understanding of a performance, because there is extensive overlap of information conveyed through the different media. At any one time the song text, dance, design, and musical structure may each refer symbolically to a different part of the complete re-creation taking place.

BIBLIOGRAPHY
Berndt, Ronald M., and Catherine H. Berndt. *The World of the First Australians.* Chicago, 1964.
Berndt, Ronald M., and E. S. Phillips, eds. *The Australian Aboriginal Heritage.* Sydney, 1973.
Ellis, Catherine J. "The Role of the Ethnomusicologist in the Study of Andagarinja Women's Ceremonies." *Miscellanea Musicologica* 5 (1970).
Strehlow, T. G. H. *Songs of Central Australia.* Sydney, 1971.

CATHERINE J. ELLIS

AUSTRALIAN BALLET. The death of Edouard Borovansky in 1959 and the disbanding of his ballet company in 1961 left the future of Australian ballet in doubt. State companies existed on a small scale and an audience had been created, but under commercial management there was neither the continuity of an established, balanced repertory nor the security of full-time employment for dancers.

Public support was enlisted for a national ballet company, and the federal government agreed to channel a subsidy through the Australian Elizabethan Theatre Trust. A controlling body, the Australian Ballet Foundation, was formed in 1962 by the directors of the Theatre Trust and the theatrical firm J. C. Williamson, Theatres Ltd., which owned theaters, costumes, scenery, and the rights to some ballets. Peggy van Praagh, the English dancer, teacher, and ballet director who had overseen the last months of the Borovansky Ballet, was appointed founding artistic director and went to Europe to talk former Borovansky principals into returning and to engage other dancers. Another British dancer and teacher, Margaret Scott, conducted classes for the remaining Borovansky soloists and corps members, who would form the nucleus of the new troupe. [*See the entry on van Praagh.*]

The Australian Ballet's first season began on 2 November 1962 with a performance of *Swan Lake* at Her Majesty's Theatre in Sydney, starring guest artists Sonia Arova and Erik Bruhn. Principal dancers were Borovansky veterans Kathleen Gorham, Marilyn Jones, and Garth Welch, as well as Caj Selling from the Royal Swedish Ballet.

The opening season included works by John Cranko (*The Lady and the Fool*) and Antony Tudor (*Les Rendezvous*). Ray Powell, who had come from the Royal Ballet on a six-month leave of absence as ballet master and decided to stay in Australia, contributed two short, comic ballets. The first commission for the company was Rex Reid's *Melbourne Cup*, a lively *ballet bouffe* set in 1861 at the Flemington Racecourse, site of Australia's most important horse-racing event. A box office, if not a critical success, the work was first danced on 16 November 1962.

The next all-Australian ballet to win national acceptance was *The Display*, a fusion of the talents of Robert Helpmann, who choreographed the work, Malcolm Williamson, who wrote the music, and artist Sidney Nolan, who designed the scenery and costumes. First performed to wide acclaim at the Adelaide Festival of Arts in 1964, *The Display*, which was inspired by the stylized mating dance of Australia's stunning lyrebird, led to the company's invitation to dance at the Commonwealth Arts Festival in Covent Garden the following year. Helpmann became the company's most durable native-born choreographer, producing the delicate Japanese ballet *Yugen* (1965), the atmospheric *Sun Music* (1968), and his tribute to the moon, *Perisynthyon* (1974). He was appointed co-artistic director with van Praagh in 1965 and, after her retirement in 1974, was the company's artistic director until 1976. [*See the entry on Helpmann.*]

Australian ballet audiences, used to the expansive, Russian-based, cosmopolitan style of the Colonel W. de Basil's Ballets Russes companies which had toured the continent in the 1930s, at first viewed the English influences brought to the Australian Ballet by van Praagh with a trace of diffidence. There was, indeed, a slight change in style, a more meticulously prepared corps de ballet, and a considerable change in repertory.

There was a difference, too, in the attitude of the company. After years of being affected by the changeable winds of commerce, the dancers had steady employment and space to rehearse, and they were no longer being bullied and cajoled into producing miracles against the clock. In this more relaxed atmosphere, the principals and soloists thrived. The vivid and moving Kathleen Gorham had an excellent showcase for her dramatic talents in *The Display;* Marilyn Jones could infuse her elegant dancing with a trace of comedy when the role suited; and the *danseur noble* Garth Welch was equally adept in lyric, classical roles and *demi-caractère* parts.

To help maintain the company's high standards and to train future dancers, the Australian Ballet School was founded in 1964 by Margaret Scott, who subsequently be-

came the school's director. Young dancers were selected by audition from all over Australia and given professional training in ballet and associated arts; the best students were offered places in the company's corps de ballet. In addition to the school's regular teachers, Australian Ballet principals have conducted classes, as have a number of international dance stars, including Vera Volkova, Alicia Markova, and Irina Kolpakova. [*See the entry on Scott.*]

In 1964 Margot Fonteyn, who had danced with the Borovansky Ballet, and Rudolf Nureyev began a long association with the Australian Ballet as guest artists. A year later, when only three years old, the company undertook its first overseas tour. The Australian Ballet made its foreign debut at the Baalbeck Festival in Lebanon, with Bruhn as guest artist, and then visited France, rehearsing and performing additions to the repertory, including Nureyev's new version of *Raymonda* and van Praagh's production of *Giselle.* At the Commonwealth Arts Festival in London, the company presented *The Display* and several short ballets. English critics were impressed by the lively, outgoing styles and the enthusiasm and vigor of the dancers. The highest praise was reserved for Danish dancer-choreographer Poul Gnatt's revival of August Bournonville's mid-nineteenth-century classic *Konservatoriet,* a high-spirited but strictly classical work set in a dancing class. Before returning to

AUSTRALIAN BALLET. *(left)* Gary Norman (Colas) lifting Marilyn Rowe (Lise) in act 2 of Frederick Ashton's version of *La Fille Mal Gardée. (right)* A scene from the 1973 film version of Rudolf Nureyev's *Don Quixote,* with Robert Helpmann (left) as the title character and Lucette Aldous as Kitri. (Photographs from the Dance Collection, New York Public Library for the Performing Arts.)

AUSTRALIAN BALLET. Kelvin Coe and Josephine Jason in *Growth*, the third movement of Robert Helpmann's *Sun Music* (1968). (Photograph by Paul Crowley; used by permission.)

Melbourne, the company revisited Paris and took part in the International Festival of Dance, where van Praagh's *Giselle*, designed by Kenneth Rowell, was awarded the Grand Prix of the City of Paris.

This successful tour was followed by many others, including one to Montreal's World's Fair, Expo 67, a coast-to-coast tour of the United States in 1970–1971, and another in 1976 as part of the American bicentennial celebrations. In 1980 the Australian Ballet's tour of China, the first such visit by a major ballet company, was seen by an estimated two hundred million television viewers. Other trips encompassed western Europe, the Soviet Union, and South America.

In the mid-1960s, when Gorham retired, the company's prominent young dancers included Janet Karin, Kathleen Geldard, Carolyn Rappel, Barbara Chambers, Gailene Stock, Karl Welander, Paul Saliba, Leonie Leahy, Josephine Jason, Warren de Maria, and the English-born Bryan Lawrence. Elaine Fifield, an established ballet star with the Borovansky Ballet, joined the company in 1964. As the Australian Ballet School developed an increasing number of dancers trained in the company's style, a large measure of fluidity became possible in casting ballets.

AUSTRALIAN BALLET. *(above)* Counterbalanced, Adrian Burnett and Stanton Welch support Justine Summers in the company's mounting of Jiří Kylián's *Return to the Strange Land*, originally created for the Stuttgart Ballet in 1975. *(below)* Welch holds Vicki Attard's hand in Graeme Murphy's *Beyond Twelve* (1980). (Top photograph by Gaica Branco; bottom photograph by James McFarlane; both used by permission.)

Expansion of the repertory was faster still. Nureyev's version of *Raymonda* received an enthusiastic welcome in Australia in 1966. His reworking of *Don Quixote*, which premiered at the Adelaide Festival of Arts on 28 March

1970, attracted worldwide interest. British composer John Lanchbery, who later became the company's musical director, arranged the Minkus score and conducted, and Barry Kay provided imaginative, eye-catching decor. Helpmann returned to the stage to mime the Knight of the Woeful Countenance, Nureyev was Basil, the romantic young barber, Ray Powell played Sancho Panza, and Lucette Aldous, a New Zealander who officially joined the troupe in 1971, danced the role of Kitri. A motion picture version of the work was released in 1973.

Frederick Ashton's version of the venerable *La Fille Mal Gardée*, first presented by the company in 1967, proved popular with Australian audiences, as did his *The Dream* and *The Two Pigeons*. In 1972 Ashton personally supervised the Australian Ballet's production of his *Cinderella*, in which he and Helpmann delighted viewers as the two Ugly Sisters. Antony Tudor visited Australia in 1969 to produce his *Pillar of Fire* and work on a new ballet, *The Divine Horsemen*, which was not successful. Igor Moiseyev's sentimental *The Last Vision*, which also premiered in 1969, did not enter the repertory.

Gradually, the nineteenth-century classics that were the mainstays of the company's repertory were refurbished, and the neoclassicism of George Balanchine and John Cranko was added. In 1968, the American modern dance choreographer John Butler created the starkly dramatic *Threshold* to the music of contemporary composers Zsolt Durko and Gracyna Bacewicz. Five years later, Glen Tetley contributed *Gemini*, a plotless ballet focusing on the dual and contrasting natures of two couples. The company also danced the works of Jiří Kylián *(Symphony in D)*, Jerome Robbins *(Afternoon of a Faun* and *The Concert)*, and Eugene Loring *(Billy the Kid)*.

Dancers who rose to prominence during the 1970s included John Meehan, Gary Norman, Carolyn Rappel, Alan Alder, and Alida Chase. Marilyn Rowe and Kelvin Coe succeeded Jones and Welch as the company's most famous partnership. In 1973 they were awarded a silver medal at the second International Ballet Competition in Moscow. Five years later, they returned to the Soviet Union as guest artists with the Bolshoi. Another young dancer from the Australian Ballet, Danilo Radojevic, became the first non-Russian to win a gold medal at the third competition in 1977.

Anne Woolliams took over the artistic direction of the Australian Ballet when Helpmann left in 1976, but after a

AUSTRALIAN BALLET. A scene from a 1981 performance of Robert Helpmann's *The Merry Widow*, with Marilyn Rowe in the title role. (Photograph reprinted from a souvenir program, 1981.)

AUSTRALIAN BALLET. Members of the company in Stanton Welch's *Red Earth* (1996). (Photograph by Branco Gaica; used by permission.)

year Woolliams resigned for the freer atmosphere of the Victorian College of the Arts. Van Praagh returned to the helm for a year, and then Marilyn Jones became artistic director. Jones formed a second performing group in 1980. Originally known as The Dancers of the Australian Ballet, it was designed to provide performing experience for young graduates of the Australian Ballet School. Now known as The Dancers Company, it is composed of final year students from the school, usually augmented by members of the main company. This successful venture was one of Jones's major contributions during her term as artistic director. [*See the entry on Jones.*]

During the late 1970s and early 1980s, the company's repertory was expanded with a number of specially commissioned, full-length works. Helpmann's *The Merry Widow* (1975), the first full-length work commissioned by the Australian Ballet, was a popular success both nationally and internationally and has remained in the company's repertory. It was followed by three more ballets created for the company: André Prokovsky's *Anna Karenina* (1979) and *The Three Musketeers* (1980), and Bruce Wells's *The Hunchback of Notre Dame* (1981), which was burdened by an overcomplicated plot and an overcrowded stage.

The development of the company suffered a major setback in 1981 when the dancers, concerned with working conditions and with what they felt were declining artistic standards, went on strike. Urgent negotiations went on for six weeks until the Australian Ballet returned in *The Merry Widow* with Marilyn Rowe in the title role. At the request of the dancers, Rowe returned from retirement as special adviser and held a caretaker position as ballet director during 1982 after Jones resigned. When Maina Gielgud took up the post early in 1983, Rowe remained as her deputy. Rowe then became director of the Dancers Company in 1984. [*See the entry on Rowe.*]

The Australian Ballet, a company of just over sixty dancers, flourished under Gielgud's direction, achieving the stability and security it lacked in the late 1970s and early 1980s. To the troupe's eclectic repertory of traditional classics and contemporary works, Gielgud introduced several ballets from Maurice Béjart, with whom she had danced in Europe, and single pieces from Nacho Duato and William Forsythe. She added more works by Frederick Ashton, George Balanchine, Jiří Kylián—whose choreography she especially admired—Kenneth MacMillan, Jerome Robbins, Paul Taylor, Glen Tetley, and Antony Tudor, and she staged new productions of *The Sleeping Beauty* and *Giselle*.

Under Gielgud, the company's repertory of ballets from European, British, and American choreographers was balanced by the work of Australians. In 1995, Gielgud appointed two resident choreographers, Stephen Baynes and Stanton Welch, from within the ranks of the company. Baynes achieved acclaim with his abstract *Catalyst* (1990) and his reflection on the classical technique, *Beyond Bach* (1995); Welch's major contributions have been *Of Blessed Memory* (1991), *Divergence* (1994), and *Madame Butterfly* (1995). Graeme Murphy, one of the country's most respected choreographers, also continued to create for the Australian Ballet. His most important piece to be commissioned during Gielgud's term as artistic director was *The Nutcracker* (1992), an iconoclastic, Australianized reworking of the traditional Christmas ballet and his first full-length piece for the company.

After a stabilizing period, Gielgud also reinstated the company's overseas touring schedule. She concentrated especially on touring in the Asia-Pacific region, particularly the Pacific Rim. The company enjoyed success in China, Japan, and the West Coast of the United States; it also made important tours to Russia, the United Kingdom, and the East Coast of the United States. Australian dancers who emerged as principals in the 1980s and 1990s included Vicki Attard, Lisa Bolte, Miranda Coney, Paul de Masson, Steven Heathcote, Greg Horsman, Ulrike Lytton, Adam Marchant, David McAllister, Lisa Pavane, Fiona Tonkin, and Christine Walsh.

Following a bizarre series of events beginning in 1993, in which Gielgud was accused of not being capable of managing the company effectively, her directorship of the Australian Ballet was brought unceremoniously to an end. At the end of 1994, the board of the Australian ballet elected not to renew her contract beyond 1996 and appointed Australian-born Ross Stretton, then assistant director of American Ballet Theatre, to lead the company beginning in 1997.

The Australian Ballet has been, from its inception, a touring repertory company. This model was inherited from the Ballets Russes companies that toured Australia in the late 1930s and was perpetuated in the 1940s and 1950s by the Borovansky Ballet. Since the late 1960s the Australian Ballet has also had in place a strongly entrenched national subscription system. As the move to unseat Gielgud grew stronger, there were suggestions that it was time to change the basic structure of the Australian Ballet to that of a company led by a choreographer. Graeme Murphy was a strong contender for the position that eventually went to Stretton. Murphy had also applied for the position of artistic director in 1982, when Gielgud was appointed. There was no structural change, however, and as Stretton prepares to take over the directorship of the Australian Ballet it remains a subscriber-driven tour-ing repertory company, and the national company of a postcolonial country located on the Pacific Rim.

[*See also* Australia, *article on* Ballet.]

BIBLIOGRAPHY
Baum, Caroline. *Artists of the Australian Ballet.* Sydney, 1989.
Brown, Ian F., ed. *The Australian Ballet, 1962–1965.* Melbourne, 1967.
Cargher, John. *Opera and Ballet in Australia.* Sydney, 1977.
Lisner, Charles. *The Australian Ballet: Twenty-One Years.* St. Lucia, 1984.
Pask, Edward H. *Ballet in Australia: The Second Act, 1940–1980.* Melbourne, 1982.
Potter, Michelle. "Such Savage and Scarlet: Maina Gielgud's Australian Years." *Dance Research* 14.1 (Summer 1996): 75–88.
Potter, Michelle. *A Passion for Dance.* Canberra, 1997.

MICHELLE POTTER
Based on material submitted by Geoffrey William Hutton

AUSTRIA. [*To survey the history of theatrical dance in Austria, this entry comprises two articles. The first article provides a general overview; the second provides a brief history of scholarship and writing.*]

Theatrical Dance

Theatrical dance became popular in Austria in the late fifteenth century; it played an important part in the university games of Conrad Celtis, who moved to Vienna in 1497 at the invitation of Emperor Maximilian I. Dance interludes figured in the school plays of the Jesuits; the dramas of Avancinus (1611–1686), for example, featured pantomimed allegorical scenes and processions. Dancing also played a major role in the sumptuous court festivals. The earliest mythological pantomimes appeared in a courtyard tournament sponsored by Maximilian II in 1560, and a similar festive pantomime followed the next year.

The first of a long line of professional court dancers was employed by Maximilian II. Many more followed, including Carlo Beccaria, a student of Cesare Negri active around 1600 in the court of Rudolf II (1576–1612), who had seen and taken dance instruction from Negri some years earlier. Italian dance teachers were prominent in the Viennese court; in 1626, Santo Ventura moved from Venice to work as dance teacher to Ferdinand II (1619–1637), and Ventura and Desiderius Scaramuzo taught dance to Ferdinand's children and other members of the court. The marriage of Ferdinand's son—the subsequent Ferdinand III (1637–1657)—to Maria Anna of Spain in 1631 saw the first dramatic musical performance at the Viennese court, which included a horse ballet, a dance celebration, and a solemn ballet.

Dance was stimulated further by Leopold I (1658–1705), who had a passion for the theater. Ballet served to glorify the royal house, with the emperor himself leading the court in performances. The ballets were in suites and were performed at the end of individual opera acts or at court celebrations. The sumptuous dance performances reached their peak in 1667 with the celebration of Emperor Leopold's betrothal to Margaret Theresa of Spain. Santo Ventura designed the court ballets and later was responsible for the ballets in the opera *Il Pomo d'Oro* (The Golden Apple). Following his death in 1677, his son Domenico served as dance master until his own death in 1697.

In 1715 Claudius Appelshoffer became dance master to the court, which also employed eight dancers, including Franz Joseph Sellier and his son Carl Joseph Sellier. Simon Pietro Levastori della Motta served as dance master from 1720 to 1732; Alexander Philebois followed in 1734. In 1723 Maria Anna Scio Philebois became the first female dancer to be hired by the Viennese court.

The shift from dilettante aristocrat to professional bourgeois performer thus was complete, with the dancers now being middle-class people displaying their art for

AUSTRIA: Theatrical Dance. An engraving dating from the early nineteenth century that depicts Marie Antoinette as a child, dancing with her brothers in a court ballet at the Imperial Palace in Vienna. The performance celebrated the marriage of Joseph II to Maria Josepha of Bavaria in 1765. (Dance Collection, New York Public Library for the Performing Arts.)

money, rather than members of the court. After 1728, ballet and pantomime were performed at the Kärntnertor Theater, as well as at the Burgtheater after 1741. Maria Theresa's reign (1740–1780) saw the complete development of dance from *divertissement* (a finale at the end of an act of opera, comedy, or tragedy) to an independent art form. Dramatic ballet was cultivated in the works of Franz Hilverding and culminated in the first tragic pantomime-ballet by Christoph Willibald Gluck and Gaspero Angiolini.

Hilverding was hired as a court dancer in 1735 and won appointment as court ballet master in 1749. In 1744 he created the ballets to music by Ignaz Holzbauer for the opera *Ipermestra* by Johann Adolf Hasse, the last opera to be performed in the emperor's private opera theater in the palace. Franz Anton Philebois began to work with Hilverding, and in 1746 they used the stories of Apollo and Daphne, Pygmalion, and Molière's *L'Avare* (The Miser) to construct ballets within operas.

Between 1752 and 1758 Hilverding created many ballets. Those with serious subjects were performed at the Burgtheater and those with popular and grotesque subjects at the Kärntnertor Theater. He was responsible for both theaters' companies as well as for performances at the emperor's palaces at Laxenburg and Schönbrunn. He also collaborated with such choreographers as Antoine-Bonaventure Pitrot, Giuseppe Salamoni, Karl Bernardi, and Pietro Sodi. Most of the members of Hilverding's two ballet ensembles were Italian, including the Tagliavini–Lenzi dance couple, Louise Bodin, Gaspero Angiolini and his wife, Maria Teresa Fogliazzi. [*See the entries on Angiolini and Bodin.*]

In 1758, Hilverding, the composer Joseph Starzer, and the solo dancer Santina Zanuzzi left for Saint Petersburg. Angiolini became the Burgtheater's ballet master, while Bernardi took over the Kärntnertor Theater. The collaboration between Gluck and Angiolini now set the course for ballet reform as Vienna became its showplace. Their treatment of the story of Don Juan, *Le Festin de Pierre* (1761), was the first ballet with a tragic ending. Angiolini used the departed Hilverding's pantomimes, which he described in his program notes as designed "to bring tears to the eyes." At Hilverding's recommendation, in 1766 Angiolini replaced him in Saint Petersburg. Hilverding had returned to Vienna in 1765, where his first work was the ballet *Il Trionfo d'Amore* (The Triumph of Love), in honor of Emperor Joseph II's wedding. Hilverding died in 1768. [*See the entry on Hilverding.*]

In 1767 Gaëtan Vestris danced in Jean-Georges Noverre's *Médée et Jason* at the Burgtheater, with Julie Bournonville as Medea. Noverre himself left Stuttgart for Vienna, where he staged his first Viennese work, *L'Apothéose d'Hercule*, with Vestris in the title role. In the next seven years Noverre took Viennese ballet to new heights. Several dancers had accompanied him from Stuttgart, including Charles Le Picq, Nancy Trancard, and eleven-year-old Marguerite Delphin. François Simonet and Leopold Frühmann acted as his assistants and also taught in the dance school Noverre founded in 1771.

Noverre's contract was not renewed in 1774, and he left for Milan, taking many of his best dancers. Angiolini returned from Saint Petersburg to succeed him but became unpopular because of a protracted dispute with Noverre. Still, his ballets enlivened many performances, although Sébastien Gallet received an imperial order to restage Noverre's ballets, which hastened Angiolini's departure. In 1776 Noverre returned briefly as lessee of the Kärntnertor Theater, now Vienna's only ballet theater. Also that year, Giovanni Antonio Sacco presided over a greatly weakened ballet ensemble that temporarily dissolved after his departure. [*See the entry on Noverre.*]

Ballet was revived briefly in the Burgtheater in 1781–1782 under the leadership of ballet master Peter Anton Crux, who had been brought from Munich; however, Emperor Joseph II (1765–1790) detested ballet, and its further development became impossible. Not until the reign of Leopold II (1790–1792) and the appointment in 1791 of Antonio Muzzarelli as ballet master was the form revived, with the company returning to its previous complement of forty dancers. This period also saw the elevation of the court theater's members to the status of civil servants.

As early as 1780, when ballet was at a standstill in the royal theaters, performances were given in a predecessor of the Theater in der Josefstadt, where a ballet by Franz Joseph Haydn was performed in 1789. In the Theater in der Leopoldstadt, founded in 1781, comic pantomime was performed. This genre flowered there after 1813 under Paolo Rainoldi; after 1825, it was also presented at the Theater in der Josefstadt, particularly by Fernando Occioni. At the Theater auf der Wieden in 1795 and 1796, some attention was given to ballet under Giovanni Battista Cecchi, who premiered his own works along with ballets by Noverre. At the Theater an der Wien after 1810, Louis Henry, Antoine Titus, and Louis-Antoine Duport all worked; after 1815, the theater became home to the famed Children's Ballet under the direction of Friedrich Horschelt. [*See* Viennese Kinderballett.]

In 1793, Salvatore Viganò and his wife, Maria Medina, began to work in Vienna. Their expressive style was received enthusiastically by the public and introduced a new era of ballet. Viganò returned frequently to Vienna; in 1801 he produced *Die Geschöpfe des Prometheus* (The Creatures of Prometheus) to the score by Ludwig van Beethoven. Giuseppe Trafieri, also active in this period, brought the solo dancer Maria Casentini to Vienna. Francesco Clerico, Gaetano Gioja, and Sébastien Gallet also worked as choreographers. In 1805 Filippo Taglioni

AUSTRIA: Theatrical Dance. A hand-tinted engraving depicting Jean Coralli in his ballet *Die Inkas*, which premiered at the Hofoper in Vienna, 1807. (Dance Collection, New York Public Library for the Performing Arts.)

debuted in Pierre Gardel's *La Dansomanie*. In 1806 Jean Coralli, who had moved to Vienna with his wife Teresa, began to choreograph. In 1808, Pietro Angiolini became court ballet master.

Although Viennese ballet's three decades as pacesetter were now over, the coming of renowned French choreographers allowed Vienna to become a center for early Romantic ballet. In 1808 Louis-Antoine Duport made his first appearance as dancer and choreographer; in the 1830s, he would lease the Kärntnertor Theater. In 1810, Louis Henry worked for the first time in Vienna, following Jean-Louis Aumer, who presided over the court opera ballet ensemble from 1814 to 1820. In 1811 Antoine Titus choreographed for the first time in Vienna.

Despite this infusion of talented dancers and choreographers, only some of Aumer's ballets and Filippo Taglioni's *Das Schweizer Milchmädchen* (The Swiss Milkmaid; 1821) found their way from Vienna to international dance stages. Taglioni's daughter, Marie, made her debut in Vienna in 1822 (the twelve-year-old Fanny Elssler then in the corps de ballet). The choreographers also included Armand Vestris, Jean-Baptiste Petit, Paolo Samengo, Luigi Astolfi, Monsieur Albert, Pietro Campilli, Giovanni Casati, and Pierre Aniel. In Amalia Brugnoli the ensemble had a leading dancer with a distinctive style.

The rapid turnover of ballet masters, however, pre-

AUSTRIA: Theatrical Dance. A scene from Luigi Astolfi's ballet *Panurge auf der Laterneninsel*, which premiered at the Kärntnertor Theater, Vienna, 1829. Here, Panurge (left) sits near a shrine, as the Lanterns, the literary quacks ridiculed in François Rabelais's books *Gargantua* and *Pantagruel*, recoil in fear. This engraving is by Johann Wenzel Sinke. (Dance Collection, New York Public Library for the Performing Arts.)

vented the formation of a specifically Viennese repertory. The demands of the Romantic age's leading ballerinas, who wanted to appear in the works that had made them famous, shaped ballet history in Vienna much as it did in other European cities. One exception was the 1838 Vienna premiere of *Der Kobold,* the first important ballet by Jules Perrot. Otherwise, it was works that enjoyed success in Paris that were allowed to enter the Vienna repertory. Ballerinas such as Therese Heberle, Fanny Elssler, and Katti Lanner reversed this direction; Elssler triumphed in Paris and subsequently returned to Vienna only for guest performances. With Vienna as their base, Josefine Weiss and her children's ballet toured extensively through Europe.

During the 1840s Auguste Hus, Bernard Vestris, and Antonio Guerra were the leading choreographers, and Gustave Carey was in much demand as a dancer. By 1848 the ballet ensemble had approximately seventy members, but political instability made continuous theater operation impossible, and a series of short-tenured ballet masters followed. The inferior quality of their compositions accelerated the ensemble's decline, reinforced by the paucity of good libretti—Romanticism had become exhausted of subjects. Fanny Elssler's departure from the stage in 1851 sounded Romantic ballet's death knell.

Even August Bournonville, who directed the ballet ensemble in 1855–1856, could not succeed in Vienna. He was overshadowed as choreographer by Paul Taglioni, who as guest director dazzled the city for the next two decades with his large-scale ballets. He was accompanied by his daughter, Marie Taglioni the younger. Another choreographer was Pasquale Borri; his naturalistic *Carnevals-Abenteuer in Paris* (Carnival Adventure in Paris; 1858) enjoyed great success. Domenico Ronzani, Giovanni Golinelli, and Giuseppe Rota also staged ballets. In the mid-1850s Carolina Pochini accepted the post of *prima ballerina;* she was followed by Claudina Cucchi, while Virgilio Calori was *premier danseur.*

In 1859 ballet master Carle Telle arrived from Berlin as deputy for Paul Taglioni. A ballet school was created in 1862, and its first teacher was Elisa Albert-Bellon. In 1870 the school was given the rank of an official institution and has operated continuously ever since. The Austrian public now called for a national ballet company, even though most of the eighty-member ensemble were Austrian. The leading positions, however, continued to be filled by Italian and French dancers.

A new era began when the company moved to the new Hofoperntheater (Royal Opera House) in 1869. Here the ballet's shape was transformed because choreographers had to fill a much larger stage. Unfortunately, expansion also brought a loss of substance as sets and crowd effects became dominant. In the Romantic era, the story had been conveyed by dancers, but now mimes carried an often flimsy plot that tended to be a pretext for displaying technique, especially the pas de deux. The corps de ballet became largely decorative.

Guglielmina Salvioni was the first *prima ballerina* of the Hofoperntheater, where she danced in the revival of Paul Taglioni's *Sardanapal* in 1869. The Viennese Bertna Linda followed, but with the arrival of Luigia Cerale, an Italian again led the ensemble. The featured mimes of this period were Katharina Abel (who was Viennese), Louis Frappart, and Julius Price.

Following the brilliant success of his pantomime *divertissement Die Puppenfee* (1888), first dancer Josef Hassreiter became ballet master in 1891. Soon the repertory was composed almost exclusively of Hassreiter ballets, which were distinctive in style and widely staged throughout Europe. Only Frappart's *Wiener Walzer* and the Italian ballet *Excelsior* were even close to Hassreiter's ballets in popularity. [*See the entry on Hassreiter.*]

The ensemble now comprised more than one hundred members, almost all graduates of the company's own school, even though Italian ballerinas such as Irene Sironi and Cäcilie Cerri remained at the top. The leading mime was Carl Godlewski, and the principal male dancer was Carl Raimund, Sr. When Gustav Mahler, who rejected Hassreiter's ballets, became director of the Hofoperntheater, it sounded the death knell of the Hofopernballett. Despite its brilliant exterior and past successes, it had become a mere amusement, notwithstanding even the success of the Johann Strauss ballet *Aschenbrödel* (Cinderella; 1908).

AUSTRIA: Theatrical Dance. Fanny Elssler as Fenella in Daniel Auber's *opéra-ballet La Muette de Portici*, at the Kärntnertor Theater, Vienna, 1832. This engraving is by Andreas Geiger after J. C. Schoeller. (Courtesy of Madison U. Sowell and Debra H. Sowell, Brigham Young University, Provo, Utah.)

With World War I and the end of the monarchy, the ballet lost its principal *raison d'être*—reflecting the splendor of the ruling house. The eventful three centuries of the Hofopernballett had come to an end.

Free Dance Movement. The stagnation of classical ballet occurred at about the same time as the birth of "free dance" *(Freier Tanz)* in central Europe, with Vienna as one of its centers. The free dancers shared an aversion to classical ballet. Their impulses also sprang from sources external to dance, particularly those of a sociopolitical nature. The change in the status of women in the late nineteenth century brought a new freedom, a new physicality, and—for dance—a new opportunity for self-development. The teachings of François Delsarte and Émile Jaques-Dalcroze were fertile for a generation with a new vision of dance. Classical ballet in central Europe was not influenced by Michel Fokine's reforms and was soon ousted by the free dancers as a relic of the old social order. Their aim was to give expression to the self and to music through natural movement.

Vienna's first free dancer was Grete Wiesenthal, a former member of the Hofopernballett. Her impetus came neither from the theories of Delsarte and Jaques-Dalcroze nor from guest performances by Loie Fuller, Isadora Duncan, Maud Allan, and Ruth St. Denis, but from the atmosphere of spiritual breakthrough fostered by the Vienna Secessionists, Austria's exponents of Art Nouveau. In Wiesenthal's dance the Vienna waltz found its ideal interpreter. Her followers included Lucy Kieselhausen and Maria Ley. [*See the entry on Wiesenthal.*]

Free dancers formed a school, beginning with Elsa Wiesenthal, in 1912. The local school for "rhythmic-plastic" expression gave performances of "Delsartismus." After World War I, Gertrude Barrison, who had appeared in Vienna since 1906, founded her own school, as did Ellen Tels, who attracted attention with her group dances. Gertrud Bodenwieser stood out from other Viennese representatives of free dance, her choreographic and pedagogical activity becoming one of the most important factors in the movement. Beside Bodenwieser, Grete Gross was a teacher at the national academy. Other schools were operated by Ellinor Tordis, Gertrud Kraus, and by Hilde Holger. From 1925 to 1935, Elizabeth Duncan ran a school in Salzburg.

The move of the Hellerau School to Laxenburg, near Vienna, in 1925 reinforced Austria's importance in the free dance movement. Dance education in this school was directed by Valeria Kratina and from 1930 to 1938 by Rosalia Chladek. In 1929 Rudolf Laban organized a "new rhythm" parade in Vienna that involved more than three thousand people, the first of his organized festivals. In the early 1930s, however, the free dance movement reached a crisis, because of the rise of Nazism, and its leaders were forced to compromise their principles. The political situa-

AUSTRIA: Theatrical Dance. Members of the Vienna State Opera Ballet look on as Willy Dirtl as Albrecht clutches the hand of Margaret Bauer as the title character in the final scene of act 1 of *Giselle*. (Photograph by Rudolf Pittner; from the Dance Collection, New York Public Library for the Performing Arts.)

tion soon led Gertrud Kraus, Gertrud Bodenwieser, and many others to emigrate.

After World War II, only such figures as Grete Wiesenthal and Rosalia Chladek, as developers of a transmittable technique, and Hanna Berger continued to offer their orientation as an alternative to classical ballet, which had undergone a decisive transformation, influenced in part by free dance. Since the 1980s a new generation of choreographers, whose works often impart a strong sociopolitical message, brought a renaissance of free dance to Austria. These manifold activities—influenced by European and American trends and also by the examples of visiting companies in the international dance festivals held regularly in Vienna since 1982—have become a vital and important aspect of Austria's cultural offerings. The leading figures are Liz King (Tanztheater Wien), Manfred Aichinger, and Nikolaus Selimov (Tanztheater Homunculus), Sebastian Prantl, Bert Gstettner, Willi Dorner, Elio Gervasi, Editta Braun, Zdravko Haderlap, and Doris Ebner and Roderich Madl.

Modern Ballet. After World War I, the Hofopernballett (Royal Opera Ballet) became the Staatsopernballett (State Opera Ballet) and began to search for a new self-image. The style it had developed during the Hassreiter era was no longer in demand, its external splendor had become threadbare, and its aesthetics were long out of date. Conditions for developing a new image, however, were not favorable, and ballet as an art form was of secondary importance in Vienna.

The history of the company up to the recent past is full of wasted opportunities and accidents. For example, the space allowed for ballet was determined by the opera's directors, and only one, Richard Strauss, gave it any support. In 1923 the ensemble came under the direction of Heinrich Kröller, who served as ballet master until 1928. His staging of *Die Josephslegende* (Joseph's Legend) represented the only influence of the Ballets Russes in Vienna. *Schlagobers* (1924) was created in collaboration with Richard Strauss.

Part of the company's illustrious past was recovered with a new Kröller version of Gluck's *Don Juan*. The new generation of solo dancers included Gusti Pichler—the second *prima ballerina* to be produced by the Vienna school (Elsa von Strohlendorf was the first)—Hedy Pfundmayr, Adele Krausenecker, Riki Raab, Tilly Losch, Toni Birkmeyer, and Willy Fränzl.

Following Kröller's departure, the Staatsopernballett was influenced more strongly by the free dancers. Sacha Leontjev—and Grete Wiesenthal and Valeria Kratina as guest choreographers—worked for the company, which had shrunk to fifty members. Margarete Wallmann (a representative of free dance who was ballet mistress from 1934 to 1938) faced the dilemma of directing an ensemble that still was being trained only in classical ballet. She exercised her talent for moving large groups in large-scale ballets with historical subjects. During this period, Julia Drapal (later a *prima ballerina*) and Carl Raimund, Jr., were solo dancers.

Erika Hanka, ballet mistress from 1942 to 1958, was a free dancer who recognized the trend toward classical ballet that characterized theatrical dance in central Europe following World War II. Her style of repertorial organization was seen in 1955 when she contrasted the Romantic *Giselle* with Boris Blacher's modern *Der Mohr von Venedig* (The Moor of Venice). Under her direction, the State Opera Ballet danced story ballets with music that often was contemporary, although it also used traditional choreography for the first time in performing excerpts from Tchaikovsky ballets. The ensemble's leading dancers included the *prima ballerina* Edeltraud Brexner as well as Margaret Bauer, Christl Zimmerl, Willy Dirtl, and Richard Adama, an American. [*See the entry on Hanka.*]

After Hanka's death, a series of ballet masters—Dimitrije Parlić, Aurelio Milloss, and Vaslav Orlikovsky—followed, but none of them was able to expand the company's repertory successfully and permanently. During the 1960s the lack of a strong choreographer could not be offset even with the staging of works by such established choreographers as Léonide Massine, George Balanchine, and Ninette de Valois. The most outstanding event of the 1960s was a collaboration with Rudolf Nureyev, who created his own versions of *Swan Lake* and *Don Quixote* for the company. The new generation of soloists included Susanne Kirnbauer, Gisela Cech, Lilly Scheuermann, Karl Musil, and Michael Birkmeyer.

Gerhard Brunner, who was director from 1976 to 1990, aimed to offset the lack of a creative leader by organizing the repertory around works created especially for Vienna by leading international choreographers. Outstanding among these productions were John Neumeier's *Josephslegende* (1977) and *Der Feuervogel* (1983), Hans van Manen's *Grand Trio* (1978), Rudi van Dantzig's *Ulysses* (1979), Ruth Berghaus's *Orpheus* (1986), and Jochen Ulrich's *Tantz-Schul* (1988). The assessment of a Viennese repertory was Brunner's special merit. Thus, the reconstruction of the original version of *Die Puppenfee* proved not only exemplary but also extraordinarily successful. Moreover, in this era, reconstructions were produced of both the solo and group choreographies of the Viennese exponents of free dance, Grete Wiesenthal, Rosalia Chladek, and Gertrud Bodenwieser. A choreographer who emerged from the ranks of the company in the 1980s is Bernd R. Bienert. From 1991 to 1993 the company was headed by Elena Tschernischova. In 1993 Anne Woolliams took over from her.

Since 1995 the Vienna State Opera Ballet has been directed by Renato Zanella. His call to head the company followed his 1994 creation of *La Chambre* and his staging of *Empty Place*. In his first season as ballet director and chief choreographer he presented an all-Stravinsky evening, with *Symphony, Movements,* and *La Sacre de Printemps,* as well as stagings of his *Konzertantes Duo, Black Angels,* and *Mata Hari*. First soloists in 1996 were Katherine Healy, Marialuise Jaska, Simona Noja, Brigitte Stadler, Ludwig Karl, Vladimir Malakhov, and Tamás Solymosi.

In Vienna, the Volksoper (Folk Opera) and the Theater an der Wien also had permanent companies to perform ballet. Between 1938 and 1944 the Volksoper had such ballet masters as Jerschik, Dia Luca, Herbert Freund, and Antony Joukowski. Dia Luca took over the management of the reconstituted Volksopernballett in 1955 and was followed by Gerhard Senft from 1973 to 1983, and Susanne Kirnbauer from 1986 to 1996, although the theater rarely put on performances exclusively devoted to ballet. Since 1996 the Volksopernballett has been directed by Kimberly Duddy. Between 1967 and 1984, the Theater an der Wien maintained its own company, which appeared in ballets by Alois Mitterhuber (who led the company until 1974) and by guest choreographers.

Dance in the Provinces. Early examples of ballet in provincial cities include the 1785 opening of the theater in Graz with a Noverre ballet and performances in Linz in the 1780s. In contrast to Graz, which has always had its own company, the cities of Linz, Salzburg, Innsbruck, and Klagenfurt, established permanent ballet companies only in the 1930s. The main task of these groups was and is to perform in operas and operettas, but they also appear in their own productions. Because of the rapid turnover of ballet masters, however, permanent repertory has been rare. Long-lasting tenures of ballet masters in these cities have been those of Andrei Jerschik, Hanna Kammer, Rein

AUSTRIA: Theatrical Dance. Christl Zimmerl as Desdemona and Willy Dirtl as Othello in Erika Hanka's *Der Mohr von Venedig* (1955). (Photograph from the Dance Collection, New York Public Library for the Performing Arts.)

Esté, Alexander Meissner, Fred Marteny, Vaslav Orlikovsky, and Peter Breuer.

Since 1990 the ballet company of Bühnen Graz, under its intendant Gerhard Brunner, has offered a first-rate repertory by renowned international choreographers—among them Frederick Ashton, László Seregi, Hans van Manen, Heinz Spoerli, Jochen Ulrich, William Forsythe, and Rami Be'er.

[*See also the entries on the principal figures mentioned herein.*]

BIBLIOGRAPHY

Alexander, Gerda, and Hans Groll, eds. *Tänzerin, Choreographin, Pädagogin Rosalia Chladek.* 4th ed. Vienna, 1995.

Amort, Andrea. "Ausdruckstanz in Österreich bis 1938." In *Ausdruckstanz: Eine mitteleuropäische Bewegung der ersten Hälfte des 20. Jahrhunderts,* edited by Gunhild Oberzaucher-Schüller. Wilhelmshaven, 1974.

Amort, Andrea. "Die Geschichte des Balletts der Wiener Staatsoper, 1918–1942." Ph.D. diss., University of Vienna, 1981.

Brown, Bruce Alan. *Gluck and the French Theatre in Vienna.* Oxford, 1991.

Brunner, Gerhard. "Wiener Ballett-Dramaturgie." In *Ballett 1968: Chronik und Bilanz des Ballettjahres,* edited by Horst Koegler. Velber bei Hannover, 1968.

Derra de Moroda, Friderica. "Franz Anton Christoph Hilverding und das Ballet d'action." In *Österreichische Musikzeitschrift* 23.4 (1968).

Dunlop MacTavish, Shona. *Gertrud Bodenwieser: Tänzerin, Choreographin, Pädagogin: Wien—Sydney.* Bremen, 1995.

Fiedler, Leonhard M., and Martin Lang, ed. *Grete Wiesenthal. Die Schönheit der Sprache des Körpers im Tanz.* Salzburg/Vienna, 1985.

Fleissner-Moebius, Elisabeth. *Erika Hanka und das Wiener Staatsopernballett.* Frankfurt am Main, 1995.

Gregor, Joseph. *Kulturgeschichte des Balletts: Seine Gestaltung und Wirksamkeit in der Geschichte und unter den Künsten.* Vienna, 1944.

Guest, Ivor. *Fanny Elssler.* London, 1970.

Haas, Robert. "Die Wiener Ballett-Pantomime im 18. Jahrhundert und Glucks Don Juan." *Studien zur Musikwissenschaft* 10 (1923): 6–36.

Haas, Robert. "Der Wiener Bühnentanz von 1740 bis 1767." *Jahrbuch der Musikbibliothek Peters* 44 (1937): 77–93.

Haider-Pregler, Hilde. *The Theatre in Austria.* Translated by Richard Rickett. Vienna, 1973.

Hauser, Peter. "Der Choreograph Aurel von Milloss und sein Wiener Wirkungsbereich." Ph.D. diss., University of Vienna, 1975.

Hirschbeck, Denny, and Rick Takvorian, eds. *Die Kraft des Tanzes: Hilde Holger; Wien, Bombay, London.* Bremen, 1990.

Jackson, George. "Das Ballett im Zeitalter Maria Theresia." In *Almanach der Wiener Festwochen 1969: Ballettfestival, 100 Jahre Staatsoper, Wiener Schule.* Vienna, 1969.

Lynham, Deryck. *The Chevalier Noverre: Father of Modern Ballet.* London, 1950.

Manor, Giora. *The Life and Dance of Gertrud Kraus.* Hakibbutz Hameuchad, Israel, 1978.

Matzinger, Ruth. "Die Geschichte des Balletts der Wiener Hofoper, 1869–1918." Ph.D. diss., University of Vienna, 1982.

Nics, Peter, and Jarmila Weissenböck, eds. *Tanz: 20. Jahrhundert in Wien.* Vienna, 1979.

Oberzaucher, Alfred. "Die Wiener Staatsoper als unumstrittenes Zentrum: Das Ballett in Österreich." In *Tanz in Deutschland: Ballett seit 1945,* edited by Hartmut Regitz. Berlin, 1984.

Oberzaucher, Alfred. *125 Jahre Ballett im Haus am Ring.* Vienna, 1994.

Oberzaucher, Alfred, ed. "Josef Hassreiter: Leben und Werk." In *Tanz-Affiche* 8.60 (1995/96).

Oberzaucher-Schüller, Gunhild. "Der Tanz in Wien im 20. Jahrhundert." In *Tanz: 20. Jahrhundert in Wien.* Vienna, 1979.

Praschl-Bichler, Gabriele. *Vom Wiener Ballett.* Vienna, 1989.

Prieler, Claudia. "Riki Raab: Zeitzeugin einer Tanzepoche." Mag. phil. dissertation, University of Vienna, 1993.

Raab, Riki. "Das k. k. Hofballett unter Maria Theresia, 1740–1780." *Jahrbuch der Gesellschaft für Wiener Theaterforschung, 1950–1951* (1952).

Raab, Riki. "Ballettreformator J. G. Noverre in Wien." *Jahrbuch des Vereines für Geschichte der Stadt Wien* 13 (1957).

Raab, Riki. *Fanny Elssler: Eine Weltfaszination.* Vienna, 1962.

Raab, Riki. "Grabstätten von Ballettmitgliedern des Kärntnertortheaters, der k. k. Hofoper und Staatsoper, Wien." *Jahrbuch des Vereins für Geschichte der Stadt Wien* 28 (1972).

Raab, Riki. *Biographischer Index des Wiener Opernballetts von 1631 bis zur Gegenwart.* Vienna, 1994.

Rice, John A. "Emperor and Impresario: Leopold II and the Transformation of Viennese Musical Theater, 1790–1792." Ph.D. diss., University of California, Berkeley, 1987.

Salmen, Walter, ed. *Mozart in der Tanzkultur seiner Zeit.* Innsbruck, 1990.

Seebohm, Andrea, ed. *Die Wiener Oper: 350 Jahre Glanz und Tradition.* Vienna, 1986.

Sommer-Mathis, Andrea. *Die Tänzer am Wiener Hofe im Spiegel der Obersthofmeisteramtsakten und Hofparteienprotokolle bis 1740.* Vienna, 1992.

Weissenböck, Jarmila. "Expressionistischer Tanz in Wien." In *Expressionismus in Österreich: Die Literatur und die Künste,* edited by Klaus Amann and Armin A. Wallas. Vienna, 1994.

Winter, Marian Hannah. *The Pre-Romantic Ballet.* London, 1974.

Zechmeister, Gustav. *Die Wiener Theater nächst der Burg und nächst dem Kärntnerthor von 1747 bis 1776.* Vienna, 1971.

ALFRED OBERZAUCHER
Translated from German

Dance Research and Publication

Folk dance research in Austria began with the work of Raimund Zoder (1882–1963), whose collection is now housed in the Austrian Folk Song Archives in Vienna. Most work today is done by researchers associated with the Austrian Folk Song Foundation and is published in the *Jahrbuch des österreichischen Volksliedwerkes.* Important essays on folk dance appear in the journal *Der fröliche Kreis,* published by the Federal Study Group on Austrian Folk Dance. This group supervises the collection of new information on folk dance; video recording has been used only in recent years. The group has also standardized folk dance terminology and computerized the process of documentation.

Nineteenth-century Austrians had little interest in theatrical dance except as it was associated with charismatic performers. The "free dance" movement in the first decade of the twentieth century led to a new kind of interest in dance as art, well documented by a flood of dance literature. When classical ballet returned to prominence after World War II, however, it still failed to attract critical attention in Vienna. It took the magnetic personality of the Russian dancer Rudolf Nureyev, who first performed in Vienna in the early 1960s, to revive public interest in ballet; his admirers and their students now make up the circle of ballet historians and critics working in Vienna.

In the mid-1970s the Institute of Theater Studies of the University of Vienna established a dance history department. Teaching concentrated on the history of dance in Vienna and on investigating the relationship between the development of free dance in central Europe and that of modern dance in the United States. Andrea Amort, Ruth Matzinger, Gunhild Schüller, Gerhard Winkler, and Gustav Zechmeister have written dissertations at the Institute of Theater Studies. Earlier, Riki Raab, a former dancer, had devoted many years to writing on Viennese dance.

The periodical *Tanzblätter* published articles on dance from 1976 to 1982. Today, however, such essays appear only in the drama journal *Maske and Kothurn* and the music journal *Österreichische Musikzeitschrift.*

GERLINDE HAID

AVANT-GARDE DANCE. In the arts, the term *avant-garde,* French for "vanguard," can be defined as the cutting edge of an emerging movement. It literally refers to the advance wing of an army, and its use in art implies a bellicose stance toward artistic institutions. The origins of the term in the artistic quest for the new at the end of the nineteenth century often lead us to identify it with the modernist abstraction of much twentieth-century art, yet there have been avant-gardes that are not abstract, for example surrealism and postmodernism.

The history of avant-garde dance is a braid in which strands from the history of the other arts are entwined. Dancers have been associated with various historical avant-garde art movements, and performances involving gesture and movement—although not always called dance—have also served these movements. Sergei Diaghilev in the 1910s and 1920s (and such competitors as Les Ballets Suédois and Soirées de Paris) and Merce Cunningham since the 1950s made the dance event the nexus for presenting avant-garde visual art, music, film, and performance in conjunction with dancing. The history of avant-garde dance can be approached variously in terms of art-world history and dance-world history.

Loie Fuller was important to the symbolists not only for her effects, which fit so well with their own aesthetic, but also because she seemed to embody a future art. Her use of the costume as a screen for brilliant lighting designs fit with the use of the scrim in symbolist theater and also heralded the magical phantasms of cinema. Her

AVANT-GARDE DANCE. Steve Paxton and Deborah Hay wield a large, unruly prop in Paxton's experimental work *The Deposits* (1965), performed on the golf course of Kutsher's Country Club in Monticello, New York. (Photograph © 1965 by Peter Moore; used by permission.)

venue was the popular stage, but her dancing created nearly abstract images. For the symbolists, motion was more truthful than language, and Fuller's work became an even more powerful "emblem of poetry" than written texts could be. She was, moreover, an artist-scientist, an innovator in the new technology of electrical stage lighting; Stéphane Mallarmé called her an "industrial achievement."

A fascination with motion, live presence, and technology continued to characterize the modern arts until World War II and to forge successive links between dance and the other arts. The Italian futurists were obsessed by mechanization and by the visual and linguistic representation of dynamism, as well as by performance techniques that emphasized gesture and sound over text. Many of their performances, even those they did not call ballets, thus could be considered dance. In using puppets and other nonhuman moving elements as the primary "performers" (for example in *Fireworks* by the futurist painter Giacomo Balla, a light show presented in 1917 as part of a Ballets Russes program), and in calling for new uses of the body (as in Filippo Marinetti's instructions for imitating the actions of inanimate objects in his "Manifesto of the Futurist Dance") the futurists extended the definition of dance in ways that remain controversial.

The Russian cubo-futurists and constructivists were similarly inspired by mechanization and by popular culture; for a short time after the 1917 revolution the avant-garde in art and politics meshed. Independent studio choreographers such as Nikolai Foregger and Vera Maya hailed industrialization with their machine dances, and those who worked on the ballet stage, such as Fedor Lopukhov and Kasyan Goleizovsky, sought amalgams of new abstract forms with folk motifs, gymnastics, and popular dancing. All of them were influenced by the work of Émile Jaques-Dalcroze, Isadora Duncan, and the German expressionist dance, as well as by the other arts in revolutionary Russia: the machine-fabricated objects that replaced fine arts; the stylized, movement-oriented theater (especially the biomechanics of Vsevolod Meyerhold), which in turn drew on circus and vaudeville; and the cinematic technique of rapid montage.

Rudolf Laban, Mary Wigman, and other dancers were associated with both expressionism and Dada and with the lively cabaret scenes that, repudiating the separation (as well as the canons) of the various high arts, mingled dancing with singing, declamation, chamber theater, and other less clearly defined performance forms. At the Cabaret Voltaire in Zurich, writers and artists joined the dancers in action, using masks and movements often sparked by a fascination with the exotica of non-European cultures as well as with the popular stage. A new kind of dance movement, developed by Wigman and her associates, inscribed expressionist iconography on the body: cramped, angular, nervous, and macabre. But there was no iconography as such for Dada; it assimilated a range of dance from the antics at Cabaret Voltaire and other soirées, to the various events that constituted the ballet-cum-film *Relâche* (1924). [*See* Relâche.]

It was a ballet, *Parade* (1917), that prompted Guillamme Apollinaire's first use of the term *sur-réaliste*. Surrealist performances of the 1920s, while too literary to be considered ballets as such, often mixed text with dance and song in a music-hall manner and used ballet dancers and acrobats in their casts. The surrealists also presented *tableaux vivants* and featured dancers in various works, from Lizica Codreanu's dances in *Le Coeur à Barbe* (1923) to Hélène Vanel's *The Unconsummated Act (Danse Macabre)*, part of Marcel Duchamp's "environment" at the Paris surrealist exhibition of 1938.

The union of dance and art with technology found its apotheosis in theatrical experiments by Oskar Schlemmer and others at the Bauhaus in the 1920s. Unlike the deliberately anarchic gestures of the Dadaists and surrealists, the Bauhaus performances were part of a utopian political program of construction. Reflecting the school's pedagogical and architectural approach, the Bauhaus dances examined and abstracted anatomic function and design, especially in relation to objects. The geometric, analytical method recalled Laban's systematization of human movement and anticipated the analytic postmodern dance of the 1970s. [*See* Bauhaus, Dance and the.]

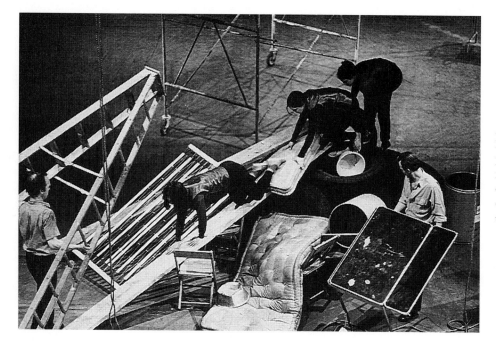

AVANT-GARDE DANCE. In Yvonne Rainer's *Room Service* (1965), performers play follow-the-leader in a sculptural environment created by Charles Ross. (Photograph © 1965 by Peter Moore; used by permission.)

AVANT-GARDE DANCE. Meredith Monk/The House at Goddard College during the filming of *Vessel*, a dance-opera about Joan of Arc. The performers standing on the hillside are Monk (foreground), Pablo Vela, Coco Pekalis, Daniel Ira Sverdlik, Linn Varney, Blondell Cummings, Signe Hammer, and Lanny Harrison. (Photograph © 1972 by Monica Mosely; used by permission.)

From the happenings of the late 1950s and early 1960s to the performance art of the 1970s and 1980s, bodily action has been a key element in a highly visual *mise-en-scène*, that is transacted in the art world (and, more recently, in the music world), rather than in the theater. This emphasis on nonverbal behavior also has been the mode in much alternative theater, from the ritual-like work of The Living Theater of Judith Malina and Julian Beck to the spectacles of Richard Foreman, Meredith Monk, Robert Wilson, and The Wooster Group.

Dance has been a feature of avant-garde art and also has renewed itself through applying the concept of the avant-garde in its own medium. The twentieth century has witnessed a series of two-pronged reactions to the resilient academic style. The first branch has been in the form of changes and innovations within the ballet institution, reaching its apogee in the work of George Balanchine and continuing in a new vein with the incursion into the ballet repertory of choreographers such as Twyla Tharp, Laura Dean, and David Gordon, who were not formed by the ballet academy. The second branch has been the continual series of avant-gardes that constitute modern dance, in which the aspiration of each new generation—if not each new artist—has been to formulate an original style of movement.

Although the forerunners of modern dance made much of their rupture with the ballet academy, it was not so much antiballet that they set out to create as a new style of theatrical dancing, often based on forms of dance other than the European classical style. They looked to non-Western dance and popular culture for alternative sources. Despite Isadora Duncan's hopes for the integration of dance into the daily lives of children and despite the use of dance by leftists in the 1930s for political organizing and for improving workers' health, historical modern dance was for the most part still conceived of as art dance. Not until the 1960s, when avant-garde dancers self-consciously examined and revealed the institution of theatrical dance, did the border between art dance and life disintegrate, as all the formal properties that constitute a dance work were called into question. Postmodern dance, at least in its early stage, was concerned not with making new forms and canons of expression, but with radically questioning the very making and breaking of forms themselves. The challenge was to the most basic theoretical assumptions of dance as art: that it is composed of special movements, rhythmically and dramatically ordered, performed by specially trained bodies, in a special venue. In terms of dance history, its aggressive program of denial allies postmodern dance, rather than modern dance, to the historical avant-garde art movements like futurism and dada.

Avant-garde dance has undergone its political moments, for example, the fusion of new ballet and revolutionary politics encouraged by Anatoly Lunacharsky in the Soviet Union and the communist agitprop dances in Germany in the 1920s, the Workers' Dance Movement in the United States of the 1930s, and the militant African-American dance movement in the late 1960s. In choosing to focus primarily on the medium of dance as an abstract art, the avant-garde choreographers of the 1950s were perhaps rebelling to some extent against the political programs of the previous vanguard generation. Consolidating, extending, and reacting to the research of their immediate forebears, the postmodern dancers were supremely conscious of their role as heirs to the avant-garde tradition. They were also well educated about the history of that role, partly through John Cage's advocacy on behalf of figures such as Erik Satie, Marcel Duchamp, and Antonin Artaud, and partly through their own involvement with contemporaries working in the other arts. They were able to step back, to look with new eyes at the dance-world institution, its inner workings, and its relation to other artworld institutions and to daily life.

Theatrical dance's internal changes have not evolved in a vacuum. The theories and practice—sometimes simply the idea—of dance have influenced twentieth-century arts, both directly and indirectly; in turn, dance has been influenced by the other arts. Moreover, the avant-garde—in dance as in the other arts, a distinctly Euro-American elite notion—has consistently tapped non-Western and folk or popular traditions. This complex cultural transaction is at the heart of the avant-garde's dilemma: its status as a cutting edge limits its appreciation to the cognoscenti, while it often embraces explicit political goals concerning mass audiences or even participants. Hence its perennial fascination with popular culture, which constitutes, on the one hand, a slap in the face of reigning high art, and, on the other, a means for mass appeal. With her arch references to popular and social dancing, done to music emblematic of past times, Twyla Tharp prefigured one aspect of this sensibility, dominant in the 1980s. Another aspect of avant-garde dance in the 1980s, the return of expressionism, primitivism, and melodrama

(epitomized in groups such as the Japanese *butō* troupe Sankai Juku and Pina Bausch's Tanztheater Wuppertal, as well as in work by young American choreographers), is clearly a response to the penchant for the analytic formalism of postmodern choreographers such as Yvonne Rainer and Trisha Brown. So, too, is the proliferation of dances about social and political identity—in regard to issues of race, ethnicity, gender, sexual preference, and age—in the 1990s. While to many it might seem that, after the self-conscious reflexiveness of postmodern dance in the 1960s and 1970s, the avant-garde has reached the end of its road, its persistent, constant renewal shows that it continues to thrive, seeking new forms and outlets.

BIBLIOGRAPHY

Banes, Sally. *Terpsichore in Sneakers: Post-Modern Dance.* Boston, 1980.

Cohen, Selma Jeanne. "Avant-Garde Choreography" (1961). In *The Dance Has Many Faces,* edited by Walter Sorell. 3d ed. Pennington, N.J., 1992.

Goldberg, RoseLee. *Performance: Live Art, 1909 to the Present.* New York, 1979.

McDonagh, Don. *The Rise and Fall and Rise of Modern Dance.* Rev. ed. Pennington, N.J., 1990.

Morrissey, Lee, ed. *The Kitchen Turns Twenty: A Retrospective Anthology.* New York, 1992.

Shattuck, Roger. *The Banquet Years.* New York, 1958.

Souritz, Elizabeth. *Soviet Choreographers in the 1920s.* Translated by Lynn Visson. Durham, N.C., 1990.

Tomkins, Calvin. *The Bride and the Bachelors.* Harmondsworth, 1968.

SALLY BANES

AVELINE, ALBERT (born 23 December 1883 in Paris, died 3 February 1968 in Asnières), French dancer, teacher, choreographer, and ballet master. Albert Aveline entered the ballet school of the Paris Opera in 1894, when he was ten years old. Upon his graduation, in 1901 or 1902, he joined the Opera's corps de ballet. Having attracted notice in a pas de cinq with Léo Staats and Gustave Ricaux in 1905, he was promoted to *premier danseur* in 1906. In 1917, he became *premier danseur étoile,* the first in many years because male dancers had not been in favor since the Romantic period. The same year he was appointed ballet master to the company and teacher in the ballet school.

Prior to World War I, Aveline danced in *La Fête chez Thérèse* (1910), set to music of Reynaldo Hahn by Madame Stichel, a ballet mistress at the Opera, and he created roles in a number of ballets by Ivan Clustine. Among them were *Les Bacchantes* and *Suite de Danses* (both 1912); *La Péri* (1913), in which he danced with Natalia Trouhanova; and *Philotis* (1914), in which he partnered Carlotta Zambelli. On active duty with the French army during the war, Aveline was wounded and taken prisoner by the Germans. After his release, he performed in the French army's theater, appearing sometimes with Zambelli and once, in a 1918 production of Charles Gounod's opera *Roméo et Juliette*, with Anna Johnsson.

Aveline continued to dance until 1934, primarily with Zambelli, appearing in *Sylvia* (1919), *La Taglioni chez Musette* (1920), and *Cydalise et le Chèvre-pied* (1923), all by Léo Staats. In 1924, he appeared with Olga Spessivtseva (becoming one of her favorite partners) in Nicholas Sergeyev's production of *Giselle*. In 1925, he created a role in Bronislava Nijinska's *Impressions de Music-Hall*, and in 1927 he danced in Michel Fokine's *Daphnis et Chloë*. Following his retirement, he remained as director of the Paris Opera Ballet School until 1950.

Aveline also became well known as a choreographer, although most of his works were academic in style. Among them were *La Grisi* (1935), *Un Baiser pour Rien* (1936), *Elvire* (1937), *Les Santons* (1938), a new version of *Le Festin de l'Araignée* (1939), and *La Chartreuse de Parme* (1939). In 1941, he produced *Jeux d'Enfants*, a ballet for schoolchildren, which was revived in 1977. He also created *La Grande Jatte*, with music by Fred Barlow, in 1950; in the following year staged his own version of Gounod's *Roméo et Juliette* with Liane Daydé and Michel Renault. In 1952, he collaborated with Serge Lifar and Harald Lander on a revival of the *opéra-ballet Les Indes Galantes;* the production was so well received that another *opéra-ballet, Oberon,* was produced in 1954.

Throughout his career, Aveline was particularly well known for his revivals, among them *Iphigénie en Tauride* (1931), *La Juive* (1933), *La Tragédie de Salomé* (1944), produced for Suzanne Lorcia; *Sylvia* (1946), for Lycette Darsonval; *Les Fêtes d'Hébé au Versailles* (1950); another *Salomé* (1954), also for Darsonval; *The Faust Ballet* (1956); and *Suite de Danses* (after Clustine).

In his 1929 book, *La danse d'aujourd'hui,* critic André Levinson observed, "One of the great virtues of Albert Aveline's choreography is the coherence and diversity of his ensembles." And upon Aveline's death, a critic for *Le Monde* wrote: "An excellent technician, with great purity and elegance of style, he illustrated better than anyone else the academic ideals of the Palais Garnier in his nobility of expression."

BIBLIOGRAPHY
Art et danse (March 1968). Features four articles on Aveline.
Levinson, André. *La danse d'aujourd'hui.* Paris, 1929.
Levinson, André. *Les visages de la danse.* Paris, 1933.
Obituary. *Le monde* (7 February 1968).
Percival, John. "Ballet School of the Paris Opera." *Dance and Dancers* (August 1978): 35–37.
Vaillat, Léandre. *Ballets de l'Opéra de Paris (Ballets dans les opéras—nouveaux ballets).* Paris, 1947.

ARCHIVE. Walter Toscanini Collection of Research Materials in Dance, New York Public Library for the Performing Arts.
MONIQUE BABSKY
Translated from French

AZERBAIJAN. Lying south of Russia, bounded by the Caspian Sea on the east, Iran on the south, and Armenia on the west, Azerbaijan was peopled by Medes and was part of the ancient Persian Empire. Successively overrun by Georgians, Armenians, Romans, Huns, and Mongols, it fell under Turkish domination, which lasted from the eleventh through the early eighteenth centuries, adopted Islam and became a Muslim state. Although it was on an important trade route during the Middle Ages, over time it fell into enduring poverty. After 1813 Azerbaijan was dominated by Russia, joining the USSR in 1922 and becoming a constituent republic in 1936 as part of Transcaucasia. With the dissolution of the USSR in 1991, it became an independent state and has since that time been in conflict with Armenia over religious issues and territorial rights.

Folk Dance. Azerbaijani folk dance is from ancient times; dancers carved in stone some ten thousand years ago may be seen on rocks in Gobystan, about fifty miles (80 kilometers) from the capital, Baku. These may represent the dance *yally,* which is still popular. It is a round dance performed during folk festivals by three groups: men, women, and children. One type of *yally* has various forms known as *kochari, uchayag, tello,* and *galadan-galaya;* another type is a dance mixed with games called *gazy-gazy, zopy-zopy,* and *chopu-chopu. Yally* is most common in the Nakhichevan region; the round dances *gyulmen khagysh-da* and *salam aleikum* occur in other regions. They are each performed by two groups of girls, as in a contest, and are accompanied with choral singing by the dancers.

Subject-motivated dances are prominent. These include *findjan-findjan, bulag-byshynda, bakhar,* and *mudja-samma,* which are distinguished by playfulness, humor, improvisation, and a competitive character. Other Azerbaijani dances are the warlike *djangi* and the athletic *zorkhana.* Many dances are performed as solos, with the dancers improvising as they try to outdo each other in technique, plasticity, and style. Melodies are composed by folk musicians and often bear the names of villages, mountains, rivers, and flowers as well as proper names. Sometimes they are named after events in the lives of the people, such as "Express Trains." The 6/8 meter is most characteristic of Azerbaijani folk dance; 2/4 occurs also, but less frequently. The melodies vary widely and may be played in quite different variations, although the main theme, the general character of the music, and the tempo remain unchanged.

Women's dancing is remarkable for its expressive arm movements, which often imitate the work of picking crops or domestic chores. Leg movements are less varied, though, consisting largely of broad circular or side-to-side motions. The style is soft, lyrical, and graceful. Men's dancing is more vigorous and is notable for its quick tempo and sharp, accented leg movements. Unlike the women, the men dance in one spot and hold their arms firmly in fixed positions.

Theatrical Dance. Ballet came into Azerbaijan in the nineteenth century and played an important part in opera, which began there in the early twentieth century. In 1920 the Azerbaijani Opera House, now named Akhundov, was opened in Baku. In 1923 Sergei Kevorkov opened a dance studio there, and in 1923 it became a ballet school. In the 1920s and 1930s many ballet classics were staged. The first national ballet, *The Maiden's Tower*, with choreography by Kevorkov and Vakhtang Vronsky, was staged in 1940. It incorporated both classical technique and indigenous folk motifs.

The talent of Gamer Almaszade, the first Azerbaijani ballerina and choreographer, was at its height in the 1940s and 1950s. [*See the entry on Almaszade.*] Her ballet *Gyulshen* (1950) marked an important development in Azerbaijani choreography. In the 1960s and 1970s the Russian ballet masters Petr Gusev, Konstantin Sergeyev, and Yuri Grigorovich worked with the Baku company. From 1972 to 1989 Almaszade headed the company, except for 1982 to 1986 when the theater was closed owing to a fire. She was succeeded by Nela Nazirova from 1989 to 1990.

During the 1960s a number of national ballets were added to the repertory by Almaszade, Rafiga Akhundova, and Nela Nazirova; Chimnaz Babaeva also choreographed for the company. Representative of such ballets was *The Thousand and One Nights*, with choreography by Almaszade and music by Fibret Amirov. It depicts a woman who personifies the night. The well-known tales are related in successive episodes, with the dance of Night used as a refrain between them. The color of the hero's costume changes, gradually turning from dark (wine-colored or green) to white to symbolize his return to vital ideals and belief in goodness. Paralleling the emotional tones of the music the choreography used various dance forms, including free plastique. For example, a bacchanal in a scene of revelry included classical dance for the corps de ballet and character dance for Night, all overlaid by an intimation of the region.

In the 1990s the company, which had had seventy dancers, was reduced to thirteen women and seven men, and from two to three performances a month to less frequently than once a month. Excerpts from *The Nutcracker* and *Giselle* were given. There was no corps de ballet, but students from the school were used for performances. Tamilla Shiralieva headed the school from 1990 to 1992; she was succeeded by Leila Vekilova.

An enterprising studio called Young Ballet of Baku organized a Festival of Terpsichore in 1987 and another in 1991. These included symposiums and competitions for young dancers. In 1990 the studio became a center for nationalistic propaganda and the development of choreography.

In the revival of nationalistic feeling since independence, there has been more interest in folk dance than in ballet. A new folk dance ensemble, Dzang, was created by Kagraman Nazirov in 1993. It later toured the United States and Canada under its new director, Khumar Zulfugarov.

BIBLIOGRAPHY
Abasova, Elmira. *Kara Karaev.* Baku, 1988.
Badalbeili, A. B., and Kubad Kasimov. *The Akhundov Opera and Ballet Theater.* Moscow, 1959.
Kashkai, Khabiba. *Azerbaidzhanskii baletnyi teatr.* Moscow, 1987.
Karagicheva, Liudmila. *Kara Karaev.* Moscow, 1994.
Roslavleva, Natalia. "How Large Is Soviet Ballet?" *Dance Magazine* (November 1963): 35–37, 58–61.
Swift, Mary Grace. *The Art of the Dance in the U.S.S.R.* Notre Dame, 1968.
Tkachenko, Tamara. *Narodnyi tanets.* 2d ed. Moscow, 1967.

K. GASANOV and VLADIMIR PLETNEV
Translated from Russian

AZUMA TOKUHO (Yamada Kikue; born 15 February 1909 in Tokyo), dancer and teacher. Azuma Tokuho is the daughter of *kabuki* actor Ichimura Uzaemon XV and Fujima Masaya, a respected member of the Fujima school. She began dance training at the traditional age of six under the strict eye of her mother and *kabuki* actor Bandō Mitsugorō VII, well known for his skill at dance. At the age of fourteen she became an actress (using the name Fujima Harue) at the Teikoku Theater, where she appeared in *kabuki*, new plays, and avant-garde theater. She began her professional dancing career with the first Shunto-kai recital in 1930. A representative dance from this period is *Kiku* (Chrysanthemum), which shows a woman at various stages of life and experiences of love, each stage likened to a certain type of chrysanthemum.

Japanese dance was marked at that time by a modernization movement led mostly by women. Tokuho became a major figure in this movement, liberally using Western music and art and in many cases collaborating with women lyricists. In 1933, her father made her head of the Azuma school of dance, which was closely associated with the Ichimura line of actors but had been dormant since the end of the Edo period (1603–1868). She then took the name Azuma Harue, which she changed to Azuma Tokuho in 1941.

Tokuho had begun working with Fujima Masaya II in 1939. Masaya would become not only her main choreographer but her husband as well. They premiered many new pieces in a series of recitals known as the Fusai-kai, which became a forum for experimenting with melding traditional Japanese dance with Western influences. Representative of this period was the dance *Shizuka Mono-*

gatari (The Tale of Shizuka), about the tragic fate of Shizuka Gozen, lover of the famous general, Minamoto Yoshitsune.

Tokuho's desire to increase knowledge of Japanese dance overseas led to Azuma Kabuki, a traveling show that toured the United States and Europe in 1954 and 1955. She considered applying for permanent residence in the United States but returned to Japan and began yearly Tokuho no Kai recitals in 1965. Among the most famous of the dances to premiere at these recitals was *Fujito no Ura* (Fujito Bay), roughly based on a play from the classic *nō*, that is itself based on a passage of the war epic *Tales of the Heike*. *Fujito no Ura* again shows how Tokuho strove to mix traditional dance with modern influences.

Although Tokuho in 1950 relinquished the title of head of the Azuma school to her son, the noted *kabuki* actor Nakamura Tomijūrō V, and the title was later passed on to her granddaughter Azuma Tokuya, she still retains an honored position within the school and among her peers.

Tokuho's most popular dances tended to be of young women who fall passionately in love, a love that controls their actions and makes them act impulsively. These kinds of dances succeeded for Tokuho, perhaps, because her private life was very much the same. Influenced by Tokuho's own style, the Azuma school also became known for its lavish costumes and vibrant dances.

[*See also* Japanese Traditional Schools; Kabuki Theater; *and the entry on Fujima Fujiko.*]

BIBLIOGRAPHY

Azuma Tokuho. *Sekai ni Odoru.* Tokyo, 1957.
Azuma Tokuho. *Odori.* Tokyo, 1967.
Azuma Tokuho. *Onna de Gozaru.* Tokyo, 1978.
Azuma Tokuho. *Odotte Odotte Hachiju-nen.* Tokyo, 1988.
Azuma Tokuho. *Onna Sammai Gei Sammai.* Tokyo, 1990.
Sugi Masaro, ed. *Buyo Shu Tokuho.* Tokyo, 1979.
Yamaura Shinkichi. *Nihon Buyo Ryuha Saiken.* Tokyo, 1970.

VIDEOTAPES.   National Theater Library, Tokyo (for performances after 1966).

MATTHEW JOHNSON

B

---◦≫◦---

BABILÉE, JEAN (Jean Gutmann; born 2 February 1923 in Paris), French dancer and ballet director. The son of a Parisian eye specialist, Jean Babilée studied at the Paris Opera's ballet school with Gustave Ricaux, Alexandre Volinine, and Victor Gsovsky. Even as a child he showed astonishing technical facility and natural grace. He was small but well proportioned, with a piquant face, high cheekbones, and hazel eyes. His exceptional *ballon* and rapid, well-positioned *batterie* suited him well for dramatic and poetic roles, though he was not a classical partner. Nevertheless, he had triumphs in the traditional repertory, including *Le Spectre de la Rose* and the Bluebird pas de deux from *The Sleeping Beauty,* in which his quivering *brisés volés* were exceptionally beautiful. Babilée always danced to express a character or an image.

Babilée's career began in Marika Besobrasova's troupe in Cannes during the German occupation of France in World War II. His first major performance took place in December 1944, in one of the Soirées de la Danse organized by Irène Lidova at the Théâtre Sarah-Bernhardt in Paris. In 1945 Babilée became a star of Roland Petit's Ballets des Champs-Élysées, in such roles as the Joker in Janine Charrat's *Jeu de Cartes* and the Young Man in Petit's *Le Jeune Homme et la Mort.* This last was Babilée's most famous role, which he later danced in New York and at the Teatro alla Scala in Milan. In 1946, he married the ballerina Nathalie Philippart; after that they frequently appeared together.

Babilée's first choreography for the Ballets des Champs-Élysées was *Amour et Son Amour* (1948). This was followed in 1949 by *Till Eulenspiegel.* After the Ballets des Champs-Élysées dissolved, he worked with Aurelio Milloss during the 1951 Maggio Musicale in Florence, creating roles in *Don Juan* and *Mystères.* In 1953 he returned briefly and unsuccessfully to the Paris Opera, dancing *Giselle* with Liane Daydé and creating the leading role in Harald Lander's *Hop-Frog.*

In 1955, Babilée produced *Balance à Trois,* perhaps his best choreography, for the Monte Carlo Opera. He repeated this ballet in 1956 with a company he formed at the Théâtre des Champs-Élysées. Even with such new creations as *Sable* and *Caméléopard,* and such principal dancers as Claire Sombert, Iovanka Biegovitch, and Dirk Sanders, the troupe did not survive long.

Babilée once again became a freelance artist, dancing at La Scala in Léonide Massine's *Mario and the Magician,* acting in films and on the stage in Tennessee Williams's *Orpheus Descending* and Jean Genet's *The Balcony,* and playing the lead in the dance drama *The Green Queen,* mounted by Maurice Béjart in 1963. In 1967 Babilée made a ballet comeback, dancing the title role in Joseph Lazzini's setting of Prokofiev's *The Prodigal Son.* This ballet earned Babilée the Gold Star for best dancer at the International Festival of Dance in Paris. In 1968 he directed and danced *Hai-Kai* for the newly formed Ballet-Théâtre Contemporain, and in 1971 he successfully staged Stravinsky's *The Soldier's Tale,* with his daughter Isabelle in the role of the Princess. During the 1972/73 season, he directed the Ballet du Rhin in Strasbourg.

Relying on his innate and exceptional physical qualities, Babilée dissipated his energies, finding no occupation that truly absorbed him. He made a move toward teaching but quickly tired of it. In 1979, at age fifty-six, he made an extraordinary return to the stage in New York, dancing in *Life,* created for him by Béjart. He subsequently danced *Life* at the Paris Opera and in 1983 for Béjart's company Ballet du XXᵉ Siècle in Brussels and during the company's Paris season at the Théâtre du Châtelet. In July 1983 he also participated as guest star in the Festival of Nervi in Italy. In 1995 the television film *Babilée '95* was produced by Klein and shown in France.

BIBLIOGRAPHY

Bland, Alexander, and John Percival. *Men Dancing: Performers and Performances.* New York, 1984.
Boll, André. *Jean Babilée.* Paris, 1966.
Clair, Sarah. *Babilée-Danse buissonnière.* Paris, 1995.
Glasstone, Richard. "Poet and Dancer." *The Dancing Times* (December 1989): 248–249.
Goldschmidt, Hubert. "A Conversation with Jean Babilée." *Ballet Review* 22 (Summer 1994): 24–47.
Lidova, Irène. *Dix-sept visages de la danse française.* Paris, 1953.
Passet, Dominique. "Jean Babilée, un retour en force." *Danser* (September 1984). Interview with Babilée.
Stoop, Norma McLain. "The Charismatic Career of Jean Babilée." *Dance Magazine* (July 1979): 64–77.
Swinson, Cyril, ed. *Dancers and Critics.* London, 1950.

IRÈNE LIDOVA
Translated from French

BABY LAURENCE (Laurence Jackson; born 25 February 1921 in Baltimore, Maryland, died 2 April 1974 in Baltimore), American tap dancer and singer. Laurence first visited New York City when he was eleven years old and started frequenting the Hoofers Club in Harlem, where he particularly studied the work of Honi Coles, the soft-shoe specialist Eddie Rector, and the sliding Raymond Winfield. Shortly after his return to Baltimore, Laurence lost both his parents in a fire, after which he was brought up by an aunt. He soon ran away back to New York, where he found work in a nightclub run by Dickie Wells, who gave him his nickname.

In the mid-1930s Laurence worked with several acts, among them the Four Buds and the Six Merry Scotchmen, later renamed the Harlem Highlanders. In the early 1940s he put together a solo act with the help of choreographer Leonard Reed and started working steadily with big bands, such as those of Count Basie, Woody Herman, and Duke Ellington. Laurence claimed to have learned most of what he knew about tap dancing from musicians. He told the jazz dance historians Marshall and Jean Stearns, "While I danced, I hummed [Charlie] Parker's solos to myself and tried to fit rhythmic patterns to them with my feet; those solos have subtle new accents that some musicians haven't heard yet." He worked as a singer with Art Tatum, of whom he said, "Every time I heard Tatum play the piano, I had a crazy impulse to move my feet as fast as he moved his fingers." When Laurence danced he mostly stayed in one spot, in which, according to Edwin Denby, he "[built] up a cascading complexity of sound."

Laurence's tapping can be heard on a record, *"Baby" Laurence—Dance Master*, recorded during his prime, 1959–1960. Many swing tappers stayed with the eight-bar time, but Laurence took tap into the complex rhythms of bebop, dancing faster and dropping his heels into multitudes of cramp rolls (four quick sounds: toe-heel, toe-heel) punctuated with slaps and slides, almost as if he were the drummer in the band.

After a lengthy illness, Laurence appeared with Count Basie at the Apollo Theater in Harlem in 1961. In the following year he performed at the Newport Jazz Festival, where he was discovered by the jazz critics. In 1965 he went into semiretirement in Baltimore but returned to New York in the fall of 1972 to perform with other dancers at the New York Jazz Museum, and in the following year he appeared at both the New York and the Monterey Jazz Festival. Frequent television appearances followed, and at the end of 1973 he appeared with Josephine Baker at the Palace in New York. One of his last appearances was with O. D. Jackson and "Bubba" Gains in a television show shown on NBC on 10 January 1974. The documentary film *Jazz Hoofer*, made by Bill Hancock in September 1973, demonstrates Laurence's concern for tap's unknown history and his desire to salvage the tradition by demonstrating the contributions of other dancers.

[*See also* Tap Dance.]

BIBLIOGRAPHY

Frank, Rusty E. *Tap! The Greatest Tap Dance Stars and Their Stories, 1900–1955.* Rev. ed. New York, 1994.

Stearns, Marshall, and Jean Stearns. *Jazz Dance.* Rev. ed. New York, 1994.

FILM.   Bill Hancock, *Jazz Hoofer: The Legendary Baby Laurence* (1973).

JANE GOLDBERG

BAKER, JOSEPHINE (Josephine McDonald; born 3 June 1906 in Saint Louis, Missouri, died 12 April 1975 in Paris), American dancer and singer. Baker was an African-American singer and dancer who became famous in Paris in the 1920s. She made her debut at the age of fourteen at the Booker T. Washington Theater in her home town, and subsequently went on tours. During this time she married first Willie Wells and then William Howard Baker, from whom, despite intervening liaisons and a pretended marriage to Count Pepito Abatino, she was not divorced until 1936. She was engaged in New York for the 1920s musical comedies *Shuffle Along* and *The Chocolate Dandies*.

Paris discovered Baker on 20 October 1925 when, with her partner Joe Alex, she appeared as the star of Noble Sissle's *La Revue Nègre* at the Théâtre des Champs-Élysées. The subject of much attention, she posed for Paul Colin, Pablo Picasso, Fujita Tsuguharu, Kees van Dongen, Man Ray, Henri Laurens, Alexander Calder, and Domergue. Colette called her a "beautiful panther." Her version of the Charleston charmed the art critic Pierre MacOrlan and the novelist F. Scott Fitzgerald. André Levinson wrote:

> Some of her poses, with her waist curved inward, her rump projecting, her arms interlaced and lifted in a semblance of a phallic symbol . . . evoke all the marvels of noble black statuary: she is no longer the dancing girl . . . she is the Black Venus who haunted Baudelaire.

By turns wanton and coquettish, Baker next dazzled Berlin. She turned down offers to perform from both Max Reinhardt and Count Henry Kessler in order to make her debut at the Folies-Bergère. Wearing a belt of bananas in "Yes, We Have No Bananas," she combined whimsical improvisation with exceptional professionalism and extraordinary radiance.

In 1926, with the help of the impresario Pepito Abatino, Baker opened a cabaret known as Chez Joséphine, the first of several. In 1927 she published her memoirs in Paris and also established the revue *Un Vent de Folie*. Baker made several films at this time, including *Une Excursion à Paris*, *La Sirène des Tropiques*, and *Princess Tam-Tam*. She made her first international tour in 1928–1929, arousing both enthusiasm and hostility (particularly in Vienna) as a "black sex symbol." In 1930 she succeeded the great star of music-hall, Mistinguett, at the Casino de Paris, presenting the revue *Paris qui Remue;* it included the song that became her signature, "J'ai Deux Amours"—"I have two loves, my country and Paris."

In 1933 Baker toured England and Europe. In 1934 she appeared in Jacques Offenbach's *La Créole* at the Bouffes-Parisiens theater and filmed *Zouzou* with Jean Gabin. In 1936 she appeared at the Winter Garden in New York in the *Ziegfeld Follies* and opened another Chez Joséphine cabaret there, on Fifty-fourth Street. She returned to the Folies-Bergère in 1937 and opened a new cabaret on the Champs-Élysées, as well as marrying her third husband, Jean Lion.

In September 1939, as World War II began, Baker starred with Maurice Chevalier in *Paris-Londres* at the Casino de Paris and appeared with him at the Théâtre aux Armées. She joined the Free French underground, volunteered with the Red Cross, revived *La Créole* in Marseille, and traveled to Casablanca to entertain French troops, where she became seriously ill with bronchitis and typhoid. After regaining her health in 1943, she performed for the armed forces in North Africa, Palestine, Corsica, and Italy, returning to Paris in 1944.

On 3 June 1947 Baker married musician Jo Bouillon at her château in the Dordogne, Les Milandes. She visited the United States in 1948 and 1949; as a result of her experiences with racial segregation there, she adopted twelve children of various races between 1954 and 1965. They became known as her "rainbow tribe."

Baker spent some time performing in Argentina in 1952. In 1956 she began a round of farewell performances in a number of countries, beginning at the Olympia in Paris. In May 1959 she returned to the Paris stage in *Paris mes Amours,* which traced her career from Saint Louis to her early conquest of Paris. She appeared at Carnegie Hall in New York in 1973 and in Monte Carlo in 1974. The principal purpose of these farewell performances was to raise money to meet her increasing expenses, the result of bringing up her large adopted family. On 8 April 1975 she opened at the Bobino Music Hall in Paris in *Joséphine,* another revue based on her life, but she died only a few days later, on 12 April.

The "black pearl" is remembered for her feline walk, her warmth, and her exceptional rhythmic spontaneity. She received France's Croix de Guerre, for her work during the war, as well as the medal of the City of Paris and membership in the Légion.

[*See also* Music Hall, *article on* French Traditions.]

BIBLIOGRAPHY

Baker, Jean-Claude. *Josephine: The Hungry Heart.* New York, 1993.
Baker, Josephine, and Jo Bouillon. *Josephine.* Translated by Mariana Fitzpatrick. New York, 1977.

BAKER. Josephine Baker was a "triple threat": dancer, singer, and actress, a star in films as well as on the stage. In this scene from *Zouzou* (1934), a film co-starring a young Jean Gabin, Baker sings about missing her island home. (Photograph from the Film Stills Library, Museum of Modern Art, New York.)

Haney, Lynn. *Naked at the Feast: A Biography of Josephine Baker.* London, 1981.
Levinson, André. *La danse d'aujourd'hui.* Paris, 1929.
O'Connor, Patrick, and Bryan Hammond. *Josephine Baker.* Boston, 1988.
Rose, Phyllis. *Jazz Cleopatra: Josephine Baker in Her Time.* London, 1989.
Wiser, William. *The Great Good Place: American Expatriate Women in Paris.* New York, 1991.

MARIE-FRANÇOISE CHRISTOUT
Translated from French

BAKST, LÉON (Lev Samoilovich Rosenberg; born 27 April 1866 in Grodno, Russia, died 27 December 1924 in Paris), Russian scenery and costume designer. Bakst was perhaps the most revolutionary of Russia's stage designers of the early twentieth century, and his name is synonymous with the successes of the Ballets Russes de Serge Diaghilev. He prepared for his career as an artist and designer by auditing courses at the Academy of Arts in Saint

BAKST. Watercolor costume study by Léon Bakst for Vaslav Nijin-sky's role in *La Péri*. (Metropolitan Museum of Art; Gift of Sir Joseph Duveen, 1922 [no. 22.226.1.]; photograph used by permission.)

Petersburg between 1883 and 1886, and subsequently worked as a magazine and book designer.

Bakst was a cofounder of *Mir iskusstva* (World of Art), a magazine published in Saint Petersburg from 1899 to 1904, collaborating closely with Serge Diaghilev, Alexandre Benois, and others with whom he prepared the decor of Diaghilev's production of *Sylvia*, which was projected for the Maryinsky Theater but never realized. Bakst's first individual efforts as a stage designer were for productions of *Le Coeur de la Marquise* (1900), *Hippolytus* (1902), and *Die Puppenfee* (1903) at the Hermitage Theater in Saint Petersburg. Thereafter, he was active in numerous dramatic, operatic, and ballet productions.

When Diaghilev launched the Ballets Russes in Paris in 1909, Bakst remained a close associate and designed much of the repertory, including *Cléopâtre* in 1909, *Le Carnaval* and *Schéhérazade* in 1910, *Le Spectre de la Rose* and *Narcisse* (1911), and *Les Femmes de Bonne Humeur* (1917). There is no question that the immediate popularity of the Ballets Russes was much indebted to Bakst's work—to his riot of colors, exotic and erotic evocations, and dynamic forms. These elements were identified above

all with *Schéhérazade*, perhaps the most provocative and audacious of the Diaghilev productions. [*See* Carnaval, Le; *and* Schéhérazade.]

At the same time, Bakst designed for Ida Rubinstein, Anna Pavlova, and other dance luminaries in Europe and the United States. His ambitious resolution of Pavlova's *The Sleeping Beauty* (New York, 1916) even included real dogs, cats, and birds for the castle onstage. Bakst also continued to keep abreast of the nontheatrical art world, publishing, for example, a long article on modern art in *Apollon*, an illustrated fine arts journal published in Saint Petersburg (1909–1910).

Of the central members of Diaghilev's World of Art group of artists, poets, musicians, and aesthetes, Bakst and Mstislav Dobujinsky were the most distinguished painters. Bakst embodied the greatest aspiration of the World of Art—the *Gesamtkunstwerk* (collective, or unified, work of art)—both in his readiness to investigate and combine various media and methods and in his propagation of the theater as the highest art form.

The history and philosophies of ancient Greece and the Orient were Bakst's major interests, as he demonstrated in many stage productions, beginning with *Hippolytus* and culminating in such famous pieces as *Hélène de Sparte* and *Daphnis et Chloé* in 1912. After his travels in Greece in 1907 with the artist Valentin Serov, Bakst concluded that the "real" Greece was not a civilization of intellectual poise and discipline but rather a highly emotional, archaic, and heathen society, an interpretation that puzzled the Paris audience of *Hélène de Sparte*. Bakst's Oriental evocations in *Cléopâtre* and *Schéhérazade* also appeared hedonistic to audiences, although his designs relied for their effect on precise formal organization and severe order. In ballets such as these, Bakst consciously used the stage space as a three-dimensional unit—as a relief rather than a pictorial plane. He replaced conventional horizontal sequences with diagonal axes and ensured that volumetric forms played a primary role onstage, even in such ethereal and seemingly simple ballets as *L'Après-midi d'un Faune*. [*See* Après-midi d'un Faune, L'.]

Bakst gave particular attention to the entire notion of costume onstage, emphasizing flexibility and liberating the dancer's movement. Indeed, what was innovative in his costumes for *Thamar, Schéhérazade,* or *Le Dieu Bleu* (1912) was not just the elaborate sensuality of the ensembles but the real emancipation and exaggeration of the body's rhythm. Bakst treated the dancer's body as the principal organizational element onstage (and also in the salon, when he turned his attention to haute couture) and hence as the determinant of the costume's expression. This inspired him to expose the body at strategic points and to extend its physical movements outward. Consequently, Bakst used the multicolored pendants, feathers, loose trousers, and veils of his creations (the unproduced

La Péri of 1911 or the costumes of the slave girls in *Cléopâtre*) as functional devices that could extend the body's reverberations outward into space.

The only criticism that was leveled at Bakst's costumes and sets was that they were visually overwhelming: "The spectacle dominates the music too much," wrote the French art critic Henri Ghéon about *Schéhérazade* in 1910 in *La nouvelle revue française*. Bakst himself was aware of this incongruity, as he implied in his essay "In the Theater No One Wants to Listen Anymore, They Just Want to Look," published in *Peterburgskaia gazeta* in 1914. Nevertheless, Bakst could also be sober and rigorous in his decorative conceptions, demonstrated by his simple, no-nonsense set and costumes for *Jeux* (1913), which, in its geometricity and minimalism, anticipated such constructivist experiments of the 1920s as Kasyan Goleizovsky's *Joseph the Beautiful,* produced in Moscow in 1925.

Among the artists and stage designers of the time, Bakst enjoyed the widest recognition, and his sensuous art influenced many young Russian designers, such as Boris Bilinsky, Erté (Romain de Tirtoff), and Simon Lissim. His contribution to dance design was transformative, his success was meteoric, and his talent burned out quickly.

By the early 1920s Bakst was repeating himself (as in Rubinstein's *Artemis Troublée* of 1922) or was producing a surfeit of rich colors and forms that tended to stifle rather than enhance the effect of the ballet. *The Sleeping Princess,* produced by Diaghilev in London in 1921, is a case in point. Although Bakst applied his rich fantasy to the six scenes and three hundred costumes of Marius Petipa's classical ballet, and though his loyal champion, dance critic André Levinson, referred to the "expert orchestration of colour and an inexhaustible wealth of decorative invention," the result was cumbersome and contrived and relied too obviously on his work for Pavlova's *The Sleeping Beauty* of 1916. Before this decline, however, Bakst's creative genius had contributed to the universal success of Diaghilev and the Ballets Russes.

[*For related discussion, see* Scenic Design. *In addition, many of the figures and works mentioned herein are the subjects of independent entries.*]

BIBLIOGRAPHY

Bakst. London, 1974. Exhibition catalogue, Fine Art Society.
Bakst, Léon. "Tchaikowsky aux Ballets Russes." *Comoedia* 15 (October 1921): 1.
Borisovskaia, Natalia. *Lev Bakst* (in Russian). Moscow, 1979.
Garafola, Lynn. *Diaghilev's Ballets Russes.* New York, 1989.
Mayer, Charles S. *Bakst: Centenary, 1876–1976.* London, 1976.
Mayer, Charles S. "The Influence of Léon Bakst on Choreography." *Dance Chronicle* 1.2 (1978): 127–142.
Potter, Michelle. "Designed for Dance: The Costumes of Léon Bakst and the Art of Isadora Duncan." *Dance Chronicle* 13.2 (1990): 154–169.
Pruzhan, Irina. *Léon Bakst: Set and Costume Designs, Book Illustrations, Paintings, and Graphic Works.* Translated by Arthur Shkarovsky-Raffé. Middlesex, 1986.
Schouvaloff, Alexander. *Léon Bakst: The Theatre Art.* London, 1991.
Spencer, Charles. *Leon Bakst and the Ballets Russes.* Rev. ed. London, 1995.

ARCHIVES.   Ashmolean Museum, Oxford. Mr. and Mrs. N. D. Lobanov-Rostovsky, London. Musée National d'Art Moderne, Centre Georges Pompidou, Paris. New York Public Library for the Performing Arts. Serge Lifar Collection, Wadsworth Atheneum, Hartford, Connecticut.

JOHN E. BOWLT

BALANCHINE, GEORGE (Georgii Melitonovich Balanchivadze; born 22 January 1904 in Saint Petersburg, died 30 April 1983 in New York), Russian-American dancer, choreographer, and company director. The leading choreographer of the twentieth century and the architect of classical ballet in America, George Balanchine dominated his art as had no other figure since Marius Petipa. The emergence of dance as an autonomous art is an essentially Western phenomenon to which Russians, Americans, and Europeans all made important contributions in the first two decades of the twentieth century. Balanchine, who came along as these contributions were being made, was not the first to make dance continuity the whole content of a ballet; he was not even the first to insist on academic classicism as the base of that continuity. But it was Balanchine who, in imposing his genius on the emerging dance epoch, explained it to the world and made it great. Recognized in his lifetime for the emblematic significance of his career, at his death he was acknowledged to have been among the foremost artists of modern times, one who, like Igor Stravinsky and Pablo Picasso, not only established new standards of expression, but also summed up and interpreted traditional values for the contemporary audience.

Balanchine's father was a composer from Georgia; his mother, of part-German ancestry, was a native of Saint Petersburg. Although known as "the Georgian Glinka," Meliton Balanchivadze's career as a composer was not a lucrative one, and he suffered several business reverses while his children were still young. He had planned a naval career for Georgi but gave up when the boy, accompanying his sister to an audition at the Imperial School of Theater and Ballet, was chosen for the ballet. The Imperial School offered free tuition and room and board. As a ballet student, Georgi wore the same uniform as a naval cadet but with insignia in the shape of a lyre. He studied with Samuil Andrianov and later with Leonid Leontiev; the mime performances of the veteran dancer Pavel Gerdt also made a deep impression. At the age of eleven, Georgi joined the pupils who appeared in ballets on the stage of the Maryinsky Theater. He danced choreography by Petipa, Lev Ivanov, Aleksandr Gorsky, Nikolai Legat, and Michel Fokine. He also acted at the Alexandrinsky Theater in plays by Anton Chekov and others.

BALANCHINE. Felia Doubrovska perches on Serge Lifar's shoulders in *La Pastorale* (1926), an early Balanchine work for Diaghilev's Ballet Russes. This pose displays Balanchine's predilection for lifts in which men partner women from kneeling positions. (Photograph from the Dance Collection, New York Public Library for the Performing Arts. Choreography by George Balanchine © The George Balanchine Trust.)

In 1921, Georgi graduated from the ballet school and entered the company, distinguishing himself as a character dancer. The following year, he formed the Young Ballet with colleagues and classmates. It became an instantaneous hit in the advanced artistic circles of Petrograd and officially launched his career as a choreographer, although he had actually begun making dances for school concerts in 1919 or possibly as early as 1917. During this period Balanchivadze supported and broadened himself by playing the piano for classes, at dance concerts, and in movie theaters; by playing, dancing, and devising entertainment in cabarets; by choreographing pantomimes and dance movement in plays and operas, and by working with experimental theater groups. The opposition of the Maryinsky authorities effectively put an end to the Young Ballet after about a year.

With a friend, the baritone Vladimir Dimitriev, Balanchivadze in 1924 organized a small group of Maryinsky dancers and singers for a summer tour of Germany. The dancers—Alexandra Danilova, Tamara Geva, Nicholas

Efimov, and Balanchivadze—wound up in Paris auditioning for Serge Diaghilev and were accepted into the Ballets Russes. Balanchivadze, whom Diaghilev renamed Balanchine, spent five eventful years as ballet master to the Ballets Russes. After Diaghilev's death in 1929, Balanchine was offered the post of ballet master at the Paris Opera but fell ill with tuberculosis. Recuperating, he worked on variety shows in London and as ballet master of the Royal Danish Ballet in Copenhagen. He organized the first season of René Blum's Ballets de Monte Carlo. In Paris, he founded Les Ballets 1933 and created its repertory of six ballets, including the first version of *Mozartiana*. After little more than a dozen performances, the company disbanded, leaving Balanchine without prospects. It was then that Lincoln Kirstein offered to bring him to the United States. [*See* Ballets 1933 *and the entry on Kirstein.*]

Although Balanchine's life's work seems from the beginning to have been impelled by a grand inevitability, much about it remains problematical, even mysterious. Conceivably, had he not from the age of thirty been obliged to deal with the relatively inexperienced American audience, Balanchine would not have developed the astonishing aesthetic range that, by the time he formed the New York City Ballet, already distinguished his work. *Concerto Barocco, Ballet Imperial* (later retitled *Tchaikovsky Piano Concerto No. 2*), *Danses Concertantes, The Four Temperaments, Symphonie Concertante, Theme and Variations,* and *Symphony in C*—all created between 1941 and 1948—typify the array of skills and resources he brought to the task of persuading the American public that classical dancing in and of itself incorporated drama and diversion, spectacle and fantasy.

The indicator of his versatility (if not the key to it) was his choice of music. From Johann Sebastian Bach to Georges Bizet, the theme is always classical expression, but the formal process of exposition is repeated in organically different terms to completely new effect. Balanchine's eclectic musical tastes were matched by a musical intelligence, professionally trained from the age of five. He might have had a concert career as a pianist or a conductor had he not chosen to choreograph; in either case, he would have wielded a broad repertory. In the same season in which he launched a new era in modern classicism with Stravinsky's *Agon*, he revived a faded image of the classicism of the Paris Opera in *Gounod Symphony*. This was followed by a ballet to the music of John Philip Sousa. Two seasons later, he was choreographing Anton Webern, and by the end of the following year he had dealt with Petr Ilich Tchaikovsky, George Frideric Handel, Gaetano Donizetti, Johannes Brahms, and Stravinsky again.

Balanchine's lack of bias in music extended to the spheres of activity in which he was willing to be engaged. He was a choreographer of opera ballets (some one hundred different productions, including operetta), of incidental music in plays, of musical comedies and revues, of film and television productions, of innumerable concert numbers and *pièces d'occasion*. With Stravinsky, he even did a ballet for circus elephants. Except for a few years in the 1930s and 1940s during which he functioned exclusively as a Broadway and Hollywood dance director, Balanchine managed to keep on making his ballets while carrying out his other work. His total output has been estimated at a herculean 425 works, the last of which, a solo variation for Suzanne Farrell, was produced only four months before he was hospitalized with his fatal illness. Of his more than two hundred ballets, a fair number consisted of remakes— old music and old themes revisited (his last *Mozartiana* was his fourth and perhaps best version of that work).

Balanchine's productivity was a manifestation of his genius. He choreographed swiftly and without strain, often completing a ballet in a week. He came to the studio having already visualized the shape and style of the dance from a study of the music; the actual steps were created on the spot, frequently with the active collaboration of the dancers. He was noted for his flexibility, his pragmatism, and for the peaceful atmosphere of his rehearsals, unclouded by creative histrionics.

From the beginning of his career, Balanchine was romantically as well as artistically involved with his ballerinas. His marriage at eighteen to Tamara Geva, his liaison with Alexandra Danilova, and his subsequent marriages to Vera Zorina, Maria Tallchief, and Tanaquil Le Clercq were only the most publicized of his many erotic attachments. In person, Balanchine was elegant, intense, candid, and enigmatic. Although he was not always in good health, he possessed great physical vitality. He had come to the United States with a damaged knee that had all but ended his dancing career; despite this handicap and the collapse of one lung (owing to persistent tubercular infection), he invariably demonstrated what he wanted from his dancers, both the steps and the partnering. In 1978, a heart attack forced him to curtail his rigorous work habits. However, neither this blow nor any of the other ailments that plagued him throughout his life had anything to do with the disease that killed him, the nature of which became known only after he died. Balanchine's malady was diagnosed as Creutzfeldt-Jakob disease, an extremely rare slow virus that is thought to have attacked his brain five years earlier, bringing about the syndrome that resulted in the sudden deterioration of his faculties in his final months. How Balanchine contracted this contagious, fatal disease is not known.

Although he lived to a precarious old age, he suffered no decline as an artist. But as the end came on, it was possible to feel that he had finished his life's work—no resource had been neglected, no avenue unexplored. That his life should have ended when his work did seems entirely consistent with the fusion of impulses that characterized life and work for Balanchine. As man and artist, he expressed himself with an undivided wholeness of inspiration. In assigning four main aspects to his legacy, we do not suggest that Balanchine assumed roles or discriminated in any way among his gifts. There was only one gift, prodigious in its very nature, which revealed itself in the following ways.

- First, as a choreographer and ballet master—the terms were for him interchangeable—he leaves two monuments: a repertory and a company. More than sixty ballets, from *Apollo* (1928) to *Mozartiana* (1981), continue to be performed by the New York City Ballet, the ensemble that he guided and, in his last decade, brought to international preeminence.
- Second, as a teacher Balanchine is remembered through the School of American Ballet, the national academy of dance, which he founded with Kirstein in 1934. From its inception, principles taught there by Balanchine had both their outlet and their origin in his choreography.
- Third, as a poet he possessed a quality of utterance unparalleled in the lyric theater.
- Last, he was a showman in the tradition of Shakespeare and Molière, Mozart and Verdi—artists whose work, although consciously shaped to please an audience, was not dominated by audience taste. He built an enlightened ballet public not by giving it what it wanted but by causing it to want what it got.

BALANCHINE. *Apollo* (1928) was revived in 1937 by the American Ballet with Daphne Vane as Calliope, Holly Howard as Polyhymnia, and Lew Christensen as the Greek god. (Photograph by Richard Tucker; used by permission of Julia Tucker. Choreography by George Balanchine © The George Balanchine Trust.)

Choreographer and Ballet Master. Just as Balanchine's powers did not decline in his last years, in his earliest extant ballets they cannot be seen to evolve. Already in the first of these, *Apollo*, the nature of his gift is completely and purely pronounced. In its most basic manifestations, it reveals itself as a gift for distillation, harmonious design, and logical progression, with a propensity for theme-and-variations structures. It is a profoundly musical gift, and its philosophical bias is classical. Because Balanchine remained true to this gift to the end of his life, *Apollo* can be looked at as a kind of manifesto, setting out the terms and predicting the direction of many later masterpieces. But Balanchine had, by the time of *Apollo*, already produced some four dozen works, five of them for Diaghilev. After *Apollo* came three more for Diaghilev, only one of which, *The Prodigal Son*, survives. Some twenty additional ballets were produced under various auspices before his departure for the United States and the creation of the next surviving work, *Serenade* (1934). What were all these lost ballets like and what was their relation to *Apollo*?

BALANCHINE. Originally created for Les Ballets 1933 in Paris, Balanchine's *Mozartiana* was revived in 1945 by the Ballet Russe de Monte Carlo, with Frederic Franklin and Alexandra Danilova in the leading roles. (Photograph from the Dance Collection, New York Public Library for the Performing Arts.)

As a student, Balanchine was trained in the world's most lavishly endowed dance academy. His formative years were spent mastering the classical repertory and absorbing the atmosphere of revitalization and experimentation that prevailed in all the arts of Russia before and for some years after the 1917 Revolution. In the opinion of a contemporary, Yuri Slonimsky, the training, the repertory, and the tests to which both were put by the searching spirit of the time were of equal importance in the development of the choreographer. Although the young Balanchine embraced a number of extreme tendencies of the avant-garde (Slonimsky says, "He tried to do everything at once"), his true direction was foreshadowed by an event in which he participated as a dancer—the production in 1922 of Fyodor Lopukhov's *Dance Symphony*. "From Ivanov through Fokine (in *Les Sylphides*) and Lopukhov to Balanchine," Slonimsky (1976) writes, "there is a thread of continuity of perception—like a line of music acquiring visible form in the plasticity of dance." Despite this thread, when Balanchine left Russia he was neither a dance symphonist nor a classicist. His work bore the marks of his classical education as well as, what appeared to contradict it, his attachment to a variety of expressionistic forms and devices. He had choreographed mostly small-scale concert pieces and needed a wider outlet for his energies. Not until he was hired by Diaghilev and given the full resources of the Ballets Russes did his career as a choreographer flourish and the world begin to take notice of it.

He worked on assignment, and his output was determined by Diaghilev's needs and preferences. The star of the company at that time was Serge Lifar for whom, on Diaghilev's orders, Balanchine constructed several vehicles. The closest of these to *Apollo*, in which Lifar found his most glorious role, were *La Chatte*, created the year before, and *The Prodigal Son* the year after. Serge Grigoriev records with satisfaction Diaghilev's decision to revert to narrative after a neoclassical period under Nijinska, thus reviving the type of ballet that had made the company's name.

Boris Kochno took the plot of *La Chatte* from Aesop's fable about a cat changed by Aphrodite into a woman and then back again. It lent itself to ironic treatment by the composer, Henri Sauguet, by Balanchine, and by the designers Naum Gabo and Antoine Pevsner, who conceived Aphrodite's temple as a geometrical setting in clear plastic. The dancers wore vinyl costumes with mica and metal accents. This was constructivism—the heralded new classicism of the machine age, and dominant mode of the avant-garde theater in postrevolutionary Russia. By the time he joined Diaghilev, Balanchine had forged a style that combined erotic freedom of movement with acrobatics drawn from the circus and the music hall; his idiom could be described as a kind of dance constructivism ex-

BALANCHINE. Kathyrn Mullowny, Holly Howard, Charles Laskey, and Elena de Rivas in the American Ballet's 1935 production of Balanchine's *Serenade*, which students at the School of American Ballet had premiered the year before. Jean Lurçat designed these costumes, which are dramatically different from the flowing tulle dresses usually associated with this ballet. (Photograph from the Dance Collection, New York Public Library for the Performing Arts. Choreography by George Balanchine © The George Balanchine Trust.)

ploring the body as a machine. Using six men in *La Chatte,* he built human pyramids and chariots for Lifar, who also danced a sensual pas de deux with his feline love. Constructivism in choreography was not new to Diaghilev; it had its roots in the folk-art rituals of *Le Sacre du Printemps* (Vaslav Nijinsky) and *Les Noces* (Nijinska). The same year that he produced *La Chatte* (1927, the tenth anniversary of the Russian Revolution), Diaghilev also presented *Le Pas d'Acier,* with Léonide Massine's gear-and-piston "factory" dances contrived as a salute to Soviet industrialism. The choreography of *La Chatte* was not mechanistic; nor was it ritualistic in the same sense as the Nijinsky–Nijinska ballets. Although we cannot define its quality with certainty, photographs reveal a wit, a sense of fantasy, an elegance of taste, and an atmosphere of inscrutability now recognized as quintessentially Balanchine.

Stylistically, *La Chatte* may have been the first identifiable "Balanchine ballet." Technically, it seems to have begun a process of cementing the sculptural connections between constructivism and classicism—the very process that would prove instrumental to the success of *Apollo.* As a prelude to *Apollo,* it also groomed Lifar in noble plastique and confirmed his exotic appeal in the timeless setting of a Greek myth. And, in providing a key role for Diaghilev's favorite classical ballerina, Olga Spessivtseva, the ballet paved the way for *Apollo's* Terpsichore.

Although to some extent an evolution from *La Chatte, Apollo* (then known as *Apollon Musagète*) marked a new stage in Balanchine's development, one that he has credited to the influence of Stravinsky. In composing the ballet, Stravinsky had sought an order based on similarity rather than contrast. As his biographer Eric White notes,

This led him to the conclusion that the music for this *ballet blanc* must be diatonic in character and that all extrinsic effects of instrumental contrast and variety should be avoided. He accordingly set aside the ordinary orchestra with its various instrumental departments because of its heterogeneous character . . . and decided to use a string orchestra.

(White, 1979)

In responding to this unity in Stravinsky's music, Balanchine found that he had made an apocalyptic discovery. "*Apollon* I look back on as the turning point in my life," he wrote in 1948. "In its discipline and restraint, in its sustained one-ness of tone and feeling the score was a revelation. It seemed to tell me that I could dare not to use everything, that I, too, could eliminate." Putting his work in perspective, Balanchine goes on to recall *Pastorale,* which he had set previously to music by Georges Auric:

[It] contained at least ten different types of movement, any one of which would have sustained a separate work. It was in studying *Apollon* that I came first to understand how gestures, like tones in music and shades in painting, have certain family relations. As groups they impose their own laws. The more

BALANCHINE. Original cast members Nicholas Magallanes, Gisella Caccialanza, and Fred Danieli link hands in *Ballet Imperial* (1941), Balanchine's tribute to the classical style of Marius Petipa and the Maryinsky Ballet. (Photograph from the Dance Collection, New York Public Library for the Performing Arts. Choreography by George Balanchine © The George Balanchine Trust.)

conscious an artist is, the more he comes to understand these laws and to respond to them. Since this work, I have developed my choreography inside the framework such relations suggest.

We need not take Balanchine's word for it. In his next surviving ballet, *The Prodigal Son* (1929), we see him working with the formal economy and poetic force characteristic of *Apollo*. If we consider *Apollo* to be the superior work, it is because its remarkable unity—its "oneness of tone and feeling"—extends to and permeates its subject. Alone among all the works of this period it is a rendition in dance of ideas about dance. *The Prodigal Son*, based on the New Testament parable, is dance constructivism in an unmodulated, almost aggressive, state. One cannot imagine the mechanical lust of the Siren, the rigid conformism and compulsive savagery of the Drinking Companions and their brutalization of the Prodigal expressed in terms of *Apollo*'s classicism. Yet the terms in which these things are expressed are no less transparent. Constructivism was not, for Balanchine, a contradiction of classicism; as *Apollo* proved, it was inherently proto-classical. Balanchine's interest in constructivism as a poetic language eventually died, and in later years he regarded *The Prodigal Son* as dated. But he apparently did not think it worth suppressing (unlike the prologue of *Apollo*), in fact, he revived it periodically as a vehicle for

star performers. It is one of several artistically distinguished, innovative works (*Le Bal, Cotillon, The Seven Deadly Sins, L'Errante*—all lost) in which he sought a way of continuing the neoclassicism of the 1920s.

Neoclassicism—not just a new twist to the style, but more emphatically a new content—incorporated sports, acrobatics, *la danse moderne*, ballroom, nightclub, and show dancing, and colloquialisms of all kinds. In this context, *Mozartiana* (1933) was perhaps an exceptional declaration, as was *Serenade* (1934), and later *Le Baiser de la Fée* (1937). These three ballets form a sequence that points toward the choreographer's eventual adoption of a pure classical idiom. In spite of his classical education, Balanchine could not accept classicism as a priori theory; he had to find the path for himself and his search for a style continued through the 1930s. It was an end in itself, and each ballet made its own discovery. We do not know what all these discoveries were, but because we know where the path led, we look back and think we see Balanchine approaching or receding from his "goal" on the strength of whether or not he used a scenario. Rather, the key element seems to have been the circumstances of production and the relative freedom accorded to the choreographer, scenario or no scenario.

Balanchine's idea of classicism then and later did not exclude dramatic circumstance. Calliope and Polyhymnia were not banished from Apollo's realm, merely eclipsed by the greater glory of Terpsichore. *Mozartiana*, a suite of dances, had a quasi-scenario heavily influenced by the designer Christian Bérard; *Baiser* had a book by Stravinsky based on a story by Hans Christian Andersen. Neither ballet has remained in repertory in its original form, but we know that both were meditations on the subject of art and classicism that allowed Balanchine to concentrate his faculties on something more than brilliant ephemera—something that deeply concerned him and his destiny. Both ballets used the music of Tchaikovsky; *Serenade*, to the choreographer's own scenario, did also and was perhaps the most far-ranging meditation of all. These three guideposts put Balanchine back in touch with his tradition at successive stages during the critical period 1933–1937. When by 1940 he returned to the proposition, so powerfully expressed in *Apollo*, that the content of classicism is the style of classicism, he was not rejecting his neoclassical experiences but consolidating them. He was ready to refocus classical style.

Balanchine was a musician's choreographer. The two composers who recur most often in his work are Tchaikovsky and Stravinsky. It was their compositions that helped him find his style and make the transition between Europe, where ballet was presumed to have died with Diaghilev, and the United States, where it was virtually unknown.

Serenade, to Tchaikovsky's "Serenade for Strings," was

Balanchine's first ballet in the New World; the milestone was accompanied by a revival of *Mozartiana*, in which Tchaikovsky meditates on Mozart. Three years later, the first American production of *Apollo* was presented with Stravinsky's study of Tchaikovsky and his era of ballet, *Le Baiser de la Fée*. According to his closest observer, Edwin Denby, the shift to "a new interest in classic coherence, limpidity and grace," that characterized Balanchine's work in the 1940s, began with *Balustrade* (1941), the controversial setting of Stravinsky's Violin Concerto in D, but the shift may actually have occurred as early as 1938, when Balanchine started work on *Concerto Barocco* to Bach's Double Violin Concerto in D Minor. The Bach ballet was finally performed in 1941 alongside another new piece, *Ballet Imperial*, set to Tchaikovsky's Piano Concerto no. 2. The pairing, which launched American Ballet Caravan, expressed the continuity of the classical tradition as a matter of pure form (Bach) and as a matter of historical record (Tchaikovsky), much as had the earlier pairings of *Mozartiana* and *Serenade* and then *Apollo* and *Baiser*.

As the subtext of *Serenade* was *Giselle* and the Romantic ballet, that of *Ballet Imperial* (1941) was Petipa, the Maryinsky Ballet, and *Swan Lake*. Typically, Balanchine was looking back and ahead at the same time, placing his own work in aesthetic and historical perspective and establishing the premise for future work. He was by now producing his choreography as formal essays on the music. The commentaries on the past lay in the depths, not on the surface; one did not have to know *Swan Lake*—or *Giselle*, for that matter—to appreciate Balanchine's ballet. The new purity of idiom was marked by the absence of those "distortions" and "modernisms" (acrobatics and other kinds of stylization) that Denby had found in Balanchine's earlier work. "His present style is not an oblique neoclassicism, it is a direct new classicism," Denby wrote in 1945. Of *Balustrade*, which preceded *Concerto Barocco* onto the stage by five months (and lasted three performances), he wrote: "I have the impression that . . . the first and last part of it, in which the movement was simple and open and made its effect directly by its dance rhythm, began definitely in the present direction; although it was the wonderfully sensual acrobatics of the middle section that delighted one part of the audience and shocked another" (Denby, 1949).

When Balanchine remade the piece in 1972, as *Stravinsky Violin Concerto*, he again used acrobatics (in Aria II). In fact, he never entirely abandoned these lucid metaphorical stylizations of the human body. The great *Agon* pas de deux is full of them. By now, though, they were not appearing as "lovely erotic interruptions" (to use Denby's term for a neoclassical tendency) but as calm images embedded in an eloquently transformed classical context. In *Agon*, Balanchine pushed classical syntax to new extremes of expression (heightening the tension of a supported balance in the adagio by having the man lie on the floor, for example). In the same season with *Agon* (1957–1958), he once again revived *Apollo*, this time in a plain constructivist-style setting, with a wooden platform. Twinned with and illuminated by *Agon*, *Apollo* had a miraculous renewal, only now *it* was the ballet of historical record while *Agon* expressed classicism as pure form.

Stravinsky, ever the illustrious mentor and collaborator, presided over the new epoch. His text in *Agon* had been a French seventeenth-century dance manual. Thirty years before, he had composed *Apollo* in homage to the masters of music and dance at the court of Versailles in the time of Louis XIV, the Sun King. In this he was conscious of the example of Tchaikovsky, who in *The Sleeping Beauty* had evoked the same Baroque image. The connections and correspondences that continued to inform Stravinsky's art were reflected in Balanchine's. Like the composer, the choreographer beheld a vision of classical dance rooted in the Renaissance, and he explored that vision in direct and indirect participation with Stravinsky. Bach inspired Stravinsky in the violin concerto; a decade later Balanchine took it and a Bach concerto as well, and from their joint inspiration laid the cornerstone of "a direct new classicism."

BALANCHINE. *Danses Concertantes* (1944), with the original-cast principals, Alexandra Danilova and Frederic Franklin, and members of the ensemble. The costumes were designed by Eugene Berman. (Photograph by Robert S. Thomas; from the Dance Collection, New York Public Library for the Performing Arts. Choreography by George Balanchine © The George Balanchine Trust.)

BALANCHINE. The plotless *Symphonie Concertante* (1947) was set to Mozart's Sinfonia Concertante in E-flat for violin and viola (K. 364). Here the dancers are Todd Bolender, Diana Adams, and Tanaquil Le Clercq. (Photograph by Walter E. Owen; from the Dance Collection, New York Public Library for the Performing Arts. Choreography by George Balanchine © The George Balanchine Trust.)

Still later, Stravinsky's interest in the Viennese serialists incited ballets to Arnold Schoenberg and Webern; his own music furnished Balanchine with a means of extending the *materia* of *Agon* into the 1960s and 1970s. Both men were attracted to American jazz. And always there was their mutual pact, so profoundly Russian, with Tchaikovsky.

Although Balanchine expressed many types of music, his most progressive theme was that which flows from *Apollo* through *Serenade* and *Le Baiser de la Fée* into the mainstream of *Concerto Barocco, Ballet Imperial,* and the other masterpieces of the 1940s, to be replenished in the rushing cataracts of *Agon*. If an evolution can be traced in these works, it is greater refinement of means. There was no appreciable difference in Balanchine's control of dance expression from one work to another; there are only changes in the method he used to achieve it, and these changes were invariably determined by the structure and momentum of the music.

In *Apollo,* the shift from constructivist to classical aesthetics is a visible process effected through plastic geometry in a clearly defined, majestically paced sequence of happenings. *Serenade* rushes, glides, or melts from one pure Euclidean configuration into another. The configura-

tions of *Concerto Barocco* are contained in a complex contrapuntal web. One can say that *Apollo* is the culminating work of Balanchine's youth, *Concerto Barocco* the first work of his maturity, and *Serenade,* which did not achieve its complete form until 1940, is the bridge between. One notes in *Serenade* the mastery of spatial dynamics and rhythmic impetus that was to sustain so many of the large-scale pieces, from symphonic "abstractions" to dramatic spectacles such as *Swan Lake* (1951), *La Valse* (1951), and *Vienna Waltzes* (1977). One sees the confidence of the craftsman who in ballet after ballet reopens the subject of classical expression, showing how forms flower from the simple to the complex. One can pinpoint the times when, with each new company he was put in charge of, Balanchine begins to turn out a secondary kind of work—the repertory piece. One can discuss higher and lower levels of repertory pieces and enumerate the categories into which they fall. What one cannot say—because one cannot see it—is anything about Balanchine's growth as an artist. The great theme ballets are an advancing stream of discovery that continually flows back on itself. He seems never to have done anything he had not done before, and yet everything he did was new.

It is not uncommon for artists to establish a pattern of recapitulation and forecast in the works they produce. What makes Balanchine exceptional is that this was the pattern in works that seemed at the time, and still do seem, unique and unrepeatable. *Agon* established a precedent for virtuosity in modern ballet. Yet it not only elaborated the seventeenth-century dance forms that were the models for *Apollo,* but also brought back constructivism in a new guise. The impersonal language of midcentury dance technicians spoke of a machine-tooled efficiency; their exploits outmaneuvered and outwitted the menace of dehumanization in the modern world. Of the Stravinsky of *Le Sacre du Printemps,* Edmund Wilson once wrote, "He does not yield to the rhythms of the machines and attempt to compete with them, to reproduce them: he opposes to them rhythms of his own, the rhythms of titanic dances" (Wilson, 1958). *Agon* was constructivism in the computer age. "It is a machine," Balanchine said at the time, "but a machine that thinks."

It is a sobering fact that Balanchine, a prodigy who at the age of twenty had been Diaghilev's ballet master, had to wait until he was past forty for recognition in his chosen country. This finally came about in 1946 when the New York City Center of Music and Drama began to house regular seasons of a company of his own making—Ballet Society, rechristened in 1948 the New York City Ballet. It is at this point that the "American Era in Balanchine Ballet" begins to fade definitively into the "Balanchine Era in American Ballet." A decade after establishing residence at the City Center, Balanchine produced his tumultuous *Apollo–Square Dance–Agon–Stars and Stripes* season, proclaiming his own ascendancy and the coming of age of

American classical dancing. He had already proved that Americans belonged in ballet; now he seemed to be saying, ballet belonged in America.

In the quarter-century that was left to him, he choreographed incessantly, as fanciful and unpredictable as ever. His only restraint was budgetary, although in the early 1960s he spent money on spectacles (*The Figure in the Carpet, A Midsummer Night's Dream*), hoping to reverse the company's reputation for austere ballets and impoverished decor. As an artistic director working in the America of craft unions and commercialized theater, Balanchine preferred to get on with bare-stage productions rather than try to continue Diaghilev's search for innovative designers. Bare stages, in any case, suited his aesthetic, and he not infrequently stripped his dancers of cumbersome costumes. The architectural and ornamental variety of his choreography acted as a kind of built-in decor.

Diversity within unity became his hallmark. His poetic language, even in such breakaway experiments as *Ivesiana* (1954) and *Episodes* (1959), was never conceived *ab initio;* it was always a reconstructed language, filled with permutations and reversals or with habitual usages refitted to a new context. Unlike some other choreographers, he was not above the habitual. He often used old steps, trusting the rhythmic contours to make them new. Through the years, he adapted this language of his to widely differing musical scores, to exigencies of repertoire, and to particular dancers. His ability to think in broad dynamic patterns enabled him to change steps in his ballets without changing the overall effect. (The fact that he often adjusted his choreography to suit different dancers should not blind us to the harm that such adjustments can do when made by persons who lack his grasp of form.) He set no priority on personal expression; change in his work came about through practical estimates of what dancers needed to dance and audiences needed to see. As time passed, though, he relaxed his formal vigilance to the extent of permitting a more rhetorical influence on choreographic patterns of thought. Thus, *Chaconne* (1976) is more contextually an eighteenth-century vision than *Concerto Barocco*, and *Vienna Waltzes* is more concerned with the times and the customs than *Liebeslieder Walzer* (1960).

A major change occurred with the expectancy and then the realization of a new home—the New York State Theater at Lincoln Center, where the company moved in 1964. Having to create on a larger scale and having to attract a new audience seemed only to make Balanchine more Balanchinean. At Lincoln Center, he produced *Jewels* (1967), a pure-dance spectacle consisting of three separate ballets linked by terms of evocation and methods of exposition. By this time, Balanchine had succeeded in restructuring the audience's idea of an evening of dance entertainment. The process of recapitulation and forecast implicit in his most progressive ballets now took hold of the repertory at large, resulting in a number of nostalgic

essays at the heart of which would be a soloist of brilliance demonstrating the latest breakthroughs in technique. However we may organize the phases of his work, whatever value we may place on the importance of certain composers or certain dancers, there is always a cyclical subcurrent to undermine the tidy pace of chronology—the eternal return of the artist to his own mystery.

The Teacher. In his devotion to classicism, Balanchine himself claimed descent from Marius Petipa. His fifty-year mission in the United States recalls Petipa's fifty-five years of imperial service in Russia, although it was greater in the weight and scope of its achievement. Balanchine came to the United States in 1933 and, with Lincoln Kirstein, immediately set about opening a school. At the time there was no institutionalized ballet in the United States (as there had been in Russia before Petipa)—no national academy, no company of stature, no native repertoire. Balanchine sensed that his immediate task would be to establish the terms in which American classical dancers would be developed. He did not invent these terms. He taught the style of ballet he had learned in Russia, emphasizing and altering certain features to reflect

BALANCHINE. The quintessential Balanchine ballerina Tanaquil Le Clercq dances a role she created in *La Valse* (1951), set to the music of Maurice Ravel. Her costume was designed by Barbara Karinska. (Photograph by Walter E. Owen; from the Dance Collection, New York Public Library for the Performing Arts. Choreography by George Balanchine © The George Balanchine Trust.)

his ideal conception of it. In so doing, he instilled a fresh classical sensibility in his American dancers, one that set them apart from classical dancers everywhere else.

In his emphases and alterations, Balanchine differed from the majority of Russian pedagogues who were then at work in the United States and in other countries. He believed that classicism was not a set of rules to be perpetuated but a body of beliefs to be examined, clarified, and renewed from generation to generation. In the classroom, he sought new standards in the execution of steps, the aim being to increase clarity and breadth of motion, sharpness of nuance, and intensity of image. Balanchine dancers became renowned for their brilliance in allegro; they also mastered an even more distinctive adagio technique. In Balanchine, allegro and adagio are not polarized but complementary, each partaking of virtues once thought exclusive to the other: fullness of volume in allegro, crispness of accent in adagio. Open backs, hips lifted free of the thighs, and fully turned-out legs that are mobilized from the thigh—these features of the Balanchine physique account for the wide-angle arabesques that are another of the Balanchine dancer's trademarks. But again the importance of these electrifying poses (which may be unsupported as well as supported) is the principle of contradistinction that governs them. Balanchine wanted his dancers to be capable of turned-out movement on the largest possible scale (particularly after the New York State Theater became their home), but he also specified that, unlike Soviet dancers, they move from the smallest possible base of support, using the least amount of visible preparation. The typical *effacé* look of his women dancers was developed in relation to pointe work that became ever more particularized, pliant, and energetic. Because Balanchine-style pointe work employs the discipline of the whole leg, the feet absorb extra energy that is ultimately expended in a display of freedom and intricacy.

BALANCHINE. The "Waltz of the Snowflakes" from *The Nutcracker*, staged by Balanchine, after Lev Ivanov, in 1954 for the New York City Ballet. (Photograph by Fred Fehl; used by permission. Choreography by George Balanchine © The George Balanchine Trust.)

BALANCHINE. The ensemble of the New York City Ballet with Maria Tallchief (center) dancing a role Balanchine created for her in *Gounod Symphony* (1958). (Photograph by Fred Fehl; used by permission. Choreography by George Balanchine © The George Balanchine Trust.)

And because the closing of the feet in fifth position is unusually tight, a *relevé* in this position becomes the narrowest of firing pins for launching broad strokes in space.

Despite innovations of this kind, Balanchine was not a revolutionary; he merely extended and strengthened the logic of classical technique. As classical technique cultivates the body's ability to sustain two or more movement ideas at once, so the tendency of classical logic is to reconcile opposites: torso and arms moving in opposition may together oppose the legs. Oppositions in direction, in rhythm, in scale, in pressure are always harmoniously integrated. Thus Balanchine, generally speaking, extended classical technique by forcing its logic to encompass new oppositions or tensions and resolve them. Throughout the ballet syllabus, contradictory and unpredictable impulses were fused in refreshing new harmonies. These harmonies were the materials out of which Balanchine forged his characteristic drama.

Balanchine's best-known specialty was the making of ballerinas, and any discussion of his technical preferences automatically assumes a feminine coloration. If there is one area of technique in which he may be said to have truly innovated, it was pointe work. No other classical school produced ballerinas who have the maneuverability of the women trained by Balanchine. This does not mean that he did not also groom male dancers. The exceptional pointe work was simply an extension of Balanchine's idea, applicable to men as well as women, that the body's weight should be projected forward and up, never allowed to settle back on the heels. Neither does his exhaustive reconditioning of technique mean that other companies representing other schools of classicism cannot dance his ballets. Dancing Balanchine well is less a matter of enunciating steps than of phrasing them dynamically. This feature was built into Balanchine's training program at every level. Even the simplest and most fundamental movements were articulated with an accent that shaped them into expressive rhythmic units. A Balanchine *barre* was a progression of such units, inculcating detail by detail stylistic emphases in a coherent pattern. A musically sensitive dancer can dance Balanchine choreography without these emphases and still succeed. However, the performance will not have the depth that is imparted when the structural core of rote movements to which the dancer returns in daily practice is thoroughly Balanchinized.

In the company classes taught by Balanchine until the last years of his life, he preferred humdrum musical accompaniment (pianists were instructed to supply "wallpaper"), the better perhaps to isolate problems of stress, cadence, and attack. As a teacher, Balanchine reached rarefied heights in company class. This was his laboratory,

BALANCHINE. *The Figure in the Carpet* (1960), set to music by George Frideric Handel, was devised in the style of an eighteenth-century court ballet. In scene 3, the Prince and Princess of Persia received foreign ambassadors. Arthur Mitchell and Mary Hinkson, a guest artist, portrayed the Oni of Ife and His Consort. (Photograph by Martha Swope © Time, Inc.; used by permission. Choreography by George Balanchine © The George Balanchine Trust.)

where he refined his material and carried out perilous experiments in anatomical possibility. Dancers' capacities, spiritual as well as physical, were put to the test. Balanchine demanded total cooperation. He wanted his dancers to be unreservedly his, but he also expected from them a degree of self-motivation and was inclined to lose interest in the ones who did not show it. The ethical basis of his teaching was a concept of service. Performing in the theater meant a dedication of one's total energies not only at the moment of performance, but also in practice and in rehearsal. To be a Balanchine disciple meant that one gave one's all in the service of an ideal and in emulation of the master who was himself a servant. Balanchine's credo may well have been inspired by the Biblical injunction to let "he that is greatest among you . . . be your servant" (*Matthew* 23.11).

Although there came into being a recognizable "Balan-

chine technique," he himself never wrote a textbook, frequently revised or reversed himself, and was fond of saying that technique, in order to grow, had to come from the stage to the classroom, not the other way around. Underlying this principle was a commitment to performance—to the ineluctable "now" of the art. Within months of the founding of the School of American Ballet, Balanchine had his students on the stage testing his precepts under performance tension, without the cover of guest stars or the comfort of proven, popular choreography. In *Serenade*, they danced steps created for them and in a sense by them: Balanchine incorporated incidents—accidental falls, a late entrance—that had occurred in rehearsal. As time went on, he absorbed, classicized, and aggrandized the gifts of his dancers and so expanded the store of classical gesture inherited from Russia. Without Balanchine there would have been an American ballet but there would not have been an American style in ballet. It was his ability to make use of the newfound characteristics of his American dancers—their emotional objectivity no less than their speed and control of complex rhythm—that accounted for the persistence of his style through five decades.

The Poet. Balanchine's musicality long confined him, in the eyes of some critics, to the status of a sophisticated music visualizer. He himself insisted that there was no dramatic rationale in his ballets and that his only inspiration was the music. Because he used, for the most part, scores that had not been composed for dancing, he was seldom contradicted. Had he commissioned more music, he would surely have been suspected now and then of harboring ideas that he wanted to express. As things stood, Balanchine's practice of appropriating pieces of the world's finest music, dealing with them as he saw fit, without the intervention of a librettist or a scene designer, and naming the result after the score—for example, *Symphony in C* (1947), *Divertimento No. 15* (1956), and *Robert Schumann's "Davidsbündlertänze"* (1980)—enabled him to represent himself to the public as little more than a piece of blotting paper whose function was to draw out the meaning of the music, adding nothing to what was there.

In fact, there is such a thing as a Balanchinean world view. Its manifestations arise from music and are sustained by music. On rare occasions, they have been defeated by music. However they are always there because Balanchine's mastery of formal and figurative gesture was indistinguishable from his moral wisdom and sensuous refinement. His famous impersonality did not require that he keep himself out of the picture; he could not have done that if he tried. (He kept *self* out of the picture, a very different thing). Between the reading of a musical score and the shaping of its counterpart in movement there fell an influence that we can only call the mind of the poet. Without it, the mind of the musician would have been incapable of creating the masterpieces that were Balanchine's.

BALANCHINE. The original cast of Balanchine's *A Midsummer Night's Dream* (1962), with Arthur Mitchell as Puck (left, foreground), Edward Villella as Oberon, and Melissa Hayden as Titania. (Photograph by Fred Fehl; used by permission. Choreography by George Balanchine © The George Balanchine Trust.)

We see the two minds working together to create the very first masterpiece, *Apollo*. In one stroke, Balanchine grasped the principle of unity in the music and applied it to the "family relations" in dance movement. In an even more astonishing stroke, he perceived that the story of Stravinsky's *Apollo* was the story in allegorical terms of the development of a particular style of movement: academic ballet. Balanchine not only invented dozens of "family relations" for key movement themes—for example, the wide *croisé* pose in fourth position fondu in which Terpsichore begins her solo—but also linked them symbolically. Terpsichore's pose and the consistency of her *port de bras* as she steps out reappear in her pas de deux with Apollo, as, seated on his thigh, she merely changes her arms in fourth position to complete the echo and accomplish that perfect fusion of wills with the god of music. It is one of the ballet's most sublime achievements.

The crystallization into metaphor tells the eye it has been right to perceive one whole and ordained meaning in dancing so musically transparent. But the metaphors that seem special to *Apollo* turn up again in reconstituted form in later ballets and work just as well. If Balanchine's entire motivation were his music, this would not be the case. *Serenade* and many of his greatest works of the 1940s fasten on *Apollo*-like images that seem to clinch some positive and sought-for connection to the earlier ballet. Yet the differences are as great as the similarities. From *Concerto Barocco* on, Balanchine's metaphors tended to be instantaneous formations rather than the climax of the incident–pattern–metaphor progression out of which *Apollo* spins its dumbfounding revelations. This progression, though, is right at the heart of *Serenade*.

A complex, shuttling weave of such progressions, *Serenade* is a study in the making of movement metaphors. Its link to *Apollo* is seen in the opening pose of the corps as it stands looking up at the moon: the upraised arm with the palm flattened and turned outward derives from Apollo's salute in answer to the summons of Zeus just before the moment of consecration, when Apollo and the Muses prepare themselves for the ascent to Parnassus. *Serenade* depicts a different kind of consecration—one of mortals, not divinities—and it entails pain and sacrifice. The first phrase of choreography tells us as much when the upraised arm contracts, the back of the wrist comes to rest against the temple, and all these young women turn away from the light. Their eyes are averted, their gaze is shielded from the vastness of the fate that awaits them. Each of them, symbolically merged in the single figure of the ballerina, will by the end of the ballet have died in order to be reborn a dancer. In the opening phrase, it is as if each is brushed by the wing of death—or the eagle wing of Zeus. On this note of prophecy, the ballet begins. Feet open to the first position, slide to the side in tendu, and close in fifth. As the music brightens, the dancers become divinely inspired; arms rise from their sides like wings,

BALANCHINE. *Don Quixote* (1965), with Suzanne Farrell as Dulcinea and Balanchine as the title character. (Photograph by Fred Fehl; used by permission. Choreography by George Balanchine © by Suzanne Farrell.)

and they break ranks and fly, branching out on their various messianic errands. There is the onrushing sense of a pattern, and within a few seconds the ballet is in the grip of an extended metaphor. So began Balanchine's magnificent American debut.

As the graduation exercises of the School of American Ballet at the end of its first term, *Serenade* commemorates a historic occasion. As a theatrical poem, it is the core experience of *Apollo* transmuted and collectivized—adolescent epiphany darkened by overtones of trauma and broadened by communal images of love, loss, and immolation. But for all its spiritual links to the earlier ballet, it does not look like *Apollo*. *Serenade* is, in the language of its day, streamlined. The nascent classicism of *Apollo*, with its blunt sensations and its slow catalytic changes, has bloomed in a new-model, high-speed, urban paradise with sleek new-model women. Only in the final section (the Elegy) does the driving force of the ballet subside to a majestic progression, as in *Apollo*.

Balanchine's endowments, which allowed him to select the right pattern of movements and set them to the right piece of music, were complemented by an ability to create happenings on the stage that were incited neither by musical perceptions nor by pure dance invention. There existed for him a kind of raw material consisting of inci-

dents or gestures that could be integrated with the dance pattern and absorbed by the technical language while remaining identifiably and emblematically his—strokes of Balanchinean wit and fancy. This sort of idiosyncratic invention formed a big part of the early ballets and, when it returns in the later ones, it is essentially filigree. But it returns as late as *Robert Schumann's "Davidsbündlertänze"* (1980). Terpsichore's foot pawing the ground like a horse, the Muses' forward-pointing fingers, the Siren's mannequin strut in *The Prodigal Son*: these and other recurrent "Balanchine phenomena" can be seen as part of a personal code of meaning even though they do not always mean the same thing in each ballet. The shielded gaze, a familiar gesture in Balanchine and one that may have been borrowed from Slavic folk dancing, occurred as early as the Hand of Fate passage in *Cotillon*, where it seems to have accompanied a *femme fatale* theme. In *Serenade*, the gesture is keyed to the more solemn theme of blind fate that makes its appearance with the entrance of a Poet who is simultaneously guided and blinded by a Dark Angel, and this conception is undoubtedly a link to Balanchine's productions about Orpheus, both the Gluck opera (1936) and the Stravinsky ballet (1948). It is a recurrent Balanchine theme, appearing also in *Le Baiser de la Fée* and *Don Quixote*. But the Sleepwalker in *Night Shadow* (or *La Sonnambula*) and the sightless or blinded women of *Ivesiana* and *Stravinsky Violin Concerto* are not in the Orphic line, seeming to inhabit a psychological realm and a quite different order of dramatic suggestion.

An important rhetorical resource for Balanchine was classical archetypes and the mythopoeic aspects of art and of the ballet. Like other masters of the modern age, but more specifically like ballet masters of every age, he generated art from art. As a rendition in dance of ideas about dance, *Serenade* is more than a sequel to *Apollo*. Like *Le Baiser de la Fée* and numerous works to come, it annexes the territory of the Romantic ballet and is governed by a tragic muse. The heroine who dies to the world in order to achieve her salvation as an artist is a modern re-creation of Giselle. She and her companions are generically dancers whose spirits (as Wilis) once waltzed tirelessly on sacred ground by the light of the moon. Balanchine takes only one or two images and a scattering of dance steps from the old ballet. In the Elegy, intimations of Orpheus and Eurydice (on whose legend the scenario of *Giselle*'s second act is partially based) are combined with echoes of Canova's statue of Psyche and Amor in the ballet's most celebrated incident: as the Poet bends low over his beloved, Destiny flares her wings and bears him away.

Although dance, dancers, and past eras of ballet remained perennial subjects, references to specific moments in classic ballets eventually disappeared from Balanchine's poetic language. Like Stravinsky's quotations from other composers, Balanchine's allusions to classic ballets and other works of art were not used opportunistically as tags; rather they were anchors embedding elements of personal iconography in a classical nexus. Even the "Sistine ceiling" moment in *Apollo* is qualified by the emphasis Balanchine gives to Terpsichore's pose: one finger touches Apollo's, the other points away and off. She is the most resonant of the various Muse, Angel, or Fate figures who move through Balanchine's ballets, propelling his heroes to immortality. The Destiny figure of *Serenade*—the woman standing pressed to a man's back who suddenly moves her arms and gives him wings—may be a vertical transcription of Terpsichore poised prone on Apollo's bent shoulders and "swimming." We feel Terpsichore's iconographic power even in its nonrepresentational form, as in the pas de deux of *Concerto Barocco* or in the Theme sections of *The Four Temperaments*.

Classicism and the modes of classicism came to occupy Balanchine's full attention, and we must imagine the muse ever at his back, directing the transition that enabled him to produce, instead of dances about ideas about dance, dances about dance, dance as idea, and even dance as pure thought. Like Stravinsky, who held that music was powerless to express meanings outside itself but that it nevertheless bore the imprint of "the things of this world," Balanchine was adamant about the intent of his ballets. But he rejected the label "abstract." "If a boy takes a girl's hand," he would say, "it is already a love story." In fact, the poetic content of Balanchine's ballets is both more and less explicit than this. It is not always the case that a pas de deux is a love story. Very often Balanchine used the form to frame a woman's portrait, with the man acting as part of her setting. In the "love" duets, there is frequently a tension between the partners or between the woman's independent will and her need for the man. Alone of male choreographers in this century, Balanchine could see women approximately as they saw themselves. And he was one of the few choreographers who could use the human body, particularly the female body, as a medium of fantasy in one work after another and never unintentionally violate its humanity. In the same way that classicism was for him a comprehensive, not a restrictive, view of his art, the pas de deux, embodying all the things he knew or thought he might discover about women, was a microcosm of his imagination. It may have been his most fruitful form of composition; there is virtually no Balanchine ballet without one. *Symphonie Concertante* (1947), the only significant example of a Balanchine ballet without a central pas de deux, was never revived by its creator. One of his rare Mozart ballets, it was superseded in repertory by *Caracole* (1952), later revised as *Divertimento No. 15*— a major classic that reaches its peak in an extended pas de deux series. *Liebeslieder Walzer*, which is built almost entirely of pas de deux, is the most penetrating study of the form, and of the waltz, that anyone has yet contributed.

During his life, Balanchine was regarded by his dancers and colleagues as a universal genius; as W. H. Auden said,

"He's not an intellectual, he's something deeper, a man who understands everything." If the classical tradition did not already exist in the dance, Balanchine would have had to invent it; as it was, he expanded it to embrace physical and metaphysical, ethical, and aethestic implications Marius Petipa never dreamed of. He did this not by loading his choreography with extraneous profundities but by respecting the limitations of the medium and the nature of the truths it was designed to convey. The nineteenth-century ballet recognized in classical ideals an implicit principle of transcendence. Balanchine retained this faith by extending those ideals into the modern era. His ballerinas were not magic sylphs and swans but recognizable healthy Americans who engendered new forms of classical perfection and displayed them as honest accomplishment. The old ballets placed the fantasy of classical style at a distance from real life; the ballerina was an unattainable vision or a languishing creature doomed to an unreal existence. Balanchine blended fantasy and reality; if his women were unattainable it was because they were too interesting to belong to any one man—were, in fact, Balanchine superwomen. In ballets such as *Rubies*, *Ballo della Regina*, and *Tzigane*, these truths are conveyed so lightly and lucidly that they are accessible to us all.

Yet there is also an enigmatic side to Balanchine's work, a blending of fantasy and reality peculiar to the mind of the all-comprehending genius to whom Auden refers. The women are not only too interesting, but also fundamentally unknowable. Classical order reveals their beauty, and classical order is the mode of perception Balanchine relies on to carry his meanings to the audience. But running through these meanings, illuminating them from inside,

BALANCHINE. The original principals, Patricia McBride and Edward Villella, in *Rubies*, the second section of Balanchine's three-part suite *Jewels* (1967). It is set to Stravinsky's Capriccio for Piano and Orchestra. (Photograph by Fred Fehl; used by permission. Choreography by George Balanchine © The George Balanchine Trust.)

BALANCHINE. In 1970, Balanchine mounted *Tchaikovsky Suite No. 3*, using his earlier work *Theme and Variations* (1947) as the fourth movement. Here, Gelsey Kirkland is seen at the center of the female ensemble. (Photograph by Fred Fehl; used by permission. Choreography by George Balanchine © The George Balanchine Trust.)

is a vein of mystical apprehension. Balanchine's religious beliefs were fixed early. His uncle was a bishop of the Russian Orthodox Church; he himself was a lifelong communicant. His ballets cannot be called religious art in the same sense in which the term is applied to the music of Bach or Handel. It is rather that, in Balanchine, religion, philosophy, aesthetics, and morality are all governed by one vision. The balance between mysticism, which requires a receptiveness bordering on the passive, and classical order, which makes vigilance a constant necessity, was a balance exactly congenial to Balanchine's nature. His ballets are journeys of wondrous unpredictability, which we can take again and again, year after year. Some of the most wondrous—*The Prodigal Son, Ballet Imperial, The Nutcracker, The Four Temperaments*—seem to contain every variety of experience. Even in the most concentrated, most austere reaches of his art, Balanchine's mind was open to paradox and ambiguity. In *Concerto Barocco, Liebeslieder Walzer, Mozartiana*, the path is steep, the air may grow thin, but the vista is never narrow.

The Showman. If American audiences, faced with a novelty called ballet, needed a Balanchine to educate them, Balanchine for his part needed to create for an audience as free of knowledge and therefore of prejudice as Americans were. By the time he settled in at the New York City Center, he had evolved an unspoken policy of appealing to this audience over the heads of critics and other guardians of taste who had been dismissive or uncomprehending of his efforts since the 1930s. The problem then was that Balanchine was too modern for connoisseurs of Russian ballet, the only known brand, and too classical for followers of modern dance, the only serious dance tradition in the United States. Both camps found him cold and superficial.

On Broadway, he raised show dancing to a new elegance and managed to attract a following, for which he was patronizingly congratulated. In his first Rodgers and Hart show, *On Your Toes* (1936), he produced a hit ballet, "Slaughter on Tenth Avenue," and in another number he pointedly satirized the Ballet Russe. To Balanchine, who was determined to put the "russe" legend behind him, the energy of American popular music and dancing was inspiring, and he proposed certain basic features of popular style as self-evident values in the ballets he was offering to the American public. His pedagogical approach to audiences, as to dancers, was based on the conviction that no lesson was worth teaching to pupils who were unwilling to learn for themselves or who relied on the explanations of "experts." At the City Center, he spent little on publicity, refused to court opinion, flouted fashion, and in general behaved as if his only obligation to the public was to put on the best ballets he could create, danced by the best dancers he could afford. A declared enemy of the star system, he was the first to bill dancers alphabetically, and he never announced casts more than a week in advance.

Frequently, Balanchine's idea of what ballet could be defied the comfortable expectations of his audience. His productions of *Firebird* (1949), *Swan Lake*, and *The Nutcracker* dismayed those who saw him as an avant-gardist. After *Western Symphony* (1954), *Square Dance* (1957, originally produced with a spiel by a caller), and *Stars and Stripes* (1958), he was accused of cynicism and jingoism. These "commercial" ballets of Balanchine contained as much Balanchine as his "advanced" ones; he did not expect the audience he was cultivating to discriminate snobbishly between them. He once complained to a journalist, "I understand people who love *Stars and Stripes* and hate *Episodes*. What I don't understand are the people who love *Episodes* and hate *Stars and Stripes*."

The sector of opinion regularly and vastly offended by Balanchine—the balletomane public nurtured on foreign companies—was much larger and more vocal in the 1960s than it had been in the 1930s. As he did not produce "the classics" and promote stars in the manner of Sol Hurok and the Royal Ballet, Balanchine was an automatic target for those who claimed that the United States had no classical ballet, that what the Royal or the Bolshoi or the Kirov companies offered was the real thing and "Balanchine-ballet" was only an offshoot. In addition, diehard anti-Balanchine opinion held that he was distorting classical technique and ruining talent as a consequence, and this opinion was supported by many professional dancers and teachers. But the growing body of dance lovers who attended New York City Ballet performances saw extensions rather than distortions in technique. For the most part, though, they were oblivious of the charges against Balanchine and of the controversy that erupted when, at virtually one and the same moment, his company was announced for the new theater at Lincoln Center and was chosen along with the School of American Ballet and al-

lied companies (San Francisco Ballet and Pennsylvania Ballet among them) to receive the first Ford Foundation grants to dance. (Balanchine's organization was denounced as a monopoly, when in fact it was the only one prepared to administer a national program to improve the quality of training and performance in American ballet.)

All this Balanchine withstood. He had worked for the great showmen of his era, from Diaghilev to C. B. Cochran and Samuel Goldwyn, and he continued to rely on the public's instinct for entertainment (he preferred the word to "art"), and on his own ability to produce it. In the end he was vindicated. But it was not until the 1970s that the controversy surrounding his name and practice died away and his pact with the great audience was sealed. This audience, which had previously endorsed isolated "hits"—*Firebird*, *Swan Lake*, the 1958 revival of *The Seven Deadly Sins*, *The Nutcracker*, and *Jewels*—now became party to large-scale "family" endeavors of the New York City Ballet: the Stravinsky, Ravel, and Tchaikovsky festivals, the panoramic productions *Union Jack* (1976) and *Vienna Waltzes*. This was Balanchine showmanship more or less splashily displayed. It was also the culmination of a series

BALANCHINE. Peter Martins and Suzanne Farrell in Balanchine's *Chaconne* (1976), set to the finale of Gluck's opera *Orfeo ed Euridice*. (Photograph by Max Waldman; used by permission. Choreography by George Balanchine © The George Balanchine Trust.)

of strategic choices begun forty years earlier by an artist for whom no audience existed and the sky, therefore, was the limit. In making himself responsible to the public for almost the whole of its knowledge of ballet, he had become a protean master—now a modernist, now a conservative, now an austere classicist, now an impassioned nineteenth-century romantic. The phases were not successive; they were simultaneous. Balanchine was an inveterate mixer: modern-classical (*Concerto Barocco, The Four Temperaments, Agon*), classical-romantic (*Serenade, La Valse*), conservative-classical-romantic (*Swan Lake, Scotch Symphony*); conservative-modern (*Allegro Brillante*), modern-romantic (*Ivesiana*), romantic-austere (*Liebeslieder Walzer*), or classical-popular (*Harlequinade, Who Cares?*). The audience learned that there were no categorical restrictions on its ability to understand and enjoy dance. One did not have to know dance history or aesthetics, although obviously the more one knew, the more one could appreciate Balanchine's learning and grasp of tradition. The way he saw classicism, as a cavalcade of eras and idioms, derived directly from exotic Maryinsky and Paris Opera spectacles such as *The Daughter of the Pharoah, La Sylphide*, and *La Bayadère*. As Petipa had done before him, Balanchine reincarnated the variety of the past and—there being no past tense in dance—projected it in contemporary terms.

Although Balanchine's ballets were not designed to teach lessons, like every great body of work they are perpetually enlightening in many ways at once. To an overeducated, puritanical audience, they teach the lesson that art is pleasure. To a mindless audience, they say that art is work. To the artist in any art, they give hope that by striving to please himself he will please others. The saga of Balanchine and his audience is an important chapter in American cultural history. His art reproaches the arts-educational system not least in the way it represents the triumph of the individual over any system whatsoever. Because Balanchine found a way to deal with the public directly, not from behind a screen of agents, packagers, and publicity men, the New York City Ballet became a force in the city's intellectual life—the only ballet company to do so. It was one of the few creative institutions in the world in whose presence people of intelligence could feel happily connected to the times in which they lived.

[*See also* American Ballet; Ballet Caravan; New York City Ballet; *and the following entries on Balanchine ballets:* Agon; Apollo; Ballet Imperial; Concerto Barocco; Cotillon; Divertimento No. 15; Don Quixote, *article on* Balanchine Production; Four Temperaments, The; Liebeslieder Walzer; Prodigal Son, The; Serenade; *and* Symphony in C.]

BIBLIOGRAPHY

Amberg, George. *Ballet: The Emergence of an American Art*. New York, 1949.

Ashley, Merrill. *Dancing for Balanchine*. New York, 1984.

Balanchine, George. "Notes on Choreography." *Dance Index* 4 (February-March 1945): 20–41.

Balanchine, George, with Francis Mason. *Balanchine's Complete Stories of the Great Ballets*. Rev. and enl. ed. Garden City, N. Y., 1977.

Balanchine, George. "The Dance Elements in Stravinsky's Music." *Ballet Review* 10 (Summer 1982): 14–18.

Balanchine, George. *By George Balanchine*. New York, 1984.

Ballet Review 11 (Fall 1983): 81–96. Symposium entitled "Staging Balanchine's Ballets."

Ballet Review 19 (Winter 1991): 61–97. Proceedings of a symposium entitled "Balanchine as Teacher."

Buckle, Richard. *George Balanchine: Ballet Master*. New York, 1988.

Choreography by George Balanchine: A Catalogue of Works. New York, 1983.

Crisp, Clement. "Balanchine's Operas." *Ballet Review* 16 (Fall 1988): 43–44.

Croce, Arlene. "Balanchine: Servant and Master." In *The New York City Ballet in Fort Worth*. Fort Worth, Texas, 1981. Souvenir program.

Croce, Arlene. *Going to the Dance*. New York, 1982.

Dance Magazine 57 (July 1983). Special issue commemorating Balanchine's work.

Daniels, Don. "Academy: The New World of *Serenade*." *Ballet Review* 5.1 (1975–1976): 1–12.

Denby, Edwin. *Dance Writings*. Edited by Robert Cornfield and William Mackay. New York, 1986.

Emerson, Jane, ed. *George Balanchine: A Reference Guide*. New York, 1987.

Garis, Robert. *Following Balanchine*. New Haven, 1995.

Gold, Arthur, and Robert Fizdale. "George Balanchine, 1904–1983." *New York Review of Books* (2 June 1983).

Greskovic, Robert. "School for Style." *Dance Theatre Journal* 1 (May 1983): 25–27.

Grigoriev, Serge. *The Diaghilev Ballet, 1909–1929*. Translated and edited by Vera Bowen. London, 1953.

Haggin, B. H. *Discovering Balanchine*. New York, 1981.

Hunt, Marilyn. "The Prodigal Son's Russian Roots: Avant-Garde and Icons." *Dance Chronicle* 5.1 (1982): 24–49.

Jordan, Stephanie. "Music Puts a Time Corset on the Dance." *Dance Chronicle* 16.3 (1993): 295–321.

Kahn, Marion Clare, and Susan Au. "Balanchine: A Selected Bibliography" (parts 1–2). *Ballet Review* 11.2 (1983): 9–11; 11.3 (1983): 97–99.

Kendall, Elizabeth B. *Dancing: A Ford Foundation Report*. New York, 1983.

Kirstein, Lincoln. *Thirty Years: The New York City Ballet*. New York, 1978.

Kirstein, Lincoln. *Ballet, Bias, and Belief: Three Pamphlets Collected and Other Dance Writings*. New York, 1983.

Kirstein, Lincoln. *Portrait of Mr. B: Photographs of George Balanchine*. New York, 1984.

Lowry, McNeil. "Conversations with Balanchine." *The New Yorker* (12 September 1983).

Lowry, McNeil. "Conversations with Kirstein." *The New Yorker* (15–22 December 1986).

Maiorano, Robert, and Valerie Brooks. *Balanchine's "Mozartiana": The Making of a Masterpiece*. New York, 1985.

Mason, Francis. *I Remember Balanchine: Recollections of the Ballet Master by Those Who Knew Him*. New York, 1991.

McDonagh, Don. *George Balanchine*. Boston, 1983.

Museum of Broadcasting. *A Celebration of George Balanchine: The Television Work*. New York, 1984.

Pierpont, Claudia Roth. "Balanchine's Romanticism." *Ballet Review* 12 (Summer 1984): 6–17.

Reynolds, Nancy. *Repertory in Review: Forty Years of the New York City Ballet.* New York, 1977.

Reynolds, Nancy. "The Red Curtain: Balanchine's Reception in the Soviet Union." In *Proceedings of the Fifteenth Annual Conference, Society of Dance History Scholars, University of California, Riverside, 14–15 February 1992,* compiled by Christena L. Schlundt. Riverside, Calif., 1992.

Scholl, Tim. "Balanchine's 'Blessed Vision.'" *Ballet Review* 19 (Summer 1991): 28–29.

Schorer, Suki. *Balanchine Pointework.* Edited by Lynn Garafola. Madison, Wis., 1995.

Shearer, Moira. *Balletmaster: A Dancer's View of George Balanchine.* London, 1986.

Slonimsky, Yuri. "Balanchine: The Early Years." Translated by John Andrews. *Ballet Review* 5.2 (1975–1976): 1–64.

Souritz, Elizabeth. "The Young Balanchine in Russia." *Ballet Review* 18 (Summer 1990): 66–71.

Stravinsky, Igor, and Robert Craft. *Dialogues.* Berkeley, 1982.

Stravinsky, Vera, and Robert Craft. *Stravinsky in Pictures and Documents.* New York, 1978.

Taper, Bernard. *Balanchine: A Biography.* New rev. ed. New York, 1984.

Vaughan, David. "Balanchine: Lost and Found." *Ballet Review* 16 (Fall 1988): 45–46.

White, Eric W. *Stravinsky: The Composer and His Works.* 2d ed. Berkeley, 1979.

Wilson, Edmund. *The American Earthquake: A Documentary of the Twenties and Thirties.* Garden City, N.Y., 1958.

ARLENE CROCE

BALASARASWATI (Tanjore Balasaraswati; born 13 May 1918 in Madras, died 9 February 1984 in Madras), Indian dancer. Balasaraswati was considered the embodiment of the Tanjore style of *bharata nāṭyam,* and in accordance with regional custom she added the name of this South Indian city to her own. She represented the seventh generation of a family primarily concerned with the performance of classical music and dance. Her ancestor Papammal, the earliest known dancer and musician in her family, performed at the Tanjore court during the eighteenth century.

Balasaraswati was the only daughter of Modarapu Govindarajulu and his wife Jayammal, an eminent vocalist. Balasaraswati and her four brothers were reared in the home of their grandmother, Veena Dhanam, where art figured prominently in family life. Two of the brothers, flutist Viswanathan and drummer Ranganathan, became noted performers and teachers in India and North America.

Mylapore Gowri Amma, a fine dancer of the period, convinced Balasaraswati's mother to train her four-year-old daughter in dance, despite a general decline of the art at the time. Jayammal engaged the dance master Kandappa Pillai, a descendant of one member of the mid-nineteenth-century Tanjore Quartet, four brothers who redefined dance traditions, codified the training system for dancers, choreographed, and composed music for repertory still performed in concert today.

Kandappa remained Balasaraswati's teacher until his premature death in 1941. An unrelenting taskmaster, he provided his only notable student with a thorough grounding in the essential elements defining the aesthetics of his style: correct placement and line of limb and gesture; proper stance, tempo, and form in each *adavu* (pure movement phrase); and grace of execution and phrasing. At the same time, Jayammal and Veena Dhanam coached her in the subtle relationship between contour of melodic line and movement. Kandappa presented Balasaraswati in her debut when she was only seven. Connoisseurs were astounded by the child's facility and maturity of interpretation in *abhinaya* (expressive mime) passages and by the clarity, precision, and grace of execution in complex *thīrmanam*s (concluding rhythmic passages).

The young prodigy began performing regularly and continued to perform for more than fifty years. Jayammal accompanied her as vocalist until the early 1960s; Kandappa acted as her dance master until his death, when his son, Kandappa Ganesan, replaced him; he was followed by his primary student, Kalyanasundaram Ramaiah. The extraordinary quality of musical accompaniment in her concerts lent a unique artistic strength to Balasaraswati and drew acclaim from established musicians in India and abroad. Uday Shankar introduced her to northern Indian audiences in 1936. The cumulative effect of an active career and continuous refinement of her art enabled Balasaraswati to reach the highest rank in her field.

Balasaraswati studied improvisation in *abhinaya* with Chinnayya Naidu and, in her thirties, with the renowned master of Kuchipudi dance drama, Vedantam Lakshminarayana Sastri. Under the aegis of the Madras Music Academy, Balasaraswati in 1953 opened a small school where she instructed young Indian girls and an occasional American student.

In 1955 Balasaraswati was the first person from South India to receive the newly established Presidential Award through the Sangeet Natak Akademi, New Delhi. In 1977 the government of India bestowed on her the title of Padma Vibhushan (Exemplary Golden Lotus), usually awarded to outstanding statesmen and scholars. She received an honorary doctorate from Rabindra Bharati University (1964), as well as numerous other public commendations. In 1973 she was elected presiding president of the Forty-seventh Music Academy Conference at Madras and honored with the title Sangita Kalanidhi (Musical Treasure).

Connoisseurs outside India were first exposed to Balasaraswati's artistry in 1961 at the East/West Music Encounter in Tokyo; by 1981, she had accepted eleven invitations to tour and teach in America and Europe. She

BALASARASWATI. One of India's most celebrated dancers, Balasaraswati epitomizes the Tanjore style of *bharata nāṭyam.* During her fifty-year career, she created more than two hundred solos and several dance dramas. (Photograph from the archives at Jacob's Pillow, Becket, Massachusetts.)

appeared in eight concerts at the Edinburgh Festival in 1963 after her first North American tour in 1962, which began at Jacob's Pillow and included a residency at Wesleyan University that was sponsored by New York's Asia Society. Her appearances inspired the formation in 1965 of the American Society for Eastern Arts in Berkeley, California, as well as that in 1976 of Asian Traditions, which that year established the Balasaraswati School of Music and Dance in Berkeley. The two institutions sponsored Balasaraswati in tours and residence programs of their own (1965, 1966, 1974, 1977, 1978) and at Wesleyan University (1968, 1980, 1981), the University of California at Los Angeles (1968), the University of Washington (1968, 1973), the California Institute for the Arts (1972), and the American Dance Festival (1977, 1978). During these years she taught hundreds of Americans and was seen by thousands in concert.

Balasaraswati's supremacy in *abhinaya* remained unchallenged. The deceptively effortless grace she employed in pure dance sections revealed her singular artistry in the exacting patterns of complex rhythmic passages. The nature of her art was not to astound but to enhance the general aim of *bharata nāṭyam:* to nourish the spectator's spiritual and aesthetic experience. The dance critic Anna Kisselgoff wrote:

The expressiveness of Balasaraswati's gestures, the depth of the emotions she registers and the concentration that pervades her figure all go beyond mere entertainment to suggest quiet ecstasy. In one flash, the sacred origins of Indian classical dance become clear.
(Kisselgoff, 1977)

Balasaraswati's dance repertory of more than 200 solos and several dance dramas was transmitted to her daughter, Lakshmi Knight, who is now a dancer in her own right and carries forward the family tradition. Balasaraswati's young grandson, Aniruddha Knight, also shows great aptitude for music and dance.

[*See also the entry on Knight.*]

BIBLIOGRAPHY

Balasaraswati. "Music and the Dance." *Quarterly Journal of the National Centre for the Performing Arts* 2 (December 1973): 41–45.

Balasaraswati. "Bharata Natyam." *Quarterly Journal of the National Centre for the Performing Arts* 5 (December 1976): 1–8.

Balasaraswati. "On Bharata Natyam." *Dance Chronicle* 2.2 (1978): 106–116.

"Balasaraswati Dances into Ecstasy." *New York Times* (9 August 1977).

Balasaraswati School of Music and Dance. *Balasaraswati: A Tribute to the Artist and Her Art.* N.p., 1986.

Higgins, Jon B. *The Music of Bharata Nāṭyam.* New Delhi, 1993.

Kisselgoff, Anna. "Asian Dance: Is It 'Ethnic' or Classical?" *New York Times* (13 March 1977).

Meri, La. "Encounters with Dance Immortals: Balasaraswati and Ragini Devi." *Arabesque* 11 (November–December 1985): 12–13.

Narayana Menon. *Balasaraswati.* New Delhi, c.1963.

Poursine, Kay. "Hasta as Discourse on Music: T. Balasaraswati and Her Art." *Dance Research Journal* 23 (Fall 1991): 17–23.

Quarterly Journal of the National Centre for the Performing Arts 13 (June 1984). Obituary for Balasaraswati with excerpts from her writings and comments by Narayana Menon and Satyajit Ray.

Van Zile, Judy, and Jon B. Higgins. "Balasaraswati's *Tisram alarippu.*" In *Performing Arts in India*, edited by Bonnie C. Wade. Berkeley, 1983.

FILMS.   *Balasaraswati* (1962). Satyajit Ray, *Krishna ni begane baro* (1976).

LUISE ELCANESS SCRIPPS

BALET COMIQUE DE LA ROYNE, LE. A court spectacle generally considered to be the first ballet, *Le Balet Comique de la Royne* was performed at the French court in the Salle de Bourbon of the Louvre on 15 October 1581. The climax to a two-week-long celebration in honor of the wedding of King Henri III's favorite, the duc de Joyeuse, to the queen's sister, Mademoiselle de Vaudemont, it was the first attempt to combine music, dance, and poetry to tell a story. Of the many festivities organized for this occasion, known from a surviving manuscript program, only *Le Balet Comique* is documented, in a book published by the king's printers, Adrian Le Roy, Robert Ballard, and Mamert Patisson, accorded a royal privilege on 13 February 1582. The fact that only this performance was recorded may be interpreted as both a recognition of its political importance and a sign of its artistic significance. Certainly it is a remarkable work, and its creators were clearly aware of its exceptional qualities.

The performance, commissioned by the queen mother, Catherine de Médicis, lasted five hours. It begins to the sound of melodious music with the arrival of the queen's gentleman, playing Ulysses, before the king's dais in the center of the Great Hall. There Ulysses recites a long speech explaining how he and his companions have, through greed, given themselves up to the evil powers of the enchantress Circe and have been transformed into wild animals. He has temporarily regained his human shape and has come to plead for his freedom. Only a greater power can overcome Circe's magic, and Ulysses is confident that Henri III has that power. Circe suddenly appears at the end of his speech and gives a resounding account of her magical powers, which she intends to deploy without pity.

The stage is set for a demonstration through music and dance of two different orders of power—the evil magic of Circe against the virtuous strength of the king. The latter's powers are displayed through a triumph of sea creatures, Sirens and Tritons, who form the suite of the gods Glau-

cus and Thetis and sing the praises of the French royal house. Twelve pages and then twelve naiads dance with joy at the prospect of enjoying the king's protection. Their dance is brutally interrupted by the sudden return of Circe, who with one stroke of her wand immobilizes the dancers. Circe departs triumphant.

Almost immediately, a thunderclap heralds the arrival of Mercury, who brings the herb moly, with which he anoints the dancers; they resume their steps as though the ballet had never been disturbed. The sound of music and dancing brings Circe back; she immobilizes the dancers once more and stays to explain how she controls all desire for change in the universe, whatever its source—natural, moral, or political. To display her power she restores movement to the dancers and to Mercury, constrains them to dance to her orders, and eventually obliges them to repair to her enchanted palace. Ulysses' companions, the powers of the sea, and Mercury are now all at her command.

A new phase of the ballet begins with the arrival of satyrs and wood nymphs disturbed by Circe's triumph. They seek the help of Pan, who has the gift of making things change. He agrees to act and, in company with Minerva, the cardinal virtues, and Jupiter, presents himself before the king. To overcome Circe, they will need his strength as well as their own powers.

When confronted by such an accumulation of forces, Circe at first appears confident. The presence of the king of France, however, is the decisive factor; the enchantress is finally overcome and is led before Henri III and forced to recognize his unassailable authority. Harmony is thus restored, and in celebration the dancers join with members of the court in a ball.

A power struggle is the dramatic center of *Le Balet Comique*, as it was to form the focus of many a tragedy. Here, however, its demonstration and resolution are achieved not through mere words but through a successful combination of speech, music, and dance. At court festivities earlier in the sixteenth century, similar combinations had been attempted—at Bayonne in 1565, for instance, and in two works of Balthazar de Beaujoyeulx, the *Paradis d'Amour* in 1572 and *Le Ballet des Polonais* in 1573. Yet these earlier efforts were not so grand in scope, so complex in design, or so successful in terms of coherence and artistic and technical ambitions.

Although Beaujoyeulx was its principal creator, *Le Balet Comique* was a collaborative effort. The king's almoner, the sieur de la Chesnaye, wrote all the poems, based on Natale Conti's *Mythologiae;* Lambert de Beaulieu, who was associated with Joachim Thibault de Courville, the founder of the Académie de Musique et de Poésie, composed the music with the aid of Jacques Salmon. The decor—mobile machines and other elements scattered around the Great Hall—was devised by Jacques Patin,

LE BALET COMIQUE DE LA ROYNE. The Four Virtues, as rendered by Jacques Patin, for this 1581 court spectacle, considered to be the first ballet. Commissioned by Catherine de Médicis as the culmination of a two-week celebration in honor of the marriage of the duc de Joyeuse and Mademoiselle de Vaudemont, the five-hour *Ballet Comique* combined music, dance, and poetry. (Courtesy of Elizabeth Aldrich.)

who also supplied the engravings for the printed text. Unfortunately, Patin's drawings do not give us a clear idea of the nature of the dancing, but the text provides much detail of the ballet figures and of the general artistic intentions of Beaujoyeulx and his colleagues.

To live up to the standards of novelty, beauty, and variety required by Henri III, Beaujoyeulx constructed a well-proportioned work that would appeal equally to the eye, the ear, and the understanding. He claimed in his preface to *Balet Comique* to achieve this balance by a judicious mix of dance and music: "blending the two together, diversifying the music with verse, lacing the poetry with music, and, most often, fusing them together." Indeed, *Le Balet Comique* is a seamless garment, and in this sense it is unique. All attempts to cut the work up into acts, interludes, scenes, or episodes have failed to convince. Contemporaries were aware of this seamlessness. In the preliminary poems to the published work, the poets Volusian and A. Costé comment on its novelty and on the unusual intertwining of music, dance, and verse, which they attribute to the knowledge Beaujoyeulx and his colleagues had of similar works in ancient Greece.

Music played a dominant role in making the work a cohesive whole. The bands of musicians in the heavenly vault and in Pan's wood remained present throughout the performance as players and dancers came and went. They accompanied the solos that alternated with larger ensembles of six, eight, or twelve voices. Sometimes as many as forty instrumentalists played together, with as many voices, to produce harmonies appropriate to a heavenly vault. The music changed with its dance function: for the *clochette* (bell dance) performed at the beginning of the ballet, the music is described as "new and full of bright gaiety," whereas during the final grand ballet, violins played fifteen different movements.

According to Claude Billard, who dedicated a poem to Beaujoyeulx, the entire concept of dancing in *Le Balet Comique* was novel, inspired by ancient Greece, where dancing and geometry had much in common. To be a choreographer at the end of the sixteenth century was to be a learned man, and Billard applauded Beaujoyeulx for his inventiveness and ingenuity, but above all for his scholarship.

The choreographer himself in his preface drew the reader's attention to the central role dancing was to play in his work: "I have given the principal title and honor to the dance." He went on to define dance as "a mixture of geometrical movements made from several people dancing together to different harmonies made by a diversity of musical instruments." The first ballet of twelve pages and twelve nymphs corresponds to this definition; they performed twelve geometrical figures before they were enchanted by Circe.

Similarly, at the end of *Le Balet Comique*, water nymphs and wood nymphs came together to dance fifteen different movements, each one calculated to bring them directly facing the king at the end of the dance. Once there, they performed a complex dance comprising forty different figures, which required them to trace geometric patterns on the floor—round, square, or triangular, of diverse size, and consisting of different steps. No sooner had the naiads completed their dance than the dryads took over "in such a manner that each observer thought that Archimedes could not better understand geometric proportions than these princesses and ladies who practiced them so expertly in this ballet."

The spectacular nature of the dancing impressed contemporaries, but almost more important were its harmonious effects. The assault on Circe's garden, toward the end of *Le Balet Comique*, was clearly a stylized struggle, reminiscent of the mock combats that had graced festivals in European Renaissance courts; however, other dances displayed a preoccupation with patterns and geometric figures. These, careful of shape and proportion, represented the harmonies that sixteenth-century poets and thinkers perceived in the heavens. These natural and moral harmonies were what Circe had sought to disrupt and what the French king had championed. His victory over Circe was at once a reestablishment of harmony in the moral and philosophical spheres and a confirmation of political concord under a strong and just monarch. The shifts from threatening disruption to peace and prosperity were played out both through the myth of Circe and, more concretely, through the complicated movements of the dance.

According to sixteenth-century theories, dance brought the world into being; from original chaos, it created the ball of stars, ensuring that the planets move in proportion and harmony. That influential role is reenacted in *Le Balet Comique* when Circe threatens to return the world to chaos. In many ways, then, the work is the culmination of artistic effort and exploration that go well back into the early sixteenth century. It is also a beginning in France, demonstrating that song, dance, word, and spectacle could be satisfactorily blended, giving rise to a new art form—the court ballet—which was to survive for almost three centuries and influence the festivities presented in European courts for many generations.

[*See also* Renaissance Dance Technique; Scenic Design; *and the entry on Beaujoyeulx.*]

BIBLIOGRAPHY

Caula, Giacomo A., ed. *Balet Comique de la Royne, 1582.* Turin, 1965.

Christout, Marie-Françoise. "Le Balet Comique de la Royne and the Ballet de Cour." Translated by Anna Kisselgoff. *Dance Chronicle* 6.3 (1983): 267–272.

Delmas, E. "*Le Balet Comique:* Structure et signification." *Revue d'Histoire du Théâtre* 2 (1970): 142–156.

Hardy, Camille. "Balet Comique de la Reine: A Primer on Subtext and Symbol." In *Proceedings of the Fifth Annual Conference, Society of Dance History Scholars, Harvard University, February 1982,* compiled by Christena L. Schlundt. Riverside, Calif., 1982.

MacClintock, Carol, and Lander MacClintock, trans. *Balet Comique de la Royne, 1581.* N.p., 1971. English translation and modern transcription of the music.

McGowan, Margaret M. *L'art du ballet de cour en France, 1581–1643.* Paris, 1963.

McGowan, Margaret M., ed. *Le Balet Comique by Balthazar de Beaujoyeulx, 1581.* Binghamton, N.Y., 1982.

Prudhommeau, Germaine. "A propos du Balet-comique de la Reine." *Recherche en Danse,* no. 3 (June 1984): 13–24.

Yates, Frances A. *The French Academies of the Sixteenth Century.* London, 1947.

Yates, Frances A. "Poésie et musique dans les *Magnificences* au mariage du duc de Joyeuse, Paris, 1581." In *Musique et poésie au XVIe siècle.* Paris, 1954. Reprinted in Yates's *Astraea* (London, 1975).

MARGARET M. McGOWAN

BALI. *See* Indonesia, *articles on Balinese Dance Traditions. For discussion in a broader context, see* Asian Dance Traditions.

BALL. The dance term *ball* (French, *bal*) is associated primarily with western European formal and ceremonial occasions for social dancing, yet the etymology of the word has deep primal associations with confrontation and battle. (These associations have long been exploited by wits and journalists who throughout the centuries have found humor in ballroom encounters and social maneuvering.) For example, both the necessary order of the event and the dancing relate to social ideals of harmony and agreement, and the term *ball* also recalls celestial bodies and the cosmos as well as the golden orb as symbols of power. On the other hand, ball participants were sometimes disorderly. Some view the term *ball* as a corruption of *brawl*—in some instances in literature the two words are used interchangeably—and in the nineteenth and early twentieth centuries country balls sometimes ended in fights. This association with social imperfections mirrored in turmoil is reflected in the term's connotations as a globular body to play with and knock about, a firearm projectile, and a pyrotechnical and military display. Such displays were commonly accompanied by a formal dancing party, and the two events, apparent disorder contrasting with ostensible order, were appreciated intellectually and poetically as one. The ballroom itself has been an arena wherein participants tacitly played with the term's duality of meanings—creation and destruction—through powerful and symbolic actions of ceremonial conduct and dancing.

BALL. A formal dance gathering. This lithograph by A. Faivre was printed in the 1860s treatise entitled *Le Cotillon* by the French writer LeBorde. (Courtesy of Elizabeth Aldrich.)

G. Desrat, author of *Dictionnairè de la danse* (Paris, 1895), defined three kinds of balls that were known internationally before the eighteenth century and that still survive but in modified forms: (1) the ball given by a head of state for representatives and dignitaries in honor of an event and by invitation, (2) the ball given by the head of an affluent private house by invitation, with guests often in costume, masks, or *en travesti*, and (3) the ball arranged by a committee for which tickets are purchased.

Historically the origin and development of balls parallels that of classical Western dance choreography and theatrical performance. According to Ingrid Brainard, *balli*, or ballets—social dances composed by dancing teachers for their elite pupils to display at court—were first recorded during the Renaissance in Italy. *Balli* necessitated careful planning and attention because the intimate gathering for these dances and the dances themselves had more elaborate programs, themes expressed by the dances, and enacted drama. The entertainment required rehearsal as well as command of the technical virtuosity and ease in performance, which were desirable in individuals—men and women—at court. Good dancing expressed the acquisition of manners and social grace. Later balls evolved from these largely nonverbal but literate and restricted entertainments. For hosts and guests alike the formal dancing party was a mirror. It both reflected and displayed individuals in the significance of the occasion; it called attention to host and guests' social power. Balls in court and among the aristocracy proliferated as a dramatic and political device to symbolize authority as the bourgeois class and commercial interests grew and tested monarchical influence. Occasions for formal dancing drew clear attention to wealth and defined status, skills, and roles of the ball participants as older power hierarchies floundered.

Places, occasions, and audiences for balls multiplied in the eighteenth and nineteenth centuries as patterns of socialization changed, owing to migrating populations, industrialization, and changes in class structure and economic life. "Public" balls, such as those conducted in pleasure gardens at Vauxhall, London (1661–1859), La Colisé, Paris (1769–1779), and the Paris Opera and other opera houses (used because they afforded more indoor space than did other existing structures), gained popularity as power shifted from the closed society of the aristocracy to the more open and mobile society of the middle class. At a public ball, where social classes mingled somewhat freely, interclass marriage as a means of social mobility became possible.

In the mid-eighteenth century balls came to be held frequently in the private, exclusive assembly rooms of urban clubs, such as, in London, those of Carlisle House in Soho Square (established 1763) and Almack's in King Street (established 1765), and in the assembly rooms of spas all over Europe, like those of Tunbridge Wells and Bath in England. At the end of the century governmental and social authority came to be rooted in the middle classes, and middle-class morality became more conservative. The private home began to rival the public arena as the most popular and respectable place for private dances. With a restricted guest list and constant vigilance provided by the host, the private ball in the home was considered an accepted place for courtship.

By the mid-nineteenth century, public halls owned by respectable volunteer and benevolent organizations, military corps, and new business enterprises (hotels, restaurants, and dancing academies) could be rented for dancing parties. These new spaces and their audiences for dance competed with those of traditional public balls at opera houses and amusement parks, places that newly conservative bourgeoisie equated with the dissipated habits of the aristocracy and with social contamination. When social respectability could be purchased with a few dance lessons and with membership in a community organization, more people became involved and balls became a conventional part of cosmopolitan and popular culture.

In the nineteenth century the term *ball* was increasingly used to grant dignity to a broad variety of dance events as well as to distinguish the greater formality of some occasions for dancing. Balls then gradually faded and were redefined in the twentieth century. Dancing parties became outmoded that had as their traditional purposes to display an individual's social exclusivity and position; to heighten interpersonal awareness and relationships through ceremony, etiquette, and certain dances; and to require a social network of elaborate organization and preparation. Twentieth-century individualism—with, paradoxically, a concomitant erosion of one's personal power—and the social alienation endemic to industrial and corporate culture redefined formal dancing parties and necessitated new dance communication forms. However, traditional society balls that place less emphasis on dancing and more on the gathering have continued among the very wealthy for charity events and debutantes. Recreational and community dance fêtes—some still called balls—are used to raise money for local causes, and others commemorate historical events or revive old dance forms.

[*For related discussion, see* Social Dance.]

GRETCHEN SCHNEIDER

BALLET. *See* Genres of Western Theatrical Dance.

BALLET CARAVAN. Although it was not the first classical company in America, Lincoln Kirstein's Ballet Caravan (later American Ballet Caravan) was groundbreaking in its aim of developing a national style of dance distinct from European, specifically Russian, antecedents. Its crusading insistence that a new kind of ballet company—modest and serious, with a fresh and unhackneyed repertory—could succeed as the model of American ballet was the troupe's most substantial contribution to dance.

Ballet Caravan was born on 17 July 1936 at Bennington College, Vermont, as a vehicle for choreographic ideas conceived by Kirstein and carried out by dancers on leave for the summer from George Balanchine's American Ballet in its association with the Metropolitan Opera. Under Kirstein's directorship, with Douglas Coudy as company manager and Lew Christensen as ballet master, the 1936 company initially consisted of thirteen dancers: Ruby Asquith, Ruthanna Boris, Gisella Caccialanza, Harold Christensen, Lew Christensen, Rabana Hasburgh, Erick Hawkins, Albia Kavan, Charles Laskey, Eugene Loring, Annabelle Lyon, Hannah Moore, and Kathryn Mullowney. The theatrical manager Frances Hawkins, whose experience included booking Martha Graham, arranged a tour of thirty-eight performances throughout New England that summer.

From the beginning, the goals of the company were ideological as well as artistic. "The Ballet Caravan is a permanent company of the first rank of young American dancers and choreographers trained in the classic tradition," Kirstein announced in a program note in 1938:

> The Caravan is unique in so much as all of its choreography is done by its own dancers . . . and because it employs as collaborators, not already recognized European designers, but only Americans of a generation parallel to the dancers. . . . The Caravan will continue to collaborate with younger American designers and musicians to find a direction for the classic dance . . . rooted in our contemporary and national preferences.

The first season's repertory included two "American subject matter" ballets: Eugene Loring's *Harlequin for President* (to music by Domenico Scarlatti) and Lew Christensen's *Pocahantas* (commissioned score by Elliott Carter), both to scenarios by Kirstein. Other works were Christensen's abstract *Errante* (to Wolfgang Amadeus

Mozart), William Dollar's *Promenade* (to Maurice Ravel), and Coudy's *The Soldier and the Gypsy* (to Manuel de Falla). Considering the inexperience of the choreographers (only Dollar had choreographed previously), their craftsmanlike work won sound acceptance but little enthusiasm. Anatole Chujoy, who saw the company in its late fall engagement at New York's Ninety-second Street YM-YWHA found "a certain a-theatricality, an overall dryness and coldness."

A second season, commencing again in July, in Philadelphia, saw the debut of Dollar's *Yankee Clipper* (commissioned score by Paul Bowles, scenario by Kirstein). The multinational spectacle was extremely popular in its day. Other experiments were Coudy's *Folk Dance* (to Emmanuel Chabrier) and Erick Hawkins's *Show Piece*, subtitled "A Ballet Work-out in One Act" (commissioned score by Robert McBride).

The reception of Christensen's *Filling Station* (commissioned score by Virgil Thomson) in Hartford, Connecticut, on 6 January 1938 was a highlight of the company's existence. Its stock characters—a gas station attendant, truck drivers, lost motorists—depicted in a "cartoon" style, were popular with audiences and received by critics with coolly favorable reviews. The artistic peak came with Loring's *Billy the Kid* (to Aaron Copland) in October of that year. The American Ballet had folded, and an enlarged Caravan had absorbed many more of its dancers, among them Marie-Jeanne (then Marie-Jeanne Pelus), who was becoming the company's leading ballerina.

Cross-country tours in 1938 and 1939 brought ballet both to American audiences unfamiliar with the Ballet Russe de Monte Carlo and to cities knowledgeable enough about the art to note with interest Caravan's new twists. These two groups formed the troupe's best audiences, although the company also appeared before houses that were disappointed not to see swans and fairy-tale trappings.

The Caravan never really caught on as a widely acclaimed company and never produced another ballet to equal *Billy the Kid*. After three and a half years, Chujoy noted that the company was "showing signs of artistic exhaustion." Wrote Kirstein, "I began to realize we'd come to the limits of our particular operation." His induction into the army in 1940 and the organization of Ballet Theatre in that year, in essence, put an end to Ballet Caravan (sometimes called American Ballet Caravan after 1939), except for its brief revival in the summer of 1940 at the World's Fair in Flushing Meadows, New York. Caravan's dancers became part of the Ford Motor Company's tribute to the motorcar, *A Thousand Times Neigh!* Two full companies of dancers were remuneratively employed, each dancing half of the eighteen-minute shows (choreographed by Dollar) that were given every hour on the hour, twelve times a day.

The company's life was extended, in a sense, when Nelson Rockefeller's interest led to a State Department "goodwill" tour of Latin America from June through October 1941. Thirty-six dancers and a staff of eleven, including

BALLET CARAVAN. William Dollar's *Promenade* (1936), set to music by Maurice Ravel. From left to right the dancers are Lew Christensen, Erick Hawkins, Rabana Hasburgh, Gisella Caccialanza, Ruthanna Boris, Annabelle Lyon, Charles Laskey, and Harold Christensen. (Photograph from the Dance Collection, New York Public Library for the Performing Arts.)

Kirstein and George Balanchine, formed the American Ballet that traveled to nine countries: Brazil, Uruguay, Argentina, Chile, Bolivia, Peru, Ecuador, Colombia, and Venezuela.

Balanchine created two of his greatest masterpieces for this company: *Ballet Imperial* (to Petr Ilich Tchaikovsky's Piano Concerto no. 2) and *Concerto Barocco* (to Johann Sebastian Bach's Double Violin Concerto in D Minor), both featuring Marie-Jeanne.

The new repertory for the tour was previewed in New York City at the Little Theater of Hunter College in late May 1941. Not able to review the works, the press in general stressed the tour's political aspects. The opening program in Rio de Janeiro consisted of *Filling Station, Ballet Imperial,* and Balanchine's *Serenade* (to Tchaikovsky). New works included Antony Tudor's *Time Table* (to Copland), *Pastorela* (a dance based on themes from Mexican folklore and choreographed by Christensen and José Fernández to music by Bowles); Dollar's *Juke Box,* a "bad work," according to Chujoy; and Balanchine's new *Divertimento,* choreographed during the tour and never performed since. Older works were *Apollo, Errante,* and *The Bat,* all three by Balanchine. "Of all of these, curiously enough," wrote John Martin in the *New York Times,* "the one that has had the greatest popular success is the Stravinsky 'Apollon Musagete.' . . . Balanchine's personal success has been great."

The overall success of the tour did not inspire wild enthusiasm—perhaps American Ballet's impact was lessened by memories of the previous summer's tour of the Ballet Russe de Monte Carlo—but the company appealed to artists and intellectuals in the cities it visited. On its return to New York in October 1941, Ballet Caravan was dissolved for the last time.

[*See also entries on the principal figures mentioned herein.*]

BIBLIOGRAPHY
Chujoy, Anatole. *The New York City Ballet.* New York, 1953.
Kirstein, Lincoln. *Blast at Ballet.* New York, 1938.
Kirstein, Lincoln. *The New York City Ballet.* New York, 1973.
Reynolds, Nancy. *Repertory in Review: Forty Years of the New York City Ballet.* New York, 1977.

ANITA FINKEL

BALLET COMPETITIONS. The first internationally oriented performance tourney for ballet dancers was organized by the Bulgarian Concert Bureau in the resort city of Varna in 1964. Implemented as a spur to local tourism, the Varna International Ballet Competition invited classically trained dancers between the ages of fifteen and twenty-eight to compete against one another in successive eliminating rounds for the receipt of diplomas, medals, and cash awards. The dancers were evaluated by an invited jury of internationally recognized authorities working within a concrete numerical point system that incorporated both objective variables relative to the specifics of dance technique and more subjective variables such as interpretation, musicality, stage presence, and overall artistry.

The initial Varna competition was sufficiently successful to warrant its repetition in 1965 and 1966. Its success also prompted other cities to follow suit, and international competitions were begun in Moscow in 1969; Tokyo in 1976 (subsequently moved to Osaka); Jackson, Mississippi, in 1979; and New York City, Helsinki, and Paris in 1984. Participants in the competitions, averaging between fifteen and twenty-five years of age, included both student and professional dancers. A competition begun in Lausanne, Switzerland, in 1973 was open exclusively to student dancers. Its featured award, the Prix de Lausanne, is a scholarship for a year of study at one of several participating international schools.

Over the years the International Theater Institute helped organize the competitions in Helsinki, Jackson, Moscow, and Varna. The proliferation of competitions, however, brought about the need for a supervising body that would coordinate the various events by arranging schedules to prevent conflicts, establish basic rules for member competitions, and generally facilitate communications. In 1986 in Jackson, the International Dance Competition Organization was formed.

Rules and regulations for the various competitions are based on mutually acknowledged common denominators. The competitions are unilaterally based upon the classic ballet repertory, although modern dance performance and instruction have been incorporated into several competitions. Usually, competing dancers prepare selections in advance from a list of variations and pas de deux designated by the competition. The New York competition, however, introduced a crucial variant in this procedure: its dancers are instructed to learn a single common pas de deux prior to the competition; then, all the contestants receive instruction in the same three pas de deux during the course of the competition—one pas de deux for each of the three rounds. With the exception of the Japanese competition, which is exclusively pas de deux, and Lausanne, which is based entirely upon solo performance, dancers compete in both solo and pas de deux categories.

In all the competitions, the dancers work through three eliminating rounds toward the awarding of medals, certificates of merit, and cash prizes scored at three ascending levels of achievement. Awards are not given automatically at each meeting of every competition, and each competition retains a single, highest award, given exceptionally. The single extra-performance citation common to all the competitions, except New York, is a special citation for original choreography.

Independent choreographic competitions developed in the middle to late 1970s. Annual choreographer competitions take place in Bagnolet and Le Vésinet in France, in Nyon in Switzerland, and at the Cologne Summer Academy in Germany. A choreography competition was also begun in Boston, Massachusetts, in 1979, although that city has a tradition of such competitions dating back to the 1940s.

Criticism has riddled the competitions since their inception. Conceptually, ballet aligns uneasily with objective mathematical analysis. Practically, the high media profiles accorded the competitions likened them unfavorably to a commercialized ballet Olympics, with inordinate and inappropriate commercial or political significance attached to success. Host cities and nations are perpetually subject to complaints of partisanship.

The organizational structure of the competitions has proved another point of contention. The Soviet bloc competitions were state funded. Nonsocialist competitions are privately sponsored, generally with a single individual responsible for concept and development: Philipp Braunschweig in Lausanne; Masako Ohya in Osaka; Doris Laine in Helsinki; and Ilona Copen and Igor Youskevitch in New York City.

Funding for competing dancers has been complicated: for example, Soviet-trained dancers at the Moscow competition progressed through a series of regional competitions toward selection for the Moscow competition and may have prepared for as long as a year in advance of the actual event, during which time they were paid by their government. European dancers have also been eligible for state support through the various opera-house systems. Dancers from the United States were personally responsible for all their expenses until 1975, when the American Ballet Competition was organized as a means of financial assistance. Also, because many dancers compete in several of the competitions, an additional concern developed over a nascent breed of competition dancers.

Despite objections, competitions have flourished as a crucial showcase for emergent talents and are carefully scrutinized by the international dance community. Winners become commercially viable both to the major companies and to the guest-performance circuit. Dancers who first received international notice via the competitions, along with their nations and the dance companies they joined, include Mikhail Baryshnikov (Soviet Union; Varna and Moscow, Kirov Ballet, American Ballet Theatre); Natalia Bessmertnova (Soviet Union; Varna, Bolshoi Ballet); Bryony Brind (Britain; Lausanne, Royal Ballet); Fernando Bujones (United States; Varna, American Ballet Theatre); Patrick Dupond (France; Varna, Paris Opera Ballet); Eva Evdokimova (United States; Moscow); Alessandra Ferri (Italy; Lausanne, Royal Ballet, American Ballet Theatre); Gen Horiuchi (Japan; Lausanne, New York City Ballet); Natalia Makarova (Soviet Union; Varna, Kirov Ballet, American Ballet Theatre, Royal Ballet); Amanda McKerrow (United States; Moscow, American Ballet Theatre); Alexandre Proia (France; New York City, New York City Ballet); Martine van Hamel (Canada; Varna, American Ballet Theatre); and Vladimir Vasiliev (Soviet Union; Varna, Bolshoi Ballet).

[*For general discussion on related forms of competition, see* Ballroom Dance Competition *and* Ice Dancing.]

BIBLIOGRAPHY

The preceding entry was prepared primarily with the application forms and information booklets provided by the competitions themselves. The following articles were also consulted.

Bland, Alexander. "Nation Dancing against Nation." *London Observer* (12 January 1969).

Dunning, Jennifer. "A Ballet Mecca in Mississippi?" *New York Times* (17 June 1979).

Dunning, Jennifer. "This Dance Competition Does More Than Give Prizes." *New York Times* (20 January 1985).

Saal, Herbert. "Footloose in Jackson." *Newsweek* (9 July 1979).

Steinbrink, Mark. "Dancers Who Have Scored Abroad." *New York Times* (8 August 1981).

Terry, Walter. "Choreographic Contest." *Saturday Review* (31 August 1968).

Terry, Walter. "Contest in Moscow." *Saturday Review* (6 August 1969).

Terry, Walter. "International Ballet: And Never the Twain Shall Meet." *Saturday Review* (19 October 1974).

Terry, Walter. "The Olympics of Ballet Crowns a New Champion." *New York Times* (8 August 1976).

Terry, Walter. "Varna Spawns a Winner." *Saturday Review* (18 September 1976).

Terry, Walter. "Ballet's Beaux and Belles." *Saturday Review* (1 September 1979).

OTIS STUART

BALLET DE COLLÈGE. Allegorical ballets prepared for important celebrations by the French secondary schools called *collèges* (now known as *lycées*) in the seventeenth and eighteenth centuries were called *ballets de collège*. Since dance was part of their education, the students were able to perform these ballets with their dance masters. The participation of European students in dances performed on major feast days—for example, the feasts of Saint Catherine, Saint Nicholas, or Epiphany—dates back to the Middle Ages. The historian Charles de Bourgueville noted that "*basses danses* and *branles* were performed in the *collèges*, ending with the tordion." This type of recreation led to dissipation, and in 1488 the administrative body took stringent measures to regulate holidays, which were said to be causes of insolence and disorder, and to forbid the student dancers from performing outside their own schools.

During the sixteenth century, however, theater was developing in the *collèges* in all the major cities of Europe. In Paris, among the most active in this regard was the Collège de Clermont, founded in 1560 and renamed Louis-le-Grand in honor of Louis XIV in 1682. Its Jesuit directors played an influential role in the development of French tragedy, which began to be accompanied by ballets in about 1618. According to Ernest Boysse, "The ballet was the principal attraction of their performances, and they poured all the resources of their imagination into it." In this they were following the contemporary enthusiasm for dance at the court and in the theater. In the *lettres patentes* for the establishment of the Académie Royale de Danse in 1661, Louis XIV defined dance as "one of the arts most useful to our nobility, not only in the time of war, in our armies [dance being one of the exercises for training the body] but in time of peace as well, in the *divertissements* of our ballets."

The Jesuits, who were the educators of the nobility, shared his sentiments. In addition to Père Ménéstrier's 1682 treatise, Père Jouvancy and Père le Jay explained the rules of the *ballet de collège* in works of their own. In 1685 Jouvancy recorded the custom of mounting *divertissements* between the acts of a tragedy to amuse the spectators:

> A place will gladly be made for dance, which is a *divertissement* worthy of a properly educated man and a useful exercise for the young. In addition, the dramatic ballet is like silent poetry, expressing in skillful movements of the body the feelings that the poets express in their movements.

In 1725 Père le Jay, the author of several ballets, stated, "Ballet is a dramatic dance that imitates, in a pleasant manner designed to please, actions of figures, movements, and gestures, and with the assistance of song, machinery, and theatrical equipment of every kind."

Ballets were performed each year, during the distribution of prizes in early August, by students of rhetoric, whose teacher was often the author of the libretto. Historical ballets, fables, and imaginative works were performed; their four sections had to comply with a prescribed structure typically associated with tragedy. Ménéstrier noted that "for the tragedy about the ruination of the Assyrian Empire, 'Dreams' was chosen as the subject of the ballet, because this collapse had been predicted in several dreams." The author then gave this scenario to the dance master, "whose job it was to draw all the choreographic consequences."

The set, probably the same one used for the tragedy, was important, the accessories numerous, the machinery (including chariots and animals) complicated, and the costumes sumptuous. The storage facilities of Louis-le-Grand were said to be much more extensive than those of the Comédie Française, if not as large as those of the Opera. The considerable expense was defrayed by gifts, fund-raising drives, municipal subsidies, and sometimes admission charges. The actors often provided their own costumes; some were purchased from the Ballets du Roi.

Costumes symbolized the characters. "The costume for Spring should be green with sprigs of flowers," Ménéstrier wrote. "The Winds are dressed in feathers because of their lightness; the Sun is dressed in gold fabric, and the Climate in four colors corresponding to the seasons."

The musical composition had a prologue, four sections, and an epilogue or general ballet. Composers included Marc-Antoine Charpentier, César Clérambault, and particularly André Campra. Appropriate music accompanied the dance; le Jay's advice to dance masters was that "it is not enough for these movements and gestures to be composed, elegant, harmonious, and pleasant to view if they do not have a specific meaning and precise significance." Dance, harmonizing with the feelings, should illustrate the characters represented:

> For the Winds, the dance should be light and rapid, characterized by frequent pirouettes that imitate the whirling of the wind. If you are painting Joy, the dance should be lively and agile, so that the feet, in their repeated leaps, seem barely to touch the earth, while the extended fingers, agitated arms, and the entire appearance of the body should express that lightness that gives pleasure.

The ballet masters were selected from among the best dancers of France, among them famous artists of the Opera such as Pierre Beauchamps, Louis Pecour, Claude Ballon, Michel Blondy, Antoine Bandieri de Laval, Malter the elder, and Louis Dupré. They gave lessons to the students, composed the ballets, and danced the more difficult roles. Accounts of the dancers do not mention Jean-Baptiste Poquelin, later known as Molière, who was a student at the Collège de Clermont from 1636 to 1641, but it is known that spectacles of this type influenced his career as a dramatist.

The performances might be given in a nearby castle or in the provinces, but they most frequently occurred in the hall of the *collège* or in the courtyard, as at Louis-le-Grand. A large stage was set up; G. Emond describes how "an immense tent was erected to cover the spectators, who filled up three amphitheaters and all the casements that looked out onto the courtyard." Originally, performances were announced to the city by drummers; later, programs were posted at crossroads and at the door of the *collège,* specifying the subject of the drama and the plot of the ballet. These programs were also distributed to the homes of guests, replacing entrance tickets.

Particularly in the provinces, where there was no other theater, the audience showed up in such numbers that people often had to be turned away, or a second performance had to be given. As many as four thousand people gathered in the main courtyard of Louis-le-Grand. At Aix-en-Provence in 1700, the crowd and the confusion were so great that the performance could not be held. Rows of seats sometimes collapsed under the weight of the spectators. Parents, dignitaries, and sometimes even the king attended.

L. V. Gofflot (1907) wrote that during wars, when the king arrived in a city that had a *collège*, a performance was organized in his honor. At Bordeaux in 1660, after their marriage, the king and queen "attended a comedy on the subject of Peace, in combination with several very amusing ballet *entrées*."

The first ballet about which we have detailed knowledge was danced in 1638 at Louis-le-Grand. The Abbé de Choisy wrote that it took place "in the courtyard of the *collège*, lighted by more than two thousand lights, in connection with the birth of Louis XIV." As often happened, circumstances dictated the ballet's subject. Thus the signing of several treaties inspired *Le Ballet de la Paix*, produced in 1698 by seventeen students and eighteen Opera dancers led by Blondy. A royal birth, graduation, coronation, or marriage were all potential subjects. *Le Ballet de la Jeunesse* was performed in honor of the duke of Burgundy in 1697, with melodies and dances by Beauchamps. *Le Ballet des Comètes* (1665) commemorated the discovery of two new comets. *Le Ballet de l'Espérance* of 1709, a "year of sterility caused by the severe winter, at a time when war was raging at its fiercest," was less pompous than the usual performances, alluding to the misfortunes of the country and stirring the hope of better times.

All the ballets were based on allegory, whether philosophical, poetic, or purely imaginary. Along with symbolic figures such as Truth, Hope, and Destiny, the Classical gods—Mercury, Mars, Pluto, Apollo, or Terpsichore—directed the activity. Some admired works were given more than once; they included *Le Ballet de la Vérité* and *Le Ballet des Jeux*, created in 1653, which contained a dance by a pair of ninepins, which in 1739 became *L'Origine des Jeux*, by Malter. In connection with the latter, the journal *Le mercure* commented, "The manner in which a large painted checkerboard was depicted on the floor of the theater, with the movements of the young warriors dressed as game pieces and little children dressed as pawns, was extremely ingenious." *Le Ballet de l'Illusion* (1672) was pleasant and amusing. *Apollon Législateur, ou Le Parnasse Réformé* (1711), which combined dancing, singing, and declamation, was a complex creation by Pecour, and the variety of its tableaux and sets was greatly admired. Human absurdity was exposed and wisdom sought in *L'École de Minerve*. *Le Temple de la Gloire* (1723), choreographed by Froment and—said *Le mercure*—"danced by the best masters in Paris and by several excellent children," ingeniously illuminated an austere subject: "Most human beings aspire to glory, but few find the right path." *Le Ballet des Saisons* (1688) repeated the theme of the seasons, which was popular with the public and had been treated

by Isaac de Benserade in 1661 for the court. Père Porée's *L'Histoire de la Danse* (1732) provided a living fresco of the origins of dance, represented by "a confused mixture of animated sallies and expressive *bourrades*," with academic "linkings of cadenced steps and ordered poses."

The enthusiasm for the *ballet de collège* was so great that it spread to schools of all kinds, seminaries, monasteries, and even convents. Gofflot (1907) tells us that "the convent of the Abbaye au Bois in Paris, which was licensed to teach girls of upper-class families, had a beautiful theater with numerous sets and costumes that left nothing to be desired in terms of elegance. The ballets were directed by Noverre, Philippe, and Dauberval." The enemies of the Jesuits, and particularly of the University of Paris, found this activity frivolous and harmful to young people, and their attacks upon it became increasingly aggressive, notably in Rector Charles Rollin's *Traité des études*, published in 1726. Père Porée answered Rollin in the program for his ballet *L'Homme Instruit par les Spectacles, ou Le Théâtre Changé en École de Vertu:*

> We do not claim in the ballet to answer the charges that have been leveled against the theater, often rightfully so. We want above all to show that it is possible to change theatrical performances into opportunities for instruction that are as useful as they are pleasant, without destroying the spectacle.

Nevertheless, the decline of the *ballet de collège* had begun. Discussing *Le Ballet de Mars*, in which the dances created by Malter required sixty performers, *Le mercure* noted in 1735 that "This is perhaps the only ballet that can now give some idea of the magnificence of the ballets that were given in the youth of the late King." Two brilliant works were created after that, however. *Le Portrait du Grand Monarque*, staged in 1748 by Dupré, used costumes borrowed from the Opera and new and beautiful sets. It was performed by the best dancers of the Opera, with a few students of the *collège* whom they had trained. Most of the dancers were masked. In 1754 *Les Spectacles du Parnasse*, created by Père du Parc, ended with a display of fireworks devised by the Ruggieri brothers. The departure of the Jesuits in 1762 extinguished a tradition that had contributed for a century and a half to the development and popularity of dance.

[*For related discussion, see* Christianity and Dance.]

BIBLIOGRAPHY

Astier, Régine. "Pierre Beauchamps and the Ballets de Collège." *Dance Chronicle* 6.2 (1983): 138–163.

Bourgueville, Charles de. *Recherches sur la ville de Caen.* Caen, 1588.

Boysse, Ernest. *Le théâtre des Jésuites.* Paris, 1880.

Choisy, Abbé de. *Mémoires pour servir à l'histoire de Louis XIV.* Utrecht, 1727.

Emond, G. *Histoire du Collège Louis-le-Grand.* Paris, 1845.

Gofflot, L. V. *Le Théâtre au Collège.* Paris, 1907.

Jouvancy, Joseph de. *De ratione discendi et docendi.* 1685.

Le Jay, Gabriel-Thomas. *Liber de choreis dramaticus.* Paris, 1725.
Ménéstrier, Claude-François. *Des ballets anciens et modernes selon les règles du théâtre.* Paris, 1682.

JEANNINE DORVANE
Translated from French

BALLET DE COUR. [*To describe the history and evolution of French court ballet, this entry comprises two articles. The first focuses on the importance of the patronage of Catherine de Médicis and Louis XIV; the second examines the influence of Italian opera and the development of the comédie-ballet.*]

Ballet de Cour, 1560–1670

A composite art form, *ballet de cour* (court ballet) was born in France toward the end of the sixteenth century in the context of a general European interest in courtly splendor. France's dowager queen, Catherine de Médicis, loved dancing, and it was she who presided over the creation and development of *ballet de cour*.

At first, dancing at court festivals such as masquerades consisted of nobles performing well-known social dances, such as the slow and dignified *pavane* or the dramatic *courante*. Everything began to change with the arrival of Balthazar de Beaujoyeulx, an Italian-born violinist and dancing master in the employ of Catherine de Médicis, and with the research of sixteenth-century humanists into evidence of classical Greek choreography. Beaujoyeulx transformed social dances into *ballets de cour*, furnishing as Guillaume Colletet, one of the first historians of ballet, wrote in *Le grand ballet des effects de la nature* (1632, p. 1), "a living image of our gestures and expression through artifice of our innermost thoughts." In addition to skill and elegance, the dancer had to try to convey the feelings of the character depicted—the misery of a pilgrim, the madness of a spirit, or the pride of Phoebus Apollo.

Beaujoyeulx's most celebrated work, *Le Balet Comique de la Royne* (1581), was an ambitious work that combined poetry, song, elaborate decor, and large numbers of dancers and musicians. Moreover, he wished to bind these elements into a harmonious whole, at the same time giving the central importance to dance. The magical powers of the enchantress Circe and the French king's victory over them were depicted in dance figures of a geometric structure intended to mirror the harmony of celestial bodies.

The performance of *Le Balet Comique de la Royne* lasted five hours, but other *ballets de cour,* such as those during the reign of Henri IV, were often less solemn and less time-consuming. Their main focus was burlesque, as indicated by such titles as *Ballet des Fous* (1596) and *Ballet des Bouteille* (1604). Developing alongside this lighthearted approach were preoccupations with the new stage machinery imported into France from Italy. This could give

effective expression to the romanesque and mythological themes that *ballet de cour* borrowed from the Italian Renaissance poets Ludovico Ariosto and Torquato Tasso, or from classical literature. *Le Ballet de la Délivrance de Renaud* (1617), for example, featured difficult, athletic, and grotesque dances alternating with noble and symbolic ballets.

This blend of the fantastic and the regal is characteristic of *ballet de cour* throughout the period under Louis XIII and into the earlier years of the reign of Louis XIV. The burlesque element was usually presented by professional dancers whose agility and power of expression could transmit the violence, madness, or strangeness of demons, half-human beings, hermaphrodites, and lunatics. The noble aspect was depicted by the king, princes, princesses, gentlemen, and ladies of the court. Their gestures and dance steps were more limited and their dances less individualistic; usually the dancers were beautifully and richly dressed, commanding as much admiration for

BALLET DE COUR. A character from *Le Ballet des Fêtes de Bacchus,* performed in 1651 in Paris. The costume design is by Henry Gissey, one of the designers at the court of Louis XIV. (Photograph from the Dance Collection, New York Public Library for the Performing Arts.)

their costumes as for the patterns and figures their feet inscribed on the floor.

In *Le Ballet de la Délivrance de Renaud*, as in *Le Balet Comique de la Royne*, the entertainment had serious moral and political intentions, demonstrating the French king's ability to overcome the powers of magic and evil. Political interest remains a constant element; indeed, many historians believe that the need to promote a powerful, lavish image of the prince and his court is at the heart of the creation of *ballet de cour*.

Cardinal Richelieu recognized the propaganda value of *ballet de cour* and exploited it on numerous occasions. His ideas transformed the ballet, giving a greater role to theatrical machinery, on which he relied to promote the astonishment, enjoyment, and the approval he sought for his various military enterprises on behalf of the French crown. Thus, in *Le Ballet de la Prosperité des Armes de la France* (1641), royal palaces and the rich woods of Arcadia are a background for the French victories at Casal and at Arras. Despite this emphasis on spectacle, *ballet de cour* had enough flexibility to stay in the vanguard of theatrical innovation; whatever developments it absorbed, it still retained dancing as its central element.

The Jesuit fathers, who from the first decade of the seventeenth century had dominated education in the towns, increasingly incorporated dancing into their formal curriculum. Pupils displayed their talents on Founders' Day, when ambitious dramatic and choreographic spectacles rewarded parents and townspeople for their financial investment. Both Louis XIII and Louis XIV paid regular visits to the Collège de Clermont, later renamed Louis-le-Grand, and on each occasion were entertained with appropriate extravagance. [*See* Ballet de Collège.]

Royal support of *ballet de cour* in France aroused interest abroad. With a French princess as queen of England and another as duchess of Savoy, it was inevitable that French artistic influence in both regions became strong. In Turin accounts of French performances were eagerly read and immediately copied. Filippo d'Aglié, who composed all the principal ballets at the Savoy court until his death in 1667, preferred to adopt noble themes that allowed him to show off his wit and sophistication. Similar borrowings were reflected in the masquerades given at the court of Charles I of England, where mythology and elegant refinement, inspired by French *ballet de cour*, replaced the learned spectacles devised by Ben Jonson for James I and his queen, Anne.

By 1640 the professionalism that had been required for the acrobatic displays of burlesque *ballets de cour* had become a significant feature of all ballet. This was due primarily to the introduction of the Italian-style proscenium arch and the raised stage into French public and private theaters, giving the spectator an entirely new perspective and obliging the dancer not only to perfect intricate foot movements but also to develop advanced technique for the whole body.

In the early years of Louis XIV's reign a taste for the spectacular became entrenched, partly as an effort to match the high theatrical standards the French royal house had adopted under Richelieu and pursued under his successor, Jules Mazarin, and partly to meet Mazarin's love of magnificence. In this period lavish decor was considered the adjunct of royalty, and skilled dancing the sign of true nobility. Louis XIV had considerable natural gifts as a dancer, enjoyed performing in public, and at times played roles of some technical difficulty. He danced several times a year (occasionally several times a week) in *ballets de cour* put on in various royal palaces; his performances before the whole court and in the presence of ambassadors and visiting dignitaries were faithfully reported in special issues of the *Gazette* and the *Mercure galant*.

Throughout the king's dancing career, the structure of *ballet de cour* remained the same. Works such as *Les Proverbes* (1654), *Hercule Amoureux* (1662), and *La Naissance de Vénus* (1665) were divided into parts (or acts) and involved thirty to fifty *entrées* organized according to a theme that ensured variety, ingenuity, and opportunities for display. A typical example, much praised for its coherence and inventiveness by contemporaries and later by historians of court ballet, is *Le Ballet de la Nuit* (1653). Designed by the duke of Nemours, and with a libretto by Isaac de Benserade, it had four equal parts and was performed seven times by Louis XIV. The first act presents nightfall with its ghostly hours, customs, and strange habits. Following a scene change there are midnight entertainments with Venus and Comus and the exploits of romanesque heroes. The third part is dominated by the Moon, her familiar spirits, and the activities of witches at their sabbath. The ballet reaches its climax with the coming of dawn and the rising sun, danced by the king himself. The political overtones are obvious, but the exact nature of the dancing is less clear. Professionals still danced side by side with nobles, among them the choreographer Pierre Beauchamps, who set down the five basic dance positions; the composer and dancer Louis de Mollier; Dolivet, renowned for his character parts; Vertpré, admired for his speed and vigorous dancing; and Jean-Baptiste Lully, who had gained the king's favor as much for his daring and supple dancing as for his musical compositions. Eyewitnesses tended to record only general impressions, but from the comments that survive, it seems that much attention was given to achieving height and speed of movement, and to increasingly complex and large ensembles. These may be the result of a general improvement in dance technique that came with the founding of the Académie Royale de Danse by Louis XIV in March 1661.

Once Louis XIV retired from the stage in 1670, interest in dancing flagged for a time, and new forms such as opera became dominant. Nonetheless, many operas featured dance, as did a number of dramas and comedies. The French dancing masters of the seventeenth century had provided a solid foundation upon which Raoul-Auger Feuillet and Jean-Georges Noverre could build classical ballet.

[*See also* Balet Comique de la Royne, Le; Ballet Technique, History of, *article on* French Court Dance; *and the entries on Beaujoyeulx and Louis XIV.*]

BIBLIOGRAPHY

Auld, Louis E. "Social Diversity in the *Ballet de Cour:* Le Château de Bicêtre." In *Theater and Society in French Literature,* edited by A. Maynor Hardee. Columbia, S.C., 1988.

Buch, David J. *Dance Music from the* Ballets de Cour, *1575–1651: Historical Commentary, Source Study, and Transcriptions from the Philidor Manuscripts.* Stuyvesant, N.Y., 1994.

Christout, Marie-Françoise. *The Ballet de Cour in the Seventeenth Century* (in French and English). Geneva, 1987.

Coeyman, Barbara. "Theatres for Opera and Ballet during the Reigns of Louis XIV and Louis XV." *Early Music* 18 (February 1990): 22–37.

Franko, Mark. *Dance as Text: Ideologies of the Baroque Body.* Cambridge and New York, 1993.

McGowan, Margaret M. *L'art du ballet de cour en France, 1581–1643.* Paris, 1963.

McGowan, Margaret M. *The Court Ballet of Louis XIII.* London, 1988.

Rice, Paul F. *The Performing Arts at Fontainebleau from Louis XIV to Louis XVI.* Ann Arbor, 1989.

MARGARET M. MCGOWAN

Ballet de Cour, 1643–1685

Upon the death of Louis XIII in 1643, Cardinal Mazarin, the king's chief minister, wanted to introduce Italian opera into France, but his desire was frustrated by the French preference for ballet. As soon as the queen's period of mourning was over, Anne of Austria viewed a performance of the ballet *Le Libraire du Pont-Neuf* (1644) at the Palais-Royal. To amuse her son, the infant king, Giovanni Battista Balbi designed grotesque dances for the Italian comedy *La Finta Pazza,* performed at the Petit-Bourbon palace. The French public, however, continued to prefer the elaborate sets and machinery by Giacomo Torelli for the ballet *Le Dérèglement des Passions* (1648) to Francesco Cavalli's opera *Orfeo* (1647). When the Parlement of Paris suspended the court entertainments and ordered the Italian troupes to leave, the ballet company took refuge outside Paris, notably in Avignon, where it performed *Les Divers Entretiens de la Fontaine de Vaucluse* (1649).

Louis XIV captivated his rebellious subjects by dancing *Cassandre* (1651) five times at the Palais-Royal, as well as *Les Fêtes de Bacchus.* Encouraged by Cardinal Mazarin and surrounded by youthful courtiers who loved brilliant entertainments, he added increasingly fantastic and spectacular ballets. According to Claude-François Ménéstrier, a contemporary writer, *Le Ballet de la Nuit* (1653) was a polished example of the genre, bringing together plot, luxury, staging, Torelli's sets and machinery, and costumes. The forty-five *entrées,* divided into four parts, made use of poetic, burlesque, mythological, allegorical, realistic, and romantic dances, in addition to mime and academic dance. This combination of the picturesque, the exotic, and the nobly elegant was characteristic of the French style. The casts included beggars, cripples, thieves, blacksmiths, hunters, Egyptians, shepherds, coquettes, gallants, Turkish warriors, astrologers, witches, demons, monsters, Nereids, Cyclops, the spirits of Fire, Air, Water, and Earth (representing the four temperaments of the human body), and the spinners of dreams. Louis XIV danced as Apollo in the traditional final grand ballet, with twenty-two dancers, including both members of the nobility and professional dancers, among them Pierre Beauchamps, Nicolas de Lorges, Des Airs, Louis de Mollier, and Jean-Baptiste Lully (who became a composer as well).

At Carnival, Louis XIV amused himself by dancing the *boutade* of *Les Proverbes* and restaging *Les Noces de Pélée et de Thétis* (1654), in which the ten ballet *entrées* were performed with Carlo Caproli's opera, which they eclipsed. This entertainment was organized by the duke of Saint-Aignan and was intended to dazzle the court, foreign ambassadors, and Parisians. Very unusual and very expensive, it brought together the best professional dancers and the most skilled noble amateurs; its machinery, sets, and sumptuous costumes are known from an illustrated book and from drawings by Torelli, Henry Gissey, and Israël Silvestre. The king enjoyed dancing the most fantastic ballets, including *Les Bienvenus* (1655), *Le Temps* (created by Louis Hesselin, 1654), and *Les Plaisirs* (1655), evoking at the Louvre the delights of both country and city. Anything could serve as a pretext for dancing. In 1656 Louis XIV danced in seven masquerades and ballets, including the often-repeated *Psyché,* in which the ladies of the court played important roles.

In the *boutade* of *La Galanterie du Temps* (1656), Lully and Beauchamps imitated the playwrights Trivelin and Scaramouche, who were irritated by this parody. French and Italian tastes come face to face in the burlesque ballet *L'Amour Malade* (1657), commissioned by Lully, and in *Les Plaisirs Troublés* (1657), commissioned by the duke of Guise from composer and dancer Louis de Mollier, Dolivet, and Beauchamps. This synthesis marked the end of the rivalry between the two styles.

Vertpré, who danced in the magnificent ballet *Alcidiane,* was a professional who also danced in *La Raillerie* (1659), in which the king appeared exclusively with professionals. Professionals alone performed the *boutade* in *Chacun Fait le Métier d'Autruy* (Everyone Does Someone Else's Job; 1659) celebrating the king's coming marriage. They also danced in the interludes for Cavalli's *Xerxes* (1660), another attempt at winning acceptance for opera. The preference for dance, however, continued to prevail in France, and the attempt to make comic or noble *entrées* follow one another more coherently, without neglecting caprice and fantasy, succeeded in 1661 in the ballet *L'Impatience* (a revealing title), given at the Louvre.

The death of Cardinal Mazarin encouraged Louis XIV to expand his near-divine prestige, gradually exalting his majesty and imposing his lavish style on all of Europe. In this apotheosis of the French monarchy, the ballet played a political role both at home and abroad. It occupied and distracted the court and the foreign dignitaries invited to these spectacles. Each was performed several times, with sets and machinery by the Vigaranis, rich symbolic costumes by Gissey and later by Jean Berain the elder, and the cheerful music composed by Lully. However, Louis complained that there were too few dancers skilled enough to perform his ballets. The Académie Royale de Danse was created to improve technique and raise the general level of both amateur and professional performers. In the ballet *Les Saisons* (1661), which had movable sets, the ladies of the court—notably Henrietta of England as Diana—rivaled the dancers, including Vertpré and Louis XIV. Male dancers in female costume, always masked, contributed to the "gallant and marvelous diversity of the *entrées*" praised by *La gazette*. A short time later Molière and Beauchamps enchanted Louis XIV with a new genre, the *comédie-ballet*, exemplified by *Les Fâcheux*. This genre flowered gradually and opened a new arena for dance.

Created in the Salle des Machines at the Tuileries, Cavalli's *Hercule Amoureux* (1662) was praised by the public for Lully's ballet *entrées*, the sets, machines that could carry sixty people, and above all, such aristocratic dancers as the princes of Condé, Guiche, and Armagnac, and the duke of Guise, as well as the professional dancers (including Louis Lestang, Desbrosse, de Lorges, Vertpré, and Ribera). The production was costly and dangerous; Louis XIV preferred a traditional ballet with *entrées* such as *Les Arts* (1663), judged by the critics to be "worthy of the gods." The cast of *Les Arts* included the king, his mistress Louise de la Vallière as a shepherdess, and his sister-in-law Henrietta of England as Pallas.

In *Le Mariage Forcé* (1664), Beauchamps as the Magician brought forth demons; as a gallant, he danced with the comedienne Du Parc, who played the wife of Sganarelle, danced by Molière. The queen played Proserpine in *Les Amours Déguisés* (1664); Vertpré was Cleopatra, the duke of Saint-Aignan was Mark Antony, Louis XIV was Renaud, and Beauchamps was La Renommée. Ménéstrier thought highly of the production's inventiveness but mentioned several inconsistencies. At Nancy, the duke of Lorraine commissioned the ballet *La Diversité des Fols*, but interest was concentrated on *Les Plaisirs de l'Île Enchantée* (1664), directed by the duke of Saint-Aignan at

Versailles in May and performed before a huge crowd. The dancers appeared each day in ring races, banquets, comic ballets, water fights, and fireworks displays that echoed the theme of this carnival. In the mythological ballet *La Naissance de Vénus* (1665), at the Palais-Royal, Henrietta of England was Venus, Saint-Aignan and Beauchamps were Castor and Pollux, Louis XIV was Alexander (in reference to the recent war), Lully was Bacchus, and de Lorges was Eurydice.

In addition to these opulent traditional *divertissements* during Carnival, the court amused itself with impromptu masquerades. Comical improvisation was never sacrificed to pomp. *Le Ballet des Muses* (1666) was an admirable blend of the noble, the comic, and the exotic, including mime, song, and male and female dances. Louis XIV, the marquis de Villeroy, and Beauchamps portrayed three nymphs. With some changes, the work remained successful. Three thousand people crowded into Versailles to applaud *Georges Dandin* (1668), a comic ballet and the centerpiece of the festival of 1668. In *Le Ballet de Flore* (1669), which gave its name to the pavilion of the Louvre where it premiered, Louis XIV, who had become known as the Sun King, and the royal *fleur de lys* were triumphant.

Burlesque continued to rival allegory. *Monsieur de Pourceaugnac* (1669), created at Chambord by professionals, rivaled *Les Amants Magnifiques* (1670), an example of total theater. The latter performance marked the departure of Louis XIV and the eventual decline of the genre. The king applauded *Le Bourgeois Gentilhomme* (1670), as well as *Le Grand Ballet de Psyché* (1671), in which seventy dance masters appeared. A council decree of 1669 had permitted nobles to dance in public on the stage, but the ballet was becoming the province of professionals. However, the tradition of public performance was revived periodically for the young princes. The dauphin, son of Louis XIV, danced in *Le Triomphe de l'Amour* in 1681 and in *Le Temple de la Paix* in 1685. At the age of eleven, Louis XV had appeared in *Les Éléments*, yet he did not share Louis XIV's predilection for dance. *Les Éléments* was directed by Claude Ballon, supervised by the aged de Villeroy. Guided by Jean-Baptiste de Hesse and surrounded by such nobles as de Courtenvaux, it drew a fleeting brilliance from the presence of young professional dancers and of Madame de Pompadour.

Nevertheless, the genre had fallen irreparably from its peak between 1653 and 1669. Under Louis XIV this blend of pure dance and action dance, of amateurs and professionals, had enjoyed a fame that was due to the quality of various performers and to public favor. It was the ideal reflection of an aesthetic that has remained memorable.

[*For further discussion, see* Académie Royale de Danse; Ballet Technique, History of, *article on* French Court Dance; *and* France, *article on* Theatrical Dance, 1581–

1789. *See also the entries on Beauchamps, Benserade, de Hesse, Louis XIV, and Lully.*]

BIBLIOGRAPHY

Auld, Louis E. "Social Diversity in the *Ballet de Cour:* Le Château de Bicëtre." In *Theater and Society in French Literature,* edited by A. Maynor Hardee. Columbia, S.C., 1988.

Auld, Louis E. "The Non-Dramatic Art of *Ballet de Cour:* Early Theorists." In *Beyond the Moon: Festschrift Luther Dittmer,* edited by Bryan Gillingham and Paul Merkley. Ottawa, 1990.

Buch, David J. *Dance Music from the* Ballets de Cour, *1575–1651: Historical Commentary, Source Study, and Transcriptions from the Philidor Manuscripts.* Stuyvesant, N.Y., 1994.

Christout, Marie-Françoise. *Le ballet de cour de Louis XIV, 1643–1672.* Paris, 1967.

Christout, Marie-Françoise. *The Ballet de Cour in the Seventeenth Century* (in French and English). Geneva, 1987.

Coeyman, Barbara. "Theatres for Opera and Ballet during the Reigns of Louis XIV and Louis XV." *Early Music* 18 (February 1990): 22–37.

Gazette de France. Edited by Théophraste Renaudot. Paris, 1643–1672.

Harris-Warrick, Rebecca, and Carol G. Marsh. *Musical Theatre at the Court of Louis XIV: Le Mariage de la Grosse Cathos.* Cambridge, 1994.

Lacroix, Paul, ed. *Ballets et mascarades de cour de Henri III à Louis XIV.* 6 vols. Geneva, 1868–1870.

La Vallière, Louis César de la Baume le Blanc, duc de. *Ballets, opéra, et autres ouvrages lyriques, par ordre chronologique depuis leur origine.* Paris, 1760.

Loret, Jean. *La muze historique (1650–1665).* 4 vols. Edited by C.-L. Livet. Paris, 1857–1878.

Ménéstrier, Claude-François. *Des ballets anciens et modernes selon les règles du théâtre.* Paris, 1682.

Pure, Michel de. *Idée des spectacles anciens et nouveaux.* Paris, 1668.

Rice, Paul F. *The Performing Arts at Fontainebleau from Louis XIV to Louis XVI.* Ann Arbor, 1989.

Schwartz, Judith L., and Christena L. Schlundt. *French Court Dance and Dance Music: A Guide to Primary Source Writings, 1643–1789.* Stuyvesant, N.Y., 1987.

MARIE-FRANÇOISE CHRISTOUT
Translated from French

BALLET DER LAGE LANDEN. In 1947 the Dutch dancers Mascha ter Weeme, Max Dooyes, Bob Nijhuis, and Florrie Rodrigo formed a company called Amsterdamse Ballet Combinatie, renamed after two months the Ballet der Lage Landen (Ballet of the Lowlands). All the founders except Rodrigo had formerly been with Ballet Yvonne Georgi. From the beginning the choice of repertory and dancers was determined by the idea that expression in dance should be more important than perfect technique. At first story ballets, both dramatic and comic, filled the repertory. The company—then under the sole direction of ter Weeme—strove to attract a large audience throughout the Netherlands.

During the eleven years of its existence the company traveled through Holland extensively, performing everywhere, even in the smallest available theaters. The dancers were hardly paid and had to do other work to earn their living. Every dime went into the productions, which considering the deplorable financial situation had a surprisingly high standard, owing to the director's impeccable taste and sense of theater. In the second year of the company's existence, an English dancer from the Sadler's Wells Company, Leo Kersley, was invited to join; after that the link with the English dance world remained strong through contributions from choreographers such as Jack Carter, Walter Gore, Andrée Howard, and Michael Holmes, and dancers including Kersley, Angela Bayley, Paula Hinton, and Norman McDowell.

The repertory also had many ballets by the Dutch choreographers Pieter van der Sloot, Dooyes, Greetje Donker, Karel Poons, and Rodrigo, whose war ballet *Verzet* (Resistance) was performed by members of the company at the ballet competition in Copenhagen in 1947. Van der Sloot and Dooyes in particular were of great importance: van der Sloot not only for his dancing qualities but also for his easygoing, lighthearted, and musical ballets; and Dooyes for his more poetic approach and his daring in the search for new dance forms.

Although public response to the Lage Landen was always very positive, the reception in the press, especially in Amsterdam and The Hague, was after the first five years definitely not so. This negativism sprang mainly from the battle over which Dutch company should receive official recognition in the form of financial support. Several dance critics made it their policy to destroy the Lage Landen, accusing it of "an English disease" and too much storytelling. In spite of enormous difficulties, the company produced the first three-act classical ballet in Holland (*Coppélia,* produced by Carter) and the first ballet to use Martha Graham dance technique (*Cortège,* 1952, created by Harvey Krekfets, better known now as the mime Adan Darius) at a time when Graham's work was almost unknown in Holland.

The Ballet der Lage Landen's most important ballets were the classics: *Coppélia* and act 2 of *Swan Lake* (choreographed by Carter), *The Nutcracker* (choreographed by Gore), *Les Sylphides* (produced by Holmes), and several well-known pas de deux. Other important creations were Dooyes's *Vlucht met Zwarte Zwanen* (Flight with Black Swans), *Straat der Verbeelding* (Street of Imagination), *Nacht van Endymion,* and *Cascade;* van der Sloot's *Garden Party, Achilles,* and *Sonatine;* Carter's *The Witch Boy, Pavana Interrumpida, Stagioni,* and *Impromptu for Twelve;* Gore's *The Lonely One* and *Street Games;* Rodrigo's *Verzet;* Suzanne Egri's *Foyer de la Danse;* and Howard's *Death and the Maiden.*

The company's most important dancers were Marie-Jeanne van der Veen, Mascha Stom, Hanny Bouman,

Panchita de Péri, van der Sloot, Martin Scheepers, and Ben de Rochemont, who excelled in the classical works, and ter Weeme, Donker, Poons, and Johan Mittertreiner as strong dramatic dancers. Bayley, Ine Rietstap, and McDowell combined both technical and dramatic qualities.

Owing to the fight for financial support, in 1959 the Ballet der Lage Landen had to amalgamate with the Ballet of the Netherlands Opera. The newly formed company, the Amsterdam Ballet, survived only two seasons, after which it was combined with the Netherlands Ballet to become the National Ballet.

[*See also* Netherlands, *article on* Theatrical Dance since 1945; *and the entry on* Weeme.]

BIBLIOGRAPHY

Schaik, Eva van. *Op gespannen voet: Geschiedenis van de Nederlandse theaterdans vanaf 1900.* Haarlem, 1981.

Sinclair, Janet. *Ballet der Lage Landen.* Haarlem, 1956.

INE RIETSTAP

BALLET DU XXᵉ SIÈCLE. This international dance company, the name of which means "Ballet of the Twentieth Century," was founded by Maurice Béjart following his creation in Brussels of *Le Sacre du Printemps* (1959), for which Béjart assembled a large corps de ballet by combining his own company Ballet-Théâtre, that of the Théâtre Royal de la Monnaie, and the Western Theatre

Ballet from England. In 1960 it became a permanent troupe that performed internationally, although it was attached to the Théâtre Royal de la Monnaie, an opera house in Brussels. This institution's director, Maurice Huisman, exempted Béjart's company from regular performances of *divertissements* for the opera.

The company recruited dancers from the companies of Janine Charrat and Milorad Miskovitch, and later from throughout the world. Béjart, the artistic director, wanted diversity of body types, races, and temperaments among his dancers. While requiring sound classical training, he increasingly sought varied abilities such as modern dance, drama, and singing. He exploited dancers' complementary talents and specific qualities, and even their defects. To meet the ever greater technical demands of Béjart's choreography, the young company constantly had to raise its level under the strict direction of Russian or Russian-trained teachers, including Asaf Messerer, Tatjana Gsovsky, Tatiana Grantseva, Nora Kiss, Menia Martinez, José Parés, Louba and Pierre Dobrievich, and Azari Plisetsky, along with teachers drawn from the company itself, such as Jacques Sausin, Robert Denvers, Jean Nuyts, Jean-Marie Limon, and Catherine Verneuil, as well as guest artists from the Paris Opera, among them Jacqueline Rayet and Rita Thalia. This transmission of a style developing in accordance with Béjart's ideas ensured continuity in a troupe that experienced frequent changes in membership and constant challenge from new produc-

BALLET DU XXᵉ SIÈCLE. Maurice Béjart's 1959 version of *Le Sacre du Printemps,* set to the score by Igor Stravinsky. The success of this large-scale endeavor, which featured a corps de ballet assembled from three companies, led to the formation of Béjart's Ballet du XXᵉ Siècle. (Photograph by Robert Kayaert; from the Dance Collection, New York Public Library for the Performing Arts.)

tions. From the very beginning this style clearly distinguished the company.

The aim of the Ballet du XXe Siècle was to speak to youth and to reach a wide public that knows little about dance, utilizing scores that mingle contemporary music, classical music, and jazz, recorded by their best interpreters. This broad appeal enables the use of large ensembles in new kinds of performance spaces, offering audiences major spectacles in which choreography is always the main element. Nevertheless, the company did not abandon experimental works that were less accessible.

In 1960 Béjart added to his established team of soloists—Michèle Seigneuret, Tania Bari, Laura Proença, Germinal Casado, and Patrick Belda—the newcomers Paolo Bortoluzzi, Duska Sifnios, Jörg Lanner, Vittorio Biagi, André Leclair, and Lothar Hofgen. He also hired novice dancers who quickly demonstrated their abilities—Itomi Hasakawa, Woytek Lowski, Lorca Massine, Robert Thomas, Victor Ullate, and Jorge Donn, who was to play an important role in the repertory. Béjart had a preference for male dance, which became an essential feature of the company, sometimes unduly eclipsing female dance. Realizing this, Béjart called on Janine Charrat for an infusion of poetic femininity. Together they produced *Les Quatre Fils Aymon,* based on a Flemish legend, and then *Les Sept Péchés Capitaux* (1961) to a score by Bertolt Brecht and Kurt Weill.

The troupe was soon invited to Paris and Venice, where it presented an extravagant spectacle with music by Domenico Scarlatti and costume and stage designs by Salvador Dali; its most noticed segment was *Gala* with Ludmilla Tcherina. Performances at Bayreuth and Salzburg and the new Cologne opera house established it as a European company. At the Baalbek Festival of 1963 it performed *Prométhée II,* starring Casado. It overwhelmed Brussels audiences, including visiting Parisians, with the provocative *La Veuve Joyeuse* (The Merry Widow), which was soon banned from performance. After that time it divided its activities regularly between seasons in Brussels and tours throughout Europe, Latin America, the Middle East, North America, Japan, and the Soviet Union (1978). In twenty years the company visited, sometimes recurringly, almost two hundred cities and more than thirty countries. It performed in a wide variety of settings, including such traditional ones as the Théâtre des Champs-Élysées, the Théâtre du Châtelet, the Théâtre de la Ville (all in Paris), the Teatro La Fenice in Venice, the Teatro alla Scala in Milan, and the City Center in New York, as well as unusual locales such as temples, amphitheaters, sports arenas, stadiums, public squares, floating rafts, simple stages set up in the desert, and the gardens of the Tuileries in Paris and the Boboli Gardens in Florence.

This demanded great adaptability of the choreographer and dancers. The fact that most of the members were

BALLET DU XXe SIÈCLE. Beatriz Margenat, Guy Braaseur, Laura Proença, and Anne Goléa in Maurice Béjart's *Cantates* (1965), set to the music of Anton Webern. This neoclassical work later formed the first section of Béjart's three-part *À la Recherche de . . .* (1968). (Photograph by Robert Kayaert; from the Dance Collection, New York Public Library for the Performing Arts.)

young, and the constant renewing of the troupe, facilitated this flexibility and sense of improvisation, shaping them into material amenable to the intentions of Béjart. Exotic locales led to the creation of new works, such as the Mexican *Fiesta,* created at the time of the 1964 Olympic Games; *Offrande Chorégraphique,* a classical-jazz duel staged for the first time in New York in 1971; and the Italian-inspired *V Comme,* set to music by Verdi (Verona, 1977), and *Light* (Venice, 1981). Additions were continually being made to a repertory that eventually comprised more than one hundred ballets, most of them staged by Béjart. In addition, the company occasionally performed works by choreographers from its own ranks, including Patrick Belda, Biagi, Lorca Massine, Micha van Hoecke, Bortoluzzi, Angèle Albrecht, and Maguy Marin. Béjart also called on the talents of Léonide Massine *(Parade),* Hans van Manen *(Symphony in Three Movements),* and Lar Lubovitch *(Marimba).*

The creative ferment and the renown of the company continually attracted both brilliant beginners (Rita Poelvoorde, Patrice Touron, Bertrand Pie, Jean-Marie Limon, Philippe Lizon, Kyra Kharkevitch, Martin Boieru, Gil Roman, and Michel Gascard) and well-known dancers (Albrecht, Maina Gielgud, Daniel Lommel, and Gérard Wilk). To create even greater interest, Béjart set strictly classical dancers, such as Iván Markó and Andrzej Ziemsky, side by side with modern dancers such as Dyane Grey-Cullert. Beginning in 1973, he also used the best dancers from his Hindu-influenced Mudra School, including Shonach Mirk, Yann le Gac, and Maguy Marin. Donn was the favorite interpreter of the Béjart style; for a time he was joint artistic director, with Lommel, while Anne Lotsy handled administration with her assistant Sonia Mandel, who replaced her in 1982.

From time to time prestigious guests were invited to perform. Some of them, such as Suzanne Farrell and Niklas Ek, stayed for several years, inspiring Béjart to create roles in *Sonate* (1971), *Nijinsky, Clown de Dieu* (1971), *Golestan* (1973), and *I Trionfi* (1974). Shorter sojourns were made by Jacqueline Rayet *(Ça Plus que Lente),* Luciana Savignano *(Ce que l'Amour Me Dit,* 1974), Rudolf Nureyev *(Le Chant du Compagnon Errant,* 1971), Judith Jamison *(Le Spectre de la Rose,* 1978), Maya Plisetskaya *(Isadora* and *Leda,* 1979), Vladimir Vasiliev *(Petrouchka,* 1977), Yoko Morishita *(Light,* 1979), Marcia Haydée *(Wien, Wien, nur du Allein,* 1982), and Jean Babilée *(Life,* 1979).

Béjart could also be inspired by the talents of an individual member of the company. He designed *Nomos Al-*

pha (1969) for Bortoluzzi, *Mallarmé III* (1973) for Albrecht, *Tombeau* (1973) for Lommel, *Séraphite* (1974) for Markó, *Clair de Lune* (1977) for Touron, and *Gaîté Parisienne* (1978) for Ullate. Roles in the classical ballets of the repertory, such as *Le Sacre du Printemps, Boléro, The Firebird,* and *Romeo and Juliet,* were assigned in alternation, making it possible to try out young talents. Sometimes the performers were drawn by lot or even selected by the public; examples were *Variations pour une Porte et un Soupir* and *Lettera Amorosa.* Béjart increasingly emphasized the unique characteristics of each member, except in certain works dedicated to the corps de ballet *(Farah, Variations Don Giovanni,* and *Neuvième Symphonie).* He demanded that the classical dancer also be a modern dancer, an actor, an acrobat, or a singer. This trend was increasingly apparent in *Notre Faust* (1975), *Le Molière Imaginaire* (1976), *Héliogabale* (1976), *La Muette* (1981), *The Magic Flute* (1981), *Wien, Wien, nur du Allein* (1982), and *The Soldier's Tale* (1983).

The complexity of the repertory, which ranged from experimental works to large thematic ballets, on several occasions made it possible to divide the company temporarily, with one section touring while the other rehearsed in Brussels. In 1976 Béjart made this practice a matter of policy when he founded a group called Yantra within the Ballet du XXᵉ Siècle. It was an experimental group with variable membership, depending on the works created; however this original project was short-lived.

In 1983 the company consisted of twenty-seven female dancers and thirty-three male dancers, all permanent, plus occasional visiting artists. Over the years the technical level of the dancing had become very high, while some members concurrently developed other stage skills. In 1987, following a disagreement between Béjart and the director of La Monnaie, the company disbanded after a June tour to Leningrad. Throughout its history, the company faithfully reflected the nonconformist influences and aesthetic peculiar to Béjart—often surprising, always fascinating, sometimes loved and sometimes condemned by critics and audiences.

[*See also* Scenic Design *and the entry on Béjart*].

BIBLIOGRAPHY

Brabants, Jeanne. "Les trois coups belge" (parts 7–8). *Saisons de la Danse*, no. 238 (September 1992): 48–50.

Christout, Marie-Françoise. "Ballet of the Twentieth Century." *Dance and Dancers* (August 1975): 38–39.

Christout, Marie-Françoise. *Le ballet occidental, XVIe–XXe siècle*. Paris, 1995.

Farrell, Suzanne, with Toni Bentley. *Holding On to the Air: An Autobiography*. New York, 1990.

Gruen, John. *The Private World of Ballet*. New York, 1975.

Hofmann, Wilfried. "Béjart and the Ballet of the 20th Century." *Dance News* (June 1975): 8.

Livio, Antoine. "Salut l'artiste." *Danser* (December 1993): 26–28.

Moffett, Luisa. "Béjart e i suoi fanno le valigie." *Balletto Oggi* (July 1987): 28–29.

Théâtre Royal de la Monnaie. *Panorama 100: Ballet du XXe Siècle*. Brussels, 1978.

Trévoux, Carole. *Danser chez Béjart, ou, Dionysos, l'odyssée d'une création*. Brussels, 1986.

MARIE-FRANÇOISE CHRISTOUT
Translated from French

BALLET IMPERIAL. Ballet in three movements. Choreography: George Balanchine. Music: Petr Ilich Tchaikovsky; Piano Concerto no. 2 in G Major, op. 44. Scenery and costumes: Mstislav Dobujinsky. First performance: 25 June 1941, Teatro Municipal, Rio de Janeiro, American Ballet Caravan. (Preview: 29 May 1941, Little Theater of Hunter College, New York.) Principals: Marie-Jeanne, William Dollar, Gisella Caccialanza, Fred Danieli, Nicholas Magallanes. Revival, staged by Frederic Franklin: 15 October 1964, New York State Theater, New York City Ballet. Scenery: Rouben Ter-Artunian. Costumes: Barbara Karinska. Principals: Suzanne Farrell, Jacques d'Amboise, Patricia Neary, Frank Ohman, Earle Sieveling. Restaged as *Tchaikovsky Piano Concerto No. 2:* 12 January 1973, New York State Theater, New York City Ballet. Costumes: Barbara Karinska. Lighting: Ronald Bates. Principals: Patricia McBride, Peter Martins, Coleen Neary, Tracy Bennett, Victor Castelli.

George Balanchine revitalized the classical heritage of Petipa and Tchaikovsky for American dancers in *Ballet Imperial*, his tribute to tsarist Russia. It is among the most symphonic of his works, with expansive, hierarchical structure, large-scale expositions, developmental sections, recapitulations, and virtuosic cadenzas for the ballerina.

The work's original frame of reference was the grandeur of the Imperial court of Russia. Balanchine choreographed it to Tchaikovsky's Second Piano Concerto, as a showcase for Marie-Jeanne, who was noted for her speed and clarity. William Dollar, Gisella Caccialanza, Fred Danieli, and Nicholas Magallanes were also featured. Mstislav Dobujinsky designed regal tutus and a sumptuous backdrop depicting an embankment along the Neva River.

When the work entered the New York City Ballet repertory in 1964, with Suzanne Farrell and Jacques d'Amboise as principal dancers, the imperial setting and tone were retained by Rouben Ter-Arutunian's new scenery and Karinska's new costumes. In 1973, Balanchine shifted the focus from the hierarchical to the musical by deleting the conventional mime passages and staging the work without scenery; Karinska's chiffon skirts replaced the formal tutus. *Ballet Imperial* was thus transformed into *Tchaikovsky Piano Concerto No. 2*, a work that alludes only to its Romantic, evocative score through powerful kinetic expressiveness.

The ballerina establishes her supremacy with her first entrance to the piano's dazzling bravura cadenza. Her decorous retinue, the corps, consolidates into shifting though distinctive geometric designs, which parallel the grandeur of the orchestral sonority. Sometimes the corps is led by the secondary female soloist, whose entrances correspond to the score's secondary theme.

As the mournful, melodic line of the second movement intensifies and diminishes, the cavalier and a line of women press forward and retreat as one unit. The cavalier embraces his ballerina, who rushes toward him, only to disappear through the line of Romantic "swans." All are reunited, however, in the spirited, folk-inspired finale.

Ballet Imperial has been staged for companies in many countries around the world, including England, Italy, Germany, Switzerland, Australia, Norway, and Mexico. In 1944 Ballet Russe de Monte Carlo mounted a production that was especially notable for the brilliant execution of the ballerina roles by Mary Ellen Moylan and Maria Tallchief. The Sadler's Wells Ballet production in 1950 featured sumptuous designs by Eugene Berman and a cast headed by Margot Fonteyn, Michael Somes, and Beryl Gray. Fonteyn was not ideally suited to her part, but Somes and Grey were much admired for their regal bearing and aristocratic manner as well as for their mastery of the technical demands of the choreography. In 1988 the work was staged for American Ballet Theatre, with new decor by Rouben Ter-Artunian, and has remained a showcase for many of the principal dancers of the company. At New York City Ballet, as *Tchaikovsky Piano Concerto No. 2*, it continues to be a repertory favorite. In the demanding role of the leading ballerina, requiring both lyricism and bravura, Merrill Ashley and Kyra Nichols have won special acclaim.

BIBLIOGRAPHY

Balanchine, George, with Francis Mason. *Balanchine's Complete Stories of the Great Ballets.* Rev. and enl. ed. Garden City, N.Y., 1977.
Choreography by George Balanchine: A Catalogue of Works. New York, 1984.
Denby, Edwin. Review. *New York Herald Tribune* (21 February 1945).
Jordan, Stephanie. "Ballet Imperial." *Dance Now* 2 (Winter 1993–1994): 28–37.
Kaplan, Larry. "Corps Choreography by Balanchine." *Ballet Review* 15 (Winter 1988): 64–75.
Kirstein, Lincoln. *The New York City Ballet.* With photographs by Martha Swope and George Platt Lynes. New York, 1973.
Kirstein, Lincoln. *Ballet, Bias, and Belief: Three Pamphlets Collected and Other Dance Writings.* New York, 1983.
Kisselgoff, Anna. Review. *New York Times* (14 January 1973).
Lederman, Minna. Review. *Modern Music* 22 (March–April 1945): 201–204.
Martin, John. Review. *New York Times* (21 February 1945).
Reynolds, Nancy. *Repertory in Review: Forty Years of the New York City Ballet.* New York, 1977.

REBA ANN ADLER

BALLET NACIONAL ESPAÑOL. Members of the company spinning in *Flamenco.* (Photograph © 1996 by Jack Vartoogian; used by permission.)

BALLET NACIONAL ESPAÑOL. Until the 1970s Spain had no full-time, government-sponsored national dance company. Although individual companies had been sponsored for cultural exchanges or had toured under foreign impresarios, no long-term planning and financial support was forthcoming for the formation of a national dance company that would encompass Spain's vast dance heritage. This lack of continuity prevented long-term development of an ongoing repertory from Spain's best choreographers and security for talented dancers.

This situation changed in the early 1970s, when the question of the formation of a national company was voiced strongly. At that moment the danced interludes (choreographed by Alberto Lorca) of the *Antología de Zarzuela* (anthology of Spanish operetta) were extracted and used as the basis for the formation of the Ballet Antología Española. Led by the principal dancers María del Sol and Mario de la Vega, this company performed to great acclaim, but administrative problems following a U.S. tour led to changes in the directorship; this was to become a pattern over the next few years. The initial policy of adding works from other famous companies, such as those led by Pilar López, Luisillo, Mariemma, and Antonio Ruiz, became confused, and the company floundered under constant changes in directors and repertory. The company withdrew as a contender for the title of Ballet Nacional Español and reverted to its original size and repertory.

With the change in artistic policies following the death of Francísco Franco, the ministry of culture offered Antonio Gades the opportunity of forming a national company in 1978. The departure of the Ballet Antología, although it had left some shaky remnants, demanded a totally fresh start and the development of a new repertory. Gades forged ahead by selecting the best dancers available to create a Spanish dance company representative of the modern age. However, following a dispute regarding Gades's personal political ambitions, he left the post of director to form anew his own company, which he had relinquished on taking up the leadership of the national company. Once again Spain's national dance company framework was crumbling.

Gades was succeeded by María de Avila, whose efforts have led to the formation of a second national company, which will represent the traditional Spanish dance heritage of the *escuela bolera*, regional dances, neoclassical dances to the music of Enrique Granados, Manuel de Falla, Isaac Albéniz, and other Spanish composers, and flamenco. A second company concentrates on classical ballet and is known as the Ballet Nacional Clásico to distinguish it from the first company. María de Avila has been assisted in this task by Angel Pericet, whose knowledge of the *escuela bolera* is unrivaled except within his own family. Both companies are still in their infancy, but their identities are becoming established. Neither has yet achieved major international status, but both hold promise. At last Spain can be proud of having not one but two dance companies to present the dancers of today and the heritage of Spain's great dancers and choreographers of the past.

[*See also the entry on Gades.*]

BIBLIOGRAPHY

Berger, Renato. "Academia Amor de Dios und Spanisches National-Ballett." *Das Tanzarchiv* 27 (March 1979): 134–141.

Lartigue, Pierre. *Antonio Gades.* L'Avant-scène/Ballet-danse, no. 14. Paris, 1984.

PHILIPPA HEALE

BALLET OF THE TWENTIETH CENTURY. *See* Ballet du XXe Siècle.

BALLET RAMBERT. *See* Rambert Dance Company.

BALLET ROYAL DE WALLONIE. *See* Charleroi/Danses.

BALLET RUSSE DE MONTE CARLO. The company, which existed from 1938 to 1962, came into being as a result of dissension in the mid-1930s between Léonide Massine, chief choreographer of Colonel Wassily de Basil's Ballets Russes, and de Basil, the company's director. Massine had long desired to hold the post of artistic director, but de Basil, wishing no rival in the company's directorate, granted him only the title of *collaborateur artistique* in 1934.

By 1937 Massine felt he could no longer work with de Basil. Some wealthy businessmen and patrons of the arts sympathetic to Massine soon founded an organization known first as World Art, and later as Universal Art, that would support a new ballet company directed by him. Prominent among the backers of the newly proposed Ballet Russe were Julius Fleischmann, heir to a fortune in yeast, liquor, and coffee; Watson Washburn, an attorney; and Sergei J. Denham, a Russian-born banker who eventually became the new company's general director. Dancers for this company would include artists specially hired by Massine or persuaded to leave de Basil.

On 19 November 1937 World Art also bought an existing company, René Blum's Les Ballets de Monte-Carlo, founded as the result of an earlier quarrel with de Basil. Blum, a director of the Monte Carlo Opera, had been associated with de Basil's company since its inception in 1932. Blum severed his connections with the Colonel in 1935 and

BALLET RUSSE DE MONTE CARLO. Léonide Massine (The Miller) and Tamara Toumanova (His Wife) in a revival of Massine's *Le Tricorne* presented in the company's 1938/39 season. This work was originally created for the Ballets Russes de Serge Diaghilev in 1919. (Photograph by Fred Fehl; used by permission.)

denied de Basil's Ballets Russes the use of the Monte Carlo Opera, where Blum established his own company in 1936. When Les Ballets de Monte-Carlo was purchased by World Art, Blum theoretically remained a co-director of the group, yet actually he had little to do with it.

Massine assumed control of the Monte Carlo troupe for a spring season at the Monte Carlo Opera, from 5 April to 15 May 1938. The company at that time had seventy dancers, and Massine's associates were Boris Kochno, *collaborateur artistique;* Jan Yazvinsky, *régisseur;* David Libidins, *directeur administratif,* and Denham, *président du conseil d'administration.* The repertory featured ballets created by Michel Fokine for Blum (among them, *Don Juan* and *L'Épreuve d'Amour*) and two new works by Massine, *Gaîté Parisienne* and *Seventh Symphony. Gaîté Parisienne,* set to an arrangement of tunes by Offenbach, concerned doings in a Second Empire Parisian café and soon established itself as one of the most popular of all Massine's choreographic comedies. *Seventh Symphony,* set to Beethoven's score, was one of Massine's allegorical "symphonic ballets." Depicting the creation and destruction of the world, it was praised for its choreographic architecture and criticized for its thematic pretentiousness.

BALLET RUSSE DE MONTE CARLO. Scene from Léonide Massine's *Saratoga* (1941), with (left to right) Nicholas Beriozoff, Vladimir Kostenko, Roland Guerard, Frederic Franklin, Alexandra Danilova, Tatiana Chamié, and Sviatoslav Toumine. (Photograph by Maurice Seymour; used by permission.)

Faced with the prospect of two rival Ballets Russes, impresario Sol Hurok attempted to reconcile them for a summer 1938 engagement in London and an autumn tour of the United States. But his efforts were unavailing and on 20 June 1938 the de Basil company opened at Covent Garden (but, for legal reasons, without de Basil's name listed as director); on 12 July 1938 Massine's Ballet Russe de Monte Carlo moved into the nearby Theatre Royal, Drury Lane. The summer season in which both companies were performing in theaters only a few blocks apart soon acquired the nickname "ballet war."

Among the leading dancers of Massine's company were Alexandra Danilova, Tamara Toumanova, Alicia Markova, Mia Slavenska, Eugénie Delarova, Lubov Rostova, Nathalie Krassovska, Jeannette Lauret, Milada Mladova, Nini Theilade, Igor Youskevitch, Serge Lifar, Frederic Franklin, George Zoritch, Michel Panaiev, Roland Guerard, Marc Platoff, Simon Semenoff, and Jan Yazvinsky. The London season included the premiere, on 21 July 1938, of Massine's *Nobilissima Visione* (known as *Saint Francis* in the United States), to a score commissioned from Paul Hindemith. Retelling medieval legends of Saint Francis in a gesturally austere manner, *Nobilissima Visione* was considered by some critics to be one of Massine's greatest works.

The Ballet Russe, as the company was usually known, became an immediate success during its first New York season, which opened 12 October 1938 at the Metropoli-

tan Opera House, and it was equally successful on the tour that followed. The company planned to give an annual spring season in Monte Carlo, a summer or early autumn season in London, and to spend the rest of autumn and winter on tour, particularly in the United States. The outbreak of World War II in September 1939 put an end to these schemes and the company hastily escaped to the States. It never visited Europe again and, from then on, it made New York City its headquarters, becoming in effect, if not in name, an American company.

Many noted dancers, American and European alike, performed with the Ballet Russe, but throughout the 1940s and into the early 1950s it was dominated by the partnership of Alexandra Danilova and Frederic Franklin. Danilova, a Russian dancer said to have the most beautiful legs in all ballet, was a ballerina of great style, wit, and sophistication. The English-born Franklin was unusually versatile, his repertory extending from *Swan Lake* and *Giselle* to contemporary comic and serious roles.

The company's early seasons were dominated by Massine's ballets. Among his most important premieres were *Capriccio Espagnol* (Monte Carlo, 4 May 1939), a choreographic collaboration with La Argentinita; *Rouge et Noir* (Monte Carlo, 11 May 1939), a symphonic ballet to Shostakovich's First Symphony with decor by Henri Matisse and a symbolic scenario about forces of destiny shaping man's life; and *Bacchanale* (New York, 9 November 1939), an elaborate surrealist work, with designs by

Salvador Dalí that depicted the deranged fantasies of Ludwig of Bavaria.

Other choreographers were also represented in the repertory. Frederick Ashton contributed *Devil's Holiday* (1939). By choreographing *Ghost Town* (1939), Marc Platoff made a historically important attempt to create an Americana ballet for the Ballet Russe. In 1940 the company took over three works from George Balanchine's defunct American Ballet: *Le Baiser de la Fée*, *Jeu de Cartes*, and *Serenade*. In addition, the company gave many Americans their first glimpses of *The Nutcracker*, in an abridged version, and the third act of *Swan Lake* (under the title of *The Magic Swan*).

After 1940 Massine's directorial authority became increasingly unstable. Several ambitious productions, both comic and serious, had been attacked by the critics and had failed at the box office, among them *Vienna—1814* (1940); *The New Yorker* (1940); *Labyrinth* (1940), another collaboration with Dali; and *Saratoga* (1941), which was universally proclaimed to be Massine's weakest effort in years. The businessmen who backed the Ballet Russe wondered whether Massine had turned from an asset into a liability, and critical taste began to find both Massine's grandiloquent allegories and his antic comedies outmoded. Finally, in 1942, Massine resigned. That same year, Hurok ceased managing the company's tours and Sergei Denham assumed full directorial responsibilities.

Between 1942 and 1944, Denham commissioned diverse works from several choreographers. Links to the Diaghilev Ballets Russes tradition were maintained by means of four ballets by Bronislava Nijinska: *Chopin Concerto* and the premiere of *The Snow Maiden* in 1942, and *Etude* and the premiere of *Ancient Russia* in 1943. The most acclaimed of these was *Chopin Concerto*, an abstraction danced to Chopin's First Piano Concerto that was a revision of a work first staged by Nijinska for the Warsaw Ballet in 1937.

Representing a somewhat different Russian balletic tradition was Igor Schwezoff's *The Red Poppy* (1943), a one-act adaptation of an evening-long ballet to music by Glière that had been hailed as a triumph of Soviet choreography at its first production in 1927. To give it topicality during World War II, Schwezoff made the villain Japanese, and the heroes were Russian, British, and American sailors.

The most significant of Denham's commissions during the beginning of his tenure as sole director of the Ballet Russe was Agnes de Mille's *Rodeo*, which received its premiere at the Metropolitan Opera House on 16 October 1942. Set to a score by Aaron Copland, de Mille's comedy about a tomboy cowgirl and some ranch hands affirmed the validity of Americana as a balletic genre and indicated how far the Ballet Russe had gone in its process of Americanization.

In the spring of 1944, the Ballet Russe became the first ballet company to dance at the City Center of Music and Drama, a former Shriners' auditorium that had been acquired by the City of New York to serve as a popularly priced cultural center. That same spring also saw a New York equivalent of the London ballet war—for both the Ballet Russe and the Ballet Theatre, which Hurok had booked into the Metropolitan Opera House, scheduled their seasons to open on 9 April 1944. Both groups were financially successful, but partisans of Ballet Theatre accused the City of New York of engaging in unfair competition with private enterprise because of the City Center's ability to offer low-cost tickets.

There were few summer engagements for ballet companies during the 1940s; however, in the summer of 1944 Denham was able to provide theatrical producer Edwin Lester with the entire Ballet Russe to serve as the dance contingent for *Song of Norway*, a musical about the life of Norwegian composer Edvard Grieg, by Robert Wright

BALLET RUSSE DE MONTE CARLO. Frederic Franklin (The Hussar) and Alexandra Danilova (The Street Dancer) in one of the company's most popular works, Léonide Massine's *Le Beau Danube*. Created in 1924 for Diaghilev's Ballets Russes, it was mounted for the Ballet Russe de Monte Carlo in 1933 and was hardly ever absent from the repertory. (Photograph from the Dance Collection, New York Public Library for the Performing Arts.)

and George Forrest. A part of Lester's annual Civic Light Opera series in California, *Song of Norway* opened in Los Angeles on 12 June 1944, moved to San Francisco on 3 July 1944, and settled down for a Broadway run at the Imperial Theater on 21 August 1944. After the show had become a success and the Ballet Russe wished to ready its own repertory for a fall season, company staff members trained and supervised a second cast of dancers to continue on in *Song of Norway*. The musical was choreographed by George Balanchine, whose contributions included Norwegian folk dances, a balletic satire to Grieg's incidental music to Ibsen's *Peer Gynt*, and, as finale, an elaborate classical ballet to an abridgment of Grieg's Piano Concerto.

Balanchine remained with the company for two more years, during which time the Ballet Russe attained the highest creative level it had known since its first seasons under Massine. An autumn engagement at the City Center began impressively on 10 September 1944 with the pre-

BALLET RUSSE DE MONTE CARLO. Ruthanna Boris, Alexander Goudovitch, and Dorothy Etheridge, members of the original cast, in George Balanchine's *Danses Concertantes* (1944), set to music by Igor Stravinsky. The fanciful costumes were designed by Eugene Berman. (Photograph from the Dance Collection, New York Public Library for the Performing Arts. Choreography by George Balanchine © The George Balanchine Trust.)

miere of Balanchine's playful *Danses Concertantes*, to a score by Stravinsky and with glittering jewel-like decor and costumes by Eugene Berman. A suite of dances for a ballerina, a *danseur*, and four sets of pas de trois dancers, the ballet was intended as a vehicle for Danilova and Franklin, who danced the premiere. But Franklin sustained an injury on the second night and for the rest of that engagement Leon Danielian appeared in the principal male role.

In addition to creating new works, Balanchine brought into the repertory revivals or new versions of ballets he had originally staged elsewhere. Thus 1944 saw the company's first performance of *Le Bourgeois Gentilhomme*, an adaptation of Molière's comedy produced by the Ballets Russes of Blum and de Basil in 1932; *Ballet Imperial*, an abstraction to Tchaikovsky's Second Piano Concerto that had been staged by the American Ballet in 1941; and *Mozartiana*, a set of mood pieces to Tchaikovsky's Fourth Suite for Orchestra that Balanchine created for his own company, Les Ballets 1933. Balanchine revived *Concerto Barocco* in 1945, an abstraction to Bach's Concerto in D Minor for Two Violins and Orchestra that had been originally produced by the American Ballet in 1941. Because Berman disliked the way in which his designs had been realized, he forbade their use, so *Concerto Barocco* was performed in black tunics against a plain backdrop. The Ballet Russe thereby instituted the now prevalent practice of dancing Balanchinian abstractions in the simplest possible settings and costumes.

Balanchine also created totally new works for the Ballet Russe. *Pas de Deux (Grand Adagio)* (City Center, 14 March 1945) was for Danilova and Franklin, to music from Tchaikovsky's *Sleeping Beauty*. *The Night Shadow* (City Center, 27 February 1946) was set to a score by Vittorio Rieti, adapted from themes by Bellini, with decor by the surrealist painter Dorothea Tanning; it was a Gothic fantasy dealing with the phenomenon of sleepwalking portrayed by Danilova, with Nicholas Magallanes, Maria Tallchief, and Michel Katcharoff. Assisted by Danilova, Balanchine produced a three-act version of Aleksandr Glazunov's *Raymonda* (City Center, 12 March 1946) that also starred Danilova and Magallanes. Audiences of the time, unused to multiact classical ballets, found *Raymonda* too leisurely in its pace, so it was soon trimmed to a one-act *divertissement*.

In 1945 the company staged Ruth Page and Bentley Stone's *Frankie and Johnny*, a rowdy bit of Americana that had been created for the choreographers' Chicago company in 1938. Considered slightly risqué in its retelling of an old popular ballad, it occasionally raised eyebrows and attracted the attention of municipal censorship boards. Also in 1945, Todd Bolender had a ballet produced for the first time by a major company when the Ballet Russe offered his *Comedia Balletica*, a revised version

BALLET RUSSE DE MONTE CARLO. Members of the ensemble in George Balanchine's *Ballet Imperial*, set to Tchaikovsky's Piano Concerto no. 2. Originally choreographed in 1941 for the American Ballet, Denham's company first mounted this homage to Russian style in 1944. (Photograph by Richard Tucker; used by permission of Julia Tucker. Choreography by George Balanchine © The George Balanchine Trust.)

of *Musical Chairs,* a playful piece to Stravinsky's *Pulcinella* suite that Bolender had originally staged at Jacob's Pillow.

Nevertheless, despite such contrasting works by other choreographers, Balanchine significantly affected company style. Long noted for the vitality of its character and *demi-caractère* dancing, the Ballet Russe developed a new sense of classical refinement as a result of dancing Balanchine's ballets. At the same time, the presence in the repertory of works by Fokine, Massine, de Mille, and Page kept the *demi-caractère* tradition alive. In casting his ballets, Balanchine both found roles for such international stars as Danilova and Franklin and encouraged such young North American dancers as Maria Tallchief, Mary Ellen Moylan, Ruthanna Boris, Patricia Wilde, Leon Danielian, and Nicholas Magallanes.

Balanchine also helped to make the Ballet Russe of interest to the dance world's intelligentsia as well as to the general public. A controversial choreographer, Balanchine, through his abstractions, divided both the public and the press into equally vocal and ardent, but opposing, camps. This dichotomy is perhaps best reflected in the attitudes of two leading dance critics, John Martin of the *New York Times* and Edwin Denby of the *New York Herald Tribune.* For Martin, many of Balanchine's ballets consisted of nothing more than "pretty mathematics," whereas Denby praised them for their "clarity and excitement" and "human naturalness of expression." Denby declared that by demonstrating that Americans "can dance straight classic ballet without self-consciousness—as naturally as people speak their native tongues—he [Balanchine] has proved that ballet can become as native an art here as it did long ago in Russia."

Events following World War II took Balanchine away from the Ballet Russe. He was invited to be ballet master at the Paris Opera and to create new works for Ballet Society, an experimental producing organization founded by Lincoln Kirstein in 1946. Loathing the drudgery of one-night stands and the unreliable standards of pickup orchestras on tour, Balanchine found both of these new opportunities more congenial to him than continued association with the Ballet Russe. He was the last resident choreographer the company was to have.

From 1946 onward, Denham commissioned ballets from an assortment of choreographers, his initial choices proving to be quite enterprising. Ruth Page's *The Bells* (1946) was a symbolic interpretation of the poem of that name by Edgar Allen Poe; and in her *Billy Sunday* (1948) she blended the spoken word with dance movement in a ballet derived from the extravagant sermons of a baseball player turned evangelist. Both productions were first presented in Chicago by Page's company before entering the Ballet Russe repertory.

On 4 March 1947 at the City Center, the Ballet Russe offered the premiere of Valerie Bettis's *Virginia Sampler*,

BALLET RUSSE DE MONTE CARLO. Leon Danielian and Ruthanna Boris in Boris's *Cirque de Deux* (1947). (Photograph reprinted from Anderson, 1981.)

thereby becoming the first classical ballet company to perform a work by a modern dancer. With music by Leo Smit, *Virginia Sampler* concerned life in a southern small town shortly after the American Revolution. If not totally successful, it was nonetheless considered an honorable experiment.

Antonia Cobos, a dancer and choreographer who combined classical ballet with traditional Spanish dance, contributed *Madroños* (City Center, 22 March 1947), a light-hearted suite of Spanish dances, and *The Mute Wife* (Metropolitan Opera House, 16 September 1949), adapted from a comedy by Anatole France. Ruthanna Boris made a successful choreographic debut with *Cirque de Deux* (Hollywood Bowl, 1 August 1947), an affectionate parody of balletic mannerisms to the Walpurgis Night music from Gounod's *Faust*.

To celebrate the tenth anniversary of its American debut, the Ballet Russe offered an autumn 1948 season at the Metropolitan Opera House that was notable for the high quality of its ensemble dancing and the brilliance of its stars, four of whom—Alicia Markova, Alexandra Danilova, Mia Slavenska, and Nathalie Krassovska—shone brightly on 18 September 1948 in a staging of Anton Dolin's *Pas de Quatre*. Changing balletic taste was evident in that revivals of Massine's *Seventh Symphony* and *Rouge et Noir* caused little stir. The most unusual of the season's novelties—unusual not in its theme, but in the circumstances of its creation—was Boris's *Quelques Fleurs* (30 September 1948), a comedy to a potpourri of pieces by Auber that told of a haughty contessa's vain attempts to lure a young man by enticing him with magic perfumes. The ballet was financed by the Houbigant perfume company, and Boris was free to use any story or theme she pleased, provided she called her work *Quelques Fleurs*, the name of a perfume that Houbigant was reintroducing on the American market.

Despite the individual excellence of some of the ballets, it gradually became apparent that Denham's commissions of the late 1940s and early 1950s did not reflect any carefully thought-out artistic policy. In 1949 Danilova staged the *divertissements* from Marius Petipa's *Paquita*, but their episodic nature failed to please audiences of the time. Also in 1949 there was a new production of David Lichine's *Graduation Ball*. Tatiana Chamié, a popular and influential teacher, created two light comedies, *Birthday* (1949) and *Prima Ballerina* (1950). As a guest artist with the company in 1950, French ballerina Yvette Chauviré revived Serge Lifar's *Mort du Cygne* and *Roméo et Juliette* and Victor Gsovsky's *Grand Pas Classique* and *Nocturne*.

In previous years, the Ballet Russe had cherished tradition and encouraged new creations. But now it had serious rivals in both aspects of ballet production. As a touring company reduced to no more than forty dancers, it could not afford to mount the classics on the lavish scale that England's Sadler's Wells Ballet had introduced to America. In addition, it was becoming apparent that America's most vigorously creative company was the recently established New York City Ballet.

The increasingly erratic nature of Ballet Russe policies led to the departure of several vital company members: Ruthanna Boris and Mary Ellen Moylan resigned in 1950; on 30 December 1951, in Houston, Danilova gave her last performance as a regular member of the company. Finally, Denham temporarily disbanded the full company. For the 1952/53 and 1953/54 seasons, only a Ballet Russe de Monte Carlo Concert Company existed. Consisting of fifteen dancers, it toured the country with one-night stands under the auspices of Columbia Artists Management, presenting a single bill of *Swan Lake* (act 2), *Cirque de Deux*, the Bluebird pas de deux, and *Gaîté Parisienne*.

A reorganized Ballet Russe made its debut during the 1954/55 season. Favorite items from the repertory were revived and there were two new productions. Antonia Cobos choreographed a dance version of Gilbert and Sullivan's *The Mikado* (Baltimore, 1 October 1954) and Massine returned to his old company to create *Harold in Italy* (Boston, 14 October 1954), a ballet in the symphonic mode set to the Berlioz score. The season's guest artist was another former member of the company, Maria Tallchief, then of New York City Ballet.

During the 1955/56 season, the company began an association with Alicia Alonso and Igor Youskevitch, who had replaced Danilova and Franklin as the most famous couple in American ballet. Alonso remained with the company until 1960, when worsening political relations between the United States and her native Cuba made it impossible for her to appear in the United States. Youskevitch continued with the Ballet Russe, as guest artist and artistic adviser, until the company's demise.

Important productions of the mid-1950s included *La Dame à la Licorne* in 1955, a ballet on a medieval theme with choreography by Heinz Rosen and decor by Jean Cocteau that had originally been produced in Munich in 1953; *Sombreros* (1955), a suite of Mexican dances that was Leon Danielian's choreographic debut; and a version by Boris Romanov of Riccardo Drigo's *Harlequinade* (1956). The company's leading female dancer was now Nina Novak, a Polish dancer who had joined the Ballet Russe in 1948 and who, after successfully dancing character and *demi-caractère* roles, received classical ones as well. She also served as ballet mistress and choreographed *Variations Classiques* (1957), an abstraction to Brahm's *Variations and Fugue on a Theme by Handel*.

The Ballet Russe, which had not had a long New York season since 1951, returned to the Metropolitan Opera House from 21 April to 4 May 1957, with Danilova, Franklin, and Danielian as guest artists. Although that engagement broke all box-office records for an American

BALLET RUSSE DE MONTE CARLO. A tableau from the company's 1948 production of *Pas de Quatre*, staged by Anton Dolin after Jules Perrot's 1845 Romantic *divertissement* featuring the four most famous ballerinas of the day. Clockwise from left, the dancers are Mia Slavenska as Carlotta Grisi, Alicia Markova as Marie Taglioni, Nathalie Krassovska as Lucile Grahn, and Alexandra Danilova as Fanny Cerrito. (Photograph by Walter E. Owen; from the Dance Collection, New York Public Library for the Performing Arts.)

company at the Met, the critics, despite their praise for stars and soloists, found that the company was artistically drifting, rather than developing, and that charge was repeatedly made in the years after 1957. New productions continued to be offered, but few were of any consequence. The most elaborate of these novelties was a three-act *Swan Lake*, staged in 1960 by Novak and Anatole Vilzak. The most durable of them has been Franklin's *Tribute* (1961), a lyrical treatment of César Franck's *Symphonic Variations* that has found its way into the repertory of other companies. The Ballet Russe repertory diminished in size and variety, and many programs were devoted to repetitions of *Swan Lake* (act 2), the one-act *Nutcracker*, and *Schéhérazade*—a triple bill that became a company trademark.

Once a popular, beloved, and financially successful troupe, the Ballet Russe now found its artistic reputation tarnished and its financial receipts dwindling. Finally, at the end of the 1961/62 season, Denham quietly disbanded his company.

Although the company's twilight years can serve as an object lesson in the necessity for a dance group to have a coherent artistic policy, the Ballet Russe de Monte Carlo was a company of genuine importance, and its best pro-

BALLET RUSSE DE MONTE CARLO. A studio portrait of Alan Howard and Nina Novak in costume for Balanchine's *Ballet Imperial*, revived in 1957. (Photograph by Maurice Seymour; used by permission. Choreography by George Balanchine © The George Balanchine Trust.)

ductions made real contributions to the art of dance. Its early years, under Massine, were marked by such light works as *Capriccio Espagnol* and *Gaîté Parisienne* and by serious efforts such as *Nobilissima Visione, Seventh Symphony*, and *Rouge et Noir*. Under Balanchine's guidance, the company championed the neoclassical abstract ballet. *Rodeo* stands as a landmark in the Americanization of ballet, and the Ballet Russe also promoted Americana with *Ghost Town, Frankie and Johnny*, and *Billy Sunday*. The company made a historically important venture into modern dance with *Virginia Sampler* and gave choreographic opportunities to Todd Bolender, Ruthanna Boris, and Antonia Cobos.

The company's diverse repertory also included works from the nineteenth century, such as *Giselle, Coppélia, Swan Lake, The Nutcracker*, and *Paquita*. From the Diaghilev era came *Les Sylphides, Petrouchka, Schéhérazade, Le Spectre de la Rose, L'Après-midi d'un Faune, Le Tricorne (The Three-Cornered Hat), La Boutique Fantasque*, and the Polovtsian Dances from Borodin's opera *Prince Igor*.

The company favored a vivid style of presentation. The-atrical projection and stage personality were highly valued. Yet the stylistic demands of each ballet were met and no dancer was allowed to violate that style. In its later years, the company was accused of having lost some of this concern for stylistic distinctiveness—yet it never lost its vitality.

Forced by World War II to make the United States its home, the Ballet Russe de Monte Carlo bridged the Old World and the New. Its roster included many glamorous European artists. Yet Americans were members of the company from the outset and, soon, most of the dancers were from the Western Hemisphere. The acceptance of American dancers into such a cosmopolitan company was hailed as a vindication of the efficacy of American ballet training. Among the important dancers from the United States, Canada, and Latin America who were members of the Ballet Russe before its reorganization in 1954 were Ruthanna Boris, Leon Danielian, Ian Gibson, Alan Howard, Anna Istomina, Robert Lindgren, Nicholas Magallanes, Milada Mladova, Mary Ellen Moylan, Lupe Serrano, Gertrude Tyven, and Patricia Wilde. After the reorganization, notable dancers from the New World included Alicia Alonso, Irina Borowska, Eugene Collins, Eleanor D'Antuono, Deni Lamont, Roni Mahler, Lawrence Rhodes, Eugene Slavin, and Andrea Vodehnal. Four important dancers of American Indian descent were at one time or another members of the Ballet Russe: Rosella Hightower, Maria Tallchief, Yvonne Chouteau, and Moscelyne Larkin. With the hiring of Raven Wilkinson in 1956, the Ballet Russe became the first touring American ballet company to employ a black dancer.

Not only did the Ballet Russe encourage American dancers, it also helped to bring ballet to American audiences. The Ballet Russe regularly toured on a scale that most later companies would not think of matching. For example, there were 188 performances in 104 cities during 1954/55, and the next season's schedule included 161 performances in 95 cities. The tours—by train before 1952 and by bus and truck after that—were arduous. Yet, thanks to a remarkable esprit de corps, the company tried to dance full-out at every performance. Danilova and Franklin served as exemplars in this—for them, no town or audience was too small or unimportant to justify cutting choreographic corners or dancing at less than peak energy. As a result, the Ballet Russe worked wonders; it gave many Americans their first glimpse of ballet, and audiences tended to like what they saw. Thus the Ballet Russe helped to make ballet an important American art. Many American dancers were inspired to study ballet because they had seen performances by the Ballet Russe; and, today, many former members of the Ballet Russe are teachers and company directors throughout America.

[*Many of the figures and works mentioned herein are the subjects of independent entries.*]

BIBLIOGRAPHY

Amberg, George. *Ballet: The Emergence of an American Art.* New York, 1949.

Anderson, Jack. *The One and Only: The Ballet Russe de Monte Carlo.* New York, 1981. Contains a complete season-by-season listing of the Ballet Russe de Monte Carlo personnel and repertory.

"Ballet Russe de Gotham." *Newsweek* (24 September 1945).

"A Conversation with Alexandra Danilova." *Ballet Review* 4.4 (1973): 32–51; 4.5 (1973): 50–60.

Danilova, Alexandra. *Choura: The Memoirs of Alexandra Danilova.* New York, 1986.

de Mille, Agnes. *Dance to the Piper.* Boston, 1952.

Denby, Edwin. *Looking at the Dance* (1949). New York, 1968.

Fay, Anthony. "Ballet Russe Retrospective." *Ballet Review* 4.6 (1974): 91–97.

García-Márquez, Vicente. *The Ballets Russes: Colonel de Basil's Ballets Russes de Monte Carlo, 1932–1952.* New York, 1990.

García-Márquez, Vicente. *Massine: A Biography.* New York, 1995.

Martin, John. *Ruth Page: An Intimate Biography.* New York, 1977.

Maynard, Olga. *The American Ballet.* Philadelphia, 1959.

Robert, Grace. *The Borzoi Book of Ballets.* New York, 1946.

Taper, Bernard. *Balanchine: A Biography.* New rev. ed. New York, 1984.

Twysden, A. E. *Alexandra Danilova.* London, 1945.

JACK ANDERSON

BALLETS AFRICAINS, LES. Founded around 1952 in Paris by the Guinean intellectual Fodéba Kéita, Les Ballets Africains was originally comprised of musicians and dancers from throughout the French colonies in Africa and the Caribbean. First known as Les Ballets Africains de Kéita Fodéba, it became the first of the African national dance companies, known as Les Ballets Africains of the Republic of Guinea, when Kéita presented the troupe to the new nation following Guinean independence in 1958.

Although not the only Guinean dance troupe of the period before independence, as the longest surviving and best known, it is considered to have pioneered the genre of African theatrical dance that has been influential both in Africa and in the West. In this genre rhythm patterns from a variety of cultures are performed in segments in choreographed works. A rhythm pattern that might be

LES BALLETS AFRICAINS. Originally an all-male troupe, Les Ballets Africains is one of the oldest folkloric companies in Africa. This photograph shows the company's emphasis on merging elements of traditional West African dances with European, specifically French, performance values. (Photograph © 1991 by Jack Vartoogian; used by permission.)

played for hours in a village celebration becomes a segment of ten minutes or less. Some pieces have elaborate stories, others are based on themes or moods such as *Serenade*. None are abstract. Both musicians and dancers are costumed. The creation of new work is a collaborative process involving all company members, who are asked to contribute songs and step patterns known to their families. After forty years Les Ballets Africains continues to find new material in the villages of Guinea. A trip in 1991 by the technical director and choreographer to seven towns in the Guinean interior for research and informal auditioning was beautifully documented on video by Guinean filmmaker Lamine Camara.

Music and dance have a central place in traditional African political and cultural life, and under the first regime after Guinean independence (1958 to 1984) were used to galvanize a new national identity. Les Ballets Africains toured in the interior of Guinea as part of the campaign leading up to independence. Kéita was elected to the Territorial Assembly of Guinea as the representative of Siguiri, his home district, and in 1957 became minister for internal affairs. In the first decade of independence he held important positions in the new government, but in 1969 he was arrested and imprisoned in the infamous Camp Boiro, never to be seen again by his family. After the death of Guinea's first president in 1984, the dissolution of the national performing arts troupes was widely expected. However, although the government no longer provides extensive administrative and financial support to national and regional troupes, Les Ballets Africains and the second national dance troupe, Le Ballet National Djoliba, have survived the transition, and along with newer ensembles, participate in national and local celebrations in addition to international touring.

Since 1986 the three most important members of the management committee of Les Ballets Africains have been Italo Zambo, director general; Hamidou Bangoura, technical director; and Kemoko Sano, choreographer. Zambo was born in Dakar in 1939 and joined Les Ballets Africains in Dakar in 1955. By the mid 1960s, Zambo and Bangoura had become the two principal male dancers and were considered to represent the artistic management of the company. Bangoura headed Les Ballets Africains from 1980 to 1986. Sano, who directed Le Ballet National Djoliba from 1973 to 1986, was asked to select ten musicians and dancers from that troupe to transfer with him to Les Ballets Africains in 1986.

From its earliest years Les Ballets Africains has toured extensively internationally in Europe, North and South America, Japan, Australia, and also in Africa. It toured West Africa in 1956 and first performed in the United States in 1959. According to Richard Long, in his book *The Black Tradition in American Dance* (1989), "The success of the Ballets Africains contributed to a widespread movement in the United States." The company was seen less outside Africa after 1973, until 1990, when it resumed a very active touring schedule under new management. In December 1991 Les Ballets Africains performed in Accra at the invitation of the government of Ghana.

Fodéba Kéita had set some of his works for Les Ballets Africains in the colonial period, notably *Minuit*, a tragic love story that Guinean Television produced with the company in 1988 in tribute to him. On international tours in 1990 and 1991 Les Ballets Africains presented a mixed bill that included older works such as *Malissadio* along with the newer *La Cloche de Hamana* (The Bell of Hamana), with which the company had celebrated the thirtieth anniversary of Guinean Independence in 1988. On tours in 1993 it presented a new evening-length work, *Silo: The Path of Life*, the story of a mother with two sons, and in 1996, *Heritage*, which combines history and legend.

BIBLIOGRAPHY

Charry, Eric. "A Guide to the Jembé." *Percussive Notes* 34.2 (April 1996).

Fleming, Bruce. "A Conversation in Conakry." *Danceview* (Autumn 1993).

Fodéba, Kéita. "About Les Ballets Africains." *Christian Science Monitor* (31 January 1959).

Kaba, Lansiné. "The Cultural Revolution, Artistic Creativity, and Freedom of Expression in Guinea." *The Journal of Modern African Studies* 14.2 (1976): 201–218.

Long, Richard A. *The Black Tradition in American Dance*. New York, 1989.

VIDEOTAPE. *Afrika Tanzt*, Insel Film (Munich, c.1963). *International Zone: AFRICA DANCES*, United Nations Television (New York, 1967). *Naitou*, Syli Cinema, Moussa Diakité (Conakry, Republic of Guinea, 1982). *Minuit*, Radio-Television Guineenne–RTG (Conakry, 1988). *Les Ballets Africains, After-Image*, Channel 4 TV (London, 1990). *Heritage*, Queensland Performing Arts Trust (Brisbane, 1996). *Dance of Guinea, Prefectures of N'Zérékouré, Lola, Macenta, Siguiri, Mandiana, Boké*, MGZIC 9-5067 to MGZIC 9-5072, Dance Collection, New York Public Library for the Performing Arts at Lincoln Center; documentation of a 1991 trip to the Guinean interior by Hamidou Bangoura and Kemoko Sano of Les Ballets Africains.

LOUISE BEDICHEK

BALLETS DE PARIS DE ROLAND PETIT. After leaving the Ballets des Champs-Élysées in 1947, the young choreographer Roland Petit set out to establish a company over which he would have complete control. With the financial assistance of Prince Alessandro Ruspoli, an Italian patron of the arts, and the prince's wife, the company made its debut on 21 May 1948 at the Théâtre Marigny in Paris. Its style was close to that of the Ballets des Champs-Élysées. It commissioned designs from leaders in the decorative world; musical scores were entrusted to contemporary French composers; and the libretti for the ballets were created by popular writers of the day. Initially Petit presented some works by Janine Charrat and Léonide Massine's *Le Beau Danube*, but gradually the company's repertory became completely dominated by Petit's own work. [*See the entry on Petit.*]

The principal dancers of the Ballets de Paris were Janine Charrat, Zizi Jeanmaire, Colette Marchand, Vladimir Skouratoff, Serge Perrault, Milorad Miskovitch, and Gordon Hamilton. Margot Fonteyn appeared as a guest artist in Petit's *Les Demoiselles de la Nuit* (Ladies of the Night, 1948; music by Jean Françaix; libretto by Jean Anouilh; scenery and costumes by Léonor Fini). Other works performed during the first season were Petit's *L'Oeuf à la Coque* (The Boiled Egg), in which Colette Marchand scored a triumph, and Charrat's *Adame Miroir*, based on a book by Jean Genet (music by Darius Milhaud; scenery and costumes by Paul Delvaux). The hit of the season, however, was Petit's version of *Carmen*, which premiered at the Prince's Theatre in London on 21 February 1949. This led to a number of opportunities for Petit in the United States, including a season in New York and offers to make Hollywood films.

The Ballets de Paris had no permanent company, and Petit assembled dancers anew for each Paris season. At the Empire Theatre in 1953 he introduced several new works, including *Le Loup* (The Wolf), *Ciné-Bijou* (Bijou Theater), and *Lady in the Ice*. The leading dancers that season included Colette Marchand, Violette Verdy, George Reich, Serge Perrault, and Hélène Constantine. In 1955, the Ballets de Paris appeared at the Théâtre des Champs-Élysées, performing Petit's *La Chambre* (The Room) and *Les Belles Damnées* (The Beautiful Damned), with Veronika Mlakar, Tessa Beaumont, and Buzz Miller. In the 1958/59 season, the company appeared at the Alhambra Theatre in Paris. From 1962 to 1964 the couturier Yves Saint-Laurent collaborated with Petit on *Maldoror*, *Violon*, and *Rhapsodie Espagnole*. The last appearance of the Ballets de Paris was on 9 March 1966 at the Théâtre des Champs-Élysées; the company performed Petit's *Éloge à la Folie* (In Praise of Folly; music by Marius Constant; libretto by Jean Cau; scenery and costumes by Niki de Saint-Phalle, Jean Tinguely, and Martial Raysse).

[*See also* France, *article on* Ballet since 1914. *Many of the figures mentioned herein are the subjects of independent entries.*]

BIBLIOGRAPHY

Beaumont, Cyril W. *Ballets of Today: Being a Second Supplement to the Complete Book of Ballets.* London, 1954.
Beaumont, Cyril W. *Ballets Past and Present: Being a Third Supplement to the Complete Book of Ballets.* London, 1955.
Lidova, Irène. *Dix-sept visages de la danse française.* Paris, 1953.
Lidova, Irène. *Roland Petit.* Paris, 1956.
Lidova, Irène. "Roland Petit." *Les saisons de la danse*, no. 6 (Summer 1968): 11–14.
Lidova, Irène. "Roland Petit." *Danse-opéra* (April 1969).
Mannoni, Gérard, ed. *Roland Petit.* Paris, 1984.
Mannoni, Gérard. *Roland Petit: Un chorégraphe et ses peintres.* Paris, 1990.
Schneider, Marcel, and Marcelle Michel. *Danse à Paris.* Paris, 1983.

IRÈNE LIDOVA
Translated from French

BALLETS DES CHAMPS-ÉLYSÉES. This French company was established on 12 October 1945 at the Théâtre des Champs-Élysées in Paris. Its founders were Roland Petit, a twenty-one-year-old dancer and choreographer; Boris Kochno, who had previously worked with Serge Diaghilev; and Irène Lidova, who had been working with Petit. Despite the brief lifespan of the company, it is remembered in the history of French ballet for its freshness and youth. [*See the entries on Kochno and Petit.*]

The Ballets des Champs-Élysées was originated in 1943/44 with the first recitals by Petit and Janine Charrat and the Soirées de la Danse (Dance Evenings) organized by Irène Lidova at the Théâtre Sarah-Bernhardt after the Allied liberation of Paris. At these evening programs the public was introduced to new young dancers, including Jean Babilée, Nina Vyroubova, Irène Skorik, Ethéry Pagava, Colette Marchand, Zizi Jeanmaire, Janine Charrat, and Roland Petit. This brilliant generation of dancers, and Petit's choreographic talent, attracted the attention of stage designer Christian Bérard, writer Boris Kochno, and Roger Eudes, the manager of the Théâtre des Champs-Élysées. This led to the creation of Roland Petit's first ballet, *Les Forains* (The Traveling Players), with libretto by Kochno, music by Henri Sauguet, and scenery and costumes by Bérard. The ballet was presented in March 1945, during one of Petit's recitals; Roger Eudes was so impressed by it that he invited Petit to establish a new company, the Ballets des Champs-Élysées, at his theater. Boris Kochno became the artistic director, and Irène Lidova served as secretary general, while Eudes shared financial responsibilities with Petit's father.

The group began with very young dancers, including Jean Babilée, Irène Skorik, Ethéry Pagava, Nathalie Philippart, Marina de Berg, Hélène Sadovska, Christian Foye, and others. The star was Ludmilla Tcherina, replacing Jeanmaire, who had joined Serge Lifar in the Nouveau Ballet de Monte Carlo. The first program, given on 12 October 1945, included the forest scene from *The Sleeping Beauty*, staged by Olga Preobrajenska; *Jeu de Cartes*, staged by Janine Charrat, and *Les Forains*. The program was a brilliant success.

The second Paris season included several new works by Petit: *Les Amours de Jupiter* (music by Jacques Ibert); *La Fiancée du Diable* (music by Jean Hubeau); *Los Caprichos*, danced by eighteen-year-old Anna Nevada; *Concert de Danse*, created by Marcel Bergé, the choreographer of the Bal Tabarin, with sets by Beaurepaire); and a revival of

Rendez-vous (music by Joseph Kosma), previously staged at the Théâtre Sarah Bernhardt.

The next success of the company occurred in April 1946 at the Adelphi Theatre in London. Babilée was the idol of the third Paris season in June 1946, when he displayed his talent in *Le Jeune Homme et la Mort*. Another event of this season was the arrival of Nina Vyroubova, who danced *La Sylphide* in the version by Victor Gsovsky. New Petit ballets followed during 1946 and 1947: *Le Bal des Blanchisseuses* (The Washerwomen's Ball); (music by Duke); *Le Portrait de Don Quichotte* (music by Petrassi); and *Treize Danses* (music by André-Ernest-Modeste Grètry, costumes by Christian Dior), the ballet in which Violette Verdy and Leslie Caron came to public attention.

At the end of 1947, Roland Petit had a dispute with the management and with Kochno and left the company. Kochno invited David Lichine and Victor Gsovsky to join the company, and Jean Robin became the director. There were two successes in 1948, choreographed by Lichine: *Création*, Lichine's ballet without music; and *Rencontre, ou Oedipe et le Sphinx* (music by Sauguet), with Leslie Caron.

In 1949 a certain lassitude set in. Petit had just founded the Ballets de Paris, which was competing with the Ballets des Champs-Élysées. Little notice was taken of the latter company's two works by John Taras, *Devoirs de Vacances* (Vacation Assignments) and *Reparateur de Radio* (Radio Repairman); however, Babilée's *Till Eulenspiegel* (music by Strauss) was a great success. The company had two brilliant dancers in Youly Algaroff and Jean Guélis, while Yvette Chauviré and Vladimir Skouratoff performed on tours, creating *Grand Pas Classique* (music by Louis-François-Marie Auber, choreography by Gsovsky). The last creation of the Ballets des Champs-Élysées was Léonide Massine's *Le Peintre et Son Modèle* (music by Georges Auric, designs by Balthus), danced by Irène Skorik and Youly Algaroff. Faced with insoluble financial problems, the group was forced to terminate its activities.

Boris Kochno and Jean Robin made several efforts to revive it. In partnership with a group of former dancers, and with the participation of Yvette Chauviré, they organized a 1950 season at the Théâtre des Champs-Élysées, consisting of several works from the older repertory, with Chauviré dancing in *Le Cygne* (The Swan) and *Suite Romantique*. New artists included Hélène Trailine, Igor Fosca, and Gérard Ohn. A more serious attempt to revive the company was made in 1951, with the help of the American choreographer Ruth Page. The season opened on 17 October 1951, at the Théâtre de l'Empire, with *La Revanche* (Revenge), a Page creation adapted from the opera *Il Trovatore*, with sets and costumes by Antoni Clavé. The principal dancers included Violette Verdy, Vladimir Skouratoff, Hélène Trailine, Sonia Arova, Jacqueline Moreau, and Leon Danielian. After this short season, the group was discontinued for good during an unsuccessful tour in Germany.

[*See also* France, *article on* Ballet since 1914; *and the entries on the principal figures mentioned herein.*]

BIBLIOGRAPHY

Beaumont, Cyril W. *Ballets of Today: Being a Second Supplement to the Complete Book of Ballets.* London, 1954.

Beaumont, Cyril W. *Ballets Past and Present: Being a Third Supplement to the Complete Book of Ballets.* London, 1955.

Brunelleschi, Elsa. "Six Dancers of the Ballets des Champs-Élysées." *Ballet* 11 (November 1951): 18–26.

Lidova, Irène. *Dix-sept visages de la danse française.* Paris, 1953.

Lidova, Irène. *Roland Petit.* Paris, 1956.

Lidova, Irène. "Roland Petit." *Danse-opéra* (April 1969).

Mannoni, Gérard, ed. *Roland Petit.* Paris, 1984.

Mannoni, Gérard. *Roland Petit: Un chorégraphe et ses peintres.* Paris, 1990.

Schneider, Marcel, and Marcelle Michel. *Danse à Paris.* Paris, 1983.

Tugal, Pierre. "Ballet in Paris, 1946–1947." *Ballet Annual* 2 (1948): 80–89.

IRÈNE LIDOVA
Translated from French

BALLETS 1933. A chamber company founded by choreographer George Balanchine and former Ballets Russes librettist Boris Kochno, Les Ballets 1933 existed largely through the patronage of Edward James, a wealthy young Englishman. During its brief life—less than four weeks of performances in June and July 1933 before small but posh audiences in Paris and London—Les Ballets 1933 provided Balanchine with his first opportunity in the West to create an entire repertory of his own. Of the six ballets presented by the company, all were by Balanchine and all were new. In the tradition of Serge Diaghilev, distinguished artists contributed the designs, and several of the works had commissioned scores.

In Paris on 7 June at the Théâtre des Champs-Élysées, world premieres were presented of *Mozartiana*, set to music of Petr Ilich Tchaikovsky, with scenery and costumes by Christian Bérard; *Les Songes*, set to music of Darius Milhaud, with scenery and costumes by André Derain; and *Les Sept Péchés Capitaux* (The Seven Capital Sins), with music by Kurt Weill, a libretto by Bertolt Brecht, and scenery and costumes by Caspar Rudolph Neher. (The last-named of these, also called *Anna Anna*, featured Lotte Lenya as the singing Anna and the beautiful Tilly Losch as the dancing Anna.) *Fastes*, set to music of Henri Sauguet, with scenery and costumes by Derain, and *Errante*, to music of Franz Schubert, with scenery, costumes, and lighting by Pavel Tchelitchev, followed on 10 June. Completing the repertory, *Les Valses de Beethoven*, with scenery and costumes by Emilio Terry, was presented on 19 June.

Balanchine had been dismissed from René Blum and Colonel W. de Basil's Ballet Russes the previous January. With Kochno (who had been Diaghilev's companion and confidant), and modestly backed by a circle of friends that included Broadway composer Cole Porter and Paris fashion designer Coco Chanel, Balanchine formed a small troupe that soon attracted the financial support of Edward James, whose real love was surrealism but who had married the "exotic" Viennese dancer Tilly Losch (for whom Balanchine created two highly unclassical ballets).

The critical reception was mixed: Virgil Thomson praised the company's "youth and new ideas"; André Levinson, an admirer of Balanchine, saw only "confusion and uncertainty"; and the "grotesque" and "German" nature of *Errante* and *The Seven Capital Sins* was found offensive by many. (According to Tchelitchev, however, *Errante*—with its stunning effects of light on fabric—received thirty-two curtain calls; clearly Balanchine was partial to the work, for he revived it at the debut of his American Ballet in 1935, again in 1941, and for Ballet Theatre in 1943.)

When some of these ballets were presented in New York in 1935, the *New York Times* critic John Martin saw in them "evidences of the decadence of the classic tradition as it is found in certain European environments, examples of what someone has aptly called 'Riviera aesthetics.'" *Mozartiana* had the longest life: Balanchine mounted it, with modifications, for the American Ballet in 1935 and for the Ballet Russe de Monte Carlo ten years later; the Danilova Concert Group was still performing it in 1956. (In 1982 Balanchine created another work to the score; he had staged a new *Seven Deadly Sins* in 1958.)

Les Ballets 1933 disbanded after a single season. Among the young dancers Balanchine had engaged who went on to important careers were Tamara Toumanova, Roman Jasinski, Lubov Rostova (Lucienne Kylberg), Natalie Leslie (Nathalie Krassovska), and Pearl Argyle. It was during the London appearance of Les Ballets 1933 that Balanchine was introduced to Lincoln Kirstein; their meeting changed both their lives and altered the history of ballet in America.

BIBLIOGRAPHY
Les Ballets 1933. Exhibition catalog, The Royal Pavilion, Brighton. Brighton, 1987.
Les Ballets 1933. Exhibition catalog, National Museum of Dance. Saratoga Springs, N.Y., 1990.
Dezarnaux, R. Review. *Liberté* (13 June 1933).
Finch, Tamara. "Les Ballets 1933." *The Dancing Times* (March 1988): 532–535.
Kirstein, Lincoln. "Entries from an Early Diary." *Dance Perspectives*, no. 54 (Summer 1973).
Lassalle, Nancy. "Beyond Les Ballets 1933." *Ballet Review* 16 (Fall 1988): 9–12.
Martin, John. Review. *New York Times* (10 March 1935).
Menuhin, Diana. "Les Ballets 1933." *Dance Research* 6 (Autumn 1988): 61–77.
Pritchard, Jane. "Les Ballets 1933." *Ballet Review* 16 (Fall 1988): 13–34.
Taper, Bernard. *Balanchine: A Biography.* New rev. ed. Berkeley, 1996.
Tyler, Parker. *The Divine Comedy of Pavel Tchelitchew.* New York, 1967.

ARCHIVES. Brighton Art Gallery and Museums. Collection Rondel, Bibliothèque de l'Arsenal, Paris. Edward James Collection, The Royal Pavilion, Brighton.

NANCY REYNOLDS

BALLET SOPIANAE. In 1960 a handful of enthusiastic young graduates from the Hungarian State Ballet Institute, along with Imre Eck, then solo dancer with the Budapest Opera Ballet, were engaged by the National Theater of Pécs in southern Hungary. The new company, named Ballet Sopianae, was given free rein in producing new and modern programs. Eck choreographed fourteen one-act ballets between January 1961 and December 1962, initiating modern ballet in Hungary. [*See the entry on Eck.*]

Eck relied on classical technique but also used jazz dance elements, acrobatic movements, exotic folklore, pantomimic gestures, realistic and naturalistic movements of daily life, and various props such as sticks, chairs, platforms, and networks of bars. Besides staging works to the music of François Couperin, Antonio Vivaldi, and other classical composers, Eck worked in close cooperation with young Hungarian composers. His works dealt with protests against cruelty and war, the problems of the younger generation, and the eternal struggle of good and evil, but they also displayed pure dance elements.

The first twelve years of the Ballet Sopianae carried the imprint of Eck's personality in both form and content, although he also allowed young dancers in the company to choreograph and welcomed both Hungarian and foreign guests to stage their productions. Sándor Tóth, one of the group's best dancers, produced *What Is under Your Head?* to music by Jószef Kincses in 1964; in a comic vein, it became a lasting success. Antal Fodor's best creation for the company was *Ballo Concertante* (music by Vivaldi, 1966). After a few other works, Fodor joined the Budapest Opera Ballet, but Tóth turned out to be an excellent collaborator and Eck entrusted him with the directorship of the group, remaining as artistic director.

While continuing as solo dancer, Tóth established himself as a choreographer between 1972 and 1974 with five short works in *Barefoot* (1973) and three one-act ballets set to music by Gustav Mahler (1974), which revealed Tóth's sense for intimate and concise forms as well as for proportional choreographic architecture. His *Five Études for Cymbale* to music by modern Hungarian composers in 1977 continued his line of mini-ballets; he later chose major forms such as Johann Sebastian Bach's second and third Brandenburg concerti and Petr Ilich Tchaikovsky's *Romeo and Juliet*, both in 1980, and a dance fantasy, *The*

Fountain of Bakhchisarai (music by Boris Asafiev), in 1982.

Other young dancers of the Ballet Sopianae also were given their chance to choreograph. The company welcomed masters and dancers from other groups, such as Gyula Harangozó (*Scene in the Czarda* and the Polovtsian Dances from *Prince Igor*, both 1970), and folk dance choreographers such as Sándor Tímár (1974), along with foreign guests. The company's ballet mistress was Zsuzsa Végvári and the leading solo dancers included Mária Bretus, Dóra Uhrik, and János Hetenyi. In the first two decades, almost all costumes were designed by Judit Gombár.

Since 1978 the company has expanded its activities by organizing the annual Pécs Summer Festival for various theatrical genres, including pantomime and music as well as dance, holding performances at various sites in and outside the town, among old ruins, in parks, and on open-air stages. Eck remained responsible for artistic management. Within three decades, the Ballet Sopianae produced or staged more than two hundred ballets, including more than one hundred by Eck, with a diverse array of subjects, styles, and choreographies, making Pécs the richest modern dance center in Hungary.

During the 1980s, the Ballet Sopianae's repertory included works by foreign guest choreographers such as Pavel Smok and Bertrand d'At, by young Hungarian choreographers such as Péter László and Katalin Lőrinc, and some of Imre Eck's important works. Sándor Tóth's *Romeo and Juliet* was premiered in 1980. The Ballet Night of February 1982 featured Eck's *A Midsummer Night's Dream* (music by Felix Mendelssohn) and Tóth's *Medeia* (music by J. Lucik) that combined classical, modern, pantomime, and elaborate stage effects into a dramatic harmony. *The Desert of Love* (music by the East Ensemble), one of Eck's last ballets, was an attempt at a lighter, jazz-style type of movement.

The company celebrated its thirtieth anniversary in 1990, opening the stage for a new generation of dancers and choreographers including István Herczog, who had spent two decades in Germany. Herczog introduced and established himself with *The Stations of Life* in March 1991 (music by Kitaro and Jarre), a journey from the embryonic state to death, and *Romeo and Juliet* (music by Serge Prokofiev) in November 1991. In 1992, Herczog became director. He started to forge a new company style by inviting several young Hungarian choreographers to work with the company. The company has also toured Europe, India, Sri Lanka, and much of the Middle East.

BIBLIOGRAPHY

Dienes, Gedeon P. "A Pécsi Balett reperteárjának koreográfiai elemzése" (A Choreographic Analysis of the Repertory of Ballet Sopianae). *Tánctudományi tanulmányok* (1967–1968): 7–28.

Dienes, Gedeon P., and Lívia Fuchs, eds. *A Színpadi tánc története Magyarországon.* Budapest, 1989.

Fuchs, Lívia. "Reminiscences and Visions." *Hungarian Dance News,* no. 3–4 (1983): 3–4.

Fuchs, Lívia. "Novelties in the Repertoire of Ballet Sopianae." *Hungarian Dance News,* no. 1 (1989): 8–10.

Kaán, Zsuzsa. "Budapest and Pécs." *Hungarian Music News,* no. 6 (1976): 5–6.

Kaposi, Edit, and Ernő Pesovár, eds. *The Art of Dance in Hungary.* Translated by Lili Halápy. Budapest, 1985.

Koegler, Horst. "Pécs" and "Pécsi Balett." In *The Concise Oxford Dictionary of Ballet.* New York, 1977, 1982.

Körtvélyes, Géza. "A magyar balettművészet tizenötéve." *Tánctudományi tanulmányok* (1961–1962): 11–24. Includes a summary in French, "Quinze années de ballet hongrois."

Kövágó, Zsuzsa. "Young Choreographers with Ballet Sopianae." *Hungarian Dance News,* no. 3–4 (1984): 2–3.

Kövágó, Zsuzsa. "B-S-E Ballet Night." *Hungarian Dance News,* no. 1 (1985): 9–10.

Peters, Kurt. "Interbalett '79 in Budapest." *Das Tanzarchiv* 27 (April 1979): 183–194.

GEDEON P. DIENES

BALLETS RUSSES DE MONTE CARLO. At various times, the Ballets Russes de Monte Carlo was alternatively known as the Ballets Russes de Colonel W. de Basil, Educational Ballets Limited, Covent Garden Russian Ballet, and Original Ballet Russe. After Serge Diaghilev's death in 1929 René Blum, director of plays and operettas at the Théâtre de Monte Carlo, was appointed director of ballet at the theater. Determined to establish a new Russian ballet company based in Monte Carlo, he approached several of Diaghilev's former associates but met with little success. In 1931, however, he made the acquaintance of Colonel Wassily de Basil, an émigré Cossack colonel who became active in the theater after settling in Paris in 1919 and who was now co-director of L'Opéra Russe à Paris, which had a sizable ballet company. In late 1931 Blum and de Basil, despite considerable differences in background and temperament, organized a company, Les Ballets Russes de Monte Carlo, and appointed George Balanchine as ballet master, Boris Kochno as artistic adviser, and Serge Grigoriev as *régisseur général.*

The first full ballet season opened in Monte Carlo on 12 April 1932. However, the dancers had already performed during the earlier opera season at a special gala for Monaco's Fête Nationale on 17 January, at which Balanchine's *Cotillon,* a delightfully light but by no means insubstantial work, was premiered, with twelve-year-old Tamara Toumanova in the leading role. Along with twelve-year-old Irina Baronova and fourteen-year-old Tatiana Riabouchinska, Toumanova had been discovered by Balanchine in the Paris studios of Olga Preobrajenska (Toumanova and Baronova) and Matilda Kshessinska (Riabouchinska). These three were to become known as the "baby ballerinas."

BALLETS RUSSES DE MONTE CARLO. *(left)* Valentina Blinova, David Lichine, and Tamara Toumanova with the corps de ballet in the company's 1932 revival of Michel Fokine's *Les Sylphides* in Monte Carlo. *(below)* Scene from George Balanchine's *Cotillon* (1932), which became a staple in the company repertory. (Left photograph by Raoul Barbà; both photographs from the Dance Collection, New York Public Library for the Performing Arts. *Cotillon* choreography by George Balanchine © The George Balanchine Trust.)

The inaugural season lasted until 5 May 1932; the repertory included some Diaghilev revivals and three ballets by Boris Romanov as well as creations by Balanchine *(Cotillon, La Concurrence,* and *Le Bourgeois Gentilhomme)* and Léonide Massine *(Jeux d'Enfants).* Among the leading dancers were Felia Doubrovska, Valentina Blinova, Leon Woizikowski, and Valentin Froman. In addition to the "baby ballerinas," other young dancers were Lubov Rostova, Hélène Kirsova, Nina Verchinina, and Olga Morosova. An important group of young men also per-

formed: David Lichine, Yurek Shabelevsky, Roman Jasinski, Paul Petroff, and Roland Guerard.

The Massine Era. Balanchine and Kochno left at the end of the year to form Les Ballets 1933 and some of the company's dancers, including Toumanova, went with them. Thereupon Massine became the Ballets Russes de Monte Carlo's ballet master. A gala on 7 March 1933 featured a revised version of his ballet *Le Beau Danube,* which had been first staged in 1924 for Étienne de Beaumont's Soirées de Paris. During the 1933 Monte Carlo ballet season Massine created *Scuola di Ballo,* a comedy to music by Luigi Boccherini arranged by Jean Françaix, and the first of his controversial symphonic ballets, *Les Présages,* to Tchaikovsky's Fifth Symphony. This work provided notable opportunities for Baronova, Riabouchinska, and Lichine, and brought forward Verchinina who, having studied with both Preobrajenska and the modern dance pioneer Rudolf Laban, injected modern dance elements into the clasical vocabulary. It also introduced a young dancer who had exceptional turning ability, André Eglevsky. Leading dancers now included Nina Tarakanova, Massine himself, and Alexandra Danilova, whose sparkling personality triumphed in *Le Beau Danube.*

The company made its London debut at the Alhambra Theatre on 4 July 1933. The London public was enchanted by the dancers, among whom Anton Dolin appeared as guest artist. Their performances, enhanced by good publicity from an enthusiastic admirer, the critic Arnold Haskell, and the news value of the "baby ballerinas," resulted in an extended season that lasted until 4 November 1933. The company was further strengthened by the return of Toumanova and other dancers after the demise of Les Ballets 1933.

In October 1933 Massine staged his second symphonic ballet, *Choreartium,* to Brahms's Fourth Symphony. Considerable critical and public discussion ensued about the validity of staging choreographic versions of symphonic music, with eminent opinions supporting both sides of the argument. The productions, however, were extremely popular with audiences.

The impresario Sol Hurok arranged to present the company in New York, where it opened at the St. James Theatre on 22 December 1933. Its resident conductors were Efrem Kurtz and Antal Dorati, who had joined the company the previous month. The New York season lasted until 14 February 1934. During this time part of the company undertook a short tour, rejoining the main group in Chicago in February, when Massine's *Le Tricorne* and Michel Fokine's *Le Carnaval* were revived. A short return engagement took place at the St. James in March, and then, as a compliment to the United States, the company staged Massine's *Union Pacific* in Philadelphia on 6 April 1934. Some dancers had returned earlier to Monte Carlo, where they opened the an-

BALLETS RUSSES DE MONTE CARLO. The company ensemble in the first movement of Léonide Massine's *Choreartium* (1933), set to Brahms's Fourth Symphony. The sets were designed by Constantin Terechkovitch and Eugène Lourié and were executed by Elizabeth Polunine. (Photograph from the Dance Collection, New York Public Library for the Performing Arts.)

nual season (7 April–3 May) under Bronislava Nijinska's direction. In London the full company appeared at the Royal Opera House, Covent Garden (19 June–10 August), an important new association resulting from the strong interest engendered by the successful 1933 engagement. Influential company friends had collected funds to enable more Diaghilev ballet revivals to be staged, and *La Boutique Fantasque, The Firebird,* and *Aurora's Wedding* were added to the repertory. Danilova's dancing enhanced these works, as did Toumanova's and Baronova's, particularly in *Aurora's Wedding.*

The next North American tour began in October 1934 in Mexico City and took the company to Toronto, California, and Vancouver. Vera Zorina was now dancing leading roles in *La Boutique Fantasque* and *Le Beau Danube.* In Chicago in March 1935 Massine staged *Le Bal* and *Jardin Public,* neither of which proved particularly successful.

The Monte Carlo 1935 spring season (4–30 April) was to be the company's last at that theater because René Blum soon resigned as artistic director. The company continued to perform as the Ballets Russes de Colonel W. de Basil. (Blum went on to create a new company, Les Ballets de Monte Carlo.)

After its regular appearance in Spain, de Basil's company appeared at Covent Garden (11 June–24 August), a season marked by Lubov Tchernicheva's appearances in revivals of Fokine's *Schéhérazade* and *Thamar.* As Serge Grigoriev's wife, Tchernicheva had traveled with the company as a teacher since its founding, but now she made a triumphant return to the stage and would continue to perform certain roles for more than ten years. Bronislava Nijinska, who was on a year's contract as choreographer, staged the very successful *Les Cent Baisers* for Baronova. Revivals were staged of Massine's *Les Femmes de Bonne Humeur,* the dancers once more demonstrating their *demi-caractère* abilities, and of *Le Spectre de la Rose.*

From 9 to 20 October the de Basil ballet performed for the first time at the Metropolitan Opera House in New York, offering New York premieres of various works, including *Choreartium* and a revival of Massine's *Le Soleil de Nuit.* The company returned to New York on 12 April 1936 after a coast-to-coast tour and revived Nijinska's *Les Noces* for four performances. The difficulties of providing the full complement of singers and musicians for the score forced the company to drop the ballet from its repertory. Nijinska also mounted her lively and popular *Danses Slaves et Tziganes.*

At Covent Garden from 15 June to 29 August 1936 Massine staged his third symphonic ballet, *Symphonie Fantastique,* for de Basil's company, with himself and Toumanova in the leading roles and with magnificent sets by Christian Bérard. As Berlioz's score was program music the ballet generated less controversy than had Massine's earlier symphonic works. David Lichine, who had

BALLETS RUSSES DE MONTE CARLO. George Zoritch and Nina Verchinina in the third movement of Léonide Massine's 1936 *Symphonie Fantastique,* set to music by Hector Berlioz. The scenery was designed by Christian Bérard. (Photograph from the Dance Collection, New York Public Library for the Performing Arts.)

already choreographed two works for the company, also earned praise for his *Le Pavillon,* and two famous dancers, Matilda Kshessinska and Lydia Sokolova, performed solos at a gala on 14 July.

Invited to tour Australia, de Basil formed a second company in August 1936. This group was formed in part by dancers from Les Ballets de Leon Woizikowski, the company that had been founded by Woizikowski when he left de Basil in 1934 and that had been beset by financial problems. The repertory for the Australian tour comprised works from the main company's repertory and two ballets by Woizikowski. The principal dancers were Valentina Blinova, Hélène Kirsova, Valentin Froman, and Woizikowski. Other leading dancers were Tamara Tchinarova, Sonia Woizikowska, Nina Youchkevitch, Igor Youskevitch, and Roland Guerard. Jean Hoyer, who with his wife, Nathalie Branitska, had been with de Basil from the beginning, was appointed *régisseur général.* This tour, which included New Zealand, lasted from 13 October 1936 to 14 July 1937 and proved to be immensely successful. The group then toured Europe until the spring of 1938 with a varying roster of dancers.

Meanwhile, the main company appeared at the Scala Theater in Berlin in October 1936 and at the Metropolitan Opera House in New York (28 October–8 November),

BALLETS RUSSES DE MONTE CARLO. *(left)* Members of the company in front of the set designed by Cecil Beaton for David Lichine's *Le Pavillon* (1936). *(right)* Anton Dolin standing over Sono Osato in the original production of Lichine's *Protée* (1938); the scenery was designed by Giorgio de' Chirico. (Photographs from the Dance Collection, New York Public Library for the Performing Arts.)

where it staged a revival of Massine's sparkling and popular *Cimarosiana*. An arduous American tour, mainly consisting of one-night stands, followed from November 1936 to April 1937 and ended with a return engagement at the Metropolitan in April 1937, which included a performance billed as the company's one-thousandth. During this tour, countless small towns across the country saw full-scale ballets for the first time. American dancers hired by the company included Anna Adrianova (Shirley Bridge) and Sono Osato, and three new English dancers were recruited from Ballet Rambert: Pauline Strogova (Prudence Hyman or Hythe), Lisa Serova (Elizabeth Ruxton), and Vera Nelidova (Betty Cuff). For the coronation season of 1937 at Covent Garden the company danced with the opera from 9 June through the month, and then on its own from 1 to 31 July. After a short break it returned for a second season, which lasted from 6 September to 9 October.

De Basil's finances were always precarious. He relied on box-office receipts and patron support, and thus the regular summer season at Covent Garden was of the utmost importance. At about this time Massine and de Basil were embroiled in disagreements over matters of title and copyright. As early as August 1936 Massine had initiated a series of "choreographic copyright" suits against de Basil as he tried to restrain the second (Australian) company

from performing his ballets. He was unsuccessful, and in July 1937 he resumed litigation. Eventually he succeeded in obtaining a complicated verdict. For some of his works in de Basil's repertory Massine was awarded exclusive ownership. However, de Basil was awarded the right to perform some of Massine's works to a certain date and was given exclusive rights to other works as the commissioning agent.

The Era of Fokine and Lichine. In June, before Massine's contract expired in September, de Basil had engaged Fokine as choreographer. Fokine, who had revived *Papillons* in Chicago in December 1936, now embarked on intensive work on his ballets staged earlier by Grigoriev and Woizikowski. He also staged a spectacular and enticing version of his *Le Coq d'Or*, with Baronova and Riabouchinska. De Basil also called on David Lichine, who created the effective dramatic ballet *Francesca da Rimini* for Tchernicheva, a charming version of *Les Dieux Mendiants* for Danilova and Shabelevsky, and *Le Lion Amoureux* for Alice Nikitina, which proved to be a minor disaster.

Massine's contract was extended to cover part of the fall and winter American tour, which opened at the Metropolitan Opera House on 22 October 1937. He gave his last performance with the company at the San Francisco Opera House on 30 January 1938. Although his departure was regrettable because he was at his peak as a choreographer and dancer, it was by no means a serious setback. The company had many fine *demi-caractère* dancers, and both Fokine and Lichine produced popular ballets during the next few seasons. Both Danilova and Toumanova left at the same time as Massine. Various other dancers went with Massine, who had been appointed artistic director of Blum's company in Monte Carlo. This soon gained the sponsorship of World Art, Inc. (later Universal Art, Inc.), creating the company known as Ballet Russe de Monte Carlo directed by Sergei Denham.

In the hope of arranging a merger with de Basil, the new company signed an agreement with him, but this was later refuted by de Basil on the grounds that he had not properly understood the document he signed. Universal Art Inc. then brought an action against him personally in London on the eve of the de Basil Ballet Covent Garden season, threatening to stop performances. They were outwitted, however, by de Basil, who resigned as director general of his company; the directorship was taken over by the triumvirate of Victor Dandré, German (Gerry) Sevastianov, who had been de Basil's executive secretary, and W. G. Perkins, a lawyer. The season went ahead under the company's new name, Educational Ballets Limited, opening on 20 June 1938 at Covent Garden. (The Denham company opened at Drury Lane on 12 July 1938, thus engendering the famed London "ballet war.") At Covent Garden Vera Nemchinova was added to the roster of ballerinas. Fokine staged *Cendrillon* for Riabouchinska, and Lichine produced *Protée*. The five nymphs in this graceful cameo represented a new generation of dancers: Sono Osato; Anna Adrianova; two Canadian girls, Alexandra Denisova (Patricia Denise Meyers) and Natasha Sobinova (Rosemary Deveson); and Lina Lerina (Jacqueline Leri). Lichine danced the title role

The company now lost Hurok's sponsorship and found that American tours were no longer possible. Under the name Covent Garden Russian Ballet it undertook a lengthy and triumphant tour of Australia and New Zealand from 28 September 1938 to 27 April 1939. Among the principal dancers were Nemchinova, Baronova, Riabouchinska, Tchernicheva, Dolin, Lichine, Shabelevsky, Jasinski, and Petroff. Denisova, Anna Volkova, and Yurek Lazowski also danced leading roles. A new Lichine ballet, *The Prodigal Son*, was presented in Sydney, with Dolin in the title role.

Upon the company's return for a six-week engagement at Covent Garden starting 19 June 1939, Fokine staged *Paganini* for actor-dancer Dmitri Rostov, Riabouchinska, and Baronova. The outbreak of World War II disrupted all plans. After a short period of confusion de Basil returned from France to resume the company's directorship and soon negotiated another Australian tour. Dolin, Baronova, and her husband, Sevastianov, left the company, but de Basil retained a long list of principals and also added Michel Panaiev and George Skibine. Serge Lifar appeared with the company as guest artist in Sydney, reviving his ballet *Icare*. Igor Schwezoff had joined as a company member, staging *La Lutte Éternelle*. Verchinina choreographed *Etude*, and ballet master Anatole Oboukhoff re-

vived a two-act *Coppélia* in Sydney in 1940. A group of talented young dancers also emerged, including Marina Svetlova, Geneviève Moulin, Tatiana Leskova, Tatiana Stepanova, Oleg Tupine, and Nicholas Orloff. The tour lasted from 30 December 1939 to 19 September 1940 and included one brilliant premiere, Lichine's *Graduation Ball*. The cultural impact on Australia of the three de Basil tours was enormous, and of those dancers who chose to remain, Edouard Borovansky and Hélène Kirsova became key figures in the development of the country's ballet.

To lessen the confusion about the Russian ballet companies, de Basil now called his company Original Ballet Russe, and it was under this name that it returned to the United States in October 1940. After a short tour it appeared in New York at the Fifty-first Street Theater from 6 November 1940 to 26 January 1941, during which time Toumanova, Baronova, and Riabouchinska appeared together for the last time. Apart from *Graduation Ball*, new productions met with mixed reactions. A premiere by Bal-

BALLETS RUSSES DE MONTE CARLO. *Paganini* (1939), Michel Fokine's ballet about the great Romantic violinist, was set to Sergei Rachmaninov's *Rhapsody on a Theme of Paganini*. Here, Irina Baronova as Divine Genius whispers to Dmitri Rostov in the title role. (Photograph by Dan Bale.)

anchine, *Balustrade*, was especially controversial. Set to Stravinsky's Concerto in D for Violin and Orchestra and with designs by Pavel Tchelitchev, it featured a role created for Toumanova.

The Final Years. In March 1941 Original Ballet Russe arrived in Cuba and immediately encountered problems. A cut in salaries led to a protest letter from seventeen dancers. Failing to reach a settlement with de Basil, they went on strike, an unprecedented action at that time, and, although the remainder of the company fulfilled the Havana season, the rest of the scheduled tour had to be canceled. The dancers were stranded for many weeks but made ends meet by taking local engagements.

Eventually de Basil found another American backer, Fortune Gallo, and took his company to North America

for open-air performances in Washington, D.C., and a tour of eastern Canada. Nana Gollner was engaged, and Leon Danielian and Kenneth MacKenzie were added to the list of male dancers. An extensive tour of the United States was planned, but de Basil and Gallo had a falling out and in November 1941 Original Ballet Russe was once more in trouble. Without Hurok or Gallo, de Basil could make no more arrangements for appearances in North America. However, by January 1942 he had negotiated a South American tour that took the company to cities in Brazil, Uruguay, and Argentina and included an important season at the Teatro Colón in Buenos Aires for six weeks starting 15 October. Original Ballet Russe remained in South America until September 1946. It appeared regularly in Rio de Janeiro, Montevideo, and Buenos Aires and was joint resident ballet company at the Teatro Colón from 28 April to 28 November 1943. In addition, the company undertook pioneering tours of other South American countries, often under extremely adverse travel and performance conditions.

BALLETS RUSSES DE MONTE CARLO. The original cast, including Nicholas Orloff as the Drummer and (standing at right) Tatiana Riabouchinska as the First Junior Girl and David Lichine as the First Junior Cadet, in Lichine's *Graduation Ball* (1940). (Photograph by Roger Wood; used by permission.)

By this time, only a handful of the earlier principals remained with the company. Riabouchinska and Lichine had left, and after the first few months Nana Gollner and Paul Petroff returned to the United States. The leading dancers now were Olga Morosova, Tamara Grigorieva, Tchernicheva, Stepanova, Leskova, Volkova, Moulin, Nina Stroganova, Jasinski, Tupine, Rostov, MacKenzie, and Vladimir Dokoudovsky. The principal conductor was Eugene Fuerst; William McDermott joined as conductor in March 1943. Several other dancers subsequently departed, including Grigorieva in 1944 and Leskova in 1945, both to settle in South America, as had Verchinina.

Few important new ballets were produced because of insufficient funds and the lack of a major resident choreographer. Those staged were primarily by Ivo Váňa Psota, a Czech character dancer who had been with de Basil from 1932 to 1937 and then again in 1941. They consisted mainly of minor tributes to individual localities and had little merit. The large standard repertory of de Basil's company was novel to South American audiences, however, and the company's influence was great both at the time it toured and in the long term through the work of the dancers who remained to teach and choreograph.

The 1943 season brought active interchanges between Original Ballet Russe and the resident Colón ballet company. Thus, several Colón principals appeared in de Basil ballets, including María Ruanova, Leticia de la Vega, Dora del Grande, Lida Martinoli, Angel Eleta, and Louis Le Bercher, while Stepanova danced in the Colón production of *The Sleeping Beauty*.

The breach with Hurok had healed enough in 1946 to allow Original Ballet Russe's return, albeit in a somewhat shopworn state, to New York for a season at the Metropolitan Opera House (29 September–23 October), a coast-to-coast tour, and a second New York season (20–29 March 1947). This tour included ballets and dancers from Marquis de Cuevas's now defunct Ballet International, among them Rosella Hightower, Marjorie Tallchief, George Skibine, and John Taras. Ballets given New York premieres were *Cain and Abel* (staged by Lichine for de Basil in Mexico in March 1946), *Camille* (choreographed by Taras for guest artists Alicia Markova and Anton Dolin), and *Yara*, a Psota work first performed in August 1946 in Brazil. André Eglevsky also appeared as guest artist, and a production of *Giselle* by Dolin featured Markova and Hightower (the latter in a debut).

Hurok proposed that the collaboration between the de Basil and de Cuevas companies be made permanent, but de Basil would not agree, wishing to retain control of his own company. He returned to Europe and, together with the European impresario Julian Braunsweg, prepared for an engagement at Covent Garden (22 July to 13 September 1947). Numerous old favorites were staged, but although Serge Grigoriev was still *régisseur général* and

BALLETS RUSSES DE MONTE CARLO. A portrait of Alicia Markova and Anton Dolin, the original Camille and Armand, in John Taras's *Camille* (1946), set to the music of Franz Schubert. (Photograph by Maurice Seymour; used by permission.)

Tchernicheva the teacher, the performances failed to live up to memories of prewar standards. Riabouchinska and Lichine opened the season with *Graduation Ball*, which was seen for the first time in London and greatly enjoyed. The leading dancers for this engagement were Morosova, Renée (Zizi) Jeanmaire, Moulin, Hélène Komarova, Jasinski, Dokoudovsky, Vladimir Skouratoff, and Paul Grinwis; soloists included Hélène Constantine, April Olrich, Moussia Larkina (Moscelyne Larkin), and Barbara Lloyd. In September, Boris Kniaseff staged two ballets, *Piccoli* and *Silver Birch*. The conductors were Anatole Fistoulari and Richard Beck.

Lack of finances and the abruptly changing cultural atmosphere of the time meant that Original Ballet Russe had no future. It had seasons in Paris and Brussels, and then de Basil took a greatly changed company on an extensive tour of Spain and North Africa (April–November 1948). This group was led by Morosova, Stroganova, Verchinina, Dokoudovsky, and Grinwis. Robert Bell (Boris Belsky), a long-time member of the company, was *régisseur* under Grigoriev. During this tour Verchinina staged two short ballets. Another new production was Antony Joukowski's folk ballet *Danzas Eslavas*. The tour ended in

Palma de Mallorca on 6 November 1948, and the company was disbanded for good.

Some of the former dancers and a few new ones were recruited by de Basil in Paris in 1949 in the hope of filming several ballets. The venture came to little: only two works, *Graduation Ball* and *Swan Lake* act 2, were rather sketchily produced by Tadié-Cinéma.

De Basil planned to resume operations with new financial backing and was in the midst of negotiations to do so when he died of a heart attack on 27 July 1951 in Paris. His associate, the designer George Kirsta, launched a new Original Ballet Russe at Wimbledon Theatre in England on 10 October 1951. This hastily rehearsed company completed a provincial tour in Great Britain before appearing at the Royal Festival Hall in London on 26 December 1951. It offered a limited repertory that included one new (and unsuccessful) production, Dokoudovsky's *Les Femmes d'Alger*. Leading dancers were Sonia Arova, Nina Stroganova, Inge Sand, Paula Hinton, Joan Tucker, Herida May, Dokoudovsky, Jack Spurgeon, and Poul Gnatt. The company moved to the Adelphi Theatre on 14 January 1952 but failed to attract audiences and closed prematurely on 26 January, never to appear again.

De Basil's ballet company provided an invaluable link between Diaghilev's Ballets Russes and the development of various major indigenous companies throughout the world. Its repertory was diverse, encompassing traditional classical works (such as *Aurora's Wedding*), many *demi-caractère* ballets (in which the company excelled), and experimental works as exemplified by Massine and Lichine. The company also played a vital role in the popularization of ballet throughout the world by its indefatigable tours of the Americas and its acclaimed seasons throughout Australia.

Creatively, it is identified with Massine's symphonic ballets, beginning with *Les Présages* in 1933, and with David Lichine's career as a choreographer. Although *Graduation Ball* is the only work of his that is still performed today, Lichine was a dance creator of considerable inventiveness. Balanchine, Nijinska, and Fokine all produced fine new ballets for the company in the 1930s. Commissioned scores were rare, but Georges Auric, Jean Françaix, Vladimir Dukelsky, Nicolas Nabokov, and Frédéric d'Erlanger were each called upon to contribute. The designers' roster was impressive and included Christian Bérard, Pavel Tchelitchev, Raoul Dufy, Jean Hugo, André Derain, Oliver Messel, Alexandre Benois, Joan Miró, Cecil Beaton, and Giorgio de' Chirico. Some of the world's greatest conductors were associated with the company over the years.

If de Basil did less for the development of choreography than did other ballet directors, he contributed much to successive generations of dancers. They keenly appreciated the opportunity to learn and dance an important repertory of Russian ballets, and their later widespread influence as teachers, artistic directors, and choreographers has been of the utmost value to the dance world.

[*Many of the figures and works mentioned herein are the subjects of independent entries.*]

BIBLIOGRAPHY

Beaumont, Cyril W. *The Monte Carlo Russian Ballet.* London, 1934.
Chujoy, Anatole. *The Symphonic Ballet.* New York, 1937.
Coton, A. V. *A Prejudice for Ballet.* London, 1938.
García-Márquez, Vicente. *The Ballets Russes: Colonel de Basil's Ballets Russes de Monte Carlo, 1932–1952.* New York, 1990.
García Victorica, Victoria. *El original Ballet Russe en América latina.* Buenos Aires, 1948.
Haskell, Arnold L. *Balletomania.* London, 1934.
Haskell, Arnold L. *Dancing Round the World.* London, 1937.
Sorley Walker, Kathrine. *De Basil's Ballets Russes.* New York, 1983.
Stokes, Adrian. *To-Night the Ballet.* London, 1934.
Stokes, Adrian. *Russian Ballets.* London, 1935.

FILMS.   The Barzel Collection, Newberry Library, Chicago, contains films made by Ann Barzel during the Ballet Russe de Monte Carlo's stay in Chicago.

KATHRINE SORLEY WALKER

BALLETS RUSSES DE SERGE DIAGHILEV. From the inception in 1909 of what was to become the Ballets Russes until his death in 1929, the Russian art critic and impresario Serge Diaghilev played a role that was more artistic than managerial. While he did not make a direct creative contribution to any of the works he presented, he was ultimately responsible for the company's artistic policy, especially after 1911, when in place of the ad-hoc ensemble that had until then appeared in western Europe under his direction, he created a full-time ballet troupe. Because he made all the final artistic decisions, he exercised greater influence on the development of ballet in his time than any of the individual creative artists who worked for him, no matter how distinguished.

First and foremost, Diaghilev was an inspirational and generative force, the cause of creativity in others. He commissioned new scores from composers such as Maurice Ravel *(Daphnis et Chloé)*, Claude Debussy *(Jeux)*, Richard Strauss *(Die Josephslegende)*, Erik Satie *(Parade)*, Francis Poulenc *(Les Biches)*, and Sergei Prokofiev *(Le Pas d'Acier, The Prodigal Son)*. Diaghilev launched the international career of Russian composer Igor Stravinsky (who had already orchestrated two of the Chopin pieces that made up the music of *Les Sylphides*) by giving him the important commission to write *The Firebird* when the composer was twenty-seven. Diaghilev introduced several major artists (painters and sculptors) to the theater, among them Henri Matisse, Pablo Picasso, Georges Rouault, Juan Gris, Georges Braque, Maurice Utrillo, Giorgio de'Chirico, Max

BALLETS RUSSES DE SERGE DIAGHILEV. Michel Fokine's *Les Sylphides* was performed during the company's first season in Paris in June 1909. In this plotless one-act ballet, set to a suite of orchestrated piano pieces by Chopin, Fokine developed major aspects of his choreographic style, including a flowing, expressive use of the upper body and a reliance on nonhierarchical spatial groupings. This photograph shows Tamara Karsavina (front, right) during a 1911 performance in London. (Photograph from the Dance Collection, New York Public Library for the Performing Arts.)

Ernst, Joan Miró, Naum Gabo, and Antoine Pevsner. Diaghilev supervised the work of the fledgling choreographers Vaslav Nijinsky, Léonide Massine, Bronislava Nijinska, and George Balanchine.

As Alexandre Benois, one of the principal collaborators of Diaghilev's early days, put it in 1954, "This powerful manipulator . . . obliged creative artists to become the obedient executants of their own ideas under his despotic sway." Diaghilev had no hesitation in rejecting the designs submitted by Picasso for *Pulcinella* or insisting that the artist revise his conception completely. He criticized

Prokofiev's music for *The Prodigal Son* and asked for changes. He even made cuts in Stravinsky's *Apollo* (though they were later restored).

An Introduction of Russian Arts and Aesthetic Coherence. Diaghilev's activities in western Europe were prompted by a desire to show the world the artistic accomplishments of his native land. In 1906 he organized a comprehensive exhibition of Russian art for the Salon d'Automne at the Grand Palais in Paris. In 1907 at the Paris Opera he presented a festival of Russian music, consisting of five concerts. In 1908 he returned to the Opera with six performances of Modest Mussorgsky's opera *Boris Godunov*—the first outside Russia—in which the title role was sung by Fedor Chaliapin. In 1909 he was back in Paris, this time at the Théâtre du Châtelet, with more Russian opera. During the same season he presented four autonomous ballets: *Le Pavillon d'Armide*, *Les Sylphides*, *Cléopâtre*, and a *divertissement*. Contrary to expectations, the success of these ballets completely eclipsed that of the

BALLETS RUSSES DE SERGE DIAGHILEV. Scene 1 of the original production of *Petrouchka* (1911), choreographed by Michel Fokine and designed by Alexandre Benois. In the three cells of the Showman's booth (upstage) are the figures of Vaslav Nijinsky as Petrouchka (right), Tamara Karsavina as the Ballerina (center), and Nicholas Orloff as the Moor (left). Standing between the latter two is Enrico Cecchetti as the Showman. (Photograph from the Dance Collection, New York Public Library for the Performing Arts.)

operas; when Diaghilev returned to Paris in 1910 for a further Saison Russe, he offered nothing but dance. Thereafter, he devoted most of his energies to ballet—his most important life achievement being to change the attitude of the West toward an art that, in its own right, had been regarded as artistically inconsequential.

Until the arrival of the Russians, Paris was unfamiliar with a conception of ballet that could command attention—one in which dance and mime were thoroughly blended. In most of Diaghilev's early productions, the traditional separation of these two elements into diversion and exposition was obliterated. In the theaters of Europe and Russia, ballet was essentially notional and abstract, the exemplification in movement of long-held principles of order, harmony, and grace. For the World of Art group, ballet was essentially narrative and affective. As a result, the formal constraints of the *danse d'école* tended to give way to a kind of expressive body language that lent the dramatic action an air of unprecedented realism.

While in both Russia and Europe the standard nonoperatic ballet filled an entire evening and was necessarily discursive in manner, virtually all of Diaghilev's productions were in one act—aimed at swiftness, boldness, and dramatic tension—even when, like *Petrouchka* (1911), they consisted of several scenes. In the case of nonnarrative works (e.g., *Les Sylphides* [1909] and *Carnaval* [1910]) or those in which situation subsumed plot (e.g., *Le Spectre de la Rose* [1911]), the ballets set out to sustain a single, unbroken mood from beginning to end. A decisive factor in the tremendous theatrical impact of *Schéhérazade* (1910), apart from its exoticism, was that its provocations and thrills were so concentrated. The constituent elements—choreography, decor, costumes, plot, music—were combined to produce an effect of aesthetic coherence.

Even when, as in the case of *Schéhérazade*, that entailed the use and severe abridgment of a symphonic poem written to a different scenario, the ideal of the *Gesamtkunstwerk* (totality; the whole artwork) dominated all of Diaghilev's endeavors, both early and late in his career. Diaghilev's belief in this ideal, shared by the entire World of Art group as well as by choreographer Michel Fokine, led him to give great importance to scenery and costumes, even in later years when the Ballets Russes was more than once on the verge of bankruptcy. Until World War I, the visual side of the company's work was dominated by two brilliant men, Alexandre Benois and Léon Bakst, the work of Bakst being one of the company's principal attractions.

Another attraction was Nijinsky. Not for many years had male dancing of such brilliance, virility, and expressiveness been seen in the West, where (Denmark excepted) ballet was regarded as an almost exclusively female pursuit. For the first time since the days of Auguste Vestris, a male dancer eclipsed the ballerinas in renown. Except for the 1921 season, when Diaghilev presented his company in continuous performances of *The Sleeping Beauty* (renamed for the occasion *The Sleeping Princess*), a male star was the main attraction of the Ballets Russes—Nijinsky being succeeded in turn by Léonide Massine, Anton Dolin, and finally Serge Lifar.

Nearly all the singers, dancers, orchestral players, technicians, and administrators who had taken part in the 1909 Saison Russe were employees of the Russian imperial theaters, and most of them members of the Maryinsky Ballet in Saint Petersburg, in which city the repertory was rehearsed. Only after the season had ended in Russia might they travel to the West and participate in, essentially, a series of gala performances. Thus the first balletic endeavors of Diaghilev were limited to the period of spring to early summer. Only by creating a permanent organization, as he did within two years, was he able to make the Ballets Russes a part of the regular European theatrical scene. Despite its new status as a full-time company, the Ballets Russes that opened in Monte Carlo, Monaco, in April 1911 was hardly different in character from what it had been before. Fokine, who had resigned from the Maryinsky, was its choreographic director (a new title), Enrico Cecchetti its principal teacher, Vaslav Nijinsky its premier danseur, and Adolph Bolm its chief character dancer. Although Tamara Karsavina did not resign from the Maryinsky, she was prepared to spend a great deal of time with Diaghilev's company.

The corps de ballet was difficult to assemble, but one was finally established with dancers from Russia and Poland, some of whom came from a touring company. The quality of the corps de ballet was always difficult to maintain, though in due course it was strengthened by dancers who left Russia after the Revolution of 1917 and by an influx of European dancers, mainly English, all of whom were given Russian names. For its debut in London in the summer of 1911, the Ballets Russes had numbered seventy-five members. Thereafter, its size varied with Diaghilev's requirements and finances, though it was never to be as large again. For his summer season in London in 1921, he had forty-one dancers; for *The Sleeping Princess*, later that year, sixty-two. During the company's final season—in London in 1929—he had fifty. From its first performance in 1909 to its last, twenty years later, Diaghilev's Ballets Russes, which by the very nature of the enterprise could never cover expenses through box-office receipts alone, depended not on courtly or governmental subvention but on the ingenuity, charm, and social connections of Serge Diaghilev.

Much connected Diaghilev's company to the Russian imperial theaters—in particular to the Maryinsky—the ballet master and chief choreographer Michel Fokine, a product of the Maryinsky school, as were his dancers Anna Pavlova, Tamara Karsavina, Vaslav Nijinsky, and Adolph Bolm. Fokine began teaching at the Maryinsky in 1902 and by 1909 the forward-looking in Russia considered him both the legitimate successor of Marius Petipa and the renewer of a moribund tradition. Although many in Paris believed that Fokine's work represented the achievements of the Russian imperial ballet company of Saint Petersburg, it was in fact untypical of that institution. Diaghilev's company, created for the West, never appeared in his native land, though unfulfilled plans had

been made for it to do so in 1912. Of the seven major Fokine ballets presented by Diaghilev in his first two Paris seasons, *Le Pavillon d'Armide, Les Sylphides,* and *Cléopâtre* were revised versions of works that had already been produced at the Maryinsky. *Carnaval,* however, was created in 1910 for a private performance in Saint Petersburg, while the *Polovtsian Dances* from *Prince Igor, Schéhérazade,* and *The Firebird* were made especially for Paris.

Changes in Direction. All these ballets embodied the reformist principles that Fokine had arrived at as early as 1905, to which the World of Art group subscribed wholeheartedly—none more so than Diaghilev. Yet by 1912 Fokine's work for the Ballets Russes was essentially at an end. Fokine departed from the Ballets Russes in 1912 because his authority had been deliberately undermined by Diaghilev's sedulous promotion of Nijinsky as a choreographer. In discarding the man who had essentially created the entire repertory of the Ballets Russes, Diaghilev seems

BALLETS RUSSES DE SERGE DIAGHILEV. Vaslav Nijinsky as the Faun and Lydia Nelidova as the Principal Nymph in Nijinsky's first ballet, *L'Après-midi d'un Faune,* Paris, 1912. Set to music by Claude Debussy and designed by Léon Bakst, it features movements that stylistically evoke the flattened figures of ancient bas reliefs. (Photograph by Baron Adolf de Meyer; from the Dance Collection, New York Public Library for the Performing Arts.)

to have been fully aware of what he was risking. Having undergone a major shift in aesthetic sensibility, however, he no longer looked to Fokine to satisfy the company's needs. Within about three years, Diaghilev became increasingly dissatisfied with a conception of ballet whose goal was either mimetic expressivity or the creation of a situational mood—and whose principal mode was narrative of a historical, mythological, or exotic kind.

Diaghilev did not suddenly discard Fokine's ballets after the choreographer's departure, if for no other reason than that the public demanded to see them. In fact, to the very end, they remained the most popular works in his repertory, especially *Petrouchka, Le Spectre de la Rose, Carnaval, The Firebird, Schéhérazade* (which Diaghilev found increasingly ludicrous), and *Les Sylphides* (which is said to have been his favorite ballet). The impulse to ally himself with the cause of aesthetic renewal, which had marked his career from its beginnings, reasserted itself in 1912 and kept him thereafter permanently in the avant-garde.

Many still believe that Diaghilev blundered in changing direction in 1912. There is something indestructible about the reputation of Fokine, a number of whose ballets survive in the repertory and in the collective memory of dance lovers. Several reasons exist for this: the historical prominence of the ballets, which reestablished the art in the West; their association with legendary dancers such as Nijinsky and Karsavina; the splendor of their music; and the brilliance and lavishness of their decor and costumes. When seen in the theater today, most of the celebrated works look lifeless. Although we continue to read about the impact they had when new, *Petrouchka* nowadays fails to move, *Le Spectre de la Rose* to enchant, and *Schéhérazade* to excite—unless to risibility. Perhaps the times are wrong for the just appreciation of the early Di-

aghilev repertory, which requires a star dancer, the great and individual personality with a more than ordinary gift for acting. Another drawback may be changes in theatrical practice; the vastly increased costs of production make it impossible to re-create with any authenticity the designs of Bakst and Benois, on which so much of the success of Fokine's works clearly depended. The greatest impediment of all may be that our interest has shifted from silent drama to choreography, of which these works now seem to contain very little. The Fokine works from the Diaghilev repertory that do survive are those that, like *Les Sylphides* and *Carnaval*, have dance as their principal feature.

Some have doubted that Diaghilev dropped Fokine because of artistic considerations, believing that his true reason was the desire to promote the fortunes of his lover, Nijinsky. In arriving at decisions of a nominally artistic nature, Diaghilev often allowed his emotions to play a significant role. Fortunately for the art he dominated from 1909 to 1929, he nearly always fell in love with the kind of talented young man who could, with education and propitious circumstances, become the instrument of his artistic will.

For many years after a premature withdrawal from the stage, Nijinsky labored under the imputation of failure as a choreographer. This view is now superseded by one that places him in the forefront of balletic innovators of the twentieth century. In the three works produced under the direct supervision of Diaghilev—*L'Après-midi d'un Faune* (1912); *Jeux* (1912, to a commissioned score by Debussy); and *Le Sacre du Printemps* (1913, to a commissioned score by Stravinsky)—Nijinsky had made a heroic effort to restore the primacy of dance to ballet. Fokine had used movement primarily to express interests more literary and psychological than spatial and kinetic—except in the merest handful of works—above all, his masterpieces, *Les Sylphides* and *Carnaval*. In Fokine's *Petrouchka*, the anguish of the protagonist is communicated by stance (turned-in feet, limp arms, stiffly held head) and mime. As its composer, Stravinsky, later complained, Fokine staged rather than choreographed the crowd scenes, leaving the corps de ballet to impersonate the many different characters, in the manner of improvisatory actors.

For Nijinsky, dance was not so much representation as embodiment. While each of his ballets was structured through sequential action, and thus had a plot of sorts, none was simply a narrative in dumb show. In *L'Après-midi d'un Faune*, the theme—that of self-discovery through sexual awareness—is the cause of dance, not a conclusion arrived at through it. While it is possible to speak of a synopsis in connection with *L'Après-midi d'un Faune*, the action of *Jeux* defies description. Contemporary accounts suggest that its theme—a metaphor of polite athletic rivalry—was the assertion through social behavior of sexual need in all its ungovernable variety. *Jeux*, which brought together twentieth-century sport and sexual mores, was danced in clothing rather than costumes (the women wore tennis dresses designed by the fashionable Parisian couturier, Paquin) and was set in an urban park. *Le Sacre du Printemps* took place before the dawn of civilization, its theme being the renewal of life—associated with the return of spring—that is implicit in death. While its argument dealt with the sacrifice of a tribal maiden to propitiate the gods of fertility, its subject was nothing less than the primal energy of the universe, a force that dance by its very nature can both invoke and bring under control.

L'Après-midi d'un Faune was received with hostility and *Jeux* with puzzlement. *Le Sacre du Printemps* was treated as if it were a deliberate attempt to outrage the sensibilities of the socially smart audience that had supported the Ballets Russes since 1909. The fearsome, deliberately ungainly choreography of Nijinsky to the polytonality and savagely elemental rhythms of Stravinsky defied polite taste. With Nijinsky's ballets, in each of which he extended prodigiously the range of balletic movement, Diaghilev as producer drew sharply ahead of many of his original admirers; if at first disconcerted, he soon decided that his task henceforth was to shape the public's taste rather than to satisfy it.

Nijinsky, though, was not to be his chief instrument of change for long—in 1913, the dancer defected to heterosexuality. Diaghilev's response, as a betrayed lover, was to fire him from the Ballets Russes. By humbling himself before Fokine and acceding to all his artistic and financial demands, Diaghilev persuaded the older choreographer to

BALLETS RUSSES DE SERGE DIAGHILEV. Members of the company in the *Polovtsian Dances* from *Prince Igor*, choreographed by Michel Fokine and designed by Nikolai Roerich, at the Metropolitan Opera House, New York, 1916. This ballet was originally presented by Diaghilev as act 2 of Aleksandr Borodin's opera *Prince Igor* in Paris in 1909. (Photograph by White Studio; from the Dance Collection, New York Public Library for the Performing Arts.)

return. The reversion to earlier principles that inevitably ensued was short-lived. While Fokine's wan *Papillons* (Butterflies; 1914) was at least the recapitulation of his masterpiece *Carnaval*, the inept *Midas* (1914) was the re-capitulation of earlier failures to re-create in dance the beauty of classical antiquity: *Narcisse* (1911) and *Daphnis et Chloé* (1912). Fokine's only real success during this period was the choreographed opera, *Le Coq d'Or* (1914), in which the dancers, performing against Natalia Goncharova's astonishing red-and-yellow backcloths in the style of Russian peasant art, mimed the action onstage as vocalists sang from the sides of the stage.

World War I and Its Effects. How Diaghilev managed to keep his company going throughout World War I is difficult to understand. Fokine had returned to Russia. Patronage was virtually nonexistent, and bookings were few. Germany and the Austro-Hungarian Empire were at war with Russia, France, Italy, the Low Countries, and Britain. Wartime Britain, though friendly, had no room for Diaghilev's company, so in 1916 arrangements were concluded with U.S. producer Otto Kahn for an American tour. Since the contract specified the participation of Nijinsky, then interned in Hungary as an enemy alien, Diaghilev had not only agreed to his return but also labored to secure his release. After a mighty effort, the dancer was allowed to travel to the United States, thus ensuring both the company's engagement and its success. Arrangements were made for a second American tour in 1916–1917; at Nijinsky's insistence, Diaghilev did not accompany the troupe. At the conclusion of the tour, Nijinsky left the company for good. In 1917, the Ballets Russes appeared in Rome and Paris. During the rest of the war, it eked out an existence in Spain, where the penniless dancers often went hungry.

While in the United States with the company, Nijinsky had choreographed and starred in Richard Strauss's *Till Eulenspiegel* (1916), the first work he created without the supervision of Diaghilev—who in fact never saw it. Successful though *Till* was, the dancer's final departure from the company in 1917 and his subsequent illness made any revival of it, or of *Jeux* and *Le Sacre du Printemps*, impossible. By then, however, Diaghilev had found in Léonide Massine not only a new lover and leading dancer but evidence of an important choreographer. In December 1913, when Massine was first spotted at Moscow's Bolshoi Theater by Diaghilev—who was impressed by his performance of the tarantella in act 3 of *Swan Lake*—Massine was trying to choose between a career in ballet and the dramatic theater. Essentially a character dancer, he was talented, ambitious, and a remarkably quick learner. Schooled by Diaghilev and his close associates (above all, Mikhail Larionov) in dance, theatrical skills, music, and art, Massine began his career as a choreographer in 1915 with *Soleil de Nuit*, an essay in the Russian folkloric style.

With *Les Femmes de Bonne Humeur* (1917), Massine revealed his theatrical mastery and a gift for seeming to express the spirit of the moment, even in a work set in eighteenth-century Venice. Seemingly contemporary in feeling, the ballet marked a reversion to the expressive and narrative principles of Fokine—one reason, no doubt, for its immediate acceptance by the Parisian audience. In *Les Femmes de Bonne Humeur*, as in later successes such as *La Boutique Fantasque* (1919), *Le Tricorne (The Three-Cornered Hat*; 1919), and *Pulcinella* (1920), Massine perfected a kind of ballet in which an often highly complicated story is told by means of movement that, for the most part, mediates between dance and mime though with lyrical interludes, especially solos, to add variety.

What principally differentiates Massine from Fokine is his attitude toward the subject matter. Massine's view of character was on the whole impersonal, his projection of it wryly comic; his bent was for satire, which he achieved through the exaggeration of gesture and the speeding up of action. In Massine's ballets, character, though based on acute observation, is inseparable from idiosyncrasy and foible; himself a performer of genius, who was invariably at his best in roles that called for a strong admixture of the grotesque, he had a gift for the translation of human oddity into movement. Fokine's approach to his subjects, by contrast, had been empathetic; his style was broad, leisurely, and naturalistic.

Massine's attitude, then, was enough to make him look innovative, even when in a work like *La Boutique Fantasque*—set in a toy shop, mostly after hours—he used hackneyed, inherently sentimental material. His *Les Femmes de Bonne Humeur* did have designs by Bakst, perhaps an unconscious acknowledgment that Massine, however different in temperament from Fokine, was working toward similar anecdotal goals. However, the Massine ballets that followed were designed by artists of a distinctly modernist sensibility: Larionov (*Contes Russes*, 1917), Derain (*La Boutique Fantasque*, 1919), Matisse (*Le Chant du Rossignol*, 1920) and Picasso, with whom he collaborated on three ballets (*Parade*, 1917; *Le Tricorne*, 1919; and *Pulcinella*, 1920).

1920s Innovations. Until the end of the company's existence, decor continued to play an important role in maintaining the popularity of the Ballets Russes. Before the war, decor was supplied largely by experienced and dedicated scenic designers, such as Léon Bakst, Alexandre Benois, and Mstislav Dobujinsky. From the time of Massine onward, decor was supplied largely by easel painters, occasionally by sculptors. With only a handful of exceptions, these were among the most important artists of the age. Through the decors commissioned by Diaghilev each season, the audiences of the Ballets Russes were able to keep up with the latest developments in art. Part of the public that supported the Ballets Russes during the 1920s did so primarily because it put them in touch with the latest artistic sensations.

In Europe, decisions about taste were no longer the perquisite of the aristocracy—but of the fashionable—of those whose chief interest was *le dernier cri* (the latest thing). To survive after 1914—and during the war years—Diaghilev was obliged to appeal to the international smart set, those who, being rich, rarefied, and easily bored, demanded constant titillation. Only once, in 1921, with *The Sleeping Princess*, did he fail to stay in the vanguard of sophisticated taste. Conscious of the need to please those who determined the cultural enthusiasms of the age, Diaghilev made it his business to woo anyone who might be of help to his company. French *couturière* Coco Chanel, for example, designed, supplied, and paid for the costumes of *Le Train Bleu* (1924), having subsidized both the orchestration of *Les Noces* (1923) and before that the revival of *Le Sacre du Printemps* (1920), with new choreography by Massine; but, appearances to the contrary, Diaghilev never confused fashion with artistic innovation.

As everyone involved in the creation of *Parade* was aware, the ballet marked the beginning of a new, innovative phase of the Ballets Russes. Given its premiere at the Théâtre du Châtelet in 1917, one month after the first performance there of *Les Femmes de Bonne Humeur, Parade* was a tacit acknowledgment that the Russian ballet had become Europeanized. Cut off from his native country by the war, Diaghilev from this point on identified his company with the cultural life of Paris, where the aesthetic standards of the age were being remade. By bringing together Erik Satie, Pablo Picasso, and Jean Cocteau (who inaugurated the work and devised its scenario), Diaghilev was giving notice that ballet was to be recognized as a significant participant in the current, *moderne* revitalization of the arts. The point was given emphasis by the manifesto in the program written by Guillaume Apollinaire.

Parade was a declaration of faith in the new, anti-Romantic sensibility that was to dominate the arts during the following decades. Picasso's cubist designs were objective rather than evocative. Satie's music (which incorporated sounds from daily life, like a clicking typewriter, as well as a Ted Snyder–Irving Berlin song) turned its back on the entire Austro-German symphonic tradition—not least, by eschewing all solemnity—to achieve a cleansing simplicity. Cocteau's scenario gave the fairground theme an air of astringency. Massine's choreography made witty, nonnarrational use of mime and gesture. At its best, in the solo for the Chinese Conjurer (a part danced by Massine himself), his contribution took a subordinate role, serving more to hold the spectacle together than to animate it with any coherent choreographic purpose. In the works that followed, though, Massine reasserted the leadership of the choreographer. With *La Boutique Fantasque* and *Le Tricorne*, he produced two of

BALLETS RUSSES DE SERGE DIAGHILEV. Lydia Lopokova and Léonide Massine as the Can-Can Dancers in Massine's *La Boutique Fantasque*, at the Alhambra Theatre, London, 1919. (Photograph reprinted from Milo Keynes, *Lydia Lopokova*, New York, 1982, p. 111.)

the most popular offerings in Diaghilev's postwar repertory, two of the best roles he ever devised for himself.

In 1921 Massine, like Nijinsky eight years before, was dismissed for having betrayed Diaghilev with a woman. Diaghilev thereupon attempted to transform one of his dancers, Tadeo Slavinsky, into a choreographer by apprenticing him to Larionov, in the way that had proved so successful with Massine; however, the result of their labors, *Le Chout*, was not encouraging. On the same program, Diaghilev presented a group of Spanish dancers in their own work, *Cuadro Flamenco*.

A Return to the Classical. Finally, Diaghilev turned not to further experimentation or novelty but to the classical foundations of the art whose scope he had been laboring to expand for more than a decade. His choice for the return to balletic essentials was Marius Petipa's *The Sleeping Beauty*, created in Saint Petersburg in 1890 and the acme of Russian imperial ballet. Hitherto seen outside Russia only in Milan and New York, and then very briefly, *The Sleeping Beauty*—ceremonial, leisurely, and aristocratic—was antithetical both to the spirit of the times and to all toward which Diaghilev had seemingly been reaching. His decision to stage the evening-length work as *The*

BALLETS RUSSES DE SERGE DIAGHILEV. Felia Doubrovska (center) as the Bride in a rooftop rehearsal of Bronislava Nijinska's *Les Noces*, at the Théâtre de Monte-Carlo, 1923. (Photograph from the Dance Collection, New York Public Library for the Performing Arts.)

Sleeping Princess at the Alhambra Theatre in London at the end of 1921 disconcerted a great many of his supporters. All they could find was a purposeless retrogression. The consensus was that Diaghilev had made an artistic blunder—a judgment strengthened by a technical mishap during the first performance, when the forest failed to rise properly at the end of act 1.

Although the 1921 version of *The Sleeping Princess* offered a feast of dancing and a magnificent spectacle, sumptuously designed by Bakst, it did not attract enough people to cover its very high costs; the deficit almost put the Ballets Russes out of business for good. As a result of the losses sustained by Diaghilev the company was in limbo for a couple of months after the last performance; for several seasons, it was then burdened with debts.

To judge the venture simply as a retreat from modernity and innovation—as Britain's avant-garde Bloomsbury group did—is to misunderstand Diaghilev's dedication to the concept of classical ballet, which was central to his dance aesthetic. To the end of his days, he was moved by the autonomous beauty and profound symbolic eloquence of the *danse d'école*. It is true that Petipa's great work represents the aesthetic antithesis of Fokine's, but so does the oeuvre of Nijinsky. From at least 1912 Diaghilev had been trying to move away from Fokine's mimetic narratives to a style of dance that, if very different in manner from the work of Petipa, represented a radical transformation of nineteenth-century classicism while maintaining its impersonality and self-sufficiency.

Only after Diaghilev's death did the significance of *The Sleeping Princess* become fully apparent. Its influence is to be found in the British production of the work mounted for the Vic-Wells company in 1939 by Nicholas Sergeyev, who worked from the same choreographic script in Stepanov notation that he had used for the Ballets Russes

in 1921. As if in homage to Diaghilev, the 1939 production was also called *The Sleeping Princess*. The successor to this production, staged in 1946 and re-renamed *The Sleeping Beauty*, inaugurated a new phase of popularity for ballet in Britain and the Americas. Despite its 1921 box office failure, Diaghilev's production was instrumental in the survival, at mid-century and thereafter, of the classical balletic traditions of the Maryinsky.

After the 1921 failure of *The Sleeping Princess*, Diaghilev's recourse was to resume his backing for new balletic forms and modes. Nevertheless, he did not discard Petipa entirely. In 1922, in scenery derived from *Le Pavillon d'Armide*, he presented a *divertissement* drawn from *The Sleeping Beauty* under the title of *Aurora's Wedding*; it remained in the repertory of the Ballets Russes until the end and served to keep the company in touch with its classical heritage. *Aurora's Wedding* was staged and partly choreographed by Bronislava Nijinska, who had left the company in 1914 after her brother was dismissed. In 1921, she returned, agreeing both to dance in *The Sleeping Princess* and to arrange some of its numbers. Nijinska's alterations of and additions to Petipa offended Sergeyev, formerly *régisseur* at the Maryinsky, who walked out on the production when Diaghilev began to edit it.

Nevertheless, Nijinska's work pleased Diaghilev, who quickly found her to be the successor to Massine as company choreographer. Nijinska remained with Diaghilev until 1925. Among the ballets she created during that time, two are enduring masterpieces: *Les Noces* (1923) and *Les Biches* (1924). Inspired by her brother's choreography, she avoided the realistic and local in favor of the ceremonial and universal. Though the nominal subject of *Les Noces* is a Russian peasant wedding, the work is conceived in terms of a ritualism that transcends specificity and achieves the archetypal. Nijinska's nonnationalistic approach to *Les Noces* proved highly sympathetic to Diaghilev.

Despite tempting offers from the Soviet government, Diaghilev never returned to his native land. If he felt any nostalgia for the irrecoverable Russia of his youth, it hardly made itself apparent in the 1920s output of his company, except perhaps indirectly. In the scenario, choreography, and overall style of the nineteenth-century *The Sleeping Beauty*, for example, there is adumbrated a monarchical view of order and grace—and to this, Tchaikovsky's original score suggests a tsarist mode; to counter this, Nijinska choreographed a Russian character dance, "Innocent Ivan and His Two Brothers," for the coda of the act 3 pas de deux. Nijinska also created a ballet to Mussorgsky's *Night on the Bare Mountain* in 1924, but it remained in the repertory only briefly. Three years later, Massine, who between 1925 and 1928 returned several times to the Ballets Russes as a freelance choreographer, made *Le Pas d'Acier* (1927), intended as a tribute to the new industrialized Russia created by Lenin; it was equally relevant to the modern world in general.

The Influence of a New Age. Nijinska's arrival as a choreographer coincided with the first, heady years of the jazz age, a period of marked social change in the West, especially in France, Britain, and the United States. In 1923 the company made Monte Carlo its home base, a resort city on the Riviera and the capital of Monaco. Thereafter, it became known as the Ballets Russes de Monte Carlo, and it identified its aims with the outlook of the smart set thronging to the Riviera each summer. The company's element of chic also resulted from the style and art of Nijinska; because of her antinaturalistic approach to choreography, she could confer a recognizably personal movement style upon subjects as remote from one another as a barnyard fable (*Le Renard*, 1922), a Molière comedy (*Les Fâcheaux*, 1924) and a vignette showing fashionable youth disporting itself on the Riviera (*Le Train Bleu*, 1924). In these, the vocabulary of classical ballet was given a new range of reference by unexpected violations of traditional syntax. It was this idiosyncrasy, above all, that made her work seem so in tune with the times. Two of her greatest successes in 1924 actually had contemporary subjects, *Le Train Bleu* and *Les Biches*. *Le Train Bleu* did not survive the departure in 1925 of Anton Dolin, for whom the acrobatic leading role was created. *Les Biches* has never disappeared for long; set in the smart drawing room of a house overlooking the Mediterranean, it is a comedy of manners (on a subject already treated, though very differently, by her brother in *Jeux*—the variousness of sexual appetite). Impersonal, allusive, equivocal, Nijinska's ballet has the wit, insight, and elegance of a play by Pierre de Marivaux, though one written in a post-Freudian age. Diaghilev's interest in the circle of French author Jean Cocteau, which included the young composers known as Les Six, yielded a score for *Les Biches* by the twenty-four-year-old Francis Poulenc that distilled the sound and rhythms of its time (including jazz); it has lasted as well as the choreography, the artistic value of neither one being in any way vitiated by their contemporaneity, irreverence, or lack of solemnity.

In 1924, Diaghilev engaged the twenty-year-old George Balanchine, a recent Maryinsky-trained Soviet émigré. During Balanchine's years with the company (1924–1929) he created ten ballets. During the same period, Massine, as a freelancer, created five and revised one—*Mercure* (1927)—originally made three years earlier for the Soirées de Paris, the company of Comte Etienne de Beaumont, one of Diaghilev's short-lived imitators and rivals in the 1920s.

In the American phase of Balanchine's career, he rejected the Diaghilevian aesthetic of the *Gesamtkunstwerk*—discarding the idea that either decor or literary theme had any necessarily significant role to play in the creation of a ballet. Above all, Balanchine was determined

BALLETS RUSSES DE SERGE DIAGHILEV. Serge Lifar (top) in the title role of George Balanchine's ballet *The Prodigal Son* (1929). Set to music by Sergei Prokofiev and designed by Georges Rouault, this dramatic ballet was Balanchine's last production for Diaghilev. (Photograph from the Dance Collection, New York Public Library for the Performing Arts. Choreography by George Balanchine © The George Balanchine Trust.)

in his later American ballets to diminish the prominence of the scenic artist. When Balanchine made his 1929 ballet *Le Bal* for Diaghilev, the choreography had to compete for attention with the brilliant surrealist sets of Giorgio de' Chirico; in *Apollo* (1928), the costumes by the naive painter André Bauchant had proved impossible to wear; in *La Chatte* (1927), the dancers had performed on a stage covered with black oilcloth. Yet Balanchine's belief in the autonomous importance of movement was, if not formed at the Ballets Russes, then strengthened there. It was also triumphantly exemplified, whatever the decorative distractions, in works such as *Apollo* and *The Prodigal Son*. These, moreover, were created under the direct supervision of Diaghilev, whose enthusiasm for them is a matter of record. Balanchine was quoted by Bernard Taper in his 1984 biography *Balanchine:* "It is because of Diaghilev that I am what I am today" (p. 121).

No more graphic demonstration exists for Diaghilev's importance to the Ballets Russes as a whole than the collapse of the entire enterprise when he died, in Venice, in 1929—despite all efforts to save it on the part of Boris Kochno, his secretary, and Serge Lifar, his last balletic protégé. For the previous twenty years, Diaghilev had sustained his company by an exercise of will. Under his rule, which was absolute, the administration and artistic policy of the Ballets Russes were indivisible. The structure of the company was a function of its creative energy, which came entirely from him. There was no one with the necessary vision, knowledge, cunning, and ruthlessness to succeed him.

[*Many of the figures and works herein are the subjects of independent entries.*]

BIBLIOGRAPHY

Baer, Nancy Van Norman. *The Art of Enchantment: Diaghilev's Ballets Russes, 1909–1929.* San Francisco, 1988.

Beaumont, Cyril W. *The Diaghilev Ballet in London.* 3d ed. London, 1951.

Benois, Alexandre. *Reminiscences of the Russian Ballet.* Translated by Mary Britnieva. London, 1941.

Buckle, Richard. *In Search of Diaghilev.* London, 1955.

Buckle, Richard. *Nijinsky.* London, 1971.

Buckle, Richard. *Diaghilev.* New York, 1979.

Calvocoressi, M. D. *Music and Ballet: Recollections of M. D. Calvocoressi.* London, 1934.

Fokine, Michel. *Memoirs of a Ballet Master.* Translated by Vitale Fokine. Edited by Anatole Chujoy. London, 1961.

Garafola, Lynn. "Looking Backward: Retrospective Classicism in the Diaghilev Repertory of the Twenties." *Proceedings of the Eleventh Annual Conference, Society of Dance History Scholars, North Carolina School of the Arts, 12–14 February 1988,* compiled by Christena L. Schlundt. Riverside, Calif., 1988.

Garafola, Lynn. *Diaghilev's Ballets Russes.* New York, 1989.

Grigoriev, Serge. *The Diaghilev Ballet, 1909–1929.* Translated and edited by Vera Bowen. London, 1953.

Harris, Dale. "Diaghilev's Ballets Russes and the Vogue for Orientalism." In *Léon Bakst, sensualismus triumf.* Stockholm, 1993.

Haskell, Arnold L., and Walter Nouvel. *Diaghileff: His Artistic and Private Life.* New York, 1935.

Kahane, Martine. *Les Ballets Russes à l'Opéra.* Paris, 1992.

Karsavina, Tamara. *Theatre Street.* Rev. and enl. ed. London, 1948.

Kirstein, Lincoln. *Four Centuries of Ballet: Fifty Masterworks.* New York, 1984.

Kirstein, Lincoln. "The Diaghilev Period." In Kirstein's *By With To and From.* New York, 1991.

Kochno, Boris. *Diaghilev and the Ballets Russes.* Translated by Adrienne Foulke. New York, 1970.

Kodicek, Ann, ed. *Diaghilev, Creator of the Ballets Russes: Art, Music, Dance.* London, 1996.

Krasovskaya, Vera. "An Anatomy of Genius." *Dance Chronicle* 13.1 (1990): 82–88.

Lieven, Peter. *The Birth of Ballets-Russes.* Translated by Leonide Zarine. London, 1936.

Lifar, Serge. *Serge Diaghilev, His Life, His Work, His Legend: An Intimate Biography.* New York, 1940.

Macdonald, Nesta. *Diaghilev Observed by Critics in England and the United States, 1911–1929.* New York, 1975.

Massine, Léonide. *My Life in Ballet.* New York, 1968.

Nijinska, Bronislava. *Early Memoirs.* Translated and edited by Irina Nijinska and Jean Rawlinson. New York, 1981.

Nijinsky, Romola. *Nijinsky.* New York, 1934.

Pastori, Jean-Pierre. *Soleil de nuit: La renaissance de Ballets Russes.* Lausanne, 1993.

Pierpont, Claudia Roth. "Maenads." *The New Yorker* (20 August 1990).

Pozharskaya, Militza, and Tatania Volodine. *The Art of the Ballets Russes.* Translated by V. S. Friedman. London, 1990.

Pritchard, Jane. "The Diaghilev Russian Ballet in Manchester." *The Dancing Times* (October 1994): 13–21.

Scholl, Tim. *From Petipa to Balanchine: Classical Revival and the Modernization of Ballet.* New York, 1994.

Sokolova, Lydia. *Dancing for Diaghilev.* Edited by Richard Buckle. London, 1960.

Svetlov, Valerian. *Le ballet contemporain.* St. Petersburg, 1912.

DALE HARRIS

BALLETS SUÉDOIS. Les Ballets Suédois was founded in Paris in 1920 by Rolf de Maré, a Swedish landowner, art patron, and amateur ethnographer. Jean Börlin, a dancer with the Stockholm Royal Opera who had worked with Michel Fokine in Sweden, was the choreographer and lead dancer. Inspired by Diaghilev's Ballets Russes, Les Ballets Suédois was initially intended to present the folk art of Sweden as translated into theater by modern artists, but for the five years of its existence its repertory was dominated by innovative works incorporating dance, mime, painting, and music that rivaled Diaghilev's avant-garde productions. Börlin, trained in a mixture of Danish Bournonville style and Italian virtuoso technique, had nearly quit dancing when he met Fokine, and his own choreographic philosophy was based on his teacher's theories of reform.

Les Ballets Suédois arose from a solo concert given by Börlin in March 1920 at the Théâtre des Champs-Elysées, in which he performed two harlequin studies, a series of Swedish airs, and two dances entitled *Derviche* and *Negro Sculpture*. Already the various directions of the company's repertory were clear. During its five-year lifespan, the company presented, primarily in Paris, twenty-four ballets that fell into three basic categories: ballets derivative of the Diaghilev style and themes, dances based on Swedish folklore, and original, avant-garde productions, often based on the folklore and popular entertainment of other cultures.

The first performance of Les Ballets Suédois took place at the Théâtre des Champs-Elysées on 25 October 1920. The premiere program consisted of *Jeux*, mounted as a tribute to Nijinsky; *Iberia*, based on Börlin's travels in Spain and North Africa but clearly reminiscent of the Massine–Falla–Picasso *Le Tricorne* (1919); and *La Nuit de Saint-Jean*, a re-creation of a Swedish folk festival. Later in the season, several more ballets were added: the sinister *Maison de Fous*; *Le Tombeau de Couperin*, to three sections from Ravel's suite; *El Greco,* built on tableaux from the works of the painter; *Derviche,* Börlin's whirling solo; *Les Vierges Folles,* another Swedish folkloric ballet, inspired by a parable; and *La Boîte à Joujoux,* with a plot nearly identical to Massine's *La Boutique Fantasque* (1919). All were choreographed by Börlin, who also reconstructed for the first season dances from Fokine's *Chopiniana.*

In later seasons other works rooted in Swedish folklore were mounted by Les Ballets Suédois: *Dansgille* (1921), *Offerlunden* (1923), and *Le Porcher* (1924). Several of the folkloric works were well received, but *Offerlunden* (The Sacrificial Grove), a ballet reminiscent of the Nijinsky–Stravinsky *Le Sacre du Printemps* (1913), was, notably, the least popular work in the company's repertory.

The most important ballets performed by the company were avant-garde collaborations with modern French composers, writers, and painters. The first of these was *L'Homme et Son Désir* (1921), a collaboration among Börlin, Paul Claudel, Darius Milhaud, and Andrée Parr. Originally, the ballet had been inspired by and planned for Nijinsky, but Diaghilev rejected Milhaud's score and the project was taken to de Maré instead. It was the story of a man in a tropical rain forest (portrayed abstractly), imprisoned by the night and obsessed by desire. The next collaboration was Jean Cocteau's play *Les Mariés de la Tour Eiffel* (1921), with music by five of the group known as Les Six (Georges Auric, Arthur Honegger, Darius Milhaud, Francis Poulenc, and Germaine Tailleferre), masks and costumes by Jean Hugo, and scenery by Irène Lagut. Cocteau was extremely pleased with the production and considered it a culmination of his experiments in *Parade* and *Le Boeuf sur le Toit.* [*See* Parade *and the entry on* Cocteau.]

Two jazz ballets were presented in 1923. *La Création du Monde,* subtitled *A Negro-Jazz Ballet,* was inspired by the then-current Paris vogue for black art from Africa and America, a fascination that had already sparked cubism and influenced much modern art and literature. Blaise Cendrars, the poet and anthologist of black folklore, wrote the ballet's scenario using African creation myths. Milhaud, galvanized by his visits to Harlem clubs, composed music for a jazz orchestra. Fernand Léger designed the costumes and masks, modeled after African ritual animal disguises, and the scenery. The characters in the ballet included gods, plants and animals, shamans and sorcerers, and the first human couple. An "American ballet," *Within the Quota,* was planned at Léger's suggestion as a curtain raiser for *La Création du Monde,* although the order of the ballets was ultimately reversed. The libretto, written by the American artist Gerald Murphy, satirized the American dream of instant success, as did the backdrop he de-

BALLETS SUÉDOIS. Jean Börlin as the Madman in his ballet *Skating Rink* (1922). Set to music by Arthur Honegger and designed by Fernand Léger, the ballet presents grotesque caricatures of people at a skating rink. (Photograph by Isaby, Paris; from the Dansmuseet, Stockholm.)

signed, which parodied the front page of a Hearst newspaper. A Swedish immigrant meets characters who are partly real, partly Hollywood stereotypes, including a Sheriff, a Cowboy, a Jazz Baby, Mary Pickford, a Colored Gentleman, and an Heiress. Cole Porter, not yet famous, wrote the piano score, and Börlin incorporated social dances such as the shimmy and the fox trot in the choreography.

Among other works presented by Les Ballets Suédois in 1924 was *La Jarre (La Giara),* a realist tale of an impoverished Sicilian village, based on a comic story by Luigi Pirandello. It was set to music composed by Alfredo Casella and had scenery and costumes designed by Giorgio de Chirico (his first ballet commission).

The final work given by the company was its most famous: *Relâche,* a Dadaist multimedia spectacle that included an appearance by Man Ray. It also included dancing without music and music without dancing; people changing clothes onstage; various film episodes, including a "cinematographic entr'acte" by Francis Picabia (who wrote the scenario for the ballet) and René Clair that has entered the avant-garde film canon; satirical music by Erik Satie; a fireman smoking and filling buckets of water; and a backdrop of 370 bright lights set in reflectors. The ballet was a burlesque that deliberately and outrageously thumbed its nose at bourgeois taste, and it was celebrated by the Parisian avant-garde for breaking down the boundaries between ballet and the music hall and between art forms. As it was also an impossible act to follow, de Maré dissolved Les Ballet Suédois shortly thereafter.

BIBLIOGRAPHY

Baer, Nancy Van Norman, ed. *Paris Modern: The Swedish Ballet 1920–1925*. San Francisco, 1995.

Banes, Sally. "An Introduction to the Ballets Suédois." *Ballet Review* 7 (1978–1979): 28–59.

Dorris, George. "Diaghilev and de Maré in Paris. "*Dance Chronicle* 15.1 (1992): 106–113.

Häger, Bengt. *Ballets Suédois*. Translated by Ruth Sherman. New York, 1990.

Marié, Rolf de, et al. *Les Ballets Suédois dans l'art contemporain*. Paris, 1931.

Modern Swedish Ballet. London, 1970. Exhibition catalog, Victoria and Albert Museum.

Svenska baletten: Les Ballets Suédois, 1920–1925. Stockholm, 1969. Exhibition catalog, Dansmuseet.

ARCHIVES. Materials on Les Ballets Suédois collected by Rolf de Maré are now in the Dansmuseet Archives, Stockholm, and in the museum of the Paris Opera.

SALLY BANES

BALLET TECHNIQUE. [*This entry comprises eight articles. The first surveys major schools of training; the following four outline basic concepts of ballet technique; and the last three survey broad categories of movement.*

> Major Schools
> Feet Positions
> Arm Positions
> Body Positions
> Directions
> Turning Movements
> Linking Movements
> Jumping Movements

These articles are supplemented by numerous articles on specific aspects of ballet technique that appear elsewhere in the encyclopedia. See, for example, the following entries: Adage; Allegro; Arabesque; Attitude; Battement; Batterie; Partnering; Pas de Deux; Plié; Pointe Work; Rond de Jambe; *and* Turnout. *For further discussion of the history of ballet technique, see* Ballet Technique, History of.]

Major Schools

As ballet historians have attempted to distinguish variety within the sphere of classicism, they have traditionally made distinctions based on nationality. References to the "French school," the "Italian school," and the "Russian school" have been prominent in discourse on dancing since the nineteenth century. References to the "English school," the "Danish school," and the "American school," have also become fairly common. Explanation of these categories might be grounded in a simple focus on the country identified in each name, but such simplification would not, in fact, represent reality. Over the years, the identities of national schools of ballet technique have become blurred.

An example of national mixture in a single school category occurs early in the history of ballet tutelage. In 1820, Carlo Blasis published his *Traité élémentaire théorique et pratique de l'art de la danse* in Milan. The information therein continues to be used today to discuss Italian balletic technique. However, prior to composing his book, Blasis actually studied exclusively in France. His next book was written in French but was intended for publication in England; translated into English, it was first published as *The Code of Terpsichore* in 1828. This French-Italian-English admixture makes labeling difficult. In his time, Blasis was an exponent of the French school of dancing, but his artistic descendants (notably in and through the literature of Enrico Cecchetti) have, in the modern world, become exemplars of the Italian school. Thus, through a process of growth and assimilation, theories of ballet technique have evolved; technical elements of one national school have become incorporated as an essential part of another.

It is therefore more useful to assess technical distinctions in terms of contemporary usage. Today, the three most common methods of training are those described by the names of the pedagogues who codified them: Agrippina Vaganova, Enrico Cecchetti, and August Bournonville.

Vaganova and the Russian School. In the 1930s, the Russian school, as we have come to know it, was beginning to be codified by Agrippina Vaganova (1879–1951). Her *Basic Principles of Classical Ballet*, translated into English in 1937, first appeared in Russia in 1934. The value of this book stems not only from its delineation of the Saint Petersburg school traditions advocated by Vaganova herself but also from its reference to methods of the French and Italian schools that were evident in pedagogy at the time. Many of these derived from the teachings of Marius Petipa (1818–1910), the French ballet master whose work brought Russia's Imperial Ballet to its magnificent climax at the end of the nineteenth century.

In the introduction to Vera Kostrovitskaya's *School of Classical Dance* (1978), a textual analysis of Soviet/Russian ballet technique, Natalia Roslavleva refers to Vaganova's legacy:

> She never denied the dependence of teaching on contemporary practice and, had she lived today, would have introduced innumerable changes into her system of training. . . . Therefore, the present system, as used and worked out by special "method departments" of the leading Soviet schools, cannot be called "the Vaganova method," though this great professor had a lot to do with its origin and development.

Much of Vaganova's early work on ballet technique concerned strength and breadth in dancing. The "well-arched back" and expansive upper torso that she stressed have remained in the Russian aesthetic and are especially noticeable in attitude and arabesque and big jumps in open leg positions. This forceful technique allowed Soviet dancers to achieve dramatic, heroic effects. Recent texts by Asaf Messerer and Nikolai Tarasov agree with Kostrovitskaya in making a distinction between small-scale and large-scale poses and movements. Reflecting the continuing aesthetic concern with large scale, texts by Russian teachers usually give specific instructions for achieving the awesome and expansive effects characteristic of the contemporary Russian school of performance.

In one sense, the Russian school has directly influenced every other variation on classical theatrical dancing in the late twentieth century, just as the French school disseminated its theories when ballet spread through Europe in the late nineteenth century. The most obvious and direct descendant of the Imperial Russian school is the classical school of dancing developed by George Balanchine in the United States. Honoring the strict principles that he learned in his youth at the Imperial Theater School in Saint Petersburg, he did not pursue the dramatic, deliberate effects of the later Soviet teachers but instead strove for speed, energy, and precision, which are the characteristics of what has sometimes been called the American school.

In England, the Russian school was but one influence on ballet technique. In 1920, the Royal Academy of Dancing was founded with five teachers, each representing a different "school": Tamara Karsavina, the Russian school; Adeline Genée, the Danish; Lucia Cormani, the Italian; Édouard Espinosa, the French; and Phyllis Bedells, the English. This organization, however, deals mostly with teaching and certification. It is the Royal Ballet and the Royal Ballet School that exemplify the aesthetic standards of the English school. Both the company and the school have strong Russian roots, embedded in the repertory of works by Marius Petipa that were set by Nicholas Sergeyev according to notations from his days as a dancer and ballet master of the Imperial Ballet in Saint Petersburg.

Cecchetti and the Italian School. Equally strong in its effect on ballet dancing in England was the work of the Italian teacher Enrico Cecchetti (1850–1928). Considered a direct descendant of Blasis, Cecchetti had worked in Russia and Poland as a ballet master and teacher and had developed his own method of teaching. After some years as the principal teacher with the Ballets Russes de Serge Diaghilev, he settled in London in 1918 and opened his Academy of Dancing, where he taught until 1923. The Cecchetti Society, established in 1922 for the express purpose of conserving his system of teaching, was incorporated into the Imperial Society of Teachers of Dancing in 1924. In the United States, the Cecchetti Council of America was formed in 1939.

Cecchetti's method of teaching, widely disseminated through the publication of technical manuals, has had a pervasive influence in England. Frederick Ashton, the dominant ballet master during the formative years of the Royal Ballet, was directly affected by Cecchetti's aesthetics, via his first ballet teacher Léonide Massine, who had regularly studied with Cecchetti. Richard Glasstone (1984) has noted the link: "In Massine's lessons with Ashton the essence of Cecchetti's mastery of the use of the upper body was thus passed on by one great choreographer to another in embryo." An accent on liveliness in the upper body and on brilliant footwork, including skimming beats and running steps, was built into the English school through Ashton's inventions based on Cecchetti-schooled technique. Since no strong Italian company existed as exemplar of the traditions established by Blasis, the work of Ashton and his English school provide the most concentrated practical evidence of Cecchetti's Italian school.

Bournonville and the Danish School. Although the original French school of ballet dancing, which was the basis for all subsequent academic technique, is no longer discrete, some of its features can be detected in the Danish school developed by August Bournonville (1805–1879), who was trained in France. Like Petipa in Russia, Ashton in England, and Balanchine in the United States, Bournonville shaped the company with which he worked, the Royal Danish Ballet, and in which he has posthumously persisted as a model. Bournonville also directly influenced Cecchetti's pedagogical work. As Erik Bruhn and Lillian Moore (1961) pointed out, Cecchetti adopted Bournonville's body positions (adding one of his own), followed most of Bournonville's arm positions, and restated Bournonville's theory about the use of opposition for the arms.

The Royal Danish Ballet continues to perform works created by Bournonville in the nineteenth century. Notably, a scene in his *Konservatoriet* (1849) depicts a typical ballet class as conducted by the great French master Auguste Vestris. The deliberate adagio and the lilting allegro combinations re-created in this classroom scene are typical of moves that characterize other Bournonville works. There is a prominent focus on legwork and footwork, with the torso and arms held quietly firm. The theory of holding the shoulders steadily down serves to maintain a calm torso, while the legs and feet execute complexities of *batterie*, *élévation*, and *ballon*. Bournonville's ballets, and subsequently his Danish-school technique, became identified with brilliance and intricacy of footwork.

International Intermixtures. In the twentieth century the Royal Danish Ballet and its associated school have worked to strengthen the overall technical range of Danish dancers. The most notable of such efforts came in 1951, when Vera Volkova, a Russian-trained dancer and an expert teacher of the Vaganova system, was invited to teach in Copenhagen. Having taught at the Sadler's Wells' Ballet School in London from 1943 to 1950, Volkova had a profound effect on both the English and the Danish schools.

Pedagogical influences have also flowed outward from Denmark and have been felt in Russia, England, and the United States. The Swedish dancer Christian Johansson, a pupil of Bournonville, became one of the foremost influences on the Russian school as the men's teacher at the Imperial Theater School in Saint Petersburg. The Danish dancer Adeline Genée (born Anina Jensen) made her career in England and, as noted, was a founding member of the Royal Academy of Dancing. More recently, the Danish dancer and teacher Stanley Williams, a protegé of Vera Volkova, has since 1964 been the principal teacher of men's classes at the School of American Ballet in New York.

The purest exponents of the French style today are the dancers of the Paris Opera Ballet. Although the Académie Royale de Danse, founded in Paris in 1661, has the longest lineage of any school, Italian methods dominated the teaching from the mid-nineteenth to the mid-twentieth century, by which time White Russian and, later, Soviet émigrés had begun to have an impact. After a period during the middle of the twentieth century in which exaggeration of every effect seemed to be the norm, the best French dancers currently convey an air of gracious refinement in all their movements. Their extremely strong techniques are notable for very high extensions for the women and exceptionally lofty elevation for the men.

[*See also the entries on the principal figures mentioned herein.*]

BIBLIOGRAPHY
Beaumont, Cyril W., and Stanislas Idzikowski. *A Manual of the Theory and Practice of Classical Theatrical Dancing: Cecchetti Method* (1922). Rev. ed. London, 1940. Reprint, New York, 1975.
Blasis, Carlo. *An Elementary Treatise upon the Theory and Practice of the Art of Dancing* (1820). Translated by Mary Stewart Evans. New York, 1944.
Blasis, Carlo. *The Code of Terpsichore: A Practical and Historical Treatise on the Ballet, Dancing, and Pantomime.* London, 1828.
Bournonville, August. *Études choréographiques.* Copenhagen, 1861.
Bruhn, Erik, and Lillian Moore. *Bournonville and Ballet Technique: Studies and Comments on August Bournonville's "Études choréographiques."* London, 1961.
Glasstone, Richard. "Changes of Emphasis and Mechanics in the Teaching of Ballet Technique." *Dance Research* 1 (Spring 1983): 56–63.
Glasstone, Richard. "Ashton, Cecchetti, and the English School." *Dance Theatre Journal* 2.3 (Autumn 1984): 13–14.
Greskovic, Robert. "Ballet, Barre and Center, on the Bookshelf." *Ballet Review* 6.2 (1977–1978): 1–56.
Kostrovitskaya, Vera, and Alexei Pisarev. *School of Classical Dance* (1978). Translated by John Barker. London, 1995. This is the official textbook of the Vaganova Choreographic Institute in Saint Petersburg.
Messerer, Asaf. *Classes in Classical Ballet.* Translated by Oleg Briansky. Garden City, N.Y., 1975.
Ralov, Kirsten, ed. *The Bournonville School.* 4 vols. New York and Basel, 1979.
Stuart, Muriel, et al. *The Classic Ballet: Basic Technique and Terminology.* New York, 1952.
Vaganova, Agrippina. *Basic Principles of Classical Ballet: Russian Ballet Technique* (1934). Translated by Anatole Chujoy. Edited by Peggy van Praagh. 2d ed. London, 1953.

CLAUDE CONYERS
Based on materials submitted by Robert Greskovic

Feet Positions

There are five positions of the feet (*positions des pieds*) that are fundamental to the execution of all ballet steps. In each, the weight of the body is distributed equally over both feet, and the legs are rotated outward from the hip joints so that the feet form a straight line (a 180-degree angle) when the heels are together.

- First (*première*) position: feet in a straight line, heels touching.
- Second (*seconde*) position: feet in a straight line, heels approximately one foot-length apart.
- Third (*troisième*) position: one foot crossed directly in front of the other, the heel of each foot touching the middle of the other.
- Fourth (*quatrième*) position: one foot forward of the other; approximately one foot-length apart, either crossed directly in front (*quatrième croisée*) or opened forward from first position (*quatrieme ouverte*).
- Fifth (*cinquième*) position: feet together, the front foot either crossed completely or as far as the first joint of the big toe of the back foot.

These positions can be executed with the heels raised and the weight resting on the balls of the feet or on the points of the toes. The raised positions are quarter point (*pied à quart*); half-point (*pied à demi*); three-quarter point (*pied à trois quarts*); and full point (*sur la pointe*).

The open positions (second and fourth) can be executed with one leg at *pointe tendue* (toes touching the floor) or extended *à la demi-hauteur* (45 degrees *en l'air*) or *à la hauteur* (90 degrees or higher *en l'air*). The raised foot placed at the ankle of the supporting leg is said to be *sur le cou-de-pied* (on the neck of the foot). The raised toe touching the knee of the supporting leg is in the *retiré* (or *raccourci*) position.

In the sixteenth century, Thoinot Arbeau (1589) described and illustrated six positions for the feet when together *(pieds joints)* and apart *(pieds larghis)*. Only slight turnout was indicated. In 1725, Pierre Rameau credited Pierre Beauchamps with systematizing the five positions of the feet, and these have remained fundamental to ballet technique. Rameau declared that these positions were invented to give a regular proportion to the steps—fourth position being useful for going forward and backward, second position for stepping sideward, and third and fifth positions for steps crossing in front or back (Rameau, 1725). As notated by Raoul-Auger Feuillet in 1700, the feet were opened outward to only a 90-degree angle in the five *bonnes positions* and turned inward or parallel in the five *fausses positions* (Feuillet, 1700). The latter were appropriate for comic or character roles but not for the noble style of theatrical or social dancing.

By 1779, the true positions, as described by Gennaro Magri, formed an obtuse angle. By 1820, however, turning the legs fully outward was deemed the first essential by Carlo Blasis, whose illustrations show a complete 180-degree turnout (Blasis, 1820). His contemporary, E. A. Théleur (1831) observed that the fifth position had entirely superseded the third position in stage dancing; Arthur Saint-Léon continued to use both third and fifth positions in his 1852 notation of classroom exercises, however.

Although all five positions are learned in contemporary classes, third position frequently is practiced only by beginners before the more demanding fifth position is mastered, or only in the *plié* sequence at the *barre*. Most ballet steps begin and end in one of the other four positions, all of which have been used effectively by themselves in choreography: in the strong, unrelenting closing to fifth position by the Death figure as he travels diagonally forward in Kurt Jooss's *The Green Table* (1932) or in the simple, expectant opening to first position by the stage filled with dancers at the beginning of George Balanchine's *Serenade* (1935).

In 1760, Jean-Georges Noverre suggested that the five positions were good to know, although the art of a great dancer was to neglect them gracefully. Théleur and Serge Lifar (1954) are two who attempted to add to the basic number and character of the positions, but their efforts failed. Since their codification in the late seventeenth century, the five positions have maintained their authority.

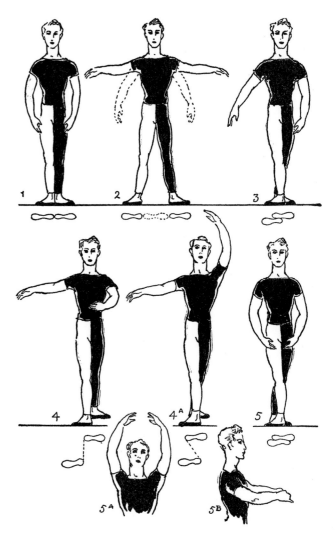

BALLET TECHNIQUE: Feet Positions. The five basic positions of the feet and the corresponding positions of the arms. (Reprinted from Kay Ambrose, *The Ballet-Lover's Pocket-Book*, New York, 1949, p. 12; used by permission of Celia Franca.)

BIBLIOGRAPHY

Arbeau, Thoinot. *Orchesography* (1589). Translated by Mary Stewart Evans. New York, 1948. Reprinted with introduction, corrections, and notes by Julia Sutton, New York, 1967.

Beaumont, Cyril W., and Stanislas Idzikowski. *A Manual of the Theory and Practice of Classical Theatrical Dancing: Cecchetti Method* (1922). Rev. ed. London, 1940. Reprint, New York, 1975.

Blasis, Carlo. *An Elementary Treatise upon the Theory and Practice of the Art of Dancing* (1820). Translated by Mary Stewart Evans. New York, 1944.

Feuillet, Raoul-Auger. *Chorégraphie, ou L'art de décrire la dance, par caractères, figures et signes démonstratifs, avec lesquels on apprend facilement de soy-même toutes sortes de dances.* Paris, 1700. Translated by John Weaver as *Orchesography, or, The Art of Dancing* (London, 1706).

Grant, Gail. *Technical Manual and Dictionary of Classical Ballet.* Rev. ed. New York, 1982.

Kostrovitskaya, Vera, and Alexei Pisarev. *School of Classical Dance.* Translated by John Barker. Moscow, 1978.

Lifar, Serge. "The Technical Evolution of Academic Dancing." *Ballet Annual* 8 (1954): 62–66.

Magri, Gennaro. *Trattato teorico-prattico di ballo.* Naples, 1779. Translated by Mary Skeaping as *Theoretical and Practical Treatise on Dancing* (London, 1988).

Noverre, Jean-Georges. *Lettres sur la danse et sur les ballets.* Stuttgart and Lyon, 1760. Translated by Cyril W. Beaumont as *Letters on Dancing and Ballets* (London, 1930).

Rameau, Pierre. *Abbrégé de la nouvelle méthode, dans l'art d'écrire ou de tracer toutes sortes de danses de ville.* Paris, 1725.

Rameau, Pierre. *Le maître à danser.* Paris, 1725. Translated by Cyril W. Beaumont as *The Dancing Master* (London, 1931).

Saint-Léon, Arthur. *La sténochorégraphie.* Paris, 1852. Translated into English by Raymond Lister (Cambridge, 1992).

Stuart, Muriel, et al. *The Classic Ballet: Basic Technique and Terminology.* New York, 1952.

Théleur, E. A. *Letters on Dancing, Reducing This Elegant and Healthful Exercise to Easy Scientific Principles.* London, 1831.

Vaganova, Agrippina. *Basic Principles of Classical Ballet: Russian Ballet Technique* (1934). Translated by Anatole Chujoy. Edited by Peggy van Praagh. 2d ed. London, 1953.

SANDRA NOLL HAMMOND

Arm Positions

Arm positions *(positions des bras)* are the basic forms that accompany ballet poses; from them, almost all ballet arm movements are derived. Unlike the five positions of the feet, the arm positions are less standardized, although each observes a gently curving line from shoulder to fingertip, except in the more extended arabesque poses. The carriage of the arms from one position to another is termed a *port de bras.* [*See* Port de Bras.]

General characteristics of the four basic arm positions used in three teaching methods—the Russian/Vaganova school, the Cecchetti method, and the Bournonville school—are as follows:

- Arms low, forming an oval in front of the body, hands almost touching, palms facing upward (preparatory position, Russian/Vaganova school; fifth position *en bas*, Cecchetti method; *bras bas*, Bournonville school)
- Arms raised in front of the body forming an oval forward of the diaphragm or the waist, palms facing the body (first position, Russian/Vaganova school; fifth position *en avant*, Cecchetti method and Bournonville school)
- Arms open to the side, at or slightly below shoulder level, very slightly rounded in the elbows, sometimes with a gentle slope downward toward the wrists (second position, all three systems)
- Arms raised above and slightly forward of the head, forming an oval, palms facing downward (third position, Russian/Vaganova school; fifth position *en haut*, Cecchetti method and Bournonville school; also known as *bras en couronne* in French systems)

Variations of these basic forms include the following:

- One arm curved low in front of the body, the other open slightly to the side (third position, Cecchetti method and Bournonville school)
- One arm curved in front of the body, the other either open to second position (fourth position *en avant*, Cecchetti method) or slightly lower (Bournonville school)
- One arm open to second position, the other either raised overhead (fourth position *en haut*, Cecchetti method) or above the shoulder (Bournonville school); this basic form is known also as *bras en attitude*
- Arms low, either curved at the sides with fingertips touching the thighs (first position, Cecchetti method) or hanging almost naturally, very slightly rounded and forward (Bournonville school)
- Arms open to the side, halfway to the height of second position (*demi-seconde* position, Cecchetti method and Bournonville school)

Bras à la lyre is a term for two quite different positions: (1) arms rounded overhead with wrists crossed (French systems) and (2) one arm overhead, the other curved in front of the body below waist level, both hands slightly overcrossing the center of the body (Bournonville school, where it also is termed "fourth position crossed").

A position used especially when the body is *en face* or at the conclusion of an *enchaînement* is sometimes called *demi-bras.* Similar positions include Arthur Saint-Léon's *bras au public* and the Bournonville "greeting arms." Usually, the arms are opened at half the height and width of second position, with the palms turned upward.

Credit for being one of the first to introduce and to lay down rules for use of the arms is given to Pierre-François Beauchamp (1636–1705?). About 1780, the five positions for the arms were described and notated for the first time in conjunction with the five positions of the feet. As recorded in Malpied's text *Traité sur l'art de la danse* (c.1785), they are:

- First position: arms extended alongside the body
- Second position: arms open to the side at shoulder height

BALLET TECHNIQUE: Arm Positions. The four basic arm positions named according to the terminology of Agrippina Vaganova. (Reprinted from Vaganova, 1953, p. 42.)

preparatory position   1st position   2nd position   3rd position

- Third position: the wrist of one arm bent and the other arm open to the side
- Fourth position: the elbow of one arm bent and the other arm open to the side
- Fifth position: one arm "quite closed in" and the other arm open to the side

The importance of the opposition of arm to leg is stressed in dance manuals from the early eighteenth century onward. In Pierre Rameau's descriptions, the raised arm (always in contrast to the forward leg) is gently rounded, with the elbow low and the hand in line with, and slightly forward of, the shoulder. The other arm is open to the side in line with the pit of the stomach. (This is an earlier version of Malpied's fourth position and today's *bras en attitude.*)

Four levels for the arms, to be used in the oppositions, were described by Gennaro Magri in 1779: *basse, a mezz'aria, alte,* and *forzatte,* or *grands bras.* The latter two were less exact than the other positions and were permitted to go above the head. Such "forced arms" could be used in tableaux or by certain characters, such as the *groteschi* playing comic roles.

As late as 1831, E. A. Théleur advised that arms raised to the "grand or highest position" (that is, above the height of the head) should "never be used unless to express grandeur, extreme voluptuousnessor in grouping." But Carlo Blasis, a contemporary of Théleur and author of several technical manuals, illustrated many poses with arms raised above head level. Blasis's drawings, however, are in agreement with Théleur's statement that "care should be taken never to permit the hands to approach each other so as to hide the body; they should rise in front, opposite the shoulders."

Thus, early in the nineteenth century the distance between the hands, even when raised overhead, was approximately the width of the shoulders rather than the few inches that is common today. And, judging from illustrations of the period, elbows were generally more extended in the positions than they became later in the century. Still commonly observed is the convention that the hands should never cross the center of the body in the standard positions of the arms or when moving from one arm position to another.

BIBLIOGRAPHY

Beaumont, Cyril W., and Stanislas Idzikowski. *A Manual of the Theory and Practice of Classical Theatrical Dancing: Cecchetti Method* (1922). Rev. ed. London, 1940. Reprint, New York, 1975.

Blasis, Carlo. *An Elementary Treatise upon the Theory and Practice of the Art of Dancing* (1820). Translated by Mary Stewart Evans. New York, 1944.

Blasis, Carlo. *The Code of Terpsichore: A Practical and Historical Treatise on the Ballet, Dancing, and Pantomime.* London, 1828.

Blasis, Carlo. *The Art of Dancing Comprising Its Theory and Practice, and a History of Its Rise and Progress, from the Earliest Times.*

Translated by R. Barton. London, 1831. Second edition of *The Code of Terpsichore.*

Grant, Gail. *Technical Manual and Dictionary of Classical Ballet.* Rev. ed. New York, 1982.

Hammond, Sandra Noll. *Ballet: Beyond the Basics.* Palo Alto, Calif., 1982.

Hammond, Sandra Noll. *Ballet Basics.* 3d ed. Mountain View, Calif., 1993.

Kostrovitskaya, Vera, and Alexei Pisarev. *School of Classical Dance.* Translated by John Barker. Moscow, 1978.

Magri, Gennaro. *Trattato teorico-prattico di ballo.* Naples, 1779. Translated by Mary Skeaping as *Theoretical and Practical Treatise on Dancing* (London, 1988).

Malpied. *Traité sur l'art de la danse.* Paris, c.1785. 2d ed., rev. and enl. Paris, c.1789.

Mara, Thalia. *Do's and Don'ts of Ballet Center Practice.* New York, 1957.

Prudhommeau, Germaine, and Geneviève Guillot. *Grammaire de la danse classique.* Paris, 1969. Translated by Katherine Carson as *The Book of Ballet* (Englewood Cliffs, N.J., 1976).

Ralov, Kirsten, ed. *The Bournonville School.* 4 vols. New York and Basel, 1979.

Rameau, Pierre. *Le Maître à danser.* Paris, 1725. Translated by Cyril W. Beaumont as *The Dancing Master* (London, 1931).

Saint-Léon, Arthur. *La sténochorégraphie.* Paris, 1852. Translated into English by Raymond Lister (Cambridge, 1992).

Théleur, E. A. *Letters on Dancing, Reducing This Elegant and Healthful Exercise to Easy Scientific Principles.* London, 1831.

Vaganova, Agrippina. *Basic Principles of Classical Ballet: Russian Ballet Technique* (1934). Translated by Anatole Chujoy. Edited by Peggy van Praagh. 2d ed. London, 1953.

SANDRA NOLL HAMMOND

Body Positions

Pierre Rameau's 1725 treatise on social dancing, *Maître à danser,* established an awareness of set positions for the body. In the first part of his work, Rameau named five basic positions for the dancer's feet (already notated by Raoul-Auger Feuillet in 1700), and in the second part, he concentrated on the use of the dancer's arms. His details for the upper body contrasted with the workings of the lower body. Their combined effect aimed toward "that opposition which is the adornment of dancing."

Sometimes called "directions of the body," body positions vary in number according to the school of instruction, the three principal ones of which are those of Enrico Cecchetti, Agrippina Vaganova, and August Bournonville. All body positions were derived, however, from common theories of design. They are all named by terms that describe the angle of the dancer's body in relation to the audience as well as the relationship of the arms and legs. All body positions can be assumed either *par terre* (on the floor) or *en l'air,* that is, either *en tendu* or *en arabesque.*

Croisé and Effacé. Like the terms describing contrasting positions of the legs in arabesque—*ouverte* (open) and *croisé* (crossed)—the terms *croisé* and *effacé* (literally, "shaded") designate basic positions for the dancer's body.

Both positions present the dancer's figure at an oblique angle to the audience—that is, along a diagonal line from stage corner to stage corner. The relationship of the legs is the dominant factor for establishing a *croisé* or *effacé* position.

Whenever the downstage leg is presented "across" the upstage leg, the dancer is holding some form of *croisé* position, with his or her legs forming a kind of X-shape crossed at the upper thighs. *Effacé* is simply an open position taken at an angle to the audience. In *effacé* positions, the legs describe the apex of a triangle, peaking at an imaginary point at the dancer's waist. Both these positions can have an accent *devant* (in front) or *derrière* (behind), depending on the direction of the working leg. The angle of the head and the relation of the arms to these positions differ for the Cecchetti and Vaganova schools, but each version involves an arrangement for the arms in which one is upcurved to the side and the other is outstretched to the other side.

À la Seconde and À la Quatrième. The body positions described as *à la seconde* and *à la quatrième* (*devant* or *derrière*) are more consistent from school to school because each comes directly out of its numbered foot position, either second (*seconde*) or fourth (*quatrième*). These numbered body positions are asymmetrical, working versions of their corresponding symmetrical foot positions. Both designs are presented *en face*, directly facing the audience, with both arms extended to the sides, in second position, and the working leg either in second position (*à la seconde*) or in fourth position (*à la quatrième*), in front (*devant*) or behind (*derrière*).

Écarté. The position designated *écarté*, meaning "separated" or "thrown widely apart," is essentially an *à la seconde* position taken at an oblique angle to the audience, with one arm usually lightly upcurved and the other extended to the side. Details of arm positions vary from school to school. The head for *écarté* faces a downstage corner: toward the downstage raised arm in the case of *écarté devant* and toward the downstage extended arm in *écarté derrière*.

Épaulé. The term *épaulé*, meaning "shouldered," is the only designation that refers specifically to the upper body, as it describes the gaze of the dancer looking at the audience over the shoulder of the downstage arm, which is extended forward while the downstage leg is extended backward, either *à terre* or *en l'air*, in arabesque. The Cecchetti school specifies an *arabesque épaulé* with the legs held *effacé derrière* and the arms held in a second arabesque line, in opposition to the legs. The Vaganova school specifies two versions: an *épaulé devant*, which is very like Cecchetti's design, and an *épaulé derrière*, where the legs are *croisé*, the dancer's back is angled to the audience, and his or her head is turned against the downstage shoulder and facing the audience.

BALLET TECHNIQUE: Body Positions. An illustration showing the eight positions of the body in classical ballet. Lines at the base of sketches indicate the angles from which positions should be viewed. (Reprinted from Kay Ambrose, *The Ballet-Lover's Companion*, New York, 1949, pp. 36–37; used by permission of Celia Franca.)

croisé devant   *à la quatrième devant*   *écarté*   *effacé*

à la seconde   *épaulé*   *à la quatrième derrière*   *croisé derrière*

BIBLIOGRAPHY

Beaumont, Cyril W., and Stanislas Idzikowski. *A Manual of the Theory and Practice of Classical Theatrical Dancing: Cecchetti Method* (1922). Rev. ed. London, 1940. Reprint, New York, 1975.

Grant, Gail. *Technical Manual and Dictionary of Classical Ballet.* Rev. ed. New York, 1982.

Stuart, Muriel, et al. *The Classic Ballet: Basic Technique and Terminology.* New York, 1952.

ROBERT GRESKOVIC

Directions

In classical ballet, any reference to directions presupposes the dancer performing to a fixed front—that is, dancing on a stage and facing an audience seated directly opposite. Any notion of directions must therefore be considered within this framework.

Most balletic movements and poses involve the simultaneous use of several different elements, such as the alignment of the hips, the rotation or inclination of the upper body, and the positioning and movements of the arms and head. In attempting to analyze and codify them, one is therefore faced with a complex situation in which the notion of direction cannot be totally divorced from that of body position and alignment and thus from the concepts of *croisé*, *effacé*, and *écarté*.

Épaulement (lit., "shouldering") refers to the direction of the shoulders and upper body vis-à-vis the audience and in relation to the direction of the hips. The term *effacé* (from *s'effacer*, to turn slightly to one side) is often used loosely (and incorrectly) as if it were synonymous with *ouverte* (open); in fact, the terms *overt(e)* and *croisé(e)* refer only to the disposition of the dancer's limbs relative to the audience. *Effacé* denotes a particular placing of the shoulders, as in *l'épaulement effacé*, in which the shoulders are rotated slightly upstage, away from the audience.

A feature of many theaters, particularly older opera houses, is the slope of the stage, known as the rake. The tradition, still current in France, of describing movement as being made *en descendant* (downward) or *en remontant* (lit., back up again) originally related to this slope. In the terminology of the English stage, the expressions *downstage* and *upstage* refer, respectively, to those areas of the stage closest to and farthest from the audience. If the dancer faces downstage, with both hips square to the audience, his or her direction is said to be *de face*.

A device used by some schools so that any instruction relating to a given direction (for purposes of teaching or rehearsing or of notating choreography can be understood quickly and clearly is to assign numbers to the corners and walls of the studio (or stage). Enrico Cecchetti numbered the corners counterclockwise from 1 to 4 and the walls from 5 to 8 (so that the downstage corner to the dancer's right is 1 and the audience is 5); the Russian school assigns the audience the number 1 and then pro-

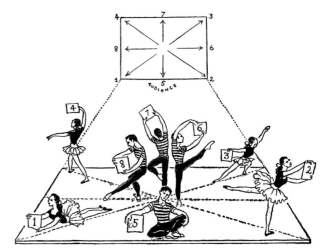

BALLET TECHNIQUE: Directions. An illustration showing the eight directions used in classical ballet to specify the relation of dancer to audience. (Reprinted from Kay Ambrose, *The Ballet-Lover's Companion*, New York, 1949, p. 38; used by permission of Celia Franca.)

ceeds clockwise, making the right-hand downstage corner number 2, the next wall 3, and so on until the left-hand downstage corner is reached at 8.

The conventions of classical ballet dictate that the dancers should think of themselves as standing in the center of a small square. Thus, when they direct their hips to one of the downstage corners, this is in fact a corner of their own imaginary squares and not of the dancing area as a whole. A dancer is then said to be standing *obliquement* (at an oblique angle to the audience). The other body directions are *à dos* (with the back to the audience) and *en profile*.

Independently of the direction faced, the dancer can move *en avant* (forward); *en arrière* (backward); *de côté* (sideways); *en tournant en dehors* (turning outward—that is, away from the supporting foot); and *en tournant en dedans* (turning inward toward the supporting foot). The dancer can make a movement *dessus* (over—meaning that the back foot is brought to the front) or *dessous* (under—the front foot moving to the back); or *devant* (at the front), *derrière* (at the back), or *en croix* (lit., in the shape of a cross, indicating that a movement—e.g., a *battement*—is executed successively to the fourth front, to the second, to the fourth back, and to the second again).

The dancer can perform *sur place* (on the spot); *en manège* or *autour de la salle* (in a circle, around the dancing area); or *en diagonale* (diagonally across it). A pose or movement can be done *à terre* (on the ground) or *en l'air* (in the air).

BIBLIOGRAPHY

Beaumont, Cyril W., and Stanislas Idzikowski. *A Manual of the Theory and Practice of Classical Theatrical Dancing: Cecchetti Method* (1922). Rev. ed. London, 1940. Reprint, New York, 1975.

Bournonville, August. *Études chorégraphiques.* Copenhagen, 1861.

Glasstone, Richard. *Better Ballet.* London, 1977.

Kostrovitskaya, Vera, and Alexei Pisarev. *School of Classical Dance.* Translated by John Barker. Moscow, 1978.

Meunier, Antonine. *La danse classique (école française).* Paris, 1931.

Prudhommeau, Germaine, and Geneviève Guillot. *The Book of Ballet.* Translated by Katherine Carson. Englewood Cliffs, N.J., 1976.

Vaganova, Agrippina. *Basic Principles of Classical Ballet: Russian Ballet Technique* (1934). Translated by Anatole Chujoy. Edited by Peggy van Praagh. 2d ed. London, 1953.

RICHARD GLASSTONE

BALLET TECHNIQUE: Turning Movements. Danish ballerina Kirsten Ralov finishes a Bournonville-style *pirouette sur la pointe.* (Photograph by Rigmor Mydstkov; used by permission.)

Turning Movements

Among the many types of turning movements in the vocabulary of classical ballet are various kinds of pirouette as well as *chaîné* turns, *soutenu* turns, *piqué* turns, *fouetté* turns, and *tours en l'air.* Most balletic turning movements, or *tours,* involve a complete revolution of the body, not just a change of direction.

Pirouettes. The most common form of *tour* in ballet is the pirouette, a whirling or spinning turn of the body while balanced on one foot. By 1820, Carlo Blasis considered pirouettes a fine and separate element of dancing. He devoted an entire chapter to them in his treatise on dance, *Traité élémentaire, théorique et pratique de l'art de la danse,* crediting Pierre Gardel and Gaëtan Vestris as their inventors. Notations from other sources, however, show that pirouettes were used at least a century earlier.

All standard variations on the pirouette that are performed today—*pirouette en dedans, pirouette en dehors, pirouette en attitude, pirouette en arabesque,* and *pirouette renversée*—were known to Blasis in 1820. Unknown at the time were the full-pointe base for balancing the turn and the smartly lifted foot (in *passé* position, beside the kneecap of the supporting leg) for shaping the turn.

Pirouettes in closed positions. Pirouettes *en dehors* (outward) and *pirouettes en dedans* (inward) are companion moves. In the former, the dancer spins in a direction away from the supporting leg; in the latter, the turn circles toward the supporting leg. Preparatory positions of the feet and legs vary. According to Blasis, the proper preparation for a *pirouette en dehors* is with the feet placed somewhere between second and fourth positions and with the legs in *demi-plié.* Such a preparation, planted in an openly turned-out stance, helps establish the turnout needed to impel and sustain the outward momentum that is this turn's distinctive characteristic. This preparation was also taught by August Bournonville and Enrico Cecchetti and is a tradition continued today by teachers schooled in their methods. For a *pirouette en dedans,* a fourth-position *demi-plié* preparation (sometimes with the back leg straight), has become traditional; both the Bournonville and Cecchetti theories favor it. The front-to-back width of the pose readies the dancer to initiate the inward accent with a kind of *grand rond de jambe en l'air* swing of the back leg to the front, which immediately lends the move its distinctive accent.

Male dancers sometimes take a second-position *demi-plié* preparation for *pirouettes en dehors,* but for female dancers, the fourth-position preparation is now standard for all pirouettes, both *en dehors* and *en dedans.* Pirouettes from fifth position, sometimes referred to as *relevé* (relifted, or raised) turns, have a character all their own. The *relevé* action itself, as the dancer rises to half pointe or full pointe, produces nearly all the momentum needed to initiate the turn: Like most turns, *pirouettes relevées* can be performed either *en dehors* or *en dedans.*

The number of pirouettes (and other turns) that a dancer is able to execute is, of course, dependent on the dancer's equilibrium and stamina, but it is also linked to a timing function called spotting. In this action, the dancer's head is held steady, with the gaze fixed on a single spot, until the last possible instant of the body's turn, when the head whips around and the gaze focuses again on the dancer's "spot." This snapping of the head not only gives multiple turns a pronounced rhythm but also prevents the dancer from getting dizzy. Spotting makes possible the feat of sustained, multiple revolutions. Individual abilities vary, but virtuoso level for a male dancer is seven or eight revolutions and for a female dancer, on pointe, about four.

Pirouettes in open positions. Standard pirouettes are those in which, after preparation, the working foot goes immediately into contact with the supporting leg—anywhere from *sur le cou-de-pied* (on the ankle, the "neck of the foot") to knee-high *passé.* Pirouettes may also be performed with an extended leg—*à la seconde, en arabesque,* or *en attitude*. Anna Friedrike Heinel, an eighteenth-century *danseuse*, is traditionally credited with perfecting the *pirouette à la seconde* (although there is evidence that it had been performed by women earlier). As the turn developed and as costuming became lighter and shorter, the working leg held *à la seconde* could be raised to hip level, creating a spectacular effect while the dancer turned.

Such pirouettes, now performed almost exclusively by men, are called *grandes pirouettes à la seconde* or just *grandes pirouettes*. In this virtuoso feat, the dancer does an extended series of *pirouettes à la seconde en dehors*, with a *relevé* to *demi-pointe* providing impetus at each turn or, sometimes, at every other turn; after the last full revolution *à la seconde*, he brings his extended foot into contact with the supporting leg and finishes the sequence with a multiple *pirouette en dehors* before a final pose. The related *grande pirouette sautée* involves tiny hops off the supporting foot as the turns are made. Both of these advanced turns can be executed with the extended leg in arabesque as well as in second position. *Grandes pirouettes à la seconde* are routinely performed in the codas of the bravura pas de deux from *Don Quixote* and *Le Corsaire*.

Pirouettes performed in open poses—*à la seconde, en arabesque*, or *en attitude*—are more difficult to sustain and are not so easily executed in multiple revolutions as pirouettes in closed, more compact positions. Pirouettes with extended legs are often done at a deliberate, adagio tempo, without spotting. The image of a dancer slowly and serenely revolving rather than spinning or whirling is what distinguishes an adagio turn from an allegro turn.

Pirouette renversé. One version of pirouette that combines something of the liveliness of an allegro turn and the calculation of an adagio turn is called a *pirouette renversé* (turned upside down; reversed). This pirouette is an *en dedans* turn that involves a strong bend in the upper body toward the working leg, which is raised in a *passé* position. The last-second follow-through by the torso in the direction of the turn has an effect similar to that of spotting with the head, as the entire upper half of the dancer's body—often with arms widespread—seems to flip over. Whereas the sharp snap of the head in multiple *pirouettes en dehors* adds sparkle to the turns, the off-center flip of the torso in a *pirouette renversé* lends the turn a distinctly weighty drama.

Chaîné Turns. *Tours chaînés déboulés* (turns in a rolling chain), *petits tours* (small turns), or just plain *chaînés* (a chain of turns) are various names for a turning movement across the floor on both feet. (The Cecchetti school of training prefers the "small turns" description, while the French and Russian schools prefer the "chain" and "rollings of a ball" images.) *Chaîné* turns are produced by stepping onto alternate feet, with each foot initiating a half turn of the body. The chain effect comes from the repeated linking of these alternating steps in a diagonal path *(en diagonale)* or in a circular direction (*en manège*, as in the ring of a riding school).

Chaîné turns can be done both on half pointe and on full pointe. Deliberate execution of a series of these half turns alternates open-position and closed-position dynamics: in the first step one foot goes to second-position width and in the next step the other foot closes up to it, creating the half turn with a first-position accent. Arm positions correspond directly to the positions of the feet—that is, the second-position step is performed with open arms, which are brought together on the first-position step. If the turns are meant to be performed rapidly, the feet and arm positions vary much less, with a consistently fine base for the feet (which are held tightly in a parallel first position, especially if the dancer is on full pointe) and a calm but firm carriage of the arms, close to the body.

Soutenu Turns. Another *tour par terre* (on the ground, or floor) on two feet is the *soutenu* (sustained) turn. Sometimes this move is called *soutenu en tournant* or *assemblé soutenu en tournant*. A full revolution can be done in two half turns—*soutenu en tournant en dedans* and *soutenu en tournant en dehors*—similar to a *chaîné* turn, or in a single movement. The impetus to start the turn, or half turn, comes from pulling the arms and an extended leg, which have been opened in preparation, to a closed position. Simultaneously, the dancer springs to fifth position, on half pointe or full pointe, and swivels around. An added impetus may be given to the turn by sweeping the arms up overhead.

To add even more impetus and sweep to *soutenu* turns, the French school of training gives the drawing in of the working foot a *demi-rond de jambe à terre* accent. Depending on the working leg, this turnabout can appear plain and simple—like a revolving, smooth column—or fancifully ornamented—like a spiraling, fluted pillar. *Soutenu* turns, and many other kinds of turning movement, are featured in Harald Lander's *Études* (1948), which is a virtual lexicon of ballet's academic vocabulary.

Piqué Turns. *Tour piqué* and *tour posé* are interchangeable names for another kind of turn *par terre*. The former term is used by the Russian school of training, the latter by the Cecchetti school. The notion of a *tour piqué* (pricked turn) relates appropriately to the sudden, sharp contact made with the stage by the foot of the dancer's working leg. Once the contact is struck, and the working leg becomes the supporting leg, the dancer revolves in a *posé* (poised) position. *Piqué* or *posé* turns can be done either *en dehors* or *en dedans* and are usually performed either on a diagonal or *en manège*. The arms tend to assist by opening on the *piqué* step onto the supporting leg and closing during the *posé* turning action.

Piqué turns have their sharpest, truest effect when they are done by a ballerina stepping crisply onto pointe. Once poised, the turns can be single or multiple in revolution, as the dancer employs the standard spotting mechanism. A striking example of the effective force of single *piqué* turns occurs in the first movement of George Balanchine's *Serenade* (1934): taking the lead from the demi-soloists, the ensemble of fifteen women performs a stagewide ring of fast-paced, space-eating *piqué* turns in a *grand manège* fifteen times over.

Fouetté Turns. As the full, formal name indicates, a *fouetté rond de jambe en tournant* is a turn that combines a whipping action with a circling of the leg. Usually done in a series without ever putting the working foot down, these turns can be done on half pointe or full pointe and with single, double, or triple revolutions. Although they can be executed either *en dehors* or *en dedans*, they are almost always done *en dehors* and usually from a multiple *pirouette en dehors* preparation and with a multiple *pirouette en dehors* finish. Perfectly done, a series of *fouetté* turns, beginning and ending with multiple pirouettes, is one of the most spectacular feats that a ballerina can perform.

Capable of performing thirty-two of these turns in a row, the Italian ballerina Pierina Legnani (1863–1923) began a tradition of virtuosity that has carried on to the present day. Having already performed thirty-two *fouettés* in *Aladdin* (London, 1892) and in Marius Petipa's *Cinderella* (Saint Petersburg, 1893), Legnani introduced them into the coda of the Black Swan pas de deux in act 3 of Petipa's *Swan Lake* (Saint Petersburg, 1895). They can still usually be seen in that pas de deux today. Most balletomanes are unable to resist mentally counting the turns while watching closely to see if the ballerina remains in complete command of her equilibrium and stays firmly planted in the spot she has chosen at center stage.

Tours en l'Air. A turn in the air, in which a dancer jumps off the floor and makes a complete revolution of the body before landing, is called a *tour en l'air*. The standard preparation is a *demi-plié* in fifth position, which is almost universally employed. Finishing positions are, however, more varied. One common landing is in fifth position with the feet reversed, as the dancer will have made a *changement de pieds* (change of feet) while turning in the air. Other familiar endings include a kneeling pose or a pose with one leg extended *à la seconde* or *en arabesque*. During the turn, the dancer's arms may remain down, in front of the body, or be raised *en couronne* (overhead, like a crown). Similarly, the legs may be held tautly, with the feet in fifth position, or, as is sometimes dictated by the Russian school, one leg may be held with the foot in *passé* position, especially if the *tour* is to finish in an arabesque pose.

Generally, although not exclusively, *tours en l'air* are performed by men, and almost always the dancer performs two revolutions, a double *tour*, although in some instances only one is called for. The dancer who can do a triple *tour* in performance is not unknown, albeit still uncommon. Edward Villella, a star of the New York City Ballet in the 1960s and 1970s, remains notable as a performer who regularly executed triple *tours* on stage.

The "Team Play" movement of Jerome Robbins's *Interplay* (1945) has a section for the cast's four men to do successive series of double *tours en l'air*. The first dancer does one double *tour;* the second does two, one after another; the third does three; and the last tops them all by doing four double *tours* in a row. Accomplished performers can usually execute this challenge, but the classical accuracy of the later turns is often sacrificed. Double *tours* also figure prominently in the male pas de quatre in the *grand pas hongrois* in *Raymonda*, in Prince Désiré's variation in the *grand pas classique* in *The Sleeping Beauty*, and in a dazzling passage for the principal male dancer in Balanchine's *Theme and Variations*.

BIBLIOGRAPHY

Beaumont, Cyril W., and Stanislas Idzikowski. *A Manual of the Theory and Practice of Classical Theatrical Dancing: Cecchetti Method* (1922). Rev. ed. London, 1940. Reprint, New York, 1975.

Blasis, Carlo. *An Elementary Treatise upon the Theory and Practice of the Art of Dancing* (1820). Translated by Mary Stewart Evans. New York, 1944.

Grant, Gail. *Technical Manual and Dictionary of Classical Ballet*. Rev. ed. New York, 1982.

Karsavina, Tamara. *Ballet Technique: A Series of Practical Essays*. London, 1956.

Messerer, Asaf. *Classes in Classical Ballet*. Translated by Oleg Briansky. Garden City, N.Y., 1975.

Vaganova, Agrippina. *Basic Principles of Classical Ballet: Russian Ballet Technique* (1934). Translated by Anatole Chujoy. Edited by Peggy van Praagh. 2d ed. London, 1953.

ROBERT GRESKOVIC

Linking Movements

Classical ballet uses several simple dance movements to link its various steps and poses, from gliding movements to little running steps. In function and use the movements resemble the conjunction in grammar: the dynamic and rhythmic structure of any *enchaînement*—two or more steps linked to form a movement phrase—depends on the correct timing and emphasis of each linking movement relative to the step or pose that immediately follows.

Pas de Bourrée. One of the most widely used linking movements is the *pas de bourrée*. Its basic form consists of three rapid transfers of weight, usually starting on the end of a musical measure and finishing on the first beat of the next measure. In allegro work, these transfers of weight are very swift. The nineteenth-century French school used a soft, unemphasized *pas de bourrée*, but the Italian school in the same period changed the movement's character: the foot was lifted sharply, which gave the movement more relief. Choreographically, this movement varies according to its context.

Pas de bourrées fall into two main categories: those that involve the feet changing place with each other *(pas de bourrées dessus* and *dessous)* and those that begin and end with the same foot in front *(pas de bourrées devant* and *derrière).* They can begin with either the front or the back foot and can also be performed *en tournant* (turning), *en dehors* or *en dedans* (outward or inward), and *en avant* or *en arrière* (forward or backward). The *pas de bourrée courru* is a light, running movement, on pointe or half pointe, that can either finish in second or fourth position *(pas de bourrée ouvert)* or be performed *suivi* (following), as an unbroken series of tiny steps in fifth position (or in a first position that is not turned out).

Glissade. A *glissade* is essentially a gliding *terre à terre* step, moving sideways from fifth position and ending in fifth position with or without having changed the feet. This step can also be performed *en avant* or *en arrière.* It often serves as a preparation to a *jeté* or an *assemblé* movement.

Chassé. The *chassé*, as its name implies, strictly speaking, is a movement in which one foot displaces the other, "chasing" it from its place. The foot thus displaced glides forward, backward, or sideways to fourth or second position, without leaving the ground. However, the Italian school sometimes uses the term *chassé* to describe a gliding movement from a closed to an open position, beginning and ending in a *demi-plié* and with the weight evenly distributed.

Coupé. In the *coupé*, one foot also replaces the other, but the feet join briefly in fifth position (on the ground, en pointe or half pointe, or in the air) before the original supporting foot is released, either to the *cou-de-pied* or to fourth or second position *pointe tendue à terre* or *dégagée.*

Temps Levé. The *temps levé* (a hop on one foot) is sometimes classed as a preparatory or a linking movement. When combined with a *chassé passé*, it forms a *demi-contretemps.* This is essentially a short anacrusis (or preparatory movement) and is a vestige of a longer form of anacrusis, the full *contretemps*—a linking movement of subtle rhythmic complexity.

Failli and Contretemps. Some schools use the term *pas failli* to describe a movement similar to a *demi-contretemps*, but involving either the joining of the feet in fifth position *en l'air*, or the raising of one leg in a low fourth position, prior to the *chassé passé.* This movement can also be beaten. There is a tendency today to use the terms *demi-contretemps* and *failli* synonymously, to indicate any linking movement that basically consists of a hop and step. However, *failli* (Fr., *faillir*, "to fail") and *contretemps* or *contratempo* (lit., "against the beat"), as well as *demi-contretemps*, were originally specific indications of the timing of these movements. *Contretemps* denoted a movement timed to anticipate the strong beat, whereas *failli* denoted a hesitation before it.

Other Linking Movements. This type of subtlety in the timing of linking movements, once a hallmark of the *danse d'école*, has been gradually eroded by the shift away from a ballet aesthetic essentially rooted in nuances of rhythmic movement and toward one increasingly concerned with subtleties of line and shape. In a classical ballet context, dancers use stylized forms of stepping *(posé* and *piqué)*, of walking *(pas marché)*, of passing the foot from front to back or vice versa *(passé)*, and of running *(pas de course* and *pas courrus)* to link movements and poses.

Other movements classed as linking or auxiliary movements include *temps relevé*, in which the dancer rises up to the *demi-pointe* or *sur la pointe* on both feet or on one; and *petits fouettés à terre en tournant*, more commonly known as *flic-flac.* The latter onomatopoeic description relates to the sharp, whipping action made against the floor with one foot as the dancer revolves on the other.

BIBLIOGRAPHY

Craske, Margaret, and Cyril W. Beaumont. *The Theory and Practice of Allegro in Classical Ballet: Cecchetti Method.* London, 1930.

Glasstone, Richard. *Better Ballet.* London, 1977.

Kostrovitskaya, Vera, and Alexei Pisarev. *School of Classical Dance.* Translated by John Barker. Moscow, 1978.

Meunier, Antonine. *La danse classique (école française).* Paris, 1931.

Prudhommeau, Germaine, and Geneviève Guillot. *The Book of Ballet.* Translated by Katherine Carson. Englewood Cliffs, N.J., 1976.

Vaganova, Agrippina. *Basic Principles of Classical Ballet: Russian Ballet Technique* (1934). Translated by Anatole Chujoy. Edited by Peggy van Praagh. 2d ed. London, 1953.

RICHARD GLASSTONE

Jumping Movements

The vocabulary of classical ballet includes a vast number and variety of jumping movements. Nevertheless, all jumping movements in ballet can be classified in one of five categories:

- Jumps from both feet, landing simultaneously on both feet (e.g., *changement de pieds, échappés sautés*).
- Jumps from both feet, landing and ending on one foot (e.g., *sissonne ouverte, entrechat trois volé*).
- Jumps from one foot, landing and ending on the same foot (e.g., *ballonés, temps levés sur le cou-de-pied*).
- Jumps from one foot, landing and ending on the other foot (e.g., *jetés, ballottés, sauts de basque*).
- Jumps from one foot, ending on both feet. This category has two subdivisions: (1) *pas assemblé*, an "assembled" movement, where the jump lands on both feet simultaneously, and (2) *pas fermé*, a "closed" movement, where the jump lands on one foot but with the other closing immediately into fifth position (e.g., *cabriole fermée*).

According to their height and character, jumps are generally divided into two main types: steps of *élévation* and *terre à terre* (lit., "ground to ground") movements. *Terre à terre* is used to describe movements performed very close to and along the floor, with the impetus and strength deriving mainly from the action of the feet (e.g., *glissades*).

In *terre à terre* steps, the dancer should seem almost reluctant to leave the ground. The latter quality contrasts with *élévation*, the term used to describe all jumps essentially directed upward, away from the ground. These can be big jumps *(grande élévation* or *grands sauts)* or small ones *(petite élévation* or *petits sauts);* they can be done traveling or *sur place;* and they can have a smooth, soaring quality or a sharp, bouncy one. All come under the general heading of *élévation* because, whether big or small, they give the impression that the performer has been temporarily released from the pull of gravity.

The varying character of different steps of *élévation* is dictated, in part, by the mechanics of specific movements; however, it is also largely dependent on the dynamics of the music. The particular musical phrasing of a series of jumps can give the impression of the dancer hovering for a moment in midair, at the peak of each jump, before landing softly in a *demi-plié* just in time to soar upward again (this is the quality known as *ballon,* the hallmark of good elevation).

In *terre à terre* jumps, the dancer's distance from the ground is only fractionally more than the length of his or her own foot; if the dancer jumps any higher than this, the movement becomes one of *petite élévation;* if the latter is embellished with beats, it comes into the category of *petite batterie* or *petits pas battus.*

Depending on the context in which they are being performed, as well as on the speed of the music, certain steps such as *glissades, brisés,* and some *entrechats* can be performed either *terre à terre* or as *petite élévation.* Here, the influence of the Soviet school, with its emphasis on soaring leaps, has sometimes tended to erode the variety and brilliance of fast footwork characteristic of the western European tradition.

The character of a jump can also vary according to the height of the raised leg. If it is thrown up only high

BALLET TECHNIQUE: Jumping Movements. These four male dancers of the Royal Danish Ballet demonstrate the extraordinary *ballon* that is a trademark of the Bournonville style. (Photograph by John Lindquist; used by permission of the Harvard Theatre Collection, The Houghton Library.)

enough to make an angle of 22.5 degrees or 45 degrees to the supporting foot—as in a *balloné*—the effect will be quite different from that obtained by thrusting the legs up to or beyond hip height, as in *grands jetés*.

During the latter part of the twentieth century, the emphasis on high leg extensions has sometimes tended to blur the differences that should exist between jumps in which the raised leg is kept low and those in which it should be well lifted.

Many jumps can be performed with a turn. These vary from the brilliant double (an even triple) *tours en l'air,* which belong essentially to the province of the male dancer, to the simple *temps levé* or *sissonne ordinaire* performed *en tournant* (basically a hop on one foot, turning in the air). Other turning jumps are *grands jetés en tournant* or *jeté entrelacé,* in which the dancer revolves in the air and interchanges legs, and *fouettés sautés,* in which the dancer moves his or her body sharply to make a half turn in the air away from the raised leg. *Entrechats* can also be performed *en tournant.*

The search for weightlessness—the desire to appear to be escaping from gravity—is the single characteristic that most strongly differentiates the development of ballet technique and the aesthetics of ballet in the nineteenth century and in much of the twentieth, in pre-Romantic ballet and "modern" or "contemporary" dance. It was, of course, the introduction of pointe work, early in the nineteenth century, that was to be the decisive factor in shaping this new aesthetic of weightlessness. However, its roots are to be found much earlier, in the search for *élévation.* The acrobatic capering of the *groteschi,* so vividly recorded by Gennaro Magri in 1778, had gradually influenced and eroded the noble style during the course of the eighteenth century. After the French Revolution, it finally supplanted the old dance forms. In the hands of pedagogues like Carlo Blasis, Christian Johannson, Enrico Cecchetti, and Agrippina Vaganova and choreographers like August Bournonville, Marius Petipa, and Michel Fokine, the leaps and tricks of the *groteschi* were refined and honed into the expressive aerial dance language of classical ballet.

The fashion for jumping *ritirate* (with the legs drawn up underneath the body) described by Magri survived in the Italian school well into the twentieth century. Margaret Craske (1930) describes many jumps in this way: of *assemblé,* she says, "While the body is in the air, bend both knees (a *plié à quart*) and bring together the flat of the toes of both feet." Vaganova (1934) deplores the practice, writing, "In order to create the impression of a higher jump, the Italians bend the knees. . . . This renders the dance a grotesque character, spoiling its classic line." The streamlined, linear aesthetic of twentieth-century ballet has gradually made these *sauts à l'italienne* almost obsolete. Although their training value is still recognized by some

BALLET TECHNIQUE: Jumping Movements. Maya Plisetskaya performs a *grand jeté* in typical Russian fashion, in act 3 of a Bolshoi Ballet production of *Swan Lake.* (Photograph from the Dance Collection, New York Public Library for the Performing Arts.)

schools, onstage such jumps are now only used for specific choreographic effect.

BIBLIOGRAPHY

Adice, G. Léopold. *Théorie de la gymnastique de la danse théâtrale.* Paris, 1859. Excerpts translated by Leonore Loft in *Dance as a Theatre Art,* edited by Selma Jeanne Cohen (New York, 1974).

Beaumont, Cyril W., and Stanislas Idzikowski. *A Manual of the Theory and Practice of Classical Theatrical Dancing: Cecchetti Method* (1922). Rev. ed. London, 1940. Reprint, New York, 1975.

Blasis, Carlo. *The Code of Terpsichore: A Practical and Historical Treatise on the Ballet, Dancing, and Pantomime.* London, 1828.

Bournonville, August. *Études chorégraphiques.* Copenhagen, 1861.

Craske, Margaret, and Cyril W. Beaumont. *The Theory and Practice of Allegro in Classical Ballet: Cecchetti Method.* London, 1930.

Glasstone, Richard. *Better Ballet.* London, 1977.

Kostrovitskaya, Vera, and Alexei Pisarev. *School of Classical Dance.* Translated by John Barker. Moscow, 1978.

Meunier, Antonine. *La danse classique (école française).* Paris, 1931.

Prudhommeau, Germaine, and Geneviève Guillot. *The Book of Ballet.* Translated by Katherine Carson. Englewood Cliffs, N.J., 1976.

Vaganova, Agrippina. *Basic Principles of Classical Ballet: Russian Ballet Technique* (1934). Translated by Anatole Chujoy. Edited by Peggy van Praagh. 2d ed. London, 1953.

RICHARD GLASSTONE

BALLET TECHNIQUE, HISTORY OF. [*To trace the history and development of ballet technique, this entry comprises three articles:*

> French Court Dance
> Ballet in the Late Eighteenth and Early
>   Nineteenth Centuries
> Ballet since the Mid-Nineteenth Century

The first article discusses the development of danse noble; *the second describes the transition and expansion of technique from French court dance into the Romantic ballet; the third focuses on the development of virtuosity and dancing* sur les pointes.]

French Court Dance

Seventeenth-century *danse noble* was the dance of serious aesthetic purport; it was the pure, classic dance of the Baroque period. The central figure in the performance of this dance, and the most influential in its development, was Louis XIV of France (ruled 1643–1715). The so-called French court dance was by no means confined to France; it was widely copied throughout Europe.

In the early 1600s, a simple and fluid dance style had begun to emerge. The first dance to be developed in the new French style was a slow *courante*, and some of its steps—"des pas coupez et entrecoupez, d'autres graves, ensemble des liaisons, et des beaux temps" (de Lauze, 1623)—seem to have provided the basis for the *danse noble* to be developed by Louis's dance masters. A new element of enormous significance was an outward rotation of the legs and feet. As this fashionable feature of standing and leisurely walking became more extreme, it was established as a fundamental component of classical dance.

Apart from the king himself, probably the most influential figure in dance development was the composer Jean-Baptiste Lully. As a composer of *ballets de cour* and *comédies-ballets*, Lully introduced into them, and into the ballroom, lively rhythms from French regional dances; the dance masters then stylized their most characteristic steps to augment the vocabulary.

The nobility, aristocracy, and gentry had two types of serious dance: first, the ballroom *danses à deux*, which were performed by one couple at a time; second, the classical, heroic, or aristocratic roles of the *ballets de cour*, the king's most famous role being that of the ancient Greek sun god Apollo.

For the upper classes, dance lessons began at a young age and were essential in preparing its members to shine in society. The ideal social presence was characterized by poise and simplicity. The carriage of the body and the turn of the head were the ultimate hallmarks of distinction. Dance masters wrote that any suggestion of affectation must be avoided. The arms were held relatively low during a dance, allowing the head, the seat of the intellect, to remain the highest point of the body.

In 1672, the king retired from the *ballets de cour*. That same year, he appointed Lully to become director of the new Académie Royale de Musique, where a company of professional dancers was soon established. The serious roles became the sole property of professionals, with female characters being danced by boys until the 1680s.

When dances were first published in notation in 1700, the technical demands of court dances continued to approximate those of many dances performed at the Académie. For example, one theater dance, "L'Allemande" (1702), with many *pas sautés* and *pas battus*, was immediately adopted as a ballroom *danse à deux*. Other theater dances showed great technical virtuosity in the male and, more gradually, in the female step vocabulary.

No technical books on dance were published in France between François de Lauze's *Apologie de la danse* (1623) and Raoul-Auger Feuillet's *Chorégraphie* (1700), but early eighteenth-century publications on dance notation and dance technique shed some retrospective light on a period when the dances, steps, and technique they describe were developed and systematized.

In *Chorégraphie,* Feuillet explains a system of dance notation that would be used less and less often later in the eighteenth century. Shortly after its appearance, however, masters began to publish manuals describing steps and their manner of performance. The most monumental of these manuals is Gottfried Taubert's *Der Rechtschaffener Tantzmeister* (1717); it was followed by the clearest text, Pierre Rameau's *Le Maître à danser* (1725), and Kellom Tomlinson's *The Art of Dancing* (1735).

The ballroom and comparably complex theater dances are choreographed from a vocabulary of *pas composés* and *temps* (step-units). The basic units, many of which have several variations, are the *pas de bourrée, de courante, de gaillarde, de menuet, de passacaille, de rigaudon, de sissonne;* the *pas assemblé, balancé, coupé, échappé, tombé;* the *temps de courante;* contretemps de chaconne, de gavotte, de menuet, *and* ballonné; glissades; chassés; jetés chassés, jetés; *and* pirouettes. In ballroom dances, pirouettes are made with the weight supported on both feet; in the theater, single and multiple pirouettes on one foot are also employed.

The single steps (transferences of weight) used in *pas composés* are a *pas marché*, a walking step usually made on [demi-] pointe, the knee well braced; a *pas glissé*, in which the ball of the foot slides along the floor; a *demi-coupé*, which combines a *plié* and *élevé* with a step; and a *demi-jeté* and a *jeté*, both of which are "ordinary" steps but made with a spring. Some step-units are composed of walking steps combined with bends and rises; others combine walking with springing steps, while some units are entirely sprung. All steps are performed with the legs rotated outward about forty degrees.

The fundamental actions used in the step-units are *pliés*, in which the knees bend and the heel, or heels, remain on the ground; *elevés*, in which the knees straighten from the bend, an action usually continued into a rise onto [*demi-*] *pointe;* and *sautés*, small springs into the air following a bend. These components have an important rhythmic function in making the meter of a dance clear. A bend followed by a rise makes up an action known as a *mouvement*, which usually serves to mark the musical upbeat and downbeat. A bend is made on the upbeat, leading to a rise on the downbeat; in a sprung *mouvement*, the bend and spring both occur on the upbeat, with the landing marking the downbeat.

Other actions are the *glissé*, a qualitative element denoting a slow, sustained step-unit; and the *tombé*, in which the body is momentarily shifted out of equilibrium and "falls" onto a free foot. Certain straight and circular low leg gestures *(ouvertures de jambe)* are made, sometimes ornamented in theater dances by a *tour (rond) de jambe* from the knee. Small rhythmic *battements*—beats of one foot around or against the other—are added to some steps *(pas battus),* and in theater dances these become very elaborate in their own right. Beats of the legs against each other are made during some springs *(entrechats trois, quatre, cinq, six,* and *huit,* and *cabriolles,* or capers).

Motions of the arms parallel those of the legs. A motion of the arm held straight from the shoulder balances a motion of a straight leg from the hip; a circular motion of the arm from the elbow, a bending and straightening of the knee; a turn of the wrist, a small spring made primarily from the ankle. Arm motions are also related to the disposition of the legs in space. Generally speaking, the arms move in a highly stylized "natural" opposition to the forward foot, the high arm being that in opposition. When the feet are side by side, the arms are elevated sideways to hip or waist level. To make the opposition, the arm is circled inward from the elbow, returning downward by the same path or through an outward circle. In some step-units, and according to the taste of the dancer, a shading of the shoulders and a turn of the head toward the raised arm may be introduced. The arms move in rhythmic sympathy with the steps, aid balance, and adorn the presence.

Descriptions of dance lessons for this period are scarce. In a first lesson (Sol, 1725), the pupil learned to rotate the legs outward to make a *plié* and an *élevé* and to walk on [*demi-*] *pointe,* the legs braced and the body steady. In technical descriptions, Rameau stressed the need for making deep [*demi-*] *pliés* before the *elevés* "without which the steps appear lifeless and dull." The student thus developed strength and control in the insteps, and a strongly centered balance.

Only the steps used in both ballroom and theater

BALLET TECHNIQUE. Entitled "Habits des nymphes de la suitte d'Orithie du balet du Triomphe de l'amour," this illustration of a professional dancer, in a costume designed by Jean Berain for *Le Triomphe de l'Amor* (1681), shows the higher arm in graceful opposition to the forward foot. The dancer's legs are characteristically turned out, his torso is centered but fluid, giving the effect of ease, vitality, and strength, and the turn of his head suggests a continuous motion rather than a static pose. (Dance Collection, New York Public Library for the Performing Arts.)

dances are described. For *pas de ballet,* Feuillets tables in *Chorégraphie* and dance scores must be consulted. The major collections of theater dances were published in 1700 and 1704 (Feuillet) and c.1714 (Gaudrau) and c.1725 (Rousseau). Although virtuosic dances for men appear in each book, the last two volumes show a rapid development in women's technique. In the last collection, women are performing *pirouettes à la seconde* of as many as one-and-a-half revolutions. Performed for a kinesthetically attuned audience, these virtuosities were not stressed by preparations and conclusions, rather, they were merely slipped into the rhythmic flow of the dance; an expert dancer should make Baroque dance appear very easy. In fact, the performance of Baroque dance is exceptionally demanding because of its subtle textures of movement and the highly developed rhythmic interplay between dance and music. It requires an inherent nobility of presence and motion, an unfaltering rhythmic sense, intellectual dexterity, quick and precise footwork, a strongly centered balance and control, and a keen awareness of spatial configuration.

Mainly through the performance of the *menuet*, ballroom dance in the old style survived until the French Revolution in 1789. Further developments in theatrical technique were not recorded during the eighteenth century, until the appearance of Gennaro Magri's *Trattato teorico-prattico di ballo* (1779).

In addition to the *danse noble*, *demi-caractère* and comic styles were seen in the theater. Notation exists for the *demi-caractère* genre, which is mentioned in the theater notices of the period, as is comic dance.

[*See also* Academie Royal de Danse; Ballet de Cour; Feuillet Notation; France, *article on* Theatrical Dance, 1581–1789; Opéra-Ballet and Tragédie Lyrique; *and* Technical Manuals, *article on* Publications, 1400–1700. *For information on French ballroom and theatrical dances, see* Anglaise; Bourée; Chaconne and Passacaille; Courante; Entrée Grave; Folia; Forlana; Gavotte; Gigue; Loure; Minuet; Musette; Passepied; Rigaudon; Sarabande; *and* Tambourin. *See also the entries on Pierre Rameau, Molière, and Lully.*]

BIBLIOGRAPHY

Annas, Alicia M. "The Elegant Art of Movement." In Annas's *An Elegant Art*. Los Angeles, 1983.

Feuillet, Raoul-Auger. *Chorégraphie, ou L'art de décrire la dance, par caractères, figures et signes démonstratifs, avec lesquels on apprend facilement de soy-même toutes sortes de dances.* Paris, 1700. Translated by John Weaver as *Orchesography, or, The Art of Dancing.* London, 1706.

Feuillet, Raoul-Auger. *Recueil de dances composées par M. Pécour.* Paris, 1700.

Gaudrau, Michel. *Nouveau recueil de dances de bal et celle de ballet, contenant un très grand nombres des meillieures entrées de ballet de la composition de Mr. Pécour.* Paris, c.1714.

Hilton, Wendy. "A Dance for Kings: The Seventeenth-Century French Courante." *Early Music* (April 1977).

Hilton, Wendy. *Dance of Court and Theatre: The French Noble Style, 1690–1725.* Princeton, 1981.

Hilton, Wendy. *Dance and Music of Court and Theater: Selected Writings of Wendy Hilton.* Stuyvesant, N.Y., 1997.

Lauze, François de. *Apologie de la danse, 1623: A Treatise of Instruction in Dancing and Deportment.* Translated by Joan Wildeblood. London, 1952.

Magri, Gennaro. *Trattato teorico-prattico di ballo.* Naples, 1779. Translated by Mary Skeaping as *Theoretical and Practical Treatise on Dancing.* London, 1988.

Rameau, Pierre. *Le maître à danser.* Paris, 1725. Translated by Cyril W. Beaumont as *The Dancing Master.* London, 1931.

Rousseau, F. *A New Collection of Dances.* London, c.1725.

Sol, C. *Méthode très facile et fort nécessaire pour montrer à la jeunesse de l'un et l'autre sexe la manière de bien danser.* The Hague, 1725.

Taubert, Gottfried. *Rechtschaffener Tantzmeister, oder Gründliche Erklärung der frantzösischen Tantz-Kunst.* Leipzig, 1717.

Tomlinson, Kellom. *The Art of Dancing Explained by Reading and Figures . . . Being the Original Work First Design'd in the Year 1724, and Now Published by Kellom Tomlinson, Dancing-Master.* 2 vols. London, 1735.

WENDY HILTON

Ballet in the Late Eighteenth and Early Nineteenth Centuries

The late eighteenth to the early nineteenth centuries were an important bridge between Baroque dance and Romantic ballet. It was a period of transition in which the old technique was assimilated by the new. Dancing masters observed the blending of once-distinct genres, the noble or serious, with the *demi-caractère*, or lighter style. Reviewers lamented the disappearance of the elegant *danse noble*, expressing amazement often mixed with shock and outrage as they described the trend toward pirouetting, soaring, hovering, high jumps, and sustained balances in which the dancer fully extended his leg from his side, and danced on tiptoe.

To the previous *terre à terre* manner was added the *ballonné* style, encouraged by such masters as Carlo Blasis, who, in his *Traité élémentaire* (1820), urged dancers to "be as light as possible. . . . I would like to see you bound with a suppleness and agility which gives me the impression you are barely touching the ground and may at any moment take flight" The suppleness and agility necessary for the expanded technical range was nurtured in rigorous classes, such as those given by Blasis at the Dancing Academy of the Teatro alla Scala in Milan. Once admitted to the academy, pupils began an eight-year course of training that included three hours of dancing and an hour of pantomime instruction "every day of the year, except the usual prescribed holidays" (Blasis, 1847).

In his books of 1820 and 1831, Blasis provides the first account of the general format for the ballet lesson, beginning with "elementary exercises" practiced with the hand first resting on something firm, and then without support. The sequence outlined by Blasis, and later detailed by Giovanni Léopold Adice (1859) was forty-eight *pliés* with the heels remaining firmly on the floor in the five positions of the feet; then, for each leg, sixty-four *grands battements* to hip level, forty-eight *petits battements* (analogous to *battements tendus*) to the side, sixty-four *ronds de jambe à terre* and the same *en l'air*, and thirty-two slow *petits battements* on the instep followed by sixty rapid ones.

Similar sequences had been described in social-dance manuals earlier in the century, including the now requisite complete 180-degree turnout. (As late as 1779, according to Gennaro Magri, turnout was sufficient if the feet formed only an obtuse angle when the heels were joined, as in first position.) The difference in training, however, was in the greater number of repetitions of the exercises expected of the professional dancer—according to Adice, 648 "gymnastic movements" before moving "to the center of the floor to repeat exactly the same exercises without holding on" (Adice, 1859 [1974]). Exhaustion was somewhat mitigated perhaps by changing to the other leg after sixteen *grands battements* to any given direction and after thirty-two *ronds de jambe en dehors* before repeating them *en dedans*.

Although Blasis advised that, to give flexibility and strength to the insteps, the five positions of the feet "should be practiced on the toes," his illustrations for such positions show the dancer only on a high three-quarter pointe. However, his contemporary, E. A. Théleur, included in his 1831 text two illustrations of women on full pointe and designated positions of the body either "resting on the balls of the feet or on the points of the toes." To gain strength on the points, Théleur suggested rising gradually, "keeping the joints of the toes perfectly straight from the commencement of the movement" and then permitting the heels to descend "in the same manner." By 1847, Blasis, in his *Notes upon Dancing*, merely mentions *genere puntato*, "dancing where much is done on the toes."

Following repetition of the elementary exercises in center floor, the lesson continued with the practice of an eighteenth-century legacy, the *temps de courante simples et composés* (single and double). The clearest account of this sequence in its nineteenth-century form is given by Léon-Michel Saint-Léon, whose description is very similar to that published by J. H. Gourdoux-Daux (1817) in his social dance manual. The rendering of the single version in Théleur's system of notation can be summarized as *plié* and *relevé* in fifth position; carry the back leg to the side and then forward, stepping to fourth position; lower the feet, and close to fifth position. Adice lamented that this venerable exercise was, by 1859, given only to young beginners, artists having rejected it as inconsequential for their training and improvement.

Coupé exercises, clearly related to earlier techniques, appear in accounts of center work, the most comprehensive being Arthur Saint-Léon's description and notation in *La sténochorégraphie* in 1852. His sequences begin with a *plié*, then a step to a given direction (the descendant of the baroque *demi-coupé*), usually onto *demi-pointe*, with the other foot *sur le cou-de-pied*. This is followed by an extension of the raised leg *à la seconde* at hip height (an expansion of the leg gesture of the previoius era) before continuing with other movements of balance. Such an extension did not go to the knee, but lifted directly from the ankle to a high attitude before unfolding. In his social dance text, Giacomo Costa (1831) termed such a movement a *développé*, or *incavazione*, and, like Théleur, specified that the supporting heel be raised from the floor during the extension and the movement be terminated with a lowering of both feet to a closed position. (*Coupé* as a cutting movement *dessus* and *dessous* was also practiced.)

Adagio combinations of *grands ronds de jambe* and *grands fouettés* are strikingly similar to those in today's technique—for instance, in the Cecchetti method and the Vaganova school. Less clearly related to contemporary technique is the *pas de chaconne*, a frequent and seemingly varied *exercise au milieu* in the early nineteenth century. Costa (1831) describes a *pas de jaconne* that is "slow and large," and also a rapid, *petit* version, both including a pirouette. Adice mentions "*temps de chaconne*, or *fouettés ballottés*," as twenty-four connected poses "beginning very slowly and accelerating progressively into the *enchaînement sauté*, all in one breath and without interruption. In all, forty *fouettés ballottés*." Possibly related is Arthur Saint-Léon's *grand ballotté, assemblé soutenu*, and double *port de bras*"—the latter are movements of the arms certainly akin to the Cecchetti second and the Vaganova fourth *port de bras*.

Multiple pirouettes were, according to Blasis's earliest books, the result of "the surprising advancement made of late years in dancing." He acknowledged that in his day the three most usual positions for turning were with the leg raised to second position, attitude, and *sur le cou-de-pied*, but he encouraged greater variety, including one of his innovations: "Turn three times round in the second position, then place the leg and the arms in the arabesque attitude (as in *arabesque à la lyre* . . . and give three or four more turns in that attitude, ending in the same." He recalled that "on one occasion, performing the part of Mercury, I took, as I turned in my pirouette, the attitude of *Mercury* by J. Bologne [Giambologna]." Clearly, the concept of the *grand pirouette* was well established early in the century, and both Théleur and Saint-Léon notate preparations (or *temps de pirouette*) for *en dehors* turns that are still used before *grands pirouettes*.

Equally impressive were the multiple beats. Blasis is most precise: "One can beat *entrechats quatre, six, huit, dix*, or even *douze*. Dancers have been known to press the number up to fourteen, but these are unpleasant *tours de force* which only provoke astonishment at the muscular strength displayed."

The variety of *entrechats* was hardly unusual, most steps having multiple forms, as even social-dance manuals attest. Costa describes numerous versions of *chassé, brisé*, and *sysson* [sic]. His extensive step vocabulary includes many terms used more than fifty years before by Magri, but often with somewhat different descriptions: *passo dello zeffiro (pas de zephire), tempi di coscia (temps de cuisse), ailes de pigeons (pistolette)*, and *flinc e flanc (flic-flac)*. Costa's *ortence*, in which the dancer jumps over his own leg, seems related to the *salto ribaltato*, one of the many virtuoso steps Magri gives for the *grotteschi*.

In his handwritten treatise, *Méthode de Vestris*, August Bournonville has provided invaluable insights into the classroom of his teacher, Auguste Vestris (c.1826). Some 105 basic exercises are listed, grouped into categories of *développé, ballotté, relevé, fouetté, plié, pirouette, temps de cuisse*, and *exercices combinés*, the last featuring various *pirouettes* and *échappés*. Lengthier and more challenging combinations of steps are found in the selections grouped as *enchaînements à 4 temps* and *temps sautés à 3/4*. Bournonville's later system of notation helps in the interpretation of step vocabulary from this important period, and his staged version of a Vestris class remains in the repertory of the Royal Danish Ballet (from *Konservatoriet*, 1849).

Numerous *enchaînements* and *entrées*, with their music, are found in four handwritten notebooks compiled by Léon-Michel Saint-Léon from 1829 to 1836, during his tenure as dance master at the Court of Würtemberg. His descriptions of ballet variations as well as his examples of *allemande, gavotte, mazurka, bolero, cachucha, kracovia,* and *menuet* and reveal an extensive movement vocabulary of *jetés, sissonnes, assemblés, entrechats, pas de bourrées, pirouettes,* and rises onto toe tip. Notations for several *enchaînements* are later provided by his son, Arthur Saint-Léon, including three versions of *brisé télémaque,* each increasing in difficulty. Théleur's notations of the popular duet "Gavotte de Vestris" closely agree with the elder Saint-Léon's written version and provide clear examples of the ways in which elementary steps were connected in dances for performance. Much more demanding technical examples occur in Saint-Léon's selections from solos and pas de deux composed by Pierre Gardel, Jean-Pierre Aumer, and Albert (François Decombe) for performances at the Paris Opera.

Practice of the positions and carriage of the arms included, according to Théleur, "forming circles by raising them in front and lowering them at the sides; then the contrary way; oppositions circles should then follow, the arms going in contrary directions to each other." Elbows were less rounded than later in the century and hands were farther apart, rising "opposite the shoulders" so as not to hide the body. The oppositions of arm to leg were practiced to the "oblique directions" but were not yet designated *croisé, effacé,* and so forth.

Adice recalled the lesson terminating with the *temps de vigueur,* such as *entrée de ronds de jambe* and *entrée de fouettés.* From such sequences, he said, dancers earlier in the century had chosen those that seemed fitting to their inclinations. The dancers gave particular attention to the task of perfecting those sequences to create for themselves their own uniquely executed type of dance. Clearly, the dancers of the early nineteenth century were ready for the expanded technical demands of Romantic ballet.

[*See also* Pointe Work; Technical Manuals, *article on* Publications, 1765–1859; Turnout, *article on* History and Aesthetics; *and the entry on Blasis.*]

BIBLIOGRAPHY

Adice, G. Léopold. *Théorie de la gymnastique de la danse théâtrale.* Paris, 1859. Excerpts translated by Leonore Loft in *Dance as a Theatre Art,* edited by Selma Jeanne Cohen (New York, 1974).

Beaumont, Cyril W., and Stanislas Idzikowski. *A Manual of the Theory and Practice of Classical Theatrical Dancing.* London, 1922.

Blasis, Carlo. *An Elementary Treatise upon the Theory and Practice of the Art of Dancing* (1820). Translated by Mary Stewart Evans. New York, 1944.

Blasis, Carlo. *The Code of Terpsichore: A Practical and Historical Treatise on the Ballet, Dancing, and Pantomime.* London, 1828.

Blasis, Carlo. *The Art of Dancing Comprising Its Theory and Practice, and a History of Its Rise and Progress, from the Earliest Times.* Translated by R. Barton. London, 1831. Second edition of *The Code of Terpsichore.*

Blasis, Carlo. *Notes upon Dancing, Historical and Practical.* Translated by R. Barton. London, 1847.

Bournonville, August. *Méthode de Vestris.* Undated manuscript located in Copenhagen, Royal Library, NKS 3285 4°.

Bournonville, August. *Etudes Chorégraphiques.* Copenhagen, 1855 and 1861.

Bournonville, August. *Vocabulaire de Danse avec les Signes d'Abréviation.* 1855 manuscript located in Copenhagen, Royal Library, NKS 3285 4°.

Bruhn, Erik, and Lillian Moore. *Bournonville and Ballet Technique.* London, 1961.

Chapman, John V. "Dance in Transition, 1809–1830." *The Dancing Times* (March 1978): 334–335.

Costa, Giacomo. *Saggio analitico-pratico intorno all'arte della danza per uso di civile conversazione.* Turin, 1831.

Encyclopédie méthodique: Arts académiques, équitation, escrime, danse, et art de nager. Paris, 1786.

Fenner, Theodore. "Ballet in Early Nineteenth-Century London as Seen by Leigh Hunt and Henry Robertson." *Dance Chronicle* 1.2 (1978): 75–95.

Flindt, Vivi, and Knud Arne Jürgensen. *Bournonville Ballet Technique.* London, 1992.

Gallini, Giovanni. *Critical Observations on the Art of Dancing, to Which Is Added a Collection of Cotillons or French Dances.* London, c.1770.

Gourdoux-Daux, J. H. *Principes et notions élémentaires sur l'art de la danse.* 2d ed. Paris, 1811. Translated by Victor Guillou as *Elements and Principles of the Art of Dancing* (Philadelphia, 1817).

Hammond, Sandra Noll. *Ballet: Beyond the Basics.* Palo Alto, Calif., 1982.

Hammond, Sandra Noll. "Clues to Ballet's Technical History." *Dance Research* 3 (Autumn 1984): 53–66.

Hammond, Sandra Noll. "Searching for the Sylph: Documentation of Early Developments in *Pointe* Technique." *Dance Research Journal* 19 (Winter 1987–1988): 27–31.

Hammond, Sandra Noll. "Steps Through Time: Selected Dance Vocabulary of the Eighteenth and Nineteenth Centuries." *Dance Research* 10 (Autumn 1992): 93–108.

Jürgensen, Knud Arne, and Ann Hutchinson Guest. *The Bournonville Heritage, a Choreographic Record, 1829–1875.* London, 1990.

Magri, Gennaro. *Trattato teorico-prattico di ballo.* Naples, 1779. Translated by Mary Skeaping as *Theoretical and Practical Treatise on Dancing* (London, 1988).

Pierce, Ken. "Saut What? Sauts in Early Eighteenth-Century Dance." *Proceedings of the Eleventh Annual Conference, Society of Dance History Scholars, North Carolina School of the Arts, 12–14 February 1988,* compiled by Christena L. Schlundt. Riverside, Calif., 1988.

Saint-Léon, Arthur. *La sténochorégraphie.* Paris, 1852. Translated by Raymond Lister. Cambridge, 1992.

Saint-Léon, Léon-Michel. *Exercices de 1829, cahier d'exercices pour LL. AA. Royalles les Princesses de Würtemberg 1830, 2me cahier exercices de 1830.* Untitled manuscript volume containing exercises of 1833, 1834, and 1836. Manuscript located in Paris, Bibliothèque de l'Opéra, Res.1137 and 1140.

Théleur, E. A. *Letters on Dancing, Reducing This Elegant and Healthful Exercise to Easy Scientific Principles.* London, 1831.

Warner, Mary Jane. "Gavottes and Bouquets: A Comparative Study of Changes in Dance Style between 1700 and 1850." Ph.D.diss., Ohio State University, 1974.
Winter, Marian Hannah. *The Pre-Romantic Ballet*. London, 1974.

SANDRA NOLL HAMMOND

Ballet since the Mid-Nineteenth Century

The development of classical ballet technique during the second half of the nineteenth century was characterized by the search for virtuosity in general and for a virtuoso technique of dancing *sur les pointes* in particular.

Whereas the early Romantic ballerinas rose only fleetingly onto toe tip in their soft satin slippers, by the early 1860s a specially strengthened pointe shoe had been developed. Although still not so hard as the modern "blocked" shoe, the new reinforced shoes made possible the development of a manner of dancing *sur les pointes* that was both more brilliant and more sustained than that of the Romantic era. [*See* Pointe Work.]

For the first time, dancers were able to *pirouette sur les pointes,* and several new types of turning movement were evolved, *en diagonale* and *en manège*. The culmination of these virtuoso feats of spinning was the performance of thirty-two *fouetté* turns on one spot. According to dance historian Ivor Guest, the first dancer to accomplish this was Maria Giuri, in 1883, in Bologna. Pierina Legnani is said to have performed thirty-two *fouetté* turns in London ten years later, in 1893, prior to introducing them in the 1895 production of *Swan Lake* in Saint Petersburg. During the last quarter of the nineteenth century, ballet skirts became shorter and shorter, to show off the new technical developments to their best advantage.

The dancers from Milan were the undisputed masters of the new, virtuoso style, and during the late 1800s several of them appeared in Russia. Their effect on the development of the Russian school was to be decisive.

The most influential of the Italians was Enrico Cecchetti, who taught technique at the Maryinsky Theater from 1890 to 1892. Apart from the example of his own technical expertise in *batterie* and pirouettes (he created the role of Bluebird in *The Sleeping Beauty*), his influence as a pedagogue was to be profound and long lasting. Writing in 1934, Agrippina Vaganova commented, "Insofar as pointes are concerned, the Italian technique has such unquestionable advantages that I subscribe to it without reservations. Cecchetti taught the dancer to rise on the pointes with a little spring, distinctly pushing off the floor. This manner develops a more elastic foot and teaches concentration of balance of the body on one spot." She then expressed her disapproval of the French manner of rising on the pointes smoothly from the very beginning of training.

Nikolai Legat has recorded how Russian dancers strove to emulate the technical tricks of the visiting Italians and how he himself was able to pass on this new expertise to his own pupils, although he regarded the Italian style as lacking finesse. Early Russian training was, however, based on the elegant French school, so that the Russian style of classical ballet that emerged was a fusion of Italian technical strength and French elegance.

Among specific points of difference between the French and Italian schools was the Italian manner of performing many leaps *ritirate*—that is, with the knees slightly bent and the soles of the feet drawn together underneath the body. This was still being advocated in the 1930s by Margaret Craske (who handed down Cecchetti's work in England and the United States), while Vaganova was decrying the practice because "it lends the dance a grotesque character, spoiling its classic line" (1934 [1953]). This search for purity of line gradually became a dominant factor in the evolution of classical ballet technique, culminating eventually in the streamlined look aspired to by late-twentieth-century dancers.

Another consequence of the consolidation of the technique of dancing *sur les pointes* during the latter part of the nineteenth century was the development of supported *adage* movements. While increased technical strength and stronger shoes enabled the ballerina to remain poised *sur la pointe* for a much greater length of time, she was unable to control and adjust her own balance in the same way as when dancing on *demi-pointe*. This resulted directly in the increased importance of the cavalier and the evolution of the classical pas de deux.

Through Rita Sangalli, Rosita Mauri, and especially Carlotta Zambelli, the influence of the Italian school of virtuosity entered the portals of the Paris Opera. In fact, by the time Antonine Meunier (1931) set out to record what she terms *la danse classique–école française,* Milan's influence had thoroughly and irrevocably permeated the French school. Zambelli had stunned blasé Parisian audiences with her whirlwind *tours déboulés,* and such Italian *tours de force* quickly became *de rigueur* at the Opera.

The true French school survived in a much purer form in Copenhagen, where many aspects of August Bournonville's choreography were rooted in the *école* of his teacher, Auguste Vestris. Under Bournonville the use of *épaulement* became more clearly defined; *batterie* flourished; and the light, *balloné* style of elevation was preserved. It is sometimes forgotten that the lightness of the Romantic ballerinas derived less from their (still minimal) dancing *sur les pointes* than from the effortlessness of their jumps—a feature that continues to characterize the Danish school. As a result of the work of Hans Beck and Valborg Borchsenius, the Bournonville school was preserved almost intact in the comparative isolation of the Royal Theater in Copenhagen until 1951. (In that year, a deliberate policy decision to broaden the technical and stylistic scope of the Danish school led to the engagement of Vera Volkova and the exposure of the Danish dancers to the distinctive Russian style, a synthesis of the old French and Italian schools.)

The determining factors in the evolution of ballet technique during most of the first half of the twentieth century were the revolt against academic principles and the search for expressive movement that characterized the thinking of the young Michel Fokine. At the same time, the new "modern expressionist" schools of dance (which had emerged partly as a direct reaction against the by then sterile pyrotechnics of the ballet) were to have a significant—albeit indirect—influence on the development of ballet technique during this period.

The trend toward a manner of dancing that was both less academic and less acrobatic was at first more apparent on stage in the work of choreographers like Fokine than it was in the ballet classroom. By 1912 much of Serge Diaghilev's ballet repertory involved no pointe work at all, and virtuosity for its own sake had been banished from the Ballets Russes's stages. Yet, the pedagogue Cecchetti still ruled the company classroom.

During the second quarter of the twentieth century the role of the traditional *maître de ballet* gradually declined as a result of the innovative classroom experiments of the new generation of Diaghilev choreographers (notably Bronislava Nijinska and George Balanchine). A more expressive and expansive use of the whole upper body gained general acceptance in the ballet classroom.

Here again, the evolution of costume went hand in hand with technical development. The gradual abandonment of the boned bodice in the early part of the twentieth century gave the female dancer much more upper-body freedom of movement. Pavel Tchelitchev's designs of allover body tights for *Ode* in 1928 presaged the universal adoption of this type of garment as the standard practice costume for all dancers.

Since the middle of the twentieth century, the dominant feature of ballet technique has been the steadily increasing emphasis placed on height of leg elevation, or leg extensions, as they are generally known. Meunier (1931) still described the correct height for an arabesque as being "*à la hauteur de la hanche*" (at hip height). By 1949, however, Serge Lifar, in his *Traité de la danse académique*, was describing the raised leg in arabesque as being "at least at hip height," while in the early 1950s Lycette Darsonval is quoted in *La grammaire de la danse* as saying that the leg should be raised "as high as possible"—a tendency very much in evidence today.

The effort required to hold the leg so high for so long has resulted generally in a shift of emphasis in training away from the intricacies of footwork and *épaulement* (once so characteristic of the *danse d'école*) and toward a bolder, more athletic style of dancing. In today's linear, streamlined ballet aesthetic, the concentration on the action of the lower leg—*le travail du bas de jambe*—that used to be such an essential feature of classical training has tended to be replaced by a greater interest in the use of the whole leg as a linear unit. The theory of a careful, harmonious balance of line between arms and legs advocated by Blasis and so clearly expounded by Cecchetti is ultimately unable to encompass the imbalance inherent in these extremes of leg elevation.

Clothing reflects people's image of themselves. During the second half of the twentieth century, the allover, unisex body tights worn by dancers become symbolic of a society in which distinctions of sex, class, and race were increasingly regarded as irrelevant. The result was a series of changes in mechanics and emphasis in contemporary ballet technique. Liberated from the restrictions of both social conventions and cumbersome costumes, male and female dancers alike use their new-found freedom to exploit to the full their bodies' athletic potential. Pushing themselves to their physical limit, both men and women raise their leg extensions as high as possible, lift their *retiré* positions right up to the knee, rise as high as they can on the three-quarter pointe on all *relevés*, and increase the range of their *cambré* movements to the maximum. In many instances, the previously specifically "male" or "female" connotations attached to such movements have been superseded by an androgynous athleticism.

However, if allover body tights finally gave dancers total freedom of movement, this stylized equivalent of balletic nudity also had the effect of revealing every detail of their physical makeup, placing the dancer's body, as it were, under a microscope. A trend followed toward greater anatomical analysis by dancers and teachers alike and toward placing much greater importance on the exact shape of a dancer's body. Where it is carried to extremes, this tendency holds within it the same threat of decadence as did the excesses of virtuosity seen in the late nineteenth century.

In Russia, the seeds of Fokine's revolt against academic dance had been sown at the turn of the twentieth century. However, subsequent historical events in that country were eventually to result in a return to an academic structure that, in many respects, could be regarded as counterrevolutionary. In the wake of the Russian Revolution, the Imperial Ballet was re-created in the image of the new, centrally planned Soviet society. Building on the work of previous generations of *maîtres de ballet*, Vaganova, the great Russian pedagogue, evolved a scientifically structured eight-year program of study, much of which still formed the basis of the Soviet school and that of its many satellites.

Until that time, little had existed outside of Russia in the way of a graduated scheme of training specially designed for children and young students. (Erik Bruhn has described how, as a child, he followed the same set daily program of Bournonville classes that his elders did.) The new Soviet school concentrated on the refinement of technical training that resulted in exquisitely controlled leaps and turns. The calculated athletic perfection of the Soviet dancers began to replace the sometimes haphazard virtuoso-bravado of their Italian-school forebears.

The Soviet system of ballet training has become the model for many schools throughout the world. Even in those establishments where it is not deliberately followed, many Soviet influences are evident. This is true particularly of the approach to exercises at the *barre*. Whereas in the Italian and French schools these exercises were simple, repetitive, and generally geared to the dynamics of allegro, the Soviet school takes a more carefully structured approach to *barre* work, with greater emphasis on controlled precision of form. Another feature of the Russian style of *barre* work is the often equal use of both legs for a single exercise, as opposed to the traditional system of treating one leg as the "working" leg and the other as the "supporting" one.

In many countries, the effect of the work of individual choreographers remains a major influence on technical development. The British school, for example, has evolved out of an amalgam of Frederick Ashton's lyricism and Ninette de Valois's academic precision. In the United States, the dominant influence has undoubtedly been that of George Balanchine, who created a style of dance rooted in academic fundamentals, but divested of the traditional conventions of stylized expression. The formal elegance of classical *ports de bras* has been replaced by a dynamic involvement of the whole body in a style of movement whose energy and speed reflect that of the American people.

[*See also* Ballet Technique *and the entries on the principal figures mentioned herein.*]

BIBLIOGRAPHY

Bruhn, Eric, and Lilian Moore. *Bournonville and Ballet Technique.* London, 1981.

Craske, Margaret, and Cyril W. Beaumont. *The Theory and Practice of Allegro in Classical Ballet (Cecchetti Method).* London, 1930.

Glasstone, Richard. "Changes of Emphasis and Mechanics in the Teaching of Ballet Technique." *Dance Research* 1 (Spring 1983): 56–63.

Guest, Ivor. "Costume and the Nineteenth Century Dancer." In *Designing for the Dancer,* by Roy Strong et al. London, 1981.

Legat, Nikolai. *The Story of the Russian School.* Translated by Paul Dukes. London, 1932.

Meunier, Antonine. *La danse classique (école française).* Paris, 1931.

Prudhommeau, Germaine, and Geneviève Guillot. *The Book of Ballet.* Translated by Katherine Carson. Englewood Cliffs, N.J., 1976.

Vaganova, Agrippina. *Basic Principles of Classical Ballet: Russian Ballet Technique* (1934). Translated by Anatole Chujoy. Edited by Peggy van Praagh. 2d ed. London, 1953.

RICHARD GLASSTONE

BALLET THEATRE. *See* American Ballet Theatre.

BALLET-THÉÂTRE CONTEMPORAIN. In 1968, the French Ministry of Culture established a national choreographic center and company in Amiens, about seventy miles north of Paris. The stated purpose of this company, Ballet-Théâtre Contemporain (Contemporary Ballet Theater), was to create modern choreography with the assistance of contemporary musicians and painters. In 1972, the company moved from Amiens to Angers, in western France, where in 1978 it was subsumed by the activities of the newly established Centre National de Danse Contemporaine.

When it was established in 1968, Ballet-Théâtre Contemporain comprised thirty dancers and was housed in the Maison de la Culture in Amiens. Jean-Albert Cartier, publicist, art critic, and organizer of exhibitions of contemporary art, served as artistic adviser; Françoise Adret, a lively woman of wit and imagination, with a bold approach to the ballet vocabulary, was choreographic director. The first performance of the company, given on 4 December 1958, included *Danses Concertantes*, set by Félix Blaska to music of Igor Stravinsky; *Salomé*, set by Joseph Lazzini to music by Francis Miroglio; *Aquathème*, set by Adret to music by Ivo Malec; and *Déserts*, set by Michel Descombey to music by Edgard Varèse.

In 1969, the repertory was expanded to include *Hai-Kai*, set by Jean Babilée to music of Anton Webern; *Eonta*, set by Adret to music by Iannis Xenakis; *Violostries*, set by Descombey to music by Bernard Parmegiani; *Cantate Profane*, set by Milko Sparemblek to music by François Bayle; *Le Soleil des Eaux* (The Sun of Waters), set by George Skibine to music by Pierre Boulez; *Dangerous Games*, set by Brian Macdonald to music by Archie Shepp; and *Hopop*, set by Dirk Sanders to popular music. Initially, the soloists included Magdalena Popa, Krassimira Koldamova, Jean Babilée, Martine Parmain, Muriel Belmondo, James Urbain, Juan Giuliano, Colette Marchand, and Don Snyder. They were later joined by Marie-Claire Carrié and Jacques Dombrowsky.

Productions in 1970 included *Astral*, choreographed by company member Juan Giuliano to music by Wojciech Kilar; *Itineraries*, choreographed by John Butler to music by Luciano Berio; and *La Legende de Cerfs*, choreographed by George Skibine to music by Béla Bartók. *Hymnen*, a collaborative work by Michel Descombey, Jacques Garnier, Alain Deshayes, and Aline Roux, set to music by Karlheinz Stockhausen, was well received by the public, if not by the critics. In subsequent years Adret contributed two major works to the repertory: *Requiem* (1971), set to music by György Ligeti, and *La Follia di Orlando* (1972),

BALLET-THÉÂTRE CONTEMPORAIN. Two soloists on the dramatic set of *Violostries*. Choreographed by Michel Descombey to music by Bernard Parmegiani, this work was first presented in 1969 during the company's second season. This photograph shows a 1972 performance at the Brooklyn Academy of Music. (Photograph from the Dance Collection, New York Public Library for the Performing Arts.)

set to a score by Gofredo Petrassi. The company toured widely in France and in other countries, appearing in London in 1971 and in New York in 1972.

By the time the company moved from Amiens to Angers in 1972, it had grown to forty-five members. Since its founding, it had performed in twenty-five cities and given more than three hundred and fifty performances, including twenty-seven premiers of works by twenty choreographers, nineteen composers, and twenty-two set designers. Its activities included discussions, film showings, courses, and public rehearsals. Its aim was to serve all the contemporary arts, and the company succeeded very well as far

as music and stage design were concerned, but it fared less well with respect to choreography.

In 1972, the company staged an Homage to Stravinsky, presenting Jacques Lecoq's *Le Renard*, Lar Lubovitch's *Sans Titre*, and Adret's *Le Rossignol*, with Itchko Lazarov, Jean-Claude Giorgini, Serge Chaufour, Thérèse Thoreaux, and Dominique Mercy as additional soloists. Other new works followed in 1973, among them *ES, le 8ème Jour*, set by Descombey to music by Stockhausen, with Lawrence Rhodes in the leading role; *Trauma*, set by John Neumeier to music by Harald Genzmer; and *Nuits*, set by Moshe Efrati to music by Xenakis. *Trauma* was the first work choreographed by Neumeier in France. From this time onward, the company turned with increasing frequency to U.S. and Canadian choreographers, staging Brian Macdonald's *Rags*, John Butler's *Kill What I Love*, and Paul Sanasardo's *Saints and Lovers*, all in 1975; Carolyn Brown's *Balloon* in 1976; and Viola Farber's *Autumn*

Fields and Louis Falco's *Cooking French*, both in 1978.

In 1978, Ballet-Théâtre Contemporain was disbanded as a result of the establishment in Angers of the Centre National de Danse Contemporarine, with Alwin Nikolais as resident teacher. After the demise of the company, Jean-Albert Cartier was instrumental in the formation of a new company in Nancy, the Ballet-Théâtre Français, but its stated purpose—to present major twentieth-century dance works, from the Diaghilev era onward—was radically different from the creative goals of Ballet-Théâtre Contemporain.

BIBLIOGRAPHY

Christout, Marie-Françoise. "A House Is Now a Home for French Arts." *Dance and Dancers* (February 1969): 33–35.

Christout, Marie-Françoise. "Paris Collections." *Dance and Dancers* (April 1969): 28–34.

Lidova, Irène. "France's New Company." *The Dancing Times* (February 1969): 251.

Petitjean, Pierre. *Backstage.* New York, 1978.

Williams, Peter. "French Revival." *Dance and Dancers* (February 1972): 25–31.

Monique Babsky
Translated from French

BALLO AND BALLETTO. The Italian term *ballo,* for "dance," has been in use since at least the twelfth or thirteenth century. It continues broadly to mean a social gathering with dance, a short choreographed composition, a traditional or regional dance with distinct choreography, or simply "dance." *Balletto* can mean "little dance," but today in Italy and Spain it usually refers to ballet. *Ballo* and *balletto* (pl., *balli; balletti*) are now used in English, however, to refer more narrowly to several categories of European social and theatrical dance from the fifteenth through the seventeenth centuries. Today in Italy many regional traditional dances are still called *balli.*

The Fifteenth Century. In the first instructional sources, the fifteenth-century Italian dance treatises, *ballo* and *balletto* seem to be used interchangeably to designate specifically choreographed court dances intended for both private and public performance. Most of those that have come down to us were composed by Domenico da Piacenza and his Jewish disciple Guglielmo Ebreo da Pesaro (also known after his conversion as Giovanni Ambrosio). In Domenico's treatise *De arte saltandi* (c.1455) and in the first (c.1463) version of Guglielmo's *De pratica seu arte tripudii* (see the entry on Guglielmo for a complete list of his works), only *ballo* is used; Antonio Cornazano, in his *L'arte del danzare* (c.1465), however, refers to each dance as a *ballo* in the choreographic descriptions but uses *ballo* and *balletto* synonymously in his theoretical introduction. In the so-called Giorgio manuscript (c.1470, one of many versions of Guglielmo's treatise), new dances and new versions of dances are called *balletti* and older dances *balli.*

Each of the fifty *balli/balletti* in the Italian repertory of the fifteenth century had its own melody, unlike the forty-four *bassedanze* in the same sources (Marrocco, 1981). Often, the musical material was borrowed from preexistent Italian or French art or popular songs (e.g., "Rostiboli Gioioso"/"Rôtibouilli Joyeux). According to Guglielmo, *ballo* music was in one of two modes (similar to major and minor keys), and the dancers were expected to adapt the style of their steps and gestures to each mode's particular qualities. Iconographic evidence suggests that the monophonic tune given for each *ballo/balletto* would in practice have been filled out with accompanying lines by experienced instrumentalists improvising in two to four parts.

The most important characteristic of the fifteenth-century *ballo/balletto,* as compared with the *bassadanza* or other dance types of the period, was that it was sectional, usually composed of a combination of two to four recognizably different *misure* (not to be confused with the *mesures* of the French *bassedanses*). Each *misura* denoted both a tempo and a mensuration (a proportional sign related to musical meter). The *bassadanza* was the slowest; the *quadernaria* was one-sixth faster; the *saltarello* was two-thirds faster; and the *piva* was twice as fast as the *bassadanza.* These *misure* may be shown to be proportionally related as 6:5:4:3. In modern practice these *misure* are normally transcribed as 6/4, 4/4, 3/4, and 4/8 or 6/8. All except the *quadernaria* (which Antonio Cornazano called a German *saltarello*) were independent dance types that could be juxtaposed in *balli.* The *quadernaria,* however, appeared almost exclusively within *balli.*

The terminology related to *misure* had both musical and choreographic meanings. For example, one *tempo di saltarello* could mean one rhythmic unit of *saltarello* music (usually one bar of compound duple meter, 6/8 or 6/4 in modern transcriptions), one dance step pattern (e.g., one *saltarello* double), or both. Changes of *misura* also provided variety and often heightened characteristic and dramatic moments in *balli.* Up to thirteen sections of *bassadanza, saltarello, quadernaria,* and *piva misure* might be freely strung together, with simple repetitions, or repetitions with melodic variation, in both a musical and a danced rondo form of considerable sophistication. With their frequent changes of *misure,* the Italian *balli* of the fifteenth century stood in marked contrast to the two "French" *balli* included in Guglielmo Ebreo/Giovanni Ambrosio's treatise (c.1474), which are in *piva misura* only.

Most fifteenth-century *balli* begin with an introductory *saltarello* (in either *saltarello* or *quadernaria misura*), probably for entering into and gaining the center of the dance space. They end in fast *piva* tempo, with the dancers responding to one another with quick leg movements and turns. The central sections of each *ballo*, normally in *bassadanza misura*, contain unique figures performed by up to twelve dancers (but most often by a couple or a trio), in side-by-side, line, square, triangular, or longways-by-couple formations.

In general, fifteenth-century *balli* express a playful affect, with approaches and retreats, circling and encircling, echoing and mirroring. Choreographic paths are usually quite clear, particularly those of Domenico da Piacenza. While there are few specific instructions for executing the steps other than their duration, there is evidence for the demonstration of male virtuosity and prowess (including flourishes, turns, and jumps; see, e.g., Guglielmo/Giovanni Ambrosio). Only a few *balli* are pantomimic. For example, "La Mercantia" (The Seller of Wares) is about a lady courted by three suitors who dances with all of them "as if they were a thousand, like someone who deals in lovers" (Cornazano, 1981).

Balli were performed in private, in the chambers of aristocratic young women; in public, at balls, by young nobles of both sexes; and, indoors and out, in costumed performance pieces *(moresche)* on grand occasions. The choreographers were honored, their creations copied into many manuscripts, and their fame attested in numerous records of great events. In the accounts of the entertainments in Florence for the visit of the pope in 1459, several *balli* were danced, including Domenico's "Rostiboli." The continued popularity of many *balli* into the sixteenth century was ensured by their high and noble status. In about 1530, the humanist Giangiorgio Trissino, for example, mentions "Rostiboli," among others, as a dance of great merit, equaling in artistry the music of Clément Jannequin, the painting of Leonardo da Vinci, and the poetry of Dante and Petrarch.

Sixteenth to Seventeenth Centuries. From the mid-sixteenth to the mid-seventeenth centuries, *balli* and *balletti* continued to appear in both social and theatrical settings, and there are many so titled in purely musical sources. In fact, *balli* and *balletti* together form the majority of the dances in the important manuals of Fabritio Caroso (1581, 1600) and Cesare Negri (1602, 1604). Although the terms *ballo* and *balletto* seem still to be used synonymously, *balletto* appears more often in the title and *ballo* in the text of the same dance. Differences between *ballo* and *balletto* emerge at the simpler end of the spectrum of dance types, where *ballo* is a group game to music (e.g., "Ballo del Piantone," a mixer), and *balletto* is used as a subtitle for specially composed one-movement dance types in sets of variations, such as *bassa*, canary, *passo e mezzo*, *pavaniglia*, and *tordiglione*.

At the more complicated end, *ballo* is used to refer to a staged dance (see below) and *balletto* designates a specifically composed variation suite made up of two to four dances of different mensurations, all based on the same musical material, except for the canary. These suites frequently begin with an untitled dance in moderate duple time and continue with one or more triple-time dance movements, concluding with the liveliest (e.g., "Nido d'Amore" in Caroso, 1600). Generally speaking, each dance within a suite conforms to a recognizable type: first (untitled), *pavan* or *allemande*; second, a *galliarde*; third, a *saltarello*; fourth, a *canario*. *Balletto* suites may have other complex structures, such as combined ternary and variation-suite form (e.g., "So Ben My Chi Ha Buon Tempo", in Negri, 1602, 1604), or rondolike variation suites (e.g., the four "Barrieras," in Caroso, 1581, 1600).

The *balletto* suite was clearly popular with sixteenth-century dancing masters. Its different movements to the same music satisfied an aesthetic involving both unity and variety, clarity and complexity; originality was subordinated to accepted traditions of step vocabulary and figures, and elegant manners and social graces were part of the choreography. The differing paths and footwork of the individual dance types within the suite served the same aesthetic. The *balletto* suite showed off the dancing couple in a reasonably demanding choreography that challenged the memory yet permitted the dancers to use what they already knew and to demonstrate their own value as beautiful adornments to a court.

The step vocabulary in the dance types that make up a *balletto* suite is explained in detail in sixteenth-century Italian manuals, as are the choreographic paths (see Sutton, 1986). More importantly, specific step patterns and paths predominate in certain dance types: the *seguito battuto ala canario* (stamped sequence as in the canary) is only used in canarylike dances in fast triple meter, usually with a dotted rhythm, most commonly in a *pedalogue* (a dialogue with the feet) between facing partners. Thus, a dance within a *balletto* whose type is not given can often be identified by its predominant kinds of steps and paths. Often, identification is further confirmed by musical motives specific to the dance type.

The small number of choreographies that include *ballo* in their title in sixteenth-century Italian manuals are, as said, either playful, gamelike dances (e.g., "Ballo del Fiore," a mixer, in Caroso, 1581, 1600), or theatrical dances (e.g., "Austria Felice," in which six nymphs present a basket of flowers and a song to visiting royalty, in Negri, 1602, 1604). Indeed, the stage *ballo*, for which there are only a half-dozen detailed choreographies extant from that time, was apparently a somewhat independent dance type that could range from simple to exceedingly complicated and virtuosic and could be danced by a male soloist, a group of one sex, or by upwards of twenty people of both sexes. The group dances often emphasized geometric patterns to be discerned from above the dance floor, used fantastic or allegorical costumes, and illustrated mythological, pastoral, or sacred subjects. It could also be composed of a sophisticated musical and choreographic interweaving of many sections and mensurations, as in Emilio de' Cavalieri's final *ballo* for the grand *intermedi* to *La Pellegrina* (1589). He provided its music, diagrams of the dancers on stage, directions for the entire *mise-en-scène,* and six sections of written instructions designed to fit more than twenty sections of music in changing mensurations. The custom of placing grand sung-and-danced *balli* and other dances in the finales of early operas—those of Claudio Monteverdi and Marco da Gagliano, for instance—became a well-established tradition in later opera and other stage spectacles and has extended through the twentieth century. [*See* Intermedio.]

Twentieth Century. The terms *ballo* (especially) and *balletto* (to a lesser extent) persist in the titles of many traditional Italian dances, whether simple and playful mixers or dances demonstrating real skill. A large number are documented in the region of Emilia-Romagna in central Italy. Some of their titles suggest their long history (e.g., "Ballo del Piantone" appears in Caroso's and Negri's manuals; "Ballo del Fiore" in Caroso's), but tracing them through the centuries in any detail is impossible without written evidence. More may come to light as research progresses.

[*See also* Social Dance, *article on* Court and Social Dance before 1800.]

BIBLIOGRAPHY: SOURCES
Alessandri, Filippo degli. *Discorso sopra il ballo.* Terni, 1620.
Anonymous. *Il Papa.* Circa 1520–1530. Manuscript located in the Dance Collection, New York Public Library for the Performing Arts (fifteen *"balletti"* and a theoretical introduction).
Anonymous. Four "balletti" from Tuscany c.1555, and a "Battaglia" (1559). In Gino Corti's "Cinque balli toscani del cinquecento." *Rivista Italiana di Musicologia* 12 (1977): 73–75.
Caroso, Fabritio. *Il ballarino* (1581). Facsimile reprint, New York, 1967.
Caroso, Fabritio. *Nobiltà di dame.* Venice, 1600, 1605. Facsimile reprint, Bologna, 1970. Reissued with order of illustrations changed as *Raccolta di varij balli.* Rome, 1630. Translated into English with eight introductory chapters by Julia Sutton, the music transcribed by F. Marian Walker. Oxford, 1986. Reprint with a step manual in Labanotation by Rachelle Palnick Tsachor and Julia Sutton, New York, 1995.
Cavalieri, Emilio de'. "Intermedio VI." In Cristofano Malvezzi's *Intermedii et concerti, fatti per la Commedia rappresentata in Firenze nelle Nozze del Serenissimo Don Ferdinando Medici et Madama Christiana di Loreno, Granduchi di Toscana.* Venice, 1591. Translated and edited by D. P. Walker as *Les Fêtes de Florence: Musique des intermèdes de "La Pellegrina."* Paris, 1963.
Cavalieri, Emilio de'. *La rappresentazione di anima e di corpo* (1600). Facsimile reprint, Bologna, 1967.
Compasso, Lutio. *Ballo della gagliarda.* Florence, 1560. Facsimile reprint with introduction by Barbara Sparti, Freiburg, 1995.
Cornazano, Antonio. *L'arte del danzare* (c.1455–1465). Manuscript located in Rome, Biblioteca Apostolica Vaticana, codex Capponiano, 203. Translated by Madeleine Inglehearn and Peggy Forsyth as *The Book on the Art of Dancing.* London, 1981.

Corso, Rinaldo. *Dialogo del ballo.* Venice, 1559. Facsimile reprint, Bologna, 1969.
Corti, Gino, "Cinque balli toscani del cinquecento." *Rivista Italiana di Musicologia* 12 (1977): 73–75.
Domenico da Piacenza. *De arte saltandi & choreas ducendi* (c. 1455). Manuscript located in Paris, Bibliothèque Nationale, f.ital.972. English translation by D. R. Wilson in *Domenico of Piacenza,* corr. ed. Cambridge, 1995.
Foligno, Seminario Vescovile, Biblioteca Jacobilli, D.I.42. Published by D. M. Faloci-Puliganano as *Otto Bassedanze di M. Guglielmo da Pesaro e di M. Domenico da Ferrara.* Foligno, 1887.
Guglielmo Ebreo da Pesaro (also known as Giovanni Ambrosio). *De pratica seu arte tripudii.* Milan and Naples (?), 1463, 1471–1474. In Paris, Bibliothèque Nationale, f.ital.973 and f.ital.476. Transcribed and translated by Barbara Sparti as *On the Practice or Art of Dancing.* Oxford, 1993. Other MS copies or versions under the same title c.1461–1510.
Jacobilli, Ludovico. *Modo di ballare.* Circa 1615. Manuscript located in Foligno, Biblioteca Jacobilli, AIII.19, ff.102–104.
Mancini, Giulio. *Del origine et noblità del ballo* (c.1623–1630). Facsimile with introduction by Barbara Sparti, Freiburg, 1996.
Negri, Cesare. *Le gratie d'amore.* Milan, 1602. Reissued as *Nuove invenzione di balli.* Milan, 1604. Translated into Spanish by Don Balthasar Carlos for Señor Condé, Duke of Sanlucar, 1630. Manuscript located in Madrid, Biblioteca Nacional, MS 14085. Facsimile reprint of 1602, New York and Bologna, 1969. Literal translation into English and musical transcription by Yvonne Kendall. D.M.A. diss., Stanford University, 1985.
Nuremburg, Germanisches Nationalmuseum, HS 8842/GS 1589 (1517). Manuscript (choreographic source) published by Ingrid Wetzel as "'Hie innen sindt Geschriben die wellschen Tenntz': Le otto danze italiane del manoscritto di Norimberga." In *Guglielmo Ebreo da Pesaro e la danza nelle corti italiane del XV secolo,* edited by Maurizio Padovan. Pisa, 1990.
Smith, A. William, trans. and ed. *Fifteenth-Century Dance and Music: The Complete Transcribed Italian Treatises and Collections in the Tradition of Domenico da Piacenza.* 2 vols. Stuyvesant, N.Y., 1995.
Venice, Biblioteca Nazionale Marciana, ital.II.34 (=4906), *Il libro di Sidrach,* c.105 (c.1474–1475). Manuscript (choreographic source) published by A. William Smith as "Una fonte sconosciuta della danza italiana del quattrocento." In *Guglielmo Ebreo da Pesaro e la danza nelle corti italiane del XV secolo,* edited by Maurizio Padovan. Pisa, 1990.
Viterbo, Archivio di Stato, Notarile di Montefiascone, Protocollo 11 (c.1480s). Manuscript (choreographic source): *fiorito* dances. Transcribed by Barbara Sparti as "Rôti Bouilli: Take Two 'El Gioioso Fiorito.'" *Studi Musicali* 24 (1996): 231–261.

BIBLIOGRAPHY: OTHER STUDIES
Aldrich, Putnam. *Rhythm in Seventeenth-Century Italian Monody.* New York, 1966.
Brainard, Ingrid. "Bassedanse, Bassadanza, and Ballo in the Fifteenth Century." In *Dance History Research: Perspectives from Related Arts and Disciplines,* edited by Joann W. Kealiinohomoku. New York, 1970.
Brainard, Ingrid. "The Role of the Dancing Master in Fifteenth-Century Courtly Society." *Fifteenth-Century Studies* 2 (1979): 21–44.
Brainard, Ingrid. "Ballo." In *The New Grove Dictionary of Music and Musicians.* London, 1980.
Brainard, Ingrid. *The Art of Courtly Dancing in the Early Renaissance.* West Newton, Mass., 1981.
Brainard, Ingrid. "The Art of Courtly Dancing in Transition: Nürnberg, Germ.Nat.Mus.Hs.8842, a Hitherto Unknown German Dance Source." In *Crossroads of Medieval Civilization: The City of Regens-

burg and Its Intellectual Milieu, edited by Edelgard E. DuBruck and Karl Heinz Göller. Detroit, 1984.

Brainard, Ingrid. "Pattern, Imagery, and Drama in the Choreographic Work of Domenico da Piacenza." In *Guglielmo Ebreo da Pesaro e la danza nelle corti italiane del XV secolo*, edited by Maurizio Padovan. Pisa, 1990.

Brooks, Lynn Matluck. *The Dances of the Processions of Seville in Spain's Golden Age*. Kassel, 1988.

Brown, Howard M. "Alta." In *The New Grove Dictionary of Music and Musicians*. London, 1980.

Castelli, Patrizia. "Il moto aristotelico e la 'licita scientia': Guglielmo Ebreo e la speculazione sulla danza nel XV secolo." In *Mesura et arte del danzare: Guglielmo Ebreo da Pesaro e la danza nelle corti italiane del XV secolo*, edited by Patrizia Castelli et al. Pesaro, 1987.

Commune di Roma Assessorato all Cultura. *La danza tradizionale in Italia, mostra documentaria*. Rome, 1981.

Daniels, Véronique, and Eugen Dombois. "Die Temporelationen im Ballo des Quattrocento: Spekulative Dialoge um den labyrinthische Rätselkanon *De la arte di ballare et danzare* des Domenico da Piacenza." *Basler Jahrbuch für Historische Musikpraxis* 14 (1990): 181–247.

Daniels, Véronique. "Tempo-Relationships within the Italian *Balli* of the Fifteenth Century: A Closer Look at the Notation." In *The Marriage of Music and Dance: Papers from a Conference Held at the Guildhall School of Music and Drama, London, 9th–11th August 1991*. Cambridge, 1992.

Esses, Maurice. *Dance and Instrumental Diferencias in Spain during the Seventeenth and Early Eighteenth Centuries*. Stuyvesant, N.Y., 1992.

Fenlon, Iain. "Music and Spectacle at the Gonzaga Court, c.1580–1600." *Proceedings of the Royal Musical Association* 103 (1976–1977): 90–105.

Feves, Angene. "Fabritio Caroso and the Changing Shape of the Dance, 1550–1600." *Dance Chronicle* 14(1991): 159–174.

Gallo, F. Alberto. "Il 'Ballare lombardo,' circa 1435–1475." *Studi musicali* 8 (1979): 61–84.

Gallo, F. Alberto. "L'autobiografia artistica di Giovanni Ambrosio (Guglielmo Ebreo) da Pesaro." *Studi musicali* 12 (1983): 189–202.

Gatiss, Ian. "Realizing the Music in the Fifteenth-Century Italian Dance Manuals." In *The Marriage of Music and Dance: Papers from a Conference Held at the Guildhall School of Music and Drama, London, 9th–11th August 1991*. Cambridge, 1992.

Ghisi, Federico. *Feste musicali della Firenze Medicea, 1480–1589*. Florence, 1939.

Heartz, Daniel. "A Fifteenth-Century Ballo: *Rôti bouilli joyeux*." In *Aspects of Medieval and Renaissance Music: A Birthday Offering to Gustave Reese*, edited by Jan LaRue. New York, 1966.

Hudson, Richard, and Suzanne G. Cusick. "Balletto." In *The New Grove Dictionary of Music and Musicians*. London, 1980.

Hudson, Richard. *The Allemande, the Balletto, and the Tanz*. Cambridge, 1986.

Jones, Pamela. "Spectacle in Milan: Cesare Negri's Torch Dances." *Early Music* 14.2 (1986): 182–198.

Jones, Pamela. "The Relation between Music and Dance in Cesare Negri's 'Le gratie d'amore' (1602)." 2 vols. Ph.D. diss., University of London, 1988.

Jones, Pamela. "The Editions of Cesare Negri's *Le Gratie d'Amore*: Choreographic Revisions in Printed Copies." *Studi musicali* 21 (1991): 21–23.

Kämper, Dietrich. *Studien zur instrumentalen Ensemblemusik des 16. Jahrhunderts in Italien*. Analecta Musicologica, vol. 10. Cologne, 1970.

Kendall, Yvonne. "Rhythm, Meter, and *Tactus* in Sixteenth-Century Italian Court Dance: Reconstruction from a Theoretical Base." *Dance Research* (Spring 1990): 3–27.

Kinkeldey, Otto. "A Jewish Dancing Master of the Renaissance: Guglielmo Ebreo." In *Studies in Jewish Bibliography and Related Subjects, in Memory of Abraham Solomon Friedus*. New York, 1929.

Kinkeldey, Otto. "Dance Tunes of the Fifteenth Century." In *Instrumental Music: A Conference at Isham Memorial Library, May 4, 1957*, edited by David G. Hughes. Cambridge, Mass., 1959.

Little, Meredith Ellis. "Saltarello." In *The New Grove Dictionary of Music and Musicians*. London, 1980.

Marrocco, W. Thomas. *Inventory of Fifteenth-Century Bassedanze, Balli, and Balletti in Italian Dance Manuals*. New York, 1981.

McGee, Timothy J. "Dancing Masters and the Medici Court in the Fifteenth Century." *Studi Musicali* 17.2 (1988): 201–224.

Meyer, Ernst Hermann. "Ballo." In *Die Musik in Geschichte und Gegenwart*. 1st ed., vol. 1, 1949–1951. Kassel, 1949–1979.

Mingardi, Maurizio. "Gli strumenti musicali nella danza del XIV e XV secolo." In *Mesura et arte del danzare: Guglielmo Ebreo da Pesaro e la danza nelle corti italiane del XV secolo*, edited by Patrizia Castelli et al. Pesaro, 1987.

Moe, Lawrence H. "Dance Music in Printed Italian Lute Tablatures from 1507 to 1611." Ph.D. diss., Harvard University, 1956.

Nagler, Alois. M. *Theatre Festivals of the Medici, 1539–1637*. New Haven, 1964.

Nettl, Paul. "Ballett." In *Die Musik in Geschichte und Gegenwart*. 1st ed., vol. 1, 1949–1951. Kassel, 1949–1979.

Nevile, Jennifer. "The Italian Ballo as Described in Fifteenth-Century Dance Treatises." *Studies in Music, Australia* 18 (1984): 38–51.

Nevile, Jennifer. "The Courtly Dance Manuscripts from Fifteenth-Century Italy." Ph.D. diss., University of New South Wales, 1992.

Nevile, Jennifer. "The Performance of Fifteenth-Century Italian *Balli*: Evidence from the Pythagorean Ratios." *Performance Practice* 6 (1993): 116–128.

Padovan, Maurizio. "La danza nelle corti itliane del XV secolo: Arte figurativa e fonti storiche." In *Mesura et arte del danzare: Guglielmo Ebreo da Pesaro e la danza nelle corti italiane del XV secolo*, edited by Patrizia Castelli et al. Pesaro, 1987.

Pirrotta, Nino, and Elena Povoledo. *Music and Theatre from Poliziano to Monteverdi*. Translated by Karen Eales. Cambridge, 1982.

Pontremoli, Alessandro, and Patrizia La Rocca. *Il Ballare lombardo: Teoria e passi coreutica nella festa di corte del XV secolo*. Milan, 1987.

Solerti, Angelo. *Musica, ballo e drammatica alla corte medicea dal 1600 al 1637*. Florence, 1905.

Sparti, Barbara. "Music and Choreography in the Reconstruction of Fifteenth-Century Balli: Another Look at Domenico's *Verçepe*." *Fifteenth-Century Studies* 10 (1984): 177–194.

Sparti, Barbara. "The Fifteenth-Century *Balli* Tunes: A New Look." *Early Music* 14 (1986): 346–357.

Sparti, Barbara. "Style and Performance in the Social Dances of the Italian Renaissance: Ornamentation, Improvisation, Variation, and Virtuosity." In *Proceedings of the Ninth Annual Conference, Society of Dance History Scholars, City College, City University of New York, 14–17 February 1986*, compiled by Christena L. Schlundt. Riverside, Calif., 1986.

Sparti, Barbara. "How Fast Do You Want the Quadernaria?" In *The Marriage of Music and Dance: Papers from a Conference Held at the Guildhall School of Music and Drama, London 9th–11th August 1991*. Cambridge, 1992.

Sparti, Barbara. "Antiquity as Inspiration in the Renaissance of Dance: The Classical Connection and Fifteenth-Century Italian Dance." *Dance Chronicle* 16 (1993): 373–390.

Sparti, Barbara. "Baroque or Not Baroque—Is That the Question? Dance in Seventeenth-Century Italy." Paper presented at the international conference, "L'Arte della Danza ai Tempi di Claudio Monteverdi," Turin, 6–7 September 1993.

Sparti, Barbara. "Rôti Bouilli: Take Two 'El Gioioso Fiorito.'" *Studi musicali* 24 (1996): 231–261.

Spohr, Helga. "Studien zur italienischen Tanzcomposition um 1600." Ph.D. diss., University of Freiburg, 1956.

Sutton, Julia. *Renaissance Revisited: Twelve Dances Reconstructed [in Labanotation] from the Originals of Thoinot Arbeau, Fabritio Caroso, and Cesare Negri.* New York, 1972.

Sutton, Julia. "Dance: IV. Late Renaissance and Baroque to 1700"; "Caroso, Fabritio"; and "Negri, Cesare." In *The New Grove Dictionary of Music and Musicians.* London, 1980.

Sutton, Julia. "Triple Pavans: Clues to Some Mysteries in Sixteenth-Century Dance." *Early Music* 14.2 (1986): 174–181.

Sutton, Julia. "Musical Forms and Dance Forms in the Dance Manuals of Sixteenth-Century Italy: Plato and the Varieties of Variation." In *The Marriage of Music and Dance: Papers from a Conference Held at the Guildhall School of Music and Drama, London, 9th–11th August 1991.* Cambridge, 1992.

Sutton, Julia, and Sibylle Dahms. "Ballo, Balletto." In *Die Musik in Geschichte und Gegenwart.* 2d. ed., vol. 1, 1994. Kassel, 1994–.

Tani, Gino. "Balletto" and "Ballo." In *Enciclopedio dello spettacolo.* 9 vols. Rome, 1954–1968.

Tani, Gino, et al. "Danza." In *Enciclopedio dello spettacolo.* 9 vols. Rome, 1954–1968.

Wilson, D. R. *The Steps Used in Court Dance in Fifteenth-Century Italy.* Cambridge, 1992.

VIDEOTAPE. Julia Sutton. *Il Ballarino (The Dancing Master),* a teaching videotape featuring a glossary of steps and three sixteenth-century Italian dances by Caroso and Negri (Pennington, N.J. 1991).

JULIA SUTTON
with Barbara Sparti

BALLON, CLAUDE (also known as Claude Balon; born 1671 in Paris; died 9 May 1744 in Versailles), French dancer, teacher, choreographer, and chancellor of the Académie Royale de Danse. Frequently but incorrectly referred to as "Jean," Claude Ballon, who achieved a spectacular dance career in the first half of the eighteenth century, was blessed with every conceivable gift at birth to pave his way. He had dazzling looks, spirit, charm, ease of manners, outstanding performing abilities, and even good family connections. His grandfather Antoine Ballon (1606–1654) had been dancing master to the queen's pages, and his father, François, had taught the pages of the *petite écurie,* a part of the magnificent royal stables.

Five portraits of Ballon have survived, representing the dancer in various roles in costumes designed by Jean Berain, ranging from the very noble *entrée* in *Amadis de Grèce* (1699) to the grotesque madman of *Le Carnaval et la Folie* (1704). These engravings project the qualities of lightness, ease, and gracefulness so characteristic of his style. Although there is no evidence for the story that the term *balon* was taken from his name, the Parfaict brothers describe him as "of a size below average, which is perhaps better fitting for the dance. He had a perfect ear, beautiful legs, and admirable arms. If one adds to this a lightness, fire, and a certain air of tenderness, which pervaded all his attitudes—especially in the pas de deux—one will not be surprised at the reputation that this dancer had acquired at the Opéra and still enjoys today."

Ballon made his debut at the Paris Opera in 1690 in *Cadmus et Hermione.* By 1700 he was "the most fashionable dancer and one of the greatest teachers" (Nemeitz, 1727). According to the *London Stage,* in 1699 he had impressed British audiences while on tour with his partner Marie-Thérèse Subligny. However, English dancer and choreographer John Weaver (1712) wrote of Ballon that "although an excellent dancer, he pretended to nothing more than a graceful motion, with strong and nimble risings and the casting of his body into several agreeable postures. But for expressing anything in Nature but modulated motions, it was never in his head." From 1702 until 1721, Ballon choreographed and recorded ballets in Feuillet notation and seven of his roles are notated in Guillaume-Louis Pecour's *Recüeil de danses* (1704). He used Feuillet notation for his ballroom dances as well, and thirteen dances published between 1712 and 1720 can be found in *Recüeil de toutes les danses . . . depuis l'année 1700.*

Ballon retired from the Paris Opera around 1712 to join the Duchesse du Maine's court at Sceaux. There, in 1714, in *Apollon et les Muses,* an *opéra-ballet,* he scored a triumph in a dance and mime scene from Pierre Corneille's *Les Horaces,* with his partner Françoise Prévost. This work is generally thought to have been a forerunner of the *ballet d'action.* In 1715 Ballon rose to the prestigious post of dancing master to the five-year-old Louis XV, and on 11 March 1719 he was appointed composer of the king's ballets. That same year he replaced Pierre Beauchamps as head of the Académie Royale de Danse. In recognition of his work with the royal family, he was named Dancing Master to the Children of France in August 1731. Upon his death, his court positions were officially passed on to his nephew, Antoine Bandieri de Laval.

Claude Ballon married Marie Dufort, a dancer at the Paris Opera, on 11 July 1696. The couple had three children, none of whom followed in his parents' footsteps. Ballon's last years were saddened by the death of his wife in July 1742 and his eldest son in January 1743. He died a year later: "On 10 May 1744, Claude Ballon, the King's dancing master was buried. He died yesterday at seventy-three years of age . . . in the presence of his son, Nicolas Ballon, Knight of the Military Order of Saint Louis, former captain of cavalry in the regiment of Picardy, Engineer-in-Chief and Usher of the King's Cabinet" (*Registre . . . de l'année 1744*).

Son Nicolas and grandson Claude Petit Darbouville were later to give up their inheritances "for being more onerous than profitable." Ballon's estate, which at some point had been considerable and had included a townhouse in Paris and a magnificent country seat nearby, had been heavily mortgaged with debts.

BIBLIOGRAPHY

Astier, Régine. "La vie quotidienne des danseurs sous l'ancien régime." *Les goûts réunis*, no. 3 (January 1983): 30–39.

Astier, Régine. "Claude Ballon, Dancing Master to Louis XIV: A Biography." In *Proceedings of the Ninth Annual Conference, Society of Dance History Scholars, City College, City University of New York, 14–17 February 1986*, compiled by Christena L. Schlundt. Riverside, Calif., 1986.

Du Bos, Jean-Baptiste. *Réflexions critiques sur la poésie et sur la peinture*. 2 vols. Paris, 1719.

Ferguson, Ian. "Who Was Monsieur Balon?" *The Dancing Times* (December 1982): 198–199.

Jal, Auguste. *Dictionnaire critique de biographie et d'histoire*. Paris, 1867.

Nemeitz, J. C. *Séjour de Paris*. Paris, 1727.

Parfaict, François, and Claude Parfaict. *Histoire manuscrite de l'Académie Royale de Musique*. Paris, n.d. Manuscript located in Paris, Bibliothèque Nationale, fr. 12355.

Rameau, Pierre. *Le maître à danser*. Paris, 1725. Translated by Cyril W. Beaumont as *The Dancing Master* (London, 1931).

Registre pour servir de seconde minute pour les sépultures de l'église royale et paroisse de Saint-Louis de Versailles pendant le courant de l'année 1744. Archives des Yvelines, Versailles.

Swift, Mary Grace. "The Three Ballets of the Young Sun." *Dance Chronicle* 3.4 (1979–1980): 361–372.

Trévoux, A. *Les divertissements de Sceaux*. Paris, 1722.

Weaver, John. *An Essay towards the History of Dancing*. London, 1712.

Winter, Marian Hannah. *The Pre-Romantic Ballet*. London, 1974.

ARCHIVE. Bibliothèque Nationale, Paris: Fichier Laborde.

RÉGINE ASTIER

BALLROOM DANCE COMPETITION. During the twentieth century this style of couple dancing evolved from popular social dances into the context of dance competitions. It has gradually become a pursuit that combines theatrical performance with sport, in some senses like modern figure skating. Courtship, the primary motivation of Western social dancing, does not dominate; instead, the competition ballroom dancer's appearance and style of movement are governed by the goal of winning.

At the present time there are two divisions in competition dancing, called International and American and differentiated by the styles in which the individual dances are performed. Each division has two categories: Standard (International) or Smooth (American), including the fox trot, waltz, tango, quickstep, and (usually) Viennese waltz; and Latin, comprising the samba, rumba, cha-cha, paso doble, and (usually) jive.

History. Ballroom dance competitions blossomed especially in England during the period of World War I. In 1921 a newspaper, the *Daily Sketch*, organized a national amateur fox trot and waltz contest judged by leading dance teachers (earlier contests had been judged by stage and ballet stars), initiating the link between teaching, judging, and competing that persists today.

In 1929 the Official Board of Ballroom Dancing was established to standardize steps, and by 1934 pupils were being tested and ranked in their expertise at a series of standardized levels, symbolized by bronze, silver, and gold medals. Britain's leadership in these developments resulted in its primacy in the ballroom dance scene; to this day the most prestigious competition in the world is the Open British Championship, held annually in Blackpool, England.

Style and Technique. The need to be noticed by the judges among a large group of dancing couples dictates the posture, style, and technique of competition ballroom dancing. Dancers seek to make their movements bigger, faster, and clearer than those around them. They often incorporate movements from other dance genres for emphatic effects and lengthened lines. Thus drops and jazz dance movements add flash to Latin dances; in standard dances, notably the waltz, steps are taken in a straight line, forward or backward, to create the longest distance between two points, as opposed to the social dance's less visible curving pattern. Lifts, in which both the woman's feet are off the floor, are not permitted in any competition dances.

The goal of being recognized also accounts for the stylized appearance of competitive dancers. Costumes are flashy and often constructed to emphasize the dancer's movements. Women wear their hair in stiff styles, often upswept to accentuate the line of the neck and head—important in the closed position of standard dances, in which the dancer is seen primarily from the back. Makeup and hair color are exaggerated to stand out in the crowd.

Standard dance competitors seek visibility by covering large amounts of space as they move. This search for "body flight" has led to a concern with the physics of how the mass of a couple can move most efficiently across the dance floor. What began as a technique based on simple walking has developed into a highly-skilled ability to maneuver, seemingly without effort, over long distances while maintaining body contact. Turning offers the greatest technical challenge, and dancers learn to accomplish progressively more difficult turns.

In the Standard dance position, the woman stands slightly toward the man's right side, with her right hipbone slightly to the right of his navel. This permits the couple to move on separate tracks; their feet are slightly dovetailed, their right sides touch, and their left sides are free. The man places his right hand outside the woman's left shoulder blade and holds her right hand in his left; she places her left hand on his upper right arm, with her arm resting along his. The elbows are generally held on a plane parallel to the floor, creating breadth in the couple's outline. This position with body contact is the only one allowed in competitive Standard dancing; in American Smooth, however, open and apart positions are allowed.

BALLROOM DANCE COMPETITION. Judges, as elegantly attired as the dancers, walk around the floor rating contestants at the Star Ball, London, 1956. (Photograph from the Dance Collection, New York Public Library for the Performing Arts.)

To achieve the goal of visual length and breadth, the dancers can vary their position somewhat. Like two flowers in a vase, they may touch at the hips but arch their upper bodies back in a spiral motion. Each couple develops an individual style, depending on their artistry, relative build (length of legs is particularly important), and the fashion of the moment.

In Latin dances couples are not restricted to a closed position and employ various open positions. The couple may face each other at arm's length, holding one hand, both hands, or crossed hands ("open position"); they may stand side by side facing the same way; or they may face each other without touching ("shine position").

Several of the Latin dances are characterized by the "Cuban motion," a rhythmic lateral movement of the pelvis and ribcage. In social versions of these dances the hip moves in opposition to the bent leg; in competition, because of the importance of long, exaggerated lines, the legs are straightened and the hip is taken onto a straight leg.

In order not to give an advantage to any of the many couples performing simultaneously, the music for each dance in a competition is played at a standardized tempo, known as "strict tempo." Couples prepare their choreography to the tempo but without knowing what piece of music will be used, unlike competitive skaters or ballet dancers who choose specific music for their performances. In general, variety and nuance are sacrificed for regularity and predictability: couples have a prepared routine, or major sequences (called "groups") of a routine, and dance those steps to whatever tune the orchestra plays.

Organization of Competitions. Competitive dancers are classified as either professional or amateur. (There are also "pro-am" competitions for couples in which one member is professional and the other amateur, usually a student.) Large contests may be further divided in the age classes Juniors (under 35) and Seniors (over 35). Open competitions accept participants from any geographic area, while closed competitions are restricted to dancers born or residing in a designated area.

The panel of judges is made up of persons who have qualified with a recognized dance organization. A complex system of marking, called the "skating system," is used. Judges look for technical competence, clean lines, ease of movement, and general visual impression. Judging at the highest level is sometimes based more on taste than on technical points, because all finalists are likely to be technically proficient.

Competitions are organized in heats, or elimination rounds. As many as twenty-five couples may dance in each heat, with half the competitors being eliminated and the other half going on to the next heat. Each individual dance has its series of heats. Thus the first round of the waltz is danced, then the first round of the fox trot, and then the remaining dances of that division. This process is repeated in successively fewer heats until only six couples remain; these are then ranked after their final performance, and the winners emerge. The heats are short, and the judges often have only ninety seconds to view all the couples in a given heat.

Dances. All the dances performed in competitions originated as popular social couple dances. They have been adapted, standardized, stylized, and assigned specific tempos. Following are descriptions of the individual Standard (fox trot, slow waltz, tango, quickstep, and Viennese waltz) and Latin dances (rumba, cha-cha, paso doble, jive, and samba).

Fox trot. Based on a rhythm of slow-quick-quick, the competitive fox trot is a stylized walk incorporating long strides and spiral twists of the body. The basic walking technique of Standard dances emphasizes moving the body's center of gravity in a smooth and continuous manner; the sequence is equally divided between the time the center is held over each leg and the time it is suspended between them. The spiral action, or contra body movement, consists of turning the opposite side toward the moving leg; it permits the couple to maintain body contact even when the movement of the dance takes the man's right foot to the left of both the woman's feet. The visual shape of the fox trot is a series of long, low scallops. The music is in 4/4 time at 30 bars per minute.

Slow waltz. Danced at 30 bars per minute, this is the slowest variant of the waltz. It is based on the box step, but in order to cover much space, it has eliminated much of the whirling traditionally associated with the waltz. Its main characteristic is rise and fall, accomplished through movement of the ankles and knees, yielding an up-and-down motion and space-covering swinging action. In the International style the couple must maintain the dance position throughout, but the American style permits steps where the partners move apart, such as an underarm turn by the woman. The music is in 3/4 time.

Tango. The last of the Standard ballroom dances added to competitions (in 1931), the competitive tango has a staccato style and emphasizes rolling the weight of the body on the foot diagonally from heel to toe (from the in-side edge to the outside edge). It moves in a flat plane, without foot or body rise. The sharp movements characteristic of the competitive tango developed from the style introduced by Freddie Camp and Alida Pasqual in 1935. Camp had the ability to accelerate explosively from stillness to vigorous action, then to reassume a static posture pregnant with expectation of the next movement. This powerful attack characterizes the International style of tango and has resulted in a change in the usual hold: the woman locks her left elbow or forearm with the man's right arm so that her left hand is underneath, rather than above. The music is in 4/4 time and is played at 33 bars per minute.

Quickstep. The name "quickstep" was coined by Florence Purcell in 1924 to distinguish this fast version of the fox trot. Danced today at 48 bars per minute, the quickstep has a basic rhythmic sequence of slow-quick-quick-slow and is characterized by hopping and skipping steps. It shows the influence of the Charleston. Maintaining body contact is especially difficult in this dance because of its speed.

Viennese waltz. The fastest of all the competitive dances at 58 bars per minute, the Viennese waltz consists basically of left and right turns traveling along the line of the counterclockwise flow of dancers around the ballroom. This movement is interrupted with fancy turns, called *fleckerals*, performed in the middle of the dance floor. The Viennese waltz has fewer variations than any other competitive dance in the Standard category and is closest to the traditional concept of the waltz.

Rumba. The competitive rumba bears little resemblance to its historical source. It is danced at 28 to 31 bars per minute in 4/4 time. Its pattern is recognizable as that of the traditional Latin dance, but over the years many drops, spins, kicks, and jazz movements have been added to intensify it. Because the speed of leg movements has become a technical point, the dance has assumed a stop-and-go quality. Cuban motion, the lateral movement of hips and ribcage, is important. To allow for the increasingly acrobatic, technically difficult movements, the tempo of the dance has been decreased over the years.

Cha-cha. The step pattern of the cha-cha (called the cha-cha-cha in Britain) developed from that of the mambo. It consists of five steps done to four beats of the music; the cha-cha *chassé* falls on the fourth beat, its accompanying hesitation, and the first count of the next measure. In a technical refinement, the dancer crosses the feet slightly on the hesitation while moving forward or backward. It is performed in both open and closed positions to a tempo of 32 to 34 bars per minute in a syncopated 4/4 rhythm; the syncopation is a defining characteristic of this dance. Judges look for good foot and leg action in coordination with lateral hip and ribcage movement.

Paso doble. In its simplest form, the paso doble is a marching dance; the basic action is step side, close together. It is a mimetic dance based on the Spanish bullfight, featuring postures and movements reminiscent of the matador, cape, and bull. It is usually performed to music in 2/4 time at 60 to 62 bars per minute but may use 3/4 or 6/8 time. Several variations have French names related to bullfighting, such as *le huit* (known as the cape due to the shape of the figure), *la passe,* and *coup de pique.*

Jive. A development of swing dancing, done to jazz and rock-and-roll in the 1940s and 1950s, the jive is a six-count basic dance performed in 4/4 time at 40 to 46 bars per minute. It differs from the social dance in that the dancers maintain a trained body position and move with great exactness. The feet are usually pointed in the kick steps, and movements tend to be very exaggerated. Lifts are not allowed in competition.

Samba. Bearing little resemblance to the traditional Brazilian samba, the competitive samba travels around the floor in a counterclockwise direction. It is danced at 48 to 56 bars per minute in 2/4 or 4/4 time. Its distinctive element is the "basic bounce," a vertical movement of the body driven by the ankles and knees. Many of the variations danced today resemble in pattern and position those of a once-popular social dance, the maxixe.

[*See also* Social Dance, *article on* Twentieth-Century Social Dance to 1960. *For discussion of other forms of competitions, see* Ballet Competitions and Ice Dancing.]

BIBLIOGRAPHY

Franks, A. H., ed. *The Modern Ballroom Dancers Handbook.* London, 1963.

Hallewell, Kit. *Blackpool, My Blackpool, 1931–1978.* Birmingham, 1979.

Imperial Society of Teachers of Dancing. *The Revised Technique of Latin American Dancing.* London, 1975.

Laird, Walter. *Technique of Latin American Dancing.* London, 1964.

Malnig, Julie. *Dancing Till Dawn: A Century of Exhibition Ballroom Dancing.* New York, 1992.

Moore, Alex. *The Revised Technique.* Kingston-on-Thames, 1982.

Moore, Alex. *Ballroom Dancing.* London, 1986.

Richardson, Philip. *A History of English Ballroom Dancing.* London, 1946.

YVONNE MARCEAU

BAMANA DANCE. The Bamana, a Mande-speaking people numbering close to three million, are subsistence farmers who live in the dry savannas of the West African country of Mali. They are also called *Bambara* by outsiders. Traditionally animists but now gradually converting to Islam, the Bamana have several initiation societies that use anthropomorphic or zoomorphic masks in annual dance rituals. In recent years, as Islam has spread, these initiation societies have declined, but some of their masks and dances have been adapted for use in secular entertainments held twice a year—in April or May, at the beginning of the planting season, and in December after the harvest.

The Bamana also perform nonmasked dances during various community and family celebrations. Like masked dances, these are usually performed by young adults and adolescents. Occasionally older men and women participate in the dances, often on an impromptu basis, their improvised choreography drawing much praise from spectators.

About every two or three years, youngsters of more or less the same age form a *flan-bolo* group, one for girls and one for boys. In some areas, several *flan-bolo*s are grouped into a larger village age-set association called a *ton.* Masked dances are assigned to individual *flan-bolo*s, the least difficult dances being performed by the youngest, and the more difficult by the oldest. A keen sense of competition exists among the internal groups of a *ton,* and rivalries are frequent between village *ton*s for recognition as the best dancers in a region.

The orchestra that accompanies Bamana dances usually consists of three or four drums made from hollowed logs, with cowhide stretched over one or both ends. The *jembe* drum, once the most important, has a long cylindrical base that flares at the top where the skin is attached. Rectangular pieces of metal edged with metal rings are attached to the top of the drum. Musicians also use xylophones and bars of metal to be tapped with metal rings attached to the fingers. Women and girls clap, often using elaborately carved oval wooden clappers known as *teggere.* The music is augmented by the sounds of beads, bells, and bits of metal that dancers tie around their ankles.

In a sense, since the 1960s there has been a profanation of some Bamana dances. Some dances that were once performed alone as part of religious ceremonies are now performed together for purposes of entertainment. In addition, these dances are presented before heterogeneous groups, including people from other villages and individuals never initiated into the societies from which the dances are derived.

Among the prominent nonmasked dances performed by the Bamana are the *bondialan, mandiani,* and *gomba.* The *bondialan* dancers carry calabashes covered with nut-containing fiber nets and wear anklets of bells and bits of metal. The *mandiani* is performed by young girls, groups of whom dance in a long line, holding either a fly whisk or piece of cloth in one hand. The *gomba,* an initiation and consecration dance, is performed by young men and consists of carefully measured steps. Women often dance with their grand flowing *boubou*s (robes) at celebrations, improvising the choreography. Clapping, raising and lowering their arms, and moving in unison, they dance in single file around and across the dance arena.

Virtually all Bamana dances are performed in the village square, except in large towns and cities where they are presented on street corners or in the middle of roads. Mali's National Folk Troupe has adapted many of these dances for theatrical presentation on the stage both in Mali and abroad.

Before dances begin in a village square, the orchestra arrives; its members tune the drums by placing the skins close to a fire to dry them out and render them taut. Performers try to make dramatic entrances or otherwise tantalize the audience by beginning their performances beyond the dance arena, slowly moving toward it. Masked dancers, often hidden by elaborate camouflage, and armatures are usually accompanied by age-set members who quickly repair and otherwise secure the camouflage.

The choreography of Bamana dances imitates both human and animal behaviors. In doing so, it extols virtue and condemns deviation from societal norms. Some of the common masked dances performed by the Bamana include the *kono*, which represents the hornbill, a seemingly foolish bird that is actually very shrewd; the *zantegeba*, which represents the baboon; the *n'tomo*, which represents humans as pristine animals; the *sigi koun*, a buffalo; and the *tyi wara*, which represents a mythical creature, half human and half animal, who taught humans how to farm. *Tyi wara* dancers wear beautifully sculptured wooden headdresses of numerous styles. Spectators are encouraged to emulate the lion's dignity, to despise the antics of the baboon, and to strive for the perfection portrayed by the *tyi wara*.

[*See also* West Africa.]

BIBLIOGRAPHY

Arnoldi, Mary Jo. *Playing with Time: Art and Performance in Central Mali.* Bloomington, 1995.

Decock, Jean. "National Folk Troupe of Mali." *African Arts* 1 (Spring 1968).

Ezra, Kate. *A Human Ideal in African Art: Bamana Figurative Sculpture.* New York, 1986.

Imperato, Pascal James. "The Dance of the Tyi Wara." *African Arts* 4 (Autumn 1970).

Imperato, Pascal James. "Last Dances of the Bambara." *Natural History* 84 (April 1975).

Imperato, Pascal James. "Bambara and Malinke Ton Masquerades." *African Arts* 13 (August 1980).

BAMANA DANCE. Two scenes from a communal event in Mali. (*above*) Young men and boys of a *ton*, an age-set association, in a dance celebrating cooperative work, hoeing a field. (*left*) Young women and girls of the *ton* sing and clap as several young men work on the field. (Photographs by Judith Gleason; used by permission.)

Imperato, Pascal James. "The Depiction of Beautiful Women in Malian Youth Association Masquerades." *African Arts* 27 (January 1994).

Zahan, Dominique. *Sociétés d'initiation Bambara.* Paris, 1960.

PASCAL JAMES IMPERATO

BANDŌ MITSUGORŌ, name used by nine generations of *kabuki* actor-dancers.

Bandō Mitsugorō I (born 1745 in Osaka, died 10 April 1782 in Edo [Tokyo]) was a handsome, versatile star who specialized as leading men *(tachiyaku)* and young lovers *(nimaime)* while also being outstanding as a dancer and female impersonator *(onnagata).*

Bandō Mitsugorō II (born 1750, died 2 October 1829), who was not related to Mitsugorō I, took his name in 1785 and mostly followed his namesake's traditions, but when the legitimate son of Mitsugorō I came of age in 1799, Mitsugorō II changed his name to Ōgino Isaburō II and handed the Mitsugorō name over to its rightful owner.

Bandō Mitsugorō III (born 1773 in Edo, died 27 December 1831 in Edo) was the son of Mitsugorō I and was one of the great actors of his day. He engaged in a famous artistic rivalry with Nakamura Utaemon III. A great dancer and actor, he brought a human dimension to his roles that influenced actors for generations to come. He was particularly adept at quick-change pieces. He founded the school of dance called *Bandō Ryū.*

Bandō Mitsugorō IV (born 1802 in Edo, died 18 October 1863 in Edo), adopted son of Mitsugorō III, rose to fame in the Kyoto-Osaka region (Kamigata), and took the name in 1832. He was a handsome, versatile player of leading men and made dance inroads in such pieces as *Sanja Matsuri.* He captured Edo's urban atmosphere when he starred in plays of lower-class life *(kizewamono).* He and Nakamura Utaemon IV had a famous rivalry. Mitsugorō IV later became Morita Kanya XI and managed Edo's Morita-za.

Bandō Mitsugorō V (born 1812 in Edo, died 6 March 1855 in Edo), Mitsugorō IV's adopted son, was known as Bandō Shuka I for most of his career.

Bandō Mitsugorō VI (born 1841, died 11 September 1873 in Tokyo), Mitsugorō V's son, was a promising female impersonator, but he died young.

Bandō Mitsugorō VII (born 1882 in Tokyo, died 4 November 1961 in Tokyo), son of Morita Kanya XII (1846–1897), was acclaimed for the care he took to make his productions authentic and for his effort to preserve *kabuki*'s traditions, about which he wrote several books. The recipient of many prestigious honors, he was one of the best dancers of his era and was considered on a par with the great Onoe Kikugorō VI, with whom he created such popular dances as *Bōshibari* and *Migawari Zazen.*

Bandō Mitsugorō VIII (born 19 October 1906 in Tokyo, died 16 January 1975 in Tokyo), the adopted son of Mitsugorō VII, spent much of his early career in Kamigata, but returned to Tokyo in 1961. His acting specialties were villains and old men. Mitsugorō VIII was the best-read *kabuki* actor of his generation and was a prolific author of theater books. He was adept at the tea ceremony, flower arrangement, and calligraphy.

Bandō Mitsugorō IX (born 14 May 1929 in Tokyo) married into the Mitsugorō family in 1955. He is especially good in the roles of old men, such as Gekizaemon in *Meiboku Sendai Hagi* and Tosa no Shōgen in *Keisei Hangonkō.* His forte is dance, especially works such as *Echigo Jishi, Renjishi,* and *Noriaibune,* in which he recaptures the spirit of old Edo. His son is the popular Bandō Yasosuke V.

[*See also* Japanese Traditional Schools; Kabuki Theater; *and* Onnagata.]

BANDŌ MITSUGORŌ. An actor specializing in villains and old men, Bandō Mitsugorō VIII appears here as the God of the Mountain in the *kabuki* drama *Momijigari.* (Photograph courtesy of Samuel L. Leiter.)

BIBLIOGRAPHY

Akasaka Jiseki, ed. *Kabuki haiyū daihyakka.* Tokyo, 1993.

Engekikai (January 1994). Special issue on *kabuki* actors.

Leiter, Samuel L. "Four Interviews with Kabuki Actors." *Educational Theatre Journal* (December 1966): 391–404.

Nojima Jusaburō. *Kabuki jinmei jiten.* Tokyo, 1988.

Toita Yasuji, ed. *Kabuki kanshō nyūmon.* 3d ed., rev. Tokyo, 1994.

SAMUEL L. LEITER

BANDŌ TAMASABURŌ, name used by five generations of *kabuki* actors.

Bandō Tamasaburō I (born 1812 in Edo [Tokyo], died 6 March 1855 in Edo), the line's founder, was better known as Bandō Mitsugorō V.

Bandō Tamasaburō II (born 1831 in Edo, died 30 May 1872 in Tokyo), the adopted son of Bandō Shuka, took the name Tamasaburō II in 1844 but finished out his career as Bandō Minosuke IV, a name he took in 1869.

Bandō Tamasaburō III (born 1883 in Tokyo, died 15 January 1905 in New York City) was the daughter of Morita Kan'ya XII. Skilled from childhood at dance, classical Japanese music, *koto* playing (a Japanese horizontal harp), flower arrangement, the tea ceremony, and other traditional arts, she chose to join the women's *kabuki* movement that briefly burgeoned during the Meiji era (1868–1912). She took the name Tamasaburō III in 1889 and in the early years of the twentieth century moved to New York City, where she taught Japanese dance.

Bandō Tamasaburō IV (born 8 March 1907 in Tokyo, died 28 March 1977 in Tokyo), adopted son of Morita Kan'ya XIII, debuted under that name in 1914 but took the name Bandō Shuka III in 1926 and in 1935 changed again to Morita Kan'ya XIV, under which he was best known. His good looks made him a popular romantic actor in roles such as Sakuramaru in *Sugawara* and Yosaburō in *Kirare Yosa*, but he was rather versatile and even played women on occasion.

Bandō Tamasaburō V (born 25 April 1950 in Tokyo), the most distinguished member of the line, is the adopted son of Morita Kan'ya XIV. His actual father was a Tokyo restaurant owner. He debuted at Toyoko Hall as Bandō Kinoji in December 1957, and became Tamasaburō V in 1964. He is perhaps the finest *onnagata*, or female impersonator, today. He first came to prominence in 1967 in the National Theater's revival of *Sakura-hime*, playing Shiragiku, although he played both this role and the lead, Princess Sakura, in later productions. His partnership in the early 1970s with Ichikawa Ebizō (later, Ichikawa Danjūrō XII), who played romantic leads opposite him, was nicknamed "Ebitama"; fans referred to his later partnership with Kataoka Takao as "Takatama." In addition to princess roles, he has excelled in such characters as Omiwa in *Imoseyama*, Yūgiri in *Kuruwa Bunshō*, Otomi

and Kasane in *Kasane*, and Agemaki in *Sukeroku*, in which parts he brings to mind the great Nakamura Utaemon V, whose style he emulates.

Tamasaburō V has also become a major figure in other forms of theater, including modern drama, Shakespeare (including such roles as Desdemona and Lady Macbeth), and ancient Greek tragedy (including Medea). Maurice Béjart choreographed a ballet for him, and in 1993 the Polish director Andrzej Wajda directed him in *Anastazja*. Tamasaburō V has branched out into directing for film and stage. He possesses a beautiful, old-fashioned-looking face, which is perfect for female parts, though he is unusually tall for an *onnagata*. Not only has his work brought many new Japanese fans to *kabuki*, but he has developed a considerable international reputation from his frequent appearances abroad. In 1990 he opened the Tokyo Conservatory, a school dedicated to teaching all facets of theatrical art.

[*See also* Japanese Traditional Schools *and* Kabuki Theater.]

BIBLIOGRAPHY

Akasaka Jiseki, ed. *Kabuki haiyū daihyakka.* Tokyo, 1993.

Bandō Tamasaburō and Sunaga Asahiko. *Tamasaburō: Butai no yume.* Tokyo, 1984.

Engekikai 52.2 (1993). Special issue: *kabuki* actors' directory.

Nojima Jusaburō. *Kabuki jinmei jiten.* Tokyo, 1988.

Toita Yasuji, ed. *Kabuki kanshō nyūmon.* 3d ed., rev. Tokyo, 1994.

SAMUEL L. LEITER

BANGLADESH. The nation of Bangladesh, which became autonomous in 1971, lies in the northeastern corner of the Indian subcontinent. Muslim Bengalis constitute the great majority of the population.

The mosaic of dance in Bangladesh encompasses the dances of tribal groups living mainly in the hilly areas, the Santhals of the tea plantations, the Kuki and Khasi peoples, and tribes from the Myanmar border. Recently many tribal and folk dances have been theatricalized for urban public performance or for export under official patronage as part of cultural delegations, a familiar pattern worldwide. In the course of this transformation, the viability of the authentic traditional performing art is often lost.

The primary dance institution in Bangladesh is the National Academy of Performing Arts, established in 1979 as a division of the Shilpakala Academy of the Bangladesh Ministry of Education. The government subsidizes the arts as an important aspect of nation-building; an arm of this policy, the Shilpakala Academy locates, studies, records, and catalogs traditional dance performances. In addition, scholars, musicians, and choreographers have been urged to stylize local dances to make them more accessible and suitable for theatrical presentation.

The government also supports the creation of choreographed compositions based on the activities of rural people, for example, the "Snake Charmer's Dance," "Fishermen's Dance," "Tea-Leaf Picking Dance," and "Wedding Dance." These greatly transformed folk-based dances are common in popular cinema and amateur theater productions. They are based not so much on folk dance as on the representation through dance and pantomime of socioeconomic activities of nonurban people. Such themes and adaptations are equally common in the popular repertory of dance groups in Calcutta, India; indeed, the dance-conscious public of Bangladesh in large part shares a cultural and linguistic heritage with the West Bengal region of India.

Another important aspect of dance in Bangladesh is the local variant of the Meitei tradition of dance, better known as Manipuri dance, common in the border region of Sylhet-Tripura. The Indian state of Manipur, north of Bangladesh, provides one of the mixed classical and folk traditions of Bangladeshi dance; Manipur is also a source of material for contemporary urban choreographers in such cities as Dhaka. [*See* Manipur.]

Important in any discussion of dance in Bangladesh is the influence of the Bauls, whose dances are closely related to their mystic religious beliefs and may be performed while in trance. Followers of the Baul tradition are found in both Hindu and Muslim communities. Such catholicity is encouraged as part of the synthesis of ethnic, cultural, and religious groups vital to the task of nation-building. Solidarity among Bangladesh's diverse communities—which include not only Hindus and Muslims but also Buddhists, Christians, and animists—is seen as necessary.

Bangladesh is still a very young nation, and the reorganization of preexisting traditional dance and music is still in an early stage. Aside from the established dance and music traditions mentioned, popular developments in dance and the other performing arts, stimulated by government support, are still emerging. Like a number of other nations, Bangladesh is in the process of developing a dance arts expression that will represent its many peoples fairly and accurately, and with aesthetic responsibility.

BIBLIOGRAPHY

Bangladesh Centre of the International Theatre Institute. *International Seminar on Cross-Cultural Contacts in Theatre, Dhaka, January 19–21, 1995.* Dhaka, 1995.
Kabir, Alamgir. "Bangladesh." In *The Sixth Festival of Asian Arts.* Hong Kong, 1981.

CLIFFORD REIS JONES

BANQUET. The connection between the leisurely consumption of food and celebration is a natural one. Documentation in the form of pictures and written descriptions exists for banquets from the early Egyptian dynasties onward. In medieval and Renaissance Europe, banquets brought companionship and relaxation after battles and tournaments. Feasts of the Christian calendar, coronations, weddings, arrivals and departures of visiting dignitaries—any event worthy of celebration at court as well as in towns and cities—could and usually did involve a festive meal, enhanced by the participation of music, theater, dance, and the decorative arts. Besides their more obvious purpose of feeding and entertaining an assembled company, banquets served to demonstrate the host's refined and educated tastes and his political power and economic supremacy (Cosman, 1976).

Medieval banquets, emulating the models set by classical antiquity and biblical repasts, emphasize the meal itself (cf. the more than twenty food episodes in *Sir Gawain and the Green Knight* described by Cosman, 1976, pp. 12ff.), surrounded by an established ritual of serving dishes and wines. Grace, in Latin, was chanted before the feasting began; fanfares announced the arrival of each course; music played by minstrels accompanied the eating of beautifully decorated dishes; jugglers, acrobats, dwarfs, and jesters entertained the diners between courses. The host, his family, and honored guests sat at the "high table," which was placed on a dais and thus was literally raised above the level of the floor of the hall. The banquet ceremonial was controlled by the household's marshal or chief usher, who, like the squires and stewards in charge of food and drink, belonged to the nobility. After the feasting, which lasted several hours, the tables were cleared away and the company united in social dancing into the wee hours.

Renaissance banquets, beginning in the mid-fifteenth century, became full-fledged theatrical spectacles with allegorical or mythological themes, written scenarios, decorations, props and machinery and involved the court's entire artistic staff of poets, musicians, dancing masters, architects, and, of course, the kitchen personnel whose culinary creativity produced cascades of sweets on mountains of crystal, pies filled with singing birds, and fountains spouting five kinds of wines in as many different directions. It is during this period that the word *entremet*—originally applied to a decorative dish of fruits, nuts, cheeses, and the like, served as a lighter fare between main courses—acquires its new meaning of "theatrical interlude," either acted, sung, or danced, not only at banquets but in the professional theater as well.

How far a cook's responsibilities for the banquets under his care could go is forcefully demonstrated by the diaries of Cristoforo di Messisbugo (1549), which list not only the events, the food courses (with recipes), and decorations but also the music and the dances that took place at the *conviti* (banquets) in Ferrara during his tenure as chief kitchen artist of the Este household.

The line of great Renaissance banquets began with the allegorical banquet *La Fête du Faisan* (Feast of the Pheasant) at Lille on 17 February 1454, given by Philip III, duke of Burgundy, for the knights of the Order of the Golden Fleece (description in La Marche, 1883–1888; see also Cartellieri, 1921). Much of the music for this spectacular event was composed by Guillaume Dufay. A festival banquet at Tours in 1457 included *entremets, morescas,* and *mommeries* as well as a mystery play (Petit de Julleville, 1880). The marriage festivities for Charles the Bold, duke of Burgundy, and Margaret of York in Bruges in 1468 included, besides the famous tournament *Le Pas d'Arbre d'Or* (The Spectacle of the Golden Tree), an elaborate banquet, as did the nuptials of Giangaleazzo Sforza, duke of Milan, and Isabella of Aragon in Tortona in 1489. Mary of Hungary gave a banquet in Binche, Belgium, in 1549 in which the great hall of the palace was transformed into an "enchanted" room, with planets and stars moving across the ceiling and raining comfits and perfumes on the assembly (Strong, 1973, p. 107). Baldassare di Belgiojoso (Beaujoyeulx), *valet de chambre* and court choreographer to Catherine de Médicis, arranged the dances and composed the music for the banquet at Chenonceau in 1577 (Ménéstrier, 1681 [1972]). Riders on horseback, cloud machines, and food courses devoted to figures from classical mythology (Hercules, Juno, Minerva) and served by correspondingly costumed noblemen and ladies were all part of the allegorical banquet, on the theme of Peace, celebrating the marriage by proxy of Marie de Médicis and Henri IV of France in Florence in 1600.

The tradition of the festival banquet continued through the seventeenth and eighteenth centuries (Israel Silvestre's engravings depict the food arrangements and spectacles presented in the palace and gardens of Versailles at banquets given by Louis XIV). Now, royal and aristocratic banquets included variants such as the German *Wirtschaft* and *Bauern Hochzeit*, in which the historical and mythological framework was replaced by a lower-class or peasant setting.

Of all the arts that embellished banquets, music was the most important. Medieval poets and music theorists such as Heinrich von Veldeke, Guillaume de Machaut, and Johannes de Groccheo speak of "music to eat by"; town bands, trumpeters' guilds, and court orchestras in the Renaissance and the Baroque period were committed to play for courtly and urban banquets, and the contract of a conductor (*maestro di cappella, Kapellmeister*) frequently included a clause that obligated him "to provide the necessary music for courtly and ordinary tables" (as in a contract signed by Georg Philipp Telemann in 1717) in addition to his other musical duties.

Especially in the seventeenth and eighteenth centuries, collections of music to enhance dining pleasure were published. These include Johann Hermann Schein's *Banchetto musicale* (1617) and the *Studenten-Schmauß* (1626), Thomas Simpson's *Taffel-Consort* (1617, 1621), Marc-Antoine Charpentier's *Airs sérieux et à boire* (1678 and later editions), Michel-Richard Delalande's *Sinfonies . . . qui se jouent ordinairement au souper du Roy* (1703), and Telemann's *Musique de table* (1733).

BIBLIOGRAPHY

Austin, Thomas, ed. *Two Fifteenth-Century Cookery-Books.* New York, 1888.

Becker-Glauch, Irmgard. *Die Bedeutung der Musik für die Dresdener Hoffeste bis in die Zeit Augusts des Starken.* Kassel, 1951.

Cartellieri, Otto. "Das Fasanenfest." *Historische-Politische Blätter für das Katholische Deutschland* 167 (1921): 65–80; 141–158.

Cartellieri, Otto. "Theaterspiele am Hofe Karls des Kühnen von Burgund." *Germanisch-Römishce Monatsschrift* 9 (1921).

Cartellieri, Otto. *Am Hofe der Herzöge von Burgund.* Basel, 1926.

Cosman, Madeleine Pelner. *Fabulous Feasts: Medieval Cookery and Ceremony.* New York, 1976.

Cotarelo y Mori, Emilio. *Colección de entremeses, loas, bailes, jácaras, y mojigangas.* Madrid, 1911.

Dent, Edward J. "Social Aspects of Music in the Middle Ages." In *The Oxford History of Music,* edited by Percy C. Buck and William H. Hadow. 2d ed. London, 1929: 184–218.

Eggebrecht, Hans Heinrich. "Festmusik." In *Riemanns Musiklexikon.* 12th ed. Mainz, 1959–.

Fenlon, Iain. "Music and Spectacle at the Gonzaga Court, c. 1580–1600." *Proceedings of the Royal Musical Association* 103 (1976–1977): 90–105.

Gerstfeldt, Olga von. *Hochzeitsfeste der Renaissance in Italien.* Esslingen, 1906.

Ghisi, Federico. *Feste musicali della Firenze Medicca, 1480–1589.* Florence, 1939.

Gundersheimer, Werner L., ed. *Art and Life at the Court of Ercole I d'Este.* Geneva, 1972.

Huizinga, Johan. *The Waning of the Middle Ages* (1924). New York, 1969.

Jacquot, Jean, ed. *Les Fêtes de la Renaissance.* 3 vols. Paris, 1956–1973.

Jacquot, Jean. "La Reine Henriette-Marie et les influences françaises dans les spectacles à la cour de Charles Ier." *Cahiers de l'Association Internationale des Études Françaises* 9 (1957): 128–134.

Krapf, Ludwig, and Christian Wagenknecht, eds. *Stuttgarter Hoffeste: Texte und Materialien zur höfischen Repräsentation im frühen 17. Jahrhundert.* Tübingen, 1979.

Lacroix, Paul. *Moeurs, usages, et costumes au moyen âge et à l'époque de la Renaissance.* Paris, 1871.

La Marche, Olivier de. *Mémoires.* 4 vols. Paris, 1883–1888.

Lazarowicz, Klaus. "Konzelebration oder Kollusion? Über die Feste der Wittelsbacher." In *Europäische Hofkultur im 16. und 17. Jahrhundert,* vol. 2, *Referate der Sektionen 1–5,* edited by August Buck et al. Hamburg, 1981.

Massialot, François. *Le cuisinier roial et bourgeois.* Paris, 1691.

Ménéstrier, Claude-François. *Des représentations en musique anciennes et modernes* (1681). Geneva, 1972.

Messisbugo, Cristoforo di. *Banchetti: Compositioni di vivande, et apparecchio generale.* Ferrara, 1549.

Minor, Andrew C., and Bonner Mitchell, eds. *A Renaissance Entertainment: Festivities for the Marriage of Cosimo I, Duke of Florence, in 1539.* Columbia, Mo., 1968.

Petit de Julleville, Louis. *Les mystères.* 2 vols. Paris, 1880.

Pontremoli, Alessandro, and Patrizia La Rocca. *Il ballare lombardo: Teoria e prassi coreutica nella festa di corte del XV secolo.* Milan, 1987.

Prunières, Henry. *Le ballet de cour en France avant Benserade et Lully.* Paris, 1914.

Rosselli, Giovanne de. *Epulario, or, The Italian Banquet.* London, 1516.

Salmen, Walter. *Der fahrende Musiker im europäischen Mittelalter.* Kassel, 1960.

Sass, Lorna J. *To the King's Taste.* New York, 1975.

Sass, Lorna J. *To the Queen's Taste.* New York, 1976.

Strong, Roy. *Splendour at Court: Renaissance Spectacle and Illusion.* Boston, 1973.

Younger, William. *Gods, Men, and Wine.* London, 1966.

Watson, Katherine F. "Sugar Sculpture for Grand Ducal Weddings from the Giambologna Workshop." In *Connoisseur* 199 (September 1978): 20–26.

INGRID BRAINARD

BARBERINA, LA (Barbara Campanini; born 1721 in Parma, Italy, died 7 June 1799 in Barschau, Silesia), Italian dancer. Campanini studied ballet at the Teatro Farnese with Antonio Rinaldi (known as Fossano), who imparted to her a brilliant technique and knowledge of pantomime. In 1739, she and Fossano went to Paris and were hired by the Paris Opera. There, her virtuosity (she was noted for performing *entrechat huit*) fascinated composer Jean-Philippe Rameau, who created four solo dances for her debut in his *opéra-ballet Les Fêtes d'Hébé* in 1739. Her pas de deux with Fossano, laced with burlesque mime, was considered enchanting. Richly rewarded performances followed at the court of Louis XV, as did leading roles in other new *opéra-ballets* of 1739: Rameau's *Dardanus* and Louis Dupré's production of Joseph Royer's *Zaïde, Reine de Granade*, which also featured Marie Sallé. Campanini's success led to Sallé's retirement. People began to refer to her as La Barberina and called her "the Flying Goddess."

La Barberina's beauty and charm attracted many admirers. Prince de Carignan, director of the Opera, made her his principal mistress, and he was followed by other highly placed admirers. For the 1740/41 season, John Rich brought her to London, where she shone in solo parts and in dances with famous partners, at court, at Lincoln's Inn Fields, and at Covent Garden. She appeared in a pantomime-ballet, *Mars and Venus,* and performed minuets and various dances, including "Tambourine," "The Italian Peasants," and "Tyrolean Dance." In 1741 and 1742 she danced in Paris and London and at the Dublin Festival. Her Terpsichore in *Les Fêtes Grècques et Romaines* caused the Parisian poet Filandre to sigh, "O incomparably beautiful Barberina, Cupid and the Graces may envy you."

Frederick the Great of Prussia saw Barberina in Paris and hired her to appear in the spring of 1744 at his Berlin Opera House, but she formed a liaison with Lord Stuart Mackenzie, and the couple fled to Venice to evade the Berlin contract. The Prussian king acted through diplomatic channels, and Barberina was brought to Berlin under military guard; she made her first appearance there on 13 May 1744. She was the unchallenged favorite of the Berlin stage until 1748, in a company that also included Jean-Barthélemy Lany, his sisters Louise-Madeleine and Charlotte, Jean-Georges Noverre, Pietro Sodi, and Marianne Cochois. The king allowed Barberina to set her own price—seven thousand reichstalers a year (Carl Philipp Emanuel Bach, the court harpsichordist, was paid three hundred reichstalers), plus five months vacation—but all contingent on her remaining unmarried.

Barberina's palace became a gathering place for the king, the nobility, and the diplomatic corps. From 1744 to 1748, she danced in a long succession of operas by Karl Heinrich Graun or by Johann Adolf Hasse. In 1748, however, she fell out of favor when Charles-Louis de Cocceji, the son of the king's chancellor, knelt at her feet on the stage and asked her to marry him. She accepted, and the king ordered her dismissed. She went to England, but in 1749 she returned to Germany and became betrothed to Cocceji, whose father considered the liaison a disgrace. The couple tried to flee, but the future husband was imprisoned for eighteen months. They married in secret, and Cocceji, a high government official, was exiled to Glogau (now Głogów), in Silesia. Barberina was forced to sell her palace in Berlin. In 1759 the couple separated; they were divorced in 1788.

Barberina purchased the Silesian castle and estate of Barschau and other properties and proved to be an outstanding administrator. The year after her divorce, in 1789, she requested that King Frederick bestow the title Countess Campanini on her; in return, she offered her castle as a charitable institution for impoverished young noblewomen. The king instead named her Countess von Barschau, and she became director of the foundation. She was given a priceless jeweled coat of arms as her letters patent; decorated with pearls and diamonds, it showed dancing cranes and the motto "Virtuti Asilum" (Haven for Virtue). She died there, but her foundation remained in existence until World War I.

BIBLIOGRAPHY

Dall'Ongaro, Giuseppe. *La Barberina.* Novara, 1987.

Heidrich, Ingeborg. *Wie sie gross wurden.* Stuttgart, 1959.

MacCormack, Gilson B. "La Barberina: A Forgotten 'Star' of the Eighteenth Century." *The Dancing Times* (December 1930):261–265.

Migel, Parmenia. *The Ballerinas: From the Court of Louis XIV to Pavlova.* New York, 1972.

Moore, Lillian. "The Adventures of La Barberina." *Dance Magazine* (December 1958):68–69, 116–117.

Olivier, Jean-Jacques, and Willy Norbert. *La Barberina Campanini.* Paris, 1910.

Winter, Marian Hannah. *The Pre-Romantic Ballet.* London, 1974.

KARL HEINZ TAUBERT

BARIS. The *baris* dance seen today preceding a Balinese *topéng* performance or in the standard repertory of the tourist revue is an embellished, virtuosic twentieth-century derivative of the ritual dance *baris gedé*. The costume elements are the same, though showier. A narrative genre, *baris melampahan*, enacted episodes from the *Mahābhārata* and *Rāmāyaṇa* in which several *baris* dancers could participate, along with a pair of story-tellers, and sometimes such female characters as a princess *(putri)*, and her lady-in-waiting *(condong)*. Just as *légong* allows dancers to use the same costume when representing any of a number of characters, *baris* performers retain uniform costumes. The *baris* dancer does not vocalize, leaving his Kawi (classical Balinese) lines and their interpretation into vernacular Balinese to his storytellers. This narrative dramatic form is rarely seen today.

The dramatic *baris* of contemporary Bali is a solo dance without any narrative element, usually accompanied by the *gamelan gong kebiar* ensemble. Perhaps the most energetic of Balinese dances, it is generally performed by adolescent boys, who engage in a dazzling array of full-circle spins and leaps heightened by the gamelan's sudden cadences *(angsel)*. The gamelan music reflects every nuance

BARIS. The young I Made Basuki Mahardikg in a pose from *baris*, an energetic dance genre traditionally performed by men. (Photograph © 1989 by Linda Vartoogian; used by permission.)

of mood and gesture, from fear and trepidation preceding battle to anger and unbridled power in conflict. The dancer must also convey calm, a sweet and seductive quality out of which emerge sudden bursts of energy. As in *barong* and *jauk*, two umbrellas *(pajeng)* at either side of the curtain are of great import. The *pajeng* signify a mystical and awesome gateway through which the characters must pass in order to get from one world to another. The *baris* dancer postures on one leg and then the other as he regards each umbrella with wonder.

Baris contains many of the essential male movements found in other Balinese dance theater forms. The styles of walking *(pejalan)* positioning of arms and hands *(agem)*, shifting of gaze *(dedeling)*, and quick, darting eye movements *(seledét)* are a few such elements. In the *agem* for *baris*, the position of the legs is mostly open and lowered to a demi-plié, while the elbows are held at shoulder level, higher than the upper arms. The fingers point up and maintain an energetic, trembling motion, called *gegirahan*.

There is an intensely close relationship between dancer and gamelan in overall phrasing and in particular accents from the *kendang* drum. The structure of modern *baris* follows a sequence of *gilak, bapang, gilak* (strong, refined, strong). The musical phrasing maintains eight beats to each gong-phrase, while the *kendang* playing alternates between stick- and hand-drumming.

Although *baris* is a male dance, girls have been known to excel at it. At the modern schools where dance is taught, *baris* is the dance boys first learn, and girls are often given at least rudimentary instruction in it.

[*See also* Asian Dance Traditions, *overview article; and* Indonesia, *article on* Balinese Ceremonial Dance.]

BIBLIOGRAPHY

Bandem, I Madé, and Fredrik Eugene DeBoer. *Balinese Dance in Transition: Kaja and Kelod.* 2d ed. New York, 1995.

Covarrubias, Miguel. *Island of Bali.* New York, 1937.

de Zoete, Beryl, and Walter Spies. *Dance and Drama in Bali* (1938). New ed. New York, 1973.

Dibia, I Wayan. "Arja: A Sung Dance Drama of Bali; A Study of Change and Transformation." Ph.D. diss. University of California, Los Angeles, 1992.

Herbst, Edward. *Voices in Bali: Energies and Perceptions in Vocal Music and Dance Theater.* Hanover and London, 1997.

Hitchcock, Michael, and Lucy Norris. *Bali, the Imaginary Museum: The Photographs of Walter Spies and Beryl de Zoete.* New York, 1995.

Holt, Claire. *Art in Indonesia: Continuities and Change.* Ithaca, N.Y., 1967.

McPhee, Colin. *A House in Bali.* New York, 1946.

McPhee, Colin. *A Club of Small Men.* New York, 1948.

McPhee, Colin. "Children and Music in Bali." In *Childhood in Contemporary Cultures*, edited by Margaret Mead and Martha Wolfenstein. Chicago, 1955.

McPhee, Colin. *Music In Bali.* New Haven and London, 1966.

McPhee, Colin. "Dance in Bali." In *Traditional Balinese Culture*, edited by Jane Belo, pp. 290–321. New York, 1970.

Ornstein, Ruby. "Gamelan Gong Kebjar: The Development of a Balinese Musical Tradition." Ph.D. diss., University of California, Los Angeles, 1971.
Tenzer, Michael. *Balinese Music.* Singapore, 1992.

EDWARD HERBST

BARONG DANCE. *See* Indonesia, *article on* Balinese Mask Dance Theater.

BARONOVA, IRINA (Irina Mikhailovna Baronova; born 28 February 1919 in Petrograd, Russia), dancer and teacher. Baronova's family moved to Bucharest, Romania, in 1920, where Irina studied ballet as a child with Madame Mazhaiskaya, who had been in the corps de ballet at the Maryinsky Theater in Saint Petersburg. As Irina's talent became obvious her family decided to move to Paris in 1928, where she attended the Collège Victor-Hugo and studied dance with Olga Preobrajenska, developing a virtuosic technique. Baronova made her debut in *Orphée aux Enfers,* a *divertissement* choreographed by George Balanchine, at the Théâtre Mogador in 1931 and was chosen by Balanchine to join the newly formed Ballets Russes de Monte Carlo at the end of 1931. At age thirteen when the season opened in April 1932 she was one of the three "baby ballerinas" (along with thirteen-year-old Tamara Toumanova and fourteen-year-old Tatiana Riabouchinska) launched by the company. She remained with it until 1939, dancing a wide variety of leading roles, including Passion in Léonide Massine's *Les Présages* and the Queen of Shemakhan in Michel Fokine's *Le Coq d'Or,* becoming acknowledged as a superb and versatile ballerina of sparkling personality and great charm.

With her husband German (Gerry) Sevastianov (Severn), company director Colonel Wassily de Basil's executive secretary, whom she had married in 1936, Baronova went to Hollywood, where she made the film *Florian* (1939). Sevastianov became Sol Hurok's promotion manager in 1939, and when he transferred to Ballet Theatre as managing director a year later, Baronova joined that company as *prima ballerina.* She danced in 1940 as guest artist with Ballet Russe de Monte Carlo, directed by Sergei Denham, and in 1945 with Massine's company, Ballet Russe Highlights; she also appeared with Original Ballet Russe, directed by de Basil, in New York and Cuba between 1940 and 1941. She made another film, *Yolanda* (1942), and in 1946 appeared onstage in Great Britain in *Dark Eyes* and with Massine in the musical play *A Bullet in the Ballet.*

In 1946, after her marriage to Sevastianov had been dissolved, Baronova married Cecil Tennant and retired from dancing. Like other dancers of her time, she had had wide-ranging ability that enabled her to be equally suc-

BARONOVA. Paul Petroff with Irina Baronova as the Prince and Princess in Bronislava Nijinska's *Les Cent Baisers,* created for the Ballets Russes de Monte Carlo in 1935 and based on a fairy tale by Hans Christian Andersen. (Photograph from the Dance Collection, New York Public Library for the Performing Arts.)

cessful in pure classical roles, such as *The Sleeping Beauty* Aurora or *Swan Lake* Odette; in comedy roles, such as Mariuccia in *Les Femmes de Bonne Humeur* or Boulotte in *Bluebeard;* or in symphonic ballets, such as *Les Présages.* Two of her greatest original roles were the Princess in Bronislava Nijinska's *Les Cent Baisers* (1935) and the Queen of Shemakhan in Fokine's *Le Coq d'Or* (1937).

Baronova lived in England until Tennant's death in 1969, when she moved to Switzerland. In 1976 she resumed teaching master classes in the United States and the United Kingdom, and in 1986 she staged Fokine's *Les Sylphides* for the Australian Ballet. She is a vice president of the Royal Academy of Dancing in London, traveling internationally for the Academy as a lecturer and coach. In 1996 she received a Nijinsky Medal from the Polish Ministry of Culture in Warsaw and an honorary Doctor of Fine Arts degree from the North Carolina School of the Arts.

BIBLIOGRAPHY
Barnes, Clive. "Irina Baronova: Lovely Legend." *Dance Magazine* (July 1961): 40–41.
Davidson, Gladys. *Ballet Biographies.* London, 1954.
Finch, Tamara. "Working with Great Choreographers: Interview with Irina Baronova." *The Dancing Times* (January 1989): 334–337.
García-Márquez, Vicente. *The Ballets Russes: Colonel de Basil's Ballets Russes de Monte Carlo, 1932–1952.* New York, 1990.
Guest, Ivor. "Baronova on the Ballets Russes." *The Dancing Times* (April 1964): 350.

"Irina Baronova Delivers a Talk to the Association of Ballet Clubs." *The Dancing Times* (January 1961): 263.

Sorley Walker, Kathrine. *De Basil's Ballets Russes.* New York, 1983.

Sorley Walker, Kathrine. "Irina Baronova: A Life in Ballet." *Dance Now* 4 (Spring 1995): 9–17.

Stocker, Hilary. "Meet Irina Baronova." *Carnaval*, no. 3 (November–December 1946): 57–59.

KATHRINE SORLEY WALKER

BAROQUE DANCE. *See* Ballet Technique, History of, *article on* French Court Dance. *For historical information on theatrical dance in western Europe, see the theatrical dance articles within individual country entries. For related discussion, see the entries on* Ballet de Cour; Masquerades; Opéra-Ballet *and* Tragédie Lyrique. *For discussion of social dance, see* Social Dance, *article on* Court and Social Dance before 1800. *For discussion of Baroque dance types, see the following entries:* Allemande; Anglaise; Bourée; Canary; Chaconne and Passacaille; Courante; Entrée; Entrée Grave; Folia; Forlana; Gavotte; Gigue; Hornpipe; Loure; Minuet; Musette; Passepied; Rigaudon; Sarabande; *and* Tambourin.

BARRE, JEAN-AUGUSTE (born 25 September 1811 in Paris, died 1896), French sculptor. Barre's chief contribution to dance history was in the form of two bronze statuettes, one of Marie Taglioni and the other of Fanny Elssler, the rival ballerinas of the Romantic period. The major part of Barre's work was devoted to portraiture in busts, statues, statuettes, and medallions. He also treated mythological and historical subjects and made decorative figures, but little of his work has been studied by art historians.

Born into a family of sculptors, Barre began his studies with his father, Jean-Jacques. In 1826 he was admitted to the École des Beaux-Arts in Paris. He produced his first recorded sculpture, *Gymnastics*, at the age of eighteen and began to exhibit his works at the prestigious Paris Salon in 1831. In the 1850s he won favor as a portrait sculptor to the court of Napoleon III; in 1852 he was elected to the Légion d'Honneur.

Barre's portrait statuettes of theatrical personalities were among his most popular works. His statuette of Elssler dancing *La Cachucha* was "the talk of Paris in the winter of 1836" (Guest, 1980), the year in which she created the dance in Jean Coralli's ballet *Le Diable Boiteux*. Elssler's statuette and that of Taglioni as the Sylphide, her most famous role, were exhibited in the Salon of 1837. They are mentioned in a review in the journal *L'artiste*, although neither is listed in the Salon's official *livret*. Both statuettes were drawn by Achille Devéria and subsequently made into lithographs that disseminated Barre's images even more widely.

Barre also executed two lesser-known statuettes of dancers. One was of the Indian dancer Amani, who appeared in Paris in 1838. The other, dating from 1861, portrayed Marie Taglioni's ill-fated protégée Emma Livry (1842–1863), who died tragically young after her dress caught fire during a stage rehearsal at the Paris Opera.

BIBLIOGRAPHY. An essay on Barre's life and work, by Marie Busco and Peter Fusco, may be found in *The Romantics to Rodin: French Nineteenth-Century Sculpture from North American Collections*, an exhibition catalog edited by Peter Fusco and H. W. Janson (Los Angeles, 1980). The exhibition included the Elssler statuette. See also Ivor Guest, *The Romantic Ballet in Paris*, 2d rev. ed. (London, 1980).

SUSAN AU

BARRIERA, TORNEO, AND BATTAGLIA are Italian words, derived from the language of chivalry, that refer to specific kinds of armed confrontation turned into knightly competition in the framework of large-scale festivals. In the sixteenth century, all three terms were used for ballroom dances that mirrored the earlier martial forms.

- A *barriera* or *sbarra* (Fr., *course à la barrière*; Ger., *Stechen*) was a contest on horseback between two knights riding along opposite sides of a barrier, lances at the ready. The object was to unseat one's opponent.
- The *torneo* (also It., *torneamento*; Eng., tournament, tourney; Fr., *tournois*; Ger., *Turnier*) in the Middle Ages was a public contest between armed horsemen in simulation of a real battle. Over time the form expanded to include individual combat on foot and on horseback and culminated in a grand, collective *mêlée*. The heraldic *devise*, which originally identified each participating knight, during the fifteenth century grew into a kind of libretto that explained the dramatic plot underlying the entire splendid affair. After the fatal accident of Henri II of France in a tournament in 1559, the process of stylization increased in pace and the *torneo* became a fully choreographed show of military and equestrian skills *(ballet à cheval)*, including specially composed music and danced interludes. Spectacular theatrical tournaments were especially popular in seventeenth-century Italy, Germany, and Austria (Timms, 1980); their French counterparts, even more stylized and strongly influenced by the court ballet, were the *carroussels* under the Bourbon dynasty. [*See* Horse Ballet.]
- *Battaglia* (Fr., *bataille*; Ger., *Schlacht*) simply means "battle," either in the sense of a serious military confrontation or stylized in the setting of a tournament.

The general preoccupation with such military spectacles led many composers to translate into their own medium the noises of battle—the fanfare signals, the booming of cannons, the cries of victors, and the laments of the defeated. The musical genre of the *bataille* or *la guerre* ("the War"), whose antecedents can be found in some Italian *caccie* ("chases," usually involving a cannon) of the fourteenth century, flourished from the late fifteenth to the eighteenth century (see Brown, 1965, for pieces published before 1600). The genre's most famous early representative is Clément Janequin's four-part *chanson* "La Guerre," written to commemorate the Battle of Marignano of 1515. Published by Pierre Attaingnant in 1528, "La Guerre" influenced many later battle pieces, among them the well-known pavane "La Bataille" printed by Tylman Susato in 1551.

The popularity of the *battaglia* during the sixteenth century is reflected in the dance collections of the period. Battle dances called *barriera*, *torneo*, and *battaglia* are included in Fabritio Caroso's *Il ballarino* (1581) and *Della nobiltà di dame* (1600), in Cesare Negri's *Le gratie d'amore* (1602), as well as in an anonymous manuscript collection now held by the Biblioteca Nazionale Centrale in Florence and dating from the second half of the sixteenth century. Later editions of Caroso (1630) and Negri (1604) also carry the dances.

The original differences between the three genres became irrelevant as they were transformed into choreographies for the ballroom. All became purely social dances, using the steps and patterns common to other *balli* and *balletti* in the collections but choreographed in such a manner as to depict the changing fortunes of warfare, from exploratory skirmishes and challenges, to approaches and withdrawals, to direct frontal attacks in which the clashing of swords was imitated by dancers clapping their partners' hands.

A strong miming element was always present. It was implied in the way steps sequences were built, as in the rapid alternation of slow and fast steps in M. Battistino's *barriera* ("Sciolta Graue della Sonata," in *Il ballarino*), or in the manner in which the body was moved in space—for example, the strong shading on alternate sides in the "Barriera" in *Della nobiltà di dame*, together with the man's cloak gesture that uncovered the sword hilt, a gesture taken directly from fencing. Mime was called for in places where words designating the actions of combat were used: *giostrare* (to joust), *schermire* (to fence, to skirmish), and *passo della picha* (the step of the spear or lance).

Caroso, in both *Il ballarino* and *Della nobiltà di dame* records *barrieras* for two dancers and for six (the "Barriera Nuova," for three couples in a circle); Negri, in *Le gratie d'amore*, demands multiples of two. The "Torneo Amoroso" by M. Battistino recorded in *Il ballarino* and the one in Negri's *Le gratie* are both for two dancers; Negri's splendid "Battaglia" is for four (two couples).

Likewise for four (all men) is Thoinot Arbeau's "Les Bouffons" (in his *Orchésographie*, 1588), a battle dance performed with swords and bucklers that makes use of the motions of hand-to-hand combat more directly than the stylized ballroom combats that come from Italy and does not really belong to the *battaglia/torneo/barriera* group but rather to the moresca family of dances, as indicated by the bells that the dancers wear at their knees and by the subtitle "Les Mattachins." [*See* Matachins.]

Only one of the extant Italian battle dances is for a large group of participants. The anonymous choreographer of the aforementioned Florentine manuscript says that his "La Bataglia Baletto" should be danced by "no less than six persons, but if there be twenty, so much the better." To begin, the men enter from one side of the hall, the ladies from the other. They arrange themselves in two lines, like two squadrons facing one another; at each end are the captains who, throughout the dance, initiate all the actions or figures, followed by the rest of the group doing the same steps as their leaders.

Structurally all the pieces of this group are small suites, changing from an initial 4/4 musical meter to two or more sections in various triple meters. (The exception is Negri's "Battaglia," in which a different sequence of meters is observed.) The melodies, short repeated phrases, move in triads, descending scales, and rapid note repetitions in the manner of trumpet signals and fife tunes. Musically closest to Janequin and Susato is the Florentine "Bataglia," in which not only the playing technique of the instruments of warfare is imitated but also the shift from higher-pitched phrases to an immediate response in a lower register, symbolizing attack and counter-attack as they are simultaneously depicted in the choreographic sequences of the dance.

Not enough work has as yet been done on the signal tunes or on the calls to arms or to retreat that were in use around 1600. Yet the fact that certain melodic formulas recur in all the dances belonging to the *barriera-torneo-battaglia* family of that time leads one to suspect that the composers, rather than copying from one another, had recourse to a standard repertory of military calls familiar to all, musicians, choreographers, and nobles, whether they were out in the field or at home in the ballroom. Until more is known, some intentional puns on combat situations that may be hidden in the battle choreographies will continue to go unrecognized.

[*For related discussion in a broader context, see also* Armed Dances.]

BIBLIOGRAPHY

Brenet, Michel. "Essai sur les origines de la musique descriptive" (parts 1–2) *Rivista Musicale Italiana* 14–15 (1907–1908).

Brown, Alan. "Battaglia." In *The New Grove Dictionary of Music and Musicians*. London, 1980.

Brown, Howard M. *Instrumental Music Printed Before 1600: A Bibliography*. Cambridge, Mass., 1965.

Engel, Hans. "Battaglia." In *Die Musik in Geschichte und Gegenwart*. Kassel, 1949–.

Ghisi, Federico. *Feste musicali della Firenze Medicea, 1480–1589*. Florence, 1939.

Inglehearn, Madeleine. "Swedish Sword Dances in the Sixteenth and Seventeenth Centuries." *Early Music* 14.3 (1986): 367–372.

McGowan, Margaret M. "A Renaissance War Dance: The Pyrrhic." *Dance Research* 3.1 (1984): 29–38.

Reese, Gustave. *Music in the Renaissance.* Rev. ed. New York, 1959.

Squire, William Barclay, et al. "Military Calls." In *The New Grove Dictionary of Music and Musicians.* London, 1980.

Strong, Roy. *Art and Power: Renaissance Festivals, 1450–1650.* London, 1973.

Strong, Roy. *The Cult of Elizabeth: Elizabethan Portraiture and Pageantry.* London, 1977.

Strong, Roy. "Festivals for the Garter Embassy at the Court of Henry III." *Dance Research* 1.2 (1983): 45–58.

Timms, Colin. "Tourney." In *The New Grove Dictionary of Music and Musicians.* London, 1980.

Wellesz, Egon. "The 'Balletto a Cavallo.'" In Wellesz's *Essays on Opera.* Translated by Patricia Kean. London, 1950.

INGRID BRAINARD

BARTENIEFF FUDAMENTALS. *See* Body Therapies, *article on* Bartenieff Fundamentals.

BARTÓK, BÉLA (born 25 March 1881 in Nagyszentmiklós, Hungary; died 26 September 1945 in New York City), Hungarian composer and ethnomusicologist. Bartók studied at the Royal Hungarian Academy of Music in Budapest. He completed his studies in 1903, joining the faculty in 1907 and remaining there until 1934. In 1940 he emigrated to the United States and was appointed research assistant in music at Columbia University in New York, where he continued to pursue his studies of folk materials.

Like composer Zoltán Kodály, Bartók undertook extensive research on Hungarian folk music. In addition to transcribing many original tunes for the piano and other instruments, he utilized folk rhythms and melodies in many of his original compositions. He had an eye for precision and completeness when recording folk phenomena. György Martin quotes him as saying, "An ideal collector of folk music has to be a polymath: he needs some education in choreography to be able to describe the connections between folk music and dances." When collecting dance music, Bartók said,

> it is important to put down the name of the dance and the movements as accurately as possible, the data about time and persons dancing, the musicians, then to note whether they sing when dancing or whether others sing; that is, only the dancers or the audience, or all sing together with the music.

Early in his career Bartók analyzed the folk dances of Transylvania and established their place in the dance cycle, a traditionally evolved, suitelike sequence displaying regional characteristics. He also discovered choreographic types behind the different names given to the same morphological movement sequence in various villages or regions. He established a method for characterizing dances, beginning with a brief description of the spatial formation and then noting the participating sexes, modes of contact between bodies, and step motifs. Bartók also noted the social context in which the dances took place, depicting concomitant phenomena such as the participants' behavior while dancing. In time he explored not only Hungarian but also Ruthenian, Serbo-Croatian, Gypsy, Arabic, and Turkish dances.

Many Hungarian folk dance choreographers have created dances to Bartók's compositions. The first was István Molnár in the 1940s and 1950s; later, choreographers working with both amateur and professional folk dance groups enriched their repertories with dances to Bartók's music. Among them were Lajos Molnár, László Náfrádi, Ferenc Novák, Antal Kricskovics, and Katalin Györgyfalvay.

Although many of Bartók's compositions have been used by ballet choreographers, he wrote only two scores specifically for ballet. Premiered on 12 May 1917 in Budapest, *The Wooden Prince* had a fairy-tale libretto by Béla Balázs that told of a prince who carves a wooden prince to win the admiration of a girl; she in turn falls in love with the doll and only later appreciates its creator. The first choreography, by Otto Zöbisch, was unsuccessful, but later attempts fared better. In 1939 Gyula Harangozó produced the definitive version, using elements of classical, character, and folk dance. Imre Eck did a version full of intensive symbolism in 1965, and László Seregi created a folk tale version in 1970 and a neoclassical one in 1981.

Bartók's *The Miraculous Mandarin* has had a tempestuous history. The melodramatic scenario by Menyhért Lengyel told of three pimps trying to kill a rich Chinese mandarin, who cannot die until the prostitute yields to his desire. After its premiere in Cologne in 1926, with choreography by Hans Strobach, the work was banned on moral grounds. The ballet was performed again on 9 December 1945, using Gyula Harangozó's choreography of 1941. A new version by Harangozó was premiered on 1 June 1956 by the Budapest Opera Ballet. Other Hungarian productions were staged by Seregi, Eck, and Iván Markó. Among the more than one hundred versions, the one most often seen in western Europe is that of Hungarian-born Aurelio Milloss, who staged it in Milan in 1942 and thereafter reproduced it for other companies in Europe and South America. To celebrate the seventieth anniversary of its premiere, a two-part "Festival of Mandarins" was organized in Budapest by the EuroDance Foundation (part one held in 1996, part two scheduled for 1997).

Many choreographers have used Bartók's concert works. In addition to the Hungarians already noted, they include Maurice Béjart, Birgit Cullberg, Peter Darrell, Eliot Feld, Kenneth MacMillan, Herbert Ross, and Hans van Manen.

BIBLIOGRAPHY
Bartók, Béla. *The Stage Works of Béla Bartók.* London, 1991.
Bartók, Béla, and Lengyel Menyhért. *A csodálatos mandarin.* Preface by Béla Bartók, Jr. and a study by Fernec Bónis. Budapest, 1993.
Körtvélyes, Géza. "Béla Bartók and the Hungarian Ballet." *Hungarian Dance News,* no. 1–2 (1981): 1–3.
Martin, György. "Bartók, Kodály, and Folk Dance Research." *Hungarian Dance News,* no. 1–2 (1983): 4–5.
Stevens, Halsey. *The Life and Music of Béla Bartók.* Rev. ed. New York, 1964.

GEDEON P. DIENES and GÉZA KÖRTVÉLYES

BARYSHNIKOV, MIKHAIL (Mikhail Nikolaevich Baryshnikov; born 27 January 1948 in Riga, Latvia), Russian-American dancer and company director. In 1966, the international dance world became aware of a singular, superlative male dancer in the Soviet Union. Upon winning first-class distinction in the junior category at the International Ballet Competition in Varna, Bulgaria, the youthful Mikhail Baryshnikov was commended as being "graceful and exceptionally mature in his technique." In 1967, the year he made his debut with Leningrad's Kirov Ballet (in the peasant pas de deux from *Giselle*), Baryshnikov attracted further attention in the West through publication in the United States of a diary of a Russian trip made by dance critic Clive Barnes. Having observed Baryshnikov in the legendary men's class taught by Aleksandr Pushkin at the Leningrad Choreographic Institute, Barnes described him as "the most perfect dancer I have ever seen."

Baryshnikov had begun his studies at about age twelve, in 1960, at the ballet school and conservatory of music attached to the opera house in his hometown of Riga. In 1964 he entered the Agrippina Vaganova Leningrad Choreographic Institute, one of the principal centers of training for professional ballet dancers in the Soviet Union. His short stature, clear, full musculature, and boyish features gave evidence that he would become a *demi-caractère* dancer, yet his exceptional technical prowess and unwavering control gave strong promise of the elegance and serenity that mark the *danseur noble.* According to Gennady Smakov (1981), Baryshnikov thus presented a peculiar problem to the Soviet system of categorizing dancers by physical type and assigning them to a set repertory of roles.

In his first years with the Kirov Ballet, Baryshnikov danced a number of featured roles, including the Bluebird in *The Sleeping Beauty* and the Youth in *Chopiniana,* as well as pas de deux from *Don Quixote* and *Le Corsaire.* His technical mastery and facility for interpretation soon made him a favorite of Soviet choreographers. Oleg Vinogradov, Konstantin Sergeyev, Igor Tchernichov, and Leonid Yakobson each created roles for him. In 1969, Yakobson made an extraordinary solo for him based on the artistry of the eighteenth-century virtuoso Auguste

BARYSHNIKOV. As a star of American Ballet Theatre during the late 1970s, Baryshnikov danced a leading role in George Balanchine's *Theme and Variations.* (Photograph © 1978 by Jack Vartoogian; used by permission. Choreography by George Balanchine © The George Balanchine Trust.)

Vestris. Created to fulfill the requirement for a work of contemporary choreography at the International Ballet Competition in Moscow (where Baryshnikov won the gold medal in the senior category), *Vestris* became for a time the dancer's signature work. He performed it during the Kirov's 1970 London season and on several special programs during his early years in the West.

In 1971 Baryshnikov created the role of Adam in *The Creation of the World,* a comic ballet mounted for the Kirov Ballet by Natalia Kasatkina and Vladimir Vasiliov. In this cartoonlike work, Baryshnikov had the chance to exercise his spectacular acrobatic abilities and to give free reign to his comic gifts. Dance historian and critic Vera Krasovskaya viewed the portrayal as a landmark in his career, coining the phrase "before Adam" to identify the years before his maturity as an artist. It was, however, his 1972 debut as Albrecht in *Giselle* that Baryshnikov himself sees as his turning point. His interpretation went against consistent Russian tradition, for he portrayed Albrecht as a warmblooded youth, a prince sincerely in love

BARYSHNIKOV. During the 1990s, Baryshnikov performed with the White Oak Dance Project. Here, in a revival of Merce Cunningham's *Signals* are (left to right) Nancy Colon, John Gardiner, Kate Johnson, Baryshnikov, and Rob Besserer. (Photograph © 1994 by Jack Vartoogian; used by permission.)

with his peasant sweetheart, rather than as the cool, unshakeable aristocrat to which Russian audiences were accustomed.

In the summer of 1974, Baryshnikov was on tour in Canada with a small group of Soviet dancers billed as Stars of the Bolshoi. On 29 June, in Toronto, he left the group and sought political asylum, following in the famous footsteps of Rudolf Nureyev and Natalia Makarova, dancers who had earlier defected from the Soviet Union in search of artistic freedom. On 27 July Baryshnikov made his debut with American Ballet Theatre in New York, dancing Albrecht to Makarova's Giselle. He spent the next four years dancing primarily, although not exclusively, with American Ballet Theatre. He danced numerous roles, almost all new to his repertory, with various works created especially for him. Twyla Tharp's *Push Comes to Shove* (1976), with its modern-dance-meets-ballet emphases was the high point of these premieres: "Nothing was as new, as different, and thank God, as inevitable as *Push Comes to Shove*" is how he described the experience in his book, *Baryshnikov at Work* (1976).

In addition to performing, Baryshnikov also undertook to stage two major, full-length productions for the company: *The Nutcracker* in 1977 and *Don Quixote* in 1978. He frequently danced the leading male roles in both these works, most often as partner to Gelsey Kirkland. His choreography for *The Nutcracker* was largely original, while his staging of *Don Quixote* relied heavily on the production by Aleksandr Gorsky that he had danced in Leningrad with the Kirov Ballet. [*See* Don Quixote, *article on* Other Productions.]

In 1978 Baryshnikov announced that he would leave American Ballet Theatre to join the New York City Ballet, giving as his reason his wish to work with George Balanchine. He made his New York City Ballet debut as Franz in *Coppélia* during the company's summer season in Saratoga Springs, in upstate New York. He remained with the company only about a year, leaving in October 1979. Although he danced numerous new roles, his hopes for creative work with Balanchine failed to materialize because of the ballet master's poor health. Jerome Robbins did use Baryshnikov in two new ballets, *The Seasons* and *Opus 19*, but neither work did more than show off the dancer as he was already known. The bulk of his repertory consisted of roles created for or identified with Edward Villella, such as the title role in *The Prodigal Son*. All his roles with the New York City Ballet were challenging and all his performances in them were distinguished, but he did not perform any role long enough to make it something of his own.

In September 1980 Baryshnikov returned to American Ballet Theatre in a dual post: as a principal dancer and as artistic director of the company. The demands on him in both these positions were to grow increasingly heavy. As a dancer, he continued to enjoy great success, despite the physical effects of a knee operation in 1982. In the spring of 1983, Twyla Tharp created a new work for him, originally called *Once Upon a Time* but later retitled as *The Little Ballet*. It showed a different Baryshnikov, the dancer of the 1980s, after *Push Comes to Shove*, and after knee surgery. He projected a dreamy quality, spiraling through ornate turns rather than hurtling through vaulting jumps. The mood was melancholy, yet mischievous; the tone finespun, yet awesomely powerful. Because of his knee trouble, his extraordinary elevation had diminished somewhat, but his intensity and clarity of movement had, if anything, increased. As a model of classical male technique, Baryshnikov remained peerless. Before him, the combined cleanliness, size, and consistency of his dancing had been unknown.

As artistic director of American Ballet Theatre, Baryshnikov faced daunting tasks. His expressed aims, to upgrade the level of ensemble dancing and to make the company independent of guest stars, were progressive but were not, in the end, entirely successful. His repertory acquisitions stressed ensemble dancing in works by master choreographers, and his treatment of familiar nineteenth-century ballets was mostly in the twentieth-century traditions of the Kirov Ballet. He staged *Giselle* for the company in 1980, as well as parts of *Raymonda* and *The Sleeping Beauty*, all with choreography more or less "after Marius Petipa." In 1983, he mounted a new production of *Cinderella*, with Peter Anastos as co-choreographer, and in 1988 he staged a complete *Swan Lake*, again billed as "after Petipa." Neither of these works was, however, a success, and each was withdrawn from the repertory after a limited number of performances. Otherwise, Baryshnikov maintained the artistic level of American Ballet Theatre by stressing cleanliness of classical technique at all levels of performance, by promoting more youthful casting in the repertory, and by introducing works by innovative choreographers such as Choo San Goh, John McFall, David Gordon, and Mark Morris. He resigned his position in 1989, having headed the company for almost a decade. [*See* American Ballet Theatre.]

Thereafter, Baryshnikov appeared on Broadway as an actor in Steven Berkoff's play based on Franz Kafka's *Metamorphosis*, the chilling tale of a man who awakes to find himself changed into a cockroach. He also continued to perform as a dancer, but he discontinued his tours with "Baryshnikov & Co.," a group who performed a concert program of ballets, in favor of working with practitioners of modern dance. In 1990 he became head of the White Oak Dance Project, a group of mature modern and ballet dancers that performed exclusively the works of choreographer Mark Morris. Eventually, the repertory of the troupe was extended to include the works of other modernists, including not only established figures such as Martha Graham, Merce Cunningham, Lar Lubovitch, David Gordon, and Paul Taylor but also such younger experimentalists as Dana Reitz.

During the early 1990s, Baryshnikov made isolated appearances as a guest artist on programs of the Martha Graham Dance Company, Feld Ballets/NY, New York City Ballet, and the Erick Hawkins Dance Company. In 1992, he was featured, alongside Twyla Tharp, in *Cutting Up*, a showcase program choreographed by Tharp, and in 1996, under the aegis of the White Oak Project, he toured a shared program of solo dances with Dana Reitz. His current interests seem to coincide with those of the postmodernist school.

BIBLIOGRAPHY

Alovert, Nina. *Baryshnikov in Russia*. Translated by Irene Huntoon. New York, 1984.

Aria, Barbara. *Misha: The Mikhail Baryshnikov Story*. New York, 1989.

Baryshnikov, Mikhail. *Baryshnikov at Work*. New York, 1976.

Croce, Arlene. "Baryshnikov among Sylphs." *New Yorker* (20 June 1983).

Croce, Arlene. "The Mysterious Baryshnikov." In Croce's *Sight Lines*. New York, 1987.

Garis, Robert. "Some Baryshnikov Questions." *Ballet Review* 10 (Summer 1982): 7–13.

Goldner, Nancy. "Who Cares about Choreography When You Can Jump Like Baryshnikov?" *Village Voice* (12 July 1976).

Kirkland, Gelsey, with Greg Lawrence. *Dancing on My Grave: An Autobiography*. New York, 1986.

Maynard, Olga. "Baryshnikov Talks to Olga Maynard." *Dance Magazine* (October 1974): 58–65.

Polanski, Roman. "Interview with Mikhail Baryshnikov." *Paris Vogue* (December 1986–January 1987).

Shearer, Sybil. "About Baryshnikov." *Ballet Review* 14 (Summer 1986): 72–74.

Smakov, Gennady. *Baryshnikov: From Russia to the West*. New York, 1981.

FILM AND VIDEOTAPE.   Baryshnikov appeared in five Hollywood films: *The Turning Point* (1977), *White Nights* (1985), and *Dancers* (1987), all directed by Herbert Ross; *Company Business* (1990); and *The Cabinet of Dr. Ramirez* (1991), directed by Peter Sellers. From 1976 onward, he appeared in numerous television specials on the Public Broadcasting Service, including *Baryshnikov at the White House* (1979), and he starred in two network specials: *Baryshnikov on Broadway* (ABC Television, 1980) and *Baryshnikov in Hollywood* (CBS Television, 1982).

ROBERT GRESKOVIC

BASEL BALLET. Located on the River Rhine, at the juncture of Switzerland, Germany, and France, the Swiss city of Basel (formerly Basle) is the capital of the canton of Basel as well as of the demicanton of Basel-Stadt. The Basler Stadttheater (Basel Municipal Theater) is the home base for an ensemble of performing groups that, since the early nineteenth century, has regularly presented seasons of opera, operetta, and drama, as well as, periodically, dance. Over the years, the significance of ballet in the program of arts offered to Basel audiences has fluctuated, depending on whether or not a competent ballet director has been in residence.

The first Municipal Theater was opened in Basel in 1834, but programs from the first hundred years indicate that dance was only occasionally performed on its stage. The generic term *ballet* was used to describe several productions mounted during the theater's first ten years, and a dance scene from *La Sylphide* was apparently performed in 1842. For decades thereafter, only such descriptions as "comedy with dance" indicate that dance did not disappear completely from the Basel municipal stage. Records show some periods with fairly frequent references to dance and other periods (for example, around

BASEL BALLET. Cathy Sharp and Chris Jensen in Heinz Spoerli's *Wir Warren—Liebeslied aus einer Schlechten Zeit* (1977). Sharp and Jensen, both Americans, made their careers in Switzerland. (Photograph © by Peter Schnetz; used by permission.)

1900) in which practically no such references can be found.

Performances by guest artists and companies from other cities, which had been a feature of programming since the opening of the theater, became common in the early decades of the twentieth century, when German interpretive dance *(Ausdruckstanz)* flourished. In the late 1920s, this style of expressive dance determined the Municipal Theater's own productions, which were choreographed by the Austrian dancer Rosalia Chladek. During the 1930s and early 1940s, performances of dance on the Basel municipal stage were only sporadic. After World War II, Heinz Rosen, a German dancer and choreographer, became ballet master at Basel, but his work was unremarkable. Not until the mid-1950s would a municipal ballet company be formed with an artist of exceptional talent at its head.

That artist was Vaslav Orlikovsky, a Russian dancer and choreographer, who assumed the post of ballet master in Basel in 1955. Under his direction, the Basler Ballett (Basel Ballet) enjoyed its first success. Orlikovsky opened his first season in Basel with a production of *Swan Lake* that brought the company recognition well beyond its regional boundaries. Hiring dancers from all over Europe, Orlikovsky assembled a large troupe whose quality far exceeded that of the ensemble at most other municipal theaters. With a strong company to call upon, he built his repertory around full-length works, including classics such as *The Sleeping Beauty, The Nutcracker,* and *Giselle* and Soviet favorites such as *The Stone Flower* (1962) and *The Fountain of Bakhchisarai* (1965). He also mounted a notable production of *Abraxas,* one of the most successful ballets of postwar Germany, and created two remarkable works in *Peer Gynt* (1956) and *The Prince of the Pagodas* (1961). His *Peer Gynt,* a ballet in three acts and ten scenes, based on a libretto by Eugen Wigeliew and set to Edvard Grieg's familiar music, was one of the Basel Ballet's earliest successes. Other productions were also acclaimed, and the company was invited to perform its *Swan Lake* and *The Nutcracker* at the Berlin Festival in 1960.

After Orlikovsky's departure in 1967, the Basel Ballet slipped into decline. Pavel Šmok, appointed ballet master in 1970, had ambitious plans for the company but was unable to arouse it from its somnolent state. It awoke with a start, however, when Heinz Spoerli arrived in 1973 and began work as resident choreographer of the company. A Basler by birth and training, Spoerli had had his first experience as a performer with the company in 1960, under Orlikovsky's direction. He had thereafter performed in a wide variety of neoclassical and modern works with companies in Cologne, Winnipeg, Montreal, and Geneva, and he had a burning desire to turn the Basel Ballet into one of the leading companies in Europe.

In short order, Spoerli rejuvenated the Basel Ballet's roster of dancers, bringing in a number of youngsters trained in the United States and Canada, and he began to rebuild the company's repertory around innovative productions of the classics and his own strikingly original works. With remarkable speed, he turned the company of some thirty-five dancers into a technically proficient troupe whose performances were characterized by consistently high quality and by an exuberant liveliness and joy in movement. After 1977, Spoerli was strongly supported in his efforts by the pedagogically and stylistically skilled work of his ballet master, Peter Appel.

Among Spoerli's early works for the Basel Ballet were *The Firebird* (1973), featuring Teresa Bacall; *Petrouchka* (1974), featuring Sheldon Schwartz; and *Flowing Landscapes* (1975), a work set to the music of Charles Ives and featuring Cathy Sharp and Mohammed Bahiri. In January 1976, *A Midsummer Night's Dream,* with Ruth Weber and Jean-Luc Chirpaz in the roles of Titania and Oberon, was Spoerli's first full-length work mounted for the company. The following September, his production of *Giselle,* based on a reexamination of the original score, was a solid hit, featuring guest artists Gaye Fulton and Jonas Kåge in the principal roles and Ruth Weber as Myrtha, Queen of the Wilis. Notable among Spoerli's many original works were two that he produced in 1977: *Opus 35,* set to music by Dmitri Shostakovich, and *Wir Waren—Liebeslied aus Einer Schlechten Zeit,* set to music by André Bauer and a text by Bertolt Brecht. These works were followed in quick succession by *Romeo and Juliet* (1977), *Ondine* (1978), *Catulli Carmina* (1979), and *The Nutcracker* (1979), along with numerous shorter ballets. Principal dancers in these and other works included Ruth Weber, Chris Jensen, Cathy Sharp, Sheldon Schwartz, Norma Batchelor, Shauna Wagner, Otto Ris, Linda di Bona, and Rudy Bryans.

The 1980s were a decade of unparalleled activity for the Basel Ballet, as Spoerli, now officially recognized as ballet director, continued to produce new works and to mount new productions for each new season. Among the highlights of the early 1980s were *Pulcinella* (1980), featuring Sheldon Schwartz and Amanda Bennett; *Till Eulenspiegel* (1980), featuring the remarkable Swiss dancer Martin Schläpfer; *Verklärte Nacht* (1982), with Sylviane Bayard and Philippe Anota; and *Orpheus und Eurydike* (1983), with Chris Jensen and Sylviane Bayard in the title roles. These were followed by *Coppélia* (1984), *John Falstaff* (1984), *Die Nacht aus Blei* (1985), a new version of *A Midsummer Night's Dream* (1985), *Broadway Show* (1986), *Swan Lake* (1986), *The Miraculous Mandarin* (1987), *La*

BASEL BALLET. Members of the ensemble in *Coppélia* (1984). Spoerli set his version of *Coppélia* in a German university town at the end of the nineteenth century; act 3 features a student ball celebrating the end of the semester. (Photograph © by Gundel Kilian; used by permission.)

Belle Vie (1987), *Orpheus* (1988), *Don Quixote* (1989), and *Les Noces* (1990). Among the principal dancers in these works were Catherine Zerara, Sophie Marquet, Victoria Mazzarelli, Gilma Bustillo, Sandy Delasalle, Chris Jensen, Serge Lavoie, Martin Schläpfer, and Charles Maple.

Under Spoerli's direction, the Basel Ballet achieved international recognition. Although his own works dominated the repertory, he took pains to bring in works by other contemporary choreographers, including Richard Kuch, Richard Gain, Riccardo Duse, Christopher Bruce, William Forsythe, Hans van Manen, and John Cranko. The Basel Ballet made its first overseas appearance in the spring of 1983 in New York, where it returned for a second season in 1988. Having appeared in numerous television productions in Switzerland and Germany, it became widely known in Europe, and it scored a spectacular success during a tour of China in 1986. Following his vision, Spoerli had created a company of rare abilities, able to dance a serious classic such as *Swan Lake,* to put modern tension into a work such as *Orpheus,* and to be equally competent in a vivacious work such as *La Fille Mal Gardée.* His departure in the summer of 1991 marked the end of the most meaningful era of dance in the history of the Basel Municipal Theater. [*See the entry on Spoerli.*]

Spoerli's successor, Youri Vámos, took on the difficult task of having to live up to an illustriously rich heritage. But he won the Basel audience from the very beginning. He is one of those rare choreographers who, through his dance language, is able to tell stories in a clear, vivid, and understandable way. He showed traditional ballets in new versions and created several new story ballets of his own. In 1996, however, Vámos left Basel in the wake of a deci-

sion by the theater management to disband the ballet company. The Basel Ballet, a fine company laboriously and creatively built up over decades, was simply given up, its rich and valuable possibilities nullified. In its place was a group working in the easy, commonplace style of the 1990s, *Tanztheater*, directed by Joachim Schlömer. Despite disappointment by Basel balletomanes at losing their local company, Schlömer's first production, *Neuschnee in Troja* (New Snow in Troy; 1996) was a big success with both audiences and critics.

BIBLIOGRAPHY

Basler Ballett. Basel, 1980.
Como, William. "Big Times for Basel." *Dance Magazine* (February 1989): 40–45.
Eckert, Heinz. *Heinz Spoerlis Basler Ballett.* Basel, 1991.
Enkelmann, Siegfried. *Ballett in Basel.* Basel, 1962.
Merz, Richard. "Vorgeschobene Argumente." *Süddeutsche Zeitung* (16 February 1996).
Pastori, Jean-Pierre. "The Emancipation of Dance in the Municipal Theatres." *Ballett International* 10 (June 1987): 12–18.
Pastori, Jean-Pierre. *Dance and Ballet in Switzerland.* Translated by Jacqueline Gartmann. 2d ed., rev. and enl. Zurich, 1989.
Sikes, Richard, ed. *Heinz Spoerli und das Basler Ballett.* Basel, 1985.
Vollmer, Horst. "Direktorenkarussell." *Tanz und Gymnastik* 51.3 (1995): 42–46.
Weiss, Fritz. *Das Basler Stadttheater, 1834–1934.* Basel, 1934.

RICHARD MERZ
Translated from German
Amended by Claude Conyers

BASQUE DANCE. The seven Basque provinces fall within the political confines of north-central Spain (Vizcaya, Guipúzcoa, Alava, and Navarra) and southwest France (Basse-Navarre, Soule, and Labourd). Basque is a non–Indo-European language. Basques have their own distinct society and culture. Music, dance, and popular poetry are of great importance, as are certain characteristic sports. There are many types of dances: ceremonial (both secular and religious, performed by men), social (line dances for men and couple dances), and spectacular dances involving a great show of strength and agility, often encompassing both ritual and audience-oriented forms. Many newer, often balletic, dances have been choreographed for men and/or women in recent decades.

References to Basque dance date from Roman times, but the first major study is J. I. de Iztueta's *Guipúzkoa'ko dantzak* (Dances of Guipúzcoa), written in 1826, which includes detailed descriptions of many Guipúzcoan dances and some of the social and aesthetic values behind them. Iztueta also transcribed the music for many of the dances, and his work is still used by scholars and choreographers.

Basque dances vary greatly by region, type, and purpose, but in all of them footwork is of primary importance. The men's dances include high kicks and turns in the air. The arms are used for balance, and implements are often carried and used to shape the movement. There is little emphasis on movement of the torso and head. Line and circle dances usually move to the right, and dances in formation (for eight, twelve, or sixteen dancers) are often performed so that the group moves to face each of four directions, ending in the starting position.

Costumes used today are usually relatively new, and by Iberian standards they are not particularly elaborate. They do, however, incorporate elements that emphasize movement: bells, ribbons that fly out, mirrors, and feathers. Most of the women's costumes are of recent origin or are reconstructions from old photographs, descriptions, or paintings.

The Biscay (Bizkaya) region offers the "Dantzari Dantza" (Dancer's Dance) of the Durango area, a suite of dances for eight men that includes stick and sword dances, followed by a chain dance into which women are incorporated, and ending with a *jota,* danced by couples in a circle. The coastal town of Lequeitio presents the Kaxarranka, in which the town documents are brought in procession to the house of the new mayor, while a single dancer dances atop the chest *(kaxa)* in which they are carried. There is also a recently reconstructed chain dance led by women, into which men are incorporated. "San Miguel de Arretxinaga," a sword dance representing the battle between good and evil, is performed in Jemein. At the end the swords are woven into a mesh on which the statue of Saint Michael is lifted.

The Guipúzcoan dances of the Goyere region form an *ezpata-dantza* (sword dance) suite. Most use some sort of implements (sticks, swords, arches, hoes, or shields) to shape the movement. The first section of the dance, *zortziko,* in 5/8 time, features fancy steps and figure changes. This is followed by the *deia* (a transition) and the quick *joko* ("play," in 6/8 or 2/4 time), in which the implements are used, still with figure changes but with less elaborate steps. In the town of Oñate, the dances in honor of Corpus Christi use somewhat similar steps and paraphernalia, but they also include castanets—not common in the Basque region. The town of Zumárraga has a type of multisectioned dance performed partially inside the church. It includes a simple long-sword dance, a short-sword dance done before the altar, and a chain dance and *jota* performed outside the church.

Both the Vizcayan and Guipúzcoan dances are usually accompanied by the *txistu,* a three-holed vertical flute, and the *damboril,* a tabor-style drum, and both instruments are played simultaneously by the same musician. Often the first *txistu* is joined by a second (usually without drum), a *silbote* (a larger *txistu*), and a snare drum.

Most of the dances from northern Alava are of recent origin or are reconstructions for couples or women. From the southern Rioja area come processional dances, stick

BASQUE DANCE. Dancers and musicians of the Basque folkloric troupe Euzkadi!. The man on the left simultaneously plays the *txistu*, a vertical, three-holed flute, and the *damboril*, a tabor-style drum. (Photograph from the Dance Collection, New York Public Library for the Performing Arts.)

dances (especially from Villabuena), and the set dances of El Ciego, at present performed by eight young women. Many Rioja dances include a clown figure. Rioja has its own version of the *jota*.

The province of Navarre has a great variety of dances. There are stick dances in Ochagavía, Cortes, and Vera de Bidasoa, and sticks are used as long-swords in Lesaca. Leiza offers a chain-dance suite, and Estella has a suite of dances for couples. The Baztan Valley has a rich assortment of *mutil-dantzak* (men's dances) done in lines without handholds or implements. The dances in Alava and Navarre use accompaniment by *txistu, txistu* group, or *gaita navarra* (a shawm-like reed instrument) in the Rioja, Ochagavía, and Estella regions.

The northernmost part of Navarre, included in the Basse-Navarre dance zone, is famous for the *jautziak* ("jumps"), line dances for men that are sometimes called and are made up of about eighteen different steps. These dances form an important part of Carnival celebrations, especially in the Valcarlos–Arneguy area. They are usually accompanied by a brass band.

Soule is considered by many the model area for Basque dancing. The region's *jautzi* dances, similar in structure to those of Basse-Navarre, are accompanied by the *txirula*, a short three-holed flute, and the *soñu*, a stringed drum. *Maskaradak* ("carnivals") in Soule include many types of dances, such as the very elaborate and balletic men's spectacular dancing with high jumps, turns in the air, and multiple *entrechats*, culminating in a *godaleta*, in which

the five main characters dance around and finally jump onto a glass filled with wine. The stock characters of the *maskaradak* are a Betty (a male dancer dressed as a woman), a Flagbearer, a "Cat Man," a Sweeper, and a Hobby-Horse. The Souletine *pastorale*, a form of outdoor popular theater dating from medieval mystery and morality plays, also includes dancing, most notably the "Satan-Dantza" (Devil's Dance), similar to the dance for the *maskaradak*.

In Labourd, little survives of the old tradition. Records indicate Carnival celebrations, quadrilles, and *sauts* ("jumps") not unlike those of Soule and Basse-Navarre. Immigrants to Labourd from the Biscay area brought many dances during and after the Spanish Civil War.

The Basque *jota*, consisting of a *fandango* in 3/8 time and an *ariñ-ariñ* in 2/4 time, is probably not of Basque origin but is widespread and extremely popular. It is still performed in all the Basque provinces in a social context and is included in most staged performances of Basque dance. It is also at the end of many suites of Basque dances, although scholars believe that it was added relatively recently. The *jota* is most often performed by couples, and the urban areas often sponsor *jota* contests, especially for younger dancers.

There are concentrations of Basques in the United States, especially in Boise, Idaho; Reno, Nevada; and San Francisco, Los Banos, Fresno, Bakersfield, and Chino, California. The *jota* is popular with all Basque groups, but much of the repertory varies according to the groups' origins and ties to Europe. The Vizcayan-oriented groups do many Durango-area dances, while the Basse-Navarrese perform *jautzi*s. Most groups include some version of the Souletine *maskaradak* and the *jota*. Accompaniment is usually by accordion or *txistu,* and dances are performed in a social context or for audience viewing. Ceremonial use of the dances is infrequent.

BIBLIOGRAPHY

Alford, Violet. "The Basque Masquerade." *Folklore* 39 (1928): 68–90.

Alford, Violet. "The Farandole." *English Folk Dance and Song Society* 1.1 (1932): 18–33.

Arrarás Soto, Francisco. "Danzas de Navarra." *Cuadernos de Etnología y Etnografía de Navarra* 8 (1971): 171–219.

Barandiarán, Gaizka. *Danzas de Euskalerri.* 3 vols. San Sebastian, 1963–1969.

Barandiarán, Gaizka. "Basque Music." In *The New Grove Dictionary of Music and Musicians.* London, 1980.

Dantzariak. San Sebastian, 1969–. Journal of the Euskal Dantzarien Biltzarra.

Dassance, L. "Les Sauts Basques et les vieilles danses labourdines." *Bulletin du Musée Basque* 3 (1926): 21–30.

de Alaiza, Candi. "Santa Grazi Pastorala." Ph.D. diss., University of California, Los Angeles, 1978.

de Alaiza, Candi. "The Ingurutxo Leiza." *Viltis* 35.2 (1976): 8–11.

de Alaiza, Candi. "The Evolution of the Basque *Jota* as a Competitive Form." In *A Spectrum of World Dance,* edited by Lynn Ager Wallen and Joan Acocella. New York, 1987.

Etxebaría y Goiri, J. L. de. *Danzas de Vizcaya.* Bilbao, 1969.

Gallop, Rodney. *A Book of the Basques.* London, 1930.

Hérelle, Georges. *La représentation des pastorales à sujets tragiques.* Paris, 1923.

Hérelle, Georges. *Études sur le théâtre basque: Le théâtre comique.* Paris, 1925.

Iztueta, Juan Ignacio de. *Danzas de Guipúzcoa* (1824). Edited by Santiago Onandía. Bilbao, 1968.

Jiménez, Joaquín. "Danzas en Alava." *Dantzariak* 3 (1972): 3–12.

Sagaseta, Miguel Angel. *La danzas de Valcarlos.* Pamplona, 1977.

Urbeltz Navarro, Juan Antonio. *Dantzak.* Bilbao, 1978.

CANDI DE ALAIZA

BASSEDANSE. The *bassedanse* (Fr., "low dance"; It., *bassadanza;* Sp., *baixa danza;* Ger., *Schreittanz, Hoftanz*), an elegant stepping dance fashionable in central Europe from the fourteenth to the second half of the sixteenth century. The name appears as early as 1340 in the *Cansos e bassas dansas* by the troubadour Raimond de Cornet. At the height of its popularity, in the mid-fifteenth century, two types of "low dance" can be distinguished: the processional *bassedanse* of Burgundy and the choreographically more intricate Italian *bassadanza.*

Burgundy. The main source for the classical Burgundian *bassedanse* is a manuscript now in the Brussels Bibliothèque Royale. It is a calligraphic masterpiece on black paper with gold and silver writing produced in the scribal workshops of the dukes of Burgundy late in the fifteenth century and containing a retrospective repertory of fifty-nine dances, with music, spanning several decades. Closely related is the manual *L'art et instruction de bien dancer,* printed in Paris by Michel Toulouze around 1488. Robert Coplande's brief treatise of 1521, *The maner of dauncyinge of bace daunces after the vse of fraunce and other places, translated out of frenche in englysshe,* is of the same lineage but does not transmit music. Also without music are the manuals by Antonius de Arena (1528) and Jacques Moderne (c. 1540) and the numerous collections of *bassedanse* choreographies from the period.

All instruction books consist of a theoretical introduction and a practical section comprising the choreographies. The introductions contain descriptions of steps as well as general rules regarding dance style, in which lightness and grace, calm simplicity of motion *(sans soy demener),* and the smallness of the steps are stressed. Prescribed for each step is the gentle rise and fall of the dancer's body that is the equivalent of the *ondeggiare* ("undulation") of contemporary Italian dance. The system of *mesures* is also explained. A *mesure* is a dance phrase composed of a variable number of steps; it must begin with a pair of single steps and end with the *branle,* a swaying sideways motion. Depending on their internal structure, the *mesures* can be *grandes, moyennes, petites, parfaites, plus que parfaites,* or *imparfaites* (see Heartz, 1958–1963, p. 301).

The introductions also deal briefly with the structural distinction between *basse danse maieur* and *basse danse mineur.* The former is the straightforward *bassedanse;* the latter is a bipartite form that begins with a lightly jumped opening passage called *pas de breban* (It., *passo brabante, saltarello,* or *alta danza*) followed by the *bassedanse* itself.

The introductions explain the letters of the step tablature used in the choreographies. All *bassedanse* manuals stress that the duration of each step is the equivalent of one musical note (the blackened breve of the tenor melody), with the exception of the single steps *(pas simples),* two of which equal one note.

The notated choreographies show a distinct tendency toward regularity of structure, which is achieved by an orderly succession of *mesures* of varying length. Within the confines of this system, merely by the carefully planned arrangement of the step sequences, the anonymous choreographers created *bassesdanses* that are expressive, emotional, tender, and of extraordinary beauty. Floor patterns are rarely given; *bassesdanses* are normally danced processionally, couple behind couple (occasionally in groups of three), with partners holding hands. All step with the same foot.

Bassesdanses of the classical Burgundian type were danced in England, France, Germany, Austria, Spain, and Portugal. In Spain a notation developed in which the let-

BASSEDANSE. A miniature from *Histoire de Renaud de Montauban* depicting a processional dance at the court of King Yon of Gascony before the marriage of his daughter Clarissa with Renaud. (Bibliothèque de l'Arsenal, Paris.)

ters of the Burgundian step tablature were replaced by linear symbols (see Brainard, 1981); abbreviations of step names and verbal descriptions in the Italian manner are also given.

Bassesdanses were social dances par excellence, designed to accommodate an unlimited number of participants. They were originally performed by the nobility and gentry at balls, banquets, and other festive occasions. Toward the end of the fifteenth century they became part of the repertory of the urban upper classes as well.

The musical accompaniment was provided by the court or town band, which usually consisted of two shawms and a sackbut. The alto shawm played the even notes of the tenor melody while the other two instruments improvised above and below that tenor. For more intimate occasions the soft instruments, such as recorder, harp, and *vielle*, were used.

Thoinot Arbeau, in *Orchésographie* (1588), gives choreographies for four *bassesdanses* in letter tablature and music for one. By this time, however, these dances bore only a remote resemblance to their Burgundian ancestors. The step speed had slowed from the one-note value of the fifteenth century to a four-measure phrase *(quaternion);* the technical execution of the steps had changed, as had the overall form, which now consisted of *bassedanse commune* and *retour de la bassedanse* (in musical sources also

called *recoupe* or *reprise*), followed by a tordion, which Arbeau calls "a kind of galliard close to the ground." The *bassedanse incommune* of the early sixteenth century had all but disappeared.

Italy. About forty *bassedanze* choreographies are transmitted in the fifteenth-century Italian manuals. They fall into three categories. The first is the *bassedanze* for two dancers (man and woman); because the couple dances mainly side by side, *bassedanze* of this kind lend themselves to performance by several couples in processional formation in the manner of the Burgundian *bassedanse*. The second category of *bassedanze* includes those that have a set number of performers, are spatially expansive, and have a floor pattern; the majority of these are intended for three dancers, others for two or four dancers, and a few for six or eight. The third category, *bassedanze alla fila* (in a line), includes dances that are usually for as many dancers as wish to participate *(in quanti si uole)*, though at times they are meant for a set number of performers. Nothing is said about the shape of the line, and some *bassedanze* of this type may have been performed in a circle rather than a straight line. They would thus conveniently bridge the gap between the iconography of the fifteenth century, in which innumerable circle dances are shown, and the dance instruction books, where circle choreographies are conspicuously absent.

Italian *bassedanze* of the fifteenth century are considerably more technically intricate than their Burgundian counterparts, making use of the full range of current steps and movements, except for the *salto* (leap or jump). Occasional *tempi di saltarello* and *salteti* (small hops or jumps) are, however, inserted into the otherwise even flow of the step sequences, imparting a buoyancy to the dance.

Bassedanze are notated choreographically only, in verbal descriptions without musical accompaniment. Only Antonio Cornazano, in his *Libro dell'arte del danzare* (1455–1465), gives three model tenors, "the best and most used of all," in even semibreves suitable for *bassedanze* and *saltarelli*. Cornazano appears to suggest that any tenor may be used for the accompaniment of any *bassadanza* so long as the musical notes correspond to the number of steps. As in Burgundy, the Italian tenors were elaborated and ornamented by the improvising band, which originally consisted of three instrumentalists. Later in the century the number was increased to five.

According to Cornazano, the *bassadanza* is always followed by a *saltarello*, a practice that would have combined a sedate main dance with a faster after-dance known since the Middle Ages. That the practice existed is confirmed by three of the eight *bassedanze* in the Foligno collection, where a concluding *saltarello* is specifically demanded. But the other five of these *bassedanze* are without *saltarello*, and there is no allusion to the pairing of *bassadanza* and *saltarello* in the other fifteenth-century dance manuals. There is little evidence to indicate that the practice was as common as Cornazano implies.

In Italy, as elsewhere in Europe, new dance types began to appear in the early sixteenth century. Yet the *bassa*, as it was then called, remained in the repertory throughout the century, although in decreasing numbers. Fabritio Caroso's *Il ballarino* (1581) contains eight such pieces; his *Della nobiltà di dame* (1600) contains three; and Cesare Negri's *Le gratie d'amore* (1602) also has three. The heritage of the preceding century is visible in the construction of their dance phrases and in traditional *bassadanza* figures, such as the circling of partners first by the right hand and then by the left, or the advance in line of direction first by the man, then by the woman. An interesting case is Caroso's "Bassa," of "Bassa et Alta, Balletto" (in *Il ballarino*), which in its opening segment bears a close resemblance to a Burgundian *grande mesure parfaite*, whereas in its entirety it is almost identical to the step sequence given in a rhymed Spanish dance description by Pedro de Gracia Dei (c.1486)—evidence that the earlier *bassadanza* was still in living memory a century later.

Only two of the late sixteenth-century Italian *bassas* are stepping dances throughout. In all others the initial 4/4 meter is followed by one or more sections in a quicker triple meter, called variously *saltarello*, *gagliarda*, or simply *la sciolta della sonata*. The old, independent "low dance" had merged with the *balletto* and was, in fact, called by that name.

[*See also* Ballo and Balletto. *For related discussion, see* Social Dance, *article on* Court and Social Dance before 1800. *For an example of Burgundian bassedanse* notation, *see* Notation.]

PRIMARY SOURCES

Arbeau, Thoinot. *Orchésographie et traicte en forme de dialogve, par leqvel tovtes personnes pevvent facilement apprendre & practiquer l'honneste exercice des dances.* Langres, 1588, 1589. Reprinted with expanded title, Langres, 1596. Translated into English as *Orchesography* by Mary Stewart Evans. New York, 1948. Reprint with corrections, a new introduction, and notes by Julia Sutton. New York, 1967.

Arena, Antonius de. *Ad suos compagnones studiantes.* Lyon, 1528. Translated by John Guthrie and Marino Zorzi in "Rules of Dancing by Antonius Arena," *Dance Research* 4 (Autumn 1986): 3–53.

Caroso, Fabritio. *Il ballarino.* Venice, 1581. Reprint, New York, 1967.

Caroso, Fabritio. *Della Nobiltà di Dame,* 1600, 1605. Reissued as *Raccolta di varij balli.* Rome, 1630. Translated into English as *Nobiltà di Dame* by Julia Sutton, Oxford, 1986. Reprint, New York, 1995.

Coplande, Robert. *The Maner of Dauncynge of Bace Daunces after the Vse of Fraunce and Other Places.* London, 1521. Edited by Mabel Dolmetsch in *Dances of England and France from 1450 to 1600* (London, 1949).

Cornazano, Antonio. *Libro dell'arte del danzare.* N.p., 1455–1465. Manuscript located in Biblioteca Apostolica Vaticana, Capponiano 203. Edited by Curzio Mazzi, "Il 'Libro dell'arte del danzare' di Antonio Cornazano," *La Bibliofilia* 17 (1915): 1–30. English translation by Madeleine Inglehearn and Peggy Forsyth, *The Book on the Art of Dancing* (London, 1981). Text and English translation by A. William Smith in *Fifteenth-Century Dance and Music* (Stuyvesant, N.Y., 1995).

Domenico da Piacenza. *De arte saltandi and choreas ducendi.* N.p., c.1455. Manuscript located in Paris, Bibliothèque Nationale, f.ital.972. Published by Dante Bianchi, "Un trattato inedito di Domenico da Piacenza," *La Bibliofilia* 65 (1963): 109–149. English translation by D. R. Wilson, *Domenico of Piacenza (Paris, Bibliothèque Nationale, MS ital. 972),* corr. ed. (Cambridge, 1995). Text and English translation by A. William Smith, *Fifteenth-Century Dance and Music* (Stuyvesant, N.Y., 1995).

Giovanni Ambrosio [Guglielmo Ebreo da Pesaro]. *De pratica seu arte tripudii.* Naples(?), c.1471–1474. Manuscript located in Paris, Bibliothèque Nationale, f.ital.476. Translated in part by Barbara Sparti in *On the Practice or Art of Dancing* (Oxford, 1993). Text and English translation by A. William Smith in *Fifteenth-Century Dance and Music* (Stuyvesant, N.Y., 1995).

Guglielmo Ebreo da Pesaro. *De pratica seu arte tripudii.* Milan, 1463. Manuscript located in Paris, Bibliothèque Nationale, f.ital.973. Translated by Barbara Sparti as *On the Practice or Art of Dancing* (Oxford, 1993).

Guglielmo Ebreo da Pesaro. *De pratica seu arte tripudii.* N.p., c.1474. Manuscript located in Siena, Biblioteca Comunale, L. V.29. Partial edition by Curzio Mazzi, "Una sconosciuta compilazione di un libro quattrocentistico di balli," *La Bibliofilia* 16 (1914–1915): 185–209.

Guglielmo Ebreo da Pesaro. *De pratica seu arte tripudii.* N.p., c.1477. Manuscript located in Florence, Biblioteca Nazionale Centrale,

Magliabecchiano XIX.88. Published by Francesco Zambrini, *Trattato dell'arte del ballo* (Bologna, 1873).

Guglielmo Ebreo da Pesaro. *De pratica seu arte tripudii.* N.p., c.1477. Manuscript located in Modena, Biblioteca Estense (formerly Palatina), ital.82.a.J.94. Published by Giovanni Messori Roncaglia, *Della virtute et arte del danzare* (Modena, 1885).

Guglielmo Ebreo da Pesaro. *De pratica seu arte tripudii.* N.p., c.1480. Manuscript located in the Dance Collection, New York Public Library for the Performing Arts, *MGZMB-Res. 72–254. Edited by Andrea Francalanci, "The *Copia di M° Giorgio del Guideo di ballare basse danze e balletti* as Found in the New York Public Library," *Basler Jahrbuch für Historische Musikpraxis* 14 (1990): 87–179.

Guglielmo Ebreo da Pesaro. *De pratica seu arte tripudii.* N.p., 1510. Manuscript located in Florence, Biblioteca Medicea Laurenziana, Antinori 13. Published by Beatrice Pescerelli, "Una sconosciuta redazione del trattato di danza di Guglielmo Ebreo," *Rivista Italiana di Musicologia* 9 (1974): 48–55.

Le manuscrit dit des basses danses de la Bibliothèque de Bourgogne. N.p., n.d. Manuscript located in Brussels, Bibliothèque Royale, 9085. Facsimile edition by Ernest Closson. Brussels, 1912. Facsimile edition, in original colors, with commentaries by Claudine Lemaire et al. Graz, 1988.

Moderne, Jacques. *S'ensuyuent plusieurs basses dances tant communes que incommunes.* Lyon, c.1540. Partial edition by François Lesure, "Danses et chansons à danser au début du XVIe siècle," in *Recueil de travaux offert à M. Clovis Brunel* (Paris, 1955).

Negri, Cesare. *Le gratie d'amore.* Milan, 1602. Reissued as *Nuove inventioni di balli.* Milan, 1604. English translation by Yvonne Kendall. Ph.D. diss., Stanford University, 1985.

Toulouze, Michel. *L'art et instruction de bien dancer.* Paris, 1488. Edited by Richard Rastall. New York, 1971.

DANCE COLLECTIONS

Ballet de la Reine de cessile. Nancy, c.1445. Manuscript located in Paris, Bibliothèque Nationale, f.fr.5699. Published by Auguste Vallet de Viriville in *Chronique de la Pucelle* (Paris, 1859). Facsimile edition in *Historical Dance* 2.5 (1986–1987): 23.

Capmany, Aurelio. "El baile y la danza." In *Folklore y costumbres de España,* vol. 1, edited by Francisco Carreras y Candi. 2d ed. Barcelona, 1934. Partial edition of a manuscript, c.1496, located in Arxiu Històric, Cervera, Fonds notarial, 3.3.

Catholicon. Venice, 1497/98. Manuscript located in Salisbury Cathedral, Chapter Library. Facsimile edition in Daniel Heartz, "The Basse Dance: Its Evolution circa 1450 to 1550," *Annales Musicologiques* 6 (1958–1963): 310–311.

Otto bassedanze di M. Guglielmo da Pesaro e di M. Domenico da Ferrara. Foligno, 1887. Published by D. M. Faloci-Pulignano from a manuscript located in Foligno, Seminario Vescovile, Biblioteca Jacobilli, D.I.42.

Smith, A. William. "Una fonte sconosciuta della danza italiana del quattrocento." In *Guglielmo Ebreo da Pesaro e la danza nelle corti italiane del XV secolo,* edited by Maurizio Padovan. Pisa, 1990. Publication of a manuscript fragment with choreographies, c.1474–1475, located in Venice, Biblioteca Nazionale Marciana, ital.II.34 (=4906), *Il libro di Sidrach,* c.105.

Stribaldi Roll. N.p., 1517. Manuscript located in Turin, Archivi Biscaretti, Mazzo 4.14. Published by F. Meyer, "Rôle de chansons à danser du XVIe siècle," *Romania* 23 (1894): 156–160.

Die wellschen tenntz. N.p., 1517. Manuscript located in Nuremburg, Germanisches Nationalmuseum, HS 8842/GS 1589. Published by Ingrid Wetzel, "'Hie innen sindt Geschriben die wellschen Tenntz': Le otto danze italiane del manoscritto di Norimberga," in *Guglielmo Ebreo da Pesaro e la danza nelle corti italiane del XV secolo,* edited by Maurizio Padovan (Pisa, 1990). Text and English

translation by A. William Smith in *Fifteenth-Century Dance and Music* (Stuyvesant, N.Y. 1995).

SECONDARY SOURCES

Baratz, Lewis Reece. "Improvising on the Spagna Tune." *American Recorder* 29.4 (1988): 141–146.

Bernstein, Harry. "Aspects of the Performance of the Fifteenth-Century Basse Danse." Master's thesis, Stanford University, 1977.

Brainard, Ingrid. "Bassedanse, Bassadanza, and Ballo in the Fifteenth Century." In *Dance History Research: Perspectives from Related Arts and Disciplines,* edited by Joann W. Kealiinohomoku. New York, 1970.

Brainard, Ingrid. *The Art of Courtly Dancing in the Early Renaissance.* West Newton, Mass., 1981.

Brainard, Ingrid. "The Art of Courtly Dancing in Transition: Nürnberg, Germ.Nat.Mus.Hs.8842, a Hitherto Unknown German Dance Source." In *Crossroads of Medieval Civilization: The City of Regensburg and Its Intellectual Milieu,* edited by Edelgard E. DuBruck and Karl Heinz Göller. Detroit, 1984.

Brown, Howard M. *Music in the French Secular Theater, 1400–1550.* Cambridge, Mass., 1963.

Brown, Howard M. *Instrumental Music Printed before 1600: A Bibliography.* Cambridge, Mass., 1965.

Brunner, W. *Höfischer Tanz um 1500 unter besonderer Berücksichtigung der Bassedanse.* Tanzhistorische Studien, 3. Berlin, 1983.

Bukofzer, Manfred F. "A Polyphonic Basse Dance of the Renaissance." In Bukofzer's *Studies in Medieval and Renaissance Music.* New York, 1950.

Castelli, Patrizia, et al., eds. *Mesura et arte del danzare: Guglielmo Ebreo da Pesaro e la danza nelle corti italiane del XV secolo.* Pesaro, 1987.

Daye, Anne. "Towards a Choreographic Description of the Fifteenth-Century Italian Bassa Danza." In *Guglielmo Ebreo da Pesaro e la danza nelle corti italiane del XV secolo,* edited by Maurizio Padovan. Pisa, 1990.

Dixon, Peggy. "Reflections on Basse Dance Source Material: A Dancer's Review." *Historical Dance* 2.4 (1984–1985): 24–27.

Gallo, F. Alberto. "Il 'ballare lombardo,' circa 1435–1475." *Studi musicali* 8 (1979): 61–84.

Heartz, Daniel. "The Basse Dance: Its Evolution circa 1450 to 1550." *Annales musicologiques* 6 (1958–1963): 287–340.

Heartz, Daniel. "Hoftanz and Basse Dance: Towards a Reconstruction of Fifteenth-Century Dance Music." *Journal of the American Musicological Society* 19 (1966): 13–36.

Hill, Simon R. "Improvising Accompaniments to the Burgundian *Bassedanse.*" In *The Marriage of Music and Dance: Papers from a Conference Held at the Guildhall School of Music and Drama, London, 9th–11th August 1991.* Cambridge, 1992.

Inglehearn, Madeleine. "A Little-Known Fifteenth-Century Italian Dance Treatise." *Music Review* 42 (1981): 174–181.

Jeschke, Claudia. *Tanzschriften: Ihre Geschichte und Methode.* Bad Reichenhall, 1983.

Marrocco, W. Thomas. *Inventory of Fifteenth-Century Bassedanze, Balli, and Balletti in Italian Dance Manuals.* New York, 1981.

Mas i García, Carles. "Le più antiche notizie di 'baxa dança' nei documenti catalani." In *Guglielmo Ebreo da Pesaro e la danza nelle corti italiane del XV secolo,* edited by Maurizio Padovan. Pisa, 1990.

Mas i García, Carles. "Baixa Dansa in the Kingdom of Catalonia and Aragon in the Fifteenth Century." *Historical Dance* 3.1 (1992): 15–23.

McGee, Timothy J. *Medieval and Renaissance Music: A Performer's Guide.* Toronto, 1985.

Meylan, Raymond. *L'énigme de la musique des basses danses du quinzième siècle.* Bern, 1968.

Meylan, Raymond. "Migration et transformation des polyphonies à armatures (Basse Danse et Hoftanz)." In *Le concert des voix et des instruments à la Renaissance: Actes du XXXIVe colloque interna-*

BATES. The gifted, one-legged tapper caught airborne in the Los Angeles production of Ken Murray's *Blackouts*, 1948. (Photograph from the collection of Rusty E. Frank.)

tional d'études humanistes Tours [1991], edited by Jean-Michel Vaccaro. Paris, 1995.

Mullally, Robert. "The Polyphonic Theory of the *Basse Danse*." *Music Review* 38 (1977): 241–248.

Polk, Keith. "Flemish Wind Bands in the Late Middle Ages: A Study in Improvisatory Performance Practices." Ph.D.diss., University of California, Berkeley, 1968.

Pontremoli, Alessandro, and Patrizia La Rocca. *Il ballare lombardo: Teoria e prassi coreutica nella festa di corte del XV secolo*. Milan, 1987.

Smith, A. William. "Una fonte sconosciuta della danza italiana del quattrocento." In *Guglielmo Ebreo da Pesaro e la danza nelle corti italiane del XV secolo*, edited by Maurizio Padovan. Pisa, 1990.

Smith, A. William, trans. and ed. *Fifteenth-Century Dance and Music: The Complete Transcribed Italian Treatises and Collections in the Tradition of Domenico da Piacenza*. 2 vols. Stuyvesant, N.Y., 1995.

Southern, Eileen. "Some Keyboard Basse Dances of the Fifteenth Century." *Acta musicologica* 35 (1963): 114–124.

Southern, Eileen. *The Buxheim Organ Book*. Musicological Studies 6, Institute of Medieval Music. Brooklyn, N.Y., 1963.

Southern, Eileen. "Basse-Dance Music in Some German Manuscripts of the Fifteenth Century." In *Aspects of Medieval and Renaissance Music: A Birthday Offering to Gustave Reese*, edited by Jan LaRue. New York, 1966.

Ward, John M. "The Maner of Dauncying." *Early Music* 4 (1976): 127–142.

Wetzel, Ingrid. "'Hie innen sindt Geschriben die wellschen Tenntz': Le otto danze italiane del manoscritto di Norimberga." In *Guglielmo Ebreo da Pesaro e la danza nelle corti italiane del XV secolo*, edited by Maurizio Padovan. Pisa, 1990.

Wilson, D. R. "Theory and Practice in the Fifteenth-Century French Basse Dance." *Historical Dance* 2.3 (1983): 1–2.

Wilson, D. R. "The Development of French Basse Dance." *Historical Dance* 2.4 (1984–1985): 5–12.

Wilson, D. R. *The Steps Used in Court Dance in Fifteenth-Century Italy*. Cambridge, 1992.

Wilson, D. R. "A Further Look at the Nancy Basse Dances." *Historical Dance* 3.3 (1994): 24–28.

INGRID BRAINARD

BATES, PEG LEG (Clayton Bates; born 11 October 1907 in Fountain Inn, South Carolina), tap dancer. Bates defies any concept of singularity by executing acrobatic turns, graceful soft-shoes, buck-and-wings, and powerful rhythm dances—all on one leg and a peg.

Bates was born into an extremely poor sharecropping family whose father deserted them when Bates was only three years old. During World War I, Bates began working in a cotton-seed ginning mill. On his third night there, the lights failed, and the twelve year old accidentally stepped into an open auger conveyer. The equipment chewed up his leg so badly that an amputation was necessary; since hospitals were then segregated in the South, the doctor performed the procedure on the family's kitchen table. Bates still wanted to dance, however. Fitted with a peg, he began observing dance steps and adapting them to his own needs.

> I was very ambitious when I was dancing. The reason for these different styles—the acrobatics, the rhythm, the legomania—was I wanted to be so good, I wanted to *surpass* the two-leg dancers! (Frank, 1994)

By the time he was fifteen, Bates was a professional tap dancer. He worked his way up from minstrel shows to carnivals, from the African-American vaudeville circuit TOBA to the white vaudeville circuits. In 1929, in Paris, he joined the revue *Lew Leslie's Blackbirds*, an African-American show featuring some of the most outstanding entertainers of the day. Bates soon returned to the United States and, throughout the 1930s, played top Harlem nightclubs, including the Cotton Club, Connie's Inn, and Club Zanzibar. In the late 1930s, he was the opening act for the *Ed Sullivan Revue*, traveled the Keith and Loew theater circuits, and appeared to great acclaim on Australia's Tivoli circuit. He performed throughout the 1940s, including dancing in the popular Los Angeles version of *Ken Murray's Blackouts*. During the 1950s, Peg Leg Bates made twenty-one appearances on Ed Sullivan's television show—more appearances than any other tap dancer.

A measure of Bates's success was the sound of his dancing, created by the unique construction of the tip of his peg; the inside was leather, the outside rubber. For the tapping, he used the sound of the leather interior, and for novelty steps—like balancing on the peg—he worked on the exterior rubber to keep from slipping. He wore a regular tap shoe on his right foot. The combination of sounds he created was unparalleled.

[*See also* Tap Dance.]

BIBLIOGRAPHY
Frank, Rusty E. *Tap! The Greatest Tap Dance Stars and Their Stories, 1900–1955.* Rev. ed. New York, 1994.
Stearns, Marshall, and Jean Stearns. *Jazz Dance: The Story of American Vernacular Dance.* Rev. ed. New York, 1994.

FILM.   Dave Davidson, *A Dancing Man: Peg Leg Bates* (1991).
RUSTY E. FRANK

BATTAGLIA. *See* Barriera, Torneo, and Battaglia.

BATTEMENT. The term *battement* (literally, "beating") refers to a group of approximately twenty ballet exercises in which the working or active leg leaves and then returns to the supporting leg. These exercises are practiced at the barre and in the center, in all directions. Their perfection allows for the execution and technical polish required for allegro and *batterie* sequences. Although *battements* are rarely performed on stage as such, they have been wonderfully displayed in George Balanchine's *Symphony in C* (1947) and Harald Lander's *Études* (1948).

In a *battement*, the leg must beat—that is, it must open and close. *Battements* can be divided into three major categories, depending on whether they work mainly the ankle, the knee, or the hip joint. The supporting leg can be straight, bent *(en fondu)*, on the ball of the foot *(demi-pointe)*, on pointe, pivoting *(en tournant)*, or in a jump *(sauté)*.

Battements exercising the ankle joint are of two types: those that move from and to closed positions (first, third, or fifth), and those that move with the working foot in *cou-de-pied* position (at the "neck" of the foot or instep).

Battement tendu simple (or *point battement*) is the extension of the foot along the floor until it is fully pointed, followed by return to the closed position. In *battement relevé*, after pointing the foot, the heel of the working leg is briefly lowered, and the foot is then pointed again; no weight is transferred. *Battement glissé (battement tendu jeté, battement dégagé)* is a quick extension of the foot to a fully extended, pointed position one to three inches above the floor. Taken to 45 degrees, it is *battement jeté;* from *pointe tendu* it is *battement tendu jeté pointé.* The strength developed from pushing along the floor is vital in jumping; for example, *battement glissé* from *demi-plié* is a useful preparation for *assemblé.*

Battement frappé sur le cou-de-pied usually begins with the working foot in *cou-de-pied* position and quickly extends in the manner of *battement glissé,* with the ball of the foot sometimes striking the floor on its way out but not on its return. In a double *frappé,* the foot, placed in *cou-de-pied* front or back, opens just enough to move to the other *cou-de-pied* position before the *glissé* action, all without losing speed and rhythm.

Battements fondus ("melted") exercise both knee joints. The working foot is placed *cou-de-pied* (either flexed or pointed), while the supporting knee is bent. The succeeding extension of the raised leg and the stretch of the supporting leg must occur simultaneously. In the same manner, the extended leg arrives back into *cou-de-pied* just as the supporting leg is at the lowest point of its bend. This exercise is for control, coordination, and strength in preparation for *adage* and jumping, depending on the movements' speed and accent. In double *battement fondu,* the supporting leg stretches as the working foot remains in *cou-de-pied* and then bends again before both supporting and working legs stretch simultaneously.

In *petits battements sur le cou-de-pied,* the working heel is lifted and placed at the instep. The foot extends slightly sideways and closes in *cou-de-pied* position behind. This placing and replacing is done repetitively, with the accent either in front or behind. The position of the working foot in *cou-de-pied* can be either relaxed or "wrapped" around the supporting ankle (heel at front, toes reaching around). The thigh of the working leg is held motionless and turned out, with all movement happening from the knee down. *Petits battements sur le cou-de-pied* teach rhythm, speed, and accuracy in placing, in preparation for precision in *batterie.* Compan (1787) stated that they could also be done while jumping *(en sautant).* When done continuously, these *petits battements* are called *serrés. Petits battements battus,* in which the pointed foot of the working leg continuously strikes the supporting heel or arch in a fluttering motion, display Odette's emotional fragility in *Swan Lake*'s act 2 pas de deux.

Still done from the lower leg but placed higher on the supporting leg, *battement frappé fouetté* involves the working foot being repetitively placed below the knee of the supporting leg, front and back.

In *battements retirés* ("drawn up"), the fully pointed working foot is drawn up the side, front, or back of the supporting leg, with the bending knee turned out, and returns to the closed position without movement of the hip girdle. Full *retiré* height is above the calf, by the knee joint. Although *retirés* are used in allegro *(retirés sautés),* their primary purpose is for placement in *adage.*

Battements that work the hip joint are of two types: those that pass through *retiré,* and those that pass through *pointe tendu.* Those from *retiré* position are *battements développés.* Done in a series in different directions, they are *développés passés.* A movement from *grand battement* to *retiré* and then to a forward or backward extension is a *grand battement jeté passé.*

Done swiftly from closed position through a *tendu, grand battement* (or *grand battement jeté*) is a balletic kick, a throwing of the working leg upward as high as possible and its return to the closed position. With a pause in *pointe tendu,* it is a *grand battement pointé.* In *battement soutenu* ("sustained"), the working leg extends outward along the floor from a bent supporting knee before closing into fifth *demi-pointe.*

Battements en ronds (fouettés battements) are thrown between fifth or third position from front to back or the reverse, thus describing a full circular arc. *Grand battements en clôche* swing swiftly back to front through first position. If a slight body inclination in the opposite direction of the leg is added, these become *battement balancés (battements en balançoire).*

Battements tendus pour la batterie are usually done on *demi-pointe;* the working leg, often with a flexed foot, passes from fifth front through first (or a small second) to fifth back (or vice versa), with the accent either front or back. The rebound experienced by beating the stretched working leg against the taut supporting one is a preparation for learning *batterie.*

[*See also* Ballet Technique, History of.]

BIBLIOGRAPHY

Beaumont, Cyril W., and Stanislas Idzikowski. *A Manual of the Theory and Practice of Classical Theatrical Dancing.* London, 1922.

French, Ruth, and Felix Demery. *First Steps.* Rev. ed. London, 1938.

Kostrovitskaya, Vera, and Alexei Pisarev. *School of Classical Dance.* Translated by John Barker. Moscow, 1978.

Stuart, Muriel, et al. *The Classic Ballet.* New York, 1952.

Vaganova, Agrippina. *Basic Principles of Classical Ballet: Russian Ballet Technique* (1934). Translated by Anatole Chujoy. Edited by Peggy van Praagh. 2d ed. London, 1953.

KENNETHA R. McARTHUR

BATTERIE. The generic term *batterie* (Fr., *battre,* "to beat"), covers all ballet jumps involving the beating together of the legs in the air. These fall into two main categories. All steps belonging to the *entrechat* family are classed as *la batterie à croisements* (crossing beats) and are characterized by an interweaving action of the feet during the course of a jump, resulting in each leg beating against the other a given number of times. However, when the beating occurs not as a result of the crisscrossing of the legs and feet, but because one leg is struck deliberately against the other at the highest point of a leap (as in a cabriole), the step comes into the category of *la batterie de choc* (striking beats).

In contemporary ballet terminology, the term *cabriole* is applied only to those jumps in the fourth front or back, or in the second position, where the supporting leg is struck against the raised leg at the height of the leap, both legs being completely straight. However, in eighteenth-century and early nineteenth-century balletic usage, the French word *cabriole* and the Italian *capriola* still covered a wide variety of leaping movements not necessarily involving beats. When a leap was embellished by the addition of a beat, it was termed either *capriola intrecciata,* or *capriola battute* (literally an interwoven or a beaten caper; hence, Emile Littré's assertion in his nineteenth-century *Dictionnaire de la langue française: "les entrechats sont des cabrioles."*

According to Gennaro Magri (1779), these *capriole* could be performed either with straight legs or *ritirate* (with the legs drawn up underneath the body). Although the more extreme forms of *ritirate* are now obsolete, some schools (notably those derived from Enrico Cecchetti and Édouard Espinosa) still teach that the *entrechat* should be performed with a degree of mobility in the knee joint, so that the crossing action is executed mainly by the feet and the lower part of the legs. In this type of *batterie* the beating takes place from the base of the calf downward and is incidental to the brilliantly interwoven footwork—hence the Italian appellation of *intreciatta* ("braided" or "interwoven"), from which the French word *entrechat* is derived.

Other schools (notably the Soviet school) advocate that the legs be kept straight during the *entrechat.* For women, the beat is performed mainly with the calves, but male dancers are required to beat with the thighs as well as the calves. In practice, the precise mechanics of the *entrechat* depend on practicalities such as the speed of the music, the height of the jump, and the shape of the individual dancer's legs. The character of the movements can be *terre à terre* or *grand élévation.*

The way the number of beats is calculated in any given *entrechat* varies from one school to another. Originally, the French school required *entrechats* to be executed both starting from and ending in a closed position of the feet, whereas the Italian style called for the step to begin from, and end in, an open position. In the French system, the counting of the movements commenced with the first opening out of the legs, whereas the Italians numbered the *entrechat* starting with the first closing action. By the end of the eighteenth century, it was already accepted practice for dancers to mix these two styles, thus commencing an *entrechat* in the French manner and finishing it *à l'italienne,* or vice versa. As a result, the logic of the original distinction between the French and the Italian manner of counting the beats gradually became blurred; this is reflected in the inconsistency of contemporary nomenclature.

Pas battu is the name given to any step embellished by the addition of a beat (e.g., *jeté battu, sissonne battue*). The term *brisé* ("broken") has come to be used almost exclusively to denote a type of traveling *pas assemblé battu.* However, according to the classic French school (as recorded by Antonine Meunier), *brisé* is the description applied to any small jumping movement interrupted by the crossing of the lower legs before landing—the beating movement produced by this crossing thus, as it were, "breaking" into the execution of the step.

The term *volé* ("flown") is usually used to describe an *entrechat* or *pas battu* finishing on one leg *(à l'italienne).* One of the most spectacular examples of this type of movement is the diagonal of *brisés volés* performed by the male dancer in the coda of the Bluebird pas de deux of the final act of *The Sleeping Beauty.*

BIBLIOGRAPHY

Beaumont, Cyril W., and Stanislas Idzikowski. *A Manual of the Theory and Practice of Classical Theatrical Dancing.* London, 1922.

Blasis, Carlo. *The Code of Terpsichore: A Practical and Historical Treatise on the Ballet, Dancing, and Pantomime.* London, 1828.

Espinosa, Édouard. *Ballet: Advanced Syllabus and Technique of Operatic Dancing.* London, 1941.

Glasstone, Richard. *Better Ballet.* London, 1977.

Kostrovitskaya, Vera, and Alexei Pisarev. *School of Classical Dance.* Translated by John Barker. Moscow, 1978.

Magri, Gennaro. *Theoretical and Practical Treatise on Dancing* (1779). Translated by Mary Skeaping. London, 1988.

Meunier, Antonine. *La danse classique (école française).* Paris, 1931.

Prudhommeau, Germaine, and Geneviève Guillot. *The Book of Ballet.* Translated by Katherine Carson. Englewood Cliffs, N.J., 1976.

Vaganova, Agrippina. *Basic Principles of Classical Ballet: Russian Ballet Technique* (1934). Translated by Anatole Chujoy. Edited by Peggy van Praagh. 2d ed. London, 1953.

RICHARD GLASSTONE

BAUHAUS, DANCE AND THE. An early twentieth-century school, the Bauhaus was formed to unify the arts, crafts, science, and technology for the creation of a new social order. Founded in Weimar, Germany, in 1919 by the architect Walter Gropius, the Bauhaus sought to create a "modern architectonic art, which, like human nature, should be all-embracing in its scope." The school attracted to its faculty such artists as Paul Klee, Wassily Kandinsky, Oskar Schlemmer, Johannes Itten, László Moholy-Nagy, Marcel Breuer, Gunta Stölzl, and Mies van der Rohe. Using as a model the relationship of medieval building lodges *(Dombauhütten)* that surrounded a cathedral under construction, the Bauhaus workshops, headed by artists and craftsmen, were given equal status.

With the founding of the Weimar Republic, post–World War I Germany experienced considerable revolutionary idealism. In this atmosphere, and breaking with the tradition of the academy and salon, Bauhaus students became apprentices to both a master of form (painting, sculpture) and a master craftsman. In addition to the workshops in form, cabinetmaking, metal, wall painting, printing, pottery, and stained glass, Gropius envisioned a stage workshop in which students would explore fundamental elements—space, body, movement, form, light, color, sound—to create an "architectonic" theater.

Initially, Lothar Schreyer, the painter and dramaturge of the expressionist *Sturm* group, was appointed head of the stage workshop. With the Bauhaus students he developed pieces that continued such expressionistic pursuits as the dissolution of language, movement, and sound into highly codified sequences implying emotive melodrama. Schreyer's approach was so at odds with the Bauhaus ideal of pure, simple exploration of form that his pro-

BAUHAUS. Oskar Schlemmer as the Turk in his first stage work, *Triadic Ballet* (1922). (Photograph with gouache and pencil 1924/1928; used by permission of the Oskar Schlemmer Theater Estate, Badenweiler, Germany.)

jected performance for the upcoming Bauhaus Week of 1923 was canceled, and his resignation soon followed. Thus in 1922 Gropius transferred the leadership of the workshop to the painter and sculptor Oskar Schlemmer, whose first dance production, *Triadic Ballet* (1922), had its premiere in Stuttgart to wide acclaim. Schlemmer inaugurated his position during Bauhaus Week with performances of *Triadic Ballet* and *Figural Cabinet* (1922).

Triadic Ballet was a dance for three dancers, and it utilized triads—form, color, space; height, depth, breadth; ball, cube, pyramid; and red, blue, yellow. It had originally been performed in 1916 in short sketches. As a visual artist, Schlemmer first created eighteen sculptural figurine costumes abstracting the functions and expressions of the human body. They varied from medieval-looking armor to exaggerated folk puppets and technological ballerinas surrounded by metal hoops and spiral disks. After the figurines were completed he modeled the floor patterns on their costumes and then added the music: first a classical potpourri and, in 1926, an original score by Paul Hindemith for player piano. Schlemmer's aim in this abstract ballet of three sections—the burlesque "Yellow," the solemn and festive "Rose," and the metaphysical "Black"—was to find the harmonic balance between the emotional, Dionysian element of dance and the rational, Apollonian formality of architectural space. As in his painting and sculpture, Schlemmer continually sought a reconciliation between the figurative and the abstract.

What most characterized these stage productions was the students' instinct for play *(der Spieltrieb)*. *Figural Cabinet*, also first performed in 1922, consisted of animated maquette (small-scale) figures satirizing the new "faith in progress and organizational-directedness" of the time. No theatrical form—religious ritual, classical theater, cabaret, variety show, or circus—was spared the workshop's desire for satire and parody. In *Meta* (1924), the student performers carried placards bearing theatrical terms, such as "conflict," "suspense," and "intermission," which they acted out. Even the famous thematic Bauhaus parties drew costumed revelers ready to engage in improvisations provoked by the stage students, while the Bauhaus jazz band provided music for the kicking, stomping "Bauhaus dance" that found its way into the stage productions.

The move in 1925/26 to the Bauhaus building in

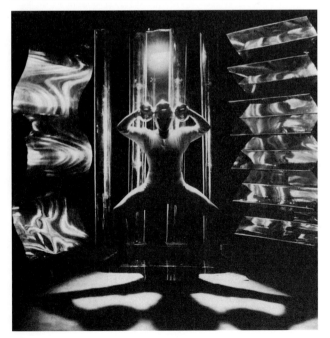

BAUHAUS. Karla Grosch in *Metal Dance*, from *Bauhaus Dances* (1929), created as part of the Dessau Bauhaus Stage Workshop. (Photoarchive C. Raman Schlemmer, Oggebbio, Italy; used by permission of the Oskar Schlemmer Theater Estate, Badenweiler, Germany.)

Dessau, with its specially designed stage, permitted Schlemmer and his students their fullest experimentation in theater. At a lecture-demonstration given in 1927, Schlemmer explained the principles of the stage workshop:

> In short, we should review its primary endeavor, which is to approach all our material from a basic and elementary standpoint. . . . It is natural that the aims of the Bauhaus—to seek the craftsmanlike-practical by thoroughly investigating the creative elements, and to understand in all its ramifications the essence of *der Bau* [from Ger., *bauen*, to build]—creative construction—have valid application to the field of theater. . . . Not the least of its functions is to serve the metaphysical needs of man by constructing a world of illusion and by creating the transcendental on the basis of the rational.   (Gropius, 1961)

The lecture-demonstration opened with a play of the curtain and lights, suggesting dramatic moods. Suddenly, a single white figure appeared, expressively gesticulating. Defining the axes and diagonals of the blackened cubical stage with his body, he proceeded to walk in and around the gridded floor to establish a three-dimensional sense of the space. This was followed by a series of "architectonic" dances illustrating the geometric relationship between the human figure and architectural space. By padding and masking the performers, Schlemmer transformed the *Tanzermensch* ("dancer") into the *Kunstfigur* ("art figure"). These marionettelike figures reiterated Gropius's themes of unification, abstraction, and standardization of form while also creating timeless characters symbolizing the humor, pathos, and dignity of the human in the new technological era.

Developing in complexity, the 1927 architectonic dance series began with *Space Dance*, in which three dancers costumed in the primary colors were assigned a related walking tempo—slow, medium, fast—to percussive accompaniment. Creating geometric puzzles on the gridded floor, they synchronized their spatial patterns of line and plane to recapitulate the design of the Bauhaus. Combining time, color, and space, each dancer became a metaphor for human temperament. To build upon the conceptual structure, spheres, wands, and a pole were added in *Form Dance*, a series of sculptural moving tableaux. *Gesture Dance* introduced social context: with bench, stool, and chair, and wearing tailcoats, white gloves, and mustaches, the dancers playfully enacted a social drama in abstract sound and gesture. (Schlemmer suggested in his diary that this piece, along with *Space Dance*, had inspired parts of Kurt Jooss's *Green Table*, which was choreographed four years after the Bauhaus troupe's performance at the 1928 Dance Congress in Essen, the home of Jooss's Folkwang Dance School.)

Chorus of Masks featured twelve dancers, each wearing masks of stereotypical expressions, "conversing" around a

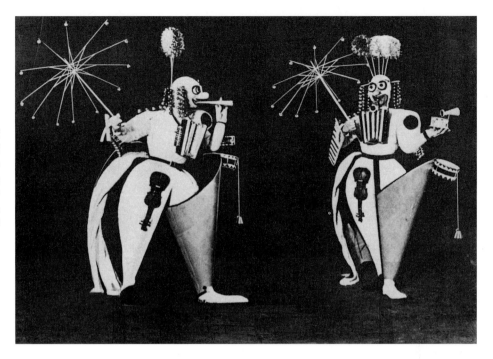

BAUHAUS. Two different views of Andreas Weininger in his *Musical Clown,* 1926. (Photoarchive C. Raman Schlemmer, Oggebbio, Italy; used by permission of the Oskar Schlemmer Theater Estate, Badenweiler, Germany.)

table in stylized gestures. To parody the architects at the Bauhaus, the dancers in *Block Play* built their own structures out of cubes, challenged the compositions of their neighbors, and finally cooperated in building a single tower around which they danced triumphantly. In the solo *Hoop Dance* the dancer was nearly camouflaged by wearing black, allowing the radiant white hoops to create optical illusions; in *Pole Dance* twelve white poles extended the limbs and central axis of the body to engage the surrounding space.

Although these are the best-known productions of the Bauhaus theater, Andreas Weininger's *Musical Clown, Equilibristrics* with its geometric props, the glass-chimed costume of *Glass Dance,* the reflective metallic properties in *Metal Dance,* and Schlemmer's "clown" acts were favorites. Students also could be found performing throughout the Bauhaus building.

"Mechanistic cabaret, metaphysical eccentricity, spiritual tightrope walking, ironic 'variété'?" Schlemmer wrote of the Bauhaus theater. Like most avant-garde theater of the 1920s, the Bauhaus stage was preoccupied with the "mechanical" in movement. However, the dancers' linear, flat movements were executed not with the harsh precision of robots but rather with a sense of soft suspension; the human element was always primary and central.

In 1929, with Nazism on the rise, Schlemmer resigned from the Bauhaus after being pressured by its new director Hannes Meyer to politicize the theater, and the stage workshop was virtually terminated. Schlemmer was soon dismissed from teaching posts and a significant body of his work was destroyed by the Nazis. The Bauhaus, forced to move to Berlin, was closed by a Nazi raid in 1933. Despite these events, the impact of the Bauhaus stage workshop was widely acknowledged. Costumes from *Triadic Ballet* were exhibited throughout the United States and Europe, and Bauhaus students scattered around the world to teach and practice their principles. Alexander ("Xanti") Schawinsky, a student whose *Circus* had been performed in 1924, was invited after World War II to join the faculty of progressive Black Mountain College in North Carolina.

Oskar Schlemmer, impressed by the notation system of Rudolf Laban (a dance contemporary with whom he had served on the committee for the Magdeburg Dance Congress of 1927), preserved many Bauhaus pieces in his own style of notation. Later reconstructions have shown that they retain their original vitality as avant-garde performance, representative of a significant cultural, historical, and artistic phenomenon. The Bauhaus pieces are timeless in content and striking in visual simplicity, and their nonnarrative structure, task activity, and minimalist style can be regarded as precursors of mixed-media theater, postmodern dance, and performance art. Schlemmer and his students integrated dance, theater, and the visual arts to celebrate the human as master architect of the stage.

[*See also* Artists and Dance, *article on* Artists and Dance, 1760–1929. *For more general discussion, see* Germany, *article on* Theatrical Dance, 1600–1945.]

BIBLIOGRAPHY
Gropius, Walter, ed. *The Theater of the Bauhaus.* Translated by Arthur S. Wensinger. Middletown, Conn., 1961.
Lahusen, Susanne. "Oskar Schlemmer: Mechanical Ballets?" *Dance Research* 4 (Autumn 1986): 65–77.

Lehman, Arnold L., and Brenda Richardson, eds. *Oskar Schlemmer.* Baltimore, 1986. Exhibition catalogue, Baltimore Museum of Art.

Maur, Karin von. *Oskar Schlemmer.* Stuttgart, 1977. Exhibition catalogue, Staatsgalerie.

Moynihan, D. S., with Leigh George Odom. "Oskar Schlemmer's *Bauhaus Dances:* Debra McCall's Reconstructions." *Drama Review* 28 (Fall 1984): 46–58.

Scheyer, Ernst. "The Shapes of Space: The Art of Mary Wigman and Oskar Schlemmer." *Dance Perspectives,* no. 41 (Spring 1970).

Schlemmer, Tut, ed. *The Letters and Diaries of Oskar Schlemmer.* Translated by Krishna Winston. Middletown, Conn., 1972.

Wingler, Hans Maria. *The Bauhaus.* Translated by Wolfgang Jabs and Basil Gilbert. Cambridge, Mass., 1969.

INTERVIEWS. Ise Gropius (Lincoln, Mass., 1980), Andreas Weininger (New York, 1979–1983), Raman Schlemmer (New York, 1982).

ARCHIVES. The Schlemmer Archive, Staatsgalerie, Stuttgart, contains costumes and notated movement scores; the Bauhaus Archive, Berlin, contains drawings and sculpture.

DEBRA McCALL

BAUSCH. Members of the Tanztheater Wuppertal in Bausch's *Kontakhof* (1978). (Photograph by Ulli Weiss; used by permission.)

BAUSCH, PINA (Philippine Bausch; born 27 July 1940 in Solingen, Germany), German dancer, choreographer, and ballet director. Born in Germany during World War II, Bausch grew up in and around her parents' restaurant and was taken to her first dance classes by restaurant patrons who happened to be theater folk and who noticed her extreme physical flexibility. At fifteen Bausch left home to study with Kurt Jooss at the Folkwang School in Essen. When she was nineteen, she moved to New York City and studied with Antony Tudor, dancing under his direction with the Metropolitan Opera Ballet. She also absorbed elements of the modern tradition from another teacher, Paul Sanasardo, a student of Anna Sokolow.

In 1961, Jooss summoned Bausch back to Germany, offering her a job. She eventually began to choreograph and was successful enough to attract the attention of the management of the theater in Wuppertal, an industrial town in the Ruhr Valley. She devised a Venusberg ballet for a production of *Tannhäuser* in 1972 and was appointed director of the Wuppertal ballet company a year later. Bausch choreographed her first work, *Fritz,* to music by Wolfgang Hufschmidt, as resident director in 1974. For a while she continued to stage dance sections of operas, choreographing a production of *Iphigenia in Tauris* in 1975 and *Orpheus and Eurydice* in 1975.

In 1975 Bausch choreographed Igor Stravinsky's *Le Sacre du Printemps;* although this work was connected to the traditional scenario, the dancing took place on a stage covered with damp soil. By this time she had begun working with designer Rolf Borzik, who became her close collaborator as her style evolved away from conventional dance and broke new ground in the evolving area of dance theater. With *The Seven Deadly Sins,* choreographed in 1976, Bausch departed entirely from dance conventions.

She introduced a rehearsal method in which she posed questions to dancers and wove their responses, verbal or physical, into a piece that included a spoken text accompanied by recorded music, both popular and classical.

Her other works with Borzik included *Bluebeard—While Listening to a Tape Recording of Béla Bartók's Opera "Duke Bluebeard's Castle", Come Dance With Me,* and *Renate Emigrates* (all 1977); *Cafe Müller* and *Kontakthof* (both 1978); and *Arien* (performed on a stage covered with ankle-deep warm water) and *Legend of Chastity* (both 1979). Borzik died of cancer at age thirty-five in 1980; Bausch's *1980—A Piece by Pina Bausch* is often interpreted as a farewell to the close friend who guided her vision. Her later works include *Bandoneon* (1980); *Walzer* (1982); *Carnations* (1982), performed on a floor of live flowers that were trampled by the dancers; *On the Mountain a Cry Was Heard* (1984); *Two Cigarettes in the Dark* (1985); *Victor* (1986); *Palermo, Palermo* (1989); *A Tragedy* (1994); and *Danzon* (1995).

Bausch's works, connected as they are to the German expressionist dance tradition called *Ausdruckstanz,* embody feelings of existential angst, anomie, and dissociation. All her works share essential similarities. They have no plot, no conventional sense of progression, no revelation of character, and no sense of any specific geographic place. They have, however, lots of atmosphere, sparks of wicked humor, and a pattern of romantic tantalization and humiliation. Bausch's works are built of brief episodes of dialogue and action often centered on a slightly surreal situation, prop, or costume: for example, in *Victor,* dancer Silvia Kesselheim pounded a steak with a mallet, then stuffed the bloody steak, and her foot, into a toe shoe and performed *bourrées* to "Adagio Lamentoso"; in *Bandoneon,* Dominique Mercy evolved from a man in a business suit into a dreamer in a ballerina's tutu.

Bausch's dancers often address the audience, directly involving them in the performance. The question-and-answer exchanges that propel Bausch's unusual rehearsal process are incorporated into the finished pieces; in *Bandoneon*, for example, each dancer was asked "What does 'Mary' suggest to you?" The answers, recited in an extended sequence, ranged from "Mary Christmas" and "marijuana" to "Mary had a little lamb." Bausch's works often contain physical interludes (seldom actual dances) that present men and women as partners or antagonists in a social dance in which need and collusion alternate uncomfortably with hostility. Bausch plays with conventions of theatrical time and pacing; a tableau may be set

BAUSCH. Scene from a revival of Bausch's *Arien* (1979) at the Brooklyn Academy of Music, New York. (Photograph © 1985 by Beatriz Schiller; used by permission.)

up with a deliberateness that suggests slow motion, only to be shattered by a parade of the full cast marching around the stage, singing and shouting.

Though seemingly constructed of disparate, random elements, Bausch's dance theater has an unmistakable integrity, clarity, and internal balance. Her work has been enormously popular throughout the world, from Germany to the United States, Japan, and South America. Perhaps because it looks technically thin, it has frequently been imitated, though the many directors and choreographers, some of them Bausch's own dancers, who have tried to recreate her effects have failed. In Germany, she has enjoyed an artistic rivalry with other women dance-theater creators of her generation, notably Reinhild Hoffman. For a time in the 1980s Bausch was probably the most influential stage artist in the world, and her work shaped that of artists as diverse as Robert Wilson, William Forsythe, and Maguy Marin. In 1984 her company was chosen to open the Olympic Arts Festival in Los Angeles.

Though critics with a predilection toward work that developed from the German expressionism of the 1930s have embraced Bausch, those inclined toward the classical tradition have railed against her. *New York Times* theater critic Clive Barnes found her "silly, empty . . . stupid, self-indulgent, [and] self-congratulatory." Even the look of her women—who perform well into their forties and dress in loose clothing, with their hair unbound—has been attacked. Barnes termed their appearance "tatterdemalion" and *New Yorker* dance critic Arlene Croce labeled Bausch "an entrepreneuse who fills theaters with projections of her self-pity . . . a little girl acting po'faced." While she is perhaps least appreciated by North American critics, Bausch has been the subject of numerous laudatory books and documentaries in the rest of the world.

Her company of performers is unique. Mostly trained as dancers, they are mature in outlook and appearance, suggesting as individuals the cosmopolitan, complex quality of Bausch's world. They often remain with Bausch over a period of decades, and when someone leaves, several hundred hopefuls attend an open audition in which they are immersed in Bausch's methods. Among the notable performers associated with Bausch's Tanztheater Wuppertal are Josephine Ann Endicott, Lutz Förster, actress Mechtild Grossmann, Silvia Kesselheim, Ed Kortlandt, Beatrice Libonati, Jan Minarik, Dominique Mercy, Meryl Tankard, and Julie Shanahan.

BIBLIOGRAPHY

Adshead-Lansdale, Janet. "Empowered Expression from Bausch and de Keersmaeker." *Dance Theatre Journal* 12 (Winter 1995–1996): 20–23.

Birringer, Johannes. "Pina Bausch: Dancing across Borders." In Birringer's *Theatre, Theory, Postmodernism*. Bloomington, 1991.

Chamier, Ille, and Ulli Weiss. *Setz dich hin und lächle: Tanztheater von Pina Bausch*. Cologne, 1979.

Erler, Detlef. *Pina Bausch*. Zurich, 1994.

Goldberg, Marianne. "Artifice and Authenticity: Gender Scenarios in Pina Bausch's Dance Theatre." *Women and Performance* 4.2 (1989): 104–117.

Hoghe, Raimund. *Bandoneon: Für was kann Tango alles gut sein?* Darmstadt, 1981.

Kaplan, Larry. "Pina Bausch: Dancing around the Issue." *Ballet Review* 15 (Spring 1987): 74–77.

Kirchmann, Kay. "The Totality of the Body." *Ballet International* 5 (May 1994): 37–43.

Kozel, Susan. "Bausch and Phenomenology." *Dance Now* 2 (Winter 1993–1994): 49–55.

Manning, Susan. "An American Perspective on Tanztheater." *Drama Review* 30 (Summer 1986): 57–79.

Mau, Leonore. *Ensemble: Pina Bausch, Das Tanztheater Wuppertal: Portraits.* Saint Gall, Switzerland, 1988.

Sanchez-Colberg, Ana. "'You Put Your Left Foot In, Then You Shake It All About . . .': Excursions and Incursions into Feminism and Bausch's Tanztheater." In *Dance, Gender, and Culture*, edited by Helen Thomas. New York, 1993.

Schaik, Eva van. "The Amused Muse." *Ballett International* (November 1995): 36–45.

Servos, Norbert. *Het danstheater van Pina Bausch.* Amsterdam, 1982.

Servos, Norbert. "Tanz und Emanzipation: Das Wuppertaler Tanztheater." *Ballett International* 5 (January 1982): 50–59.

Servos, Norbert, and Gert Weigelt. *Pina Bausch Wuppertal Dance Theater, or, The Art of Training a Goldfish: Excursions into Dance.* Cologne, 1984.

Wehle, Philippa. "Pina Bausch's Tanztheater: A Place of Difficult Encounter." *Women and Performance* 1 (Winter 1984): 25–36.

FILM. Klaus Wildenhahn, *What Are Pina Bausch and Her Dancers Doing in Wuppertal?* (BRD, 1982).

ANITA FINKEL

BAVARIAN STATE BALLET (Bayerisches Staatsballett), formerly known as the Munich State Opera Ballet or the Bavarian State Opera Ballet. Munich, the capital of Bavaria, enjoyed various forms of dance entertainment for many years before ballet was introduced at court in the sixteenth century. At first, the Bavarian court opera ballet was directed almost exclusively by Italian or French ballet masters. The first important date in Munich's ballet history is 29 January 1781, the date of the premiere of Mozart's opera *Idomeneo, Rè di Creta,* for which Peter Legrand arranged the ballets in the final *divertissement.* In 1792 the official theater ballet school opened under the direction of a ballet master named Crux. Three years later, the Italian dancer and choreographer Salvatore Viganò and his wife, the Spanish ballerina Maria Medina, appeared at Munich's Hoftheater in Viganò's production of *La Fille Mal Gardée.* Male members of the audience greatly appreciated Madame Viganò's spirited dancing and revealing costumes, although some viewers considered the entire display to be vulgar or even obscene.

The National Theater opened in 1818, and it is in this house—burned down, bombed, and rebuilt several times—that the Bavarian State Opera's ballet company performs to the present day (with occasional performances at the Old Residence of Cuvilliés Theater, reconstructed from its original design of 1753). Here the Taglionis appeared as guests in 1825. Friedrich Horschelt was ballet master from 1820 to 1829 and again from 1839 to 1847, and it was under him that the Romantic ballet flourished, with Fanny Elssler and Lucile Grahn as guest stars. Grahn enjoyed Munich so much that she decided to stay, winning appointment as ballet mistress from 1869 to 1875. She was responsible for the bacchanale in the Munich premiere of Wagner's opera *Tannhäuser* and for the first productions of Delibes's *Coppélia* and *Sylvia.*

The next ballet master at Munich to attract wide attention was Heinrich Kröller. From 1917 to 1930 he staged many noteworthy premieres, including Richard Strauss's *Die Josephslegende,* Béla Bartók's *The Wooden Prince,* Igor Stravinsky's *Petrouchka* and *Pulcinella,* Ernst Krenek's *Mammon,* and John Alden Carpenter's *Skyscrapers.* From 1939 to 1944 Pia and Pino Mlakar were especially active; among other productions, they revived *Jocko, the Brazilian Ape,* created by Filippo Taglioni for his daughter Marie in 1826, and they premiered Richard Strauss's *Verklungene Feste,* an extended version of his *Couperin Suite,* in 1941. The Mlakars were the first directors to engage an official notator, Albrecht Knust, for their ballets.

After World War II, the Munich State Opera Ballet for many years followed a shaky course, shifting from one extreme to another under ballet masters and directors who had very different aesthetic aims. Those who made the strongest impressions on the company included Marcel Luipart (1945–1948), who choreographed the world premiere of Werner Egk's *Abraxas* in 1948, although it was considered so scandalous that it was banned after only a few performances; Victor Gsovsky (1950–1952), responsible for Boris Blacher's *Hamlet* (1950), Jean Schneitzhoeffer's *La Sylphide* (1951), and Georges Auric's *La Chemin de la Lumière* (1952); Alan Carter (1954–1959), who mounted the first German productions of Benjamin Britten's *Prince of the Pagodas* (1958) and Hans Werner Henze's *Ondine,* (1959); Heinz Rosen (1959–1968), with the Carl Orff triptych of *Carmina Burana, Catulli Carmina,* and *Trionfo di Afrodite* (1959–1960); John Cranko (1968–1970), in addition to his Stuttgart obligations; Ronald Hynd (1970–1973); Lynn Seymour (1978–1980); Edmund Gleede (1980–1984); and Hynd again (1984–1986), when he produced Offenbach's *Le Papillon* (1984). After Hynd's resignation the company was run by Annette Page as deputy director, with Stefan Erler and Alexander Minz as ballet masters.

In 1990, Konstanze Vernon was appointed artistic director, and the company's official name was changed to the Bavarian State Ballet. For many years the leading ballerina of the company, Vernon (with her husband, Fred Hoffmann) had in 1987 established the Heinz Bosl Foundation to further the careers of young dancers. [*See the entry on Bosl.*] She had also been director of the Munich Ballet Academy. Since Vernon assumed directorship, the company's roster of dancers and its repertory have made rapid progress, resulting in many invitations to tour abroad, including a fortnight at the New York State Theater in 1993.

The repertory of the Bavarian State Ballet is now firmly based on the classics: Frederick Ashton's *La Fille Mal Gardée, Giselle* (both Peter Wright's classical version and Mats Ek's modern one), Ray Barra's *Don Quixote* and *Swan Lake,* Wright's *The Sleeping Beauty,* and John Neumeier's *The Nutcracker.* These are supplemented by Cranko's *Onegin* and Neumeier's *A Midsummer Night's Dream.* Emphasis is laid on regular collaborations with such renowned European choreographers as Hans van Manen and Jiří Kylián, but the repertory also features works by American choreographers, including George Balanchine, Jerome Robbins, Twyla Tharp, Peter Martins, Lucinda Childs, and Robert La Fosse. Other guest choreographers have included Uwe Scholz, Youri Vámos, Angelin Preljocaj, and Stefan Thoss. From the company, Davide Bombana has emerged as the most promising junior choreographer.

The company roster for the 1996/97 season listed Vernon as artistic director; Cherie Trevaskis, Davide Bombana, and Thomas Mayr as ballet masters; and Stefan Erler in charge of the opera ballet. Principal dancers were Kiki Lammersen, Elena Pankova, Judith Turos, Anna Valladolid, Kirill Melnikov, and Oliver Wehe; in addition, there were eight soloists, nine demi-soloists, and a corps of thirty-three dancers. The company is now scheduled to perform regularly at the Prinzregenten Theater as well as at the National Theater and the Cuvilliés Theater.

BIBLIOGRAPHY
Friess, Hermann, et al. *Ballett-Theater.* Munich, 1963.
Koegler, Horst. "München." In *Friedrichs Ballettlexikon.* Velber bei Hannover, 1972.
Mlakar, Pia, and Pino Mlakar. *Unsterblicher Theatertanz: 300 Jahre Ballettgeschichte der Oper in München.* Wilhelmshaven, 1992.

HORST KOEGLER

BAXTER, RICHARD (died 1747), Anglo-French comic dancer. Baxter was almost certainly of English birth, but he made his main career as a comic dancer in France. His appearances in London were essentially those of a foreign visitor.

Nothing is known of Baxter's training. He first appeared in London at Drury Lane on 22 August 1702, when he performed an "Italian Night Scene" with his usual French partner, Monsieur Sorin (Surreine, Serene). His fame was that of a Harlequin dancer (indeed, he was commonly known as "the English Harlequin"). His performances were in the characters of the *commedia dell'arte;* the night scenes in which he specialized exploited the simple conceit of pretended darkness with a variety of dexterous physical tumbles and pranks.

The comic duo of Sorin and Baxter made appearances of varying lengths at Drury Lane and Lincoln's Inn Fields each year until 1705. Thereafter, they did not return to the London stage for ten years. Baxter danced with Louis Nivelon's company at the Saint-Germain fair. When, in 1711, the troupe disbanded, the players were reorganized and shortly thereafter placed under the leadership of Sorin and Baxter as Le Nouvel Opéra-Comique de Baxter et de Sorin.

Richard Steele, of the influential journal *The Spectator,* finally managed to bring them back to London in 1716 after their troupe disbanded. Their repertory was more varied than on their earlier visit, with not only their usual night scenes, but longer pieces, such as *La Guinquette, or Harlequin Turn'd Tapster; La Caprice;* and *The Whimsical Death of Harlequin.*

They had a certain importance in England that went beyond the provision of lightweight entertainment: John Weaver saw in them the degenerate remains of the noble scenical dance that had flourished as a form of serious art in ancient Greece and Rome, providing him with the first material for his important experiments in dramatic dance. For Weaver they represented the continuity of an important tradition: "The Remains indeed of these surprizing Performances of the *Pantomimes* are to be found still in *Italy,* but sunk and degenerated into Pleasantry and ludicrous representations of *Harlequin, Scaramouch,* Columbine, Pierot, &c." (Weaver, *History of the Mimes and Pantomimes,* 1728).

The rest of Baxter's career was a disappointment. He returned to France and toured with Sorin until 1721, subsequently setting up another company and managing the Opéra-Comique. When this failed, Baxter seems to have left the stage, although he made at least one more professional appearance in London, as Harlequin in *Perseus and Andromeda* in 1762. Baxter died in 1747.

Baxter represented in London—more brilliantly than any other contemporary dancer—the tradition of the Paris fairs in which the formulaic and actorish conventions of Italian *commedia dell'arte* were subtly transmuted into the abstract stuff of dance. It was in this form that Italian comic traditions were to vitalize European dance in the late eighteenth century.

BIBLIOGRAPHY
Goff, Moira. "Dancing Masters in Early Eighteenth-Century London." *Historical Dance* 3.3 (1994): 17–23.
Highfill, Philip H., Jr., et al., eds. *A Biographical Dictionary of Actors, Actresses, Musicians, Dancers, Managers, and Other Stage Personnel in London, 1660–1800.* Carbondale, Ill., 1973–.

Ralph, Richard. *The Life and Works of John Weaver.* London and New York, 1985.

Rosenfeld, Sybil. *The Theatre of the London Fairs in the Eighteenth Century.* Cambridge, 1960.

RICHARD RALPH
with Moira Goff

BAYADÈRE, LA. Russian title: *Bayaderka.* Ballet in four acts, seven scenes, and an apotheosis. Choreography: Marius Petipa. Music. Léon Minkus. Libretto: Marius Petipa and Sergei Khudekov. Scenery and costumes: Ivan Andreyev, Mikhail Bocharov, Petr Lambin, Andrei Roller, Matvei Shiskov, and Heinrich Wagner. First performance: 23 January 1877, Maryinsky Theater, Saint Petersburg. Principals: Ekaterina Vazem (Nikia), Lev Ivanov (Solor), Maria Gorshenkova (Gamzatti), Christian Johansson (Dugmanta, rajah of Golconda), Nikolai Golts (The Great Brahmin), Pavel Gerdt *(grand pas de deux).*

The libretto of *La Bayadère* was influenced by that of *Sacountala,* a two-act ballet staged by Lucien Petipa at the Paris Opera in 1858. The libretto for this work, written by Théophile Gautier, was based on the drama *Abhijñānaśakuntala* by Kālidāsa, the fifth-century Indian dramatist and epic poet. The main ideas of this masterpiece of Sanskrit drama, which tells the love story of King Dusyanta and the nymph Śakuntalā, were reinterpreted by Marius Petipa and Sergei Khudekov in the four acts and seven scenes of *La Bayadère,* and a tragic denouement was added.

The action takes place in ancient India. The love between Nikia, a *bayadère* (dancer and singer, keeper of the sacred flame in a Hindu temple), and Solor, a wealthy *kṣhatriya* (a warrior of the royal caste), incites the wrath of their powerful enemies, the Great Brahmin, who is in love with Nikia, and the Rajah Dugmanta, whose daughter Gamzatti (or Hamzatti) is Solor's fiancée. Nikia dies when she is bitten by a snake hidden in a basket of flowers presented to her by Gamzatti at a religious festival. Only in the world of dreams, the Kingdom of the Shades, does Solor meet the shadow of his beloved. But Solor's marriage to Gamzatti is not to be: an earthquake destroys the temple, and all its occupants are buried alive under the debris. In an apotheosis, the shadows of Nikia and Solor meet again.

La Bayadère is a moving story of the anguished and restless soul of a woman fiercely defending her right to love. The poetic and dramatically convincing part of Nikia—as revealed in the dialogue scenes with Solor, the Great

LA BAYADÈRE. Matilda Kshessinska and Pavel Gerdt in the *grand pas de deux* from the Kingdom of the Shades scene. Kshessinksa made her first appearance as Nikia in this ballet on 3 December 1900 at a benefit performance for Gerdt at the Maryinsky Theater, Saint Petersburg. Anna Pavlova danced the third variation in the Kingdom of the Shades. (Photograph from the Dance Collection, New York Public Library for the Performing Arts.)

Brahmin, and Gamzatti, and culminating in the subtle and sinuous snake dance—is one of Marius Petipa's supreme achievements. The score by Minkus, although not musically profound, is eminently danceable and is well suited to conveying the characters' moods of sadness and joy. The dramatic story line unfolds against the background of a lavish extravaganza, replete with exotic, atmospheric dances that exhibit Petipa's rich imagination and compositional gift.

A case in point is the famous Kingdom of the Shades scene. Often performed on its own as an independent ballet, this scene is an excellent example of Petipa's choreographic symphonism and use of vivid imagery. It opens with one of the most remarkable entrances for a corps de ballet in the entire balletic repertory: one by one, thirty-six dancers, dressed in white tutus with gauzy white scarves cascading from the head down, swim into view from a cleft in a rock set in the background. Flowing slowly down an incline to the stage floor, they move forward by a combination of step, *arabesque penchée*, *posé cambré*, *port de bras*, a two-phrase theme hypnotically repeated again and again until the dancers gradually fill the whole of the stage. Many critics have likened this ethereal spectacle to a spreading mist or billowing clouds. But the most striking aspect of the passage is its serene lyricism, an enchanting, dreamlike quality suggesting the vision of the grieving Solor.

After its premiere at the Maryinsky Theater in Saint Petersburg, *La Bayadère* almost never left the repertory, undergoing only slight modifications in successive subsequent revivals in 1884, 1900, 1920, and 1941. The 1941 revival, which is still running, was mounted by Vladimir Ponomarev and Vakhtang Chabukiani. This is a three-act variant, in which the *grand pas* of the original final act (the wedding of Solor and Gamzatti) is danced in act 2 and from which the apotheosis is dropped; the ballet now ends with the Kingdom of the Shades scene. Act 1 also features additional dances and more choreographic development in Solor's role.

A landmark in the stage record of *La Bayadère* was Aleksandr Gorsky's version for Moscow's Bolshoi Theater, which had its premiere on 25 January 1904. Liubov Roslavleva danced Nikia and Mikhail Mordkin was Solor. At this time, Gorsky made only small changes in Petipa's choreography, and his rendition was staged again in 1907 and 1910. But in 1917 Gorsky produced a new version of his own with new decor and costumes by Konstantin Korovin, who based his designs on paintings and sculptures from ancient Indian temples. Dancing figures on old bas-reliefs and poses of bronze statues also influenced the patterns of Gorsky's new dances. Korovin's use of Indian motifs and forms extended to his costume design for the shades, although here some critics felt he had upset the poetic lyricism of the scene in which the dancers had previously always worn white tutus. In 1923, Petipa's choreography for the shades was reinstated by Vasily Tikhomirov, along with the traditional costumes.

La Bayadère has been repeatedly produced by leading ballet companies all over the former Soviet Union. Natalia Makarova staged the complete ballet for American Ballet Theatre in 1980, Rudolf Nureyev mounted it for the Paris Opera Ballet in 1992, and Dawn Weller produced it for PACT Ballet in Pretoria, South Africa, in 1996. The Kingdom of the Shades scene has been put on by many ballet companies around the world.

BIBLIOGRAPHY

Benois, Alexandre. *Reminiscences of the Russian Ballet.* Translated by Mary Britnieva. London, 1941.

Croce, Arlene. "Makarova's Miracle" (1974). In Croce's *Afterimages.* New York, 1978.

Krasovskaya, Vera. *Russkii baletnyi teatr vtoroi poloviny deviatnadtsatogo veka.* Leningrad, 1963.

Lopukhov, Fedor. "Bayaderka." In *Marius Petipa: Materialy, vospominaniia, stati,* edited by Ana Nekhendzi. Leningrad, 1971.

Lopukhov, Fedor. "Khoreograficheskaya stsena 'Teni' v balete Bayaderka." In Lopukhov's *Khoreograficheskie otkrovennosti.* Moscow, 1972.

Petipa, Marius. *Russian Ballet Master: The Memoirs of Marius Petipa.* Edited by Lillian Moore. Translated by Helen Whittaker. London, 1958.

Reynolds, Nancy, and Susan Reimer-Torn. *Dance Classics.* Pennington, N.J., 1991.

Roslavleva, Natalia. "Treasure from the Past." *Dance and Dancers* (May 1989): 25–28.

Scherer, Barrymore. "Maligned Minstrel: Putting in a Good Word for Ludwig Minkus, Composer of *La Bayadère.*" *Ballet News* 1 (May 1980): 22–23.

Sirvin, René. "Special Bayadère." *Danser* (October 1992): 34–36.

Souritz, Elizabeth. *Soviet Choreographers in the 1920s.* Translated by Lynn Visson. Durham, N.C., 1990.

Wiley, Roland John, trans. and ed. *A Century of Russian Ballet: Documents and Accounts, 1810–1910.* Oxford, 1990. Includes an extract from Ekaterina Vazem's memoirs and the libretto of *La Bayadère,* with editorial notes.

VICTOR V. VANSLOV
Translated from Russian
Amended by Claude Conyers

BAYANIHAN PHILIPPINE DANCE COMPANY.
The performances of the Bayanihan Philippine Dance Company are the prime cultural export of the Republic of the Philippines. The company, whose name denotes team spirit or an atmosphere of unselfish cooperation, has its roots in the initiative taken by Francisca Reyes Aquino and Jorge Bocobo in the 1920s to foster a renewal of the local arts, especially in folk song and dance. With Aquino's aid, the Philippine Women's University (then Philippine Women's College) set up an informal program of collecting and preserving native dances and music, regional costumes, and native crafts. The Filipiniana Folk Music and

Dance Committee was organized informally, and occasional dance recitals were performed by students.

In 1954 the Philippine Women's University Dance Group, Bayanihan's predecessor, participated in the Asian Folk Dance and Music Festival in Dacca. This was the first serious attempt to present Philippine folk dance on the international stage. In 1956 a theatrical presentation of folk dances was well received at an international convention in Manila. Encouraged, in 1957 the Philippine Women's University established the Bayanihan Folks Arts Center to host the presentations of a newly organized group, the Bayanihan Philippine Dance Company.

After its initial world tour, the Bayanihan's offerings evolved from simple folk dances into stylized, theatrical dance suites comparable to presentations by the Ballet Folklórico of Mexico or Russia's Moiseyev Dance Company. The person responsible for this was Lucrecia Reyes Urtula (with the cooperation of Libertad Fajardo and Lourdes Villaflor during the company's formative years), Bayanihan's choreographer and dance director—a pioneer in the research of tribal dances on both Luzon Island and in the southern Philippines.

As a pioneering dance troupe, the Bayanihan has enjoyed numerous distinctions, including that of being the first Philippine group to dance for Russian audiences. Its many awards include the top award at the Brussels Exposition in 1958 for *Glimpses of Philippine Culture;* the Special Critics' Award for Folk Ensemble at the 1960 Fêtes des Nations in Paris; and the Ramón Magsaysay Award from the Rockefeller Foundation.

BIBLIOGRAPHY

Alejandro, Reynaldo Gamboa. *Philippine Dance: Mainstream and Crosscurrents.* Quezon City, 1978.
The Bayanihan Experience. Manila, 1987.
Lardizabal, José, et al., eds. *Bayanihan.* Manila, 1987.
Usopay, Cadar H. "The Bayanihan: How Authentic Is Its Repertoire?" *Solidarity* (December 1970): 45–50.
Williams, Peter. "The Air Was Touched with Tangerine." *Dance and Dancers* (March 1960): 14–19.

REYNALDO GAMBOA ALEJANDRO

BAYLIS, NADINE (born 15 June 1940 in London), British scenery and costume designer. Simplicity of means and sensitivity to the needs of the choreography are the outstanding attributes of Baylis's designs for dance. Her work, done principally for Ballet Rambert and the choreographers associated with that company, belongs to the type of stage design that serves the dance rather than competes with it.

Baylis made her first stage designs while a student at the Central School of Art and Design in London. Her association with Ballet Rambert began in 1965 with Norman Morrice's *Realms of Choice.* Her designs for Glen Tetley's *Ziggurat* (1967), which Morrice called "our first new-wave ballet," were a guiding element in the company's new direction. Baylis's austere style accorded well with the Ballet Rambert's new emphasis on modern dance. Her use of materials, colors, and textures displayed both imagination and sensitivity. She herself has noted that her earlier use of "steel and chrome and perspex and things like that" gave way to softer materials when she perceived a trend toward a more romantic style of choreography.

The dance critic and historian John Percival wrote of Baylis's costume designs, "She is perhaps unmatched at dressing dancers down (putting them in almost nothing to look marvellous)." She rarely makes costume sketches, preferring to work out her designs directly on the dancer's body. "I cannot work it out two-dimensionally. I can only work it out three-dimensionally like a sculptor," she has said.

Baylis has designed many ballets for Tetley, notably *Ziggurat* (famous for its open-mesh tights) and *The Tempest* (1979), which reflected her interest in Japanese and Chinese stage design. Sir John Tenniel's classic illustrations for Lewis Carroll's *Alice in Wonderland* provided the inspiration for her much-acclaimed costumes for Tetley's dreamlike *Alice* (1986), created for the National Ballet of Canada. She has also worked frequently with Morrice and Christopher Bruce.

Beginning in the 1980s, she has increasingly broadened the range of her assignments beyond Ballet Rambert. She and Tetley have continued their longtime association with *Orpheus* (1987) for the Australian Ballet and *Oracle* (1994) for the National Ballet of Canada. Her European work has included Michael Corder's *Romeo and Juliet* (1992) for the Norwegian National Ballet, and London Contemporary Dance Theatre's *The Phantasmagoria* (1987), which cochoreographers Robert Cohan, Darshan Singh Bhuller, and Tom Jobe based on the illusionistic magic shows of the late eighteenth and early nineteenth centuries. In the United States, she has collaborated with Val Caniparoli and Ben Stevenson.

BIBLIOGRAPHY

Baylis, Nadine. "Designing in the Third Dimension: Nadine Baylis Talks to Dance and Dancers." *Dance and Dancers* 29 (April 1978): 30–32.
Crisp, Clement, et al., eds. *Ballet Rambert: Fifty Years and On.* Rev. and enl. ed. Ilkley, England, 1981. Contains a chronology of works by Baylis for the Ballet Rambert.
Gow, Gordon. "Nadine Baylis: Designer." *The Dancing Times* 69 (July 1979): 637–639.

SUSAN AU

BEATON, CECIL (born 14 January 1904 in London, died 18 January 1980 in Salisbury), British photographer, stage designer, playwright, and author. As a child, Beaton first became interested in ballet when he was taken to see

Serge Diaghilev's Ballets Russes. He received his first camera at the age of eleven and often imitated theatrical photographs. As a stage designer, he was self-taught. His first stage design, for a production of Ben Jonson's *Volpone*, was made while he was a student at Cambridge University in 1923. His first published photograph appeared in *Vogue* magazine in 1924. In 1926 he met Diaghilev, whose praise of his photographs encouraged Beaton to open a studio in London. Although he gained fame for his fashion and society photographs, his subjects also included dancers, such as Tilly Losch, Alexandra Danilova, Serge Lifar, Margot Fonteyn, and Rudolf Nureyev.

Beaton first worked professionally as a stage designer for Charles B. Cochran's revue *Streamline* (1934). In 1936 he designed his first ballet, Frederick Ashton's *The First Shoot*, which was a sketch in a Cochran revue, *Follow the Sun*. Beaton designed a number of Ashton's ballets, notably *Apparitions* (1936; revised in 1949), *Illuminations* (1950), *Picnic at Tintagel* (1952), and *Marguerite and Armand* (1963). This last brought together for the first time his interests in photography and stage design, with its use of images projected onto backcloths.

Beaton also designed ballets for George Balanchine, David Lichine, and John Taras, as well as plays, operas, musical comedies, and British and Hollywood films. Although most successful as a period designer, Beaton liked the challenge of designing ballets, stating in an interview, "The problem is to keep the stage empty enough: the dance should decorate it."

BIBLIOGRAPHY. Beaton published many volumes of memoirs, containing choice tidbits about dancers, ballets, and stage design. More specialized works include his *Ballet* (London, 1951); "Designing for Ballet," *Dance Index* 5 (August 1946): 184–204; and "Scenery and Costume Design for the Ballet," *New York Times* (29 July 1956). Simon Fleet wrote a definitive article "Cecil Beaton as Ballet Designer," in *Ballet Annual* 4 (1950): 79–81. Charles Spencer's *Cecil Beaton* (New York, 1995) is an excellent study of his stage works, with an extensive bibliography. James Danziger, ed., *Beaton* (New York, 1980), provides information on other aspects of his life and reproduces many of his photographs. The authorized biography *Cecil Beaton* was written by Hugo Vickers (London, 1985).

Susan Au

BEATS. *For discussion of beating movements in ballet, see* Battement; Batterie.

BEATTY, TALLEY (born c.1923 in New Orleans, died 29 April 1995 in New York City), American dancer, choreographer, and teacher. Over a career that spanned nearly six decades, Beatty came to be acknowledged by dance critics as one of America's most brilliant dancers and choreographers. He began his dance studies at age eleven in the late 1930s under the tutelage of Katherine Dunham and was a principal dancer with her company for several years as well as a teacher of the Dunham technique. After becoming an independent dancer in 1945, he performed in filmmaker Maya Deren's *A Study in Choreography for Camera* (1945), in a revival of *Show Boat* (1946), in Syvilla Fort's *Procession and Rite* (1947), and in Helen Tamiris's *Inside U.S.A.* (1948).

In 1947 Beatty formed his own company, called Tropicana. For the company premiere he created *Southern Landscape,* a dance about the plight of African Americans in the South after the Civil War. The second section, "Mourner's Bench," a poignant solo performed by Beatty, became a landmark performance event. The company disbanded in 1955, after which Beatty began to devote his time to solo concerts and to choreograph for companies in the United States and abroad.

Beatty choreographed more than fifty ballets, and many of his dances have become American classics. Among his most notable dances were *The Road of Phoebe Snow* (1959); *Come and Get the Beauty of It Hot* (1960), which included the popular pieces "Congo Tango Palace" and "Toccata"; *Montgomery Variations* (1967); and The *Stack-Up* (1983), created for the Alvin Ailey American Dance Theater. His Broadway credits included *Don't Bother Me, I Can't Cope* (1972) and *Your Arm's Too Short to Box with God* (1976).

BEATTY. Talley Beatty in his dance *Southern Landscape,* outdoors at Jacob's Pillow, 1948. (Photograph by Eric Sanford; from the archives at Jacob's Pillow, Becket, Massachusetts.)

Beatty felt deeply about inequitable conditions in American society. Many of his dances were personal statements about alienation, racial discrimination, and the hardships of urban life. His choreography employed abstract design rather than narrative gesture to explore themes and tell stories. The movement vocabulary was fast, exuberant, explosive, and driven by the rhythm of the music. Dance phrases contained aerial, grounded, and spiraling movements that combined leaps, leg extensions, backward torso arches, and suspended body turns. His choreography, considered by dancers to be technically challenging as well as physically demanding, requires proficiency in ballet and modern and jazz dance. He was known as a perfectionist and an unusually stern taskmaster, and being able to perform his work is regarded as a significant achievement.

An essential aspect of Beatty's ability was his musicality. He identified nuances in syncopation and counterpoint and urged dancers to listen to the rhythm in order to learn movements and to understand the emotional messages in the music. Beatty was drawn to the work of American composer Duke Ellington, with whom he collaborated on several ventures, including two television specials, *A Drum Is a Woman* (NBC, 1956) and *Black, Brown, and Beige* (CBS, 1974). *Ellingtonia,* his tribute to Duke Ellington, premiered at the American Dance Festival in 1994.

In 1988, after fifty years in the dance world, Beatty received national recognition for his contributions by being selected as a choreographer for the American Dance Festival's preservation project, The Black Tradition in American Modern Dance, initiated to examine, heighten public awareness of, and preserve the master works of black choreographers. In 1993 Beatty received the Samuel H. Scripps / American Dance Festival Award for lifetime achievement in modern dance.

BIBLIOGRAPHY

Cohen-Stratyner, Barbara Naomi. "Beatty, Talley." In *Biographical Dictionary of Dance.* New York, 1982.

Dunning, Jennifer. "Talley Beatty, Who Depicted Inner-City Life in Dance, Dies." *New York Times* (1 May 1995).

Jamison, Judith, with Howard Kaplan. *Dancing Spirit.* New York, 1993. See pages 75–77.

Long, Richard. *The Black Tradition in American Dance.* New York, 1989. See pages 132–134.

Nash, Joe. "Talley Beatty." In *African American Genius in Modern Dance,* edited by Gerald Myers. Durham, N.C., 1993.

MELANYE P. WHITE-DIXON

BEAUCHAMPS, PIERRE (also known as Beauchamp; born October 1631 in Paris, died 1705 in Paris), French dancer, dancing master, choreographer, and composer. Pierre Beauchamps (often erroneously referred to as either Pierre-François or Charles-Louis Beauchamps) almost singlehandedly shaped and refined the concept of ballet and developed classical technique and style. He was a vital link in a long line of musicians and dancing masters that can be traced back to the early sixteenth century. His grandfather Christophe Beauchamps was a Parisian violinist; his uncle Pierre held the coveted position of violinist of the king's chamber; and his father, Louis, who inherited that position upon Pierre's death, was a much respected dancing master. The younger Pierre's mother, Denise Héron, was the granddaughter of Jean Henry, yet another violinist. On his paternal side, Beauchamps was related to Molière, who played an important part in his life, and all told his family provided some forty violinists to the king's chamber. Additionally, through the marriage of his sister, Catherine, his family tree was further strengthened by an alliance with the Blondys. [*See the entry on Michel Blondy.*]

Music was part of Pierre's life from his earliest years, and he soon became a proficient violinist. Who his official dance teacher was remains unknown. In 1648, "Le sieur Beauchamps" appeared for the first time in the program of the court ballet *Le Dérèglement des Passions,* thus beginning a career that would span three decades. Most likely, when Louis XIV came to power in 1661, Beauchamps was appointed intendant of the king's ballets or held that position unofficially.

His closest collaborator was the composer Jean-Baptiste Lully, whose career closely paralleled Beauchamps's. Lully, who began as a dancer, collaborated on the choreographies of a few works by Beauchamps, who, in turn, composed some of the dance tunes in Lully's scores. As a consequence, it becomes difficult to separate these two artists' contributions to ballet at either the court or the Paris Opera. "These two great men," wrote François Raguenet in 1702, "brought [ballet] to a high degree of perfection which no one in Italy or any other part of the world has ever exceeded and might never exceed."

Beauchamps also worked frequently with Molière, including on the latter's 1661 play, *Les Fâcheaux* (The Bores), for which he composed his first complete ballet score and conducted the orchestra.

In his dual capacity as music composer and choreographer, Beauchamps was entrusted in 1669 with the production of ballets presented by the Jesuits in their colleges. In 1672, he went from the court to the newly founded Paris Opera. First hired by Pierre Perrin, for whom he choreographed *Pomone,* Beauchamps was to devote the rest of his career to working with Lully. Although he formally retired upon the latter's death in 1687, he continued to choreograph the *ballets de collège* at the Jesuit Collège Louis-le-Grand until at least 1697.

Beauchamps perhaps is best known as a dancing master. Pierre Rameau, in his *Le maître à danser* (1725), credits him with the regulation of arm movements and the codification of the five basic feet positions that were to become the foundation of classical ballet technique. Some of Beauchamps's students—Jean Favier, Anne-Louis Lestang, Claude Marc Magny, and Michel Blondy—rose to great prominence in the theater, and one of Beauchamps's private students was Louis XIV.

In 1680, Beauchamps was appointed chancellor of the Académie Royale de Danse, replacing its first director, François Galand du Désert. Beauchamps was then living at 5 rue de Bailleul in the Petit Hôtel d'Aligre and moved the academy from the Louvre to his home. Free dance classes were held each Thursday for professional dancers and noble amateurs alike. Possibly during these sessions, Beauchamps began to show the system of dance notation that he is credited with inventing around 1680.

In 1687, he received unofficial privileges from the chancellery to engrave dances in this notation, although he never bothered to publish his system. In 1704, four years after the publication and success of Raoul-Auger Feuillet's *Chorégraphie*, which made extensive use of a notation system to record dance patterns, Beauchamps filed a petition against the royal privileges that had been granted to Feuillet in 1699. To establish his claim, Beauchamps produced five volumes of his own notation, including the *Chaconne de Phaëton* (1684), together with the testimonies of twenty-five French and foreign dancing masters. He lost his case, however, which might indicate that his system was significantly different from Feuillet's. He died seemingly in obscurity one year later. Pierre Beauchamps never married, and he seems to have lived quietly with his sister Louise, to whom he left an enormous fortune consisting of several houses and a vast collection of paintings.

Beauchamps is known to have been fond of drawing, and his interest in art led him to befriend a number of well-known artists, including Charles Lebrun and Jean Berain. His collection of works by Italian masters was famous in Europe; it was often visited by tourists. Many of these paintings hang in the Louvre today. In 1707 the whole Beauchamps estate was donated by Louise to Joseph Marchand and his wife, Marie-Geneviève Contugy. Regrettably, no inventory of the collection was ever made.

[*See also* Académie Royale de Danse; Ballet de Collège; Feuillet Notation; *and the entry on Lully.*]

BIBLIOGRAPHY

Astier, Régine. "Pierre Beauchamps and the Ballets de Collège." *Dance Chronicle* 6.2 (1983): 138–163.
Astier, Régine. "Louis XIV, premier danseur." In *Sun King: The Ascendancy of French Culture during the Reign of Louis XIV.* Washington, D.C., 1992.
Astier, Régine. "When Fiddlers Danced to Their Own Tunes: The Beauchamps Scores." In *The Marriage of Music and Dance: Papers from a Conference Held at the Guildhall School of Music and Drama, London, 9th–11th August 1991.* Cambridge, 1992.
Beauchamps, Pierre. *Recherches sur les théâtres de France.* 3 vols. Paris, 1735.
Bonnet, Jacques. *Histoire générale de la danse, sacrée et profane.* Paris, 1723.
Derra de Moroda, Friderica. "Chorégraphie, the Dance Notation of the Eighteenth Century: Beauchamp or Feuillet?" *Book Collector* 16 (Winter 1967): 450–476.
Despréaux, Jean-Étienne. *Mes passe-temps: Chansons suivies de l'art de la danse.* Vol. 2. Paris, 1806.
Fleck, Stephen H. *Music, Dance, and Laughter: Comic Creation in Molière's Comedy-Ballets.* Paris, 1995.
Harris-Warrick, Rebecca, and Carol G. Marsh. *Musical Theatre at the Court of Louis XIV.* Cambridge, 1995.
Hastings, Baird. *Choreographer and Composer.* Boston, 1983.
Howell, John. "Pierre Beauchamps, Choreographer to Molière's Troupe du Roy." *Music and Letters* 76 (May 1995): 168–186.
Kunzle, Régine [Astier]. "Pierre Beauchamps: The Illustrious Unknown Choreographer." *Dance Scope* 8 (Spring–Summer 1974): 32–42; 9 (Fall–Winter 1974–1975): 30–45.
Kunzle, Régine [Astier]. "In Search of L'Académie Royale de Danse." *York Dance Review,* no. 7 (Spring 1978): 3–15.
Le Cerf de la Viéville, Jean-Laurent, seigneur de Freneuse. *Comparaison de la musique italienne et de la musique françoise.* 3 vols. Paris, 1704–1706.
Loret, Jean. *La muze historique* (1650–1665). 4 vols. Edited by C.-L. Livet. Paris, 1857–1878.
Mercure de France (1673 and 1677).
Parfaict, François, and Claude Parfaict. *Histoire manuscrite de l'Académie Royale de Musique.* Paris, n.d. Manuscript located in Paris, Bibliothèque Nationale, fr.12355.
Raguenet, François. *Paralèle des Italiens et des François, en ce qui regarde la musique et les opéra.* Paris, 1702. English translation by J. E. Galliard (1709) published in *Source Readings in Music History,* edited by Oliver Strunk (New York, 1950).
Rameau, Pierre. *Le maître à danser.* Paris, 1725. Translated by Cyril W. Beaumont as *The Dancing Master* (London, 1931).
Richardson, Philip. "The Beauchamp Mystery" (parts 1–2). *The Dancing Times* (March–April 1947).

ARCHIVE. Bibliothèque Nationale, Paris: Laborde Fichier, VIII, nos. 3185, 3195.

RÉGINE ASTIER

BEAUJOYEULX, BALTHAZAR DE

BEAUJOYEULX, BALTHAZAR DE (Baldassare da Belgiojoso; born early sixteenth century in Italy, died c.1587 in Paris), Italian-French choreographer. Although Beaujoyeulx was of Italian origin, he has been called the first French choreographer. In his ballet designs he moved away from dependence on the social dances that dominated court festivities throughout the first half of the sixteenth century to compose intricate dance patterns that set large groups of dancers in a structured dramatic framework.

Beaujoyeulx came to France from Savoy in 1555 in the employ of the maréchal de Brissac. His reputation as violinist was so substantial that, on his arrival in France, he was immediately engaged by Queen Catherine de Médicis and became musical tutor to her sons.

Beaujoyeulx's first royal commission was probably the *Paradis d'Amour,* a ballet danced at the wedding of Marguerite de Valois and Henri de Navarre in August 1572. Little is known about this ballet; Simon Goulart noted in his *Memoirs on the State of France under Charles IX* that its focus was a choreographed battle, with Protestant nobles playing the roles of devils while Catholic princes danced as angels.

In 1573 Beaujoyeulx designed *Le Ballet des Polonais*, created to honor the Polish ambassadors who had come to Paris to seek an heir to the throne of Poland. For this performance, sixteen nymphs representing the provinces of France enacted a complicated ballet, in the words of a contemporary observer, Brantôme, "of such strange invention that through all the twists and turns, the intertwinings and blending of steps and sudden stops, it was astonishing that not one lady of the company fell into error."

Beaujoyeulx's supreme contribution to the history of dance came at the end of his career with *Le Balet Comique de la Royne*, which he created for the marriage of Henri III's favorite, the duc de Joyeuse, to the queen's sister in October 1581. The work was on a much larger scale than anything tried before in France. Although the performance lasted five hours, Beaujoyeulx managed to fuse dance, music, and recitation into a harmonious whole. He was clearly influenced by the poetic and musical experiments of the Académie de Musique et de Poésie, yet he gave the major role to dance. The movements and figures, he claimed, had been calculated to mirror the motions of the celestial spheres so that good influences might be drawn down from heaven to earth. The climax of the spectacle showed twelve naiads (danced by a princess and duchesses) performing forty different dance figures.

Accuracy, proportion, knowledge, and inventiveness set Beaujoyeulx apart from his contemporaries. His name survives while others' do not because he was conscious that he was the creator of new forms. He responded readily to demands for a choreography that matched the desires of the Valois court for a new aesthetic. There is no mention of Beaujoyeulx in the archives after 1581.

[*See also* Balet Comique de la Royne, Le; *and* Ballet de Cour, *article on* Ballet de Cour, 1560–1670.]

BIBLIOGRAPHY

McGowan, Margaret M. *L'art du ballet de cour en France, 1581–1643.* Paris, 1963.

McGowan, Margaret M., ed. *Le Balet Comique by Balthazar de Beaujoyeulx, 1581.* Binghamton, N.Y., 1982.

MARGARET M. McGOWAN

BEAUMONT, CYRIL (Cyril William Beaumont; born 1 November 1891 in London, died 24 May 1976 in London), dance historian, critic, technical theorist, bookseller, publisher, and translator. Raised in London in the cultured middle class, at nineteen Beaumont abandoned his scientific studies to pursue a career in bookselling. Beaumont's bookshop in London dealt initially in literary classics, but after his interest in dance was stimulated by Diaghilev's Ballets Russes, his stock of dance books superseded that of general literature. By 1920, his shop had become an internationally known center of dance literature, and it remained so until it closed in 1965.

Beaumont influenced the development of twentieth-century English ballet and dance writing and exercised his role as mentor to numerous well-known English dancers and dance writers. His first major ballet project was the codification of the Cecchetti system in *A Manual of the Theory and Practice of Classical Theatrical Dancing*, written in 1922 with Stanislas Idzikowski. In the same year he founded the Cecchetti Society to disseminate and monitor the master's style and teaching methods.

Beaumont, aware of the lack of historical dance records, sought to rectify this in his *Complete Book of Ballets* (1937) and in its three supplements (1942, 1954, and 1955), which document the most significant ballets from the end of the eighteenth century to the 1950s. The provision of detailed records of ballets and their creators is Beaumont's most extensive contribution to dance. He described and assessed the theme, plot, design, choreography, and performance of ballets that he unearthed from archives and libraries.

Beaumont was chairman of the Cecchetti Society from 1922 to 1970, editor of the *Dance Journal* from 1924 to 1939, ballet critic of the *London Sunday Times* from 1950 to 1959, and chairman of the ballet section of the London Critics' Circle from 1951 to 1961. In 1950, he was named to the Légion d'Honneur for his studies in French history, and in 1962 he was awarded the Order of the British Empire. He published more than forty books on dance, as well as numerous articles in books and periodicals.

BIBLIOGRAPHY

Adelman, Katherine M. "The Critical Writing of Cyril W. Beaumont." Master's thesis, York University, 1982.

Beaumont, Cyril W., and Stanislas Idzikowski. *A Manual of the Theory and Practice of Classical Theatrical Dancing.* London, 1922.

Beaumont, Cyril W. *Michel Fokine and His Ballets.* London, 1935.

Beaumont, Cyril W. *Complete Book of Ballets.* London, 1937.

Beaumont, Cyril W. *Supplement to Complete Book of Ballets.* London, 1942.

Beaumont, Cyril W. *The Ballet Called Giselle.* 2d rev. ed. London, 1945.

Beaumont, Cyril W. *Ballet Design: Past and Present.* London, 1946.

Beaumont, Cyril W. *The Ballet Called Swan Lake.* London, 1952.

Beaumont, Cyril W. *Ballets of Today: Being a Second Supplement to the Complete Book of Ballets.* London, 1954.

Beaumont, Cyril W. *Ballets Past and Present: Being a Third Supplement to the Complete Book of Ballets.* London, 1955.

Beaumont, Cyril W. *Bookseller at the Ballet: Memoirs, 1891 to 1929.* London, 1975.

Beaumont, Cyril W. "Forty Years' Writing on the Ballet." *Ballet Annual* 6 (1952): 69–78.

"Cyril W. Beaumont: 70th Anniversary Supplement." *Dance and Dancers* 12 (December 1961): 21–27.

KATHERINE M. ADELMAN

BECK, HANS (born 31 May 1861 in Haderslev, Denmark, died 9 June 1952 in Copenhagen), Danish dancer, director, and ballet master. Hans Beck was eighteen when August Bournonville died. Although he was not personally taught by the old master (who retired from teaching the year Beck was to enter his class), it was to Bournonville that Beck owed his ideals as a dancer, teacher, choreographer, and ballet master. Thus even as the Danish Ballet entered an experimental new century under Beck's leadership (1894–1915), the company remained dedicated to the Bournonville tradition. Beck's efforts to maintain the repertory and technique of his predecessor were sometimes criticized as provincial; nevertheless, Beck's faith and foresight preserved both Bournonville's genius and Danish ballet's national character.

The effort of preservation began as early as 1893, with Beck's creation of the teaching method known as *Bournonville-skolen.* Using exercises developed by Bournonville and steps from Bournonville ballets, Beck assembled six lessons, one for each working day of the week. The *skolen* became the foundation of the company's training and of the children's school at the Royal Theater. It remained in place until 1951, when Vera Volkova brought the Vaganova method to the curriculum.

Beck was the third ballet master of the Royal Danish Ballet, following Bournonville, after Ludvig Gade and Emil Hansen. Beck had been a celebrated dancer who made his debut in 1871 with Bournonville in the audience two days before he died. Beck took over the company and continued to dance until 1910; it was a difficult period, when the government was cutting funding for ballet and a new bourgeois audience preferred frivolous programs. He had to sacrifice many details in the Bournonville repertory and was forced to make hundreds of abridgments of the old works. Today, it is the Beck editions of Bournonville that are performed at the Royal Theater in Copenhagen.

While western European state companies surrendered to the new Russian ideals, Beck, supported by the Danish press, resisted the influences of modernism and Diaghilev. During his leadership only two works from the non-Danish repertory were staged in Copenhagen—a successful *Coppélia* (1896) and *Les Millions d'Arlequin* (1906). A version of his setting of *Coppélia* is still performed today, more than a century after its creation.

Of Beck's choreography only one work, *The Little Mermaid* (premiered 26 December 1909), has had lasting importance. Based on Hans Christian Andersen's fairy tale and set to music by Fini Henriques, the choreography was inventive and delicate in the Bournonville style. The famous statue in Copenhagen's harbor is a memorial to its ballerina, Ellen Price, who had been Bournonville's favorite dancer.

In one respect Beck was a pioneer. In the first decade of

BECK. Hans Beck, c.1889, as Emil in "The Reel" scene of Bournonville's vaudeville-style ballet *The King's Volunteers on Amager* (1871). Beck created such a sensation with this lively number that when he switched parts to play Edouard in a 1905 production of the ballet, he continued to perform in "The Reel." In subsequent productions, the character Eduoard has been included in this scene. (Photograph by Emil Hohlenberg; from the Royal Library, Copenhagen.)

the twentieth century, he allowed Danish court photographer Peter Elfelt (1866–1931) to film various solo and corps dances from the repertory. Not only do the films give us our purest insight into the Bournonville style, they also show Beck's enormous qualities as a dancer. The line of great Danish male dancers, which includes Børge Ralov, Erik Bruhn, and Peter Martins, can be traced back to Hans Beck.

Throughout his career, Beck was also involved with a large school for social dancing.

BIBLIOGRAPHY

Anderson, Jack, and George Dorris. "A Conversation with Svend Kragh-Jacobsen." *Ballet Review* 5.4 (1975–1976): 1–20.

Beck, Hans. *Fra livet og dansen.* Copenhagen, 1944.

Veale, Tom G. "Bournonville Preserved: The Story of Hans Beck." *Dance Magazine* (August 1965): 52–53, 64–65.

ARCHIVE.   Theater History Museum, Copenhagen.

ALLAN FRIDERICIA

BECK-FRIIS, REGINA (born 1940 in Stockholm), Swedish dancer, choreographer, and teacher. Beck-Friis entered the Royal Swedish Ballet School in 1949 and, after graduating in 1957, she became a member of the company. As a soloist she danced the Queen Mother in *Swan Lake,* Berthe in *Giselle,* and various roles in the ballets of George Balanchine, Antony Tudor, and Birgit Åkesson.

Beck-Friis, who studied medieval and Renaissance dance with her mother, the musician Birgitta Nordenfelt, taught historical dance at the State Dance College in Sweden. With Beck-Friis's help and encouragement, a group of students at the college formed the Saltarelli Ensemble (named after a fifteenth- and sixteenth-century court dance) to re-create early European dances. The troupe appeared in Margot Fonteyn's television series *The Magic of Dance,* which was first shown in England in 1979.

Beck-Friis became a choreographic assistant to Mary Skeaping at the Drottningholm Court Theater in 1964 and later worked independently, creating dances and ballet interludes for many operas and *opéra-ballets* at Drottningholm, among them *Orpheus and Eurydice* (1971), *Le Carnaval/Mascarade* (1975), the comic *opéra-ballets Platée* (1978) and *Proserpin* (1980), the ballets *Pygmalion* and *Don Juan* (1985). For the court theater at Ulriksdal, Confidencen, she revived *Opportunity Makes the Thief* (1989), a ballet-pantomime based on Swedish folklore and originally staged by Louis Gallodier, ballet master at the Gustavian Ballet in 1785. Beck-Friis used a well-known tragedy in Swedish circus history for *Elvira Madigan* (1992), performed by the Royal Swedish Ballet.

Beck-Friis has developed dances for Swedish and Canadian television programs about Renaissance culture and music. In 1980, with Magnus Blomkvist and Birgitta Nordenfelt, she published *Dansnöjen genom tiderna* (Dance Entertainment through the Ages).

BIBLIOGRAPHY
Beck-Friis, Regina. *En afton med Drottningholmsbaletten.* Stockholm, 1972.
Beck-Friis, Regina, et al. *Dansnöjen genom tiden.* Stockholm, 1980.
                                                    ANNA GRETA STÅHLE

BEDAYA. *See* Indonesia, *article on* Javanese Dance Traditions.

BEDELLS, PHYLLIS (born 9 August 1893 in Bristol, died 2 May 1985 in Henley), British dancer and teacher. The first important British ballerina of the twentieth century, Bedells studied with Malvina Cavallazzi, Alexander Genée, Adolph Bolm, Enrico Cecchetti, and Anna Pavlova. At age thirteen she made her debut at the Prince of Wales Theatre, London, in *Alice in Wonderland.* She began her career at the Empire Theatre in 1907, dancing in supporting roles, first to Adeline Genée (whom she considered her mentor), and then to Lydia Kyasht. When Kyasht's contract ended in December 1913, Bedells became the *prima ballerina* at the Empire—the first British dancer to hold this position.

After her contract at the Empire expired in 1915, Bedells appeared in many West End musical revues. On 5 February 1918 she married Ian MacBean. In 1920 she danced in a season of opera at the Royal Opera House, Covent Garden, and then in a season of ballet with Laurent Novikoff.

In the same year she became a founding member of the Association of Operatic Dancing of Great Britain (later the Royal Academy of Dancing). Along with Genée, Tamara Karsavina, Lucia Cormani, and Édouard Espinosa, Bedells drew up the association's first syllabus and was an important participant thereafter, evaluating candidates and, after Espinosa resigned, setting the examinations. Bedells was also one of the original members of the Camargo Society in 1930, serving with P. J. S. Richardson as its treasurer and dancing in most of its programs.

After further West End appearances, Bedells danced with Anton Dolin in the 1926/27 London Coliseum season, and then with her own company in 1928. In 1931 she was guest artist for the Vic-Wells (now Royal) Ballet. Bedells retired from the stage after a farewell performance at the London Hippodrome on 8 November 1935. She then became an important teacher, first in Bristol and later in London; she closed her school in 1966. She remained active in the Royal Academy of Dancing all her life, receiving its Queen Elizabeth II Award in 1958 and becoming a Fellow in 1971. Her autobiography, *My Dancing Days,* was published in 1954.

At a time when the British public considered that the only good dancers were foreign, Bedells, a vivacious and spirited performer with an impeccable technique, blazed the trail for native-born British dancers. Though pressured to do so, she refused to disguise her origins under a Russian or French name, as was common at the time. Richardson summed up her importance as a dancer, when, reviewing her farewell performance, he wrote:

> What a wonderful tonic the precept and example of Phyllis Bedells proved. . . . How hopeless it seemed at one time for an English dancer to even try to succeed. . . . We who are old enough to remember such things understand how much the present secure position of native ballet in England is due to [her] inspiring influence.   (Richardson, 1935)

BIBLIOGRAPHY
Bedells, Phyllis. *My Dancing Days.* London, 1954.
Borgnis, Jennifer. "The Forgotten Ballerina." *Dance and Dancers* (May 1982): 24–27.
Genné, Beth Eliot. "Openly English: Phyllis Bedells and the Birth of British Ballet." *Dance Chronicle* 18.3 (1995): 437–451.
Guest, Ivor. *The Empire Ballet.* London, 1962.

Guest, Ivor. *Ballet in Leicester Square.* London, 1992.

Sorley Walker, Kathrine. "The Camargo Society." *Dance Chronicle* 18.1 (1995): 1–114.

BETH ELIOT GENNÉ

BEDOUIN DANCE. The word *bedouin* means "man of the desert" in Arabic; it refers to nomadic herding peoples (sheep, camels, horses) of the Middle Eastern deserts from the Sahara to Iraq. Throughout the region, the bedouins are known to be stern and proud, striving for freedom, believing in courage, dignity, honor, and hospitality.

Ancient Arabic sources indicate that dance has, since earliest times, occupied an important place in bedouin life, enhancing such occasions as family festivities, religious celebrations, pilgrimages to saints' tombs, and social gatherings. The great historian Ibn Khaldūn (1332–1406) describes bedouin music before the seventh-century CE advent of Islam: "Most [Arab] music was in the light rhythm that is used for dancing and marching, accompanied by *duff* [drum] and the [oboelike] *mizmār.* It causes emotion and makes the serious-minded feel light." The conjunction of dancing and marching in this quotation still describes the nature of the dance practiced in bedouin society.

The most common dance in bedouin society is a simple communal dance; the movement aspect is social, functional, and general rather than individual. It is characterized by movements in which the trunk is treated as a single unit, by a limited play of the body in space, with a stiffness, sternness, strength, and weight. Typical bedouin movement patterns and body attitude grew out of the concepts and conditions of desert life and are similar to dances that characterize a noncomplex society.

The *daḥīyah* dance is the chief element of all festivities and social gatherings in the vast area from Egypt to Iraq. It is accompanied by voice only; no musical instruments are used. In the Sinai desert, at any given moment of a gathering or a festival, the men will form a line and chant "daḥīyah, daḥīyah," accompanying themselves by clapping their hands. This allows the dancers a few minutes to get organized and into the mood; it also informs the women, who are seated at a distance, that the men are about to dance. Then, in a muffled voice with a pronounced nasal timbre (in the minor mode), the poet-musician intones the traditional tune of the dance as he improvises verses. This is called *bidʿah* ("invention") in Arabic.

Standing side by side and clapping their hands, the dancers, keeping their feet close to the ground, take small steps forward and back. After each line of the sung verses, they intone a uniform refrain: "rahānī gowl ar-ridah." The meaning of this refrain is obscure, although some believe that *rahānī* and *ridah* are the names of the demon's sons. The dance takes place in darkness, reaching its climax in front of an unmarried woman, who is clad entirely in black. She faces the row of men, brandishing a sword or a stick. Taking large steps and making broad jumps, she waves her sword or stick at the dancers, who alternately move toward and away from her, driven back by her sword.

Although this young woman is supposedly anonymous, all the participants know who she is and pretend to ignore her identity to protect her honor. In bedouin society, the participation of a young woman in the dance is not uncommon. In some places, men and women even perform whole dances together, as in the *daḥīyah* dance of southern Yemen, in which three dancers perform within a circle of dancers. The leader faces the other two dancers, a man and a woman. From around the circle two groups alternate singing a verse and then all join in the chorus. In Iraq, the poet-musician, leading a row of male dancers, invites a young woman to join the dance. She agrees to do so only if she is rewarded with improvised verses in which the poet-musician praises her beauty. Only then does she deign to take part in the dance. This woman is unmarried and unveiled, so that she can be observed by the potential candidates for her hand in marriage.

More complex dances are performed among bedouin groups living on the fringe of the deserts. R. B. Serjeant (1951) describes a dance called *al-shabwānī,* which is accompanied by two kettle drums and a frame drum. The poets and two singers stand in the center of two rows (lines) of performers, while the drummers stand at the end of the rows. While the singers sing, the poets walk from row to row, extemporizing as they do so. When they have finished, the members of one row advance to the opposite row, with their hands unclasped, and leap when they reach it. They then return to their original position while the other row performs the same action. This alternating pattern is performed either once or twice.

The bedouin communal dances differ from certain types of solo dances in which the torso is treated as two units, and the body's motion is basically a twisting or shaking of the hips. Some of the dancers in this second category are either professional wandering dancers or seamen, who live on the margin of bedouin society.

[*See also* Egypt, *article on* Traditional Dance; *and* Iran.]

BIBLIOGRAPHY

Abdullah, A. "Dancing East of Suez." *The Dancing Times* (June 1938): 274–278; (July 1938): 400–403.

Chottin, Alexis. *Corpus de musique marocaine.* Paris, 1931.

Chottin, Alexis. *Tableau de la musique marocaine.* Paris, 1939.

Christensen, Dieter. "Tanzlieder der Hakkari-Kurden: Eine materialkritische studie." *Jahrbuch für Musikalischevolks und Völkerkunde* 1 (1963): 11–47.

Hickmann, Hans. "Quelques considérations sur la danse et la musique de danse dans l'Égypte pharaonique." *Cahiers d'histoire égyptienne* 5 (1953).

Hickmann, Hans. "La danse aux miroirs." *Bulletin de l'Institut d'Égypte* 37 (1954–1955).

Lane, Edward W. *An Account of the Manners and Customs of the Modern Egyptians.* London, 1836.

Serjeant, R. B., ed. *Prose and Poetry from Ḥaḍramawt.* London, 1951.

Shiloah, Amnon. "Ibn Hindu: Le médecin et la musique." *Israel Oriental Studies* 2 (1972): 447–462.

Shiloah, Amnon. *The Theory of Music in Arabic Writings.* Munich, 1979.

Villoteau, C. A. *De l'état actuel de l'art musical en Égypte.* Paris, 1809.

AMNON SHILOAH

BEETHOVEN, LUDWIG VAN (baptized 17 December 1770 in Bonn, died 26 March 1827 in Vienna), German composer. Of Beethoven's vast output of musical compositions, only a few were written specifically for use in dance, although much of his work has been used by choreographers of later generations. The works that he did write for dance are, however, notable, especially his two scores for ballets, one a court ballet and one a Romantic rendition of a classical Greek story.

Beethoven's court ballet, the *Ritterballett* (Ballet of Knights), was conceived by Count von Waldstein in close collaboration with a dancing master, Herr Habich from Aix-la-Chapelle. It had its first production on 6 March 1791 at the Bonn Redoutensaal. At that time Beethoven's name was not even mentioned in conjunction with the production; the count, who may have contributed a few melodic phrases, was credited as the composer.

The music of the *Ritterballett* is not ballet music proper; it is music for a pageant, meant to be performed by members of the court, probably with spoken texts between the individual dances, which were done by guests wearing Old German fancy dress. The score, which has no opus number, consists of eight pieces: (1) a march, (2) a German song—which may be considered the connecting link, functioning as a sort of entr'acte, the strophes of which correspond to Beethoven's later adaptation of Schiller's "Ode to Joy"—(3) a hunting song, (4) a love song, (5) a war song, (6) a drinking song—a setting of the medieval song "Mihi est propositum in taberna mori"—(7) a German dance, and (8) a coda.

Theatrical performances of the *Ritterballett* have been relatively rare, as the work is more a curiosity of dance and music history than one with strong audience appeal. Rudolf Laban choreographed the work for the Congress of Dancers in Magedeburg, Germany, in 1927. Giuseppe Urbani produced another version at the Bonn Municipal Theater in 1962, and Dia Luca staged another for the opening of the 1970 Vienna Festival.

Beethoven's other significant dance piece was *Die Geschöpfe des Prometheus* (The Creatures of Prometheus; op. 43), written in 1800–1801. This heroic-allegorical ballet in two acts was choreographed by Salvatore Viganò and was first performed on 28 March 1801 at the Burg-theater in Vienna, more formally known as the Kaiserlich Königliche Hof-Theater nächst der Burg. According to the playbill, the cast included Herr Cesari as Prometheus, Frau Brendl as Terpsichore, Frau Cesari as Melpomene, Gaetano Gioja as Bacchus, and Fraulein Casentini and Herr Viganò as children; the performers who filled the roles of Apollo, Amphion, Arion, and Orpheus were not listed. The libretto has been lost, so all attempts at reconstruction have been based on the theater bill and Beethoven's score, which consists of an overture, an introduction, and sixteen individual numbers. Beethoven himself arranged the piano score.

Commenting on the music for *The Creatures of Prometheus,* Humphrey Seale has remarked that

the dances . . . are real ballet music in that they are not symphonically constructed but mostly fall into short sections in contrasting moods and tempi which follow the stage action. . . . *Prometheus* was certainly an important step forward, not only for Beethoven himself, but [also for] the whole history of ballet music. (Seale, 1958)

Although the Vienna production was a great success, with the public if not with the critics, Beethoven did not care for it, apparently feeling that Viganò had not done his best work. Still, the ballet was performed sixteen times in 1801 and thirteen times in 1802. Thereafter it was not presented until 1813, when Viganò produced a "mutilated version" at the Teatro alla Scala in Milan, using only four of the score's original pieces and adding other compositions by Beethoven, Josef Weigl, Franz Joseph Haydn (parts of *The Creation*), and Viganò himself.

Important later revivals include those by Serge Lifar (Paris Opera Ballet, 1929), Ninette de Valois (Vic-Wells Ballet, 1936), Aurelio Milloss (Maggio Musicale Fiorentino, 1956), Erich Walter (Düsseldorf, 1966), and Frederick Ashton (Royal Ballet, Bonn, 1970). Richard Strauss used parts of the score for the 1924 Vienna Festival production of *Die Ruinen von Athen* (The Ruins of Athens), on which he collaborated with Hugo von Hofmannsthal and for which the choreography was done by Heinrich Kröller.

In various instrumental arrangements, Beethoven's works have lent themselves to individual dances and sets of dances (marches, polonaises, écossaises, minuets, contradances, ländlers, and so on) for ballroom use. Among the many ballets choreographed to his concert repertory, however, relatively few have enjoyed a long lifespan. Among the more important are the following: Fedor Lopukhov's *The Magnificence of the Universe* (1923), set to Symphony no. 4 (op. 60); a segment of the Walt Disney animated film *Fantasia* (1940), set to Symphony no. 6 (op. 68); Kurt Jooss's *Company at the Manor* (1943), set to the Spring Sonata (op. 24); Antony Tudor's *La Gloire* (1952), set to the *Coriolan, Leonore III,* and *Egmont* overtures (opp. 62, 72a, 84); Maurice Béjart's *Ninth Symphony* (1964; op. 125); Paul Taylor's *Orbs* (1966), set to three string quartets (opp. 127, 130, 133); Hans van Manen's *Grosse Fuge* (1971), an orchestral version of opus 133, and *Adagio Hammerklavier* (1973), set to Sonata no. 29 (op. 106); Dennis Nahat's *Celebrations and Ode* (1984), set to Symphonies no. 7 (op. 92) and no. 9 (op. 125); James Kudelka's *Pastorale* (1989), set to Symphony no. 6 (op. 68); Uwe Scholz's *Seventh Symphony* (1991); and Anne Teresa De Keersmaecker's *Ert* (1992), set to the string quartet known as the Great Fugue (op. 133).

BIBLIOGRAPHY

Gockel, Eberhard. "Beethoven und das Ballett." *Das Tanzarchiv* 18 (1970).

Goldschmidt, Harry. *"Die Geschöpfe des Prometheus* nebst der Musik zu einem *Ritterballet.*" In Goldschmidt's *Beethoven: Werkeinführungen.* Leipzig, 1975.

Kendall, Alan, and Basil Lam. "Ludwig van Beethoven." In *Heritage of Music*, edited by Michael Raeburn and Alan Kendall, vol. 2, *The Romantic Era*, pp. 23–45. Oxford and New York, 1989.

Kerman, Joseph, Alan Tyson, et al. "Beethoven, Ludwig van." In *The New Grove Dictionary of Music and Musicians*, edited by Stanley Sadie, vol. 2, pp. 354–414. London, 1980. Includes a complete list of works and an exhaustive bibliography.

Searle, Humphrey. *Ballet Music: An Introduction.* New York, 1958.

HORST KOEGLER

BEHLE, ANNA (born 1876 in Stockholm, died 1966 in Göteborg), Swedish dancer, teacher, and pioneer of modern dance in Sweden. Behle became interested in dance after seeing Isadora Duncan perform in Stockholm in 1906. She had been educated at the Music Academy in Stockholm, but after meeting Duncan, she studied at Duncan's school in Grünewald, combining courses there with studies under Émile Jaques-Dalcroze in Geneva. She took a diploma under Jaques-Dalcroze and opened a school in Stockholm, an event that marked the beginning of modern dance in Sweden.

Painters, opera singers, theater directors, and even Margaret of Connaught, the crown princess of Sweden, with her friends and two of her children became pupils at the Behle school. Behle gave performances with her students, created many dances, gave public lectures, and wrote about new dance methods.

From this school emerged many professional dancers and teachers, often after further studies on the continent with Mary Wigman and others. In 1916 Behle turned her talents to early dance forms and recreated *Den Fångne Cupido*, one of the famous mid-seventeenth-century court ballets from the reign of Queen Christina. Subsequently, Mary Skeaping based her ballet, *Cupid Out of His Humor* (1956), on the same material. Behle had such great influence on theatrical life in Sweden because she also taught her Duncan-Dalcroze classes to large numbers of students at the Royal Drama School and at the Music Academy.

BIBLIOGRAPHY

Boman, Birgit. *Isadora Duncan och den svenska barndansen.* Stockholm, 1986.

ARCHIVE. Behle's unpublished memoirs are held in the archives of the Dansmuseet, Stockholm.

ANNA GRETA STÅHLE

BÉJART, MAURICE (Maurice Jean Berger; born 1 January 1927 in Marseille), French dancer, choreographer, and director. Béjart is one of the most innovative, respected, and controversial ballet masters in Europe. He is the son of the philosopher and university administrator Gaston Berger, a self-educated man who became a teacher and then general chief of universities in Marseille. Studious and frail as a child, Béjart was enrolled at the age of fourteen in the ballet school of the Marseille Opera because doctors prescribed physical exercise.

In 1945, after graduating from the Lycée de Marseille and the Faculty of Philosophy in Aix-de-Provence, Béjart abandoned his studies, his home, and his name (taking as a pseudonym the surname of Molière's wife). He went to Paris, where he studied ballet with Léo Staats, Lubov Egorova, and Madame Rousanne (Sarkissian). During his early years as a performer, he danced in a number of galas and toured with Solange Schwarz, Janine Charrat, Roland Petit, Yvette Chauviré, and Lycette Darsonval. He was a principal dancer with Mona Inglesby's International Ballet from 1949 to 1950, dancing Siegfried in 239 performances of *Swan Lake*. In 1950 he joined the Royal Swedish Ballet, where he made his first choreographic efforts, staging *L'Inconnu* and *The Firebird* (1950), both of which were filmed.

In 1953, following a tour of duty in the French Army, Béjart joined the critic Jean Laurent in founding Les Ballets Romantiques, subsequently renamed Les Ballets de l'Étoile after the Paris theater where the company performed. Employing the talents of Solange Schwarz, Tessa Beaumont, Dirk Sanders, and Marie-Claire Carrié, Béjart choreographed a number of ballets—some poetic, some comedic. His *Symphonie pour un Homme Seul* was the first ballet to be choreographed to *musique concrète* (taped music prepared from myriad recorded sounds, not necessarily instrumental). With a score by electronic music pioneers Pierre Schaeffer and Pierre Henry, it opened on 26 July 1955. Béjart, in the leading role, played an isolated contemporary man whose despair and alien-ation are deepened by a haunting confrontation with an egocentric and aggressively erotic woman (Michèle Seigneuret). Béjart—who had been profoundly influenced by meeting Martha Graham—

BÉJART. Paolo Bortoluzzi balances on Jorge Donn's back with the assistance of other dancers from the Ballet du XXe Siècle in Béjart's 1964 staging of *The Firebird,* his second treatment of Igor Stravinsky's famous score. (Photograph by Studio Verhassel; from the Dance Collection, New York Public Library for the Performing Arts.)

suddenly revealed a complex personality and discovered a style that combined classic and modern vocabularies. His intricate and subtle weaving of the classical idiom with modern, jazz, and acrobatic motifs was further developed in such works as the psychoanalytic *Voyage au Coeur d'un Enfant* (1955); *Haut Voltage* (1956), with Milorad Miskovitch, Hélène Trailine, and Laura Proença; *Le Teck* (1956), to a score by jazz musician Gerry Mulligan; and *Prométhée* (1956), an evocative retelling of the familiar myth.

In 1957 Béjart's troupe changed its name to Le Ballet-Théâtre de Paris. In that year he created *Sonate à Trois* set to Béla Bartók's *Sonata for Two Pianos and Percussion.* Based on Jean-Paul Sartre's play *No Exit,* the work featured Béjart, Tania Bari, and Seigneuret as three people forced to live together in a room from which there is no escape. For Belgian television, Béjart staged his version of *Pulcinella* (1957), an antic ballet in which Bernard Daydé's costumes and sets complemented Igor Stravinsky's lively score, and *Orpheé* (1958), an esoteric fresco performed by Janine Monin and Germinal Casado, in which themes Béjart subsequently developed in detail appear in outline.

Innovative, optimistic, and a tireless worker, the Béjart of the late 1950s expressed himself in a burst of youthful daring, stripping away nonessentials and relentlessly exploring new relationships between nonmusical sound and music. His choreography showed a disconcerting emphasis on second position, and *port de bras.* In 1959 he was lured to Brussels, where Maurice Huisman, director of the Théâtre Royal de la Monnaie, home of the Brussels

Opera, commissioned *Le Sacre du Printemps.* Finally provided with a large corps de ballet, Béjart altered the plot (replacing the sacrifice of a virgin into the life-affirming ritual mating of a chosen maid and a young man) and eschewed sets and traditional costumes. In three weeks he staged a savage paean to sensual drive and adolescent vitality that has been restaged many times, particularly by the Paris Opera, where it was awarded the Prize of the University of Dance and the Young Critics' Prize (1960). This brilliant success led to Béjart's dancers remaining in Brussels as Ballet du XXe Siècle (Ballet of the Twentieth Century), with Béjart as director.

Béjart, whose dramatic gifts and charismatic stage presence had captivated audiences and critics, gradually withdrew from dancing; he turned his energies to choreography and to developing a troupe of carefully selected dancers representing a wide variety of temperaments, nationalities, races, and body types. The company has gained fame for its extraordinary ebullience, physical beauty, and athleticism, and performed almost constantly throughout the world. A strict taskmaster, Béjart continually challenged his dancers by creating a hybrid universe of action, transforming steps, borrowing from both modern and exotic techniques. Béjart often choreographed for large groups of male dancers, and his company had more male than female dancers. Occasionally, men and women were used interchangeably, as in the erotic *Boléro* (1960), which Béjart created in three versions—one with a male soloist and female corps, another with a female soloist and male corps, and an all-male version.

Béjart's electric choreography has often sparked controversy. For the bacchanale in Wagner's *Tannhäuser*, staged for the Brussels Opera in 1961, Béjart prescribed explicitly sexual movements (as well as costumes simulating nudity), which many observers found offensive. Béjart's surrealistic staging of Offenbach's *Tales of Hoffmann* (1962), with sets by Casado, featured a pulsating lung in a rib cage that opened and closed, a huge eye suspended from the ceiling, and a dancing ostrich. In 1963 Béjart returned to Paris, where he wrote and staged the musical show *La Reine Verte*, starring Jean Babilée and actress Maria Cesareso. This avant-garde work, with music by Pierre Henry, was unenthusiastically received by the press.

When Béjart produced *La Veuve Joyeuse* (The Merry Widow) in Brussels in 1963, he transformed the Viktor Leon–Leo Stein operetta into a spectacular blend of dance, songs, and cinema. He added scenes such as the heroine dancing on a corpse-strewn battlefield and socializing with beggars, which prompted the authors' heirs to bring legal action. Béjart's concern with the total-theater concept of dance is also evident in his version of Hector Berlioz's opera *La Damnation de Faust*, staged at the Paris Opera in 1964. The main roles were doubled, with dancers Cyril Atanassoff, Christiane Vlassi, and Jean-Pierre Bonnefous paralleled by singing counterparts. *Neuvième Symphonie*, set to music by Beethoven, employed eighty dancers representing the nations of the world, a full orchestra, and chorus and soloists; it premiered at the cavernous Cirque Royal (Royal Circus) in Brussels on 28 October 1964. It has since been danced in sports stadiums, circus tents, and great halls throughout the world, captivating audiences with its joyful vision of universal freedom and brotherhood.

The Royal Circus was also the site of the initial presentation of *Romeo and Juliet* (1966), set to music by Berlioz, in which Shakespeare's tragedy was rearranged to illustrate Béjart's pacifist sentiments and his philosophy of the world's redemption through love. The principal roles, created by Paolo Bortoluzzi and Laura Proença, have been danced by various members of the company, including Jorge Donn, Suzanne Farrell, and guest artist Itomi Hasakawa; the work has been restaged for Bolshoi stars Ekaterina Maximova and Vladimir Vasiliev. The work received the Prix de la Fraternité in Paris in 1966 for its statement against racism and for peace. *Messe pour le Temps Présent*, first performed at the papal palace in Avignon as part of the Avignon Festival of the Arts in 1967, reflects Béjart's spiritual ideals. Elements of Eastern mysticism are evident in this long work, which occasionally ended with members of the audience sitting in silent meditation with the cast.

During the 1968 Olympic Festival in Grenoble, Béjart paid homage to Petipa in *Ni Fleurs, Ni Couronnes*, set to music by Tchaikovsky. *Baudelaire* (1968) used psychedelic lighting, amplified sound effects, and a pastiche of music from Wagner to pop in an impressionist exegesis of the nineteenth-century French poet's visions, dreams, and love affairs. Later that year, Béjart choreographed *À la Recherche de . . .*, a triptych that opens with dancers practicing classical ballet steps to music by Anton Webern. Its second section, *La Nuit Obscure*, starred Béjart in a theatrical interpretation of the Spanish mystic San Juan de la Cruz's *Dark Night of the Soul*. In the concluding section, *Bhakti*, based on Hindu religion and philosophy, Béjart used dance movements and positions from India.

Hoping to work with actor-director Jean Vilar and conductor-composer Pierre Boulez, Béjart then considered accepting the directorship of the Paris Opera Ballet. He changed his mind when Vilar withdrew from the project, but he frequently worked at the Paris Opera as a guest, creating an abstract version of *The Firebird* in 1970 with Michaël Denard and Paolo Bortoluzzi in which he used Stravinsky's music but discarded the traditional Fokine scenario. Also for the Paris Opera, Béjart restaged *Serait-ce la Mort?*, with Dominique Khalfouni and Jorge Donn, and *Life*, with Babilée and Elisabeth Platel.

In 1970 Béjart became head of the Mudra (a Hindi word meaning "gesture") Centre in Brussels, which was funded by several foundations. At this international training school for the performing arts, he helped to develop dancers for his company and oversaw works in progress. In 1978, Mudra Afrique was established in Dakar, Senegal. Administrative obstacles resulted in the abandonment of plans to open a Mudra school in Paris in 1981.

In *Le Chant du Compagnon Errant* (1971), Béjart depicts Gustav Mahler's alternately sad, joyous, and somber music

BÉJART. Robert Denvers clasps Suzanne Farrell's hand in *Nijinsky, Clown de Dieu* (1971), Béjart's dreamlike portrait of the dancer Vaslav Nijinsky. (Photograph © 1972 by Jack Vartoogian; used by permission.)

BÉJART. Yann le Gac and Maurice Béjart kneel in *Notre Faust* (1975), Béjart's autobiographical work that combines material from various sources. (Photograph by Dupont; from the Dance Collection, New York Public Library for the Performing Arts.)

as a clash between a tormented young man and his other self, in which the subtle balance changes with the performers. Inspired by Vaslav Nijinsky's remark, "I appear as a clown to make myself better understood. . . . I think that a clown is only perfect when he expresses love, otherwise he is no longer a clown of God," Béjart created *Nijinsky, Clown de Dieu,* a dreamlike portrayal of the great roles, personal torments, and religious yearnings that shaped Nijinsky's life. A large cast, headed by Donn, Bortoluzzi, and Farrell, first presented this ambitious work on 8 October 1971 at the Forest National Auditorium in Brussels. Despite a lukewarm critical reception, the ballet has since drawn appreciative audiences in other large venues.

Such productions reflect Béjart's goal of making his ballets accessible to as many people as possible and attracting new converts to dance from among those more comfortable in a sports arena than in an opera house. Béjart has been warmly supported by the heterogeneous international audience he enjoys provoking (in works such as his outrageous version of Verdi's *La Traviata* [1973]) and moving (in emotional works such as *Ce que l'Amour Me Dit* [1974] and *Ce que la Mort Me Dit* [1978], both to Mahler's music). Offbeat choreography, paradox, and a penchant

to shock characterize other works, including *Stimmung* (1972); *Le Marteau sans Maître* (1973), to a score by Boulez; *Pli Selon Pli* (1975); and *Héliogabale* (1976). In 1980 the hermetic experimental creation *Casta Diva* inaugurated the Institut de Recherche et de Coordination Acoustique Musique in Paris.

Béjart has been strongly influenced by locale. Persepolis suggested the Sufi mysticism of *Golestan* (1973); Florence inspired *I Trionfi di Petrarcha;* and Venice provoked the capricious *Acqua Alta* after his troupe performed on the Grand Canal and the Piazza San Marco during dance festivals in 1975 and 1981. *Light,* to a blend of Vivaldi and California pop music, is also dedicated to Venice. In *Notre Faust* (1975), a largely autobiographical work, Béjart daringly combined material from Goethe, Bach, tangos, drama, and various choreographic styles; the choreographer—returning to the stage at forty-eight—embodied first the young Faust and then Mephisto, while Mephisto becomes the young Faust, danced by Yann le Gac. *Dichterliebe* (1978) is a musical patchwork depicting an artist (played by Jorge Donn) obsessed by his fantasies. A stunning male ensemble dance to Indonesian music highlights *Les Illuminations* (1979).

For *Eros-Thanatos* Béjart wove together eighteen previous works to form a riveting, seamless full-evening ballet. It begins with the climactic mating ritual from *Le Sacre du Printemps* and concludes with the complete *Boléro. Wien, Wien, nur du Allein* (1982) evokes the anguish of life under totalitarianism. Made for guest artist Marcia Haydée—to music associated with Vienna, from Beethoven to Alban Berg—the work depicts a group of men and women trapped in the ruins of a bomb shelter. Political and social themes are also evident in *La Muette,* set to music by Gaetano Donizetti, which was created for the one hundred fiftieth anniversary of the Théâtre Royal de la Monnaie. In honor of the tricentenary of the Comédie Française in 1976, Béjart staged *Le Molière Imaginaire,* a sprawling dance theater work that combined Béjart's dance company with the acting company from the Mudra school. Béjart's penchant for spectacle also led him to stage a number of operas, including in 1981 Mozart's *The Magic Flute* and *Don Giovanni,* and Strauss's *Salome.* Béjart has been constantly inspired by the performers in his company, including Casado, Bari, Donn, and Shonach Mirk, and by such illustrious guest stars as Vladimir Vasiliev—who danced Béjart's version of *Petrouchka*—Maya Plisetskaya *(Leda),* and Marcia Haydée, for whom he created *The Divine: An Homage to Garbo,* about the daydreams of an aspiring actress. *Les Chaises* (premiered in Rio de Janeiro, 1980) was ignited by the performances of Haydée and John Neumeier. In 1986 Béjart created *Kabuki* for the Tokyo Ballet and Eric Vu-An.

He has always viewed his dancers as his collaborators, saying, "Choreography, like love, is made by couples. Since I began I've been perpetually creating the same ballet, journal of friendships, my loves, and my discovery of the universe. That's why it's difficult to judge one of them in isolation—you have to know all of them."

The company of La Monnaie was always loyal to Béjart. Following a disagreement between Béjart and the theater's director, the company disbanded after a June 1987 tour to Leningrad. For nearly twenty-seven years it had consistently reflected the nonconformist aesthetic of its founder. After the dissolution, Béjart founded the Béjart Ballet Lausanne, which made its debut on 21 December 1987 at the Théâtre Beaulieu. Among the most important works of this period were *1789 . . . et nous* (1989), *Ring um den Ring* (1990) after Richard Wagner, *Le Mandarin Merveilleux* (1992), *Lear-Prospero* (1994) after Shakespeare, and *Journal* (1995). In 1994 Béjart was elected to the Académie des Beaux-Arts of the Institut de France. In 1992 he founded at Lausanne (as he had Mudra in Brussels) the École-Atelier Rudra Béjart Lausanne (a two-year course), with Michel Gascard as *directeur-adjoint*.

Among Béjart's many awards and honors are the Hammarskjöld Prize (1973), the Erasmus Prize (1974), and the Prize of the Society of Dramatic Authors (1980). He has written two plays, *La reine verte* (1963) and *La tentation de Saint-Antoine* (1967); a novel, *Mathilde, ou Le temps perdu* (1963); and a number of autobiographical essays, including *L'autre chant de la danse* (1974), *Un instant dans la vie d'autrui* (1979), and *Béjart par Béjart* (1979). Increasingly attracted to film and television, Béjart has staged cinematic versions of *Le Danseur* (1968), *Bakhti, Molière Imaginaire*, and *Je Suis Né à Venise*. He has experimented with every type of spectacle, but dance is his preferred language. "For me," Béjart has stated, "dance is a tool for expressing myself totally, for being, breathing, living, becoming myself."

[*See also* Ballet du XXe Siècle.]

BIBLIOGRAPHY

Béjart, Maurice, et al. *Danser le XXe siècle*. Paris, 1977.
Béjart, Maurice. *Béjart par Béjart*. Paris, 1979.
Béjart, Maurice. *Le ballet des mots*. Paris, 1994.
Boccadoro, Patricia. "Béjart's Return." *Dancing Times* (February 1995): 445–449.
Christout, Marie-Françoise. *Maurice Béjart*. Rev. ed. Paris, 1987.
Cirillo, Silvana, ed. *Corpo, teatro, danza: Béjart, Blaska, Petit*. Brescia, 1981.
Como, William. "Maestro of Spectacle." *Dance Magazine* (May 1987): 84–89.
Livio, Antoine. *Béjart*. Lausanne, 1969.
Mannoni, Gérard. *Maurice Béjart*. Paris, 1991.
Pastori, Jean-Pierre. *De Diaghilev à Béjart*. Lausanne, 1993.
Scheier, Helmut. "Maurice Béjart." *Ballett-Journal/Das Tanzarchiv* 35 (February 1987): 14–17.
Whyte, Sally. "A Traveller through Dance." *Dance and Dancers* (March 1990): 16–17.

MARIE-FRANÇOISE CHRISTOUT
Translated from French

BELARUS. The territory within the republic of Belarus was, until the demise of the Soviet Union in 1991, the Belarussian Soviet Socialist Republic. It has some 80,300 square miles (208,000 square kilometers) and a population of about 10 million. It has also been called White Russia, Byelorussia, and Belarussia. Part of Poland until acquired by the Russian Empire in the partitions of Poland (1772, 1793, and 1795), its population is mainly White Russian, one of Europe's major Slavic groups. From the sixth century CE, the Slavs displaced the Balts in settling this region. Their economy was based on agriculture but along the rivers trade soon became important. Principalities were formed and, by the tenth century, came under the rule of Kiev to form the loosely structured realm of Kievan Rus, which lasted until the mid-twelfth century.

With the Christian conversion of Kiev in 988, Eastern Orthodoxy became the dominant religion. In the thirteenth and fourteenth centuries, Belarussian territory came under Lithuanian control. When Lithuania merged with Poland in 1569, Roman Catholicism became the elite religion. Polish influences increased during the seventeenth and eighteenth centuries; the peasantry continued to speak Belarussian while the aristocracy spoke Polish. Town populations consisted mostly of Jewish merchants and artisans. Even after the partitions of Poland, this social structure remained under Russian rule and into the twentieth century.

Folk Dance. We owe to the perseverance of the people the preservation of a number of ancient folk rites, festivals, and games that have been maintained in Belarus into the twentieth century. Popular among them were "The Marriage of Tsareshka," "The Walk with a Goat," and "The Zazyulys Game." The round dances preserve links with pre-Christian agricultural and family rites. They are known for their wide variety of compositional patterns, movements, and tempos. The slow dances contain combinations of moving figures like spiral, snake, stream, and gate along with ornamental arm patterns and elements of pantomime. The quick dances feature virtuoso solo stunts and lightning movements. Some variants of round dances from the fourteenth through the sixteenth centuries also survive, including *kolo, paduschechka*, "Hare," "Sparrow," and "Little Goose." In addition to dances with definite patterns, improvisation is also in evidence. In some solo and group dances the participants use improvisation, expressing their feelings and moods in spontaneous movements. Traditional folk dances are varied in theme and often imitate work, natural phenomena, and animals. The mood is generally cheerful, and the prevailing rhythm is 2/4. The dances are performed mainly by couples or groups, although there are some solo dances. There is little difference between men's and women's dances.

In the nineteenth century, Belarusian folk dances began to assimilate elements of various urban ballroom dances, such as the quadrille and the polka, although strongly influenced by local tradition and stylistically distinct. The

BELARUS. Women of the Hungarian State Folk Ensemble, 1956, in an agrarian dance from Belarus, which depicts the planting, growing, and harvesting of the potato crop. (Photograph by Ferencné Bartal; reprinted by permission from Rezso Varjasi and Vĺue Horváth, *Hungarian Rapsody: The Hungarian State Folk Ensemble*, Budapest, 1956.)

trend has continued into this century. Improvised solo dances are often accompanied by the singing of four-line songs, which are sometimes improvised also. Even before World War II, Belarus had professional folk dance companies. The company of the Belarussian Republic was founded in 1953; Aleksandr Opanasenko and Semen Drechin were its most prominent leaders. Other important groups are the Folk Choir of Belarus, whose first leader was Petr Akulenok, and the Khoroshki company, founded in 1973 by Valentina Gaevaya.

Theatrical Dance. The first professional actors and dancers in Belarus were the clowns of the twelfth century. Dance was also an element in folk dramas of the seventeenth century and in the puppet theater called *batleika*. In the eighteenth century, serf theaters with ballet companies, which staged pantomimes, pastoral and mythological ballets, and *divertissements*, were created on large estates and in cities. Some serf theaters had their own schools and their own choreographers, of whom Antoni Loiko was one. Some of the serf dancers later appeared on the stages of the imperial theaters. In the 1740s, Maurice Pion led a private ballet company of Belarussian dancers in Vitebsk, but there was no established professional theater until after the 1917 October Revolution. The first bal-

lets were staged in the 1920s by K. Aleksiutovich at what is now the Yanka Kupala Theater.

The Opera and Ballet Theater of Belarus was founded in 1933 in Minsk, the capital. The first ballet produced was the classic Soviet ballet *The Red Poppy* (1927), with choreography by Lev Kramarevsky. The first national ballet was *The Nightingale* (1940), choreographed by Aleksei Yermolayev, to a libretto by Yuri Slonimsky and Mikhail Kroshner. In this ballet a fury of folk hatred is symbolized by a snowstorm. Using a traditional device, the hands of the dancers beat out the storm with brightly colored, embroidered towels. A circle of people dressed in bright costumes presses tightly around the enemy forces dressed in black, arresting their movements and forcing them to clamber up one another to form fantastic pyramids. In the end the snowstorm dancers annihilate the hostile forces. The dance of anger turns into a dance of victory and celebration.

Other ballets on traditional and modern themes were choreographed by Aleksei Andreev and Otar Dadishkiliani, whose *Alpine Ballade* tells the love story of two fugitives from a Nazi death camp. Classical ballets are also staged. The chief choreographer since 1973 is Valentin Elizariev. His *Till Eulenspiegel* (1978) is danced to a score by Evgeny Glebov and has a strongly patriotic tone; the enemy is represented by a monster that resembles at once a gigantic spider, a terrible, many-handed idol, and an animated swastika. IIis most recent ballet is *Rogneda* (1995). The company has toured widely. Among the leading soloists, all trained in the Minsk ballet school that opened in 1945, are Ludmila Brzhozovskaya, Nina Pavlova, Viktor Sarkisian, Yuri Troyan, Vladimir Ivanov, Vladimir Komkov, and Serge Pestekhin.

[*See also the entry on Elizariev.*]

BIBLIOGRAPHY
Churko, Yulia M. *Belorusskii balet.* Minsk, 1966.
Churko, Yulia M. *Belorusskii baletnyi teatr.* Minsk, 1983.

YULIA M. CHURKO
Translated from Russian

BELGIUM. [*This entry comprises two articles on dance in Belgium. The first article explores the history of theatrical dance; the second discusses dance education.*]

Theatrical Dance

Belgium became an independent state in 1830 when it seceded from the Netherlands. Today most of the population belongs to one of two major ethnic groups—the Dutch-speaking Flemings in the north and the French-speaking Walloons in the south; there is a small German-speaking group in eastern Belgium. In 1993 Belgium became a federal state with four areas: Flanders, Wallonie,

Brussels, and a German-speaking region. Each has its own government that provides grants for cultural projects. Prior to independence, domination by a succession of foreign powers hampered the development of a definitively Belgian dance tradition.

Early History. In 1384 the group of medieval states that is now Belgium came under the rule of the dukes of Burgundy. During this rich and prosperous time, *moresca* dances were performed by court-appointed minstrels, and pantomimes were presented at lavish celebrations. Mary of Burgundy, who reigned from 1477 to 1482, supported the arts and invited musicians to teach and perform at her courts in Brussels and Mechelen.

Margaret of Austria, who ruled the Low Countries at the beginning of the sixteenth century, compiled a handbook describing forty-nine *bassesdanses*. After Belgium passed to the Spanish branch of the Habsburg family in 1516, Flanders became the center of Belgian cultural and political life. Flemish music grew in popularity throughout Europe, particularly in Spain, leading to an exchange of court musicians.

In the town of Binche in 1549, Mary of Hungary, regent of the Netherlands and sister of Charles V of Spain, organized a feast to celebrate the conquest of the Incas in Peru. One of the highlights was a dance in which the performers painted their faces and wore yellow and red costumes and feathered headdresses; they carried baskets of oranges, which they tossed to the audience. The dance was so successful that it became a part of the Belgian folk tradition, and the folk dance troupe Les Gilles des Binches traces its roots to this 1549 festival.

In Antwerp in 1551, the composer and calligrapher Tylman Susato published *Het derde musyck boexcken* (The Third Dance Music Book), which contained music for rounds, *bassesdanses*, *pavanes*, *galliardes*, and *allemandes*, as well as one *saltarello*. Also popular at the time were *carolles*, in which children stood two by two in a circle; one child held a tambourine, which another child struck, while all the participants sang and made foot rhythms accentuated by the ringing of bells. Most of the music for these dances was provided by composers whose names are no longer known, but prominent musicians occasionally wrote for dance; Orlande de Lassus, for instance, wrote part of the score for *Le Ballet des Polonais*, commissioned by Catherine de Médicis for the Polish ambassadors and produced in Paris in 1573.

Although Flanders remained a part of the Spanish Empire until 1713, French cultural influences began to permeate it in the seventeenth century. During the reign of Louis XIV of France (1643–1715), Jesuits in Belgium staged French lyric dramas into which dances were woven. Although no dance schools existed in Brussels at the time, in 1606 a guild called Saint Job was organized to teach a wide range of subjects, including dance. For many years Belgian artistic life centered around the guild, but Saint Job's influence waned at the end of the seventeenth century with the arrival of troupes of predominantly French actors and dancers, who introduced Belgian audiences to opera and ballet.

Early Theatrical Dance. *La Selva sin Amor,* staged in Brussels in 1629, was the first opera presented in Belgium. Five years later *Le Ballet des Princes Indiens* was performed at the court, with members of the nobility dancing roles; at the wedding of Philip IV of Spain in 1650, the *ballet de cour Le Ballet du Monde* was performed. The performing arts continued to gain in popularity, leading to the construction of the Grand Théâtre in Brussels in 1682. Seventeen years later the Théâtre de la Monnaie (Theater of the Mint) was built there.

In Ghent, capital of Flanders, a government-sponsored visit by French actors, musicians, and dancers in 1696 led to the creation of the Académie Royale de Musique. The academy's first major production, the ballet *L'Europe Galante,* was staged in 1706, nine years after its premiere in Paris.

The seventeenth century was a turbulent time in Belgium. Invading armies occupied the area for short periods, and in 1713 Spain ceded the region to the Austrian Habsburgs. Although French dance forms continued to gain in popularity, English country dances were taught in Brussels by a number of teachers; in Ghent, Robert d'Aubat also led and taught dances.

During the reign of Empress Maria Theresa (1740–1780), Flanders once again prospered. When the empress visited the Low Countries in 1741, dancers performed a *divertissement, Le Bouquet de la Reine,* and the historical ballet *Les Athéniens.* A heroic ballet, *Le Retour de la Paix,* was staged in honor of the empress's visit to Brussels in 1749. During this period Karel van Lotharingen, the governor of Flanders, organized a number of feasts in which comic ballets were staged.

Maria Theresa was succeeded by her son Joseph II (1780–1790), whose zeal in enforcing the religious and social reforms of the Enlightenment met stiff resistance in Belgium. Censorship was widespread, and theatrical works could not be performed without official permission. In 1789 the Belgians rebelled, but the Austrian emperor Leopold II regained control of Flanders a year later. In 1792 and 1794 the region was invaded by the French, who ultimately forced the Austrians out of Belgium. Theatrical works such as *Mucius Scaevola, Guillaume Tell,* and *Les Victimes Cloîtrées,* which focused on the revolt against Austria, sometimes provoked riots in the streets of Brussels. The area remained under French control until the defeat of Napoleon at Waterloo in 1815.

In 1808 the French dancer-teacher Auguste Vestris and the dancer-choreographer Louis Duport served as judges for a dance competition held in Brussels. In 1816, a year after the Congress of Vienna united Belgium and the United Provinces as the Kingdom of the Netherlands, a permanent corps de ballet was established at the Théâtre de la Monnaie. Three years later, in 1819, Jean-Antoine Petipa was engaged as *premier danseur* and ballet master. Within months he produced his first major work, *La Kermesse*, a ballet set at a Flemish carnival. Petipa created *La Naissance de Vénus et de l'Amour* in 1821, and in 1826 he founded the Conservatory of Dancing, where his sons Lucien and Marius started their training.

The opera *La Muette de Portici,* for which Petipa choreographed the dances, focused on the rise of nationalism that led Belgium to declare its independence in 1830. A constitutional monarchy was set up in 1831, and Prince Leopold of Saxe-Coburg became king of Belgium. To celebrate the successful revolution, Petipa created the ballet *Le 23, 24, 25, et 26 Septembre.* [*See the entry on Jean-Antoine Petipa.*]

Enthusiasm for dance continued to grow during the next decade. The Austrian ballerina Fanny Elssler came to Brussels in 1843 to dance the title roles in *La Sylphide* and *Giselle.* The Royal Opera, founded in Ghent in 1841, added a dance academy in 1848. However, Petipa left Brussels in 1844, and by the 1850s dance had begun to lose its status as an independent art form in the region. The only new choreography was created for opera productions, and in some cities, such as Ghent, operas were mounted without dance.

In Brussels, administrative chaos and political quarrels at the Théâtre Royal de la Monnaie took precedence over artistic advancement. Dance virtually disappeared from Monnaie productions until 1886, when at the opera of Ghent, Voitus van Hamme, a former dance master, became the theater's director in 1886. The same year, *Pierrot Macabre* was staged by Théodore Hannon to the music of Pietro Lanciana. Van Hamme resigned in 1891. From 1900 until 1914 the Théâtre Royal de la Monnaie focused primarily on opera, although Isadora Duncan appeared there several times, and in 1910 Diaghilev's Ballets Russes performed.

After World War I, a resident ballet company was formed at La Monnaie with Sacha Sarkoff, Josette Cerny, Felyne Verbist, and Tylda Amand. Over the next three decades, fifty-six ballets were staged, beginning with Michel Fokine's *Schéhérazade* in 1919. Leonid Katchourovsky, who served as ballet master from 1934 to 1940, choreographed *Aurora's Wedding, Boléro,* and other works for the company.

In Antwerp, a small ballet company was founded in 1923 by Sonja Korty, who had danced two seasons with the Ballets Russes. Vladimir Karnetzky directed the company from 1934 to 1940.

Because Belgium did not have a strong ballet tradition, most of the dancers and choreographers who worked

BELGIUM: Theatrical Dance. Anastasie Gauthier in a *divertissement* from Giacomo Meyerbeer's grand opera *Robert le Diable.* This lithograph, dated 1841, ten years after the opera's premiere in Paris, appears in *Galerie des artistes dramatiques des théâtres royaux de Bruxelles.* (Dance Collection, New York Public Library for the Performing Arts.)

there came from other countries. In 1933 Madame Akarova created dances for the company Onze Tijd, directed by the Dutchman Johan de Meester. The dance company of the Théâtre Royal de la Monnaie performed under the directorship of François Ambrosiny, beginning in 1904.

In 1936 a Belgian dancer, Paul Grinwis, made his debut with the opera company in Ghent. Ten years later he danced with Colonel de Basil's Original Ballet Russe and then joined the company of the Grand Opera House in Bordeaux, for which he choreographed *La Nuit Impure, Symphonie Fantastique, La Méprise,* and *Sinfonietta.* He worked in Australia in 1951 and from 1954 to 1961, dancing with the Borovansky Ballet and choreographing *Les Trois Diables, Les Chats, Parades, La Mort d'un Matador,* and *Les Amants Éternels* for the company. After touring the United States with Le Grand Ballet du Marquis de Cuevas, he returned to Europe, opening his own school in Ghent in 1974.

Elsa Darciel (also known as Elsa Dewette) was one of the first Belgian dancers to be influenced by Isadora Duncan and the school of expressive dance. Darciel was in her teens when she saw Duncan perform in Brussels in the early 1920s. In 1933 she went to Essen, Germany, to study dance at the Folkwang Schule. She toured Belgium extensively, helping to spark interest in modern dance.

Léa Daan, another important figure in expressionist dance in Belgium, took classes during the 1920s with Francesca D'Aler and studied in Germany with Albrecht Knust, Rudolf Laban, and Kurt Jooss. In 1931 she opened a school in Antwerp, and three years later she founded a dance company. The company, Dansgroep Léa Daan, received awards at the International Dance Competition in Berlin in 1936 and in Brussels in 1939. Beginning in 1946, Daan conducted movement classes for actors in Ghent and Brussels. She disbanded her company in 1956.

A third Belgian dancer to focus on expressionist dance was Isa Voos, who in 1937 founded a company with which she toured the country. One of the first choreographers to stress Belgian themes, she created *The Faithful Shepherd* (1937) and *Farmers' Dances* (1938). Her other works include the avant-garde *Klachte der Levenden* (1938), and *Live* (1938), which had no musical score.

In 1947 Valentina Belova, who had danced at the Flemish Royal Opera House in Antwerp, founded Ballet Belges, the first autonomous Belgian ballet company, with herself as prima ballerina and Michael Charnley as premier danseur. The troupe had a short life, and in 1949 Belova formed the Chamber Ballet Company, which she turned over to Jaak van Luyt in the early 1950s. In 1957 van Luyt founded a dance studio out of which there developed a small dance company, Danstoneel. Van Luyt also served as choreographer at the Flemish Royal Opera House for the 1961/62 season.

At the beginning of the 1950s dance had yet to find a large following in Belgium. Occasional all-ballet evenings were presented at the Flemish Royal Opera House, with works by non-Belgian ballet masters Karoly Zsedény (1949–1950 season), Jacques Milliand (1951–1958), and Leonid Katchourovsky (1958–1962). From 1947 to 1953 dance festivals were organized regularly, but they did little to help build an audience.

Some important steps were taken in the mid-1950s when the Soviet dancer and teacher Nicholas Zvereff accepted an invitation to teach in Belgium. In 1954 Jean-Jacques Etchevery of the Paris Opera Comique became ballet master at the Théâtre Royal de la Monnaie, where he choreographed *Les Bals de Paris*, a production for which eleven Belgian composers wrote the music. Etchevery remained in Brussels for five years, staging such works as *Pélleas et Mélisande, Candide, Symphonie Fantastique,* and *Francesca da Rimini.* French dancer and choreographer Joseph Lazzini, who was director of ballet at the Théâtre Royal in Liège from 1954 to 1957, staged *Le Chasseur Maudit, La Fille Mal Gardée, Remords,* and *Ode des Ruines.* [*See the entry on Lazzini.*]

One of the most successful Belgian dancers of the 1950s was Marie-Louise Wilderijckx. She made her debut in the ballet company of the Royal Flemish Opera in 1956 and became a soloist in 1960, dancing leading roles in *Judith, The Triumph of the Spirits,* and *Spookkar.* After studying in Leningrad she returned to Belgium, where from 1966 to 1968 she worked with Louise Delvaux at the Royal Opera House in Ghent. She joined the Ballet van Vlaanderen as a principal in 1970.

The first Belgian-based company to attract a large, enthusiastic audience was the Ballet du XXe Siècle, founded in 1960 by Maurice Béjart. The company achieved worldwide fame with its "total theater" spectacles, which featured classical dance, songs, dialogue, striking costumes, spectacular scenery, and special effects. Though Béjart created most of the repertory, other choreographers (including Janine Charrat, Anton Dolin, Léonide Massine, and Aurelio Milloss) also worked with the company. The dancers came from many countries, and glamorous guest artists appeared frequently. Along with regular seasons in Brussels, the company made a number of successful tours throughout the world. Threatened with financial cuts, Béjart left Brussels in 1987. [*See Ballet du XXe Siècle and the entry on Béjart.*]

The following year Mark Morris was appointed director of dance at the Théâtre Royal de la Monnaie. Béjart had taken his dancers with him to Lausanne, and Morris chose to use dancers from his own company along with others trained in modern dance. The residency was accompanied by extensive tours. In 1991 Morris choreographed *The Hard Nut,* his own version of *The Nutcracker,* and *The Death of Klinghoffer,* an opera by John Adams. [*See the entry on Morris.*]

Influenced by modern dance from the United States, a company called Saltatina emerged in 1962 in Brussels with Lut van Campenhout as its choreographer and artistic director. Jazz dance became popular in physical education classes and in recreation centers, from which several amateur companies developed. In 1966 the Ballet de Wallonie was formed in Charleroi (now known as Charleroi/Danses). This troupe has gained international status, as has the Antwerp-based Koninklÿk Ballet van Vlaanderen, founded in 1969. [*See Charleroi/Danses.*]

Since the early 1980s, a new form of dance emerged in Belgium, influenced, in part, by experiments in the United States as well the neoexpressionist movement in Germany and new developments in France. A major force in dance experimentation disappeared when Béjart left Belgium. However, new initiatives emerged and pushed the development of dance in other directions. In 1973, Plan K was founded in Brussels by Frédérick Flamand. The goal was to create a dialogue among different art forms. In 1979, La Raffinerie du Plan K was organized as an international center for multi-arts research. A second center, located in Brussels, was called Plateau. Here training and performing spaces were made available and new dance forms encouraged. Dancers such as Pierre Droulers, Michèle Noiret, Nicole Moussoux, Patrick Bonté, José Besprosvany, Avi Kaiser, Thierry Smits, and Diane Broman developed their choreographic skills at Plateau. Guest teachers such as Steve Paxton encouraged creativity and, as a result, choreographer Patricia Kuypers developed her work in contact improvisation.

Anne Teresa De Keersmaeker, who studied at Mudra (a school in Brussels directed by Béjart) from 1978 through 1980, was important for her work in Brussels. After studying in New York in 1981, De Keersmaeker choreographed a work to the music of Steve Reich. In 1983 she founded her company, Rosas. De Keersmaeker's early work was strongly rhythmic, repetitive, and abstract. In later works she added emotional overtones to her characteristic mathematical structures. Several of her works have been filmed: *Violin Phase* (1986, to the music of Eric Pauwels), *Achterland* (1990, filmed in 1994) *Ottone Ottone I & II* (1991), *Rosa* (1992), *Amor Constante, Mas alla de la Muerte* (1994, set to music by Thierry de Mey). In 1988,

BELGIUM: Theatrical Dance. Members of the Ballet du XXe Siècle in Maurice Béjart's *Les Vainqueurs* (1969), a work that combined Hindu initiation rites with the legend used in Richard Wagner's opera *Tristan und Isolde*. (Photograph from the Dance Collection, New York Public Library for the Performing Arts.)

De Keersmaeker received a Bessie Award and in January 1992 her company, Rosas, became the resident company at the Théâtre Royal de la Monnaie.

In the French community, from 1991 on, the major impulses came out of Charleroi/Danses, Centre Chorégraphique de la Communauté Française de Belgique (the successor of the Ballet de Wallonie) with Frédérick Flamand as artistic director. The company's aims are to produce or co-produce contemporary dance works, to organize a Biennial International Dance Festival, to present Belgian and foreign companies, and to train professional dancers. From 1989 to 1994, Flamand, along with the Italian artist Fabrizio Plessi, produced three works that studied the relationship between man and technology *(The Fall of Icarus, Titanic,* and *Ex Machina)*. Aiming to break down the walls among various artistic disciplines, Flamand choreographed *Moving Target* in collaboration with two New York architects, Elizabeth Diller and Ricardo Scofido.

Another product of the Mudra school was Michèle Anne de Mey. She danced in Anne Teresa De Keersmaeker's first concerts but eventually went her own way in the French-speaking community of Belgium. De Mey has choreographed works for the Kaaitheater in Brussels, for Charleroi/Danses, and became resident choreographer for Brussels's Théâtre Varia. Her early works, *Balatum* (1984) and *Face à Face* (1986), were inspired by minimal, repetitive movements. Her later works, such as *Sinfonia Eroica* (1990) and *Sonatas 555* (1994), show a fast fluidity of movement.

In the Flemish community, modern dance started to develop under the guidance of the Festival de Beweeging, located in Antwerp. From this emerged a number of Flemish choreographers such as Karin Vyncke, Alain Platel, Marc Vanrunxt, and Bert van Gorp. Some critics referred to the style of these choreographers as "anti-dance."

Under the auspices of the international dance festival Klapstuk, the Merce Cunningham Dance Company, as well as modern dance choreographers Susanne Linke, Maguy Marin, Jan Fabre, and Trisha Brown, gave new impulse to the developing dance groups in Belgium. Two choreographers came out of Fabre's productions: Eric Raeves and Wim Vandekeybus (who ultimately founded his own company, Ultima Vez). The major theme in Vandekeybus's work is the study of chaos and conventionalism in society. Klapstuk also co-produced performances and among those appearing was the American dancer Meg Stuart.

Dance also plays an important role in the cultural life of the German-speaking part of Belgium. Cie Irène K plays a leading role in its development. The cultural centers in Belgium's leading cities have started to program dance and, in the realm of classical modern dance, Paleis (in Brussels) has presented internationally renowned modern dance companies.

BELGIUM: Theatrical Dance. Marina Nicoloau, David Campos Cantero, and Vinciane Ghyssens with the Royal Ballet of Flanders in Valery Panov's 1984 version of *Romeo and Juliet*. (Photograph by J. M. Bottequin; from the Dance Collection, New York Public Library for the Performing Arts.)

Other dance troupes and organizations are dedicated to preserving the centuries-old folk dances that once thrived in Belgium. De Volksdanscentrale voor Vlaanderen is adapting folk dances for community organizations. Other groups, such as Verbond voor Vlaamse Volkskunst, are reconstructing Flemish dances. The Nationale Jeugddienst voor Volksdanse has compiled many dances from different countries.

[*See also* Royal Ballet of Flanders *and the entries on Jeanne Brabants and André Leclair.*]

BIBLIOGRAPHY

Acocella, Joan. "Anne Teresa De Keersmaeker." *Dance Magazine* (March 1988): 42–45.

Aelbrouck, Jean-Philippe van. *Dictionnaire des danseurs: Chorégraphes et maîtres de danse à Bruxelles de 1600 à 1830*. Brussels, 1994.

Avermaete, Roger. *Lea Daan*. Antwerp, 1976.

Bonte, P., and N. Mossoux. *L'intime, l'étrange*. Brussels, 1992.

Brabants, Jeanne. "Les trois coups belge" (parts 1–12). *Saisons de la Danse* (February 1992–February 1993).

Garske, Rolf. "Trees in the Desert." *Ballett International* 7 (June–July 1984): 20–23.

Geens, Frans, et al. *Dansen uit Vlaanderen*. Schoten, 1991.

Houtte, J. A. van. *Geschiedenis van de Nederlanden*. Utrecht, 1972.

Hrvatin, Emil. *Jan Fabre, La Discipline du Chaos, le Chaos de la Discipline*. Paris, 1994.

Hughes, David. "Post-Structuralist Dance." *Dance Theatre Journal* 8 (Summer 1990): 28–31.

Isnardon, Jacques. *Le théâtre de la Monnaie*. Brussels, 1890.

Kaplan, Peggy Jarrell. *Portraits of Choreographers*. New York, 1988.

Kempen, J. "Dans en ballet." *Mens en Taak* 4 (1975).

Kerkhoven, Marianne van. "The Dance of Anne Teresa De Keersmaeker." *Drama Review* 28 (Fall 1984): 98–104.

Kuypers, Patricia, et. al. "Dossier Filmer la Danse." *Nouvelles de Danse* 26 (1996).

Loo, Anne van. *Akarova: Entertainment and the Avant-Garde, 1920–1950*. Brussels, 1988.

Mallems, Alex. "The Belgian Dance Explosion of the Eighties." *Ballett International* 14 (February 1991): 18–27.

Marievoet, Tilly, et al. *Zeg kwezelken wilde gij dansen? Volkdans in Vlaanderen*. Tielt, 1978.

Monsieur, Jeanine. "Théâtre et danse en communauté française de Belgique, d'un corps à l'autre." *Nouvelles de Danse* 18 (January 1994).

Moore, Lillian. "The Petipa Family in Europe and America." *Dance Index* 1 (May 1942): 72–84.

Sorgeloos, Herman. *Rosas album*. Amsterdam, 1993.

Straeten, Edmond Vander. *La musique aux Pays-Bas le XIXe siècle* (1867–1888). 8 vols. New York, 1969.

Théâtre Royal de la Monnaie. Paris, 1949.

Uytterhoeven, Michel. "14 moments de danse en Flandre: Politique de la danse, 1982–1995." *Nouvelles de Danse* (Winter 1995): 5–16.

Vaccarino, Elisa. *Altre scene, altre danze: Vent'anni di balletto contemporaneo*. Turin, 1991.

Verstockt, Katie. "Belgian Prospects." *Ballett International* 12 (November 1989): 22–25.

Vervaeke, Luc. *Inventaris van het balletleven aan de Vlaamse academies*. Louvain, 1972.

LUC VERVAEKE

Dance Education

The major ballet school in Belgium is the Municipal Institute for Ballet (Het Stedelijk Instituut voor Ballet). Founded in 1961, The Municipal Institute replaced the ballet school of the Royal Flemish Opera that was founded in 1951. The Municipal Institute conducts dance classes at kindergarten and elementary school levels and offers a thorough training program at the secondary school level. Some of the institute's graduates are selected for the Royal Ballet of Flanders; others may go to other companies or continue their education.

Dance and other performing arts were also taught at Mudra, a school founded in Brussels in 1970 and directed by Maurice Béjart. Its aim was to attract students of different races and nationalities, to expose students to different styles, and to stimulate new developments in dance. Mudra offered training in set construction, voice, lighting, theater, and rhythm. However, the school was abandoned when Béjart left Belgium.

In 1995 the Autonome Hogeschool Antwerpen was created from the former Rijksleergang voor Danspedagogiek (National Institute for Dance Pedagogy). Its director is Aimé de Lignière and the institute provides a certification program for dance teachers to teach in the government-subsidized dance academies that are found in most cities.

In September 1995, Anne Teresa De Keersmaeker started a school of contemporary dance called P.A.R.T.S. (Performing Arts Research and Training Studios). The school offers a full-time education program for dancers and choreographers interested in modern dance. Teachers include former members of the Trisha Brown Dance Company and Pina Bausch's Tanztheater Wuppertal. Improvisation is taught by former members of William Forsythe's Frankfurt Ballet. Additionally, modern dance classes are taught in Brussels at Plateau, a center for training and performing. Other efforts to promote modern dance are located in the city of Louvain with the assistance of the organizations Klapstuk and Dansconcept. Technique teachers in Louvain include Luc Vervaeke, Marie-Anne Schotte, Mia Vandeghinste, and Jan Nuitten.

Musical theater training can be obtained at the conservatory in Brussels and, at the secondary school level, a similar school has opened in Oostende. In Ghent, d'Oude Kapel presents classes in multicultural dance forms. The center also has an extensive dance research library strong in ethnic dance forms. Another research library is owned by the organization Contredanse and is located at the Maison du Spectacle–la Bellon in Brussels. Also in Brussels, Het Vlaams Theater Instituut has a video and research library. Research in the field of dance is coordinated by the Belgian dance university association, located at the Vrije Universiteit in Brussels. Other dance-related organizations include Jeugd en Dans, which promotes dance as an art form.

BIBLIOGRAPHY
Vervaeke, Luc. *Inventaris van het balletleven aan de Vlaamse academies*. Louvain, 1972.

LUC VERVAEKE

BELIZE. Bordered by Mexico to the north, Guatemala to the south and west, and the Caribbean Sea to the east, Belize has about 8,900 square miles (23,000 square kilometers), with a chief port at Belize City and a capital at Belmopan. In the 1600s, Belize was founded by buccaneers—sea raiders of the Spanish ships bringing New World treasure to their king—but the British in Jamaica soon came there for timber. Although Spain long protested their presence in New Spain, British Honduras remained a colony of the British Empire until 1964, when internal self-government was granted. Because of Guatemala's claim to the territory, through Spain, full independence came only in 1981, after negotiation by Spain and Britian.

The main ethnic groups include the following: Creoles (53 percent), of mixed West African and British ancestry; *mestizos* (30 percent), descended from the Spanish and the Maya; Garifuna, or black Carib (7 percent), descended from escaped African slaves and Island Caribs from Saint Vincent; and Maya (8 percent), farmers and villagers whose ancestors had lived for thousands of years in the region before Europeans arrived (Maya also live in Mexico, Guatemala, and Honduras). Today, large numbers of Salvadoreans (2 percent) are resettled in Belize. Each group performs traditional dances as well as borrowed dances with various origins. Annual performances of local dances are staged in Belize City, and Belize regularly participates in the Carifesta programs, at which dance groups from throughout the Caribbean meet and perform.

Belize's Mayan people came from villages in the Petén region of Guatemala and the Mexican state of Quintana Roo, mostly arriving as refugees from the wars of the late nineteenth century. Accounts of their early life in Belize record bullfights and other festivities. During these events, their *mestizada* dance was performed; in it they mock the mestizos by both costume and dancing. An older Mayan dance is the Deer Dance, a hunting dance performed only by men. By the early 1980s only a few men in the southernmost Mayan villages of Belize were able to perform this dance. It requires the use of the Mayan marimba, a shorter and presumably older marimba than the popular three-part Latin American instrument.

During a *serenada*, at which a young Mayan woman is feted by her friends and family, the marimba is played from before dawn until night. The elders shuffle to the marimba music, the tempo of which ranges from a German-derived schottische to a fast Mexican *corrida*. The younger generation dances to reggae and other popular Caribbean music.

The Creoles of Belize are the majority group of the country, descendants of British colonists and African slaves brought to the mainland by the British from the West Indies, especially Jamaica. In the late nineteenth century, after slavery was abolished, the dance groups of Belize City still used regional or tribal names brought from Africa. Stilt dancing and other uniquely African dance types have been recorded throughout Belize's history. By the early 1980s, however, even very rural Creole villages no longer produced African-style drums or drummers. Modern commercially influenced dance forms include reggae and the *brukdown* (from "break down"), a particularly Belizean dance that combines a Spanish feeling with a Caribbean two-beat.

Currently, the most active dance traditions in Belize are those of the Garifuna, who maintain a diverse repertory of both secular and sacred dances. Traditional Garifuna religious rites require drumming, singing, and trance dancing.

[*See also* Caribbean Region *and* Garifuna Dance.]

BIBLIOGRAPHY

Acuña, René. *Farsas y representaciones escénicas de los mayas antiguos.* Mexico City, 1978.

Bancroft, Hubert H. *The Native Races of the Pacific States of North America.* 5 vols. New York, 1874–1876.

Barrera Vásquez, Alfredo. *Los mayas: Historia, literatura, teatro, danza.* Merida, 1987.

Conzemius, Eduard. *Ethnographical Survey of the Miskito and Sumu Indians of Honduras and Nicaragua.* Bureau of American Ethnology, Bulletin 106. Washington, D.C., 1932.

Gann, Thomas, and J. Eric Thompson. *The History of the Maya.* New York, 1931.

Thompson, J. Eric. *Ethnology of the Mayas of Southern and Central British Honduras.* Chicago, 1930.

CAROL JENKINS

BELLE AU BOIS DORMANT, LA. *See* Sleeping Beauty, The.

BELLONA. The small neighboring Pacific islands of Bellona and Rennell (formerly Mungiki and Mungaba) are at the southeastern tip of the Solomon Islands east of New Guinea. The two share a Polynesian culture and language—whereas the larger islands of the Solomons are Melanesian—and they were converted to Christianity in 1939. Seventh-Day Adventists and South Seas Evangelical Church missions there have prohibited dancing since that time. Some 2,500 people live on the two islands.

Older islanders, however, can still perform the traditional dance repertory, consisting of seventeen dances (Rossen and Colbert, 1981). One additional dance, used as a game in the 1930s, is now forgotten. Most dances are performed by men, but there is one women's dance (the *mu'aabaka*) and one mixed dance (the *pati*). According to the people of Bellona, the dances were the same on Rennell.

In the two islands, dances are choreographed in advance by a poet-composer and performed in unison by twenty to thirty singers. They may be unaccompanied or accompanied by hand-clapping or the sounding board. The person who beats the rhythm also leads the singing. The temporal structure consists of song-dance suites with a number of sections, including introduction, main body of dances, and ending, with several to many songs in each section. The name of a dance and its parts are the same as the names of the songs sung (e.g., *'ungu pati*, "introductory" *pati*).

BELLONA. Men and women perform the mixed-sex *okeoke pati* (i.e., "ending" *pati*). The traditional costume, seen here in 1977, includes a fan tucked in the back of a dance mat that is worn around the waist. (Photograph courtesy of Jane Mink Rossen.)

All dances are based on a large repertory of movements of the arm and hand, called *'aaunga*, which are shared by men and women. Women's dances and men's introductory dances are performed standing in place or walking with measured steps. In subsequent sections of the men's dances, other leg movements such as running, step-hop, and leaping are employed. The language has more than seventy terms for arm movements and twenty for leg movements. Many of the arm movements express particular words of the poetic text that forms the basis for the dance.

Some dances begin with procession in a column to the dancing place (the *mu'aabaka* and the *makosa'u*). Some dances are performed holding fans *(mako tu'u)* or weapons *(mako hakapaungo, mako ki te nga'akau)*. Circular and linear formations are used. In one singing game, a linked chain of dancers moves in a spiral pattern. Two of the dances *(mako tu'u* and *ngongole)* are from Tikopia, another Polynesian island in the Solomons, and were assimilated in the local repertory in the 1920s.

Bellona and Rennell were populated by Polynesians in outrigger canoes who, according to oral tradition, arrived twenty-five generations before the 1960s from 'Ubea (possibly Uvea or Wallis Island west of Samoa). These ancestors brought with them certain song dances still performed in the archaic 'Ubean language. In one, the *suahongi*, two different song dances are performed simultaneously and coordinated in an organized manner (Rossen, 1978; Folkways FE 4274). This dance suite requires two song leaders and two dance leaders.

Dancing was formerly performed on the ceremonial grounds during men's rituals for tattooing, food distribution, and group visiting, as well as at the women's *mu'aabaka*, a celebration of the maturity of a high-status woman. Since World War II, the men's dances have been performed only out of context, for visiting dignitaries, anthropologists, and tourists, and at Pacific music and dance festivals. Women, however, do not usually perform on these occasions. Male dancers wear traditional apparel during performances, including a fan, dancing mat, loincloth, and headdress; the last two are made of tapa (barkcloth), dyed to a mustard-yellow shade with turmeric.

[*For discussion in a broader context, see* Oceanic Dance Traditions *and* Polynesia.]

BIBLIOGRAPHY

Rossen, Jane Mink. "The Suahongi of Bellona: Polynesian Ritual Music." *Ethnomusicology* 22 (September 1978): 397–439.

Rossen, Jane Mink, and Margot Mink Colbert. "Dance on Bellona, Solomon Islands: A Preliminary Study of Style and Concept." *Ethnomusicology* 25 (September 1981): 447–466.

Rossen, Jane Mink. *Songs of Bellona Island* (na taunga o Mungiki). 2 vols. Danish Folklore Archives, Copenhagen, 1987.

RECORDING. *Polynesian Dances of Bellona (Mungiki), Solomon Islands* (Folkways FE 4274, 1978).

JANE MINK ROSSEN

BELLY DANCE. *See* Danse du Ventre. *See also* Algeria; Egypt, *article on* Traditional Dance; *and* Ouled Naïl, Dances of the.

BELSKY, IGOR (Igor' Dmitrievich Belskii; born 28 March 1925 in Leningrad), dancer, choreographer, and teacher. Belsky graduated from the Leningrad Ballet School in 1943 and from the acting department of the Institute for Theater Arts in 1957. From 1943 to 1963 he danced with the Kirov Ballet, where he excelled as a character dancer and actor, especially of grotesque dance and pantomime. The clarity of his dancing enabled him to portray essential human character, often torn by dramatic conflicts. His temperament and intuition as an actor were best revealed in his finest roles: Shurale in Leonid Jacobson's *Ali-Batyr* of 1950 (later called *Shurale*), and Nur-Ali in Rostislav Zakharov's *The Fountain of Bakhchisarai*. Belsky was chief choreographer of the Maly (now Modest Mussorgsky) Theater in Leningrad from 1962 to 1973, of the Kirov Ballet from 1973 to 1977, and of the Leningrad Music Hall from 1979 to 1992, when he became artistic director of the Vaganova Ballet Academy. In 1946 he became a teacher of character dance at the Leningrad Ballet School, where he remained until 1956, and from 1962 to 1964 and since 1966 he has been a teacher in the choreographic department of the Leningrad (now Saint Petersburg) Conservatory. He became a professor there in 1982.

Along with Yuri Grigorovich, Belsky led a new trend in Soviet ballet, beginning in the late 1950s, that asserted the primacy of musical interpretation. His first ballet, *The Coast of Hope*, performed at the Kirov Theater in 1959, was a manifesto of that trend, a romantic poem of Soviet man's loyalty to his country, faithfulness to his beloved, and courage that overcomes all obstacles. The dances were innovative in their treatment of a modern theme and incorporated elements of athletic and work movements. Belsky's attempt at poetic representation of modern realities in that ballet was developed in *Leningrad Symphony* (1961), set to the first movement of Dmitri Shostakovich's Seventh Symphony; it portrayed Soviet man's staunch spirit in wartime, his exploits on the battlefield, and his moral integrity. [*See* Leningrad Symphony.]

Belsky adopted Fedor Lopukhov's idea of a "dance symphony" and imaginatively interpreted it in his own heroic productions, such as Shostakovich's Eleventh Symphony (1966) and *The Gadfly* (1967), both for the Maly Theater, and *Icarus* (1974) for the Kirov. His innovation was his interpretation of heroism as man's natural desire and the full expression of his moral potential. Belsky's satirical talent was revealed in *The Little Humpbacked Horse* at the Maly Theater in 1963; the fairy-tale subject was rich in allusion. [*See* Little Humpbacked Horse, The.] Belsky proved to be a modern artist in his interpretation of the classics. His staging of *The Nutcracker* at the Maly Theater in 1969 was an interesting attempt to approach E. T. A. Hoffmann's original.

Belsky was named People's Artist of the Russian Federation (1966) and received the State Prize of the USSR (1951).

BIBLIOGRAPHY

Barnes, Clive. "Kirov Ballet Backdrop." *Dance Magazine* (September 1961): 40–47.

Belsky, Igor. "Zametki khoreographa." *Sovetskaia muzyka*, no. 3 (1964).

Chistiakova, V. V. "Bereg nadezhdi: Balet o sovremennosti." *Leningradskaia pravda* (27 June 1959).

Krasovskaya, Vera. "Balet-simfoniia." *Sovetskaia kul'tura* (5 August 1961).

Kremshevskaia, G. D. "Master kharakternogo tantsa." *Vechernii Leningrad* (1 July 1955).

Roslavleva, Natalia. "New Choreographer in Leningrad." *Dance and Dancers* (March 1961): 14–15.

Shmyrova, T. "Igor Belskii." *Sovetskii balet*, no. 3 (1983).

ARKADY A. SOKOLOV-KAMINSKY
Translated from Russian

BENESH MOVEMENT NOTATION was created by Rudolf Benesh, an accountant who was also a gifted artist and musician. His wife, Joan, was a dancer with the Sadler's Wells Ballet in the late 1940s; her attempts to write down dance steps and to decipher her own notation inspired him to invent a reliable way of notating movement. Benesh used his knowledge of perspective in art and of rhythm in music, creating a system that could be adapted to all forms of human movement and be easily understood by people all over the world. Benesh notation has been developed into a rich language that embraces classical ballet, all forms of contemporary dance, opera, and theater productions. Its use also extends to other fields; its ability to record and analyze functional movement proves a great asset for physiotherapists and anthro-

pologists; it has been used to record Indian dance, gymnastics, folk dances, and even the opening procession at the Olympic Games.

Benesh movement notation is a language of signs set on a five-line matrix similar to the musical stave. The horizontal lines define the areas of the body and the vertical lines are similar to the bar-lines of the musical score. These signs can be built up from a simple solo into a complex work just like an orchestral score. Not only can the notation record a complex series of movements for the individual dancer, but it can also cope with any number of bodies. Benesh notation is also relatively easy to learn; students can usually read and write solo parts and simple group scores within a few months of study, which suffices for staging much of the classical ballet repertory.

Benesh launched his system publicly in 1955, defining choreology as "the scientific and aesthetic study of all forms of human movement by movement notation." Ninette de Valois introduced the use of Benesh notation to the Royal Ballet Company and School in London, in the same year. In 1960 the Royal Ballet was the first company to appoint a professional choreologist. Benesh founded the Benesh Institute of Choreology in 1962. The main aims of the institute are to train choreologists and teachers, to coordinate technical developments, and to maintain a growing library of movement scores and protect the notation for future generations. The institute also functions as a registration body for choreographic scores, thus providing copyright protection. Over the years many major dance companies worldwide have adopted the system and employ Benesh choreologists (some twenty-six dance companies employ full-time choreologists), who are responsible for recording new works or reconstructing revivals. The adoption of Benesh notation by dance companies throughout the world is due largely to Sir Kenneth MacMillan's commitment to the use of the language. Among other choreographers who have used Benesh no-

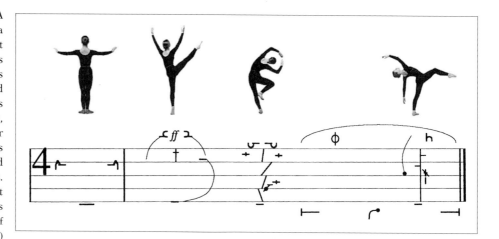

BENESH MOVEMENT NOTATION. A short sequence composed of a starting position and a four-count movement phrase. Body actions are plotted within the stave; details of rhythm, phrasing, and dynamics appear above; and notes concerning spatial direction, location, and pathway appear below. The first movement is performed very strongly (*ff*), and the last is phrased over two counts. The ф identifies the missing beat and the curved line indicates continuity of phrasing. (Courtesy of the Benesh Institute, London.)

tation are John Neumeier, Peter Wright, Glen Tetley, John Cranko, Angelin Preljocaj, Roland Petit, Richard Alston, Christopher Bruce, and David Bintley. More than a thousand scores have been produced.

To notate a new piece, choreologists attend rehearsals and record the whole work in detail over many sessions, building up the score in the studio, step by step, day by day. The final score can then be used to confirm details at later rehearsals, or teach a role to dancers new to the part, or revive a work years later when only a few of the original dancers are available to reconstruct the steps. While conserving all the detail and style of work, Benesh notation still allows for individual interpretation by the dancers. In a revival it can save a great deal of time to teach the steps first; the choreographer can then spend time perfecting style and interpretation, whether for the original company or another one halfway around the world.

A number of choreologists are freelancers, often working with one choreographer so that they specialize in his or her style of dance; this is especially useful in contemporary dance, which can require far more detailed analysis than classical ballet. They may also work in musicals or in opera or television. Some notators teach at the institute. Some are teachers or examiners for dance organizations; they may work on the publication of a new syllabus, for example, or use the notation for their own school show. Examiners may also use the notation to make notes about a student's technique, thus leaving more time to comment on style and quality of movement.

Benesh notation can also be a useful tool for studying a choreographer's style or unique way of using music. In 1994 the Benesh institute drew up an agreement for the educational use of scores. The agreement, signed by over 250 choreographers and score owners, enables the institute to grant permission for the use of specified scores on their behalf, thus making extracts of choreographic works more immediately accessible for use as a study resource in schools and universities. A major development in progress is the computerization of the system to provide professional choreologists and students of notation with a "word processor" for writing and editing notation scores.

[*For related discussion, see* Notation.]

BIBLIOGRAPHY

Benesh, Rudolf, and Joan Rothwell Benesh. *Reading Dance: The Birth of Choreology.* London, 1977.

Benesh Institute. *Benesh Movement Notation Catalogue.* London, 1986.

Cunliffe, Elizabeth. *Classical and Contemporary Syllabus Readers' Course Material.* London, 1990.

Dail-Jones, Megan Llinos. "A Culture in Motion: A Study of the Interrelationship of Dancing, Sorrowing, Hunting, and Fighting as Performed by the Warlpiri Women of Central Australia." Master's thesis, University of Hawaii, 1984.

Dransch, Detlef, et al. *Choreoscribe: A Graphics Editor to Describe Body Position and Movement Using Benesh Movement Notation.* Waterloo, Ont., 1986.

Grau, Andrée. "Dreaming, Dancing, Kinship: The Study of *Yoi,* the Dance of the Tiwi of Melville and Bathurst Islands, North Australia." Ph.D. diss., Queen's University of Belfast, 1983.

Jones, Julie. "The Sega of Mauritius." Master's thesis, Queen's University of Belfast, 1980.

Kipling-Brown, Ann, and Monica Parker. *Dance Notation for Beginners.* London, 1984.

McGuinness-Scott, Julia. *Movement Study and Benesh Movement Notation.* Oxford, 1983.

Parker, Monica. *Benesh Movement Notation Elementary Solo Syllabus with Text.* London, 1996.

Pilkington, Linda. *Syllabus of Professional Examinations in Cecchetti Method Recorded in Benesh Movement Notation.* Rev. ed. London 1996.

Pilkington, Linda. *Syllabus of Professional Examinations of the Cecchetti Method Recorded in Benesh Movement Notation.* London, 1984.

Ralov, Kirsten, ed. *The Bournonville School.* 4 vols. New York, 1979.

The Royal Academy of Dancing Children's Examination Syllabus in Benesh Movement Notation. Revised by Julie Jones. London, 1982.

Ryman, Rhonda. *Royal Academy of Dancing Children's Examination Syllabus Recorded in Benesh Movement Notation.* Waterloo, Ont., 1991.

Ryman-Hughes, Robyn, and Rhonda S. Ryman. "MacBenesh: A 'Word Processor' for Choreologists." *The Choreologist,* no. 31 (Winter 1985): 25–30.

TANIA INMAN

BENIN REPUBLIC. *See* Sub-Saharan Africa. *For discussion of dance traditions within the diaspora of the peoples of Benin, see* Brazil, *article on* Popular and Ritual Dance. *For discussion of traditional costumes worn in Benin, see* Costume in African Traditions.

BENNETT, MICHAEL (Michael Bennett DiFiglia; born 8 April 1943 in Buffalo, died 2 July 1987 in Tucson), American director and choreographer. A two-year-old Bennett, nicknamed Mickey, made his performance debut as a bongo toddler in a dance recital in Buffalo, New York, and won his first prize before the age of five, singing "I'm Looking over a Four Leaf Clover" for *The Uncle Jerry Show* on radio. Bennett studied tap, jazz, and modern dance and appeared on local television and in summer stock as a youngster. The elaborate entertainments he produced at Hutchinson Technical High School (1957–1959) affected his grades so adversely that he transferred to Bennett High School, dropping out altogether in September 1960 to dance the role of Baby John in a European touring production of the musical *West Side Story.* Many years—and several Tony awards—later, he received an honorary diploma from Bennett High School.

After the twelve-month tour in Europe, he became a chorus boy in New York City, appearing in *Subways Are for Sleeping* (1961); *Nowhere to Go But Up* (1962), where he was assistant choreographer to Ronald Field; *Here's Love* (1963); and *Bajour* (1964). During this period, Bennett danced in Lee Theodore's *The Cornerstone*, broadcast on WCBS-TV's *Look Up and Live* on 5 April 1964. A year later, he met his future wife Donna McKechnie as a performer on NBC-TV's top-forty celebrity party *Hullabaloo*. Other television work included dances for *The Ed Sullivan Show*, *Hollywood Palace*, and *The Dean Martin Show*. In 1965, he staged the musical numbers for the Universal film *What's So Bad about Feeling Good?*, along with notable summer productions in Wallingford, Connecticut. Bennett also served as unofficial "play doctor" and assistant choreographer for *How Now, Dow Jones?*, *Your Own Thing*, and *By Jupiter*.

His first solo assignment as choreographer was for *A Joyful Noise* (1966), with director Edward Padula. Reporting for *The Boston Globe* on the out-of-town tryout at Massachusetts's Storrowton Music Fair, Kevin Kelly called Bennett "a major Broadway discovery." Although *A Joyful Noise* closed after twelve performances on Broadway at the Mark Hellinger Theater, Bennett gained his first Tony nomination in 1967 for the dances. At twenty-five, he received a second Tony nomination as choreographer for *Henry, Sweet Henry*, a 1967/68 musical adaptation of Nora Johnson's novel *The World of Henry Orient*, with direction by George Roy Hill. Writing about the production in the *New York Times*, Clive Barnes called Bennett "the most hopeful new name around Broadway dance."

Bennett's third Tony nomination for choreography came in conjunction with his first Broadway hit, *Promises, Promises* (1968/69), the David Merrick musical production based on Billy Wilder's Academy Award-winning film *The Apartment* (1960). For *Promises*, Bennett was collaborating with some of Broadway's best: Neil Simon, book; Burt Bacharach and Hal David, score; and Robert Moore, direction. Bennett's act 1 finale for *Promises*, "Turkey-Lurkey Time," earned him lifelong respect from Simon. During the following season, on *Coco* (1969), Bennett continued his association with headliners and gained adulation by Coco Chanel, the production's real-life heroine, for his sensitive preliminary research on her fashion-industry career in Paris. With a score by Alan Jay Lerner and André Previn, *Coco* offered special challenges caused by star Katharine Hepburn's lack of experience in musicals. For his boisterously inventive staging, Bennett received another Tony nomination. His fifth came in 1970 for choreography in *Company*, the Stephen Sondheim (music and lyrics) collaboration with George Furth (book) that was directed and produced by Harold Prince. Among the achievements in *Company* were the exploration of contemporary urban relationships, Bennett's solo for featured performer Donna McKechnie, and his fiercely expressive use of straw hats and canes in "Side by Side by Side."

Hired as co-director with Prince and as choreographer for *Follies* (1971), Bennett created dazzling numbers for principals (Alexis Smith, Dorothy Collins, Gene Nelson, and John McMartin), cameo turns for "old dolls" like Yvonne DeCarlo and Ethel Shutta, and a drifting landscape of ghostly figures from the *Ziegfeld Follies* canon. With *Follies*, playwright James Goldman and composer Stephen Sondheim conjured a theater-of-the-past memoir without nostalgia, often criticized for cynicism. Nevertheless, Bennett finally won two Tonys, for choreography and for co-direction.

As president of Plum Productions Inc., Bennett produced and directed his first nonmusical offering. The script for *Twigs* (1971), four one-act plays by George Furth, centered on three daughters and their mother, who were all brilliantly acted by Sada Thompson. Neil Simon hired Bennett to direct his poignant *God's Favorite* for the 1973/74 season on Broadway. Bennett won his third Tony for choreography in *Seesaw* (1973), a musical collaboration by Cy Coleman and Dorothy Fields that was so changed in out-of-town tryouts that program credit for writing was also given to Bennett when the show reached New York. *Seesaw* also won the 1974 Tony award for best book.

Bennett was briefly director of *Thieves*, which opened in New York on 7 April 1974, but he was already deeply involved with preliminary collaborations on the work that changed his life and altered forever the method for evolving Broadway musicals. *A Chorus Line*, with a score by Marvin Hamlisch and Edward Kleban, had a text initially assembled by James Kirkwood and Nicholas Dante from two twelve-hour talk sessions by a group of theatrical dancers. Fusing elements of music, dance, and self-relevatory verbal confessions, Bennett transformed the narrative from one of harsh artistic perseverance in the theater to that of a universal metaphor for human effort and achievement. Among other awards, Bennett received a 1976 Pulitzer Prize for the script.

Developed as a workshop under the auspices of Joseph Papp's New York Shakespeare Festival, *A Chorus Line* opened officially at the Public's Newman Theater on 21 May 1975. Within six weeks (2 July 1975) the production was moved uptown to the Shubert Theater, where it eventually became the longest-running Broadway show (until overtaken by *Cats* in June 1997). By 1988, it had grossed more than $260 million. Bennett became a millionaire and had also assigned 1 percent rights for royalties and subsidiaries to the original cast members. Caught up in a Broadway fairy tale, he married the show's star, Donna McKechnie (their marriage in Paris on 4 December 1976 ended in divorce), and drove around the Times Square area for some time in a white Rolls Royce.

For almost five years, Bennett was involved with auditioning and rehearsing national, international, and new Broadway ensembles for *A Chorus Line*. He signed a contract with Universal Pictures for the film rights but withdrew in 1979 because of his disillusionment with Hollywood and his unwillingness to devote three more years to this one project. The film was eventually made without his collaboration, but it was carefully timed so that it would not interfere with the popularity of live productions.

While his next venture was certain to be an anticlimax, Bennett's vision for *Ballroom*—a musical version of Jerome Kass's *Queen of the Stardust Ballroom*—was an evocative use of aging former Broadway chorus dancers. Romance among the middle-aged had limited box-office appeal, yet the show completed a three-month Broadway run and a successful national tour. Bennett shared a Tony with Robert Avian for best choreography, for *Ballroom*, during the 1978/79 season.

Another financial blockbuster, *Dreamgirls*, was created by Bennett in a series of workshops in the building he had purchased in 1978, at 890 Broadway. Based on a rhythm and blues trio that strongly resembled Motown's Supremes, *Dreamgirls* was the quintessentially integrated musical: even Robin Wagner's visually kinetic scenery moved to the conductor's baton. With a score by Henry Krieger and book by Tom Eyen, *Dreamgirls* opened on 20 December 1981, ran for more than fifteen hundred performances on Broadway and was successfully replicated in Los Angeles and on tour. For it, Bennett shared his seventh Tony for choreography with Michael Peters. (At the time of Bennett's death in 1987, *Dreamgirls* was playing again on Broadway in a revival production.)

During the last years of his life, Bennett continued to lead workshop projects. *Scandal*, a musical about a woman's search for identity through a series of affairs with both sexes, was abandoned in January 1985. Later that year, Bennett was the director for *Chess*, a British production by Tim Rice with Bjorn Ulvaeus and Benny Andersson of the ABBA pop group, but he withdrew in January 1986 because of failing health. He sold 890 Broadway for $15 million and moved to Tucson, Arizona, for treatment until his death from AIDS.

Considered one of the most talented artists of the musical theater during the twentieth century, Bennett put the dancer back at center stage. His former building at 890 Broadway retains a creative heritage as headquarters for both American Ballet Theatre and Eliot Feld's Ballet Tech. Bennett's long-time associate Robert Avian summed up their stylistic amalgamation of ballet, modern, and jazz dancing, "We could go from A to Z because of our combined techniques, and that's probably our particular contribution to Broadway choreography." Bennett made major contributions to the theater with his workshop-based method for developing material for Broadway stages, along with the innovative musical-*verité* form—an integrated, concept-based format featuring darkly realistic undertones, but with "heart." The creative powerhouse behind the landmark production *A Chorus Line* main-

tained that above all, "a show has to offer an audience hope."

ARCHIVES. Dance Collection and Theater Collection, New York Public Library for the Performing Arts.

CAMILLE HARDY

BENNINGTON SCHOOL OF THE DANCE. The first center for the study of modern dance in America, the Bennington School, in its nine summer sessions from 1934 to 1942, brought together most of the prominent figures and divergent viewpoints in the young art as it was coming of age. Although conceived fundamentally as a training ground for dance students and teachers, the school quickly became a haven for most of the leading modern dancers of the period, a laboratory for experienced and neophyte choreographers, a major production center attracting audiences and critics to festival programs of new work, a tryout site prior to New York premieres, and an arena for collaborative experiments in which the arts of music, drama, design, and poetry were assembled in the service of dance.

Most of the school's sessions were held under the auspices of Bennington College, a small, private liberal arts college for women located in the foothills of Vermont's Green Mountains in the town of Bennington. The School of the Dance was a self-supporting, autonomous enterprise that used the college facilities. Bennington College, which opened in 1932, was founded on principles of progressive education—a philosophy that espoused doing as a potent form of learning. Modern dance was perfectly attuned to this educational philosophy; it was the method by which the art was learned and transmitted.

The school's three founders were Martha Hill, its director, who taught dance at Bennington College and New York University; Mary Josephine Shelly, its administrative director, a physical education teacher and administrator at New College, Columbia University; and Bennington College's president, Robert Devore Leigh.

The Bennington School of the Dance held six-week sessions on the Bennington College campus in the summers from 1934 through 1938. Its success in consolidating and strengthening the various elements of modern dance led Hill and Shelly to embark on an ambitious plan for an enlarged school of the arts. In 1939 the School of the Dance held a single session at Mills College in Oakland, California, aimed at bolstering dance in the West before the proposed expansion. Back in Vermont, in 1940 and 1941, the Bennington School of the Arts (as it was then called) offered programs in dance, directed by Hill; music, directed by Otto Luening; drama, directed by Francis Fergusson; and theater design, directed by Arch Lauterer. All these people were Bennington College faculty members. However, a new theater promised by the college failed to materialize, and the alliance among the arts had mixed success. In 1942 the last of the summer dance sessions, reduced in scope, was offered as part of the Bennington College Summer Session in the Arts, which comprised dance, government, economics, science, and graphics and plastic arts. The reasons for its cessation were the onset of war, a change in the college calendar, which kept the college in session during the summer, and a certain loss of momentum and focus.

When beginning the school, Hill and Shelly enlisted as the core faculty Martha Graham, Doris Humphrey, Charles Weidman, and Hanya Holm—known as the Big Four. All but Holm, who made her East Coast debut at Bennington in 1936, had established substantial choreographic careers by 1934. Bennington was a major source of support for these and other artists, and for Graham especially. (Not included at Bennington were such artists as Helen Tamiris, Agnes de Mille, Katherine Dunham, Lester Horton, and Pauline Koner.) They had available to them the time, opportunity, and resources to make new works; food and housing for themselves and their dancers; a pool of apprentice dancers from which to enlarge their own groups; and designers and composers with whom they could collaborate. Thus, Bennington's approach served as a model for and a precursor of the fellowships, commissions, and residencies for choreographers and their companies that were established during the decade that followed.

Forty-two dances were premiered at six of the Bennington College sessions, including sixteen dances choreographed by the Big Four: Martha Graham's *Panorama, Opening Dance, Immediate Tragedy, American Document, El Penitente, Letter to the World,* and *Punch and Judy;* Doris Humphrey's *New Dance, With My Red Fires, Passacaglia in C minor,* and *Decade;* Charles Weidman's *Quest* and *Opus 51;* and Hanya Holm's *Trend, Dance Sonata,* and *Dance of Work and Play.*

Twenty-six new dances were composed by other choreographers: Ethel Butler; Merce Cunningham; Jane Dudley, Sophie Maslow, and William Bales (the Dudley-Maslow-Bales Trio); Jean Erdman; Erick Hawkins, who danced at Bennington in the world debut of Lincoln Kirstein's Ballet Caravan in 1936, and returned in 1938 to make his debut with Martha Graham; and Esther Junger, Eleanor King, Louise Kloepper, José Limón, Anna Sokolow, and Marian Van Tuyl. Most of the dances had original scores written by musicians in residence, such as Vivian Fine, Ray Green, Louis Horst, Hunter Johnson, Harrison Kerr, Norman Lloyd, Robert McBride, Jerome Moross, Alex North, Lionel Nowak, Harvey Pollins, Wallingford Riegger, Gregory Tucker, and Esther Williamson.

Over the course of the years, the faculty included Louis Horst, a pioneering teacher of dance composition and

music director for Graham; John Martin, the first dance critic of the *New York Times* and a champion of modern dance; Bessie Schönberg, Hill's assistant; the composer-accompanist Norman Lloyd; and the stage designer Arch Lauterer, who designed and supervised productions and transformed the 150-seat College Theater and 500-seat Vermont State Armory into suitable performance spaces.

The school's students were mainly dance teachers who came to Bennington to study with the masters. Approximately one thousand people attended the Bennington sessions. From this crucible, modern dance spread to every corner of America, its influence far greater than the number of firsthand participants would suggest. Inspired at the source, teachers returned to their classrooms and communities with what they had learned at Bennington and began to teach new dance forms and to book engagements for the modern dance companies. The school was the catalyst for a touring network that performed under the auspices of college physical education departments and came to be known as the gymnasium circuit.

The curriculum emphasized technique and composition. Technique was taught by Graham, Holm, Humphrey, Weidman, and their associates, and by Hill and Schönberg. Dance composition was taught by Louis Horst, Hill, and Schönberg. There were laboratories and workshops in choreography, music for the dance, and stage design and production, and even a few courses in dance history, criticism, and notation. By 1940, subjects included ballet, tap, and folk dance. Rigor, discipline, form, systematic method, and historical models were considered prerequisites for dance composition. Individual creativity was encouraged; an amorphous style and mode of self-expression were not.

Faculty and student rosters included not only leading dancers and teachers, but their protégés as well, such as William Bales, Merce Cunningham, Jean Erdman, Nina Fonaroff, Eve Gentry, Anna Halprin, Erick Hawkins, Ann Hutchinson, Pearl Lang, Welland Lathrop, Katherine Litz, Iris Mabry, Barbara Mettler, Alwin Nikolais, Nona Schurman, and Sybil Shearer. Among the students were the educators Ruth Alexander, Helen Alkire, Ruth Bloomer, Alma Hawkins, Truda Kaschmann, Louise Kloepper, Marian Knighton, Eleanor Lauer, Gertrude Lippincott, Ruth Murray, Barbara Page, Esther Pease, Helen Priest, Muriel Stuart, Virginia Tanner, Betty Lynd Thompson, Theodora Wiesner, and Mary Ann Wells.

The school nurtured emerging new talents with choreography fellowships in 1937 and 1938 to Esther Junger, Eleanor King, Louise Kloepper, José Limón, Anna Sokolow, and Marian Van Tuyl.

The Bennington period was one of consolidation and growth, rather than revolution. There, modern dance evolved from a concert to a theater form. The jagged, raw movement of its early years gave way to movement that was more refined and lyrical, and stark abstractions yielded to consciously programmatic dances that attempted to integrate costumes, stage design, music, the spoken work, poetry, and movement. The solo form and the solo recital gave way to large group works; for example, Humphrey's *With My Red Fires* called for forty-six dancers. Dance groups became dance companies. Although Bennington was not a seedbed of politically radical dance, many of the works composed and performed there were charged with the concerns of the time—the threat to liberty and life, the rise of fascism, the hypocrisy of war, the search for meaning in the American past—and with the elusive goal of harmony in human relations.

The Bennington School was shaped by a dark but regenerative time in history—the Depression, recovery and the New Deal, and a looming world conflagration. It was a shelter for artists and students and a banner that won for modern dance legitimacy and wider acceptance. It fostered commitment, purpose, experimentation, collaboration, study, growth, and the systematic transmission of

BENOIS. Costume sketch in watercolor, pen, and pencil for the Ballerina in Michel Fokine's *Petrouchka*, which was originally presented by Serge Diaghilev's Ballets Russes at the Théâtre du Châtelet, Paris, 1911. (Dance Collection, New York Public Library for the Performing Arts.)

these values. The school took on a mythic dimension for those who were part of it and for others who followed them. It succeeded beyond the hopes of its founders as a rallying point for a vital, new American art. In 1948 the Bennington concept was reborn at Connecticut College as the American Dance Festival.

[*See also* American Dance Festival *and the entries on the principal figures mentioned herein.*]

BIBLIOGRAPHY
Anderson, Jack. *The American Dance Festival.* Durham, N.C., 1987.
Kriegsman, Sali Ann. *Modern Dance in America: The Bennington Years.* Boston, 1981.

SALI ANN KRIEGSMAN

BENOIS, ALEXANDRE (Aleksandr Nikolaevich Benua; born 4 May 1870 in Saint Petersburg, died 9 February 1960 in Paris), Russian-French painter and scenery and costume designer. Benois's artistic bloodlines ran very deep. He was the grandson of Alberto Cavos, who designed the Maryinsky Theater in Saint Petersburg and Moscow's Bolshoi Theater, the son of Nikolai Benois, academician and architect; and the uncle of Eugene Lanceray and Zinaida Serebriakova, both talented artists and designers.

From 1885 to 1890 Benois attended the Karl von May Academy in Saint Petersburg, where he met some of the future members of the *Mir iskusstva* (World of Art) group, including Serge Diaghilev (in 1890). In 1887 and 1888 he audited courses at the Academy of Arts, Saint Petersburg, and in 1890 traveled in Germany. From 1890 to 1894 he studied law at Saint Petersburg University, before taking up the curatorship (through 1899) of Princess Maria Tenisheva's collection of modern European paintings and drawings. In 1896 he organized a Russian section for the Munich Secession, made his first trip to Paris, and began to paint scenes of Versailles, a favorite artistic theme for the rest of his life.

In 1898, as Diaghilev's closest colleague and mentor (as he would have us believe), Benois helped to form the World of Art group, becoming a regular contributor to its magazine and exhibitions and establishing himself as an authority on seventeenth- and eighteenth-century French and Italian culture. From 1899 onward he illustrated many books and published numerous scholarly essays, including his *History of Russian Painting in the Nineteenth Century* (1901–1902). From 1907 to 1916 he edited the journal *Starye gody* (Bygone Years), and from 1918 to 1926, the year of his immigration to Paris, he was the curator of paintings at the Hermitage. Thereafter he continued to paint, design, and publish.

Born into the Saint Petersburg intelligentsia, Benois was profoundly affected by the cult of opera, ballet, and drama. His boyhood dream was to become a stage de-

BENOIS. Design for Le Chambre du Negre, a scene in Michel Fokine's *Petrouchka*. In addition to designing the costumes and scenery, Benois assisted Igor Stravinsky with the libretto. (Photograph by E. Irving Blomstrann; from the Dance Collection, New York Public Library for the Performing Arts.)

signer, a penchant inherited from his mother, a professional musician and avid theatergoer. Before his first extensive study-trip abroad in 1890, he saw one of the first performances of *The Sleeping Beauty* as well as *The Queen of Spades* and several other productions of ballet and opera. Falling in love with the theater immediately, Benois was attracted to its oscillation between the real and unreal and its evocation of the fairy-tale world. Consequently, he accepted with alacrity Diaghilev's invitation to work on designs for a never-realized production of *Sylvia* at the Maryinsky Theater in 1901.

Benois made his professional debut as a stage designer in 1902 with *Cupid's Revenge*, followed in 1903 by the Maryinsky production of *Götterdämmerung*. Although some critics, including Diaghilev, felt that his concept was unimaginative, others praised Benois for creating the impression of real life. This attention to historical detail became the distinguishing feature of his stage sets and costumes.

The turning point in Benois's career came with the 1907 Saint Petersburg production of *Le Pavillon d'Armide*, in which he presented a luxurious but also factually correct rendering of Versailles in the age of Louis XIV. Diaghilev's response—"This must be shown in Europe"—prepared the way for the successful Paris production in 1909. Of this Benois wrote, "In the Saint Petersburg version I had been worried by the neighbourhood of lilac, pink, and yellow. . . . These defects I now corrected." With his innate sense of measure and elegance, Benois emerged from this first Paris season as the artistic director of the newly formed Ballets Russes de Serge Diaghilev, praised for his designs for *Le Pavillon d'Armide* and *Les Sylphides*. [*See* Pavillon d'Armide, Le; *and* Sylphides, Les.] Until 1911 Benois was a prime mover of Diaghilev's company, working closely with Michel Fokine, Vaslav Nijinsky, and Tamara Karsavina in particular. His most audacious presentation, *Petrouchka*, presented by Diaghilev in Paris in 1911, however, led to a breach of trust that eventually alienated Benois from Diaghilev.

Nevertheless, his interpretation of *Petrouchka* (for which he claimed also to have written the libretto) was his greatest success in ballet design. The subject of *Petrouchka* was very close to Benois, and, in creating its sets and costumes, he evoked memories of his Saint Petersburg childhood, when Punch-and-Judy shows were still part of the city's culture. Benois returned to this ballet many times, regarding it as his own property, and it is not surprising that he was deeply offended when, at the dress rehearsal of *Petrouchka* in 1911, he saw that his representation of the juggler had been changed by Léon Bakst. The incident provoked his rift with the Ballets Russes. [*See* Petrouchka.]

However, Benois continued to work intermittently with Diaghilev, designing the 1914 production of *Le Rossignol* and the 1927 production of *Le Coq d'Or*. He was also active in other companies throughout his career, including the Antique Theater in Saint Petersburg (1907) and the Moscow Art Theater, where he was artistic director from 1909 onward. In fact, Benois continued to design ballets, operas, and dramas until the 1950s, often reworking earlier motifs and adjusting them to the needs of the new piece. A case in point is his repetition of Italian Baroque architecture: it is a feature of his designs for *Le Pavillon d'Armide* as well as for several productions of *Giselle*, and it appears as late as Bronislava Nijinska's *Les Noces de Psyché et de l'Amour* in 1928.

André Levinson wrote of Benois's *Le Pavillon d'Armide*, "It is not the luxurious and capricious dream of the colorist. . . . It is the recreation of the past." Benois was, indeed, a diligent archivist and rarely achieved the flights of fancy characteristic of Bakst. On the other hand, his artistic vision encompassed an enormous diversity of ballets, from *Les Fêtes* in 1912 (not produced) to *Sémiramis* in 1934 at the Paris Opera and from *La Dame aux Camélias* in 1923 for Ida Rubinstein in Paris to *The Sleeping Beauty* in 1953 at the Teatro alla Scala, Milan.

[*For related discussion, see* Scenic Design. *In addition, many of the figures and works mentioned herein are the subjects of independent entries.*]

BIBLIOGRAPHY

Benois, Alexandre. *Reminiscences of the Russian Ballet*. Translated by Mary Britnieva. London, 1941.
Benois, Alexandre. *Memoirs*. 2 vols. Translated by Moura Budberg. London, 1960–1964.
Benois, Alexandre. *Moi vospominaniia*. 5 vols. in 2. Compiled by N. I. Aleksandrova et al. Moscow, 1980.
Buckle, Richard. "Thoughts on Alexandre Benois." In *Alexandre Benois, 1870–1960: Drawings for the Ballet*. London, 1980. Exhibition catalog, Hazlitt, Gooden & Fox.
Crisp, Clement, et al. "*Giselle* Revived." *Dance Research* 13 (Winter 1995): 47–61. Benois's designs for the 1924 production of *Giselle*, with a translation from his notebooks.
Etkind, Mark. *Alexandre Nikolaevich Benois* (in Russian). Leningrad, 1965.
Etkind, Mark. *A. N. Benua i russkaia khudozhestvennaia kul'tura*. Leningrad, 1989.
Garafola, Lynn. *Diaghilev's Ballets Russes*. New York, 1989.
Pozharskaya, Militza, and Tatania Volodine. *The Art of the Ballets Russes*. Translated by V. S. Friedman. London, 1990.
Schouvaloff, Alexander. *Set and Costume Designs for Ballet and Theatre*. London, 1987.
Wiley, Roland John. "Alexandre Benois' Commentaries on the First Saisons Russes" (parts 1–8). *The Dancing Times* (October 1980–May 1981).
Wiley, Roland John, trans. and ed. *A Century of Russian Ballet: Documents and Accounts, 1810–1910*. Oxford, 1990.

ARCHIVES.   N. D. Lobanov-Rostovsky, London. Russian Museum, Leningrad. Mademoiselle Anna Tcherkessovna, Paris.

JOHN E. BOWLT

BENSERADE, ISAAC DE (born 1612 in Lyon-la-Forêt, died 20 October 1691 in Gentilly), French poet and librettist. De Benserade is best known as librettist of the ballets of Louis XIV. A member of the inner circle of the court, he found in the ballet fertile ground for cultivating his distinctly original talent. In *Cassandre* (1651), his first *ballet de cour*, he blended flattery and irony in verses that evoked the ugliness of the marquis de Genlis and the erudition of the marquis de Montglas, but only rarely the low social status of professional dancers. He had attained full command of his powers in *Le Ballet de la Nuit* (1653), also created for Louis XIV. Portraying the Rising Sun, the fifteen-year-old monarch alluded to his coming of age in Benserade's verses: "I no longer belong to myself; I belong to the universe."

Benserade also alluded to the amorous intrigues of such court figures as the duc de Damville and to the political role of the duke of York, brother of Charles II and later James II of England. He himself danced in *Les Proverbes, Le Temps*, and *Les Noces de Pélée et de Thétis* (1654); *Les Plaisirs* and *Les Bienvenus* (1655); and *Psyché* (1656). The role of Cupid, written for the marquis de Villeroy, emphasized the latter's youth, and that of Neptune, the fickleness of the duc de Guise. Jean-Baptiste Lully's talents were praised in *L'Amour Malade* (1657).

Benserade collaborated in masquerades as well as ballets. A loyal courtier, he cried out with Louis XIV in *L'Impatience* (1661), the year in which the king assumed full power, "Let us hasten where desire beckons." He evoked the king's glory and love for Louise de La Vallière ("Before such beauty, I artfully conceal This godlike pomp on which my being rests") and sang the praises of Henrietta of England, duchesse d'Orléans, in *Les Saisons* (1661). He stylized the troubled military career of the renegade prince de Condé in the role of Alexander in *Hercule Amoureux* (1661). The court nobility was the focus of *Les Amours Déguisés* (1664) and *Les Plaisirs de l'Île Enchantée* (1664), in which Benserade also praised the duc de Saint-Aignan, an expert organizer and protégé of the king. Molière was cited in *Les Muses* (1666).

The ailing Benserade relinquished his post as official poet with *Flore* (1669), in which Louis XIV made his last stage appearance. Benserade heralded his decision in a dedicatory rondeau in which he punned, "This duty is not crowned with glory, regardless of one's talents for the crown."

Although too old and weary to keep up with court intrigues, Benserade was still in demand as a poet. He contributed to *Le Triomphe de l'Amour* (1681), in which he paid homage to the dauphin, the dauphine, and Mademoiselle de Nantes in one last demonstration of his refined sense of irony.

By then, Benserade had written twenty-four *ballets de cour,* extolled the king in more than sixty roles, and artfully portrayed the court with its politics and passions, erotic as well as intellectual. With Vincent Voiture and Pierre Corneille, he was considered one of the three leading French poets of his day. Charles Perrault wrote that "the blow he dealt to the character rebounded on the individual, and the result was double pleasure."

[*See also* Ballet de Cour.]

BIBLIOGRAPHY

Christout, Marie-Françoise. *Le ballet de cour de Louis XIV, 1643–1672.* Paris, 1967.
Harris-Warrick, Rebecca, and Carol G. Marsh. *Musical Theatre at the Court of Louis XIV: Le Mariage de la Grosse Cathos.* Cambridge, 1994.
Isherwood, Robert M. *Music in the Service of the King.* Ithaca, N.Y., 1972.
Prunières, Henry. *Le ballet de cour en France avant Benserade et Lully.* Paris, 1914.
Silin, Charles I. *Benserade and His Ballets de Cour.* Baltimore, 1940.

MARIE-FRANÇOISE CHRISTOUT
Translated from French

BERAIN, JEAN (born 4 June 1640 in Saint-Mihiel, Lorraine, died 24 January 1711 in Paris). French engraver, costume, scenery, and stage machinery designer. Berain made a name for himself as an engraver, publishing collections of ornamental designs for such artisans as gunsmiths and locksmiths. His reputation was such that in 1671 he was asked to work for Louis XIV, and in 1674 he succeeded Henry Gissey as *dessinateur de la chambre et du cabinet du roi* (designer of the king's chamber and office). By then he was already doing commissions for the theatrical performances at the French court, apparently having begun as a costume designer for opera performances. Among other commissions Berain designed the dancers' costumes for the *divertissements* of Jean-Baptiste Lully's *tragédies lyriques* (lyric tragedies) and for the composer's two "ballets," *Le Triomphe de l'Amour* and *Le Temple de la Paix,* created respectively in 1681 and 1685 at Saint-Germain-en-Laye and Fontainebleau. He continued his work at the Paris Opera, replacing Carlo Vigarani in 1680, after which he also created the sets and the machinery.

Until 1707, when it became apparent that he could no longer design, Berain was in charge of the staging for all the lyric works performed in Paris and at the royal residences. Among other works he staged the first *opéra-ballets,* Pascal Colasse's *Les Saisons* (1695), and André Campra's *L'Europe Galante* (1697). Generally greatly admired by the public, many of his creations were quickly disseminated by engravings and through numerous copies of his designs, executed by his workshop for enthusiasts. The artists who assisted him included his son, known as Jean Berain *fils* (born 1674), who had the most important role. In 1698, Berain *fils* was already working on performances given at the court, and he succeeded his father at the Paris Opera and in the king's service. He seems to have continued working until his death in 1726. Lacking his father's talent, he was obliged to call on other artists, such as Claude Gillot, with whom he collaborated on the performances of *Le Ballet des Éléments,* danced at the Tuileries Palace in 1721 by the young Louis XV.

Numerous drawings by Jean Berain and his son survive in European and American collections, and from them we can evaluate the output of these two artists. In his cos-

BERAIN. A costume study for a male dancer by Jean Berain, a designer known for his use of decorative and symmetrical motifs. (Metropolitan Museum of Art, New York; The Elisha Whittelsey Collection, The Elisha Whittelsey Fund, 1963 [63.525.10]; photograph used by permission.)

tumes and stage sets the elder Berain was inspired by the achievements of his predecessors, Gissey, Ludovico Burnacini, Giacomo Torelli, and Vigarani, but he achieved a personal style characterized by attention to balance and elegance. He liked to make use of decorative motifs, frequently in symmetrical arrangements, paying particular attention to their design and imparting to it a grace that heralded developments in the plastic arts in France during the first half of the eighteenth century. A better set designer than inventor of elaborate machinery, he assigned a leading role to lighting, creating skillful effects. He also adapted stage space to the expression of the actors, which allowed them to work with greater freedom. His costumes were tastefully embellished, and the fabrics and accessories that he chose created an impression of great richness that dazzled the public and served as models for those designed, less successfully, by Berain *fils*. Despite its shortcomings, the son's work helped to perpetuate the father's considerable influence on the art of staging in France and in other European countries.

[*For related discussion, see* Costume in Western Traditions, *overview article.*]

BIBLIOGRAPHY

La Gorce, Jérôme de. *Berain, dessinateur du Roi Soleil.* Paris, 1986.
La Gorce, Jérôme de. *Lully, un âge d'or de l'Opéra Français.* Paris, 1991.
Levinson, André. "Berain and the French Costume Tradition." *Theatre Arts Monthly* (March 1929).
Sowell, Debra Hickenlooper. "Jean Berain and Costume Design in *Le Triomphe de l'Amour.*" In *Proceedings of the Fifth Annual Conference, Society of Dance History Scholars, Harvard University, February 1982,* compiled by Christena L. Schlundt. Riverside, Calif., 1982.
Tessier, André. "Berain, créateur du pays d'opéra." *La revue musicale* (1 January 1925).
Weigert, Roger-Armand. *Jean I Berain: Dessinateur de la chambre et du cabinet du roi, 1640–1711.* Paris, 1936.

JÉRÔME DE LA GORCE

BÉRARD, CHRISTIAN (Christian-Jacques Bérard; born 20 August 1902 in Paris, died 13 February 1949 in Paris), French painter and designer. Bérard was already well established as a painter in 1930 when he became involved in the neohumanism movement, which sought to restore a sense of spirituality and humanity to painting, something that was generally lacking in contemporary art forms. The movement's preoccupation with human personality led most of its artists toward stage design.

At the urging of Boris Kochno, Bérard designed his first work for the theater, a short ballet, *La Nuit* by Serge Lifar, for Charles B. Cochran's 1930 revue at the London Pavilion. Compared to the fussiness of much of the period's stage design, Bérard's showed a unique sense of theater. His simple arrangement of gray gauzes to represent a lonely street created the poetic atmosphere needed for that ballet.

The same simplicity on a far grander scale was evident in the next ballet that Bérard designed—George Balanchine's *Cotillon* (1932; for Colonel de Basil's Ballets Russes de Monte Carlo)—when elegant ballroom dancers moved against a series of red-lined theater boxes set in a white wall. In this and in what he did for Balanchine's *Mozartiana* (for Les Ballets 1933), when the dancers' black-and-white costumes had a simplified rococo grandeur, Bérard revealed a great affinity for the couturier's art, which was unusual for stage designers at the time. All dresses were molded to the body to enhance the dancers' lines; at the same time, the color, silhouette, and choice of material perfectly conveyed the nature of each particular role. Bérard always worked closely with dressmakers, and many of his ideas had considerable influence on fashions of the 1930s.

What Bérard designed for Léonide Massine's symphonic ballets—*Symphonie Fantastique* (1936; for de Basil's Ballets Russes) and *Seventh Symphony* (1938; for Sergei Denham's Ballet Russe de Monte Carlo)—seemed to be a return to his former work as a painter, especially in the landscape scenes that, with extreme simplication, evoked a mood by showing ruined classical architecture against a wide expanse of sky. His black-and-red ballroom scene for *Symphonie Fantastique* with the ladies in swirling, white Romantic dresses introduced the color—red—that he would feature in most of his subsequent designs.

The color red became a focal point in ballets that otherwise were virtually in monochrome, especially in two major works for Les Ballets des Champs-Élysées, of which Bérard was co-director with Boris Kochno when it was founded in 1944. For Roland Petit's *Les Forains* (1945), Bérard's masterly arrangement of a cart, poles, and a large piece of red cloth as a fit-up stage evoked the perfect atmosphere of a place in which itinerant players might perform; it was one of the masterpieces of postwar ballet design. In David Lichine's *La Rencontre, ou Oedipe et le Sphinx* (1948), a suspended, scarlet-fringed platform (on which the Sphinx, with towering white wings, awaited her prey) and a red chair were the only points of color in an otherwise monochrome Theban landscape.

Although he worked extensively in the theater, Bérard's only other ballet designs were for Massine's *Clock Symphony* (1948; Sadler's Wells Ballet) and revisions of his own previous designs, such as the dresses from *Mozartiana* for Balanchine's *Caracole* (1952; New York City Ballet). His work still inspires ballet designers with its innate taste, simplicity, and creation of atmosphere.

BIBLIOGRAPHY

Beaton, Cecil, and Philip James. *Christian Bérard: An Exhibition of Paintings and Décors.* Exhibition catalog. London, 1950.
García-Márquez, Vicente. *The Ballets Russes: Colonel de Basil's Ballets Russes de Monte Carlo, 1932–1952.* New York, 1990.
Harris, Dale. "Christian Bérard." *Architectural Digest* (April 1989).

Hastings, Baird. *Christian Bérard: Painter, Decorator, Designer.* Exhibition catalog. Boston, 1950.

Kochno, Boris. *Christian Bérard.* Translated by Philip Core. New York, 1988.

PETER WILLIAMS

BERBER DANCE. *See* Morocco; North Africa; *and* Tunisia.

BERETTA, CATERINA (born 8 December 1839 in Milan, died 1 January 1911 in Milan), Italian ballet dancer and teacher. The daughter of a mime, Catarina Beretta studied with Auguste Hus in the ballet school of the Teatro alla Scala in Milan. She was soon called to Paris, where in 1855 she delighted the public with the original style of her interpretation of *Le Diable à Quatre* and *Jovita, ou Les Boucaniers Mexicains,* both by Joseph Mazilier. Théophile Gautier, impressed by her technical capabilities, described her performance in *Le Diable à Quatre* in these words:

> She does not blur a single movement of her *jetés battus;* she jumps energetically, if not to a great height; she covers the stage with speed and agility; and in *posés renversées,* she attempts positions that are so off-balance that they would break the back of a dancer who does not have the suppleness and acrobatic elasticity that distinguish Mlle Beretta. Her *double tour sur la pointe* on the left leg, executed with a dazzling rapidity, aroused much applause.   (Gautier, as given in Guest, 1986)

Notwithstanding the general appreciation, she received some negative reviews (see Jürgensen, 1995) for her interpretation of the Spirit of Autumn in *The Four Seasons,* a *divertissement* from Giuseppe Verdi's *Les Vêspres Siciliennes,* choreographed by Lucien Petipa.

In the years that followed, Beretta appeared in Milan as the protagonist of *Shakespeare, ossia Un Sogno di una Notte d'Estate* (1856) by Giovanni Casati and also performed in Rome (1857). Between 1857 and 1871 she danced on numerous occasions and always as prima ballerina at the Teatro Regio in Turin. She alternated her appearances in Turin with performances at La Scala, at Teatro La Fenice in Venice, and at the Teatro Pagliano in Florence, always gaining great acclaim for her acrobatic virtuosity.

During the summer of 1859 Beretta danced, along with Efisio Catte, in a revival of *Rodolfo* by Pasquale Borri at La Scala. Earlier in the season she had played the main role in *Gabriella la Fioraia* (Gabriella the Flower Girl), also by Borri, at La Fenice. On that occasion, shortly before the outbreak of the Second War for Italian Independence against the Austrian domination of Milan and Venice, she incited a reaction from the Austrian police because she had pinned red and green flowers on her white costume (the colors of the Italian independence movement).

In 1861 Beretta performed at the Teatro Pagliano in *Pedrilla e Rosetta, ovvero Un Peccato di Desiderio* (Pedrilla and Rosetta, or A Sin of Desire), by her husband Lorenzo Viena. Over the next two decades she gave numerous performances at the major theaters in Italy, appearing in such works as *Zoraide, o La Schiava Circassa* (Zoraida, or The Circassian Slave), also by her husband, at the Teatro San Carlo in Naples; *La Semiramide del Nord* (Semiramide of the North), by Hippolyte Monplaisir, at La Scala; *Leonilda, ossia La Fidanzata del Filibustiere* (Leonilda, or The Pirate's Fiancée), by Paul Taglioni, at La Fenice; and *Loreley,* by Monplaisir, at La Scala. She also appeared at Her Majesty's Theatre in London in 1863 and 1864.

Beretta was one of the most famous Italian dancers of her day, acclaimed by critics and historians alike. One contemporary, Gino Monaldi, recalled her as

> a very strong ballerina who achieved miracles in her art, overcoming with admirable grace the major difficulties she faced, as though they were a game, a simple amusement. Although her face was not beautiful, she compensated by having a wonderful shape, worthy of any statue of ancient times and modern, of which she would take advantage by dancing a kind of polka dressed as a man, sure of promoting the public's enthusiasm to the highest degree.   (Monaldi, 1910)

Beretta was also highly respected as a teacher. In 1877 she was invited to Saint Petersburg to act as *maîtresse de ballet* at the Maryinsky Theater. Upon her return to Italy, she opened a school in Milan in 1879, and from 1905 to 1908 she directed the school at La Scala. Among her students were Pierina Legnani, Anna Pavlova, Vera Trefilova, and Tamara Karsavina.

BIBLIOGRAPHY

"Beretta, Caterina." Obituary notice. *Il mondo artistico* (4 January 1911).

Cambiasi, Pompeo. *La Scala, 1778–1906.* Milan, 1906.

Gautier, Théophile. *Gautier on Dance.* Translated and edited by Ivor Guest. London, 1986.

Guest, Ivor. *The Ballet of the Second Empire.* 2 vols. London, 1953, 1954.

Guest, Ivor. *The Romantic Ballet in England.* London, 1954.

Jürgensen, Knud Arne. *The Verdi Ballets.* Parma, 1995.

Karsavina, Tamara. "Carissima Maestra." *The Dancing Times* (November 1964): 66–67.

Lifar, Serge. *A History of Russian Ballet* (1950). Translated by Arnold L. Haskell. New York, 1954.

Lo Iacono, Concetta. "Minima choreutica: Fasti e dissesti del ballo italiano sul declino dell'Ottocento." In *Musica senza aggettivi: Studi per Fedele d'Amico,* edited by Agostino Ziino, pp. 391–421. Florence, 1991.

Monaldi, Gino. *Le regine della danza nel secolo XIX.* Turin, 1910.

Rossi, Luigi. "Beretta, Caterina." In *Dizionario del balletto.* Milan, 1994.

ARCHIVE. Walter Toscanini Collection of Research Materials in Dance, New York Public Library for the Performing Arts.

CLAUDIA CELI
Translated from Italian

BERGAMASQUE. The *bergamasque* (It., *bergamasca*, *bergamasco*; Eng., *bergomask*; Fr., *bergamasque*) was an Italian dance or dance song originating (c.1430) in northern Italy, in the mountainous district of Bergamo, then part of the fifteenth- and sixteenth-century Venetian Republic. With only musical evidence and no surviving dance descriptions or choreographic records, it is impossible to reconstruct the original dance movement precisely; it can be conjectured only by analogy, by rhythmic interpretation of the scores, and by context.

The earliest score, Giacomo Gorzanis's *Saltarello dito il Bergamasco* (1564), seems to suggest a lighthearted skipping pattern. The next two musical examples, Filipno Azzaiolo's music for texts written in Bergamascan dialect (1589), reveal two very different rhythmic and harmonic patterns. None of the three relates to the duple rhythms set in four-bar phrases, usually complete in a twelve- or sixteen-bar sequence, that appear in the seventeenth century and continue well into the eighteenth. Barbetta's *Moresca quarta deta la Bergamasca* (1585) provides one early link to the *moresca*, but this piece does not imply the use of the movements we associate with this dance from Thoinot Arbeau's description in *Orchesographie* (1588).

Bergamascas abound in the seventeenth century, particularly in the Italian musical literature, occurring primarily as chordal guitar accompaniments in an age that favored the guitar as the instrument for accompanying dance. Instrumental variations also exist, as do keyboard variations and some versions for violin and some for lute. A few examples occur in French sources, while John Bull, among others, wrote English bergomask music. The best-known German *bergamasque* is found in the quodlibet of Johann Sebastian Bach's *Goldberg Variations* (1742): it is the descant tune associated with the folk text "Kraut und Rüben" (Cabbage and Beets).

The *bergamasque* appears to have been widespread in European theatrical culture during the Baroque era. Shakespeare mentions one in act 5, scene 1, of *A Midsummernight's Dream* (1595). In it, Theseus denies the need for an epilogue to the delightful play-within-the-play, and instead accepts Bottom's offer "to hear a bergomask dance between two of our company" (1.361). It seems implied that two persons dance while a text is being sung, perhaps in Bergamascan dialect; however, no instructions, music, or song text survive, and "hear a . . . dance" may be a joke.

Gregorio Lambranzi includes a *bergamasco* in his *New and Curious School of Theatrical Dancing* (1716), in which he gives a musical sample and instructions for a cobbler to appear with his handiwork and show how well he sews the leather "alles nach dem musicalischen Takt."

Contextually, the *bergamasque* appears to be a Baroque manifestation of a masked *commedia dell'arte* dance, often with song, poking fun at the rustics of a hilly, landlocked region of Italy where intermarriage and poor diet produced a high incidence of mental retardation and physical abnormalities, such as goiters, which were seen as comic distortions. The development of the comical prototype (for example, circular globes on the base of the mask representing a goiter) spread widely and probably detached itself from the original image, retaining primarily the rustic, comic, and mime elements.

Nineteenth-century *bergamasque* music, such as Claude Debussy's *Suite Bergamasque*, is unrelated to the earlier dance form; instead, it evokes an antique, pastoral, or comic mood.

BIBLIOGRAPHY
Hudson, Richard. "Bergamasca." In *The New Grove Dictionary of Music and Musicians*. London, 1980.
Moe, Lawrence H. "Dance Music in Printed Italian Lute Tablatures from 1507 to 1611." Ph.D. diss., Harvard University, 1956.
Nettl, Paul. "Die Bergamaska." *Zeitschrift für Musikwissenschaft* 5 (1923): 291–295.

EMMA LEWIS THOMAS

BERGER, AUGUSTIN (Augustin Ratzesberger; born 11 August 1861 in Boskovice, Czechoslovakia, died 1 June 1945 in Prague), Czech dancer, choreographer, and pedagogue. A student of Marie Hentazová and Giovanni Martini, Berger began his professional career at Prague's Teatro Salone Italiano and later traveled with Martini to Sweden under a one-year contract. From 1876 to 1880 he was a soloist at the Stavovské Theater, and for the following two years he partnered Aenea, known as *La Mouche d'Or* (The Golden Fly), performing with her in Paris, Toulouse, Barcelona, and Milan. In 1883, after a successful yearlong stint at the New Czech Theater in Prague, he accepted a contract as a soloist at the Prague National Theater. By 1884, already at the head of the ballet ensemble, Berger was asserting himself as a choreographer and pedagogue. From 1900 to 1910 he was ballet master of the court opera in Dresden and was also guest choreographer at the Teatro alla Scala in Milan. Apparently being considered as a successor to Petipa, in 1905 Berger was invited to Saint Petersburg, but his projected staging of Léo Delibes's *Sylvia* was canceled.

Between 1910 and 1912 Berger was artistic director of the Warsaw Ballet; among his pupils was Stanislas Idzikowski. During this period he also produced a spectacular ballet version of *Carmen* at the Alhambra in London. Berger returned to the Prague National Theater as ballet master during the years 1912–1923. In 1923 he went to the Metropolitan Opera Ballet in New York, where he served as ballet master from 1926 to 1932. While there he choreographed ballets for the standard opera repertory— *Aida*, *Carmen*, *Faust*—all of which featured the Metropolitan's *prima ballerina* Rosina Galli.

Berger, a virtuoso dancer of the Italian school, could perform dazzling jumps and *batterie*. He created many stage characters and retained his strength and flexibility until late in life; at the Prague National Theater he performed 1,873 times. Among his partners were Giulietta Paltrinieri, Enriquetta Grimaldi, and Luigia Cerale. Berger was a demanding and strict teacher who trained several notable dancers, among them Anna Korecká, the first Czech *prima ballerina*, and Ivo Váňa Psota.

Berger also had an important influence on the development of Czech ballet. He made the dancers of the Prague National Theater into a unified, disciplined, highly professional company, and his work as a choreographer and librettist inspired the creation of national ballets, among them, *A Christmas Eve Dream* (1886), *The Tale of Fortune Found* (1889), and *Rákoš Rákoczy* (1891). Berger's choreography was not particularly innovative but rather represented the typical ballet aesthetics of his time: elaborately staged productions with large crowds of extras, numerous stage effects, and skillfully arranged tableaux and apotheoses. Among these was the second act of *Swan Lake*, which he choreographed in 1888 on the occasion of Tchaikovsky's visit to Prague.

[*See also* Prague National Theater Ballet.]

BIBLIOGRAPHY

Hájek, Ladislav. *Paměti Augustina Bergra*. Prague, 1942.
Novák, Ladislav. *Stará garda Národního divadla*. Prague, 1937.
Rey, Jan. "Change and Growth in Czechoslovakia." *Dance and Dancers* (October 1960): 14–17.
Schmidová, Lidka. *Československý balet*. Prague, 1962.

VLADIMÍR VAŠUT
Translated from Czech

BERIOSOVA, SVETLANA (Svetlana Nikolaevna Beriosova; born 24 September 1932 in Kaunas), Lithuanian-British ballet dancer, teacher, and coach. Svetlana Beriosova is the daughter of the dancer and ballet master Nicholas Beriozoff and his first wife. At the age of three, Beriosova left Lithuania with her mother to join Beriozoff in Paris, where he was working for René Blum's Ballets de Monte Carlo. In 1939 Beriozoff went with the Blum company to the United States, leaving his wife and child in Paris. At the outbreak of World War II, he immediately sent for them, and they sailed from Genoa to New York on the last refugee-bearing ship to leave Europe.

From 1940 to 1947 Beriosova remained in the United States, receiving her first ballet lessons from her father at age ten and then being sent to the newly opened Vilzak-Schollar School in New York. Her mother had died shortly after their arrival in America, and since her father was constantly on tour, Ludmilla Schollar "mothered" the young dancer until her father remarried.

Schollar was also a formative influence in Beriosova's early training, implanting in her a Russian grandeur of movement that was to characterize her dancing throughout her career.

Beriosova made some appearances in her youth as the child with a skipping rope in Léonide Massine's *Le Beau Danube*. Her first major role was in March 1947 with the Ottawa Ballet, when she danced the full-length version of *The Nutcracker*. She was then not yet fifteen.

When Beriozoff returned to Europe in 1947 to join Le Grand Ballet de Monte Carlo, directed by the Marquis de Cuevas, Svetlana went with him, going on with him to join the Metropolitan Ballet in England later that year. With that company she revealed her ballerina potential, creating leading roles in John Taras's *Designs with Strings*, first performed on 6 February 1948 in Edinburgh, and in Frank Staff's *Fanciulla delle Rose*, first performed on 10 June 1948 in London. In May 1950 she joined Sadler's Wells Theatre Ballet, a subsidiary company of the Sadler's Wells Ballet that served as a training company for young dancers and choreographers and was based at the Sadler's Wells Theatre. Her first role there was Odette in *Swan Lake*, act 2, which she had danced with much success with the Metropolitan Ballet. Other roles quickly followed in ballets by Frederick Ashton, George Balanchine, John Cranko, and Andrée Howard—a favorite was the Chatelaine in Howard's *La Fête Étrange*—as well as in the classics. When the company toured the United States in 1951, Beriosova and Elaine Fifield were its ballerinas.

In 1952 Beriosova moved on to the Sadler's Wells Ballet (which later became the Royal Ballet) at Covent Garden. There she made her debut as the Lilac Fairy in *The Sleeping Beauty* on 3 July. In September she triumphed in *Coppélia* and followed this with an enchanting Aurora in *The Sleeping Beauty* on 1 June 1954. She danced her first Odette-Odile, which was to become her greatest role, at Covent Garden on 19 February 1955, partnered by John Field. She danced her first Giselle, with Philip Chatfield, on 28 April 1956. Standing more than five feet six inches, she was tall for a ballerina of her generation, but eventually she found an ideal partner in Donald MacLeary. With him, she developed her Odette-Odile into a performance of great nobility, and their *Swan Lake* was rated by many as superior to that of Margot Fonteyn and Rudolf Nureyev. By birth, early training, and temperament the most "Russian" of Royal Ballet dancers, Beriosova was a natural choice for the role of the Tsarevna in the 1954 revival of *The Firebird*, a performance recorded on film (*The Royal Ballet*, 1959).

Cranko created for her the leading roles in *The Prince of the Pagodas* (1957) and *Antigone* (1959); Kenneth MacMillan cast her as the Fairy in his first version of *Le Baiser de la Fée* (1960); Ashton gave her the title role in

BERIOSOVA. The aristocratic poise of Beriosova made her excel in the classic roles in the Royal Ballet. She is seen here as Princess Aurora in *The Sleeping Beauty*. (Photograph from the Dance Collection, New York Public Library for the Performing Arts.)

his *Persephone* (1961), which included speaking the French text as well as dancing. When Bronislava Nijinska came to the Royal Ballet to revive *Les Biches* (1964) and *Les Noces* (1966), she and Beriosova established immediate rapport, and the ballerina became an ideal interpreter of the roles of the Hostess in *Les Biches* and the Bride in *Les Noces*.

In 1968, when Ashton cast Beriosova as Lady Elgar in *Enigma Variations*, she showed another facet of her talent. At the zenith of her performing career she took, not a ballerina role, but that of a mature woman—a loving, caring wife. Another true portrait of womanhood was her creation of the Tsarina in MacMillan's *Anastasia* in 1971.

Beriosova retired in 1975 but continued to teach and, especially, to coach.

BIBLIOGRAPHY
Franks, A. H. *Svetlana Beriosova: A Biography*. London, 1958.
Woodcock, Sarah C. *The Sadler's Wells Royal Ballet*. London, 1991.

MARY CLARKE

BERIOZOFF, NICHOLAS (born 16 May 1906 in Kaunas, Lithuania, died 18 February 1996 in London), dancer, ballet master, and teacher. A Lithuanian who was later granted British citizenship, Nicholas Beriozoff started his ballet training about 1920 in Prague, where he studied with Kasimir Remislavsky and began performing at the National Theater while he was still a teenager. He eventually became a full-fledged member of the ballet company, specializing in character parts. Toward the end of the 1920s, he and his wife, the dancer Maria Morskaya, left Czechoslovakia and spent two years as freelance performers in France and Germany. In 1932, compelled by Beriozoff's obligation to military service, they returned to Lithuania and settled in Kaunas. Their daughter, Svetlana Beriosova, was born at this time.

Upon completion of his military service, Beriozoff was appointed principal dancer at the Lithuanian National Ballet, then headed by Vera Nemchinova and Anatole Oboukhoff, both former members of the Ballets Russes de Serge Diaghilev. Beriozoff excelled in character roles and became acquainted with the Russian classics and some of Michel Fokine's ballets. In 1935 he joined René Blum's Ballets Russes de Monte Carlo, establishing himself as an authority on the works of Marius Petipa and Fokine.

After a severe knee injury ended his dancing career, Beriozoff became a ballet master, working for Ballet International (1944), Le Grand Ballet du Marquis de Cuevas (1947), the London Metropolitan Ballet (1948), Teatro alla Scala in Milan (1950–1951) and London's Festival Ballet (1951–1954). For London's Festival Ballet, he revived *Les Sylphides*, *Petrouchka*, *Schéhérazade*, and the Polovtsian Dances from *Prince Igor* before returning to the de Cuevas company in 1956. As ballet director of the Stuttgart Ballet from 1957 to 1960 he rigorously concentrated on the classics, laying the foundations upon which his successor, John Cranko, was able to build one of the world's finest ballet companies.

After returning once again to the de Cuevas troupe in 1961–1962 and serving as ballet master of the Finnish National Ballet from 1962 to 1964, Beriozoff spent the years 1964–1971 in Zurich, where he repeated his Stuttgart success by fashioning a repertory based on the nineteenth-century classics and the Fokine ballets of the Diaghilev repertory. He also mounted his own versions of *Ondine* (1964), *Romeo and Juliet* (1966), and *Cinderella* (1967).

After the death of his first wife, Beriozoff married the Stuttgart dancer Doris Catana. He worked at the San Carlo Opera, Naples, in 1971. During the late 1970s he was head of the ballet department at Indiana University, Bloomington, and continued to be in great demand all over the world as a ballet master. An experienced craftsman rather than a genuine creator, Beriozoff was known for his firm authority and affable manners, qualities that have endeared him to scores of dancers who have collaborated with him all over the globe. One of his last stage appearances was as the Old Sage in a Zurich production of *Le Sacre du Printemps* a few months before his death.

BIBLIOGRAPHY

Anderson, Jack. "Who Is a Ballet Master? Nicholas Beriozoff, Chef de Ballet of the Zurich State Opera Ballet, Discusses the Qualifications." *Dance Magazine* (January 1968): 54–57.

Clarke, Mary. "Nicholas Beriozoff." *The Dancing Times* (March 1996): 549.

Franks, A. H. *Svetlana Beriosova: A Biography*. London, 1958.

Wilson, G. B. L. "Beriozoff at 75." *The Dancing Times* 71 (July 1981): 689.

Merrett, Sue. "Beriozoff at 85." *The Dancing Times* (August 1991): 1033.

HORST KOEGLER

BERK, FRED (Fritz Berger; born 25 January 1911 in Vienna, died 26 February 1980 in New York City), teacher, producer, researcher, author, and performer. Born to Jacob Berger, a dairy owner, and Henrietta Blau Berger, Berk became an authority on Jewish dance and was an important influence on young modern dancers in the 1950s in New York City.

Although born into an Orthodox Jewish family, religion was less interesting to him than opera, which was a diversion from his work, beginning when he was fourteen, as an apprentice goldsmith. Back problems from hunching over his workbench sent him to a doctor who suggested dance as a remedy. Berk had seen a performance by Gertrud Kraus in a Vienna park; he chose her studio to begin his dance studies.

Berk trained and performed in the expressionist modern Kraus Dance Troupe from 1931 to 1933; he then taught in his own studio and performed own works until the Nazi annexation of Austria (1938) forced him to flee in 1939. In 1934 Berk had won the bronze medal for his anti-Hitler solo, *The Tyrant*, awarded by Austria's Ministry of Public Education and the City of Vienna with the International Archives of the Dance. He had also performed in Holland, Italy, and Switzerland. Successfully fleeing the Nazis, he reached England in 1939 and Cuba in 1940. In Cuba he performed for two years with another Kraus dancer, Claudia Vall Kauffman. During this period he was stricken with his first bout of arthritis.

In an interview for his 1985 biography *Victory Dances*, Berk said that it was only when he arrived in the United States in 1941, during the Holocaust, that he realized the importance of a positive Jewish identity. Through dance he developed a deep and ongoing commitment to Jewish culture and to Israel that would affect audiences, the professional dance world, and countless students for several decades throughout the United States.

In New York City, Berk was reunited with Katya Delakova, also a dancer from Kraus's troupe. They formed a professional duo and performed together for seven years. Their first program, "Make Way for Tomorrow," on 23 January 1944, combined American and Jewish folk music and dance. They toured extensively to Jewish community centers (JCCs) all over the country; colleges (Black Mountain College in North Carolina and Colorado College with dancer Hanya Holm); universities (University of Wisconsin at Madison); Madison Square Garden, the United Nations, the Museum of Natural History, and Carnegie Hall in New York; rallies and conferences for Jewish causes (including the Jewish Theological Seminary and Mordecai Kaplan's Society for the Advancement of Judaism); Yiddish theaters; and, in the summer, New York State's Catskill Mountain resorts—called the "Borsht Belt" circuit.

In the 1940s Berk and Delakova started the Jewish Dance Guild performing group; they did programming and taught student rabbis at New York's Jewish Theological Society, and in 1949 toured the new State of Israel (where Delakova settled).

Back in New York, in the 1950s Berk became the unequaled master of Israeli folk dance, setting the standards for teaching and staging it. His change of emphasis—from performing to teaching, directing, and producing—was in part the result not only of losing his partner, but of arthritis in his hip and unsuccessful surgery. Berk was left with a drastic limp, marking him an unlikely dance master. Forced to heighten his skills in articulating dance, he unwittingly enhanced his stature and his career developed.

Berk created and directed the Jewish Dance Department at the Ninety-second Street YM-YWHA in New York City, developing courses in the pedagogy of Israeli folk dance, teaching all levels of Israeli folk dance, bringing its creators from Israel for special workshops, and creating and directing several performing groups. His showcase company was the Hebraica Dance Company. Until his death he directed the Israeli Dance Festival in New York every spring, first at Hunter College, then at Carnegie Hall, and then at the Felt Forum and Philharmonic Hall at Lincoln Center, with hundreds of Jewish youths participating through youth groups.

Berk's efforts in the Jewish community crystallized much of what was happening in American Judaism in this thirty-year period. As part of its recovery from the Holocaust, the American community began to identify with Israel—which was itself a new reality for Judaism. For Berk this meant that Israeli folk dance and dances with Jewish themes would have increasing import for the early baby-boom students and for audiences from all sectors of Judaism. He functioned nationally through programs he created, often under the Israeli-sponsored American Zionist Youth Foundation (AZYF); at Hillels on campuses and JCCs nationwide; at summer camps (especially, for twenty-five years, at Camp Blue Star in North Carolina); but primarily at the Ninety-second Street Y.

From 1968 until his death, Berk directed the AZYF's Israel Folk Dance Institute and through it led summer study tours of folk dancers to Israel. The AZYF also published his books, including *The Jewish Dance, The Chasidic Dance, Dance of the Jewish People,* and *100 Israeli Folk Dances,* and it sponsored a small publication, *Hora,* which Berk edited. Berk's thirteen recordings of Israeli folk dance music were considered the best in both the United States and Israel for their superb musicality and the concisely written instruction manuals that accompany each.

Berk also participated fully in the life of modern dance in New York City, serving as a nexus for young choreographers through an innovative program he created called The Stage for Dancers. In the postwar United States, too few resources and too little encouragement existed for the arts and the performing arts, so Berk created a three-year series that provided stipends for performers in concerts that combined dancers from a variety of modern dance styles and New York studios. Performances took place at the Brooklyn Museum, Alwin Nikolais's Henry Street Playhouse, the Cooper Union, and the Masters' Institute.

Dance Magazine said that Berk's programs had

a healthy air of adventure and discovery . . . In the 10 years he's lived in America, the Austrian born Mr. Berk viewed with no little astonishment and finally with ire the spectacle of capable dancers practicing their craft in studios year after year. . . . "I got bored with seeing the dancers sit around their studios and I decided something must be done to get them on stage."

Berk co-founded the first professional dance company for children, the Merry-Go-Rounders, with the seminal modern dancer Doris Humphrey. His *Holiday in Israel* suite was a staple of the Merry-Go-Rounders' programming and toured throughout the New York City area to schools and community centers.

For a brief period in the late 1970s, Berk lived in Israel. His work in New York, primarily during the 1950s development of modern dance and the reemergence of Jewish and Israeli folk dance, had earned him a valued reputation as a master teacher and producer. Berk was also renowned as the leading authority on the subject he had come to love, Jewish and Israeli folk dance.

BIBLIOGRAPHY

Berk, Fred. *Jewish Folk Dance Book.* New York, 1948.
Berk, Fred. *The Jewish Dance.* New York, 1960.
Berk, Fred. *Ha-Rikud: The Jewish Dance.* New York, 1972.
Berk, Fred, ed. *The Chasidic Dance.* New York, 1975.
Berk, Fred, and Lucy Venable. *Holiday in Israel.* New York, 1977.
Berk, Fred, and Susan Reimer, eds. *Machol Ha'am: Dance of the Jewish People.* New York, 1978.
Ingber, Judith Brin. "Fred Berk: The Metamorphosis of a European Dancer, 1939–1949." *Dance Chronicle* 7.1 (1984): 1–32.
Ingber, Judith Brin. *Victory Dances: The Story of Fred Berk, a Modern Day Jewish Dancing Master.* Tel Aviv, 1985.

JUDITH BRIN INGBER

BERKELEY, BUSBY (William Berkeley Enos; born 29 November 1895 in Los Angeles, died 14 March 1976 in Palm Desert, California), American dance director of film-spectacles. The name of Busby Berkeley is practically synonymous with the genre of film-spectacle. From 1930 to 1962, Berkeley was involved in the creation of fifty-four Hollywood films, most of which were musicals. Typically he was dance director, but he also directed or co-directed several films and made a few personal appearances. Although as dance director he worked with a variety of directors (notably Lloyd Bacon and Mervyn Le Roy), the films on which he worked have become known as Berkeley films—or Busby Berkeley musicals—a testimonial to the importance of his contribution.

Prior to his career in Hollywood, Berkeley was a student at a military academy, and he worked in a shoe factory. In 1917, when the United States entered World War I, he enlisted, became an entertainment officer, and gained a reputation for his innovative drill routines. After his return to civilian life in 1918, Berkeley acted in, directed, or produced a wide range of dramatic and musical productions. Despite his lack of formal training as a dancer, by 1930 Berkeley had become recognized as one of Broadway's principal dance directors, with twenty-one musicals to his credit.

Berkeley's first motion picture, *Whoopee* (1930), featured Eddie Cantor. Following this, he made seven films before his first big success, *42nd Street,* which starred Ruby Keeler and Dick Powell, with Ginger Rogers in a lesser role. As a result of the commercial and critical acclaim of *42nd Street,* Berkeley was able to get the financial support he needed to create his elaborate numbers (then costing approximately $10,000 per minute of screen time). His greatest period of innovation, 1933 to 1937, was also his greatest period of productivity. Among the films he created during these years were *Gold Diggers of 1933, Footlight Parade* (1933), *Dames* (1934), *Fashions of 1934, Wonder Bar* (1934), *In Caliente* (1935), *Gold Diggers of 1935, Gold Diggers of 1937, Varsity Show* (1937), and *Hollywood Hotel* (1937).

After 1937, Berkeley's opportunities in Hollywood were not as frequent and his budgets were considerably reduced. In 1942, as director, he introduced moviegoers to Gene Kelly opposite Judy Garland in *For Me and My Gal.* The last film on which he worked, as second-unit director, was *Jumbo* (1962), for which he staged Rodgers and Hart songs.

By 1965, there was a revival of interest in Berkeley's work. In that year he appeared in person at showings of his films, sponsored by both Albert Johnson, director of the San Francisco Film Festival, and Raymond Rohauer, curator of New York's Gallery of Modern Art. Following these events, Berkeley, his wife, and Ruby Keeler ap-

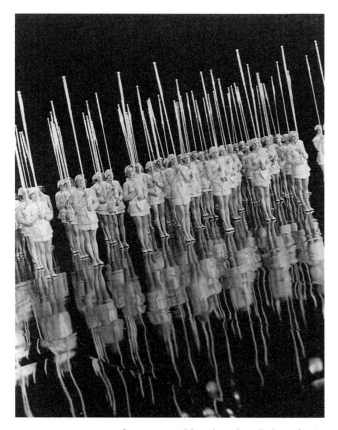

BERKELEY. An army of women wielding long-handled spades in *Gold Diggers of 1937* betray Busby Berkeley's experience choreographing military drill routines. (Photograph from the Film Stills Library, Museum of Modern Art, New York.)

peared at showings of his films throughout Europe and the United States.

In January 1971, the stage musical *No, No Nanette*, starring Ruby Keeler, opened on Broadway, with Berkeley as supervising producer. This highly successful revival of the 1925 musical was Berkeley's swan song.

Berkeley's Ziegfield-style theatrical spectacles presented a large number of glamorous young women, chosen for appearance rather than for dancing skills, in extravagant and revealing costumes. Amid sets that often employed devices such as revolving platforms and hydraulic lifts, these women performed precision routines (incorporating soft shoe and tap) based on geometric formations.

In his Hollywood work, Berkeley's choice of dancers, costumes, and movement vocabulary remained essentially the same, and he continued to employ moving platforms. Nevertheless, from the beginning of his career in the still-youthful motion picture industry, Berkeley understood some of the important differences between stage and screen and proceeded to exploit them. Although he knew nothing about cinematic technique prior to his work in Hollywood, he boldly set about using it to make his staging more spectacular.

Some of Berkeley's dance numbers were solemn—often these were patriotic or glorifying to the military, for example, "Remember My Forgotten Man" in *Gold Diggers of 1933*, which featured a male chorus of war veterans who were among the Depression's unemployed, or the finale of "Shanghai Lil" in *Footlight Parade,* in which hundreds of sailors were seen in formation marching with placards that formed first the flag and then a portrait of President Franklin Delano Roosevelt. Sexual fantasy was, however, clearly their most dominant theme. Scantily clad chorus girls were a characteristic feature of a Berkeley number. Perhaps the most sensational in this regard was "No More Love" in *Roman Scandals* (1933), an Eddie Cantor and Ruth Etting film, in which women appeared to be nude (in fact, for part of the shooting, they were) with only long wigs covering their private parts.

Berkeley also used props and cinematic devices to convey sexual innuendoes. In "The Lady in the Tutti-Frutti Hat" from *The Gang's All Here* (1943), an Alice Faye and Carmen Miranda film, images of enlarged bananas became obviously phallic when a group of chorus girls held them in front of themselves, raising and lowering them in choreographed succession. In *Dames,* Berkeley used a mobile camera to travel to forbidden places: under women's ball gowns (in "I Only Have Eyes for You") and through the crotches of a line-up of girls with straddled legs (in the "Dames" number). Also, in the "I Only Have Eyes for You" number, a vaginal metaphor was suggested

BERKELEY. Large pieces of artificial fruit were featured in "The Lady in the Tutti-Frutti Hat" in *The Gang's All Here* (1943). Berkeley often used overhead camera angles to create two-dimensional kaleidoscopic designs. (Photograph from the Film Stills Library, Museum of Modern Art, New York.)

when a screen-sized eye gradually opened by means of an "iris-out" device. Despite his blatant manner of dealing with sexuality, Berkeley's numbers were not erotic; they were rendered both asexual and highly entertaining by their frenetic pace, multiplication of look-alike women, and outrageously bad taste.

Although some dance numbers in Berkeley's films did advance the plots—"You're Getting to Be a Habit with Me" occurs during a rehearsal scene in *42nd Street* and is integrated into the film's dramatic action—this was clearly not Berkeley's primary concern. Berkeley, in fact, stated: "I did the dance numbers and the director did the story, and sometimes I'd even forget who was directing." More characteristically, Berkeley's numbers were nonnarrative spectacles or narratives based on the song lyrics of the number rather than on the plot of the film. These numbers were introduced into the plot when a character had a daydream or when the show, around which so many of the plots revolved, opened. In the latter case, however, after the curtain went up, it was made very clear that the show being presented was, in fact, one that could never fit or be performed on a proscenium stage.

While Berkeley was not concerned about integrating his numbers into the film plots, he was concerned about preserving their integrity. From the beginning of his career in Hollywood, he recognized a danger, that dance numbers could be interrupted by cutaways or rechoreographed in the cutting room (resulting from the common procedure of shooting from two or three camera angles and then allowing the editing department to edit the best "takes" as they saw fit). To prevent this he demanded, and was given, complete control of the numbers he created.

Berkeley realized his numbers through a highly organized and efficient process of planning. Starting from a very clear mental image of the completed number, he filmed each shot from only one angle and claimed never to have had a retake in his career or to have eliminated more than six feet of film. While Berkeley's policy of no retakes did lead to isolated examples of visible flubs by dancers or camera personnel, these examples are phenomenally few in number. To appreciate this, one has only to think about the possibilities for error in light of some seventy-five production numbers that Berkeley worked on, the length of the numbers (sometimes as long as twelve or thirteen minutes), the length of some takes (as long as seven minutes), the extent of camera movement (the minstrel number in the 1941 *Babes on Broadway*, for example, had thirty-eight camera moves and was filmed in one continuous take), the large number of performers in each production (sometimes hundreds), and the nature of the precision dance routines and geometric formations that obviously required a high degree of collective coordination.

Berkeley's cinematographic trademarks were his overhead shots and his close-up shots; both kinds of shots had been used in musical numbers earlier, but never to the extent, or with the skill, used by Berkeley. Typically, Berkeley's overhead shots were filmed from a height of sixty feet or higher, sometimes requiring holes to be drilled through a studio's ceiling. Berkeley used the overhead shot to maximize the visual possibilities for his geometric forms and drill-like precision choreography, transforming performers into two-dimensional patterns. In one of the best examples of these effects, the "By a Waterfall" number in the 1933 *Footlight Parade* (one of several aqua ballets created by Berkeley), circular, serpentine, snowflake, and floral designs were created by swimmers. Primarily because of such kinetic abstractions, Berkeley has been referred to as a creator of "pure" (or avant-garde) cinema.

Berkeley's use of close-ups can be seen as an extension of the cameo lighting in theatrical productions. He used a variety of close-up shots though his most frequent one, perhaps, was a tracking shot past the faces of chorus girls. When Berkeley was criticized for making women anonymous by using them interchangeably in large groupings, he countered by saying that he also used close-ups to personalize them. In fact, however, the close-ups did not individuate Berkeley's chorus girls; the women had been chosen for their all-of-a-kind vacuous glamour, and seeing them at close range simply made this more obvious. (The camera moves so quickly and smoothly past each face that one is hard-pressed to find the face of the few who later became stars.)

Berkeley is known for his use of close-ups of disembodied heads: these shots were effective because they made his performers look startlingly surreal. At the beginning of "The Lullaby of Broadway" in *Gold Diggers of 1935*, singer Wini Shaw's head is not only disembodied but also grows larger, thus heightening the surrealistic effect. In the "Polka Dot Polka" number in *The Gang's All Here*, tiny disembodied heads bob around as they sing. In this case—for which "head shot" and "close-up" are certainly not synonymous terms—the faces of chorus girls are both surreal images and modular design elements.

In addition to the manipulation of dancers and platforms, to maximize the kinetic possibilities of his film-spectacles, Berkeley's numbers used cutting strategies, moving cameras, and props that appeared to propel themselves. To create dramatic cross-screen movement, Berkeley juxtaposed reverse-angle shots; to exaggerate movement toward and away from the camera, he cut from long shot to close-up and vice versa, without going through medium shot. He sometimes combined angled shots with reverse camera motion to create the illusion of dancers falling toward each other. In the "Dames" number in *Dames*, he combined an overhead shot with reverse camera motion to achieve the effect of dancers flying into the camera lens.

BERKELEY. In this scene from *Wonder Bar*, Berkeley cleverly used mirrors to create the illusion of a cast of thousands. (Photograph from the Film Stills Library, Museum of Modern Art, New York.)

Whereas Berkeley's overhead shots emphasized the two-dimensional reality of the film screen, his extensive use of the moving camera fostered the motion picture's capacity for creating an illusion of three-dimensional plastic space. Sometimes this effect was achieved when the camera moved forward into space (through a tunnel formed by straddled legs); at other times it was achieved when the camera moved from a tight shot backward, gradually revealing a previously unseen panorama. Highly kinetic effects also were achieved through the counter-movements of platforms, performers, and camera.

Berkeley achieved the kind of camera movement he desired through varied means. He invented a monorail to transport a crane camera for the rapid yet smooth effect he sought in "The Lullaby of Broadway" for *Gold Diggers of 1935*. In *Jumbo*, some of the filming was done on a trapeze, while the finale to the 1953 Esther Williams vehicle, *Easy to Love*, was filmed from a helicopter.

Berkeley's numbers also used props that seemed self-propelling. In "The Words Are in My Heart" number for *Gold Diggers of 1935*, for example, pianos appeared to waltz. They were actually pushed by men hidden beneath them.

Ever alert to new possibilities for making his numbers more spectacular, and constantly grappling with the limited focal range of the camera with its single "eye," Berkeley used a variety of cinematic devices to emphasize the size of his sets and the large numbers of dancers in each production. He cut from one area to another to expand the actual space that dancers could use and he used a wide-angle lens to give the illusion that his sets were larger than they were. In addition, some of his kaleidoscopic images were generated with mirrors. In the "Don't Say Goodnight" number in *Wonder Bar*, an octagonal mirrored set made groups of eight dancers look like thousands and dramatically enlarged the appearance of the sound stage on which it was performed.

[*See also* Film Musicals, *article* on Hollywood Film Musicals.]

BIBLIOGRAPHY

Delamater, Jerome. *Dance in the Hollywood Musical.* Ann Arbor, Mich., 1981.

Fumento, Rocco, ed. *42nd Street* (screenplay). Madison, Wis., 1980.

Pike, Bob, and Dave Martin. *The Genius of Busby Berkeley.* Reseda, Calif., 1973.

Rubin, Martin. *Showstoppers: Busby Berkeley and the Tradition of Spectacle.* New York, 1993.

Steinke, Gary Lee. "An Analysis of the Dance Sequences in Busby Berkeley's Films: *42nd Street, Footlight Parade,* and *Gold Diggers of 1935.*" Ph.D. diss., University of Michigan, 1979.

Thomas, Tony, and Jim Terry, with Busby Berkeley. *The Busby Berkeley Book.* Greenwich, Conn., 1973.

NANCY BECKER SCHWARTZ

BERLIN OPERA BALLET (Ballett der Deutschen Oper Berlin), also known as the German Opera Ballet. The Berlin Opera Ballet traces its history from the opening in 1912 of the Deutsches Opernhaus, built to satisfy the civic opera needs of the prospering citizens of Charlottenburg, then an independent city just beyond the walls of the imperial capital. Ballet, however, functioned only as an adornment of opera productions, and its status hardly improved when the company became attached to Berlin as the Municipal Opera (Städtische Oper) from 1925 to 1933. Dance attracted no more attention when the Nazis restored the company's former name in 1933.

During World War II, the Deutsches Opernhaus was bombed late in 1943, forcing the company to shift its activities to the former Theater des Westens, where it resumed operations in 1945, again called the Berlin Municipal Opera. In 1963, when the Berlin Wall was built, the company moved back to its former site on the grounds of the Municipal Opera, where the rebuilt opera house opened its doors as the German Opera of Berlin. In effect, it became the state opera of West Berlin.

An early postwar success was Janine Charrat's production of Werner Egk's *Abraxas* (1949), which was danced more than one hundred times. [*See Abraxas.*] The company prospered when Tatjana Gsovsky took over as ballet mistress and chief choreographer in 1957, producing such long-running pieces as *Hamlet* and *The Moor of Venice,* both starring Gisela Deege and Gert Reinholm. Gsovsky also invited Mary Wigman to stage her much-admired production of Stravinsky's *Sacre du Printemps* and Dore Hoyer to choreograph the climactic Dance around the Golden Calf in Arnold Schoenberg's opera *Moses and Aaron,* which was kept in the repertory for almost ten years.

Although Gsovsky continued until 1966 as artistic director, Gert Reinholm assumed day-to-day operations of the company in 1963. He sometimes stepped back, as when Kenneth MacMillan was appointed director of ballet from 1966 to 1969, or during the one season of John Taras's reign (1971/72), but he never really abandoned control. He was also very much behind the temporary activities of the so-called Berliner Ballet, which he and Gsovsky directed during the 1950s and part of the 1960s as a touring group, featuring the repertory and the dancers of the opera house together with guest artists.

After Gsovsky began to focus on teaching in the mid-1960s, Reinholm invited guest choreographers of international caliber to Berlin, putting special emphasis on newly staged versions of the classics (*Giselle,* by Antony Tudor; *Swan Lake* and *The Sleeping Beauty,* by Kenneth MacMillan; *The Nutcracker,* by Rudolf Nureyev; *La Fille Mal Gardée* and *Coppélia,* by José Parés). In 1987, Lucinda Childs choreographed the full-length *Light Explosion.* The repertory has included a strong contingent of works by George Balanchine, Kurt Jooss, Hans van Manen, and, more recently, Valery Panov. The company is particularly strong in dramatic works, a consequence of the lasting influence of Gsovsky and her literary orientation.

When Reinholm retired at the end of the 1989/90 season, Peter Schaufuss took over the reins as artistic director. During his tenure, he staged the three Tchaikovsky classics—*The Nutcracker, The Sleeping Beauty,* and *Swan Lake*—in quick succession for the 1992/93 season, in commemoration of the centennial of the composer's death. Thoroughly disillusioned about his conspicuous lack of success, Schaufuss left his post in the midst of the following season. Ray Barra, who was then appointed acting artistic director, was unable to lift the company's morale, which was by then very low, or to effect a significant change in the company's artistic standing. The future of the company is now in the hands of Richard Cragun, who was appointed artistic director for the 1996/97 season and given a three-year contract.

BIBLIOGRAPHY

Deutsche Oper Berlin. *Funfundzwanzig Jahre Deutsche Oper Berlin: Eine Dokumentation der Premieren von 1961 bis 1986.* Berlin, 1986.

Deutsche Oper Berlin. *Dreißig Jahr Deutsche Oper Berlin 1961–1991.* Beiträge zum Musiktheater, vol. 10 (1990/91). Berlin, 1991.

Huwe, Gisela, ed. *Die Deutsche Oper Berlin.* Berlin, 1984.

Koegler, Horst. "Berlin." In *Friedrichs Ballettlexikon.* Velber bei Hannover, 1972.

HORST KOEGLER

BERMAN, EUGENE (Evgeny Gustavovich Berman; born 4 November 1899 in Saint Petersburg, died 14 December 1972 in Rome), Russian artist and designer. Berman lived in Saint Petersburg until 1908, when he left to travel in Germany, Switzerland, and France with his family. Returning to Russia in 1914, he studied with the painter Pavel Naumov and the architect Sergei Gruzenberg. In 1920 he emigrated to Finland and then to Paris, where he lived until 1935, studying with Maurice Denis and Édouard Vuillard at the Académie Ranson. A close friend of Christian Bérard and Pavel Tchelitchev, Berman had his first group exhibition at the Galérie Druot, Paris, in 1924.

In the late 1920s Berman was particularly attracted to Italian Renaissance and Baroque art and architecture, an interest that informed many of his later set and costume designs. His work in the 1930s was influenced by Salvador Dali and Giorgio De Chirico, which became manifested in fantastic imagery, often with bizarre distortions in scale. In 1930 in New York Berman had his first American one-man exhibition. After he made his debut as a stage designer for the second Hartford (Connecticut) Music Festival in 1936, he was, thereafter, very active in ballet.

Berman was one of the last representatives of Russia's "silver age" and, like Alexandre Benois, continued the exquisite eclecticism of the *Mir iskusstva* (World of Art) group. Magic, illusion, and enchantment were the qualities he demanded from stage design and, with his brother Leonid and Pavel Tchelitchev, he reacted sharply against the abstract, geometric tendencies of the 1920s and 1930s. A romantic at heart, Berman adapted his many sources of inspiration (the architecture of Bernini, the drawings of Guercino, and the paintings of Raphael and Caravaggio) to the ballets he designed, producing haunting landscapes in timeless perspectives. His decors and costumes were often provocative, as, for example, for George Balanchine's *Concerto Barocco* (1941), with its swirling acanthus-leaf bodices, and Antony Tudor's *Romeo and Juliet* (1943), interpreted as an Italian Renaissance tapestry come to life.

Berman always maintained close relationships with Russian artists and dancers. He collaborated with Serge Lifar on *Icare* (1938) in Monte Carlo, and one of his most disturbing designs was for Frederick Ashton's *Devil's Holiday* (1939), produced by the Ballet Russe de Monte Carlo in New York with Alexandra Danilova and Simon Semenoff in the lead roles. Berman's oversized heads, ruined columns, and unending wastelands became leitmotifs in many of his ballet designs, including his much-discussed *Giselle* produced by Anton Dolin for Ballet Theatre in 1946.

In 1972, which was to be the year of his death, Berman returned to stage design after a long absence. His design that year for Balancine's *Pulcinella*, produced by the New York City Ballet for the Stravinsky Festival, was among his greatest triumphs.

[*See also* Scenic Design. *In addition, many of the figures and works mentioned herein are the subjects of independent entries.*]

BIBLIOGRAPHY
Amberg, George. *The Theatre of Eugene Berman.* New York, 1947.
Delarue, Allison. "The Stage and Ballet Designs of Eugene Berman." *Dance Index* 5 (February 1946): 4–24.
Eugene Berman. Buenos Aires, 1950. Exhibition catalog, Instituto de Arte Moderno.
"Eugene Berman." *Dance Magazine* (May 1973).
Tobin, R. L. B. "Homage to Berman." *Opera News* (December 1957).
Tuggle, Robert. *Eugene Berman: Drawings for the Stage.* New York, 1989.

JOHN E. BOWLT

BERNERS, LORD (Gerald Tyrwhitt-Wilson; born 18 September 1883 in Arley Park, Bridgnorth, England, died 19 April 1950 in Faringdon House, Berkshire, England), English composer, writer, and painter. Berners, who inherited the title to one of England's oldest baronies on the death of an uncle in 1919, was educated at Eton and subsequently served the British Diplomatic Service as an unpaid attaché. He was virtually self-taught as a composer and published some early piano pieces as Gerald Tyrwhitt. While serving at the British embassy in Rome, he met Igor Stravinsky and the Italian composer Alfredo Casella, who encouraged him to give up diplomacy and devote more attention to music. He became a close friend with Igor Stravinsky, who later described him as "an amateur, but in the best and literal sense." He wrote five original scores for ballet, which were choreographed by Frederick Ashton and George Balanchine.

His ballet association began after his one-act opera, *Le Carrosse du Saint Sacrement*, was staged in Paris in 1923. His *Funeral March for a Rich Aunt*, for piano, was choreographed and performed by solo dancer Penelope Spencer for the same program as Ashton's debut ballet, *A Tragedy of Fashion, or The Scarlet Scissors.* Serge Diaghilev invited Berners to compose *The Triumph of Neptune* (1926), George Balanchine's pantomime-fantasy with traditional English toy-theater designs, for which Berners wrote comparable dances such as a schottische, polka, waltz, and hornpipe; the dancers included Alexandra Danilova, Lydia Sokolova, Serge Lifar, and George Balanchine. The music was reworked by David Bintley as *Punch and the Street Party* for the Sadler's Wells Royal Ballet in 1979.

Luna Park (1930) was Balanchine's contribution to a London theater revue, featuring Alice Nikitina as a one-legged woman and Lifar as a six-armed man. Ashton, attracted to the music and inspired by the paintings of Edgar Degas, reworked it as *Foyer de Danse* (1932) for Alicia Markova. Berners was a friend of the writer Gertrude Stein and proposed to Ashton the ballet *A Wedding Bouquet*, based on one of her stories; first produced by the Vic-Wells Ballet in 1937, the successful comedy-ballet has, since the 1960s, been frequently revived in the Royal Ballet repertory.

Berners set his selection from Stein's text for a mixed chorus costumed onstage. In wartime touring, the singers were replaced by a speaker, an expedient that was later continued; the chorus was restored on only a few occasions at Covent Garden and sang from outside the proscenium. It remains arguable whether the wider range of choral color and texture is outweighed by the gain in verbal clarity achieved with spoken words, but the music's charm and vivacity remain, along with the composer's own designs, as prime elements in the ballet's continuing success.

Berners's two later Ashton scores were for ballets that, for reasons usually ascribed to subject matter, not music, failed to outlast their first productions: *Cupid and Psyche* (1939) and *Les Sirènes* (1946). Berners was essentially lightweight, writing within the idiom of diatonic tune-and-accompaniment, sometimes with unexpected anti-Romantic twists of melody or harmony and with a facility for affectionate parody of older models. He was on occasion dubbed "the English [Erik] Satie," but any resemblance was less a matter of music than a shared fondness for quirky titles, such as *Fragments Psychologiques* and *Red Roses and Red Noses*.

Berners composed piano pieces, songs, and a few works for orchestra. He completed nothing after *Les Sirènes*, which like *Cupid and Psyche* remains unpublished. He also composed music for the films *Halfway House* (1943), *Champagne Charlie* (1944), and *Nicholas Nickleby* (1946). Berners painted decorative watercolors, and wrote six novels. He also wrote his own epitaph:

> Here lies Lord Berners, One of the learners.
> His great love of learning may earn him a burning,
> But praise to the Lord, he seldom was bored.

BIBLIOGRAPHY

Berners, Lord. *First Childhood*. London, 1934.
Berners, Lord. *A Distant Prospect*. London, 1945.
Goodwin, Noël. "The Berners Bouquet." *Dance and Dancers* (November 1983): 24–26.
Henry, Leigh. "Lord Berners' New Ballet: *The Triumph of Neptune*." *Musical Standard* 28.4 (1926): 202.
Hussey, Dyneley. "The Music of Lord Berners." *The Dancing Times* (January 1947): 183–185.
Sitwell, Osbert. *Left Hand, Right Hand*, vol. 4, *Laughter in the Next Room*. London, 1949.
Steyn, Mark. "Berners at the Ballet." *The Dancing Times* (October 1983): 31–33.
Stravinsky, Igor, and Robert Craft. *Memories and Commentaries*. Berkeley, 1960.

NOËL GOODWIN

BERNSTEIN, LEONARD (born 15 August 1918 in Lawrence, Massachusetts, died 14 October 1990 in New York City), American composer, conductor, pianist, and writer. Bernstein's original blend of popular song, jazz, and blues with Jewish, black, Latin, and other folk elements helped to create a new American style of theater music. His contributions to dance include three ballet scores for Jerome Robbins and the scores for the musicals *On the Town* and *West Side Story*.

After graduating from Harvard University in 1939, Bernstein attended the Curtis Institute of Music in Philadelphia. He was named assistant to Boston Symphony Orchestra conductor Serge Koussevitzky in the summer of 1942, then became assistant conductor to Artur Rodzinski of the New York Philharmonic Orchestra for the 1943/44 season. His successful surprise debut with that orchestra on 13 November 1943, substituting for an ailing Bruno Walter, was followed quickly with virtual overnight success as a composer, first with the *Jeremiah Symphony* in January 1944 (which was awarded the New York Music Critics' Circle Award) and then with the ballet *Fancy Free* in April.

With its timely story of young American sailors trying to shoehorn a lifetime of fun into a brief shore leave, *Fancy Free* was a complete success. Its opening—a bartender listens to blues and jazz singer Billie Holiday on the jukebox just before three sailors explosively enter—established the urban American milieu of the 1940s as completely as the opening of *Petrouchka* caught the flavor of early nineteenth-century Saint Petersburg. The work was such a success that Robbins and Bernstein would not let the idea go. With the help of libretticists and lyricists Betty Comden and Adolph Green and director George Abbott, they developed the story into a new musical comedy, *On the Town*, which opened 28 December 1944 for a run of more than four hundred performances. The work contained several extended dance sequences, including the "Imaginary Coney Island" ballet. Sono Osato starred in the entirely danced role of Ivy Smith.

Another Robbins-Bernstein collaboration, *Facsimile*, was presented by Ballet Theatre on 24 October 1946 at the Broadway Theater. The score is more symphonic, although a strong jazz element is found in its middle section. As in *Fancy Free*, a prominent piano part contributes to the score's "blues" aspects. Although *Facsimile* failed to generate the enthusiasm of the earlier ballet, its theme of alienation was one that Bernstein used in several subsequent works, including his 1949 symphonic commentary on W. H. Auden's *The Age of Anxiety*, the one-act opera *Trouble in Tahiti* (1952), and its much later continuation, *A Quiet Place* (1983).

By 1950, when Robbins choreographed *Age of Anxiety* (to Bernstein's Symphony no. 2 for Piano and Orchestra), he and Bernstein were already working on the project that eventually became *West Side Story*. In 1953 Bernstein again collaborated with Comden, Green, and Abbott on the lively *Wonderful Town*, which used boogie-woogie and Latin rhythms in its dance sequences choreographed by

Donald Saddler. In 1956 *Candide* was praised for its brilliant score and lyrics (John Latouche and Richard Wilbur), but Lillian Hellman's book was found leaden and subsequently reworked.

In early 1946 Bernstein noted in a journal that Robbins had suggested to him the idea of "a modern version of *Romeo and Juliet* set in slums at the coincidence of Easter-Passover celebrations" and which concerned conflict between Jews and Roman Catholics. Arthur Laurents was brought in as librettist, and Stephen Sondheim joined them as lyricist in 1955. *West Side Story* opened on 26 September 1957 in New York City and was instantly received as a masterpiece of American musical theater. The blending of classical, modern, and jazz vocabularies by both composer and choreographer worked to create a brilliant unity of music and dance, with the latter even more closely integrated than before into the fabric of the work, especially in such scenes as the dance in the gym and the rumble. Latin dance rhythms, already strongly felt in *Fancy Free*, were especially important in this work.

In 1958 Bernstein was named the first American-born music director of the New York Philharmonic Orchestra, and for the ensuing decade his other interests took a back seat. After leaving the Philharmonic in 1969, he set to work on *Mass*, a multimedia theater piece for singers, dancers, and players, which first premiered at the opening of the Kennedy Center for the Performing Arts in Washington, D.C., on 14 July 1971; it was choreographed by Alvin Ailey. Long interested in combining theatrical, popular, and liturgical modes in symphonic scores (as in his three symphonies, especially the *Jeremiah* and the *Kaddish*), Bernstein drew extensively on black gospel and rock styles in addition to the Jewish and American vernacular forms he had used before. Despite the composer's claim of equality among the performance elements of *Mass*, however, the music and the inherent drama of the text put dance in the background.

Bernstein also combined Broadway and black styles in the musical *1600 Pennsylvania Avenue* (4 May 1976), which was choreographed and co-directed by George Faison, but this collaboration with Alan Jay Lerner closed after just one week.

Bernstein and Robbins collaborated once again on *Dybbuk*, also known as *Dybbuk Variations*, with a scenario based on the Yiddish play by S. Ansky. Commissioned by New York City Ballet and first performed on 16 May 1974, it was not a success. The score—Bernstein's most austere ballet music—drew heavily on elements from the Kabbalah and other Jewish mystical writings; indeed, the composer claimed that every note was arrived at by a qabbalistic or other mystical manipulation of numbers. Robbins commented on the ballet, "I think Lennie and I had

different ideas. He took the dramatic side, I took the abstract. They're parallel paths that don't converge."

But *Dybbuk* was typical of Bernstein's dramatic and eclectic approach to dance music. At his best, he molded disparate elements into striking and effective compositions that, like the ballet scores of his friend and mentor Aaron Copland, supported the dance fully while maintaining their own musical integrity.

BIBLIOGRAPHY
Bernstein, Leonard. *Findings*. New York, 1982.
Burton, Humphrey. Leonard Bernstein. New York, 1994.
Cone, Molly. *Leonard Bernstein*. New York, 1970.
Edmunds, John, and Gordon Boelzner. *Some Twentieth-Century American Composers*. Vol. 2. New York, 1960.
Fluegel, Jane, ed. *Bernstein Remembered*. New York, 1991.
Garebian, Keith. *The Making of West Side Story*. Toronto, 1995.
Goodwin, Noël. "Street Side Story." *Dance and Dancers* (November 1990): 12–13.
Gottlieb, Jack. *Leonard Bernstein: A Complete Catalogue of His Works*. New York, 1988.
Secrest, Meryle. *Leonard Bernstein*. New York, 1994.
Tobias, Tobi. "Bringing Back Robbins's *Fancy*." *Dance Magazine* (January 1980): 60–62, 69–77.

GEORGE DORRIS and KENNETH LaFAVE

BERRY BROTHERS, family of three brothers whose mixture of the cakewalk strut, tap dancing, thrilling acrobatics, and amazing cane work made them one of the most exciting acts on the entertainment circuit. Members included **Ananais "Nyas" Berry** (born 1915 in New Orleans, Louisiana, died 6 October 1951 in New York City), dancer known as the "king of the strut"; **James Berry** (born c.1917 in New Orleans, died 1964 in New York City), dancer, comedian, and singer; and **Warren Berry** (born 25 December 1922 in Denver, Colorado), dancer and acrobat. Their act, which remained virtually unchanged for more than twenty years, can be seen in the film *Lady, Be Good!* (1941).

The Berry Brothers began their career in the early 1920s, with young Ananias and James billed as "The Miniature Williams and Walker," since they molded their act after the most famous African-American team of the day, Bert Williams and George Walker. By the mid-1920s, the Berry family had moved to Hollywood; by the late 1920s, the Berry Brothers had hit the big time. In 1929, James and Ananias opened as a duo with Duke Ellington at Harlem's Cotton Club, and for the next four-and-a-half years the notorious night spot remained their home base. Between engagements at the Cotton Club, they were also featured in such prestigious overseas productions as the African-American revue *Lew Leslie's Blackbirds of 1929* in London. On 27 December 1932, the brothers opened New York City's Art Deco movie palace, Radio City Music Hall.

In 1934, Ananias left the act to marry the entertainer Valaida Snow, at which time Warren was drafted into the act. James taught him the routines, move for move. Ananias's marriage did not last, however, and he talked James and Warren into moving to Hollywood. The Berry Brothers—now Ananias, James, and Warren—enjoyed tremendous success in a newly formed trio and appeared extensively throughout the United States and Europe on stages, in clubs, and in film.

In 1938, at the downtown Cotton Club, a legendary confrontation took place between the Berrys and another great dance act of the era, the Nicholas Brothers. To compete with the other act, the Berrys devised an unbeatable finish, in which Ananais and James ran up two side stairways onto an elevated balcony and took a flying leap twelve feet out, over the heads of the entire Cab Calloway orchestra playing below. Warren, meanwhile, down on the stage, completed a flip-flop twist and, on the last note of the music, all three dancers simultaneously landed on the stage in splits. "People talked about that for a long time!" recalled Warren Berry (Frank, 1994). The act stayed together until Ananias's untimely death at the age of thirty-nine. Warren suffered a hip injury, and by 1951 the act dissolved. The brothers' film appearances were in *Panama Hattie* (1942), *Boarding House Blues* (1948), and *You're My Everything* (1949).

[*See also* Tap Dance.]

BIBLIOGRAPHY
Frank, Rusty E. *Tap! The Greatest Tap Dance Stars and Their Stories, 1900–1955.* Rev. ed. New York, 1994.
Stearns, Marshall, and Jean Stearns. *Jazz Dance: The Story of American Vernacular Dance.* Rev. ed. New York, 1994.

RUSTY E. FRANK

BESSMERTNOVA. Possessing a soft lyrical quality, Bessmertnova was an ideal interpreter of classical roles. She appears here as the title character in *Giselle*, act 2. (Photograph by Larisa Pedenchuk; courtesy of Columbia Artists Managment, Inc., New York.)

BESSMERTNOVA, NATALIA (Natalia Igorevna Bessmertnova; born 19 July 1941 in Moscow), Russian ballet dancer. Bessmertnova studied dance at the children's studio of the Moscow Young Pioneers' Palace under Helena Rosse, who noticed her abilities and advised her to become a professional. In 1953 Bessmertnova entered the Moscow School of Choreography, studying with Maria Kozhukhova until her death in 1959 and then with Sofia Golovkina, who accurately assessed her talent and versatility. After graduation in 1961 Bessmertnova joined the Bolshoi Ballet. She made her debut in Agrippina Vaganova's version of Michel Fokine's *Chopiniana,* an appropriate vehicle for romantic soaring leaps, long line, and mysterious, distant beauty. On 20 November 1963 Bessmertnova created the title role in Leonid Lavrovsky's production of *Giselle.* She worked on the ballet under the guidance of Galina Ulanova but gave it a fundamentally new interpretation. Renouncing genre details, Bessmertnova brought features into the work's first-act realism that identified it with the second act's fantasy—even as a peasant girl her Giselle seemed to be a fairy possessed with the love of dance—thus creating a consistent emotional image.

Bessmertnova's first role for Yuri Grigorovich, the company's chief choreographer and her husband, was Shirien in his *Legend of Love* (1965). She gave a subtle presentation of the ballet's tragic theme; her portrayal was graphic, mysterious, and filled with piquant exoticism. She also danced Grigorovich's Phrygia in *Spartacus* and Masha in *The Nutcracker* in 1968. In his version of *Swan Lake* in 1969 Bessmertnova presented Odette-Odile in a distinctive way: rather than opposing the White Swan and the Black Swan, she portrayed a consistent image that nevertheless embodied the agonizing contradiction between earthly passion and romantic dream. In 1975 Bessmertnova danced Tsarina Anastasia in *Ivan the Terrible,* the first role that Grigorovich choreographed especially for her. Her other creations for Grigorovich were Valentina in *The Angara* (1976), Juliet in *Romeo and Juliet* (1979), and the title role in *Raymonda* (1984). Most notable was her Rita in *The Golden Age* (1982). The protagonist of this ballet lives on two planes: as a variety dancer and as a plain girl. In the intricate twists and turns of the adventure story, Bessmertnova revealed the internal drama of an actress seeking ordinary human happiness and escaping from the deceptive but alluring footlights of the stage into the world of simple human feelings. In

1989, for a special program honoring the choreographer Kasyan Goleizovsky, she danced in his impassioned pas de deux *Melody,* set to Antonín Dvořák's "Songs My Mother Taught Me," which she had first performed in 1966.

Bessmertnova's style was a synthesis of the Saint Petersburg school, with its keen sense of the Romantic tradition combined with a solid technical background, and the Moscow school, with its vivid national characteristics, broad scope, and dramatic expressiveness in movement. A ballerina of great range, she danced the entire classical repertory of the Bolshoi and also all significant modern productions. To each of her roles she gave an original interpretation. Put on pension in 1989 she left the Bolshoi in 1995.

Bessmertnova received first prize at the International Ballet Competition in Varna in 1965. She was named People's Artist of the USSR in 1976. She was awarded the Anna Pavlova Prize in Paris in 1970, the State Prize of the USSR in 1978 for the role of Valentina in *The Angara,* and the Lenin Prize in 1986.

BIBLIOGRAPHY

Atlas, Helen V. *Natalia Bessmertnova.* Brooklyn, 1975.
Avaliani, Noi, and Leonid Zhdanov, comps. *Bolshoi's Young Dancers.* Translated by Natalie Ward. Moscow, 1975.
Daniels, Don. "Girl Hunt: World Trade and the Ballerina." *Ballet Review* 21 (Summer 1993): 13–20.
Demidov, Alexander P. *The Russian Ballet: Past and Present.* Translated by Guy Daniels. Garden City, N.Y., 1977.
Demidov, Alexander P. "Garmonia Tvorchestva." *Ogonek,* no. 7 (February 1984).
Demidov, Alexander P. "Zolotoy vek Natalia Bessmertnova." *Teatralnaia Zhizn* 11 (June 1984).
Demidov, Alexander P. *A Bolshoi Ballerina: Natalia Bessmertnova.* Translated by Yuri S. Shirokov. London, 1986.
Lvov-Anokhin, Boris. *Mastera Bolshogo Baleta.* Moscow, 1976.

ALEXANDER P. DEMIDOV
Translated from Russian

BETTIS, VALERIE (born 20 December 1920 in Houston, died 26 September 1982 in New York City), American dancer and choreographer. Bettis began training in her native Houston, Texas, with Rowena Smith and studied for a brief period with Tina Flade, herself a pupil of Mary Wigman. From 1937 to 1940 she studied and performed in New York with Hanya Holm and made her professional debut in Holm's *Trend* (1937). In 1941 she made her debut as a choreographer at Carnegie Hall in New York City. In addition to presenting solos and group works with her various companies (Valerie Bettis Theater/Dance Company and Dancers' Studio), Bettis was active on Broadway and in television and film. She appeared in "Railroads on Parade" at the 1939 New York World's Fair and achieved popular success in the Broadway revue *Inside U.S.A.,* in which she danced the "Tiger Lily" number choreographed by Helen Tamiris. She followed this with appearances in *Great to Be Alive* and *Bless You All* in 1950. Bettis also enjoyed a career as an actress, replacing Lotte Lenya in *The Threepenny Opera* in 1955 and also appearing in George Bernard Shaw's *Back to Methuselah,* as well as various television dramas.

Her choreographic credits for work outside the concert stage include *Beggar's Holiday* (1946), *Two on the Aisle* (1951), *Peer Gynt* (1951), and *Ulysses in Nighttown* (1958). She also choreographed dance sequences for Rita Hayworth in the films *Affair in Trinidad* and *Salome.* Beginning in the 1940s, Bettis was instrumental in creating dance for the major television networks. In 1947 she became the first modern dancer to choreograph for a ballet company when she staged *Virginia Sampler* for the Ballet Russe de Monte Carlo.

As a performer, Bettis was noted for her dynamic stage presence. She based a number of her dances on dramatic literature: *Yerma* (1946, after Federico García Lorca), *A Streetcar Named Desire* (1952) and, *The Golden Round* (1955, based on *Macbeth*). Throughout her career, Bettis explored the dramatic and expressive capacities of dance by incorporating texts into her work. Her first endeavor in this vein was *The Desperate Heart* (1943), set to a poem by John Malcolm Brinnin. The best known and most successful of these compositions was *As I Lay Dying* (1948), based on the novel by William Faulkner. Bettis's other dances include *Triptych* (1941), *And the Earth Shall Bear Again* (1942), *And Dreams Intrude* (1944), *Facts and Figures* (1945), *Dramatic Incident* (1945), *Domino Furioso* (1948), *It Is Always Farewell* (1949), *Circa '56* (1956), *The Closed Door* (1959), *Early Voyagers* (1960), *Songs and Processions* (1964), *He Who Runs* (1964), and *Inventions of Darkness* (1964).

BIBLIOGRAPHY

Amer, Rita F. "*The Desperate Heart:* A Dance of Images." *Dance Notation Journal* 4 (Spring 1986): 31–35.
Anderson, Jack. *The One and Only: The Ballet Russe de Monte Carlo.* New York, 1981.
Lloyd, Margaret. *The Borzoi Book of Modern Dance.* New York, 1949.
Simpson, Herbert. "Valerie Bettis: Looking Back." *Dance Magazine* (February 1977): 52–66.

THOMAS CONNORS

BEY, HANNELORE (born 6 November 1941 in Leipzig), German dancer. Bey received her first instruction in dance at the age of ten in Leipzig, followed, from 1956 to 1961, by intensive training at the Gret Palucca school in Dresden. Tom Schilling engaged her for the State Theater in Dresden from 1961 to 1965. After a year of studies at the Leningrad ballet school (where she trained with Nina Belikova and rehearsed with Aleksandr Pushkin), Schilling brought her as a soloist to East

Berlin's Komische Oper in 1966. After receiving a diploma at the 1965 International Ballet Competition in Varna, Bey earned the third prize and a bronze medal in 1968 and, together with Roland Gawlik, her partner for many years, the honor "Meilleur Couple du Concours."

Esteemed for her poetic imagination and her faultless technique, Bey advanced to the position of *prima ballerina* of the dance theater of the Komische Oper and became one of the leading ballet personalities in East Germany. With time she also developed into the perfect interpreter of Schilling's work. He created a number of roles for her, including Gretchen in *Abraxas* (1965), the Girl in *La Mer* (1968), the title role in *Undine* (1970), Juliet in *Romeo and Juliet* (1973 and 1983), Hanna in *Schwarze Vögel* (1975), Titania in *The New Midsummer Night's Dream* (1981), and Ottilie in *Wahlverwandtschaften* (Elective Affinities; 1983, after the novel by Goethe). She demonstrated her extraordinary comic talent in such works as Schilling's *Match* (1971), John Cranko's *Jeu de Cartes* (1969), H. Wandtke's *Der Alptraum einer Ballerina* (1973) and O. Winogradow's *La Fille Mal Gardée* (1974). She married Frank Bey, ballet master at the Metropoltheater in Berlin.

BIBLIOGRAPHY

Gommlich, Werner. *Hannelore Bey—Roland Gawlik.* Berlin, 1977.

Regitz, Hartmut. "Die 'Schwarzen Vögel' an der Berliner Komischen Oper." *Das Tanzarchiv* 2 (November 1975): 368–370.

HARTMUT REGITZ

BHARATA NĀṬYAM. Indrani, a well-known dancer versed in several styles of classical Indian dance, in a pose from *bharata nāṭyam*. (Photograph from the archives at Jacob's Pillow, Becket, Massachusetts.)

BHARATA NĀṬYAM. *Bharata nāṭyam* is the solo dance tradition of the *devadāsī*s (female temple dancers) of the state of Tamil Nadu in South India. [*See* Devadāsī.] It was formerly also known as *dāsiāṭṭam* ("dance of servants"). *Bharata nāṭyam* was performed mainly in the temples of the god Śiva in Tamil Nadu, and to a lesser extent in the temples of the states of Andhra Pradesh and Karnataka in South India. The genre evolved between the thirteenth and fifteenth centuries CE, when Muslim invaders destroyed the temples of North India, defiled the dancers, and drove the arts from the temples of the north to the south. It attained its present form in the first quarter of the nineteenth century. Four famous brothers (the Thanjavur or Tanjore Quartet: Ponnaiyah, Chinnaiya, Sivanandan, and Vadivelu), authorities on dance and music who served in the court of King Sarfoji II of Thanjavur in Tamil Nadu, gave this style its present format and repertory and also codified it.

Within the scope of *bharata nāṭyam* are all three aspects of Indian dance, *nṛtta*, *nṛtya*, and *nāṭya*. Pure and rhythmic, *nṛtta* features varied patterns but does not depict any idea, mood, or story. *Nṛtya*, a combination of rhythmic and expressive dance, tells a story, depicts a mood, or narrates an incident, all with the help of symbolic hand gestures, appropriate facial expressions, and corresponding steps. *Nāṭya* is pure storytelling, stressing the dramatic aspect of the dance.

The sequence in a *bharata nāṭyam* performance is harmoniously balanced among these three aspects. First, *alarippu* (the invocation) and *jātīśvaram* (rhythmic patterns) fall into the category of *nṛtta*. Next, *śabdam*, which intersperses rhythmic sections with phrases that praise and describe a king or deity, and *varṇam*, the longest and most complex segment, constitute *nṛtya*. The *varṇam* is a song addressed to a god or hero. Each line, after being interpreted several times in different ways, is concluded with a rhythmic passage, danced to chanted or recited syllables or to combinations of musical notes. These constitute the first part of the program. The second half of the typical program presents *padam*s, *javali*s, *krithi*s, and *ślokam*s, all of which belong to the *nāṭya* category. A *padam* is a love lyric, usually erotic in mood, portraying such emotions as hope, despair, jealousy, anger, and ecstasy. A *javali* is of the same genre but lighter in nature, and both the melody and rhythm are more lilting. *Krithi*s are entirely devotional and glorify a deity, as do the *ślokam*s, which are somewhat shorter. In the concluding number, the *tillānā*, a cascade of pure rhythm, displays the dancer's mastery of the rhythmic aspect. The program may conclude with a verse addressed to a deity or king.

The student of *bharata nāṭyam* begins her training with practice of the *adavu*s, or basic dance units, which range from eighty to one hundred. These are steps for the feet combined with hand gestures, with the addition, wherever appropriate, of body bends and eye and neck movements. Next the student learns *thīrmanam*s (concluding movements); usually repeated three times, they bring to a conclusion a rhythmic passage consisting of a series of *adavu*s. Such rhythmic passages form the body of *alārippu, jātīśvaram,* and *tillānā,* the dances in the *nṛtta* category.

The lines of the body, which are very important to the dance, have a noble, almost geometrical angularity and a harmonious, well-balanced symmetry. From the standing position, the body is lowered to achieve the basic stance, the *aramandi* or *ayatamandalam*. In this stance the knees are bent and turned out widely and the heels come close together, with the feet pointing outward. The arms are usually stretched to the side to their fullest extent, and in certain movements, especially in the *thīrmanam*s, the body must be curved completely. The torso is sometimes held erect and sometimes inclined. The footwork, forceful and precise, requires hard and exact contact with the floor.

The symbolic hand gestures used in the *nṛtya* and *nāṭya* sequences are taken from a second-century text called *Abhinaya-dārpaṇa* (The Mirror of Gesture) and are called *hasta*s or *mudrā*s. There are twenty-eight one-handed *hasta*s *(asamyukta)* and twenty-three two-handed *hasta*s *(samyukta)*. [*See* Mudrā.]

The literary content of the songs to which *bharata nāṭyam* is danced comes from songs in classical Sanskrit or from songs in Tamil, Telugu, and Kannada, modern southern Indian languages. Some of the composers are anonymous, but many songs are taken from the ecstatic compositions of the great saint-composers of southern India. These songs are set to the classical southern Indian Karnatic mode and are performed by an ensemble of musicians conducted by the *nattuavanar*, the guru or preceptor of the dancer. The guru sets the rhythm with a pair of cymbals and chants or recites the rhythmic passages. In addition to a singer and a percussionist playing the two-headed drum *(mridangam)*, there may be one or more instrumentalists playing the *vīnā* (a stringed instrument), flute, or violin. Other, less important instruments are the *mukhavīna, kanjīra,* and *ghaṭam* (a clay pot drum). The *tamboura* provides the drone accompaniment.

In the past, the costume of the *devadāsī*s was a sari draped over a pair of pajamas or pantaloons, with one end passed between the legs and tucked into the waist. The modern costume is more tailored, with close-fitting pantaloons. A decorative pleated fan in the front is joined to the legs, and a blouse with a veil draped over it covers the torso. The costumes are made of silk, and jewels adorn the dancer from head to toe. Bells *(shalangai)* worn around the ankles are an essential feature of the performance.

[*See also* Asian Dance Traditions, *overview article;* Costume in Asian Traditions; India, *article on* History of In-

dian Dance; *and the entries on Balasaraswati, Chandrashekhar, Dhananjayan, Gopal, Indrani, Kermani, Knight, Krishnamurtha, Lakhia, Mansing, Samson, Sarabhai, Sarukkai, and Valli.*]

BIBLIOGRAPHY

Arudra. "The Transfiguration of a Traditional Dance." *Sruti* (Madras), nos. 27–28 (December 1986–January 1987): 17–36.

Bowers, Faubion. *The Dance in India.* New York, 1953.

Gaston, Anne-Marie. *Śiva in Dance, Myth, and Iconography.* Delhi, 1982.

Higgins, Jon B. *The Music of Bharata Natyam.* New Delhi, 1993.

Khokar, Mohan. *Traditions of Indian Classical Dance.* 2d ed., rev. and enl. New Delhi, 1984.

Kliger, George, ed. *Bharata Nāṭyam in Cultural Perspective.* Manohar, 1993.

Massey, Reginald, and Jamila Massey. *The Dances of India: A General Survey and Dancer's Guide.* London, 1989.

Ragini Devi. *Dance Dialects of India.* 2d rev. ed. Delhi, 1990.

Sarabhai, Mrinalini. "The Eight Nayikas." *Dance Perspectives,* no. 24 (1965).

Sarabhai, Mrinalini. *Understanding Bharata Natyam.* 3d ed. Ahmedabad, 1981.

Tyer, E. Krishna. "A Note on the Repertory from Alaripu to Tillana." In *Classical and Folk Dances of India,* by Mohan Khokar et al. Bombay, 1963.

Visvanathan [Knight], Lakshmi. *Bharatanatyam: The Tamil Heritage.* Madras, 1984.

Walker, Benjamin. *The Hindu World.* 2 vols. London, 1968.

Rɪᴛʜᴀ Dᴇᴠɪ

BHUTAN is a kingdom of 1.3 million people in almost two thousand square miles (47,000 square kilometers), located on the eastern slopes of the Himalayas. Bounded by the Tibetan autonomous region of the People's Republic of China to the north and east, and the Indian states of Sikkim, Bengal, and Assam to the east and south, it remains the only country where Tantric Buddhism (Vajrayāna) is the state religion. Although culturally similar to Tibet, Bhutan has its own distinctive social and political characteristics. The country is divided into *dzongs*, imposing provincial fortresses that serve as centers of administration and religious monasticism. Many of these thirty *dzongs* sponsor yearly festivals of several days' length that feature ritual dance. The dates and contents of these festivals vary. The origin and style of the dancing can be traced to Padmasambhava, the eighth-century Indian saint who introduced Tantric, or Esoteric, Buddhism to Bhutan and Tibet.

According to tradition, Padmasambhava first performed a ritual dance to ward off evil and thereby consecrated the site of the first Buddhist monastery in Tibet. He subsequently performed similar rites at the sites of several Bhutanese temples. For example, he was summoned to exorcise the misfortune which had befallen the kingdom of Bumthang when the king had destroyed the temple of its guardian deities. To pacify the angry spirits, the great

BHUTAN. Dancers and musicans from the royal court in *Deer Dance*, a dance drama depicting the story of the Tantric sage Padmasambhava who, while riding on a deer, stopped the demon of the wind. (Photograph from the archives of The Asia Society, New York.)

Tantric master transformed himself into eight different manifestations, both wrathful and peaceful, which performed the eight forms of dance necessary to quell the negativity. This event not only instituted the tradition of ritual dancing in Bhutan but popularized the Dance of the Eight Manifestations throughout Bhutan. In this dance the performers, garbed in the robes and masks of the eight manifestations of Padmasambhava, grant blessings to the public.

Bhutanese ritual dance can be classified into three categories: religious dance that is performed by monks; religious dance that is performed by lay people; and the dance performed by oracles. Prayers precede and follow the dances performed by monks, which depict the principle Tantric deities and protectors. Dancing solo or in groups, the monks appear majestic and colorful in boots and long brocade robes that are similar to Tibetan costumes. Their movements are graceful, with measured steps, hops, and turns, the most typical of which is the step-hop, performed with the raised knee turned out. The dancers who perform the most sacred dances are often required to meditate for several years on the deity they will portray. One such dance, dedicated to Mahakala, the principle protective deity of Bhutan, is said to have saved the country from invasion. The seventeenth-century Shab Drung, who united the religious principalities and clan territories that comprised the country, performed the dance of Mahakala to successfully avert six attacks—as he danced, he burned a list of names of Bhutan's foes. Another dance that is traditionally performed to dispell negativity is the Black Hat Dance, performed by Tantric adepts. This dance, found in most Himalayan Buddhist cultures, also plays an important apotropaic role—a safeguard from evil—in the festivals of Bhutan. The dancers, dressed in long robes and huge black hats topped by peacock feathers, stab and destroy a dough effigy that symbolizes evil. [*See* Black Hat Dance.]

Dramnyen Chotse, performed by lay dancers dressed as the ancient monastic bodyguard of the ruling Buddhist sect of Bhutan, also celebrates the victory over hostile forces. Through their slow and stately movements, the dancers re-enact the subjugation of the local spirits of a pilgrimage place by the founders of their sect. They are accompanied by the *dramnyen*, a long-necked plucked lute, an instrument generally found in secular use. The musicians for the lay dancers are usually separated from the musicians for the monastic dancers. The musicians for the monk dancers are of two groups: the brass musicians and percussionists, who play continuously, and the wind instrumentalists, who play intermittently. Sometimes they are separated spacially, with the continuous music makers seated around the dance area in the courtyard and the others positioned on the roof.

The most famous name in Bhutanese dance is the great saint and ancestor of the present king, Padmalingpa (1450–1521). He is renowned as a treasure discoverer, for he found previously hidden religious texts, and precious information was revealed to him in his dreams. For example, while on a dream visit to the Buddha fields of Padmasambhava, he observed celestial dances that he subsequently taught to his students. These dances most often depict heavenly acrobats and attendants performing dazzling athletic movements. The "Pacham" is danced barefoot by young masked lay performers who execute backbends and high head-to-knee split jumps, representing heroes and heroines in their celestial realms. Another dance represents the heavenly beings known as *gings* celebrating their victory over the serpent spirits that tried to prevent Padmalingpa from recovering a treasure from the sea. The masked dancers run through the audience drumming and tapping people on the head with their drumsticks, thereby destroying negativity and bestowing blessings. Typical of the dances performed by laymen, the dancers are barefoot and wear short colorful skirts of Bhutanese origin, and the dance is not accompanied by prayers. Some of Padmalingpa's dances resemble the dances of the village oracles. The oracles perform as a part of their divinatory experience, dancing when they become possessed by the spirits who speak through them. These dances are not performed as part of the yearly festivals.

Padmalingpa's son also transmitted dances from the realm of Padmasambhava, such as "Damitse Ngacham," another drum dance in which monks, wearing animal masks that signify the twelve years in the cycle of the lunar calendar, perform the twenty-one holy poses.

Throughout the year the ritual dancers prepare for the festivals, practicing steps with the required grace and strength. The lay dancers who perform generally remain at the *dzongs* between the ages of eighteen to thirty-five, thereafter returning to their native villages to become farmers. Before the yearly festival, a rehearsal of the

BHUTAN. Performers from the royal court in a masked sword dance. (Photograph from the archives of The Asia Society, New York.)

BHUTAN. Performers from the royal court sound hand-held drums in a ritual dance of blessing. (Photograph by Diane Glazer; from the archives of The Asia Society, New York.)

dances is presented without masks or costumes. All the performers, including the musicians, perform before the senior teachers and the lay public, who are allowed to attend.

There are also dances that are considered too sacred to present to the public, such as a dance executed by senior monks to initiate novices. Yet all Bhutanese ritual dances share the same fundamental purpose—the transformation of the minds of the dancers and viewers. The deities represented are the manifestation of the enlightened mind, which overcomes the attachment to ego and bestows the blessings of wisdom and compassion.

[*See also* Costume in Asian Dance.]

BIBLIOGRAPHY

Aris, Michael. "Sacred Dances of Bhutan." *Natural History* 89 (March 1980):28–37.
Gordon, Beate. "United States Tour of the Royal Dancers and Musicians." *Druk Losel* 2.4 (February 1981); 3.1 (May 1981).
Jaffrey, Madhur. "Buddhist Dance Spectacular in a Medieval Kingdom." *Asia* 2 (March–April 1980):16.
Olschak, Blanche, et al. *Bhutan*. London, 1971.
Shaw, Brian. "Bhutan: Land of the Dragon People." In *Seventh Festival of Asian Arts*. Hong Kong, 1982.
Singh, Nagendra. *Bhutan*. New Delhi, 1978.
Tulku, Mynak R. *The Dances, Songs, and Sports of Bhutan*. Pamphlet published for the coronation of the king, 2 June 1974.
Tulku, Mynak R. *The Sacred Dance-Drama of Bhutan*. New York, 1979.

FILM AND VIDEOTAPE. *The Royal Dancers and Musicians from the Kingdom of Bhutan* (Asia Society). "Masked Dance-Drama of Bhutan" (Asia Society).

LIN LERNER

BIAGI, VITTORIO (born 24 May 1941 in Viareggio), Italian dancer and choreographer. Having begun his dance training in Genoa, Biagi completed his studies at the ballet school of the Teatro alla Scala in Milan, where his principal teachers were Esmée Bulnes, Asaf Messerer, and Tatjana

Gsovsky. He joined the corps de ballet at La Scala in 1958 and remained with the company until 1960, when he left to join Maurice Béjart's Ballet du XXᵉ Siècle in Brussels. With Béjart's company, he danced leading roles in *Boléro* (1960); *Gala* (1961); *Mathilde, Le Cygne, Divertimento*, and *Ninth Symphony* (all in 1964); and *Venusberg* (1965). In 1966 Biagi was appointed *premier danseur étoile* at the Opéra-Comique in Paris and made his debut as the Prince in *The Nutcracker*. His other classical roles included *Les Sylphides, Graduation Ball, Flower Festival in Genzano*, Flemming Flindt's *The Lesson*, and David Lichine's *La Mer*.

During his last years in Brussels, Biagi choreographed such works as *Jazz Impression* (1964), for Marie-Claire Carrié and Patrick Belda; *Le Faune* (1965); and *La Nuit de Walpurgis* (1966). In 1968 he choreographed *L'Enfant et les Sortilèges* and *Platée* for producer Louis Erlo, who appointed him artistic director at the Lyon Opera House in 1969. Biagi's *Requiem*, set to the music of Hector Berlioz, was well received that year; in the next eight years, he choreographed at least four ballets each season.

In 1973 André-Philippe Hersin pointed out that Biagi's choreographic vocabulary was influenced by Béjart: "Biagi is, above all, a storyteller; his bountiful lyricism is what allows his talents to blossom." During his stay in Lyon, Biagi mounted new versions of *Romeo and Juliet* and *Alexandre Nevksy*, to Sergei Prokofiev's music; *Les Sept Péchés Capitaux*, to the score by Kurt Weill; and *Les Noces* and *Le Sacre du Printemps*, to scores by Igor Stravinsky. He also choreographed to contempory music, mounting *Page Blanche and Page Noire* (1972) on a score by Bernard Parmegiani and François Bayle. In 1976 he used jazz for a *Hamlet* in which the lead role is Death, clothed in white, like a clown.

Biagi left France in 1977 to work in Italy, first with Aterballetto and then, in 1978, with his own company, Danza Prospettiva, for which he mounted old ballets and created new ones, such as *Requiem senza Parola* (1980) and *Don Juan* (1982). From 1982 to 1986, he was artistic director and ballet master of the Teatro Massimo in Palermo, keeping his own group active in the meantime. Since leaving Palermo Biagi has worked with the Compania Teatrale de Torino and the Nuevo Balletto di Roma. Among his later works are an *Homage to Stravinsky, Passion selon Saint-Jean*, and *Requiem de Verdi*.

BIBLIOGRAPHY

Doglio, Vittoria, and Elisa Vaccarino. *L'Italia in ballo*. Rome, 1993.
Gould, Susan. "Perspectives." *Dance Magazine* (June 1976): 95.
Hersin, André-Philippe. "Le ballet de Lyon." *Saisons de la danse*, no. 55 (June 1973).
Lidova, Irène. "Paris." *Dance News* (April 1981).
Lidova, Irène. "Il Biagi francese." *Balletto* (September 1983).
Ottolenghi, Vittoria. "Il figliol prodigo." *Balletto* (September 1983).
Testa, Alberto. "Il 'Leonardo' di Biagi." *Danza e danza* (April 1990): 9.

MONIQUE BABSKY
Translated from French

BIAS, FANNY (born 3 June 1789 in Paris, died 6 September 1825 in Paris), French ballet dancer. Fanny Bias entered the Paris Opera Ballet School as a child and received her entire training there under the direction of Jean-François Coulon. In 1806, shortly before her graduation, she caught the eye of ballet master Pierre Gardel, who described her as a "well-developed young woman with a pretty face." She joined the Paris Opera Ballet in 1807 and soon captured the attention of critics. The journalist Léon Pillet, who later became director of the Opera, wrote, "This charming student bids fair to be an excellent dancer of the *demi-caractère* type. She has made a brilliant beginning, and her success is deserved." In 1808 Bias was made a *double* (demisoloist), in 1813 a "replacement," and in 1818 a *grand sujet* (first-rank soloist).

In 1819 the *Almanach des spectacles* noted that "Fanny skims the floor with her delicate feet. The bee is heavier, a breeze less agile." G. Le Flaneur noted in 1821, in a text reprinted in *Ces demoiselles de l'Opéra* by "a longtime enthusiast," that "her face and her back are artificial, but her pretty arm and her leg, the very model of Venus, owe nothing to artifice and shine by their natural grace." In 1821 Bias appeared at the King's Theatre in London. An engraving of the time shows her on pointe, a feat that was novel at the time. Ivor Guest quotes John Ebers as saying, "She performed beautiful little half-steps, which, more than any other, correspond to the epithet 'twinkling.'"

Two of Bias's best-known parts were in ballets made in 1820: Louis Milon's *Clari, ou La Promesse de Mariage* and Jean-Louis Aumer's *Les Pages du Duc de Vendôme*, in which she danced opposite Émilie Bigottini. She also scored a success as one of the Stepsisters in Monsieur Albert's production of *Cendrillon* (Cinderella) in 1822. She fell ill late in 1823 but reappeared on the stage in September 1824, only to abandon the theater several months later. When she died, the *Courrier des théâtres* (September 1825) mourned her as "the dancer who had most completely inherited the talent of Mme Gardel" and lauded

her character, her morals, the goodness of her heart, and the eminent merit which enabled her to shine among companions from whom it is so difficult to stand out, all qualities which made Mlle Fanny Bias dearly cherished by everyone who knew her.

BIBLIOGRAPHY

Ces demoiselles de l'Opéra par un vieil abonné. Paris, 1887.
Guest, Ivor. *The Romantic Ballet in Paris*. 2d rev. ed. London, 1980.

MONIQUE BABSKY
Translated from French

BIBIENA FAMILY. Galli (da) Bibiena was the family name of eight northern Italian architects and painters who dominated southern and central European theater design from the late seventeenth through the later eighteenth century. At the apex of their activities, in the first and second quarters of the eighteenth century, no court with a taste for late Baroque spectacle could afford to be without their services, which included festival, funeral, and ecclesiastical as well as theatrical design and decoration. In an era notable for peripatetic Italian artists, the Bibiena were perhaps the most widely traveled of all. From Lisbon to Saint Petersburg and throughout northern Italy they roamed almost as continually as the performers for whom their assemblages were intended. Fittingly for the multilevel coordination and restrictive deadlines of their ephemeral arts, collaborations among Bibiena family members were frequent. Because their talents and methods were passed from fathers to sons and nephews, collaborations also spanned generations. And, much as their contemporaries sometimes found it difficult to separate their efforts, in the face of slender documentation and widespread alterations to their buildings, modern scholars cannot readily resolve authorship among the hundreds of extant drawings associated with the family.

If their individual identities are often elusive, the deliberately collective family style is not. Bibiena trademarks include soaring arches and vaults delicately poised on clusters of slender columns; encrustations of brackets, coffers, caryatids, and entablature enrichments; sweeping curvilinear balconies, balustrades, parapets, and entablatures; and inventive stage machinery. Although these components originated in ancient Greece and Rome, in Renaissance and Baroque architecture, garden design, and stage scenery, and in the two-dimensional arts of *capriccio* and *quadratura* (painted architecture in perspective), the combinations wrought by the Bibiena family were singularly active and compelling.

The most important Bibiena innovation was the *scena per angolo* (or *veduta per angolo*), theater scenery composed at an oblique angle to the audience. Based on two-point perspective rather than the one-point perspective inherited from the Renaissance, the *scena per angolo* was visually intelligible from many parts of an auditorium, unlike single-focus perspective, which provided only spectators in the center with a satisfactory view. The Bibienas' theatrical designs arose in the artistic ferment of the emergent Age of Reason, and their "democratization" of the theater setting, as Diane Kelder has aptly called it, coincided with the rises of the public theater (with which the Bibiena were deeply involved in Italy) and of populist art (for example, that of William Hogarth), of *opera seria* (with which Bibiena designs frequently were associated), of the tragic actor and actress, and of the virtuoso dancer.

At the same time, however, most of the Bibienas' clients and the inventions they designed for them were thoroughly aristocratic. The Bibiena readily responded to courtly demands from centers of persistent absolutism, privilege, and conservative theology—exactly the loca-

tions where the preference for Italianate Baroque art lingered. Despite the Bibienas' *scena per angolo* innovation, the one-point perspective stage set also remained integral to their work. Contemporary Italian art closest to the spirit of their creativity—such as Giovanni Battista Tiepolo's frescoes in the Palazzo Labia in Venice (c.1744–1745), Carloni and Lecchi's fresco at the Villa Lecchi in Mortirone (1746), and Luigi Vanvitelli's staircase at Caserta (begun 1750)—hardly expressed the viewpoint of the common man or the rationalist intellectual. Magnificence, not reform, predominated.

The inventor and propagator of the *scena per angolo* was Ferdinando Bibiena (born 18 August 1656 in Bologna, died 3 January 1743 in Bologna), who, with his brother Francesco (born 12 December 1659 in Bologna, died 20 January 1739 in Bologna), founded the dynasty. Ferdinando and Francesco Bibiena, sons of the *quadraturista* Giovanni Maria Bibiena (born 1625 in Bibbiena, died 1665 in Bologna), were educated as painters but devoted themselves largely to stage design after their appointments in 1680 to the court of Ranuccio II Farnese of Parma. From there, their fame spread. Francesco worked throughout northern and central Italy, then, in the early eighteenth century, journeyed to eastern France and Vienna. Ferdinando, who remained with the Farnese for a quarter century, also covered wide areas of Italy and then moved, in 1708, to Barcelona under Charles III; in 1711, when the Spanish monarch became the Holy Roman emperor Charles VI, he moved to Vienna. Also in 1711 Ferdinando published *L'Architettura civile*, in which the *scena per angolo* was formally presented and described.

From Vienna Ferdinando's four sons, Alessandro (born in 1686, probably in Parma, died 5 August 1748 in Mannheim), Giovanni Maria (born 19 January 1694 in Piacenza, died c.1777 in Naples), Giuseppe (born 5 January 1695 in Parma, died 1757 in Berlin), and Antonio (born 1697 in Parma, died 28 January 1774 in Milan), fanned out into northern Europe and for the most part remained there, except for Antonio, who returned to Bologna in 1751. The accomplishments of Giuseppe were summarized in a volume of sumptuous gravings entitled *Architecture, e prospettive dedicate alla maesta di Carlo Sesto*, published in Augsburg in 1740. Lavish as these compositions were, they foreshadow the clarity and rectangularity of neoclassical architecture, as did other Bibiena designs of the later eighteenth century. A son of Francesco, Giovanni Carlo Sicinio (born c.1720, probably in Bologna, died 20 November 1760 in Lisbon), was royal architect to King Joseph I of Portugal. A son of Giuseppe, Carlo (born 1721 in Vienna, died 1787 in Florence), worked across northern Europe.

BIBLIOGRAPHY

Drawings by the Bibiena Family and Their Followers. London, 1991. Exhibition catalog.

Hadamowsky, Franz, ed.. *Die Familie Galli-Bibiena in Wien.* Vienna, 1962.

Kelder, Diane. *Drawings by the Bibiena Family.* Philadelphia, 1968.

Kelder, Diane. "Galli Bibiena Family." In *Macmillan Encyclopedia of Architects.* New York, 1982.

Mayor, Alpheus Hyatt. *The Bibiena Family.* New York, 1945.

Muraro, Maria Teresa, and Elena Povoledo, eds. *Disegni teatrali dei Bibiena: Catalogo della mostra.* Venice, 1970.

Myers, Mary L. *Architectural and Ornament Drawings: Juvarra, Vanvitelli, the Bibiena Family, and Other Italian Draughtsmen.* New York, 1975.

GERALD L. CARR

BIBLE, DANCE IN THE. Many verbs in biblical Hebrew relate to dance, indicating that it was widespread in the ancient Near East and that choreography was highly developed in the ancient kingdoms of Judah and Israel: *hagag* ("to dance in a circle"), *savav* ("to encircle," "to turn about," "to circumambulate"), *raqad* and *pizzez* ("to skip"), *qippes* and *dilleg* ("to jump"), *kirker* ("to whirl," "to pirouette"), *pasah* ("to limp"), *hyl* or *hll* ("to perform a whirling dance"), and *siheq* ("to dance," "to play").

Hagag appears in *1 Samuel* 30.16 and *Psalms* 42.5. In *Psalms* 118.27, *hag*, its derived noun, refers to the circular procession on Sukkot: "Make a procession with branches up to the horns of the altar." Circumambulation of the altar also is referred to by *savav* in *Psalms* 26.6: "I shall wash my palms with innocence so that I may walk in the procession around Your altar, O Lord." In *Jeremiah* 31.22, the verb refers to the bride's walk around the bridegroom; according to folklorists, the walk creates a *cordon sanitaire* that protects the bridegroom from demons.

The funeral rite of dancing in a circle around the coffin (in Ladino, *rodeamentos;* in Hebrew, *haqqafot*) is well known among Sephardic Jews. The rite is referred to by *savav* in *Ecclesiastes* 12.5: "When a person goes to his eternal home, the mourners in the street participate in the circumambulations."

Curt Sachs (1937) distinguishes between skip dances, which use either foot, and jump dances, which require the dancer to leave the ground with both feet at the same time; he contends that Hebrew is unique in distinguishing between the two terms. Hebrew scriptures characterize the *riqqud* ("skip dance") as the activity of rams (*Psalms* 114.4–6), calves (*Psalms* 29.6), and he-goats (*Isaiah* 13.21)—similes that suggest that the skip dance was regarded as an imitation of these animals' gamboling and romping. The only clear reference to the jump dance is in *Isaiah* 35.6, in which the prophet says that after Israel's redemption by God, "the lame will jump *(yedalleg)* like a hart, and the tongue of the dumb shall sing a joyous song."

The verb *kirker* is mentioned twice in the account in *2 Samuel* about King David's dancing in the procession that brought the Ark of the Covenant to Jerusalem: "David was whirling with all his might" (6.14) and "David was skipping [*mepazzez*] and whirling [*mekarker*]" (6.16).

Muslims on pilgrimage to Mecca walk around the Kaʿbah, dragging one foot behind the other. Such a limping dance (in Hebrew, *pissuah*) is attributed to the priests of Baʾal in *1 Kings* 18.26.

The most frequently used Hebrew term for "dance" is *mahol*, derived from the verbal root *hll* ("to whirl"); literally, it means "whirling." *Judges* 21.21 and the *Song of Songs* 7.1 use this term to refer to the whirling dance of the nubile maiden who exhibits herself to prospective marriage partners. In *Exodus* 15.20, *Judges* 11.34, and *1 Samuel* 18.6–7, 21.12, and 29.5, *mahol* is a dance performed by women celebrating a military triumph. Association of the term with chanting and instrumental music in *1 Samuel* lends support to Jack M. Sasson's theory (1973) that *mahol* is related to, and semantically equivalent to, the Akkadian *mēlultu*, which in turn corresponds to the Greek *hyporchēma*, a multimedia performance that included instrumental music, dance, choral singing, and mime. The Hebrew *siheq*, which usually means "play," is used to mean "dance" in *1 Samuel* 18.7, *2 Samuel* 6.21, *1 Chronicles* 13.8 and 15.29, and in *Jeremiah* 31.4.

In Hebrew scriptures, dancing is most often associated with worship, but the New Testament links it to worship only in *1 Corinthians* 10.7, which, following the Septuagint, anticipates Sasson's (1973) interpretation of *Exodus* 32.6 as a reference to dancing. In *Matthew* 11.17 and *Luke* 7.32, Jesus compares those of his generation who do not respect him and John the Baptist to children who hear music and do not dance.

According to *Matthew* 14.6–11 and *Mark* 6.22–28, the dancing of Herodias's daughter Salome at Herod Antipas's birthday feast so pleased Herod that he swore he would grant her heart's desire. Prompted by her mother, Salome asked for and received the head of John the Baptist on a platter. In *Luke* 15.25, music and dancing characterize the festive welcome given the prodigal son upon his return.

The New Testament's dance terminology (in Greek) comprises the verb *paizō* ("to play," "to dance") in *1 Corinthians* 10.7, the noun *chōros* ("dance") in *Luke* 15.25, and the verb *orcheomai* ("to dance"); these are used in all the New Testament passages cited above.

[*For related discussion, see* Christianity and Dance; Israel, *overview article; and* Jewish Dance Traditions.]

BIBLIOGRAPHY

Adams, Doug, and Diane Apostolos-Cappadona, eds. *Dance as Religious Studies.* New York, 1990.

Bayer, Bathja. "Dance in the Bible: The Possibilities and Limitations of the Evidence." In *The Bible in Dance: Papers Presented at the International Seminar on the Bible in Dance,* edited by Doug Adams. Jerusalem, 1979.

Caquot, André. "Les danses sacrées en Israël et à l'entour." In *Les danses sacrées,* edited by Jean Cazeneuve. Paris, 1963.

Gruber, Mayer I. "Ten Dance-Derived Expressions in the Hebrew Bible." *Biblica* 62 (1981).

Manor, Giora. "The Bible as Dance." *Dance Magazine* (December 1978): 55–86.

Oesterley, W. O. E. *The Sacred Dance.* Cambridge, 1923.

Sachs, Curt. *World History of the Dance.* Translated by Bessie Schönberg. New York, 1937.

Sasson, Jack M. "The Worship of the Golden Calf." In *Orient and Occident: Essays Presented to Cyrus H. Gordon,* edited by Harry A. Hoffner. Kevelaer, 1973.

MAYER I. GRUBER

BICHES, LES. Ballet in one act. Choreography: Bronislava Nijinska. Music: Francis Poulenc. Scenery and costumes: Marie Laurençin. First performance: 6 January 1924, Théâtre de Monte Carlo, Ballets Russes de Serge Diaghilev. Principals: Vera Nemchinova, Anatole Vilzak, Bronislava Nijinska, Lubov Tchernicheva, Lydia Sokolova, Nicholas Zvereff, and Leon Woizikowski.

Having been delighted by Francis Poulenc's witty *Trois mouvements perpétuels,* Serge Diaghilev commissioned him to write the music for a kind of contemporary *fête galante* for the Ballets Russes. Poulenc wrote an evocation of the Jazz Age and also found an intriguingly ambiguous title for the new ballet: *Les Biches. Biche* is a French word meaning "doe"; it is also a term of endearment and slang for "prostitute." The score was ready by the fall of 1923.

A loosely connected series of solos, pas de deux, and group scenes, the ballet is a subtle and ironic commentary on high society of the 1920s. Nothing was to be obvious in this "ballet of atmosphere." Designer Marie Laurençin used delicate pastel shades to suggest a drawing room on the Riviera, while picturing the does of the title on the drop curtain. Her stylized cocktail dresses and chic beachwear give the work an air of wanton sophistication.

Bronislava Nijinska, fresh from choreographing the somber *Les Noces,* infused *Les Biches* with an air of stylishness and gaiety. She choreographed a ballet that has become a milestone in the history of twentieth-century dance. What at first looked like an amusing satire proved to be the forerunner of a new style later called neoclassi-

LES BICHES. David Blair (front) as the leading Athlete flexing his muscles in the Royal Ballet's 1964 revival of Bronislava Nijinska's lighthearted ballet satirizing social manners and displays of sexuality. (Photograph by Donald Southern; from the Dance Collections, New York Public Library for the Performing Arts.)

cism. In an article about *Les Biches* written in 1930, Frederick Ashton, a student of Nijinska and one of her greatest admirers, noted that "the whole ballet is new, and yet it is, at the same time, composed entirely of classical movement with a new expression."

Les Biches was the product of Nijinska's encounter with the school of Marius Petipa during her work on *The Sleeping Beauty.* Taking the classical repertory of steps as her starting point but using an inventive *port de bras,* flexed arms, a new kind of *pas de bourrée,* variations of *épaulements* and pointe, and asynchronous movements of the torso and legs, she developed new possibilities for classical technique. The work was a triumph for Nijinska, who viewed it as a twentieth-century equivalent of *Les Sylphides.*

Nijinska's dancing was praised at the premiere, as was Vera Nemchinova's work in the difficult role of the Girl in Blue. After the premiere, the chorus was eliminated from subsequent performances given in Paris and from almost all revivals except that by the Dance Theatre of Harlem.

[*See also the entry on Nijinska.*]

BIBLIOGRAPHY

Ashton, Frederick. "A Word about Choreography." *The Dancing Times* (May 1930): 124–125.

Baer, Nancy Van Norman. *Bronislava Nijinska: A Dancer's Legacy.* San Francisco, 1986.

Barnes, Clive, et al. "Les Biches." *Dance and Dancers* (January 1965): 11.

Haskell, Arnold L. *Some Studies in Ballet.* London, 1928.

Migel, Parmenia. "Bronislava Nijinska: The Artistic Genius behind *Les Biches.*" *Dance Magazine* (December 1982): 98–106.

Nijinska, Bronislava. *Early Memoirs.* Translated and edited by Irina Nijinska and Jean Rawlinson. New York, 1981.

Poulenc, Francis. *Correspondence, 1915–1963.* Edited by Hélène de Wendel. Paris, 1967.

Sokolova, Lydia. *Dancing for Diaghilev.* Edited by Richard Buckle. London, 1960.

GUNHILD OBERZAUCHER-SCHÜLLER
Translated from German

BIG APPLE. An American social dance popular in the 1930s, the Big Apple originated in and got its name from an African-American nightclub in Columbia, South Carolina, which had once been a synagogue. As Katrina Hazzard-Gordon has noted, the Big Apple may have had its roots in a pre-1860 dance type from the plantations of South Carolina and Georgia known as a "ring shout."

Although the dates for its origination and development are not clear, the Big Apple was discovered and became popular nationwide in the mid-1930s. In 1936 a white local college student, Billy Spivey, along with Donald Davis and Harold Wiles, visited Fat Sam's Big Apple nightclub in Columbia. The visitors became entranced with a dance being performed in a semicircle by young African Americans. To swing music and the shouting of steps by a "caller," as in a square dance, each dancer would perform the designated step in the middle of the circle, this being his or her chance to "shine." The movements included currently popular jazz steps, such as Truckin', Suzy Q, and Peckin'. Reportedly, the dance concluded with the dancers closing in, at the leader's behest, arms raised up, shouting "Praise Allah!"

Spivey brought the lively dance back to his circle of friends, who embraced it. They began demonstrating the dance locally and undoubtedly added to its movement vocabulary. During the two to three years that the Big Apple was popular, upward of one hundred steps were associated with it, including Shag, Swing, Black Bottom, Charleston, Organ Grinder, Goin' to Town, Itches, Leapfrog, Kickin' the Mule, and Peelin' the Apple. The dance's popularity soon spread across the state, an area already well populated with enthusiastic Shag dancers. Spivey wrote a companion song called "The Big Apple Swing." The dance was also commonly done to Tommy Dorsey's "Marie" and "Dipsy Doodle."

In September 1937 sixteen young South Carolinians, winners of a Big Apple contest, performed at the Roxy Theater in New York City for three weeks of standing-room-only performances. Among the dancers were Spivey and many of his original performance group, known as the Big Applers. This successful engagement fanned the flames of the Big Apple craze, which soon spread nationwide. According to dance historian Lance Benishek, the Big Apple, along with the Charleston and the Twist, was one of the three biggest dance fads in the United States. For the next year, until the dance's popularity began to

BIG APPLE. The original Big Applers, c.1935. Betty Henderson and Kenneth Clarke, the center couple, perform a Charleston step as they "shine." From left to right, Billy Spivey, Dottie Eden, Maxine Martin, and Creighton Spivey look on and clap out the rhythm. (Photograph by Lance Benishek; used by permission.)

fade, a number of the Big Applers did nightclub and theater circuit tours, often performing with the top big bands of the swing era.

During this period numerous articles about the Big Apple were published, including a four-page spread in *Life* magazine marveling that this dance phenomenon had been adopted by Arthur Murray, Ivy League college students, and high society matrons. The Big Apple was also depicted in several feature films, short subjects, and musicals. Whitey's Lindy Hoppers added the Big Apple to their repertory in 1937 in a theatrical version choreographed by Frankie Manning, who several decades later taught his rendition to a new generation of enthusiasts.

Benishek and colleague Catherine A. Rudenick have been active in researching and reconstructing the Big Apple with the help of several of the original South Carolina Big Applers, notably Betty Wood.

BIBLIOGRAPHY

Benishek, Lance, and Cathy Rudenick. "Historic Dance Ensemble Swaps Dances in South Carolina." *Dancing USA* (July–August 1993).

Hazzard-Gordon, Katrina. *Jookin': The Rise of Social Dance Formations in African-American Culture.* Philadelphia, 1990.

"1937 Closes with Big Apple: New Version of Old Square Dance Dominates Holiday Parties." *Life* (20 December 1937).

FILMS.   *Start Cheering* (1938), collegiate musical with Jimmy Durante, includes a scene in which a crowd of people perform the Big Apple at a dance. Frank Capra's *You Can't Take It with You* (1938), feature film starring Jimmy Stewart and Jean Arthur, contains a brief but charming Big Apple first performed by several ragamuffin children and then attempted by Stewart and Arthur. Whitey's Lindy Hoppers and the Cootie Williams Orchestra appear in an unidentified movie excerpt from the 1940s, part of the Ernie Smith Jazz and Film Dance Collection (social dance reel) in the Moving Image and Recorded Sound Collection, Schomburg Center for Research in Black Culture, New York Public Library.

INTERVIEW.   Lance Benishek, by Cynthia R. Millman (16 June 1995).

CYNTHIA R. MILLMAN

BIGOTTINI. The famed French dancer as a peasant girl in the 1820 ballet *Clari,* choreographed by her brother-in-law Louis Milon for the Paris Opera. (Courtesy of Madison U. Sowell and Debra H. Sowell, Brigham Young University, Provo, Utah.)

BIGOTTINI, ÉMILIE (born 16 April 1784 in Toulouse, died 28 April 1858 in Passy), French ballet dancer. The daughter of a struggling Italian actor who had drifted to France, Émilie Bigottini studied at the ballet school of the Paris Opera. She was a student and protégé of Louis Milon, ballet master at the Opera (Théâtre des Arts), who was married to her half-sister, Louise. Tall, thin, supple, and elegant, her expressive face framed in dark hair, Bigottini made her first public appearance in 1799 at the Théâtre de l'Ambigu-Comique in Milon's staging of *Pygmalion.* She joined the corps de ballet at the Opera in 1801 and was soon cast in the role of Amor in Pierre Gardel's *Psyché.* Three years later she was promoted to soloist.

Bigottini's dramatic power and popularity with audiences led to starring roles in many new ballets, including *Paul et Virginie* (1806) and *La Vestale* (1808), both choreographed by Gardel. Nevertheless, her dancing lacked polish and definition. Jean-Georges Noverre, who felt that she was too negligent of the upper portion of her body and that she did not follow the music with sufficient closeness, wrote in 1807, "She is still only a replacement, well built and svelte, with an interesting physiognomy." Noverre added, however, that Bigottini "is a dancer to whom time will assign a leading position at the Opera."

Bigottini's greatest triumph came in 1813—one year after she was promoted to principal dancer: Milon gave her an opportunity to display her remarkable gifts as a mime in *Nina, ou La Folle par Amour* (Nina, or The Woman Made Insane by Love), which contained a mad scene that was a forerunner of the scene that ends act 1 in *Giselle.* This was followed by *L'Épreuve Villageoise* (The Village Test; 1815), and *Le Carnaval de Venise* (1816), both by Milon.

A favorite dancer of Napoleon I, Bigottini had a number of famous lovers and admirers, including Napoleon's stepson Eugène de Beauharnais; General Géraud-Christophe-Michel Duroc, by whom she had two children; and the Comte de Fuentès, by whom she had one daughter.

After the Napoleonic Wars, Bigottini was a guest artist at the Congress of Vienna (1814–1815). She returned to Paris to dance in a number of ballets and opera *divertissements*, such as *Prosperine* (1818) and *Olympie* (1819), both by Pierre Gardel. She delighted audiences by dancing in boy's attire in *Les Pages du Duc de Vendôme* (1820) and *Alfred le Grand* (1822), two ballets by Jean-Louis Aumer. Also in 1822 she danced the title role in Monsieur Albert's *Cendrillon* (Cinderella) and in Gardel's *Aladin*. In December 1823, after starring in *Aline, Reine de Golconde* and *Le Page Inconstant*, Bigottini retired while still at the height of her powers. A benefit was held in her honor on 18 December 1823, and two days later a critic wrote in the *Journal de Paris*, "The grace, delicacy, and expressiveness which animated all her gestures will make it difficult to match her in the role." Bigottini's portrait hangs in the Hall of Dance at the Paris Opera.

BIBLIOGRAPHY

Bouvier, Félix. *La Bigottini: Une danseuse de l'Opéra.* Paris, 1909.
Guest, Ivor. *The Romantic Ballet in Paris.* 2d rev. ed. London, 1980.
Migel, Parmenia. *The Ballerinas: From the Court of Louis XIV to Pavlova.* New York, 1972.
Moore, Lillian. "Forgotten Dancers of the Nineteenth Century." *Dance Magazine* (December 1953): 25–30.
Noverre, Jean-Georges. *Lettres sur les arts imitateurs en général et sur la danse en particulier.* Paris, 1807.

BILLY THE KID. Eugene Loring's American folklore ballet *Billy the Kid* (1938) was set to an original score by Aaron Copland. Loring (left) appears as the title character, with Lew Christensen (center) as Sheriff Pat Garrett, and Fred Danieli as Alias. (Photograph from the Dance Collection, New York Public Library for the Performing Arts.)

ARCHIVE. Walter Toscanini Collection of Research Materials in Dance, New York Public Library for the Performing Arts.

MONIQUE BABSKY
Translated from French

BILLY THE KID. Ballet in one act. Choreography: Eugene Loring. Music: Aaron Copland. Libretto: Lincoln Kirstein. Scenery and costumes: Jared French. First performance: 16 October 1938, Chicago Civic Theater, Ballet Caravan. Principals: Eugene Loring (Billy), Marie-Jeanne (Mother, Sweetheart), Lew Christensen (Pat Garrett), Todd Bolender (Alias).

Created for Ballet Caravan, *Billy the Kid* became the most popular and enduring work in the company's repertory. Eugene Loring, who came to ballet by way of the theater, approached the drama of this legendary outlaw's life not as pure dance, but as a mixture of ballet and expressive stylized gesture.

The episodic narrative, more symbolic than specifically factual, unfolds against the backdrop of the open prairie. Following the prologue, which features pioneers marching as if to push back the frontier, the violent life and death of William H. Bonney (Billy the Kid) is depicted in a series of tableaux: the accidental murder of his mother; Billy's string of slayings triggered by her death; his relationship with Pat Garrett, the sheriff who befriends and later kills him; his affair with a Mexican sweetheart, danced by the same woman who plays his mother; and his death and funeral. As Lincoln Kirstein observed, the ballet concludes as it began, "not with Billy's personal finish, but with a new start across the continent. Billy's lonely, wildfire energy is replaced by the group force of the many marchers" (Kirstein, 1938).

Loring incorporated many ingenious theatrical devices and expressive motifs into *Billy the Kid*. All of Billy's victims, for example, are portrayed by a single character, Alias, who appears in many guises as a variation on a type. Alias is always shot in silence, which Loring believed to be the most violent sound (Reynolds, 1977). Before Billy fires, he executes an emotionally charged double pirouette to express his combustible fury. Also, the dreamlike figure of Billy's sweetheart dances on pointe to emphasize her idealistic presence in this gritty reality.

The ballet was received enthusiastically at its premiere and was hailed as a convincing study of the epic American West. Decades later, it is still considered by many to be the best of the ballets dealing with American folklore.

Billy the Kid was filmed with effective camera techniques and spatial design for the *Omnibus* television series in 1953, with John Kriza in the title role. Since entering the repertory of Ballet Theatre on 8 December 1940, the work has been revived several times. In 1988, on the eve of the fiftieth anniversary of the ballet's premiere, a new revival was presented by the Dance Theatre of Harlem and later that year by the Joffrey Ballet.

BIBLIOGRAPHY

Balanchine, George, with Francis Mason. *Balanchine's Complete Stories of the Great Ballets.* Rev. and enl. ed. Garden City, N.Y., 1977.

Clarke, Mary, and Clement Crisp. *The Ballet Goer's Guide.* New York, 1981.

Denby, Edwin. *Looking at the Dance* (1949). New York, 1968.

Hodgins, Paul. *Relationships between Score and Choreography in Twentieth-Century Dance.* Lewiston, N.Y., 1992.

Kirstein, Lincoln. "About *Billy the Kid.*" *Dance Observer* 5 (October 1938): 116.

Kirstein, Lincoln. *Blast at Ballet.* New York, 1938.

Kirstein, Lincoln. *Thirty Years: The New York City Ballet.* New York, 1978.

Martin, John. "The Dance: *Billy the Kid.*" *New York Times* (28 April 1939).

Maynard, Olga. "Eugene Loring Talks to Olga Maynard." *Dance Magazine* 40 (July 1966): 35–39; 40 (August 1966): 52–53.

Maynard, Olga. "Eugene Loring's American Classic: The Legend of Billy the Kid." *Dance Magazine* (December 1979): 70–71.

Philp, Richard. "Billy the Kid Turns Fifty." *Dance Magazine* (November 1988): 36–50.

Ramey, Phillip. "Copland and the Dance." *Ballet News* 2 (November 1980): 8–13.

Reynolds, Nancy. *Repertory in Review: Forty Years of the New York City Ballet.* New York, 1977.

FILM AND VIDEOTAPE.   *Ballet Caravan* (1938–1940). "Billy the Kid," *Omnibus* (WCBS-TV, New York, 1953). Eugene Loring, "American Ballet Theatre" (1976).

REBA ANN ADLER

BINTLEY. Richard Cragun embraces Sabrina Lenzi in Bintley's *Edward II* (1995). Based on the play by Christopher Marlowe, with music composed by John McCabe, this work was created for the Stuttgart Ballet. (Photograph by Felipe Alcoceba; used by permission.)

BINTLEY, DAVID (David Julian Bintley; born 17 September 1957 in Huddersfield, England), dancer, choreographer, and director. Bintley shares a birthday with Sir Frederick Ashton, whose choreographic inventiveness and shrewd eye for detail in revealing character have significantly influenced Bintley's development, both as an artist and as a choreographer. As a character dancer Bintley enjoyed particular success as Widow Simone in *La Fille Mal Gardée,* as the myopic Stepsister in *Cinderella,* (dancing Ashton's own role), and as a much-praised Petrouchka. He is a true character artist, exploring motivation, never content with caricature. After studying with Audrey Spencer and Dorothy Stevens, Bintley went through the Royal Ballet upper school at a time when it reflected the virtues of Cecchetti training and the influence of the Ashton ballets. Both of these aimed at a natural grace in the carriage of head and arms and in the neatness of the footwork. Ashton sought to show every position clearly, but within a flow of movement that is seamless. His best works epitomized this "English style," as do Bintley's, the most notable of which are *Allegri Diversi, Galanteries, Brahms Handel Variations,* and *Tombeaux*

(which was widely regarded as one of his most beautiful pieces), his culminating eulogy of the style, created as he left the Royal Ballet in 1993.

From the outset Bintley was determined to be a choreographer and was full of ideas for projects. His first venture, at the age of sixteen, was to choreograph Igor Stravinsky's *The Soldier's Tale.* Remarkably soon after joining Sadler's Wells Royal Ballet in 1976, he revealed his characteristic flair for atmosphere in *The Outsider* (1978), *Meadow of Proverbs* (1979), and *Night Moves* (1981). His ability to inflect the classical vocabulary with accents all his own was shown in a trilogy, to music by Polish-born Sir Andrzej Panufnik: *Homage to Chopin, Adieu,* and *Polonia.* These small-scale successes, most of them well worth keeping in the repertory, led to his first full-length ballet in 1982, *The Swan of Tuonela,* based on the Finnish epic the *Kalevala,* using well-chosen music by Jean Sibelius. *The Snow Queen* followed, to music by Modest Mussorgsky, and then in 1989 *Hobson's Choice,* with an exuberant score commissioned from Paul Reade. Both in the theater and on television, this is probably the best loved of Bintley's ballets.

Almost as popular was *"Still Life" at the Penguin Café*, a threnody for extinct animals and birds that makes its ecological point with tremendous wit and style. It was created for Covent Garden, where for a period Bintley was resident choreographer. In 1993 he went freelance. He mounted his own *Sylvia* in Birmingham, England, which was resented by some who had wanted a revival of Ashton's. In San Francisco, where Bintley's version of *Job* had been welcomed, he used the music of Dmitri Shostakovich for *The Dance House*. In 1995 a fifteen-minute ovation greeted his three-act *Edward II* in Stuttgart; it was based on Christopher Marlowe's play, with music composed by John McCabe. In 1995 he succeeded Sir Peter Wright as director of the Birmingham Royal Ballet and his first creation for his company was a box office hit, *Carmina Burana*, based on the 1936 composition by Carl Orff. His first full-length ballet for them was an adaptation of Thomas Hardy's Wessex novel *Far from the Madding Crowd*, using the same composer and designer as *Hobson's Choice*, with similar success. In 1996 he set a new one-act work to Duke Ellington's jazz version of *The Nutcracker*, designed (as was *Tombeaux*) by Jasper Conran. Bintley's roots in the musicality of the "English style" and his awareness of contemporary English theater have given him strengths that stake his claim to being one of the liveliest and most innovative of choreographers, leading ballet into the twenty-first century.

BIBLIOGRAPHY

Bintley, David. *"Sylvia." Dance Now* 2 (Summer 1993): 4–9.

Goodwin, Noël. "A Matter of Form." *Dance and Dancers* (February 1989): 24–25.

Gradinger, Malve. "Interview with David Bintley." *Ballett International* 1 (January 1995): 32–34.

Macaulay, Alastair. "Twilight of the Gods: Bintley after Ashton." *The Dancing Times* (December 1988): 228–231.

Mackrell, Judith. "David Bintley." *Dance Theatre Journal* 6 (Spring 1989): 6–9.

Rigby, Cormac. *"Tombeaux." Dance Now* 2 (Spring 1993): 49–53.

Rigby, Cormac. "Fatal Distractions: David Bintley's *Far from the Madding Crowd." Dance Now* 5 (Spring 1996): 2–6.

Woodcock, Sarah C. *The Sadler's Wells Royal Ballet.* London, 1991.

CORMAC RIGBY

BIRMINGHAM ROYAL BALLET. *See* Royal Ballet.

BISMARCK ARCHIPELAGO. *See* Papua New Guinea, *overview article.*

BJØRNSSON, FREDBJØRN (born 10 September 1926 in Copenhagen, died 19 December 1993 in Copenhagen), Danish dancer and teacher. Bjørnsson belonged to the group of very talented young male dancers who, trained by Harald Lander, emerged as prominent members of the Royal Danish Ballet in the late 1940s. Bjørnsson entered the ballet school of the Royal Theater in Copenhagen in 1935. He became a member of the company in 1945 and a principal dancer in 1949.

At first Bjørnsson, exhibiting a tremendous joyfulness in his dancing and a disarming charm in his acting, was the gamin of the ballet. His main roles in this genre were as Franz in *Coppélia*, the First Junior Cadet in *Graduation Ball*, and a Bandit in Roland Petit's *Carmen*. Later Bjørnsson developed into a marvelous character dancer distinguished by a warm soul and wonderful humor, as, for example, when he played Doctor Coppélius or the General in *Graduation Ball*. He also danced more serious character parts, such as the Ballet Master in Flemming Flindt's *The Lesson* and in *Petrouchka*. In his younger years Bjørnsson often danced with Inge Sand, and he became a member of her small troupe, which in the late 1950s, as the Royal Danish Ballet's ambassadors abroad, created an interest in Danish ballet that proved to be very valuable to the larger company.

Bjørnsson's specific domain, which he shared with his wife, Kirsten Ralov, was August Bournonville. In this repertory, Bjørnsson was always a stunning artist. He danced Gennaro in *Napoli* with fervor and, later, the mime character part of the Macaroni Vendor. In *Kermesse in Bruges* he was first a young, handsome Carelis, later a clumsy, funny Gert, and finally a witty Butler. His portrayals of characters in Bournonville ballets ranged from lead to small mime roles, which he illuminated with artistic feeling. Perhaps his greatest achievement in the Bournonville repertory was as Diderik, a lovable troll, in *A Folk Tale*. This highly original creation demonstrated how much the personal creativity of the interpretive artists has enriched the Bournonville tradition.

Bjørnsson also taught Bournonville, especially in the United States and Canada, and he staged a number of his ballets. He acted in productions of the Royal Theater and created some minor ballets. In 1961 he was awarded a Danish knighthood. In 1990 he retired, both as a director and a dancer.

BIBLIOGRAPHY

Cunningham, Kitty. "Watching Bournonville." *Ballet Review* 4.6 (1974): 24–31.

Fanger, Iris M. "The Royal Danish Ballet's Kirsten Ralov." *Dance Magazine* (November 1979): 71–77.

Fridericia, Allan. "New Danish Ballets." *The Dancing Times* (December 1957): 121.

Hollander, Michael. "Walter Terry with Inge Sand and Fredbjørn Bjørnsson." *Dance Observer* (December 1956): 152.

Kragh-Jacobsen, Svend. *Twenty Solodancers of the Royal Danish Ballet.* Copenhagen, 1965.

Williams, Peter. "Dilemma in Denmark." *Dance and Dancers* (August 1955): 8–9.

ERIK ASCHENGREEN

BLACHE FAMILY, French family of musicians, dancers, and choreographers. The origins of the family may lie in Italy, with Giacomo Blache, known to have been a violinist in the royal chamber orchestra in Parma in the mid-eighteenth century. He was joined in Parma by Mimi Blache, known as dancer in Bologna, and by Enrico Blache, also known to have been a dancer. In the same period, another Blache was recorded as principal male dancer at the Prussian court from 1750 to 1778. His son, Jean-Baptiste Blache, is the best-known member of the family, followed by two of his own sons, Frédéric and Alexis.

Jean-Baptiste Blache (born 17 May 1765 in Berlin, died 24 January 1824 in Toulouse), ballet dancer and choreographer. Jean-Baptiste received his first dance training from his father, who considered him exceptionally talented. In the belief that there were no competent teachers in Prussia, his father sent him, when he was only eleven years old, to Paris to study with the elder Jacques-François Deshayes at the Académie Royal de Danse. In 1781, at age sixteen, Jean-Baptiste Blache entered the corps de ballet at the Paris Opera and danced with this company until 1786, when he left to become a principal dancer and ballet master in several cities in southern France, dividing his time between Montpellier, Bordeaux, Lyon, and Marseille. At Montpellier in 1787 he mounted the comic *Les Meuniers* (The Millers), which was so successful that he presented it everywhere he went. It brought him unusually large royalties, which he used to support his two marriages and his thirty-two children. Arthur Saint-Léon noted that by "using a series of comic prototypes, Blache succeeded in reaching all tastes, and no one was more successful at this than he" (Saint-Léon, 1852). He was an excellent violinist and arranged practically all the music for his own ballets.

Blache succeeded Jean Dauberval in Bordeaux, where he remained for many years, except for periods in Lyon and Marseille. In Bordeaux he mounted *L'Amour et la Folie, Daphnis, Le Temps Fait Passer l'Amour, Apelles et Campaspe, L'Amour au Village, La Noce Villageoise, Les Traqueurs, La Fête Indienne, Lisbeth et Muller, ou La Fille du Soldat,* and *Médée et Jason.* With *La Fille Fugitive, ou La Laitière Polonaise* (1825) he was the first to put roller skates on dancers.

In Lyon, Blache mounted *Almaviva et Rosine* (1805), which Louis Duport restaged at the Paris Opera in 1806 as *Le Barbier de Séville, ou Figaro.* It contained a pas de huit in which four dancers symmetrically reproduced the movements of four other dancers, as if in a mirror. Duport presented this ballet in 1809 in Saint Petersburg, where he was then living. One of Blache's sons staged it in 1821 in Paris, at the Théâtre de la Porte-Saint-Martin, along with *Haroun al-Raschid* in 1817, which had been given in Lyon in 1805. Other creations in Lyon included *Les Ven-* *dangeurs* (The Grape Gatherers), *La Chaste Suzanne, Zéphire et Borée,* and *Cila et Glaucus.*

Blache's debut as a choreographer at the Paris Opera was thwarted by the incumbent directors, Pierre Gardel and Louis Milon. But thanks to his son, who was able to break the contract he had signed with the Théâtre de la Porte-Saint-Martin, a two-year contract was signed in 1824. Jean-Baptiste decided to mount *Mars et Vénus, ou Les Filets de Vulcain,* originally staged in 1909 at Bordeaux, and he commissioned new music by Jean Schneitzhoeffer (the future composer of *La Sylphide*). Rehearsals did not begin until 1825, and the premiere took place on 29 May, 1826. The principals were Lise Noblet, Pauline Montessu, and Geneviève Gosselin, plus Antoine Paul (as Airy Spirit) and Monsieur Albert. Because *Mars et Vénus* was very favorably reviewed by the Paris critics, Blache could have mounted other works, but, at the age of sixty, he preferred to retire to Toulouse. Two of his older sons had inherited some of his gifts and were able to demonstrate their own talents or restage their father's ballets in France and Russia.

Frédéric Blache (Frédéric-August Blache; born 1791 in Marseilles, death date unknown), ballet master. Frédéric Blache was his father's assistant and mounted his productions at the Théâtre de la Porte-Saint-Martin in Paris, where he was ballet master from 1815 to 1825. Frédéric presented mostly pantomime ballets, as a result of the presence of the dancer Charles-François Mazurier, for whom he created *Polichinel Vampire* (1823), *Jean-Jean,* and *Milon de Crotone* (both 1824). His *Jocko, ou Le Singe du Brésil* (Jocko, or The Monkey from Brazil) in 1825, danced by Mazurier and Joseph Mazilier, was widely plagiarized by both dancers and acrobats. In 1827, he was ballet master at the Théâtre de l'Ambigu-Comique, where he mounted *La Landwer* (1828) and *Cocambo,* a pantomime *divertissement* in two acts, in 1829. At the floating Théâtre Nautique in 1834 he created a one-act comic tableau entitled *Le Nouveau Robinson.*

Alexis Blache (Alexis-Scipion Blache; born 1792 in Marseille, died 1852 in Bordeaux), ballet teacher and choreographer. Little is known of Alexis Blache other than that he studied and worked with his father. In 1830 he succeeded his father in Bordeaux and also worked in Lyon, Marseille, and Saint Petersburg (1832–1836).

In his *Histoire du ballet russe* (1950), Serge Lifar judged him unfavorably:

After Didelot, Blache proved to be a poor teacher and a poor choreographer. He lacked the burning flame of Didelot. He made his debut in the spring of 1932 with *Don Juan, ou L'Athée Puni* [Don Juan, or The Chastised Atheist] to music that he himself had composed. This was followed by *Fête Espagnole* and a ballet of his father [*La Force de l'Amour*], and another ballet based on Dauberval [*Télémaque dans l'Île de Calypso*]. There was also a major four-act ballet, *Soumbeka, ou La Prise de Kazan,* in which, despite luxurious staging and numerous sets, Blache's debut as a choreographer was not very successful.

Nevertheless, Alexis Blache subsequently mounted such ambitious works as *Gustav Vasa, Amadis de Gaule,* and *Don Quichotte et Sancho Pança.*

BIBLIOGRAPHY

Guest, Ivor. *The Romantic Ballet in Paris.* 2d rev. ed. London, 1980.

Lifar, Serge. *A History of Russian Ballet* (1950). Translated by Arnold L. Haskell. New York, 1954.

Michel, Marcelle. "Apothéose et décadence de la danse classique sous la Révolution et l'Empire." Ph.D. diss., Sorbonne, 1955.

Saint-Léon, Arthur. *Portraits et biographies.* Paris, 1852.

Winter, Marian Hannah. *The Pre-Romantic Ballet.* London, 1974.

MONIQUE BABSKY
Translated from French

BLACHER, BORIS (born 19 January 1903 in Niuchuang, Manchuria, died 30 January 1975 in Berlin), German composer. Although born in the Manchurian port city of Niuchuang (now Yingkou) and raised in Revel (now Tallinn), Estonia, Blacher was imbued with a strong sense of German identity by his parents. He went to Berlin in 1922 to study architecture and mathematics. From 1924 to 1926 he studied composition with Friedrich Ernst Koch at the Berlin Academy of Music, and from 1927 to 1931 he studied musicology with Arnold Schering, Friedrich Blume, and Erich von Hornbostel at the University of Berlin.

After working in Berlin as a freelance composer and arranger, he was appointed lecturer in composition at the Dresden Conservatory in 1938, but he fell out of sympathy with the Nazis and returned to Berlin the following year. At the Berlin Academy of Music he was appointed professor in 1948 and was director of the (West) Berlin Academy of Music from 1953 to 1970. Elected as a regular member of the West Berlin Academy of Arts in 1955, he became director of its music section in 1961 and was president of the academy from 1968 through 1971.

In great demand as a teacher of composition in Germany and abroad, Blacher had many students, including Francis Burt, Gottfried von Einem, Giselher Klebe, and Aribert Reimann. He was married to the pianist Gerti Herzog.

His commissioned ballets include *Hamlet* (choreography by Victor Gsovsky, Munich State Opera, 1950), *Chiarina* (choreography by Jens Keith, Berlin Municipal Opera, 1950), *The First Ball* (music adapted from Friedrich von Flotow, choreography by Janine Charrat, Berlin Municipal Opera, 1950), *Lysistrata* (choreography by Gustav Blank, Berlin Municipal Opera, 1951), *The Moor of Venice* (choreography Erika Hanka, Vienna State Opera, 1955), *Demeter* (choreography by Yvonne Georgi, Schwetzingen-Hanover, 1964), and *Tristan* (choreography by Tatjana Gsovsky, German Opera Ballet, 1965). To these must be added his ballet-opera *Prussian Fairy Tales* (choreography by Gustav Blank, Berlin Municipal Opera, 1952). In addition, several of his concert pieces have been choreographed, including his *Paganini Variations* of 1947 (choreography by Todd Blender, Cologne, 1963; and by Giuseppe Urbani, Florence, 1969) and *Concertante Musik* of 1937 (choreography by Richard Adama, Hanover, 1971).

Blacher's aggressive, bouncy rhythms attracted choreographers during the 1950s and early 1960s. Much concerned with the metrical and rhythmic organization of music and with developing his own system of "variable meters," he has been compared to Erik Satie and Igor Stravinsky in his pursuit of parody, satire, and generally of a terse, spare style.

BIBLIOGRAPHY

Grimm, F. K. "Boris Blacher als Ballettkomponist." *Die Bühnengenossenschaft* 10 (October 1959).

Henrich, Heribert, ed. *Boris Blacher, 1903–1975: Dokumente zu Leben und Werk.* Berlin, 1993.

Stuckenschmidt, Hans Heinz. "Wege zu Boris Blacher." In *Boris Blacher.* Berlin, 1973. Exhibition catalogue, Berlin Academy of Arts.

Stuckenschmidt, Hans Heinz. *Boris Blacher.* Berlin, 1985.

Stürzbecher, Ursula. "Boris Blacher." In Stürzbecher's *Werkstattgespräche mit Komponisten.* Cologne 1971.

HORST KOEGLER

BLACK CROOK, THE. Spectacle in four acts. Choreography: David Costa. Music: Thomas Baker. Libretto: Charles M. Barras. Costumes: M. Phillipe, Madame Costa. First Performance: 12 September 1866, Niblo's Garden, New York City. Principals: Marie Bonfanti, Betty Regal, Rita Sangalli.

This four-act extravaganza helped both to create and to satisfy the American demand for theatrical spectacle that dominated the latter half of the nineteenth century. Popular tunes of the day were arranged into a score that had additional melodies by Giuseppi Operti. The costumes included armor by Granger of Paris, and the sets, designed by more than a dozen scenic artists, featured properties by S. Wallis, gas contrivances by C. Murray, calcine lights, by C. Seward of London, and machinery by John Fronde and Benson Sherwood. The first performance lasted five and a half hours.

Often referred to as the progenitor of musical comedy, *The Black Crook* fused music, drama, and dance into a grandiose entertainment that capitalized on northern prosperity following the Civil War. Native predecessors for this new genre existed in the ballad opera tradition as well as in specific amusements, such as *The Naiad Queen* (21 April 1841), *Faustus, or The Demon of Dragonfels* (13 January 1851), and *The Seven Sisters* (26 November 1860), all of which played in New York City. The novelty and significance of *The Black Crook* lay in its emphasis on dancing and on the introduction of *coryphées* who wore pink tights, or fleshings.

The plot centers on the activities of Hertzog, the Crook himself, in his attempts to deliver a human soul to Zamiel, the Arch Fiend. Toward this end, Hertzog frees the young painter Rudolph from imprisonment and entices his obedience with false promises of gold. During their travels, Rudolph saves the life of a dove, a disguise of Stalacta, Queen of the Golden Realm. She champions Rudolph and arranges for him to marry his beloved Amina.

Not unlike the birth of opera, which developed out of Renaissance attempts at classical reconstructions, *The Black Crook* came into being by accident. Henry C. Jarrett and Henry Palmer had imported a French ballet ensemble for a spring engagement of *La Biche au Bois* at New York's Academy of Music. They also had purchased some scenery and costumes from Astley's Amphitheatre in London. After a fire made the academy unusable, Jarrett and Harry Palmer went to William Wheatley and asked to use the theater Niblo's Garden. Wheatley was preparing to produce a turgid melodrama, largely borrowed from the plot of Carl Maria von Weber's opera *Der Freischutz*, and the three men decided to merge the two projects. It was a shrewd decision. At a cost of $50,000, *The Black Crook* was the most expensive theater venture of its day yet was so popular that those first collaborators made fortunes. By 1895 the show had been revived eighteen times in New York City alone, with productions often highlighted by appearances of Bonfanti, Pauline Markham, or a member of the Kiralfy family.

Along with its sequel, *The White Fawn* (opened 17 January 1867 at Niblo's Garden), this spectacle inspired numerous imitations. Long after extravaganza became unfashionable, *The Black Crook* continued to attract crowds. By 1929, when it was presented in Hoboken, New Jersey, with choreography by Agnes de Mille, the work's leg-

THE BLACK CROOK. A print showing the Kirafly brothers in the final tableau of act 3 of the 1866 extravaganza at Niblo's Garden, New York. This popular, long-running production helped introduce ballet in America and influenced developments in vaudeville, music hall, and variety theater. (Courtesy of Barbara Barker.)

endary appeal had at last evaporated; but as recently as 1954, events surrounding the drama's tantalizing evolution provided the plot outline for the Broadway musical *The Girl in Pink Tights.*

The interpolation of the ballets was the major theatrical departure of *The Black Crook,* but several other innovations were introduced as well. This was the nation's first leg show, evidenced both in the corps de ballet and in the Amazon marches, which became a fixture on musical stages for three decades. The mixing of ballet and acrobatics also continued as a tradition in both vaudeville and legitimate theaters. Elaborate scenic transformations—particularly for Stalacta's grotto and the golden realm—along with magical stage effects (flying chariots, gilded clouds, angels) set a standard against which later extravaganzas were measured. Due to its unusually long first run, *The Black Crook* initiated the practice of updating, refurbishing, and adding new material or performers in order to prolong the production's attractiveness. Subsequent revivals continued to increase the size of the cast until a roster of more than one hundred was commonplace in American musicals.

As a whole, the enterprise represented a curious amalgamation of several tenets of European Romanticism. The plot was indebted to Goethe's *Faust* and to the German melodramatic genre. The exotic locales (the Hartz Mountains and fairyland) as well as the supernatural beings were in keeping with ballet practices in France, Denmark, and Russia. Even the method of arranging a score primarily from the existing music of several composers was common for the ballet in Continental opera houses. Chance and Yankee ingenuity succeeded in merging all these elements, enlarging the scale, and adding a happy ending to bring about the debut of a new form.

[*See also* United States of America, *article on* Musical Theater.]

BIBLIOGRAPHY

Barker, Barbara. *Ballet or Ballyhoo: The American Careers of Maria Bonfanti, Rita Sangalli, and Giuseppina Morlacchi.* New York, 1984.

Berson, Misha. *The San Francisco Stage.* 2 vols. San Francisco, 1989–1992.

Bordman, Gerald. *American Musical Theatre: A Chronicle.* New York, 1978.

Freedley, George. "*The Black Crook* and *The White Fawn.*" Dance Index 4 (January 1945): 4–16.

Mates, Julien. "*The Black Crook* Myth." *Theatre Survey* 7 (May 1966): 31–43.

Odom, Leigh George. "The Black Crook at Niblo's Garden." *Drama Review* 26 (Spring 1982): 21–40.

CAMILLE HARDY

BLACK HAT DANCE. A Buddhist ceremony from Tibet and Bhutan, the Black Hat Dance is one of the *chams* (a mystery dance drama) performed in monasteries at religious festivals. Tibetan oral tradition claims that Palgyi Doije, a Buddhist hermit of the ninth century, disguised himself in the dress of a black-hatted magician and performed a ritual dance to attract the attention of the anti-Buddhist king Lang Dharma. Then, drawing a bow and arrow from his long wide sleeves, he shot the king.

Some Tibetans believe that the imposing *cham* dancers, dressed in dark gowns and wearing huge black headdresses, represent shamanistic pre-Buddhist Bon priests. However, Tibetan scholars state that these dancers personify Tantric adepts, gods as imagined in meditation. In *Tibetan Religious Dances,* René de Nebesky-Wojkowitz claims there is little similarity between the Black Hat costume and the traditional attire of the Bon priests.

Those chosen for the important role of Black Hat dancers must be Tantric practitioners who exhibit a high degree of meditative realization. They have their own dance master, and their lead dancer must be a high *lama* (teacher) who is often the abbot of the monastery where the *cham* is performed.

According to Snellgrove and Richardson (1968), since 1959, when the People's Republic of China put down the Tibetan independence movement, these rituals have rarely been performed in Tibet. They are preserved in Bhutan, however, and in Tibetan monasteries in exile.

The dancers' impressive outfits demand a majestic style of movement. The unmasked performers wear a heavy, dark-colored brocade robe with wide funnel-like sleeves decorated with broad stripes of yellow and red silk, a poncho, dark-colored felt boots, an apron emblazoned with the embroidered head of a wrathful deity, bone ornaments such as bracelets, a wig formed in a topknot of human or yak hair, and a large broad-brimmed multileveled black hat decorated with a miniature skull, a mirror, and peacock feathers. The headdress symbolizes the world of existence, with the cosmic mountain at the center surmounted by the sun and moon.

The varying dances within the *cham* ceremony are named according to the dancers' costumes, not the ritual which is being performed. For example, the Black Hat dancers begin the first part of the ceremony with the "Dance of Golden Libation," an offering to the local spirits. Each performer carries in his right hand a chalice, which an attendant fills with beer or tea. As seen by Michael Aris in Bhutan, the dancer bends one knee, lifts the other foot, and turns a low, full circle. As he executes his slow, majestic turning-and-hopping movements, the contents of the chalice are sprinkled on the ground as an offering to the gods of the land. The dancers may also take part in the rites of exorcism—the symbolic killing of a dough effigy of a demon and the final processional in which a different malevolent figure is burned or thrown out. In the *cham* ceremony of the deity Dorje Phurba, the Black Hat dancers carry the sacred dagger *(phurba),* the emblem of the deity, which cuts through the false conception of the substantiality of the ego. They also carry a skull cup representing impermanence. Thus the Black Hat Dance and other *cham* dances present, in a mesmerizing way, a multileveled display of the symbols of inner consciousness.

BIBLIOGRAPHY

Aris, Michael. "Sacred Dances of Bhutan." *Natural History* 89 (March 1980):28–37.

Nebesky-Wojkowitz, René de. *Oracles and Demons of Tibet: The Cult and Iconography of the Tibetan Protective Deities*. The Hague, 1956. Reprint, Graz, 1975.

Snellgrove, David L., and Hugh E. Richardson. *A Cultural History of Tibet*. New York, 1968. Reprint, Boulder, 1980.

LIN LERNER

BLAIR, DAVID (David Butterfield; born 27 July 1932 in Halifax, England, died 1 April 1976 in London), British dancer. A dancer of unusual versatility and charm, Blair began his training at the age of eight with Amy Ibbetson in Halifax and entered the Sadler's Wells Ballet School in 1946. He joined the Sadler's Wells Theatre Ballet in 1948, where he danced the virtuoso leading roles in *Coppélia* and *The Nutcracker* and such disparate characters as Captain Belaye in John Cranko's rollicking *Pineapple Poll* (1951) and the poetic Harlequin in his *Harlequin in April* (1951).

Having joined the Sadler's Wells Ballet in 1953 and been promoted to principal in 1955, Blair performed with equal distinction in classical and *demi-caractère* roles. As a gracious and confident *danseur noble*, he partnered Violetta Elvin, Nadia Nerina, and, briefly, Margot Fonteyn (succeeding Michael Somes) in *The Sleeping Beauty*, *Swan Lake*, *Giselle*, and *Cinderella* and created one of the seven cavaliers in Frederick Ashton's *Birthday Offering* (1956). His *demi-caractère* roles included the Bluebird in *The Sleeping Beauty*, the Miller in *Le Tricorne*, Prince Ivan in *The Firebird*, and the title roles in *Petrouchka* and *The Rake's Progress*. He created the title role in Cranko's first full-evening ballet *The Prince of the Pagodas* (1957), Mercutio in Kenneth MacMillan's *Romeo and Juliet* (1965), and—at his most memorable and most endearing—the bounding, ebullient Colas in Ashton's *La Fille Mal Gardée* (1960).

Blair staged several of the classics in Atlanta, Georgia, before mounting act 2 of *Swan Lake* (1966), the entire *Swan Lake* (1967), and *Giselle* (1968) for American Ballet Theatre. He took a brief leave of absence (1968–1970) from the Royal Ballet (formerly the Sadler's Wells Ballet) and retired from dancing in 1973 to become a teacher with the Royal Ballet New Group. He died of a heart attack at age forty-three, only months before he was to assume the position of director of the Norwegian National Ballet. Blair was made a Commander of the Order of the British Empire in 1964.

BIBLIOGRAPHY

Bland, Alexander. *The Royal Ballet: The First Fifty Years*. London, 1981.

Crisp, Clement, ed. *Ballerina: Portraits and Impressions of Nadia Nerina*. London, 1975.

Terry, Walter. *Great Male Dancers of the Ballet*. Garden City, N.Y., 1978.

Woodcock, Sarah C. *The Sadler's Wells Royal Ballet*. London, 1991.

BARBARA NEWMAN

BLANGY, HERMINE (born c.1818, probably in Paris; died before 1890 in New York), French dancer. Noted for her "intellectual" dancing and considered to be one step below Fanny Elssler, Blangy introduced *Giselle* and other Romantic ballets to a number of American cities.

Blangy was said to be the daughter of a Parisian singer and the sister of another woman dancer. Paris Opera contracts exist for Hermine Blangy from 1832 to 1841. During the years 1838, 1839, and 1842 to 1845, Blangy also performed Romantic roles in Vienna. In May 1845 she danced *Giselle* at the Royal Theater in Munich, followed by summer engagements at Bordeaux and Nantes.

Blangy arrived in America on 15 June 1846. Initially engaged to perform with the Ravel Family, a company of pantomimists, gymnasts, and rope dancers, she made her debut at Niblo's Garden in New York City on 7 July 1846, as Calista in *The Vengeance of Diana* and in a "Neapolitan Dance." Later she performed in *Giselle* and *La Sylphide*.

Leaving the Ravels, she went to Boston's Howard Athenaeum in October 1846 to star in *Giselle*, *La Chatte Métamorphosée en Femme*, and *Bohemian Polka*. Engagements followed at Philadelphia's Arch Street Theatre, in Pittsburgh, and at Palmo's Opera House in New York. When Blangy introduced *Giselle* in New Orleans on 28 December 1846, veteran showman and theater historian Noah Ludlow declared "I never witnessed finer acting than was displayed by this artist in . . . *Giselle*." Her program also included a *fandango*, "La Viennoise," and an excerpt from *La Tentation*. After performing in Mobile, Alabama, and Havana, Cuba, she danced the role of Donna Francisco Camilla in *L'Illusion d'une Peintre* at the American Theatre in New Orleans. During a May engagement in Philadelphia, she added the role of Zelia in *Le Lac des Fées*. Engagements followed at the Park Theatre in Buffalo, and in Boston, where she was injured while performing in June 1847.

In August, Blangy danced at Philadelphia's Walnut Street Theatre. She then went south by Ohio riverboat, stopping for engagements in Cincinnati and Louisville. She caused a great sensation at the Théâtre d'Orléans in November 1847 when she danced the part of Helena in the Meyerbeer opera *Robert le Diable*. Blangy then left for Cuba, returning to Philadelphia in February 1848, where she danced the role of Florinda in *Le Diable Boiteux*.

Blangy was one of the last performers to appear at New York's Park Theatre, in mid-March 1848. During the period 1848–1850 she appeared in Boston, in New York at the Broadway Theatre and at Niblo's Garden, and in Buffalo, Saint Louis, New Orleans, Philadelphia, Louisville, Cincinnati, Baltimore, and Richmond. Her new roles included Hattie in *La Vivandière*, Helen de Wardech in *The Devil's Violin*, Ambroisine in *The Pet of the Village*, Miranda in *La Fille de Marbre*, Aurora in *Les Fleurs Animées*, and Azarine in *The Child of the Air*. In 1849 an American source said her partner Eugene Durand, a dancer from Madrid, was her husband.

Her last known American engagement was in Charleston, South Carolina, from 27 January to 8 February 1851. A critic for the Charleston press summarized her art by saying: "That which was, a few years since, nothing but an exhibition of loose flouncing and posturing to excite the passions of the vulgar has now been converted, by an exquisite combination of nature and art, into a shifting tableau of grace and intelligence."

BIBLIOGRAPHY

Guest, Ivor. *The Romantic Ballet in Paris.* 2d rev. ed. London, 1980.

Ludlow, Noah M. *Dramatic Life as I Found It.* St. Louis, 1880.

Swift, Mary Grace. *Belles and Beaux on Their Toes: Dancing Stars in Young America.* Washington, D.C., 1980.

ARCHIVES. Dance Collection, New York Public Library for the Performing Arts.

MARY GRACE SWIFT

BLANK, GUSTAV (born 28 October 1908 in Altenbögge, Westphalia, died 25 March 1987 in Munich), German dancer, teacher, choreographer, and ballet master. Gustav Blank studied dance with Rudolf Laban and Kurt Jooss at the Essen Folkwang Schule and with Victor Gsovsky and Evgenia Eduardova in Berlin. As a dancer at the Berlin State Opera from 1933 to 1949, he excelled in character roles and was especially admired in Spanish dances. Eventually he was appointed soloist and assistant ballet master. During the war he performed in a touring company for German troops all over Europe. After World War II he took over the former Eduardova ballet school in West Berlin and built it into one of the city's foremost schools.

As ballet master at the West Berlin Municipal Opera from 1949 to 1957, Blank choreographed the first local productions of *Lysistrata* (1951), *Prussian Fairy Tale* (1952), and *Renard* (1954), all conspicuous successes. He was ballet master at the Hamburg State Opera from 1959 to 1962, after having choreographed several works there, including the first German production of *Mario and the Magician* (1957) and *Don Quixote* (1957), to music by Jacques Ibert, followed by other ballets, including the first local production of *The Sleeping Beauty* (1958).

Blank settled in Munich in 1962, where he was head of the ballet department at the Academy of Music from 1962 to 1974 and continued to teach at his private school. He was one of the most respected teachers of the post–World War II generation of German dancers. He was awarded the German Dance Prize in 1986, on which occasion a festschrift was published in his honor.

BIBLIOGRAPHY

Gockel, Eberhard, et al. *Festschrift für Gustav Blank.* Special issue of *Ballet-Journal / Das Tanzarchiv* (1986).

Nevill, Timothy, trans. *Ballet and Dance in the Federal Republic of Germany.* Bonn, 1988.

HORST KOEGLER

BLASIS, CARLO (Carlo de Blasis; born 4 November 1795 in Naples, died 15 January 1878 in Cernobbio), Italian dancer, choreographer, ballet master, and writer. Blasis was the son of Francesco Antonio de Blasis, a musician; he had two sisters, Virginia, a singer, and Teresa, a pianist. The family immigrated to France and adopted the name Blasis, dropping the noble *de* for political reasons.

Blasis studied the humanities and the arts in Marseille, where he made his debut in 1814. He continued to study dance with Jean Dauberval in Bordeaux, where the family had moved and where he first performed at the Grand Théâtre in the 1816–1817 season. He made his Paris Opera debut on 17 July 1817 in a pas de deux with choreography by Pierre Gardel. He was a guest performer in 1818 at Teatro alla Scala, Milan, in ballets by Salvatore Viganò, and the following year at the Teatro La Fenice in Venice. His debut as a choreographer, at La Scala in 1819 with *Il Finto Feudatario* (The False Lord), was not a success. In April 1820 he published his first book on theory, *Traité élémentaire*, which he had begun in Paris; thereafter he alternated between dancing and writing. He went on tour from 1821 to 1826 in northern Italy and then, in 1827, to London, where he composed several choreographic works and published *The Code of Terpsichore*. In February 1832 he married the ballerina Annunciata Ramaccini, his partner on stage. As a dancer, Blasis was praised more for his expressiveness than for his technique.

In 1835 Blasis composed three dances for the Teatro della Pergola in Florence and then went on to the Canobbiana in Milan. In November 1837 he and his wife were appointed to teach graduate students at the La Scala ballet school, where their contract was renewed until 1850. In London in 1817, where he had gone to stage other ballets at Covent Garden and at the Saint James Theatre, he published *Notes upon Dancing*. After completing an engagement at La Scala he resumed his travels. In 1856, after a stint in Paris, he was a teacher and choreographer at the Warsaw Opera, where he staged works from his repertory; only *Faust* remained in the repertory for long, the Poles preferring the French style. In 1858 he went to the Teatro de São Carlos in Lisbon. In 1859 he returned to Paris, where in 1860 he composed *divertissements*. Between 1861 and 1863 he was a guest choreographer and teacher at the Bolshoi in Moscow. He returned to Milan in October 1864 to devote himself to writing, and in 1866 he settled down in Cernobbio on Lake Como in his villa, called "La Carcanina" after his daughter Luisa, also briefly a ballet dancer. Blasis died suddenly of a stroke on 15 January 1878.

None of Blasis's ballets has survived. Nevertheless, it is worth remembering *Leocadia* (1833), *Gli Amori di Adone e Venere* (1835), *La Ninfa Eco* (1849), *Faust* (1861), and the *divertissements* from many operas (*Mosè*, by Gioacchino Rossini, 1840; *Macbeth*, by Giuseppe Verdi, 1849; *Il Profeta*, by Giacomo Meyerbeer, 1852; and *La Favorite*, by Gaetano Donizetti, 1856). Descriptions of these ballets are scant. We know that in *Leocadia*, which dates from 1833 and was last performed in public at the 1834 Carnival in Modena, Blasis was already showing signs of fatigue as a dancer.

Blasis made a controversial attempt to transpose Goethe's *Faust*. He was aware of Goethe's poem as early as 1835, when he proposed his ballet; the Theater Museum at La Scala in Milan has a manuscript by Blasis containing the notes on an ambitious ballet entitled *Mephistopheles, or The Evil Spirit*. He published a description of his pet project in the March 1843 issue of the newspaper *La Fama*, but none of it got beyond the draft stage. However, the notes, introduction, ballet program, and attached drawings give a good understanding of his training in culture and the humanities. Meanwhile, on 12 February 1848, Jules Perrot staged his own *Faust* at La Scala. Though unable to realize his dream of staging *Mephistopheles*, Blasis was nevertheless able in Warsaw in 1856 and in Moscow in 1861 to stage a *Faust*. Although Blasis claimed the Moscow *Faust* as his own, his scenario clearly repeats the general features of Perrot's production.

Blasis played a fundamentally important role in the history of ballet as a teacher and a theoretician. His background in poetry, music, and the figurative arts helped him to achieve his ideal of beauty through the language of the classics and academic learning. Launching a new methodology, he devoted all his efforts toward directing the newborn Romantic ballet along classical lines. Blasis's teaching was adopted throughout the world and was passed on from pupil to pupil. His method passed to Giovanni Lepri, and from Lepri to the great Enrico Cecchetti; thus the technique that would become the training method for the modern ballet dancer was perfected.

[*See* Ballet Technique, History of, *article on* Ballet in the Late Eighteenth and Early Nineteenth Centuries; *and* Technical Manuals, *article on* Publications, 1765–1859. *See also entries on the principal figures mentioned herein.*]

BIBLIOGRAPHY

"Blasis, Carlo." In *Enciclopedia dello spettacolo*. Rome, 1954–.

Blasis, Carlo. *An Elementary Treatise upon the Theory and Practice of the Art of Dancing* (1820). Translated by Mary Stewart Evans. New York, 1944.

Levinson, André. *Meister des balletts*. Potsdam, 1923.

Moore, Lillian. "Carlo Blasis." In Moore's *Artists of the Dance*. New York, 1938.

Perugini, Mark E. "Carlo Blasis, Master of Masters" (parts 1–2). *The Dancing Times* (September–October 1927).

Puttke, Martin. "The Straight Line Is Godless." *Ballet International* 1 (January 1995): 26–31.

Regli, Francesco. *Strenna: Letterario-poetico-musicale*. Turin, 1855.

Regli, Francesco. *Dizionario biografico*. Turin, 1860.

Slonimsky, Yuri. *Klassiki khoreografii*. Moscow, 1937.

Souritz, Elizabeth. *Carlo Blasis in Russia, 1861–1864*. Studies in Dance History, vol. 4.2. Pennington, N.J., 1993.

Sowell, Debra H. "'Virtue (almost) Triumphant' Revisited." *Dance Chronicle* 18.2 (1995): 293–301.

Testa, Alberto. *Discorso sulla danza e sul balletto*. 3d ed. Rome, 1981.

Testa, Alberto. *Storia della danza e del balletto*. 3d ed. Rome, 1994.

ALBERTO TESTA
Translated from Italian

BLASKA, FÉLIX (born 8 May 1941 in Gomel, Belorussian Soviet Socialist Republic), French ballet dancer, choreographer, and company director. Félix Blaska studied with Yves Brieux at the Paris Conservatoire, where he won first prize in 1960. He then joined the Marquis de Cuevas's company for its last season, when he performed in *The Sleeping Beauty*. Following that, Blaska danced with Roland Petit's company, the Ballet du XXᵉ Siècle, from 1962 to 1969, creating parts in *Les Chants de Maldoror* (1963), *La Silla* (1963), *Les Chemins de la Creation* (for television, 1965), and *Éloge de la Folie* (1966).

In 1966, Petit gave Blaska his first ballet to mount—*Octandre*, to music by Edgard Varèse; *Les Affinités Electives*, to music by Patrice Mestral, followed in 1967. In 1967 Blaska also took part in a televised revival of *Le Jeune Homme et la Mort*. For Ballet-Théâtre Contemporain's first season in 1968, Blaska choreographed *Danses Concertantes* to music by Igor Stravinsky.

Blaska soon formed his own group, which first appeared at the Chatillon Festival in June 1969. Four of his ballets—*Electro-Bach*, to music by J. S. Bach arranged by Walter Carlos; *Sensemaya*, to music by Silvestre Revuelta; *Equivalences* (later titled *Bakyla*), to music by Jean-Claude Eloy; and *Iniciativas*, to music by Luis de Pablo—won critical favor. Anne M. Duvernoy wrote in *Art & Dance*, "the choreographic language of Felix Blaska is spontaneous, clear, and uninterrupted. The movement is never gratuitous[;] it unfolds and continuously refreshes itself."

In 1970 Blaska choreographed *Deuxième Concerto* to music by Sergei Prokofiev, for the Marseille Opera; Claire Motte and Georges Piletta were the guest artists. The year

1970 also brought two more Blaska triumphs: his first season for the Théâtre de la Ville in Paris, where he choreographed *Ballet pour Tam-Tam et Percussion* to music by Jean-Pierre Drouet, and a pas de deux for Jacqueline Rayet and Georges Piletta from a sonata for two pianos by Béla Bartók.

Blaska then toured widely with his company before finding a base at Grenoble's Maison de la Culture in 1972. There he created *En Blanc et Noir,* to music by Claude Debussy; *Ya Sin,* to music by J. P. Drouet; and *Contre,* to music by Luciano Berio, among others. For the Paris Opera in 1973, Blaska choreographed two pieces for an evening of Varèse works: *Poem Électronique* for Wilfride Piollet and *Arcana* for Jean Guizerix and Georges Piletta. Such works prompted André-Philippe Hersin to describe Blaska as "the most inventive and talented of his generation." In 1974 Blaska distinguished himself with *Linea, O King,* and *Agnus* for a Berio evening in Grenoble; *Fusion,* for the Royan festival, to the music of Carlos Roqué Alsina; and another Paris season with *Comoedia,* to the music of Stravinsky, and *Transitory.*

Also in 1974, Blaska choreographed *L'Homme aux Loups* to music by Marius Constant—a surreal fantasy about a man who becomes the victim of his own hallucinations. The dance marked the first change from Blaska's previous vivid and lively choreography. He was much criticized in 1976 for *Le Fou d'Elsa,* which was based on the poems of Louis Aragon. In 1977, Blaska completely changed both his company and his choreographic style; only a few ballets—such as *Electro-Bach,* which was danced without pointe shoes—remained in the repertory.

During another stay in Paris, Blaska met the Pilobolus Dance Theater and subsequently created a duet for himself and Martha Clarke. It was presented first in April 1979 after he had joined the Pilobolus group for one season in San Francisco; the duet also was performed that month in France. Blaska then dissolved his own company to continue studying and working in the United States. He founded the newly born Crownest group with Clarke in 1978. During the group's 1982 season in Paris, critic Lise Brunel of *Le matin* wrote, "In associating with Martha Clarke, Félix Blaska seems to have found a new source of vitality and choreographic invention that draws upon a sure and balanced technique that doesn't fear either strength or softness."

Blaska has served in the dual role of collaborator and performer in many of Clarke's more recent works, including *The Garden of Earthly Delights* and the touring product of *Vienna: Lusthaus.* He also collaborated on *Miracolo d'Amore* and performed in *Endangered Species.* Beside his work with Clarke, Blaska has continued to collaborate with Pilobolus. In 1990 he returned to France to create *Charlotte,* to music by Arvo Pärt), based on Elisabeth Kübler-Ross's book *On Death and Dying,* for Ballet du Nord in Roubaix.

BIBLIOGRAPHY

Bonis, Bernadette. "La retour en force de Félix Blaska." *Danser* (March 1990): 18–19.

Bourcier, Paul. "Danser aujourd'hui." In Bourcier's *Histoire de la danse en Occident.* Paris, 1978.

Brunel, Lise. *Nouvelle danse française.* Paris, 1980.

Cirillo, Silvana, ed. *Corpo, teatro, danza: Béjart, Blaska, Petit.* Brescia, 1981.

Diénis, Jean-Claude. "Félix Blaska." *Saisons de la danse,* no. 77 (October 1975): 23–25.

Fargue, François. "Ballet d'Avignon." *Saisons de la danse,* no. 265 (February 1995): 18.

Goodman, Saul. "Felix Blaszka: Brief Biography." *Dance Magazine* (February 1965): 50–51.

Koenig, J. F. *La danse contemporaine.* Paris, 1980.

Lidova, Irène. "Félix Blaska." *Saisons de la danse,* no. 104 (May 1978): 10–11.

Monique Babsky
Translated from French

BLISS, ARTHUR (Arthur Drummond Bliss; born 2 August 1891 in London, died 27 March 1975 in London), English composer. Music for dance formed a small but significant part of Bliss's work in four original scores for ballet: *Checkmate* (1937), *Miracle in the Gorbals* (1944), *Adam Zero* (1946), and *The Lady of Shalott* (1958). The first three were for the Vic-Wells Ballet and Sadler's Wells Ballet, the last for the San Francisco Ballet. In his 1970 autobiography Bliss wrote, "I have always found it easier to write 'dramatic' music than 'pure' music. I like the stimulus of words, or a theatrical setting."

Bliss graduated in music from Cambridge University in 1913. After army service in World War I from 1914 to 1918, he explored various forms of music, often with a jazz element, which put him among leading British composers of the next two decades. From 1923 to 1925, he lived in Santa Barbara, California, where he met and married his wife Trudy, née Gertrude Hoffman. His first connection with ballet came when *Rout,* composed in 1920 for soprano singing of wordless vocalises, with an instrumental ensemble, was reorchestrated at Serge Diaghilev's invitation for performance as a musical interlude during the 1926 programs of the Ballets Russes.

A further arrangement of *Rout,* for voice and two pianos, became the basis of one of the earliest ballets by Ninette de Valois. First performed in 1928 by students of her Academy of Choreographic Art in London, it was described by dance historian Mary Clarke (1955) as "an attempt to portray in a dance built up of groupings and what was then called 'futuristic' movement, frequently of a contrapuntal nature, the revolt of modern youth against the conventions of the older generation." It was revised and further performed by the Camargo Society and the emergent Vic-Wells Ballet until 1932.

De Valois turned to Bliss when a new ballet was needed for her company's first foreign tour, to Paris in 1937. A theme of chess pieces personified in dramatic conflict was devised by the composer following a dinner party with Tamara Karsavina at which "the discussion turned on the drama of games, and the idea of the pitiless queens in chess leapt from someone's brain to become the starting-point of the ballet." Descriptive music for a large orchestra in twelve numbers, with assertive rhythms and bright instrumentation, was a major element in the ballet's success then and since.

After a stint teaching at the University of California in Berkeley from 1939 to 1941 and as director of Music for the British Broadcasting Corporation from 1942 to 1944, Bliss composed the music for Robert Helpmann's *Miracle in the Gorbals* (1944). A dance drama surrounding a Christ figure reborn in city slums, it had a powerful effect on wartime ballet audiences, many of whom were new to the medium. Tonality is given dramatic purpose in the music, which also relates theme to character in the course of an overture and seventeen numbers. It incorporates such forms as rondo, waltz, and passacaglia with variations and achieves an almost revivalist religious fervor with the spirituals and jazz elements used in a "Dance of Deliverance for a Young Girl" rescued from suicide.

Helpmann was again the choreographer for *Adam Zero* (1946), in which the allegorical theme of a human life cycle is related to the process of creating a ballet. Bliss composed a score of sixteen numbers; its outstanding features include a forceful rhythmic impulse at the start and the expressive character of the seasonal dances tracing Adam's life cycle before and after his awakening to love. The jazzlike idiom of a nightclub scene anticipated aspects of the Leonard Bernstein musical *West Side Story* (1957) by more than a decade.

The Lady of Shalott in 1958 was composed for Lew Christensen and the San Francisco Ballet on commission for the May T. Morrison music festival at the University of California. "Using Tennyson's poem as a pretext," wrote the *San Francisco Chronicle* (4 May 1958),

> Sir Arthur has woven together a rich and sumptuous theater piece. . . . It is full of medieval color, it is highly effective in its contrasts of court life and folk life, and it is suffused throughout with a kind of enigmatic, pathetic lyricism. The score is very brilliant, wonderfully orchestrated and finely shaped.

The ballet, however, had few performances.

Pieces by other choreographers have been based on Bliss's concert works, of which he published more than 120. They include Kenneth MacMillan's *Diversions* (1961), to Music for Strings composed in 1935; John Neumeier's *Frontier* (1969), to the 1927 Quintet for Oboe and Strings, and Robert de Warren's *Royal Offering* (1977), which used *A Colour Symphony* of 1922. Bliss was knighted in 1950 and appointed Master of the Queen's Music in 1953. He published his autobiography, *As I Remember,* in 1970.

BIBLIOGRAPHY

Bliss, Arthur. *As I Remember.* Rev. ed. London, 1989.

Clarke, Mary. *The Sadler's Wells Ballet: A History and an Appreciation.* London, 1955.

Craggs, Stewart R. *Arthur Bliss: A Bio-Bibliography.* New York, 1988.

Crisp, Clement. "The Ballets of Arthur Bliss." *Musical Times* 107 (August 1966): 674–675.

Easterbrook, Giles. *Arthur Bliss: Supplement to the Catalogue of Complete Works.* Sevenoaks, Kent, 1982.

Foreman, Lewis. *Arthur Bliss: A Catalogue of the Complete Works.* Sevenoaks, Kent, 1980.

Goodwin, Noël. "Bliss at the Ballet." *Dance and Dancers* (August 1991): 19–21.

NOËL GOODWIN

BLOK, LUBOV (Liubov' Dmitrievna Blok; born 17 [29] December 1881 in Saint Petersburg, died 27 September 1939 in Leningrad), ballet historian. Readers acquainted with Russian poetry know Lubov Blok primarily as the "beautiful lady" *(prekrasnaya dama)* who inspired much of the poetry of her husband, the symbolist poet Aleksandr Blok (1880–1921). The daughter of the famous chemist Dmitri Mendeleev (author of the periodic table) and an aspiring actress, Lubov Mendeleeva married Blok in 1903. She became a pseudo-divinity in Saint Petersburg's rarefied intellectual circles the following year, when her husband's important early collection, *Verses to the Beautiful Lady,* appeared.

Little was known of Blok's life after the period of her vertiginous celebrity in Russian letters (roughly at about the time of World War I and the Russian Revolution) until the publication of a substantial volume of her writings in dance history in Moscow in 1987: *Classical Dance: Past and Present (Klassichesky tanec: Istoriia i sovremennost).* The volume contains studies Blok wrote in the 1930s, the most important being "The Origins and Development of the Technique of Classical Dance," which examines the ancient origins of classical dance, the development of professional dance, and the evolution of ballet in Italy, France, and Russia. The volume also includes Blok's material for a dictionary of French ballet terms (from the seventeenth to the twentieth centuries), and a number of articles—among them, writings on Charles-Louis Didelot's ballets, the restaging of *Swan Lake,* Agrippina Vaganova's classes, classical variations, and Kirov ballets of the late 1930s. The majority of the manuscripts that comprise the volume are held in Moscow's Bakhrushin State Theatrical Museum, where they have been housed presumably since Blok's death.

In his introduction to *Classical Dance*, Vadim Gaevsky sees innovation in Blok's use of visual sources as keys to the history of dance, comparing her work on the iconography of the Didelot ballet, notably, to the fundamentally philological approach taken by her most illustrious predecessors in the field of dance writing in Russia: André Levinson and Akim Volynsky. More importantly, Blok's history departs fundamentally from standard dance-historical practice. Rather than focus on choreographers and their ballets, on performances and performers, Blok is primarily concerned with the academy of classical dance: it's schools, pedagogues, and pupils.

Blok subtitles her main work, "The Origins and Development of the Technique of Classical Dance," an "attempt to systematize." Reflecting her father's passion for orderly tables, she offers several of her own. The French and Italian schools are neatly divided by epoch and predominant style, for example; the author later proposes an "artistic genealogy" of dance pedagogues from Pierre Beauchamps to Vaganova and Boris Shavrov. The tables and charts suggest the degree to which Blok infused her studies with a scientist's passion for precision and completeness, qualities that distinguish all her work.

Blok's observations on Vaganova's classes offer an invaluable, learned glimpse into the workings of the master teacher's studio. As Blok puts it, "to attend Vaganova's class is to be allowed into the very heart of the laboratory" (Blok, 1987, p. 441). Despite her admiration, however, Blok holds nothing sacrosanct. She finds Vaganova's students too concerned with turns, too "acrobatic," and editorializes on the state of dancing in Leningrad in the late 1930s: "It's high time the Leningrad ballet started dancing more precisely" (p. 447). Blok is expectedly, as a passionate defender of the academy, hardest on Michel Fokine and the influence of the Diaghilev ballet on the Russian school. Fokine's principles are, for Blok, naive and uninformed. Paradoxically, Blok feels that the reduction of classical dance to a kind of naturalism in the Fokine period revealed the true nature (and value) of classicism (p. 330).

Hindsight has shown Blok to be a ballet visionary as well as a perceptive interpreter of its history. In her passionate defense of the Saint Petersburg school, she campaigned for the development of the "abstract" or "pure-dance" ballet that George Balanchine would popularize in the decades after her death. Writing in Leningrad in the heyday of the Soviet *drambalet* (drama ballet), she saw the future in the work of Fedor Lopukhov, a proponent of "symphonic ballet." Blok ends her history with an expression of hope for the future of ballet: "We have every right to hope that the 'symphonizing' of dance, the liberation of dance from subservience to the laws of the dramatic spectacle, will become a subject of debate very soon—very, very soon" (p. 343).

BIBLIOGRAPHY

Blok, Lubov D., *Klassichesky tanec: Istoriia i sovremennost* [Classical Dance: Past and Present]. Moscow, 1987.

Gaevsky, Vadim M. "Istorik baleta L. D. Blok" [The Dance Historian L. D. Blok], introduction to Blok's *Klassichesky tanec: Istoriia i sovremennost*, pp. 7–22. Moscow, 1987.

TIM SCHOLL

BLONDY, MICHEL (born 1670 or 1676 in Paris, died 6 August 1739 in Paris), French dancer, teacher, choreographer, and dance academician. Although his obituary, published in *Le Mercure de France* in August 1739, stated Blondy's age as "almost seventy," his death certificate, dated 7 August 1739, noted that "[today] Monsieur Michel Blondy, about sixty-three years old and husband of Marie-Nicole (Thérèse) Dugas[t], was buried . . . having died yesterday . . . in the presence of François-Louis Malter, [dance] academician, friend of the deceased. [Monsieur Blondy was] 'pensionnaire du Roi' and composer at the Royal Academy of Music" (Archives de la Seine, Paroisse de Saint-Micolas du Chardonnet).

Michel Blondy was born into a large family, the son of Antoine Blondy, a Parisian dancing master, and of Catherine Beauchamps, sister of Pierre Beauchamps, Louis XIV's court choreographer and dancing master. Not only was Michel nephew to Beauchamps but he was also related to Pierre Marchand and Claude Desmatins, both famous musicians of the king's chamber. With these formidable allies backing his natural gifts as a dancer, Blondy could not but succeed. *Le Mercure*, which retraced his career in 1739, called him "one of the most beautiful dancers ever to appear." Jean-Étienne Despréaux wrote that "he surpassed Pecour," and the Parfaict brothers called him "the greatest dancer in Europe" for character dances. He studied with Pierre Beauchamps and was dancing in court ballets as early as 1685. He joined the Paris Opera at the same time as Claude Ballon, with whom he shared principal roles.

In 1728 Blondy replaced Guillaume-Louis Pecour as dance director of the Paris Opera, a prestigious position he held until his death. His first ballet, *La Princesse d'Élide*, opened on 20 July 1728 and received the compliments of *Le Mercure*, which found "the new Director worthy of [his] appointment." Other ballets choreographed by Blondy and reviewed by *Le Mercure* included *Les Fêtes Vénitiennes* (1721) (he had already choreographed the 1710 version as a replacement for Pecour, who was ill), *Callirhoé* (1732), *Isis* (1732), *Jephté* (1732), *Le Ballet des Sens* (1732), *Scylla* (1732), *Les Fêtes Grècques et Romaines* (1733), *Les Éléments* (1734), and *Iphigénie en Tauride* (1734). Blondy also appeared as a dancer in court ballets composed by his colleague Claude Ballon, and he choreographed some ballets at the Jesuit Collège Louis-le-Grand, including *Le Ballet de la Paix* (de Ryswick; 1698), *Apollon Législateur* (with Pecour, 1711), *Le Ballet de la Paix* (d'Utrecht; 1713) *Le Tableau Allegorique des Moeurs* (1714), *L'Empire de la Sagesse* (1715), and *L'Empire de la Mode* (with Malter the elder, 1731).

As dance master, Blondy is known to have taught the prince of Conti and Mademoiselle de Montpensier, the dowager queen of Spain. However, his best student was Marie Camargo. Perhaps out of sympathy for his uncle Beauchamps, who is reputed to have developed the system of dance notation for which Raoul-Auger Feuillet took credit, Blondy is said to have forbidden his pupils to study Feuillet's *Chorégraphie.* Blondy was listed among the dance academicians in 1719, when Ballon was chancellor of the Académie Royale de Danse.

On 7 May 1701 Blondy married the daughter of a captain of archers, Marie-Nicole Thérèse Dugast, who was still a minor. Two daughters, Catherine and Angelique, were born of this union. Blondy is also known to have had an illegitimate daughter, Mademoiselle d'Azincourt, who had a fleeting, if not too glorious, career at the Paris Opera.

Blondy died a well-off and well-considered man, an unusual fate for a dancer of his time. His obituary nevertheless reminded *Le Mercure* readers that he was "advantageously replaced at the Opera by Dupré, this incomparable dancer who unites all the perfections."

BIBLIOGRAPHY
Astier, Régine. "Pierre Beauchamps and the Ballets de Collège." *Dance Chronicle* 6.2 (1983).
Despréaux, Jean-Étienne. *Mes passe-temps: Chansons suivies de l'art de la danse.* Vol. 2. Paris, 1806.
Ferguson, Ian. "Notes on the Blondy Family." *The Dancing Times* (February 1983): 368–369.
Mercure de France (January 1720): 197–198; (February 1720): 182, 186; (April 1729): 776–777; (August 1739): 185. The last is an obituary.
Noverre, Jean-Georges. *Lettres sur la danse, sur les ballets et les arts,* vol. 4, *Observations sur la construction d'une salle de l'Opéra de Paris et programmes de ballets.* St. Petersburg, 1804.
Parfaict, François, and Claude Parfaict. *Histoire manuscrite de l'Académie Royale de Musique.* Paris, n.d. Manuscript located in Paris, Bibliothèque Nationale, fr.12355.
Rameau, Pierre. *Le maître à danser.* Paris, 1725. Translated by Cyril W. Beaumont as *The Dancing Master* (London, 1931).
Winter, Marian Hannah. *The Pre-Romantic Ballet.* London, 1974.
RÉGINE ASTIER

BLUEBELL, MISS (Margaret Kelly; born 24 June 1912 in Dublin), dancer, choreographer, and administrator, founder of the Bluebell dance troupes. Bluebells, or Bluebell Girls, are tall and slender, usually British, and wear feathered headdresses, jeweled G-strings, silver high-heeled shoes, tan fishnet tights, and little else beyond their gleaming smiles. Often they become Bluebells because they have grown too tall for classical ballet. They have been chosen not just for dancing ability but for their ability to project a distinct personality. Since the 1930s, they have been an institution in Paris, their traditional home, and elsewhere on the world's supper entertainment circuit.

Their founder, the remarkable Miss Bluebell, was born Margaret Kelly in poverty in Dublin, Ireland. She never knew her parents. At three weeks she was fostered to Mary Murphy, a spinster, who raised her. A doctor, impressed by the infant's striking blue eyes, nicknamed her "Bluebell." After the Easter Uprising of 1916, Mary Murphy moved to Liverpool, England, to the West Derby district, and worked as a hospital ward maid. At the age of eight, Bluebell began dancing lessons to help strengthen her frail physique and was found to have a remarkable aptitude. Her first professional appearance was in a pantomime, *Babes in the Wood,* at Newquay, Cornwall, in southwest England, when she was twelve. At fourteen, she joined a touring Scottish concert party, the Hot Jocks, and nine months later auditioned for Alfred Jackson, who ran several troupes of dancers in European cities. Bluebell became one of a thirty-strong precision line—The Jackson Girls—at the Scala Theater in Berlin.

The Jackson Girls performed for five months of the year at the Scala and toured during the other months. Bluebell danced in Copenhagen, Budapest, Barcelona, and at the London Coliseum. In 1930, Jackson sent her to Paris as a summer replacement at the Folies-Bergère, the international mecca of music hall entertainment, celebrated for its *mannequins nus.* The wholesome Jackson Girls were carefully segregated from the nude showgirls and lived in conventlike quarters. In 1931, Jackson made Bluebell dance captain at the Folies, but the financial crisis of that year caused his association with the theater to be terminated, and he was replaced by the American Buddy Bradley and his troupe.

Bluebell parted from Jackson, and after an unfortunate interlude at the Casino de Paris, was asked to form her own dance line at the Folies by Paul Derval, its administrator. After a brush with Mistinguett, the temperamental Folies star, Bluebell moved to cine-variety at the Paramount, and her new team, "Les Blue Bell Paramount Girls," became the sensation of Paris. Noting that Bradley used tall girls, she had made hers even taller, at least five feet, nine inches, a policy she adhered to throughout her career. No longer dancing, she became a full-time administrator and accepted Derval's invitation to form a second troupe for the Folies, an engagement that lasted until World War II. Other Bluebell dance companies had toured most European countries during the 1930s, with the exception of Nazi Germany.

In March 1939, Bluebell married Marcel Leibovici, a Romanian musician who was half-Jewish, and he became her business manager. When World War II began, her troupes were disbanded and the British girls were sent home. Only a team in Italy remained, but when Mussolini allied with Hitler in 1940, some of the British girls were imprisoned. During the 1940 Nazi invasion of France, Bluebell's husband left Paris for the south; she was interned for several months but was eventually able to claim neutrality as an Irish citizen. Her husband was arrested, however, in Marseille and sent to a concentration camp. Later he escaped, and Bluebell hid him in an attic until the liberation in 1944, facing the risk of execution if caught. She was repeatedly asked to mount shows for German troops but always declined.

After the war, Bluebell severed her association with Derval, who had toed an anti-Semitic line during the Nazi occupation of France, and joined the Lido, opened in 1946 by Joseph and Louis Clerico. New Bluebell troupes were recruited and began touring again, spreading farther around the world. In the 1950s, Las Vegas was impressed by a Bluebell line performing at the Stardust. In the 1960s and 1970s, Bluebell became responsible for the dancers in the spectacular Las Vegas shows staged by Donn Arden at the MGM Grand, now Bally's. She was trapped in the hotel during a disastrous fire in November 1980 and narrowly escaped with her life.

Bluebell had some five hundred dancers in her employ throughout the world, but her operational center was the Lido in Las Vegas, which in 1977 was remodeled as the most spectacular nightclub in the world, with an ice rink, pool, elevators, moving platforms, and a sinking dining floor. Still active, each Bluebell Girls show is designed to run for four years—as a nonstop kaleidoscope of color, music, and light—designed to appeal to patrons of any nationality.

Bluebell continued actively until after her eightieth birthday, when declining health necessitated her retirement.

[*See also* Music Hall, *article on* British Traditions.]

BIBLIOGRAPHY
Castle, Charles. *The Folies-Bergère.* London, 1982.
Perry, George. "Fifty Years in the Front Line." *London Sunday Times Magazine* (23 August 1981).
Perry, George. *Bluebell.* London, 1986.

GEORGE PERRY

BLUM, RENÉ (born 13 March 1878 in Paris, died 28 September 1942 in transit to Auschwitz), French impresario. Blum was the youngest son of a Jewish family from Alsace that settled in Paris. His elder brother, Léon, became the first Socialist premier of France in 1936. A cultured man of the highest integrity, René Blum was coeditor of the literary magazine *Gil Blas* in 1910 and of *La section d'or,* devoted to cubist art, in 1912. He was one of the founders of Le Club des Amis du Septième Art (the Ciné-Club de France) and helped to organize the influential Paris Exposition des Arts Décoratifs in 1925. During World War I he did valuable work in preserving French art treasures.

After a pilot season in 1923 Blum became director of plays and operettas at the Théâtre de Monte-Carlo in 1924. He was appointed director of ballet at that theater in 1929. Toward the end of 1931, with Colonel Wassily de Basil, Blum launched the Ballets Russes de Monte Carlo, of which he was artistic director until 1935, when disagreements with de Basil came to a head. Blum then formed the René Blum Ballets de Monte Carlo, a company that was renamed Ballet Russe de Monte Carlo in 1938, after Blum entered into a sponsorship agreement with World Art, Inc. (subsequently known as Universal Art, Inc.).

Blum visited the United States in 1940 but returned to Paris, where he was arrested on 12 December 1941 during a roundup of Jewish intellectuals under the German occupation. He was detained at Compiègne and Drancy until 23 September 1942, when he was included in a convoy for Auschwitz. He died during the journey.

[*See also* Ballets Russes de Monte Carlo.]

BIBLIOGRAPHY
Bernard, Marcelle Tristan, et al. *René Blum, 1878-1942.* Paris, 1950.
Davis, Janet Rowson. "René Blum: A Centenary Tribute." *The Dancing Times* (March 1978): 330–331.
Davis, Janet Rowson. "René Blum, 1878–1942." In *Proceedings of the Eleventh Annual Conference, Society of Dance History Scholars, North Carolina School of the Arts, February 12–14, 1988,* compiled by Christena L. Schlundt. Riverside, Calif., 1988.
Detaille, Georges, and Georges Mulys. *Les Ballets de Monte Carlo, 1911–1944.* Paris, 1954.
García-Márquez, Vicente. *The Ballets Russes: Colonel de Basil's Ballets Russes de Monte Carlo, 1932–1952.* New York, 1990.
Huisman, Georges. "René Blum." *Ballet Annual* 7 (1953): 49–50.

KATHRINE SORLEY WALKER

BODENWIESER, GERTRUD (born 3 February 1890 in Vienna, Austria, died 10 November 1959 in Sydney, Australia), choreographer and dancer. Bodenwieser studied classical ballet with Carl Godlewski between 1905 and 1910. In about 1910 she began to develop her own modern dance style, which was influenced by François Delsarte, Émile Jaques-Dalcroze, Rudolf Laban, and Isadora Duncan. The music and painting of the early 1920s inspired Bodenwieser, as did the findings of Sigmund Freud. His development of psychoanalysis was the impetus for her *Dreams—Dream of Fear and Dream of Desire.* Her *Burning Bush* was based on a painting of that name, by expressionist painter Oskar Kokoschka (1886–1980).

Bodenwieser made her first public appearance as a dancer in Vienna on 5 May 1919 in a program of six dances that she had choreographed: "Burletta" and "Silhouette" (music by Otto Reinhold); "Hysterie" (music by Max Reger); "Spanish Dance" (music by Anton Rubinstein); "Cake-Walk" (music by Claude Debussy); and "Groteske" (music by Sergei Rachmaninoff). Bodenwieser had greater success with her dance group, founded in 1922, than with her solo dance evenings. Her all-female group was made up exclusively of her students. At first she taught only in her own school in the Vienna Konzerthaus, but in 1920 she began teaching mime and dance at the Vienna State Academy of Music and Dramatic Art, where she became a professor in 1928. In 1934, when plans were made for a government examination for dance teachers, Bodenwieser worked out the curriculum. In 1938, with the German annexation of Austria, her teaching and creative work in Europe was ended for political reasons and she was obliged to emigrate. She took her group to Australia where she continued to teach, choreograph, and direct a company that consisted increasingly of Australian dancers.

Bodenwieser's early major works include the 1924 group dance *Dämon Maschine* (Demon Machine), a study of the dehumanizing aspects of mechanization, set to the music of Lisa M. Mayers. This work won first prize in a 1931 dance competition in Florence and was performed when her troupe toured Japan in 1934 and the United States in 1936. Hilde Holger, who performed with Bodenwieser, has described *Dämon Maschine* thus:

> We were four dancers who formed a solid group, with Bodenwieser dancing the part of the Demon. She dominated us four human beings till each of us became a part of a machine—thrusting, pushing, screwing, till we automatically stopped. This kept the large audience of the Great Koncerthaus in Vienna spellbound.

Bodenwieser's *Wer will Frau Wahrheit herbergen?* (Who Wants to Shelter Madame Truth?, 1930) was the first of her six dance dramas based on an old German play by Hans Sachs.

Europe was already burdened by the political pressure of National Socialism (in power from 1933 to 1945 in Germany), when in 1936 she choreographed her second dance drama, *Die Masken des Luzifer* (The Masks of Lucifer). Intrigue, terror, and hatred were its principal themes, reflected in the music of Marcel Lorber, a pianist and composer who had worked with Bodenwieser for many years.

In May 1938 Bodenwieser, her composer, and six dancers traveled to South America to appear in Bogotá. A second group of her students traveled with the London Casino Revue to Australia. In 1939 Bodenwieser went to New Zealand, where, during a demonstration performance before the YWCA Physical Education Committee, she defined creative dance as "expressing an adventure of the soul in a given form." In August 1939 Bodenwieser and her students were reunited in Sydney. She quickly founded a school and by September 1942 was able to present a dance evening exclusively with her own students. Using Sydney as her base, she made numerous tours throughout Australia and South Africa in the course of her career.

Cain and Abel (1940), with music by Lorber, was one of the first works Bodenwieser choreographed after emigrating. It was influenced by human losses and by impressions of her new homeland. Her fourth dance drama, *O World*, with music by Alexander Tcherepnin, was created shortly before the end of the war, in 1945, and was centered around quotations from works by the Hindu philosopher Jiddu Krishnamurti.

Bodenwieser's first satirical dance drama was *The Life of the Insects* (1949). Her last and perhaps most important work was *Errand into the Maze* (1954), with music by Gian-Carlo Menotti, in which she turned her back on symbolism and the use of allegorical figures and concentrated on life and humanity.

BIBLIOGRAPHY

Bodenwieser, Gertrud. *The New Dance*. Sydney, 1969.
Denton, Meg Abbie, and Genevieve Shaw. "Gertrud Bodenwieser: *The Demon Machine.*" *Dance Notation Journal* 4 (Spring 1986): 21–29.
Forster, Marianne. "Reconstructing European Modern Dance: Bodenwieser, Chladek, Leeder, Kreutzberg, Hoyer." In *Dance Reconstructed*, edited by Barbara Palfy. New Brunswick, N.J., 1993.
Grayburn, Patricia, ed. *Gertrud Bodenwieser: A Celebratory Monograph on the 100th Anniversary of Her Birth*. Guildford, 1990.
Lämmel, Rudolf. *Der moderne Tanz*. Berlin, 1928.
MacTavish, Shona Dunlop. *An Ecstasy of Purpose: The Life and Art of Gertrud Bodenwieser*. Dunedin, N.Z., 1987.

GABRIELE SCHACHERL

BODENWIESER TECHNIQUE.

BODENWIESER TECHNIQUE. All exercises used in the Bodenwieser system, as developed by Gertrud Bodenwieser, were intended to lead to the harmonic development of the body, giving it the highest degree of strength, elasticity, suppleness, and endurance. Advanced students and teachers of the system were expected to know the value of the exercises performed. Exercises designed to stretch the spinal column, counteract lordosis and kyphosis, and strengthen legs, feet, and abdominal muscles were included. The technique was intended to improve general health as well as the artistic development of the individual, and it was designed to suit children, adolescents, and adults alike.

Classes led to the analysis of movement, starting with a simple movement based on the laws of Rudolf Laban, François Delsarte, Émile Jaques-Dalcroze, and other great teachers of natural dance styles. Bodenwieser understood these principles so completely that she has been considered the finest interpreter of Laban principles ever to present his philosophy in theater form, rising high above the often banal and insensitive approach used by other disciples of this great master of movement.

Having taught a basic movement until the degree of perfection she required was achieved, Bodenwieser would then build onto the basic structure an increasingly complex series of variations; linking steps would turn a static composition into a dynamic one, leading from there into the advanced jumping and leaping style for which much of her choreography was famous. Classes usually ended with improvisation and compositional dance practice.

Students were expected to know the history of dance, the theory of music, and folk and national dance steps, which were often incorporated into class in a stylized form. Visits to art galleries, concerts, drama theater, and other dance performances were part of the careful preparation of each dancer. Above all, Bodenwieser believed in developing the personality of each artist, which she would then use within the framework of her masterpieces for the stage.

Turned-out feet were never allowed in the Bodenwieser technique, although turning out from the hip in certain jumping and leaping movements was required. Change-of-weight movements, separate exercises for the different parts of the body (now known as isolations) with special attention to pelvic and hip movements, arm movements involving circles, figure eights (very much taking into account the Delsartean law of successive movement), turning and jumping preparation and training, balance exercises, body waves (undulations), realization of music, falls, impulse, and solo and group improvisation and dance composition all somehow fit into a ninety-minute class that, however exhausting, would leave the student exhilarated and light of heart and mind.

The technique, as well as several of Bodenwieser's choreographies based on it, has been perpetuated by successive generations of protégées—in particular, Shona Dunlop McTavish in Australia, Bettina Vernon and Evelyn Ippen in Europe, and Carol Brown in England.

BIBLIOGRAPHY
Bodenwieser, Gertrud. *The New Dance.* Sydney, 1969.
Forster, Marianne. "Reconstructing European Modern Dance: Bodenwieser, Chladek, Leeder, Kreutzberg, Hoyer." In *Dance Reconstructed,* edited by Barbara Palfy. New Brunswick, N.J., 1993.
MacTavish, Shona Dunlop. *An Ecstasy of Purpose: The Life and Art of Gertrud Bodenwieser.* Dunedin, N.Z., 1987.

DENISE PUTTOCK

BODIN, LOUISE (Lucia Geoffroy, also spelled Geffroy or Joffroy; *fl.* 1747–1764), Viennese dancer and singer. Born of Italian parents, Louise Bodin was active in Vienna during the eighteenth century, when ballet had won a permanent place in European musical theater, largely owing to the work of Franz Hilverding. In 1752 Louise and her husband, Pierre Bodin, joined the city's Burgtheater as principal dancers; Pierre (or Pietro) had been dancing in Naples since 1747. Louise also was hired as a singer; she was particularly successful in the Komische Oper, which was very popular at the time.

A celebrated ballerina—her salary was three times that of composer and contemporary Christoph Willibald Gluck—Louise Bodin became the focal point of ballet in Vienna as a result of her liaison with Count Giacomo Durazzo, general manager of the Hoftheater. Her subsequent partnership with Gaspero Angiolini culminated in his ballet *Don Juan* (1761), set to music by Gluck, in which she danced the principal female role.

In March 1764, Louise Bodin left Vienna with the count. The date and place of her death are unknown.

BIBLIOGRAPHY
Brown, Bruce Alan. *Gluck and the French Theatre in Vienna.* Oxford, 1991.
Raab, Riki. "Das k. k. Hofballett unter Maria Theresia, 1740–1780." *Jahrbuch der Gesellschaft für Wiener Theaterforschung, 1950–1951* (1952).
Winkler, Gerhard. "Das Wiener Ballett von Noverre bis Fanny Elßler." Ph.D. diss., University of Vienna, 1967.
Zechmeister, Gustav. *Die Wiener Theater nächst der Burg und nächst dem Kärntnertor von 1747 bis 1776.* Vienna, 1971.

GUNHILD OBERZAUCHER-SCHÜLLER
Translated from German

BODY POSITIONS. *For discussion of body positions in ballet, see* Ballet Technique, *article on* Body Positions.

BODY THERAPIES. [*To survey various ways of optimizing body movement for therapeutic purposes, this entry comprises six articles:*

An Overview
Alexander Technique
Bartenieff Fundamentals
Feldenkrais Method
Ideokinesis
Skinner Releasing Technique

The first article presents common elements in movement-related treatments. The companion articles focus on five popular types of therapy. For related discussion, see Dance Medicine *and* Kinesiology.]

An Overview

The vertical relationship of the body to gravity is fundamental to our images of dancing and to our concept of a human being. Body therapy is a term coined in the 1970s to group a variety of specialized approaches to body education that deal with improving the adaptation of the body to gravity and fostering movement efficiency and ease. The disparate approaches that can be defined as body therapies developed quite independently of each other and do not necessarily share techniques or even assumptions about what causes dysfunction in body usage. What they share are teaching methods that emphasize self-awareness and self-direction, a concern with underlying principles of movement and learning, perception of the body as a system and its movement as a pattern or organization of responses, and an assumption that the body and the mind are intimately interconnected.

Beginning with the period of cultural change now referred to as the "sixties"—the countercultural and sexual revolution, the new interest in Eastern philosophies and disciplines, and the development of the human-potential movement in psychology—there has been a rapid multiplying of body-related educational and therapeutic methods. Once separate, even antagonistic, schools of thought have been combined and recombined as individual practitioners develop their own applications and certain values and ideas are transmitted without necessarily being incorporated in a specific school of thought.

Founders. The roots of most body therapy practice can be found in the methods and ideas of a few people whose work developed in the last hundred years and who in some way—through writing, teaching, or the establishment of training programs—institutionalized their methods. These people include Frederick Matthias Alexander (The Alexander Technique); Irmgard Bartenieff (Bartenieff Fundamentals); Moshe Feldenkrais (The Feldenkrais Method: Awareness Through Movement and Functional Integration); Alexander Lowen (Bioenergetics); Charlotte Selver (Sensory Awareness); Lulu Sweigard (Ideokinesis); and Ida Rolf (Structural Integration). In turn, the sources of these methods, through the education of their founders and their mentors—Wilhelm Reich, Rudolf Laban, Mabel Elsworth Todd, and Elsa Gindler—reach into European and American science, psychology, physical education, and dance in the first half of the twentieth century. Significantly, the field of body therapy still attracts, can even be defined by, people who want to integrate these fields or, in turn, want to apply body-therapy knowledge in them. There is also a tradition of self-education that derives from some of these original innovators—and many of them held convictions that went against the conventional wisdom of their times.

Their times were ripe for a new perspective on the body. Humankind's perception of itself was being altered by natural science, through the theories of Charles Darwin, and by psychology through the psychoanalytic theories of Sigmund Freud. Ideas of physical education and dress reform for women were beginning to assert themselves around the turn of the twentieth century, and modern dance, symbolized by the barefoot, uncorseted Isadora Duncan, was growing in the United States and Europe. The role of the body as the mere vehicle for the higher faculties was being brought into question.

Reich and Lowen. Wilhelm Reich, a disciple of Freud, was perhaps the first person in the new field of psychoanalysis to consider the body important to diagnosis and cure. He used the phrase "body armoring" to describe the chronic, patterned contraction of the musculature to repress unacceptable emotion. His analysis of character is concerned with the way different types of psychological problems are revealed in the state of the body, and his therapeutic method involved the physical release of emotionally caused tensions.

Alexander Lowen, a student and patient of Reich in the 1940s, became a physician; he further developed Reich's concepts into a method called Bioenergetics, which incorporates direct work on the body into the practice of psychotherapy. The ideas of Reich and Lowen may seem more applicable to the field of *dance therapy*, defined by the American Dance Therapy Association as "the psychotherapeutic use of movement to further the emotional and physical integration of the individual." The physical practices of Bioenergetics were developed in conjunction with psychiatry and are used as a means to a psychotherapeutic goal, while body therapy is construed to be educational. However, Lowen developed Bioenergetics exercises partially to solve the problem of maintaining body balance after the end of therapy, and the concerns such as breathing and the flow of energy through the body are similar to those in other body therapies. Important also are the ideas that tension and dysfunction may have an emotional source and, conversely, that changes in tension, function, and body alignment carry with them changes in sensation, feeling, and self-image. These changes are important to the kind of learning body therapists favor, even though body therapy begins with the functioning of the body.

Rolf. Ida Rolf (1896–1979) was a chemist with a doctorate from Columbia University; she studied the structure of phospholipids before personal health problems turned her attention to the relationship of structure and function in the human body. She felt that in human bodies, as in the organic substances she viewed under her microscope, there was a specific organization to structure that determined or constituted, in a sense, behavior. She posited that structural distortion and muscle imbalance, caused as much by accidents as any psychological source, could be corrected by direct manipulation of the connective tissue between the muscles and the bones. The goal is to bring the body into a more structurally efficient relationship with gravity. Her therapy, Structural Integration (commonly known as Rolfing), was the method that evolved. It is traditionally performed in a series of ten specific sessions—unlike other body therapies, which do not specify the length of time for study or which favor ongoing study. While most body therapy uses touch, the touch is usually gentle and guiding. Rolfing involves strong manipulation. It does share fundamental values with other body therapies, however. In Rolf's words, "It is through the creation of an appropriate *relationship* to three-dimensional space that we can be freed to a higher and more truly human functioning. It, therefore, becomes imperative not only to study the effect of gravity, but also to understand structural relations in people in terms of gravity" (see Ida Rolf, "Gravity: An Unexplored Factor in the More Human Use of Human Beings," in Kogan, 1980).

Todd and Sweigard. The efficient use of structure was also of great interest to Mabel Elsworth Todd and her protégée Lulu Sweigard. Todd was a professor at Teachers College, Columbia University, and the author of *The Thinking Body* (1937). "The ideas expressed in this book," she wrote in the preface, "have been derived from more than thirty years' experience in teaching bodily economy. They are based on the concurrent study of physics, mechanics, anatomy, and physiology. . . . Mechanical balance is provided for the organism, else it could not have survived its primary encounter with gravity, momentum, and inertia as they were met upon emergence from the water." Her teaching was concerned with "the psychophysical mechanisms involved in the organic reaction to the problem of resisting gravity in the upright position." Todd's interest in the psychophysical aspects of movement led her to develop a teaching method in which efficient use of the body was activated not by conscious control of muscles but through stimulating the nervous system with imagination based on knowledge of the underlying anatomy.

Among Todd's students was Lulu Sweigard (1895-1974), who organized and further developed Todd's ideas as a teacher at the Juilliard School in New York and in her book, *Human Movement Potential: Its Ideokinetic Facilitation* (1974). Convinced of the effectiveness of Todd's teaching, Sweigard set herself the task of validating the results through research. What she found were "nine lines of movement," nine specific ways, in location and direction, that the mechanical balance, or alignment, of the body was improved. The term *ideokinesis* links the two key processes of her method: *ideo* means "the idea of the stimulator of the process"; *kinesis* means "the physical movement induced by the stimulation of the muscles" (Martha Myers, "Todd, Sweigard, and Ideokinesis," in Myers and Pierpont, 1983). Ideokinesis is practiced in the "constructive rest position," which was designed to minimize the effects of gravity and the strain on the muscles. The teacher often uses touch to specify the location of the imagined action and to indicate its direction.

Feldenkrais. The Israeli Moshe Feldenkrais (1904–1984) was a physicist (with undergraduate degrees in mathematics and engineering and a black belt in judo) before an injury to his knee turned his attention to self-cure. Study of anatomy, neurophysiology, learning theory, and biochemistry contributed to the evolution of Functional Integration, in which the practitioner works one-on-one with the client using gentle manipulation, and Awareness Through Movement, which is taught verbally in group lessons. Feldenkrais's first book, *Body and Mature Behavior,* was published in 1949, and he taught and trained many teachers in the United States and Israel.

"Feldenkrais's approach to reeducation emphasizes: drawing on early developmental patterns of human mobility; providing more accurate data on spatial relationships of parts of the body; bringing habitual motor patterns to conscious attention; developing a more articulate spine; and establishing more organic breathing patterns" (see Martha Myers, "Moshe Feldenkrais and Awareness through Movement," in Myers and Pierpont, 1983). Feldenkrais was particularly interested in the elements of strain, habit, attention, and awareness in learning. Awareness Through Movement lessons include minute motions of one or perhaps two joints of the body to focus the students' attention on the most subtle changes in the quality of the movement and in the responses of the rest of the body. Feldenkrais considered the kind of learning-to-learn that can occur through the perception of movement patterns as a blueprint for learning in general:

> There are few intellectual processes that can be divorced from the awareness of being awake. Being awake means knowing if we are standing, sitting, or lying. It means that we know how we are oriented relative to gravity. When thinking in words, we are logical and think in familiar categories that we have thought, dreamed, read, heard, or said sometime before. Learning to think in patterns of relationships, in sensations divorced from the fixity of words, allows us to find hidden resources and the ability to make new patterns, to carry over patterns in relationship from one discipline to another.
>
> (Feldenkrais, 1981)

Gindler and Jacoby, Selver and Brooks. Sensory Awareness, the work of Charlotte Selver and her colleague Charles Brooks, originated in Germany. Elsa Gindler and Heinrich Jacoby were Selver's teachers in Berlin before World War II, when schools of breathing, dance, and gymnastics abounded. While most written material by Gindler and Jacoby was lost in the bombing of Berlin, the roots of their work can be traced back to a student of François Delsarte, Genevieve Stebbins, the author of *Dynamic Breathing and Harmonic Gymnastics* (1892). Selver emigrated to the United States in 1940, where she has been allied with the Esalen Institute in California and associated with Alan Watts and Frederick Perls.

Sensory Awareness is fundamentally concerned with developing human potential and self-expression, and puts at the center of its practice the kinesthetic awareness that either underlies or is produced by other methods. Selver and Brooks write: "We build upon sensations, whose cultivation has been so long neglected in our education that they no longer come easily. . . . In general, the work may be described as the gradual unfolding and cultivation of sensibility, of greater range and delicacy of feeling, which brings about concurrently the awakening of our innate energies. This we practice through the *activity of sensing*" (see Charles Brooks and Charlotte Selver, "Sensory Awareness: Theory and Practice," in Kogan, 1980). During simple activities, such as lying down, sitting, standing, and walking, and in exercises focusing on touch and breathing, "we gradually sort out what is perception and what is image."

Laban and Bartenieff. The blossoming of physical education and modern dance in Germany during the first part of the twentieth century also influenced Irmgard Bartenieff (1900–1981), the creator of Bartenieff Fundamentals. In Germany, Bartenieff was a dancer and a student of Rudolf Laban, whose theories about the dynamics and spatial organization of movement continue to affect the fields of dance notation, education, and therapy. Bartenieff became a physical therapist in New York City after leaving Germany at the start of World War II. The Laban perspective she brought to the scientific knowledge of physical therapy generated the development of Bartenieff Fundamentals. The Fundamentals developed within the broader context of the development of Laban's ideas in the United States, first at the Dance Notation Bureau and then at the Laban/Bartenieff Institute of Movement Studies. The name Laban Movement Analysis is used to incorporate the related areas of Effort, Space Harmony, Bartenieff Fundamentals, and Labanotation. [*See also* Labanotation; Laban Principles of Movement Analysis; *and the entry on Laban.*]

When Bartenieff worked with polio patients, she found that Laban's ideas about the three-dimensional organization of movement in space could explain the disruption of movement patterns from isolated muscle paralysis, while the physical-therapy model of single joint action could not. Laban's ideas about the importance of intention and dynamics in movement gave Bartenieff ways of motivating and mobilizing her patients.

Bartenieff Fundamentals is a collection of movement principles exemplified in movements and movement combinations that come from physical-therapy exercises and childhood developmental movement patterns. Particular attention is paid to how the movement is done: initiation, spatial intent, breathing, shift of weight, and flow of movement through the body. "Fundamentals is an evolving series of movement sequences that deal with mobiliz-ing the body efficiently in its environment and preparing it to perform as wide a range of movement qualities and shapes as possible" (see Martha Myers, "Irmgard Bartenieff's Fundamentals," in Myers and Pierpont, 1983).

Alexander. Frederick Matthias Alexander (1869–1955) was not a scientist, a physical educator, or a dancer, yet the Alexander Technique was the first to appear of all the methods discussed here and one that has continued to the present day in a direct line of teachers and schools in England and the United States. Alexander, an Australian actor who discovered the principles of his technique from self-observation, is a model of the self-education he promoted and that is a motivating idea in body therapy in general. He defined and wrote about some basic principles of body usage and the attitude that would allow the student to generate such usage for himself.

Primary control is a key principle of the technique. This refers to a particular use of the head and neck in movement of the body, a use that allows a lengthening of the spine in all activity. Other key "directions" stimulate lengthening and widening of the back and freeing of the legs in the hip joints.

Inhibition was the word Alexander used to describe the process by which one decides *not* to perform habitual movement patterns. To Alexander, the key to continual improved usage—and to learning—was the human capacity to respond in new ways, and the technique involves awareness of habitual movement patterns as well as learning to choose new responses. The educator John Dewey and the writer Aldous Huxley were among the students and admirers of Alexander.

Body Therapies and Learning. The methods of developing the use of the body, as discussed here, are all fundamentally different from traditional Western physical education and dance training, which rely on the imitation and repetition of specific exercises and forms. When many people with little previous training and with bodies of all shapes and sizes began to study dance in the 1960s and 1970s, especially in universities in the United States, the body therapies began to be considered useful alternatives in dance and movement education. Where ballet, for example, selects its talent young and weeds out the unfit over time, body therapy is democratic; it assumes unused capacities in all people and offers them a substratum for any physical activity. These methods are also used by dancers to overcome specific physical problems and as a philosophical basis to more traditional methods of dance training.

Body therapy takes as its premise that movement restrictions and inhibitions begin as children are socialized and learn to adapt their body behavior to the demands of other people and to their physical environments. Body-therapy techniques reawaken the kinesthetic sense so that students may learn to distinguish between what they are doing and what they *think* they are doing. Ways of doing this include the common practice of lying down to minimize the normal effects of gravity, breath control, drawing attention to sensation, doing movements in a small range or very slowly, and using touch to aid the student in perceiving the structure and orientation of the body and to suggest how the use of the body might change.

The developmental movement patterns of early childhood—the way a child progresses from lying down, to sitting, creeping, crawling, standing, and walking—are also important to the work of body therapists. These coordinations, along with the accompanying breathing patterns, are the basis of subsequent motor activities and cognitive development. In some methods, developmental coordinations are incorporated in the movements; in others, the progression of the human body to vertical—both ontogenetically and phylogenetically—is basic to the theories of how that vertical posture might be improved. The issue at the center of body therapy is how human beings—animals standing on their hind legs—can best adapt to that precarious and flexible position by using that which sets them apart from other animals, their brain.

Body therapy, no matter what specific method, looks at the body as an integrated system and movement as a pattern of relationships among interconnected parts and functions. The perspective that informs body therapy is general rather than focused, rather like that of the city planner, who looks at the whole, while the developer looks only at the plot on which he wishes to build.

Concerned with a systemic effect, body-therapy practice bypasses the cerebral cortex and conscious control of the muscles by using methods such as imagery and touch that directly affect the nervous system. In most methods, there is an emphasis on not-doing: on *not* willing, pushing, or straining to achieve a correct position or pose. In body-therapy methods, the emphasis is on paying attention, allowing, and discovering. Such practice requires and teaches self-awareness as well as an attitude toward learning that is quite different from the traditional trying to accomplish.

Such an attitude, although learned through physical practice, is not confined to it. The values fostered by body therapy are, as well, central to the purpose of movement in education: to develop the mind's capacity to perceive relationships, discriminate, conceptualize, and organize, and to build trust in oneself and a sense of mastery over one's actions. Body therapy encourages choice, responsibility, and individual validity. If one accepts the notion that how one learns something shapes what is learned, then one can imagine body therapy influencing not only education, but dance style and aesthetics.

BIBLIOGRAPHY

Alexander, Frederick Matthias. *The Resurrection of the Body.* New York, 1974.

Barteineff, Irmgard, and Dori Lewis. *Body Movement: Coping with the Environment.* New York, 1980.

Brooks, Charles V. W. *Sensory Awareness: The Rediscovery of Experiencing.* New York, 1974.

Dowd, Irene. *Taking Root to Fly.* New York, 1981.

Exiner, Johanna, et al. *Dance Therapy Redefined.* Springfield, Ill., 1994.

Feldenkrais, Moshe. *The Elusive Obvious.* Cupertino, Calif., 1981.

Kogan, Gerald, ed. *Your Body Works: A Guide to Health, Energy, and Balance.* Berkeley, 1980.

Lowen, Alexander. *Bioenergetics.* New York, 1975.

Myers, Martha, and Margaret Pierpont. "Body Therapies and the Modern Dancer." *Dance Magazine* (August 1983).

Payne, Helen, ed. *Dance Movement Therapy: Theory and Practice.* London, 1992.

Rolf, Ida. *Rolfing: The Integration of Human Structures.* New York, 1977.

Sweigard, Lulu E. *Human Movement Potential: Its Ideokinetic Facilitation.* New York, 1974.

Todd, Mabel Elsworth. *The Thinking Body.* New York, 1937.

Youngerman, Suzanne. *Body Education/Therapy Systems: Introductory Bibliography.* New York, 1980.

MARGARET PIERPONT

Alexander Technique

The Alexander Technique is based on the discoveries of Frederick Matthias Alexander (1869–1955). It is a means of noninterference with the postural reflexes during activity, which can be self-applied to obtain greater ease and flexibility.

An actor, Alexander suffered from hoarseness when performing. Doctors were unable to help him. After months of self-study he observed that as he started to speak he pulled his head back and down, depressed his larynx, and sucked in breath through his mouth. Trying to eliminate each of these habits separately, he recognized that if he did not pull his head back and down, all of the other symptoms decreased and his voice improved. Noticing that his entire body was affected by this movement of his head, he hypothesized a dynamic relationship between the head and the body in movement. His method of preventing interference with this dynamic relationship has come to be known as the Alexander Technique.

The technique must be experienced to be understood. Through verbal instructions and a light touch, an Alexander teacher guides the student's head in a forward and upward direction in relation to the body, encouraging the rest of the body to follow. This exceedingly small forward and upward movement changes the balance of the head so that the muscles of the neck release, producing in turn a lengthening of the torso and limbs and a widening of the trunk as the student begins an activity. This prevents the inevitable pattern of excess tension in the rest of the body that results from pulling the head back and down. The effect is facilitation and strengthening of the righting reflexes, better coordination, and easier breathing, along with clearer perception of performance and of the self in relation to the environment. As the kinesthetic sense improves and attention expands, the student can perceive bad habits more clearly and, once observed, can restructure them as desired.

It is this ability to change that has benefited many performers in the arts. Dancers find this technique a means to more flexibility, better balance and control, more energy, greater dynamic range, fewer injuries, and longer performance life. Application of Alexander's discoveries can radically change the teaching of dance by providing new tools for the study of all movement.

Research verifying Alexander's discoveries was performed by Frank Pierce Jones at Tufts University and is summarized in his *Body Awareness in Action* (1979).

More than two thousand teachers of the technique and at least sixty-five teacher-training courses are located around the world. The first Society of Teachers of the Alexander Technique was formed in England (STAT). Today there are affiliated Societies in Canada (CANSTAT), the United States (NASTAT), Australia (AUSTAT), Denmark (DFLAT), Germany (GLAT), Israel (ISTAT), South Africa (SASTAT), Switzerland (SVLAT), The Netherlands, and Brazil (ABAT). Alexander Technique International (ATI) is an organization of teachers, students, and friends of the technique who embrace the diversity of the international Alexander community and work to promote international dialogue.

The Alexander Technique Association of New England (ATA) was formed in 1975, after the death of Dr. Frank Pierce Jones, to encourage further scientific and scholarly research into the technique and to maintain and develop the Jones collection of material about the technique, which is housed in the Archives for Special Collections at Tufts University in Cambridge, Massachusetts.

BIBLIOGRAPHY

Alexander, F. Matthias. *Man's Supreme Inheritance* (England, 1910). Long Beach, Calif., 1988.

Alexander, F. Matthias. *Constructive Conscious Control of the Individual.* New York, 1923.

Alexander, F. Matthias. *The Use of the Self.* New York, 1932, 1984.

Alexander, F. Matthias. *The Universal Constant in Living.* New York, 1941.

Alexander, F. Matthias. *Alexander Technique: The Essential Writings of F. Matthias Alexander* (formerly titled *The Resurrection of the Body*), edited by Edward Maisel. New York, 1969, 1974, 1990.

Jones, Frank Pierce. *Body Awareness in Action*, Rev. ed. New York, 1979.

LUCY VENABLE

Bartenieff Fundamentals

Irmgard Bartenieff founded an original approach to movement analysis and movement training based on her experience as a dancer, choreographer, student of Rudolf Laban, physical therapist, research pioneer in cross-cultural analysis of dance style, and prime mover in the field of dance therapy. She developed the Bartenieff Fundamentals in the 1950s in part out of her work in the rehabilitation of polio patients, to which she applied Laban's concepts of dynamism, three-dimensional movement, and mobilization. To this basic Laban framework, which looked at the elements of movement and expressivity in terms of effort and space, Bartenieff added an awareness of the importance of effective body patterning.

Bartenieff Fundamentals is not a system of set exercises; it is an approach to basic body training that deals with principles of anatomical function within a context that encourages personal expression and full psychophysical functioning, viewing both as integral to total body mobilization. Bartenieff's approach always asks, What is the individual actually doing, and how does this differ from what he or she desires to do? The search for a variety of possible new patterns leads to personal insights as well as to more efficient and fluent movement.

Bartenieff said, "Body movement is not a symbol for expression, it *is* the expression. Anatomical and spatial relationships create sequences of effort rhythms with emotional concomitants. The functional and the expressive are one in the human being." While most body therapies stress release of excess tension and efficient joint functioning, few take into account the feelings and emotions expressed by movement. Bartenieff Fundamentals insists on training that goes beyond anatomical function, and views the process as a personal adventure. This leap from the anatomical to the expressive is particularly important for the dancer who wants both to prolong a performance career by maximizing body function, and to enhance emotional projection.

Fundamentals uses the entire framework of Laban movement analysis to develop efficiency and expressiveness in movement. This is accomplished by approaching each new understanding of body function through phrases of movement that incorporate change in the relationships among body, effort, and space. Effort deals with movement quality and taps its emotional resources. Space is seen as an intentional pathway through which movement proceeds to its goal. When anatomical connections, emotions, and spatial intent are coordinated, both dancer and viewer experience movement as a whole.

The technique emphasizes "mobility process" rather than muscle strength. A focus on muscle strength—common in training for dance, sport, and rehabilitation—tends to fragment motion into isolated, repetitive, two-phase movements, such as flexion and extension. Mobility process, however, uses muscle groups in sequence within a whole movement phrase.

Bartenieff's approach pays particular attention to phrasing, and above all to internal preparation for movement and to moments of initiation, since these determine the entire process and the path that a given movement will take. As an action moves from initiation to its main phase, exertion, Fundamentals teaches that the dancer must follow lines in space, and complete the expressive statement, in order to increase mobility. This attitude encourages continual adjustments in weight shift, which are especially important for dancers who repeatedly try to make only "the right shape." Fundamentals also recognizes that each movement creates its own rebound, from which the next movement follows (the Laban principle of exertion/recuperation).

Fundamentals uses basic exercises formulated according to developmental principles (for example, femoral flexion and extension; pelvic shift in the lateral and sagital planes, that is, left-to-right and front-to-back; gradated rotation in the global proximal joints, the hips and shoulders) to establish proper function of the major muscle groups. These basic exercises are then organized into larger movement sequences requiring full interplay of all these components. For example, mobilization of weight shift from the pelvic floor provides security for moving out through space; gradated rotation in the hip joints improves turnout and range of motion.

Fundamentals yields an understanding of broad principles of movement: total body connectedness; breath support that integrates torso and limbs; and dynamic alignment. The system effectively addresses the dancer's needs for balance, alignment, and coordination.

BIBLIOGRAPHY

Bartenieff, Irmgard, Martha Davis, and Forrestine Paulay. *Four Adaptations of Effort Theory in Research and Teaching.* New York, 1970.

Bartenieff, Irmgard, with Martha Davis. *Research Approaches to Movement and Personality.* New York, 1972. See especially, "Effort-Shape Analysis of Movement: The Unity of Expression and Function."

Bartenieff, Irmgard, with Dori Lewis. *Body Movement: Coping with the Environment.* New York, 1980.

Myers, Martha, and Margaret Pierpont. "Body Therapies and the Modern Dancer." *Dance Magazine* 57 (August 1983).

VIDEOTAPE. Peggy Hackney, "Discovering Your Expressive Body: Bartenieff Fundamentals in Dance Training" (1981).

PEGGY HACKNEY

Feldenkrais Method

Born in former Russian Poland in 1904, Moshe Feldenkrais emigrated as a young man to Palestine, afterward studying in France, where he took his doctorate in physics and became an associate of the 1935 Nobel Prize–winning physicist Frédéric Joliot-Curie. Feldenkrais was an outstanding *judoka* (judo black belt) and soccer player until he suffered a serious knee injury. In Britain during World War II, while working on antisubmarine warfare, he consulted a Glasgow surgeon and was told that an op-

eration on his injured knee would have only a fifty-fifty chance of success, so Feldenkrais resolved to teach himself to walk anew. He steeped himself at the same time in the literature on anatomy, physiology, psychology, and anthropology. Out of this he developed his own method that reeducates the neuromuscular system. Feldenkrais succeeded in healing himself.

Returning to Israel after the war, he decided to devote himself to teaching his new technique. This method employs a manipulative and a group exercise technique. The manipulative technique (Functional Integration) is done by a practitioner or teacher physically manipulating each student. It is individualized to fit the particular needs of each student and was the first technique that Feldenkrais developed. In Israel it is still called an "individual lesson." The group exercise (Awareness Through Movement) was designed to reproduce the effect of the manipulative "individual lessons" for a number of people at one time. The "group lessons" are given in verbal directions by the practitioner or teacher.

The Feldenkrais Method is based on a specific definition of "maturity," which contends that an individual retains the capacity to break up previous experiences and re-form them into a pattern most suitable to present circumstances; conscious control effectively becomes the overriding servomechanism of the nervous system. In that sense, maturity is an ideal state in which the uniqueness of human beings and their capacity to form new responses or to learn have reached their ultimate perfection. The method postulates that the body should be so organized that it can initiate any movement—forward, backward, up, down, to the right, left, or turning—without sudden change in the rhythm of breathing, without clenching of teeth or stiffening of the tongue, tightening of the neck muscles, or fixation of the eyes. Efficient movement should be effortless; the Feldenkrais Method teaches one how to move effortlessly. The intensity of mobilization in an effortless action is the same throughout the musculature, and the stress in each muscle is proportional to its cross section.

One feature of the technique that is unusual for dancers is the absence of drill. Never is the subject instructed to make that "extra try," and in fact straining for effect is expressly discouraged, for to be able to tell differences in exertion, one must first reduce the exertion. By encouraging the pupils to do less well than they might, the method produces both the mental ease that is necessary for the reduction of useless effort and the sensation that one could do better, thus smoothing progress. This is not the same as relaxation, however, for relaxation can be maintained only when doing nothing.

For the dancer, the Feldenkrais Method must be used as an adjunct, not a substitute, for dance technique classes. It can correct the way the dancer uses the body in small ways (i.e., the habit of moving two or three vertebrae as a block in rotation, flexion, or extension). This in itself may not be noticed—it is too delicate a movement to differentiate in dance technique class—but the dancer will notice an improvement in, for example, the number of pirouettes (where each vertebra in turn moves, though quickly) or the height of jumps (where each vertebra assists in absorbing the compression stress and thus helps to prepare for the next upward thrust).

Flexibility is also noticeably increased, because Feldenkrais exercises are designed to work on the relaxation of antagonist muscles during an action, rather than to emphasize the strength of agonist muscles; this is done by making the antagonist muscles work very hard at first. The depth and ability to breathe during movement is increased, thus making any vigorous movement easier. The exercises allow one to change those often unnoticed habits of holding the breath on an inhalation during a particular phase of movement.

The Feldenkrais Method requires that the dancer's skill to observe through the kinesthetic sense remains alert—thus emphasizing a useful direction of thought. It is this that actually interested Feldenkrais when he originated his method—real thinking leads directly to efficient, useful, purposeful movement; that is, you do what you intend to do. Feldenkrais felt that this was the measure of true intelligence.

BIBLIOGRAPHY

Feldenkrais, Moshe. *Body and Mature Behaviour.* New York, 1949.
Feldenkrais, Moshe. *Awareness through Movement.* New York, 1972.
Feldenkrais, Moshe. *The Elusive Obvious.* Cupertino, Calif., 1981.

ARCHIVES. Feldenkrais Guild Archives, San Francisco. Leistiko Resources Archives, San Francisco.

NORMA LEISTIKO

Ideokinesis

Ideokinesis is a process of imagining movement. The term was adopted in 1974 by Lulu E. Sweigard (1895–1974) to describe her way of teaching, evolved after nearly fifty years of working with dancers, athletes, and musicians in New York. The aim of ideokinesis is to engage the mind in the creation of precise concepts of body movement, which enhance patterns of habitual neuromuscular activity. These patterns provide elements of standing, walking, or dancing.

Sweigard received a master's degree from Teachers College, Columbia University, in 1927. She was profoundly influenced there by Mabel Elsworth Todd, a self-taught student of anatomy, physiology, physics, and psychology. Todd began teaching "bodily economy" in the early 1900s. Her conviction that all movement begins in the mind led her to develop her "psycho-physiological" approach to the teaching of movement. To achieve an appropriate movement response, she taught students to concentrate on the idea of the movement only, while attending to such components as the directional pathway and goal of the movement within the body. All voluntary "holding" of posture or "gripping" of muscles was discouraged as a source of interference with the learning process.

These concepts provided the groundwork for the research projects and educational approaches developed by Todd's students, who included Barbara Clark and Laura Huelster, as well as Sweigard.

Sweigard began testing Todd's hypotheses about posture by conducting a long-term X-ray study of five hundred subjects. The results of this study were presented in her thesis, "Bilateral Asymmetry in the Alignment of the Skeletal Framework of the Human Body," for which she received her Ph.D. from New York University in 1939. This, as well as later studies, led her to the conclusion that posture is an expression of habits of body mechanics. These habits are sustained by established patterns of nervous system activity and can be changed only by educating the student to establish new patterns of mental activity. Her insistence that education, rather than therapy or exercise training, is the key to change in postural and movement habits often put her at odds with her contemporaries.

In the practice of ideokinesis, the movement to be visualized is precisely located in the body, spatially and directionally, and its timing and dynamics are indicated. The highly specific nature of the "lines-of-movement" to be visualized enables the student to change patterns of activity in isolated muscle groups, as well as throughout the body as a whole, to make subtle adjustments in normal muscle usage, as well as major shifts in muscle length and tension patterns. Having found that inefficient neuromuscular patterns come into play as soon as a person begins moving, Sweigard often asked her students to initiate ideokinesis while lying down quietly, so as to avoid interference from those ingrained patterns. A position in which no muscle work is required to counter the pull of gravity is called the constructive rest position (CRP). To assume this position, one lies supine with the hip, knee, and ankle joints flexed so that the soles of the feet are flat on the supporting surface; the feet may be either parallel or turned slightly inward. The normal curves of the spine that exist when standing upright must be retained. Thus, the small of the back (lumbar spine) and the back of the neck (cervical spine) are slightly elevated from the supporting surface. The arms may lie across the chest so that the elbows are in line with the hip joints, or they may be adjusted to a position of greater ease (for example, placed by the sides with hands on the abdomen).

The student is then instructed to visualize movement traveling along delineated pathways within the body. The condition of the individual student's musculoskeletal system determines the specific lines of movement to be visualized at a particular time. For example, if the lumbar spine arches too high off the ground because of overactive, short muscles in this area (the erector spinae and quadratus lumborum muscles), one might practice visualizing a line of movement to lengthen the spine downward by imagining the sacrum gliding slowly and smoothly along the ground toward the feet. Since the imagery suggests movement that is opposite to that produced by activity in the low back muscles, these muscles will tend to be inhibited from contracting and allowed to elongate as long as this ideokinetic practice is continued.

While still visualizing a line of movement, the student can perform other activities. For example, one might continue visualizing lengthening the spine downward, by letting the sacrum hang while walking up a flight of stairs.

Ideokinesis is practiced not only as a means of refining the functioning of the musculoskeletal system, but also as a means by which performing artists can expand their repertory of movement choices. A change in the concept of movement produces a change in its performance, which in turn changes the form of the body.

BIBLIOGRAPHY

Dowd, Irene. *Taking Root to Fly: Seven Articles on Functional Anatomy.* New York, 1981.

Dowd, Irene. "Ideokinesis: The Nine Lines of Movement." *Contact Quarterly* 8 (Winter 1983): 38–46.

Dowd, Irene. *Taking Root to Fly: Ten Articles on Functional Anatomy.* 2d ed. New York, 1990.

Dowd, Irene. *Taking Root to Fly: Articles on Functional Anatomy.* 3d ed. New York, 1995.

Myers, Martha. "Todd, Sweigard, and Ideokinesis." *Dance Magazine* (June 1980).

Sweigard, Lulu E. *Human Movement Potential: Its Ideokinetic Facilitation.* New York, 1974.

Todd, Mabel Elsworth. *The Thinking Body.* New York, 1937.

Todd, Mabel Elsworth. *The Hidden You.* New York, 1953.

Todd, Mabel Elsworth. *Early Writings, 1920–1934.* New York, 1977.

IRENE DOWD

Skinner Releasing Technique

The Skinner Releasing Technique is a kinesthetic discipline for training dancers, developed in the 1960s by Joan Skinner, a professor of dance at the University of Washington. It relies on poetic imagery to convey data to the neuromuscular system. This information relates directly and obliquely to four kinesthetic principles underlying Skinner Releasing Technique: multidirectional alignment, multidirectional balancing, autonomy, and economy in movement.

The technique views correct alignment as a dynamic process of continuous adjustment to changes of weight in space; it is a crucial foundation upon which the fundamental and qualitative potential of a dancer rests. Balance is seen as a multidirectional, multidimensional experience in space, without reference to a single center of the body or a concept of "upness" or "downness." Only necessary muscles with the necessary expenditure of energy are used to achieve the greatest freedom of movement. Furthermore, breathing remains unbound by the effort of moving. Integration of these principles results in the releasing of excessive tensions that impede movement, and it makes available new sources of strength, energy, and flexibility for the dancer.

Joan Skinner describes in her mimeographed class notes of April 1973 the appearance of an Skinner Releasing Technique-trained dancer: "Movement seems to be more skeletal than muscular. The muscles appear to be lengthened and wrapped around the bones rather than contracted or gripped. The joints give the appearance of having space in them and the relationship to gravity is similar to the suspension of a dust particle in a shaft of light."

Students develop skill in using imagery while moving or still, in lying, sitting, or standing positions. Imagery is carefully selected according to one's kinesthetic experience and progresses from simple to complex, gross to fine, and one-dimensional to multidimensional. As one experiences greater involvement with the imagery, kinesthetic perceptions are heightened and an eventual streamlining of effort in movement results.

As a child, Skinner studied with Cora Belle Hunter, a former graduate student of Mabel Ellsworth Todd at Teachers College, Columbia University. After graduating in dance from Bennington College and performing with the Martha Graham and Merce Cunningham dance companies, Skinner studied the Alexander Technique in New York from 1953 to 1954. She continued to perform, teach, and study, earning a master's degree in dance from the University of Illinois in 1964. By this time the formalization of the kinesthetic principles was underway and students of the work began calling it "releasing." Since that time, Skinner's surname has been attached to her particular approach to distinguish it from the proliferation of other "release" techniques.

Skinner Releasing Technique has been taught mostly to college-age and professional dancers. Although sophisticated dance training is its main purpose, SRT has been used experimentally in therapeutic settings and in special classes for young children, pregnant women, parents with their children, and seniors. There is a Skinner Releasing Technique Teacher Certification Program for introductory and ongoing work held every other summer under the auspices of the University of Washington, Division of Dance, in Seattle. There is also an ensemble of dancers and musicians.

BIBLIOGRAPHY

Davidson, Robert. "Transformations: Concerning Music and Dance in Releasing." *Contact Quarterly* (Winter 1985).

Davis, Bridget Tone. "Releasing into Process: Joan Skinner and the Use of Imagery in the Teaching of Dance." Master's thesis, University of Illinois, Urbana, 1974.

Dempster, Elizabeth. "Interview with Joan Skinner." *Writings on Dance*. Victoria, Australia, 1995.

Skinner, Joan, Bridget Davis, Sally Metcalf, and Kris Wheeler. "Notes on the Skinner Releasing Technique." *Contact Quarterly* (Fall 1979).

Skura, Stephanie. "Releasing Dance: Interview with Joan Skinner." *Contact Quarterly* (Fall 1990).

ROBERT DAVIDSON

BOGDANOV FAMILY, Russian family of dancers who flourished during the nineteenth century. Notable members were the father, Konstantin, and his daughter, Nadezhda.

Konstantin Bogdanov (Konstantin Fedorovich Bogdanov; born c.1808, died 1877 in Moscow?), dancer, teacher, and ballet impresario. Bogdanov graduated from the Moscow Theater School in 1827 and perfected his technique under the tutelage of Charles Didelot in Saint Petersburg. Bogdanov had made his debut at the Petrovsky Theater in Moscow in 1823, when he danced a *pas sabotière* in a *divertissement* by Adam Glushkovsky. He partnered some of the leading ballerinas of the Moscow ballet, including his wife, Tatiana Karpakova, and gave a long string of memorable performances at Moscow's Bolshoi Theater, notably as the Count in Glushkovsky's 1832 revival of *Satan with All His Devices, or The Lesson of the Sorcerer*, created in 1825 by Didelot and the dancer known as Auguste; Gurn in Félicité Hullin-Sor's 1837 revival of Filippo Taglioni's *La Sylphide;* and the Duke in Théodore Guérinot's 1839 revival of Hullin-Sor's *Rosalba, or The Masked Ball*. He also performed Russian, Tatar, and Spanish folk dances, minuets, and other character dances. In the decade between 1839 and 1849 he was Glushkovsky's successor as chief *régisseur* of the ballet troupe of the Bolshoi Theater.

Until 1846 Bogdanov taught at the Moscow Theater School as well as in his own private ballet school, which was attended by his sons and his daughter, Nadezhda. From 1848 to 1850 Bogdanov toured the provinces with his own ballet troupe, appearing in Yaroslavl, Kostroma, Kaluga, Tula, Kursk, Kharkov, Odessa, and Kiev. The repertory on that tour was made up of excerpts from the Romantic ballets staged by Bogdanov especially for his daughter. He appeared with his daughter in some of the ballets, such as *La Sylphide*, in which he danced the role of James. Bogdanov's private venture as a ballet impressario was one of the first successful attempts in Russian theater to introduce the public of the provinces to the art of ballet.

Nadezhda Bogdanova (Nadezhda Konstantinovna Bogdanova; born 2 [14] September 1836 in Moscow, died 3 [15] September 1897 in Saint Petersburg), dancer. After having received her training from her father, Bogdanova began appearing on the professional stage at the age of ten. She then joined her father on the 1848–1850 tour through the Russian provinces. Following the advice of Fanny Elssler, who thought highly of the young ballerina's gifts, Bogdanova was accompanied by her father to Paris to complete her formal dance education. On the journey, in 1850, she appeared in various cities in Poland, Germany, and France.

Between 1850 and 1855 Bogdanova lived in Paris, where she attended the ballet school of the Paris Opera for three years, later perfecting her technique under Joseph Mazilier. She made her debut in 1851 as Kathi in the Paris premiere of Arthur Saint-Léon's ballet *La Vivandière*. She also appeared with Fanny Cerrito in 1853 at the Opera in Mazilier's *Orfa* and in 1855 performed the mime role of Hélène in Filippo Taglioni's ballet in Giacomo Meyerbeer's opera *Robert le Diable*. Bogdanova's talents were acclaimed by the Paris public and critics alike; Théophile Gautier, Jules Janin, and Daniel Auber all remarked on her idiosyncratic performing style. In 1854 and 1855 Bogdanova made guest appearances in Vienna, Berlin, and Warsaw, but for patriotic reasons refused to appear in a Paris performance following the fall of Sevastopol at the end of the Crimean War and terminated her contract with the Opera.

Back in Saint Petersburg she appeared in 1856 in the leading role in *Giselle* at the city's Bolshoi Theater. Russian ballet critics praised her for her tender lyricism, her natural, unaffected manner, the warmth and sincerity of her interpretations, and her uncanny ability to subordinate technical virtuosity to the larger task of projecting an integral and poetic image of the choreographer's overall concept.

Bogdanova's peak achievements are associated with the Romantic repertory. In the opinion of two leading dance scholars, Cyril W. Beaumont and Vera Krasovskaya, Bogdanova is among the best interpreters of Giselle in ballet history. On the Saint Petersburg stage she also created important roles in Jules Perrot's *La Esmeralda, Gaselda, ou Les Tziganes*, and *Faust*, all in 1856; Antoine Titus's revival of Filippo Taglioni's *La Sylphide* in 1857; and Perrot's *Le Délire d'un Peintre, ou Le Portrait Animé* in 1860. She was the first Russian ballerina to appear in the title role of Perrot's *La Débutante*, in 1857, and Saint-Léon's *Météora*, in 1861.

In 1862 and 1863 Bogdanova danced in Moscow. In 1864 she stopped her appearances at the Imperial Theaters and the following year went to Paris to appear at the Opera in act 1 of *Giselle*. In 1866 and 1867 she danced at the Warsaw Opera House as well as making highly successful guest appearances in Berlin, Hamburg, Budapest, and Naples. Late in 1867, at the height of her powers, she suddenly retired from the stage. She was officially retired from the Imperial Theaters in 1875, following fundamental creative differences with Saint-Léon, who exerted considerable influence on the management.

BIBLIOGRAPHY

Guest, Ivor. *The Ballet of the Second Empire.* London, 1974.

Guest, Ivor. *Jules Perrot: Master of the Romantic Ballet.* London, 1984.

Krasovskaya, Vera. *Russkii baletnyi teatr: Ot vozniknoveniia do serediny XIX veka.* Leningrad, 1958.

Krasovskaya, Vera. "Tantsovshchitsa Nadezhda Bogdanova." *Ucheniye Zapiski Nauchnogo-Issledovatel'nogo Instituta Teatra i Muziki* 1 (1958).

Roslavleva, Natalia. *Era of the Russian Ballet* (1966). New York, 1979.

Saint-Léon, Arthur. *Letters from a Ballet Master: The Correspondence of Arthur Saint-Léon.* Edited by Ivor Guest. New York, 1981.

Wiley, Roland John, trans. and ed. *A Century of Russian Ballet: Documents and Accounts, 1810–1910.* Oxford, 1990.

VALERY A. KULAKOV
Translated from Russian

BOLENDER, TODD (born 17 February 1919 in Canton, Ohio), American ballet dancer, choreographer, and company director. As a youth, Bolender began his dance training by studying acrobatic tap dancing in his hometown. In 1936 he went to New York, where he studied at the School of American Ballet and with Chester Hale, Edwin Strawbridge, Hanya Holm, and Anatole Vilzak. His first professional experience was with Ballet Caravan, which he joined in 1937, creating the roles of Alias in Eugene Loring's *Billy the Kid* and the State Trooper in Lew Christensen's *Filling Station* (both, 1938). Subsequently, Bolender danced with the Littlefield Ballet in Philadelphia and went on American Ballet Caravan's South American tour in 1941. In 1942, back in New York, he danced in the New Opera Company production of *Rosalinda*, choreographed by George Balanchine. Bolender next danced with Ballet Theatre, in 1944, and appeared as guest artist with the Ballet Russe de Monte Carlo in 1945. He joined Ballet Society at its inception in 1946 and continued with the company when it became New York City Ballet in 1948.

Among the many roles that Bolender created in Balanchine ballets were Phlegmatic in *The Four Temperaments* (1946), the only male role in *Symphonie Concertante* (1947), and the man who dances the Sarabande in the first pas de trois of *Agon* (1957). He also originated roles in several Jerome Robbins ballets, including *Age of Anxiety* (1950), *Fanfare* (1953), and *The Concert* (1956). Bolender was an exceptionally musical dancer, as his roles in *The Four Temperaments* and *Agon* attest, and he was also capable of vivid comedy characterizations, such as the cigar-smoking Husband in *The Concert* and the Leader of Percussion in *Fanfare.*

In 1943 Bolender co-founded American Concert Ballet, with William Dollar and Mary Jane Shea, and for it choreographed his first ballet, *Mother Goose Suite,* to music by Maurice Ravel. In 1945, he used music by Igor Stravinsky for his second work, called *Musical Chairs* at its premiere

BOLENDER. The ensemble of the Harkness Ballet, a repertory company active from 1965 to 1975, in a revival of Todd Bolender's *Souvenirs.* Set to music by Samuel Barber, this work was originally created for the New York City Ballet in 1955. (Photograph from the Dance Collection, New York Public Library for the Performing Arts.)

on a program at the Jacob's Pillow Dance Festival but retitled *Comedia Balletica* when it was mounted for Ballet Russe de Monte Carlo later that year. For Ballet Society and the New York City Ballet, Bolender mounted no fewer than eleven of his works, including *The Miraculous Mandarin* (1951), to the score by Béla Bartók; *Souvenirs* (1955), to music by Samuel Barber; *The Still Point* (1956), to music by Claude Debussy; and *Creation of the World* (1960), to the score by Darius Milhaud. *The Still Point,* his most frequently performed ballet, was first presented as *At the Still Point* by a modern dance company, the Dance Drama Company of Emily Frankel and Mark Ryder, in 1955. Bolender also choreographed for musical comedy, opera, and television.

In the early 1960s, Bolender began a new phase of his career when he accepted the first of several jobs he has held as director of a ballet company. He filled this post at the Cologne Opera from 1963 to 1966, at the Frankfurt Opera from 1966 to 1969, and at the State Opera of Istanbul from 1977 to 1980. Bolender's choreographic works during these years were few, but in 1972 he accepted Balanchine's invitation to return to New York City Ballet to create two works, *Serenade in A* and *Piano–Rag–Music*, for the company's ground-breaking Stravinsky Festival.

In 1980 Bolender became artistic director of the Kansas City Ballet, which later became the State Ballet of Missouri. Among the works he created for this company are *Classical Symphony* (1982), to the well-known score by Sergei Prokofiev; *Grand Tarentella* (1983), to music by Louis Moreau Gottschalk; and *Folktale* (1984), using Stravinsky's score for *Le Baiser de la Fée.* He also set several works to the music of George Gershwin, including *Concerto in F* (1984), *An American in Paris* (1987), and *Celebration* (1989).

BIBLIOGRAPHY

Barzel, Ann. "Todd Bolender: A Decade in Kansas City." *Dance Magazine* (October 1991): 36–37.

Chujoy, Anatole. *The New York City Ballet.* New York, 1953.

Denby, Edwin. *Dance Writings.* Edited by Robert Cornfield and William MacKay. New York, 1986.

Hastings, Baird. "Tribute to a Trio." *Ballet Review* 22 (Summer 1994): 8–9.

Kirstein, Lincoln. *The New York City Ballet.* With photographs by Martha Swope and George Platt Lynes. New York, 1973.

Reynolds, Nancy, and Susan Reimer-Torn. "The Still Point." In *Dance Classics.* Pennington, N.J., 1991.

WILLIAM JAMES LAWSON

BOLERO is a genre of Spanish dance developed in the eighteenth century, when dancing masters combined indigenous Spanish dances. Performed primarily in theatrical contexts but also, to a lesser degree, in social ones, bolero was eventually codified in academic form as *es-*

BOLERO. A late eighteenth-century engraving by Marcos Téllez entitled *Campanelas de las Seguidillas Boleras.* The *campanela* (or *campanilla,* "little bell") consists of a jump on the supporting leg while the gesture leg makes a small circle in the air. Both dancers are using castanets. (Courtesy of Javier Suarez-Parares.)

cuela bolera, or classical Spanish dance. The word *bolero* also denotes a type of musical composition.

History. There is some uncertainty regarding the origin of bolero, but scholars agree that it arose between 1750 and 1780. According to Fernando Sor (1778–1839), a guitarist, composer, and early writer on the subject, a dancer named Bolero modified the *seguidilla* to create a new style that became known as the *seguidilla bolera;* the adjective soon became the noun designating the dance and its musical accompaniment.

The early bolero was based on an ancient Spanish dance, the *seguidillas manchegas,* which was performed in 3/4 time. To the rhythmic pattern of the *seguidillas* were added steps and movements from other Spanish dances, including the *fandango, polo,* and *tirana,* as well as turns from *chaconnes* and *bureos.* The bolero then constituted a kind of rapid *seguidillas,* in which any codified dance step could be used. The music for the bolero differs from that of the *seguidillas* in that the former has a slower tempo but more notes per measure.

The importance of the bolero and its eventual ascendancy in the world of Spanish dance were due at least in part to historical factors. The late eighteenth century had been a nationalistic era in Spain, when the middle and upper classes were split between those who followed foreign trends—pejoratively called *currutacos*—and the defenders of native customs, or *majos*. For social dancing, the former favored imported *menuets, passepieds,* and *contredanses,* imports from France; the last also embraced the indigenous *fandangos, tiranas,* and especially the *seguidillas.* The *majos* recognized the newly created bolero as a showy variation of the *seguidillas* and a potential vehicle for their ideology. After a period of controversy, both literary and social, the bolero was accepted at society balls.

In the last years of the eighteenth century, while the bolero was still popular as a social dance for amateur performers, its choreography was enriched and the genre was introduced in theaters. Professional dancers added a series

BOLERO. *Pistolees de las Seguidillas Boleras* (Pistolea Steps in the Seguidillas Boleras), a late eighteenth-century engraving by Marcos Téllez. After the arrival of the Bourbon dynasty in 1700, Spain's upper classes adopted foreign fashions. That these trends belatedly reached the general population is evident in the outdated men's hats and woman's headdress seen here. (Courtesy of Javier Suarez-Parares.)

of modifications to make it a virtuoso dance and increase its dramatic impact. The new steps were, however, viewed by many as a scandalous perversion of the original bolero.

A professional dancer from Murcia named Requejo responded to public criticism by codifying the bolero to make it less offensive. His version increased the distance between the dancers, eliminated violent movements, and prohibited raising the elbows above the shoulders or the hands above the head.

During the first decade of the nineteenth century, a law was promulgated in Spain that required theatrical dance companies to include specialists in "national dance." As a result, the number of professional bolero dancers grew rapidly. Famous male dancers included Josef Roxo, Joseph Molina, Sandalio Luengo, Antonio Cairón, Antonio Ruiz, Pablo Ciprés, and Manuel Guerrero; noteworthy female performers were Paula Luengo, María Vives, Rafaela Saldoni, Mariana Castillo, Teresa Baus, Antonia Molina, and the celebrated Petra Cámara.

In the 1840s, the Spanish academic bolero was included in the European tours of Dolores Serral and Mariano Camprubi. Before this, however, the bolero as it had been danced before Requejo's codification arrived in France during the Napoleonic wars. The dancers employed by the French used unrefined techniques disapproved by the school of Requejo, including what Fernando Sor characterized as

> gestures that only belong to certain dances of the Gypsies, Bohemians of Spain. Cabrioles and splits are included, and to further denigrate it they . . . stamp flat-footed on the floor several times in succession.

A talented French dancer, Fernanda LeFebvre, formed a troupe of both French and Spanish dancers, which became very popular.

It was this French-influenced bolero—systematized by the French dancer Antonio Cairón in 1820 and described, albeit erroneously, by Carlo Blasis in 1828—that the most important figures of the dance world disseminated throughout Europe. During the nineteenth century, various schools of bolero were current in different parts of Europe: a Romantic style predominated on the stages of Paris and London; a nationalist style arose, based in revivals of the musical drama *zarzuela;* and a traditional or authentic Spanish style persisted in Spain's provincial theaters.

The tradition of the bolero was carried into the twentieth century as an academic form of the *escuela bolero.* Many touring Spanish dance companies today include boleros in their theatrical programs.

Music. The *seguidilla manchega,* out of which the bolero grew, was accompanied by compositions for solo voice and guitar, with a beat of 162 to 164 beats per minute. The *seguidilla bolera* had a slower beat of about

130 beats per minute, and the nineteenth-century bolero was even slower, with 95 to 100 beats per minute. As the tempo slowed, more musical variation and ornamentation were added. The music is in 3/4 time or some other ternary time signature.

The text of bolero songs has four lines of seven, five, seven, and five syllables, followed by three lines of five, seven, and five syllables. The musical phrases correspond to the lyrics in a strictly systematized manner. The early boleros were accompanied, like the *seguidillas*, by solo voice and guitar, but as the bolero moved into the theater, a purely instrumental style of composition was adopted. The theatrical compositions are distinguished by an extended introduction, whereas the original bolero had only a minimal harmonic and rhythmic introduction.

History of Its Choreography. The first attempt to codify the steps of the bolero in written form was Antonio Cairón's treatise, published in Madrid in 1820. He described how to adapt the dance to the music and its general choreographic structure but revealed little about the steps themselves. The bolero was said to consist of three verses *(coplas)*, each divided into three choruses *(estribillos)* and two *pasadas*. The steps of the chorus could be simple or double, depending on the time available and the number of repetitions to be performed. Cairón wrote:

> The first *estribillo* that is danced in the first verse is called the *paseo*, because it is usually a simple and low step, serving only to demonstrate the skill of the *braceo*, which is what the art of moving the arms is called.   (Cairón, 1820)

One element that must be considered in reconstructing the early bolero is the accompaniment provided by the dancer's castanets. An article in *Allgemeine musikalische Zeitung* of 27 March 1799 included transcriptions of two boleros for violin, with the castanet part clearly indicated; there was also an illustration showing how to hold the castanets.

Fernando Sor's article on bolero in the *Encyclopédie pittoresque de la musique* (Paris, 1835) gave a better explanation of the steps, informed by Sor's expertise as a guitarist and his experience as a composer for ballet. Sor also provided very useful diagrams of the dancer's spatial movements.

Iconographic sources also help with the reconstruction of the historic bolero and its costume. As early as 1790, a Madrid printer issued a series of five prints that depicted the different steps of the bolero; these were reproduced by Suárez-Pajares and Carreira (1993). Judging by the quality of the prints and their extensive advertising, they must have been widely distributed.

[*See also* Escuela Bolera.]

BIBLIOGRAPHY

Asenjo y Barbieri, Francisco. *Las castañuelas.* Madrid, 1879.
Bailar en España. Madrid, 1990.
Blasis, Carlo. *The Code of Terpsichore: A Practical and Historical Treatise on the Ballet, Dancing, and Pantomime.* London, 1828.
Borrull, Trinidad. *La danza española.* 3d ed. Barcelona, 1965.
Caballero Bonald, José Manuel. *El baile andaluz.* Barcelona, 1957.
Cairón, Antonio. *Compendio de las principales reglas del baile.* Madrid, 1820.
Capmany, Aurelio. *Un siglo de baile en Barcelona.* Barcelona, 1947.
Carretero, Concepción. *El baile.* Seville, 1981.
Carretero, Concepción. *Origen, evolución y morfología del baile por sevillanas.* Seville, 1985.
Estébanez Calderón, Serafín. *Escenas andaluzas.* Madrid, 1847.
Fernández de Rojas, Juan. *Carta de Madama Crotalistris sobre la segunda parte de la Crotalogía.* Madrid, 1792.
Fernández de Rojas, Juan. *Carta gratulatoria y de Pascuas.* Vitoria, 1792.
Fernández de Rojas, Juan. *Crotalogía o ciencia de las castañuelas.* Barcelona, 1792.
Fernández de Rojas, Juan. *Ilustración, adición o comentario a la Crotalogía.* Valencia, 1792.
Fernández de Rojas, Juan. *Impugnación literaria a la Crotalogía erudita.* Valencia, 1792.
Fernández de Rojas, Juan. *Libro de moda.* Madrid, 1795.
Iza Zamácola, Juan Antonio de. *Colección de las mejores coplas de seguidillas, tiranas y polos que se han compuesto para cantar a la guitarra.* Madrid, 1790.
Iza Zamácola, Juan Antonio de. *Elementos de la ciencia contradanzaria.* Madrid, 1796.
Jeffery, Brian. *Fernando Sor: Composer and Guitarist.* 2d ed. Soar Chapel, South Wales, 1994.
Manfredi Cano, Domingo. *Bailes regionales.* 2d ed. Madrid, 1959.
Marinero y María José Ruiz, Christina. "La escuela bolera: Coreología." In *Encuentro internacional "la escuela bolera."* Madrid, 1992.
Matteo. *The Language of Spanish Dance.* Norman, Okla., 1990.
Mota, Alejandro. *El triunfo de las Castañuelas.* 2d ed. Madrid, 1792.
Otero Aranda, José. *Tratado de bailes españoles.* Seville, 1912.
Rodríguez Calderón, Juan Jacinto. *Bolerología.* Philadelphia, 1807.
Rojo de Flores, Felipe. *Tratado de recreación instructiva sobre la danza su invención y diferencias.* Madrid, 1793.
Sepúlveda, Ricardo. *El corral de la pacheca.* Madrid, 1888.
Sor, Fernando. "Le Bolero." In *Encyclopédie pittoresque de la musique.* Paris, 1835.
Suárez-Pajares, Javier, and Xoán M. Carreira. *The Origins of the Bolero School.* Studies in Dance History, vol. 4.1. Pennington, N.J., 1993.
Udaeta, José de. *La castañuela española: Origen y evolución.* Barcelona, 1989.

JAVIER SUÁREZ-PAJARES
Translated from Spanish

BOLGER, RAY (Raymond Wallace Bolger, born 10 January 1904 in Dorchester, Massachusetts, died 15 January 1987 in Los Angeles), American dancer. The lean and limber Bolger claimed he could dance only the waltz at his high school graduation, so he watched classes to learn social dancing, was shown his first tap step by a shoe salesman, learned additional steps from a night watchman who had been a dancer, and finally studied with the Russian-trained Senia Russakoff, for whom he kept books in exchange for ballet lessons.

Initially known as an "eccentric" dancer (according to Bolger, this means one who does the unexpected in expanding on known steps), he gained fame as a dancer, mime, actor, and satirist. His uncanny sense of timing and instinct for line and gesture led critic John Martin to call him a true *commedia dell'arte* performer, whose laughs were timed to motor impulses. Typical "Bolgerisms" were his soft shoes, rubbery legs, disjointed limbs, subtle weight shifts, and the superb expressiveness in his hangdog contours and borzoi-like body.

Aside from a few appearances in Yiddish theater in Boston, Bolger's first professional performances were in 1922 with the Bob Ott Musical Comedy Repertory Company, where he remained for two years. In 1924 he played the Rialto in New York City as part of a team (with Ralph Sanford) and then as a single act. He was first seen on Broadway in *The Passing Show of 1926* and subsequently spent several years on the vaudeville circuit. Thereafter he appeared in more than a dozen Broadway shows, including *Heads Up* (1929), *George White's Scandals* (1931), and *Life Begins at 8:40* (1934). Bolger's own favorites were *On Your Toes* (1936), in which the number "Slaughter on Tenth Avenue" (to music by Richard Rodgers) brought attention to both Bolger and choreographer George Balanchine; *By Jupiter* (1942), in which Bolger was the timorous husband of the Amazon Hippolyta; and *Where's Charley?* (1948), a musical version of *Charley's Aunt*, also choreographed by Balanchine, for which Bolger won the Antoinette Perry Award—the "Tony"—and the Donaldson Award.

Bolger appeared in many films, few of which took advantage of his talents, though he will always be remembered as the seemingly rubber-legged Scarecrow in the 1939 movie classic *The Wizard of Oz*. There was also a film version of *Where's Charley?* (1952), choreographed by Michael Kidd. Bolger played in nightclubs as well, and was seen on television in his own show about a hoofer, "Where's Raymond?" (1953–1955), and in an hourlong comedy-variety series, "Washington Square" (1956–1957). His last stage appearances were in *All American* (1962) and *Come Summer* (1969), in which he worked with the choreographer Agnes de Mille.

Bolger, who choreographed most of his own dance routines, stressed the importance of form and theme in capturing and holding an audience. Once a movement idea had been expressed, he created his own unique counterpoint, via his feet.

BIBLIOGRAPHY

Barzel, Ann. "Ray Bolger's Thursday." *Dance Magazine* (April 1954): 34–37.

Current Biography. New York, 1942.

Frank, Rusty E. *Tap! The Greatest Tap Dance Stars and Their Stories, 1900–1955.* Rev. ed. New York, 1994.

DAWN LILLE HORWITZ

BOLM, ADOLPH (Adol'f Rudol'fovich Bolm; born 25 September 1884 in Saint Petersburg, died 16 April 1951 in Hollywood, California), Russian-American dancer, teacher, and choreographer. Bolm was the son of the first violin and assistant conductor of the Mikhailovsky Theater in Saint Petersburg. At age ten, he was admitted to the Imperial Ballet School, where he studied with Platon Karsavin and Pavel Gerdt. Graduating in 1903, he entered the corps de ballet of the Maryinsky Theater, becoming a soloist two years later. He became disenchanted with the Maryinsky's bureaucracy and artistic stagnation and turned his sights abroad, first as a student avid for knowledge of Western art and music, then as a performer.

In 1908, Bolm appeared with Lydia Kyasht in her debut at London's Empire Theatre; in 1908 and 1909, he partnered Anna Pavlova on her first tours of Scandinavia and central Europe, which also proved his mettle as an organizer. He participated in Serge Diaghilev's 1909 season of Russian ballet and opera in Paris, becoming, until 1917, a mainstay of Diaghilev's Ballets Russes and, after Vaslav Nijinsky, its most prominent male personality. Lacking the elegance and technical finesse of a pure classicist, Bolm made his mark in character and mime roles. He was an outstanding interpreter of Michel Fokine's choreography, his most famous creations being the Chief Warrior in the *Polovtsian Dances* from *Prince Igor* (1909), Pierrot in *Le Carnaval* (1910), Ivan Tsarevich in *The Firebird* (1910), the Moor in *Petrouchka* (1911), Darkon in *Daphnis et Chloë* (1912), and the Stranger in *Thamar* (1912). Under Diaghilev's aegis, Bolm also created his first choreography, for the operas *La Fête d'Hébé* (Monte Carlo, 1912), *Khovantchina* (Paris, 1913), and *May Night* (London, 1914), and the "underwater" act of *Sadko* (Madrid, 1916).

Diaghilev's apparent unwillingness to further Bolm's choreographic ambitions, coupled with an injury during the Ballets Russes' second American tour, where Bolm shared the artistic direction with Nijinsky, caused Bolm to leave the troupe in 1917 and settle permanently in the United States. In that year, he formed the Ballet Intime, a chamber ensemble of twelve dancers including Michio Ito, Roshanara, and, later, Ruth Page. The company toured extensively during the next three years, and Bolm created numerous choreographic miniatures and *divertissements* for it. In 1918, he choreographed "Falling Leaves," starring Flora Revalles, for *Miss 1917*, a Charles Dillingham and Florenz Ziegfeld production, and he staged *Le Coq d'Or* at the Metropolitan Opera House, appearing as King Dodon. The following year, also at the Met, he mounted *Petrouchka*, dancing the title role.

The year 1919 saw the first of Bolm's undertakings in Chicago, which became his base for most of the 1920s, and the first of his numerous collaborations with American artists. *The Birthday of the Infanta*, produced for the Chicago Civic Opera with music by John Alden Carpenter

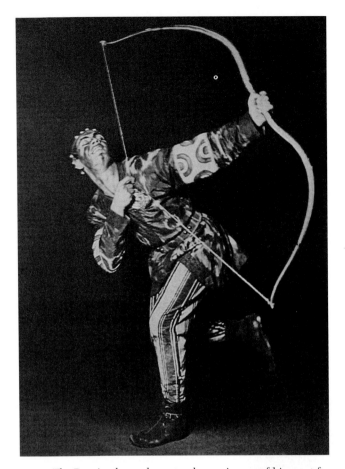

by Alexandre Tansman, 1926), and *A Garden Party* (music by Léo Delibes, 1926), in addition to numerous *divertissements*. In 1925 he staged *Le Coq d'Or*, *Petrouchka*, and several of his own works at the Teatro Colón in Buenos Aires.

His Adolph Bolm Ballet, which at various times featured Ruth Page, Agnes de Mille, Vera Mirova, and Elise Reiman, with Louis Horst as "pianist-leader," toured extensively in the middle and late 1920s. In 1928, at the Library of Congress, Bolm choreographed *Apollon Musagète*—the first production to Igor Stravinsky's famous score—*Pavane pour une Infante Défuncte* (music by Maurice Ravel), *Arlecchinata* (music by Cassanea de Mondonville), and *Alt-Wien* (music by Beethoven), all with designs by Nicolas Remisoff, Bolm's leading collaborator of the 1920s.

Three years later, in Hollywood, Bolm choreographed "Le Ballet Mécanique," to music by Alexandre Mossolov,

and designs by Robert Edmond Jones, was followed in 1922 by *Krazy Kat*, a "jazz pantomime" to a commissioned score by Carpenter, with designs by George Herriman (creator of the comic strip on which the ballet was based), and by *Danse Macabre*, an experimental film directed by Dudley Murphy. Also in 1922, Bolm became ballet master of the Chicago Civic Opera and opened his first school.

Appointed ballet master by Chicago Allied Arts in 1924, he entered on a period of intense activity, creating before the demise of that organization in 1927 such one-act ballets as *L'Enlèvement* (music by W. A. Mozart, 1924), *Foyer de la Danse* (music by Emmanuel Chabrier, 1924), *El Amor Brujo* (music by Manuel de Falla, 1925), *The Rivals* (music by Henry Eichheim, 1925), *Mandragora* (music by Karol Szymanowski, 1925), *Parnassus on Montmartre* (music by Erik Satie, 1926), *Reverie* (music by Frédéric Chopin, 1926), *Visual Mysticism* (music by Aleksandr Scriabin, 1926), *Christmas Carol* (music by Ralph Vaughan Williams, 1926), *The Tragedy of the Cello* (music for *The Mad Genius,* the first of several film ventures that included *The Men in Her Life* and *The Corsican Brothers* (both 1941). Although mangled in the editing room, Bolm's paean to the machine was restaged that year at the Hollywood Bowl as *The Spirit of the Factory.* Other works mounted by him at the Hollywood Bowl were *Les Nuages* (1931), *Schéhérazade* (1936), *Bach Cycle* (1936), and *The Firebird* (1941), in addition to dances for the operas *Carmen* (1936), *The Bartered Bride* (1936), and *Prince Igor* (1939).

Between 1933 and 1936, as ballet master of the San Francisco Opera, Bolm revived several of his older works, including *Le Ballet Mécanique* (1933); he mounted *Le Coq d'Or* (1933) and *Schéhérazade* (1935); and he choreographed *Danse Noble* (music by J. S. Bach, 1934), *Rondo Capriccioso* (music by Felix Mendelssohn, 1935), and *Lament* and *Consecration* (both to Bach, 1935), in addition to dances for many operas. He also served as the first official director of the San Francisco Opera Ballet School.

Joining forces with Ballet Theatre, Bolm danced Pierrot in Fokine's *Le Carnaval* during the troupe's 1940 inaugural season and also choreographed *Peter and the Wolf* (music by Sergei Prokofiev). In 1942–1943, he served as the company's *régisseur général,* and in 1945 he staged a new version of *The Firebird* with designs by Marc Chagall. Two years later, he choreographed his last major ballet, *Mephisto,* to music by Franz Liszt, for the San Francisco Civic Ballet. He died in 1951 in Hollywood, his home since the 1930s.

As a dancer, Bolm exemplified the Ballets Russes style at its best. In the *Polovtsian Dances,* wrote Cyril W. Beaumont, "He danced with a gusto and an elemental ferocity that was thrilling to watch"; in *Le Carnaval,* his Pierrot "was a tragic figure thrust outside the world of beauty and gaiety which he longed to enter." Alone of his émigré generation, Bolm reveled in the diversity, industrial spirit, and creative potentialities of his adopted country, allying himself from the start with progressive forces in American music, art, and dance. His taste in music was catholic, and like his most inspired creations—*Le Ballet Mécanique, Krazy Kat,* and the semi-abstract Bach cycle—it revealed a temperament attuned to modernism in its less radical forms. Above all, Bolm was a great popularizer of ballet. He brought Fokine's choreographic legacy and Diaghilev's tradition of living collaborations to the American heartland, shaping the tastes of a generation of dancers, choreographers, and audiences.

BIBLIOGRAPHY

Amberg, George. *Ballet: The Emergence of an American Art.* New York, 1949.
Beaumont, Cyril W. *Bookseller at the Ballet: Memoirs, 1891 to 1929.* London, 1975.
Bolm, Adolph. "A Dancer's Days." *Dance Magazine* (August–October 1926).
Bolm, Beata. "Adolph Bolm: Danseur et chorégraphe." *Archives Internationales de la Danse* (July 1935): 77–80.
Dougherty, John. "Perspective on Adolph Bolm" (parts 1–3). *Dance Magazine* (January–March 1963).
Levy, Suzanne Carbonneau. "The Russians Are Coming: Russian Dancers in the United States, 1910–1933." Ph.D. dissertation, New York University, 1990.
Prevots, Naima. *Dancing in the Sun: Hollywood Choreographers, 1915–1937.* Ann Arbor, Mich., 1987.

ARCHIVE.   Adolph Bolm Papers, Syracuse University.

LYNN GARAFOLA

BOLSHOI BALLET. The theater now known as the Bolshoi Academic Theater of Opera and Ballet in Moscow opened on 19 January 1825. For many years the Bolshoi Ballet was considered also to have been founded on that date, and its centenary was celebrated accordingly. Long before 1825, however, theatrical companies in Moscow had dancers among their members. These troupes were run by private entrepreneurs but were eventually taken over by the government. From the 1770s onward there was a line of continuity, and historians now consider the Bolshoi Ballet to have been founded in 1776, when regular ballet performances began at the Znamensky Theater under the auspices of the Englishman Michael Maddox and Prince Petr Urusov.

In 1780 Maddox became sole owner of the company, for which he built the Petrovsky Theater, named after Petrovskaya (now Petrovka) Street, which runs alongside the present Bolshoi Theater. The Petrovsky staged productions incorporating drama, opera, and ballet. The ballet masters were Italian, invited from abroad, including Francesco and Cosimo Morelli and Pietro Pinucci in the 1780s and 1790s; Giuseppe Solomoni replaced Francesco Morelli in 1800. The company, initially seven dancers and one ballet master, was augmented greatly in 1794 when it was joined by performers trained at the Moscow Orphanage, where ballet classes had been given since 1773. Among these new members was Gavrila Ivanov-Raikov, a popular performer of dance comedies, which, along with Russian folk dances, were much favored by the Moscow public. Less popular were serious ballets, in particular Solomoni's stagings of works by Jean-Georges Noverre. Moscow's ballet differed from that of Saint Petersburg by gravitating toward folk themes and comedies; its audience favored character dancing and dramatic works over pure dance. Moscow's ballets reflected the everyday life of the city, where national roots remained strong. In contrast to Saint Petersburg, with its cosmopolitan courtiers and officials, the tenor of Moscow life was set by the ancestral Russian nobility and the rich merchants; university circles were linked to the theater.

Nineteenth Century. In 1805 the Petrovsky Theater was destroyed by a fire, and in 1806 the directorate of the

Imperial Theaters formed a company in Moscow that included the members of the Petrovsky Theater along with serf dancers who had been sold by rich landowners. For a number of years, however, there was no permanent building. The wooden Arbat Theater, which opened in 1808, was burned during Napoleon's invasion in 1812. But the Moscow company staged its own ballets along with productions brought from Saint Petersburg, in particular those by Ivan Valberkh, who worked in Moscow in 1807, 1808, and 1811. Adam Glushkovsky was the leading ballet master and teacher of the company from shortly before its evacuation in 1812 until 1839. He staged performances in a variety of genres, ranging from the melodramatic ballets favored in Moscow to the patriotic divertissements with national dances that were popular during and after the Napoleonic war. Divertissements also were staged by Isaac Ablets, whose *Festival in the Maryina Grove* (1815) remained in the repertory until 1872. Of special significance were Glushkovsky's ballets based on works of Aleksandr Pushkin. He produced *Ruslan and Ludmila* in 1821 and brought Charles Didelot's *The Prisoner of the Caucasus* (1823) to Moscow from Saint Petersburg. *Ruslan and Ludmila*, rich in stage effects, spectacular changes of scenery, and national dances, was in the repertory for over ten years.

The Bolshoi Theater, built by the architect Osip Bovet (possibly Beauvais), was a splendid edifice with an excellently equipped stage. It opened in 1825 with the prologue *The Triumph of the Muses* and the three-act ballet *Cinderella*, staged by Félicité Hullin-Sor. The French ballerina had arrived in Moscow when Romantic ballet was emerging in Europe. She transferred Parisian productions to the Bolshoi, introducing Russian audiences to *La Sylphide* in 1837. This production starred Hullin-Sor's finest pupil, Ekaterina Sankovskaya, who was regarded as the very symbol of romanticism. Reviewers wrote that her dancing conveyed what was rarely encountered in ballet—an idea. They pointed out that, in contrast to Marie Taglioni, Sankovskaya lent a lively play of earthy passions to her fantasy characters. Other Bolshoi stars in the mid-nineteenth century included Théodore Guerinot, Nikita Peshkov, Yrca Mathias, Konstantin Bogdanov, Tatiana

BOLSHOI BALLET. The company in Kasyan Goleizovsky's 1933 version of the *Polovtsian Dances* from the opera *Prince Igor*, by Aleksandr Borodin. (Reprinted from Cyril Beaumont, *Ballet Design: Past and Present*, London, 1946, p. 145.)

Karpakova, and Fedor Manokhin. Thus began Moscow's theatrical dynasties: the Bogdanovs, Karpakovs, and Manokhins; later the Yrmolovs and the Domashovs. Fanny Elssler toured Russia twice between 1848 and 1851, appearing in *La Fille Mal Gardée, Giselle, Catarina,* and *Esmeralda.*

In 1853 the Bolshoi Theater was destroyed by fire, an event interpreted by the public to symbolize the end of an epoch. Shortly afterward Mathias left Moscow and Sankovskaya quit the stage. Russia was fighting the disastrous Crimean War, and the theater did not reopen for three years. The new building was designed by Alberto Cavos. Among the dancers who appeared there in the next few decades were Praskovia Lebedeva; Olga Nikolaeva, famous for her national dances; Nadezhda Bogdanova, who also toured widely; Anna Sobeshchanskaya; Polina Karpakova; Sergei Sokolov; and Ivan Yrmolov, along with the mimes Vasily Geltser, Fedor Reinshausen, and Wilhelm Wanner.

The traditions of the Bolshoi took shape in the early decades of the nineteenth century. The dramatic prevailed over the lyric; great attention was paid to plot and overt action. Comedy turned into *ballet bouffe* and tragedy into melodrama. The Moscow ballet was distinguished by vivid colors, dynamic changes of events, and individualized characters. Classical canons were often infringed upon in order to bring out a full spectrum of emotions. Dance technique was not refined, but relied instead on strength and outward effect. The latter half of the nineteenth century marked the artistic decline of the Bolshoi Ballet. From 1861 to 1864 the company and school were headed by the elderly Carlo Blasis. Although his productions were considered old-fashioned, he groomed ballerinas such as Sobeshchanskaya and Karpakova. Ballets by Arthur Saint-Léon, especially *The Little Humpbacked Horse,* with its Russian characters and folk dances, were well liked. The Moscow company attempted to promote

its own choreographer, Sergei Sokolov, by having him stage *The Fern, or Midsummer Night* in 1867. This provoked numerous comments in the press because it was based on a Russian theme but was structured on the model of Saint-Léon; its dramatic content was drowned in innumerable divertissements. Two years later Marius Petipa staged *Don Quixote* at the Bolshoi. This differed markedly from the subsequent production in Saint Petersburg, where many of its abundant national dances were replaced with classical variations and ensemble numbers.

During the 1870s the Bolshoi Ballet was led by the Austrian Julius (Wentzel) Reisinger, and until 1882 by the Belgian Joseph Hansen. The first *Swan Lake* was choreographed by Reisinger in 1877; it was unsuccessful, as was Hansen's revival three years later. *Swan Lake* was performed thirty-nine times before it was dropped in 1882, to be replaced by the Saint Petersburg version in 1901. In 1881 the newspaper *Moskovskie Vedomosti* noted, "Our society is rather indifferent to ballet today." About a third of the productions failed to meet their expenses; receipts ranged from 125 to 200 out of a possible 1,100 rubles. In addition, the Bolshoi always received less financial and artistic support from the directorate of the Imperial Theaters than did the company in the capital, Saint Petersburg. The mediocrity of successive choreographers and their contempt for Moscow's traditions also weakened the company. Then the reform of 1882 reduced the company by half, to 115 dancers. To make matters worse, most character dancers and mimes were dismissed, although they were the pride of the Moscow theater.

There were also more general difficulties. Beginning in the 1860s the ballet theater had lost its link with the other arts. Romanticism had been superseded by critical realism, a trend in Russian art and literature that was alien to ballet. Psychological, philosophical, and political writing was in favor. Aleksandr Ostrovsky's plays realistically depicted modern life. The painters of the group known as "The Wanderers" believed that art should explain life and comment on it. Program music was valued, as were the large-scale folk operas of Modest Mussorgsky. In ballet, however, reality was expressed not through the representation of the everyday world but through the embodiment of spiritual life in abstract forms. This was accomplished by Petipa and Lev Ivanov, in collaboration with Tchaikovsky and Glazunov, when profoundly meaningful classical ensembles appeared in ballets like *Swan Lake.* But the main line of the development of Russian ballet at this time was in the direction of pure dance, devoid of acting. Small wonder, then, that the Bolshoi lost its way and its standards deteriorated.

Aleksei Bogdanov, who led the company from 1883 to 1889, sought to bring Petipa's ballets to Moscow. Simultaneously, taking local interests into account, he staged a ballet on a Russian theme, *Svetlana, the Slavic Princess*

BOLSHOI BALLET. Olga Lepeshinskaya as Kitri and Aleksei Yermolayev as Basil in Rotislav Zakharov's staging of *Don Quixote,* after Marius Petipa, c.1940. (Reprinted from Bellew, 1956, p. 144.)

BOLSHOI BALLET. Olga Lepeshinskaya as Assol, a young girl who dreams that a seaman aboard a red-sailed ship will take her away, with the corps de ballet in *Crimson Sails*, 1943. Choreographed in 1942 by Nikolai Popko, Lev Pospekhin, and Aleksandr Radunsky, the ballet caused a controversy in the Soviet press because of its romantic theme. (Photograph from the Dance Collection, New York Public Library for the Performing Arts.)

(1886). He failed in both. The Spaniard José Mendes led the Bolshoi from 1889 to 1898, staging a number of ballets with spectacular effects but mediocre choreography. However, he was a good teacher who developed a company of good dancers, including Adelina Giuri, Liubov Roslavleva, Ivan Clustine, and Nikolai Domashov. The careers of Ekaterina Geltser and Vasily Tikhomirov began in the late 1890s.

Twentieth Century. In 1898 the directorate of the Imperial Theaters sent Aleksandr Gorsky to Moscow, and the Bolshoi entered a brilliant new era. Gorsky arrived the year that the Moscow Art Theater was founded by Konstantin Stanislavsky and Vladimir Nemirovich-Danchenko. Savva Mamontov's Private Opera staged productions designed by Mikhail Vrubel, Viktor and Apollinary Vasnetsov, Konstantin Korovin, and Valentin Serov. Fedor Chaliapin was singing in Moscow. Symbolism was the dominant trend in poetry. The World of Art group introduced avant-garde ideas from the West and promoted the idea of a new international culture. All of this activity influenced the young choreographer, who determined to overcome the stalemate in the Moscow ballet. In fact, his predilections were in accord with the traditions of the company, and his opportunity arrived just as the Petipa era ended and the development of all Russian ballet abruptly changed direction.

Aleksandr Gorsky. For more than twenty years, almost all the ballets staged at the Bolshoi were under Gorsky's direction. His ideal was a ballet drama with consistently developing action and dances illustrating that action, with a historically authentic background. All of his ballets were created in collaboration with an artist, usually Korovin, and every image was born of an interaction between choreography and scenography. In his efforts to reform the ballet, Gorsky drew close to the ideas of Michel Fokine, although the latter, working for Serge Diaghilev, had much greater independence. Leading the Bolshoi, Gorsky had to reckon with the demands of the directorate and the ballet stars as well as the need to preserve the traditional repertory. He had to make numerous compromises, and the number of productions in which he fully implemented his original conceptions was small. Further-

BOLSHOI BALLET. The company ensemble with Galina Ulanova (seated at center, on the left) in act 1, scene 4, of Leonid Lavrovsky's version of *Romeo and Juliet*. The Lavrovsky production, the first Soviet one using Sergei Prokofiev's score, was originally set on the Kirov Ballet in 1940. It became part of the Bolshoi repertory in 1946. (Photograph from the Dance Collection, New York Public Library for the Performing Arts.)

more, some of his finest works were short-lived, while those to which he attached less significance remained in the repertory. *Gudule's Daughter* (1902), based on the theme of Victor Hugo's *Notre-Dame de Paris*, was the work that Gorsky valued most of all, but it was performed only fourteen times in three seasons. In this "mimodrama" (Gorsky's term) the focus was on mass scenes showing the destitute, insurgent people. The heroine was depicted as the victim of human cruelty and stupidity. In *Salammbô* (1910) there were tense dramatic scenes, such as the visit of Salammbô to Matho's tent, her seduction, and the scene of her parting with the dying Matho.

Not all dancers were suited to Gorsky's ballets. He was most attracted to Sofia Fedorova, a character dancer who nevertheless danced the title role in his version of *Giselle*, as well as to Mikhail Mordkin, Alexandra Balashova, and Vera Karalli, who studied with him. But he had difficulty dealing with his two leading dancers, Ekaterina Geltser and Vasily Tikhomirov, both of whom advocated the preservation of the old ballets and virtuosic dance (they

had been trained in Saint Petersburg). His problems with Geltser, who was a fine dramatic dancer, sometimes diminished, as when he staged *Salammbô* for her. But he could find no common ground with Tikhomirov, who recognized only classical ballet. When the choreographer modernized ballets in order to achieve outward veracity, and when he remade Petipa's ensembles (e.g., in *La Bayadère* the scene of the shades was choreographed in Indian style), Geltser and Tikhomirov joined in protest.

There was considerable dispute about Gorsky's work in his lifetime, and even today there is no consensus. It is indisputable, however, that his productions, picturesque and luxuriantly decorated, and his dancers, full of life and dramatic power, were much admired by audiences in Moscow.

Post-revolution. In 1917 the country entered a new era. In 1918 Moscow became the capital of the Soviet Union, and the Bolshoi changed. Thanks to the greater importance given to the designer, productions had become more picturesque. Dance was now influenced by forms from the East and from antiquity and pervaded by pantomime that was livelier, more natural. In the dance of Geltser, Tikhomirov, and Mordkin a new style had grown out of the interaction between the traditions of the schools of Moscow and Saint Petersburg. The former, with its full-blooded life, juicy colors, rich gamut of choreographic patterns, and broad scope, took on a more classical and abstract character. Tikhomirov inculcated an academic as well as a manly manner of dance among his pupils, who included Laurent Novikoff, Alexandre Volinine, and Leonid Zhukov.

The decade of the 1920s in the USSR was a time of intensive exploration of new subjects and forms in art. Academic ballet stirred heated debates. Many people denied the value of traditional culture, claiming that ballet, as a creation of the old system, was useless to the people of the new era. More than once the Bolshoi was threatened with closure. However, government policy, upheld in particular by the Commissar of Enlightenment, Anatoly Lunacharsky, was to preserve the classical heritage. In these years most of the Bolshoi ballets were staged by Gorsky. For the first anniversary of the revolution he produced *Stenka Razin;* the story of the peasant rebel of the seventeenth century was considered appropriate for the times. In 1919 Gorsky staged *The Nutcracker* and in 1920 a new version of *Swan Lake.* His *Giselle* (1918 and 1922 revisions) emphasized the social aspect of the drama. As leading dancers, Geltser and Tikhomirov were joined by Viktorina Kriger and Margarita Kandaurova. Now Gorsky worked primarily with younger dancers, such as Maria Reisen, Viktor Smoltsov, and especially Anastasia Abramova, Valentina Kudriavtseva, Nina Podgoretskaia, and Lubov Bank, who were dubbed "the four." In the latter half of the decade they were joined by Asaf Messerer, Mikhail Gabovich, and Nikolai Tarasov. The mime traditions were preserved by Vladimir Riabtsev and Ivan Sidorov.

Experimental groups. Operating outside the academic theaters were Nikolai Foregger, with his "mechanical dances," and followers of Isadora Duncan as well as creators of various kinds of plastique dance and satirical programs. Among these, a conspicuous place was held by the Moscow Chamber Ballet of Kasyan Goleizovsky, which was remarkable for its high professional standards. Goleizovsky brought his innovations in dance language and composition to the Bolshoi in 1925 when he was invited to produce *Joseph the Beautiful.* Starting with the biblical story, he opposed the spiritual element, personified by the young Joseph, to the inhuman power of tyranny, epitomized by the pyramid of Pharaoh. The production was innovative in form: the constructivist principle of the designer, Boris Erdman, enabled groups of dancers to be placed on stages at different levels, while the costumes allowed the body full freedom. Goleizovsky's choreographic fantasy was revealed in unusual postures and movements that conveyed a wide range of emotional nuances, from pathetically meaningful to bordering on the grotesque.

Goleizovsky's work was supported by the young dancers and opposed by those dedicated to tradition. One of his chief detractors, Tikhomirov, staged a revival of *Esmeralda* for Geltser in 1926. The following year he produced *The Red Poppy* jointly with Lev Lashchilin. The ballet reflected some of the leading trends at the end of the 1920s and the beginning of the 1930s: a return to tradition, which had been rejected by the rebels of the early postrevolutionary years, and an interest in the psychology of the individual after a period of fascination with the lofty, abstract categories of revolution, the universe, war and peace, and the people. *The Red Poppy* was the first full-length ballet to present positive modern characters (the Soviet ship captain; the Chinese dancer Tao-Hoa). Its creators preserved the form of a nineteenth-century ballet with divertissements, pantomime scenes, and *féerie* (Tao-Hoa's dream), but modernized some parts, borrowing from related arts and show dance. The sailors' dance "Yablochko" (Little Apple), by Lashchilin, marked the first experiment in mass heroic dances, and it became one of the main innovations in the 1930s. The trend toward psychological detail, manifest in the characterization of Tao-Hoa, brought *The Red Poppy* closer to choreographic drama, which would become the main balletic genre in a

BOLSHOI BALLET. Aleksandr Lapauri as Khan Girei and Raisa Struchkova as Maria in act 2 of *The Fountain of Bakhchisarai,* c.1948. This ballet, choreographed by Rostislav Zakharov in 1934, is based on a poem by Aleksandr Pushkin that tells a dramatic story of love, abduction, jealousy, and death. (Photograph reprinted from Bellew, 1956, p. 31.)

few years. The production yielded generous box-office returns, which helped the Bolshoi to settle its financial problems, but it also evoked a polemic in the press and had quite a few opponents; a critic remarked, "One should not make a statue of a Red Army soldier out of whipped cream." Despite its modern content, *The Red Poppy* still used the same old pas de deux and waltzes of flowers.

The 1930s. The most significant Bolshoi productions of this decade were full-length dramatic ballets based on literary classics. This was historically logical. The experiments of the 1920s were not fully in line with the official demand for comprehensibility. Ballet was required to portray real life, and meaning was identified with the existence of a plot. The action developed from a clearly defined conflict and the presentation of familiar characters from Shakespeare, Pushkin, or Gogol ensured audience involvement. Pantomime conveyed the story, while dance was presented only where it was natural in everyday life, at balls and festivals. Dance was thus deprived of its meaningfulness and its metaphor.

Bolshoi choreographers worked on topical material, usually comedy. Among them were Igor Moiseyev and a group consisting of Aleksandr Radunsky, Nikolai Popko,

BOLSHOI BALLET. Maya Plisetskaya as Odette and Yuri Kondratov as Prince Siegfried with the corps de ballet in act 2 of *Swan Lake*, c.1947. This production was staged by Asaf Messerer after Aleksandr Gorsky's version of the original Lev Ivanov production. (Photograph reprinted from Bellew, 1956, p. 112.)

and Lev Pospekhin. *The Football Player*, staged by Moiseyev and Lashchilin in 1930, contained spectacular dances based on sports as well as comic episodes set in a department store. Moiseyev's *Three Fat Men* (1935) described a popular uprising against a triumvirate of rulers. A modern children's fairy tale, it contained some fascinating dances (a peddler of toy balloons swept away by the wind, kitchen boys in the palace). Suok, who sneaked into the palace disguised as a doll, was performed by the young Olga Lepeshinskaya, a playful and agile virtuoso. Radunsky with Popko and Pospekhin staged *Svetlana* for her in 1939. The plot of a Soviet girl tracking down a saboteur was similar to those of many plays and motion pictures of those years; the character of the cheerful, energetic, brave girl who felt equal to men was typical; and the lifelike pantomime scenes and melodramatic episodes with striking stage effects were familiar.

For the Bolshoi at this period the assimilation of achievements from elsewhere was important. The Bolshoi had begun to assume the status of the country's leading theater, and a number of changes were made to bolster its position. The dancers Marina Semenova, Aleksei Yermolayev, Petr Gusev, and Sergei Koren and the choreographer Rostislav Zakharov were transferred from Leningrad, and several teachers from the Leningrad school, Elisaveta Gerdt among them, were also moved to Moscow. The repertory included ballets favored in Leningrad: Vasily Vainonen's *The Flames of Paris*, Za-

BOLSHOI BALLET. Galina Ulanova as Mireille de Poitiers in act 3 of *The Flames of Paris*, c.1955. This ballet, set in Revolutionary France, was originally choreographed by Vasily Vainonen in Leningrad in 1932. (Photograph reprinted from Bellew, 1956, p. 42.)

kharov's *The Fountain of Bakhchisarai,* and Fedor Lopukhov's *The Bright Stream.* The first two became Moscow favorites. In *The Flames of Paris* Yermolayev presented a distinctive interpretation of the main character, giving the dance forcefulness and daring. He danced a variation holding an ax as if fighting his way through enemy ranks. In *The Fountain of Bakhchisarai* the heroine was danced by Galina Ulanova when she came to the Bolshoi at the end of World War II. The Girei Khan was one of Gusev's finest creations.

World War II and after: Lavrovsky, Zakharov, and Vainonen. During the war the Bolshoi was evacuated to Samara (then Kuibyshev), where it stayed until the autumn of 1943. Along with its classical repertory the company gave the premiere of *Crimson Sails* (1942) by Popko, Pospekhin, and Radunsky. Simultaneously, part of the company continued to perform in Moscow in the building of the Bolshoi Filial Theater, which was the second stage for the company from 1924 to 1959.

In 1944 Leonid Lavrovsky was appointed chief choreographer of the Bolshoi. That year he staged *Giselle* in Moscow and two years later *Romeo and Juliet.* Starring Ulanova, these ballets held pride of place in the Bolshoi repertory. Ulanova's Juliet intuitively followed the music, rising above the historically concrete. She personified the lofty lyrical element in bitter conflict with cruelty, stupid-

ity, and fanaticism. This theme had great appeal in these years of severe ordeal, when people suffered under the totalitarian regime and then faced mortal combat with the Nazis, but it did not lose its significance later.

Throughout the postwar decade Zakharov and Vainonen staged ballets at the Bolshoi along with Lavrovsky. Zakharov's *Cinderella* was staged as a brilliant spectacle, loud and jubilant like a victory salute—it was 1945. In Zakharov's *The Bronze Horseman* (1949) the central scene of the flood was depicted with amazing authenticity, but the philosophical theme of Pushkin's poem (collision between the interests of the state represented by the Horseman, that is, Peter the Great, and the man in the street) was absent. In these years the strength of the Bolshoi was not so much its productions as the skill of its dancers. Along with Ulanova, Lepeshinskaya, Radunsky, Sofia Golovkina, Yuri Kondratov, Valentina Galetskaya, and Nadezhda Kapustina, new members included Maya Plisetskaya, Raisa Struchkova, Marina Kondratieva, Vladimir Preobrajensky, Yuri Zhdanov, Nikolai Fadeyechev, Yaroslav Sekh, and Vladimir Levashev. The conductor Yuri Fayer (1890–1971) played a major role in the company's development.

In 1954 great hopes were held out for the new ballet that Sergei Prokofiev composed for the Bolshoi, but in Lavrovsky's staging of *The Tale of the Stone Flower* scenes of

BOLSHOI BALLET. Nina Timofeyeva as the Mistress of the Copper Mountain and Ekaterina Maximova as Katerina in act 3 of *The Stone Flower*, choreographed by Yuri Grigorovich. This Soviet ballet premiered in 1954 and was presented on the company's first tour of the United States in 1959. (Photograph reprinted from a Bolshoi Ballet souvenir program, 1959.)

village life and oppression of the workers were in the foreground. The theme of an artist's quest for an ideal (embodied in the "beauty of stone") had vanished. By this time a protest against illustrativeness, false realism, and poverty of dancing had arisen in Soviet ballet. Works staged in Leningrad attached a more essential role to dance, and some of them were transferred to Moscow, for example, Leonid Yakobson's *Shurale*. In 1956 an attempt was made to return Moscow choreographers to the theater. However, neither Moiseyev's *Spartacus* nor Radunsky's new staging of *The Little Humpbacked Horse* to a score by Rodion Shchedrin was a success. The turning point came with Yuri Grigorovich's *The Stone Flower* to Prokofiev's score, staged first in Leningrad in 1957 and brought to Moscow in 1959. Here the essential element was not twists and turns of external action but a philosophical theme: the unquenchable thirst for knowledge. The Bolshoi received Grigorovich's *Legend of Love* in 1965.

It soon became clear that the new trend that emphasized the priority of dance—represented first by Lopukhov, Yakobson, and Goleizovsky, then by Grigorovich and Igor Belsky—had emerged victorious. Neglected genres and forms were revived, and the language of dance was enriched. Some of the talented advocates of dramatic ballet began to revise their views. Lavrovsky, for example, staged a number of one-act ballets at the Bolshoi: *Paganini* in 1960 and *Night City* in 1961. For a short time the one-act ballet, in which it was easier to experiment, was popular. Natalia Kasatkina and Vladimir Vasiliov proved gifted choreographers with *Geologists* (1964) and *Le Sacre du*

Printemps (1965), for which they devised a new libretto. Goleizovsky returned with *Scriabiniana* (1962) and *Leili and Medzhnun* (1964).

The 1960s to 1995: Yuri Grigorovich. In 1964 Yuri Grigorovich became chief choreographer of the Bolshoi. Quite logically the repertory and performance manner reflected his favored themes and style. One may also speak of harmony between the choreographer's artistic character and the objective tasks facing the company. In addition to the works he brought from Leningrad, Grigorovich choreographed many original ballets at the Bolshoi: *Spartacus* (1968); *Ivan the Terrible* (1975); *The Angara* (1976); *Romeo and Juliet* (1979); and *The Golden Age* (1982). He also produced his own versions of the Tchaikovsky ballets and *Raymonda*. After the mid-1980s he created no new works or productions. His works were distinguished by the stylistic integrity championed by choreographers of the early twentieth century, primarily Fokine; at the same time, Grigorovich relied on large classical ensembles reminiscent of Petipa's grand ballet. His productions emphasized dance throughout but had a uniform language, unlike Petipa's ballets, which were based on contrasts of pantomime and dance, and also unlike the dramatic ballets of the 1930s, where integrity was present but dance was absent. His productions were spectacular and monu-

BOLSHOI BALLET. From left to right, Galina Ulanova, Nikolai Fadeyechev, and Raisa Struchkova in a 1960 performance of Michel Fokine's *Chopiniana*, known outside Russia as *Les Sylphides*. (Photograph by Albert E. Kahn; reprinted from his *Days with Ulanova*, London, 1962, p. 44.)

mental; the choreographer's personal theme conveyed a social message.

The ballets of Grigorovich, which tended to focus on a hero torn by contradictory passions, starred Vladimir Vasiliev, Mikhail Lavrovsky, Maris Liepa, Yuri Vladimirov, Aleksandr Bogatyrev, and Viacheslav Gordeyev. Leading female roles were danced by Natalia Bessmertnova, Ekaterina Maximova, Maya Plisetskaya, Nina Timofeyeva, and Nina Sorokina. Plisetskaya's personal creative theme—the drama of a freedom-loving and strong-willed woman—demanded productions especially designed for her. These included Alberto Alonso's *Carmen Suite* (1967) as well as her own ballets *Anna Karenina* (1972), *The Seagull* (1980), and *The Lady with a Lapdog* (1986). Also, Vasiliev choreographed for the Bolshoi *Icarus* (1971), *These Charming Sounds* (1978), *Macbeth* (1980), and *Aniuta* (1986). Most of the company members have been graduates of the Moscow ballet school, such as Nina Ananiashvili, Irek Mukhamedov, Andris Liepa, Aleksei Fadeyechev, and Yuri Posokhov, but some were trained in Leningrad (Timofeyeva, Ludmila Semenyaka), Perm (Nadezhda Pavlova), and Kiev (Nina Semizorova). As the 1980s waned the Bolshoi began to lose some of its best dancers, to companies abroad (Mukhamedov went to London) and even to the Kirov Ballet (Andris Liepa), primarily because of the stagnant atmosphere within the company, with no new ballets by Grigorovich and very few by guest choreographers. In 1994 a campaign was begun in the press and in ballet circles to induce Grigorovich to resign. The director of the Bolshoi Theater,

BOLSHOI BALLET. Stanislav Vlasov holds Ludmila Vlaslova aloft in *The Doves*, choreographed by Vladimir Varkovitsky and Stanislav Vlasov. This one-handed lift is typical of the Bolshoi's acrobatic partnering style. (Photograph reprinted from a Bolshoi Ballet souvenir program, 1966.)

BOLSHOI BALLET. Mikhail Lavrovsky and Natalia Bessmertnova in Agrippina Vaganova's *Diana and Acteon*, set to music by Ricardo Drigo. (Photograph reprinted from a Bolshoi Ballet souvenir program, 1962.)

Vladimir Kokonin, and Vladimir Vasiliev were especially active in this movement. After nearly a year of infighting Grigorovich capitulated, and in March 1995 Vasiliev was named joint director with Kokonin of the Bolshoi Theater—comprising the opera, ballet, and theater companies—with Viacheslav Gordeyev and Aleksandr Bogatyrev heading the ballet. After this there were several premieres: in 1995 a revival of Leonid Lavrovsky's *Paganini* and a new ballet, *Snowflake and the Seven Dwarfs*, choreographed by Henrik Mayorov; in 1996 a revival of Lavrovsky's *Romeo and Juliet*. Vasiliev's intent is to shore up the theater's finances and to internationalize the ballet company's repertory.

The style of the Bolshoi has been shaped by its repertory. Gradually, as the dance element was intensified in the 1960s, the emphasis on mime began to diminish. Because later ballets have been choreographed in the language of classical dance touched with national color, character dances in pure form have largely survived only in the nineteenth-century repertory. The style is also determined by the company's official status as the country's

BOLSHOI BALLET. The corps de ballet in a formation from *Giselle*, act 2. The classical precision seen here reflects the company's emphasis on pure dancing over dramatic elements. (Photograph by Larisa Pedenchuk; courtesy of Columbia Artists Management, Inc., New York.)

leading theater. It is significant that both the Bolshoi Theater and the Kremlin Palace of Congresses, where the company also performed from 1961 to 1990, have offered their stages for many sociopolitical events. In this capacity the company has addressed its art not only to followers of specific trends but also to a mass audience of varied tastes and interests. This need to appeal to a broad public has precluded consideration of the theater as an experimental center. In the selection of themes and the choice of means of expression, general accessibility and attractiveness to the masses must be taken into account—hence the spectacular stage effects, the dynamism and clarity of the story ballets, and the ability of the dancers to address the public directly through virtuosic dancing and expressive acting. The Bolshoi has assumed its present significance in the course of two centuries, gaining and losing, borrowing and creating. In our day it embodies many important features of modern reality.

[*Many of the principal figures mentioned herein are the subjects of independent entries.*]

BIBLIOGRAPHY

Avaliani, Noi, and Leonid Zhdanov, comps. *Bolshoi's Young Dancers.* Translated by Natalie Ward. Moscow, 1975.
Bellew, Hélène. *Ballet in Moscow Today.* Greenwich, Conn., 1956.
"The Bolshoi Saga." *The Dancing Times* (April 1995): 673.
Bolshoi Teatr. *Istoriia. Opera. Balet.* Moscow, 1986. Photoalbum.
Bolshoi Teatr SSSR. *Sezony s 1974 po 1980.* Moscow, 1987.
The Bolshoi Theatre. Moscow, 1990. In English and Russian.
Chernova, Natalia. *Ot Geltser do Ulanovoi.* Moscow, 1979.
Churova, Marina, ed. *Bolshoi Teatr SSSR*, vol. 1, *Sent. 1969–1970*; vol. 2, *August 1970–1971, Sent. 1971–1972*; vol. 3, *Sent. 1972–1973, 1973–1974.* Moscow, 1973–1981.
Churova, Marina, ed. *Segodnia na stsene Bol'shogo Teatra, 1776–1976: K 200-letiiu Bol'shogo Teatra.* Moscow, 1976.
Collins, Richard. *Behind the Bolshoi Curtain.* London, 1974.
Garafola, Lynn. "Vladimir Vasiliev: Champion of Perestroika." *Dance Magazine* (November 1990): 50–53.
Greskovic, Robert. "The Bolshoi: The Picture Changes." *Ballet Review* 4.5 (1973): 35–49.
Greskovic, Robert. "The Grigorovich Factor and the Bolshoi." *Ballet Review* 5.2 (1975–1976): 1–10.
Greskovic, Robert. "After the Golden Age." *New Dance Review* 1 (June–July 1988): 18–22.
Greskovic, Robert. "The Bolshoi: Of Mime and Men." *Ballet Review* 18 (Fall 1990): 35–54.
Gozenpud, A. A. *Muzykalnyi teatr v Rossii: Ot istokov do Glinki.* Leningrad, 1959.
Grosheva, Elena A. *Bolshoi Teatr soiuza SSR.* Moscow, 1978.
Kinnear, Alex. "Instability at the Bolshoi." *Dance International* 22 (Winter 1994–1995): 10–13.
Krasovskaya, Vera. *Russkii baletnyi teatr: Ot vozniknoveniia do serediny XIX veka.* Leningrad, 1958.
Krasovskaya, Vera. *Russkii baletnyi teatr vtoroi poloviny deviatnadtsatogo veka.* Leningrad, 1963.
Krasovskaya, Vera. *Russkii baletnyi teatr nachala dvadtsatogo veka*, vol. 1, *Khoreografy*; vol. 2, *Tantsovshchiki.* Leningrad, 1971–1972.
Lunacharskii, A. V., and I. V. Ekskuzovich, eds. *Moskovskii Bolshoi Teatr, 1825–1925.* Moscow, 1925.
Lvov-Anokhin, Boris. *Mastera Bolshogo Baleta.* Moscow, 1976.
Manning, Emma. "War at the Bolshoi." *Dance Australia* (June–July 1995): 44.
Moore, Lillian. "The Bolshoi Ballet at Home and Abroad." *Dance Magazine* (April 1959): 35–43.
Pokrovsky, Boris, and Yuri Grigorovich. *The Bolshoi: Opera and Ballet at the Greatest Theater in Russia.* New York, 1976.
Slonimsky, Yuri, et al. *The Bolshoi Ballet Story* (in English). Moscow, 1959.
Souritz, Elizabeth. *Soviet Choreographers in the 1920s.* Translated by Lynn Visson. Durham, N.C., 1990.

Swift, Mary Grace. *The Art of the Dance in the U.S.S.R.* Notre Dame, 1968.

Verdy, Violette. "Violette Verdy on the Bolshoi." *Ballet Review* 15 (Summer 1987): 15–38.

ARCHIVES. Bolshoi Museum, Moscow. Bolshoi Theater, Moscow. Central State Archive of Literature and Art, Moscow.

ELIZABETH SOURITZ

BOMBAY FILM MUSICALS. *See* Film Musicals, *article on* Bollywood Film Musicals.

BONFANTI, MARIE (Anna Maria Felicita Bonfanti; born 16 February 1845 in Milan, died 25 January 1921 in New York City), musical theater dancer. Best known for her work in musical theater in the United States where she was variously known as Marie or Maria, Bonfanti had trained in Milan privately with Carlo Blasis and at his school at the Teatro alla Scala. On 3 January 1860 she made her debut in Vercelli, Italy. In 1863 she left Italy and, after engagements in Lyon and Paris, became one of the featured dancers at Covent Garden, London. In the spring of 1865 she appeared in Madrid in *Masaniello* to great acclaim. A marriage proposal ensued, but her mother, fearing that a morganatic marriage would end her career, had her sign a contract to appear in the United States.

Bonfanti came to New York as the *prima ballerina assoluta* in her 12 September 1866 American debut at Niblo's Garden Theatre in *The Black Crook.* This thinly plotted melodrama, the prototype for nineteenth-century American musical spectacles, combined elaborate scenery, lavish costumes, variety artists, European ballerinas, and scantily clad show girls. Scandalous and enormously popular, *The Black Crook* was revised regularly throughout the nineteenth century. Although Bonfanti danced in many operettas and ballets, she is most closely associated with this production. Not only did she remain with it throughout its initial run, but she appeared regularly in revivals, both in New York and on nationwide tours. She brought to this role a ladylike modesty and an understated, precise technique based on Blasis's principles. A writer for the *New York Clipper* of 5 January 1867 noted her appeal as follows: "She is slight of figure and softly bland of features. Her style of dancing is in accordance with the elegance of her person; it is full of grace, buoyant and elastic, avoiding all exertions of other artists who seem to think the ballet is a school of gymnastics."

A star from the beginning to the end of her career in the United States, Bonfanti insisted in all her contracts on *prima ballerina assoluta* billing. She concentrated on maintaining her technical excellence and returned to Milan each summer for two months of training.

BONFANTI. A portrait of the Italian-born ballerina in costume for the "Pas de Demons" that she danced in *The Black Crook*, a spectacle staged at Niblo's Gardens, New York, in 1866. (Photograph from the Theater and Music Collection, Museum of the City of New York.)

Following the close of *The Black Crook* on 4 January 1868, Bonfanti appeared in a similar production, *The White Fawn*, which ran for 175 performances. She toured Chicago, Philadelphia, and Boston before returning to New York on 1 January 1869 for the opening of *The Tammany*, a musical revue. In December 1869 she traveled to San Francisco to appear at the Opera House in the musical spectacle *Robinson Crusoe*. On 12 December 1870 Bonfanti and her partner Giovanni Novissimo returned to Niblo's for a revival of *The Black Crook*.

In the spring of 1872, on her first tour of the southern United States, she met George C. Hoffman, scion of a wealthy and socially prominent New York family, and they were married in August 1872 in Paris. The couple remained in Europe for the following theatrical season, Bonfanti fulfilling engagements in England. Their daughter Sophia was born at Lake Como, Switzerland, on 14

July 1873. Hoffman, fearing parental disapproval, kept his marriage and child a secret. For the next two years Bonfanti divided her time between performances in New York City and touring productions of spectacles. In November 1875 she appeared in yet another *Black Crook* revival, with the Kiralfy family at New York's Grand Opera House.

Bonfanti's husband died in 1876, and his creditors sued Bonfanti's father-in-law for the debts the younger Hoffman had incurred. New York newspapers publicized the lawsuit and the clandestine marriage. Bonfanti retired for a brief time, returning to the stage on 27 September 1876 in Augustin Daly's production of *Life* at the Fifth Avenue Theatre in New York. The play featured her as the Spirit of the Sun in "The Snow Ballet."

Her performing career lasted another fifteen years. She danced in the musical comedies *The Devil's Auction* (1876), *Baba* (1877), and *Around the World in Eighty Days* (1878). She also danced with the Strakosh Opera Company in 1879, and she appeared in *Humpty Dumpty* (1879–1881), a burlesque musical revue, at Booth's Theatre in New York and in the Boston Theatre Company's *Voyagers in Southern Seas* (1880/81). In the 1885/86 season, Bonfanti was *prima ballerina* at the Metropolitan Opera House in New York.

Much of Bonfanti's later career was spent on tour. In 1882 she performed seven months of one-night stands with the Kiralfy brothers' *Black Crook* company. She also toured for seventeen months (1888–1890) in a production of *The Twelve Temptations*. In 1892 Bonfanti retired from the stage and in 1897 opened a dancing school in New York City. She taught until 1916. Among her pupils were many prominent New York society people as well as professional actors and dancers. Bonfanti died of pneumonia in Roosevelt Hospital in New York City in 1921.

Bonfanti bridged an important period in the history of American theatrical dance. She brought the traditions of Carlo Blasis and La Scala to the United States and refused to alter them to suit the American taste in theatrical dancing. Throughout her career she maintained the highest technical standards and kept ballet alive in the most unlikely surroundings. In later life a strict, conservative teacher, Bonfanti instilled in her American pupils a love for ballet and a respect for its traditions.

[*See also* Black Crook, The.]

BIBLIOGRAPHY
Barker, Barbara. "The Dancer vs. the Management in Post–Civil War America." *Dance Chronicle* 2.3 (1978): 172–187.
Barker, Barbara. "Maria Bonfanti and the Black Crook, New Orleans, 1872." *Theatre Journal* 31 (March 1979).
Barker, Barbara. *Ballet or Ballyhoo: The American Careers of Maria Bonfanti, Rita Sangalli, and Giuseppina Morlacchi.* New York, 1984.
Barzel, Ann. "European Dance Teachers in the United States." *Dance Index* 3 (April–June 1944): 56–100.
Freedley, George. "*The Black Crook* and *The White Fawn.*" *Dance Index* 4 (January 1945): 4–16.
Moore, Lillian. "The Metropolitan Opera Ballet, 1883–1851." In Moore's *Echoes of American Ballet*. Brooklyn, 1976.
Odell, George C. D. *Annals of the New York Stage.* Vols. 8–13. New York, 1936–1938.

ARCHIVE.   The Bonfanti Collection, containing playbills, contracts, photographs, sheet music, and manuscript material, is located in the Dance Collection of the New York Public Library for the Performing Arts.

BARBARA BARKER

BON ODORI, or *bon* dancing, is part of a Japanese festival for the dead known as O-bon, held annually for three days in mid-July. Traditionally performed outdoors, *bon odori* begins in the early evening and generally follows a religious ceremony to honor ancestors. The dancing is usually done in a circular formation (either a single circle or several concentric circles) around a small tower atop which musicians perform. Community participation is encouraged, and the dances are frequently simple enough that watching several repetitions of the movement pattern allows a spectator to join the dance group easily.

The legend of how *bon* dancing originated in India is related in early Buddhist religious texts. Because of his meritorious actions, Mauggallena (Jpn., Mokuren), a disciple of the Buddha, was granted the power to see beyond the surface reality of the world. Using this power, he observed his mother condemned to a world of suffering and hunger because of the ill deeds she had performed during her life. Mauggallena tried to aid his mother by sending her a bowl of rice, but each time she attempted to eat it, it burst into flames. Seeking advice from priests, Mauggallena was told to feed the priestly ancestral spirits on the fifteenth day of the seventh month. When he did so, his mother was freed from her suffering and danced. Mauggallena was so happy that he, too, danced for joy, and people around him joined in the excitement and dancing.

Buddhists in India continued to celebrate this event and, as Buddhism spread to China and Japan, so did the festival. Around the sixth century it is believed to have reached Japan, where it became enmeshed with indigenous festivals.

Movements used in *bon* dances are usually simple and involve both locomotor patterns and arm movements. The footwork is made up of stepping (in almost all directions), touching a part of the foot to the ground without putting any weight on it, and small turns. There are few jumps or other forms of elevation. Arm gestures are more elaborate—they may be literal pantomimic motions, such as those of shoveling coal, or purely abstract movements that serve decorative purposes. (Some of the abstract gestures may originally have had literal meanings, but these have been lost over time.) The dancers' hands are relaxed, with fingers generally held close together, as in most theatrical forms of Japanese dance. Some dances involve the manipulation of accessories such as fans, hats, parasols, or small towels.

Dances and the sung texts that accompany them are frequently regional or national in character and reflect local occupations and historical events. Coal-mining and fishing dances are common in some areas, as are songs about wars that Japan has fought. In some areas of Japan, *bon* dancing has taken on a carnival-like atmosphere, with hundreds of people dancing in the streets and some dancers wearing masks. In other areas a more ritualistic aura has been retained. In still others more complex dances are performed and more elaborate costumes are used.

As Japanese emigrated to other parts of the world, they brought their traditional religious celebrations with them. Today, *bon* dancing may be seen not only in Japan but also in other locales where groups of Japanese reside. Modernization and transplantation have brought about many changes in *bon odori*, ranging from the incorporation of upbeat, disco-influenced choreography to the use of *bon* dancing for commercial purposes.

[*See also* Japan, *articles on folk and ritual dance; and* Okinawa.]

BIBLIOGRAPHY

Ashikaga Ensho. "Notes on Urabon ('Yu Lan P'en Ullambana')." *Journal of the American Oriental Society* 71.1: 71–75.

Duyvendak, J. J. L. "The Buddhistic Festival of All-Souls in China and Japan." *Acta Orientalia* 5: 39–48.

Malalasekara, G. P. *Encyclopedia of Buddhism.* Ceylon, 1961–. Vol. 3, pp. 274–280.

Van Zile, Judy. *The Japanese Bon Dance in Hawaii.* Honolulu, 1982.

JUDY VAN ZILE

BOQUET, LOUIS (Louis-René Boquet; born 1717 in Paris, died 7 December 1814 in Paris), French painter, costume and scenery designer. Boquet began his career as a master fan painter. After 1751 he began designing the costumes and supervising their manufacture for French court entertainments. By the end of the 1750s he was invited to do the same work at the Paris Opera, succeeding Jean-Baptiste Martin. His position at the court, however, was more important, for he was also ordered to work on the properties and sets needed for performances. Boquet also supplied costume models for productions mounted in Stuttgart by the famous choreographer Jean-Georges Noverre, who was a strong influence on his style.

Boquet was initially inspired by the examples of his predecessors Jean Berain, Claude Gillot, and Martin, while respecting the conventions they had adopted to characterize various theatrical roles. Using traditional motifs for the costumes of furies, zephyrs, and tritons, he arranged them with greater lightness, giving little impor-

tance to embroideries and other decorative elements. This return to greater simplicity was also accompanied, during the 1770s, by a search for historical accuracy. Under the impetus of Noverre and the actor Henri-Louis Lekain, Boquet thus contributed to the transformation of stage costuming that occurred at the end of the eighteenth century. His early work, still marked by the grace of rococo art, remains the most charming of all his styles, as revealed by numerous extant drawings, several of them done for operas by Jean-Philippe Rameau.

BIBLIOGRAPHY

Beaumont, Cyril W. *Five Centuries of Ballet Design.* London, 1939.

Fischer, Carlos. *Les costumes de l'Opéra.* Paris, 1931.

Michel, Marianne R. *Les étapes de la création: Esquisses et dessins de Boucher à Isabey.* Paris, 1989.

Tessier, André. "Les habits d'opéra au XVIIIe siècle." *Revue de l'art* (January–March 1926).

Thienen, Frithjof van. "Louis René Boquet." In Thienen's *Ballettkultur und Lebensform.* Graz, 1967.

JÉRÔME DE LA GORCE
Translated from French

BORCHSENIUS, VALBORG (Valborg Jørgensen; born 19 November 1872, died 5 January 1949 in Copenhagen), Danish dancer and teacher. Borchsenius taught the Bournonville tradition to dancers of the Royal Danish Ballet, who, from the 1930s through the 1950s, both at home and abroad, won acclaim both for themselves as well as for August Bournonville (1805–1879). She came to the ballet school at the Royal Theater in Copenhagen as a student in the late 1870s and was one of Nora's children in the first performance of Henrik Ibsen's *A Doll's House* in 1879. Her teachers at the school were Daniel Krum and Emil Hansen, and in 1888 Borchsenius made her debut as the Eskimo Girl in Bournonville's *Far from Denmark*. In 1891 she danced *La Sylphide*, the first of a long series of leading parts in Bournonville ballets. Typical of her dancing was its respect for tradition. She was Astrid in *Waldemar*, Hilda in *A Folk Tale*, Sigyn in *The Lay of Thrym*, Ragnhild and Kirsti in *A Wedding Festival at Hardanger*, Svava in *The Valkyrie*, and Celeste in *The Toreador*. Her partner in most of these ballets was Hans Beck. She became a principal dancer in 1895 and retired in 1918.

Borchsenius was a blond, smiling dancer. She was more full-figured than is customary today, but in films of the Royal Danish Ballet from 1902 through 1906 she exhibits a fantastic yet natural *ballon*, a lightness of movement. For her last performance, as Swanilda in *Coppélia*, she danced her favorite role outside the Bournonville repertory.

Borchsenius was away from the theater for a few years in the 1920s, but she later returned to teach young students. In addition to being head of the mime school, which Harald Lander established in 1941, in the 1930s and 1940s she and Lander staged many of the Bournonville ballets that are still performed today. Other companies have since restaged them many times over—but with the Borchsenius and Lander versions as their models. Early on, Borchsenius began to write down the Bournonville ballets; she continued to do so systematically for the last twenty years of her life. Given Bournonville's ongoing influence on the company, her notations have come to be regarded as the core of the Royal Danish Ballet's tradition.

[See also Royal Danish Ballet.]

BIBLIOGRAPHY

Kragh-Jacobsen, Svend, and Torben Krogh, eds. *Den Kongelige Danske Ballet.* Copenhagen, 1952.

ERIK ASCHENGREEN

BORIS, RUTHANNA (born 17 March 1918 in Brooklyn), American dancer, choreographer, and teacher. Boris studied ballet at the Metropolitan Opera Ballet School and with Leon Fokine; she studied Spanish dancing with Helen Veola. She made her solo debut with the Metropolitan Opera Ballet in *Carmen* in 1935 and was soloist with Ballet Caravan in the 1936/37 season, creating the title role in Lew Christensen's *Pocahontas* (1936). She was featured with Paul Haakon in Agnes de Mille's dances for *Hooray for What!* (1937) and with André Eglevsky in the *Ziegfeld Follies* at the San Francisco World's Fair in 1940. From 1937 to 1942 she was *prima ballerina* at the Metropolitan Opera Ballet. From 1943 to 1950, she performed a wide range of classical and contemporary ballet roles as soloist and principal dancer for Serge Denham's Ballet Russe. Cool and precise in her interpretations of the classics and the Balanchine repertory, Boris excelled in roles that utilized her talents for both broad and subtle comedy.

For the Ballet Russe, Boris choreographed *Cirque de Deux* (1947), in which she danced with Leon Danielian, and *Quelques Fleurs* (1948) for Danielian and Mary Ellen Moylan. For the New York City Ballet, she created her most popular ballet, *Cakewalk* (1951), a comic romp depicting the antics and sentiments of an American minstrel show, as well as *Kaleidoscope* (1952) and *Will-o'-the-Wisp* (1953).

Boris toured with her husband, Frank Hobi, and with Stanley Zampakos in a small concert group from 1954 to 1956. As *prima ballerina* and director of the Royal Winnipeg Ballet for the 1956/57 season, she choreographed *Roundelay, Le Jazz Hot,* and *The Comedians* (all 1956) and revived *Cirque de Deux.*

Boris created dances for the Broadway musical *Two on the Aisle* (1951) and danced in the 1958 Broadway revival of *Annie Get Your Gun.* From 1965 to 1983 she was associate professor of drama and director of dance at the University of Washington in Seattle. She later worked as a family counselor in San Francisco.

BIBLIOGRAPHY

Anderson, Jack. *The One and Only: The Ballet Russe de Monte Carlo.* New York, 1981.

Barzel, Ann. "Ballerina: Savante." *Dance Magazine* (August 1947): 12–13.

Moore, Lillian. "The Metropolitan Opera Ballet Story." *Dance Magazine* (January 1951): 20–48.

Reynolds, Nancy, and Susan Reimer-Torn. "Cakewalk." In *Dance Classics.* Pennington, N.J., 1991.

Tracy, Robert, and Sharon DeLano. *Balanchine's Ballerinas: Conversations with the Muses.* New York, 1983.

Wyman, Max. *The Royal Winnipeg Ballet: The First Forty Years.* Toronto, 1978.

LELAND WINDREICH

BORNEO. *See* Indonesia, *article on* Dance Traditions of the Outlying Islands.

BOROVANSKY, EDOUARD (born 24 February 1902 in Prerov, Czechoslovakia, died 18 December 1959 in Sydney, New South Wales), Australian dancer, choreographer, and administrator. Borovansky began his dancing career in the corps de ballet of the Prague National Theater. After studying in Paris with Olga Preobrajenska and Lubov Egorova, he joined Anna Pavlova's touring company in 1916 and visited Australia in 1929, playing mostly *demi-caractère* roles. From 1932 to 1939 he was a soloist with various of the Ballets Russes companies managed by Colonel W. de Basil, returning to Australia with the Covent Garden Russian Ballet in 1938. With the German occupation of his homeland and the imminent outbreak of war, he decided to stay in Australia. In 1939 he founded a ballet school in Melbourne with his wife, Xenia Smirnoff, daughter of Alexandra Nikolaeva, a niece of Victor Dandré, and a classical dancer and teacher.

Borovansky's students matured quickly under his driving pressure. He trained them to become stage dancers, not to gain certificates or graduate as teachers. After some charity performances the company gave its first professional performance at the Comedy Theatre in Melbourne for two nights in 1940, as the Borovansky Australian Ballet. (It later became known simply as the Australian Ballet.)

After this, studio performances continued with the aid of the Melbourne Ballet Club, which built a small stage in Borovansky's studio. Two highly successful seasons at the Princess Theatre in 1942 proved that there was a large audience eager for ballet in Melbourne. Unable to engage overseas companies during the war, J. C. Williamson Theatres, Ltd., Australia's major theatrical management organization, hired the Borovansky Ballet in 1943. During the

1940s and 1950s the company regularly toured Australia and New Zealand under the commercial management of the Williamson organization. Margot Fonteyn, Michael Somes, Rowena Jackson, and Bryan Ashbridge appeared as guest artists in 1957, and John Cranko and David Lichine staged works for the company.

The association with the Williamson organization continued, with several long interruptions, until Borovansky's death from a stroke in 1959. Peggy van Praagh came from England to direct the company, which was finally dissolved at the very end of the 1960/61 season. She later returned to direct the Australian Ballet, with a strong nucleus of Borovansky dancers.

With his driving force, Borovansky formed a highly professional team of dancers. Despite setbacks due to commercial management and lack of continuity, the company justified his confidence in its ability. The first two ballerinas trained at his school, Edna Busse and Rachel Cameron, both left at their peak. He was fortunate that two accomplished Australian dancers and choreographers, Laurel Martyn and Dorothy Stevenson, were summoned home from England at the outbreak of war and joined him.

In his search for male dancers, then scarce in Australia, Borovansky was rewarded by two youngsters whose families had emigrated from Europe, Martin Rubinstein and Vassilie Trunoff, who later made a success in London. Several refugees from the de Basil companies who had stayed in Australia were enlisted, notably Tamara Tchinarova. Hélène Kirsova had started her own company in Sydney in 1941 and won an instant following, but its competition ended when it was disbanded in 1944, leaving Borovansky a bonus of several leading dancers: Peggy Sager, Hélène Ffrance, Strelsa Heckelman, and Paul Hammond.

The repertory, which grew to more than ninety ballets, included several of Borovansky's own entertaining, light-hearted ballets, four short-lived Australian works, and one tribute to his homeland, *Vltava*—all of which have been laid aside—some restagings, two works by Laurel Martyn, one by Dorothy Stevenson, and other originals. Most of the decor came from a collaboration with the talented William Constable. Kurt Herweg was the principal musical director.

Borovansky left three brilliant young dancers, Kathleen Gorham, Marilyn Jones, and Garth Welch, to the Australian Ballet as well as the nucleus of a corps of dancers and a receptive audience.

[*See also* Australia, *article on* Ballet.]

BIBLIOGRAPHY
Bartram, Judy. "Edouard Borovansky: Repertoire and Dancers, 1939–43." *Brolga* no. 1 (December 1994): 30–40.
García-Márquez, Vicente. *The Ballets Russes: Colonel de Basil's Ballets Russes de Monte Carlo, 1932–1952.* New York, 1990.
Pask, Edward H. *Ballet in Australia: The Second Act, 1940–1980.* Melbourne, 1982.
Salter, Frank. *Borovansky: The Man Who Made Australian Ballet.* Sydney, 1980.

GEOFFREY WILLIAM HUTTON
Amended by Michelle Potter

BORRI, PASQUALE (born 1820 in Milan, died 20 April 1884 in Desio), Italian ballet dancer and choreographer. Pasquale Borri studied with Carlo Blasis at the ballet school of the Teatro alla Scala in Milan. In 1838 he made his debut there in *Meleagro, ossia La Vendetta di Diana* by Antonio Monticini. He remained at La Scala, as *primo ballerino di rango francese*, until 1842, when he left to pursue his career elsewhere in Italy and abroad.

In 1843, Borri performed as a principal dancer in Emmanuele Viotti's *Le Nozze di Bacco e Arianna* at the Teatro La Fenice in Venice. He also appeared in Livio Morosini's *Festa della Rosa* during the 1843/44 Venetian Carnival season. From 1844 to 1848 he was under contract to the Hoftheater in Vienna. He then returned to Italy and performed in Tommasao Casati's *Odalisa, o La Figlia del Soldato* at the Teatro Grande in Trieste during the 1848/49 season and in Domenico Ronzani's *Zelia, ossia Il Velo Magico* and Jules Perrot's *Faust* at La Fenice, in 1850 and 1851, respectively. In 1853, Borri danced in Naples and in the 1853/54 Carnival season again at La Scala. In 1854, he again appeared in Perrot's *Faust*, in a production staged by Ronzani at the Kärntnertor Theater in Vienna, as partner to the famous American ballerina Augusta Maywood. The elegance, vigor, and vitality of Borri's dancing earned him the admiration of audiences everywhere, of his colleagues and partners, and, perhaps most important to him, of Carlo Blasis, his former teacher.

Borri was no less successful in choreography, in which he sought the right harmony and balance between mime and dance. Among his early works were *Rübezahl* (1848), mounted at the Kärntnertor Theater in Vienna; *La Ninfa dell 'Acqua* (The Water Nymph; 1849), produced at the Teatro Comunale in Trieste; and *La Vivandiera* (1851), staged at the Teatro La Pergola in Florence. In 1852 he danced in *La Vivandiera* with the virtuosa Amalia Ferraris in the title role, and in 1854 at La Scala he danced in it with Carolina Pochini and Efisio Catte. Enamoured of Pochini as both an artist and a woman, Borri created *Scintilla, or Il Demone Seduttore* for her in 1860, the year in which they married. This ballet, set to music by Paolo Giorza, was produced at La Scala, where it enjoyed as many as twenty-nine performances. It was produced again the same year at Her Majesty's Theatre in London.

One of Borri's best-known works was *Die Gauklerin* (The Juggler). Set to music by Giorza, it was mounted at the Hoftheater in Vienna in 1856 and was subsequently restaged numerous times. As *La Giocoliera*, it was produced at the Teatro La Fenice in Venice later that same year, in 1856, with Adeline Plunkett; it was then given at La Scala in 1857 and 1859, in Trieste in 1860, and at the Teatro di Apollo in Rome in 1861. As *L'Étoile de Messine* (The Star of Messina), it was presented at the Paris Opera in 1861, with music by Nicolò Gabrielli and with Amalia Ferraris and Louis Mérante in the leading roles. In Genoa, Borri mounted it again in 1864, as *La Giocoliera*, with his wife, Pochini, in the ballerina role. This ballet, which displayed Pochini's grace, agility, and precision, was also praised by the critics. According to Borri's contemporary, Francesco Regli, it recalled "the grandiosity of [Salvatore] Viganò and the vitality of [Louis] Henry."

In the years after 1860, while Romantic themes were declining, naturalism and decadency were beginning to appear. At the same time the political unification of Italy and the new copyright laws brought with them the birth of a nationally distributed ballet repertory. In this new situation, Borri's ballets appealed to the taste of new middle-class audiences and obtained lasting success. *Rodolfo* (La Scala, Milan, 1858), one of his most popular works, was set to music by Giorza and was based on a libretto taken from the famous serial novel *Les mystères de Paris* by Eugène Sue. *Carnevals-Abenteuer in Paris* (Hoftheater, Vienna, 1858; La Scala, 1859, as *Una Avventura di Carnevale*) was also widely appreciated for its bohemian atmosphere. Subsequently, while *grand opéra* was gaining popularity in Italy, Borri followed the growing taste for grandiose productions with such ballets as *Nephte, o Il Figliuol Prodigo* (La Pergola, Florence, 1868). With *La Dea del Valhalla* (1870) he brought on the stage of La Scala for the first time the gods of Germanic mythology, predating by many years the arrival of Richard Wagner's *Ring of the Niebelungs*.

From 1875 to 1878, Borri served as director of the ballet company and school at the Wielki Theater in Warsaw. There, he produced some of his earlier ballets again, such as *The Juggler*, and choreographed *The Warden and the Ward* (1877). His works were generally not well received in Warsaw, perhaps because his choreography was not attuned to the prevailing taste (see Pudełek, 1981). For the 1879/80 season, he returned to Vienna, where he staged, in 1880, his last work, *Der Stock im Eisen*, to music by Franz Doppler.

In his career Borri partnered some of the most celebrated dancers of his age: Fanny Cerrito, Marie Taglioni, Rosina Gusmann, and his wife, Caroline Pochini. His ballets were performed by such stars as Amalia Ferraris, Amina Boschetti, Caterina Beretta, Claudina Cucchi, Adeline Plunkett, Virginia Zucchi, and Enrico Cecchelti, and were still in the repertory of Italian theaters at the end of the nineteenth century.

BIBLIOGRAPHY

Blasis, Carlo. *Notes upon Dancing, Historical and Practical.* Translated by R. Barton. London, 1847.

Celi, Claudia. "Il balletto in Italia." In *Musica in scena: Storia dello spettacolo musicale,* edited by Alberto Basso, vol. 5., pp. 89–138. Turin, 1995.

Guest, Ivor. *The Ballet of the Second Empire.* London, 1974.

Guest, Ivor. *The Divine Virginia: A Biography of Virginia Zucchi.* New York, 1977.

Hansell, Kathleen Kuzmick. "Il ballo teatrale e l'opera italiana." In *Storia dell'opera italiana,* vol. 5, pp. 175–306. Turin, 1987.

Pudełek, Janina. *Warszawski balet w latach 1867–1915.* Kraków, 1981.

Regli, Francesco. *Dizionario biografico: Dei piu' celegri poeti ed artisti melodrammatici, tragici e comici . . . che fiorirono in Italia dal 1800 al 1860.* Turin, 1860.

Reyna, Ferdinando. "Tre grandi italiani del baletto." *La Scala* (November 1958): 35–41.

Ruffin, Elena. "Il ballo Teatrale a Venezia nel secolo XIX." *La danza italiana* 5–6 (Autumn 1987): 151–179.

Sasportes, José. "Invito allo studio di due secoli di danza teatrale a Venezia (1746–1859)." In *Balli teatrali a Venezia (1746–1859).* Milan, 1994.

Tintori, Giampiero. *Duecento anni di Teatro alla Scala: Cronologia opere–balletti–concerti, 1778–1977.* Gorle (Bergamo), 1979.

CLAUDIA CELI
Translated from Italian

BOSL, HEINZ (born 21 November 1946 in Baden-Baden, died 12 June 1975 in Munich), German ballet dancer. Heinz Bosl received his training at the children's ballet school of the Bavarian State Opera in Munich with Erna Gerbl, Kitty Wirthmüller, and Helen Kraus-Natschewa, participating from the very beginning as a supernumerary in the ballet productions of the company. Upon graduation in 1962 he became a member of the Bavarian State Opera Ballet. He was appointed soloist in 1965 and continued to study with Leonide Gonta, Gustav Blank, Michel de Lutry, and Suse Preisser. Gifted with a rather tall body of ideal proportions, naturally turned out, with strong legs and a finely arched instep, as well as highly developed musicality, he quickly established himself as one of the foremost German *danseurs nobles* of his generation.

Encouraged by ballet directors Heinz Rosen, John Cranko, and Ronald Hynd, Bosl acquired all the appropriate roles of the traditional repertory and was an especially engaging Romeo and an effectively world-weary Onegin in Cranko's ballets. Cranko was so impressed with Bosl that he invited him to appear with the Stuttgart Ballet in Moscow and Leningrad. His finest role was Günther, the cavalier in John Neumeier's *The Nutcracker,* which brought out all Bosl's inherent noble qualities, including his sensitively attuned partnering, which from 1973 on made him Margot Fonteyn's favorite partner in her worldwide tours. When he died from cancer in 1975, he was not yet thirty years old. In an affectionate and appreciative obituary, Fonteyn summed up his qualities as a dancer:

> Heinz possessed a remarkable, very clean, correct, and effortless technique. His pirouettes seemed to be different from any other dancer I know. His long, elegant legs skimmed the air with great speed but seemed to have a certain difficulty in gaining the necessary gravity to return to the floor. Indeed he leapt very fast, to descend very slowly—a phenomenon which I tried hard to achieve when I was young, and which I nonetheless considered impossible until I saw Heinz.   (Fonteyn, 1975)

After Bosl's death, a foundation carrying his name was established in Munich to help talented young German dancers at the start of their careers.

BIBLIOGRAPHY

Fonteyn, Margot. "Heinz Bosl." Obituary notice. *Ballett 1975*. Berlin, 1975.
Niehaus, Max. *Heinz Bosl* (in German). Munich, 1975.

HORST KOEGLER

BOSNIA-HERZEGOVINA. *See* Yugoslavia.

BOSTON BALLET. A neighborhood school in the Boston suburb of Malden was the birthplace of the Boston Ballet. The school was in the home of company founder E. Virginia Williams. Using her students, she began the company, then called the New England Civic Ballet, in 1958. At the outset, Williams was also the principal choreographer. Her style was lyrical, and she showed great sensitivity to the individual qualities of her dancers. Among her works were *The Young Loves* (1958), *Sea Alliance* (1964), *The Green Season* (1965), and *Sospiri* (1973).

By 1950, Williams had opened a school in Boston and had presented her students at the Boston Opera House. In 1959 her young company appeared at the first Northeast Regional Ballet Festival in Scranton and Wilkes-Barre, Pennsylvania. They won immediate acclaim. At a subsequent festival they garnered the attention of George Balanchine and Lincoln Kirstein, and at their recommendation, the company was one of seven to receive a Ford Foundation grant in 1963. By 1965 the company's name had become the Boston Ballet.

This funding enabled Williams to broaden her dancers' range by exposing them to modern dance choreographers, among them, Talley Beatty, John Butler, Ze'eva Cohen, Merce Cunningham, Louis Falco, Geoffrey Holder, Pearl Lang, Anna Sokolow, Paul Taylor, and Norman Walker. The Boston Ballet also began to develop a strong nucleus of Balanchine ballets. As the company grew in size and texture, it began to perform nineteenth-century works, such as *Giselle, Swan Lake,* and *The Sleeping Beauty,* all

tastefully staged by Williams. She also developed resident choreographers: Samuel Kurkjian, Bruce Wells, and Ron Cunningham. New choreographers were encouraged through the Vestris Prize Competition begun in 1969, and the company widened its exposure to new audiences by giving free summer performances at Boston's Hatch Shell.

In 1980, the Boston Ballet became the first American company to tour in China. Upon its return, the company began a U.S. tour with Rudolf Nureyev as guest artist. That same year, Williams invited former New York City Ballet ballerina Violette Verdy to become associate artistic director. She became artistic director when Williams retired in 1983, but after Williams's death in 1984, Verdy remained only a month and then resigned, leaving Bruce Wells as interim director.

The fortunes of the Boston Ballet changed radically with the 1985 arrival of Bruce Marks as artistic director. Marks had had a substantial performing career with American Ballet Theatre and the Royal Danish Ballet. In 1976 he and Danish-born ballerina Toni Lander, who was then his wife, had gone to Salt Lake City, where Lander became ballet mistress of Ballet West and Marks became co-director, then director. He had done a certain amount of choreography but soon discovered that his prime inter-

BOSTON BALLET. Robert Steele and Laura Young in George Balanchine's *Donizetti Variations*. (Photograph by John Lindquist; used by permission of the Harvard Theatre Collection, The Houghton Library. Choreography by George Balanchine © The George Balanchine Trust.)

ests were fund-raising and "selling" his company to the community. In this he was the antithesis of the self-effacing Williams.

When Marks reached Boston, he began assembling a strong staff, which included Anna-Marie Holmes as associate director, Sydelle Gomberg as director of the company's reorganized school, and Frank Bourman as director of an educational outreach program called CITYDANCE. To house this expanded activity, along with a far more complex administrative structure, Marks spearheaded the $7.5 million fund-raising drive that ultimately provided the organization with a home of its own. For the first time, the company also acquired a single theater, the 3,625-seat Wang Center.

The company's repertory is structured in substantially the same fashion as it was under Williams, with an underpinning of nineteenth-century ballets, most of them staged by Holmes. A notable exception was the 1990 production of *Swan Lake*, staged by former Bolshoi Ballet artists Natalia Dudinskaya and Konstantin Sergeyev. Marks has continually engaged members of the "cutting edge" choreographic elite, such as Bill T. Jones, Ralph Lemon, Susan Marshall, Bebe Miller, Mark Morris, and Twyla Tharp, as well as the durable Merce Cunningham. The former emphasis on Balanchine ballets has somewhat diminished, but the search for new choreographers continues in a project named the International Choreography Competition.

Although the Boston Ballet school is large, and there is a second company, Boston Ballet II, directed by Laura Young, much of the first company's personnel is recruited from elsewhere. Williams's fiercely regional loyalty has been supplanted by a more international outlook and scope. The Boston Ballet has also become an influential model for other regional companies in the United States.

[*See also the entries on Williams and Marks.*]

BIBLIOGRAPHY
Fanger, Iris M. "The Fearsome First Ten Years: Boston Ballet Tunnels Out." *Dance Magazine* (October 1973): 63–67.
Fanger, Iris M. "Boston Ballet." *Boston Sunday Herald Magazine* (26 February 1989).
Hering, Doris. "The Marks Magic." *The World and I* (January 1994).
Taper, Bernard. *The Arts in Boston.* Cambridge, Mass., 1970.
Tobias, Tobi. "E. Virginia Williams and the Boston Ballet." *Dance Magazine* (June 1976): 47–58.

DORIS HERING

BOTSWANA. *See* Southern Africa. *See also* !Kung San Dance.

BOURDELLE, ÉMILE-ANTOINE (born 30 October 1861 in Montauban, died 1 October 1929 in Paris), French artist. Bourdelle's drawings and sculptures of Isadora

Duncan and Vaslav Nijinsky were never meant to be portraits in the sense of physical likenesses, but they provide something rarer and more difficult to achieve: the creative response of one artist to another. The two great dancers appear in Bourdelle's major work on a dance theme, the sculptures for the façade of the Théâtre des Champs-Élysées in Paris.

Born in the south of France, Bourdelle studied art in Toulouse before going to Paris in 1884. There he studied at the École des Beaux-Arts and in the studio of Auguste Rodin. His early works were described as Dionysian, but by 1900 the Apollonian qualities of balance, harmony, and synthesis had begun to characterize his work. It is for these qualities that his work is prized.

He first saw Isadora Duncan dance in 1909 and made many sketches of her, mostly from memory. She was the principal figure in his early sketches for the relief *La Danse*, destined for the Théâtre des Champs-Élysées. Later he added a second figure, another Isadora, but finally he replaced it with the male figure of Nijinsky, whom he had sketched in ballets such as *Narcisse*, *Carnaval*, and *Le Spectre de la Rose*. Duncan was also the primary inspiration for the theater's frieze *Apollon et Sa Méditation* (The Meditation of Apollo). Bourdelle stated, "Toutes les muses, au théâtre, sont des gestes saisis durant l'envol d'Isadora Duncan. Elle fut là ma principal source." [All my muses at the theater are really gestures that I perceived during Isadora's leaps. She was my principal source there.] (Jianou, 1975).

The theater façade was executed between 1910 and 1913, unusually quickly for Bourdelle. He made numerous preliminary sketches for these sculptures as well as many action sketches of both dancers.

[*See also* Prints and Drawings.]

BIBLIOGRAPHY. An excellent introduction to Bourdelle's life and work is provided by Ionel Jianu and Michel Dufet, *Bourdelle*, 2d ed. (Paris, 1975), which includes an extensive bibliography. A more specialized work, Claude Aveline and Michel Dufet's *Bourdelle et la danse: Isadora et Nijinsky* (Paris, 1969), concentrates on his dance sketches and the sculptures for the Champs-Élysées. *Bourdelle et la critique de son temps*, by Carol-Marc Lavrillier and Michel Dufet (Paris, 1992), includes writings by Bourdelle. The reader may also consult Denise Basdevant, *Bourdelle et le Théâtre des Champs-Élysées* (Paris, 1982).

SUSAN AU

BOURMEISTER, VLADIMIR. *See* Burmeister, Vladimir.

BOURNONVILLE, ANTOINE (born 19 May 1760 in Lyons, France, died 11 January 1843 in Fredesborg, Denmark), dancer, choreographer, and ballet master. Bournonville was the son of Jeanne Evrar, a professional ballet dancer. His sister, Julie Alix de la Fay, was one of the most famous dancers in Europe for her work under Jean-Georges Noverre. As a child Bournonville studied with Noverre, who arranged for him to dance at the Paris Opera. Bournonville performed as a popular soloist in Paris and later in London, until King Gustav III of Sweden, founder of the Royal Swedish Opera, invited him to join the Stockholm-based company. An extremely accomplished and elegant *danseur noble*, Bournonville was the subject of a famous portrait by the Swedish artist Per Krafft.

During his ten years in Stockholm, Bournonville created three short ballets and several *entrées* and *divertissements*. The ballet *Fiskarena* (The Fishermen), choreographed in 1789, was reconstructed in 1971 by Mary Skeaping and Ivo Cramér for the eighteenth-century Drottningholm Theater outside Stockholm.

Bournonville was well known in the European artistic community. He maintained a lifelong correspondence with Charles-Louis Didelot, a French dancer, choreographer, and teacher who played a key role in the development of Russian ballet, and Pierre Gardel and Louis-Jacques Milon were his close friends.

In 1792 Bournonville was granted a leave of absence from the Swedish Opera. He traveled to Copenhagen, where he was invited to perform, and on 17 April 1792 the name Bournonville appeared on a Danish ballet poster for the first time. Known as a supporter of the French Revolution, Bournonville was not asked to join the Royal Danish Ballet until 1795. He then became a soloist and, during the next twenty-four years created leading roles in almost every ballet choreographed by Vincenzo Galeotti. Bournonville also staged some of his own works, including *Landsbymøllerne i Provense* (1803, originally presented in Stockholm in 1785), *Den graeske hyrde* (c.1805), and *Den Galante Gartner* (1808). He also choreographed a number of *divertissements* and *entrées*. Bournonville was appointed ballet master of the Royal Danish Ballet in 1816, but he was not successful in this capacity and resigned in 1823.

Antoine Bournonville had three children with his first wife, the gifted Danish dancer Mariane Jensen (1767–1797). His son August Bournonville, also important in the history of ballet, was born during Antoine's second marriage, to Lovisa Sundberg (1776–1859).

[*See also* Royal Danish Ballet; Sweden, *article on* Theatrical Dance, 1771–1900; *and the entry on* Galeotti.]

BIBLIOGRAPHY

Bournonville, Antoine. *Dagbøger fra 1792.* Edited by Julius Clausen. Copenhagen, 1924.
Fridericia, Allan. *August Bournonville.* Copenhagen, 1979.
Ralov, Kirsten, ed. *The Bournonville School.* 4 vols. New York, 1979.

ALLAN FRIDERICIA

BOURNONVILLE, AUGUST (born 21 August 1805 in Copenhagen, died 30 November 1879 in Copenhagen), Danish dancer, ballet master, and choreographer. Bournonville was the son of the French-born dancer Antoine Bournonville and his Swedish housekeeper and companion, Lovisa Sundberg. The couple did not marry until 1816, when Antoine Bournonville was to take over some of the late ballet master Vincenzo Galeotti's duties as director of the Royal Danish Ballet.

Life. The only one of the six Bournonville children to display an active interest in dance, August began by imitating the movements of pupils who came to take classes at the Bournonville home. His formal training started at age seven. He later wrote in his autobiography, *My Theater Life*, "It was decided that my father should take me with him to the Court Theater, where the ballet school was located at the time. And so that I should not become flawed by *frivolous* character dancing, I was made to do serious exercises which at first seemed rather tiresome." August worked directly under his father's supervision until his talent and enthusiasm caught the eye of old Galeotti, and on 2 October 1813 he made his stage debut in the Italian master's Nordic ballet *Lagertha*. Bournonville was small for his age, a clever mime, and a fine singer. He received drama coaching from some of Denmark's leading actors and performed children's roles in many plays and comic operas, most notably in Adam Oehlenschläger's *Håkon Jarl* and in L. C. Caignez's *Judgment of Solomon*, where he was praised for his "grace, innocent liveliness and filial piety."

His theater schedule made regular academic schooling impossible, so Bournonville was enrolled in an afternoon course taught by a divinity student and eventually became first in his class. Through his father's excellent library, Bournonville also became familiar with the works of Voltaire and Rousseau, the plays of Corneille, Racine, and Molière, and Diderot's great *Encyclopédie*. A true child of the Danish Romantic era, he pored over the Danish historian Peter Suhm's *Nordic Tales* and the works of Ludvig Holberg and Oehlenschläger. The latter's legendary characters, in particular, permanently colored his imagination and provided him with models of the heroic ideal, as did his admiration of the young Napoléon Bonaparte. August was also subject to strong parental influences: his mother endowed him with the middle-class virtues of clearheadedness, prudence, and piety, along with a keen interest in Scandinavian folklore; his father imparted to him a love of art, respect for dancing as a profession, a cosmopolitan outlook, and an admiration for individual freedom and for nobility conferred by merit rather than by birth.

As an adolescent, Bournonville had to choose among the theatrical arts. A dramatic career was ruled out when he developed a stammer, and even though his tenor voice was fine enough to excite the admiration of Gioacchino

BOURNONVILLE, AUGUST. Since its creation, *La Sylphide* (1836), a Romantic ballet set in the Scottish Highlands, has never left the repertory of the Royal Danish Ballet. To publicize a new production in 1882, images of Anna Tyschsen as the Sylphide and Hans Beck as James were superimposed against a backdrop of a bosky dell designed by Valdemar Gyllich for act 2. (Photomontage c.1882 by Leopold Hartmann; from the Royal Library, Copenhagen.)

Rossini, he chose to devote his energies to dance. This decision was prompted by his father's example, by the universality of the art, and by the virtuoso performances of touring guest artists such as Filippo Taglioni and his wife. His mind made up, Bournonville's artistic education intensified. He studied French and music in earnest, while drawing opened his eyes to the beautiful and the picturesque, two qualities later applied to his ballets. His exceptional gifts prompted his father to petition King Frederick VI for a travel stipend. His request was granted, and on 2 May 1820, the Bournonvilles left for Paris to spend the next six months "perfecting themselves in their profession."

In Paris, August was introduced to his father's old friends and colleagues and avidly observed ballet classes and performances. He was impressed by Pierre Gardel and Auguste Vestris but was especially taken with the teaching style of Georges Maze. His sponsors expected him to make considerable progress and hoped that the elder Bournonville would bring back compositions to renew the Royal Theater's aging dance repertory, but they were disappointed on both counts. Antoine Bournonville was not a choreographer of Galeotti's caliber, and, while August's progress was evident, he still lacked strength and maturity. [*See the entry on Antoine Bournonville.*]

In 1823 Antoine Bournonville retired as director of dancing and was replaced by Pierre Larcher. Between 1820 and 1824, August Bournonville grew in body and gained independence of mind. He progressed in his technical studies; as a member of the ballet company, he appeared in works composed by his father and the dancer Poul Funck. Bournonville continued to expand his knowledge by studying mythology and figure painting; he read the classics in French translation, while Greek and Roman antiquity opened up a new world to him. The young dancer was ambitious and foresaw little future for himself at the Royal Theater. His father's system was "tasteful and correct," but in his eyes it had become "reactionary." Bournonville set his sights on the Continent; through the theater management he asked and received Frederick VI's permission to return to Paris for fifteen months, supported solely by his theater salary, which was paid to him in advance, and on 27 April 1824 he left for France.

The ballet world Bournonville encountered on his arrival was different from that he had known in 1820. The influence of Maximilien Gardel and Louis-Jacques Milon was waning, while Jean-Louis Aumer's was rising. The male dancer, however, was still predominant, and this was vital to Bournonville's development as an artist. Gardel, unable to teach him, recommended Vestris as the master best suited to his needs. Bournonville preferred Maze, but he did not want to offend a man of Gardel's importance, so he began to study with "the god of dance." He soon became delighted with Vestris. Bournonville's impatience was his worst stumbling block, but he soon became a "model of application" and earned his teacher's satisfaction with his enthusiasm and industry. After little more than a year of unflagging effort, he was judged ready for his examination. After training almost six hours a day in the heat of a Parisian summer, Bournonville fell seriously ill. On 10 March 1826, restored in strength and spirit, he finally faced his long-awaited test.

Before a jury that included Gardel, Milon, and Jean-Baptiste Blache, Bournonville danced excerpts from *Le Jugement de Pâris* and *Nina, ou La Folle par Amour*. The jury voted unanimously to allow him to make his debut at the Opera, which he did on 5 April in a pas de trois in Milon's *Nina*. On 19 June he signed a contract as *double de la danse* in the Opera company.

While dancing at the Opera, Bournonville absorbed everything Parisian life, art, and theater had to offer. He became friends with the leading literary and artistic figures of the day, including Adolphe Nourrit, the celebrated tenor who later wrote the libretto for the French version of *La Sylphide*. His dance colleagues included Monsieur Albert (François Decombe), Antoine Paul, Jules Perrot, and Marie Taglioni. Bournonville often danced with Taglioni in the years preceding her legendary triumph as the Sylph. He wrote of the experience: "When dancing with her, she lifted one up from the earth, and her divine dancing could make one weep. I saw Terpsichore realized in her person." Bournonville subsequently trained all his female pupils after the ideal of Marie Taglioni.

BOURNONVILLE. Inspired by a visit of a troupe of Spanish dancers to Copenhagen, *The Toreador* (1840) was a two-act ballet set to music by Edvard Helsted. In 1884, the character dancer Adolph Frederick Lense first appeared in the role of Mr. William, a rich Englishman who places a bet against Alonso, the toreador. (Photograph 1899 by Sophus Juncker-Jensen; from the Royal Theater Archive and Library, Copenhagen.)

During a leave of absence from the Opera in the winter of 1827–1828, Anatole Petit engaged Bournonville to appear with the dancers Albert, Constance Petit, Louis F. Gosselin, Caroline Brocard, and a young Englishwoman, Louisa Court, in a series of guest performances at the King's Theatre in London. Bournonville was infatuated with his partner, Court, and together they scored a success in the tarantella from Petit's *Le Sicilien*. Offstage, however, the worldly and ambitious Court rejected Bournonville's marriage proposal.

After his return to Paris in April 1828, Bournonville was disappointed when he was not promoted in rank as quickly as he desired. He renewed his contract with the Opera but also opened negotiations with the Danish Royal Theater. Bournonville was anxious to perform in his native land, but he did not wish to return permanently except on his own terms. He asked that he be made leading male dancer, *maître de perfection* or *maître à danser de la cour*, and that he be able to retire with a pension after eighteen years of service. The management found these terms so excessive that they refrained from telling the king of his request. Meanwhile, Bournonville also investigated opportunities in Vienna, Bordeaux, and Berlin.

In the spring of 1829, Albert fell ill and Bournonville stepped in to replace him. He was then given the coveted rank of *premier remplacement demi-caractère*, starting 1 July 1829. The agreement included a short leave of absence, which he used to pay a visit to Denmark.

Upon his arrival in Copenhagen in early August 1829, Bournonville found the Royal Ballet in a deplorable state, but he managed to whip it into good enough shape to showcase his talents in a series of guest appearances. On 1 September, Bournonville displayed his virtuosity in his own mythological *divertissement, Gratiernes Hyldning* (Acclaim to the Graces). During this stay he also mounted Aumer's *La Somnambule* (the character of Edmond was to become one of his most memorable roles) and presented his first original ballet, the semiautobiographical pantomimic idyll *Soldat og Borde* (Soldier and Peasant). The success of *La Somnambule* led the theater administration to reopen negotiations with Bournonville about returning home to head the Royal Danish Ballet.

Art was not the only reason Bournonville wished to return to his native land. During his visit he had become engaged to a beautiful Swedish girl, Helene Frederikke Håkansson. With the prospect of a new professional and personal life, Bournonville no longer found Paris as pleasant as he had previously, and, in return for some financial concessions, he was released from his contract with the Opera.

On 29 April 1830 Bournonville danced in *La Somnambule* as a member of the Royal Danish Ballet, and on 30 June he was married. The marriage lasted nearly fifty years and produced seven children, two of whom pursued artistic careers; his daughter Augusta was a serious student of ballet and piano, while her sister Charlotte was for many years an opera singer at the Danish Royal Theater. The latter's published memoirs are important sources of information about the ballet master's home and theater life.

August Bournonville was blond and blue-eyed, five feet seven inches tall, with an oval face, a long, prominent nose, and a rather small, sardonic mouth. He evaluated himself in his autobiography:

> As a dancer I possessed a considerable measure of strength, lightness, precision, brilliance, and—when I was not carried

away by the desire to display bravura—a natural grace, developed through superb training and enhanced by a sense of music. I also had a supple back, and my feet had just enough turnout for me to be appreciated by even the severest master. The difficulties which I have worked hard to surmount . . . were all connected with *pirouettes* and the composure necessary in slow *pas* and attitudes. My principal weaknesses were bent wrists, a swaying of the head during *pirouettes*, and a certain hardness in my elevation. . . . I danced with a manly *joie de vivre*, and my humor and energy have made the same impression in every theatre. I delighted the audience, and before they admired me, they liked me.

Bournonville's self-description was borne out by theater chronicler Thomas Overskou, who wrote to a friend in 1830:

> Of his charm, grace, lightness and brilliant technique in jumps as well as in *pirouettes* and beautiful movements, you have—and can have—no idea until you have seen him. And even when you have seen him, your conception of his stage productions could not be complete; for every time he dances, one finds his dancing more beautiful. Indeed, in the connoisseurs'

BOURNONVILLE. Soon after his return from a lengthy stay in Naples, Bournonville choreographed *Napoli* (1842), a three-act ballet considered by many to be his masterpiece. In a 1988 performance, Heidi Ryom as Teresina is shown executing a featherlight *grand jeté*. To her right stand Johan Kobborg, Rose Gad, and Nikolaj Hübbe; on the bridge at the back stand students from the Royal Danish Ballet School. Many famous Danish dancers made their first stage appearance as children on the *Napoli* bridge. (Photograph © 1988 by David Amzallag; used by permission.)

opinion, even in his father's prime we never saw such graceful yet effective dancing on our stage. When a dancer is such an artist, dancing is more than a mere feast for the eye.

(Neiiendam, 1965).

Besides appearing as leading male soloist, Bournonville faced two other main tasks: rebuilding the Royal Theater's dance repertory and training a corps de ballet capable of doing justice to it. During the early years he experimented with choreography, mainly staging such French ballets as *Hertugen af Vendômes Pager* (1830), based on Aumer's *Les Pages du Duc de Vendôme* (1820), and *Paul og Virginie* (1830), based on Gardel's *Paul et Virginie* (1806), which he translated for the Danish stage. His duties also involved the staging of dances for plays and operas. Cast lists for these early works already include the names of artists who would faithfully serve Bournonville and his repertory as super dancers or mimes for the next thirty to forty years—Adolf Stramboe, Carl Fredstrup, Andreas Füssel, and Ferdinand Hoppensach. To their ranks would later be added another generation, among them Ferdinand Hoppe; Axel and Petrine Fredstrup; Adolf, Edvard, and Laura Stramboe; Harald Scharaff; Ludvig Gade; Georg Brodersen; and the Price family.

Throughout his career, Bournonville drew inspiration for his ballets from literary works, both ancient and modern; from popular trends in music and dance as evidenced in his work *Tyrolerne* (The Tyrolians; 1835); and from notable events as in *Zulma, eller Krystalpaladset* (The Crystal Palace) and *Fædrelandets Muser* (National Muses). All these sources served directly as subject matter or indirectly as the impetus for a ballet's creation.

An 1831 sequel to *Soldier and Peasant, Victors Bryllup, eller Fædrene-Arnen* (Victor's Wedding), was followed by Bournonville's first full-length original ballet, *Faust,* based on Johann Wolfgang von Goethe's poem. The following season produced another French-inspired work, *Veteranen, eller Det Gaestfrie Tag* (The Veteran), and an unsuccessful revival of Galeotti's once-popular ballet *Romeo og Giulietta* (Romeo and Juliet). This season also marked the end of Bournonville's ballet adaptations and witnessed the debut of his next major ballerina, Lucile Grahn.

In 1835 Bournonville presented his romantic, patriotic ballet *Waldemar,* based on Bernhard Severin Ingemann's popular novel about the monarch who unified the Danish kingdom. It became the country's "national ballet," and Bournonville was given the official title of *Balletmester.* The role of Princess Astrid was a perfect vehicle for the sixteen-year-old Grahn, who, to Bournonville's annoyance, also used it to exploit the virtuosic pointe work she had seen when she accompanied the Bournonvilles to Paris on a study trip the previous summer. On that trip they saw Marie Taglioni in *La Sylphide,* and Bournonville wished to present Grahn in the same part. The Paris

BOURNONVILLE. *A Wedding Festival at Hardanger* (1853), a ballet based on Norwegian tales, was extremely popular during Bournonville's lifetime, although it was criticized for lack of continuity between the stories of two pairs of lovers. In a performance in 1903 Clara Rasmussen appeared as the Bride and Christian Christensen was her Bridegroom. (Photograph 1903 by Peter Elfelt; from the Royal Library, Copenhagen.)

score, however, was too expensive for the Royal Theater, and Bournonville had no time to learn the roles, so he commissioned new music from a young nobleman in Denmark, developed the character of James for himself, and devised new dances. On 28 November 1836 he premiered what has, ironically, become the most frequently performed Bournonville ballet, *Sylfiden* (La Sylphide). Grahn became the public's darling, but her ambition grew, as did her dislike of Bournonville's feelings for her, and she demanded leave to study in Paris. When she overstayed a leave abroad in 1839, she was dismissed by the Royal Danish Theater.

During these years Bournonville kept abreast of new trends in art by traveling to Berlin (1836), London and Paris (1838), and Stockholm in 1839. Here, he and some Danish dancers made guest appearances at the invitation

BOURNONVILLE. In his memoirs, Bournonville said that *A Folk Tale* (1854) was his best work. In 1952, almost a hundred years after its creation, an all-star cast of principals and solo dancers of the Royal Danish Ballet appeared on stage together: at left, Kirsten Simone as Hilda and Erik Bruhn as Junker Ove; in the pas de sept (from left to right), Inge Sand, Fredbjørn Bjørnsson, Mona Vangsaa, Børge Ralov, Margrethe Schanne, Stanley Williams, and Mette Mollerup. (Photograph by Rigmor Mydtskov; used by permission.)

of his Swedish pupil, Christian Johansson. The year 1839 also saw the death of Bournonville's patron Frederick VI and the triumphal return to Copenhagen of the famous sculptor Bertel Thorvaldsen. Thorvaldsen had a strong influence on Bournonville's aesthetic ideas, providing models for the noble Nordic heroes who peopled ballets such as *Waldemar*, *Valkyrien* (The Valkyrie), *Thrymskvilden* (The Lay of Thrym), and *Arcona*. Bournonville's first "Italian" ballet, the 1839 *Festin i Albano* (Festival in Albano), is a tribute to Thorvaldsen's genius.

Grahn's roles were taken over by young Augusta Nielsen, for whom Bournonville created the part of the ballerina Celeste in *Toreadoren* (The Toreador; 1840). He designed this work to contrast the beauties of "native" Spanish dancing with the more "artificial" classical

French school—a style eminently suited to Nielsen's ladylike grace.

The loss of Lucile Grahn resulted in demonstrations against Bournonville by her supporters. The most notorious of these occurred on 14 March 1841, when Bournonville was jeered at his entrance in *The Toreador*. He addressed the Danish king from the stage, in the heat of the moment, and for this crime of *lèse-majesté*, he incurred a sentence of house arrest, commuted to six months of forced leave without pay.

Bournonville used this extended vacation to seek fresh artistic inspiration, to investigate job possibilities, to assess the state of European ballet, and to attempt to gain an international reputation. In Paris he witnessed rehearsals for *Giselle* and admired the lightness, elevation, and strong pointe work of Carlotta Grisi. Bournonville himself danced successfully at the Teatro San Carlo in Naples and Teatro alla Scala in Milan, but he found that, on the whole, conditions for dance and for choreographers compared quite unfavorably with those in Denmark. In October 1841 he returned home to resume his duties.

On 29 March 1842 the Danish ballet master displayed the first fruit of his journey, *Napoli, eller Fiskeren og hans*

Brud (Naples, or The Fisherman and His Bride), which became his most enduring original work. This ballet about the test and triumph of true love, set against a backdrop of Bourbon Naples peopled with colorfully clad Danes, won the accolades of the intelligentsia and ordinary theatergoers alike.

Following the 1843 premiere of another national ballet, *Erik Menveds Barndom* (The Childhood of Erik Menved), in which his eldest daughter, Augusta, made her stage debut, Bournonville learned of his father's death in his eighties. During his son's final visit with him, Antoine Bournonville had asked to see him perform his recent success, *Polka Militaire*, based on a dance Antoine himself had once done. When the impromptu performance had ended, Bournonville *père* delivered his final judgment: "You have true genius, my boy."

Success equal to that of *Napoli* eluded Bournonville in most of the works he choreographed during the 1840s. In this decade the leading female roles were danced by Augusta Nielsen and by Caroline Fjeldsted, a vivacious, conscientious, and gifted mime who steadfastly served the Danish Ballet for almost a quarter of a century.

Bellman, eller Polskdansen paa Grönalund (Bellman, or The Dance at Grönalund), a minor but charming work set to music of the eighteenth-century Swedish bard Carl Michael Bellman, was well received when it premiered in 1844, but *Kirsten Piil, eller To Midsommerfester* (1845), precursor of *Et Folkesagn* (A Folk Tale) in its fascination with folk legend and the magic and mystery of Midsummer's Eve, failed to capture the public's imagination. The same fate was shared by *Rafael* (1845) and by *Den Nye Penelope* (The New Penelope; 1847) and *Den Hvide Rose, eller Sommeren i Bretagne* (The White Rose; 1847).

In 1848 Bournonville was about to retire from dancing and was uncertain about his future course. Denmark was in crisis, and the art-loving King Christian VIII had just died. Early in the year Bournonville gave a series of farewell performances in his most popular roles; on 31 March he made his final dancing appearance, in *Waldemar*.

While as an artist Bournonville remained aloof from political statement, as a citizen he did watch duty in the city as a member of the King's Volunteers, served as a translator for the foreign ministry, and organized patriotic charitable events. He also worked to raise the social standing of dancers: he set up an academic program for children in the Royal Ballet School, and in 1869 he secured the ballet's private pension fund, the first of its kind in Europe. In 1849 the Royal Danish Ballet was removed from royal jurisdiction and placed under the ministry of culture. It now had to fight for parliamentary funding, and Bournonville was its stalwart champion.

For the 1848 Royal Theater centenary, Bournonville devised an occasional piece, *Gamle Minder, eller En Laterna Magica* (Old Memories), in which Augusta Nielsen made her last appearance on the stage, and the young members of the Price dynasty their first. In the late 1840s, the Price brothers and their wives, all entertainers at Copenhagen's popular theaters, had asked Bournonville to give their children private ballet lessons. He grudgingly agreed and began to instruct Juliette and her sister Sophie as well as their cousins, Amalie and her brother Julius. Bournonville, impressed with their gifts, composed a series of small *pas* for the young people to dance as part of their family's performances. Among his compositions for the Prices were *La Ventana*, later expanded and taken into the repertory of the Royal Theater, and *Pas de Trois Cousines*, remembered today only through a beautiful lithograph showing Bournonville's "Nordic Graces" in this dance. He was quick to spot the talent of Juliette, the pupil who came closest to approximating in her dancing the ideal of Marie Taglioni.

These years of domestic and foreign political conflict saw the creation of some lighthearted morale-boosters

BOURNONVILLE. The Señorita in *La Ventana* (1856) has been a favorite role of Danish ballerinas ever since Bournonville, shocked by the "lascivious Spanish dancers" who crowded Europe's stages, created his own "non-lascivious" *divertissement* to music by Hans Christian Lumby and Vilhelm Christian Holm. Ellen Price de Plane, seen here *sur la pointe* with castenets in hand, first appeared in the role in 1902. (Photograph 1907 by Peter Elfelt; from the Royal Library, Copenhagen.)

BOURNONVILLE. The subtitle of *Far from Denmark* (1860) is *A Costume Ball on Board*, for act 2 of this vaudeville-ballet takes place at such a ball on the quarterdeck of a Danish frigate anchored off the coast of South America. In 1920, the Chinese-style pas de cinq was danced by (from right to left) Inger Andersen, Holger Mehnen, Kaj Smith, Bente Høorup-Hassing, and (in *plié*) Karl Merrild. (Photograph 1920 by Peter Newland; from the collection of Erik Merild, Copenhagen.)

such as *Konservatoriet, eller Et Avisfriere* (1849)—in which Juliette Price became an overnight success—and *Kermessen i Brügge, eller De Tre Gaver* (Kermesse in Bruges; 1851). The Great Exhibition of 1851 sparked *The Crystal Palace*, and a trip to Norway the colorful and dramatic folk ballet *Brudefærden i Hardanger* (A Wedding Festival in Hardanger; 1853). In an attempt to dispel the sorrows of the 1853 cholera epidemic, Bournonville called up trolls, legends, and midsummer enchantment to weave what he called "my most perfect and finest choreographic work," *A Folk Tale*.

By the time Bournonville's engagement at the Royal Theater ended in 1855, he had again become disillusioned with conditions there and decided to make another bid for international fame as a choreographer, this time in Vienna. He signed a one–year contract as ballet master at the Imperial Opera, starting 1 July 1855; however, theatrical intrigue, a hostile director, and an unsympathetic public combined to make his stay bitter. He staged some of his older works with varying degrees of success; his

grandiose fairy-tale ballet *Abdallah* actually did fairly well, owing in part to the magnificent decor.

Bournonville then returned to Copenhagen by way of Paris and signed a five-year contract with the Royal Theater. He began composing new works, and inspiration came from far and wide. His stay in the Austro-Hungarian Empire proved material for *I Karpatherne* (In the Carpathians; 1857), one of the first ballets to feature ordinary working men (in this case, gold miners) as the leading characters. An Alexandre Dumas tale supplied part of the theme for *Blomsterfesten i Genzano* (Flower Festival at Genzano; 1858). Norwegian writer Bjønstjerne Bjønnsson's works lent peasant realism to *Fjelstuen, eller Tyveaar* (The Mountain Hut, or Twenty Years; 1859), while a world cruise by a Danish naval officer combined with the ballet master's own love of the sea to produce *Fjernt fra Danmark, eller Et Costumebal Ombord* (Far from Denmark, or A Costume Ball on Board; 1860). Before his contract expired in 1861, Bournonville was able to realize the dream of fashioning a great Norse ballet, *The Valkyrie*, replete with Viking chieftains and gods of Valhalla.

The multifaceted choreographer then moved on to Sweden to accept a three-year appointment as intendant for the stage at the Royal Opera in Stockholm. This time his efforts were concentrated on opera and drama; his aim was to ensure better productions and ensemble acting through a more unified approach to dramatic material, with emphasis on stage direction. During his tenure Bournonville was responsible for the production of more than fifty plays and operas at Swedish theaters.

On his return to Copenhagen in 1864 Bournonville was invited to restage some of his old ballets in the Royal Theater's repertory. He also devised a new Italian ballet, *Pontemolle: Et Kunstnergilde i Rom* (1866), and was subsequently engaged on a yearly basis until his final retirement in 1877. Still obsessed with Norse mythology, Bournonville joined forces with the celebrated composer Johan Peter Emilius Hartmann to create a balletic treatment of the Eddas, *The Lay of Thrym* (1868).

As a *metteur-en-scène* of opera, Bournonville recognized the importance of Richard Wagner's works. Between 1869 and 1875 he was responsible for introducing Danish audiences to *Lohengrin, Die Meistersinger,* and *Tannhäuser*.

The 1870s were preoccupied with planning for a new Royal Theater. While building was being completed in 1874, Bournonville took advantage of a travel grant for writers and visited Russia. He was warmly welcomed in Saint Petersburg by his colleague Marius Petipa and by his former pupil Christian Johansson. Bournonville greatly admired the Maryinsky's magnificent decor and its corps of dancers, some two hundred strong, but he deplored the shortness of the female dancers' skirts and the "acrobatic extravagancies" of some of the choreography.

The new Danish theater opened in 1874, and the Ballet's offering was the grand-scale, heroic *Arcona*. In 1876, Bournonville undertook his last work for the Royal Theater, a souvenir of his Russian journey entitled *Fra Siberien til Moskau* (From Siberia to Moscow). This gave him a chance to utilize some of the charming native dances he had admired; the work also served to display the talents of his last ballerina, the Swede Maria Westberg.

As Bournonville's theatrical activity decreased, his writing became more prolific. The first volume of his memoirs, called *My Theater Life* (Danish, *Mit Theaterliv*), had been published in 1848, the second volume in 1865, and the third in 1877–1878. His "literary testament" was his means of keeping his artistic memory alive. On retirement Bournonville moved out to his country home at Fredensborg, the summer residence of the Danish royal family.

On 27 November 1879, Bournonville attended the 150th performance of *Waldemar* at the Royal Theater; the following evening, he witnessed the debut of the young dancer Hans Beck in *Polka Militaire*, which he himself had composed. On 30 November, August Bournonville was returning from church to his daughter's home in Copenhagen when he collapsed. Shortly afterward, he died. His funeral was attended by rich and poor alike. He is buried in Asminderød Cemetery near Fredensborg.

The Bournonville Heritage. Bournonville cherished no illusions about the survival of his ballets. During his final seasons at the Royal Theater, he polished what he considered to be his finest works. These included *Far from Denmark, Flower Festival at Genzano, A Folk Tale, Kermesse in Bruges, Konservatoriet, Napoli,* and *The King's Volunteers on Amager,* which are still danced; and *Waldemar, The Valkyrie, The Toreador, The Lay of Thrym, Arcona, Pontemolle, A Wedding Festival in Hardanger, The Mountain Hut, or Twenty Years,* and *From Siberia to Moscow,* all eventually dropped from the repertory. Other works that were not being performed at the time, such as *La Sylphide* and *La Ventana,* also survived. On Bournonville's retirement, this heritage was given into the safekeeping of his trusted pupil and colleague Ludvig Gade (1823–1897).

In the years following Bournonville's death, the Royal Danish Ballet's repertory consisted exclusively of his ballets. The parts, however, were not written down in detail. Bournonville had left annotated musical scores and descriptive scenarios of his works, but the roles continued to be passed on from dancer to dancer in time-honored fashion. Gade's successor, Emil Hansen (1843–1927), in an attempt to pass on the works in as pure a form as possible, began to record dances from some of the ballets; however, there began a swift decline. The situation was exacerbated by the fact that the Royal Danish Ballet was giving fewer and fewer performances during the late nineteenth century. When Hansen retired in 1894, the young Hans Beck,

BOURNONVILLE. Based on stories from the Icelandic sagas, *The Lay of Thrym* (1868), in four acts and a final tableau, was Bournonville's most ambitious ballet. The characters are well-known figures in Nordic mythology: Thrym the giant, a force of chaos; Loki the trickster; Thor the thunderer, the most powerful of the gods; the beautiful goddess Freia (Freyja); and her brother Freir (Freyr). Absent from the repertory since 1905, the ballet was reconstructed in 1990 by Elsa-Marianne von Rosen. The dancers seen here are Lloyd Riggins as Freir and Silja Schandorff as Freia. (Photograph © 1990 by David Amzallag; used by permission.)

who had grown up in the school but had not been trained personally by Bournonville, took over, and the preservation of the Bournonville works became his primary task. Although Beck did not possess Bournonville's choreographic genius, Beck's spirited but determined character, coupled with a respect for tradition and a sense of esprit de corps, enabled him to see and do what was necessary to ensure the continued existence of the master's works and style. This era marked the birth of the "Bournonville tradition."

One of Beck's chief problems was the transmission of mime roles—those rhythmic and picturesque poses, gestures, and movements that linked action and dancing to create what Allan Fridericia calls "a poetic-dramatic unity." Bournonville ballets required a special type of actor-dancer endowed with singular dignity, grace, and a strong personality rather than only a brilliant technique. As economic cutbacks occurred, experienced artists re-

BOURNONVILLE. *The King's Volunteers on Amager* (1871) was Bournonville's last vaudeville-ballet. The plot involves a corps of military volunteers stationed on the island of Amager, south of Copenhagen, when Denmark was at war with England. In the farmhouse where the volunteers are billeted, four of them dance a lively reel with local girls. (Photograph 1918 by Peter Newland; from the collection of Erik Merild, Copenhagen.)

tired, and public interest in this type of ballet lessened, mimetic nationalistic works such as *Waldemar, The Valkyrie,* and *The Lay of Thrym* were dropped. Beck tried to get his artists to record their roles for posterity, but he was forced to recompose mimed scenes to bridge gaps in the tradition, not merely to oblige changing tastes.

Beck also interpolated into some of the ballets variations he composed to music from other Bournonville works. The best known are in the third act of *Napoli.* Knud Arne Jürgensen, a Dane who collaborated on a number of Bournonville reconstructions, compared Beck's traditional *Napoli* variations (danced to music from Bournonville's *Abdallah*) with reconstructed Bournonville steps to the same piece of music. The study revealed four apparent differences between the approaches of the two choreographers: Bournonville had a step for almost every musical beat, while Beck's fewer steps are spread out over many beats; in Bournonville, the accent goes down on the first beat, but with Beck, the jumps go up, usually landing on the second or third beat of each bar; Bournonville's floor patterns are smaller and more symmetrical than Beck's; and Bournonville's use of smaller phrases and combinations achieves a mounting choreographic intensity, as opposed to phrases in Beck's variations, which become longer toward the end of the dance. This led Jürgensen to conclude that the change of phrasing in Bournonville dancing might date from the time of Beck's leadership (1894–1915) rather than from the Fokine era in the 1920s and 1930s, as was previously assumed. Research is currently being done to clarify these points.

At the heart of Beck's conservation plan lay the training of future generations of dancers to perform Bournonville's works. Drawing on the memories of veteran dancers, he began the codification of hundreds of combinations and *pas de théâtre* used by Bournonville into a series of training exercises for the barre and center floor. The result has come to be known as the "Bournonville schools" or classes, one for each day of the week. This training system was employed exclusively in the Danish Ballet School into the 1930s. Despite Beck's successful efforts to increase the number of performances per season, he was powerless to halt changing public taste. His retirement in 1915 signaled a long eclipse of the Bournonville repertory.

During the 1920s some Bournonville works were presented, but some seasons in the 1930s saw none of these classics. In 1932 Harald Lander was appointed ballet master, and he began seriously to steer the Royal Danish Ballet into the mainstream of twentieth-century dance by introducing Russian training. During World War II, with the help of former dancer Valborg Borchsenius, the main Bournonville ballets were given new productions, though some of the vital mime scenes were omitted or abridged.

In 1950 the first ballet festival was held in Copenhagen, and the world began to become aware of the delights of this unique Danish heritage. Scholarly studies of Bournonville's works began to be undertaken, and dancers such as Erik Bruhn, Toni Lander, Flemming Flindt, Kirsten Ralov, Hans Brenaa, and Fredbjørn Bjørnsson started to dance, stage, and teach his works abroad. Today interest is greater than ever, and the use of film and videotape has made it possible to experiment with new ways of staging Bournonville works while remaining faithful to their original spirit and style.

Bournonville Style. Bournonville wanted dancing to look as natural as breathing—unforced and free, mirroring the rhythms of nature and expressing an unconscious joy in living. In the words of Erik Aschengreen,

> His steps are put together in such a way that the dancers remain in high spirits and their joy spills out over the footlights. . . . Bournonville wanted dance to be the expression of beauty and grace. To the ideals of the French school he added, besides this . . . desire for harmony, a clear assertion of a spontaneous joie de vivre. There are in Bournonville's ballets the loveliest variations and *soli* which we may characterize simply as small pieces in which the step composition in itself induces contagious joy.   (Aschengreen, 1974).

Bournonville was selective in the steps he chose to embody his choreographic ideas. Many of the same steps can

BOURNONVILLE. Frank Andersen in a 1979 performance of *From Siberia to Moscow* (1876), Bournonville's final work, set in the imperial court of Russia. Anderson is seen here in act 2, scene 5, as one of two English jockeys symbolizing the river Thames in the allegorical *divertissement* representing four major rivers of Europe: the Rhône, the Guadalquivir, the Thames, and the Rhine. (Photograph © 1979 by Jack Vartoogian; used by permission.)

be found in the vocabularies of the French, Italian, and Russian schools, but it is the way in which they are linked together, then phrased and nuanced, that makes them Bournonville's own. Hallmarks of the Bournonville style include a seemingly never-ending flow of movement; the illusion of incredible lightness, brilliance, and ease lent by the contrast of softly rounded arms held in a low position while the feet are executing swift and intricate steps; unexpected changes of *épaulement* and direction; an open, almost affectionate manner of addressing the audience; a wealth of transition steps that serve as preparations for big jumps; landings from jumps serving merely as a springboard for the next movement; and creative use of the stage, where Bournonville artists dance their way from point to point, constantly traveling up- and downstage and on the diagonal.

Among the favorite steps Bournonville used to achieve these effects are the instantly recognizable *attitude effacée,* the *grand jeté en avant en attitude, grand jeté en attitude en tournant, attitude effacée sautée, ronds de jambe en l'air sautés;* myriad *batterie* steps such as *brisés, entrechats, sissonnes,* and *assemblés;* and pirouettes—many done from second position, *en attitude* or *sur le cou-de-pied*—with characteristic *port de bras.*

The look (the "motion-profile," as critic Tobi Tobias calls it) of these steps has, of course, changed over the years. As Russian training, with its emphasis on strength and extended line, was introduced and as the short, rounded ballerina of Bournonville's day gave way to the taller, slimmer dancer of today, Bournonville's choreography kept pace. The evolution of the pointe shoe added another dimension to female dancing. The handing down of this transient art was made somewhat easier by the publication in 1979 of *The Bournonville School,* Kirsten Ralov's recording of the daily classes in French terminology, Labanotation, and Benesh notation, with accompanying music.

[*See also* Bournonville Composers; Royal Danish Ballet; *and the entries on the following Bournonville works:* A Folk Tale; Kermesse in Bruges, *and* Konservatoriet. *In addition, many of the figures mentioned herein are the subjects of independent entries.*]

BIBLIOGRAPHY

Aschengreen, Erik. "The Beautiful Danger: Facets of the Romantic Ballet." *Dance Perspectives*, no. 58 (Summer 1974).

Aschengreen, Erik. "August Bournonville: A Ballet-Poet among Poets." *CORD Dance Research Annual* 9 (1978): 3–21.

Aschengreen, Erik, et al., eds. *Perspektiv på Bournonville.* Copenhagen, 1980.

Aschengreen, Erik. "Bournonville Style and Tradition." *Dance Research* 4 (Spring 1986): 45–62.

Bournonville, August. *Études chorégraphiques.* Copenhagen, 1861.

Bournonville, August. *Efterladte Skrifter.* Copenhagen, 1891.

Bournonville, August. *Breve til barndomshjemmet/Lettres à la maison de son enfance.* 3 vols. Edited by Svend Kragh-Jacobsen and Nils Schiørring. Copenhagen, 1969–1978.

Bournonville, August. "The Ballet Poems of August Bournonville: The Complete Scenarios." Translated by Patricia McAndrew. *Dance Chronicle* 3.2 (1979)–6.1 (1983).

Bournonville, August. *Mit Theaterliv.* 3 vols. Copenhagen, 1848–1878. Translated and edited by Patricia McAndrew as *My Theatre Life* (Middletown, Conn., 1979).

Bournonville, Charlotte. *Erindringer fra hjemmet og fra scenen.* Copenhagen, 1903.

Bournonville, Charlotte. *August Bournonville: Spredte minder.* Copenhagen, 1905.

Bournonville, Charlotte. *Skyggerids af gamle minder.* Copenhagen, 1906.

Bruhn, Erik, and Lillian Moore. *Bournonville and Ballet Technique.* London, 1961.

Christensen, Charlotte, et al. *Billedhuggeren og Balletmesteren: Om Thorvaldsen og Bournonvilles Kunst.* Copenhagen, 1992. Includes English translation of the major essays.

Fog, Dan. *The Royal Danish Ballet, 1760–1958, and August Bournonville: A Chronological Catalogue.* Copenhagen, 1961.

Fridericia, Allan. *August Bournonville.* Copenhagen, 1979.

Georg, Anders, and Soren Dyssegaard, eds. *The Royal Danish Ballet and Bournonville: Centenary in Honour of August Bournonville.* Copenhagen, 1979.

Getz, Leslie, comp. *August Bournonville and the Royal Danish Ballet: A Bibliography of English Language Sources.* Palo Alto, Calif., 1984.

Glasstone, Richard. "Dance Research and Bournonville." *The Dancing Times* (April 1985): 594.

Guest, Ann Hutchinson, ed. *"The Flower Festival in Genzano": Pas de Deux.* New York, 1987.

Guest, Ivor. *The Romantic Ballet in Paris.* 2d rev. ed. London, 1980.

Guest, Ivor. "Perrot and Bournonville." *The Dancing Times* (November 1988): 138–139.

Hallar, Marianne, and Alette Scavenius, eds. *Bournonvilleana.* Translated by Gaye Kynoch. Copenhagen, 1992.

Horosko, Marian. "Bournonville's Joys—Briefly." *Ballet Review* 16 (Fall 1988): 62–66.

Jürgensen, Knud Arne. *The Bournonville Ballets: A Photographic Record, 1844–1933.* London, 1987.

Jürgensen, Knud Arne. "Is the *Flower Festival Pas de Deux* by Bournonville and Paulli?" *Dance Research* 12 (Autumn 1994): 66–113.

Kragh-Jacobsen, Svend. *Ballettens blomstring ude og hjemme.* Copenhagen, 1945.

Kragh-Jacobsen, Svend, and Torben Krogh, eds. *Den Kongelige Danske Ballet.* Copenhagen, 1952.

Kragh-Jacobsen, Svend. *The Royal Danish Ballet: An Old Tradition and a Living Present.* Copenhagen, 1955.

LaPointe, Janice D. M. "Creative Integration: A Selective Study of August Bournonville and His Musical Collaborators." *Dance Research Annual* 16 (1987): 87–97.

Moore, Lillian. "Bournonville's London Spring." *Bulletin of the New York Public Library* (November 1965).

Nørlyng, Ole, and Henning Urup, eds. *Bournonville: Tradition–Rekonstruktion.* Copenhagen, 1989. Includes English summaries.

Ralov, Kirsten, ed. *The Bournonville School.* 4 vols. New York, 1979.

Sayers, Lesley-Anne. "Bournonville Our Contemporary." *Dance Now* 1 (Winter 1992–1993): 58–63.

Teatervidenskabelige studier. Vol. 2. Copenhagen, 1972. Collection of essays on historical and technical aspects of Bournonville's works.

Terry, Walter. *The King's Ballet Master.* New York, 1979.

Veale, Tom G. "The Dancing Prices of Denmark." *Dance Perspectives,* no. 11 (1961).

ARCHIVES.   Danish Royal Theater, Copenhagen. Drottningholm Archives, Stockholm. Fryklund Samling, Music History Museum, Stockholm. Lillian Moore Collection, Dance Collection, New York Public Library for the Performing Arts. National Archives, Copenhagen. Royal Library, Copenhagen. Theater History Museum, Copenhagen.

PATRICIA MCANDREW

BOURNONVILLE COMPOSERS.

Among the sixteen composers who wrote music for August Bournonville's ballets were a few who wrote some of the most outstanding ballet scores from the Romantic period in Europe. In many instances Bournonville, led by a deep musical intuition, tapped these composers' hitherto unexplored talents in ballet music.

Johannes Frederik Fröhlich (1806–1860), the first composer to collaborate with Bournonville, was an exponent of early Romantic ballet music with its strong emphasis on neoclassical elements. Fröhlich's first ballets, such as *Waldemar* (1835), were somewhat uneven in their formal conception. These early works, however, contain many of those dramatic qualities that were later expressed in *The Childhood of Erik Menved* (1843): a strong rhythmical verve, full thematic development, and clearly defined dramatic characterizations.

Edvard Mads Ebbe Helsted (1816–1900) developed into a fine ballet composer with a particular understanding of Bournonville's aesthetic ideals. Unlike Fröhlich, Helsted contributed music for ballets based on foreign street life, such as *The Toreador* (1840), *Napoli* (1842), and *Flower Festival in Genzano* (1858), which are all characterized by rich local color and an extraordinary variety of dance types worked out in a classical idiom. Helsted is thus primarily remembered for his lively music to some of Bournonville's many travelogues, although he also wrote one significant score in the national historic genre, *Kirsten Piil* (1845). Helsted's finest contribution, however, was his Greek mythological ballet *Psyche* (1850), Bournonville's unorthodox attempt at a new and more natural mime-drama. Here, Helsted's score came closest to Bournonville's aesthetics and academic ideals. Written in the musical style of Felix Mendelssohn(-Bartholdy), it differs from the traditional ballet music of the time by avoiding regular phrases of identical length. In this work Helsted demonstrated a fine sense of melody together with a mature technique for thematic development.

The ballet music of Niels Wilhelm Gade (1817–1890) and that of his father-in-law, Johan Peter Emilius Hartmann (1805–1900), was written almost exclusively for historical and mythological ballets. Bournonville noticed Gade's lyricism with its refined instrumentation and in 1840, when Gade was twenty-three years old, asked him to write the music for the action-packed section of the national-mythological prologue *National Muses.* Two years later, Gade was commissioned to write the music for the Blue Grotto scene in the second act of *Napoli.* The results were not totally satisfactory, most probably due to Bournonville's wish to incorporate François Humbert Prüme's popular *La Mélancolie* for solo violin and orchestra. As a result, this act contains as much music by Prüme. It is interesting to imagine what this act might have become, had Bournonville allowed Gade to write the entire score.

With the music for the first and third acts of *A Folk Tale* (1854), Gade initiated a new era in Danish ballet music. Now the traditional structures gave way to a free and more balladlike musical idiom within a new and more specific Danish folk flavor. Because Gade was one of the composers who could best release the weightlessness and inner poetry of Bournonville's choreography, the dances in *A Folk Tale* are alternately characterized by a strong rhythmical conciseness and a refined pastoral sonority.

A Folk Tale represents some of the finest interaction ever between the delicate lyricism of Gade and the dark Nordic romantic sonority of Hartmann, whose spritely and bewitching music for the ballet's second act marked the real beginning of Bournonville's most fruitful and enduring collaboration with a composer. The writer of numerous overtures and melodramas based on plays by Adam Oehlenschläger, the most important literary figure of Danish Romanticism, Hartmann was thoroughly familiar with ancient Nordic myths and legends. Thus he was an ideal choice to compose the scores for Bournonville's *The Valkyrie* (1861), *The Lay of Thrym* (1868), and *Arcona* (1875). For these ambitious ballets Hartmann wrote powerful and illustrative music that brilliantly supports the grandiose mythological scenarios. Hartmann's music for *The Valkyrie* contains an extraordinary richness of symphonic themes. Characters in the ensemble dances are identified by the use of a leitmotif technique that points to a Wagnerian influence. In the solo dances, however, the music is still evocative of early French ballet music.

In *The Lay of Thrym* Hartmann continued to develop the art of identifying characters and situations with specific themes. By his characteristic rhythms, based on triplets, fully developed harmony, and prolific use of minor dominant chordal structure, Hartmann reaches his artistic peak, which leads toward the future development of Nordic Romantic composers, including Edvard Grieg. However, Hartmann's last ballet score, for *Arcona*, is somewhat stagnant; the extended thematic layout needed to unify the complex plot works against the melodic development. *Arcona* was notable mainly for the many new and surprising stage effects that were made possible with the opening of Copenhagen's new Royal Theater in 1874.

The last Bournonville composer to work within the historical Nordic genre was Peter (Arnold) Heise (1830–1879). For the ballet about a seventeenth-century Danish sea hero, *Cort Adeler in Venice* (1870), Heise wrote a charming score, with fine, soft instrumentation that emphasized the ballet's various local colors. *Cort Adeler* differs from most of Bournonville's other ballets in that it eschewed the widespread practice of interweaving numerous popular folk songs into the score. Nonetheless, the ballet attracted little attention, probably due to its vaudeville quality. Heise's music still stands as a distinguished example of the fine ballet composer he might have become had Bournonville recognized his potential sooner.

Both *Faust* (1832) and *Don Quixote* (1837), the two Bournonville ballets that were based on classical literature, were provided with scores of only minor importance. Philip Ludvig Keck (1790–1848), faced with the demanding task of composing a three-act ballet on Johann Wolfgang Goethe's *Faust*, was unable to deliver more than an arrangement of pieced-together fragments from contemporary operas and ballets. Keck's failure is even more regrettable because Bournonville was one of the first European choreographers to attempt to stage a ballet based on *Faust*.

Johann Wilhelm Ludvig Zinck (1776–1851) was a composer who could easily deliver a reliable piece of popular theater music. His score for *Don Quixote* is such an example. However, the score was close to the French vaudeville tradition and was too frail to support the complex action of the ballet.

Holger Simon Paulli (1810–1891) was the most prominent of the composers who wrote for Bournonville's numerous lighthearted ballets that showed foreign street life and original fantasies. A fine craftsman, Paulli produced euphonious and truly appropriate ballet music. He was able to avoid the prevailing tendency of stringing together a hodgepodge of local dance tunes, although he did borrow from several sources to conjure up the settings for such popular ballets as *Napoli* (1842), *Konservatoriet* (1849), *Kermesse in Bruges* (1851), and the second part of *Flower Festival in Genzano* (1858). Indeed, Paulli is the Bournonville composer whose music has survived most extensively in the repertory.

Other composers within this genre were Herman Severin Løvenskjold (1815–1870), August Henrik Winding (1835–1899), and Emil (Wilhelm Emilius Zinn) Hartmann (1836–1898), son of Johan Peter Emilius Hartmann. In Løvenskjold's striking music for *La Sylphide* (1836), the twenty-year old composer showed an astonishing maturity and great richness in his melodies. As a dramatic composer he was less accomplished, although he did collaborate on the allegorical fantasy *The New Penelope* (1847) with considerable success.

For the realistic ballet *The Mountain Hut* (1859), Hartmann and Winding each wrote an act. Winding's music in the first act is characterized by rather free forms and a striking rhythmical variety prompting Bournonville to complain in his diary about the music of the younger generation. Bournonville also had difficulty with Hartmann's brilliantly colorful orchestrations for the dramatic second act.

The rest of the Bournonville composers worked exclusively in the genres of vaudeville-ballets, *divertissements,* single dances, and tableaux. Here the dominant figure is Hans Christian Lumbye (1810–1874) who provided the music for *La Ventana* (1854). Lumbye, the leading Danish dance composer of the nineteenth century, provided Bournonville with a treasure of lively dances that were incorporated into larger vaudeville-ballets or performed as single dances. Lumbye's talent for delivering a roaring, galloping finale whenever needed benefited Bournonville throughout his professional life.

Toward the end of the 1860s, with Paulli devoting all his time to conducting, Bournonville turned to Andreas Frederik Lincke (1819–1874), Vilhelm Christian Holm (1820–1886), Christian Florus Balduin Dahl (1834–1891), and Carl Christian Møller (1823–1893) to provide arrangements for his works. All were talented musicians with the Royal Theater orchestra and or the Tivoli Gardens orchestra; but none changed the ballet music traditions established by Paulli. Bournonville's last musical collaborators thus made only minor contributions to Danish ballet music.

[*For related discussion, see* Music for Dance, *article on* Western Music, 1800–1900.]

BIBLIOGRAPHY

Bruun, Kai. *Dansk musiks historie.* 2 vols. Copenhagen, 1969.
Jürgensen, Knud Arne. "The Bournonville Composers." In *The Bournonville Heritage: Piano Scores.* London, 1991.
Jürgensen, Knud Arne. *The Bournonville Tradition. The First Fifty Years, 1829–1879.* London, 1997.
Nørlyng, Ole. "Bournonville og hans musikalske medarbejdere." In *Perspektiv på Bournonville,* edited by Erik Aschengreen et al. Copenhagen, 1980.
Schiørring, Nils. "Bournonville and the Music to His Ballets." In *Theatre Research Studies.* Vol. 2. Copenhagen, 1972.
Schiørring, Nils. *Musikkens historie i Danmark,* vol. 2, *1750–1870.* Copenhagen, 1978.

KNUD ARNE JÜRGENSEN

BOURRÉE. The term *bourrée* (also spelled *bourée*) usually refers to a type of aristocratic court dance and music popular in France and other European countries during the seventeenth and eighteenth centuries. French folk dances called *bourrées* have also been known from the Renaissance to modern times.

Several writers of French dictionaries (Furetière, 1701; Richelet, 1732; Compan, 1787) mention that the *bourrée* was believed to come from the French province of Auvergne. It probably came from provincial regions to the French court in the middle or late sixteenth century. Its reception must have been favorable, for by the early sev-

enteenth century the elegant royal *ballets de cour* included dance *entrées* entitled *bourée* (for example, in *Le Ballet de la Délivrance de Renaud,* 1617).

The *bourrée* was one of several dance types—including *menuet, passepied, gavotte, sarabande, loure, rigaudon,* and others—that were refined and changed to suit aristocratic taste by artists working under the French king Louis XIV (reigned 1653–1715). It became a joyful, gay courtship dance for a couple, full of confidence and the enjoyment of life. The dancers, moving with a graceful and strongly centered carriage, used swiftly flowing steps to form a variety of floor patterns in the geometric figures common to French court dancing of the period. There was less ornamentation and subtle footwork than in many of the other popular court dances. The tempo was fast for the time ($\downarrow$ = 80–92 M.M. in a time signature of 2 or ¢). The music is in duple meter on all levels and has a quarter-note upbeat, with many phrases four or eight bars in length; a syncopation is also common in the music.

Many different steps were used in *bourrées,* but the most common was the *pas de bourrée,* a step-unit performed to one measure of music. It consists of a *demi-coupé* (a step with *plié* and *élevé*) followed by two *pas marchées* (two plain steps without change of elevation). The *pas de bourrée* could begin on either foot (giving right–left–right or left–right–left) and thus was useful whenever a change of leading foot was desired. The third of the three steps was sometimes taken with a tiny leap (*demi-jeté*) for added liveliness. A form of the *pas de bourrée* is still used today in ballet, and varieties of it occur in many folk dances.

Bourrée entrées occurred frequently in French Baroque ballets and operas. The team of composer Jean-Baptiste Lully and choreographer Pierre Beauchamp, created many *bourrées* and other dance *entrées* in their theatrical works from the 1650s until Lully's death in 1687. The *bourrée* continued to be a popular *entrée* until the mid-eighteenth century, appearing in the works of French composers such as André Campra, Marc-Antoine Charpentier, André Cardinal Destouches, Jean-Féry Rebel, and Jean-Philippe Rameau. The chief choreographer and ballet master at the Paris Opera from 1687 to 1729 was Guillaume-Louis Pecour, and fourteen of his *bourrées* have survived in choreographic notation. Included are three for the theater, originally danced by such illustrious performers as Marie-Thérèse Subligny, Mademoiselle Guiot, Claude Ballon, and François Dumoulin.

During the same period (c.1650–1750) the *bourrée* was also well loved as a social dance at court. It was popular both as a piece for one couple dancing alone (*danse à deux*) and, from about the 1680s, as a *contredanse,* with several couples dancing at once. The *danses à deux* were through-composed pieces performed by one couple at formal ceremonial balls while the assembled court watched. *Contredanses* often followed the *danses à deux* and were easier to perform, since a continually repeating four-bar step formula was used and the figures were less complex.

Many *bourrées* survive in choreographic notation. In addition to numerous *contredanses*, there are thirty theatrical and social dances, composed by choreographers residing both in France (Pecour, Raoul-Auger Feuillet, Jacques Dezais, and Ballon) and in England (Mister Isaac, Anthony L'Abbé, and Jean-Jacques Rousseau). "La Bourée d'Achille," by Pecour, was one of the best-loved social dances and is still enjoyed today in beginning classes on French court dancing. The thirty *bourrées* range in technique from very easy to extremely difficult. Two anonymous pieces that probably date from before 1700 use generally rounded figures, and almost all step-units are *pas de bourrée*. The early eighteenth-century *bourrées* contain angular, more complex geometrical figures and a great variety of step-units, with *bourrée* step accounting for less than half of them.

The characteristic phrase structure and rhythms of *bourrée* music were exploited by Baroque composers of many countries. *Bourrées* appear often in keyboard and orchestral suites, coming after the more traditional overture, *allemande*, and *courante*, but before the *gigue*, or *giga*. Many reflect the joyful quality of the dance, although the well-known theorist and composer Johannes Mattheson wrote in 1739 that "their quality is primarily contentedness and pleasantness; at the same time they have an unconcerned or relaxed quality; they are a little careless, comfortable, and yet not disagreeable" (*Der vollkommene Capellmeister*, p. 225). *Bourées* may be found in the music of Johann Caspar, Ferdinand Fischer, Johann Kreiger, Nicolas-Antoine Lebègue, Jean-Henri d'Anglebert, Henry Purcell, and Johann Sebastian Bach. The *bourrée* continued to be used by composers of the later eighteenth century but as a topic for development within the course of a larger work such as a symphony, rather than a separate piece entitled *Bourrée*. An example is the opening of Mozart's Symphony in G Minor, no. 40 (K. 550), which is *bourrée*-like.

Little is known of the history of the *bourrée* as folk dance, but, according to Claudie Marcel-Dubois (1949), in the mid-twentieth century various dances of that name were still being performed in French provincial regions such as Bourbonnais, Berry, Marche, Limousin, Velay, Morvan, Charolais, Languedoc, Angoumois, Jura, and Savoy.

[*For related discussion, see* Ballet Technique, History of, *article on* French Court Dance.]

BIBLIOGRAPHY

Hilton, Wendy. *Dance of Court and Theatre: The French Noble Style, 1690–1725*. Princeton, 1981.

Marcel-Dubois, Claudie. "Bourree." In *Die Musik in Geschichte und Gegenwart*. Kassel, 1949–.

Witherell, Anne L. *Louis Pécour's 1700 Recueil des dances*. Ann Arbor, Mich., 1983.

MEREDITH ELLIS LITTLE

BOVT, VIOLETTA (Violetta Trofimovna Bovt; born 9 May 1927 in Los Angeles), dancer. Bovt moved to the USSR in the 1930s with her parents, who were of Russian extraction. In 1935 she entered the Bolshoi Theater ballet school, where she studied with Elisaveta Gerdt, Maria Kozhukhova, and Viktor Semenov. Upon graduation in 1944 Bovt joined the Stanislavsky and Nemirovich-Danchenko Music Theater Ballet, where she was a principal dancer for thirty-five years. Her first leading role was in Vladimir Burmeister's *Lola* in 1946. She was guided in her work by the pioneering principles of dramatic realism laid down by Konstantin Stanislavsky and Vladimir Nemirovich-Danchenko. To realize the dictum of the "dancing actor" proclaimed by their theater, she did research in libraries and museums and at exhibitions, seeking to create persuasive and authentic characters onstage. Bovt's probing interpretation of Odette-Odile was seen in Burmeister's 1953 version of *Swan Lake*. For the same choreographer she created roles in *The Coast of Happiness* (1948), *La Esmeralda* (1950), and *Jeanne d'Arc* (1957). She also danced leading roles in Aleksei Chichinadze's *Don Juan* (1962) and *Francesca da Rimini* (1964) and Natalia Ryzhenko and Viktor Smirnov-Golovanov's *Dreamers* (1976). In these years Bovt also toured widely in Europe, Asia, and South America. While still performing she began to teach, and she continued to work as a coach with the company after retiring from the stage in 1979. In 1983 she staged Burmeister's *La Esmeralda* at the Omsk Musical Theater. She was named People's Artist of the USSR in 1970. Bovt returned to live in the United States in 1987.

BIBLIOGRAPHY

Granovskaiia, G. *Violetta Bovt*. Moscow, 1972.

Imbert, Charles. "*Le lac aux cygnes* par les Ballets Soviétiques." *Danse* (July 1956): 10–11.

Souritz, Elizabeth. "Pictures at an Exhibition." *Dance Magazine* (February 1964): 81.

GALINA V. INOZEMTSEVA
Translated from Russian

BOWMAN, PATRICIA (born 12 December 1908 in Washington, D.C.), American dancer and teacher. Bowman was the star of musicals and occasionally the ballerina of a classical company. She successfully bridged two eras of ballet, two worlds of dance. She had the training and attributes of a classical ballerina and gave the large public of popular entertainment a hint of what tasteful ballet is. She appeared in cinema-house stage shows and Broadway musicals, and with ballet companies and symphony orchestras; all the while she was an uncompromising classical dancer. In the manner of her day she often arranged her own dances, designed the costumes, and chose the music; but dances were also choreographed for her by Michel Fokine, Léonide Massine, and Mikhail Mordkin for her appearances in vaudeville or ballet companies.

Bowman studied dance in Washington, D.C., with Paul Tchernikoff and Lisa Gardiner, alumni of the Anna Pavlova Company. In New York she studied intensively with Fokine, later in Europe with Nikolai Legat, Lubov Egorova, and Margarete Wallmann. Her professional career started in 1920 in *George White's Scandals*, but next she was in the Lewisohn Stadium and on tour in the summer of 1927 with a company headed by Michel and Vera Fokine. After a brief period partnering Tony DeMarco that fall in ballroom dances, she returned to ballet. Later that year, partnered by Nicholas Daks, she was *prima ballerina* at the Strand Theater in New York and later at the Roxy in the same city. In her second year at the Roxy, Massine was choreographer as well as her partner. When Radio City Music Hall opened, Bowman was *prima ballerina*, and she held that position on and off for the next eight years. One of her most popular dances there was based on the nineteenth-century *La Sylphide*. She also danced Fokine's *Dying Swan* and pieces he made especially for her: *Tennis* (music by Léo Delibes) and *Persian Angel* (music by Modest Mussorgsky). Among her partners were Daks, Charles Laskey, and very often Paul Haakon.

In 1938 Bowman danced with the Mordkin Ballet in New York City, and on tour she danced *Swan Lake, Giselle, The Goldfish*, and *Voices of Spring*. In 1939 she danced in the Lewisohn Stadium in a program of Fokine ballets— *Schéhérazade, Le Spectre de la Rose*, and *Tennis*. She was *prima ballerina* of Ballet Theatre's first season, 1940. In 1941 she returned to musicals, partnered by Haakon or George Zoritch. For the next sixteen years Bowman danced in theaters all over the United States, Canada, and London in musicals and operettas, as guest artist with symphony orchestras, and as star of stage shows in cinema theaters. For many summers she danced principal roles in operettas in the Saint Louis Municipal Opera and the Dallas Starlight Theater. In the late 1940s she was guest artist with the Chicago Opera, dancing Ruth Page's choreography in *Lakmé, Carmen*, and *Halka*. In 1957 she retired to teach until 1977, when she married Albert Kaye, moved to Nevada, and became a consultant to a ballet group.

BIBLIOGRAPHY

Barzel, Ann. "People's Ballerina." *Dance Magazine* (January 1947).
Gruen, John. "Patricia Bowman." *Dance Magazine* (October 1976): 47–62.
Gruen, John. *People Who Dance: Twenty-Two Dancers Tell Their Own Stories*. Princeton, N.J., 1988.
Ware, Walter. *Ballet Is Magic: A Triple Monograph—Harriet Hoctor, Paul Haakon, Patricia Bowman*. New York, 1936.

ANN BARZEL

BOYARCHIKOV, NIKOLAI (Nikolai Nikolaevich Boiarchikov; born 27 September 1935 in Leningrad), Russian dancer and choreographer. Boyarchikov graduated from the Leningrad ballet school in 1954. He made his debut as a dancer at Leningrad's Maly Opera House in the role of Eros in Konstantin Boyarsky's revival of Michel Fokine's ballet of the same name. Thereafter, Boyarchikov took leading roles in classical ballets and created several roles in contemporary ballets. In 1967 he graduated from the choreography department of the Leningrad Conservatory. In 1971 he was appointed chief choreographer of the Perm Opera and Ballet Theater, and in 1977 he became the chief choreographer of the Maly Opera House.

Boyarchikov made his debut as a choreographer in 1964 at the Maly. In the ballet *The Three Musketeers*, with its humorous subtitle *Almost According to Dumas*, the choreographer first articulated the basic principles of his aesthetic, which he has been developing ever since. He reinterprets the tradition of creating ballets based on literary classics. In his ballets the plot, which is barely outlined, becomes the starting point for the action, which reveals the intrinsic meaning of the event and makes it archetypal.

With the production of *The Queen of Spades* in 1968 for the Leningrad Chamber Ballet and *Tsar Boris* for the Perm Theater (1975; Maly Theater, 1978), Boyarchikov began a new stage in his development, first adapting the works of Aleksandr Pushkin for ballet and then going on to other literary classics that until then had seemed out of bounds to the art form. At the same time he was instrumental in giving new life to Sergei Prokofiev's music on the ballet stage. After *The Queen of Spades* and *Tsar Boris*, using the scores Prokofiev originally composed for film and drama, Boyarchikov turned to the ballet *Romeo and Juliet*, in which he emphasized the romantic motifs as conceived by the composer. In the 1970s and early 1980s at the Maly Boyarchikov worked with young composers as he continued to adapt for the stage literary works that did not lend themselves easily to conversion into dance. In extending the boundaries of the genre of choreographic productions he gave their subjects a contemporary interpretation.

In the mythological *Hercules* (1980), and in the balletic tragedies *The Robbers* (based on Schiller's *Die Raüber*; 1983) and *Macbeth* (based on Shakespeare's play; 1984), the choreographer asserted his own poetics of theater ballet. Its uniqueness lay in the priority given to theatricality, which dominated all components of the performance, and in the wealth of dance vocabulary, especially in solo dances. Inherent in Boyarchikov's productions are concentrated action, use of a wide variety of expressive plastique, a search for new forms of *mise-en-scène,* and vividness of descriptive detail couched metaphorically. These principles were taken up by choreographers all over the country, for example, Vladimir Salimbaev in Perm and Valery Kovtun in Kiev.

At the end of the 1980s and into the 1990s Boyarchikov returned to other classics of Russian literature, staging *The Marriage* (1986), after Nikolai Gogol; *Quiet Flows the Don* (1988), after Mikhail Sholokhov; and *Petersburg* (1992), after Andrei Bely. In *Quiet Flows the Don* Boyarchikov produced a vast epic in which every character represented both a specific psychological personality and a moral or social force that determined the events in the ballet. In 1989 Boyarchikov attended the International Choreographers Program at the American Dance Festival in Durham, North Carolina. That experience led him to invite Betty Jones, a pioneer member of José Limón's company, to stage Limón's *There Is a Time* in Leningrad, the first occasion that a modern dance work was produced in the Soviet Union by a foreign company member. Boyarchikov's policy of expanding the Maly's international repertory has continued with the visit in 1995 of Howard Sayette from the United States to stage a revival of *Les Noces.*

BIBLIOGRAPHY

Chernova, Natalia. *Ot Geltser do Ulanovoi.* Moscow, 1979.

Ilicheva, Marina. "Boyarchikov." *Teatralnaia Zhian,* no. 5 (1988).

Krasovskaya, Vera. "Ballet Changes, Shakespeare Endures." *Ballet Review* 19 (Summer 1991): 71–80.

Kusovleva, T. "Tyminsky A. Dnevnik ushedshego s ploshchadi." In *V konze vosmidesiatych na leningradskoy szene.* Leningrad, 1989.

Lvov-Anokhin, Boris. "Ottochenyi do simvola." *Teatr,* no. 4 (1978).

McDonagh, Don, and Catherine Edmunds. "A Conversation with Nikolai Boyarchikov." *Ballet Review* 20 (Winter 1992): 58–63.

Skliarevskaia, Inna. "Introducing Nikolai Boyarchikov." *Ballet Review* 20 (Winter 1992): 52–57.

NATALIA Y. CHERNOVA
Translated from Russian

BRABANTS, JEANNE (born 25 January 1920 in Antwerp), Belgian teacher and choreographer. Brabants's father taught gymnastics and acrobatics in the city of Antwerp. Jeanne and her sisters Jos and Annie all played important roles in the development of dance in Belgium.

Jeanne's father sent her to dance school, intending that she would take over his gymnastics club. She took classes in the Laban-oriented school of Léa Daan in Antwerp. Beginning in 1934 she performed solo dances with Daan's company, and in 1935 she received a certificate from the school to teach the Laban system. After receiving a degree

in physical education in 1938, she took classes with Kurt Jooss and Sigurd Leeder at Dartington Hall, London, in 1939.

In 1941 Brabants formed her own school and company. She also took classes in classical ballet with André van Damme and later continued to improve her skills with Olga Preobrajenska in Paris and at seminars in London, Leningrad, and Copenhagen.

When Jeanne's sisters joined the company—Jos in 1942 and Annie in 1943—it was possible to create larger works with different choreographic flavors. Jos choreographed primarily pieces with folkloric elements, such as *Sousta* (1951) and *Jota* (1954). In 1954 the dancer Jaak van Luyth (J. van der Maat) joined the group, and his presence further changed the output of the company. During the 1950s the company had financial difficulties, but with the rise of television it was able to survive by performing for various shows. In 1955 Ravel's *Boléro* was produced for Belgian television. During the same decade, works by Leeder were staged for the company: *The Cage* (1954), with music by Aram Khachaturian, and *Prélude* (1954), with music by Frédéric Chopin.

Brabants's school grew steadily over the years, training dancers who were often engaged by the ballet company of the Royal Flemish Opera, founded in 1923. Brabants closed the school in 1958 to take on other commitments in the ballet school of the Royal Flemish Opera. When this school emerged as the Municipal Institute for Ballet in 1961, she was appointed director. She received an award for the best choreography at the International Ballet Competition in Varna in 1968. When the Royal Ballet of Flanders was created, she became its director and produced a range of works characterized by their purity and condensed use of movement. [*See* Royal Ballet of Flanders.]

Some of Brabants's most important creations are *Poëma* (1975), *Cantus Firmus* (1968), *Dialoog* (1971), *Presto, Vivo e Lento* (1972), *Amelia* (1973), *Pierlala* (1974), *Elegie* (1975), *Een Dag aan het Hof van Bourgondie* (1964), *Salvé Antverpia* (1974), *Ulensoiegel de Geus* (1976), and *Grand Hotel* (1977). After she retired as director from the Royal Ballet of Flanders in 1984, Brabants created the company Danza Antiqua (1988), which specializes in reconstructing Renaissance and Baroque dances.

BIBLIOGRAPHY

Barbier, Rina. *Van operaballet naar Ballet van Vlaanderen.* Antwerp, 1973.

Barbier, Rina. *The Royal Ballet of Flanders, 1970–1980.* Brussels, 1980.

Barbier, Rina. *Dans voor waarden: Over Jeanne Brabants.* Antwerp, 1990.

Brabants, Jeanne. "Trees in the Desert." *Ballett International* 7 (June–July 1984): 20–23.

Brabants, Jeanne. "Les trois coups belge: Jeanne Brabants raconte" (parts 1–12). *Saisons de la Danse* (February 1992–February 1993).

LUC VERVAEKE

BRADLEY, BUDDY (Clarence Bradley; born 25 July 1905 in Epps, Alabama, died 17 July 1972 in New York City), American dance teacher, coach, and choreographer for stage, screen, cabaret, and television. Most of Bradley's professional career was spent in England and Europe, and little is recorded of his American work. This problem is shared by other African-American choreographers of his generation, such as Leonard Harper, Clarence Robinson, and Addison Carey. In addition, the date and place of his birth are uncertain, as is the date of his stage debut.

Bradley grew up in Harrisburg, Pennsylvania, and later, after his mother's death, moved to Harlem in New York City, where he lived in a boardinghouse for performers. His early influences included Dancing Dotson and Jack Wiggins, dancers on the black vaudeville circuit; precision dancers Rufus Greenlee and Thaddeus Drayton, who were fellow rooming-house boarders; and the inventive Eddie Rector. In the mid-1920s, after working as an elevator operator, Bradley took a chorus job in a musical revue at Connie's Inn in upper Manhattan. Subsequently he taught routines to white performers at the West Forty-sixth Street studios of impresario Billy Pierce and began his early transition from performer to teacher-choreographer.

Although British musical comedy star Jessie Matthews referred to him as "my tap teacher and choreographer of all my musicals," Bradley often received no public recognition for his work. He was not credited, for example, with staging routines for individual American stars (including Mae West, Gilda Gray, Ruby Keeler, Adele and Fred Astaire, Lucille Ball, and Eleanor Powell) or for the shows he doctored or completely rechoreographed (including Busby Berkeley's *Greenwich Village Follies* of 1928 and Clifton Webb's "High Yaller" routine from *The Little Show* of 1929).

Bradley first went to London with Lew Leslie's *Blackbirds* in 1926. The following year he staged Jessie Matthew's numbers in C. B. Cochran's revue *One Damn Thing after Another*. After returning briefly to the United States, he went back to London, where he worked with Matthews in many of her stage shows and movies, including both the stage and film versions of *Evergreen* (1930 and 1934, respectively) and her last musical show, the revue *Sauce Tartare* (1949). He arranged the dances for *Cochran's 1931 Revue* and *Words and Music*, both by Noël Coward, and he worked with Frederick Ashton—Bradley contributing the tap and jazz routines and Ashton the ballets—in many shows for Cochran and others, including Jerome Kern's *The Cat and the Fiddle* (1932), the revues *Ballyhoo* (1932) and *After Dark* (1933), *The Flying Trapeze* (1935), in which he staged Jack Buchanan's numbers, *Follow the Sun* (1935), and *Floodlight* (1937). In 1932 Bradley and Ashton collaborated on a jazz ballet, *High Yellow*, presented by the Camargo Society, with Alicia Markova in the leading role; it was perhaps the first ballet company to present work by a musical theater choreographer—and the first to present the work of a black choreographer.

Bradley maintained a school in London from 1933 to 1967 and used his students as the nucleus of his troupe of Buddy Bradley Girls, who appeared in movies and later on television. His last work for the London musical theater was Sandy Wilson's *Divorce Me, Darling* (1965). He also continued to choreograph for individuals, as he had done decades earlier. In 1967 with Dorothy Bradley, his wife, pupil, and muse, he returned to New York City, where he remained until his death.

Bradley's genius was to infuse simplified, African-American steps with the prevailing musical comedy style of the era to create a mix that was enticing in its black references but easy for white dancers to learn. In their book *Jazz Dance* (1968), Marshall and Jean Stearns described his style as "a blend of easy tap plus movements from the Afro-American vernacular, put together with an overall continuity and rising to a climax." Dorothy Bradley characterized him as "the Duke Ellington of dance" because of his smooth, tasteful, and sophisticated choreography.

BIBLIOGRAPHY

Stearns, Marshall, and Jean Stearns. *Jazz Dance*. New York, 1968.
Thornton, Michael. *Jessie Matthews: A Biography*. London, 1975.
Vaughan, David. *Frederick Ashton and His Ballets*. London, 1977.

BRENDA DIXON GOTTSCHILD

BRANLE (also Fr., *bransle, brallo, bralle, brale*; Med. Lat., *branlus*; Eng., *bransle, brawl[e], braul[e], bralle[e], brangle[e], brangill, brantl[e]*; It., *brando*; Basque, *branlou*; Sp., *bran*). Derived from the French verb *branler*, the term *branle* is used for both a dance step and a group-dance type of France and its northern-European neighbors (e.g., the Low Countries). The continuous histories of the step and type can be traced back to at least the fifteenth century. Randle Cotgrave (*Dictionarie of the French and English Tongues*) gives both meanings:

> Bransle: a totter, swing, or swindge; a shake, shog, or shocke; a stirring, and uncertain and inconstant motion; . . . also, a brawl, or daunce, wherein many (men, and women) holding by the hands sometimes in a ring, and otherwise at length, move all together. (Cotgrave, 1611)

Cotgrave's two senses of *branle* are clear and valid for the early sources (fifteenth and sixteenth centuries), which place the *branle* step not in the *branle* dance but in the *bassedanse*—a quite different genre. The basic steps in late sixteenth-century *branles* were termed instead simples and doubles; they closely resemble the basic footwork in today's *branles*, now termed "*branle* steps."

Many *branles* are danced in various parts of modern France: in some areas they represent an apparently unbroken folk tradition that goes back at least to the Renaissance or even to the Middle Ages (as in the Pays Basques); elsewhere they are revivals of traditions that were only briefly interrupted in the first half of the twentieth century as a result of urbanization and the widespread cultural destruction wrought by the two world wars. They were revived with the aid of those who could still remember them from childhood or youth (Guilcher, 1963, 1984).

Modern *branles* are not only representative of a long tradition in France and contiguous countries, they are essentially the French manifestations of a huge international family of circle/line "folk" dances of great but unknown age from all over Europe and the Middle East. They are still danced in rural and village milieus in the Balkan and Muslim countries surrounding the Mediterranean Sea and in parts of Scandinavia. Pictorial, literary, and musical evidence traces the French type back to the medieval *carole, estampie, rondeau*, and *farandole* of France, Provence, and the Low Countries. Attempts to go even further back lead only into the misty realms of unrecorded history. Nor can the precise geographic area from which these kinds of dances originated be identified. It is possible that traders and invaders such as the Phoenicians, Greeks, Romans, or Turks, who navigated the Mediterranean or followed ancient land routes, spread this type of dance everywhere they stopped. Documentation is, however, too sketchy to provide a continuous narrative throughout the centuries or across national boundaries. When viewed from the perspective of the ancient past, it is clear that there is some kind of connection between today's branles and their other European counterparts and similar dances of antiquity. Such recognition does not make it possible to reconstruct ancient Greek, Roman, Egyptian, or Hebrew dances with any certainty, however.

The generic names of today's circle/line dances vary with the country or region to which they belong: *khoro* (Bulgaria), *kolo* (Montenegro), *choros* and *syrtós* (Greece), *pentozali* (Crete), *hora* (Romania), *horon* (Turkey). They all share the following characteristics with the *branle:*

1. *Circle/Line Formation:* Sometimes, the number of dancers determines whether a formation is a circle or a line—that is, the circle is closed if there are many dancers and open if there are just a few—or if the formation is to be socially prescribed (eastern European and Arabian dances do not mix sexes, making separate lines or circles necessary). Those dances that are entirely symmetrical (i.e., their predominant movement is equally to the left and right) tend to be circular and without a leader; asymmetrical dances usually have a leader who calls or indicates a new section or improvises a solo while the others do a simpler, repeated step pattern.

2. *Linkage among the Dancers.* Dancers hold hands, join little fingers or elbows, or place their hands on neigh-

bors' shoulders. Linkage is also maintained by grasping belts, handkerchief corners, hoops, garlands, or sword hilts and points; by taking different holds with the right and left hands; and/or by forming a double chain in which women join hands in an inner circle and men join hands in an outer circle. In the last of these, both may interlock with the clasped hands of one sex behind the backs of the other (a figure known in American square-dance, Big-Circle, and running-dance calls as "the ladies bow and the gents know how"). Dancers may also drop hands to clap them or to pivot round, or both, and resume hands for other actions. Circles or lines without holding hands are also possible; the linkage among the dancers is then made apparent by maintaining equidistant positions along the circle. The dancers may also break the circle to form independent couples, trios, two-couple sets, and so on.

3. *Emphasis on Repeated Footwork.* Whether footwork is simple or complex, attention is called to it in most cases, while torsos are kept upright and quiet (the degree of torso movement varies with the place of origin); arms may be down, or shoulder height, and also quiet, but arms may also move from one position to another as part of the dance (coordination between hands and feet may either be very simple or difficult enough to pose a real challenge to the dancers).

4. *Movement.* Movement is usually in the same direction at the same time. Moving in opposite directions from, or alternating steps with, a partner is done frequently but not preponderantly. While sideways motion along a circle is dominant, the dancers may move into the circle and out (i.e., straight or diagonally forward and backward); they may turn and progress facing in the line of direction or away from it. *Branles* are not normally figure dances.

5. *Meter.* The dances are performed either in single meter, with simple or compound subdivisions, or in mixed meter; they are played or sung or both; and the accompanying instrumentation depends on the supposed geographic region of origin and on either the instruments available or perceived to be associated with the dancers' imagined social class. The tunes may be preexistent or newly invented. The rhythm of the feet may be identical to the basic beat, slower than the basic beat (e.g., one step to four beats), or may subdivide it; the feet and hands may or may not stamp out or clap a rhythm (i.e., supply a percussive accompaniment to or with the music).

6. *Other Musical Characteristics.* Extremes of tempo are available. The rhythmic patterns of the repeated footwork may be short or long, hypnotically repetitive of small rhythmic units, or combined into longer phrases. Phrases of music usually coincide with phrases of dance and are normally, but not always, regular.

7. *Repetition/Variation.* The dominant compositional principle is repetition, whether of tiny step units or of long step combinations. A corollary principle is variation

Tabulature du branle couppé Charlotte.

Air du branle couppé   *Mouuements requis pour*
appellé Charlotte.   *dancer ce branle.*

Pied largy gaulche.
Pied droict approché.   Ces quatre pas
                                főt vn double
Pied largy gaulche.   a gaulche.
Pieds ioincts.
Pied en l'air gauche.
Pied en l'air droict.

Pied largy droict.   Ces quatre pas
Pied gaulche approché. főt vn double
Pied largy droict   a droict.
Pieds ioincts.
Pied largy gaulche   Ces quatre pas
Pied droict approché.   font vn double
Pied largy gaulche.   a gaulche.
Pieds ioincts.

BRANLE. The music and dance instructions for the mixed *branle* "Charlotte," as notated in Thoinot Arbeau's *Orchésographie* (1588). (Dance Collection, New York Public Library for the Performing Arts.)

on the basic step pattern and/or variation of the music of the dance, which is always repetitive. Individual variation is allowed at all times, everywhere, but must not impede the direction of the group or require different music.

8. *Milieu.* The dance milieu may be indoors or outdoors, but the dances are seen normally as part of "rural" life, its combined calendar of planting and harvesting, of the Catholic and Orthodox church year, and of festive gatherings at weddings and christenings. They are, thus, the property of country folk or peasants. The dances are social in function and usually celebratory (whether sacred or secular); they may be games (such as mixers or crack-the-whip or kissing dances) or serious and ritualistic beginnings and endings of gatherings. All moods are possible, though indeed pleasure, joy, vigor, and flirtatious playfulness are the chief affects expressed.

9. *Nonrepresentational Expression.* The dances may be completely nonrepresentational, concentrating on rhythmic, hypnotically repeated footwork, or they may mimic the gestures of an animal (e.g., a horse), a human activity (washerwomen at work), a plant or flower (pea or *margueritotte* [marguerite]) or a class of people (hermits). If set to a song, they are frequently titled by its incipit (e.g., "Charlotte").

The earliest written description of *branles* as dance types thus far found is in Antonius de Arena (1528). In his playful macaronic verses he makes it clear that university students (i.e., young gentlemen) were active participants at balls given by the upper classes in town or city, and that branles took up much of the program at these festive affairs. He refers to *branlos simplos* (simple, or single, *branles*), *branlos duplos* (double *branles*), and mentions *branlos decopatos* (probably the *branles coupés,* or mixed-meter *branles,* described later by Thoinot Arbeau [1588, 1589, 1596]). Arena, however, gives no full choreographies and no music. Arena specifies forward and backward movement in *branles,* while Arbeau indicates sideways motion. A satisfactory resolution of this seeming conflict has not yet come forth, but because modern branles permit all four directions, there may, in reality, have been no conflict at all, simply omissions by the authors.

Arbeau's *Orchésographie,* the principal French manual of the sixteenth century, is the richest available source of Renaissance *branles.* He begins by explaining:

> All musicians are in the habit of opening the dancing at a festival by a double *branle,* which they call the common *branle,* and afterward they play the single *branle* and the gay *branle* and at the end the *branles* of Burgundy, which some people call the *branles* of Champagne. The order of these four varieties of *branle* is determined by the three different groups taking part in a dance; the elderly, who dance the double and the single *branles* sedately; the young married folk, who dance the gay *branle;* and the youngest, like yourself, who nimbly trip the *branles* of Burgundy. (Arbeau, 1589/1967, p. 129)

Arbeau describes twenty-four types of *branles* of duple and triple meters and regular or irregular phrase lengths. With an ingenious method of intabulation, most of his branles are easy to reconstruct with the music. Some involve only walking ("Simple Branle," "Double Branle"), some running ("Gay"), some jumping ("Montarde"), and some miming as in the "Branle des Lavandières" [Washerwomen]; some are in mixed meter (e.g., "Adrian") and have mixed choreographic motives and purposes (e.g., the "Gavotte," a kissing dance). Many *branles* are named for their supposed place of origin (e.g., "Escosse" [Scottish], "Poitou"). The identification with locality has persisted throughout the history of the dance type; indeed, a sense not only of locality but of French nationalism pervades the known history of the branle. During its long heyday at the French court (from Francis I to Louis XIV), the custom remained to begin a ball with a series of *branles* and to perform *branles* supposedly from the provinces and related principalities—as well as from more exotic places (e.g., "Branle de Malte" [Malta])—in "native" costume, in *balets* and other court entertainments.

Arbeau's *branles* are distinguished from the circle dances discussed above by just two features: they are always circles of couples (partners), and they always move first to the left with the left foot and travel to the left.

There are brief references to *branles* in some Spanish and Italian sources of the same period. Among them is Baldassare Castiglione, in *Il cortegiano* (1518–1528). He warns that *brandi* should not be danced in public because they do not befit a courtier. Later, however, Cesare Negri (1602; 1604) describes royalty dancing in a *brando* for eight in Milan in 1574. He cites another *brando* done twenty years later by eighty-two dancers at once in a *mascherata* danced before Don Juan of Austria. Negri includes four *brandi* among his choreographies but does not identify one for such a large crowd. Negri's *brandi* are group figure dances containing circles but not dominated by them; they are much more complicated in structure than Arbeau's branles and are multisectional, with corresponding changes in meter and dance type. They have not yet yielded the secret, if there is one, of how they differ from similar dances Negri called *balli* (e.g., "Brando di Cales" [Calais]).

In Spain, Juan de Esquivel Navarro (1642) described the *bran de Inglaterra* (England) as one of the old dances the dancing masters had to know, even though the dances were no longer practiced. In England, *branles* were mentioned throughout the sixteenth and into the seventeenth century; one manuscript of the group from the Inns of Court (Bodleian Library, Douce 280, c.1606) gives abbreviated verbal step cues only for "The French Brawles," clearly a circle dance.

France was indeed where *branles* continued to be popular through the seventeenth century. F[rançois] de Lauze devotes a large part of his *Apologie de la danse* (published in London, 1623) to branle steps and choreographies. They are, however, incomplete, with major omissions as to the sequences of steps, and without music; despite the valiant efforts by many, authentic reconstruction may not be possible from de Lauze's text, even though he supplies major information with regard to the changes of style and deportment that were taking place in the transition between Renaissance and Baroque dancing (e.g., increasing turnout and rising on the toes). Marin Mersenne, in his *Harmonie universelle* (1636–1637), briefly characterizes the six types of *branles* usually done at balls: "One can do an infinite number of branles for each of these types, and . . . one can add as many others as one desires, for example, the *Passepieds de Bretagne*." He is even less informative than de Lauze, unfortunately.

Huge collections of dance music from the sixteenth and seventeenth centuries—from France, the Netherlands, England, and Germany—provide a large musical repertory of branles that reflects both the popularity of the dance type with the educated classes and the hunger of newly literate amateur musicians for comparatively easy material. In the ensemble collections of *danseries* by Pierre Attaingnant, Jean d'Estrée, Claude Gervaise, and Michael Praetorius, the lute collections by Jean-Baptiste Besard and Thomas Robinson, and keyboard collections such as the Fitzwilliam Virginal Book are any number of branles and other dances of the period. Whether this music was truly intended for dancing is another matter: professional dance musicians, iconography reveals, did not play from written music but had a memorized repertory on which they freely improvised. Furthermore, many branles in these collections are not represented in Arbeau's manual (e.g., "Branles de Village") or do not fit the choreographies he gives.

Branles continued to be danced in high society in France in the late seventeenth and eighteenth centuries, according to accounts of elaborate ballroom protocol at court, such as Pierre Rameau's *The Dancing Master* (1725). Rameau recounts a successional leadership pattern for the dances that was determined by rank; he implies that *branles* were group dances still, but provides no choreographies, and the small handful by others indicates that the dance type was falling out of favor (e.g., Raoul-Auger Feuillet's fourth collection of ballroom dances from 1706 includes "Le Cotillon," for which the music is subtitled a *branle*). Feuillet describes this as a dance for two couples in a verse-refrain form; it uses figures perhaps borrowed from English country dance: Forward and Back, Siding, Four-Hands Round, and Eight-Hands Round. Although these figures are found much earlier, in Negri, for example, and in fifteenth-century *ballo* choreographies, they were, by the eighteenth century, associated with English country dance, the newest rage on the continent. The step vocabulary is very small, and Feuillet says this dance is easily learned without special instructions. He and other French dancing masters were not entirely happy with the new fad for simple dances, but while country dances persisted and were transformed into *contredanses* in the eighteenth century, then metamorphosed still further into *cotillons* and *quadrilles*, branles again retreated to the countryside, which has, in recent years, revealed an extensive repertory to ethnologists.

BIBLIOGRAPHY: SOURCES

Anonymous. *Le manuscrit dit des basses danses de la bibliothèque de Bourgogne*. In Brussels Bibliothèque Royale. MS 9085. Facsimile reprint, Brussels, 1912; also Geneva, 1975.

Arbeau, Thoinot. *Orchésographie et traict en forme de dialogve, par leqvel tovtes personnes pevvent facilement apprendre & practiquer l'honneste exercice des dances*. Langres, 1588, 1589. Facsimile reprint, Langres, 1988. Reprinted with expanded title as *Orchésographie, metode, et teorie en forme de discovrs et tablatvre povr apprendre a dancer, battre le Tambour en toute sorte & diuersité de batteries, Iouët du fifre & arigot, tirer des armes & escrimer, auec autres honnestes exercices fort conuenables à la Ieunesse*. Langres, 1596. Facsimile reprint, Geneva, 1972.

Arbeau, Thoinot. *Orchesography*. 1589. Translated into English by Mary Stewart Evans. New York, 1948. Reprint with corrections, a new introduction, and notes by Julia Sutton, and representative steps and dances in Labanotation by Mireille Backer. New York, 1967.

Arena, Antonius. *Ad suos compagnones studiantes.* Lyon, 1528. Translated by John Guthrie and Marino Zorzi in *"Rules of Dancing* by Antonius Arena." *Dance Research* 4 (Autumn 1986): 3–53.

Coplande, Robert. *The Maner of Dauncynge of Base Daunces after the Use of Fravnce & Other Places.* Printed at the end of Alexander Barcley's *The Introductory to Write and to Pronounce French.* London, 1521. Facsimile reprint, Flansham, Sussex, 1937. Also reprinted in John Ward's "The manner of dauncynge." *Early Music* 4 (1976): 128–129.

Lauze, F[rançois] de. *Apologie de la danse, 1623.* Translated by Joan Wildeblood, and with original text, as *A Treatise of Instruction in Dancing and Deportment.* London, 1952.

Manuscripts of the Inns of Court. Located in Bodleian Library, Rawl.Poet.108, ff.10v-11r; British Library, Harley 367, pp. 178–179; Bodleian, Douce 280, ff.66av-66bv (202v-203v); Bodleian, Rawl.D.864, f.199v, ff.203r-204; Royal College of Music, MS 1119, title page and ff.1–2, 23v-24r; Inner Temple, Miscellanea vol. 27.

Mersenne, Marin. *Harmonie universelle* (1636–1637). Facsimile reprint, Paris, 1963. English translation of Book 2 by J. B. Egan. Ph.D. diss., Indiana University, 1962.

Negri, Cesare. *Le gratie d'amore.* Milan, 1602. Reissued as *Nuove invenzione di balli.* Milan, 1604. Translated into Spanish by Don Balthasar Carlos for Señor Condé, Duke of Sanlucar, 1630. Manuscript located in Madrid, Biblioteca Nacional, MS 14085. Facsimile reprint of 1602, New York and Bologna, 1969. Literal translation into English and musical transcription by Yvonne Kendall. D.M.A. diss., Stanford University, 1985.

Toulouse, Michel. *L'art et instruction de bien dancer.* Paris, c.1488. Facsimile reprint, London, 1936. Reprint ed., New York, 1971.

BIBLIOGRAPHY: OTHER STUDIES

Challet-Haas, Jacqueline. *Dances from the Marais Nord Vendéen: Kinetograms and Music.* 2 vols. St. Peter, Jersey, 1977.

Guilcher, Jean-Michel. *La traditon populaire de danse en Basse-Bretagne.* Paris, 1963.

Guilcher, Jean-Michel. *La tradition de danse en béarn et pays basques français.* Paris, 1984.

Heartz, Daniel. "Sources and Forms of the French Instrumental Dance in the Sixteenth Century." Ph.D. diss., Harvard University, 1957.

Heartz, Daniel. *Preludes, Chansons, and Dances for Lute Published by Pierre Attaingnant, Paris, 1529–1530.* Neuilly-sur-Seine, 1964.

Heartz, Daniel. *Keyboard Dances from the Earlier Sixteenth Century.* American Institute of Musicology, Corpus of Early Keyboard Music, 8. Dallas, 1965.

Heartz, Daniel. "Basse danse" and "Branle." In *The New Grove Dictionary of Music and Musicians.* London, 1980.

Jones, Pamela. "The Relation between Music and Dance in Cesare Negri's 'Le gratie d'amore' (1602)." 2 vols. Ph.D. diss., University of London, 1988.

Lesure, François. "Branle." In *Die Musik in Geschichte und Gegenwart.* 1st ed., vol. 2, 1952. Kassel, 1949–1979.

Tani, Gino. "Brando" and "Branle." In *Enciclopedio dello spettacolo.* 9 vols. Rome, 1954–1968.

JULIA SUTTON
with Patricia Weeks Rader and Margaret Pash

BRAVO, GUILLERMINA (born 13 November 1923 in Chacaltianguis, Veracruz), Mexican dancer, choreographer, and teacher. One of the most important choreographers of Mexican theatrical dance, Bravo first studied folk dance at the National School of Dance in Mexico City, directed by Nellie and Gloria Campobello. From 1936 to 1942 she studied music at the National Conservatory. In 1939 she went to study ballet in the studio of Estrella Morales, where she was discovered by the American dancer and choreographer Waldeen. Between 1940 and 1945, she danced with the Ballet de Bellas Artes. Subsequently Bravo built up a modern dance group, naming it Ballet Waldeen in honor of her American teacher.

In 1946 the composer Carlos Chávez called on Bravo to found and direct, with Ana Mérida, the Academy of Mexican Dance, which opened in 1947 with a teaching program including the techniques of modern dance and the investigation of indigenous dance. In 1948 she left to found the Ballet Nacional de México, an independent center for teaching modern and contemporary dance, which became the most advanced company of its type in Latin America. Bravo, as artistic director, renewed the didactic, technical, and artistic aims of the company, maintaining up-to-date techniques, artistic procedures, teachers, and internal forms of organization and teaching. The Ballet Nacional de México has produced many of the most important Mexican dancers and choreographers; the company has founded the National Contemporary Dance Center in Querétaro, a beautiful colonial city in the center of the country.

Guillermina Bravo stopped performing in 1960. As a teacher, she incorporated Martha Graham's techniques into the instruction given at the Ballet Nacional de México; later, through the study and application of various contemporary modes, she developed a method of the company's own. As a choreographer, she has moved through distinct and varied stylistic and conceptual stages, has had experience with all types of dance production, and has choreographed for theater productions, musical comedy, and drama. Her choreographic work may be classified into categories, with key works mentioned in each. Direct incorporation of themes, plastic images, and stories in a musical structure occurred in *Quartet Opus 59, No. 3* (1946), *The Blackbird* (1947), and *Motive Power* (1949). There was a series of nationalistic and realistic works on social themes—*Memorial to Zapata* (1951), *The Sterile Cloud* (1954), *Dance without Tourism* (1955), *The Demagogue* (1956), and *Braceros* (1957). Nonrealist works with magico-ritual themes derived from native communities include *Images of a Man* (1958), *The Paradise of the Drowned-Tlalocan* (1960), *Dances of Spells* (1961), and *The Baptism* (1962). Works exploring multiple uses of groups, trios, and quartets and didactic themes are exemplified by *Commentaries to Nature* (1967). Two analyses of the inner life, with erotic and dream themes, are *Melodrama for Two Men and One Woman* (1970) and *Act of Love* (1970). Bravo explored stage space through geometric forms in *Outline for a Funeral March* (1963) and *Mexican Ball Game* (1968). Her compositions for soloists in the Ballet Nacional de México include *Dance for a Dead Boy* (1973), *Dance for a Youth* (1974), *Dance for a Ballerina Who Turns Into an Eagle* (1974), *Lament for a Tragic Event* (1975), *Sketch for a Bull* (1980), *Lioness Hunter* (1979), and *A Chimera* (1982). Reality and fantasy are opposed in *Homage to Cervantes* (1973). Some works construct visual designs according to general, universal, or scientific elements or subjects, such as *Epicenter* (1977), *The Calling* (1983), and *Four Reliefs* (1983). Finally, there are complete designs of monumental theatrical dimensions: *The Comics* (1981), *Life Is a Dream*, in collaboration with Federico Castro and Jaime Blanc (1981), *Cantata to Hidalgo* (1983), *Reportage of Our Country* (1984), *Homage to Tamayo* (1986), and *Borgia Codix* (1992).

Bravo has also choreographed more than twenty theatrical productions; every year an association of theater critics awards the Guillermina Bravo Prize for the best stage choreography. In addition to developing technical teaching programs for dance and choreography, Bravo has given numerous courses and lectures. Her works have been observed and assessed by noted critics in the United States and Europe. In 1979 Guillermina Bravo became the first woman to receive the National Prize for Art, the highest award of its kind given by the government of Mexico.

[*See also* Mexico, *article on* Theatrical Dance.]

BIBLIOGRAPHY

Dallal, Alberto. "Death in the Work of Guillermina Bravo." In *Proceedings of the Seventh Annual Conference, Society of Dance History Scholars, Goucher College, Towson, Maryland, 17–19 February 1984*, compiled by Christena L. Schlundt. Riverside, Calif., 1984.

Dallal, Alberto. *Fémina-danza.* Mexico City, 1985.

Dallal, Alberto. *La mujer en la danza.* Mexico City, 1990.

Dallal, Alberto. *La danza contra la muerte.* 3d ed. Mexico City, 1993.

Garske, Rolf. "Dance in Mexico: Interviews with Mexican Choreographers." *Ballett International* 9 (March 1986): 14–29.

Horosko, Marian. "Standards: Brava Bravo." *Dance Magazine* (October 1994): 62–63.

Luger, Eleanor R. "Choreography as Geography: Guillermina Bravo's Dances of Mexico." *Dance Magazine* (February 1982): 68–71.

Tibol, Raquel. *Pasos en la danza mexicana.* Mexico City, 1982.

ALBERTO DALLAL

BRAZIL. [*To survey the dance traditions of Brazil, this entry comprises four articles:*

Ritual and Popular Dance

Ballet

Modern Dance

Dance Research and Publication

The first article explores Native American dances, African-Brazilian ritual dance, and European and African social dances; the second and third articles focus on the history of theatrical dance; the fourth provides a brief history of scholarship and writing.]

Ritual and Popular Dance

Claimed in 1500 by the Portuguese, Brazil began to be colonized in the sixteenth century, when Roman Catholic missionaries were sent to convert the indigenous peoples. They were fought, enslaved, and removed from the coastal regions first, then progressively inland; many died from epidemics. From the sixteenth to eighteenth centuries, France, Britain, Spain, and the Netherlands were also settling colonies in the Caribbean and on the northeastern coast of South America. The consolidation of the vast Portuguese region led to it becoming the seat of the monarchy from 1808 to 1821 and an independent empire in 1822. Development was accomplished by slave laborers transported from Africa to work on plantations and in the shipping, milling, and mining regions after the demise of the indigenous coastal peoples. In 1888, the abolition of slavery alienated the planters, leading to the formation of the Republic of Brazil in 1889. Since that time, many European immigrants have come to the country, especially from central and southern Europe and the Mediterranean rim. Today's population, of mainly Portuguese-speaking Roman Catholics, is some 150 million. There are also many Afro-Brazilian religions as well as some fundamentalist Protestant sects.

Since the 1940s Hollywood films of Busby Berkeley and Walt Disney, the mention of Brazilian dance may still conjure up images of Carmen Miranda and her stylized version of the samba. But Brazil is also the land of the *coco, jongo, maracatú, marujada, carimbó,* the *fandango,* and a host of other dramatic, processional, and social dances. Many of these less-traveled forms have remained regionalized and still cluster around the saints' days, movable feasts, and solstice markers regulated by the archaic church calendar inherited from Portugal. The cyclical nature of Brazilian folk and popular celebrations, a characteristic of preindustrial societies, is one of the most paradoxical features of a country that ranks among the most rapidly industrializing.

Brazilian dance may be grouped into several major categories. Native American dances sometimes include elements resulting from contact with the Portuguese during the early colonial period. Dramatic and allegorical dances are often part of street processions, including that of Carnival. There is Afro-Brazilian ritual dance, and finally, social dances of European, African, and mixed origin.

Although some social dances, such as the fandango, stem directly from Portuguese sources, the major genres of Brazilian popular dance since the eighteenth-century *lundú* either originated among Brazil's black population or have been transformed by contact with African-Brazilian dance aesthetics. Centuries of the slave trade with Central and West Africa, especially in present-day Angola, Congo, Nigeria, and Benin, and the subsequent concentration of

BRAZIL: Ritual and Popular Dance. Samba school dancers at the Carnival in Rio de Janeiro. (Photograph © 1980 by Johan Elbers; used by permission.)

blacks in coastal urban areas, left a deep and constantly renewing impact on Brazil. With a population of at least 40 million people of African descent, Brazil ranks as the second largest black country in the world (after Nigeria).

The first great wave of Africans brought to Brazil were Kongo-Angolans from Portuguese West Africa. Their organization in the seventeenth century into church-sponsored *irmandades* (religious brotherhoods) under the patronage of certain black Catholic saints and images of the Virgin resulted in musical and choreographic forms that lie at the heart of much Brazilian popular culture. The Portuguese policy of permitting and even encouraging the maintenance of African practices, albeit in a Christianized context, led to the formation of the *irmandades* during the early colonial period. In the seventeenth century these societies, especially those connected with the Brotherhood of the Rosary, incorporated elements of Kongo kingship into worship of the Virgin. Kongo kings and queens of these societies were elected and crowned every year; the dances that accompanied their coronations were known as *Con-*

gadas, Congos, cucumbis, ticumbis, or *turundus,* depending on the region. They are the beginning of the great stream of Kongo-Angolan processional music and dance that continues to permeate the modern street carnivals of Recife and Rio de Janeiro.

The *Congadas* were simultaneously processions, dances, and theatrical performances, consisting of several sections. The first typically opened with the entrance of the dancers and arrival of the king. The royal procession paraded through the streets, dancing outside the church and the houses of dignitaries. The second section, known as the embassy, sometimes represented the struggle between Dom Henrique, a Christianized king of the Congo, and Queen Jinga, an Angolan monarch whose army was defeated and who converted to Christianity in the early seventeenth century. The final part of the *Congada* was danced in honor of the Virgin of the Rosary and hence was a celebration of the triumph of Christ.

To this day in northeastern Brazil there are dances, such as the *cambinda de Paraíba,* that derive directly from the colonial coronations of the Kongo kings. Typically they are performed on 6 January, the Day of the Kings, an important part of the annual cycle of Christmas and Epiphany celebrations. Here one can see how the church calendar was Africanized and how Kongo-Angolan elements came to dominate street processions in urban Brazil.

One fascinating aspect of Africanization in Brazil is that the dances celebrating African kingship are based on medieval Portuguese sources. The Iberian experience as a medieval multireligious frontier society, and the Christian Portuguese struggle there with the Muslims, provided the model for popular culture in early colonial Brazil, with its large population of Native Americans and later, African slaves. The most immediate sources for the *Congada* are Portuguese parish dances for the Feast of Epiphany, which featured the election of kings and queens for the day who paraded with their retinue; and the *mourisca*, a dance representing combat between Portuguese Christians and the Islamic Moors. The *mourisca* had a dramatic structure identical to the Afro-Brazilian *Congada*, whose second section represented a struggle between two Kongo groups. In the *mourisca*, an embassy of Moors approach a Christian group and offer them conversion to Islam in exchange for treasure and marriage with Turkish princesses. Their offer is rejected, battles ensue, and the Muslims are defeated and convert to Christianity. The victor and the vanquished then celebrate the triumph of Christ together.

In some areas of Brazil's northeast, *Congadas* have been combined with nautical themes and maritime battles. The resultant street epics are known as *cheganças, marujadas,* and *nau catarinetas.* Given their multiple sources and successive levels of transformation, it is not surprising to find Kongo kings, Turkish princesses, and Portuguese sailors dancing and parading side by side.

Many of these archaic saints' day and Epiphany celebrations were channeled into the modern, urban pre-Lenten Carnival. The Carnival held in Recife, in the state of Pernambuco, is perhaps the most interesting from a folkloristic perspective. Its oldest level is the *maracatú*, directly descended from the *cambindas;* it echoes the coronation of the Kongo kings, with its court, special drum rhythms, and royal umbrellas. In the mid-to-late nineteenth century military bands were added to the Recife Carnival, and a new type of swinging brass band music known as *frevo* emerged, sounding something like early jazz. Although *frevo* is derived from European marches and polkas, much of the dancing that accompanies it originates in *capoeira*, an Angolan martial art that was banned in the Recife Carnival. Some of the *capoeira* steps and movements passed directly into street dancing, with no significant change except for the addition of a decorative umbrella that disguised the true origins of the dance routines. Other steps, especially the cross-legged *tesoura* (scissors), are clearly related to choreographic elements found in the older *Congadas.* Angolan forms thus cut across several genres of African-Brazilian street dance.

Although it is mainly a twentieth-century creation, Rio's Carnival, perhaps the most famous, unites several great streams of Brazil's Kongo-Angolan inheritance. The *Carnaval samba* is a convergence of the dramatic and allegorical dances described earlier with regional forms of the *batuque,* an African-style ring dance found all over Brazil. Under various names and with many regional variations in musical accompaniment, choreography, and configuration (circle, line, solo, and couple dance), the *batuque* is a direct descendant of a ring dance found among many groups in the border area between lower Zaïre and Angola. Among the Luba, for example, it is known as *mbenga* and *lutuku.* In this dance, a single soloist or several dancers perform in the center of a ring of potential soloists who sing and clap an accompaniment. The soloist chooses a replacement from this ring by touching his or her stomach with an *umbigada,* a light pelvic thrust. (This may also be expressed as a light touch on the leg or foot of the intended replacement.) In the Brazilian state of Maranhão, this dance is called *tambor-de-crioula;* in Rio Grande do Norte, *zambê* or *bambelô;* in Pernambuco, *coco de roda;* in Bahia, *samba de roda,* or ring samba; in Minas Gerais, *caxambú;* in the state of Rio de Janeiro, *partido alto;* and in São Paulo state, *jongo.*

Whether brought to Rio by Bahían migrants as samba or based on local varieties of *partido alto* and *jongo,* this dance is inextricably bound up with the city of Rio de Janeiro. Samba was transformed and took to the streets of Rio by way of the *ranchos,* processions associated with the Christmas cycle, especially the Day of the Kings (6 January). Like other processional forms in Brazil, the *ranchos* underwent a process of "Carnivalization," in this case evolving into the *escolas de samba,* or samba schools. It has been said that the only difference between the *ranchos* and the samba schools is the presence of the samba itself. Many features of the modern schools are directly traceable to the post-Christmas *ranchos.* These include their processional form; their organization into *alas* (wings), groups of dancers wearing identical costumes; their allegorical and thematic structure; the figures of *pastores* and *pastoras* (shepherds and shepherdesses), as well as the *porta-estandarte* and the *mestre-sala,* a couple who "dance" the school's standard in the procession.

As the *ranchos* evolved in Rio under the influence of Bahians living in that city, the date of their performance was moved from 6 January to the pre-Lenten period, a change that is seen as a de-Christianizing gesture. In its carnivalized form, samba has achieved worldwide fame. Every year new *sambas-enrêdos* (allegorical sambas) are composed, usually with historical themes, for the year's Carnival parade.

The *batuque* stands behind another important series of social dances that culminates in the *samba de gafieira,* or dance-hall samba, a nonprocessional couple dance. The

BRAZIL: Ritual and Popular Dance. *(top left)* A Bahían dancer, in the first part of an *orô* performance, as an initiate before possession. *(left)* An initiate lies in trance at the feet of the *orixá* Iansan. *(top right)* Bahían dancers bow forward in a ritual performance. (Top left photograph by Andy Young; others by Pierre Verger; all used by permission.)

Brazilian slaves' African dances, such as the *batuque,* had influenced the colonists as early as the eighteenth century. White Brazilians took elements of this social dance, including its rhythm and *umbigadas,* and combined them with movements derived from the Iberian fandango, including the classical Spanish posture with one hand on the forehead and the other on the hip. This mixed form, called the *lundú,* had by the end of the eighteenth century become something of a national dance. It may be thought

of as the first African-based dance to be accepted by Brazilian society as a whole, following a trajectory from slave origins to acceptance by the Brazilian elite.

By the mid-nineteenth century touring companies of Portuguese, Spanish, and French origin had introduced a number of European social dances to Brazilian cities, especially Rio de Janeiro. The rhythmic structure of one of these dances, the polka, resembled the *lundú,* leading to the peculiarly Brazilian fusion *polca-lundú,* a couple dance. The separation of dancers in the *batuque* and *lundú*—they were joined only momentarily by the *umbigada*—was now ended. The *polca-lundú* gave rise to the *maxixe,* another couple dance that reached its peak of popularity in Brazil around World War I; it is rhythmically similar to the Cuban *habanera* and Argentine tango. Many early sambas recorded around 1920 owe much to the *maxixe* and are in tango rhythm.

Possibly aided by the expansion of Rio's Carnival, the samba replaced the *maxixe* as the national dance of Brazil in the 1920s. Its street associations spilled over into popular, non-Carnival forms; anyone who has heard popular music from Rio can feel its march-like, 2/4 foundation rhythm.

Perhaps no popular culture is as organized around Carnival as is Brazil's, but the street is only one important domain of Afro-Brazilian dance. Much of sacred dance in Brazil is based on direct Yoruba origin or has been modeled on Nagô (Brazilian-Yoruba) sources. There are a number of Angolan-based religions in Brazil, but the prestige form is inarguably Candomblé, of Yoruba and Fon origins. This religion is based on the worship of *orixás*, anthropomorphized nature deities. Since the *orixás* were syncretized with Roman Catholic saints, the dance-based festivals honoring the Yoruba gods are often held on the days dedicated to the corresponding saints. In parts of Brazil, Oxóssi, the Yoruba *orixá* of the forest and hunt, is honored on 20 January, Saint Sebastian's Day; Iêmanjá is syncretized with the Virgin of the Immaculate Conception, whose day is 8 December. In Salvador, festivals for Xangô are held during the *festas juninas,* which mark the summer solstice. During the Carnival cycle in that city, the Candomblés are quiet, and some of its members form processional groups called *afoxês,* dancing in the streets while honoring the *orixás.* Thus, even within Candomblé, one can see the regulatory impact of the church calendar.

During public ceremonies known as *orô,* the Yoruba gods come down to their "children," the initiated worshipers who dance until they reach the state of possession trance. The *orô* is divided into two parts: the first salutes and calls the *orixás* and is meant to induce trance. In the second part of the *orô,* the possessed initiates return to the dance floor after being dressed in the clothing, colors, and emblems associated with their deities; their stereotyped movements and gestures reenact myths associated with the Yoruba and Fon gods. Some important choreographic elements are the symbols and *oshê* (dance wands) associated with each *orixá* and held by the adepts while in trance. Oxóssi holds a wrought-iron bow and arrow; Xangô, a double-headed ax; Oshún, a mirror, and so on.

Candomblé served as a model for the Angolan Brazilians, who organized rituals for their own deities, the *nkisi,* along similar lines. Angolan Candomblé has its own distinctive dances and drum rhythms. Since World War II, a new syncretic religion called Umbanda has been spreading elements of Yoruba sacred dance all over Brazil. Originating in the urban south, it is a conscious attempt to create a national popular religion and mythology based on Yoruba, Kongo-Angolan, Native American, and spiritualist sources. Like all Afro-Brazilian religions it is danced, and much of its symbolism and choreography derives from Candomblé. In its public ceremonies, the Umbanda "entities" come down to possess their "mediums," or initiates, who act out their stories in dance. As in Yoruba tradition, the presence of the gods is signaled by dressing their pos-

sessed "children" with the insignia, necklaces, and artifacts associated with each deity. Umbanda has reached sections of the country, such as Amazonia, with relatively few African-based traditions, and sometimes even paves the way for the arrival of Bahían-style Candomblé.

Whether in the form of dramatic, Carnival, or ritual dance, most of the great expressions of Afro-Brazilian culture are centered in urban enclaves along the Brazilian coast, but Brazil also has a number of European-based popular and folk forms. Most of these figured and couple dances are found in the *sertão,* the arid region of the northeastern interior, where they are associated with the cattle-rearing economy of the rural *vaqueiros* (cowboys). In Brazil, as in the Caribbean islands, some of these folk forms originated in the court and salon dances in vogue in France at the end of the eighteenth century, diffusing to other parts of western Europe and to the American colonies. "Newer" dances, such as the *xotis* (schottische), mazurka, and *quadrilha* (quadrille) were introduced by the European touring companies and dance masters who also brought the polka in the mid-nineteenth century. These dances still survive in folklorized form in rural areas of northern and northeastern Brazil, much as they do in provincial western Europe, especially in France. Throughout the northeast the *quadrilha,* once a salon dance, is now a popular regional form associated with the *festas juninas,* the cycle of folkloric celebrations centered around Midsummer Day, 24 June. The *dança do lelê* of Maranhão is another European-based figured dance.

Other couple dances, such as the *xaxado, arrasta-pé,* and *baião,* are grouped under the term *forró,* the name applied to rural northeastern dance; these are strongly associated with the cattle-rearing *sertão.* The instrumental ensemble that accompanies them usually includes an accordion, triangle, and *zabumba* (bass drum). The last two instruments are part of the "Turkish music" complex that arrived in France via eastern Europe after their wars with the Ottoman Empire in the seventeenth and eighteenth centuries. From there this ensemble traveled to Portugal, the Azores, and northeastern Brazil. On the central and far southern coasts of Brazil, it is still possible to find dances marked with strongly Portuguese figures. In a fishing village on the southern coast of Rio de Janeiro state, the *ciranda de Paraty* is a combination of a circle dance of Portuguese and possibly Native American origin, Portuguese couple and *sapateo* dances (the latter featuring foot percussion), and elements of the quadrille. In the interior of São Paulo state, the fandango is composed of several sections that alternate between simple ring formations and intense *sapateos,* accompanied by hand-claps and castanets. The *fandango do Paraná,* from the far southern coast, is a suite of several movements which are either danced or feature *sapateos.*

BRAZIL: Ritual and Popular Dance. Three dancers wield swords in *Maculele*, a theatrical work based on a sugar-plantation dance from Bahía incorporating elements of martial arts, staged by Jelon Vieira for his New York–based company DanceBrazil. (Photograph © 1988 by Linda Vartoogian; used by permission.)

On the island of Marajó in the far north of the country, eighteenth-century *lundús* and typically nineteenth-century polkas and mazurkas are still performed. In the neighboring state of Pará the most important regional form is the *carimbó*, whose choreography exhibits Portuguese, Native American, and Afro-Brazilian elements. It is especially associated with local celebrations of Midsummer's Day.

The *bumba-meu-boi* is a dramatic dance in processional form and an important element in the *festas juninas* of the city of Sao Luiz do Maranhão on the northern coast. It is a mixed genre with identifiable Portuguese, African, and Native American elements. Variations, found all over Brazil, include the *boi-bumbá* (Pará), *boi-calemba* (Rio Grande do Norte), and *boi-de-mamão* (Santa Catarina). This dance has deep roots in Brazil's cattle-rearing economy, and all variants culminate in the death and resurrection of a bull or an ox, sometimes brought back to life by a Native American *pajé* (shaman).

Given Brazil's mixed heritage, it is not surprising to find forms with dance elements from all three major sources of Brazilian popular culture. As one moves into the interior, especially in northern and northeastern Brazil, Native American features become more pronounced. The term *caboclo*—a person of mixed Portuguese, Native American, and sometimes African ancestry—is also applied to Native American elements in Afro-Brazilian contexts, both ritual and secular. The close contact and shared condition of slavery among Africans and native peoples in early colonial Brazil gave rise to a number of creolized forms. Native themes have penetrated the heart of the most Afro-Brazilian institutions, including Carnival, Umbanda, and Candomblé. During Carnival in Recife and Rio de Janiero, it is not uncommon to find groups of blacks dressed as Native Americans, with such names as Caboclinhos in Recife, and Cacique de Ramos in Rio. This theme echoes across the Americas: similar motifs may be seen during Carnival in New Orleans and in Port-of-Spain, Trinidad.

Caboclos play an important role in Umbanda, where these Native American spirits come down to possess worshipers just as the African ones do. The Native American spirits dance with stereotyped gestures that represent the forest and the hunt and often shoot imaginary arrows. *Caboclos* appear in rural Candomblés in the state of Bahía, but even in the coastal capital of Salvador the *caboclos* are considered the "owners of the Earth," and special dances are performed for them in the Ketu Candomblés. It is especially in the Angolan houses that one finds elements of Native American Brazil fused with Kongo-Angolan rhythms and dance. There is even a *samba de caboclo*, a ritual dance that has certain features in common with the recreational samba, including the *umbigada* pelvic movement.

Long before Native American elements entered the Afro-Brazilian world, however, they had fused with Portuguese culture in the earliest days of European contact with coastal indigenous groups. Probably the first truly Brazilian cultural manifestations were the Roman Catholic priests' religious plays, forerunners of the *autos*, the religious dramas of a later date. The Jesuit authors of these plays incorporated Native American elements, including dance, into their structure.

Throughout Brazil dances with strong Native American elements are still to be found, sometimes in conjunction with Iberian or with Afro-Brazilian styles. On the coast of the northeastern state of Ceará there is a dance called *torém*, said to be a remnant of indigenous Tremembé culture. It is a circle dance, a common Native American configuration observed in Brazil as early as the sixteenth century by Jean de Léry, a French traveler who left some of the earliest descriptions of Native American song and dance. As recently as the late 1930s, a team organized by musicologist Oneyda Alvarenga documented the *praiá*, a masked dance of the indigenous Pankararu, from the interior of the coastal state of Pernambuco. At that time, the dance costumes included some Roman Catholic symbols. The language and presumably the culture of the Pankararu are now believed to be extinct.

Other dances with varying degrees of Native American influence include the *catira*, the *cateretê*, and the *cururu*. The *catira*, found in São Paulo, Minas Gerais, and the Rio area, is a group dance, with men and women forming two rows. They clap and stamp their feet to the sound of the accompanying guitars. The *cateretê* is a variation of the *catira* with songs in the Tupi language. The *cururu* developed under Jesuit influence. Dancers form a circle around a guitarist and two singers who improvise verses. The dance is guided by a dance master, a probable influence from formal European court traditions. The *cururu* is still performed in the interior of several Brazilian states, including Goiás, Mato Grosso, and São Paulo.

To see Native American dance in pure form one must travel far into the Brazilian interior. The region of the Upper Xingu is today one of the last preserves of indigenous culture still in relatively pristine condition. Dance is still linked to ritual activity. The *kuarup* intertribal ceremonial cycle is the most important ritual event of the Upper Xingu. In this ceremony, very long flutes are played to drive away the spirits of the dead. This cycle of music and dance celebrates the dead of the previous year and closes the period of mourning.

In 1988 an international team of musicologists documented ritual songs and dances of the Kayapó Indians of the Tocantins region in the southwest of Pará state in the far north of Brazil. They live in what is known as the "Legal Amazon," and their territories are officially delimited by the state. The whole region is in danger of being flooded by a hydroelectric project. Nevertheless, it is possible to go from the modern city of Belém to Kayapó territory in a few hours and to witness the ritual dances of the *takak*, an elaborate naming ceremony that has been revived by the Kayapó as a way of preserving their identity in an environment that is ever more threatening.

[*See also* Capoeira; Congo Dances; *and* Samba.]

BIBLIOGRAPHY

Bastide, Roger. *The African Religions of Brazil.* Translated by Helen Sebba. Baltimore, 1978.

Benjamin, Roberto, and Osvaldo Meira Trigueiro. *Cambindas de Paraíba.* Rio de Janeiro, 1978.

Browning, Barbara. "The Daughters of Gandhi: Africanness, Indianness, and Brazilianness in the Bahian Carnival." *Women and Performance,* no. 14–15 (1995): 151–169.

Cabral, Sérgio. *As escolas de samba.* Rio de Janeiro, 1974.

Faro, Antonio José. "Brazil: The Fight to Save a Rich Folk Dance Heritage." In *Beyond Performance: Dance Scholarship Today,* edited by Susan Au and Frank-Manuel Peter. Berlin, 1989.

Faro, Antonio José. "The Spanish Influence in the Folkloric Dances of Southern Brazil." In *Proceedings of the Fourteenth Annual Conference, Society of Dance History Scholars, New World School of the Arts, Miami, Florida, 8–10 February 1991,* compiled by Christena L. Schlundt. Riverside, Calif., 1991.

Ferretti, Sérgio, et al. *Tambor de crioula.* Rio de Janeiro, 1981.

Goldwasser, Maria Júlia. *O palácio do samba.* Rio de Janeiro, 1975.

Guillermoprieto, Alma. *Samba.* New York, 1990.

Katz, Helena. *Brazil Discovers the Dance Discovers Brazil.* Sao Paulo, 1994.

Kiefer, Bruno. *A modinha e o lundú.* Porto Alegre, 1977.

Léry, Jean de. *Viagem à terra do Brasil.* 4th ed. São Paulo, 1967.

Lévi-Strauss, Claude. *Tristes Tropiques.* Translated by John Weightman and Doreen Weightman. New York, 1977.

Lody, Raul G. *Afoxé.* Rio de Janeiro, 1976.

Moura, Roberto. *Tia Ciata e a pequena África no Rio de Janeiro.* Rio de Janeiro, 1983.

Oliveira, Maria Goretti Rocha de. *Danças populares como espetáculo público no Recife de 1970 a 1988.* Recife, 1993.

Omari, Mikelle Smith. *From the Inside to the Outside: The Art and Ritual of Bahian Candomblé.* Los Angeles, 1984.

BRAZIL: Ritual and Popular Dance. Women from the Balé Folclórico de Bahía in *Afixirê.* This well-regarded company presents staged versions of traditional dance genres. (Photograph © 1996 by Linda Vartoogian; used by permission.)

Pinto, Tiago de Oliveira. "'Making Ritual Drama': Dance, Music, and Representation in Brazilian Candomblé and Umbanda." *World of Music* 33.1 (1991): 70–88.

Pinto, Tiago de Olivera. "The Pernambuco Carnival and Its Formal Organizations." *Yearbook for Traditional Music* 26 (1994): 20–38.

Ribeiro, Maria de Lourdes Borges. *O jongo.* Rio de Janeiro, 1984.

Schreiner, Claus. *Musica Brasileira: A History of Popular Music and the People of Brazil.* New York, 1993.

Thompson-Drewal, Margaret. "Dancing for Ogun in Yorubaland and in Brazil." In *Africa's Ogun: Old World and New,* edited by Sandra T. Barnes. Bloomington, 1989.

Verger, Pierre. *Orixás: Deuses iorubás na África e no Novo Mundo.* Salvador, Brazil, 1981.

wa Mukuna, Kazadi. *Contribuição bantu na música popular brasileira.* São Paulo, 1978.

Zaretsky, Irving I., and Cynthia Shambaugh. *Spirit Possession and Spirit Mediumship in Africa and Afro-America: An Annotated Bibliography.* New York, 1978.

MORTON MARKS

Ballet

Classical ballet is highly respected and admired in Brazil. The great majority of dance academies throughout the country teach ballet courses and present annual recitals in which children and adolescents dance on pointe, wearing tutus. Many Brazilians believe classical ballet is the only effective technique with which to train dancers. In the cities of Belo Horizonte, Brasilia, Campinas, Curitiba, Porto Alegre, Recife, Rio de Janeiro, Salvador, and São Paulo, which are the main dance centers of the country, modern dance (particularly Martha Graham's method) and other techniques, including American jazz dance, Spanish flamenco, and Brazilian *capoeira*, are often taught along with ballet in dance academies. In the rest of the country, however, most academies teach only ballet.

The introduction of ballet in Brazil is linked to the Portuguese court, when in the early nineteenth century, to escape the Napoleonic Wars, royal families of Orleans and Braganza fled Lisbon to settle in Rio de Janeiro, then Brazil's colonial capital. Responding to Portuguese cultural preferences, ballet, music, and opera companies from Europe and Russia began touring Brazil. When independence from Portugal was declared in 1822, foreign companies continued to arrive. Don Pedro I, who was legitimizing his own new role as Brazil's emperor, became a notable aficionado of ballet. Great ballet masters from Europe had already migrated to Brazil, and they were responsible for the development of classical ballet there. In 1811 the Spanish ballet teacher Louis Lacombe (1786–1833) arrived in Rio de Janeiro, where he was joined in 1815 by a group of dancers from the French Opera Academy led by Auguste Toissant; they performed in Brazil until 1821. The first Brazilian ballerina to study

with these European masters, Lacombe and Toissant, was Estela Sezefreda (1810–1874). Anecdotes recount the story of Sezefreda's imprisonment in 1825 as an anarchist; her act of throwing lemons against the emperor's carriage, during Carnival festivities, was declared seditious.

In Rio, theaters were built to host European ballet companies. The Teatro Lirico, in existence from 1909 to 1934, welcomed Serge Diaghilev's Ballets Russes in 1913 and again in 1917. Anna Pavlova and her company danced there in 1918 and 1928, and Colonel Wassily de Basil's Original Ballets Russes performed there in 1942, 1944, and 1946.

Some touring European dancers decided to stay in Brazil for various reasons, primarily to escape World War I and World War II. With few opportunities for performance, these dancers opened schools and formed ballet companies, particularly in Rio de Janeiro, then the nation's capital, and in São Paulo, a growing urban center enriched by wealth from the coffee plantations. Under the influence of foreign dancers, the first state-sponsored local ballet companies were created. During the 1920s, 1930s, and 1940s, Brazil housed a great number of eminent foreign ballet dancers who had a common background in Russian technique.

In 1927, the Russian ballerina Maria Oleneva (1896–1965) went to live in Rio de Janiero; she had toured South America with Pavlova's company, returned as a soloist, and joined Léonide Massine's dance company in Argentina. In Rio, she began teaching ballet, and almost ten years later, in 1937, she founded the Municipal Ballet of Rio de Janeiro, the official state-run company.

In 1939, the Czechoslovakian dancer Vaslav Veltchek (1896–1947), a successful choreographer and ballet master in Paris, was invited to organize with Oleneva the official ballet season in Rio de Janeiro. When World War II began, Veltchek, who was Jewish, could not return to Europe. He moved to São Paulo; there he married the Brazilian ballerina Marília Franco and was named director of the city's official school and dance company, later called Ballet Company of the City of São Paulo. The company, however, was not officially instituted by the government until 1968, long after Veltchek's death.

The Polish dancer Halina Biernacka (born 1914) danced with Bronislava Nijinska in the Warsaw Ballet in 1933. She arrived in Brazil in 1941, founded her own dance company in São Paulo, and became responsible for the *mise-en-scène* of many Brazilian productions of ballet classics, including *Swan Lake, Les Sylphides,* and *Giselle.*

Tatiana Leskova, born in 1922, studied classical ballet in Paris with Lubov Egorova. She joined the international tour of the Original Ballets Russes. With the start of World War II in 1939, she decided to stay in South America. Leskova moved to Rio, where she became a director of the Municipal Ballet of Rio de Janeiro. There she was responsible for staging works such as *Swan Lake, Coppélia,* and *Giselle.* She was also very important as a master teacher, training such great ballerinas as Marcia Haydée.

The Russian dancer Eugenia Feodorova (born 1926) went to Brazil in 1954, invited by choreographer and dancer Dalal Aschar to work as a ballet mistress at the Municipal Ballet of Rio de Janeiro. Feodorova was a specialist in the teaching methods of Agrippina Vaganova.

The Brazilian ballerina María Carmen Brandão (1902–1992) was also a leading presence in the panorama of ballet in Brazil. After studying at La Scala Ballet in Milan, under the stage name of Carmen Lydia, Brandão performed successfully as a soloist in São Paulo and Rio de Janeiro. During this period she had a passionate and much publicized affair with the writer Oswald de Andrade (1890–1954). She retired to a convent for some years, then reappeared on the dance scene during the 1940s, becoming one of the first Brazilian ballet mistresses. In her dance academy in São Paulo important ballerinas and choreographers were initiated, among them Marika Gidali, founder and director of Ballet Stagium.

Until the 1970s, Brazilian ballet was influenced almost exclusively by the Russian method. At that time, through the efforts of Dalal Aschar—dancer, choreographer, then director of the Municipal Ballet of Rio de Janeiro, and a friend and admirer of Margot Fonteyn—Brazil became acquainted with the British Royal Academy of Dance method. Since that time this method has grown in popularity and is utilized by many Brazilian ballet academies to grade their students.

Another significant characteristic of ballet in Brazil is the use of authentic national themes. Many companies have tried to add innovation to their repertories by creating specifically Brazilian choreography; using themes from Brazilian culture, they nevertheless maintain strong references to classical ballet technique. This tradition has persisted from the time of Maria Oleneva and Veltchek's *Maracatu Dances*—based on a Brazilian regional dance and choreographed in the 1930s on pointe—to Dalal Achcar's *Amazonian Forest,* choreographed in 1975 to music by Brazilian composer Heitor Villa-Lobos.

Another important initiative in the Brazilian dance scene was the Ballet of the Fourth Centennial. In 1954, to celebrate the quadricentennial of the city of São Paulo, the state government created a company based on artistic collaboration between dancers and visual artists. The Hungarian dancer Aurelio Milloss, who had his career in Italy during and after World War II, was invited to become artistic director. The company was responsible for

BRAZIL: Ballet. Fátima Berenguer and Marcos Napoleão of the Bahía Ballet in Luis Arrieta's *Orixá,* a balletic tribute to the spirits personified in Brazilian ritual dance. (Photograph by Omar G Studio; courtesy of the Bahía Ballet.)

productions, which included innovative set and costume designs created by important Brazilian visual artists. It also used regional themes and national music. Although the Ballet of the Fourth Centennial ceased performing only a few years later because of a lack of official funding, it bequeathed important contributions to dance in Brazil.

It is important to acknowledge the large number of Brazilian ballerinas who have acquired world fame and built international careers. Among them are Marcia Haydée of the Stuttgart Ballet in Germany, and Laura Proença of Maurice Béjart's Ballet du XXᵉ Siècle. Other famous artists who have danced the classical repertory in Brazil and abroad include Ady Ador, Cecilia Botto, Beatriz Consuelo, Elionora Oliosa, Berta Rosanova, and Edith Pudelko during the 1950s and 1960s, and since then, Ana Botafogo, Nora Esteves, and Cecilia Kerche. They and their colleagues who dance today are appreciated by in-

BRAZIL: Ballet. Members of the Bahía Ballet in Luis Arrieta's *As Bodas* (*Les Noces*) at the Balé Teatro Castro Alves, Bahía. (Photograph by Omar G Studio; courtesy of the Bahía Ballet.)

ternational choreographers both for their technique and their musicality.

BIBLIOGRAPHY

Achcar, Dalal. *Ballet: Arte, técnica et interpretação.* Rio de Janeiro, 1980.

Barsante, Cássio Emmanuel. *A vida ilustrada de Tomás Santa Rosa.* Rio de Janeiro, 1993.

Faro, Antonio José. *Pequena história da dança.* Rio de Janeiro, 1986.

Faro, Antonio José. *A dança no Brasil e seus construtores.* Rio de Janeiro, 1988.

Faro, Antonio José. "Leskova Back at the Helm of Rio's Municipal Ballet." *Dance Magazine* (June 1988): 10–11.

Faro, Antonio José. "Carmen Miranda Wouldn't Know the Place." *Dance Magazine* (November 1991): 86–88.

Faro, Antonio José. "Hard Times for Dance in Brazil." *Dance Magazine* (October 1991): 24.

García-Márquez, Vicente. *The Ballets Russes: Colonel de Basil's Ballets Russes de Monte Carlo, 1932–1952.* New York, 1990.

Haydée, Marcia, and Telma Mekler. *Marcia Haydée: Uma vida para a dança.* Rio de Janeiro, 1994.

Portinari, Maribel. *História da dança.* Rio de Janeiro, 1989.

Sorley Walker, Kathrine. *De Basil's Ballets Russes.* New York, 1983.

Sucena, Eduardo. *A dança teatral no Brasil.* Rio de Janeiro, 1988.

KATIA CANTON and MARÍLIA DE ANDRADE

Modern Dance

The development of modern dance in Brazil began after 1910 with exposure to foreign dancers. In 1916 Isadora Duncan performed in Rio de Janeiro and São Paulo. She became a major influence in the Modernist movement in Brazil, which gathered visual artists, writers, and performers and was officially launched in 1922. Its theme was the assimilation and adaptation of modern foreign culture according to Brazilian ways; its symbolic motto was *anthropofagy*, which means "cannibalism."

Brazilian dancers, some of whom received their training abroad, became the forerunners of modern dance in Brazil. Chinita Ullman from Rio Grand do Sul studied with Mary Wigman in Germany and returned to Brazil in 1931. Initially Ullman began performing in solo choreographies but later formed a duet with the Italian dancer Carletto Thieben. They traveled all over Latin America until the late 1940s, when Chinita Ullman opened a school in São Paulo, where she taught Wigman's principles; she retired from dance in 1954.

Although Ullman was the first dancer to launch modern dance in Brazil, Nina Verchinina is considered the first major figure in this field. After dancing with the Original Ballets Russes and working independently in Argentina in the late 1940s and early 1950s, Verchinina settled in Rio de Janeiro in 1954. She choreographed for the Municipal Ballet of Rio de Janeiro, working with Brazilian composers and national themes. In the 1960s Verchinina stopped choreographing and opened her own school. She was a major dance educator until her death in 1995. Her dancing style juxtaposes a solid foundation of Russian ballet technique with strongly modernist and expressionistic tones. [*See the entry on Verchinina.*]

Another important educator who settled in Brazil was the Polish dancer Yanka Rudzka, who arrived in São Paulo in 1950, opened a school, and later moved to Bahía. There she became a pioneer in dance education at the university level. In 1957 she instituted a course in modern dance at the Federal University of Bahía (UFBA) that included general principles of modern dance but also focused specifically on Brazilian movement research.

The French dancer Renée Gumiel is also important in the history of Brazil's modern dance. Gumiel had been a student of Kurt Jooss, and since the late 1950s, when she settled in São Paulo, she has been expanding Brazilian dance with interdisciplinary concepts. Gumiel was influenced by the connection among dance, theater, and the visual arts recognized by French artists of the 1920s, such as Jean Cocteau. She opened a school in São Paulo that continues today. She also continues to perform and choreograph her own works, which consist mainly of solos.

The development of modern dance in Brazil owes much to the efforts of Lourdes Bastos and to Helenita Sa Erp. Bastos studied with José Limón in New York and and is responsible for the modern dance courses at the school of the Municipal Ballet of Rio de Janeiro. Helenita Sa Erp created dance courses that are part of the curriculum of the physical education department at the Federal University of Rio de Janeiro. In São Paulo, the Hungarian dancer Maria Duschenes popularized the Laban method in the late 1950s. Ruth Rachou and Clarisse Abujamra brought to São Paulo their experience with Martha Graham's technique, which they had studied in Graham's school in New York City. Klaus Vianna, who settled in São Paulo during his later years (he died in 1992), was a major researcher of the holistic movement in kinetic anatomy. He trained many experts in the field.

The growth of modern dance in Brazil was due not only to the work of educators but also to the strengthening of its major private dance companies—Stagium and Cisne Negro of São Paulo, and Corpo of Belo Horizonte. These companies were created in the 1970s and shared as a common objective the development of Brazilian themes and elements, along with a high level of technical skill. They are all funded by private sponsorship.

Stagium, inaugurated in 1971, is the most politicized company. Founded by a couple, Marika Gidali and Decio Otero, the company's main aim was to make dance accessible to the masses. Performing in public spaces and in small villages in Brazil, Stagium choreographed dances that embodied the essence of Brazilian culture. Some typical examples of their works are *Kuarup*, which portrays

BRAZIL: Modern Dance. *(left)* Two dancers of Grupo Corpo in *Nazareth*. *(right)* Scene from the dance-theater work *A Floresta do Amazonas* (The Amazon Forest), a production of Ballet Stagium with choreography by Décio Otero and direction by Márika Gidall. (Left photograph by José Luis Pederneiras; right photograph © 1973 by Gerson Zanini; both used by permission.)

native Brazilians; *Coisas do Brasil* (Things from Brazil); *Batucada,* based on a Brazilian rhythm; *Pantanal;* and *Choros.* The company has celebrated its twenty-fifth anniversary and continues.

Corpo originated in 1975 in the city of Belo Horizonte. Two brothers, Rodrigo and Paulo Pederneiras, began researching themes and movements that could be translated into a Brazilian dance. Its first production, *Maria, Maria,* using music from Brazilian pop singers Milton Nascimento and Fernando Brandt, was based on the theme of Brazilian womanhood. The company quickly grew in popularity and became an instant success all over the country. Its second hit, *Ultimo Trem* (Last Train), also used popular music by Nascimento and Brandt. Corpo is the most internationally acclaimed Brazilian dance company. It has invested heavily in technical and choreographic research. Rodrigo Pederneiras, its choreographer, was recognized worldwide in 1985, when he created *Prelude,* which is based on Chopin's music and utilizes a mixture of ballet and Brazilian gestures. Under the general direction of Paulo Pederneiras, with Fernando Velloso, the

set designer, and Freusa Zechmeister, the costume designer, Corpo is recognized as one of the world's most important modern dance companies.

Cisne Negro was founded in 1977 by Hulda Bittencourt, the director of her own dance school. Its performers were recruited from the Bittencourt school and from the physical education department of the University of São Paulo. They combine dance technique with physical strength. From its inception, Cisne Negro's hallmark was to invite the best independent choreographers working both in Brazil and internationally to create special works for the company. Therefore, the company has a varied repertory, including modernist pictures of day-to-day life, such as *Iribiri,* choreographed by Sonia Motta; poetic and intimate works, such as *Do Homem ao Poeta* (From Man to Poet), based on the poetry of Pablo Neruda and choreographed by Luis Arrieta; and kinetic, abstract works, such as the remarkable pas de deux *Gadget* by Victor Navarro. The company also uses guest artists in their ballets, among them Ana Botafogo, star of the Municipal Ballet of Rio de Janeiro, and Fernando Bujones. Cisne Negro has been touring internationally since 1985.

BRAZIL: Modern Dance. *(top)* Members of Cisne Negro in a lighthearted work. *(bottom)* Deborah Colker's *Velox* (1995) with Paulo Mantuano, Tatiana France, and Mariana Toledo. (Top photograph courtesy of Cisne Negro; bottom photograph by Cafi, courtesy of Deborah Colker.)

BIBLIOGRAPHY
"Ballet Stagium: Brazil's Contemporary Company." *Dance Magazine* (September 1990): 26–27.
Barnes, Clive. "Dance with a Latin Accent." *Dance and Dancers* (February-March 1991): 28–31.
Botafogo, Ana, and Suzana Braga. *Ana Botafogo: Na magia do palco.* Rio de Janeiro, 1993.
Deresiewicz, William. "Grupo Corpo Brazilian Dance Theater." *Dance Magazine* (February 1991): 116–118.
Faro, Antonio José. *Pequena história da dança.* Rio de Janeiro, 1986.
García-Márquez, Vicente. *The Ballets Russes: Colonel de Basil's Ballets Russes de Monte Carlo, 1932–1952.* New York, 1990.
Garcia Mendes, Miriam. *A dança.* São Paulo, 1985.
Johnson, Robert. "Stagium Battles Social Ills." *Dance Magazine* (March 1991): 13–14.
Katz, Helena. *O Brasil, descobre a dança descobre o Brasil.* São Paolo, 1994.
Marques, Isabel A. "A Partnership Toward Art in Education." *Impulse* 3 (April 1995): 86–101.
Navas, Cássia. *Imagens da dança em São Paulo.* São Paulo, 1987.
Navas, Cássia, and Linneu Dias. *Dança moderna.* São Paulo, 1992.
Portinari, Maribel. *História da dança.* Rio de Janeiro, 1989.
Sorley Walker, Kathrine. *De Basil's Ballets Russes.* New York, 1983.
Sucena, Eduardo. *A dança teatral no Brasil.* Rio de Janeiro, 1988.

KATIA CANTON

Dance Research and Publication

Dance in Brazil has been relatively unexplored by academic researchers, many of whom are independent artists seeking either the development of new artistic forms or the preservation of Brazilian regional dances and folk traditions. With few exceptions, they receive little official support, work with a limited budget, and are isolated from one another. Nevertheless, this situation is beginning to improve with the recent development of university courses that in the future will enhance the development of the field.

Two major state universities have undergraduate courses in dance—the Federal University of Bahía (UFBA) and the State University of Campinas, São Paulo (UNICAMP). UFBA has offered a bachelor's degree in dance since 1957, when the course was founded by Yanka Rudzka, a Polish dancer who studied with Harald Kreutzberg. UNICAMP's program was founded in 1985. The university also created an experimental dance laboratory for students, under the direction of choreographer and psychologist Marília de Andrade.

Both schools have advanced studies and innovative approaches for the education of dancers, integrating the techniques of Brazilian popular dances with more formal techniques such as classical ballet and modern dance. The curriculum also includes courses in dance education, performance, and choreography. Both also offer the only graduate programs—a master's degree in arts with specialization in dance at UNICAMP; a specialization in choreography at UFBA.

Some private institutions in Brazil have created undergraduate courses in dance, among them the Faculdade de Artes de Curitiba, in Paraná; the Faculdade de Dança do Rio de Janeiro; the Faculdade de Dança de Santos and the Faculdade Marcelo Tupinambá both in São Paulo. A center for dance research in the department of semiotics has also been established at the Catholic University (PUC) in São Paulo.

Publications in dance are relatively few in Brazil. Between 1978 and 1992 a monthly magazine called *Dançar* was Brazil's only dance periodical; it was discontinued for financial reasons. Some fifty books have been published focusing on dance history, education, and techniques. More than 70 percent of these were published privately. There are essentially three kinds: studies in the history and development of folk and popular Brazilian dances, such as samba and ritual festivities; broad studies in the history of dance worldwide, including dictionaries; and books on dance theory, education, and techniques.

Books on popular and folk dance make up the majority. Their most frequent subjects are *folguedos*, *frevo*, *capoeira*, and other African-derived Brazilian dances. A notable example in this field was authored by the great modernist writer Mário de Andrade, who compiled an in-depth study in three volumes of popular dances in the different regions of Brazil.

In the field of dance history, some books have been authored by dance researchers Antonio Jose Faro, Cassia Navas and Linneu Dias, Maribel Portinari, and Eduardo Sucena. These authors deal mainly with the international panorama of dance but also focus on aspects of the development of modern dance in Brazil. Books on ballet have been written by Dalal Aschar, Luis Ellmerich, and Clarice Pinto.

In the category of dance theory and education, a few publications discuss Rudolf Laban's teachings; his is the most respected and best-known method of dance education in Brazil. Authors and educators Isabel Marques, Analivia Cordeiro, Cybele Cavalcante, Claudia Hamburguer, and Regina Miranda have published manuals and books on the subject, based on their research and methods of teaching dance.

The most important dance publishing phenomenon has been the appearance of books written by important Brazilian choreographers, dance educators, and critics. Through their personal experiences they have presented detailed accounts of dance studies, both in Brazil and internationally. The dance educator Klaus Vianna has transcribed his innovative ideas on the process of the body in motion. Choreographers and dancers Marilena Ansaldi, Ana Botafogo, and Lia Robatto have recounted their works as dancers and creators. Critic and historian Katia Canton has analyzed narrative, specifically fairy tales, to confront the aesthetic codes and values embodied in dance choreographies in many countries.

These publications, although very few—considering the great number of Brazilian dancers and dance lovers—indicate a positive trend. Together with the development of university courses, they may represent the beginning of a new era for dance research in Brazil.

BIBLIOGRAPHY

Achcar, Dalal. *Ballet: Arte, técnica et interpretação*. Rio de Janeiro, 1980.
Andrade, Mário de. *Danças dramáticas do Brasil*. São Paulo, 1959.
Ansaldi, Marilena. *Atos: Movimento na vida e no palco*. São Paulo, 1994.
Arruda, Solange. *A arte do movimento: As descobertas de Rudolf von Laban e a ação humana*. São Paulo, 1988.
Botafogo, Ana. *Na magia do palco*. Rio de Janeiro, 1993.
Canton, Katia. *The Fairy Tale Revisited*. New York, 1994.
Canton, Katia. *E o príncipe dançou: O conto de fadas, da tradição oral à dança contemporânea*. São Paulo, 1994.
Carneiro, Edison. *Folguedos tradicionais*. 2d ed. Rio de Janeiro, 1982.
Cordeiro, Analivia, et al. *Método Laban: Nível básico*. São Paulo, 1989.
Ellmerich, Luís. *História da dança*. 3d ed. São Paulo, 1969.
Ellmerich, Luís, and Clarice Pinto. *Manual do balé*. Rio de Janeiro, 1972.
Faro, Antonio José. *Pequena história da dança*. Rio de Janeiro, 1986.
Katz, Helena. *O Brasil, descobre a dança descobre o Brasil*. São Paolo, 1994.
Navas, Cássia, and Linneu Dias. *Dança moderna*. São Paulo, 1992.
Portinari, Maribel. *História da dança*. Rio de Janeiro, 1989.
Robatto, Lia. *Dança em processo: A linguagem do indizível*. Salvador, 1994.
Sucena, Eduardo. *A dança teatral no Brasil*. Rio de Janeiro, 1988.
Vianna, Klauss. *A dança*. São Paulo, 1990.

KATIA CANTON and MARÍLIA DE ANDRADE

BREAK DANCING. Hip-hop—the wild-style world of graffiti, break dancing, and rapping—started in the mid-1970s as an underground current in New York City. After the film *Flashdance* (1983) was released, hip-hop moved from the streets of New York into the international mainstream of high art, fashion, and entertainment.

Break dancing (also known as rocking), is a form of competitive, acrobatic, and pantomimic dancing. It began as a game or friendly contest in which black and Hispanic teenagers outdid one another with outrageous physical contortions, spins, and backflips, wedded to a fluid, syncopated, circling, rocking motion executed close to the ground. Through breaking, all the pleasures, frustrations, hopes, and fears of adolescence are symbolically played out in public spaces. It is a way of inscribing one's identity in public through a flamboyant display of personal style, encompassing wit, virility, and physical skill.

The original format of the dance was quite fixed. Each person's turn begins with an entry, a hesitating walk that allows him time to get in step with the music and take his place "onstage." Next the dancer "gets down" to the floor to do the footwork, a rapid, slashing, circular scan of the floor by sneakered feet, while the hands support the body's weight and the head and torso revolve at a slower speed. Acrobatic transitions such as headspins and flips serve as bridges between the footwork and the freeze, an improvised pose or movement that is a flash of pure personal style, as intricate, witty, insulting, or obscene as possible. The sequence closes with an exit—either a spring back to vertical or a special movement that returns the dancer to the outside of the space. Solo turns can be extended indefinitely by inserting more footwork, spins, and freezes.

BREAK DANCING. Young dancers of the Rock Steady Crew perform in a schoolyard in 1983. (Photograph © 1983 by Jack Vartoogian; used by permission.)

Breaking is related to various forms of street rhetoric; its two primary modes are the taunt and the boast, and it is danced primarily by boys. The dance form is a synthesis of traditional African-American movements (including elements from the Lindy, Charleston, *capoeira,* and their ancestors), Asian martial arts, and images from contemporary American popular culture. It is inextricably tied to rap music, which is itself part of the African-American tradition. In rapping, the disc jockey spins and "scratches" instrumental disco records (that is, plays the disks as musical instruments by spinning them back and forth on the turntable to repeat and distort sections of the recording) while the MC (master of ceremonies) speaks over the music in a singsong narrative, often teasing out an epic boast peppered with incantatory nicknames and nonsense syllables. Breaking is also tied to subway graffiti both in terms of personnel and its comic book imagery, flamboyant style, transgressive intent, and celebration of individual identity.

The term *breaking* has been widened to include various forms of street and social dance, including electric boogie, robot dancing, popping, puppet (all of which involve pantomime moves and discrete isolations of body parts), and wave-style (a fish dive, in the manner of Yanvallou, a Haitian Vodun possession dance); many of these forms originated in California.

Costumes vary for the individual dances: electric boogie dancers usually wear more elegant garb, including white gloves, than pure break dancers, who wear T-shirts and net overshirts to improve traction for their spins. The overall look is one of militarized athleticism. Sneakers with wide, colorful laces and special hats play an important role. Hip-hop culture has special slang to refer to dance moves, graffiti lore, social roles, and value judgments. Originally, break dancers competed for one another's "colors"—T-shirts with crew insignia. Onlookers judged competitions by consensus. Organized into groups, or crews, according to family or neighborhood ties, break dancers, or b-boys, ranged in age from eight to sixteen; younger boys learned from older boys in a system of apprenticeship.

As breaking moved from the streets to the clubs and concert halls, its form and meaning changed. It was transformed from a folk form to a theatrical one. By 1983 competitions were sponsored by discos or film producers and carried large stakes—cash awards, film roles, the possibility of tours and television specials. Performances stressed acrobatic transitions and deemphasized the freeze; various other dances were incorporated into pure breaking, and the routines were choreographed. The age and skill of professional break dancers increased. While the dance gained theatrical brilliance, it lost much of its original urgency and vitality, as well the richness of its social meaning. By the 1990s, it had all but disappeared.

[*See also* Social Dance, *article on* Social Dance since 1960.]

BIBLIOGRAPHY

Banes, Sally. "To the Beat, Y'All: Breaking Is Hard to Do." *The Village Voice* (22 April 1981).

Banes, Sally. *Writing Dancing in the Age of Postmodernism.* Hanover, 1994.

Fresh, Mr. *Breakdancing.* New York, 1984.

George, Nelson, Sally Banes, Susan Flinker, and Patty Romanowski. *Fresh: Hip Hop Don't Stop.* New York, 1985.

Hager, Steven. *Hip Hop: The Illustrated History of Break Dancing, Rap Music, and Graffiti.* New York, 1984.

Holman, Michael. *Breaking and the New York City Breakers.* New York, 1984.

Tolley, Julie, and Ramsay Burt. "Strut Your Funky Stuff! Body-popping, Jazz and Funk in the North of England." *New Dance,* no. 26 (Autumn 1983): [8]–11.

FILMS.   Charlie Ahearn, *Wild Style* (1982). Adrian Lyne, *Flashdance* (1983). Stan Lathan, *Beat Street* (1984). Tony Silver, *Style Wars* (1983).

SALLY BANES

BRENAA, HANS (Hans Brun Brenaa; born 9 October 1910 in Copenhagen, died 14 April 1988 in Copenhagen), Danish dancer, teacher, and director. Brenaa began his training in 1917 in a private school with Christian Christensen, a dancer from the Royal Danish Ballet. A year later he was accepted into the Royal Ballet School. He made his stage debut at the age of nine, partnering Margot Lander in a children's pas de deux in the Danish folk play *Elverhøj* (The Elfin Hill), choreographed by Poul Funck. Brenaa grew up with daily Bournonville training organized by Hans Beck; among his important teachers was Valborg Borchsenius. This education influenced Brenaa profoundly, first as a dancer and later as a teacher and director. After graduating in 1929, Brenaa made his formal debut in a ballet by Børge Ralov, *Enken i Spejlet* (The Widow in the Mirror), in which he danced the part of White Groom. Among his early roles was Eros in *Psyche* by Nini Theilade.

In 1938, when the Royal Danish Ballet staged *Swan Lake* for the first time (act 2 only), Brenaa was Siegfried, again partnering Margot Lander. In the premiere of Harald Lander's *Étude* (later *Études*) in 1948, Brenaa appeared as one of the leading males. In the late 1930s, Brenaa studied in Paris with Lubov Egorova, as did other dancers from the Royal Danish Ballet at that time. For a while he danced in Egorova's company, Ballets de la Jeunesse, in Paris. In 1945, Brenaa was appointed principal dancer of the Royal Danish Ballet; in 1949 he made his debut as director, collaborating with Egorova on *Aurora's Wedding,* which introduced classical Russian style to the Bournonville- and Lander-dominated Danish repertory.

Brenaa appeared for the last time with the Royal Danish Ballet in 1955, as the General in David Lichine's *Graduation Ball.* He then became a teacher and a director, mainly of Bournonville productions. He was a connoisseur of the Bournonville style and had a remarkable memory for steps. Brenaa's knowledge and experience enabled him to combine well-remembered parts of the ballets with his own choreography in August Bournonville's style. He also remembered solos that had not been danced for many years. Brenaa was a vital contributor to Allan Fridericia's 1967 Danish television production on the Bournonville curriculum, a series of lecture-demonstrations for each day of the week.

In 1971, Brenaa choreographed and directed *Les Millions d'Arlequin* with music by Riccardo Drigo, for the Tivoli Gardens Pantomime Theater. Sets and costumes were by Bjørn Wiinblad. Brenaa produced the following Bournonville ballets and *divertissements* for the Royal Danish Ballet: *Kermesse in Bruges* (1957 and 1978), *La Sylphide* (1967), *Konservatoriet* (1968), *The King's Volunteers on Amager* (1970), *Far from Denmark* (1973), *La Ventana* (1979), and *William Tell Divertissement* (1980). All were still in the repertory at the time of the Bournonville Festival in 1992.

Brenaa officially retired from the Royal Danish Ballet in 1975 but was a guest artist on several occasions. He also produced Bournonville ballets for other major companies, including the Metropolitan Opera Ballet in New York, the Joffrey Ballet, the Paris Opera Ballet, the Scottish Theatre Ballet, the Dutch National Ballet, and the Opera Ballet in Budapest.

BIBLIOGRAPHY

Anderson, Jack, and George Dorris. "A Conversation with Svend Kragh-Jacobsen." *Ballet Review* 5.4 (1975–1976): 1–20.

Jackson, George. "Falling in Love Again." *Dance View* 9 (June 1992): 31–37.

Schønberg, Bent. *Hans Brenaa: Danish Ballet Master.* Translated by Joan Tate. London, 1990.

Tomalonis, Alexandra. "Bournonville's Gifts." *Dance View* 9 (June 1992): 42–54.

EBBE MØRK

BRIANTZEV, DMITRI (Dmitrii Aleksandrovich Briantzev; born 18 February 1947 in Leningrad), Russian dancer and choreographer. Upon graduation in 1966 from the Leningrad ballet school, where he had trained under Nikolai Zubkovsky, Briantzev joined the company now called Moscow Theater of Classical Ballet. He remained there as a dancer, first under Igor Moiseyev's and then Yuri Zhdanov's direction, until 1977. In 1977 Briantzev graduated from the choreography department of the Lunacharsky Theater Technicum in Moscow.

The first two important works that Briantzev choreographed were for television. Working with the cinema director Aleksandr Belinsky, he made *Galatea* (1977), based on *My Fair Lady,* to variations by Timur Kogan on music by Frederick Loewe, and *Old Tango* (1979), based on the film *Peter,* to music by Kogan. Both works were created for Ekaterina Maximova and had great success, revealing Briantzev's talent for comedy. In 1979 the Kirov Ballet invited him to stage *The Hussar's Ballad,* based on Aleksandr

Gladkov's popular comedy *Long, Long Ago (Davnym davno)*, about a young girl who, during the war of 1812, disguises herself as a man and fights in the army. Briantzev remained at the Kirov from 1981 to 1985, staging a new version of *The Little Humpbacked Horse* to the score by Rodion Shchedrin in 1981.

In 1985 Briantzev was appointed chief choreographer of the Stanislavsky and Nemirovich-Danchenko Musical Theater in Moscow. Before this, Briantzev had been considered a choreographer of comic, lively dances, often tinged with acrobatics. For the Stanislavsky, however, he had to take into consideration the company's traditions, its present state, and his own potential. The company had been founded by Vladimir Burmeister, whose works had all been highly dramatic, a trend that dominated Soviet ballet from the 1930s to the 1950s. Mime and pantomime prevailed in these works, and the company's dancers were also good actors. Apart from Burmeister's version of *Swan Lake*, the famous Russian classical ballets were not in the company's repertory. By the time Briantzev came to the company, Burmeister's choreography had become obsolete, and no works of importance had been staged by his successors after his death in 1971.

Briantzev enriched the repertory by bringing in classical pas de deux and variations from old ballets. He also choreographed several one-act ballet comedies: *Bravo, Figaro!* (1985), to music by Rossini; *The Cowboys* (1988), to music by George Gershwin; and *Nine Tangos and . . . Bach* (1995), to music by Astor Piazzolla and Bach. He also tried his hand at ballets with strong dramatic content, and even monumental, multiact tragedies: *Optimistic Tragedy* (1985), based on Vsevolod Vishnevsky's play about the 1918–1921 civil war in Russia, to music by Mikhail Bronner; *Othello* (1994), to music by Aleksei Machavariani; and *The Haunted Ballroom* (1995), to music by Chopin. In 1994 Briantzev became director of the Saint Petersburg Chamber Ballet. He was awarded the title of People's Artist of the Russian Federation in 1989.

BIBLIOGRAPHY
Belova, Ekaterina. "Geroini baletov Dmitriia Briantzeva." In *Voprosy teatra*, no. 13. Moscow, 1993, 54–81.
Belova, Ekaterina. "Prizrachnoe schaste 'Pechalnogo Bala.'" *Balet*, no. 6 (1995): 3–5.
Belova, Ekaterina. *Rakursy tantsa, televisionny balet*. Moscow, 1991, 47–87.
Lutskaya, Elena. "Yago tango ne tansuet." *Teatr*, no. 7–8 (1994): 27–37.
ELIZABETH SOURITZ

BRIANZA, CARLOTTA (born 1867 in Milan, died c.1930 in Paris), Italian dancer. Brianza was trained at the Teatro alla Scala in Milan, where tradition holds that she was a student of Carlo Blasis. In fact, Blasis moved to Cernobbio to devote himself to writing one year before Brianza's birth and died in January 1878; Youtchewsky (1935) may be correct in stating that Brianza actually studied with Madame Viganò Kazatti, Cesare Coppini, and Virginia Zucchi's teacher La Montani. Brianza made her debut as *prima ballerina* at La Scala in Luigi Manzotti's *Excelsior* and in 1883 toured the United States in the Kiralfy brothers' production of that ballet. Her reputation spread as she starred in the Paris production of *Excelsior* at the Eden Theatre.

The Russian phase of Brianza's career began in 1887 with a successful debut at the Arcadia Theater in Saint Petersburg, where she again appeared in *Excelsior*. She was offered a contract with the Imperial Theaters, which she postponed fulfilling for one year owing to an intervening commitment in Italy. In 1889 Brianza debuted at the Maryinsky Theater in Lev Ivanov's *The Tulip of Haarlem* (with Pavel Gerdt) and quickly became one of the most acclaimed ballerinas in Russia. She went on to create the leading roles in Marius Petipa's *The Sleeping Beauty* (1890)—her most renowned achievement—and *Kalkabrino* (1891). She was also noted for her interpretation of Jules Perrot's *Esmeralda*. Her contract included appearances in Moscow, where she appeared with Ivan Clustine in *Pygmalion*.

In 1891 Brianza returned to western Europe and was engaged by the Imperial Opera in Vienna, but the company dismissed her in 1892 for refusing to dance a secondary role in *Excelsior* in a last-minute program change. As *prima ballerina* at La Scala in 1895, Brianza appeared in Louis Mérante's *Sylvia* and Emilio Graeb's *Nozze Slave*; then at the Teatro La Fenice in Venice she appeared in *Tanzmärchen* by Franz Gaul and Josef Hassreiter. In 1896 she danced in Ferdinando Pratesi's *Day Sin*, as well as in *Coppélia* and *The Sleeping Beauty*; in 1900 she danced in Manzotti's *Sieba* and Hassreiter's *The Red Shoes*. In the 1903/04 season, she danced in the Paris Opera productions of *Lakmé* and *Manon*.

After Brianza retired from the stage, she taught in Paris. Serge Diaghilev brought her out of retirement in 1921 to assist Bronislava Nijinska in setting *The Sleeping Princess*; Brianza played the role of Carabosse in the London production. Little is known of Brianza's final years; she is said to have committed suicide in Paris between 1930 and 1935.

Brianza was one of several Italian-trained ballerinas (including Virginia Zucchi and Pierina Legnani) who dominated the Russian Imperial Theaters toward the end of the nineteenth century. In Russia, she was acclaimed for the purity of her strong classical technique, and her virtuosity was appreciated in the demanding role of Aurora. Vera Krasovskaya (1972) noted contemporary reports that Tchaikovsky did not care for dramatic dancers, preferring grace and generalized feeling to detailed acting, a predilection that accounted for his admiring Brianza over Zucchi. Krasovskaya also discussed the suitability of Brianza's style, more musically than dramatically expressive, to the lyrical role of Aurora. While the

Italian virtuosi influenced the Russian style, the reverse was also true; according to Milloss (1954), the Russian historian Aleksandr Pleshcheyev wrote in 1890 that Brianza had been influenced by the Saint Petersburg school, revealing more softness and expressiveness than her compatriots.

BIBLIOGRAPHY

Guest, Ivor. *The Divine Virginia: A Biography of Virginia Zucchi.* New York, 1977.

Ivchenko, Valerian [Svetlov, Valerian]. "Les étoiles étrangères en Russie." *Archives internationales de la danse* (October 1934): 126–128.

Krasovskaya, Vera. "Marius Petipa and *The Sleeping Beauty*." Translated by Cynthia Read. *Dance Perspectives*, no. 49 (1972).

Milloss, Aurelio. "Brianza, Carlotta." In *Enciclopedia dello spettacolo.* Rome, 1954–.

Wiley, Roland John. *Tchaikovsky's Ballets.* Oxford, 1985.

Wiley, Roland John, trans. and ed. *A Century of Russian Ballet: Documents and Accounts, 1810–1910.* Oxford, 1990.

Youtchewsky, N. "Quelques mots sur Carlotta Brianza." *Archives Internationales de la danse* (October 1935): 120.

DEBRA HICKENLOOPER SOWELL

BRINSON, PETER (born 6 March 1923 in Llandudno, Wales, died 7 April 1995 in London), Welsh writer, lecturer, company director, and dance historian. After earning first class honors in politics, philosophy, and economics at Oxford in 1948, Brinson began writing for films and television, thus inaugurating a career as a specialist in cultural politics. For ten years, starting in 1954, he lectured on ballet at Oxford, Cambridge, and London universities. In 1964 he founded Ballet for All, a small company of dancers and actors that he directed in programs exploring the history of theatrical dance for young people. With the assistance of consultants such as Ivor Guest and Mary Skeaping, Ballet for All was a model of dance scholarship presented as entertainment. In the eight years of its existence, the company served to build audiences for dance throughout Britain.

Awarded a Council of Europe Research Fellowship in 1961, Brinson surveyed dance resources in European libraries to compile his book *Background to European Ballet.* From 1971 to 1982 he served as director of the British and Commonwealth Branch of the Gulbenkian Foundation, a position that he used not only to aid ballet companies in the United Kingdom but also to initiate pilot projects, such as the founding of the English Society for Dance Research. From 1975 to 1980 he was chairman of a national inquiry into the state of dance in education.

Brinson's long-standing concern with social problems was strengthened by his work at Gulbenkian on community arts programs. In 1982 he became head of research and community development at the Laban Centre. Located in the underprivileged southeast section of London, next to Goldsmiths' College, an associated institution, the Laban Centre offered Brinson both an academic setting and an opportunity for fieldwork. His course in the sociology of dance, an original concept, included both theoretical and practical aspects, with the aim of preparing graduates for activities that would encourage community participation. His special concerns included work with the youth subculture and with minority groups.

Since 1987 Brinson served as consultant to the Laban Centre and the Hong Kong government. In 1988 Brinson represented the United Kingdom at the conference, "Beyond Performance: Dance Scholarship Today," held in Essen, Germany and sponsored by the International Theatre Institute. He was chairman of the National Inquiry into Arts and the Community and was editor of *International Working Papers on Dance*, which began publication in London in 1990.

BIBLIOGRAPHY

Brinson, Peter, and Joan Wildeblood. *The Polite World.* London, 1965.

Brinson, Peter. *Background to European Ballet.* New York, 1966.

Brinson, Peter, and Clement Crisp. *Ballet for All.* London, 1970.

Brinson, Peter. *Dance as Education: Towards a National Dance Culture.* Falmer, 1991.

Brinson, Peter, ed. *International Working Papers on Dance.* London, 1991–.

Ralph, Richard, ed. *Dance Research* (Peter Brinson Memorial Issue) 15.1 (Summer 1997).

van Praagh, Peggy, and Peter Brinson. *The Choreographic Art.* London, 1963.

SELMA JEANNE COHEN

BRNO BALLET. The history of ballet in Brno, Czechoslovakia, dates from 25 December 1913, when the old theater Na Veveří staged *The Veil of Pierrette*, the ballet pantomime of Ernő Dohnányi, with choreography by Hana Vojáčková. The development of ballet in Brno continued uninterrupted after World War I, when the newly independent Czechoslovak Republic created favorable conditions for the cultural development of the nation.

The company's distinguishing characteristic in the period between the two world wars was a progressive, modern repertory oriented to national and Slavic artists. Between 1925 and 1935 Máša Cvejičová choreographed ballets to scores by Igor Stravinsky, Sergei Prokofiev, and Bohuslav Martinů. Cvejičová also produced the first Soviet ballet in Czechoslovakia, *The Red Poppy*, in 1935. This progressive policy did not change even after Ivo Váňa Psota, who had been a soloist and between 1928 and 1932 director of the company, returned in 1936 as director and choreographer, having in the interim been a member of the Ballets Russes de Monte Carlo. Psota's *chef-d'oeuvre* was the world premiere of Prokofiev's *Romeo and Juliet* in 1938; Psota and Zora Šemberová danced the title roles.

Psota immigrated to the United States in 1941, but he returned in 1947 and within a short time had formed a first-rate company, with which he staged premieres that earned Brno recognition as a ballet capital. Psota's death in 1952 was a serious blow. [*See the entry on Psota.*] Several directors followed him before Luboš Ogoun took over in 1961, bringing an upsurge of creativity to the ensemble with such works as his setting of Dmitri Shostakovich's *Leningrad Symphony* in 1962.

After Ogoun's departure in 1964, Miroslav Kůra, Rudolf Karhánek, and Jiří Němeček followed as directors. Beginning in 1977, the company was directed by Olga Skálová, a student of Psota's who had a wide range of experience as a ballerina in both the classical and Soviet repertories. Primary choreographers were Ogoun and Daniel Wiesner. After the so-called "velvet revolution" in 1989, Ogoun again became director, until 1991, when the position was given to Zdeněk Prokeš.

The National Theater in Brno (the former State Theater Brno) is the second largest and artistically strongest company (after the Prague National Theater Ballet) in the Czech Republic. It comprises around sixty dancers. The theater also has a smaller group of about fifteen dancers for performances of operettas and musicals.

[*See also* Czech Republic and Slovak Republic, *article on* Theatrical Dance; *and the entries on Ogoun, Kůra, and Němeček.*]

BIBLIOGRAPHY
Almanach 90 let stálého českého divadla v Brně. Brno, 1974.
Brno State Theater. *Almanach 66–69.* Brno, 1969.
Putování Múzy Thálie. Brno, 1984.
Schmidová, Lidka. *Československý balet.* Prague, 1962.
Windreich, Leland. "Brno State Theater Ballet." *Ballet Review* 23 (Fall 1995): 9–13.

VLADIMÍR VAŠUT
Translated from Czech

BROWN, CAROLYN (Carolyn Rice; born 26 September 1927 in Fitchburg, Massachusetts), American dancer. Brown's first dance teacher was her mother, Marion Rice, who taught according to Denishawn principles in their hometown of Fitchburg. Brown did not intend to become a professional dancer, however; instead she attended Wheaton College as a philosophy major and earned a bachelor's degree in 1950. In the spring of 1951, while living in Denver, Colorado, with her husband Earle Brown she studied dance with Jane McLean. Merce Cunningham and John Cage came through Denver on tour, and Cunningham gave a master class that Brown attended. Brown then decided that she wanted to dance, and in the fall of 1952 she and her husband moved to New York, where she enrolled in dance classes at the Juilliard School. She also studied with Cunningham. (Earle Brown soon began to work with Cage on a taped-music project.)

In the spring of 1953 Brown performed for the first time with Cunningham, in *Suite by Chance,* and that summer she was one of the group that went with Cunningham to Black Mountain College in North Carolina. Their performances that summer marked the beginning of the Merce Cunningham Dance Company as a regularly constituted group. As Cunningham's partner for the next two decades, Brown danced in nearly every piece he choreographed. She left the Juilliard School but continued to study ballet with Margaret Craske and Antony Tudor.

Brown's purity of line and coolly patrician demeanor rivaled those of any classical ballerina of her time; coupled with her deeply felt commitment to the work, these characteristics made her the ideal interpreter of Cunningham's choreography. (She was also an excellent teacher of his technique.) When she left the company in 1972, many saw it as the end of an era, and indeed several works in his repertory (among them *Walkaround Time* and *Second Hand*) have not been performed in their entirety since.

Brown also danced in John Cage's 1960 *Theatre Piece* and in Robert Rauschenberg's *Pelican* in 1963. Her own choreographies include *Balloon,* for the First New York Theatre Rally in 1963; *Car Lot,* for the Manhattan Festival Ballet in 1967; *House Party,* for Among Company in 1974; *Circles,* for the Maryland Dance Theatre in 1975; and *Balloon II,* for Ballet-Théâtre Contemporain in 1976. Her film *Dune Dance* was completed in 1978. She received the *Dance Magazine* Award in 1970 and a Guggenheim Fel-

CAROLYN BROWN. A member of Merce Cunningham's company for twenty years, Brown leaps here in *Winterbranch* (1964). The costume, a dark sweat suit and face paint, is of Robert Rauschenberg's design. (Photograph © by Jack Mitchell; used by permission.)

lowship for choreography and filmmaking in 1982. From 1980 to 1982 she was dean of the Dance Division at the State University of New York at Purchase.

BIBLIOGRAPHY
Brown, Carolyn. "McLuhan and the Dance." *Ballet Review* 1.4 (1966): 13.
Brown, Carolyn. "On Chance." *Ballet Review* 2.2 (1968): 7.
Brown, Carolyn. Untitled essay in *Dance Perspectives* (Summer 1968).
Brown, Carolyn. "Merce Cunningham." In *Merce Cunningham*, edited by James Klosty. New ed. New York, 1986.

DAVID VAUGHAN

BROWN, TRISHA (born 25 November 1936 in Aberdeen, Washington), dancer, choreographer, and founding member of Judson Dance Theater and Grand Union. One of the key postmodern choreographers, Trisha Brown has developed a choreographic style that makes use of verbal wit and deadpan physical humor, problem-solving strategies, improvisatory structures, logical systems, unusual spaces, the protocol of the performance situation, syncopated rhythms, and her own movement style, which is vigorous, fluid, multifocal, and flexible. She was one of the founding members of the Judson Dance Theater and of the improvisational group Grand Union. In 1970 she formed the Trisha Brown Company.

Brown received a bachelor's degree in dance from Mills College in Oakland, California, and also studied at the American Dance Festival with Louis Horst, Anna Halprin, and Robert Dunn. She has taught at Mills College, Reed College, and New York University.

Brown's earliest dances, such as *Trillium* (1962), a solo, and *Lightfall* (1963), a duet with Steve Paxton, were partial improvisations that allowed for naturally forceful actions and interactions, flyaway movements, perchings, and stillnesses. A number of her dances created during the 1960s dealt with the physical act of falling or with images of flight. Others were task performances in which the movements and, often, language were produced by prescribed goals for the performers and, occasionally, for the audience. In *Rulegame 5* (1964), for example, five performers were instructed to negotiate their way along a multilevel course by talking to each other and making any necessary mutual adjustments. For the improvisational *Yellowbelly* (1969), Brown urged the audience to heckle her and egged them on to shout louder.

In 1968 Brown began to construct a series of equipment pieces. In dances such as *Planes* (1968), *Man Walking Down the Side of the Building* (1970), and *Walking on the Wall* (1971) she used external support systems such as ropes, pulleys, mountain-climbing gear, and a giant pegboard to create the illusion of natural movement in situations that changed the relation of the performers to weight and gravity. Brown also explored unusual spaces and surfaces in other works, such as *Improvisations on a*

TRISHA BROWN. The choreographer in her solo *Water Motor* (1978). (Photograph © 1978 by Johan Elbers; used by permission.)

Chicken Coop Roof (1963); *Roof Piece* (1971), in which dancers stationed on roofs in lower Manhattan relayed movements along a twelve-block area; and various versions of *Group Primary Accumulation* (1973), performed on park benches, in an outdoor plaza, and on rafts in a lagoon.

Brown is interested in the tension between the clarity of a movement idea and its physical distortion. This can be seen in *Roof Piece* and in such dances as *Discs* (1973), in which three performers interrupt the movements of another, or *Drift* (1974). A more subtle distortion takes place in Brown's various accumulation pieces, such as *Accumulation* (1971), a solo for Brown that roots her to one spot while she repeats discrete gestures of different body parts according to a mathematical system.

Brown continued to use conceptual systems to order such dances as *Locus* (1975), in which a numerical code was assigned to the alphabet, a corresponding code was assigned to points on an imaginary cube in space, and an autobiographical text provided clusters of points on the cube, which the dancer had to move through, touch, look at, or jump over. The matter-of-fact gesturing and joint articulation of the accumulation pieces gave way in Brown's dances of the late 1970s to complex aerial movements.

BROWN. From left to right, Trisha Brown, Stephen Petronio, Lisa Kraus, and Eva Karczag in Brown's *Opal Loop*, with a cloud installation by Fujiko Nakaya. (Photograph © 1981 by Johan Elbers; used by permission.)

Brown has also used accumulation as a choreographic structure. *Line Up* (1976–1977) included various earlier short pieces in an exploration of the boundaries between order and disorder. In a conglomerate work, *Accumulation with Talking plus Water Motor* (1978), Brown tells several stories simultaneously while splicing two different dances together, interrupting the stationary *Accumulation* (1971) with *Water Motor* (1978), originally a separate, brief solo packed with fleeting images. *Accumulation with Talking* was first performed in 1973.

After nearly twenty years of presenting dances without theatrically expressive elements such as special costumes or lighting and, for the most part, without music, Brown began in 1979 to collaborate with other artists. In *Glacial Decoy* (1979), Robert Raushchenberg's black-and-white photographic images slid across a series of immense screens that served as a backdrop, while his white, translucent, fluted dresses swirled around the dancers' bodies. There was a slippery quality in the dance's flyaway movements, as two dancers darted on- and offstage from the wings, as if propelled by invisible forces, while two other dancers performed their phrases in the center of the stage. Finally, as all four repeated their material simultaneously, viewers could grasp the entire choreographic structure, which had previously been shown in spatial fragments.

In 1980 Brown choreographed *Opal Loop*, which was presented with sculptor Fujiko Nakaya's *Cloud Installation #72513*, a sculpture made of fog. The clouds concealed and revealed the dancers, clothed in richly iridescent costumes, as they worked their way forward in a narrow, raw loft space. The movements, a series of shrugs, flings, and jerks, looked like reflex actions, but in fact were planned, repeatable dance phrases built into a movement loop or endless phrase, giving the dancing a liquid appearance.

In *Son of Gone Fishin'* (1981) the choreography was engulfed in a sea of music (Robert Ashley's *Atalanta*). Sculptor Donald Judd's massive green and blue backdrops rose and fell behind the dancers, who moved in and out of canon, sometimes arriving at clear, steady, momentary unison as their bodies rippled with small, sudden movements alternating with steady, centered, luxurious motions that seemed to flow beyond the boundaries of the body.

Brown's work has evolved from a concern with objects and the tasklike use of equipment to the production of dances with a legibility that promotes a feeling of object-like permanence and stability, to dances whose fluidity, water imagery, and rapid phrasing defy categorization. In the 1980s and 1990s, her major works such as *Set and Reset* (1983), *Lateral Pass* (1985), *Newark* (1987), *Astral Convertible* (1989), *Foray Forêt* (1990), and *For M. C.: The Movie* (1991) extended her artistic collaboration with such visual artists as Rauschenberg, Judd, and Nancy Graves and composers Laurie Anderson, Peter Zummo, and Richard Landry. These pieces are characterized by unusual, off-balance movements and supports; surprising interactions between the dancers and moving sets; and witty references to earlier Brown dances. Although her early inclination seems to have evolved into its opposite, in the 1980s and 1990s Brown has returned to the theme of one of her earliest dances, *Trillium*, whose rules were that she "could stand, sit, or lie, and ended up levitating."

After contributing the dances to director Lina Wertmuller's production of Georges Bizet's *Carmen* in 1986 (in which she also performed), Brown became interested in working with already existing musical scores. The result was *M.O.* (1995), a fifty-five-minute dance to Johann Sebastian Bach's *Musical Offering,* in which Brown created intricate choreographic structures to counterpoint the complex rhythms of the composer's canons and ricercares. In *Twelve Ton Rose* (1996), she choreographed to a number of Anton Webern's short dodecaphonic chamber-music pieces (the dance's title punningly refers to the music's twelve-tone rows), devising complex, shifting correspondences between the dancers and the instrumental voices. Her other works from the 1990s include *One Story as in Falling* (made for the French dance company of Dominique Bagouet), later reworked for her own dancers as *Another Story as in Falling.* Brown's solo *If You Couldn't See Me* (1994), which the choreographer danced entirely with her back to the audience, was transformed in 1996 into a duet, *You Can See Us,* for Brown and Mikhail Baryshnikov.

Brown's company has toured extensively, performing throughout the United States, Europe, and Asia. Brown is also an accomplished graphic artist, whose drawings have been shown in many exhibitions, including the Venice Biennale. Brown has received five fellowships from the National Endowment for the Arts and two Guggenheim fellowships, among many other grants. The government of India named her Artist in India in 1970. In 1987 she received both the *Dance Magazine* Award for "twenty-five years of sustained innovation," and the Laurence Olivier Award (London's equivalent to New York's Tony awards) for the year's most outstanding achievement in dance. In 1988 Brown was named a Chevalier dans l'Ordre des Arts et des Lettres by the French government, and she won the Prix de la Danse de la Société des Auteurs et Compositeurs Dramatiques in 1996. In 1991 she received a MacArthur Foundation Fellowship, and in 1994 the Samuel H. Scripps Award at the American Dance Festival. Brown was appointed to the National Council on the Arts by President Bill Clinton in May 1994.

BIBLIOGRAPHY

Banes, Sally. *Terpsichore in Sneakers: Post-Modern Dance.* 2d ed. Middletown, Ct., 1987. Includes a bibliography.

Brown, Trisha, and Yvonne Rainer. "A Conversation about *Glacial Decoy.*" *The Village Voice* (10 October 1979).

Goldberg, Marianne. "Trisha Brown: All of the Person's Person Arriving." *Drama Review* 30 (Spring 1986): 149–170.

Kaplan, Peggy Jarrell. *Portraits of Choreographers.* New York, 1988.

Sears, David. "A Trisha Brown-Robert Rauschenberg Collage." *Ballet Review* 10 (Fall 1982): 47–51.

Sommer, Sally R. "Equipment Dances: Trisha Brown." *Drama Review* 16 (September 1972): 135–141.

Vail, June. "Moving Bodies, Moving Souls: Trisha Brown Company in Stockholm, 1989." In *Proceedings of the Fifteenth Annual Conference, Society of Dance History Scholars, University of California, Riverside, 14–15 February 1992,* compiled by Christena L. Schlundt. Riverside, Calif., 1992.

FILM AND VIDEOTAPE.   *Water Motor* (dir. Babette Mangolte, 1978). *Making Dances* (Blackwood Productions, 1979). "Dancing on the Edge" (WGBH–TV, Boston, 1980). "Trisha and *Carmen*" (WGBH-TV/WNET-TV, 1987).

SALLY BANES